# 10,000
# VITAL RECORDS OF
# WESTERN NEW YORK

1809–1850

# 10,000
# VITAL RECORDS OF
# WESTERN NEW YORK

## 1809–1850

*Fred Q. Bowman*

GENEALOGICAL PUBLISHING CO., INC.

*Baltimore* 1988

# NOTE

These records are drawn from the marriage and death columns of five western New York newspapers published prior to 1850. Birth announcements were not published in these early journals. Fortunately, many of the marriage and death notices made mention of birth years, birthplaces, and parents' names.

In this book bridegrooms and all those who were subjects of death notices are listed in alphabetical order. Marriage officials are identified in the appendix. All other persons mentioned in the text are listed in the index.

Towns of residence are by no means confined to western New York. Communities in the rest of the state as well as New England and the Mid-West are frequently identified. Occasionally found are references to "West Florida," California, "Burmah," China, "Owyhee" (Hawaii), Argentina, Gibralter, and Greece, to name but a few of the more distant places.

The numbers given in parenthesis at the end of each entry are source citations. The first number (see map overleaf) identifies the newspaper; the remaining numbers (following the dash) refer to the month and day of publication, and less frequently the year of publication. Unless given in the citation, the year of issue of the newspaper is that of the vital record itself.

Except for *surv by* (survived by) and *inf s* (infant son) the abbreviations used here are those commonly found in genealogical writings. Unless otherwise noted all cities, towns, villages, and hamlets referred to are in New York. For the locations and histories of these communities and their related counties see especially J. H. French's *Gazetteer of the State of New York*, 1860.

*Fred Q. Bowman*

THE FIVE WESTERN NEW YORK NEWSPAPERS OF VITAL RECORD REVIEW

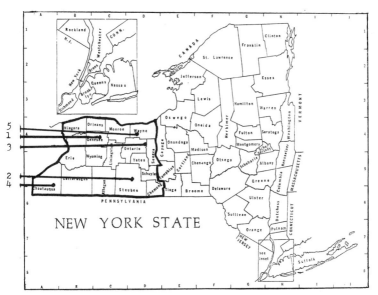

NEW YORK STATE

Western New York as outlined above covers an area more than
twice that of Connecticut and Rhode Island combined.

| Citation code number | Publication town | Newspaper title | Date span of review | Number of vital records secured |
|---|---|---|---|---|
| 1 | Batavia | Republican Advocate | 3/19/22-12/31/50 | 729 |
| 2 | Bath | Steuben Farmers Advocate | 1/5/31-12/31/50 | 1221 |
| 3 | Geneva | Geneva Gazette | 6/21/09-12/31/27 | 4975 |
| 4 | Jamestown | Jamestown Journal | 7/21/26-12/31/50 | 1117 |
| 5 | Palmyra | Wayne Sentinel (Palmyra Register, 1817-21) | 3/16/17-9/25/44 | 2014 |

Geneva lies on the border between central and western
New York. Vital records, 1828 through 1850, from the
Geneva Gazette will appear in the forthcoming book,
10,000 Vital Records of Central New York, 1824-1850.

1.    ____, Aaron of Waterloo m 12/29/24 Lydia Cross of Junius in J  (3-1/19/25)
2.    ____, Chauncy, 40, d 4/22/43 in Mayville (4-4/27)
3.    __ket, David m 11/21/24 Harriet Beebe in Canandaigua (3-12/1)
4.    __lock, David of Utica m Martha S. Ketchum of Jericho, L.I., NY, "after
      the order of the Society of Friends" (4-9/5/45)
5.    ____, Dinah, "at least 116 years old", a black woman and native of Bucks
      Co., PA, formerly the property of Mr. Langhorne, d 4/23/10 in the Bucks
      Co. Alms House (3-5/23)
6.    ____, John, 59, State Librarian and proprietor of the Albany Reading Room,
      d 8/21/23 in Albany (3-8/27)
7.    ____, Thomas, 71, m 2/3/23 Mrs. Lewis, 65, in Benton (3-3/12)
8.    Abbey, Samuel (Capt.) m Margaret Miller in Penn Yan (3-6/6/27)
9.    Abbey, W. W. m 12/4/31 Clarissa Houghton in Macedon (5-12/27)
10.   Abbot, Abiel (Rev.), 60, D.D., of Beverly, MA d on board a ship from Cuba
      to NYC (3-6/18/28)
11.   Abbot, Ezra, 76, d 2/24/33 in Busti; a native of Ridgebury, CT; surv by
      "an aged consort" ("Editors of Rutland, Vt, Danbury, Conn. and of ...
      New York City will confer a favor ...")  (4-2/27)
12.   Abbot, Ezra m 11/17/37 Mary Bush in Busti; Emry Davis, Esq. (4-11/22)
13.   Abbot, Martha, 22 mo., dau of Ezra, d 3/24/41 in Jamestown (4-3/31)
14.   Abbot, Stephen S. m 2/5/45 Emma D. Frank, only dau of William, in Busti;
      Rev. E. R. Swain. All of Busti. (4-2/14)
15.   Abbott, A. J., attorney, of Batavia m 9/20/48 M. J. Beach of Fowlerville
      in F.; Rev. H. W. Smuller (1-10/17)
16.   Abbott, A. S. m 9/25/43 L. M. Bullock in Busti; Rev. E. R. Swain (4-9/28)
17.   Abbott, William H. of Roscoe, IL m 11/6/45 Mercy Ann Arms of Jamestown
      in J.; Rev. E. J. Gillett (4-11/14)
18.   Abeel, John N. (Rev. Dr.), 42, one of the pastors of the Reformed
      Protestant Dutch Ch. of NYC, d 1/19/12 in NYC (3-2/5)
19.   Abel, Jacob C. m Mary Chase in Milo (3-6/6/27)
20.   Abel, William H. m 12/12/50 Sarah F. Van Amburg, both of Savonia, in S.;
      Rev. J. C. Mallory (2-12/25)
21.   Abell, James (Rev.) of Oswego m Laura G. Bogue in Clinton (3-4/22/29)
22.   Aber, Aaron m 3/26/50 Elizabeth Ann Cornwell, both of Bath, in B.; Rev.
      J. C. Mallory (2-4/6)
23.   Aber, Anna, 53, wf of Nathaniel, d 2/13/50 in Bath (2-2/20)
24.   Aber, T. J. m 5/1/50 Samantha B. Bramble in Bath; Rev. L. Merrill Miller.
      All of B. (2-5/8)
25.   Abery, Benjamin of Brutus, Cay. Co., m 8/21/22 Cynthia Hastings of
      Canandaigua in C. (3-9/18)
26.   Acher?, Chester m 6/25/44 Elizabeth Coon; Rev. William M. Ferguson.
      All of Palmyra. (5-7/3)
27.   Acker, Joseph, 9 mo., s of David, d 9/17/26 in Seneca (3-9/20)
28.   Ackley, Charles, "about 28, colored man", d 2/8/36 in Jamestown (4-2/10)
29.   Ackley, James of Palmyra m 1/1/35 Betsey Lumbard of Lyons in Sodus (5-1/9)
30.   Acocks, Phebe, 52, wf of Maj. William, d 12/21/31 in Jamestown (4-12/28)
31.   Adams, Abijah, editor of the Independent Chronicle, d in Boston, MA
      (3-6/5/16)
32.   Adams, Ann Eliza (Miss), 22, d 4/30/45 in Bath (member of New Presby. Ch.
      and of the choir) (2-5/7)
33.   Adams, Asahel m Esther Lee in Italy, NY (3-5/14/28)
34.   Adams, Asahel, 61, father of Messrs. John and David, d in Lyons (3-9/17/28)
35.   Adams, Barnabas of Williamson m 5/17/37 Ellen Hicks of Palmyra; Rev. Sears
      (5-5/26)
36.   Adams, Chauncey, 19, m Susanna Adams, 34, both of Middlesex, in Gorham
      (3-12/4/11)
37.   Adams, Cornelia, only surviving ch. of Rev. Adams, d in Syracuse (3-12/30/29)
38.   Adams, Daniel of Batavia m 2/4/49 Rosanna Stickney of Barcelona, Chaut. Co.
      in B.; Esquire Goodrich (1-2/13)

39. Adams, Daniel P., late editor and proprietor of People's Press, m Maria
    Seaver in Batavia (3-12/23/29)
40. Adams, David m 3/6/24 Mary Corning in Batavia; D. Tisdale, Esq. (1-3/12)
41. Adams, David, formerly of Batavia, m 1/2/26 Hannah Perrine in Lyons; Rev.
    Hubbell (1-1/13)
42. Adams, Earle m Deborah Gifford in Ellery; J. Winchester, Esq. (4-1/3/27
43. Adams, George, inf s of B. C. Adams, d 9/19/24 in Batavia (1-9/24)
44. Adams, George P., 4 mo., only s of Rev. J. W., d in Syracuse (3-12/9/29)
45. Adams, George Smith, inf s of B. C. Adams, d 2/19/26 in Pembroke (1-2/24)
46. Adams, Hannah, 45, wf of William, d 2/9/39 in Palmyra (5-2/22)
47. Adams, Harriet Maria, inf dau of O. G., d 8/30/24 in Batavia (1-9/3)
48. Adams, Harvey m 11/18/30 Eliza Scott of Rome, NY in R (5-11/26)
49. Adams, John m 9/14/17 Arva L. Brown in Prattsburgh (3-9/24)
50. Adams, John of Canandaigua m Rebecca Hamilton in Manchester (3-3/1/20)
51. Adams, Maria, 35, wf of Daniel, d 7/23/46 in Batavia (1-7/28)
52. Adams, Oliver G., 33, d 10/20/25 in Batavia (1-10/21)
53. Adams, Peter B., Esq., 85, bro of Pres. Adams, d in Quincy, MA (3-7/30/23)
54. Adams, Samuel H., 28, d 2/27/49 at the home of his father in Painted Post
    (member Indep. Order of Odd Fellows; only son of aged parents; surv by
    parents and sisters) (2-3/7)
55. Adams, Sarah, 62, mother of Mrs. A. B. Johnson and sister-in-law of Pres.
    John Q. Adams, d 8/3/28 in Utica (3-8/13)
56. Adams, William m Lurany Beach in East Bloomfield (3-1/2/22)
57. Adams, William m Harriet Cassleman in Harmony; Rev. Hinebaugh (4-9/29/42)
58. Adams, William H., Esq. m Elisa J. Clark in Canandaigua (3-11/26/17)
59. Adamson, William, a native of England, d 7/3/19 "of opisthetonos" in Geneva,
    NY (3-7/7)
60. Addicot, Mary Ann, 5, dau of Henry, d 8/26/44 in Palmyra (5-9/25)
61. Addison, Robert (Rev.), 72, pastor of Episc. Ch. in Niagara, d near N (3-10/21)
62. Adgeton, William m 5/16/44 Calista Avery, both of Palmyra in P; Rev.
    Griswold (5-5/22)
63. Adriance, James m 11/28/26 Delia Bouton in Hector (3-11/29)
64. Agin, David m 7/19/41 Euphemy Bayles of Lyons in Palmyra; Rev. Shumway
    (5-7/28)
65. Aiken, Hellen H., 13 mo., dau of Rev. S. C., d in Utica (3-8/1/27)
66. Aiken, James m 3/8/31 Adeline Cook in Palmyra; Elder Roe of Newark (5-3/18)
67. Ailsworth, Daniel m 10/17/33 Betsey Perkins, both of Galen; Jesse Fifield,
    Esq. (5-10/25)
68. Ainsworth, D. W. C. m 5/3/45 Aurelia J. Cole in Prattsburgh; Rev. William
    Andruss. All of Prattsburgh (2-5/14)
69. Ainsworth, De Witt C., 21, d 3/17/47 in Prattsburgh (member of Lyceum)
    (2-3/24)
70. Ainsworth, Isaac, 53, d 3/8/40 at his home in Prattsburgh (one of the
    earliest settlers in P; surv by "a family") (2-3/18)
71. Akenhead, Adam, 25, d in Lyons (3-5/9/27)
72. Akin, George, 22, formerly of Auburn, d 7/14/35 in Natchez, MS (5-8/21)
73. Akin, Grace, 38, wf of Elijah, d 1/12/35 in Carroll (4-1/14)
74. Akin, Lucinda, 34, wf of John H., d 1/31/43 in Carroll (4-2/16)
75. Albritt, George m 10/11/38 Mary McCumber in Palmyra; I. E. Beecher, Esq.
    All of Palmyra (5/10/19)
76. Alcock, _____, 4 mo., ch of W. Alcock, d 8/6/27 in Geneva (3-8/8)
77. Alden, Hiram (Dr.), formerly of Chaut. Co., d 11/26/38 in Detroit, MI
    (4-1/2/39)
78. Alden, Lewis, 18, s of Benjamin, d 3/14/49 in Howard (2-3/28)
79. Alden, Richard of Alden, PA- m Betsey Newman of Ashville in A; I. S. Fitch,
    Esq. (4-2/7/27)
80. Aldrich, Albert m 2/27/40 Marietta Osband, dau of Rev. Wilson Osband;
    Rev. Jonas Dodge. All of Arcadia (5-3/4)
81. Aldrich, Charles m 11/25/21 Mrs. Allen in Palmyra; A. Spear, Esq. (5-12/12)
82. Aldrich, David S., merchant, m 4/12/41 Catherine T. Sexton, dau of Pliny.
    All of Palmyra (5-4/14)
83. Aldrich, George m Polly Patten; Elisha Slocum, Esq. (5-11/28/17)
84. Aldrich, Jared C. M. m Mahitable Thrasher in Farmington (5-1/12/20)
85. Aldrich, Nathan, 58 d in Farmington (3-11/18/18)
86. Aldrich, Nathan m Betsey Estelow in Farmington (5-1/12/20)
87. Aldrich, Oren, Esq., 51, late supervisor of town of Lyons, d 4/13/23 in L
    (3-4/23)

4

88. Aldrich, Rebecca, 68, wf of Nahum, d 4/30/43in Busti at the home of
George Stoneman while there visiting (a native of "Pomfort, Conn and
emigrated to this county nearly 40 years ago") (4-5/4)
89. Aldrich, Rudolphus m 8/2/41 Mrs. Catharine Nottingham in Bath; H. Pier,
Esq. (2-8/4)
90. Aldrich, Seth m Jane Kempshall in Canandaigua (3-7/9/28)
91. Alexander, Aro Carmi of Belfast, Alleg. Co., m 9/27/43 Julia Ann Carpenter
of Ellington in E; Rev. W. Waith (4-10/5)
92. Alexander, Daniel m Charlotte Scofield, both of Harmony, NY in Sugargrove,
PA (4-1/27/42)
93. Alexander, Jonathan, 79, d 8/8/42 in Jamestown (4-8/11)
94. Alexander, Moses, 95, m 4/11/31 Mrs. Frances Tompkins, 105, in Bath; Rev.
D. Smith (2-4/20 and 1-4/29)
95. Alexander, William, Esq., 37, d 1/21/13 in Herkimer (3-2/17)
96. Alger, Matthew m 3/17/24 Louisa Fay in Bethany; Henry Rumsey, Esq. All of
Bethany (1-3/19)
97. Allcott, Amos, formerly of Ballston Spa, d 3/4/24 in Batavia (his obit from
the Rochester Telegraph of 3/2 included) (1-3/5) (age 40 at death)
98. Allen, _____, 1 mo., dau of Augustus F., d 8/27/37 in Jamestown (4-8/30)
99. Allen, Abner H., merchant, m 8/28/45 Pauline E. Wescot; Rev. Gillet. All
of Jamestown (4-9/5)
100. Allen, Almiron W., 23, s of Nathaniel, Esq., d 1/12/29 in Richmond (3-1/21)
101. Allen, Amos m 6/8/26 Parmelia Graton in Batavia; D. Tisdale, Esq. (1-6/9)
102. Allen, Augustus F., merchant, of Jamestown m Margaret Cock of NYC in NYC
(4-10/19/36)
103. Allen, Betsey, wf of Nathaniel, Esq., d 6/9/26 in Richmond (3-6/14)
104. Allen, Dana H. m 10/31/36 Martha J. Budlong of Jamestown; Rev. E. J. Gillet.
All of J (4-11/2)
105. Allen, Daniel m 12/23/33 Matilda Hoag of Farmington in Palmyra; Frederick
Smith, Esq. (5-12/27)
106. Allen, Dascum, merchant, of Jamestown m 11/14/39 Susan W. Darling of
Dunkirk in D; Rev. Smith (4-11/20)
107. Allen, David, Esq., 47, attorney and late state senator, d 5/11/20 in
Lansingburgh, Renss. Co. (3-5/24)
108. Allen, David G. m Betsey Mariah Winans in Milo (3-6/18/28)
109. Allen, Edward F. m 2/11/44 Hannah M. Tinney in Palmyra; Rev. D. Harrington.
All of Palmyra (5-2/14)
110. Allen, Elisha, 46, d 9/13/30 in Jamestown (4-9/15)
111. Allen, Ephraim, "a young married man", d in Scipio, Cay. Co. (suicide by
hanging) (3-5/1/16)
112. Allen, Ethan B. (Gen.), 48, d 4/19/35 in Batavia (5-5/1)
113. Allen, Eunice (Miss), 80, d 7/18/18 in Deerfield, MA ("In ... 1746, at the
Barr's fight so called in Deerfield, she had a tomahawk struck in her
head by an Indian ...") (5-8/25)
114. Allen, Fluvia F., 37, wf of Sumner, d 5/10/44 in Poland, NY (4-5/17)
115. Allen, Gain R. m 12/31/43 Arelia? Potter, both of Perinton, Monroe Co.,
at the Meth. Chapel in Palmyra; Rev. Ferguson (5-1/3/44)
116. Allen, Gideon of Providence m Catharine Van Ness in Jerusalem (3-7/22/29)
117. Allen, Gideon of Yates Co. m Sally Larrowe in Wheeler (3-12/23/29)
118. Allen, Gilbert (Deacon), 80, d 1/6/16 in Morristown, NJ and "on the
Wednesday following Elizabeth Allen, his wife" (3-1/31)
119. Allen, Harriet Mariah, 1 yr., dau of Draper, d 7/30/32 in Palmyra (5-8/1)
120. Allen, Henry P. m 1/9/32 Ann Maria Havens; B. H. Hickox. All of Palmyra
(5-1/10)
121. Allen, Israel B. m 6/24/40 Eliza Ann Van Hoosen; Rev. Goodell. All of
Howard (2-7/1)
122. Allen, Jane, 1 yr., only ch of Joseph and Sophia K., d 3/2/37 in East
Palmyra (5-3/10)
123. Allen, Jesse of Harmony m 3/2/43 Laura Way of Busti in B; D. Williams, Esq.
(4-3/23)
124. Allen, John R. m 1/7/44 Olive Knight in Jamestown; Rev. Dodge of Mayville
(4-1/12)
125. Allen, John W. P. m Lois Grant in Rome, NY (3-5/2/27)
126. Allen, Joseph, Jr. m 10/12/43 Julia A. Galloway in Palmyra; Rev. H. Fuller.
All of P (5-10/18)
127. Allen, Julia A., wf of Nicholas of Villanova, d in Macedon (3-5/7/28)

5

128. Allen, Juliette, wid of Elisha and mother of A. F. and D. Allen, merchants, of Jamestown d in J (With her husband "at an early period of the settlement of this county" she came from VT and remained in J) (4-10/16/39)
129. Allen, Lydia (Mrs.), 55, mother of late Lt. Commander W. H. Allen. d 1/7/23 in Hudson (3-1/22). "W. H. Allen of the U.S. Navy" (5-1/29)
130. Allen, Marvin m 11/20/36 Mary Gardner, both of Farmington, in Palmyra; Frederick Smith, Esq. (5-11/25)
131. Allen, Nathaniel (Maj.), 51, of Richmond, NY d 12/22/32 in Louisville, KY (5-1/23)
132. Allen, Peter, youngest s of Nathaniel, Esq., d in Richmond (3-5/24/26)
133. Allen, Phillip S., 39, eldest s of Stephen, Esq., d 1/4/29 in NYC (surv by wf and 3 ch of Geneva) (3-1/14)
134. Allen, Sally, 35, wf of Isaac, d 11/27/39 in Clear Creek (4-12/11)
135. Allen, Solomon M., "professor of languages in the College", d in Middlebury, VT ("His death was caused by falling from the new college edifice") (3-10/15/17)
136. Allen, Sumner (Capt.) of Poland, NY m Mrs. Harriet Evans of Westfield in W; Z. C. Young, Esq. (4-5/30/45)
137. Allen, Theophilus (Capt.), 68, d in Bristol (3-2/13/28)
138. Allen, William, city attorney, Utica, m 9/18/43 Mary P. Hallock, dau of Nicholas, at the home of William Schram in Poughkeepsie (4-9/28)
139. Allen, William E., inf s of Draper, d 2/1/35 (5-2/13)
140. Allerton, Townsend m 2/1/38 Ann Chapin in Bath; Rev. Wheeler. All of Bath (2-2/7)
141. Alley, George, merchant, m 2/4/40 Abagail Graves, dau of Charles, Esq., in Howard (2-2/5)
142. Allin, Josiah, 69, d 11/27/48 in Prattsburgh (one of the original settlers of P; for many years a trustee of Franklin Academy (2-12/20)
143. Alling, Lucy Maria, 14, youngest dau of Stephen and Amanda, d 11/2/43 in Port Gibson (5-11/8)
144. Alling, Stephen m 12/10/20 Amanda Finney; Frederick Smith, Esq. (5-12/20)
145. Alling, Talbot B., 34, d 2/12/24 in Elba (1-2/20)
146. Alling, Y. S., about 55, d 2/3/31 in Sodus (5-2/18)
147. Alma, Chauncy of Buffalo m 1/27/41 Caroline M. Morehouse of Le Roy in LR; Rev. Brown (1-2/2)
148. Alsop, Robert, 62, d 3/27/44 at his home in Williamson (5-4/3)
149. Alverson, Richard m 8/8/13 Laura Lewis in Seneca; Oren Aldrich,Esq. All of Seneca (3-8/18)
150. Alvord, Elisha of Lansingbirgh m Eliza C. Vandoren of Owasco in Utica (3-1/14/29)
151. Ament, William, Esq., 35, d in Dansville (3-3/3/19)
152. Ames, Erastus, Jr. of Cohocton, 23, killed 1/27/31 "by the fallof a tree" (2-2/2)
153. Ames, Robert B. of Livonia m Peggy Wilkin in Geneseo (3-3/29/20)
154. Ames, Zebulon, 80, d 8/4/23 in Junius (member, Meth. Episc. Ch.) (3-8/20)
155. Amidon, Lucy, 31, wf of Shepherd Amidon, d 6/18/49 in Greenwood (2-7/4)
156. Amidon S. Shepherd, Esq., formerly of Greenwood, m 7/31/50 Betsey Maria Razey of Almond in Hartsville; C. C. Purdy, Esq. (2-8/7)
157. Amsdell, William of Albany m 7/9/23 Abigail -illard? of Benton in Albany (3-7/16)
158. Amsden, _____ (Dr.), s of Simeon, d in Hopewell (3-9/13/26)
159. Amsden, Alonzo K. of Rochester m 2/19/46 Harriet Love Williams of Batavia at St. James Ch. in Batavia; Rev. James A. Bolles (1-2/24)
160. Amsden, Isaac of Seneca m Mrs. Diadama Lockwood in Canandaigua (3-7/28/13)
161. Amsden, John, Jr. m 1/23/33 Ann Parker in Palmyra; Rev. B. Hickox (5-1/30)
162. Anable, Russell, 24, late of Geneseo, d near the head of Seneca Lake (3-6/11/28)
163. Anderson, Elias, 33, bro of Mrs. D. D. Waite, d 1/1/45 in Tecumsah, MI (1-1/21)
164. Anderson, Josiah m 2/6/22 Mary Johnson in Geneva; J. Field, Esq. All of Seneca (3-2/20)
165. Anderson, Stephen, 85, formerly of Rochelle, father of Mrs. D. D. Waite, d 2/15/44 in Le Roy (1-2/20)
166. Anderson, William m 9/3/29 Lydia Wing; Rev. E. W. Martin (3-9/9)
167. Anderson, William, 58, formerly of Le Roy and bro of Mrs. D. D. Waite, d 8/7/46 in Tecumsah, MI (1-8/18)

6

168. Andrews, _____, inf ch of Jared, d 4/4/22 in Clyde (Galen) (3-4/10)
169. Andrews, Appleton, 55, d in Farmington (3-12/20/15)
170. Andrews, Charles M. L., formerly of Saratoga Springs, m 9/15/36 Leah
     Mallory in Macedon; D. Osband, Esq. All of Macedon (5-9/23)
171. Andrews, Chester of Bethel, Ont. Co. m 8/21/26 Elizabeth Stewart of
     Junius (3-8/30)
172. Andrews, Deloss m 7/3/36 Hannah Matteson in Busti; E. Davis, Esq. All of
     Busti (4-7/6)
173. Andrews, Eber m 1/9/25 Hannah Fisk in Attica; Rev. Brown (1-1/21)
174. Andrews, Elnathan, Esq., 44, d 11/23/15 in Ithaca (3-12/6)
175. Andrews, F. C., Esq. of Reading m Euphema Smith of Bath in B; Rev. Isaac
     Platt (2-6/2/41)
176. Andrews, Ichabod, 73, d 7/18/40 in North Reading (2-7/22)
177. Andrews, John, about 50, formerly of Pennsylvania, d 10/31/24 in Geneva
     (3-11/10)
178. Andrews, John T. (Maj.) m 4/2/32 Eliza Andrews, both of Reading, in R;
     H. L. Arnold, Esq. (2-4/11)
179. Andrews, Mary (Mrs.), 49, d in Canandaigua (3-2/4/18)
180. Andrews, Samuel m 11/7/22 Aleymena Leach in Lyons; Rev. Pomeroy (3-11/27)
181. Andrews, Samuel G. of Rochester m 11/30/25 Ann F. Swan in Aurora (3-12/21)
182. Androus, Alceymena E., 31, wf of Samuel, d in Lyons (3-11/25/29)
     Alceymena d 11/11/29 (5-11/27)
183. Andrus, Charles m Mary Crosby in Bristol (3-1/20/30)
184. Andrus, Patrick m Maria Goss, both of Oriskany (3-5/2/27)
185. Andrus, Warren m 9/30/23 Lorinda L. Barnes in Lyons (3-10/22)
186. Angel, Abiah m 5/1/36 Lucy Parker in Marion; F. Smith, Esq. (5-5/6)
187. Angus, Andrew, 21, s of Walter, d 4/10/28 in Benton (3-4/16)
188. Angus, John of Geneva m 9/19/27 Deborah Smalley of Palmyra in P; Rev.
     Martin (3-9/26)
189. Anis, Thomas m Sarah Bruce in Junius (3-1/21/18)
190. Annabal, Phebe, 25, wf of Caleb, d 1/3/41 in Milo (2-1/13)
191. Annin, Henry R., about 19, s of Judge Annin, d 4/16/14 in Cayuga
     (3-5/4)
192. Annin, Joseph, Esq. of Cayuga, 47, d 6/3/15 in Onondaga (3-6/14)
193. Annin, Joseph m 11/27/17 Sally Waddum in Phelps; Rev. Moser (3-12/10)
194. Annin, Matilda, 13, dau of Hon. Joseph, d 10/11/13 in Cayuga
     (3-10/20)
195. Annis, S., wf of Joseph, Esq., d 3/9/12 in Cayuga (3-3/18)
196. Ansberger, Jacob m Harriet Hoxter, both of Fayette; Rev. Lane (3-6/6/27)
197. Ansley, Adam m 3/27/11 Betsey Naggs near Geneva; Rev. Wilson (3-4/3)
198. Ansley, Albert m 2/28/22 Prudence Clark in Seneca; Anthony Gage, Esq.
     (3-3/6)
199. Ansley, William, Jr. m 3/12/29 Catharine Cromwell, dau of Benjamin, in
     Seneca; Rev. Smith of Benton (3-3/18)
200. Anthony, Charles E., 23, d 12/8/48 in Bath (2-12/13)
201. Antis, Eliza, 11, dau of William, d in Canandaigua (3-12/23/18)
202. Antis, Mary, 20, dau of William, d 7/27/29 in Canandaigua (3-8/5 and
     5-7/31)
203. Antis, Robert m Mary Ann Gibbs in Canandaigua (3-6/6/27)
204. Applegate, John, Esq., 48, d "in Enfield near Ithaca" (3-12/28/25)
205. Applegate, William F. m 12/20/31 Elizabeth Gardner, both of Macedon,
     in Palmyra; F. Smith, Esq. (5-12/27)
206. Archer, Thomas L. of Rochester m Laura Lacy of Chili, NY in C (3-1/14/29)
207. Arden, Mary (Mrs.), 91, d in NYC (3-2/26/17)
208. Armington, Emily, inf dau of Henry and Aurelia, d 8/23/40 in Palmyra
     (5-8/26)
209. Arms, Israel m 5/15/20 Sally Axtell in Sodus (3-5/24)
210. Armstrong, _____, ch of Mr. Armstrong, d "in the Canandaigua Lake"
     (3-8/23/15)
211. Armstrong, _____, 3 yrs, dau of Francis, d in Geneseo (3-5/2/27)
212. Armstrong, Ackerson of Pulteney m 11/18/41 Eliza Wheeler, dau of the Hon.
     Grattan H. Wheeler, in Wheeler; Rev. Gaylord (2-12/1)
213. Armstrong, Alida, wf of Gen. John A., late Secretary of War, d 12/24/22
     in Red Hook (5-1/29/23)
213a. Armstrong, James A. m 1/23/23 Nancy McPherson in Seneca; Rev. Axtell
     (3-1/29)

7

214. Armstrong, John m 3/9/17 Mary Barrow, both of Seneca (3-3/12)
215. Armstrong, John of Seneca m Sarah Embree of Milo in M; Rev. Axtell
    (3-1/2/22)
216. Armstrong, M. V. of Stafford m 2/7/50 Betsey A. Owen of Attica; Rev.
    Morgan (1-8/20)
217. Armstrong, Mahala, wf of M. V., d 4/14/49 in Stafford (1-4/17)(d age 36)
218. Armstrong, Matthew m Sally Sherman; Elisha Slocum, Esq. (5-11/28/17)
219. Armstrong, Nathan m Polly Deusenbery in Cohocton (3-12/22/19)
220. Armstrong, Robert d 10/4/10 in Pulteneyville (3-10/10)
221. Arnold, Alanson m 9/10/20 Betsey Clark in Farmington; Rev. Chaise
    (5-9/13)
222. Arnold, Alonzo W. m 12/30/41 Eunice B. Lord, both of Ellery in Jamestown;
    George W. Parker, Esq. (4-1/6)
223. Arnold, Benjamin d 1/12/16 in Homer ("instantaneously killed inthe act of
    felling a tree") (3-1/31)
224. Arnold, Caroline, 14, dau of Isaac, d in Macedon (3-8/6/28)
225. Arnold, George G. m Charlotte Crafts in Middlesex (3-11/28/27)
226. Arnold, Henry C. m 3/26/33 Eliza Knight in Jamestown; Rev. Gillet (4-4/3)
227. Arnold, Isaac N., attorney, of Chicago, IL m 8/ 4/41 Harriet Augusta
    Dorrance, dau of the late Dr. Trumbull Dorrance of Pittsfield, MA,
    in Batavia; Rev. James A. Bolles, pastor of St. James Episc. Ch. (1/8/10)
228. Arnold, Israel (Capt.) of Middlesex m 11/7/13 Penelope Brown, dau of
    Benjamin, of Benton in B; George Green, Esq. (3-11/10)
229. Arnold, Joseph S. m 5/21/43 Mary Phillips in Ellery; Rev. H. Smith. All
    of E (4-5/25)
230. Arnold, Kezia, 51, wf of Charles, formerly of Fairfield, Herk. Co., d 9/8/33
    in Chautauqua (4-9/18)
231. Arnold, Loring, 21, hatter, d in Penn Yan (3-1/20/30)
232. Arnold, Lyman of Avoca m 1/8/50 Mary Jane McNeil of Wheeler in W; Rev.
    H. Spencer (2-1/23)
233. Arnold, Reynolds of Jamestown m 1/3/39 Sarah Ann Cole of Hamburgh, Erie
    Co., in H; William Hamilton, Esq. (4-1/16)
234. Arnold, Richard m 9/19/32 Minerva Knight in Jamestown; Rev. Gillet (4-9/26)
235. Arnold, Stephen d "lately" in the State Prison in NYC ("the subject of
    much newspaper and legislative discussion") (3-1/1/12)
236. Arnott, _____ (Mr.) of Panama, NY m 5/27/41 Mrs. Nancy Hazard in
    Jamestown; Rev. Gillett (4-6/2)
237. Arrowsmith, Sidney of Monroe Co. m 9/20/41 Lucinda Cady of Cohocton in C;
    Rev. James Brownson (2-11/17)
238. Arthur, William of Ellicott m 11/9/34 Polly Bostwick of Busti in B; Rufus
    Pier, Esq. (4-11/12)
239. Asbury, Francis, Senior Bishop, Meth. Episc. Church in U.S.A., d 3/31/16
    in the home of George Arnold, Esq. in Spotsylvania, VA (3-4/17)
240. Ashley, _____ (Mrs.), about 90, d 4/10/41 in Bethany (1-4/27)
241. Ashley, William F., one of the publishers of the Western Argus, m 2/19/36
    Eliza Jane Denton in Lyons; Rev. Hubbell. All of Lyons (5-3/4)
242. Ashmun, Eli P., late a senator in Congress, d 5/10/19 in Northampton, MA
    (3-6/2)
243. Asper, John m Maria Biles in Bath (3-6/27/27)
244. Aspinwall, Augustus, 21, M.D., d in Genoa, NY (3-3/12/28)
245. Aspinwall, Gilbert, Esq., merchant, d in NYC (3-10/6/19)
246. Astor, William R., son of John Jacob, Esq., m 5/20/18 Margaret Armstrong,
    dau of Gen. Armstrong, in the home of the latter; Rev. McMurray (3-6/10)
247. Atkins, Christopher m 2/4/29 Martha Townsend in Ithaca (3-2/25)
248. Atkins, Elisha T. m Margaret M. Marther in Bath (3-9/9/29)
249. Atkinson, _____ (Brevet Brig. Gen.) d 7/11/42 at Jefferson Barracks near
    St. Louis (2-7/20)
250. Atwater, Amos A. m Julia Bartholomew in Williamson (5-8/25/18)
251. Atwater, Jeremiah (Dr.) of New Haven, CT m Maria Thompson of Scituate, MA
    in New Haven (3-7/6/14)
252. Atwater, Thomas of Sodus m 3/2/31 Harriet Conner of Williamson in W;
    Rev. Allen (5-3/11)
253. Atwell, Elisha B., 29, d in Waterloo (3-10/8/28)
254. Atwell, Joseph m Phoebe Moe in Lima (3-3/29/20)
255. Atwell, Michael m Wealthy Stoddard in Gaines, Orl. Co. (3-11/30/25)

8

256. Atwood, Alvah J. m 2/28/36 Mary Northrup, dau of R. K., Esq., in
     Ontario, NY; William A. Fuller, Esq. All of O (5-3/4)
257. Aulls, Ephraim m 10/13/50 Mary Bryant in Bath; Rev. Wright. All of Bath
     (2-10/16)
258. Aumick, John m Jane Gillis in Ovid (3-7/21/19)
259. Austin, Benjamin, 68, d 5/4/20 in Boston (presumably NY) (3-5/24)
260. Austin, Jemima, 30, wf of Francis, late of Queensbury, Warren Co., d in
     North Junius (3-11/5/28)
261. Austin, Zebell, 30, dau of William, d 10/25/30 in Newark, NY (5-11/12/30)
262. Auten, Catharine (Mr.) (sic) d in Dresden (3-5/20/29)
263. Averell, Elisha (Gen.) d 8/21/21 in Manchester (buried with Masonic honors)
     (5-8/22)
264. Averill, John R. m Clarissa Palmer in Farmington; Joshua Van Fleet, Esq.
     (5-6/6/21)
265. Averill, Marilla, 51, wf of Gideon of Davenport, IA, d 8/16/43 in
     Sinclairville, NY (4-8/31)
266. Avery, Alfred of Ledyard m 1/28/34 Mary Jane Underhill of Genoa, Cay. Co.,
     in G (5-2/7)
267. Avery, Caleb m Abigail Cole in Palmyra (5-6/14/20)
268. Avery, Daniel, Esq., 56, "candidate for senator", m Freelove Mitchell, 16,
     in Aurora (3-10/29/23)
269. Avery, Henry K., merchant, m 3/4/23 Eliza L. Adams, both of Lyons, in L;
     Rev. Brace (3-3/19)
270. Avery, Parthenia, 43, wf of Cyrus, formerly of Wethersfield, CT, d 9/12/30
     in Lyons (5-9/24)
271. Avery, Sylvanus, 17, d 6/15/17 in Phelps ("drowned in Dickinson's mill
     pond") (3-7/9)
272. Avery, Thomas., 15, d in Groton "from eating wild cherries which had been
     in rum and cider" (3-11/22/15)
273. Axtell, Daniel m Sally Axtell, both of Friendship, Alleg. Co., in F
     (3-10/29/28)
274. Axtell, Henry (Maj.), 80, d 4/6/18 in Mendham, NJ (3-4/22)
275. Axtell, Henry, 55,.D.D., d 2/11/29 in Geneva. His oldest dau, Rebecca,
     age 30, d 2/14. Both were buried in the same grave. (He b in
     Mendham, NJ in 1773; grad from Princeton in 1796; settled in Geneva,
     NY by 1804. Co-pastor of Presby. Ch. with Rev. Jedediah Chapman in
     1812. On death of latter in 1813 Dr. Axtell became sole pastor)
     (3-2/18 and 5-2/20)
276. Axtell, John m Sally Bennet in Geneva; Rev. Orin Clark (3-9/8/19)
277. Axtell, Martha, 36, wf of Hiram,d in Canandaigua (3-11/12/28)
278. Axtell, Phebe, 89, relict of late Maj. Henry and mother of late Rev. Henry,
     d 7/6/29 "near Seneca" ("She was a.subject of the religious revival in
     Morris Town (N.J.) in ... 1764") (3-7/22)
279. Axtell, Phoebe Ann C., 16, second dau of Rev. Henry, d 4/6/22 in Geneva
     (3-4/10). She d 4/5 (5-4/17)
280. Axtell, Silas (Col.), 54, of Mendham, NJ, bro of Henry of Geneva, NY,
     d 9/29/23 in Zanesville, Ohio while on a trip with his wife to visit
     a son living near Columbus, Ohio (3-11/12)
281. Ayers, John m 2/16/15 Polly Cowing in Seneca; Rev. Axtell (3-2/22)
282. Aylsworth, John R., 17, s of Levi D., d in Phelps (3-11/28/27)
283. Ayrault, Lyman m Eunice H. Mills, formerly of Canandaigua, in Pike, Alleg.
     Co. (3-4/2/23)
284. Ayres, John m 7/4/29 Kazia Clark in Palmyra; Rev. Gear (3-7/15 and 5-7/10)
285. Ayres, Lewis of Ithaca m 11/2/24 Rebecca Osborn of Geneva in G; Rev. Dr.
     Axtell (3-11/10)
286. Ayres, Peter m Harriet Capell, both of Milo, in Benton (3-4/8/29)
287. Ayres, Samuel, Esq., 59, d at his home in Mason Co., VA (lived many years
     in Chaut. Co., NY; surv by wf and ch) (4-10/28/29)
288. Babbet, Anna, 26, wf of "Mr. Babbet", d 3/23/22 (3-3/27)
289. Babbit, Elias, 3 yrs, s of John, d 4/3/22 in Geneva (3-4/10). Elias age 6
     at time of death (5-4/17)
290. Babbit, Roswell, Esq., 32, d 5/15/22 in Saratoga (3-6/5)
291. Babbit, Sally, 63, wf of Isaac, formerly of Barre, MA, d in Busti, NY
     (4-3/29/44)
292. Babbit, Simon, 18, m 12/18/17 Polly Savage, 16, children (sic) of
     Nathaniel and Olive Babbit; Rev. R. Fairbanks (3-1/7/18 and 5-12/24/17)

9

293. Babbitt, Jacob, Jr., 38, d 10/11/30 in Alabama, NY (formerly of Irasburg, Orleans Co., VT) (1-10/22)
294. Babbitt, Roswell, Esq. m Pamelia Stephens, both of Rochester, in Lowville (5-3/31/18)
295. Babbitt, Roswell, Esq. of Rochester d 5/18/22 in Ballston Springs (age blurred: either 50 or 80) (1-5/31)
Babcock. See Bobcock also.
296. Babcock, Asa (Capt.) m 8/16/24 Mercy Adams; Charles Woodworth, Esq. All of Elba (1-8/20)
297. Babcock, Barber of Jamestown drowned 1/3/33 while trying to cross the lake on ice at Fluvanna (4-1/9)
298. Babcock, Benjamin d 5/11/19 in Lyons (3-5/19)
299. Babcock, Brayton (Dr.) of Scottsville m Eunice Smith of Avoca at the Meth. Episc. Church in A; Rev. N. Hoag (2-9/9/40)
300. Babcock, Dennis m 9/10/48 Dorcas Pease; Elder M. Colman. All of Elba (1-9/12)
301. Babcock, James m 10/23/47 Catharine Van Gelder; Rev. L. Merril Miller. All of Bath (2-10/27)
302. Babcock, Jared R. m 9/23/45 Adelia H. Mann, dau of David, Esq., in Westfield; Rev. T. P. Tyler of Fredonia (4-10/3)
303. Babcock, John C. m 8/5/41 Celestia Benham in Penn Yan; Rev. O. Miner (4-8/19)
304. Babcock, Lavina, 19, dau of Henry, d 11/19/41 in Busti (4-12/2)
305. Babcock, Lucy, wf of Capt. Asa, d 6/15/24 in Elba (1-6/18)
306. Babcock, Phebe, 41, wf of Samuel, d 3/26/27 in Geneva (3-3/28)
307. Babcock, Samuel d 2/20/27 in Geneva (3-2/21)
308. Babcock, Sarah (Mrs.), 63, d in Caton (2-10/13/41)
309. Babcock, William, Esq., merchant, m 11/13/24 Mary Tuell, both of Penn Yan in P Y; Joel Dorman, Esq. (3-11/24)
310. Babcock, William, Esq., about 50, d 10/20/38 in Penn Yan (2-10/24)
311. Bachman, George m 1/20/25 Sally Hendricks, both of Fayette; Rev. Lane (3-2/2)
312. Bachman, Henry, 23, d 11/21/32 in Pulteney (2-11/28)
313. Bachman, Jacob m Hannah Susanna Sine Jolly in Fayette (3-9/3/28)
314. Bachman, William m Hannah Huff in Fayette (3-1/16/28)
315. Bachus, Namon S. of Groton, Tompkins Co., m 12/17/39 Hannah A. Spear, dau of Deacon Stephen of Macedon, in M; Rev. A. W. Stowell (5-12/20)
316. Backenstose, Frederick, 44, d 3/14/16 in Geneva "having resided in it 21 years" (3-3/20)
317. Backenstose, George, 45, bro to Joseph of Geneva, d in Fort Hawkins, GA (3-1/5/20)
318. Backenstose, Jacob, 44, d 3/4/13 (a resident of Geneva; surv by wf and 11 small ch) (3-3/10)
319. Backenstose, James Carter, 9 mo, s of Henry, d 9/3/27 in Geneva (3-9/5)
Backus. See Bockus also.
320. Backus, Albert, 21, of Rochester, NY, second s of late Dr. Azul Backus, pres. of Hamilton College, d 2/24/19 in Montpelier, France (3-6/9)
321. Backus, Azel (Rev.), D.D., 50, pres. of Hamilton College in Oneeida Co., d 12/26/16 (3-1/8/17)
322. Backus, Frederick F. (Dr.) of Rochester m Rebecca Fitzhugh, dau of Col. F., in Williamsburgh (3-11/11/18)
323. Backus, John of Newark, NY m 10/9/38 Theodosia Patterson of Painted Post; Rev. Hotchkin (2-10/17)
324. Backus, Timothy, about 55, d 5/16/45 in Lockport (formerly of Batavia) (1-5/20)
325. Backus, William W., merchant, m 6/20/27 Mary Ann Ainsworth in Utica (3-7/11)
326. Bacon, _____, 1 yr, ch of Horace, d 10/29/38 in Jamestown (4-10/31)
327. Bacon, Asa, 75, of Junius, Sen. Co., d 9/6/18 in New Lebanon, Columbia Co. (3-9/16)
328. Bacon, Edward m Eliza McBurney, dau of Judge McBurney, in Bath (3-11/17/19)
329. Bacon, Isaac M. of Bigflat, Chemung Co., m 12/11/45 Emily A. Gardner of Corning at the Corning Hotel in C; Rev. Dr. Graves (See also marr. of Asher Barnard this date) (2-12/17)
330. Bacon, J. W., Esq., attorney, of Waterloo m 12/16/21 Mrs. M. C. Smith, dau of Lewis B. Sturges, Esq. of Auburn, in Auburn (3-1/16/22)

331. Bacon, James, 22 or 32?, d 10/10/20 in Palmyra (5-10/11)
332. Bacon, Joseph m Laura Case in Canandaigua (3-10/1/17)
333. Bacon, Ruth Amy, 15, dau of Noah, d 4/10/41 in Bath (2-4/14)
334. Bacon, Truman m 3/10/25 Mrs. Martha Harmon in Pembroke (1-3/18)
335. Bacon, William m Virginia S. Thornton in Bath (3-12/25/22)
336. Badgeley, Albert m Mary Kimball in Harmony; D. Williams, Esq. (4-8/31/43)
337. Badgeley, Ichabod, 23, of Geneva d 5/4/27 in Phelps (3-5/9)
338. Badger, Almond m 12/1/33 Elizabeth Dolloff, both of Poland, NY, in P;
    Rev. W. R. Babcock (4-12/4)
339. Badger, Harvey of Elmira m 9/20/41 Louisa Potter, dau of Hiram, sheriff
    of Steuben Co., in Bath; Rev. Frazer (2-10/6)
340. Bagnell, William (Capt.), 37, d in Cohocton (3-9/10/28)
341. Bailey, Erastus, 56, d 7/20/49 in York, Livingston Co. (1-7/31)
342. Bailey, James m Jerusha Cooley in Milo (3-7/21/19)
343. Bailey, Lewis m 6/7/45 Delia Hollenback of Wayne in W; Rev. Mallory. All
    of Wayne (2-7/2)
344. Bailey, Reuben, 42, m 4/26/18 Hildah Barritt, 29, in Penfield "after a
    long and tedious courtship" (5-5/19)
345. Bailey, S. Joseph of Dover, MI m 10/28/41 Celinda Reeves, dau of Luther
    of Palmyra, in P (5-11/10)
346. Baily, Martin m 1/22/26 Margaret Banker in Hector (3-2/8)
347. Baily, Richard, 11 mo, s of Thomas and Lorinda, d 2/6/50 in Bath (2-2/13)
348. Baily, Wright m 1/19/41 Margaret Bowdoin, both of Tyrone, in T; Elder
    Ketchum of Barrington (2-1/27)
349. Bainbridge, Joseph (Capt.) of U. S. Navy d 11/17/24 in NYC (3-12/1)
350. Bainbridge, Mahlon of Romulus m 6/16/29 Roenna Burnett of Phelps in P;
    Rev. A. D. Lane of Waterloo (3-6/24)
351. Baker, A. H., merchant, of Panama, NY m 11/28/39 Hannah Wiltsie, only
    dau of Capt. Thomas, in Harmony; Rev. Cross (4-12/4)
352. Baker, Andrew m Armenia Graves in Howard (3-4/1/29)
353. Baker, Anna, inf dau of Maj. Henry, d 9/4/29 in Jamestown (4-9/9)
354. Baker, Armenia, 27, consort of Andrew, Jr., d 8/30/35 in Howard (2-9/9)
355. Baker, B. Franklin of Republic, Ohio m 10/12/47 Mary Brundage, dau of
    William of Urbana, in U; Rev. L. W. Russ (2-10/13)
356. Baker, C. Steele (Rev.) of the Genesee Conference, m 4/14/47 C. Lasira
    Hall of Buffalo in Wales, NY; Rev. H. N. Seaver (1-4/20)
357. Baker, Caleb of Canisteo m 11/13/42 Emeline Stephens of Greenwood in G;
    E. Stephens, Esq. (2-11/23)
358. Baker, Calvin of Oakfield m 10/22/45 Mrs. Ann Scofield of NYC in NYC
    (1-11/4)
359. Baker, David J., Esq. of West Bloomfield m 10/9/19 Sarah T. Fairchild of
    Waterloo in W; Rev. Axtell (3-10/20)
360. Baker, Ebenezer of Hammondsport m 9/6/40 Harriet Tyler of Pulteney in P;
    John Gload, Esq. (2-9/16)
361. Baker, Ebenezer C. m Marcia B. Stafford in Lansingburgh (3-1/21/29)
362. Baker, Edy m 12/30/41 Lilly Bump in Cameron; J. K. Ketcham, Esq. (2-1/5)
363. Baker, Hannah, 24, wf of James, d 5/18/32 in Palmyra (5-5/23)
364. Baker, Hiram of Bellevue, Ohio m 7/17/36 Catharine Hagaman of Macedon in M;
    Rev. Miner (5-8/19)
365. Baker, James W. of Norwalk, Ohio m 8/7/43 Arathusa D. Berry of Fredonia
    in F; Rev. E. Loomis (4-8/10)
366. Baker, Joseph, 72, a Rev. soldier and father of Roswell, d 9/5/26 in
    Phelps (3-9/13)
367. Baker, Joseph of Wheeler m 4/3/32 Susannah Buskirk of Cohocton in C;
    Abraham I. Quackenbush, Esq. (2-4/11)
368. Baker, Lyman W. m 2/11/30 Asenith Warner in Manchester; David Howland, Esq.
    (5-2/19)
369. Baker, Mariah (Miss), 23, formerly of Palmyra, d 12/12/29 in Manlius,
    Onon. Co. (3-12/30 and 5-12/25)
370. Baker, Norman C. of Lenawee Co., Mich. Terr. m Harriet Robinson of
    Northville, Wayne Co., M. T., (both formerly of Manchester, NY) in
    Northville (5-2/5/36)
371. Baker, Samuel m Catharine Hammond in Bath (3-9/2/18)
372. Baker, Sargent, 83 (a Rev. soldier) killed by lightning 6/24/28 in his
    house in Hector (member of Meth. Episc. Ch.) (3-7/2)

11

373. Baker, Seneca m Phoebe Smith in Elmira (3-1/29/17)
374. Baker, Sophia (Miss), 25, d in Canandaigua (3-2/10/19)
375. Balcom, Jesse of Palmyra m 9/15/36 Martha Ann Reed of Farmington in F;
     Rev. Hall of Victor (See marr. of William Balcom this date) (5-9/23)
376. Balcom, Uriah of Erwin m 9/8/40 Jane Besley, dau of Samuel, Esq, in
     Campbell; Rev. Smith (2-9/16)
377. Balcom, William of Palmyra m 9/15/36 Rhoda Reed of Farmington in F;
     Rev. Hall of Victor (See marr. of Jesse Balcom this date) (5-9/23)
378. Baldwin, Abigail, 59, wf of Benjamin, formerly of Windham, Greene Co.,
     d 12/29/40 in Dexterville (4-1/6/41)
379. Baldwin, C. C., Esq. of Worcester, MA, "librarian of the Antiquarian Soc.
     was killed a few days since while travelling in Ohio, by the upsetting
     of a stage coach. His travelling companion, Isaac Southgate, Esq. of
     Leicester (MA?) was badly injured." (2-9/16/35)
380. Baldwin, David m 1/28/45 Jane L. Tracy in Sinclairville (Both of S.)
     (4-2/7)
381. Baldwin, Grant B. m 3/7/16 Myrilla Sayre, dau of James, in Elmira
     (3-3/13)
382. Baldwin, Grant B., Esq., 48, d 1/25/40 in Elmira (formerly first judge
     of the Tioga Co. courts, postmaster of Elmira, and state assemblyman)
     (2-2/5)
383. Baldwin Guy m Polly Chase in Milo (3-11/25/29)
384. Baldwin, Hannah, 37, wf of Augustin U., d 6/14/41 in Westfield, Chaut. Co.
     (1-6/22)
385. Baldwin, Isaac (Maj.) m 11/27/12 Mrs. McDowell; Jacob Keefe, Esq.
     (3-12/9)
386. Baldwin, Isaac (Col.), 51, d 11/23/15 in Elmira (3-12/6)
387. Baldwin, Isaac, merchant, m 1/25/16 Alice Dunn in Elmira; Rev. Simeon R.
     Jones. All of Elmira (3-1/31)
388. Baldwin, Isaac, Esq., 65, d 12/22/18 at his home in Pompey, NY (3-1/27/19)
389. Baldwin, J. Davis of Elmira m 11/10/46 Elizabeth T. Maxwell, dau of
     S. H., Esq. of Corning, in C; Rev. W. Van Zandt (2-11/18)
390. Baldwin, James M., 21, midshipman, U. S. Navy, d "lately" in NYC "from
     wounds received on Lake Champlain on the memorable 11th of September."
     (3-8/16/15)
391. Baldwin, John, Esq. of Moscow, NY m Pamela Sage in Geneseo (3-12/27/15)
392. Baldwin, Jonas C. (Dr.), 58, d in Onondaga (3-3/28/27)
393. Baldwin, Lathrop m Sally Griswold in Elmira (3-11/12/17)
394. Baldwin, Mary, 29, wf of Alfred, d in Benton (3-6/24/29)
395. Baldwin, Silas m 3/22/27 Zemanda Stull in Southport (3-4/25)
396. Baldwin, Thomas P., Esq., attorney, of Palmyra m 10/8/18 Mrs. Eleanor
     Cuyler formerly of Phelps in Phelps; Rev. Townsend (3-10/14 and
     5-10/13)
397. Baldwin, William m 4/20/34 Jane N. Dutcher, both of Jamestown, in J;
     Rev. Colman (4-4/23)
398. Baldwin, William J. m 10/22/40 Catharine Dow in Bath; Rev. Wing. All
     of Bath (2-10/28)
399. Ball, Aaron, 63, d 12/10/44 in Prattsburgh (2-12/18)
400. Ball, Adaline M., 39, wf of Calvin S., d 8/24/49 in Pompey, Onon. Co.
     (1-9/4)
401. Ball, Benjamin m 11/12/35 Eunice Burge in Wayne; Rev. George E. Delavan
     (2-11/25)
402. Ball, Gideon, Sr., 66 (a Rev. soldier) d 11/27/26 in Seneca (3-11/29)
403. Ball, John m 8/10/50 Nancy Stacey, both of Batavia; Rev. J. K. Cheesman
     (1-8/13)
404. Ball or Bull?, Walter m 7/20/29 Mary Scott in Benton; S. G. Gage, Esq.
     (3-8/19)
405. Ballard, Alpheus R. m 2/17/50 Emeline Cooper, both of Wheeler, in Bath;
     Rev. B. R. Swick (2-2/27)
406. Ballard, Elizabeth (Miss), 17, d 4/28/28 in Seneca (3-5/28)
407. Ballard, Franklin m 8/3/23 Ann Lewis in Geneva; R. Hogarth, Esq. All
     of Seneca (3-8/6)
408. Ballard, Jane, 13 mo, only child of James, d (date and place of death
     lacking) (1-3/10/26)
409. Ballentine, William of Monroe Co., m 12/31/29 Mary R. McAuley of
     Seneca (3-1/20/30)

410. Baltze, Louis m 7/11/30 Mathalane Shuler in Lyons; William Voorhies, Esq.
(5-7/16)                                                    (3-1/6/30)
411. Bamborough, William m 12/31/29 Elizabeth Coleman in Benton; Rev. Smith ∧
412. Bancker, Henry S. m 8/10/26 Maria Saibley in Canandaigua (3-8/23)
413. Bancroft, B. B. m 4/25/29 Penelope Green, both of Seneca, in Junius;
James Scott, Esq. (3-4/29)
414. Bancroft, Laura, consort of Willard, d 5/4/23 in Sodus (3-5/28)
415. Bancroft, Mary, 49, consort of Thadeus, d 9/15/13 in Sodus ("a mother")
3-9/29)
416. Bancroft, Thomas, Esq. m 1/1/23 "Mrs. Merill" in Ontario, NY (5-1/22)
417. Bancroft, Willard m 12/5/22 Laura Smith in Sodus (3-12/25)
418. Banister, Harwood m 6/21/12 Elsy Boyd in Phelps; William Barnet, Esq.
(3-6/24)
419. Banks, Daniel (Rev.), pastor of Presby. Ch. of Potsdam, d in P (3-9/19/27)
420. Bannister, Christopher m 11/24/29 Rebecca Simmons, dau of Capt. A., in
Phelps (3-12/2)
421. Bannister, Theodore (Col.), 42?, d 9/23/18 in Phelps ("interred with
military and masonic honors")  (3-9/30 and 5-10/6)
422. Banyar, Goldsbrow, Esq., 90, d 11/11/15 in Albany (3-11/29)
423. Barber, ____ (Mr.), 84, d in Penn Yan (3-3/1/26)
424. Barber, Asa m 10/2/28 Abbey Cowles, both of Geneva; Rev. Dr. Axtell
(3-10/8)
425. Barber, Hannah (Mrs.), 48, d 1/31/22 in Middlesex (3-2/13)
426. Barber, Ira of Middlesex m Lydia Belknap in Benton (3-1/6/30)
427. Barber, John, Sr., 82, d 6/24/40 in Adrian (a Rev. soldier; "member of
a Congregational or Presbyterian church for more than 50 yrs.")
(5-7/15)
428. Barber, Jonathan m 11/16/45 Adaline Burns of Cameron in C; Elder D.
Smith (2-11/26)
429. Barber, Lemuel, 79, d in Naples, NY (3-2/3/19)     late
430. Barber, Phoebe (Miss), 17, d 11/7/22 in the home of /Judge Nicholas near
Geneva (3-11/20)
431. Barber, Robert, 41, printer, d 5/31/12 in Albany (3-6/24)
432. Barber, William, 18, m 2/1/22 Betsey Boyle, 45, (prob. in Scipio) (5-2/13)
433. Barclay, Peter m Hannah Henry in Junius (3-7/9/28)
434. Barcley, Barton m Clarissa Tilden in Lyons (3-4/23/28)
435. Bardin, Nathan, 96, /of Bloomfield d 5/19/29 at the poor house in Hopewell
(3-6/3)
436. Bargow?, George, "an eminent mathematician born in England but for many
years a resident of New York City", d 6/18/12 in NYC (3-8/5)
437. Baright, Stephen m Matilda R. Woodruff in Ithaca (3-9/19/27)
438. Barker, ____ (Mrs.), wf of William, d 10/21/18 in Geneva (3-10/28)
439. Barker, Abiel m Roxana Rush in Olean (3-4/14/19)
440. Barker, Alden (Capt.) of Rochester m 12/29/36 Mrs. Fidelia Barnhart, dau
Aretus Lapham of Palmyra in P; Frederick Smith, Esq. (5-12/30)
441. Barker, Cecilia Ann, 9, only ch of L. Barker, d in Rochester (1-4/27/41)
442. Barker, Comfort T. d in Auburn (3-10/6/19)
443. Barker, James A. m Rebecca Rogers in Waterloo (3-8/15/27)
444. Barker, Josiah of Phelps m 8/14/22 Betsey McInstry of Junius in
Montezuma; Rev. Elisha House (3-8/21)
445. Barker, Lucinda, 28, wf of Silas, d 6/7/18 in Penfield (surv by husband
and 5 small ch; "Editors of the Pittsfield (MA) and Berkshire Star
are requested to publish the above (5-6/30)
446. Barker, Samuel m Elizabeth Kenny, both of Romulus, in Fayette (3-9/17/28)
447. Barker, Phineas of Jamestown m Orinda Blanchar (sic) of Ellery in E
(4-3/2/31)
448. Barker, Phineas of Jamestown m 1/4/38 Harriet Blanchard of Ellery in E;
William H. Fenton, Esq. (4-1/10)
449. Barker, Samuel Augustus (Gen.), 64, d 11/19/19 in Beekman, Dutchess Co.
(a Rev. soldier and, later, a member of the legislature) (3-12/8)
450. Barker, Samuel S. m 12/8/31 Mary Ann Eggleston in Palmyra; Rev. E.
Blakesley (5-12/13)
451. Barker, Sarah, 23, wf of Samuel S. and dau of Ezra Crandall, d 7/16/30
in Palmyra (5-7/23)
452. Barlow, Mary, wf of Nathan, Esq., d in Canandaigua (3-10/22/28)

13

453. Barlow, Ruth, 62, relict of late Joel, Esq., d "at Kalorama" (3-6/17/18)
454. Barlow, Shazette (sic), 14 mo, dau of Ahaz, d 2/9/32 in Jamestown
(4-2/15)
455. Barnaby, Ambrose d 1/8/29 in Fredonia (4-1/14)
456. Barnard, Abner (Dr.) of Lockport m 5/20/29 Harriet Jane Hepburn of
Perinton in Pittsford; Rev. A. Mahan (5-6/12)
457. Barnard, Albert of Buffalo m 4/28/40 Elizabeth A. Jenkins of Port Gibson
in P G; Rev. C. M. Butler (5-4/29)
458. Barnard, Asher of Corning m 12/11/45 Abigail Gardner of Newville, Steuben
Co., at the Corning Hotel in Corning; Rev. Dr. Graves (See also marr.
of Isaac M. Bacon this date) (2-12/17)
459. Barnard, D. D. (Hon.) of Rochester m 11/15/32 Catharine Walsh, dau of late
Dudley, Esq. of Albany, in Albany (5-11/28)
460. Barnard, Eliza, 5, dau of Foster, d 11/18/19 in Geneva (3-12/1)
461. Barnard, Ebenezer S. m Elizabeth B. Copps in Vienna (3-7/30/28)
462. Barnard, Evelina, 22,dau of Foster, d 9/18/22 in Geneva (3-9/25)
463. Barnard, Foster, Jr. m 6/19/17 Maria Hall in Geneva; Rev. Axtell (3-6/25)
464. Barnard, Hannah, 70, a celebrated preacher in the Society of Friends,
d 11/26/25 in Hudson (3-12/7)
465. Barnard, Samuel (Dr.), 50, d 9/4/15 in Sodus (3-9/13)
466. Barne, Claudius Victorius Boughton m 9/7/41 Mary Helen Wade in Franklinville; Rev. W. C. Gillam. All of F (5-9/29)
467. Barnes, Chauncy of West Bloomfield m 6/7/18 Lydia Fairchild of Geneva
in G; Rev. Axtell (3-6/10)
468. Barnes, David (Rev.), 80, d 4/26/11 in Scituate, ME in the 57th year of
his ministry there (3-6/26)
469. Barnes, David m 2/6/23 Olive Spencer, dau of Capt. Truman Spencer, in
Benton; Rev. Axtell (3-2/12)
470. Barnes, Eben m Mary Hinds in Palmyra; William N. McLean, Esq. (5-2/12/23)
471. Barnes, Edmund (Dr.), 54, d 11/10/30 in Le Roy (1-11/12)
472. Barnes, James, Jr. of Seneca m 10/16/17 Laura Spencer, dau of Capt.
Truman Spencer of Benton, in B; Rev. White (3-10/22)
473. Barnes, James, Sr., 76, d 10/7/27 in Seneca ("a native of Ireland and
for many years ... a member of the Associate Reformed Church.")
(3-10/17)
474. Barnes, Martha, 17, dau of James, d 12/12/11 in Seneca (3-12/18)
475. Barnes, Olive, 27, wf of David and dau of Capt. T. Spencer of Benton,
d 3/20/28 in Seneca (3-4/2)
476. Barnes, Roxana, 60, wf of Sherman, Esq. d 3/26/42 in Lyons (5-4/6)
477. Barnes, William, 10 yrs, only s of Joseph, d 7/19/23 in Benton (3-8/6)
478. Barney, Caroline, 10 mo, dau of Nelson, d 4/1/42 in Bath (2-4/6)
479. Barney, Ely, 35, d 9/11/09 in Geneva (3-9/13)
480. Barney, Ephraim m Ruth Holmes in Wheeler (3-6/25/28)
481. Barney, Luther, Esq., 87, d 9/30/44 in Ellery (4-10/11). Luther b 1757 in
Norwich, CT; served in navy in Rev.; taken prisoner by British;
recaptured and pressed into service by French; released "through the
personal interference of the generous and noble Lafayette"; after the
Rev. moved first to VT and then to Cayuga Co., NY where he remained
about 20 yrs prior to his move to Newstead, Erie Co.; spent last 13
yrs of life in Ellery (4-10/18)
482. Barney, Milo m 3/28/44 Laura Wilbur, both of Ellery; Rev. H. Smith (4-4/19)
483. Barney, Nathan m 4/28/35 Ann McWhortle in Avoca (2-5/6)
484. Barney, Nelson of Otsego m 8/6/35 Phylancy T. Beckwith of Bath in B;
Rev. Platt (2-9/16)
485. Barney, Nicholas m Lucy Osborn in Canandaigua (3-10/28/18)
486. Barney, Philance T., 35, wf of Nelson, d 10/5/50 in Bath (2-10/9)
487. Barney, Samuel m Eliza Bemus, dau of Thomas, Esq., in Harmony (4-2/7/27)
488. Barney, Thomas H. of Wheeler m 1/8/45 Lucy Rice, dau of Oliver, Esq. of
Avoca in A; Elder Tuttle (2-1/15)
489. Barney, Vincent G. of Rushville m Nancy Connet in Moravia (3-3/3/24)
490. Barnhart, Christian, 57, d 1/13/35 in Palmyra (5-1/16)
491. Barnhart, Euphanie, 47, wf of Christian, d 2/19/23 in Palmyra (5-2/26)
492. Barnhart, Isaac of Macedon m 8/21/43 Mrs. Ann Wooster of Ontario, NY in O
(5-8/30)
493. Barnhart, Job of Macedon m 7/9/34 Fidelia Lapham, dau of Aretus, in
Palmyra; F Smith, Esq. (5-7/11)

494. Barnhart, Job, 22, formerly of Macedon, d 8/22/35 in Cold Water, MI
(5-9/18)
495. Barns, Ann, 20, wf of Eben, d 4/9/22 in Palmyra (5-4/10)
496. Barns, Eben m 1/16/22 Ann Boyle, both of Palmyra, in P (5-1/23)
497. Barns, H. (Rev.) of the Meth. Church m Martha Moore in Ithaca (3-7/4/27)
498. Barns, John F. of Perry m 1/20/33 Clarissa Camp of Jamestown in Ellicott;
R. Pier, Esq. (4-1/23)
499. Barns, Nathaniel, 40, d 3/20/33 in Ashville (4-3/27)
500. Barns, Orris m 1/12/39 Amanda Burlingham in Ashville; L. Lakin, Esq.
(4-1/30)
501. Barns, Rachel, 88, relict of Ebenezer, d 3/15/18 in Blanford, MA  (3-4/15)
502. Barnum, _____, inf ch of Thomas P., d 5/30/29 in Canandaigua (5-6/12)
503. Barnum, Harriet Augusta, 26, wf of Philo B., d 7/11/35 in Auburn (5-7/24)
504. Barnum, Lucy, 63, consortof Isaac, d 6/29/42 in Prattsburgh (member of
Baptist Church (2-7/6)
505. Barnum, Philo B., publisher of the Gospel Messenger, m 9/2/30 Augusta
Foster of Auburn in A; Rev. Dr. Rudd (5-9/17)
506. Barnum, Thomas B., Esq., late editor of the Erie Observer and formerly
of the Ontario Freeman, d in Farmington, Mich. Terr. (5-8/15/32)
507. Barr, John m 1/5/22 Abigail Jones, both of Manchester in M; Peter
Mitchell, Esq. (5-1/23)
508. Barr, John W., 20, d 2/9/26 in Elba (1-3/10)
509. Barret, Harriet, 30, wf of Cornelius, d 12/8/48 (prob. in Bath) (2-12/13)
510. Barret, Moses, physician, of Charlemont, MA m 11/26/39 Fanny A. White,
late principal of the Female Dept. of Palmyra High School in Palmyra;
Rev. Shumway (5-12/13)
511. Barrett, _____, inf ch of Maj. Samuel, d in Jamestown (4-7/5/26)
512. Barrett, Harris, 30, d 8/28/30 in Lyons (5-9/3)
513. Barrett, Henry of the firm of Barrett, Baker & Co. of Jamestown d 1/9/36
in Havana, Cuba where he had gone for his health.  En route from
Charleston, SC to Havana he had been weakened still farther "by the
fatigues of a perilous shipwreck." (4-2/24)
514. Barrett, Lucy (Mrs.), 82, mother of Samuel, Esq, d 7/16/38 in Jamestown
(4/7/18).  Born in Worcester, MA in 1757; After her marriage moved to
Paris, NY where she spent most of her life.  For past 7 yrs lived with
son Samuel in Jamestown; member Bapt. Ch.  Husband and 3 children
pre-deceased her.  Survived by three children  (4-7/25)
515. Barrett, Samuel H. of Jamestown m 9/16/44 Maria Louisa Spencer, youngest
dau of Rev. E. M. Spencer, in Westville, Otsego Co.; Rev. E. M. Spencer
(4-9/27)
516. Barrett, William E. m 5/29/45 Laura A. Wescot in Jamestown; Rev. E. J.
Gillett (4-6/6)
517. Barron, James (Commander) m Mary Ann Wilson, dau of J., Esq., in
Portsmouth, VA (3-12/9/29)
518. Barron, William of Seneca m 4/30/18 Sally Waters of Fayette in F;
Squire Pixley (3-5/26)
519. Barrows, Isaac, 49, d 10/13/43 at the home of his brother (not named)
in Jamestown (4-10/19)
520. Barrows, Lucy (Mrs.), 44, d 9/16/18 in Farmington (5-10/27)
521. Barrows, Mary, 3 yrs, d 9/13/41 in Jamestown (See also death of Mercy
Barrows) (4-9/23)
522. Barrows, Mercy, 3 yrs, d 9/13/41 in Jamestown (Presumably Mercy is the
the same person as Mary immediately above) (4-9/30)
523. Barrows, Robert m Mrs. Jemima Warren in Canandaigua (3-5/24/20)
524. Barstow, Charles R. m Charlotte Coburn in Nichols, Tioga Co. (3-4/30/28)
525. Barter, James C., one of the publishers of the St. Lawrence Gazette,
m 1/17/27 Eliza Harwood in Hopkinton; Rev. Pettibone (3-1/31)
526. Bartholf, Julia (Mrs.) d 5/11/24 in Batavia (1-5/14)
527. Bartholf, Peter m 1/16/25 Margaret Van Horn in Batavia; C. Carpenter, Esq.
(1-1/21)
528. Bartholomew, Daniel, 84, (a Rev. soldier) d 11/22/42 in Bradford (2-12/14)
529. Bartholomew, Eli W. m 8/19/30 Hannah Brockway, both of Williamson, in W;
D. Grandin, Esq. (5-8/27)
530. Bartleson, Enos, one of the editors of the Monmouth (NJ) Inquirer,
m 12/8/29 Elizabeth Ann Lloyd in Freehold, Monmouth Co., NJ; Rev.
Roy (5-12/18)

15

531. Bartlet, Jesse m Bathia Babcock in Bath (3-11/26/17)
532. Bartlet, John of Chautauqua m 10/28/32 Molly Briggs of Stockton in
      Ellery; Almon Ives, Esq. (4-10/31)
533. Bartlet, Josiah, Esq. d 1/29/13 in Albany (a state assemblyman from
      Montgomery Co.) (3-2/17)
534. Bartlet, Samuel, 77, m Elizabeth Forbush, 70, in Sempronius (3-8/11/19)
535. Bartlet, Warren of Elmira m Letty Caldwell in Southport (3-9/30/29)
536. Bartlett, Sylvanus m 2/18/32 Isabel Van Duzer in Williamson; D. Poppino,
      Esq. (5-2/21)
537. Barto, Henry D., Esq. m 2/28/19 Prudence Jagger in Trumansburgh (3-3/10)
538. Barton, Andrew G., 15, d 5/22/41 in Bath (surv by parents, 1 sister, and
      1 bro) (2-5/26)
539. Barton, Chester m 7/4/46 Eliza Vangelder in Bath; Arnold D. Read, Esq.
      (2-7/22)
540. Barton, H. H. m 3/29/42 Lydia Jane Lane, 2nd dau of Col. C., merchant,
      in Lima; Rev. Schuyler Seager. All of Lima (5-4/6)
541. Barton, James C. of Carroll m 1/25/35 Lovira Ann Brainard of Napoli, NY
      in N; David Hathaway, Esq. (4-2/4)
542. Barton, James L., s of Benjamin, Esq. of Lewiston, m 4/23/17 Sally M.
      Horner in Buffalo (3-5/7)
543. Barton, Leonard of Carroll m 7/3/36 Emeline Fargo of Gerry; Joseph Wait,
      Esq. (4-7/6)
544. Barton, Samuel, s of Benjamin, Esq., m 4/1/19 Harriet S. Fairbanks, dau
      of Joshua F., Esq., in Lewiston (3-4/14)
545. Barton, Stephen, 36, d in Marion (3-7/9/28)
546. Bascom, Ansel, Esq., attorney, of Seneca Falls m Elizabeth Sherwood, dau
      of Isaac, Esq., in Skaneateles (3/9/19/27)
547. Bass Abigail (Mrs.), 60, wid of late Samuel of Randall, MA, d 2/1/49 at
      the home of Lyman Kidder in Darien (1-2/20)
548. Bassell, Alanson m Sarah Ann Lord in Barrington (3-11/12/28)
549. Basset, Isaac of Avoca m 7/27/42 Sally Lyle of Montgomery Co. in Avoca;
      Rev. S. Pitt (2-8/3)
550. Bassett, David B. m 7/8/28 Almira Foster, both of Geneva, in G; Elder
      Martin (3-7/16)
551. Bassett, John C. m 2/9/45 Mary T. Germond of Hunt's Hollow, Alleg. Co.,
      in Kennedyville; A. D. Read, Esq. (2-2/19)
552. Bassett, Sheldon of Hector m 12/7/26 Eliza Ruscoe of Starkey in S; Rev.
      Samuel White (3-12/13)
553. Bassy, Elias m 8/8/29 Lucinthia Wilber in Williamson; Robert Alsop, Esq.
      (5-8/14)
554. Bate, John of Williamstown, MA m Mary Ann Bass of Bozrah, CT/"after a  in Bozrah
      courtship of one hour" (3-9/1/19)
555. Bateman, Thankful, wf of Eleazer, Esq., d 7/16/20 in Perinton (5-7/26)
556. Bates, _____, inf s of Stephen, Esq., d in Gorham (3-10/1/17)
557. Bates, _____, 77, wf of Phineas, Esq., d in Canandaigua (3-6/11/28)
558. Bates, Benjamin m 2/9/17 Betsey Beavers in Geneva (3-2/19)
559. Bates, Elvira, wf of Alvah, d in Ellington Center (4-2/2/43)
560. Bates, George C. formerly of Canandaigua, m 5/25/36 Mrs. Ellen Marion
      Walcott in Detroit, MI (5-6/3)
561. Bates, Horace m Mary Nichols in Rochester (3-12/30/18)
562. Bates, James m Amanda Yerrington in Syracuse (3-1/14/29)
563. Bates, Joseph m 4/10/25 Harriet Wilkie in Attica; Rev. Brown (1-4/22)
564. Bates, Marble m 2/4/24 Ascenith Hawes in Covington; Rev. True. All of C
      (1-3/26)
565. Bates, Morgan, editor of the Chautauque Republican, m 12/8/28 Janet M. Cook,
      dau of Dr. Robert, in Argyle, Wash. Co.; Rev. George Mairs, Jr.
      (4-12/24)
566. Bates, Nathaniel m Bellona Gannet in Palmyra (5-1/13/19)
567. Bates, Orlando of Ridgeway, Orleans Co., m 2/25/30 Irene Spear, dau of
      Abraham, Esq. of Macedon, in M;Rev. Powell (5-2/26)
568. Bates, Phebe Jane, 22 mo, dau of P. P. Bates, Esq., d in Canandaigua
      (3-7/17/22)
569. Bates, Phineas, Esq., 83, 85, or 88 (blurred), d 11/22/29 in Canandaigua
      (Emigrated to C in 1789) (5-11/27).  Phineas, Esq. father of Messrs.
      Stephen and Phineas P. and one of the earliest settlers in the area
      (3-11/25)

16

570. Bates, Sarah Cornelia (Miss), 18, dau of P. P., Esq., d 2/7/26 in
     Canandaigua (3-2/15)
571. Bates, Susan, 29, wf of Philo, d in Hopewell (3-12/9/29)
572. Bates, Truman m 2/25/16 Mary Franklin in Benton (3-3/6)
573. Batterson, Cyrus A., 26, d 11/20/32 in Rochester (formerly of Palmyra)
     (5-11/28)
574. Batty, Jonathan, Esq. m Amy Comstock, dau of Jared of Farmington, in F
     (5-5/12/19)
575. Baxter, William m 5/19/16 Laura Chase in Seneca; Eli Bannister, Esq.
     (3-5/22)
576. Bayard, William M., Esq., formerly of Palmyra, m 7/14/35 Ramania Danniell
     of Louisville, KY in Seneca Falls; Rev. George Dashiell (5-7/17)
577. Bayles, William m 2/18/35 Jane Hamilton, both of Urbana, in U; Obediah
     Wheeler, Esq. (2-2/25)
578. Bayly, Richard M. of the house of Messrs. Colt,and Bayly, merchants,
     of Geneva m 7/17/17 Harriet Swift, oldest dau of Reuben, Esq. of
     Waterloo, in W; Rev. Axtell (3-7/23)
579. Beach, Abner, 74, formerly of Colebrook, CT, d in Hopewell (3-4/16/28)
580. Beach, Alvah m Clarissa Willard in Bloomfield (3-2/18/18)
581. Beach, Charles C., 38, printer, a native of Vermont and for several years
     publisher of the Gazette on the Island of Jamaica, d 9/12/26 in
     Buffalo, NY (3-9/27)
582. Beach, Clarissa Tirzah, inf dau of Jefferson Beach, d in Jamestown
     (4-3/22/44)
583. Beach, Cornelia (Mrs.), 17, dau of late Ira Pratt of Bath, d in
     Marcellus (3-9/26/27)
584. Beach, Elias m 2/26/18 Lucinda Gardner, both of Geneva, in G; Rev. Axtell
     (3-3/4)
585. Beach, Elias Hervey, 13 mo, s of Elias, d 7/17/27 in Geneva (3-7/25)
586. Beach, George m Gehiel Caykendall, both of Ulysses (3-7/21/19)
587. Beach, Jarvis T. of Lodi m 9/21/26 Mary Potter of Hector in H; Rev.
     Thomas Lounsbury of Ovid (3-10/4)
588. Beach, John H., Esq of Auburn m 3/7/11 Christina Campbell of Albany in
     Auburn; Rev. D. Higgins (3-4/17)
589. Beach, Mary, 52, wf of Israel B., d in East Bloomfield (3-3/23/14)
590. Beach, Nathaniel, 23, formerly of Canandaigua, d in Bloomfield (3-10/13/19)
591. Beach, Thomas J., inf s of Jefferson, d 8/22/41 in Jamestown (4-8/26)
592. Beach, William A. m Cornelia R. Pratt in Prattsburgh (3-7/4/27)
593. Beadle, Thomas, about 58, d 4/6/14 in Junius "leaving a wife and a number
     of children" (3-4/13)
594. Beadle, Thompson m 5/5/24 Nancy McGowen in Junius (3-5/19)
595. Beal, John, Esq. m 3/15/37 Melissa J. Sandford, both of Palmyra, in P;
     Rev. Heustice (5-3/17)
596. Beal, William of Michigan m 3/10/31 Rachael Comstock of Farmington in
     Rochester; J. D. Thompson, Esq. (5-4/15)
597. Beales?, A. (Mr.), a Christian preacher, m 11/7/22 Dolly Deane? in
     Williamson (print indistinct on original) (5-11/13)
598. Beals, _____, ch of Josiah, d in Phelps (3-8/23/15)
599. Beals, _____, 2 yrs, s of James, d in Canandaigua (3-8/13/17)
600. Beals, Abraham of Port Gibson m Stella Seely of Lyons in Palmyra (3-6/25/28)
601. Beals, Ezra R. m 1/27/31 Catharine Katner in Wheeler; James Wheeler, Esq.
     (2-2/9)
602. Beals, James m Hila Rawson in Angelica (3-10/21/18)
603. Beam, John of Sodus m 11/24/31 Mrs. Clarissa Miles in Palmyra; Rev.
     B. H. Hickox (5-11/29)
604. Beam, John m 8/15/41 Desdemona Wallace, both of Sodus; L. E. Beecher, Esq.
     (5-8/18)
605. Beaman, Henry C. of Jersey m 11/18/32 Martha Rowley, dau of John S. of
     Bath; H. W. Rogers, Esq. (2-11/28)
606. Beaman, Isaac (Rev.) of Chautauqua Co. m 11/24/42 Sally Hoyt of Marion
     in M; John McLouth, Esq. (5-12/14)
607. Beaman, James m Eunice Chase in Prattsburgh (3-2/5/17)
608. Beaman, Mary, 7 yrs, d 3/20/35 in Bath (3-2/25)
609. Bean, _____, wf of George, d 7/17/28 in Phelps (3-7/23)
610. Bean, George m 11/2/28 Almira Kimball in Geneva; E. Hastings, Esq.
     (3-11/19)

17

611. Beard, Joseph m 11/18/13 Zilpha Howley in Lyons; John Brown, Esq. All of
     Lyons (3-12/8)
612. Beardsley, James of Auburn, late editor of the Louisiana (New Orleans)
     Advertiser, m Charlotte A. Hopkins in Pompey, Onon. Co. (3-5/14/28)
613. Beardsley, John W. of Big Flat m Elizabeth Carpenter in Havana, NY
     (3-11/26/28)
614. Beardsley, Livingston Crannell, 22, editor and publisher of The Canadian,
     d 9/14/25 in Niagara (3-9/28)
615. Beatie, David m 2/16/29 Dorothy Trumbull of Seneca; Eurotus Hastings, Esq.
     (3-2/18)
616. Beaton, _____ (Mrs.), 88, d in St. John's Madder market, Norwich; a
     native of Wales and commonly called the Freemason from her having,
     while hidden, learned that secret ("she was a singular old woman
     as the secret died with her") (3-11/1/09)
617. Bean, _____ m Cordelia Cary in Ontario, NY (5-3/18/31)
618. Beatty, William m 4/9/22 Martha Beaden in Geneva; Jacob Dox, Esq. (3-4/17)
619. Beaumont, A. L., Esq. m 8/24/29 Clarissa G. Holley, 2nd dau of Hon. Myron,
     in Lyons; Rev. L. Hubbell (3-8/26 and 5-8/28)
620. Bebee, Miles m Lima Brockelbank in Canandaigua (3-2/25/29)
621. Beck, N. F., Esq. (Adjutant Gen.) m Anna Maria Walton in Schenectady
     (3-7/11/27)
622. Beck, Nicholas F., Esq., 33, adjutant general of State of NY, d 6/27/30
     in Albany (4-7/14 and 5-7/9)
623. Becker, Peter of Gorham m 12/2/19 Lucy Ball of Seneca; Rev. Merrill
     (3-12/22)
624. Beckwith, A. B. of Bath m 9/29/40 Martha C. Thompson of Painted Post
     in P P; Rev. John Smith (2-10/7)
625. Beckwith, Amasa, 51, d 8/14/32 in Windham Co, CT (2-9/5)
626. Beckwith, Arilla Jane, 11, dau of Amasa of Bath, d 12/6/31 in Prattsburgh
     (2-12/21)
627. Beckwith, Cynthia Ann, 2 yrs, dau of Nathaniel, d 7/17/18 in Palmyra
     (5-7/21)
628. Beckwith, Cynthia Ann, 15, dau of late Nathaniel H., d 1/30/35 in
     Palmyra (5-2/6)
629. Beckwith, Elijah, late of Bath, NY, m 7/30/35 Ann Wyatt of Bangor, ME
     in Bangor (2-9/2)
630. Beckwith, George Whitfield, 10 mo, s of George, d 8/18/32 (5-8/22)
631. Beckwith, Henry m Patience Dean in Southport (3-9/3/28)
632. Beckwith, Nathaniel H. (Capt.) of Palmyra m 1/13/23 Sophia Birchard
     of Lima in L (5-1/22)
633. Beckwith, Nathaniel, 5, s of Col. N. H., d 2/19/32 in Palmyra (5-2/28)
634. Beckwith, Oscar, 4, s of Nathaniel H., d 4/3/21 in Palmyra (5-4/4)
635. Beckwith, Sheldon m Betsey McHenry in Southport (3-1/9/28)
636. Beckwith, Wilson m 4/28/36 Mary J. Post, both of Palmyra (5-4/29)
637. Beckwith, Richard B. m 8/2/40 Martha Ann Lee; E. Bacon, Esq. All of
     Erwin (2-8/19)
638. Beddoe, Johnstone, 23, d 3/7/28 at the home of his father in Jerusalem,
     NY (epilepsy) (3-3/26)
639. Beden, _____ (Mrs.), 94, d 10/7/26 in Geneva (3-10/11)
640. Beden, Calista, 4, dau of Smithfield, d 4/15/22 in Wolcott (3-5/1)
641. Bedient, Ira S. of Jamestown m 1/28/45 Catharine T. Carpenter of Busti
     in B; Rev. E. R. Swain (4-1/31)
642. Beebe, Ira of Chester, Warren Co., m 5/31/45 Laura Ann Warren of Schroon,
     Essex Co., in S; Rev. S. Wood (4-6/20)
643. Beebe, Joseph L, of Seneca Falls m 3/4/34 Jane Aurelia Chapin of Tyre,
     Sen. Co., in Tyre; Rev. Lane (5-3/7)
644. Beebe, Joseph S. of Palmyra m 3/5/29 Mary Ann Crosby of Phelps in P;
     Rev. Strong (3-3/11 and 5-3/6)
645. Beebe, Mary Ann, consort of Joseph L., late of Palmyra, d 10/7/30 in
     Seneca Falls (5-10/22)
646. Beebe, Rachel, 15, dau of Gabriel, d in Canandaigua (3-9/17/17)
647. Beebe, Sarah, 99, relict of Zaccheus, d 5/11/15 in Bern ("was in the
     marriage state 66 years, and remained a widow 15 years") (3-5/31)
648. Beebee, Amon, 79, (a Rev. soldier) m 5/31/29 Mrs. Warson, 56, in Clymer;
     William Rice, Esq. (4-6/10)

649. Beecher, Welthy, 28, wf of Randal F. and dau of John Donahe(sic), d 4/23/45 in Howard (2-4/30)
650. Beeden, John m 5/13/27 Lavina Garrison, dau of William, in Benton, All of B (3-6/6)
651. Beedon, William E. m 11/27/28 Sarah Tailor in Seneca; Samuel Gage, Esq. (3-12/3)
652. Beeman, Almon, Esq. of Addison m 4/16/38 Elmira Bostwick of Hornellsville in Angelica; Rev. Nathaniel F. Bruce (2-4/25)
653. Beeman, William M. m 12/16/48 Elizabeth Fisher in Italy, NY; Rev. B. C. Smith (2-12/27)
654. Beement, Erastus of Ulysses m Elnor Himrod of Hector in H (3-1/17/16)
655. Beers, David Booth, 39, merchant, d in Ithaca (3-1/5/20)
656. Beers, Silas d 7/22/29 in Starkey ("an old ... farmer of that town") (3-7/29)
657. Beers, William P., Esq., clerk of the city and county of Albany, d 9/13/10 in Fairfield, CT (3-9/26)
658. Beeton, John m 1/29/26 Julia Dickinson in Benton; S. G. Gage, Esq. All of Benton (3-2/8)
659. Begley, Hugh, about 40, d 6/11/19 in Geneva (3-6/16)
660. Begole, Devan m 9/11/49 M. C. Wallace, dau of James, Esq., in Cohocton; Rev. A. Adams. All of C (2-9/19)
661. Beitharz, J. J. (Rev.) of Fayette m 10/31/26 Sarah Bergstroser of Romulus in R; Rev. Whillers (3-11/15)
662. Belden, Elizabeth (Miss), 21, d 6/e/27 in Gorham (3-6/6)
663. Belden, George, merchant, of Marion m 3/2/31 Mary Putnam of Walworth in Marion; Rev. Boyle (5-3/18)
664. Beldin, Riley m 11/1/29 Louisa Pullman, dau of Joseph, Esq., in Sodus; Elder Allen (5-11/27). Surname is Belding in 3-11/25)
665. Belding, Clarissa (Miss), 19, dau of Azor, d 6/24/27 in Gorham (3-6/27)
666. Belding, Esther, consort of Selah, d 8/23/16 near Geneva (3-8/28)
667. Belding, Sidney m 1/4/44 Mary Ann Winchester in Fredonia; Allen Hinckley, Esq. (4-1/26)
668. Belding, William, about 26, s of Selah, d 3/16/27 "in Seneca (Castle street)" (3-3/28)
669. Belknap, Giles N. m 4/4/41 Eliza M. Frost in Stockton; Rev. Hunter (4/4/7)
670. Bell, Abram L. m 5/8/28 Sarah Backenstose, dau of late Frederick, both of Geneva, in Seneca; Rev. Nesbit (3-5/14)
671. Bell, Amos of Cortland Co. m 6/15/42 Eliza Ann Ruger of Urbana in U; J. Larrowe, Esq. (2-7/6)
672. Bell, Benjamin, 2 yrs, s of Benjamin P., d 1/25/43 in Jamestown (4-2/2)
673. Bell, Elizabeth, 62, wf of William, d 4/17/46 in Orange (2-5/5)
674. Bell, John M. of Geneva m 12/3/27 Sarah Giraud of Manchester in Vienna, NY; Thomas Smith, Esq. (3-12/5)
675. Bell, Sarah (Miss), 20, d in Palmyra (3-11/16/25)
676. Bell, Sarah Ann, 14 mo, dau of Benjamin P., d 10/16/39 (prob. in Jamestown) 4-10/23)
677. Bellamy, Samuel (Col.), 74, d in Auburn (3-4/1/29)
678. Bellas, George m 12/13/46 Jane Aber in Bath; Elder Ira Brown. All of B (2-12/16)
679. Bellen, John (Rev.), late of St. John's Church in Canandaigua and formerly from England, d 3/2/30 in Albany (5-3/19)
680. Bellis, George C. m 5/10/47 Jane Aber in Bath; Rev. H. Spencer. All of B (2-5/12)
681. Bellows, Ora (Mr.) d 8/29/20 in Upper Sandusky (Ohio?) ("of the firm of Stone, Bellows, and Hendee"; formerly of Palmyra) (5-9/20)
682. Bellows, William H., 3 yrs, s of Isaac, d 9/18/41 in Prattsburgh (2-9/29)
683. Beman, Mumford m 5/12/25 Harriet Phelps in Attica (1-5/13)
684. Beman, Mumford m 12/25/25 Harriet Phelps; Stephen Griswold, Esq. All of Stafford (1-1/6/26)
685. Beman, Seth m Mrs. Elsey Pritchard in Canandaigua (3-12/3/17)
686. Bement, David m 1/8/29 Eliza Bird in Palmyra; Frederick Smith, Esq. All of Manchester (probably) (5-1/9)
687. Bement, Edward m Lydia Bird in Manchester; David Howland, Esq. (5-6/11/30)
688. Bement, Hiram m 12/2/29 Harriet Persons in Manchester; Esq. Van Fleet (5-12/25) also (3-12/30)

19

689. Bement, Mary (Mrs.), 94, d 4/2/42 in Manchester (5-4/6)
690. Bement, William E. m 12/13/43 Laura Ann Newell in Manchester Center;
    J. N. Granger, Esq. All of M C (5-12/20)
691. Bemis, Benjamin, 83, father of J. D., Esq. of Canandaigua, d 3/9/27 in
    Worcester, MA (3-3/28)
692. Bemus, David m Bethiah Van Nostrand in Clymer (4-4/25/27)
693. Benedict, _____ (widow), 101, d in Leicester (3-9/19/27)
694. Benedict, Abraham (Deacon), 99, d 8/27/45 in Elba (a native of Norwalk,
    CT; fought in Rev. from CT; among first settlers in New Lisbon, Otsego
    Co., NY) (1-9/23)
695. Benedict, Isaac m 9/13/45 Mary Hall in Ashville; Rev. T. D. Blin (4-9/26)
    (See marr. of John Hall same date).
696. Benedict, John Churchill, 1 yr, s of Hiram, d in Ashville (4-8/2/26)
697. Benedict, John T., formerly of Otsego, m 2/11/39 Mrs. Betsey Benedict,
    wid of Isaac, of Elba"after an acquaintanceship of about thirty years
    and a pleasing and interesting courtship of about thirty minutes",
    at the house of Marlin Scofield in Elba; Rev. Emmons (1-2/14)
698. Benedict, Mary (Miss), 42, dau of Eleazer of Danbury, CT, d 8/24/20 in
    Penfield (5-8/30)
699. Benedict, Oscar F. m 4/20/47 Maria S. Bennet, both of Alexander, in A;
    Rev. J. S. Barrie (1-4/27)
700. Benedict, Salon d in Busti (4-2/6/39)
701. Benedict, Samuel, 92, (a Rev. soldier) d in Harmony (4-7/4/45)
702. Benedict, Sarah, 90, wf of Samuel, d 3/17/45 in Ashville. ("Her husband,
    92, with whom she has lived seventy years still survives.") (4-3/28)
703. Benham, Beacher m 12/19/16 Nancy Dickson in Gorham (3-1/8/17)
704. Benham, Catharine Calista, 19 mo, dau of David and Sally, d 3/24/33 in
    Walworth (5-4/3)
705. Benham, David m Sally Moore in Canandaigua (3-3/26/17)
706. Benham, James, 6, s of S., d 4/17/42 in Jamestown (4-4/21)
707. Benham, Mary (Mrs.), 40, d in Hopewell (surv by husband and 7 ch)
    (3-8/8/27)
708. Benham, Silas m Laura Reed in Canandaigua (3-1/6/27)
709. Benjamin, Elijah P., merchant, of Geneva m 5/28/27 Margaretta L. Crooke,
    dau of John of Poughkeepsie, in P; Rev. Dr. Reed (3-6/6)
710. Benjamin, John m 11/26/46 Lydia Campbell in Bath; Rev. E. B. Fuller.
    All of B (2-12/2)
711. Benjamin, Maria (Miss), 23, dau of Samuel, formerly of New Jersey,
    d 5/14/47 in Bath (2-5/26)
712. Benjamin, Orson, Esq. m Mary Kibbe, dau of William, Esq., in Canandaigua;
    Rev. Onderdonk (3-10/1/17)
713. Benjamin, Walter of Waterloo m Arraminta Palmer in Fayette (3-12/23/29)
714. Bennet, Alcalie m 2/25/46 Harriet M. Goff, both of Howard, in H ; Rev.
    Sawyer (2-3/4)
715. Bennet, Anna, 35, wf of Phineas, late of Ithaca, d in Hector (3-6/3/29)
716. Bennet, Daniel of Howard m 1/20/47 Maroa (sic) Rose of Burton, Ohio in
    Howard, NY; Rev. L. Rose (2-1/27)
717. Bennet, George of Seneca m 3/1/15 Sally Lum of Geneva in G; Rev. Axtell
    (3-3/8)
718. Bennet, Josiah (Dr.) m Ruth Reeves in Williamson (3-12/2/18)
719. Bennet, Samuel m Martha Ann May in Milo (3-1/21/29)
720. Bennet, William, 101, d in Pennsylvania ("He built the first keel-boat
    that ever floated on the Susquehanna") (3-5/13/12)
721. Bennett, Abraham H., one of the editors of the Penn Yan Herald,m 10/4/18
    Desdemona Kidder in Penn Yan (3-10/14)
722. Bennett, Abraham H., 45, an editor of the Penn Yan Democrat, d 5/13/42
    in Penn Yan (5-5/25)
723. Bennett, Asa (Deacon), 47, d 11/9/25 in Homer (3-11/30 and 3-12/14)
724. Bennett, Dolphas. printer, of Utica m Sila Sessions, dau of Amasa, Esq.,
    in Marcellus (3-11/19/28)
725. Bennett, George, 16, d in Nunda (3-5/30/27)
726. Bennett, Henry, 15, s of Joseph, d 9/26/29 in Geneva (3-9/30)
727. Bennett, Henry T. m 11/13/45 Eliza Jane Wood in Bath; Rev. L. W. Russ.
    All of Portage, Alleg. Co. (2-11/19)
728. Bennett, Hiram, Esq. m 5/1/50 Eliza Doty in Hornellsville; Rev.H.
    Pattengill. All of H. (2-5/15)

20

729. Bennett, James, 71, d in Bethany (a Rev. soldier) (3-12/29/19)
730. Bennett, James, 68?, d in Junius (3-5/16/27)
731. Bennett, John L. m 7/6/42 Amanda Benham in Penn Yan; Rev. O. Miner
     (4-7/21)
732. Bennett, Louisa, about 35, wf of Reuben, d 12/19/30 in Lyons (5-12/24)
733. Bennett, Lydia (Mrs.), 74, consort of late James, d 6/28/25 in Bethany
     (mother of 16 ch.; "14 reared to manhood") (1-7/1)
734. Bennett, Myron H. m 9/26/43 Mary E. Fish, dau of Isaac, Esq., in Williamson;
     Rev. C. P. Merwin (5-10/4)
735. Bennett, Orson, 36, d in Auburn (3-3/1/26)
736. Bennett, Orval m 5/27/46 Delia Beals in Batavia; Rev. B. Sunderland. All
     of Batavia (1-6/2)
737. Bennett, Trumbull L., M.D., of Lima m 7/17/50 Elizabeth S. Paine, dau of
     Maj. E. L. of Canisteo; Rev. D. Nutten of Bath (2-7/24)
738. Bennett, Valentine of Hamburgh m 10/7/17 Mary Kibbe, dau of Gaius (3-10/22)
739. Bennett, Wiliam H. of SC drowned 1/16/13 in Litchfield, CT along with
     William Ensign of Litchfield, "both young men belonging to Mr. Morris'
     School" (Both fell through the ice on the Great Pond while fishing)
     (3-1/20)
740. Bennett, Willis m Mariah Tuthill, dau of Capt. Samuel, in Southport,
     Tioga Co. (3-11/30/25)
741. Bennitt, James C. m Anna Mabee in Wayne (a double ceremony with John
     Bennitt marrying Polly Smith, which see) (3-7/26/15)
742. Bennitt, John m Polly Smith in Wayne (see marriage of James C. Bennitt
     in #741) (3-7/26/15)
743. Benoy, Clarissa (Mrs.) d in Bloomfield (3-2/5/17)
744. Benson, Demmon of Hector m Olive Black in Wyalusing, PA (3-1/21/29)
745. Benson, James, 57, d 6/6/39 in Palmyra (5-6/7)
746. Benson, Jane Sophia, 11 mo, d 6/23/22 in Palmyra (5-6/26)
747. Benson, Peleg m 3/3/31 Hannah Washburn in Carroll (4-3/9)
748. Bent, Hartwell, Esq., 40, d 5/2/44 in Randolph (4-5/10)
749. Bentley, Alexander m 1/25/43 Lavantia Norton in Poland, NY (4-1/26)
750. Bentley, Elnathan m 6/29/26 Diantha Wilcox in Palmyra (3-8/2)
751. Bentley, John, Jr., 43, d in Ellery (4-9/5/32)
752. Bentley, Nancy, 65, wf of Uriah, Esq. d in Busti (4-4/26/44)
753. Bentley, Simeon m 1/22/39 Alice Gifford in Busti; L. Lakin, Esq. (4-1/30)
754. Bentley, William m 7/12/40 Betsey Crosby in Cohocton; Constant Cook, Esq.
     All of C (2-7/22)
755. Benton, Alonzo, 19, d 9/28/41 in Urbana (2-10/6)
756. Benton, Betsey, 19, wf of Henry, d 7/3/09 in Seneca (3-8/2)
757. Benton, Chester H. m 2/26/24 Sarah R. Sloan in Seneca; Rev. Dr. Axtell
     (3-3/3)
758. Benton, David, 81, formerly of Ontario Co., d 3/7/45 in Brownstone,
     Jackson Co, Indiana (a native of CT and a pioneer settler in western
     NY; arrived in Ontario Co. in 1790) (2-4/2)
759. Benton, James B., 11 yrs, s of George, d in Lyons (3-10/17/27)
760. Benton, Mary, 80, wf of Levi, formerly of Benton, NY, d 8/1/27 in New
     Trenton, IN (3-8/29)
761. Benton, Norman m 6/15/42 Mary D. Daniels in Bath; Rev. O. Frazer. All
     of B (2-6/22)
762. Benton, Sarah (Mrs.), 60, mother-in-law of Moses H. Lyon, d in Bath
     (3-12/7/25)
763. Berdan, David m Harriet M. Cannon, both of Phelps, in Lyons (3-10/22/28)
764. Berger, John of Romulus m 11/1/27 Almira Gardner of Seneca in S; Rev. Dr.
     Axtell (3-11/7)
765. Berry, _____, 36, wf of William, d 3/23/27 in Seneca (3-3/28)
766. Berry, Charles H., Esq. , 11/14/50 Frances Hubbell in Corning; Rev. A. L.
     Brooks. All of C (2-11/27)
767. Berry, Ephraim, merchant, m 7/16/26 Maria Van Nostrand, both of Ashville,
     in Ashville; Isaac S. Fitch, Esq. (4-7/19)
768. Berry, John, Jr. m 2/24/29 Mrs. Hannah Flower, both of Seneca (3-3/4)
769. Berry, Richard m 6/10/47 Susan Bedell in Le Roy; Rev. D. C. Houghton
     (1-6/22)
770. Bertine, Louisa, 18, d 4/16/42 in Bath (2-4/20)
771. Betts, Peter m Anna Sisson in Benton (3-5/28/28)

21

772. Betts, Seth m 11/16/37 Jane Hopkinson, both of East Palmyra, in E P;
     Rev. S. W. Wooster (5-11/22)
773. Bidleman, Joseph m 11/30/25 Polly Mondy in Elmira (3-12/21)
774. Bidwell, Eli, Jr. m 3/4/47 Louisa Dudley, dau of Benjamin F.; Rev. L.
     Merril Miller. All of Bath (2-3/10)
775. Bidwell, Eli, Sr., 61, d 11/22/49 in Bath (b in East Hartford, CT 9/20/1788;
     at age 17, with an older brother, came to Prattsburgh area; has lived
     in Bath 36 yrs) (2-11/28)
776. Bidwell, George H., editor and proprietor of Dansville Republican,
     m 5/3/46 Mary E. Moses of Hartford, CT in Christ Ch., Hartford;
     Rev. Burgess (2-5/20)
777. Bidwell, Harriet, 59, wf of Capt. E. R., d 4/3/49 in Rochester (2-4/11)
778. Bidwell, Phineas m 9/20/32 Tryphena Robbins in Palmyra; M. W. Williams, Esq.
     (5-9/26)
779. Bidwell, Porter m Vesta Slayton in Middlesex (3-6/18/28)
780. Bidwell, Rebecca G., 8 yrs, youngest dau of Capt. Edwin R., d 1/26/47
     in Bath (2-1/27)
781. Bidwell, Rodolphus, 84, father of Eli of Bath, NY, d 5/29/40 in East
     Hartford, CT (2-6/10)
782. Bidwell, William E. of Bath m 9/29/50 Sarah M. Brown of Cleveland
     (state not given) in Mud Creek; Rev. J. C. Mallory (2-10/9)
783. Bigelow, Daniel, 47, d in Fayette (3-9/30/29)
784. Bigelow, F. S. of Pavilion m 5/27/49 Emeline M. Wait, dau of Judge Ira
     of Bethany, in B (1-6/5)
785. Bigelow, Hannah, wf of John, d 10/11/31 in Manchester (5-10/18)
786. Bigelow, Horace m 1/17/40 Mary Moore, both of Macedon, in Palmyra;
     Frederick Smith, Esq. (5-1/22)
787. Bigelow, Horace m 1/29/45 Almira Sturgess in Batavia; Rev. Sunderland.
     All of Batavia (1-2/4)
788. Bigelow, Ira m Elizabeth Ames in Livonia (3-4/12/15)
789. Bigelow, Thomas m Ann Cornwell in Bath (3-7/9/28)
790. Bignall, ____, 63, wf of Buliff, d in Junius (3-10/8/28)
791. Biles, Hezekiah S. of Bath m 2/27/47 Olive S. Griswould of Penn Yan in
     Bath; Rev. L. Merrel Miller (2-3/3)
792. Biles, Lewis d 9/11/41 at his home in Bath (2-9/15)
793. Biles, William A., about 25, d 12/27/45 in Bath (2-12/31)
794. Bill, E. B. m A. Van Clief in Seneca Falls; Rev. Orton (3-8/22/27)
795. Billings, ____ (Mrs.), wf of Dr. James A., d 5/4/26 in Elba (1-5/5)
796. Billings, Benjamin, age blurred, d at his home in Macedon (a Rev. officer)
     (5-1/17/38)
797. Billings, Benjamin, Jr. m 4/21/31 Mary Glover in Macedon; F. Smith, Esq.
     (5-5/6)
798. Billings, James A. (Dr.) of Batavia m 4/19/24 Juliana Hinckley of Rochester
     in R; Rev. F. H. Cuming (1-4/23)
799. Billings, Jonas S., merchant, of Batavia m 10/31/24 Betsey Selleck of
     Greenfield, Sara. Co. in Saratoga; Elder Lamb (1-11/19)
800. Billings, Louisa, 34, dau of William, d 7/27/36 in East Palmyra (5-7/29)
801. Billings, Lucy Mariah, 13, dau of William, d 4/14/31 in Palmyra (5-5/6)
802. Billings, Mary Urilla, 16, dau of Dr. James A. of Batavia, d 8/13/47 at
     the home of her uncle, J. T. Hathaway, Esq. in Buffalo ("Dr. Billings
     has had the misfortune to lose two daughters in the verge of womanhood.")
     (1-8/17)
803. Billings, William, Sr., about 55, formerly of Palmyra, d 10/2/38 in
     Canandaigua, Lenawee Co., MI (5-11/17)
804. Billington, Matthias L. m 9/27/35 Mary Wentworth in Kennedyville; George
     Wheeler, Esq. (2-9/30)
805. Bills, Isaac C. m 2/3/22 Hannah Selby, both of Palmyra, in Farmington;
     P. Mitchell, Esq. (5-2/20)
806. Bingham, Charles B. m 10/23/34 Abigail Tice in Palmyra; Rev. Shumway.
     All of Palmyra (5-10/24)
807. Bingham, Morgan L. m 12/30/41 Lydia Ann Tice, both of Palmyra, in P;
     Rev. Hurlburt (5-1/12/42)
808. Bingham, Thomas, Jr. of Riga m 11/24/25 Almira E. Galusha in East Bloomfield
     (3-12/14)
809. Birch, Joshua E. R. (Dr.), 40, of NYC d "on his passage from New York City
     to Teneriffe for ... his health..." (3-3/27/16)

810. Birch, William H., 38, d 1/24/35 (5-1/30)
811. Birchard, Mortimer N. of Moscow, Liv. Co. m 8/18/36 Louisa J. Gregg, formerly of Palmyra, in Perry, Gen. Co.; Rev. Clark (5-8/26)
812. Birchard, Norton B., 27, s of Asahael, Esq., d 11/3/34 at his home in Lima (5-11/14)
813. Bird, Charles of Elmira m Mary Ann Kennedy, dau of Dr. John P., in Covington, PA (3-4/25/27)
814. Bird, George J. of Canisteo m 4/23/49 Nancey Daggert of Cameron in C; Rev. David Smith (2-5/2)
815. Bird, Ira R. (Capt.) m 8/12/33 Caroline E. Beecher in Westfield (1-8/27)
816. Birdsall, ____, wf of Hon. John,d in Mayville (4-5/22/33)
817. Birdsall, Betsey, wf of Samuel, Esq. of Waterloo, d in Owego (3-12/15/19)
818. Birdsall, Horace of Ovid m 9/16/29 Dorcas Flagler of Palmyra in P; Rev. Gear (5-9/18 and 3-9/23)
819. Birdsall, John (Hon.), judge of the 8th circuit, m Ann Whiteside in Mayville (3-8/1/27)
820. Birdsall, Lewis A. (Dr.) m Mary Jane Lee, dau of Dr. Joshua, in Milo (3-12/28/25)
821. Birdsall, Phebe Jane, 16, only ch of Daniel, d 11/1/42 in Macedon (5-11/9)
822. Birdsall, Sutton Sylvester, 4, s of Sutton and Eliza, d 2/16/40 in Palmyra (5-2/19)
823. Birdsall, Sylvester, 1 yr 9 mo, s of Sutton, d 5/11/29 in Palmyra (5-5/15)
824. Bishop, ____, 103, a native of Saybrook, CT, d in Berkshire, Tioga Co. (3-9/19/27)
825. Bishop, A. D. of Jamestown m 8/9/33 Emeline Jenner of Ashville in Harmony (both formerly from Essex Co., NY); Z. Ward, Esq. (4-8/14)
826. Bishop, Edison of Montezuma m Semantha Leonard, dau of Deacon P.of Morris Co., NJ, in Waterloo (3-6/11/28)
827. Bishop, Harvy m Mary Puffer in Junius (3-9/9/29)
828. Bishop, John m 6/3/41 Eliza Ann Haskins in Troupsburgh; Thomas W. Baley, Esq. All of T (2-6/16)
829. Bishop, Seymour Lawrence, 2 yrs, s of Elijah and Amy, d 8/6/42 (prob. in Jamestown) (4-8/11)
830. Bishop, William (Dr.) m Lucretia McCullock in Painted Post; Rev. D. Higgins (2-10/24/32)
831. Bissel, Anna, 64, wf of Moses, d in Canandaigua (3-2/21/16)
832. Bissell, Josiah, Jr., 45, of Rochester d 4/5/31 in Seneca Falls (4-4/20 and 5-4/15)
833. Bixbe, William, 49, d 5/25/31 in Marion (5-5/27)
834. Bixby, Simon ofHornby m 7/9/49 Phebe T. Lake of Bath in B; Rev.B. R. Swick (2-7/11)
835. Bixby, William H., 32, d 5/28/46 in Bath (2-6/3)
836. Black, David m 1/14/30 Mary Wilkie in Seneca; Rev. Nesbit. All of Seneca (3-1/20)
837. Black, David, a late graduate "of Middlebury College, Vt.", d 3/12/43 in Sheridan (4-3/23)
838. Black, Henry, Esq. of Orange Co. m Eliza Gray of Greene Co. and dau of Henry Brown, merchant, of Bluehill, ME (underlining in original) (2-4/7/41)
839. Black, Hugh m 3/8/27 Nancy Rice, dau of "Mrs. Mary Rice", in Seneca; Rev. Dr. Axtell (3-3/14)
840. Black, Ja____?, 63, d 3/8/23 in Geneva (3-3/12)
841. Black, James, Esq. of Yarmouth, England m 1/26/29 Tereza Machi of Athens, Greece in Egina, Greece; Rev. Jonas King ("She is the person addressed by Lord Byron in his poem 'Maid of Athens, here we part/Give, oh give me back my heart...'") (5-6/12)
842. Black, Jeremiah m 9/5/26 Eliza Warden, both of Bath, in Cohocton; Rev. Clary (3-9/20)
843. Black, John (Capt.) m 2/7/28 Mary Haynes, oldest dau of Nathan, in Seneca; Rev. Nisbet (sic) (3-2/13)
844. Black, John (Capt.), 30, s of Aaron, d 9/28/28 in Seneca (3-10/1)
845. Black, Moses of Seneca m 1/20/20 Mary McMasters of Benton in B; Rev. Axtell (3-1/26)

23

846. Black, William, s of Hugh, m 4/5/21 Isabella Rippey (sic), dau of John,
     in Seneca; Rev. Axtell (3-4/11)
847. Black, William d 8/25/24 near Geneva "at an advanced age" (3-9/1)
848. Black, William, late of Ireland, m Laura Hurd, dau of Thomas, Esq., in
     Jersey (3-6/18/28)
849. Black, William G., 9 yrs, s of Jeremiah, d 11/21/41 in Bath (2-11/24)
850. Blackman, Abel, 72, d 3/18/43 in Newark, NY (5-3/22)
851. Blackman, Adeline, wf of Ransom of Newark, NY, d 6/30/30 in Newark
     (5-7/2)
852. Blackman, Cyrenius C. m Sabrina Denio in Palmyra (3-12/20/15)
853. Blackman, David m 1/22/29 Deborah Beals, dau of B. Beals, in Macedon.
     All of M (5-1/30)
854. Blackman, Elisha m Dorcas Wheeler in Palmyra (3-12/20/15)
855. Blackman, Ransom m 6/6/30 Adeline Miller (probably in Newark, NY); Rev.
     Peter Kanouse?. All of Newark (5-6/18)
856. Blackman, Ransom, 39, d 12/31/41 in Newark, NY (5-1/5/42)
857. Blackman, Robert R. m Phebe Bateman in Perinton; Rev. J. Irons (5-11/28/17)
858. Blackmarr, Adoniah 74, d 10/21/18 in Ontario, NY (5-10/27)
859. Blackmer, ____, 4 yrs, a dau of Mr. S. of Canandaigua, d 5/24/15
     ("burnt to death by her clothes taking fire") (3-6/7)
860. Blackmer, Alice (Mrs.), 48, d in Palmyra (3-2/3/13)
861. Blackmore, Henry of Richmond m Elizabeth A. Hayes in Bristol (3-2/3/30)
862. Blain, Gideon m Sally Bryant in Romulus (3-1/6/30)
863. Blain, John m 6/23/22 Lucy Hodge in Ovid; Ledlie (sic) Dunlap, Esq.
     (3-7/3)
864. Blair, A. E. (Dr.), 22, d 11/12/32 in Kennedyville (2-11/14)
865. Blair, Eli, 40, and Abby, his wife, 36, d 10/4/31 in Lyons (5-10/11)
866. Blake, Francis, Esq. (Hon.), 43, d in Worcester, MA (3-3/12/17)
867. Blake, Henry I. (Capt.) of U. S. Artillery m Gertrude B. Truax in Albany
     (3-2/28/16)
868. Blakeley, Horace S., 28, d 3/5/20 in Phelps (3-3/8 and 5-3/15)
869. Blakeley, Melvin, 18, d 5/30/27 in Geneva (3-6/13)
870. Blakeman, Phebe Ann, 6, dau of Joel, Esq., d 4/17/22 in Galen (3-5/1)
871. Blakesley, Jane M., 34, wf of Dr. J. M., d 8/7/46 in Rochester (1-8/14)
872. Blakesly, Lorenzo m 12/21/45 Roxana Wright of Poland, NY in Rendolph,
     Catt. Co.; A. G. Bush, Esq. (4-12/26)
873. Blanchard, Charles, Esq., 32, attorney, formerly of NH, d 4/17/11 in
     Batavia (3-5/1)
874. Blanchard, Elijah m 9/14/42 Rhoda Tyler in Bath; Henry Pier, Esq.
     (2-9/21)
875. Blanchard, Gabriel m 3/19/22 Hannah Henries; Jacob Dox, Esq. All of
     Geneva (3-3/27)
876. Blanchard, William of Ellery m 1/4/38 Laura Messenger of Ellicott in E;
     William H. Fenton, Esq. (4-1/10)
877. Blany, John, 103, d 5/1/35 in Sandy Hill (5-5/15)
878. Blatchford, Samuel (Rev.), D.D., 60, d 3/7/28 in Lansingburgh "in the
     41st year of his ministry (3-4/2)
879. Blazdell, Polly (Mrs.) d of dropsy in Portsmouth, NH ("She had been tapped
     since Nov. 1805 more than two hundred times and more than eleven
     hogsheads of water drawn from her.") (3-6/16/19)
880. Bleecker, Anthony, Esq., 56, d 3/13/27 in NYC (3-3/28)
881. Bleecker, Elizabeth (Mrs.), 86, d in Albany (3-12/25/11)
882. Bleecker, Elizabeth (Mrs.), 64, d 3/14/18 in Albany (3-3/25)
883. Bleecker, Gerritie, 75, relict of the late J. L., d in Albany (3-8/25/13)
884. Blish, John H. m 11/8/24 Venera Anderson in Stafford; Rev. Anson
     (1-11/12)
885. Bliss, George W., one of the editors of the Pantheon, m 5/1/31 Sarah
     Maria Overton, both of Westfield, in W (4-5/18)
886. Bliss, John, 35, d in Avon (3-1/3/16)
887. Bliss Nathan of Farmington m Elizabeth Spoor of Hector in Phelps
     (3-11/15/15)
888. Bliss, Peletiah, 33, one of the proprietors of the Troy Post, d in
     Troy (3-10/14/18)
889. Bliss, Zenas (Rev.) m 5/2/35 Eliza Chamberlain in Fredonia; Rev. William
     Bradley (4-5/13)
890. Blithe, James, 69, d 10/24/27 in Pulteneyville (5-10/29)

891. Blodget, Arba (Mr.), about 47, killed 11/28/37 "by the falling of ...
earth upon him while engaged in digging sand." (4-11/29)
892. Blodget, Howard B., Esq., 43, d 6/21/37 in Clymer (4-6/28)
893. Blodget, John W. m 5/23/41 Jane Crandall in Busti; Rev. S. Baker. All
of B (4-5/26)
894. Blodget, Rebecca (Mrs.) d in Gorham (3-9/16/18)
895. Blodget, William (Col.), formerly of Providence, RI, d in Hartford, CT
(3-5/23/10)
896. Blodgett, George W. of Le Roy m Sophia Gould in Canandaigua (3-11/25/18)
897. Blodgett, Henry, 14, s of Hon. Heman, d 2/10/48 in Alexander (1-2/15)
898. Blodgett, Sally (Mrs.), 34, d 10/27/24 in Alden, Erie Co. (1-11/19)
899. Bloget, Bethsheba, 50, wf of Maj. Rufus, d 3/8/13 in Pulteney, Steuben
Co. (3-3/17)
900. Blood, Allen, 38, d 10/31/38 in Bath (2-11/14)
901. Blood, Asa (Capt.), 63, d 9/1/49 at his home in Bath (member, Episc. Ch.)
(2-9/5)
902. Blood, Charles, Esq. of Bath m 3/31/46 Ellen M. Fisk of Geneseo in G;
Rev. Pierpont (2-4/15)
903. Blood, Charles, 1 yr, s of Mrs. Ellen Blood, d 7/28/50 in Bath (2-7/31)
904. Blood, Daniel, 48, formerly of Carlisle, MA, d 8/18/26 in Carroll
(4-8/30)
905. Blood, Indiana, 56, wf of late Capt. Blood, d 11/24/49 at the home of
T. C. Thompson in Ithaca (2-12/5)
906. Blood, Isaac, 82, formerly of Bath and father of Capt. Asa Blood of Bath,
d 7/18/42 in Cohocton (2-7/20)
907. Blood, Samuel F., formerly of Bath, m 9/22/41 Lydia S. Cole of Howard
in H; Rev. William Goodell (2-9/29)
908. Bloodgood, Eliza, wf of Francis, Esq., d in Albany (3-11/25/18)
909. Bloom, Ephraim, 100, d 12/17/28 in Lansing, Tompkins Co. Served in
French War 2 yrs and in the Rev. War for 3 yrs in the U. S. Armory
in Pennsylvania; lived past 40 yrs in Tompkins Co., NY (one of the
first settlers there). Ephraim is father of "Gen. Bloom who was
wounded in the War of 1812". Surv by 4 ch, 61 gr. ch. and 110 gr gr ch
(3-12/31)
910. Bloom, Henry (Gen.), 50, sheriff of Tompkins Co., d 9/11/18 in Lansing
(3-9/23).
911. Bloomfield, _____ (Gen.) d 10/3/23 in Burlington, NJ (a Rev. officer;
"commander at the N.Y. station at the commencement of the late war")
(3-10/15)
912. Blossom, Abigail M., 19, dau of late Ezra of Blandford, MA and niece of
Col. William Blossom of Canandaigua, d 7/5/30 (5-7/9)
913. Blossom, Enos, 75, d in Onondaga (3-11/16/25)
914. Blossom, Isaac, 66, d 5/6/29 in Manchester (5-5/15)
915. Blossom, Isaac, 47, d in Manchester (3-5/20/29)
916. Blossom, Isaac B. m 3/23/37 Anna H. Ford, dau of Phineas, in Batavia;
Elder William W. Smith (1-3/30)
917. Blossom, Seth, 82, d 3/6/46 in Batavia (1-3/10)
918. Bly, Daniel m Phoebe Gardner in Canandaigua (3-6/11/17)
919. Boardman, Isaac m 7/7/40 Mary Dixon of Dixon's Ferry, IL (2-8/5)
920. Boardman, William, formerly of Geneva, m Alida Pruyn in Albany (3-5/14/28)
921. Boarland, Hiram of Waterloo m Betsey Davis, dau of John, of Seneca in S;
Samuel G. Gage, Esq. (3-7/9/23)
922. Bobcock, Lovina, 18, wf of Worden, d 2/24/40 in Ellery (4-2/26)
Bockus. See also Backus.
923. Bockus, Charles m 1/12/26 Carolyn Matilda Mallory, formerly of Batavia,
in Gananoque, Upper Canada at the house of Col. Stone; Rev. Arch Deacon
Stuart (1-2/17)
924. Bodine, John C., 64, one of the early settlers of Tyrone, d in T (2-1/2/50)
925. Bodine, Lewis m 4/13/40 Maria Read in Mud Creek; Ira Nash, Esq. (2-4/22)
926. Bogart, Caroline, 2 yrs, dau of Peter J. and Susan, d 5/21/37 in NYC
(5-6/2)
927. Bogart, Henry (Dr.), 29, s of John, Esq. of Albany, d 8/18/17 in New
Orleans (3-10/15)
928. Bogart, John, 77, of Washington, Richland Co., Ohio (a Rev. soldier)
d in Auburn, NY ("The fatigue of his journey ... the probable cause
of his death.") (3-9/17/28)

929. Bogert, Alexander Hamilton, 22, s of H. H., Esq. of Geneva, d 10/1/26 in Albany (3-10/18)
930. Bogert, Alida, 70, consort of Nicholas and dau of the late Rev. Johannes Ritzema, d (death date and place lacking in original) (3-4/14/13)
931. Bogert, David Ritzema, Esq. m 12/5/15 Margaret Morton in NYC (3-12/20)
932. Bogert, Eliza, 26, consort of Nicholas, d 11/4/14 in NYC (3-11/16)
933. Bogert, Eugene, merchant, m Eliza Ann Beck, dau of William, in NYC ((3-8/27/28)
934. Bogert, Gerrit, Esq. d 2/9/20 in Albany (3-3/15)
935. Bogert, Isaac, Esq., 78, father of H. H., Esq. of Geneva, d 9/24/18 in Albany (a Rev. officer) (3-9/30)
936. Bogert, Jacobus, 77, d 10/22/11 in NYC (3-11/6)
937. Bogert, James, Sr., 73, d 2/1/11 in NYC (3-3/13)
938. Bogert, Jane, 8, dau of H. H., Esq., d 9/4/13 in Geneva (3-9/8)
939. Bogert, John, 18, s of Rodolphus B., attorney, d 8/17/23 in NYC (3-8/27)
940. Bogert, John Ritzema, 3 yrs, s of Rudolphus, d 12/21/29 in NYC (3-12/30)
941. Bogert, John Shankland, 20 mo, s of Dr. Stephen V. R., d 8/24/28 in Geneva (3-8/27)
942. Bogert, Nicholas, 88, d 1/29/14 at his home in Beekmantown, Dut. Co. (3-2/9)
943. Bogert, William (Capt.), 38, late one of the proprietors of the Geneva Gazette, d 3/25/18 in NYC "after a lingering illness of 20 months" (3-4/8)
944. Bonaparte, Jerome Napoleon m Susan May Williams, dau of late Benjamin, in Baltimore (3-11/18/29)
945. Bonham, Charles m 9/18/38 Mary B. Goodwin in Campbell; Rev. Hotchkin (2-9/26)
946. Bonham, William, Esq. m 2/16/41 Eliza Cook in Campbell; Elder A. Abell (2-2/24)
947. Bonney, Jethro m Abigail Genung in Milo (3-2/27/22)
948. Bonney, P. H. (Deacon) of Jamestown m 1/29/40 Sybil Covey, dau of Deacon Amos of Fenner, Mad. Co., in F; Rev. A. P. Mason (4-2/26)
949. Boofman, John m 12/25/17 Caroline Waterman in Farmington (5-12/31)
950. Boogher, Christina (Mrs.), 61, relict of late Frederick, d 2/10/30 in Clyde (5-2/26)
951. Boogher, Frederick d in Seneca "leaving a large family in a helpless situation." (3-2/9/14)
952. Boogher, Frederick m 4/13/23 Ann Herrington "at the Glass Factory" (3-4/16)
953. Boon, David of Ithaca m 2/17/40 Jane Race of Painted Post; Edward Bacon, Esq. (2-3/25)
954. Boorman, ____, inf dau of Brazilla, d 3/31/22 in Geneva (3-4/3)
955. Booth, David m 10/23/17 Ann Darrow, both of Waterloo, in W; Rev. Axtell (3/11/5)
956. Booth, David of Junius m 11/6/23 Mrs. Lots Crittenden of Phelps in P; Rev. Axtell (3/11/19)
957. Booth, Isaac L. m Mary Ann Sherwood in Junius (3-1/9/28)
958. Booth, Rowland m 9/24/40 Susannah H. Keith, both of Farmington, in Palmyra; F. Smith, Esq. (5-9/30)
959. Booth, Sarah (Miss), 33, late of Palmyra, d 7/28/36 in Ashtabula, Ohio (5-8/5)
960. Booth, Sharon (sic) m Mrs. Ann Wilder of Bristol in Farmington(3-11/15/15)
961. Booth, William A., merchant, m 2/4/29 Alida Lucretia Russel, dau of late Charles, Esq. of Morristown, in NYC; Rev. Cox (3-2/18)
962. Boots, William, about 50, d 2/23/13 in Romulus (3-3/3)
963. Borden, Ambrose of Howard m 7/6/41 Loisa Stewart of Pulteney in Wheeler; Levi Grey, Esq. (2-7/7)
964. Borden, Azariah m 6/6/41 Sally Rose in Howard; Rev. Smith (2-6/9)
965. Borden, Eliza (Mrs.), 25, dau of Henry Mesick, d 1/8/40 in Howard (2-1/15)
966. Borden, George Isaac, 12, oldest s of Isaac and Eliza C., d 5/16/41 in Hornellsville (2-6/23)
967. Borden, John m 4/14/42 Caroline Andrus in North Cohocton; Simeon Holmes, Esq. (2-4/20)
968. Borrekens, ____ (Mrs.), consort of Mr. Borrekens of the house of Borrekens & Co., Troupville, Great Sodus Bay, NY, d 4/15/10 (3-5/2)

969. Borrowe, Samuel (Dr.), 29, d 3/5/27 in Geneva (a grad of Yale College; moved to Geneva in 1824; funeral at home of S. Colt, Esq.) (3-3/7)
970. Borrowe, Samuel, 62, father of Dr. Borrowe late of Geneva, deceased, d 3/28/28 in NYC (3-4/2)
971. Borst, Joseph m 7/5/38 Nancy Ward in Erwin; C. K. Miller, Esq. (2-7/18)
972. Bortle, Eleanor (Mrs.), 70, "the first white person that settled in Geneva" died "in February last in Schoharie" (3-7/24/11)
973. Bortle, Eliza, 22, d 12/19/21 in Palmyra (5-12/26)
974. Bortle, James m Hannah Scudder in Victor (3:11/22/15)
975. Bortles, Francis m 9/3/34 Emily Lilly, both of Palmyra, in P; Rev. Howell (5-9/5)
976. Bortles, Harriet Elizabeth, inf dau of J. H., d 7/27/36 in Palmyra (5-7/29)
977. Bortles, Jacob H. of the firm of Willcox and Bortles, booksellers, m 3/5/34 Mary Colt, dau of Maj. Joseph, at Zion Ch. in Palmyra; Rev. Staunton. All of Palmyra (5-3/7)
978. Boss, Washington G. m 1/1/44 Adelia A. Glass in Jamestown; S. Jones, Esq. (a double ceremony - see Henry B. Glass this date) (4-1/12)
979. Bostwick, _____, wf of Maj. Bostwick, d 9/5/19 in Geneva (3-9/8)
980. Bostwick, Hiram m 1/1/27 Ann McCornell, both of Auburn; Rev. William W. Bostwick (3-1/10)
981. Bostwick, Mercy, 61, oldest sister of H. W. Bostwick, Esq., d 8/24/49 in Corning (2-9/5)
982. Bostwick, William, 59, d 6/25/25 in Auburn (1-7/1)
983. Bostwick, William W. (Rev.) of Bath m Mary Lewis, dau of Ozias, in Litchfield, CT; Rev. Stone (3-5/7/28)
984. Bosworth, John (Capt.) of Phelps m Mrs. Anna Markham of Farminton in F; Zurial Brown, Esq. (5-9/16/40)
985. Bosworth, Seth W. m Catharine Pond in Farmington (3-12/26/27)
986. Both, Elder (Mr.), 45, m 12/12/32 Phebe Smith, 20, of Addison in A; Elder D. Shart (2-12/26)
987. Botsford, Elijah, 65, d in Jerusalem, NY (3-5/20/29)
988. Botsford, Emma Aurelia, 8 mo, dau of Luther H., d 2/14/35 in Carroll (4-2/18)
989. Boughton, Abijah, 57, m 1/29/26 Charlotte Robinson, 27, in Ovid (3-2/8)
990. Boughton, Abraham m Mrs. Ruth Brace in Victor (3-11/22/15)
991. Boughton, Amos H. m 12/26/24 Deziah Wolcott, dau of Erastus, in Elba; Elder S. Whitcomb (1-12/31)
992. Boughton, Claudius V., 47, d 11/10/31 in Vienna, NY (5-11/22)
993. Boughton, Enos, 73, formerly of Victor, Ontario Co. "and the first settler west of Oneida", d in Lockport (3-10/24/27)
994. Boughton, Morris of Michigan m 12/10/43 Lucretia Culver of Williamson in W; Rev. O. Moses (5-12/20)
995. Boughton, Newel m 9/20/26 Phebe Chase in Pembroke, both of P; Rev. H. Wallis (1-9/22)
996. Bouton, Henry H. of Avoca m 12/31/44 Laura S. Willys of Howard in Avoca; Rev. Samuel T. Babbitt (2-1/22/45)
997. Bowdish, Gideon, 82, d in Waterloo (3-7/1/29)
998. Bowdish, James m 1/21/40 Laura Hine in Palmyra; Rev. Stowell. All of P (5-1/22)
999. Bowdish, William m 10/20/24 Eleanor Burnet in Junius (3-11/1)
1000. Bowdoin, James (Hon.), 60, only s of late Gov. Bowdoin of Massachusetts and late ambassador from the U. S. to the Court of Spain, d in Boston, MA (3-11/6/11)
1001. Bowen, George T. m 1/1/44 Angeline Dunbar, both of Frewsburg, in Carroll; Rev. O. D. Hibbard (4-1/12)
1002. Bowen, L. E. (Col.) m 10/29/46 E. A. Perry, both of Troupsburgh, in Greenwood; L. Smith, Esq. (2-11/11)
1003. Bowen, Moses m 2/4/40 Adelia Briggs in Painted Post (2-3/25)
1004. Bowldner?, Susan (Miss), 23, d 9/6/20 in Palmyra (5-9/13)
1005. Bowman, Brooks (Dr.) of Oak Orchard m 2/27/24 Emily Ward of Riga; Rev. Darwin (1-3/12)
1006. Bowman, Elizabeth, 23, d in Urbana (3-10/15/28)
1007. Bowman, Joseph C. m 11/22/24 Sarah Patrick in Batavia; D. Tisdale, Esq. (1-11/26)
1008. Bowne, Robert, 73, member of the Society of Friends, d in NYC (3-8/12/18)

1009. Boyd, _____, ch of Robert, d in Canandaigua (3-2/14/16)
1010. Boyd, Hamilton, 44, d 10/20/22 in Albany (3-10/30)
1011. Boyd, John m 4/20/31 Prudence Wilcox, both of Wheeler, in Bath; Rev.
      D. Higgins (2-5/4)
1012. Boyd, Martin m 4/13/34 Diana Davis in Carroll; R. Pier, Esq. (4-4/16)
1013. Boyd, Sarah, 49, wf of James I., d 1/1/16 near Geneva (3-1/17)
1014. Boylan, Daniel C. m Sally Arnet, late of Orange County, in Southport
      (3-4/16/28)
1015. Boyle, Francis m 1/22/42 Sally M. Phelps of Sodus in S; Alexander B.
      Williams, Esq. (5-2/9)
1016. Boylen, William of Harlem m Isabel Aull of Caledonia; Rev. William
      McLaren ("Rochester Democrat please copy") (1-9/4/49)
1017. Boynton, Jonathan m Mahala Tibbetts, both of Lyons, in Ontario, NY
      (3-1/14/29)
1018. Boynton, Lorenzo m 4/18/39 Philura Main of Ontario, NY in Walworth;
      Rev. A. Hopkins (5-4/26)
1019. Brace, _____, inf s of Charles, d in Bath (3-11/4/29)
1020. Brace, Elisha m Laura Scudder in Victor (3-11/22/15)
1021. Brace, Elizabeth, 37, wf of Charles, d 10/8/41 in Bath (2-10/12)
1022. Brace, William B. of Ottawa, Lasalle Co, IL m 6/17/49 Alvira Strait of
      Bath at the Meth. Episc. Ch. in B; Rev. S. Walden (2-6/20)
1023. Bradish, Curran, formerly of Macedon, m Roby S. Comstock, dau of Darius,
      Esq., of Logan, Lenawee Co., MI, in L (3-4/8/29 and 5-4/3/29)
1024. Bradish, Hannah, 76, relict of Col. John deceased, d 12/5/28 in Macedon
      (5-12/19)
1025. Bradish, James (Dr.), 65, formerly of Hampshire Co., MA and father of
      John, Esq. of Utica, d 9/18/18 in Floyd (3-10/7)
1026. Bradish, Luther, Lt. Gov. of NY, m 11/19/39 Mary E. Hart, dau of Peter G.,
      in NYC; Rev. Dr. Hawks (4-12/4)
1027. Bradish, Nancy, wf of Calvin, d 9/23/39 in Lenawee Co., MI (was formerly
      of Macedon, NY) (5-10/4)
1028. Bradle, Chester m 1/25/26 Eliza Morrison in Dansville (3-2/8)
1029. Bradley, Alonzo F., 26, merchant, d 9/21/50 in Delavan, WI (From the
      Delavan Express: "He was married on the 11th of September 1848, thus
      leaving ... a lone widow in two short years..." (1-11/5)
1030. Bradley, Betsey Tiffany, 34, wf of Col. Edwin D., formerly of Jamestown,
      NY, d 8/21/39 in Green Creek, Seneca Co., Ohio (4-9/11)
1031. Bradley, Bristol m 12/24/40 Cornelia Abbot in Westfield; Rev. Hopkins.
      All of Westfield (4-1/6/41)
1032. Bradley, Daniel (Capt.) of Middlebury m 3/2/26 Mrs. Electa Foster of
      Batavia; Rev. Spencer (1-3/3)
1033. Bradley, Dorcas, 22, wf of Zera, d in Bath (3-9/19/27)
1034. Bradley, Edwin D. m 11/6/31 Betsey Tiffany in Jamestown; Rev. Eddy (4-11/9)
1035. Bradley, Joseph T. m Margaret Van Buren in Canandaigua (3-3/20/22)
1036. Bradley, Mary Ann, 32, consort of Zera and dau of George Wheeler, Esq.,
      d 9/13/41 in Bath (2-9/15). She d 9/1 (2-9/22)
1037. Bradley, Sturges, 84, d 10/22/49 at the home of his son (not named)
      in Bath (2-10/31)
1038. Bradley, Thomas of Phelps m 11/17/18 Luanna Bradley of Lyons (3-11/18)
1039. Bradley, William m 5/30/43 Rosetta Young, both of Westfield, in Ripley;
      Rev. Orton (4-6/15)
1040. Bradley, Zera m Mary Ann Wheeler in Bath (3-6/11/28)
1041. Bradt, Anthony m 11/20/42 Eliza Lee in Busti; G. W. Parker, Esq. (4-11/24)
1042. Bradt, James, 2 yrs, s of Mr. Bradt, d 7/26/24 (prob. in Geneva) (3-7/28)
1043. Bragaw, Samuel J. of RI m 4/11/43 Elizabeth E. Hawkes of Palmyra in P;
      Rev. W. H. Douglas (5-4/19)
1044. Brainard, John G. C., Esq., 32, poet and editor of the Connecticut Mirror,
      d in New London, CT (3-10/15/28)
1045. Brainard, Seymour of Attica m 3/16/26 Anna Sherman of Middlebury, late of
      Lanesboro', MA, in Middlebury, NY (1-3/17)
1046. Bramble, John m Rhoda Cole in Prattstown (3-4/30/17)
1047. Brang, Conrad m Phoebe Venorman in Elmira (3-1/29/17)
1048. Brannach, Consider m 4/30/25 Mary Husted in Elba; J. Wilford, Esq.
      (1-5/6)
1049. Brayton, J. A., principal of the Ontario Female Seminary, m Mrs. Mary
      Winne in Canandaigua (3-10/8/28)

28

1050. Breck, Elizabeth, 67, wf of Joseph of Bath (sic), d 6/28/50 in Bath
(She had come to Bath to visit her son A. Y. Breck "and was taken
sick the day she intended to start for home"; member "Presbyterian
Church, Constitutional of Bath"; surv by husband, 8 ch, and 19 gr ch)
(2-7/10)
1051. Breck, Marcia Ann, 28, wf of George W., d 12/13/48 in Bath (buried in
Vienna, NY) (2-12/20)
1052. Breck, Samuel P. of Branch Port, Yates Co., m 9/19/39 Mary R. Baldwin
of Palmyra at Zion Ch. in Palmyra; Rev. C. M. Butler (5-9/20)
1053. Breed, Philip S., 22, bro of W. and J. C. of Jamestown, d 4/13/36 in
Carroll ("epileptic or fallen fits") (4-4/20)
1054. Brees, John m Mary Ann Trusdell in Elmira (3-1/29/17)
1055. Brees, John, 90, d in Elmira (3-4/15/29)
1056. Brewer, Henry, 69, d in Fayette (3-8/5/29)
1057. Brewer, John of Huntsville, Ohio m 11/1/32 Mrs. Mary Hussey of Palmyra
in P; Rev. B. H. Hickox (5-11/14)
1058. Brewer, Thomas d 5/6/23 in Annapolis, MD (a Rev. War pensioner)
(3-5/14)
1059. Brewster, Charles, merchant, late of Boston, d 12/10/25 (prob. in
Rochester) (3-12/21)
1060. Brewster, Morgan L. of Waterloo m Mrs. Sarah Kendig in Fayette
(3-5/27/29)
1061. Brewster, William R., merchant, of Canandaigua m 5/12/29 Elizabeth
R. Mott, dau of Samuel of NYC, in NYC; "his honor the Mayor"
(5-5/22 and 3-5/27)
1062. Bridges, George W., 1 yr, s of James W., d 6/25/26 in Bellona (3-7/5)
1063 Bridgman, Louisa H., 21, wf of Lewis H., d 10/23/35 in Coventry,
Chen. Co. (2-11/11)
1064. Briese, Norman d 2/1/25 in Geneva (3-2/2)
1065. Briggs, Alanson m 12/15/22 Mary Sloan in Junius (3-1/8/23)
1066. Briggs, Alanson E. m 4/24/50 Betsey E. Hilton in Prattsburgh; Rev.
B. C. Smith (2-5/1)
1067. Briggs, Alva m 1/31/41 Ischa Leonard in Arcadia; Rev. I. C. Goff
(5-2/10)
1068. Briggs, Henry of Avoca m 9/28/45 Hannah Whiting, only dau of James, Esq.,
in Cohocton; Dan H. Davis, Esq. (2-10/22)
1069. Briggs, John R., Jr. m 9/7/42 Margaret R. Pierce in Westfield; A. L.
Wells. All of Westfield (4-9/15)
1070. Briggs, Joseph T. of Benton m Miss A. Andrews in Middlesex (3-7/9/28)
1071. Briggs, Joshua m Eunice Andrews in Middlesex (3-1/19/20)
1072. Briggs, Lyman, 12, d 9/10/19 in Geneva (3-9/15)
1073. Briggs, Mary (Miss) d in Middlesex (3-3/31/19)
1074. Briggs, Robert m 10/24/16 Lydia Hall (prob. in Middlesex); Enoch Bordwell
Esq. All of Middlesex (3-10/30)
1075. Briggs, William of Bath m 8/20/38 Celia Towle in Hawley, Orleans Co.;
Rev. Perkins. All of Hawley (2-8/29)
1076. Briggs, William R. m Martha Willson in Middlesex (3-6/30/19)
1077. Briggs, William T. of Palmyra m 11/20/33 Clarinda? Farr of Sodus; Rev.
Buck (5-11/29)
1078. Brigham, James Risley, 22, s of James, Esq. of Dunkirk, d 7/26/43 in
Pittsburg, PA (4-8/17)
1079. Brigham, Jeremiah, about 45, formerly of Palmyra, d 3/1/37 in Port
Miami, Ohio (5-3/31)
1080. Brigham, John (Col.) of Nunda m Eliza Ayer in Rochester (3-12/28/25)
1081. Brigham, Mary (Mrs.), 75, d 3/29/28 at the poor house in Hopewell
(3-4/16)
1082. Brigham, Samuel m 11/3/39 Emily Ann Street in Palmyra; Frederick Smith,
Esq. All of Penfield (5-11/8)
1083. Bright, Michael (Gen.), 51, d in Philadelphia, PA (3-3/18/12)
1084. Brigs, John, 71, d in Bigflat (3-3/12/28)
1085. Brinckerhoff, John, 30, d in Sempronius (3-10/10/27)
1086. Brink, Amanda (Miss), 15, d 10/27/45 in Urbana (2-11/5)
1087. Brink, Charles m 11/28/41 Nancy Hallock in Erwin; C. K. Miller, Esq.
(2-12/8)
1088. Brink, George W. of Clarendon, Orleans Co., m 9/10/48 Sophia Bridges
of Elba (1-9/12)

29

1089. Brink, James L. m 3/3/47 Harriet A. Pratt, both of Mud Creek, in M C
(2-3/17)
1090. Brink, Joseph of Ovid m Harriet Pease in Peatown (3-2/3/19)
1091. Brinkerhoff, Henry I. of Wayne, Steuben Co. m Catharine Bevier of Owasco
in O; Rev. McNeal (3-11/7/27)
1092. Brinkerhoff, J. L. m 1/18/15 Charlotte Troup, dau of Col. Robert, in NYC
(3-2/1)
1093. Brisbane, George, Esq. of Batavia m 12/17/48 L. I. Whitehouse in Brooklyn;
Rev. W. H. Davis (1-1/16/49)
1094. Brisbee, Gain, 24, d 10/23/21 in Farmington (5-10/31)
1095. Bristol, Ira of Jamestown m 1/3/31 Nancy Warner of Erie, PA in E; Rev.
McCreedy (4-1/12)
1096. Bristol, John (Dr.) m 2/8/44 Mary Anne Birdsall, both of Pittsford, in P;
Rev. Hammond (5-2/14)
1097. Bristol, Lathrop S., 38, d 3/14/42 (death place not given) (5/3/23)
1098. Bristol, Reuben of Newark, NY m 2/10/31 Polly Watrous in Lyons; Rev. I.
Hubbell (5-2/25)
1099. Bristol, W. H. of Deposit, Dela. Co. m 10/5/48 Mary A. Worthington, dau
of G., Esq. of Batavia; Rev. Dr. James A. Bolles (1-10/10)
1100. Brisze, ____, inf s of Stephen,d 3/28/19 in Geneva (3-4/7)
1101. Britton, Richard m Eliza Stewart "in Jersey" (3-6/24/29)
1102. Brizse, Henry m 9/10/15 Phebe Dobbin in Geneva; Jacob Dox, Esq. (3-9/13)
1103. Brizse, Mary Jane, 11 mo, dau of Henry, d 5/23/27 in Geneva (scalded to
death) (3-5/30)
1104. Broadhead, William H. m 10/29/45 Lucy Cobb in Jamestown; Rev. S. W.
Parks. All of Jamestown (4-10/31)
1105. Brock, Finton m 10/17/22 Thankful Phelps in Williamson; Rev. J. Kinney
(5-10/23)
1106. Brockenborough, Austin (Lt.) of the U.S. Army m 12/19/26 Mary Skinner
Brown, dau of Maj. Gen. Brown, in Washington, D.C. (3-1/5/27)
1107. Brockway, Abel m Betsey Crane in Williamson; Rev. Howell R. Powell
(5-12/24/17)
1108. Brockway, Abner m 4/3/42 Mary Ann White in Wheeler; Seth Wheeler, Esq.
All of Wheeler (2-4/6)
1109. Brockway, Azuba, 66, wid of late Gamaliel, d 3/28/13 in Seneca (3-4/14)
1110. Brockway, Gamaliel, 62, d 8/17/09 in Seneca (3-8/23)
1111. Brockway, Hannah, wf of George, d 3/25/13 in Seneca (3-3/31)
1112. Brockway, Walter m 10/20/41 Dolly Beal, both of Wheeler,in W (2-10/27)*
1113. Broderick, Patrick of Starkey m Catharine Starks in Waterloo (3-4/29/29)
1114. Bromfield, Abraham m 2/23/31 Elvira Parker in Palmyra; Rev. A. E.
Campbell (5-2/25)
1115. Bronson, Esther (widow), 78, d in Bloomfield (3-11/19/17)
1116. Bronson, Gilbert m Phebe Cole in Howard (3-1/22/17)
1117. Bronson, Ira of Geneva m 9/15/16 Mary Crittenden of Phelps in P;
Philetus Swift, Esq. (3-9/18)
1118. Bronson, Thomas of Oswego m 12/25/22 Harriet Peters of Canandaigua; S. T.
Kibbe, Esq. (3-1/8/23)
1119. Bronson, William m Rachael Van Wormer in Cohocton (3-12/22/19)
1120. Brookfield, William of Philadelphia m 8/15/13 Emma Lalliet of Cayuga in C;
Rev. Woodruff (3-8/18)
1121. Brookins, Clark m Mary Ann Halstead, both of Alexander, in A; Rev. R. L.
Waite (1-1/4/38)
1122. Brookman, Samuel of Seneca Falls m Betsey Conner of Fayette in Waterloo
(3-12/9/29)
1123. Brooks, ____ (Mrs.), wf of Gen. Micah, d 3/26/25 in East Bloomfield
(3-4/13)
1124. Brooks, Barbara, 70, d in Phelps; Samuel Brooks, 40, d in Phelps; Moses
Brooks, 37, d in Phelps (All three of one family) (3-3/24/13)
1125. Brooks, David B. m 1/19/45 Nancy Pelton in Kennedyville; A. D. Read, Esq.
All of Bath (2-1/29)
1126. Brooks, Henry, 26, s of Birdsey of Brooks, Oakland Co., MI d 10/25/47
in Fairport, NY (2-11/3)
1127. Brooks, James G., Esq.. editor of the Morning Courier m Mary Elizabeth
Aiken, formerly of Geneva, in NYC (3-2/4/29)
1128. Brooks, Micah (Gen.) of Brooks Grove, Liv. Co. m 9/23/33 Elizabeth Chatter
(or Chatten) of Salem, Wash. Co. in S; Rev. W. Whiting (5-10/11)

* Officiating: Seth Wheeler, Esq.

30

1129. Brooks, Walter R. of Ashville m 10/20/42 Susan E. Curtis of Mayville in M; Rev. Dodge (4-10/27)
1130. Brooks, William C. m Lucinda Hopkins in Elmira (3-2/13/28)
1131. Broom, John (Hon.), 72, Lt. Gov. of NY, d 8/8/10 in NYC (3-8/22)
1132. Brotherson, P. C. H., Esq., Cashier of the Niagara Suspension Bridge Bank, m 9/13/38 Cynthia R. Scovell, dau of Seymour, Esq. of Lewiston,in L (5-9/21)
1133. Broughton, Urial m 10/28/32 Mrs. Naomi York in Bath; Henry W. Rogers, Esq. (2-10/31)
1134. Brower, John W., 15, a son of William, drowned 6/17/10 in the Hudson River "just south of Albany" (3-6/27)
1135. Brower, Mary, 64, relict of Theophilus and dau of late Nicholas Bogert, d 3/14/19 in NYC (3-3/24)
1136. Brower, Theophilus, 65, d 11/11/18 in NYC (3-11/25)
1137. Brown, ____, inf s of Barney, d in Bath (3-11/16/25)
1138. Brown, Abner m 6/2/44 Betty Stoddard in Jamestown; R. Lennox, Esq. (4-6/14)
1139. Brown, Alfred, 22, d in Nunda (3-5/2/27)
1140. Brown, Alva E. m 10/9/50 Sarah H. Hamilton, youngest dau of William, Esq., in Bath; Rev. Almon Gregory, rector of St. Thomas Ch. All of Bath. (2-10/16)
1141. Brown, Ann Ellen, 23 mo, youngest dau of Ezra W., d 12/12/42 in Marion (5-12/14)
1142. Brown, Anna, 39, consort of Daniel, d 3/26/13 in Benton (3-5/5)
1143. Brown, Anna (Mrs.), 82, mother of S. A., Esq. of Jamestown, d 8/10/37 in Hebron, CT (4-8/30)
1144. Brown, Asahel of Shelby, Orl. Co. m 11/11/45 Orilla M. Peck of Avoca in A; Rev. H. Spencer (2-11/26)
1145. Brown, Augustus m Pamelia Irons in Palmyra (3-1/21/18 and 5-1/14/18)
1146. Brown, Benjamin H. (Col.) of Rochester m Julia E. Morgan in Hartford, CT (3-12/7/25)
1147. Brown, Charles m 4/20/31 Dinah Freeman in Batavia; Rev. Gray (1-4/22)
1148. Brown, Charles C., Esq. m 9/6/43 Eliza J. Hoskins in Jamestown; Rev. E. J. Gillett. All of J (4-9/7)
1149. Brown, Charles Leslie, 3 mo, s of George M. of Bath, d 4/29/42 (2-5/4)
1150. Brown, Chester, Esq. of Waterloo m Elizabeth Force of Oppenheim, Mont. Co. in O (3-10/28/18)
1151. Brown, Daniel, 84, father of S. A. Brown, Esq. of Jamestown, d in Hebron, CT (In Rev. War served 6 yrs as Deputy Commissioner General "with the rank of Colonel") (4-6/20/32)
1152. Brown, Daniel B., Esq., 41, attorney, d 7/7/22 in Batavia (lived in B "since January 1804") (1-7/12)
1153. Brown, Edmund (Dr.) m Harriet H. Woodward in Cameron (3-4/30/28)
1154. Brown, Emmet E. of Cameron m 8/14/31 Mary Laughry of Canisteo in C; H. D. Millard, Esq. (See also marriage of Charles Laughry this date) (2-8/24)
1155. Brown, Ephraim (Dr.), 39, d 5/11/26 in Batavia ("lived many years in this place") (1-5/12)
1156. Brown, Ezekiel m 9/10/09 Betsey Wilson in Marcellus (3-9/13)
1157. Brown, Frances Ann, inf dau of Nelson, d 6/2/32 in Macedon (5-6/11)
1158. Brown, Francis of Rochester m 2/25/16 Jane Penfield, dau of Daniel, Esq., in Penfield (3-3/13)
1159. Brown, Francis m Loisa Hill, both of Palmyra, in P (5-6/30/18)
1160. Brown, Francis (Rev.), D.D., President of Dartmouth College, d 7/27/20 in Hanover, NH (5-8/23)
1161. Brown, G. W., Esq. of Batavia m 7/15/44 Angeline Gennette Britton of Elba in E; Rev. Dr. Corwin (1-8/13)
1162. Brown, George m Hannah Swarthout in Ovid (3-10/14/29)
1163. Brown, George M. m 4/22/35 Caroline Griswold in Bath (2-4/29)
1164. Brown, Guy R. of Le Roy m 12/1/47 Elizabeth Alton of Covington in Batavia; Rev. D. C. Houghton (1-12/7)
1165. Brown, Hannah, 23, wf of John, d 4/12/28 in Seneca (3-5/28)
1166. Brown, Helden (sic), wf of Thomas, d 4/20/39 in Hinchinbrook, Lower Canada (5-5/10)
1167. Brown, Heman of Bethany m 2/10/42 Sophia A. Conklin of Middlebury in M; Rev. R. Richardson (1-2/15)

31

1168. Brown, Henrietta, dau of Ebenezer, Esq., d in Penn Yan (3-8/13/28)
1169. Brown, Henry C. of NYC, 28, d 9/13/30 in Lockport (5-9/24)
1170. Brown, Henry O. of Portage m Olive Everess in Pike (3-10/10/27)
1171. Brown, Jacob, 62, d 4/19/24 in Stafford (1-4/23)
1172. Brown, James, 33 or 38, d 11/17/20 in Ridgeway (surv by wf; no mention
      of ch) (5-11/29)
1173. Brown, James m 9/17/24 Eliza Kane in Pembroke (1-9/17)
1174. Brown, James F., attorney, formerly assistant teacher at Palmyra High
      School, d 6/1/39 in Rochester (5-6/14)
1175. Brown, Jesse of Lyons was murdered 1/4/12 in Sodus ("shot through the
      head by Samuel Warren of Sodus"; Brown had been deputized "to assist
      a person in arresting Warren for a breach of the peace.") (3-1/8)
1176. Brown, John, Esq. m 7/29/13 Rebecca Tibbets in Lyons; Rev. ___ orus?
      All of Lyons (3-9/1)
1177. Brown, John m Mary Hayden in Palmyra (3-1/17/16)
1178. Brown, John A. of Elba m 5/11/25 Betsey Cash of Evans, Erie Co.; Aaron
      Salisbury, Esq. (1-5/20)
1179. Brown, John M. of Seneca m 8/17/28 Mary Jane Dickerson of Bellona;
      Samuel Gage, Esq. of B (3-8/27)
1180. Brown, John W. of Pembroke m 1/1/38 Roxana L. Noble of Batavia in Batavia;
      Rev. R. L. Waite (1-1/4)
1181. Brown, Jonathan m 12/24/28 Eliza Bradley in Painted Post (3-1/7)
1182. Brown, Joseph of Geneva, NY m 11/5/26 Lorinda Silsbee of Pittstown. PA
      in P; Rev. Gildersieve of Wilkesbarre, PA (3-11/15)
1183. Brown, Lucien of Cohocton m 5/10/38 Susan Besley, dau of Samuel, Esq.,
      in Campbell (2-5/16)
1184. Brown, Lucius H. m 7/31/45 Mrs. Harriet Hubbard, dau of Philip Cook, Esq.,
      in Cohocton; Rev. Wilson (2-8/6)
1185. Brown, Mark m Rose Waters in Colchester, CT ("after a courtship of 35
      years, their having had 15 children and 8 grand-children. It was
      high time for the old couple to get married.") (3-6/30/19)
1186. Brown, Mathew of Rochester m Mary Ann Burhans at Black Rock (3-1/14/29)
1187. Brown, Miriam Agnes, 16 mo, dau of S. A. and P. O. Brown, d 7/21/41 in
      Jamestown (4-7/22)
1188. Brown, Myron W. of Thurston m 12/11/50 Calcina E. Stewart of Campbelltown
      in C; Rev. J. C. Mallory (2-12/25)
1189. Brown, Nathan, Jr. m 8/17/41 Elizabeth Le Fevre in Ellington; Rev. E. J.
      Gillett (4-8/19)
1190. Brown, Nelson m Nancy Tucker in Palmyra; Rev. L. Camburn (5-11/28/21)
1191. Brown, Nelson m 3/4/38 Almina Watkins in Ellington; Elder E. Beardsley.
      All of Ellington (4-3/7)
1192. Brown, Paul S. m 4/1/27 Rebecca Lobdell in Palmyra (3-4/25)
1193. Brown, Ransom m 1/14/21 Hannah Washburn in Palmyra (5-1/17)
1194. Brown, Rassalas, A.M., of Warren m 1/20/41 Elizabeth L. Sill of Pleasant
      Township, Warren Co., PA (4-2/10)
1195. Brown, Robert m Temperance Dorman in Milo (3-5/28/28)
1196. Brown, Royal of Phelps m 7/9/18 Irene Moss of Waterloo in W; Rev. Bacon
      (3-7/15)
1197. Brown, Samuel, 17, s of Phineas, d 10/2/18 in Ontario, NY (5-10/6)
1198. Brown, Samuel m Betsey Cary in Prattsburgh (3-6/14/26)
1199. Brown, Samuel m Letty Rogers in Jerusalem, NY (3-4/23/28)
1200. Brown, Samuel R., 42, "for some time past a resident of Auburn, d near
      Cherry Valley. Author of Western Gazateer (sic), History of the Late
      War, ... (3-10/1/17)
1201. Brown, Silas m Mary Howland in Farmington (3-3/10/19 and 5-3/3/19)
1202. Brown, Simon m Rebecca Slocum in Waterloo (3-7/15/29)
1203. Brown, Stephen m 3/4/30 Ann Bennett in Marion; Elder Allen (5-3/10)
1204. Brown, Sylvester, merchant, m Elizabeth Hawley in Caledonia (3-4/8/18)
1205. Brown, William m 8/24/23 Eliza Kendal, both of Geneva (3-8/27)
1206. Brown, William Henry Harrison of Cameron m 1/19/40 Jane Townsend, dau of
      Uriah of Dresden; Rev. Smith Beers (2-2/12)
1207. Browne?, John m 6/11/40 Louise Stautice, both of Arcadia, in Palmyra;
      Rev. A. H. Stowell (5-6/17)
1208. Brownson, John W. (Dr.) d 11/20/24 in Gainesville (1-12/17)
1209. Brownson, Morton m 2/15/42 Harriet J. Taft in Lyons; Rev. Ira Ingram
      (5-2/23)

32

1210. Bruce, Archibald (Dr.), 42, d in NYC (3-3/11/18)
1211. Bruce, Arthur m 2/10/20 Isabella Hogg in Geneva; Rev. Clark ("baeth frae the land o' Cakes") (3-2/16)
1212. Bruce, Arthur, 38, keeper of the Washington House, d 7/10/27 in Geneva (3-7/11)
1213. Bruce, Eli (Dr.), 37, d 9/24/32 (of cholera) in Lockport (5-10/3)
1214. Bruen, Eleazer, 14, s of Gabriel, d 6/24/22 in Benton (accidentally shot 6/15 by a hunting companion) (3-7/3)
1215. Bruen, Matthias, pastor of the Bleecker Street Presby. Ch., d in NYC (3-9/23/29)
1216. Brumfield, Erastus m 10/27/41 Amy Brockway in Palmyra; Rev. G. R. H. Shumway. All of Palmyra (5-11/3 and 4-11/11)
1217. Brumfield, James, 94, father of James I. and Andrew D., formerly of Dutchess Co., d 12/18/44 in Westford, Ots. Co. (a Rev soldier) (5-1/3)
1218. Brumfield, Richard m 3/18/41 Electa Eggleston, both of Palmyra; Rev. R. Mann (5-3/24)
1219. Brundage, Alfred of Urbana m 7/3/42 Sarah Jane Lee, dau of David R., in Bath; Rev. Babcock (2-7/6)
1220. Brundage, Benjamin m Mary Read in Pleasant Valley (3-3/26/17)
1221. Brundage, Charles of Belfast m Caroline Dautremor____? in Angelica (3-8/19/29)
1222. Brundage, Ira m 5/18/50 Delia Robinson in Bethany; D. L. Worthington, Esq. All of Bethany (1-5/28)
1223. Brundage, James M. m 1/7/46 Jerusha Davis, both of Urbana, in Wayne; Elder Mallory (2-1/14)
1224. Brundage, Jesse, s of Capt. Abram of Bath, m 12/30/30 Sarah Wheeler, dau of Hon. Grattan H. of Wheeler, in W; Rev. D. Higgins (2-1/5/31)
1225. Brundage, Polly, 52, wf of Capt. Abram, d in Urbana (3-5/14/28)
1226. Brundage, Robert L., Esq. of Hornellsville m 5/26/46 Hannah A. Van Sickle of Greenwood in G; Rev. Northrop (2-6/10)
1227. Brunson, Amos, Jr. m Caroline Peck of Prospect, CT in Bloomfield, NY (3-10/17/27)
1228. Brunson, James m Mary Thrall in Olean (3-2/10/19)
1229. Brunson, Robert m 4/20/26 Lovisa Cowles in Geneva; Rev. Dr. Axtell (3-4/26)
1230. Brush, Charles m 5/24/21 Sarah Ann Hollett, dau of Mr. Peregrine Hollett, in Bethel; Rev. Wright (3-5/30)
1231. Brush, Charles of Bethel m 4/20/26 Laura Earll of Seneca, dau of Jephthah, in Seneca; Rev. Nisbet (sic) (3-4/26)
1232. Bruyn, Johannes, Esq., 63, d 2/5/14 in Shawangunk, Ulster Co. ("late a Senator in the Legislature and a judge of the common pleas in Ulster County") (3-3/2)
1233. Bryan, David, about 25, late of Bath, d 12/9/34 in Rensselaerville, Albany Co. (2-1/7/35)
1234. Bryan, Mary L., dau of J. B. Bryan, Esq., d 2/26/43 in Penfield (5-3/8)
1235. Bryan, William G., attorney, of Batavia m 2/24/48 Ruth Beardsley of York at the home of Mr. Stocking in York; Rev. H. W. Smuller (1-2/29)
1236. Bryant, George, 40, d in Waterloo (3-6/11/28)
1237. Bryant, Joshua m 11/17/41 Mary Jane Allerton in Bath; Rev. Beebee (2-12/8)
1238. Bryner, Eliza Ann, dau of R. W., d in Penn Yan (3-8/13/28)
1239. Buchan, Edward Wise, Esq., 39, d 2/22/14 at Fort Fayette (Lt. and commander in the British Navy - interred with military honors - commanded the "Lady Prevost" and "was severely wounded, ultimate cause of his death, in the memorable action of 10 Sept 1813 on Lake Erie." (3-4/13)
1240. Buchanan, Elizabeth, 50, wf of William, d 4/1/22 in Junius (3-4/10)
1241. Buchanan, William, 81, d in Bath ("one of the first settlers in that town") (3-8/6/17)
1242. Bucher, Catharine (Mrs.), 70, d in Painted Post (3-3/11/29)
1243. Bucher, Henry, 35, d in Painted Post (3-7/8/29)
1244. Buck, _____, ch of James, d in Waterloo (3-8/13/28)
1245. Buck, _____, ch of Roswell, d in Jamestown (4-10/23/39)
1246. Buck, Addison N. m 6/21/18 Sabrina Short, dau of Theophilus, in Manchester; Peter Mitchell, Esq. All of M (5-7/7). Married in Farmington (3-7/1)

1247. Buck, Daniel m Julia Ann Emans in Bucksville, Cay. Co. (3-5/2/27)
1248. Buck, Daniel, 45, d 3/20/29 in Palmyra (3-4/15 and 5-4/3)
1249. Buck, Elizar m Amanda Hildruth in Arcadia (3-12/30/29)
1250. Buck, Harriet, 36, wf of Roswell, d in Jamestown (4-7/9/34)
1251. Buck, James m 7/6/23 Mary McCollum in Waterloo; Rev. Lane. All of
       W (a double ceremony - see John Clark, Jr.) (3-7/16)
1252. Buck, James m Jane McCowlan in Junius (3-11/26/28)
1253. Buck, John (Capt.) m Ruth Bunce in Elmira (3-1/29/17)
1254. Buck, Justus, 55, and Hannah, 58, his wife, d in Junius ("both buried in
       in one grave, leaving a large family") (3-10/8/28)
1255. Buck, Miner m Elinor Thomas in Ovid (3-2/7/16)
1256. Bick, Zina J. m Eunice Hopkins in Palmyra (3-6/10/18 and 5-6/2/18)
1257. Buckanan, Walter, 18, m 8/15/17 Sally Hamilton, 17, in Lansing, Tompkins
       Co.; Rev. Kelsy (3-8/27)
1258. Buckbee, John of Benton m Ann Townsend of Ovid in O (3-3/13/22)
1259. Buckbee, John, 33, d in Penn Yan (3-6/13/27)
1260. Buckingham, Joseph of Pulteneyville m 10/3/32 Eveline West in Macedon;
       Rev. B. H. Hickox (5-10/10)
1261. Buckley, Abel B. of Milo m 11/13/26 Cathalina Bogert, dau of Isaac, of
       Dresden in D; Rev. Eddy of Penn Yan (3-11/15)
1262. Buckley, F. C. of Walworth m 5/5/36 Louisa Delano of Canandaigua; Rev.
       Greene (5-5/13)
1263. Buckley, Hugh m 12/31/09 Mary Barton in Cayuga (3-1/17/10)
1264. Buckley, Mary, wf of Col. Robert, d 7/6/17 in Benton (3-7/9)
1265. Buckner, George (Capt.), 69, (a Rev. officer) d 11/18/28 in Brayfield,
       Caroline Co., VA (3-12/24)
1266. Budd, Charles A. (Lt.) of U. S. Navy d 3/22/27 in NYC ("performed a
       gallant part with Macdonough in the Battle of Plattsburgh") (3-4/4)
1267. Budd, John m Mary Vail, both of Enfield, Tompkins Co., in Fayette
       (3-2/18/29)
1268. Budlong, Benjamin, 56, d 7/2/44 in Olean, Catt. Co. (His bro Samuel
       preceded him in death by two months. "Twenty five years since, while
       travelling on the St. Lawrence on the ice", he, his wife, their
       infant dau, "now Mrs. Allen", and sister-in-law all fell into the
       river. He pulled himself out and personally rescued all the others)
       (4-7/12)
1269. Budlong, Lawrence, 5, s of Benjamin, d 9/20/34 (4-9/24)
1270. Budlong, Philetta, 48, wf of Col. Judiah E., d 6/28/45 in Carroll
       ("among the earliest settlers of Jamestown") (4-7/11)
1271. Buel, Ichabod, late of Ridgeway, Gen. Co., d in a shipwreck on board the
       brig "Clotilda", "near Cape Henry" (3-2/18/18)
1272. Buell, Maria, 34, wf of Rev. A. K., d 9/19/35 in St. Catherines (5-11/6)
1273. Buell, Mary (Mrs.), 88, d 6/6/46 in Batavia (1-6/16)
1274. Bugby, Lyman of Attica m Mary T. Moffitt in Cazenovia (1-6/17/25)
1275. Bulkley, Levi m 12/15/29 Emeline Goddard in Phelps; Rev. Strong (3-12/23)
1276. Bull, Hannah, 57, wf of Asher, d 2/26/13 in Pulteney, Steuben Co.
       (surv by "a numerous family") (3-3/3)
1277. Bull, Horace H., 34, d 3/2/13, "five days after the death of his mother",
       in Pulteney, Steuben Co. (3-3/17)
1278. Bull, John, 51, d in Utica (3-7/25/27)
1279. Bull, Joshua m Sarah Buck, both of Buffalo, in Williamsville (3-8/21/16)
1280. Bull, Susan, inf dau of Col. William H., d 2/17/32 in Bath (2-2/22)
       Bull, Walter. See Ball, Walter.
1281. Bull, William H. m 9/20/29 Sarah Whiting, dau of Col. John, at the M. E.
       Ch. in Bath; Rev. William Bostwick (3-9/23)
1282. Bullis, Abraham (Dr.) m 5/13/40 Lydia P. Lapham in Macedon; A. D. Gage,
       Esq. All of Macedon (5-5/20)
1283. Bullock, David, 45, d in Schuyler (3-5/2/27)
1284. Bullock, John W. m 2/10/42 Jane Olmsted, both of Lyons; Rev. Nathan
       Baker (5-2/23)
1285. Bullock, Norvis m "Miss Smith" in Perinton (5-4/17/22)
1286. Bump, James, Jr., late of Hector, d 3/18/13 in Geneva (a soldier in
       the U.S. Army) (3-3/24)
1287. Bump, Joseph m 5/4/31 Betsey Phillips in Bath; Henry W. Rogers, Esq.
       (2-5/11)
1288. Bunce, David L., 44, d 2/13/26 (3-2/15)

34

1289. Bundy, Peter of Otsego m 6/24/47 Charlotte J. French of Bath in B; Rev. E. B. Fuller (2-7/14)
1290. Bunnel, Azubah, 41, consort of Col. Abner, d 12/10/22 in Canandaigua (3-1/1/23)
1291. Bunnel, Dennis D. m _____ Durand in Canandaigua (3-2/18/18)
1292. Bunnell, _____, a ch of Miles, d in Canandaigua (3-1/6/13)
1293. Bunt, John, 13, d 1/20/13 in Geneva (3-1/27)
1294. Burbank, Laura A., wf of Solomon M. and dau of William P. Irwin, Esq. of Sodus, d 7/5/43 in Marion, Wayne Co. (5-8/2)
1295. Burbank, Solomon M. of Newark, NY m 6/3/40 Laura Ann Irwin of Sodus in S; Rev. Jacob Burbank (5-6/17/40)
1296. Burch, Jeremiah m 7/5/30 Lucinda Smock in Lyons; Rev. Jones (5-7/16)
1297. Burger, Anson of Hopewell m 8/14/31 Celista Lemunion of Manchester at the National House in Palmyra; A. R. Tiffany, Esq. (a double ceremony - see John Cole) (5-8/16)
1298. Burgess, Annis, 25, wf of John, d 10/11/22 in Batavia (1-10/18)
1299. Burgess, Merrick m Ann Brown in Benton (3-4/17/22)
1300. Burgis, Allison (Rev.), D.D., 74, d 3/20/27 in Trenton, NJ (3-3/28)
1301. Burhans, Hezekiah, attorney, of Philadelphia m 5/16/30 Elvina Scovell of Modina; Rev. Savage (5-5/21)
1302. Burk, Horace of Italy, NY m 3/27/47 Sarah Ann Noble of Prattsburgh in P; Rev. J. K. Tuttle (2-4/7)
1303. Burke, John of Buffalo m Harriet Bradish of Jamestown in J; Rev. Parmely (4-5/26/41)
1304. Burket, Mary, 50, wf of William, d 9/15/45 in Bath (2-9/17)
1305. Burley, Elijah of Bath m 9/7/41 Cornelia Quant of Cameron in C; _____ Ketcham, Esq. (2-9/15)
1306. Burley, Hannah, 26, wf of Daniel, d 5/13/45 in Bath (2-5/21)
1307. Burley, John (Capt.) of Attica m 4/26/25 Martha Stebbins of Bennington in B; Elijah Carpenter, Esq. (1-5/6)
1308. Burley, William m 9/17/32 Susan Carnahan in Cameron; S. Willard, Esq. (2-9/19)
1309. Burley, William m 3/8/46 Anna Merfields, both of Bath, in Thurston; J. S. Depue, Esq. (2-3/11)
1310. Burlingame, Julia Ann, wf of Rev. A. H., pastor of the Bapt. Ch. in Palmyra, and dau of Nathan and Hannah Calhoon, d 6/25/41 at the home of her father in Pittsford, Monroe Co. (surv by a husband and one young ch) (5-7/7)
1311. Burlinggame, William (a Rev. soldier) d "at an advanced age" in Newtown (3-3/26/28)
1312. Burlingham, Philip m 12/5/39 Mrs. Cynthia Montgomery in Jamestown (4-12/18)
1313. Burnell, Madison, Esq., attorney, m 2/17/41 Sarah Spurr in Jamestown; Rev. Gillet. All of J (4-2/24)
1314. Burnes, Abel, 34, of the firm of Marshall, Chapin & Co., papermakers, recently from Massachusetts, d 8/7/26 in Waterloo (3-8/16)
1315. Burness, J., 115, a native of Scotland, d in Canada (served in the Battle of Culloden in 1745) (3-1/29/23)
1316. Burnet, Albert, 20, s of Gen. Burnet, d in Phelps (3-5/21/23)
1317. Burnet, George B. m 9/5/30 Abigail Craw, both of Galen, in Arcadia; Hezekiah Dunham, Esq. (5-9/17)
1318. Burnet, John (Maj.), 85, father of Gen. William, d 12/26/24 in Phelps (Maj. Burnet a Rev. soldier) (3-1/5/25)
1319. Burnett, Horace m 7/28/42 Delinda Smith, both of Macedon, in Palmyra; Frederick Smith, Esq. (5-8/10)
1320. Burnham, George W., merchant, of Avoca m 2/1/35 Caroline Silsbe, dau of James, Esq. of Avoca, in A; Rev. Bronson (2-2/4)
1321. Burns, Leonard m 9/22/16 Margaret Passage; Eli Bannister, Esq. All of Seneca (3-9/25)
1322. Burns, Peter m Eunice Henman in Canandaigua (3-2/18/18)
1323. Burns, Robert of Geneva m 12/25/28 Rebecca Fisher of Rushville in R; Lemuel Morse, Esq. (3-12/31)
1324. Burnside, James (age blurred) d 2/8/40 in Kennedyville (2-2/12)
1325. Burr, Freeman, about 60, formerly of Conway, MA, d 1/27/23 in Gorham (3-2/5/23)

1326. Burr, George N. of Batavia m 2/17/25 Miranda Foster of Elba in E;
      Rev. C. Colton (1-2/18)
1327. Burr, George N., 30, d 4/29/25 in Batavia (1-5/6)
1328. Burr, Mary, 23, dau of Joseph of Batavia, d 2/8/25 in NYC (1-2/25)
1329. Burrall, Erastus W., 36, d in Palmyra (3-8/6/28)
1330. Burrall, Thomas D., Esq. of Geneva, attorney, m 8/25/13 Charlotte
      Davies of Poughkeepsie in P; Rev. Reed (3-9/8)
1331. Burrall, Thomas D., Esq. of Geneva m 1/24/22 Sarah J. Mann, dau of
      late Dr. Mann of Hudson, in H; Rev. Read of Poughkeepsie (3-1/30)
1332. Burrel, Catharine, 20, dau of Edward, d 7/30/29 in Seneca ("No. 9")
      (3-8/5)
1333. Burrel, Isaac m 6/23/19 Margaret Burrel in Seneca; Rev. White(3-7/7)
1334. Burrel, Thomas (Capt.) of "No. 9" (in Seneca?) m 1/1/23 Mary Hall in
      Seneca; Rev. Axtell (3-1/15)
1335. Burrell, Arnold m Catharine Bennet in Ulysses (3-2/7/16)
1336. Burrett, Harvey (Dr.) m 12/13/31 Ann Babcock in Campbelltown; Rev.
      Smith (2-1/11/32)
1337. Burrington, Leander m 7/30/32 Lurena Walker in Kennedyville "after a
      courtship of an hour and a half"; E. F. Warren, Esq. (4-8/8)
1338. Burroughs, David of Shelby m 4/7/22 Mrs. Deborah Leonard of Batavia;
      Rev. Calvin Colton (1-4/12)
1339. Burroughs, David, Esq., 46, of Shelby (for several years supervisor
      for that town) d 10/10/22 in Shelby (1-10/25)
1340. Burrows, Almira, 30, wf of Ransom, d 6/2/40 in Jamestown (4-6/10)
1341. Burrows, Joseph A. m 12/22/42 Rowena L. Osband, dau of Rev. Wilson
      Osband, in Arcadia; Rev. G. Osband. All of Arcadia (5-12/28)
1342. Burt, Calvin m Betsey Covey in Harmony (4-1/10/27)
1343. Burt, George, merchant, m 9/23/23 Mary Pratt in Buffalo (3-10/8)
1344. Burt, Thankful, 22, dau of Oliver of Napoli, NY (formerly of Southampton,
      MA) d 8/15/33 in Busti (4-8/21)
1345. Burt, Timothy, Esq., 38, d 2/28/11 in Canandaigua (3-3/13)
1346. Burtch, _____, wf of Malcolm C., d in Junius (3-10/1/28)
1347. Burtio, William, 56, d in Canandaigua (3-7/15/29)
1348. Busenbark, John, 20, d 1/21/23 in Waterloo (3-1/29)
1349. Bush, Florena, 39, wf of Selden F., d in Busti (4-3/22/44)
1350. Bush, Gilbert, "aged xcviii years" d 11/19/24 in Geneva (3-12/8)
1351. Bush, Henry m 5/12/11 Rachael De Witt in Geneva (3-5/22)
1352. Bush, Hiram m Mary Laraby, both of Busti; George Martin, Esq. (4-3/30/36)
1353. Bush, John of Reading m 10/16/49 Huldah A. Bennett of Urbana in U;
      Rev. B. R. Swick (2-10/24)
1354. Buskerk, Zachariah m Rhoda Shays, wid of late celebrated Gen. Shays,
      formerly of Massachusetts, in Sparta (3-5/20/29)
1355. Bussey, Thomas m 2/23/32 Harriet Kelly (5-3/6)
1356. Bussy, Sabra, 12, d in Palmyra (3-3/24/13)
1357. Busti, Paul, Esq., late Agent General of the Holland Land Co. (all
      lands in NY west of Genesee River), d 7/23/24 in Philadelphia, PA
      "at an advanced age" (3-8/11)
1358. Butler, _____ (Mr.) m 7/31/42 "Miss Emerson", both of Avoca; Rev. O.
      Johnson (2-8/3)
1359. Butler, Alva m 1/27/38 Letitia Boyer in Bath; Rev. Wisner. All of
      Bath (2-2/7)
1360. Butler, Burr of Palmyra m 11/5/22 Maria Payne of Vienna, NY in
      Phelps; Rev. Brace (3-11/13). Maria of Phelps (5-11/6)
1361. Butler, C. N. of Jamestown m 7/3/39 M. A. Storey of Harmony in H;
      Rev. Gray (4-7/10)
1362. Butler, Charles, Esq., attorney, of Geneva m 10/12/25 Eliza A. Ogden,
      dau of Abraham late of Walton, Dela. Co., deceased, in W; Rev.
      Hedley (3-10/19)
1363. Butler, Charles H., 4, s of Charles, d 9/17/36 in Jamestown (4-9/21)
1364. Butler, David m Hannah Giltson in Canandaigua (3-11/15/15)
1365. Butler, Harlow of Busti m 3/11/39 Maria Sprague of Jamestown in J;
      Rev. Parmely (4-3/13)
1366. Butler, James, Jr., 20, d 5/5/44 at the home of his father in Laona (sic)
\*     (4-5/10)
1376. Butler, John, 90, d 6/5/12 in Benton (3-6/24)
1377. Butler, Joseph m Rebecca Newton in Canandaigua (3-12/17/17)
\* Numbers 1367-1375 inadvertently omitted.

1378.  Butler, Joseph m 12/24/40 Catharine Royer in Bath; H. Pier, Esq. (2-12/30)
1379.  Butler, Mary Jane, 4, dau of G. J., d 6/10/41 in Jamestown (4-6/17)
1380.  Butler, Mary O., 4, only dau of A. R. and Orville L. of Milwaukee, WI, d 6/29/49 in the home of Dr. Butler in Alexander (1-7/3)
1381.  Butler, Nancy Adelaide, 1 yr, dau of C.N. and M. A., d 2/4/42 in Jamestown (4-2/10)
1382.  Butler, Richard (Deacon), 77, d 1/2/39 in Busti (served for many years as deacon of the Cong'l. Ch. in Jamestown)(4-1/9)
1383.  Butler, Samuel m 1/24/39 Elizabeth M. Rice in Jamestown; Rev.Chapin (4-1/30)
1384.  Butler, Sarah Jane, 2 yrs, dau of Charles, d 3/1/33 in Jamestown (4-3/6)
1385.  Butler, Solendia, 2 yrs, dau of Solomon S. and Mary E., d 2/10/42 in Busti (4-2/17)
1386.  Butler, William m Esther Miles in Seneca; Rev. Axtell (3-12/22/13)
1387.  Butler, William, about 60, uncle of the Attorney General of the U.S., d 3/11/35 in Deposit, Dela. Co., "late a temporary resident of Bath" (2-3/18)
1388.  Butter, Gould of Jamesville m Bethia Dodge in Lyons; Rev. Pomeroy (3-2/27/22)
1389.  Butterfield, Martin of the firm of Sexton and Butterfield m 10/5/35 Nancy May of Westminster, VT in Palmyra, NY (5-10/9)
1390.  Butterfield, Richard m 10/30/22 Charity Deyoe, both of Geneva; Rev. Lane (3-11/13)
1391.  Button, Samuel m 3/14/33 Melissa Morey? in Harmony; T. S. Bly (or Ely), Esq. (4-3/27)
1392.  Butts, James, Jr. m 12/31/44 Ruthany Fessendon in Gerry; R. Lennox, Esq. (4-1/3/45)
1393.  Butts, Pardon, 24, m 12/25/17 Ruth Lomiston?, 44, in Farmington (5-12/31)
1394.  Buzzell, Polly, 3, dau of Dr. S. D. and Roba, d 7/28/39 in Harmony (4-7/31)
1395.  Buzzell, Roba, 35, wf of Dr. S. D., d 5/8/42 in Poland, NY (4-5/19)
1396.  Byrne, Jane, 83, d in NYC (3-12/20/15)
1397.  Byrne, John (Rev.), 84, rector of Richmond, Upper Canada, m 11/1/24 Ann Eyneuf, 11, (sic), dau of "Mr. Eyneuf", late schoolmaster of Richmond (3-12/22)
1398.  Cady, Jabez m 10/11/23 Sibel Church in Troupsburg (3-11/12)
1399.  Cady, Jane, 22, wf of Ichabod and only dau of William Clark, d 11/26/42 in Carroll (4-12/1)
1400.  Cady, Marvin I., 28, "candidate for the ministry in the Protestant Episcopal Church", d 9/15/23 in Geneva (3-9/17)
1401.  Cain, Charles R. m 11/23/50 Lorinda E. De Lano, both of Batavia; Rev. S. M. Stimson (1-12/3)
1402.  Cain, Henry, 84, m Mrs. Maxwell, 96, in Glasgow (presumably in Scotland) (sixth marr. of bridegroom, ninth of the bride) (3-2/8/15)
1403.  Cain, Joseph L. of Wayne m 1/27/50 Nancy Tyler of Mud Creek in Wayne; Rev. A. C. Mallory (2-2/6)
1404.  Caldwell, Charles William, s of William, d in Cameron (3-4/15/29)
1405.  Caldwell,, James W. m 4/2/43 Clarissa F. La Due of Chautauqua in C; Rev. Holland of Delanti (4-4/6)
1406.  Caldwell, Thomas m Mary Ann Shaw of Williamson in Ontario, NY; Jonathan Boynton, Esq. (5-2/13/22)
1407.  Calhoon, Erastus R. of Vienna, NY m 7/11/44 Lucinda Newton of Palmyra at the Bunker Hill Hotel in P; F. Smith, Esq. (5-7/17)
1408.  Calhoon, Harriet E., 22, wf of Erastus R., d 10/12/43 in Palmyra (5-10/18)
1409.  Calhoun, Erastus R. m 9/19/41 Harriet Drake in Palmyra; F. Smith, Esq. (5-9/22)
1410.  Calhoun, Mary, 62, wf of James, d 4/4/42 in Williamson (5-4/13)
1411.  Calkin, Elbert m 1/2/26 Elsa Wolcott; Rev. S. Whitcomb. All of Elba (1-1/6)
1412.  Calkin, H. M. of Henrietta m 11/6/50 Sarah Ann Todd of Pittsford in P; Rev. W. M. Ferguson (1-11/12)
1413.  Calkins, Ira of Pulteney m 12/20/31 Harriet Whiting of Bath in B; Rev. Parker (2-12/28)

1414. Calkins, John C. of Avoca m 1/30/49 Abigail Mack of Bath in B; Rev.
L. Miller (2-2/7)
1415. Calkins, John K., 55, d 3/21/47 in Bath (2-3/24)
1416. Cambell, Samuel m Elizabeth Tolsday in Campbelltown (3-7/15/29)
1417. Camburn, Jacob m Rebecca Champron in Palmyra (5-1/12/20)
1418. Camburn, Joseph m Roxcenia Shadduck in Palmyra (5-12/16/18)
1419. Cameron, _____, 4 yrs, dau of Dugald, Esq., d in Bath (3-5/16/10)
1420. Cameron, Charles, 8, s of Dugald, Esq., d in Hornellsville (3-10/21/29)
1421. Cameron, Charles, 22, s of late Dugald, d 8/8/32 in Hornellsville
(to be interred in Bath "by the side of his Father and Mother")
(2-8/15)
1422. Cameron, Dugald (Hon.), 52, assemblyman from Steuben Co., d 3/20/28 at
his lodgings at Bements Recess in Geneva (born in Invernesshire,
Scotland; arrived in U.S. in January 1795; settled immediately in
Bath, NY and remained there permanently). "His wife, son, brother,
and his wife's sister arrived a few days before his death." For
many years he served as agent for the Pulteney estate. (3-4/9)
1423. Cameron, Duncan, Esq., 54, late candidate for Senator, d in Athol.
(3-11/26/28)
1424. Cameron, Elizabeth, 40, consort of Dugald, Esq., d 10/1/22 in Bath
(surv by husband, children, and mother) (3-10/9)
1425. Cameron, Ewen, father of Dugald, Esq. of Bath, d 4/22/32 in Prattsburgh
(funeral at Meth. Chapel in Bath) (2-4/25)
1426. Cameron, George m 6/26/31 Betsey Pauling in Bath; Henry W. Rogers, Esq.
(2-7/6)
1427. Cameron, Jane, 65, wf of Charles, Esq., d 2/28/41 in Greene, Chen. Co.
(2-3/3)
1428. Cameron, Jennet (Mrs.) d in Bath (3-12/9/18)
1429. Cameron, John A. m 10/20/33 Harmony Hitchcock in Jamestown; Rev. W. R.
Babcock (4-10/23)
1430. Cameron, Joseph K. of Jamestown m 10/19/37 Elmira E. Lindsey of Stockton
in S (4-11/15)
1431. Camfield, Ebenezer m Mariam Mills in Urbana; Rev. T. P. Clark (2-5/5/46)
1432. Camp, Ambrose m 9/8/39 Phebe Jane Mills, both of Macedon, in Palmyra;
F. Smith, Esq. (5-9/20)
1433. Camp, Clark of Lee Center, Lee Co., IL m 8/23/47 Louisa Partridge of
Batavia at the Bapt. Ch. in Batavia; Rev. S. M. Stimson (1-8/31)
1434. Camp, Edgar m Hannah Carrier in Holland, Erie Co. (3-1/21/29)
1435. Camp, George Avery, 15, nephew of Col. Hermon of Trumansburgh, d 7/7/27
in Geneva (3-7/11)
1436. Camp, Hermon, merchant, of Trumansburgh, Tompkins Co., m 4/4/27 Mary
Caroline Cook, oldest dau of David, Esq., in Geneva; Rev. Dr. Axtell
(See also marriage of Charles A. Cook this date) (3-4/11)
1437. Camp, Nathan, Esq., 37, d 5/19/19 in Owego (3-6/2)
1438. Campbell, _____, inf s of Christopher, d 3/4/19 (3-3/17)
1439. Campbell, Ascha (Col.) d 3/14/25 in Campbelltown (3-3/30)
1440. Campbell, Aurelia Roy, 2 yrs, dau of Rev. Alfred E, d in Palmyra
(3-9/10/28)
1441. Campbell, Benjamin, merchant, m 2/5/23 Sophronia Ensworth, dau of Dr.
Azel; Rev. Mulligan. All of Rochester (5-2/19)
1442. Campbell, Ebenezer of Busti, 46, d in Pittsburgh (presumably in PA)
(4-6/19/33)
1443. Campbell, Henry F., 28, "town supt. of common schools of Batavia,
formerly of Putney, VT, d 4/22/47 in Batavia (1-5/4)
1444. Campbell, Hiram m 7/22/21 Amelia Ann Edwards, both of Seneca, in
Junius; P. A. Baker, Esq. (3-7/25)
1445. Campbell, J. M., Esq., formerly editor of the Genesee Republican,
m 3/8/48 D. McNaughton of Caledonia in C (1-3/21)
1446. Campbell, John of Jamestown m 11/27/31 Sally M. Bush of Busti in B;
R. Pier, Esq. (4-11/30)
1447. Campbell, John, about 66, d 2/15/45 in Bath (2-2/19)
1448. Campbell, John, 76, d 6/12/45 in Thurston (2-6/18/45)
1449. Campbell, John L., 27, "lately from Pennsylvania", d 8/24/09 in
Geneva (3-8/30)
1450. Campbell, Luther m 5/30/40 Elizabeth Burton in Greenwood; B. S.
Brundage, Esq. (2-6/3)

38

1451. Campbell, Mary Ann, 2 yrs, dau of Archibald, d 3/25/22 (3-3/27)
1452. Campbell, Nathaniel m 6/24/21 Lucretia Murray in Victor (3-7/25)
1453. Campbell, Permillia (Miss), 20, dau of John, d 10/10/42 in Bath
       (member, Presby. Ch.) (2-10/26)
1454. Campbell, Robert, Esq., 76, d 2/17/17 in Campbell Town, Steuben Co.
       (3-3/5)
1455. Campbell, Robert, 1 mo, s of John, d 3/26/42 in Bath (2-3/30)
1456. Campbell, Robert, Sr., 84, d 6/27/49 at the home of his son, Charles W.,
       Esq. in Bath (Born in the Parish of Galston, Ayreshire, Scotland,
       1/1/1765; lived in NYC 1794-96; in 1796 settled in Bath; original
       member, Presby. Ch., Bath) (2-7/4)
1457. Campbell, S. Miner of Campbelltown m 9/18/45 S. Louisa Burton, dau of
       G. E. of Prattsburgh,in P; Rev. B. C. Smith (2-9/24)
1458. Campbell, Sarah (Mrs.), 56, late of Batavia, d 9/18/48 in Hamilton,
       Ohio (1-10/3)
1459. Campbell, Sylvanus m 7/16/31 Electa Hunt in Howard; John D. Collier,
       Esq. All of H. (2-8/24)
1460. Campbell, Thomas, 42, formerly of Philadelphia and bro of late Mrs.
       Elizabeth Powell of Geneva, d 1/21/28 in Nashville, TN (surv by wf
       and 7 ch) (3-2/20)
1461. Campbell, William, 23. of Oxford, NY, formerly of Albany, d 10/2/10
       in Geneva (3-10/10)
1462. Campbell, William m 3/20/18 his former wife Mrs. Anna Campbell in
       China Grove; Rev. Fiddle (3-4/29)
1463. Campbell, William, Esq. of NYC m 8/26/33 Maria Starkweather, dau of
       Samuel, Esq., in Cooperstown (1-8/27)
1464. Canfield, _____ (Mrs.), 74, d 7/21/25 in Batavia (1-7/22)
1465. Canfield, Augustine m 5/19/24 Mrs. Electa Lewis, both of Alexander,
       in A (1-5/21)
1466. Canfield, Cyrenus W., Esq., attorney, 25, d 12/7/24 in Batavia (Funeral
       in St. James Ch.; Rev Lucius Smith officiating) (1-12/10)
1467. Canfield, Harvey m Sally Root in Canandaigua (3-2/18/18)
1468. Canine, Harrison, 15, m Eliza Plough, nearly 12, in Lexington, KY
       ("A long life to them. Mrs. Canine, 12 years hence, will be a spruce
       girl. The parties may be grandfather and grandmother ere they are
       thirty. Kentucky expects every man to his duty." - from a Kentucky
       newspaper) (5-9/18/29)
1469. Canius, Harrison, 15, m Eliza Plough, nearly 12, in Lexington, KY
       (3-9/23/29)
1470. Cantine, Christina, relict of the late Moses I., Esq., formerly one of
       the editors of the Albany Argus, d 11/25/23 in Kinderhook (3-12/10)
1471. Cantine, J. J. C., late editor of the Cortland Journal, m 7/20/28 Ruth
       Bull of Caroline, Tompkins Co., in C (3-8/13)
1472. Cantine, Moses I., Esq., senior editor of the Albany Argus and a state
       printer, d 1/24/23 in Albany (3-1/29 and 5-2/5)
1473. Cantine, Moses, Esq., 74, d in Marbletown, Ulster Co. (3-7/25/27)
1474. Capron, Austin, 25, formerly of Palmyra and son of William P. of
       Macedon, d 8/5/38 in Michigan City, IN (5-8/24)
1475. Capron, Elias W. "of Sodus Bay Phalanx" m 6/12/44 Rebecca M. Cooper,
       dau of Griffith M., of Williamson; "by themselves" (5-6/19)
1476. Capron, Eunice, 90, wid of late Samuel and mother of William P., d 3/7/33
       in Macedon (member of Episc. Ch.) (5-3/20)
1477. Capron, George of Macedon m 10/20/41 Tabitha Frances Stoddard of
       Windham, CT in W; Rev. J. E. Tyler (5-11/3)
1478. Capron, Samuel, 74, formerly of Norwich, CT, d 12/11/18 in Palmyra
       (surv by wf and ch) (5-12/23)
1479. Capron, Seth M. of Oneida Co., m Caroline Amelia Scofield in NYC
       (3-5/9/27)
1480. Capron, Tabitha Frances, wf of George and dau of late Wait Stoddard of
       Windham, CT, d 3/15/42 in Macedon, NY (surv by her mother (5-3/23)
1481. Card, John m Sylvia Scovell in Palmyra (5-11/20/22)
1482. Card, Stephen, Jr. m 3/7/41 Louisa Card, dau of Timothy, in Harmony;
       M. Norton, Esq. (4-3/31)
1483. Carey, Ananias, 70, d in Benton (3-4/1/29)
1484. Carey, David m 3/1/29 Ann Maria Ware, both of Geneva, in Marcellus
       (3-3/4)

39

1485. Carleton, _____ (Rev.) m 2/18/36 Jane Sherman in Palmyra; Rev. Lucky
(5-3/4)
1486. Carlisle, _____, about 6 yrs, dau of David, d 3/27/14 in Geneva ("her
death occasioned by a large log falling on her") (3-3/30)
1487. Carlton, Sally (Mrs.), 26, d 1/27/17 in Geneva (3-1/29)
1488. Carman, William m Mary Ann Davison in Almond (3-5/16/27)
1489. Carnahan, Henry m 2/25/31 Susan Fluent in Cameron; D. G. Skinner, Esq.
(2-3/2)
1490. Carner, Hiram P. m 2/29/32 Lydia A. Cole in Bath (2-3/7)
1491. Carothers, Hiram B. of Manchester m 12/21/29 Lucy Robinson of Phelps
in P; Rev. Farley (5-2/5/30)
1492. Carpenter, Abigail, 24, wf of George and dau of Azor Belding, Esq.,
d 10/31/28 in Hopewell (3-11/12)
1493. Carpenter, Ahaz F. of Dexterville m 7/7/42 Mary Ann Jackson in Wattsburgh;
Rev. Rowland (4-7/14)
1494. Carpenter, Anderson, 50, d in Bath (killed by the fall of a tree)
(3-3/19/17)
1495. Carpenter, Chauncy of Covington, KY m 4/17/43 Catharine C. Stoneman of
Harmony in H; Rev. W. R. Brooks (4-4/27)
1496. Carpenter, Clement, Esq., attorney, of Batavia m 1/23/25 Eliza Ann
Ganson, dau of James, Esq. of Le Roy, in L R; Rev. Lucius Smith
(He was appointed justice of the peace in Batavia in 1822) (1-1/28)
1497. Carpenter, Elijah m 10/28/13 Elvira Baldwin, dau of Capt. William,
in Elmira; Hon. Caleb Baker, Esq. All of Elmira (3-11/10)
1498. Carpenter, J. E. m 5/8/50 Elizabeth Waite, both of Le Roy, at the home
of Chester Waite, Esq. in Le Roy (1-5/21)
1499. Carpenter, Joseph, 48, d in Elmira (3-6/3/29)
1500. Carpenter, Joseph of Lancaster, Erie Co., m 7/4/37 Cynthia Rogers of
Williamson in W; C. Bateman, Esq. (5-7/7)
1501. Carpenter, Joseph, a member of the Friends' Society and formerly of
Dutchess County, d 6/22/44 in Macedon ("Poughkeepsie papers please
copy") (5-6/26)
1502. Carpenter, Lott C. of Palmyra m 10/1/40 Caroline S. Underhill of
Macedon in M; I. E. Beecher, Esq. (5-10/7)
1503. Carpenter, Monroe m 10/3/41 Emily Greenleaf in Gerry (4-10/7)
1504. Carpenter, Samuel D. m 10/20/42 Laura Wakeman in Port Gibson; Rev.
Fuller (5-10/26)
1505. Carpenter, Sarah, mother of Jesse, Esq., d in Elmira (3-6/13/27)
1506. Carpenter, Stephen C. m 5/12/36 Ambaline Aldrich, both of Macedon, in M;
F. Smith, Esq. (5-5/13)
1507. Carpenter, Stephen D. m Emeline Britton in Harmony (4-10/14/41)
1508. Carpenter, W. L., editor of the Dunkirk Beacon, m 1/10/37 Frances
Bristol, dau of Josiah W., in Dunkirk; Rev. T. Stillman. All of
Dunkirk (4-1/25)
1509. Carr, Asaph m 3/9/47 Cordelia A. Handy, both of Corning, in Elmira (2-3/24)
1510. Carr, Henry of Junius m 1/12/32 Susan Powell of Galen in Alloway
(5-1/24)
1511. Carr, John m Lucy Sanger in Canandaigua (3-5/20/18)
1512. Carr, John of Bulley Hill m 12/25/45 Sally Smith, late of Rochester,
in Bath; Elder Rutherford (2-12/31)
1513. Carr, Mills m Sarah Spencer in Catlin (3-4/1/29)
1514. Carr, Smith m Betsey Whitney in Milo; Hezekiah Townsend, Esq. (3-4/17/22)
1515. Carr, Thomas (Gen.), a member of Congress, d in South Carolina
(3-8/8/27)
1516. Carrier, Amariah m 1/31/44 Jerusha Hager; Rev. H. Smith (4-2/16)
1517. Carrier, John of Syracuse m 3/29/32 Sophronia Farewell of Lyons (5-4/11)
1518. Carroll, Angeline (Mrs.), 47, sister of Mrs. Isaac Gardner of Palmyra,
d 6/29/43 in NYC (5-7/12)
1519. Carroll, Charles, 56, formerly of Maryland, d 10/28/23 in Groveland
(3-11/5)
1520. Carroll, Charles, 6 yrs, only s of Judge Carroll, d in Groveland (3-2/3/30)
1521. Carroll, Charles H., Esq. of Williamsburgh, Ont. Co. m 5/9/20 Alida Maria
Van Rensselaer, dau of Jeremiah, Esq., of Utica in U (3-5/24)
1522. Carroll, William m 4/15/38 Mary Green, both of Jamestown, in J; Rev.
Aylworth (4-4/18)

1523. Carruthers, Katurah D., 22, wf of Cameron and dau of James Bowlby,
      d 12/8/46 in Bath (2-1/13/47)
1524. Carson, _____, 4 mo, dau of Peter, d in Canandaigua (3-8/8/27)
1525. Carson, Porter m 12/8/25 Lucinda Stevens in Canandaigua (3-12/21)
1526. Carson, Wilson B. m 1/19/26 Lydia Shepherd in Batavia; Rev. C. Colton
      (1-1/20)
1527. Carter, Amasa m Hannah Emmons in East Bloomfield (3-1/13/30)
1528. Carter, John, Esq., 69, d in Providence (presumably in RI) ("one of the
      most accurate and scientific printers in the U.S. and Proprietor of
      the Providence Gazette which he edited upwards of 45 years ... born
      in Philadelphia and served his apprenticeship with Benjamin
      Franklin... He was postmaster 20 years.") (3-9/21/14)
1529. Carter, John, 66, (a Rev. soldier) d 9/17/25 in Bennington (1-9/23)
1530. Carter, John, 86, (a Rev. soldier) d 10/24/45 in Seneca Falls (grand-
      father of Capt. E. R. Bidwell of Bath)(2-11/5)
1531. Carter, Nathaniel H., Esq., one of the editors of the New York Statesman
      and author of Travels in Europe, d 1/22/30 in Marsailles, France
      (5-3/5)
1532. Carthart, William, 15, m Clara Crandall, 14, in Dover, Dutchess Co.
      (3-11/7/10)
1533. Carvalho, Emanuel Nunez (Rev.), "Pastor of the Hebrew Congregation of
      Philadelphia (state not given), d in P (3-4/30/17)
1534. Cary, Ebenezer (Dr.), 71, d in Dutchess Co. (3-6/7/15)
1535. Cary, Ebenezer (Capt.), 67, d 5/15/25 in Batavia (1-5/20)
1536. Cary, Hiram m Miss Reynolds in Prattsburgh (3-1/30/28)
1537. Cary, Joseph m 5/20/26 Harriet Sweet in Prattsburgh (3-6/14)
1538. Cary, Joshua m 1/23/23 Elizabeth Dodd "near the Glass Factory"
      (probably the Geneva area); Rev. Axtell (3-1/29)
1539. Cary, Lucinda, 25, dau of late Ebenezer, Esq. and niece of the Hon.
      Trumbull Cary, d 1/2/49 in Batavia (1-1/16)
1540. Case, David m 10/27/19 Catharine Youmans, both of Romulus, in R; Rev.
      Brown (3-11/3)
1541. Case, George of Penn Yan m 4/19/28 Eliza Backenstose, dau of late
      Frederick, of Geneva in Seneca; C. Shekell, Esq. (3-4/30)
1542. Case, George m 5/25/50 Harriet Graves in Howard; Rev. L. Rose. All of
      Howard (2-6/12)
1543. Case. John, Jr. of Bath m 2/19/47 Adaline Rector of Rome, NY in North
      Dansville; Rev. E. H. Walker (2-7/7)
1544. Case, Joseph A. m 5/22/31 Patty Fairbank, dau of Pearley, in Busti
      (bride and groom from B); E. Davis, Esq. (4-5/25)
1545. Case, Warner W. m 11/27/16 Susan P. Leonard in Bridgeport (West Cayuga);
      Rev. Axtell (3-12/18)
1546. Case, William m 1/15/32 Catherine Lefurgey (prob. in Sodus) (5-1/24)
1547. Cass. Erastus m 12/24/20 Parmelia Grimes, both of Farmington, in F
      (5-12/27)
1548. Cassada, John H. m Sally Bovier in Southport (3-5/20/29)
1549. Cassedy, Quintilian, 38, a native of Ireland, d in Waterloo (3-4/30/28)
1550. Cassida, Robert, 64, d in Elmira (3-7/2/17)
1551. Cassin, John (Capt.) of U.S. Navy d in Charleston, SC (3-4/10/22)
1552. Cater, John m 11/18/21 Polly Bush in Farmington; Daniel Allen, Esq.
      All of New Salem Village (5-11/21)
1553. Cathcart, William m 11/17/24 Pamela Chase in Pembroke; Rev. Hugh Wallis
      (1-11/26)
1554. Catlin, Brant, s of Judge Catlin, m 12/4/11 Peggy Bennet, dau of Ephraim,
      in Charlestown; Elder James _____ds? (3-12/25)
1555. Catlin, James m 1/10/14 Hulda Stanley, dau of Seth, in Seneca; Rev.
      Merrill (3-1/19)
1556. Catlin, Levi m Almira Sprague in Waterloo (3-11/25/29)
1557. Catlin, Phineas, Esq., 68, d 1/31/27 in Catharine (one of the earliest
      settlers in Tioga Co.) (3-2/21)
1558. Catlin, Putnam, 1 yr, s of William, Jr., d 5/25/21 in Geneva (3-5/30)
1559. Caton, Deborah, 65, wf of Elder John, d in Romulus (3-3/18/29)
1560. Caward, Ann (Miss), 20, dau of George, d 7/30/29 in Seneca (3-8/5)
1561. Caward, Elizabeth, 26, dau of George, d 1/8/30 in Seneca (3-1/20)
1562. Caward, George m Hannah Clark in "No. 9"(prob. in Geneva area)
      (3-1/30/28)

41

1563. Caykendall, John m Susan R. Baldwin in Milo (3-2/3/30)
1564. Cerio?, Hilliard of Lyons m 7/4/42 Melissa Turner of Arcadia at the
        home of Silas Hyde in Arcadia; Rev. K. Townsend (5-7/13)
1565. Chadwick, Alvah m 11/14/24 Sophronia Ashley of Pembroke in P; Elijah
        Flint, Esq. (1-11/19)
1566. Chadwick, Sarah, 66, wf of Elder Jabez, d 1/15/45 in Bath (2-1/22)
1567. Chaffer, Ephraim C. m Jane Blair in Italy, Ont. Co. (3-1/14/29)
1568. Chainholt, Martin m Rosana Vanornam in Canandaigua (3-4/2/17)
1569. Chamberlain, _____ (Mr.), 62, d in Lyons (3-10/1/28)
1570. Chamberlain, Angeline, 25, late of Bath, wf of W. W., d 4/14/40 in
        Livonia, Liv. Co. (2-4/22)
1571. Chamberlain, Angeline, 4 mo, dau of Henry W. and Angeline, d 8/21/40
        in Howard (2-8/26)
1572. Chamberlain, Betsey, 50, consort of Hon. Calvin T., d 2/27/45 in Cuba,
        Alleg. Co. (2-3/12)
1573. Chamberlain, Charles m 9/15/19 Pamela Dean in "No. 9 (Geneva area?);
        Rev. Axtell (3-10/6)
1574. Chamberlain, Eslhon, 51. wid of late Joseph, d 8/22/45 in Bath (2-9/3)
1575. Chamberlain, Franklin m Hannah Burt in Fayette (3-6/11/17)
1576. Chamberlain, Henry W. of Bath m 2/14/38 Angeline Bacon, dau of Cole S.,
        in Howard; Rev. Wheeler (2-2/21)
1577. Chamberlain, John, late of VT, m 4/2/29 Mary McCullough, wid of late
        John, Esq.; C. Shekell, Esq. (3-4/15)
1578. Chamberlain, Jonathan, 35, d 7/17/26 in Batavia (1-7/21)
1579. Chamberlain, Lewis m 1/16/17 Maria Hicks in Fayette (3-1/22)
1580. Chamberlain, Major m 7/11/22 Betsey Shed in Byron (1-7/12)
1581. Chamberlain, Rhoda Amanda, 12. d 2/11/45 in Bath ("for past two years
        a member of the Meth. Episc. Church") (2-3/5)
1582. Chamberlain, William m Elizabeth Herbert in Fayette (3-1/13/30)
1583. Chamberlin, Aaron m Catharine Viles in Fayette (3-6/3/29)
1584. Chamberlin, Enoch?, Jr. m 4/25/25 Catharine Van Ri_____?, both of
        Fayette in Waterloo; Rev. Lane (3-5/11)
1585. Chambers, James (Lt.) of the U.S. Army, "a young man", d 10/10/09 at
        Fort Columbus, NY (3-11/1)
1586. Chambers, William (Dr.) d 7/22/27 in NYC ("celebrated for his cure for
        intemperence ... left a recipe for the medicine") (3-8/1)
1587. Champion, Edmund of Macedon m 12/29/29 Delia Durfee of Palmyra in P;
        Rev. Eustace (See also the marr. of Capt. Harvey Cobb this date)
        (5-1/1/30 and 3-1/6)
1588. Champion, Thomas J. m 12/20/28 Almira Sutland, both of Palmyra, in
        Pittsford; Rev. Elder Tinney (5-12/26)
1589. Champlin, Charles d 10/20/19 in Sodus (3-11/3)
1590. Champlin, David D., 33, d 3/5/24 in Bethany (1-3/12)
1591. Champlin, James d in Ithaca (3-5/16/27)
1592. Champlin, Volentine m 1/8/32 Phebe Wilbur in Macedon; J. F. Packard, Esq.
        (5-1/17)
1593. Chandler, Albert, Esq. ("Rec. Clerk of the House of Assembly of Mich.")
        of Constantine, MI m Eliza Frances Abbott, dau of Robert, Esq. of
        Detroit, in Detroit (5-3/7/38)
1594. Chandler, Charles m Mary Bishop in Lodi (3-9/19/27)
1595. Chandler, Daniel H., Esq. m 12/24/24 Mary Stark at St. James Ch. in
        Batavia; Rev. Lucius Smith. All of Batavia (1-12/24)
1596. Chapin, Amelia, 17, dau of Col. Cyrenius, d 8/15/18 in Geneva (5-9/1)
1597. Chapin, Andrew, one of the proprietors of the iron foundry in Wolcott,
        d 2/4/26 in W (3-2/15)
1598. Chapin, Asahel (Rev.) m 1/1/40 Catharine Southland, dau of J., Esq.,in
        Jamestown; Rev. Z. M. Palmer. All of Jamestown (4-1/8)
1599. Chapin, Charles, 24, only s of Israel, Esq., d in Gorham (3-10/15/17)
1600. Chapin, Cyrenius (Dr.). 66, d in Buffalo (4-2/28/38)
1601. Chapin, Daniel m 5/27/22 Peggy Savacool, both of Batavia (1-5/31)
1602. Chapin, Diantha, 1 yr., dau of Vistus, d in Bath (3-2/13/28)
1603. Chapin, Graham H., Esq., 45, of Rochester, d 9/3/43 in Mount Morris
        (formerly lived in Lyons, Wayne co., and served as Dist. Attorney,
        Surrogate, and member of Congress) (5-9/13)
1604. Chapin, Henry m 2/9/32 Cynthia Chapin, dau of Henry, Esq. (5-2/14)
1605. Chapin, Israel, 70, d 8/31/33 in Hopewell (5-9/13)

1606. Chapin, Joseph m 6/26/50 Elizabeth _____att?, both of Campbell, in C;
       Rev. R. M. Beach (2-7/17)
1607. Chapin, Lucy, 85, d 2/11/50 in Bath (2-2/20)
1608. Chapin, Luther?, Esq. of Savannah, NY m 6/11/34 Mrs. Ann Jones of Lyons
       in L (5-6/27)
1609. Chapin, Lydia, 3 yrs, dau of Silas, d 3/19/23 in Geneva (3-3/26)
1610. Chapin, Maria (Miss), 17, dau of Col. Cyrenius, d 7/15/18 in Geneva
       (surv by parents and sisters) (3-8/19/18)
1611. Chapin, Moses, Esq., first judge of Monroe Co., m Mrs. Lucy T. Kibbe
       in Canandaigua; Rev. A. D. Eddy (3-11/15/26)
1612. Chapin, O. N. (Rev.) of Freedom, Portage Co., Ohio m Sarah B. Hobart
       of Busti in B; Rev. Morgan (4-5/19/42)
1613. Chapin, Oliver, 56, d 7/12/22 in Bloomfield (formerly of Salisbury, CT;
       one of the first settlers in Bloomfield) (5-7/31)
1614. Chapin, Pulaski (Col.), 31, s of Hon. Ezra of Prattsburgh, d 7/4/46
       in P (sermon by Rev. James H. Hotchkin at Presby. Ch.; surv by
       parents, a brother, and sisters) (2-7/15)
1615. Chapin, Ralph of the firm of H. and R. Chapin, merchants, m 11/12/29
       Eliza C. Morse in Canandaigua; Rev. Wheeler (3-11/25 and 5-11/27)
1616. Chapin, Sally, 21, d in Venice, NY (3-6/6/27)
1617. Chapin, Samuel, Jr., Esq. of Livonia m 9/4/27 Eliza Armstrong of Seneca
       in S; Rev. Todd (3-9/12)
1618. Chapin, Seth m 9/29/16 Mrs. Sylvia Holmes, dau of Cyrenius Chapin;
       Rev. Henry Axtell. All of Geneva (3-10/2)
1619. Chapin, Seth, 36, d 11/11/26 in Buffalo (3-11/29)
1620. Chapin, Silas of Geneva m 10/10/15 Deborah Dorsey, dau of Daniel, of
       Lyons in L; Rev. Lawrence Riley (3-10/18)
1621. Chapin, Silas, 18 mo, s of Silas, d 12/30/22 in Geneva (3-1/1/23)
1622. Chapin, Sophia (Mrs.), 39 or 59, wf of Henry, d in Gorham (3-1/30/22)
1623. Chapin, Spencer of the firm of Cameron and Chapin m 5/30/14 Eliza
       Seymour in Canandaigua (3-6/8)
1624. Chapin, Thaddeus, 63 or 68, d 3/7/30 in Canandaigua (one of the
       earliest settlers of that town) (5-3/19)
1625. Chapin, Timothy, 85, (a Rev. soldier), formerly of Springfield, MA,
       d 12/11/44 in Howard (2-12/18)
1626. Chapin, Volneyof Ogdensburgh m Cloe Sloan in Rochester (3-11/11/29)
1627. Chapman, _____, inf ch of John T., d 12/12/13 in Geneva (3-12/15)
1628. Chapman, _____, inf s of J. T., d 2/17/17 in Geneva (3-2/19)
1629. Chapman, _____, 16, of Penfield drowned 7/4/20 in Irondequoit Bay,
       town of Brighton, Ont. Co. (5-7/26)
1630. Chapman, Andrew F. m 3/4/47 Mary E. Hicks, both of Benton, in B;
       Rev. H. Spencer (2-3/10)
1631. Chapman, Daniel (Dr.), now editor of the Western Argus, m 10/24/32
       Elizabeth A. Gorgas, dau of Joseph, Esq. of Pennsylvania, in
       Lyons, NY; Rev. L. Hubbell (5-10/31)
1632. Chapman, George H., merchant, of North Urbana m 9/10/50 Amanda M.
       Walling of Cohocton in C; Rev. L. W. Russ of Hammondsport (2-9/18)
1633. Chapman, Heman m 3/3/16 Levina Swarthout, both of Benton, in B (3-3/13)
1634. Chapman, James m Mary Cronkite in Ithaca (3-9/19/27)
1635. Chapman, Jedidiah (Rev.), 72, Assoc. Pastor of Presby. Ch., Geneva,
       d 5/22/13 in Geneva (was ordained in his 21st year at Orangedale, NJ
       "where he labored 40 years ...") (3-5/26)
1636. Chapman, John C., 7, s of William, d 6/24/36 in Macedon (5-7/1)
1637. Chapman, Josiah B., Esq., "for many years sheriff of Seneca County",
       d 3/21/27 in Ovid (3-3/28)
1638. Chapman, Nathan, 69, d 4/6/27 in Geneva (3-4/11)
1639. Chapman, Noah, 47, d in Busti (4-5/11/31)
1640. Chapman, Palmyra, 41, wf of Ezekiel J., d 7/31/26 in Livonia (3-8/16)
1641. Chapman, Roswell R., 72, d 11/16/49 in Bath (2-11/21)
1642. Chapman, Sally B., 56, wf of Guy R., d 1/9/49 in Wheatland, Monroe Co.
       (1-1/16)
1643. Chapman, Thomas, 11 mo, s of Thomas, d 8/2/22 (3-8/7)
1644. Chapman, William E., one of the editors of the Oxford Gazette, m
       Harriet Selleck in Ulysses (3-9/23/29)
1645. Charles, _____, ch of Lewis Charles, d in Canandaigua (3-2/14/16)

43

1646. Charlesworth, William m 9/29/22 Mary Jackson; Rev. Kelly.  All of
      Geneva (3-10/2)
1647. Chase, _____ m Catharine Winship in Benton (3-2/19/17)
1648. Chase, A. B. (Rev.) of Cameron m 9/17/50 Elizabeth B. Towle of Howard in
      Bath; Rev. B. R. Swick (2-10/2)
1649. Chase, A. J. m 7/14/43 Charlotte Mabbet in Fredonia; Allen Hinckley, Esq.
      All of Fredonia (4-8/17)
1650. Chase, Asa m 2/23/35 Sarah Bogardus in Bath; Rev. Bostwick (2-3/4)
1651. Chase, Asa T. m 12/30/41 Betsey Ann Phelps in Manchester; Rev. A. H.
      Burlingame (5-1/5/42)
1652. Chase, Austin, 1 yr, s of George and Mary A., d 10/28/42 in Jamestown
      (4-11/3)
1653. Chase, Charles m 11/14/33 Orpha Bancroft in Walworth; John Stevens, Esq.
      All of Walworth (5-11/29)
1654. Chase, Christopher, 49, d in Ontario, NY (3-12/9/18)
1655. Chase, Clark, 51, of Palmyra d 7/27/21 in Chatham, Col. Co. (5-8/22)
1656. Chase, Edmund (Capt.) m Hannah Brown in Manchester (3-2/13/28)
1657. Chase, Elisha m 1/1/22 Margery Smith (3-1/16)
1658. Chase, Eliza Jane, 8 mo, only dau of John and Eliza, d 3/22/42 in
      Carroll (4-3/31)
1659. Chase, Francis, 32, d in Newton, NH of hydrophobia (3-7/10/16)
1660. Chase, Harriet O., wf of Charles and dau of Nathaniel Bundy, Esq.,
      d 9/5/49 in Cameron (2-9/12)
1661. Chase, Henry of Waterloo m 2/21/31 Caroline Page of Phelps in Palmyra;
      Rev. A. E. Campbell (5-2/25)
1662. Chase, Horace of Medina, Orleans Co., m 11/30/31 Amanda Turner, dau of
      Capt. Noah of Macedon, in M; Rev. B. H. Hickox (5-12/6)
1663. Chase, Ira m Lucy Wynship in Jerusalem, NY (3-7/1/18)
1664. Chase, Isaiah m Amanda Hoyt in Carroll; Rev. Adams (4-3/13/39)
1665. Chase, Job m Martha Miller in Palmyra (3-12/10/17)
1666. Chase, Obed G. m 12/31/44 Amy W. Sherman, oldest dau of Nicholas of
      Busti,in B; G. W. Parker of Jamestown (4-1/3/45)
1667. Chase, Philip d in Waterloo (3-4/23/28)
1668. Chase, William d 7/9/43 in Williamson (5-7/19)
1669. Chatfield, John, merchant, of Pembroke d 4/22/25 in Batavia (1-4/28)
1670. Chatfield, John, merchant, of Batavia, m 5/8/26 Mary Ann Moore of
      New Lebanon Springs; Rev. Taggert (1-5/19)
1671. Chatfield, Miranda, 19, wf of John, merchant, of Pembroke and dau of
      Capt. Samuel F. Geer of Batavia, d 4/10/25 in Pembroke (1-4/15)
1672. Chatfield, William Henry, 4, s of John and Mary Ann of Batavia,
      d 8/28/46 (1-9/1)
1673. Chauncey, Anna (Mrs.), 83, mother of Commander Chauncey, d 7/27/29 at
      the Navy Yard, Brooklyn (5-8/7)
1674. Cheedell, John H. of Auburn m Metila Cook, dau of Philip, Esq., in
      Cohocton (3-2/13/28)
1675. Cheeny, Susannah, about 26, wf of William, d 8/11/18 in Palmyra
      (5-8/18)
1676. Cheeny, Walter S., M.D., m 3/12/50 Louisa Falls at the cottage of
      Judge Denniston in Prattsburgh; Rev. B. C. Smith (2-3/20)
1677. Cheeny, William m 11/23/19 Abbey Jane Stocking in Palmyra; Ira Selby,
      Esq. (5-12/1)
1678. Cheesman, Nicholas m Catharine Garrison in Hector (3-2/7/16)
1679. Cheney, Daniel (Capt.) m 2/20/31 Amanda Parkhurst of Chautauqua in C
      (4-3/2)
1680. Cheney, Polly, 71, d 4/20/36 in Ellery (4-4/27)
1681. Cheney, Stephen of Batavia m 8/16/32 Electa Allen of Le Roy in
      Batavia; C. M. Russell, Esq. (1-8/21)
1682. Cheney, William m Susan Davidson, both of Palmyra, in P (3-6/3/12)
1683. Cherry, Jasper of New Jersey m 11/20/25 Dorothy Kane in Ithaca (3-11/30)
1684. Cherry, John, merchant, m 10/31/11 Alcinoe Baldwin, dau of Maj. Isaac,
      in Elmira; Henry Wells, Esq. All of Elmira (3-11/6)
1685. Cherry, Samuel (Maj.) (a Rev. veteran) d about 11/12/25 in Oswego
      ("was at the battles of Saratoga, Monmouth, and Yorktown - at the
      latter place he fought by the side of Gen. La Fayette") (3-11/30)
1686. Chesebro, Charles, 23, d in Canandaigua (3-6/13/27)

1687. Chester, _____ (Rev. Dr.), pastor of the 2nd Presby. Ch., Albany, d 1/12/29 "in Philadelphia" (3-1/21)
1688. Child, Asa, 47, printer and formerly editor of the Montgomery Republican at Johnstown, d 3/19/27 in NYC ("a brother to William, editor of the Seneca (NY) Farmer) (3-4/4)
1689. Child, Caroline Cleveland, 6, only dau of Elias and Lyvonia, d 7/4/48 in Batavia (1-7/11)
1690. Child, Jonathan, Esq. of Bloomfield m 5/7/18 Sophia E. Rochester, dau of Col. Rochester, in Rochester (3-5/20)
1691. Child, Luther, formerly of Bradford, m 1/10/41 Angeline Coates of Bradford in B; Elder Wall of Tyrone (2-1/20)
1692. Child, William H., publisher of the Skaneateles Telegraph, m Susan Hill in Waterloo (3-12/23/29)
1693. Childs, _____, 1 yr, ch of Joel, d 9/11/22 in Geneva (3-9/18)
1694. Childs, Amasa, M.D., of Waterloo m Larissa Southwick, dau of David, Esq., in Junius (3-11/26/28)
1695. Childs, Daniel, 51, "was shot by Augustus Hall (in Tyrone) about a year since. After a lingering and painful existence for many months, he died on the 4th inst. (in Tyrone)" (2-5/18/31)
1696. Childs, David W. of Utica, 45, attorney, d 7/27/26 in Pittsfield, MA (Left a will,with his charitable bequeathments listed in the obit) (3-8/16)
1697. Childs, Timothy m Catharine Adams in Wayne (3-4/9/17)
1698. Childs, Timothy (Dr.) d 2/25/21 in Pittsfield, MA (5-3/21/21)
1699. Childs, Ward of Lewiston m 10/10/22 Martha Washington Stevenson of Canandaigua in C (3-10/30)
1700. Childs, William H., merchant, of Niagara Falls m 4/15/28 Laura Amsden of Phelps in P (3-4/16)
1701. Chipman, Darius, 75, d 4/23/32 in Middlebury (1-4/24)
1702. Chissom, Ephraim m 8/7/15 Sally Miller in Benton; Elijah Spencer, Esq. (3-9/13)
1703. Chissom, George of Wheeler m 7/28/38 Ruth Williamson, dau of David of Wheeler (and recently of Medina. Mont. Co.) in Wheeler; Rev. McKenney (2-8/1)
1704. Chittenden, Jairus of Victory, Cay. Co., m 11/26/22 Mary Eliott of Waterloo in W; Rev. Lane (3-12/4/22)
1705. Chittenden, William E. (Rev.) of Bellville, IL m 4/24/45 A. E. Smith of Prattsburgh in P.; Rev. A. Kneeland (2-5/14)
1706. Chris?, Sally, about 20, died by suicide 4/2/12 at Benton (3-4/8)
1707. Christie, John (Col.), about 26, d 7/15/13 "at camp near Fort George" (23rd Regiment, U.S. Infantry; formerly Lt. Col. of the 13th, and one of the Inspectors General of the army) (3-7/28)
1708. Christopher, Joseph m Mary Ann Howell in Rochester (3-10/29/28)
1709. Chrystie, Thomas (Maj.), late of the U.S. Army, d in NYC (3-11/15/15)
1710. Chubbock, John m 1/31/47 Frances B. Rathbun in Howard; Rev. L. Rose. All of Howard (2-2/17)
1711. Church, Adonijah, 40, d 6/2/22 in Wolcott (surv by wf and several ch) (3-7/3)
1712. Church, Alden m 2/4/24 Polly Hough in Covington; Rev. True. All of C (1-3/26)
1713. Church, Angelica, 57, wf of John B., Esq. and dau of late Gen. Philip Schuyler of Albany, d in NYC (3-3/23/14)
1714. Church, Caleb C. of Lockport m 10/13/36 Christina A. Fisher of Newark, NY in Palmyra; Rev. G. R. H. Shumway (5-10/14)
1715. Church, Charles, brother-in-law of Col. C. Southerland of Geneva, d 9/22/28 at Black Rock (3-10/1/28)
1716. Church, Edwin F. of Bath m 12/26/49 Catharine Andrus of Ithaca in I; Rev. Henry (2-1/9/50)
1717. Church, ?Enos Galusha Levi, s of Alonzo, d 5/17/41 in Walworth (5-6/2)
1718. Church, Irving W., 9, s of Warner, d 9/5/44 in Palmyra (5-9/11)
1719. Church, Mary Zelina, 1 yr, dau of Chauncy, d 4/13/43 in Jamestown (4-4/20)
1720. Churchill, C. Dyer m 7/22/45 Sarah Rubles, both of Ellington, in Gerry; Rev. R. Punnell (4-8/1)
1721. Churchill, Charlotte, 38, consort of Josiah Churchill, Esq., d 3/17/26 in Bethany (1-3/17)

45

1722. Civer, William H., printer, m 8/13/45 Melissa Jane Cooley, dau of
      Edwin A., Esq. All of Attica (1-8/19)
1723. Clackner, Hannah, 42, wf of John B., d 8/1/31 in Palmyra (5-8/5)
1724. Clackner, Hannah, 3, dau of John S., d 2/11/32 in Palmyra (5-2/14)
1725. Clackner, John F. m 9/8/31 Mrs. Elizabeth Walker in Palmyra (5-9/20)
1726. Clackner, Lydia, 15, d 12/--/30 in Palmyra (5-12/17)
1727. Clapp, David m 2/3/22 Sylva (sic) Fox in Canandaigua (3-2/20)
1728. Clapp, Henry, 26, of Kempville, Upper Canada d 3/6/35 in Ransomville,
      Niag. Co. (5-3/13)
1729. Clapp, Luther m 9/8/23 Lydia Smith; R. Hogarth, Esq. All of Geneva
      (3-10/1)
1730. Clapper, Peter, 16, of Bethlehem south of Albany, apprentice of Mr.
      ?Jonathan Kidney   and son of late Mr. Clapper,d in or near Albany
      (3-6/27/10)
1731. Clark, _____, 5, s of Samuel, d in Canandaigua (3-12/6/15)
1732. Clark, _____, inf dau of Gaius, d 3/10/19 (3-3/17)
1733. Clark, _____, inf dau of Rev. Orin Clark, d 8/9/26 in Geneva (3-8/16)
1734. Clark, _____, 8 mo, ch of Gaius, d 7/7/27 in Geneva (3-7/11)
1735. Clark, _____, 9 mo, ch of Hiram, d in Geneva (3-9/5/27)
1736. Clark, _____, wf of Calvin, d 3/14/32 in Bath (2-3/21)
1737. Clark, _____ (Mrs.) d 2/5/33 in Jamestown (small-pox) ("This is the
      first case where this disease has proved fatal in our town  and we
      hope that He who governs the destinies of the human race may so
      order that it shall be the last.") (4-2/6)
1738. Clark, _____ (Mr.) m Jemima Moody of Am_____? (5-9/27/37)
1739. Clark, Albert, s of _____ius? C., d 9/11/17 in Geneva (3-9/17)
1740. Clark, Asahel, Esq., 57, attorney, d 11/22/22 in Glens Falls (3-12/18)
1741. Clark, Ashbery of Wheeler m 9/3/45 Eliza  Ann Budd, dau of Joseph, in
      Monticello (2-10/1)
1742. Clark, Austin, 23, d in Owego (3-10/8/28)
1743. Clark, Benjamin (Maj.), 63, d in Naples, NY (3-5/9/27)
1744. Clark, Benjamin, about 45, of Marion, Wayne Co., d 6/21/41 (suicide)
      (2-7/14)
1745. Clark, Beulah, 48, consort of Capt. William and mother of Mrs. Eddy of
      Canandaigua, d 2/9/27 in Utica (3-2/21)
1746. Clark, Caleb, 80, d in Canandaigua (3-8/26/18)
1747. Clark, Caleb m Elizabeth Taylor in Rushville (3-7/30/28)
1748. Clark, Charles R. of Wheeler m 2/26/42 Sarah Bailey, dau of Nicholas
      of Urbana, in U; John Randel, Esq. (2-3/2)
1749. Clark, Chloe, 61, consort of John, d 3/11/25 in Geneva (3-3/16)
1750. Clark, Dexter m Mary Rankin in Ovid (3-12/17/17)
1751. Clark, Elbriton F. m 10/3/40 Georgianna Short, both of Victor, in
      Palmyra; F. Smith, Esq. (5-10/7)
1752. Clark, Elihu L. of Palmyra m 9/11/34 Isabella Bean of Walworth in W;
      Rev. G. Osband (5-9/26)
1753. Clark, Eliza, 26, wf of Rev. Orin Clark, rector of Trinity Ch., Geneva,
      d 5/4/21 (3-5/9 and 5-6/6)
1754. Clark, Elizabeth, 34, consort of Alonzo, d 5/24/46 in Darien (1-6/2)
1755. Clark, Erasmus B., editor of the Seneca Falls Journal, m 1/20/30
      Prudence Darrow in Seneca Falls (3-2/3/30)
1756. Clark, Erastus, Esq., 57, d in Utica (3-11/16/25)
1757. Clark, Ezekiel of Jerusalem, NY m Polly Youngs (prob. in Benton)
      (3-2/13/28)
1758. Clark, Freeman m 5/2/44 Lydia Robinson; Rev. D. Harrington. All of
      Palmyra (5-5/8)
1759. Clark, George W., about 30, formerly of Bath and s of Jonas, Esq.,
      d 5/31/42 in Naples, Ont. Co. (2-6/8)
1760. Clark, Harvey m 12/30/30 Rhoda Tice in Palmyra; Rev. A. E. Campbell
      (5-12/31/30 and 5-2/4/31)
1761. Clark, Henry, Esq., 28, attorney, d in Ithaca (3-3/5/17)
1762. Clark, Hiram m 6/4/26 Mercy Brockway in Geneva; Rev. E. W. Martin.
      All of Geneva (3-6/7)
1763. Clark, Hiram G. m 5/15/47 Mary C. Bardeen, both of Prattsburgh, in P;
      Rev. Chapman (2-6/2)
1764. Clark, Horace m Parmelia Miles, both of Gorham, in G (3-4/8/18)

1765. Clark, Horace, 30, merchant, s of Ezekiel of Utica, d in Rodney, MS (3-2/23/29)
1766. Clark, Ira C. (Hon.), 46, member of county court, d (date and place not given) (Born in North Salem; moved to Prattsburgh from Manlius in 1824) (2-8/19/40)
1767. Clark, Israel W., 38, printer, formerly of Cooperstown, d in Rochester (3-10/1/28)
1768. Clark, James m Polly Baley in Romulus (3-6/24/18)
1769. Clark, Jerome S., 8 mo, s of J. A. and Caroline, d 9/11/41 inBatavia (1-9/21)
1770. Clark, Jesse, Esq. m 7/23/17 Lucinda Pixley, dau of Joseph, Esq., in Waterloo; Rev. O. Clark (3-8/6)
1771. Clark, John, 52, d 4/25/13 in Canandaigua (3-5/5)
1772. Clark, John m Sally Lock in Bath (3-11/19/17)
1773. Clark, John, Sr. m 4/19/26 Mrs. Sental in Trinity Church; Rev. Stone (3-4/26)
1774. Clark, John, merchant, of Rushville m Olive Jackson, dau of late Giles of Berkshire, MA and his 26th child ("Out of this number 22 have been married and most of them have large families. The oldest daughter was married upwards of 52 years ago.") (3-11/15/26)
1775. Clark, John, "Pioneer Agent", of Geneva m 9/10/29 Mary Lee (see footnote)*
1776. Clark, John, 49, d in Bath (3-9/23/29)
1777. Clark, John, Jr. m 7/6/23 Cynthia Buck in Waterloo; Rev. Lane. All of Waterloo (a double ceremony - see James Buck) (3-7/16)
1778. Clark, John L. m 10/13/42 Martha A. Flower in Palmyra; Rev. N. W. Fisher. All of Palmyra (5-10/19)
1779. Clark, Jonathan (deacon), 90, father of Joseph P. of Batavia, d 1/5/46 in Washington, NH (served 8 yrs. in Rev. War; moved permanently to Batavia, NY, then a wilderness, about 1804; member of Batavia Cong'l. Ch. 40 years) (1-3/10)
1780. Clark, Joseph, 71, d 8/7/20 in Ontario, NY (5-8/9)
1781. Clark, Levi m 5/3/43 Fulena Truacs in Williamson; Rev. Octavus Mason (5-5/10)
1782. Clark, Lucy, 31, wf of William H., d 3/10/46 in Batavia (1-3/17)
1783. Clark, Margaret, 16, dau of Peter, d in Catharine (3-1/13/30)
1784. Clark, Maria, 20, wf of Maltby C., d 4/15/22 in Palmyra (5-4/17)
1785. Clark, Mary A. Mills, 20, wf of Jonathan, d 8/30/46 in Bath (2-9/9)
1786. Clark, Mary S., 10, niece of Mrs. Davidson and dau of Thomas B. Clark of NYC, d 3/23/16 at the home of James Davidson, Esq. in Geneva (3-3/27)
1787. Clark, Matthew M. m Hetty Trowbridge in Waterloo (3-4/23/28)
1788. Clark, Moses B. m Betsey Baley in Lancaster, Sen. Co. (3-6/30/19)
1789. Clark, Myron H. m Zilpha Watkins, dau of Andrew, in Naples, NY (3-1/27/30)
1790. Clark, Oliver, 76, d 1/20/43 in Palmyra (5-2/1)
1791. Clark, Oren (Rev.), rector of Trinity Ch., Geneva, m 5/17/15 Eliza Ann Rutgers of Geneva in Trinity Ch.; Rev. Welton (3-5/24)
1792. Clark, Orin (Rev.), rector of Trinity Ch., Geneva, m 6/3/22 Susan L. Nicholas, dau of late Hon. Judge Nicholas, at White Springs Farm near Geneva; Rev. Dr. McDonald (3-6/5). Correction: Rev. Norton (3-6/12)
1793. Clark, Oren (Rev.), D.D., rector of Trinity Ch., Geneva, m 10/1/27 Sarah L. McComb, dau of John N. of NYC, at St. John's Chapel in NYC; Rt. Rev. H. U. Onderdonk, Bishop Elect of Pennsylvania (3-10/10)
1794. Clark, Orin (Rev.), 40, D.D., rector of Trinity Church, d 2/24/28 in Geneva (3-2/27). (His obituary appeared in this newspaper dated 3/12 - not genealogically significant)
1795. Clark, Otis Bronson, 6, s of Jesse, Esq., drowned 7/20/28 in Waterloo (3-7/30)
1796. Clark, Peter, 23, d 12/22/31 in New Haven, CT (refrained from eating proclaiming himself a reprobate) The editor states that there "seems to be a rash of this type of suicide in the U.S.A. at this perticular time. It is indeed full time that these frequent cases of insanity and suicide, the effect of sectarian zeal, should become the subject of pointed rebuke, if not of judicial inquiry"(5-1/10/32)
1797. Clark, Phebe, wf of Samuel, d in Junius (3-10/8/28)
* 1775 addendum: Mary Lee is dau of Francis of Benton; m in B; Rev. Eddy (3-9/16)

1798.   Clark, Philander m 6/12/28 Anna Van Dine, both of Middlesex, in
        Geneva; C. Shekell, Esq. (3-6/18)
1799.   Clark, Philo of Port Gibson m 9/12/41 Elizabeth Fitzgerald of Manchester
        in M; Rev. A. H. Burlingame (5-9/22)
1800.   Clark, Richard, 50, d in Romulus (3-8/27/28)
1801.   Clark, Richard L. of NYC m 1/29/35 Julia I. Fenton, dau of J. S.,Esq.
        of Palmyra, in P; Rev. Shumway (5-1/30)
1802.   Clark, Rosanna (Mrs.), 40, d 9/29/25 (1-9/30)
1803.   Clark, Samuel, Esq., attorney, of Waterloo m 1/3/25 Caroline _____
        of Auburn in A (3-1/19)
1804.   Clark, Samuel m Mrs. Jane Ingalls in Seneca Falls (3-2/3/30)
1805.   Clark, Samuel S. d in Benton (3-8/8/27)
1806.   Clark, Samuel W., 53, printer and formerly editor of the Bee, d 8/16/32
        in Hudson (2-9/5)
1807.   Clark, Stephen m 2/5/35 Ann Hathhorn in Palmyra; A. Salisbury, Esq.
        (5-2/13)
1808.   Clark, Susan R., wf of Rev. O., rector of Trinity Ch., and dau of late
        Hon. John Nicholas, d 7/31/26 in Geneva (3-8/2)
1809.   Clark, Thomas, Sr., 99, m 8/30/49 Mrs. Phebe Aspell, 72, wid of late
        Richard, in Starkey; Rev. J. Dodge. All of Starkey (2-9/12)
1810.   Clark, Timothy (Rev.), 78, d 4/11/41 in Le Roy (1-4/27)
1811.   Clark, William m Harriet Moore in Canandaigua (5-3/31/18)
1812.   Clark, William, about 10 mos, s of Gaius, d 5/25/21 (prob. in Geneva)
        (3-5/30)
1813.   Clark, William m 1/31/22 Susan Upson in Wolcott; Rev. Clark. All of
        Wolcott (3-2/13)
1814.   Clark, William E. of Geneva m 12/14/28 Eliza G. Frisbee of Lewiston
        in Albion; Rev. Lewis Cheeseman (3-12/31)
1815.   Clark, William H. m 9/8/40 Sybil A. Swan in Marion; Rev. Isaac C. Goff
        (5-9/16)
1816.   Clarke, Adam (Rev. Dr.) d in England (2-11/7/32)
1817.   Clarke, Adolphus m Sally Loring in East Bloomfield (3-12/26/27)
1818.   Clarke, James M. of Baldwinsville m 5/24/35 Eunice Harrison of Jamestown
        in J; Abner Lewis, Esq. (4-5/27)
1819.   Clarke, Theodore F., 19, s of late James C. and Eliza A. of Newburgh,
        d 4/3/50 in Poughkeepsie (2-4/10)
1820.   Clarke, William P. m Roby Eldridge in Jamestown; Rev. Peet (4-10/8/34)
1821.   Clarkson, Mathew (Gen.), 67, d 4/20/25 in NYC (3-5/4)
1822.   Clary, John, 43, d 9/2/27 in Geneva (3-9/12)
1823.   Clason, Isaac, 63, merchant, d 3/1/15 in NYC (3-3/15)
1824.   Clauchery, Alexander m 8/6/28 Sarah Jane Martin, both of Junius; Rev.
        Lane (3-8/27)
1825.   Cleaveland, Andrew W. of Naples, NY m 1/1/45 Almyra Goodrich of South
        Bristol in Cohocton; Dan H. Davis, Esq. (2-1/8)
1826.   Cleaveland, Josiah, 73 (a Rev. soldier) d in the town of Western, NY
        (5-1/24/32)
1827.   Cleaveland, Levi m Meriam Parish in Salem, Wash. Co. (3-3/11/29)
1828.   Clemmons, Alva, 20, d 10/5/22 in Geneva (3-10/9)
1829.   Clemons, John T. m 10/26/09 Jane Black in Geneva (3-11/1)
1830.   Clemson, Samuel (Dr.), Deputy Commissioner of the Port of Big Sodus Bay,
        m 6/5/34 Fanny S. Franklin late of Geneva in Sodus (5-6/27)
1831.   Clerc, Laurent of La Balme, France m 5/3/19 Elizabeth C. Boardman of
        Whitesborough, NY at the home of Benjamin Prescott, Esq. in Cohoes;
        Rev. Butler (Both deaf and dumb; he a principal instructor in the
        Asylum for the Deaf and Dumb in Hartford, CT; she a pupil there)
        (3-5/12)
1832.   Cleveland, Ephraim, Jr. (Capt), 42, d in Naples, NY (3-3/22/15)
1833.   Cleveland, Henry, 21, d 2/4/47 in Prattsburgh (2-2/10)
1834.   Cleveland, John m 7/12/46 Nancy Berry at Doty's Corners; G. G. Babcock,
        Esq. All of South Dansville (2-7/22)
1835.   Cleveland, Lucy C., consort of Stephen B. and dau of Joseph Huntington
        of Norwich, CT, d in West Bloomfield, NY ("married only ten months -
        left an infant son four weeks old") (5-4/14/18). Her middle name
        is Coit in 3-4/15.
1836.   Cleveland, Marcia, 44, d 5/5/42 in Hammondsport (2-5/11)

1837. Clifford, Samuel R., 53, d 7/13/49 in Chicago, IL (formerly of Le Roy, NY (1-7/31)
1838. Clift, Joseph, 76, d in Brutus ("killed by a kick from a horse") (3-5/30/27)
1839. Clinton, Charles A., Esq. m Catharine Hone, dau of John, Esq., in NYC (3-5/16/27)
1840. Clinton, De Witt (His Excellency) m 4/31/19 Catharine Jones, dau of late Dr. Thomas of NYC, in NYC (3-5/5)
1841. Clinton, George, Jr., Esq. d in NYC (3-9/27/09)
1842. Clinton, George W., Esq. of Albany m 5/15/32 Laura Catherine Spencer, dau of Hon. John C., in Canandaigua (5-5/23)
1843. Clinton, George Washington, only son of the late Vice President Clinton, d at his home near Wapping Creek, Dutchess Co. (3-4/14/13)
1844. Clinton, Maria, wf of his Excellency Gov. Clinton, d 8/6/18 at Mount Vernon near NYC (3-8/12 and 5-8/11)
1845. Clisbe, Addison (Mr.), 26, d 11/9/32 in Bath (2-11/14)
1846. Clisbe, Ira, Esq. of NYC m Eliza M. Camp, dau of late William, in Owego (3-10/24/27)
1847. Clisbee, James m 1/25/35 Sarah Linkletter in Howard; Rev. S. T. Babbitt (2-3/4)
1848. Clizbe, Phoebe, 38, wf of Joseph, d 3/29/49 in Avoca (2-4/4)
1849. Close, Abraham m 1/29//31 Rhoda Holcomb in Galen; William Voorhies, Esq. (5-2/4)
1850. Close, Gideon of Half Moon, Saratoga Co., m 5/5/25 Matilda Moe, dau of Capt. John of Covington; Rev. Anson (1-5/13)
1851. Close, James m Sarah Hammond in Penfield (5-1/17/21)
1852. Close, John, about 38, d 2/6/32 in Rose (5-2/14)
1853. Closson, Alice, 43, wf of Dr. Samuel, d 10/27/32 in Sodus (5-10/31)
1854. Co_____, Minor m 7/30/38 Harriet De Witt in Bath; Rev. Wheeler. All of Bath (2-8/1)
1855. Coary, Moses of Ovid m Mrs. Mary Clark in Romulus (3-1/27/30)
1856. Coates, Le Roy m 9/14/42 Matilda Knapp in Jamestown; Rev. Cook (4-9/22)
1857. Coates, Prudence (Mrs.), 80, mother of Mrs. S. A. Brown of Jamestown, d in Springfield, Ots. Co. (4-7/29/41)
1858. Coates, Solomon of Oneida Co. m 2/7/47 Lucia Guptyl of Batavia; Rev. Babcock (1-2/16)
1859. Coates, Leonard G. m 7/5/47 Nancy W. Grant in Bath; Rev. H. Spencer. All of B (2-7/7)
1860. Coats, Nancy Whiting, 27, wf of Leonard and dau of Col. Stephen Grant, d 12/12/50 in Bath (2-12/18)
1861. Cobb, E. S. m 1/28/23 Cornelia Parish, dau of Capt. J., in Canandaigua (3-2/12)
1862. Cobb, Eli m 8/11/29 Sarah Dexter in Marion; Marvin Rich, Esq. (5-8/14)
1863. Cobb, Freeman m Polly Harris, both of Palmyra, in P (3-6/3/12)
1864. Cobb, Harvey (Capt.) m 12/29/29 Ann Durfee in Palmyra; Rev. Eustace (See also the marr. of Edmund Champion this date) (5-1/1/30)
1865. Cobb, Harvey, 44, formerly of Palmyra, d in Hudson, Lenawee Co., MI (5-6/8/42)
1866. Cobb, Louisa H. (Miss), 36, d 2/5/43 in Cazenovia (member of Bapt. Ch. in Palmyra) (5-3/1)
1867. Cobb, Orin m 9/30/32 ?Unsuna Terrill in Middlebury (1-10/10)
1868. Cobb, Rensselaer m 9/21/36 Mary Gibson in Palmyra; Rev. G. R. H. Shumway (5-9/30)
1869. Cobb, Samuel m 1/1/15 Lois Lamphier in Bath; Rev. D. Higgins ( a double ceremony - see Jacob Smellagen) (3-1/18)
1870. Cobb, Sheldon B., 3 yrs, s of Adam B. and Thetis, d 3/7/41 in Jamestown (4-3/17)
1871. Cochran, Gertrude (Mrs.), 88, sister of late Gen. Schuyler, d in Palatine, Mont. Co. (3-3/31/13)
1872. Cochrane, R. E. (Lt.), 4th Infantry, U. S. Army, m 12/19/43 Sally T. Beall, dau of Tam'l (sic) T. of Bardstown, KY, at Fort Smith, AR (4-1/26/44)
1873. Cock, Samuel m 12/12/22 Charlotte Ann Vincent, both of Reading, in R; Rev. Adgate (3-12/18)
1874. Codding, George, 33, d in Bristol (3-3/13/16)

49

1875. Codding, Sarah, 83, relict of late George, Esq., d in Bristol (3-2/18/18)
1876. Codding, Sarah H., 33, wf of William T., d in Bristol (3-12/6/15)
1877. Codington, Samuel O. of Geneva m Patty White of Dresden in D.; Rev. O.
       Clark (3-1/14/18)
1878. Coe, Anna, 55, wf of Canfield, d 12/21/22 in Auburn (3-1/1/23)
1879. Coe, Chauncey H., 40, d 4/24/35 in Canandaigua (5-5/1/35)
1880. Coe, Elsey, 48, wf of Cyrus, d 5/20/42 in Jamestown (4-6/2)
1881. Coe, James (Rev.), ·D. D., 63,d in Troy "in the 30th year of his ministry"
       (3-8/7/22)
1882. Coe, John R., 23, second son of late Rev. Dr. Coe of Troy, d 9/30/23
       in Whitehall (3-10/22)
1883. Coe, Mathew, Jr. m 2/28/22 Ruth Deyo (prob. in Seneca); Elder Goff
       (3-3/6)
1884. Coe, Sarah, 48, wf of John, d 4/28/12 in Catharinetown (surv by husband
       and 7 ch) (3-5/20)
1885. Coffee, John (Gen.), 61, d 7/7/33 at his home near Florence, AL (5-8/9)
1886. Coffin, Robert S., the Boston bard, d 5/7/27 in Rowley, MA (3-5/23)
1887. Coffman, Abraham, 8 mo, s of Norris, d 8/2/31 in Bath (2-8/24)
1888. Coggshall, William, "a convict sentenced to 4 years imprisonment" d in
       the state prison in Ontario, NY (3-12/10/17)
1889. Cogsdill, William of NYC m Nancy Parks in Phelps (3-11/15/15)
1890. Cogswell, George of Marshall, MI m 10/23/44 Celeste A. Stone of Batavia
       at St. John's Ch., Batavia; Rev. Allen Steele (1-10/29)
1891. Cogswell, William, 22, d 4/28/26 in Alexander (formerly from Canterbury,
       NH) (1-5/5)
1892. Cogswell, William F. m 10/30/50 Louisa Patterson of Alexander in A; Rev.
       A. Kidder (1-11/5)
1893. Colbrate, Hugh of Palmyra m 3/26/44 Anna S. Colvin of Macedon in M;
       F. Smith, Esq. (5-3/27)
1894. Colbrath, William m 7/8/13 Olive Picksley, both of Gates, in Phelps
       (3-7/14)
1895. Colbrath, William d 3/18/30 in Palmyra (5-3/26)
1896. Colburn, Warren, 40, author of treatises on arithmetic and algebra,
       d in Lowell, MA (4-10/23/33)
1897. Colburn, Z. A. of Bethany m 9/11/48 Martha Bishop of Middlebury in M;
       Rev. J. Elliot (1-9/19)
1898. Colcord, Phineas, 19, s of Joseph, d 4/14/42 in Cameron (2-4/20)
1899. Colden, John, Jr. of Macedon m 6/20/34 Rachel Smith of Marion in
       Palmyra; F. Smith, Esq. (5-6/27)
1900. Cole, Abner, Esq. of Geneva m 10/14/10 Fanny B. Lawrence of Randolph,
       Morris Co., NJ in Randolph (3-11/7)
1901. Cole, Abner, Esq., formerly of Palmyra, d 7/13/35 in Rochester (5-7/17)
1902. Cole, Alexander H. m Eliza Way in Milo (3-9/16/29)
1903. Cole, Allen, Esq., 34, d in Jerusalem, NY (3-12/23/29)
1904. Cole, Caleb, about 50, a stranger, d 5/7/38 at the home of Amos Preston
       in Dansville ("a tin pedlar from one of the eastern states")
       (2-6/6)
1905. Cole, Daniel W., M.D., of Oswego m 12/25/26 Philura Bostwick, dau of
       late William of Auburn, at St. Peter's Ch., Auburn; Rev. Dr. Rudd
       (3-1/10/27)
1906. Cole, Eleanor H. (Miss), 20, dau of Dr. J. Cole, d 1/19/29 in Auburn
       (3-1/28/29)
1907. Cole, Elijah and Reuben, twin brothers of China, ME m Elizabeth and
       Mary ·Jones, twin sisters and daus of Edward of Brunswick, ME, at
       the Friends' Meeting House in Durham (3-10/26/25)
1908. Cole, Elijah, 34, d 10/31/42 in Phelps (5-11/9)          and 5-2/13)
1909. Cole, Elizabeth, 19, dau of Luther, d 1/28/22 in Canandaigua (3-2/20▲
1910. Cole, Elizabeth, 55?, wid of late Samuel of Baltimore, MD, d 7/5/38
       in Palmyra (5-7/11)
1911. Cole, Erastus of Palmyra m 1/2/21 Deborah Mudge of Wolcott in Palmyra
       (5-1/10)
1912. Cole, Ezra, 69, d 4/30/21 in Benton ("one of the first settlers of the
       county") (3-5/16)
1913. Cole, Franklin m 1/1/47 Hannah Mariah Clark in Howard; W. B. Rice, Esq.
       (2-1/6)

1914.  Cole, George W. of Palmyra m 8/29/29 Maria Waters of Lyons in L; Rev.
       L. Hubbell (5-9/4). Maria Waterous (3-9/9)
1915.  Cole, Hezekiah M., 37, formerly of Oneida Co., d in Howard (3-8/19/27)
1916.  Cole, James B., 29, formerly of Bath, d in Jackson, MI (2-9/31/42)
1917.  Cole, James L., Esq., 24, a poet "known by the library world under
       'Adrian'" d 2/8/23 in Canandaigua (5-2/26). ("His career was
       arrested by a fatal malady ... which had already consigned to the
       tomb a mother and sister") In this obituary his final poem (8 lines)
       is posted. (3-2/19)
1918.  Cole, John m 8/14/31 Priscilla Lemunion, both of Manchester, at the
       National House in Palmyra; A. R. Tiffany, Esq. (a double ceremony -
       see Anson Burger) (5-8/16)
1919.  Cole, Joshua m Innocent Durfee in Williamson (5-2/11/18)
1920.  Cole, Luther m 10/3/22 Sarah Rumney in Canandaigua; Rev. Johns (3-10/16)
1921.  Cole, Luther, 55, d 10/11/24 in Canandaigua (3-10/20)
1922.  Cole. M. S. (Dr.) m 7/9/29 Susan Powley of Sheffield, MA in Greece,
       Monroe Co.; Rev. Sampson (3-7/22)
1923.  Cole, Marcus m 3/29/32 Rosannah Beals in Palmyra; Rev. Osband of
       Canandaigua (5-4/11)
1924.  Cole, Mary, 42 wf of Luther, d 4/11/19 in Canandaigua (3-4/21)
1925.  Cole, Nancy Maria, 1 yr, d 4/2/22 in Geneva (5-4/17)
1926.  Cole, Nathan m Anna M. Goble in Jerusalem, NY (3-6/24/18)
1927.  Cole, Samuel J., 20, youngest s of late Samuel of Baltimore (presumably
       the village in the town of Preble, NY) d 10/10/38 in Palmyra (he
       one of the publishers of the Palmyra Whig) (5-10/12)
1928.  Cole, Sarah (Mrs.), oldest dau of Edward of Boston, d in Canandaigua
       (3-5/23/27)
1929.  Cole, Sophrona, relict of late Hezekiah M., d 5/11/40 in Howard
       (2-5/13)
1930.  Cole, William Ninde, one of the editors of the Wayne County Whig, of
       Lyons m 5/16/43 Emily W., dau of Ovid of NYC, in NYC; Rev. George B.
       Cheever (5-5/24)
1931.  Colegrove, Herman C. of Ulysses m Malvina Mullen of Hector in Jackson-
       ville (3-7/15/29)
1932.  Colegrovem James, 45, d in Hector (3-5/30/27)
1933.  Colegrove, William J. of Norwich, PA m 1/20/41 Eunice Wright of Bath
       in B; George Wheeler, Esq. (2-1/27)
1934.  Coleman, Celesta, 21, dau of Ambrose, d 10/15/48 in Le Roy (1-10/31)
1935.  Coleman, Cornelius C., 35, d 8/5/41 in Palmyra (5-8/11)
1936.  Coleman, Henry R. of Benton m 2/7/28 Caroline Squires of Seneca in
       Geneva; Rev. J. Gillmore (3-2/20)
1937.  Coleman, Spencer, Esq., formerly of Bloomfield, NY, d 4/21/23 in
       Detroit, MI (3-6/4)
1938.  Coleman, William, 63, senior editor of the New York Evening Post,
       d 7/13/29 in NYC (4-7/22)
1939.  Coles, Ann Maria, 21 mo, dau of Alva, d 4/2/22 (prob. in Geneva)
       (3-4/10)
1940.  Colgrove, George m 4/22/40 Emma A. Robinson in Addison; A. F. Lyon,
       Esq. All of Addison (2-4/29)
1941.  Colhard, Asa, Esq., sheriff of Albany Co., d 10/5/31 in Rensselaerville
       (2-10/12)
1942.  Collar, Elvira (Miss), 24, d 7/31/26 in Middlebury ("lately from
       Berkshire County, Mass.") (1-8/4)
1943.  Collar, Thomas m 4/3/31 Hannah Rowley in Bath; H. W. Rogers, Esq.
       (2-4/6)
1944.  Collier, Barbara, 35, wf of John A., Esq. of Binghamton, d 8/2/26 at
       the home of D. Woodcock, Esq. in Ithaca "while travelling for her
       health." (3-8/16)
1945.  Collier, Hamilton m Cecilia Merrill in Binghamton (3-10/3/27)
1946.  Collier, John A., Esq. of Binghamton m Lydia Ann Shepard in Elmira
       (3-10/24/27)
1947.  Collins, Eliza (Mrs.), 42, d 8/12/17 in Bloomfield (3-9/3)
1948.  Collins, George, inf s of John, d 3/18/25 (3-3/23)
1949.  Collins, Graves m Polly Belcher in Binghamton (3-1/14/29)
1950.  Collins, Hester Naomi, inf dau of Moses P., d 8/10/22 in Wolcott
       (3-8/21)

51

1951. Collins, Isaac, 71. d 3/21/17 in Burlington (printer and bookseller; member of Society of Friends)(3-4/9)
1952. Collins, Joseph J., 22. d in Ithaca (3-9/23/18)
1953. Collins, Martin, about 55, d 7/30/47 in Bath (2-8/4)
1954. Collver, Elias B., about 25, s of Phineas, d 8/12/26 in Hector (3-8/23)
1955. Collyer, Jacob of Milo m Hannah Potter in Benton (3-1/9/28)
1956. Collyer, Joel, 52, d in Cohocton (funeral sermon by Rev. Clary) (3-8/19/29)
1957. Colson, Henry m 8/19/32 Nancy Grow in Elba (1-8/21)
1958. Colt, Jabez, 60, bro of late Joseph of Palmyra, d 11/29/32 in NYC (5-12/5)
1959. Colt, Joseph, Esq., 64, d 2/4/31 in Palmyra (one of the oldest residents of this town) (5-2/11)
1960. Colt, Joseph Henry, 6 wks, s of Joseph S., Esq., d 6/11/32 in Palmyra (5-6/13)
1961. Colt, Joseph S. of Palmyra m 9/30?/30 Henrietta L. Peckham of Albany at St. Peter's Episc. Ch., Albany; Rev. Dr. Lacy (5-10/8)
1962. Colt, Judah, Esq., 71, bro of late Joseph of Palmyra, d (date and place not given) (Deceased was first sheriff and first treasurer of Ontario Co.) (5-10/24/32)
1963. Colt, Lucretia, about 50, consort of Capt. Elias, d 1/11/13 in Phelps (3-1/20)
1964. Colt, Susan Ann (Miss), 23, only ch of Gen. Samuel of Geneva, d 11/13/23 in NYC ("Her remains will be brought to this village for interment.") (3-11/19)
1965. Colton, Abby N., 28, wf of Rev. Calvin, d 2/2/26 in Batavia ("She was principal of a Ladies School"; funeral services in Presby. Ch., Batavia, with burial in Moscow, NY) (1-2/3). She d 2/1 (3-2/15)
1966. Colville, Walter, 9, s of William, Jr., d in Forestville (4-4/6/43)
1967. Colvin, David S. (Dr.) m 12/31/27 Harriet Eliza Morgan, dau of Peter B. of Poughkeepsie, in Syracuse; Rev. Barlow (3-1/16/28)
1968. Colvin, Jonathan B. of Tinicum, PA m 9/30/24 Margaret Gillimand of Fayette in F (3-10/13)
1969. Colvin, Zina H., Esq. m 9/21/18 Susan S. Barton, dau of Maj. Benjamin, in Lewiston (3-10/7)
1970. Combs, Mitchell McCarty m 2/3/23 Elmira Heath in Geneva; J. Field, Esq. (3-2/5)
1971. Combs, William m 12/31/29 Clorinda Gere in Seneca; Cephas Shekell, Esq. (3-1/6/30)
1972. Compton, Catharine, 13, dau of James, drowned 8/22/39 in the millpond in Jamestown "while playing upon the floating logs" (4-8/28)
1973. Compton, Hannah (Mrs.), 64, d 4/25/41 in Orange (2-5/12)
1974. Compton, Hannah Louisa, 15, dau of Peter, d 4/19/41 in Orange (2-4/28)
1975. Compton, Jane, 26, wf of Jonathan, d in Fayette (3-8/15/27)
1976. Compton, Jonathan m 3/5/29 Elizabeth Plate in Geneva; C. Shekell, Esq. All of Fayette (3-3/11)
1977. Compton, Reuben m 2/17/25 Margaret Cary at the Glass Factory (in or near Geneva); Rev. Nisbet (sic) (3-3/16)
1978. Comstock, Aaron, 77, d 4/12/15 in Half Moon, Saratoga Co. (a Rev. officer) (3-4/19)
1979. Comstock, Adam, 80 (a Rev. patriot) d 4/10/19 in Saratoga Co. (3-5/5)
1980. Comstock, Daniel m Mrs. Roxcenia Harris in Palmyra (5-6/14/20)
1981. Comstock, Heman N. (Dr.), 56, d 8/20/18 in Wayne, Steuben Co., (3-9/9)
1982. Comstock, Hezekiah d "last week" in Bethany (formerly from Connecticut) (1-7/29/25)
1983. Comstock, Joseph of Farmington d 8/5/21 in Lockport (5-8/8)
1984. Comstock. Laura, 28, wf of Moses, d in Utica (3-11/23/25)
1985. Comstock, Milo m _____ Perry in Palmyra (3-12/10/17)
1986. Comstock, Nathan, 55, formerly of Macedon, d 9/28/29 in Lockport (3-10/14 and 5-10/9)
1987. Comstock, Orville m Jane Gurlinghouse in Richmond (3-5/27/29)
1988. Comstock, Sarah, 27, wf of Edwin P., d 11/14/31 in Batavia (she was formerly of Chenango Co.) (1-11/25)
1989. Concannon, Luke (Right Rev.), 69. Consecrated Bishop of New York by the "present Sovereign Pontiff, Pius the 7th", d 6/19/10 at Naples (3-10/17)

1990. Condit, _____, 7, ch of "Mr. Condit", d 9/9/26 in Geneva (3-9/13)
1991. Cone, Eli, late of Marcellus, Onon. Co., d "in August last in the
      Indiana Territory" (3-1/29/17)
1992. Cone, Mary, consort of Eli, d 2/26/13 in Marcellus (3-3/24)
1993. Cone, Salmon m Nancy Kenyon in Locke (3-10/10/27). See #1994.
1994. Cone, Thomas of Locke m Rachel Goodrich in Painted Post (3-/10/10/27).
      See #1993.
1995. Conklin, Ambrose m 9/14/50 Lucy E. Fluent, both of Addison, in Bath;
      Rev. B. R. Swick (2-9/18)
1996. Conklin, Augustus G. m 2/18/47 Asenith Hawley, both of Middlebury;
      Rev. J. S. Barris (1-2/23)
1997. Conklin, Samuel (Capt.), 62, formerly of Fayette, d in Gorham (3-9/28/25)
1998. Conkling, Vincent m Sally Mathews in Southport (3-12/9/29)
1999. Connel, Philip M. m 11/30/12 Jane Wynkoop; Rev. Simeon R. Jones.
      All of Elmira (3-12/9)
2000. Connelly, John m Sally Ann Ellsworth, both of Milo, in Benton (3-10/28/29)
2001. Conner, Alexander, about 22, d in Bath (2-9/15/41)
2002. Conner, Charles W., 36, cashier of Newburgh Branch Bank in Ithaca,
      d 10/29/25 (3-11/16)
2003. Conner, Garret, Esq. m 8/30/46 Clarissa Morse, both of Elba, "on Pine
      Hill"; Rev. G. S. Corwin (1-9/1)
2004. Connolly, John (Right Rev.) , Bishop of the Roman Catholic Church of
      NYC, d 2/6/25 in NYC (3-2/23)
2005. Contoraman, Samuel of Howard d 1/8/38 ("hung himself in his own chamber")
      (2-1/10)
2006. Converse, Betsey, wf of John P., d 2/2/17 in West Cayuga (3-3/5)
2007. Cook, _____, wf of Bates, Esq. d in Lewiston (3-12/8/19)
2008. Cook, _____, 2 yrs, ch of Nathaniel, d in Canandaigua (3-10/1/28)
2009. Cook, Adaline (Miss), 21, d 4/21/47 in New Berlin, Chen. Co. (had been
      a teacher in Bath for 2½ yrs.) (2-5/12)
2010. Cook, Adam, 96, d 6/8/17 in Greenbush ("His wife, 94, performed ...
      the last pious office of closing his eyes - after having lived
      together as husband and wife ... sixty-nine years.") (3-6/18)
2011. Cook, Albert of Chautauqua m 12/29/44 Sarah Brown of Ellery in E;
      Rev. Halliday (4-2/14/45)
2012. Cook, B. Gordon, merchant, of Gorham m 1/17/33 Ehoda Cole of Benton
      in B; Rev. Gaylord (5-1/30)
2013. Cook. Bates, Esq., late comptroller of NYS, d 5/30/41 in Lewiston
      (2-6/9)
2014. Cook, Benjamin C., Esq., attorney, of Cohocton, Steuben Co., m 8/6/26
      Harriet Todd of Worcester, Ots. Co. in W (3-8/30)
2015. Cook, Betsey (Miss), 24, dau of David, of Phelps d 5/30/19 in P
      (3-6/2)
2016. Cook, Charles A., Esq. m 4/11/27 Anna Maria Cook, oldest dau of late
      Rev. Henry, pastor of the Presby. Ch. in Metuchen, NJ; Rev. Dr.
      Axtell (3-4/11). (See also marr. of Hermon Camp this date).
2017. Cook, Comfort, 88, formerly of Hartwick, Ots. Co., d 1/29/45 in Bath
      (2-2/5)
2018. Cook, Daniel of Covert m Phebe Bishop in Bath (3-9/2/29)
2019. Cook, Daniel P. (Hon.), late a member of Congress from IL, d in Kentucky
      (3-11/7/27)
2020. Cook, Edmund m 4/14/42 Zyporah Chapman in Canisteo; Elias Stephens, Esq.
      (2-4/20)
2021. Cook, George m 1/7/16 Sophia Van Riper in Fayette; Rev. Henry Axtell
      (3-1/10)
2022. Cook, Hannah, 43, wf of David, Esq. of Mendham, NJ, d 11/6/17 in
      Geneva (lived in G about 22 yrs; member of Presby. Ch.; surv by
      husband and 6 ch) (3-11/12)
2023. Cook, Henry A., 24, oldest s of David, Esq. of Geneva, NY, drowned 7/25/19
      in the Mississippi River while "passing up-river from Harrisonville
      (about 30 miles below St. Louis, Missouri Territory) to Bridgewater"
      (3-9/15)
2024. Cook, J. m 9/29/45 M. Sneatman, both of Wheeler, in W; Rev. J. Strough
      (2-10/8)
2025. Cook, John d in Albany (3-4/29/18)

2026. Cook, John, Esq., attorney, of Angelica m Sally Chittenden of Litchfield, CT; Rev. W. Bostwick (10/22/28)
2027. Cook, Lyman m Sally Winchell in Pompey (5-4/4/21)
2028. Cook, Maranda (Mrs.), 51. wf of Sheldon, Esq., d 4/9/47 in Batavia (1-4/20)
2029. Cook, Moses of Phelps m 7/31/36 Roxina Carlow of Hopewell, Ont. Co., in Palmyra; F. Smith, Esq. (5-8/5)
2030. Cook, Nehemiah m "recently" Helen Ann Billson of Kennedyville; Rev. Brown (2-12/2/46)
2031. Cook, Orsell, Esq., attorney, m 1/31/39 Ann Maria Tew, both of James-town, in J; Rev. Parmely (4-2/6)
2032. Cook, Paul C., Esq. m 3/18/41 Margaret Rosenkrans in Cohocton; Rev. Platt (2-3/24)
2033. Cook, Philander m 12/23/39 Sarah Putnam in Panama; Rev. Gray (4-1/1)
2034. Cook, Philip, Esq., 82, d 7/16/46 in Avoca, Steuben Co. "where he had resided for the last 26 years" (2-7/22)
2035. Cook, Rebecca, 21, second dau of Rev. Henry, deceased, of New Jersey, d 2/23/28 in Geneva (3-2/27)
2036. Cook, Stephen of Centerville, Alleg. Co., formerly of Palmyra, m 7/11/35 Charlotte Hale of Canandaigua in West Avon; Rev. R. Kearney (5-7/17)
2037. Cook, Sybel, wf of Titus R. and dau of late Capt. William Hall, of Phelps, d 2/25/23 in Scauys (sic) (3-3/5)
2038. Cook, Titus of Scauys (sic) m 6/19/23 Saphrona Kennedy, dau of Capt. John of Mendon, in M (3-7/16)
2039. Cook, William A. (Capt.) of Bath m 12/28/41 Ellen C. Cook of Pike, Alleg. Co., in P; Rev. William Conklin (2-1/12)
2040. Cooke, George F., the celebrated comedian, m Mrs. V. M. Benn, dau of James Bryden, keeper of the Tontine Coffee House in NYC, in NYC (3-7/10/11)
2041. Cooke, George Frederick, Esq., 36, "the celebrated tragedian", d 9/26/12 in NYC (3-10/21)
2042. Cooke, Merit, 56, d 12/24/44 in Pomfret (4-1/3/45)
2043. Cooley, Anthony of Seneca m 10/30/22 Polly Emerick of Fayette; P. A. Barker, Esq. (3-11/13)
2044. Cooley, George m 3/25/30 Harriet C. Piper in Palmyra; William Willcox, Esq. (See marr. of Luke Wells this date) (5-3/26)
2045. Cooley, James m Mary Bruyn in Milo (3-3/12/28)
2046. Cooley, James, Jr., s of James, d 4/9/21 in Seneca (3-4/11)
2047. Cooley, Phoebe, 73, wf of John, d in Canandaigua (3-6/11/17)
2048. Cooly, Isaac m Stella Beckwith, dau of Samuel, in Southport (3-12/30/29)
2049. Coon, _____ (Mr.), about 55, d 7/9/27 in Benton (3-7/11)
2050. Cooper, Anthony of Troupsburgh m Mrs. Mary Wygant in Erwin (3-7/22/29)
2051. Cooper, Asa, 69, d 5/5/14 in Prattsburgh, Steuben Co. (3-5/11)
2052. Cooper, Benjamin Franklin, Esq. of Utica m Mary Ann Brantley, dau of Rev. W. T., in Philadelphia (state not given) (3-10/21/29)
2053. Cooper, Charles m Abigail Roberts in Ridgeway, PA (3-1/27/30)
2054. Cooper, Christopher, Jr. m 5/3/46 Ester Hammon of Cohocton in Avoca; John L. Robords, Esq. (2-5/5)
2055. Cooper, Daniel, about 80, d 7/30/47 in Bath (2-8/4)
2056. Cooper, David m 9/5/13 Betsey Avery, both of Junius, in Phelps; Joseph Hall, Esq. (3-9/8)
2057. Cooper, Elias (Rev.), 58, rector of St. John's Church, Yonkers, West. Co., d in Yonkers (3-1/31/16)
2058. Cooper, Elizabeth, 8, second dau of Richard F., Esq. of Cooperstown, d 10/14/11 in Geneva, "her clothes having accidentally caught fire from a candle on the preceding evening" (3-10/16)
2059. Cooper, Enoch, 42, d 10/7/32 in Palmyra (5-10/10)
2060. Cooper, Hannah R. (Miss), 26, d 1/26/49 in Bath (2-2/7)
2061. Cooper, James (Maj.), 60, d 2/13/11 in Fishkill, Dutch. Co. (3-3/13)
2062. Cooper, James Byron, s of Griffith of Williamson, m 9/6/43 Sarah W. Rogers, dau of John of Marion, in M; William Danforth, Esq. (5-9/13)
2063. Cooper, John m 3/27/17 Maria Smith, both of Fayette (3-4/16)
2064. Cooper, John m 1/15/23 Bethsheba Decker, both of Manchester, in Palmyra; William A. McLean, Esq. (5-1/22)
2065. Cooper, John (Rev.), 61, pastor of the Bapt. Ch. in Preston Hollow, Albany Co., d in Rensselaerville (3-10/21/29)

2066. Cooper, John (Rev.), 61, pastor of the Bapt. Ch. at Preston Hollow, Albany Co. d in Rensselaerville (3-10/21/29)
2067. Cooper, Laura Ann, wf of Thomas J. (formerly of Palmyra, NY) d 10/2/41 in Palmyra, MI (5-10/13)
2068. Cooper, Robert m Sophia Miller in Canandaigua (3-7/9/28)
2069. Cooper, Silas, ?83, d 12/31/29 in Arcadia (5-1/16/29)
2070. Cooper, Thomas, 67, d 2/26/46 in Bath (2-3/4)
2071. Cooper, William, Esq. (Hon.) of Cooperstown d 12/22/09 in Cooperstown (3-1/3/10)
2072. Coots, Henry C. m 9/26/41 Mary Miller; Harlow Smith, Esq.  All of Bath (2-9/29)
2073. Copp, Edward m 1/22/40 Jane Bemus, both of Ellery, in Ashville; M. Norton, Esq. (4-2/12)
2074. ?Coppeck, Juliet Jane, 22 mo, dau of F., d 8/19/30 in Palmyra (5-8/20)
2075. Coppock, William R. of Palmyra m 5/3/31 Mary Barlow of Minaville, Mont. Co. in Minaville (5-5/13)
2076. Corbit, John m Hannah Buckingham in Hornby (3-10/14/29)
2077. Corbitt, Thomas, 76, (a Rev. soldier) d in Bath (3-1/14/29)
2078. Corby, Merrit of Michigan m 7/27/36 Jane Gibson of Wayne Co., NY in Jamestown; S. Jones, Esq. (4-8/3)
2079. Corby, Samuel m 4/2/20 Hannah Franklin in Lyons; John Tibbitts, Esq. (5-4/5)
2080. Corey, Joseph of Marion m 2/21/36 Sally Cranston of Ontario, NY (5-3/11)
Ccrey, Moses.  See Coary, Moses.
2081. Corlay, Joseph of St. Louis (state not given) m 12/25/40 Maria Del Refugio Antonina Mucia Isadora Johanna Bernard De Jesu Solares Covian of New Mexico in St. Louis (2-1/20/41)
2082. Cornell, John, Esq. of Nichols m Harriet Hurd, dau of Ebenezer, Esq., in Amenia, Dutchess Co. (3-10/8/28)
2083. Corning, Alexander H., s of Rev. Alexander and nephew of Erastus of Albany, m Indiana Blood, dau of Capt. Asa of Bath, in Napolian, MI (2-2/3/47)
2084. Corning, Jasper m Abigal Kibbe, dau of Isaac, Esq., in Buffalo (3-9/17/17)
2085. Corning, Andrew m 1/11/43 Mary Calhoon in Williamson; Rev. George Wilkinson (5-1/18)
2086. Cornwall, Ansel A. m 1/27/40 Martha Brewer, both of Pulteneyville, in P; Daniel Poppino, Esq. (5-2/5)
2087. Cornwell, J. W. m Maria Youngs in Benton (3-5/2/27)
2088. Cornwell, William (Dr.) m 7/27/17 Sally Chidsey, dau of Col. Augustus, in Benton; Rev. Farley.  All of Benton (3-7/30)
2089. Corse, Richard, 27, formerly editor of the Hudson Whig, d in Leyden, MA (3-5/7/23)
2090. Corter, James m Mary Payne in Pulteney (3-2/13/28)
2091. Corwin, ____, an inf ch of Isaac, d 10/1/28 in Geneva (3-10/15)
2092. Corwin, Abel, "cashier of the bank at Ithaca", m Margaret Poillon in NYC (3-9/19/27)
2093. Corwin, Isaac m 11/27/23 Mary Ann Todd, both of Seneca, "near the Glass Factory"; Rev. Dr. Axtell (3-12/3)
2094. Cory, Benjamin, editor of the Chenango Republican, m Leafa Balcom in Oxford (3-10/3/27)
2095. Coryell, Jane, 25, consort of V. M. and dau of Dugald Cameron, Esq., d 4/17/25 in Bath (3-4/27)
2096. Cosart, Caroline (Mrs.) d 1/7/39 in Palmyra (5-1/11)
2097. Cosart, E. C. (Maj.) of Palmyra m 8/27/40 Ann M. Hill of Rushville in R; Rev. G. R. H. Shumway (5-9/2)
2098. Cosart, Enoch m 10/29/35 Caroline Osborne in Palmyra; Rev. Shumway (5-11/6)
2099. Coss, Joseph m 11/29/32 Delin Butler in Bath; Henry W. Rogers, Esq. (2-12/5)
2100. Cost, ____, ch of Capt. E., d in Phelps (3-8/23/15)
2101. Cost, Elias m 9/16/28 Mrs. Fanny Oaks, wid of late Thaddeus, both of Phelps, in P; Rev. Lane of Waterloo (3-9/17)
2102. Cost, Jacob, 81, father of Col. Elias of Phelps, d 2/20/27 in Newtontrap, MD (3-3/14)
2103. Cost, Jesse m Cynthia Beggerly in Manchester (3-4/29/29)

2104. Coster, Henry A., Esq., 62, merchant, d in NYC (3-1/26/20)
2105. Cotton, Edward m 1/9/45 Phebe Ann Eggleston in Bath; Rev. Ferris
      (2-2/5)
2106. Cotton, Henry G., Esq., attorney, m 3/8/31 Maria McBurney, both of
      Painted Post, in Bath; Rev. David Higgins (2-3/9)
2107. Cotton, Maria, 28, wf of Henry G., Esq. and dau of late Thomas McBurney,
      d 1/29/32 in Painted Post (2-2/1)
2108. Cotton, Sarah (Mrs.), 64, dau of Deacon Amos Hawley, d 7/18/43 in
      Brooklyn, Jackson Co., MI (4-8/3)
2109. Cotton, Silas m 12/31/45 Sarah Ann Mack in South Dansville; Rev. S. S.
      Brown. All of Dansville (2-1/7/46)
2110. Cotton, William Henry, 3 yrs, only s of E. Cotton, d 3/23/49 in
      Patchinsville (2-4/4)
2111. Couch, Ira, merchant, of Jamestown m 9/9/33 Caroline E. Gregory of
      Ellicottville in E; Rev. Vining (4-9/11)
2112. Couch, Walter Scott, 3 mo, s of Ira, d 8/22/36 (4-8/24)
2113. Coudery, Franklin, editor of the Hamilton Recorder, m 11/28/19 Amanda
      Munger in Moscow, NY (3-12/22)
2114. Coughrin, Joshua m 5/4/25 Betsey Peck in Attica (1-5/6)
2115. Courter, Phebe (Mrs.), 23, late of Palmyra, d in Schenectady (5-10/3/32)
2116. Coutry, Erastus m 7/17/21 Henrietta Cook in Galen; James Dickson, Esq.
      All of Galen (3-7/25)
2117. Covell, Edward, 35, M.D., d 12/27/26 in Wilkesbarre, PA (3-1/17/27)
2118. Covell, Orrin m Mrs. Susan Fish in Napoli, NY (4-4/22/29)
2119. Coventry, Charles (Dr.) of Utica m 4/23/29 Clarissa Butler, oldest dau
      of Hon. Medad and sister of C. Butler, Esq. of Geneva, in Stuyvesant,
      Columbia Co. (3-5/20)
2120. Covert, ____ (Mrs.), 79, consort of Tunis, Sr., d 10/1/18 in Ovid
      (3-10/21)
2121. Covert, David m Mrs. Anna Vandorn in Ovid (3-1/16/22)
2122. Covert, Jacob m Catharine Starret in Ovid (3-3/11/29)
2123. Covert, Peter I. m Mrs. Sally Seeley in Ovid (3-1/16/22)
2124. Covey, John m Patience Eggleston in Harmony (4-1/10/27)
2125. Covil, George, 37, of Phelps d in Cleveland, Ohio (3-10/14/29)
2126. Covil, Willis m 7/1/47 Mary Custor in South Dansville; Rev. J. Selsmer.
      All of South Dansville (2-7/14)
2127. Cowan, Alexander M. (Rev.) of Skaneateles m 9/6/24 Mary Sherwood, third
      dau of Isaac of Geneva; Rev. Dr. Axtell (3-9/8)
2128. Cowan, Charles m Sally Lamphier in Bath (3-9/2/18)
2129. Cowan, George W. m 8/26/30 Sally Maria Covell in Carroll; Rev. Isaac
      Eddy (4-9/1)
2130. Cowan, George W. m 9/29/33 Esther L. Covell, both of Carroll, in
      Jamestown (4-10/2)
2131. Cowan, Sally, 72, relict of Ephraham (who d 1/19/22 in Westport,
      Essex Co.) d 7/31/44 in Carroll (She was born 10/6/1771 in Cambridge,
      Wash. Co.; lived in Carroll 22 yrs.; member Cong'l. Ch. 30 yrs.)
      (4/8/9/44)
2132. Cowant, Smith, 33, d in Pulteneyville (5-9/26/21)
2133. Cowden, Orson W. m 1/1/44 Rosanna Klock; Rev. H. Smith (4-2/16)
2134. Cowden, Truman C. of Poland, NY m 1/1/43 Phebe Ann Hazzard in Levant;
      S. B. Winsor, Esq. (4-1/5)
2135. Cowden, William of Poland, NY m 1/8/43 Amelia Harrington of Fluvanna;
      A. Brown, Esq. (4-2/2)
2136. Cowdin, Mary S., 20, dau of A. Cowdin, Esq., d 8/27/48 in Batavia
      (funeral at Presby. Ch. (1-8/29)
2137. Cowen, John m 2/6/23 Sally Harding in South Williamson; Rev. Kinney
      (5-3/5)
2138. Cowen, Nelson of Mansfield, Tioga Co., PA m 7/17/38 Emeline Whitney,
      dau of Abraham I., Esq. of East Painted Post, in E. P. P. (2-7/25)
2139. Cowing, Albert m 3/3/25 Sally Torrance in Seneca; Rev. G. Laning
      (3-3/9/25)
2140. Cowing, James of Seneca m 11/13/12 Mrs. Margaret Clark of Reading, wid of
      Rev. Phineas (3-12/9)
2141. Cowing, James, 81, m 7/13/21 Mrs. Editha Fullington, 63, both of Seneca;
      Richard Hogarth, Esq. of Geneva (his fourth and her fifth marriage)
      (3-7/25 and 5-8/1). (married 7/18 in 5-8/1)

2142. Cowing, James, 88, (a Rev. soldier) d 4/8/29 in Seneca (one of the earliest settlers in this town) (3-4/15)
2143. Cowing, John (Capt.), 72, (a Rev. soldier) d in Jamestown (born in Northampton, MA; in 1827 moved his family to western NY; lived in Jamestown continuously from 1830) (4-9/11/33)
2144. Cowing, John K., merchant, m 3/13/37 Sedate Foote, both of Jamestown, in J; Rev. Gillett (4-3/15)
2145. Cowing, Luther m 4/11/24 Mrs. Edith Babcock in Stafford (1-4/30)
2146. Cowing, Ruth, 49, wf of Capt. Calvin, d in Jamestown (4-8/24/36)
2147. Cowles, Josiah m 11/2/23 Hannah Hicks, both of Geneva, in G; Rev. Axtell (3-11/5)
2148. Cowles, Louisa Osborne (Mrs.), 22, d 3/25/50 in Batavia (surv by husband and an inf ch aged 8 months; funeral at Bapt. Ch.)
2149. Cowls, William M. m 2/12/48 Louisa A. Osborn, both of Batavia, in B; Rev. Stimson (1-2/15)
2150. Cox, _____, dau of Thomas, d in Williamstown, MA (3-1/14/29)
2151. Cox, James m 5/9/24 Polly Wyman in Shelby; Stephen Hill, Esq. (1-5/14)
2152. Cox, Sabra (Miss), 20, niece of Mr. Eddy, d 7/2/18 in Geneva (3-7/8)
2153. Coy, Joseph F. of Elba m 12/23/24 Mrs. Lovisa Randall of Stafford in Batavia; C. Carpenter, Esq. (1-12/24)
2154. Coykendall, Jonathan B. m 1/18/20 Elizabeth West; Jacob Dox, Esq. (3-1/19)
2155. Cradell (sic), Archibald S. m Betsey Ann Strait in Elmira (3-8/29/27)
2156. Crager, William m Bet____ ?Burick in Lyons (3-5/11/25)
2157. Cragg, William m 6/29/43 Jane Wake in Williamson; Rev. Clark A. Smith (5-7/5)
2158. Cramer, William m 7/30/43 Mary Shepherd in Harmony; Rev. Pember (4-8/24)
2159. Cranch, Richard (Hon.), 85, d in Quincy, MA (3-11/6/11)
2160. Crandal, Daniel, 50, d 11/15/36 (5-11/18)
2161. Crandall, Alvin m Electa Horton in Gerry; Rev. Barr. All of Gerry (4-10/5/31)
2162. Crandall, Charles m 10/4/45 Louisa Willson in Sugargrove, PA; Rev. Todd. All of Sugargrove (4-10/17)
2163. Crandall, David P. m Catherine Bradt, dau of "Mr. Bradt", late sheriff of Albany Co., in Sennett (3-4/1/29)
2164. Crandall, Jacob R. m 9/27/41 Julia Ann Cook in Palmyra; Rev. Brittan. All of Palmyra (5-9/29)
2165. Crandall, Joseph Daniel, 21 mo, s of ?Adovestus and Ann P. of Palmyra, d 4/1/43 (5-4/5)
2166. Crandall, P. Milford of Canandaigua m 5/18/42 Celista M. Calhoun, dau of Nathan, Esq., in Pittsford; Rev. A. H. Burlingame of Palmyra (5-5/25)
2167. Crandall, Rensselaer m 10/30/32 Mary W. Burrell, both of Palmyra, in Canandaigua; Rev. Kearny (5-11/14)
2168. Crandall, William m 3/9/30 Rebecca Rawson in Macedon; Rev. Powell (5-3/10)
2169. Crandall, William B., formerly of Batavia, d in Wesley City, Tazewell Co., IL (1-2/14/39)
2170. Crane, Charles Giles, 13 mo, s of Lyman, d in Jamestown (4-8/16/26)
2171. Crane, Daniel, 56, d 4/2/13 in Benton (3-4/14)
2172. Crane, Elizabeth, 81, mother of Lyman, d in Jamestown (4-7/25/38)
2173. Crane, Gilbert m Electa Pratt in Manchester (5-12/1/19)
2174. Crane, Jacob m Parmilla Perkins in Williamson; Rev. Howell R. Powell (5-12/24/17)
2175. Crane, Jeremiah, 70, d 5/13/31 in Jamestown (4-5/18)
2176. Crane, John m 4/27/28 Maria Turk, dau of Capt. Abram, in Geneva; C. Shekell, Esq. All of Geneva (3-4/30)
2177. Crane, Joseph N. m 10/10/49 Helena Ann Mitchell, dau of John B., Esq., at the Presby. Ch. in Wayne; Rev. L. M. Russ of Hammondsport (2-10/24)
2178. Crane, Laura (Miss), 15, dau of Lyman, d 12/20/34 in Jamestown (4-12/24)
2179. Crane, Nelson, 20, d 4/14/42 in Jamestown (4-4/21)
2180. Crane, Stephen m 1/12/25 Clarinda Daw in Elba; John Lamberton, Esq. (1-1/21)
2181. Crane, Susan, 22, d 11/8/25 in Canandaigua (3-11/30)
2182. Crane, ?Zebina m 1/16/44 Hannah P. Peed (or Peeb) in Williamson; Rev. C. A. Smith (5-1/31)

2183. Cranmer, _____, wf of Dyer, Esq., d in Wheeler (3-6/11/28)
2184. Crawford, Andrew, 76, d in Jamestown (a Rev. soldier) (4-5/29/39)
2185. Crawford, Benjamin m 6/6/19 Laurena Hatch in Middlesex; _____ Comstock, Esq. (3-6/9)
2186. Crawford, David, about 21, d 8/21/31 in Cohocton (2-9/7)
2187. Crawford, Gilbert H. (Rev.) m Jane Elliott in Le Roy (3-6/24/29)
2188. Crawford, W., 60, m Elizabeth Dickerson, 16, in Sullivan Co. (3-5/11/14)
2189. Crawford, William J. of Alabama, NY m 1/1/50 F. E. Brown, dau of John A., Esq. of Elba in Pine Hill; Rev. Corwin (1-1/8)
2190. Crippen, Henry m 1/8/40 Mary Ann Altenburg in Jamestown; S. B. Winsor, Esq. (4-1/15)
2191. Crissey, Jason m Roxana Windsor, dau of Elder Windsor, in Stockton (4-9/5/32)
2192. Crissey, Stephen m 5/10/41 Sevila Palmiter, dau of P., Esq., in Jamestown; Rev. Chapin (4-5/12)
2193. Critchet, Ezekiel T. m Betsey Southwell in Junius (3-5/9/27)
2194. Crittenden, Edgar, 67, m Sarah Hurd, 65, in Gorham (3-12/7/25)
2195. Crittenden, Experience, wf of Inmer, d 2/4/26 at the Old Castle (Seneca) (3-2/8)
2196. Crittenden, Fortescue W. m 9/23/29 Caroline Merrill, dau of Capt. Nathaniel, in Geneva; Rev. Strong of Phelps (3-9/30/29)
2197. Crittenden, Inmer d 12/16/26 at Old Castle, town of Seneca (3-12/20)
2198. Crittenden, Noah m 1/9/28 Lucinda Starkweather of Seneca in S (3-1/16)
2199. Crittenden, Samuel m 11/2/13 Dorcas Craft, wid of late Edward, Esq., in Gorham; J. French, Esq. (3-11/17)
2200. Crittenden, Samuel, 81, d 6/1/16 at Old Castle near Geneva, NY (3-6/5)
2201. Crittenden, Solomon m 11/8/09 Polly Tippetts at the Old Castle (3-11/15)
2202. Crittenden, William A. m Lydia P. Smith in Gorham (3-6/27/27)
2203. Crocker, Wickham R., 11 mo, s of Dr. Wickham R. and Jane R., d 7/24/50 in Cameron (2-7/31)
2204. Croghan, _____ (Lt. Col.), "late of the Army", m 5/8/17 Serena Livingston in NYC; Bishop Hobart (3-6/4)
2205. Cromwell, Isaac, about 60, d 9/3/23 in Seneca near the Glass Factory (3-9/10)
2206. Cromwell, John W., merchant, of Fishkill Landing, Dutch. Co. m 10/5/36 Louisa Brumfield, dau of A. D. of Palmyra; Rev. G. R. H. Shumway (5-10/7)
2207. Cromwell, Orin d in Romulus "as a consequence of drinking cold water" (3-8/25/19)
2208. Cronk, Jacob, 26, d in Jerusalem, NY (3-3/12/28)
2209. Cronk, Solomon d in Cambridge, NY "of a wound of the hand, by the cut of a scythe" ("he married two sisters with each of whom he lived alternately a week at a time. He had 26 children, 13 by each wife, all 28 of whom attended his funeral") (3-11/22/15)
2210. Crookes, John, 47, editor of the Mercantile Advertiser d in NYC (3-7/8/18)
2211. Crosby, Darius, Esq., senator-elect for the southern district of this state, d 11/17/18 at his home in Somers, West. Co. (3-12/9). He died 12/3 (5-12/16)
2212. Crosby, Eli, 64, d 1/27/43 in Newfane, VT (4-2/9)
2213. Crosby, Eliakim of Poland, NY m 2/22/44 Angeline Emory of Ellery at the Jamestown House in J; Rev. E. J. Gillet (4-3/1)
2214. Crosby, Lucy Ann, 39, wf of Eliakim, d 1/1/44 in Poland, NY (4-1/12)
2215. Crosby, Samuel C. m 12/15/41 Mary Ann Foote, dau of Hon. E. T., in Jamestown; Rev. E. J. Gillett (4-12/23)
2216. Crosby, Timothy m 5/5/22 Mary Kinney in Attica; Rev. Hibberd (1-5/10)
2217. Crosby, William, 27, one of the editors of the Auburn Gazette, formerly from Boston, d 12/27/17 in Auburn (3-1/7/18). Age 28 (5-1/7/18)
2218. Crosby, _____, 18 mo, s of Henry S., d 9/13/16 (prob. in Geneva) (3-9/18)
2219. Cross, Anna (Mrs.), 71, d 8/11/25 in Stafford (1-8/19)
2220. Cross, Asa m 1/28/40 Catharine Bowlsby in Bath; Rev. Platt (2-2/5)
2221. Cross, Ellena (Miss), 26, dau of Edward, d in Middlesex (3-9/30/29)
2222. Cross, Joel m Abigail Colburn in Batavia; Daniel Tisdale, Esq. (1-9/2/25)
2223. Cross, John m 8/25/31 Louise Perkins, dau of Capt. John, in Pulteney. All of P (2-8/31)

58

2224. Cross, John J. of Seneca Falls m 1/1/43 Harriet E. Brooks of Lysander, Onon. Co. in Seneca Falls (5-1/11)
2225. Cross, Sophia, 42, wf of E. T. of Buffalo and dau of Jabez Otis of Westfield, MA, d 8/7/50 in Buffalo (1-8/13)
2226. Cross, Walter m 8/26/49 Jane Parsons, both of Byron, in Bergen; Samuel Richmond, Esq. (1-9/4)
2227. Cross, William of Stafford m 9/8/22 Harriet Bollard of Byron in B (1-9/13)
2228. Cross, William C. m 6/1/26 Eliza Bigelow in Bethany; Rev. E. Spencer (1-6/16)
2229. Crosset, William, 66, one of the earliest settlers in Livingston Co., d in Geneseo (3-12/23/29)
2230. Croswell, Edwin, Esq., editor of the Albany Argus, m 9/15/24 Catharine Adams, dau of John, Esq., in Catskill (3-9/22)
2231. Crouch, Andrew J. m 9/19/41 Charlotte Van Deusen in Jamestown (4-9/23)
2232. Crouch, Caleb, 54, d 8/21/42 at his home in Cohocton (2-8/31)
2233. Crough, Henry (Capt.) of Cohocton m 4/22/15 in Marcellus, Onon. Co. ("was made prisoner 17 September, sent to Quebec, and on his return home was seized with small-pox") (3-5/24)
2234. Crow, William of Bath m 6/11/45 Emily L. Angel of Cameron in C; Rev. Ferris (2-7/2)
2235. Crowell, Calvin, 18, s of Solomon, Sr., d 6/26/41 (5-6/30)
2236. Crowell, John F. of Geneva m 8/13/28 Eliza Starks of Waterloo in W; Rev. Lane (3-8/27)
2237. Crowell, Solomon, Jr. of Palmyra m 1/1/44 L. D. C. Manley of Canandaigua in C; Rev. U. Clark (5-1/3)
2238. Cruger, Hannah, 40, consort of Daniel, Esq., formerly of Bath, d 12/7/31 in Syracuse (2-12/14)
2239. Cruger, Jefferson m 12/17/31 Mary Sherwood in Poughkeepsie; Rev. C. C. Cuyler (2-1/4/32)
2240. Cruger, Washington m 7/23/31 Jane Ann Brown of Poughkeepsie in P; Rev. A. Perkins (2-1/4/32)
2241. Crumb, Augustus Charles, 4 mo, s of David, d 7/6/23 in Geneva (3-7/9)
2242. Crumb, Waitstill (Deacon), 73, d in Cherry Creek (4-1/26/44)
2243. Crutch, Ambrose L. m Nelle Hendrix in Cohocton (3-3/11/29)
2244. Cruthers, Burdette of Branford, Upper Canada, formerly of Palmyra, NY, m 9/22/35 Irena Stringer of Marion ("This Mr. C. is the same whose death was erroneously advertised in this paper in July last. The gentleman is doubtless conscious of the difference between being dead and married." (5-9/25)
2245. Cuffee, Paul, 59, "a very respectable man of color and a native of Africa", d 9/7/17 in West Port (3-10/1)
2246. Cullum, Horace of Meadville, PA m 10/1/35 Mary Bemus of Jamestown in J; Rev. Taylor (4-10/7)
2247. Culp, Henry H. m Bethia Brown in Elmira (3-6/20/27)
2248. Culver, Adeline G., 23, wf of James H., d 2/18/31 in Jamestown (4-2/23)
2249. Culver, Austin B., 7, s of John, d 9/8/43 (fractured skull, kick of a horse) (4-9/14)
2250. Culver, Daniel, Sr., 78, d in Reading (one of the first settlers in this town) (3-7/1/29)
      Culver, Elias B. See Collver, Elias B.
2251. Culver, George M. m 11/15/25 Nelly Shutts in Milo (3-7/12/26)
2252. Culver, Lawrence m Patty Brunning in Ovid (3-2/7/16)
2253. Culver, Stephen, 40, m Elizabeth Kent, 24, in Palmyra; Rev. Benjamin Bailey (5-5/12/19)
2254. Culver, Stephen, Esq. of Newark, NY m 6/9/42 Helen Mar Salisbury, dau of Hon. Ambrose of East Palmyra, in E. P.; Rev. E. B. Fuller (5-6/15)
2255. Cuming, Caroline A., wf of Rev. F. H., d in Rochester (3-1/9/28)
2256. Cuming, Francis H. (Rev.) m 1/31/22 Caroline A. Hurlburt, dau of J. W., Esq. of Auburn, in St. Peter's Ch., Auburn; Rev. Smith (3-2/6)
2257. Cumings, _____, inf ch of Simeon, Esq., d 8/22/24. Also: "This morning another child of Mr. S., aged 2 years and 8 months" (1-8/27)
2258. Cumings, Horace m 12/7/43 Lucy G. Thompson in Palmyra; Rev. Fisher. All of Palmyra (5-12/13)
2259. Cumings, Samuel P., 2, s of Chauncey, d 2/20/40 in Palmyra (5-2/26)

2260. Cumming, John N. (Gen.), 69, d in Newark, NJ (a Rev. soldier; "fought by the side of Washington") (3-7/25/21)
2261. Cummings, Betsey, 23, d 3/26/20 in Geneva (3-3/29)
2262. Cummings, Jacob m Lucinda Mace in Milo (3-3/24/19)
2263. Cumpton, Cornelius m Jane Sebring in Ovid (3-1/16/22)
2264. Cunningham, Henry, Esq., 35, late member of the state assembly, d 7/25/26 in Johnstown, Mont. Co. (3-8/2)
2265. Currier, Samuel (Capt.) m Clarrissa Gilbert in Pittsford,("she being only his fifth wife") (5-4/14/19)
2266. Curtenius, Peter (Maj. Gen.), 55, d in NYC (3-4/9/17)
2267. Curtis, _____ (Miss), 16, dau of Alpheus, d 9/11/21 (5-9/12)
2268. Curtis, Albert (Dr.) of Arcadia m 10/27/30 Mary A. C. Lilly of Palmyra; Rev. A. E. Campbell (5-10/29)
2269. Curtis, Chloe A., 24, wf of Hiram W., d in Jamestown (4-4/4/27)
2270. Curtis, Elihu S. of Rochester m 1/24/27 Mary Garner of Geneva in G; Rev. Dr. Axtell (3-1/31)
2271. Curtis, George W. m 9/29/47 Isabel Swarthout in Wayne; Rev. S. C. Mallory. All of Wayne (2-10/6)
2272. Curtis,Hiram m 12/1/22 Miss Warren; William A. McLean, Esq. (5-12/11)
2273. Curtis, Spencer m 5/18/43 Rhoda Lamphier of Busti in B; Rev. Hinebaugh (4-6/15)
2274. Curtis, Zenas m 9/10/09 Amy Rathbun in Marcellus (3-9/13)
2275. Curtiss, Alfred A., 27, s of Azor, d 12/9/47 in Le Roy (1-12/21)
2276. Curtiss, Amelia, 25, wf of Samuel F. and dau of Robert Boyd of Benton, d in Penn Yan (3-5/27/29)
2277. Cutiss, Samuel F. of Penn Yan m Emily Lewis in Benton (3-10/21/29)
2278. Curwan, Nathan m 5/8/21 Sephronia Porter; James Field, Esq. (3-5/16)
2279. Cushing, _____ (Mrs.), 55, wf of John, d 3/10/48 in Le Roy (1-3/21)
2280. Cushing, Seth, Classical Tutor at Middlebury Academy, m 9/4/25 Perisses Thomas in Attica; Elder E. M. Spencer, principal of Middlebury Acad. All of Middlebury (1-9/9)
2281. Cushing, Zattu (Hon. Judge), 69, d 1/11/39 in Fredonia (a pioneer settler of Chautauqua Co.; came from Oneida Co. about 1806) (4-1/24)
2282. Cushman, Consider (Mr.), 63, d 7/14/18 in Benton (3-7/29)
2283. Cushman, David, Esq., 34, d 2/3/32 in Savannah, NY (5-2/14)
2284. Cushman, Hiram m 7/4/24 Marian Stewart, both of Bethany; Rev. Hurd (1-7/9)
2285. Cutler, Abraham m Catharine Young in Ovid (3-2/21/16)
2286. Cutler, Luther, 68, d 8/17/50 in Girard, Branch Co., MI (formerly of Batavia, NY) (1-9/3)
2287. Cutter, Abdilla, formerly of VT, d 4/16/39 in Palmyra (5-5/3)
2288. Cutterback, _____ (Mr.) m Catherine Spanbeck in Perinton (5-4/17/22)
2289. Cutting, Lucius m 10/3/41 Eunice Salisbury in Gerry (4-10/7)
2290. Cuyler, Benjamin, Esq., 29, attorney, d 6/30/26 in Aurora, Cayuga Co. (3-7/12)
2291. Cuyler, Catherine, 75, relict of late Henry, Esq., d 1/28/18 in Greenbush (3-2/11 and 5-2/11)
2292. Cuyler, George (Col.) of his Brittanic Majesty's 11th Regiment of Foot and brother of late Maj. William Howe Cuyler of Palmyra, NY, d 11/11/18 in London, England (5-3/31/19)
2293. Cuyler, George W. (Maj.), attorney, of Palmyra m 9/12/31 Caroline Porter, dau of Chauncey, Esq. of Pittsford, Monroe Co., in P; Rev. B. H. Hickox (5-9/20)
2294. Cuyler, Glen, Esq., 85, d 9/1/32 in Aurora, Cayuga Co. (5-9/12)
2295. Cuyler, James, 35, d 1/28/11 in Greenbush (3-10/9)
2296. Cuyler, John L., Esq. of Lockville m 8/9/31 Elizabeth C. Marsh, dau of E. C., Esq. of Aurora, Cayuga Co., in Aurora; Rev. S. Smith (5-8/12)
2297. Cuyler, Mary Eliza, 4, second dau of William H. and Eliza, d 2/6/40 in Palmyra (5-2/12)
2298. Cuyler, Richard G. (Col.), 33, d 4/13/32 in Palmyra (5-4/25)
2299. Cuyler, William H. of Palmyra m 5/21/33 Eliza Akin of Owasco, Cayuga Co. in Owasco; Rev. B. H. Hickes of Rochester (5-5/29)
2300. Cuyler, William Howe (Maj.), 37, late of Palmyra and principal aid-de-camp to Maj. Gen. Hall, was killed 10/9/12 at Black Rock by a cannon shot from the British batteries (3-10/21)

2301. Dabole, Mary, wf of Ansen, d 12/21/41 in Prattsburgh (a native of Litchfield, CT; moved to Prattsburgh in 1822; she is defined as "a mother") (2-12/29)

2302. Daboll, Nathan, Esq., author of a "valuable system of arithmetic", d in Groton, CT (3-4/15/18)

2303. Dagget, David P. m 5/6/21 Ruth Hildreth; John Tibbits, Esq. (5-5/16). (This news release is a correction of an earlier one dated 5/9 wherein the groom was erroneously identified as "David Patterson")

2304. Daggett, Alonzo, 8, an adopted son of William M. Eddy, drowned 7/28/34 in Jamestown "while bathing in the Creek" (4-7/30)

2305. Daggett, Betsey, 4, dau of Levi, d 3/22/31 in Bath (2-3/23)

2306. Daggett, Levi, 67, d 5/13/35 (5-5/15)

2307. Daily, George m 11/25/30 Sarah R. Pound, both of Farmington, in Macedon (5-12/10)

2308. Daily, Jane, 15, d in Elmira (3-1/13/30)

2309. Daily, John W. m 1/23/42 Charlotte Hill in Lyons; C. O. Hoffman, Esq. All of Arcadia (5-2/9)

2310. Daily, Samuel C. of Waterloo m Mary Brownell of Junius in Vienna (3-4/29/29)

2311. Dains, Eliza (Miss), 19, d 8/1/22 in Milo (3-8/14)

2312. Daken, Samuel D., Esq. of Utica m Mary Mumford, dau of Thomas, Esq., in Cayuga (3-9/19/27)

2313. Dana, Cyrus, Esq. of Owego m Elizabeth C. Stockwell in Binghamton (3-10/3/27)

2314. Dana, Thomas, 96, d in Utica (3-9/17/17)

2315. Danforth, Asa (Gen.), 73, a Rev. officer and one of the first settlers in Onondaga Hollow, d in O. H. (3-9/16/18)

2316. Danforth, Flavel of Busti m 9/7/43 Harriet Parsons of Sharon, MI in Sharon; Rev. A. Corning (4-9/28)

2317. Danforth, Lavina, wf of Deacon Thomas, d 4/10/30 in Busti (her age posting blurred: possibly 42) (4-4/21)

2318. Danforth, Lavinia, 8, dau of Deacon Thomas, d 7/13/33 in Busti (4-7/17)

2319. Danforth, Loring m 9/28/42 Louisa M. Mills in Homer; Rev. Platt (4-10/13)

2320. Danforth, Thomas of Busti m 1/13/31 Mrs. Sarah Hoar of Napoli, NY; Rev. Wilcox (4-2/2)

2321. Danforth, Williston, 19, d 1/20/43 in Busti (4-1/26)

2322. Daniels, Catherine, 2, dau of Norman, d 2/27/41 (prob. in Bath) (2-3/3)

2323. Daniels, Edwin M., merchant, of Geneva m 5/6/28 Sarah Ann Coffin of NYC in NYC; Rev. Dr. Matthews (3-5/21)

2324. Daniels, Jesse m 8/16/22 Rebecca Snook, both of Phelps, in Geneva; Jacob Dox, Esq. (3-8/21)

2325. Daniels, Kendrick m 9/5/50 Sarah H. Warren, second dau of Col. Phineas, in Avoca; Rev. William Bradley. All of Bath (2-9/11)

2326. Daniels, Noble, 42, d 7/18/49 in Morganville (1-7/31)

2327. Darling, Ezra m Lois Moore in Canandaigua (3-3/26/17)

2328. Darling, Solomon m Nancy Kast in Penfield (5-4/21/18)

2329. Darrin, Daniel, 91, (a Rev. soldier) d 11/4/38 in Troupsburg, Steuben Co. (surv by "a large circle of relatives") (2-12/12)

2330. Darrow, _____, inf dau of Jared, d (date and place not given) (3-4/10/22)

2331. Darrow, John P., 75, d 3/10/48 in Stafford (1-3/21)

2332. Darrow, Samuel G. of Pembroke m 3/7/24 Orinda Darrow of Alden in A; "Esqr. Badger" (1-3/19)

2333. Dart, Eliza, 37, wf of Jonathan, formerly of Palmyra, d 9/6/31 in Shelby, McComb Co., Mich. Terr. (5-9/27)

2334. Dascam, Jennet, dau of Henry, d 8/22/26 (prob. in Geneva) (3-8/23)

2335. Daskam, Charles C., 4, s of Nathan, d 1/17/30 in Geneva (he fell into a vessel of boiling water) (3-1/20)

2336. Daskam, John Henry, inf s of Nathan, d 4/1/22 in Geneva (3-4/3)

2337. Daskam, Sylvia, inf dau of Nathan, d 10/2/24 in Geneva (3-10/6)

2338. Dauby, Augustine G., editor and printer of the Rochester Gazette, m 1/21/18 Mary E. Parmele in Utica (3-2/4 and 5-2/11)

2339. Dauphin, William, 45, m 1/24/18 Paulina Thompson, 16, in Angelica "after a long and tedious courtship of sixty minutes" (3-2/11)

2340. Davenport, Amelia (Mrs.), 24, d in Canisteo (3-3/17/19)

2341. Davenport, Ephraim, 28, d in Macedon (5-8/9/39)

2342. Davenport, Ephraim m 12/14/43 Amelia Emery in Ellery; Rev. H. Smith (4-2/16/44)
2343. Davenport, Ira of Hornellsville m 2/25/24 Lydia Cameron, oldest dau of Dugald of Bath, in Bath; Rev. Higgins (3-3/3)
2344. Davenport, Nathaniel, 84, d 11/22/15 in Ulysses (3-12/6)
2345. Davenport, Susanna, 59, consort of Squire Davenport, formerly of Danville, VT., d 10/1/24 in Junius (3-10/13)

Daves. See also Davis,

2346. Daves, _____ (Mrs.), 31, wf of Hon. John P. and sister of C. W. Henry of Geneva, d 6/9/27 in Newbern, NC (3-7/11)
2347. Davids, Elizabeth, 2, dau of John, d 6/11/22 in Batavia (1-6/14)
2348. Davidson, David, 71, d 4/1/50 in Monterey (2-4/17)
2349. Davidson, Elizabeth, 53, consort of James, d in NYC (3-8/9/09)
2350. Davidson, Isaac m Laura Rathbone in Avon (3-3/29/20)
2351. Davidson, Isaac, Jr. m Clary Field, both of Palmyra, in P (3-6/3/12)
2352. Davies, Ann, 20, second dau of Rev. Dr. Davies, president of Hamilton College, d in Clinton (3-6/27/27)
2353. Davies, Charles, prof. of math., m 12/11/24 Mary Ann Mansfield, dau of Col. Jared, at West Point; Rev. Charles P. McIlvaine (3-10/19/24)
2354. Davies, John m prior to 6/20/34 Sarah ?Barber, both of Palmyra, (prob. in Palmyra); F. Smith, Esq. (5-6/27)
2355. Davies, Maria, wf of William, Esq., d 11/18/15 in Poughkeepsie (3-11/29)
2356. Davies, Maria H., 22, dau of William, Esq., d 8/2/17 in Poughkeepsie (3-8/13)
2357. Davies, Polly, wf of Capt. William of Poughkeepsie, d 7/23/14 in P (3-8/3)

Davis. See also Daves.

2358. Davis, _____ (Mrs.) d in Canandaigua (3-2/22/15)
2359. Davis, _____ (Mrs.). 31, wf of James J., d 9/24/24 in Geneva (3-9/29)
2360. Davis, _____ m 11/1/29 Louisa Perry in Williamson (3/11/25 and 5-11/27)
2361. Davis, _____ (Mrs.), 83, d 4/8/41 in Bergen (1-4/27)
2362. Davis, Abner m 4/28/25 Christiana Lester in Newport (1-4/28)
2363. Davis, Asahel (Rev.) of Geneva m Matilda Merrell of Utica in U; Rev. A. G. Baldwin (3-2/25/18)
2364. Davis, Calvin L. m Amelia Sanford in Elmira (3-10/24/27)
2365. Davis, Caroline Anne Jane (Miss), youngest dau of Gen. George R. of Troy, d 6/4/39 in Jamestown (funeral at home of Thaddeus W. Patchin, Esq.) (4-6/5)
2366. Davis, Daniel O., "late of Batavia", m Delia De Forrest, dau of William, Esq. of York, Upper Canada, in York, U. C. (1-3/18/25)
2367. Davis, Elihu A. m 4/10/42 Sarah Strickland in Walworth; Rev. Daniel Lyon (5-4/20)
2368. Davis, George (Dr.), late surgeon of U. S. Navy, d in NYC (3-8/26/18)
2369. Davis, George m 1/21/30 Elizabeth Williams in Romulus; S. B. Chidsey, Esq. (3-1/27)
2370. Davis, Hannah, 24, d in Canandaigua (3-11/28/27)
2371. Davis, Hetty, 24, consort of Dr. James, Jr. and oldest dau of Dr. John Delamater of Palmyra, d 5/29/36 in Vienna, NY (5-6/10)
2372. Davis, Hobart E. of Essex, CT m 6/21/49 Catherine Victoria Parsons, dau of David, Esq. of Batavia, in B; Rev. Byron Sunderland (1-6/26)
2373. Davis, Isaac, merchant, "of the late firm of Norton and Davis", d in Canandaigua (3-11/12/17)
2374. Davis, James, 2, s of J. Davis, d 10/25/22 in Geneva (3-10/30)
2375. Davis, Jesse m Huldah Barnes in Jerusalem, NY (3-8/8/27)
2376. Davis, John m 11/21/43 Miranda Fairbanks (prob. in Jamestown); Rev. E. J. Gillett (4-11/24)
2377. Davis, Jonathan m 9/25/28 Mary Baloo in Geneva; E. Hastings, Esq. (3-10/8)
2378. Davis, Joseph, Jr., 17, d 1/6/25 in Batavia (1-1/7)
2379. Davis, Louisa M. (Miss), 18, dau of William, Esq., d 4/28/24 in Poughkeepsie (3-5/19)
2380. Davis, Lucy, 26, wf of Aaron, d in Geneseo (3-9/19/27)
2381. Davis, Lydia (Mrs.), 59, of Lockville d in Canandaigua (3-2/3/30)
2382. Davis, Mary, 17, dau of Samuel, d in Le Roy (1-3/10/26)
2383. Davis, Paul (Rev.), 66, (a Rev. soldier) d in Carroll (formerly preached in New Salem, MA; later formed several churches in Bapt. denom; "has preached in Chaut. Co. past 9 yrs."; surv by wf and ch; funeral at

home of his son, Simeon C.; "Printers in Worcester, Mass. are
requested to insert ...") (4-1/3/27)

2384. Davis, Paul H. of Ridgeway, Orleans Co. m 5/26/44 Charlotte Spear,
youngest dau of Denison Stephen Spear, in Macedon; Rev. D. Harrington
(5-6/5)

2385. Davis, Sally, 23, dau of Emry, d 9/8/39 in Busti. In this release
these four additional deaths are reported (the first three are Emry's
children and the fourth his grandchild): (1) Sally, 23, wf of Solon
Bush, d 9/8; (2) Lucinda, 21, wf of Ransom Smith, d 11/17; (3) James,
3, d 9/5; and (4) Oscar, 4 yrs., s of Solon Bush, d 9/21 ("Printers
in Brattleboro, Vt. are requested to insert the above") (4-11/20)

2386. Davis, Samuel, a stage driver in Batavia, d 8/25/33 in Batavia ("His
parents reside in Sterling, Cayuga Co.") (1-8/27)

2387. Davis, Seth (Rev.) of Seneca Falls m 11/30/32 Mary Emeline Thayer, dau
of Levi of Palmyra, in Zion Church, Palmyra; Rev. B. H. Hickox
(5-12/5)

2388. Davis, Susan (Mrs.), about 70, mother of William H. of Batavia, d 4/17/47
in Standstead, Lower Canada (1-4/27)

2389. Davis, Thomas m 3/17/16 Nancy Lewis, both of Phelps; Jacob Dox, Esq.
(3-3/20)

2390. Davis, William, Esq. of Poughkeepsie m Alice Antill of Orange Co.;
Rev. Reed (3-4/29/18)

2391. Davis, William, merchant, of Batavia m Miss Emeline Williams of Tolland,
CT (1-10/25/22)

2392. Davis, William, 54, formerly of Washington Co., NY, d 9/12/32 in Marion
(surv by wf) (5-9/19)

2393. Daw, B. F. of Pavilion m 9/5/48 C. M. Capron of Fowlerville in F; Rev.
H. W. Smuller (1-10/17)

2394. Dawly, John m 9/30/30 Polly Frank in Busti; Hon. E. T. Foote (4-10/6)

2395. Dawson, Jane (Mrs.), 48, d 4/25/45 in Bath (2-5/7)

2396. Day, A. B. of Livonia m _____ Cyrene of Bloomfield in Bristol (3-1/20/30)

2397. Day, Betsey, 47, wf of late Nathaniel, d 8/14/41 in Palmyra (5-8/18)

2398. Day, Cornelius m 2/20/42 Mary Baxter at the Bapt. Ch. in Palmyra;
Rev. A. H. Burlingame (5-2/23). See #2402.

2399. Day, Edward (Dr.) m Sally Ann Hayt in Romulus (3-9/17/28)

2400. Day, Elijah of Waterloo m "week before last" Mrs. Ann Swift in Lyons
(3-4/8/29)

2401. Day, Eliza, 25, wf of Elijah, d 7/15/26 in Waterloo (3-7/26)

2402. Day, Ezra P. m 2/20/42 Mary C. Baxter at the Bapt. Ch. in Palmyra;
Rev. A. H. Burlingame (5-3/2). See #2398.

2403. Day, Hiram T., 30 or 50 (blurred), late editor of the Lyons Advertiser
and brother of one of the editors of the Buffalo Journal, d 8/16/26
in Lyons (3-8/30)

2404. Day, Margaret Maria, 23, wf of Jackson, d 5/21/42 in Howard (2-6/8)

2405. Day, Moses, 66, d 10/2/28 in West Springfield, MA (5-10/17)

2406. Day, Moses m 11/27/36 Matilda Fisher, both of Palmyra, in P; Frederick
Smith, Esq. (5-12/2)

2407. Day, Nelson m 10/30/31 Jane Ammerman, both of Canandaigua, in Lockville
(5-11/29)

2408. Day, William (Capt.) m 4/15/18 Eleanor Van Dyck, dau of late James, in
NYC (3-4/29)

2409. Dayton, Hezekiah, Esq., 62, d 12/1/18 in Butternuts (3-12/23)

2410. Dayton, Hiram of Olean m Betsey Bennett in Rushford (3-4/14/19)

2411. Dayton, Ruth (Mrs.), 37, d 11/1/24 in Alden, Erie Co. (1-11/19)

2412. Dean, Benjamin m 6/5/18 Thankful Robins in Benton "after a courtship
of about thirty minutes"; Rev. Farley (3-6/17)

2413. Dean, Benjamin m 9/9/27 Ann Eliza Critchell in Benton; Elder Chase
(3-9/12)

2414. Dean, Eliza, wf of Robert, d in Middlesex (3-5/30/27)

2415. Dean, Jesse H. m 1/1/40 Phebe Russell in Jamestown; E. F. Warren, Esq.
(4-1/8)

2416. Dean, John m 7/4/25 Sarah Blake in Batavia; D. Tisdale, Esq. (1-7/8)

2417. Dean, Paul D., merchant, of Bradford, PA, m 9/12/44 R. Cordelia J.
Crooker, dau of George A. S. Crooker, Esq., in Rutledge, Catt. Co.;
Rev. William Waith (4-9/20)

2418.  Dearborn, _____, Major Gen (Excellency) of the U. S. Army, m Mrs. Sarah
       Bowdoin, wid of late Hon. James, Esq., in Boston (state not given)
       (3-12/1/13)
2419.  Dearborn, Henry (Gen.), 78, a Rev. soldier and an officer in the War of
       1812, d 6/6/29 at his home in Roxbury (3-6/17 and 5-6/19)
2420.  Dearborn, Sarah Bowdoin, 65, wf of Gen. Dearborn, d in Boston (both her
       husbands were U. S. ministers to foreign courts) (3-6/21/26)
2421.  Deare, Lewis, 37, printer, d 10/17/17 in New Brunswick, NJ (3-11/5)
2422.  Debow, Gerret m Maria H. Thurber in Canandaigua (3-6/6/27)
2423.  Debow, John, 7, s of John, d 4/4/22 in Clyde (Galen) (3-4/10)
2424.  De Bow, John of Batavia m 11/11/24 Fanny F. C. Knowles of Stafford in
       S; S. S. Skinner, Esq. (1-11/19)
2425.  De Bow, Margaret, 87, relict of John, d 9/16/41 in Stafford (1-9/21)
2426.  Decker, Alexander m 12/30/40 Almira L. Allison, both of Urbana, in
       Bath; Henry Pier, Esq. (2-1/13/41)
2427.  Decker, Betsy, about 45, d 1/27/45 in Bath (2-1/29)
2428.  Decker, David, 67, d in Galen (3-10/8/28)
2429.  Decker, Henry H. of Arkwright m 6/27/43 Catherine J. Edwards of
       Ellington in E; Elder W. Shephard (4-7/13)
2430.  Decker, Hezekiah m 9/26/49 Jane Smith, dau of Charles, in Bath; Rev.
       L. M. Miller. All of Bath (2-10/10)
2431.  Decker, John S. m 9/15/33 Betsey Hammond in Palmyra; F. Smith, Esq.
       (5-9/20)
2432.  Decker, Polly, wf of Richard, d 7/24/22 in Phelps; also her infant
       child at the same time (5-7/31)
2433.  Decker, Seymour m Rebecca Hultz in Canandaigua (3-1/14/29)
2434.  Decker, Sidney S. d 8/25/49 in Havana, NY (2-9/5)
2435.  Decker, Uri m Experience M. Baker in Manchester (3-3/11/29)
2436.  D'Garmo, Jones, merchant, of Detroit m Catharine H. Annin, dau of late
       Judge Annin of Cayuga, in Onondaga (3-4/8/18)
2437.  Degolier, Eliza, 22, d in Penn Yan (3-10/21/29)
2438.  De Golyer, Cordelia, dau of Rensselaer, d 4/18/22 in Clyde (3-5/1)
2439.  De Graw, George W. m 10/31/46 Mary Jane Bigsby in Barrington; Rev.
       P. Shedd (2-11/11)
2440.  Dekey, Thomas B. of New Jersey m 3/12/29 Sarah E. Cowdrey, dau of
       Col. John of Waterloo, in Goshen, Orange Co. (3-4/15)
2441.  Delamater, R. D., merchant, of Hudson, Col. Co. m 5/1/27 Cathalina
       Bogert, dau of H. H., Esq., in Geneva; Rev. Dr. Axtell (3-5/2)
2442.  Delamater, Richard C., 39, d 8/10/29 in Dresden, Yates Co. (lately
       removed from Hudson, NY; member of Presby Ch.; surv by wf and two
       infant children; funeral in Geneva from home of his father-in-law;
       H. H. Bogert, Esq. officiating) (3-8/12)
2443.  Delamatter, Clarissa, 29, wf of George C., d 8/6/39 in Jamestown
       (4-8/7)
2444.  D'Lamatter, G. Clinton, Esq. m 7/3/43 Jane Tisdale in Jamestown;
       Rev. S. W. Parks (4-7/6)
2445.  D'Lamatter, Ruth (Mrs.), 26, d 11/23/42 in Jamestown (4-11/24)
2446.  D'Lamatter, Thomas J., 24, d 4/6/31 in Busti (4-4/13)
2447.  D'Land, Edwin B. of Busti m 12/29/31 Amelia Towsley of Westfield in W;
       Rev. Parmalee (4-1/4/32)
2448.  De Land, Edwin Russel, 11 mo, s of William F. and Eunice A., d 9/29/44
       in Jamestown (4-10/4)
2449.  Deland, Mary, 66, wf of Deacon William, d 9/23/39 in Busti (funeral in
       Cong'l. Meeting House in Jamestown (4-9/25)
2450.  Deland, Washington m Sally Ann Moore, both of Panama, NY, in P (4-11/7/38)
2451.  De Land, William (Deacon), 72, d 7/24/43 in Busti, NY (born in Sandisfield,
       MA 1/16/1771; lived in New Marlborough, MA until age 27 and then moved
       to Vernon, NY where he remained until 1811. That year moved to Busti
       area where he helped to construct the first buildings; appointed
       deacon of Cong'l. Ch. there in 1817 (4-7/27)
2452.  Delano, Francis m 11/8/38 Lydia Garfield in Busti; Rev. Parmely
       (4-11/14)
2453.  Delano, Martha, 55, wf of Israel and dau of Judge William Rogers, d
       8/8/32 in Macedon (5-8/22)
2454.  Delano, Reuben, Jr., 40, d in Skaneateles (3-9/30/29)
2455.  Delany, _____, inf dau of James, d in Canandaigua (3-9/10/17)

2456. Delavan, Elizabeth M., consort of Henry W., Esq. of Albany, d 10/15/22
       in Philadelphia (state not given) (3-10/30)
2457. Delbridge, James G. m 10/21/41 Harriet Ware in Stafford; Rev. Gideon
       Laning (1-11/2)
2458. De Leany, Thomas m "sometime since" Rachel Metzger, both of Junius;
       Rev. L. Merkel (3-5/14/17)
2459. De Long Harry m 9/23/40 Mary Ann Tolbert, both of Wayne; Henry Pier,
       Esq. (2-9/30)
2460. D'Miner, Homer m 3/27/31 Amanda Hall in Prattsburgh; Rev. Rudd (2-3/30)
2461. Deming, Alfred J., merchant, of Williamson m 1/10/19 Harriet St. John
       of Sodus in S; Rev. Seba Norton (5-1/13)
2462. Deming, Alfred J. (Maj.), 34, d in Sodus (3-3/28/27)
2463. Deming, Charles, Esq., 48, d 4/25/16 in Catherinestown ("interred with
       Masonic honors") (3-5/8)
2464. Deming, Charles Augustus, 14 mo, s of Dr. Fenn Deming, d in Westfield
       (4-12/31/28)
2465. Deming, David (Gen.) d in Colchester, CT (3-6/20/27)
2466. Deming, Fenn, Esq. of Westfield (formerly postmaster there) d 11/10/34
       in Lewiston, IL (4-11/12)
2467. Deming, Harriet (Miss), 21, dau of late Dr. Deming of Westfield,
       d 7/23/43 at the home of Orlando McKnight in Sandusky, Ohio (4-8/10)
2468. Deming, J. P. H., M.D., m 10/24/42 Mary Bortles, both of Palmyra, in P;
       Rev. M. Cook of Lyons (5-10/26)
2469. De Mott, Abraham of Reading m 9/6/18 Jane Hogarth, dau of late John,
       of Ovid in O (3-9/16)
2470. De Mott, Daniel m 1/20/25 Widow Huggins in Pembroke; Benjamin Stetson,
       Esq. (1-1/28)
2471. Denio, Cotton m 2/23/24 Mrs. Debo____ (one line of type missing) in
       Batavia; Rev. C. Colton (1-9/24)
2472. Denison, William H. m Caroline Turner, dau of Enoch, Esq., in Sodus
       (3-5/20/29)
2473. Dennis, Humphry m 1/12/17 Mrs. _____ Bailey in Ulysses (3-1/29)
2474. Dennis, John m 5/13/41 Amanda Taylor in Jasper; B. S. Brundage, Esq.
       All of Jasper (2-6/16)
2475. Dennis, John P. of Middlesex, Ont. Co. m 8/11/33 Susan Hunt of Palmyra
       in P; Frederick Smith, Esq. (5-8/16)
2476. Dennis, Joseph, Esq., editor of the Port Folio, d 1/7/12 in Philadelphia,
       PA (3-1/22)
2477. Dennis, Simeon m 11/24/36 Ann Capron, both of Manchester, in M; Rev.
       Shumway (5-11/25)
2478. Dennis, Stephen m 1/10/28 Elizabeth Perrine in Cayuga; Rev. Barton
       (3-1/30)
2479. Dennison, Lawton of Richmond, Ont. Co. m Polly Dibble of Cautia, Tioga
       Co. at Olean Point (3-4/8/18)
2480. Dennison, R. S. C. m 11/22/49 Mary Bissell in Batavia; Rev. Stimson.
       All of Batavia (1-11/27)
2481. Denniston, Edward D. m 5/25/26 Mary Jones, both of Benton, in B (3-6/7)
2482. Denny, William m Patty Root in Bloomfield (3-7/25/21)
2483. Denton, Elijah m Polly Simpson in Ovid (3-3/17/19)
2484. Denton, Francis Granger m 10/6/49 Almira Wilcox in Batavia; S. Wakeman,
       Esq. All of Batavia (1-11/20)
2485. Deolf, Ezra (Maj.), 102, formerly of Tolland, CT, d 9/16/11 in Hopkinton,
       NH (an officer in the "Indian and French Wars and a Revolutionary
       patriot") (3-9/25)
2486. Deppen, John m Diana Links in Romulus (3-1/20/30)
2487. De Pue, Elijah m 8/7/15 Sylvia Crane in Benton; Elijah Spencer, Esq.
       (3-9/13)
2488. Derby, _____, child of John K., d 10/20/39 (prob. in Jamestown)
       (4-10/23)
2489. Derick, James m 11/5/46 Jane Van Alst, both of Stafford, in Batavia;
       Rev. W. K. Babcock (1-11/10)
2490. De Riemer, Elsie, 75, relict of late Peter, d in Poughkeepsie (3-11/11/18)
2491. Dering, Nicholl H., M.D., of NYC m Frances Huntington, second dau of
       Henry, Esq., in Rome (presumably Rome, NY) (3-6/28/26)
2492. Derr, George (Capt.) d in Gorham (3-7/21/19)

65

2493. Dervel, Daniel of Bristol, Ont. Co. m 2/11/47 Mrs. Lucia Ann Strickland of Bath in Kennedyville; Rev. J. Case (2-2/17)
2494. Devereaux, Elisha, 70, d 2/5/27 in Busti (4-2/7)
2495. Devereux, Luke, formerly of Utica, d 10/20/17 in Natchez (presumably in Mississippi Terr.) (3-3/18/18)
2496. Devoe, William m 10/22/43 Nancy Carpenter; Elder Bullock (4-10/26)
2497. Devore, Silas m Mary Ann Genung in Milo (3-12/26/27)
2498. Dewey, Daniel (Hon.), "one of the Judges of the supreme judicial court" of Massachusetts, d 5/26/15 in Williamstown, MA ("within a little more than two years this commonwealth has been deprived by death of four judges of the same court, viz Judges Sedgwick, Parsons, Sewall, and Dewey.") (3-6/21)
2499. Dewey, Darwin H., 21. "a member of the Senior Class in Middlebury College, Vt.", d 7/1/41 in Jamestown (member of First Presby. Ch. of Jamestown) (4-7/8)
2500. Dewey, Jeremiah, Jr. m Eleanor McUmber; Frederick Smith, Esq. All of Manchester (5-1/9/29)
2501. Dewey, L. H., printer, of Sackets Harbor, Jeff. Co. m 12/29/40 Harriet Y. Merriam of Auburn in A; Rev. Hopkins (2-1/13/41)
2502. Dewey, Timothy m Sally Flint in Cohocton (3-12/22/19)
2503. De Witt, Daniel of Bath m 1/13/47 Eliza Stephens of Chenango Co. in Bath; Rev. L. Merril Miller (2-1/20)
2504. De Witt, Horace m 4/22/18 Judith Bronk, both of Milo, in Geneva; Jacob Dox, Esq. (3-4/29)
2505. De Witt, Jacob d 9/27/12 at his home near Geneva (3-9/30)
2506. De Witt, Jacob m 4/17/14 Elizabeth Nicholson in Junius; Esq. Pixley (3-4/20)
2507. De Witt, John, D.D., of New Brunswick (presumably in NJ) m 9/20/25 Anna M. Bridgen in Albany; Rev. Ferris (3-9/28)
2508. De Witt, Simeon, Esq., Surveyor General of NY, m 10/29/10 Susan Linn, dau of Rev. Dr. William Linn, in Greenwich; Rev. Rewan (3-11/28)
2509. De Witt, Susan, wf of Simeon, Esq. of Albany and second dau of late Dr. Linn of NYC, d 5/5/24 in Philadelphia (state not given) "while on a visit to her friends" (3-5/19)
2510. De Witt, Thomas (Rev.) of Fishkill m 10/11/26 Eliza Annn Waterman, youngest dau of Jedediah, Esq.; Rev. Dr. Murray (3-10/18)
2511. De Wolf, James m 1/21/20 Elizabeth Lounsbury, both of Elmira, in Albany (3-2/2)
2512. Dexter, Daniel S. of the U. S. Navy d 10/10/18 in Erie, PA (commandant of the naval station on Lake Erie; a native of RI) (3-10/28)
2513. Dexter, Jabez B., 51, d 4/27/13 in Geneva (had lived there for 22 yrs) (3-5/5)
2514. Dexter, Norman m Abigail Riker in Big Flat (3-3/12/28)
2515. Dexter, Samuel of Boston, "democratic candidate for Governor at the late election in Massachusetts", d at the home of his son (not named) in Athens, NY (3-5/15/16)
2516. Dexter, Samuel of Boston, s of late Hon. Samuel, m 5/19/16 Augusta Amelia Provost of Greenville, NY in G (3-5/29)
2517. Dexter, Windsor, formerly of Chaut. Co., NY, d 8/16/41 in Fort Wayne, IN (4-9/9)
2518. Dey, _____ (Dr.), late of Romulus, d "a few days since" in New Jersey (3-8/15/10)
2519. Dey, Alexander H. m 3/20/42 Augusta Stewart in Penn Yan; Rev. Miner (4-3/31)
2520. Dey, Benjamin, Esq., about 60, d 3/24/22 in Romulus (a native of NJ; among the earliest settlers in Seneca Co.) (3-3/27)
2521. Dey, Benjamin P., 28, s of late Dr. Philip, d 3/20/19 in Romulus (3-3/24)
2522. Dey, Catharine, wf of Anthony, Esq., d 1/20/19 in NYC (3-2/3)
2523. Dey, David D., 18, s of David of Romulus, d 10/17/16 ("during a short apprenticeship at this Office ...") (3-10/23)
2524. Dey, Jane, 68, wid of Dr. Philip, d in Romulus (3-8/29/27)
2525. Dey, John, 18, s of David, d 3/9/15 in Romulus (3-3/15)
2526. Dey, John P. of Romulus m 10/12/16 Phoebe Van Brunt of the Narrows, Long Island, NY in "The Narrows" (3-10/30)
2527. Dey, Mary, 5, dau of Anthony and Hannah, d in Romulus (3-8/29/27)

66

2528. Dey, Peter, 8 mo, s of Ben, Esq.,d in Ithaca (3-8/1/27)
2529. Dey, Peter J. m 7/13/20 Maria Shepherd in Seneca; Abner Woodworth, Esq. (3-8/2)
2530. Dey, Teunis of Romulus m 2/18/16 Susan Dey of Fayette in F; Rev. Young (3-2/21)
2531. De Zeng, Arthur N., 32, bro of William S. of Geneva, d 1/1/30 in Clinton, Ohio (3-1/20)
2532. De Zeng, Evelina Throop, 3 yrs, dau of Maj. William S., d 12/3/23 in Geneva (3-12/10)
2533. De Zeng, William S., merchant, m 1/7/17 Caroline Rees, dau of Maj. James, in Geneva; Rev. Clark (3-1/8)
2534. Dibble, Charles W. m 12/31/49 Olive Emeline Leonard, dau of Alonzo, in Batavia; Rev. Byron Sunderland. All of Batavia (1-1/8/50)
2535. Dible, Rachel, 64, wf of Peter, d in Mayville (4-4/27/43)
2536. Dick, Samuel, Esq., 72, d 11/16/12 in Salem, NJ ("a revolutionary character of eminence") (3-2/10/13)
2537. Dickerson, Elizabeth, 46, wf of Lyman and dau of James Barnes of Seneca, d 12/20/27 in Gorham (3-1/2/28)
2538. Dickerson, Heman G. m Mary L. Griswold in Lyons (3-10/22/28)
2539. Dickerson, Lyman of Bethel m 11/6/23 Mrs. Elizabeth Moore at the home of her father James Barnes; Rev. Axtell (3-11/19)
2540. Dickerson, Lyman B. m 1/24/31 Sarah Ford in Clyde; Rev. Salisbury (5-2/4)
2541. Dickerson, Thomas of Fairport m 2/13/39 Charlotte Leonard, dau of Cyrus of Palmyra,in P; Rev. Shumway (5-2/15)
2542. Dickerson, William m Electa Banister in Phelps (3-8/7/16)
2543. Dickinson, ____, inf ch of William, d 2/28/31 in Batavia (1-3/4)
2544. Dickinson, Abner m 9/23/27 Tamor Coles in Geneva; Rev. Martin. All of Geneva (3-9/26)
2545. Dickinson, Alva m 12/1/11 Amanda Crane, both of Benton, in B; E. Spencer, Esq. (3-12/11)
2546. Dickinson, Amos B. C. m 12/1/44 Anna Jones, both of Bath, in B (2-12/18)
2547. Dickinson, Charles m 8/31/26 Susan Gates in Geneva (3-9/6)
2548. Dickinson, Edward, inf s of E. A., d 10/6/44 in Jamestown (4-10/11)
2549. Dickinson, Eli m Mrs. Pullen in Phelps; Rev. Mosher (3-9/30/18)
2550. Dickinson, John m Sally Hart in Hopewell (3-5/11/25)
2551. Dickinson, Patrick P., 37, d in Brighton (3-5/30/27)
2552. Dickinson, Renald m 10/24/47 Lucy V. Noble in Bath; Rev. S. W. Alden. All of Urbana (2-11/3)
2553. Dickinson, Walter, 58, d 4/10/50 near Jefferson (2-4/17)
2554. Dickinson, William A. m 11/1/25 Melinda Russell in Batavia; Rev. Colton. All of Batavia (3-11/16). Elinda Russell in 1-11/4.
2555. Dickinson, William m 3/25/27 Nancy Baker in Lima (3-4/25). Nancy Barker in a restatement of this entry (same newspaper, same date)
2556. Dickman, Thomas, Esq., 73, d in Greenfield, MA ("an industrious veteran of the Massachusetts Press, an apprentice of the celebrated Benjamin Eden of Boston, and the typographical instructor of the Editor of the Advocate") (2-1/19/42)
2557. Dickson, James (Dr.) d 9/8/34 in Clyde (5-9/26)
2558. Dickson, Thomas (Col.), 49, d 1/22/25 in Queenston, Upper Canada (for many years collector of that port and a magistrate of that Province) (3-2/2)
2559. Didama, Affi, 51, wid of Dr. Simon Didama, d 12/26/18 in Trenton, Oneida Co. (3-1/6/19)
2560. Diffenbaugh, Benjamin m 8/31/44 Levina T. Pickett of Erie, PA in Erie; Rev. A. M. Reed of Jamestown (4-9/6)
2561. Dike, Flanders m Lucy Harris in Palmyra (3-5/14/28)
2562. Dildine, Levi m 1/23/45 Mary Boyd; Rev. P. Olney. All of Pulteney (2-2/19)
2563. Dill, Samuel, Esq. m 10/21/18 Deborah Field, dau of Peter, in Auburn; Rev. Lansing (3-10/28)
2564. Dinnin, Betsey, 37, wf of James, d 7/17/35 in Jamestown (4-7/22)
2565. Dinnin, James R. m 8/12/44 Cynthia Schoonmaker in Jamestown; Rev. Owen Street. All of Jamestown (4-8/16)
2566. Disbrow, Bradley d 11/1/25 in Waterloo (3-11/30)

67

2567. Disbrow, Ira of Barrington, Yates Co. m 12/26/44 Mary Jane Hause of
Tyrone, Steuben Co.; Rev. Rowlet (2-1/1/45)
2568. Disbrow, Simon (Capt.), 43, of Rochester d 3/5/35 in Hollidaysburgh,
PA (surv by wf and 4 ch in Rochester) (5-3/27)
2569. Divan, John m Olive Bacon in Reading (3-9/23/18)
2570. Divine, David m Mrs. Hannah Kies in Junius (3-10/22/28)
2571. Divine, Lemuel C. P. of Orangeville m 10/7/48 Sophrona Lewis of Batavia
in B; Rev. S. M. Stimson (1-10/10)
2572. Dixon, John, Esq. of Westfield, NY m 5/23/43 Sarah A. Preston of
Palestine, IL in P (4-6/15)
2573. Dixon, Matthew m 10/27/25 Eliza Robson in Seneca; Rev. Merrill (3-11/9)
2574. Doane, Elisha, 60, d in Mentz (3-6/6/27)
2575. Doane, George W. (Rev.) of Trinity Ch. m Mrs. Eliza G. Perkins in NYC
(3-10/7/29)
2576. Doane, Jonathan, 63, d in NYC (for several years a resident of Geneva)
(3-11/25/18)
2577. Dobbin, _____, a child of Justus, d 7/13/11 in Geneva (3-7/17)
2578. Dobbin, Charles, 32, d 2/17/17 in Victor ("of a malignant pneumonic
disease") along with his wife, Mary, age 31, "and an infant child
of premature birth. All enclosed in one coffin.") (3-3/12)
2579. Dobbin, Henry Wisner, 20, s of Col. Hugh W., d 3/20/16 in Junius
(3-4/10)
2580. Dobbin, Hugh W. (Gen.) of Junius m 11/20/17 Mrs. Martha Sears of West
Bloomfield in W. B. (3-12/17)
2581. Dobbin, Margaret, 45, wf of Col. H. W., d (date and place not given)
(surv by husband and children) (3-3/9/14)
2582. Dobbin, William W. of Junius m 2/5/15 Julia Ann Larzelerf; Rev. Axtell
(3-2/8)
2583. Dobbs, Anna (Mrs.), about 82, d 12/20/45 in Thurston (2-12/24)
2584. Dockerell, Sara (Mrs.), 24, d 10/6/18 in Canandaigua (3-10/21)
2585. Dodd, Edward, 53, "a native of Northumberland county, Eng. but a
resident of this country 22 years", d 11/11/22 near Geneva (surv by
wf and 6 ch) (3-11/20)
2586. Dodd, John m 5/28/14 Graty Taylor in Phelps; Joseph Hall, Esq. (3-6/1)
2587. Dodge, Amos m Polly Robinson in Batavia; Rev. C. Colton (1-4/28/26)
2588. Dodge, Evens W. m Lavina Knap; Elisha Slocum, Esq. (5-11/28/17)
2589. Dodge, John R., pastor of the First Bapt. Ch. in Brockport, m 6/4/29
Harriet M. Winchester, author of "Hesselrigge" and other poems
under the signature of "Amica Religionis", in Batavia; Rev. Joseph
Elliot (3-6/17)
2590. Dodge, Nehemiah m 9/26/20 Fanny Beebe, both of Pompey, Onon. Co., in
Palmyra; Frederick Smith, Esq. (5-10/4)
2591. Dodge, Warren m Permelia Church in Romulus (3-12/26/27)
2592. Dodge, Warren, 33, d 8/24/49 in Wayne (2-9/12)
2593. Dolbear, Rufus m 7/27/37 C. M. P. Lawrence, only dau of Rev. A. B.,
in New Orleans (presumably in Louisiana); Rev. A. B. Lawrence.
All of New Orleans (5-8/18/37)
2594. Dold, Matilda (Miss), 14, d 8/30/22 in Geneva (3-9/4)
2595. Doleby, Dillings D. m Mary Bennott in Howard, Steuben Co. (3-2/10/19)
2596. Dollbee, Jonathan, 61, (a Rev. soldier) d 8/10/23 in Junius (3-8/20)
2597. Dolly, Christopher, 73, d 3/1/49 in Howard (2-3/14)
2598. Donahue, James of NYC m 8/5/46 Martha Berry of Marshall, MI in Batavia;
Rev. J. Parker (1-8/11)
2599. Donegan, Elijah m 11/18/28 Mohent Buchanan in Geneva; E. Hastings, Esq.
(3-11/26)
2600. Doolittle, Edward m Sally Williams in Canandaigua (3-1/16/22)
2601. Doolittle, Edwin m 1/1/33 Adaline Amsbury in Jamestown; Rev. Gillet
(4-1/9)
2602. Doolittle, Jesse, merchant, of Ithaca m 3/13/28 Harriet E. McBurney,
dau of Thomas, Esq. of Painted Post, in P. P.; Rev. E. G. Gear
(3-4/9)
2603. Doolittle, Jesse, 38, merchant, d 12/21/31 in Painted Post (2-12/28)
2604. Doolittle, Solomon m 2/21/27 Caroline Saterly, both of Hector; Rev.
E. W. Martin (3-2/28)
2605. Doolittle, Sylvester m Catharine Gould in Utica (3-1/21/29)

2606. Dorchester, James D. m 9/14/17 Clarissa Backenstose, both of Geneva;
Rev. Henry Axtell (3-9/17)
2607. Dorchester, Mark (Capt.), 34, d 9/16/29 in Marcellus (3-9/30)
2608. Doremus, Ann (Miss), 18, dau of Deacon Doremus, of Romulus d 9/18/22
at the home of Miss McKay in Geneva (3-9/25)
2609. Dorman, Joel (Dr.) m "within a few days past" Olive Lawrence in Snell
(See also marr. of Abraham Townsend) (3-11/1/09)
2610. Dorman, John Lawrence, 1 yr, s of Dr. Joel, d 4/2/22 in Jerusalem, NY
(3-4/17)
2611. Dormand, Gilbert, 41, d 3/20/23 in Jerusalem, NY (3-4/2)
2612. Dorr, Louisa M., 23, wf of Dr. James D. Dorr, d 9/11/47 in Bath (2-9/15)
2613. Dorrance, George, 90, d in Brutus (3-5/30/27)
2614. Dorrin, John, 69, of Geneva d 9/9/34 in Buffalo (5-9/26)
2615. Dorsay, Cecilia M. (Mrs.), 24, dau of Dr. John D. Higgins, d 8/8/42
in Bath ("She lost a  son aged 6 months on the 22nd of July.")
(2-8/10)
2616. Dorsey, Andrew of Lyons m 5/14/11 Ruth Shekell of Phelps in P (3-5/22)
2617. Dorsey, Daniel, 66, a native of Maryland and "a migrant to this country
in the year 1801", d 5/16/23 in Lyons (a Rev. soldier; 38 years "in
communion with" the Meth. Episc. Ch.; surv by "a wife of nearly equal
age with himself and twelve children all of whom except three have
now families of their own") (3-5/21)
2618. Dorsey, Thomas E. of Lyons m 3/21/19 Sophia Hecox of Paris, Oneida Co.
in P (3-3/31)
2619. Dorsey, Upton m 9/2/15 Ann Sterret in Lyons; Rev. Pomeroy. All of
Lyons (3-9/13)
2620. Doty, _____, ch of John, d in Ovid (3-8/13/28)
2621. Doty, Elijah, Esq., about 60, d 2/5/22 in Porter, Niag. Co. (3-2/20)
2622. Doty, Elizabeth, 10, dau of Abel, d 8/22/43 in Charlotte Center (4-8/31)
2623. Doty, George d 10/3/28 at Flint Creek in Seneca town (3-10/8)
2624. Doty, Jacob m 9/18/31 Sarah Maria Moore in Canisteo; Rev. Bowers
(2-10/4)
2625. Doty, Nathaniel R. m 12/23/24 Anna Loomis in Attica; Rev. Amos P. Bowen.
All of Attica (1-1/7/25)
2626. Doty, Warner m 1/25/32 Fanny Reed in Carroll; Rev. Eddy. All of Carroll
(4-2/1)
2627. Doubleday, William B. of New Hartford m Emilia Sherrill of Rome, Oneida
County in R (3-1/21/29)
2628. Doubleday, William James, inf s of U. F., editor of the Cayuga Patriot,
d 10/12/22 in Auburn (3-10/23)
2629. Dougherty, James m 5/11/43 Charity P. Clarke in Westfield; J. E. Chapin,
Esq. All of Westfield (4-5/25)
2630. Douglas, George m Eliza Metcalf in Gorham (3-3/11/29)
2631. Douglas, Isaac, s of Stephen of Mexico, Oswego Co., d in Mexico ("had
been a resident of Catskill for about four years where he applied
himself to theological studies ...") (3-7/21/19)
2632. Douglass, Albert m Jane E. Taylor in Urbana; Rev. T. P. Clark (2-5/5/46)
2633. Douglass, Asa (Maj.), 72, d in Richmond, MA (a Rev. officer) (3-5/13/12)
2634. Douglass, James B., merchant, m Cornelia L. Brower in Albany (3-9/1/13)
2635. Dow, John (Hon.) of Reading m 2/14/27 Temperance Leake of Hector; Rev.
Lanning (3-2/28)
2636. Dow, Lorenzo (Rev.) m Lucy Dolbear of Montville (CT?) in Hebron, CT
(3-5/3/20). Lucy Boulbear in 5-5/17.
2637. Dow, Peggy, wf of Lorenzo, d 1/6/20 near Hebron, CT (3-1/26)
2638. Dowd, Heman, 29, d 10/27/50 in Batavia at the home of his father
(name not given) (1-11/12)
2639. Downing, Sarah S. (Miss), 19, dau of Nathaniel, d 6/11/33 in Vermont,
Oneida Co. (Editors of Massachusetts papers are requested to copy
the above) (5-6/19)
2640. Downing, Thomas m 7/4/41 Delphena S. Parks, both of Palmyra, in Walworth;
Rev. Bennett (5-7/14)
2641. Downs, Beach of Huntington, CT m Henrietta Remer, dau of Abraham, in
Seneca Falls (3-11/22/28)
2642. Dows, John m Adriana Maria Cooke, dau of late John, Esq. of Albany, in A
(3-3/18/29)
2643. Dowse, William, Esq., Congressman from 15th dist. of NY d in Cooperstown
(3-3/17/13)

69

2644. Dox, Abraham, merchant, m 11/4/11 Ann C. Nicholas, dau of the Hon. John, Esq., near Geneva; Rev. Chapman (3-11/6)
2645. Dox, Elizabeth R., 11, dau of late Jacob, Esq. and gr dau of Maj. Rees, d 11/14/28 in Geneva (3-11/19)
2646. Dox, Garrit L., late of Geneva, m 1/9/17 Magdalena Bogart, dau of Gerrit, Esq. of Albany, in A (3-1/22)
2647. Dox, Jacob, Esq. m 2/26/16 Mary Ann Rees, dau of Maj. James, in Geneva; Rev. Clark (3-2/28)
2648. Dox, Jacob (Col.), 35, attorney, d 1/15/23 in Geneva ("In 1810 removed to Geneva from Albany (his native place) where he has served as justice of the peace and other town offices"; surv by wf and 3 ch) (3-1/22 and 5-1/22)
2649. Dox, Myndert M., Esq., 42, late collector of the Port of Buffalo, d 9/8/30 in Buffalo (a Capt. in U. S. Army in War of 1812) (5-9/17)
2650. Dox, Peter P., Esq., 29, postmaster of Albany, d 11/29/15 in Albany (3-11/29)
2651. Dox, Rebecca Ann, 9, dau of Thomas, d 10/25/22 in Seneca (3-10/30)
2652. Dox, Sabina (Miss), 43, dau of Peter, Esq., late of Albany d 2/11/26 in Geneva (3-2/15)
2653. Doyle, Samuel, 50, d in Bath (3-7/23/17)
2654. Dozen, Charles m 7/19/37 Rachel Cogswill, both of Michigan, in Palmyra (5-7/21)
2655. Drake, Amanda P., 36, wf of Allen, d 5/29/47 in Jasper (2-6/9)
2656. Drake, Asa m Phebe Potter in Benton; Rev. Farley, Esq. (3-1/20/19)
2657. Drake, Barnabas, 33, d 10/31/28 in Palmyra (3-11/12 and 5-10/31)
2658. Drake, Joseph H. of Wheeler m 10/7/49 Catharine Caster of Prattsburgh in P (2-10/17)
2659. Drake, Joshua of Palmyra m 10/6/41 Agnes Green, dau of John N. of Macedon, in M; Rev. Shumway (5-10/13)
2660. Drake, Luther m 11/10/38 Charlotte Johnson; Rev. Case (2-12/5)
2661. Drake, Mable, wf of Gideon, d in Lyons (3-3/31/13)
2662. Drake, Nelson, produce merchant, m 3/24/41 Della C. Duggan, oldest dau of Nathaniel, Esq.; Rev. G. R. H. Shumway. All of Palmyra (5-3/31)
2663. Drake, Ruhama, 59, wf of Deacon Drake, d 4/30/50 in Jasper (2-5/15)
2664. Drake, Sally, 40, wf of John, d in Lyons (3-6/12/22)
2665. Drake, Samuel, 64, d 5/5/26 in Batavia (1-5/5)
2666. Drake, Sarah S., 29, wf of G. W., d 3/12/48 in Le Roy (1-3/21)
2667. Draper, Dyer B. m 2/25/19 Hannah G. Clemons, both of Geneva, in G; Rev. Axtel (3-3/3)
2668. Draper, Gideon (Rev.) m 6/28/12 Elizabeth Cornice in Lyons (3-7/8)
2669. Draper, Philip N. (Dr.), 30, d in Manchester (3-12/26/27)
2670. Draper, Salmon m Loretta Wood in Dansville; Rev. S. S. Brown. All of Cohocton (2-11/18/46)
2671. Drew, John, Esq. m 4/30/26 Malinda Jones in Orangeville; Stephen King, Esq. (1-5/5)
2672. Driggs, Roswell of Tonawanda m Margaret Barnes of Buffalo in Williamsville (1-12/16/25)
2673. Drinkwater, Henry, Esq., cashier of the Bank of North America, d in Philadelphia (3-10/30/22)
2674. Driscoll, John of Palmyra drowned 8/22/40 in Albany ("At the State Street bridge Mr. Cavanaugh, a deranged person of Westmoreland, Oneida Co., under charge of Messrs. Stevens and Fuller, on his way to the Lunatic Asylum became refractory and attracted a crowd whose weight broke the draw and precipitated the crowd twenty feet below where the water was twelve ft. deep..." Those drowned were: James Hinman, constable, Albany; John Driscoll (above); John Lyon, Albany; H. S. Hoffman, Fultonville; Charles Kittle, Albany; Roderick Davidson, Albany; William L. Morey, VT; John Hendree, Jr., Albany; Mr. Cavanaugh (above); Orrin J. Fuller, Rome, NY; Samuel Fisher, Albany; Smith Mathews, Troy; Joseph Welch, Albany; James Van Buren, German Flats; Thomas McDowell, Albany; John Riordon, Albany; a boy named Wood; Mr. Jones, Albany; and a son of Mr. Chamberlain presently from Canada) (2-9/2)
2675. Driscoll, Joshua, 34, formerly of Palmyra, d 8/9/35 in Auburn (5-10/2)
2676. Drown, _____, 12. son of Samuel, d in Canandaigua (3-2/3/13)
2677. Drum, Henry, 29, d 5/17/42 in Arcadia (5-5/25)

2678. Drum, John W. m 8/21/39 Elizabeth Hazen, both of Manchester, in Palmyra;
Rev. Shumway (5-8/23)
2679. Dryer, _____ (Mrs.) d "at an advanced age" in Junius (3-9/6/26)
2680. Dubois, Edward m 5/20/37 Silvena Wolcott, both of Macedon; I. E. Beecher,
Esq. (5-5/26)
2681. Dubois, Jacob D. m 12/18/28 Eliza Van Riper in Fayette; Rev. Dr. Axtell
(3-12/24)
2682. Ducaler, Abraham m 7/4/29 Lucine Aldrich in Manchester; David Holland,
Esq. All of Manchester (5-7/10)
2683. Dudley, Charles E. (Hon.) d 1/23/41 in Albany (5-1/27)
2684. Dudley, Eleanor (Mrs.), 54, d 3/4/16 in Canandaigua (3-3/13)
2685. Dudley, Jeremiah, Esq., 85, d 11/10/38 in Bath (2-11/14)
2686. Dudley, William, 23, s of Deacon John, d 9/25/45 at the home of his
father in Bath (2-10/1)
2687. Duel, William m 11/14/38 Maria Garlock, both of Marion, in Palmyra;
F. Smith, Esq. (5-11/17)
2688. Duester, Abraham m Lusina Aldrich in Manchester (3-7/15/29)
2689. Duggan, Elizabeth (Mrs.), 80, d 10/8/35 in Palmyra (funeral at Presby.
Ch.) (5-10/9)
2690. Dummer, Edward m 4/13/28 Mrs. Olive ?Duffey in Geneva; Rev. G. Laning
(3-4/23)
2691. Duncan, Alexander of Canandaigua m Sarah Butler of Providence, RI in
New Haven (state not given - there is a New Haven in Oswego Co., NY)
(3-10/24/27)
2692. Duncan, Sarah Jane, 24, wf of Rev. William C., editor of the Southwestern
Baptist Chronicle, and oldest dau of Lyman Coss of NYC, d 7/8/47 in
New Orleans (1-8/3)
2693. Dunforth, Asa (Gen.), 73, d in Onondaga (a Rev. officer) (5-9/22/18)
2694. Dungan, Marsha (Miss), 19, dau of late Dr. Dungan of Canandaigua, d in
Romulus (3-12/23/18)
2695. Dungan, Samuel (Dr.), 42, d 11/6/17 in Canandaigua (3-11/19)
2696. Dunham, David m 7/1/30 Mary Hillman in Arcadia; Elder William Rowe
(5-7/16)
2697. Dunham, Spencer, 2, s of Timothy, d in Gorham (3-8/23/15)
2698. Dunham, Zenas (Mr.), 32, d 9/12/23 in Waterloo (3-10/1)
2699. Dunkison, Mary Ann, 35, of Seneca, "a disorderly person", d at the
poor house in Hopewell (3-4/1/29)
2700. Dunlap, Earnest A., Esq., clerk of Seneca Co., d 11/30/27 in Ovid
(3-12/12)
2701. Dunlap, Ernest, 5 mo, s of late E. A., deceased, d in Ovid (3-4/9/28)
2702. Dunlap, George m Nancy Ketchum in Ovid (3-9/17/28)
2703. Dunlap, James (Dr.), 70, d in Philadelphia (state not given) (3-4/21/19)
2704. Dunlap, Robert, nearly 70, m 6/29/17 Anna Williams, 20, in Pulteney,
Wayne Co.; Rev. Lazel (3-7/16)
2705. Dunn, Daniel, Esq., 53, d 9/12/42 in Lyons (an early resident of that
town) (5-9/21)
2706. Dunn, Ebenezer m Sarah Dickinson in Penfield (5-1/17/21)
2707. Dunn, George, 56, m Patty Runyan, 22, in Hector; John Spencer, Esq.
(3-3/15/20)
2708. Dunn, Hiram m Charlotte Clark in Reading (3-11/30/25)
2709. Dunn, James, 32, of the firm of Douglas and Dunn, Albany, d 10/20/29
in NYC (5-11/6)
2710. Dunn, Martin, M.D., of Dundee m 4/22/39 Lucina Fairbanks, dau of Rev.
Ira of Benton, Yates Co., at the Franklin House in Geneva; Rev. W. P.
Davis (5-4/26)
2711. Dunn, Thomas m Rachael Satterlee in Elmira (3-10/14/29)
2712. Dunnet, Christiana (Mrs.), 30, d 2/20/19 in Ovid (3-3/3)
2713. Dunnett, Andrew m 12/14/09 Christiana Harris, dau of Jacobus, in
Lancaster, Sen. Co.; Esq. Sebring. All of Lancaster (3-1/10/10)
2714. Dunning, Anna (Mrs.), wf of Martin and sister of William Platt of
Batavia, d 5/19/24 in Black Rock ("Her remains, together with her
infant child, were brought to this place (Batavia) and interred on
Friday last (5/22)" (1-5/28)
2715. Dunning, Henry (Col.), 84, (a Rev. officer) d near Easton, MD (3-10/21/18)
2716. Dunning, Jehiel m 1/29/31 Katharine Servis in Pittsford; A. Purdy, Esq.
All of Pittsford (5-2/18)

71

2717. Dunning, Josiah, 86, (a Rev. soldier) d 2/27/42 in Sodus (formerly of Vermont) (5-3/9)
2718. Dunning, Martin m 1/6/23 Anna Platt, both of Batavia; William H. Tisdale, Esq. (1-1/10)
2719. Dunning, Martin m 10/15/28 Lydia Bridge in Palmyra; Rev. Campbell (3-10/22 and 5-10/17)
2720. Dunscomb, Edward, Esq., 60, d 11/12/14 (prob. in Geneva) (3-12/7)
2721. Dunton, Ebenezer m 2/20/34 Ann Palmiter in Jamestown; Rev. Gillet (4-2/26)
2722. Duparcq, William, A.M., m 3/8/35 Juliet Osborn; Rev. S. T. Babbitt. All of Howard (2-3/18)
2723. Dupont, Victor, Esq. of Brandywine Hundred d 2/6/27 in Philadelphia (had been for many years a member of the Delaware legislature and a director in the Bank of the United States (3-2/14)
2724. Durfee, _____ (Mrs.), 46, wf of Stephen, d 9/14/29 in Palmyra (5-9/18)
2725. Durfee, _____, inf s of Elihu, d 1/24/31 in Palmyra (5-1/28)
2726. Durfee, Edward, 21, d 3/1/41 in Palmyra (5-3/3)
2727. Durfee, Elihu of Palmyra m 11/29/37 Maria Howland of Walworth at the Friends Meeting House in Macedon (5-12/6)
2728. Durfee, George m Pamilla Stark, both of Palmyra, in P (3-6/3/12)
2729. Durfee, Heely of Palmyra m 12/22/30 Abigail ?Rees of Marion in M; Rev. Burbank (5-12/24)
2730. Durfee, Isaac F., Esq. m 2/25/41 Mrs. Anna Hoag in Macedon; Durfee Osband, Esq. All of Macedon (5-3/17)
2731. Durfee, Job (Capt.) d in Palmyra (3-2/24/13)
2732. Durfee, Lucy, 35, wid of late Abel, d 10/5/36 in Palmyra (5-10/14)
2733. Durfee, Maria Louisa, oldest dau of Philo, d 3/23/43 in Buffalo (5-4/5)
2734. Durfee, Nathan m Arlow Franklin in Palmyra (3-1/17/16)
2735. Durfee, Pardon d in Palmyra (3-5/14/28)
2736. Durfee, Permilla, 25, wf of William, d 6/17/34 in Palmyra (5-6/27)
2737. Durfee, Philo of the firm of Clapp and Durfee m 2/12/33 Mary White, dau of Dr. James; Rev. Jesse Townsend. All of Palmyra (5-2/20)
2738. Durfee, Sarah, 46, wf of Stephen, d in Palmyra (3-9/23/29)
2739. Durfee, Stephen m Minerva Kingman in Palmyra (3-12/10/17)
2740. Durfee, Stephen, about 24, s of Lemuel, d 8/6/18 in Palmyra (5-8/11)
2741. Durfee, Stephen of Palmyra m Sarah Fuller of Scipio in S (5-2/13/22)
2742. Durfee, Stephen of Palmyra m 12/30/30 Mary Bristol of Macedon at the Friends Meeting House, Macedon (5-12/31)
2743. Durfee, Stephen, 7, s of Elihu, d 1/15/35 (5-1/16)
2744. Durfee, Sydney S. m 12/18/28 Sophia Rogers, dau of William, Jr., in Palmyra; Frederick Smith, Esq. All of Palmyra (5-12/19)
2745. Durfee, William m 11/25/21 Catherine Cole in Palmyra (5-11/28)
2746. Durfie, Hervey m 10/30/20 Betsey Dagget in Palmyra (5-11/1)
2747. Durham, Ashley D. m 4/27/43 Phidelia Truesdel, both of Harmony, in H; Rev. Hinebaugh (4-5/4)
2748. Durham, James, merchant, m Sophia D'Labar in Newtown (3-9/26/27)
2749. Durkee, David M. m 3/26/43 Abba J. Forsyth, both of Ripley, in Westfield; T. B. Hopkins (4-4/6)
2750. Durkee, John m 10/12/50 Adeline Erwin, both of Bath, in Hammondsport; Rev. Wilson (2-10/16)
2751. Dustin, Stephen m 4/1/22 Mary Ann Cole; William H. Tisdale (1-4/5)
2752. Dutcher, Reuben m Ruth Williams in Lyons (3-1/27/30)
2753. Dutcher, William A. of Geneva m 1/21/40 Mary Woods, dau of late William, Esq., in Bath; Rev. Isaac W. Platt (2-1/29)
2754. Dutten, Ebenezer, 49, d 8/10/15 in Canandaigua (3-8/23)
2755. Dutton, Austin m 2/4/16 Sarah Stone in Pittsford (3-2/21)
2756. Dutton, Joseph F., 74, d 4/10/31 in Chautauqua (1-4/22)
2757. Dutton, Maria, 23, wf of Austin, d 4/10/15 in Seneca (surv by her husband only) (3-4/19)
2758. Duzenbury, Elisha m 4/18/22 Polly McNiel in Phelps (3-4/24)
2759. Dwight, James S., 55, d 3/20/22 in Springfield, MA (3-4/10)
2760. Dwight, Timothy, 81, m Arietta Lincoln, 75, in Gardiner, KY ("Both of them have lost a leg and he is so deaf that he has to use an ear trumpet and the bride is so blind that she cannot see an inch before her nose!") (5-7/2/30)

2761. Dwinnell, Israel of Rochester m Polly Hecox in Lyons (3-10/28/29)
2762. Dyckman, Jacob, M.D., commissioner of health, secretary of the N.Y.
    Literary and Philosophical Soc., and one of the trustees of the
    College of Physicians and Surgeons, d 12/5/22 in Kingsbridge
    (3-12/18)
2763. Dyer, Jareb (sic) (Dr.), about 60, d 2/5/13 in Middlesex (3-2/10)
2764. Dyer, Patrick m 3/2/47 Mary Towner, both of Bath, in Avoca; Rev. J.
    Strough (2-3/10)
2765. Dygert, John of Avoca m 12/8/50 Aurissa V. Merril of Howard in Bath
    (2-12/18)
2766. Dygert, Samuel of Canisteo m 7/27/50 Mary Ann Dygert of Cameron in C;
    Rev. David Smith (2-8/14)
2767. Dygert, Walter m 11/24/50 Rhoda Willis; Rev. N. Sawyer. All of Bath
    (2-12/4)
2768. Dykins, Elias S. m Emily Bennet in Bath (3-1/13/30)
2769. Dykins, Jedediah, 63, d in Elmira (3-5/2/27)
2770. Dysinger, Elizabeth (Mrs.) d 2/14/26 in Fayette (3-3/1/26)
2771. Eams, Kittredge, formerly of Carroll, d "while on his way from
    Cincinnati to New Orleans" (4-10/8/34)
2772. Earl, James m 10/1/29 Elizabeth Clary; Cephas Shekell, Esq. All of
    Geneva (3-10/7)
2773. Earl, Jephthah m Eliza Hutchinson in Benton (3-8/5/29)
2774. Earl, Morris of Penn Yan m 12/26/28 Emiline Clark of Rushville in R.
    (3-1/7/29)
2775. Earll, Amos, 15 mo, d 8/3/16. Also Daniel Earll, 2, d 8/13. Both
    died in Seneca and both are sons of Jephthah Earll (3-8/28)
2776. Earll, Benjamin m 5/5/25 Lorinda Osborn in Attica (1-5/6)
2777. Earll, Ira, Esq., attorney, of Attica m 5/27/24 Mary Ann Hayden, dau of
    Strong Hayden, Esq. of Bennington,in B; Rev. Smith of Batavia (1-5/28)
2778. Earll, Stephen m Ann Eliza Evans in Benton; S. G. Gage, Esq. (3-2/11/29)
2779. Eason, Mary, 16 mo, dau of Hart, d 8/17/47 in Canisteo (2-8/25)
2780. Eastman, Alexander H., 2 yrs, s of "Mr. Eastman", d in Rochester (3-8/29/27)
2781. Eastman, John L. (Dr.) m 2/23/19 Sally R. Sandford in Ovid; Rev. Porter
    (3-3/10)
2782. Eastman, Oliver of Auburn m Esther Hopkins in Brutus (3-1/14/29)
2783. Easton, Liba L. m Magdalena Clawson in Fayette (3-2/13/28)
2784. Eaton, Aura B., wf of Prof. Amos Eaton "of the Rensselaer School",
    d 12/18/26 in Troy (3-1/5/27)
2785. Eaton, Benjamin, 84, (a Rev. Soldier) d 5/28/47 at the home of his
    only brother in Urbana (he was born in Massachusetts; emigrated at age
    25 to Painted Post; for past 8 years a member of the Presby. Ch. in
    Hammondsport) (2-6/23)
2786. Eaton, Benjamin of Bath m 11/21/50 Mrs. Mercy Yost of Cameron in Gibson
    (2-11/27)
2787. Eaton, Elizabeth, wid of Gen. William, d in Auburn (4-6/15/31)
2788. Eaton, Mary, about 45, consort of Benjamin, d 9/7/47 in Bath (2-9/15)
2789. Eaton, Stephen, 59, d 2/23/19 in Perinton (5-3/3 and 3-3/10)
2790. Eaton, Timothy Dwight, 21, adjunct prof. in the Rensselaer School and
    son of Prof. Amos Eaton, d in Troy (3-11/26/28)
2791. Eaton, William m Amelia Sanger in Canandaigua (3-2/25/29)
2792. Ebberts, Catharine, 20, wf of John, d in Waterloo (3-8/6/28)
2793. Ebert, John H. m Catharine Stewart in Waterloo; Dr. McDonald (3-12/28/25)
2794. Ebert, John H., 30, d in Waterloo (3-11/28/27)
2795. Eckley, Thomas, 13, only s of Thomas of Phelpstown, Ont. Co., d 8/4/12
    in Newark, NJ (3-9/30/12)
2796. Eddy, _____ (Mr.) m Mary Miller in Palmyra (5-1/23/22)
2797. Eddy, Amelia Ann, 2 yrs, dau of Joseph, d 9/1/21 in Williamson (5-9/12)
2798. Eddy, Cyrenus C. of Williamson m 12/21/42 Cornelia S. Miller of Marion
    in M; Rev. Clark H. Smith (5-12/28)
2799. Eddy, Eli, about 45, "Teacher of a Select School", d 9/4/32 in Bath
    (2-9/5)
2800. Eddy, Enoch m Milly Glover in Phelps; Thomas Smith, Esq. (3-11/3/19)
2801. Eddy, George P. of Marion, s of Rev. David, m 5/16/33 Catharine H.
    Rowe, dau of Rev. Epicratus, deceased, in Palmyra (5-5/22)
2802. Eddy, Hiram S. of Sherman m 2/7/39 Elizabeth L. Hawley, only dau of Col.
    Alpheus, in Jamestown; Rev. Parmely (4-2/13)

73

2803. Eddy, Isaac (Rev.), 59, d 6/26/33 in Jamestown (funeral in Presby. Ch.)
He was born in Middleborough, MA; a lineal descendant of Pilgrims.
His parents, when he was age 6, moved the family first to Woodstock
and later to Sherburne and Pittsfield, all in VT. Isaac, with his
older bro, was apprenticed at Woodstock to a clothier. At Pittsfield
he served as deacon and was later ordained at age 42 (Royalton Assoc.
of Cong'l. Ministers). Prior to 1825 a minister at Locke, Cay. Co.
Cong'l. minister in Jamestown until 1830. (surv by children) (4-7/3)

2804. Eddy, Jane, widow, 68, d 1/21/40 in Marion (a suicide by hanging)
(5-1/29)

2805. Eddy, John m Polly Barnhart in Palmyra (5-11/28/21)

2806. Eddy, John of Pittstown m 2/3/22 Mary Miller of Palmyra; Rev. Spacer
(5-2/6)

2807. Eddy, Laran S. (Mr.), 22, of the firm of Eddy and Clark of Palmyra
d 10/31/33 in Macedon at the home of his father (5-11/1)

2808. Eddy, Mary, 27, wf of John and dau of Hezekiah Miller d 1/16/32 in Lyons
(funeral at Bapt. Meeting House in Macedon) (5-1/17)

2809. Eddy, Otis, 56, of Ithaca d 9/5/43 in Sincairville at the home of his
son (4-9/7)

2810. Eddy, Safford of Jamestown m Ann Alida Abeel of Hanover in H (4-2/26/34)

2811. Eddy, Samuel, 78, d 11/29/21 in Williamson (a Rev. soldier) (5-12/5)

2812. Eddy, Samuel m 10/14/28 Achsah Maria Tucker in Marion (5-10/17). Achsay
Maria Tucker in 3-10/22.

2813. Eddy, Thomas, 70, d in NYC (3-9/26/27)

2814. Eder, John of Newtown m Mercy Pfouts in Pine Creek, PA (3-9/26/27)

2815. Edget, Lovett m Joanna Lesieur in Pulteney (3-12/22/19)

2816. Edgett, George m 3/27/41 Sarah J. Jones of Howard in H; J. Whiting, Esq.
(2-4/7)

2817. Edington, Philip m 4/5/25 Magdalena Fiero, dau of William, in Seneca;
Rev. Nesbit (3-4/6)

2818. Edmonds, Lucy, 45, wf of John L., d 1/4/43 in Busti (surv by husband
and 6 ch) (4-1/5)

2819. Edmons, John m 10/24/17 Lucy Stodard in Ontario, NY (5-11/28)

2820. Edmonson, William (Col.), 68, d in Abington, VA (a Rev. soldier who, with
rank of major, fought in the Battle of King's Mountain with three of
his brothers, two of whom were there killed) (3-10/12/22)

2821. Edmonston, James of Vienna m 6/6/32 Mary Danielson of Butternuts, Otsego
Co.; Rev. Goodrich (5-11/28)

2822. Edmunds, I. O., "Resident Graduate of the Hamilton Literary and Theological Institute, m 1/15/40 Philena Spear, dau of Deacon A. Spear of
Macedon; Rev. W. I. Crane of Hartland (5-1/22)

2823. Edmunds, James, Jr. of Hartland, Niag. Co. m 9/23/30 Cordelia Spear
of Macedon in M; Elder Robert Powell (5-10/8)

2824. Edsell, Charles m Mary Miller, dau of Capt. S., in Jackson, PA (3/4/16/28)

2825. Edson, Calvin, the Living Skeleton,d "recently" in Randolph, VT. "By a
post mortem examination it was ascertained that a tapeworm 15 feet in
length, was the cause ... of his ultimate death." (5- 10/3/32). Same
source dated 10/24: "Calvin Edson ... is still alive and being
exhibited in Portland, Maine."

2826. Edson, Harvey of Pinegrove, PA m 1/6/41 Mary Jane Van Deusen, dau of
John of Busti, in B; M. Norton, Esq. (4-1/13)

2827. Edson, William m 8/16/32 Isabella Wilson in Jamestown; R. Pier, Esq.
(4-8/22)

2828. Edwards, _____ (Miss), 80, d in New Jersey (3-10/25/09)

2829. Edwards, _____, wf of Jeremiah, d "at an advanced age" in Benton
(3-11/28/27)

2830. Edwards, _____, wf of Hon. Ogden Edwards and oldest dau of Daniel
Penfield, Esq., d in NYC (3-1/21/29)

2831. Edwards, _____, inf s of Hon. George C., d 1/8/32 in Bath (2-1/11)

2832. Edwards, Alexander, formerly of Bath, m 10/2/49 Elizabeth McCurdy of
Dansville in D; Rev. Jesse Edwards (2-10/10)

2833. Edwards, George C., Esq. m 5/21/12 Hannah Carpenter in Elmira; Rev.
Simeon R. Jones. All of Elmira (3-6/3)

2834. Edwards, Ira m 10/22/43 Mary Chapman, dau of Rev. Joseph; Rev. Hogaboom.
All of Arcadia (5-10/25)

2835. Edwards, Ira P. m 5/11/45 Margaret Dawson in Pulteney; Rev. Sagar. All of Bath (2-8/13)
2836. Edwards, Jephtha W. m Esther Emmons in Romulus (3-2/3/30)
2837. Edwards, Jeremiah m Mrs. Martha Clark in Benton (3-3/12/28)
2838. Edwards, Joseph of Syracuse m 12/10/27 Susan Gleason of Geneva in G; Rev. Dr. Axtell (3-12/12)
2839. Edwards, Martha Ann, 18, dau of George and Martha, d 8/27/50 in Batavia. "Hampton (Northampshire, Mass.) Gazette copy" (1-9/3)
2840. Edwards, Pierpont (Hon.) m Polly Tucker in Bridgeport, CT ( 3-10/21/18)
2841. Edwards, Samuel T., 24, d 3/31/40 in Bath (2-4/1)
2842. Edwards, Timothy E., 29, d 11/30/25 in Ithaca. ("The wife and an infant child of the deceased died about three weeks since.") (3-12/19/25)
2843. Edwards, William m 2/14/22 Maria Fitzhugh, dau of late Peregrine, Esq., in Sodus; Rev. Orin Clark (3-2/20/22)
2844. Eggleston, Aaron, 60, d in Utica (3-12/26/27)
2845. Eggleston, Charles Payne, 3 yrs, s of Dr. J. S., d 11/6/30 in Palmyra (Dr. J. S. thanks friends and neighbors for their kindness and "particularly Gain Robinson, M.D., for his friendly and faithful attendance") (5-11/12)
2846. Eggleston, Henry Fenton, s of Dr. J. S., d 1/8/41 (5-1/13)
2847. Eggleston, John m 9/18/49 Harriet Emerson in Bath; Elder Swick. All of Bath (2-10/17)
2848. Elderkin, Hiram , 18 mo, s of Dr. Vine Elderkin, d 9/18/30 in Ashville (4-9/22)
2849. Elderkin, Ira m 6/15/43 Phoebe Ann Rockwell; S. Jones, Esq. (4-6/22)
2850. Eldred, _____ (Mrs.), 35, wf of Cooper Eldred d 8/21/31 in Cohocton (2-9/7)
2851. Eldrid, Ann Eliza, 6, d 10/24/21 in Palmyra (5-10/31)
2852. Eldrid, Daniel m Eliza Johnson in Fayette; Rev Martin of Geneva (3-4/15/29)
2853. Eldridge, James m 4/24/45 Roena Preston in Elba; Rev. J. A. Bolles. All of Elba (1-4/29)
2854. Eldridge, Jonathan, 32, m Rachel Ketchum, 56, in Bath; Rev. Powers (3-12/24/17)
2855. Ellas, _____, inf dau of Henry, d 8/5/27 in Bath (3-8/15)
2856. Ellas, Francis S., "Assistant Teacher in the Clinton Institute", Onon. Co., m 5/9/38 Sarah E. Hoyt, formerly of Buffalo, in Stamford, CT; Rev. Todd (2-5/23)
2857. Ellas, George H. of Decatur m 2/26/50 Phebe Bronson of Urbana in U; Rev. George Hood (2-3/6)
2858. Ellas, George S. (Maj.) of Bath m 6/16/41 Amanda D. Loomis of Rushville in R; Rev. Gelston (2-6/23)
2859. Ellas, Henry, 36, of Bath d 9/5/35 in Huron Village, Ohio (2-9/23)
2860. Ellas, Josiah Young, about 18 mo, s of Alva, Esq., d 9/9/31 in Bath (2-9/14)
2861. Ellas, Mary, about 36, wf of Henry, d 4/18/35 in Kennedyville (2-4/22)
2862. Ellet, William H., M.D., of NYC m 12/3/31 Elizabeth F. Lummis, dau of Dr. William N. of Maxwell, Gen. Co., in NYC; Rev. John A. Clark (5-12/27)
2863. Ellicot, Joseph, late agent for the Holland Land Co. at Batavia, d 8/19/26 "at the New York Asylum" (3-8/30)
2864. Ellicott, Andrew, 67, Professor of Mathematics at the Military Academy, d 8/23/20 at West Point (5-9/13)
2865. Ellicott, Benjamin, Esq., 63, formerly a member of Congress, d in Williamsville, Erie Co. (3-12/26/27)
2866. Ellicott, John B., Esq. of Batavia m Helen Griffith, dau of Dr. Thomas, deceased, of New Jersey, in NYC; Rev. William Berrigan (3-2/13/22)
2867. Ellicott, John of Chili, NY m 8/7/50 Mary Russell of Stafford at "Genesee House" (perhaps in Batavia); Rev. J. K. Cheesman (1-8/13)
2868. Elliott, Ruth d in Friendship; also two of her children (3-2/10/19)
2869. Elliott, Samuel H. (Rev.) of Woodbridge, CT m 10/9/44 Marcia Lorette Harvey, dau of Col. C. R. of Somerville, NJ, in S; Rev. Dr. Messler (4-10/25)
2870. Ellis, _____ (Dr.) of Auburn m 12/27/09 Lucy Phelps, dau of Rev. Phelps, of Geneva in G; Rev. Phelps (3-1/3/10)
2871. Ellis, Edmond m 9/18/42 Roxanna Fay in Portland; Rev. La Hatt (4-9/29)
2872. Ellis, Eugene, 10 mo, s of Ella (sic) and Jane, d 9/3/49 in Bath (2-9/5)

75

2873. Ellis, George, about 23, d 12/17/41 (prob. in Bath) (2-12/22)
2874. Ellis, John (Dr.), 13 yrs (sic), s of Jason, d 12/15/41 in Bath (2-12/22)
2875. Ellis, John A. m 9/19/41 Mahitabel Agur; John Randel, Esq. All of Urbana
       (2-9/22)
2876. Ellis, Simeon of Benton m 11/14/22 Elizabeth Gray of Milo in M (3-11/27)
2877. Ellis, Thomas, merchant, of Attica m 1/9/25 Marian McEntee of Perry in
       Perry; Rev. Brown (1-1/21)
2878. Ellis, William m Rachel Davis, both of Seneca, in Geneva; S.G. Gage, Esq.
       (3-6/3/29)
2879. Ellison, John m 6/21/15 Charlotte Minzie of Geneva in G; Jacob Dox, Esq.
       (3-6/28)
2880. Ellsworth, Gardner m 1/30/23 Sally Hurley (5-2/5)
2881. Ellsworth, John m 5/6/19 Mrs. Thirza Squier, both of Geneva; Jacob Dox,
       Esq. (3-5/12)
2882. Elmendorf, Conrad J., a Rev. soldier, d in Kingston (3-6/20/27)
2883. Elmore, John m Esther Umstead in Phelps; Rev. Mosher (3-1/21/18)
2884. Elston, Cornelius m 3/8/31 Julia Deland, both of Busti, in B; Rev. Isaac
       Eddy (4-3/16)
2885. Elsworth, Levi m 2/10/31 Isabella McIntyre in Sodus; Robert Alsop, Esq.
       (5-2/18)
2886. Elsworth, Ransom m 1/27/20 Eliza Prentis in Benton (3-2/9)
2887. Elty, E., and Mrs. McKinney, and Mrs. Camp, the two latter being sisters,
       were all interred in one afternoon (date not given) in Auburn
       (3-1/13/13)
2888. Ely, David G. of the firm of Beckwith and Ely m 10/9/33 Ruth S. Marvin
       in Palmyra; Rev. Jesse Townsend (5-10/11)
2889. Ely, Edward B. m 9/24/15 Fanny Avery in Ulysses; Rev. James Reynolds
       (3-9/27)
2890. Ely, Giles S., merchant, of Palmyra m 10/13/32 Caroline A. Hoe, dau of
       Robert of NYC, in NYC; Rev. Cyrus Mason (5-10/31)
2891. Ely, James, merchant, of Owego m Cynthia Bundy, dau of E., in Elmira
       (3-10/22/28)
2892. Ely, Joseph N., formerly of Palmyra, m 2/28/43, "in the form of the
       Society of Friends", Hannah M. Robbins, both of NYC, in NYC (5-3/15)
2893. Ely, Richard M., about 38, merchant, d 2/11/28 in Penfield (3-2/13)
2894. Ely, Ruth (Mrs.), 35, d 7/17/44 in Palmyra (member of Presby. Ch.;
       "from childhood a resident among us") (5-7/24)
2895. Emerson, Amos m 4/18/50 Helen Cornelia Eggleston in Bath; Rev. J. K.
       Tuttle. All of Bath (2-5/22)
2896. Emerson, John M. m 1/27/31 Ruby Blackman (2-2/2)
2897. Emerson, Joseph m 3/14/47 Harriet Jaquay, late of Hamilton, Madison Co.,
       in Thurston; Rev. T. McElhana (2-3/17)
2898. Emerson, Joseph, 60, d 2/7/49 in Bath (2-2/14)
2899. Emerson, Marilla, 46, wf of Joseph, d 1/18/47 in Bath (2-1/27)
2900. Emerson, William (Rev.), 42, pastor of the First Church, Boston, d 6/11/11
       in Boston, MA (3-6/26)
2901. Emmet, Thomas Addis, Esq., 65, attorney, d 11/14/27 in NYC while on duty
       in circuit court (3-11/21)
2902. Emmons, Carlos (Hon.) of Springville, Erie Co. m 10/21/47 Mrs. Caroline
       Powers, wid of late Rev. Philander of the Genesee Conference, in
       Bath; Rev. S. W. Alden (2-10/27)
2903. Emmons, Joseph, lately of NYC, m 3/4/12 Elizabeth Huston, dau of John,
       in Geneva; Rev. Phelps (3-3/11)
2904. Emmons, Lucy, 21, consort of Rev. George and youngest dau of Capt. Asa
       Babcock of Elba, d 4/19/45 in Barre, Orleans Co. (1-4/29)
2905. Emott, Melissa, consort of Hon. Judge Emott, d in Poughkeepsie (3-2/16/20)
2906. Emsen, William d 2/18/11 at the Glass Factory near Geneva (3-2/20)
2907. Engelbrecht, Conrad, 60, a native of Germany and father of Mr. Engelbrecht
       of Geneva, NY, d 2/2/19 in Frederickstown, MD (lived in F nearly
       40 yrs.; an elder and treasurer of the Lutheran Church in Fredericks-
       town (3-2/24)
2908. English, Clarinda E., 30, wf of Charles, d 8/16/32 in Stafford (1-8/21)
2909. Enos, Henry m Sarah Crandall in Almond (3-5/16/27)
2910. Ensign, Washington m 6/28/25 Tamma Huested, both of Batavia, in B
       (1-7/1)
2911. Ensworth, _____ m Catharine Henion in Waterloo (3-11/25/29)

2912. Ensworth, Dyer m Catharine Henyon in Waterloo (3-11/4/29)
2913. Ensworth, James T. of Jamestown m 4/27/45 Emeline Lewis, dau of the Hon.
        A. of Panama, NY, in P; Rev. C. R. Chapman (4-5/2)
2914. Ensworth, Mason C., 25, s of Dr. Azel, d 5/27/20 while traveling from
        Kingston, Upper Canada to his father's home in Rochester (5-5/31)
2915. Ensworth, Russell m Ann Brockway in Palmyra (3-1/17/16)
2916. Erants, John of Fayette d in Fayette (3-9/6/26)
2917. Errickson, Aaron of Rochester m Hannah Bockover of Lyons in Milo
        (3-9/19/27)
2918. Erway, Ira of Barton, Tioga Co. m 3/5/41 Louisa Monell of Bath; Rev.
        Dunham (2-4/14)
2919. Erwin, Arthur, Jr. m Frances Maria McKeen in Painted Post (3-3/12/28)
2920. Erwin, John A., inf s of Gen. F. E., d 4/13/41 in Painted Post (2-4/21)
2921. Erwin, Robert m 8/29/16 Betsey Lott, both of Phelps; Philetus Swift,
        Esq. (3-9/4)
2922. Erwin, Samuel, Esq., oldest s of Gen. F. E., m 8/7/50 Amelia Shaw in
        Painted Post; Rev. Youngs. All of Painted Post (2-8/14)
2923. Eschenberg, John, Esq. of Germany, merchant, m 6/2/24 Eliza Rodney,
        second dau of late Caesar A., Esq., in Buenos Ayres (sic) (3-8/18)
2924. Essex, James, 20, midshipman in U. S. Navy and a native of Lexington,
        KY, d in Darien, GA (3-3/10/19)
2925. Estelow, _____ (Mr.), one of the oldest settlers of Macedon, d 4/26/26
        in Macedon (3-5/3)
2926. Esterly, George m 3/4/32 Jane Lewis, dau of Joseph, in Penfield. All
        of Williamson (5-3/14)
2927. Esterly, Robert m 4/6/31 Amanda Blakely in Sodus; Elder M. Allen
        (5-4/15)
2928. Etleson, George G. m 12/17/30 Hannah Drake in Lyons; Rev. Hubbell
        (5-12/24)
2929. Eustis, William (Hon.), Secretary of War, m Caroline Langdon, dau of
        late Judge Langdon, in Portsmouth, NH (3-11/7/10)
2930. Evans, Benjamin, Esq. of Mayville, Chaut. Co. m 6/13/22 Susan Shippey
        of Batavia; Rev. Calvin Colton (1-6/14)
2931. Evans, David E., Esq. of Batavia m Catharine Brinckerhoff of Albany
        in A (3-8/1/27)
2932. Evans, Elizabeth, 19, only dau of David E., Esq., d 1/16/48 in Batavia
        (1-1/18)
2933. Evans, John E., Esq. of Painted Post m Ann Hempsted in Bath (3-1/30/28)
2934. Evans, Leonard, 80, d in Fall River (prob. in Massachusetts) (a Rev.
        pensioner) (5-1/24/32)
2935. Evans, Lewis m 11/3/25 Anna Hoyt in Batavia; Daniel Tisdale, Esq.
        (1-11/4 and 3-11/16)
2936. Evans, Lucy, 31, consort of David E. Evans, Esq., d 9/24/24 in Batavia
        (1-10/1)
2937. Evans, Oliver, Esq., 64, d 4/16/19 in NYC (3-4/28)
2938. Evans, Ross m Mary Tudor in Buffalo (3-1/14/29)
2939. Everson, Bruce, merchant, m 1/28/41 Lucy Crowell in Palmyra; Rev. T. S.
        Brittan. All of Palmyra (5-2/3)
2940. Ewer, Alwyn (Capt.), 32, d 3/31/26 in the Pacific Ocean (of the ship
        "Criterion" of Nantucket - killed by a whale) (3-9/13)
2941. Failing, George m 10/23/30 Sally Lemoreau in Lyons; Rev. Alverson
        (5-11/12)
2942. Fairbank, Joshua A., 25, drowned 3/27/41 in Kennedyville (4-3/31)
2943. Fairbanks, Eleazer (Rev.), 68, d 5/14/20 in Pulteneyville (3-5/24 and
        5-5/17)
2944. Fairbanks, Leland m 12/9/45 Sarah Corbin in Poland, NY; Ames Fuller,
        Esq. All of Poland (4-12/19)
2945. Fairbanks, Rufus P., 50, d 2/29/21 in Pulteneyville (5-5/2)
2946. Fairbanks, Russel m Lucy Merriman, dau of Sylvester, in Friendship,
        Alleg. Co. (3-5/2/27)
2947. Fairbanks, Sarah, 77, relict of the late Rev. Eleazer, d 6/9/36 in
        Williamson (5-6/17)
2948. Fairchild, James of Oberlin, Ohio m 11/29/41 Mary F. Kellogg, dau of
        Titus, formerly of Jamestown, in Minden, Caiborne Parish, LA
        (4-1/6/42)
2949. Fairchild, Joseph, 44, d 3/5/13 (surv by wf and 7 ch) (3-3/10)

77

2950. Fairchild, N. of Ogdensburgh m Julia Strong, dau of John W., Esq., in Rochester (3-6/20/27)
2951. Fairchilds, A. H. m Sarah Loverhill in Lyons (3-6/10/18). Susan Loverhill (5-6/2/18)
2952. Fairchilds, Abiathar V. m 8/29/22 Betsey Fox of Victor in Lyons; Rev. Pomeroy (3-9/11 and 5-9/4)
2953. Fairfield, Joseph m 4/16/47 Ellen B. Thomas of Alexander; Rev. Babcock (1-4/20)
2954. Falconer, Patrick, Esq. m 11/28/44 Martha T. Hallock in Dexterville; Rev. O. Street (4-11/29)
2955. Faling, Jacob, 19, d in Palmyra (3-11/17/19)
2956. Fall, Daniel d in Mendon (surv by wf and 6 ch) (3-4/29/29)
2957. Falson, Jerusha, 37, d in Italy, NY (3-7/9/28)
2958. Fanning, Zeraviah, wf of Phineas, d 8/22/18 in Palmyra (5-9/8)
2959. Farely, Polly, 53, wf of Millins, d 10/1/48 in Le Roy (1-10/31)
2960. Farewell, Charles m 12/29/42 Mary Holling in Pulteneyville; A. Cornwall, Esq. (5-1/4/43)
2961. Fargo, John of Geneva m 4/12/32 Amelia Rhodes of Lockport in Rochester (5-5/2)
2962. Fargo, Russell of Benton m 9/10/28 Mary Chapman of Ovid, dau of John, Esq., late Sheriff of Seneca Co., deceased, in Ovid; Rev. Thomas Lounsbury (3-9/17)
2963. Faribault, Joseph N., Esq., about 35, formerly of Montreal and late Prof. of French in Geneva College, d 8/17/27 in Plattsburgh (3-9/12)
2964. Farley, George W. m Caroline Smock in Lyons (3-7/18/27)
2965. Farney, George m Sally Ann Wheeler in Ovid (3-1/16/22)
2966. Farnham, Adalaide (Miss), 22, dau of Caleb, d 8/14/42 in Bath (2-8/17)
2967. Farnham, Charles, 22?, d in Elmira (3-9/30/29)
2968. Farnham, Martha Augusta, 20, dau of Deacon Aaron, d 5/31/43 in Hardwick, VT ("She had lived in Chautauqua Co., NY many years") (4-6/22)
2969. Farnham, Samuel (Judge), about 50, d 7/13/22 in Williamson (5-7/17)
2970. Farnsworth, Jeremy, 15 mo., d in _____ (original posting partly illegible) (3-7/7/13)
2971. Farr, Reuben of Jamestown m 9/25/33 Rebecca Campbell of Busti in B; R. Pier, Esq. (4-10/2)
2972. Farrar, Lysander, Esq., attorney, m Melissa M. Keyes in Jamestown; Rev. E. J. Gillett. All of Jamestown. (4-8/14/39)
2973. Fassett, John of Tyrone m 10/22/46 Ann Ellison in Reading; Rev.B. Hurd (2-11/11)
2974. Faulkner, _____, inf s of J. W., d in Bath (3-3/10/19)
2975. Faulkner, Daniel P., formerly of Geneva, s of John of Urbana, drowned "in January last near the falls of Ohio" (3-6/25/28)
2976. Faulkner, Horton m 8/29/41 Susan Prentiss, both of Ontario, NY, in Pulteneyville (a double ceremony - see marriage of Martin Terwilliger) A. Cornwall, Esq. (5-9/8)
2977. Faulkner, James (Dr.) of Bath m Minerva Hammond in Bath (3-6/17/12)
2978. Faulkner, Morgan L., merchant, of Clyde m 11/15/28 Caroline Mount of NYC at the home of R. Mount near Waterloo; Rev. Lane (3-11/19)
2979. Faunce, Jeduthan L. m 4/19/46 Deborah Weeks in Batavia; A. Cowdin, Esq. All of Bethany (1-4/28)
2980. Favor, Joseph (Col.), 47, d 9/30/48 in the home of J. R. Bond in Mount Morris (deceased formerly of Lockport) (1-10/31)
2981. Fay, Anna, 40, wf of Europe Fay and dau of Isaac Foster of Holliston, MA, d 4/26/35 in Carroll (Printers in New Hampshire and VT are asked to insert this notice) (4-5/6)
2982. Fay, Clinton S. m Almira Clark in Portland; Rev. La Hatt (4-3/3/42)
2983. Fay, Levi (Dr.) m 10/25/18 Bathsheba Gaines in Prattstown (3-11/4)
2984. Fayette, Julius Raymond, printer, d near Cambridge, MA ("... had lived for some time in Canandaigua (NY) which place he left about a month ago') (3-2/14/16)
2985. Feagles, John of Lyons m 10/19/22 Julia Ann White of Romulus (3-10/30)
2986. Featherly, Charles, 1 yr, s of Peter, d 3/17/25 in Geneva (3-3/30)
2987. Featherly, George, 19, oldest s of Henry, d 1/20/30 in Geneva (3-1/27)
2988. Felch, Cheever d 3/27/27 in NYC ("late editor of Coram's Champion, formerly of the New Hampshire Farmers Advocate, and the Port Folio") (3-4/4)

78

2989. Fellows, Eleazer of Carroll m 11/5/35 Betsey Cook of Pinegrove in
Pinegrove (4-11/11)
2990. Fellows, Jonathan m Catharine M. Sly, both of Painted Post, in P. P.
(3-11/12/23)
2991. Felshaw, Willard H. m 1/2/31 Naomi Pratt, both of Sodus, in Sodus
(5-1/14)
2992. Felt, Sylvester, about 58, d in Bushnell's Basin (state not given -
probably Pennsylvania) (5-1/14/31)
2993. Feltus, Henry J. (Rev.), D.D., 53, rector of St. Stephen's Church,
d in NYC (3-9/10/28)
2994. Fennow, Samuel of Tyrone, Steuben Co., m 4/18/41 Ann Eliza Bunnell
of Canandaigua in C; Rev. Thompson (2-4/21)
2995. Fenton, Bicknel D. m 9/21/43 Cordelia A. Ide in Ellery; Rev. H.
Smith. All of Ellery (4-10/5)
2996. Fenton, Catharine (Miss), 18, third dau of Joseph S., d 3/1/36 in
Palmyra ("funeral at the Presbyterian House") (5-3/4)
2997. Fenton, Elliott Barrett, 8 mo, youngest s of R. F., d 4/12/42 in
Jamestown (4-4/14)
2998. Fenton, Jane W., 20, wf of R. E., d 2/2/42 in Frewsburgh (4-2/3)
2999. Fenton, Josiah J. of Buffalo m 10/5/36 Frances Ann Conklin of Geneva
in G; Rev. Abeel (5-10/14)
3000. Fenton, Marcus of Jamestown m 10/24/32 Mary Johnson of Ashville in A;
Rev. E. J. Gillet (4-10/31)
3001. Fenton, R. F. (Maj.) of Jamestown m 6/9/33 Marianne A. Lawrence of
Jaffrey, NH "at church" in Jamestown; Rev. E. J. Gillet (4-6/12)
3002. Fenton, Reuben E., merchant, m 2/5/40 Jane Frew, dau of John, Esq.,
in Frewsburgh; G. Swift, Esq. All of Carroll. (4-2/12)
3003. Fenton, Reuben E. m 6/12/44 Betsy Scudder in Carroll; Rev. O. D. Hibbard.
All of Carroll. (4-6/14)
3004. Fenton, Sabra (Miss), 22, dau of William H., Esq., d 5/21/45 in
Dexterville (4-5/30)
3005. Fenton, Sally Ann, 32, wf of Maj. R. F. and sister of the Messrs Tews
of Jamestown, d 7/11/32 in Jamestown (surv by husband, two ch,
parents, brothers, and sisters, none named) (4-7/11)
3006. Fenton, Sarah Ann Tew, 2 yrs 6 mo, youngest dau of R. F. Fenton,
d 8/27/39 in Jamestown (4-8/28)
3007. Ferguson, John m Laura Lockwood in Murray, Genesee Co. (5-9/29/18)
3008. Fergy, Andrew of Brighton m 11/5/39 Isabella Adams in Palmyra; Rev.
Shumway (5-11/15)
3009. Ferre, Asenith, 43, wf of Gideon, d in Canandaigua (3-7/9/17)
3010. Ferrington, Noah, 19, late of Rutland, Jefferson Co., d (date and
place not given) (5-7/26/20)
3011. Ferris, A. J., 26, s of Hon. James C., d 11/3/49 at the home of his
father (name not given) in the village of Wyoming (1-11/13)
3012. Ferris, A. P., Esq. m 10/20/47 Catharine Reed, dau of Capt. Reed, at St.
Thomas Church in Bath; Rev. Corson. All of Bath (2-10/27)
3013. Ferris, Benjamin m Sabra Stone, dau of Asahel, Esq., in Naples, NY
(3-3/11/29)
3014. Ferris, F. of Howard m 9/29/45 A. Shaver of Avoca in A; Rev. J. Strough
(2-10/8)
3015. Ferris, Florinda, 24, wf of James, d 8/15/26 in Jamestown (4-8/23)
3016. Ferris, Israel, 78, of Milo m Mrs. Norris, 74, of Tyrone in Barrington
(3-8/26/29)
3017. Ferris, Lemuel H. of Bath m 3/14/50 Eliza Ann McDowell of Howard in
Avoca; Rev. H. Spencer (2-3/27)
3018. Ferris, Lewis G., M.D., of Mount Morris m 1/2/40 Sophronia Holmes, dau
of Simeon, Esq., of Cohocton in C; Rev. A. Chase (2-1/15)
3019. Field, Alfred T. of Canandaigua m Eliza Martin in Avon (3-10/22/28)
3020. Field, Darius m 9/12/49 Maria Knickerbocker (possibly in Cohocton);
Rev. A. Adams (2-9/19)
3021. Field, David J (or Jr.?) m 7/4/16 Electa Hastings, both of Geneva;
Rev. Henry Axtell (3-7/10)
3022. Field, H. F. (Capt.) m Elizabeth B. Jones in Sweden, Tioga Co. (3-1/14/29)
3023. Field, Hannah, 64, consort of David, d 8/22/13 in Geneva (3-8/25)
3024. Field, Hannah, 27, wf of David of Geneva, d 7/3/15 at the home of
Ebenezer Chittenden in Phelps (3-7/12)

3025. Field, Nancy (Mrs.), 40, consort of Calvin, d 1/19/26 in Batavia
(1-1/20)
3026. Field, Pliny A., Esq., 35, of Black Rock d 5/31/17 (drowned in Niagara
River opposite Black Rock; surv by wf and 2 ch) (3-6/11)
3027. Field, Richard, 29, senior editor of the _Recorder_, d in Catskill
(3/12/26/27)
3028. Field, Sophia, 22, dau of David, d 7/9/12 in Geneva (3-7/15)
3029. Field, Thomas Jefferson m Louisa A. Chapman, dau of Dr. Elisha, of
Marcellus in Syracuse (3-6/6/27)
3030. Field, William m 2/2/14 Phila Field in Geneva; Rev. Axtell (3-2/9)
3031. Field, William, 48, d 9/11/29 in Geneva (3-9/16)
3032. Fields, _____, 6, "a child of Oliver of Phelps", d 8/18/16 (3-8/21)
3033. Fields, Arnold m Cyrene Cole in Howard (3-9/10/17)
3034. Fields, Elias, 40, d in Elba (1-8/23/22)
3035. Fife, Hiram of Bath m 4/19/49 Matilda Smith of Elmira at the Methodist
Parsonage in Elmira; Rev. H. N. Seaver (2-4/25)
3036. Filch, Edward of Buffalo m 9/14/42 Jane Grawbadger of Savannah, NY in
Lyons; Charles O. Hoffman, Esq. (5-9/21)
3037. Fillmore, Joseph F. of Palmyra m 4/4/43 Harriet J. Adams of Phelps in P;
Rev. John Baggerly (5-4/12)
3038. Fina, Nehemiah L. of Greenfield, PA m 1/31/41 Lucena Weaver, dau of A.
Weaver of Clymer; Rev. L. Rathbun (4-2/3)
3039. Finch, Caleb, 40, d 10/22/30 in Newark, NY (5-11/12)
3040. Finch, Calvin, 45, d in Onondaga, NY (3-11/16/25)
3041. Finch, Calvin m Caroline S. Nash in Spencer (3-1/14/29)
3042. Finch, Daniel G., 44, d 2/26/42 in Tecumseh, MI (an early settler there;
had formerly lived in Palmyra, NY) (5-3/23)
3043. Finch, Elizabeth, 40, wf of Daniel G., formerly of Palmyra, d in
Tecumseh. MI (5-4/12/39)
3044. Finch, Elsy Elizabeth, inf dau of Daniel G., d 8/10/33 in Palmyra
(5-8/16)
3045. Finch, Eugene, 7 mo, s of Daniel G., d 8/11/31 in Palmyra (5-8/12)
3046. Finch, Samuel m Lorany Green in Milo (3-4/23/28)
3047. Finley, Nathan, about 35, d 12/17/32 in Arcadia (5-12/19)
3048. Finn, Ananias m Rebecca Tice in Elmira (3-2/3/19)
3049. Finn, Ananias, 27, d in Phelps (3-5/9/27)
3050. Firman, James of Sugargrove (in Pennsylvania?) m 10/10/35 Susan Phelps
of Busti in B; Rev. Graves (4-10/14)
3051. Fish, _____, ch. of Cyrus of Jamestown, drowned "while playing near a
pond" (4-5/31/44)
3052. Fish, Chauncey m 3/26/44 Phebe Jane Cottrell in Williamson; Charles G.
Richards, Esq. All of Williamson. (5-4/3)
3053. Fish, David m 5/29/46 Sally L. Smith, both of Cohocton, in C; Rev. S. S.
Brown (2-6/3)
3054. Fish, Harry m 1/29/35 Polly Russell, both of Williamson; Rev. Fillmore
(5-2/6)
3055. Fish, Job, 50, d 3/31/22 in Palmyra (5-4/10)
3056. Fish, Juriel, 77, d 12/28/21 in Farmington (5-1/16/22)
3057. Fish, Louisa, 22, wf of E. H. and dau of William Dewey, d 2/16/44 in
Batavia (1-2/20)
3058. Fish, Minerva M., 26, dau of Libbeus, Esq., d 4/14/41 in Batavia
(1-4/27)
3059. Fish, Resolved m 1/14/21 Philena Shadduck in Palmyra (5-1/17)
3060. Fish, Sheldon, Esq. m 1/14/38 Almira G. Stetson, both of Jamestown, in J;
Rev. Gray (4-1/17)
3061. Fish, Stephen, 30 (blurred, possibly 80), d in Williamson (3-3/28/27)
3062. Fish, Thomas m 5/17/42 Adelia Hart in Canandaigua; Solomon C. White,
Esq. (5-5/25)
3063. Fish, Whitehead, Esq., 51, d in NYC (3-7/14/19)
3064. Fisher, _____ (Mrs.), about 65, wf of Adam, d 2/7/26 in Geneva (3-2/15)
3065. Fisher, Adam m 12/17/26 Huldah Blackford in Seneca (3-12/27)
3066. Fisher, Anna, 20, consort of Henry, d 2/26/13 "near Geneva" (surv by
husband) (3-3/3)
3067. Fisher, Christian m 2/21/22 Chloe Steele; Jacob Dox, Esq. All of Geneva
(3-2/27)

3068. Fisher, Ebenezer d in Vermont ("While hiving a swarm of bees one of them stung hom on the end of the nose and ... it occasioned his death in about thirty minutes...") (3-7/31/11)
3069. Fisher, Hannah, 80, wid of late George, Esq. (a Rev. War "Patriot"), d 3/21/29 in Montezuma, NY (5-3/27)
3070. Fisher, Henry, 49, d 9/27/28 near Geneva (3-10/1)
3071. Fisher, Herman m 2/17/24 Miss Sally Palmer, both of Elba, in E; Rev. Salmon Hebard (1-2/20)
3072. Fisher, Howard of Palmyra m 10/2/43 Sarah Maria Hubbard of Farmington in Palmyra; Rev. Fisher (5-10/4)
3073. Fisher, John m 11/5/22 Jane Lewis in Geneva; Jacob Dox, Esq. (3-11/20)
3074. Fisher, John, 69, d 3/15/47 in Rathboneville at the home of his son-in-law, Gen. R. Rathbone (2-3/31)
3075. Fisher, Josiah m 11/8/40 Emily Williams in Charlotte; Rev. James Schofield (4-11/11)
3076. Fisher, Libbeus, Esq. m 2/17/30 Rebecca Vaughan in Batavia; C. Carpenter, Esq. (1-2/26)
3077. Fisher, Peter of Farmington m 11/18/10 Lydia Oakley, dau of Jonathan of Seneca; S. Whedon, Esq. (3-12/26)
3078. Fisher, William, 74, d 9/17/24 in Batavia "after a lingering illness of nearly 30 years" (1-9/17)
3079. Fisher, William m Ellen Hannibal in Ithaca (3-5/14/28)
3080. Fisk, Amos d in Bath (surv by wf and 5 small ch) (3-8/29/27)
3081. Fisk, Francis A. of Bath m 1/27/46 Mary S. McHenry of Elmira in E; Rev. P. H. Fowler (2-2/4)
3082. Fisk, Harvey (Rev.) m 2/17/29 Anna Mary Plumb, sister of Mr. J. Plumb formerly of Geneva, in Lodi, Erie Co.; Rev. Spencer (3-3/4)
3083. Fisk, Harvey (Rev.), 31, brother-in-law to Alvin Plumb of Jamestown, d 3/5/31 in NYC (Deceased b in VT; grad from Hamilton College, 1826; theological educ at Princeton; at time of death had chargeof a classical institution at Woodbridge, NJ; NJ Sunday School Journal almost wholly "the production of his pen") (4-3/30)
3084. Fisk, Jabez m Catharine Tinbrook in Elmira (3-10/6/19)
3085. Fitch, Asahel m 12/17/15 Charlotte Squier in Seneca Falls; Rev. Wells (3-1/3/16)
3086. Fitch, Ira H. m Philena Johnson, both of Harmony, in Ashville; Rev. Leonard (4-3/16/31)
3087. Fitch, Isaac, 14 mo, s of Clark, d in Ashville (4-10/22/28)
3088. Fitch, Jabez, Esq., 78 (a Rev. officer) d 1/5/29 in Saratoga (3-1/21)
3089. Fitch, James (Capt.), 32, d in Auburn (3-1/17/27)
3090. Fitch, Rufus, 79, (a Rev. soldier) d 4/29/35? (date blurred) in Ashville (surv by children) (4-5/6/35? - date blurred)
3091. Fitch, William of Buffalo m 9/12/37 Julia F. Rumsey of Stafford in S; Rev. Bolles (1-10/5)
3092. Fitts, Benjamin of Ontario, NY m 7/4/42 Aurilla Bristol of Palmyra in P; Rev. Wilson Osborn (5-7/6)
3093. Fitzgerald, Evin m 12/6/32 Hepsebeth Cooper, both of Manchester, in M; Rev. Gideon Osband (5-12/12)
3094. Fitzhugh, Bennett C. See Fitzhugh, Rennet C.
3095. Fitzhugh, Henry m Elizabeth Carroll, dau of late Charles, Esq., in Groveland (3-12/26/27)
3096. Fitzhugh, Peregin, Esq., formerly of Maryland and aide-de-camp to Gen. Washington in the Rev. War, d 11/28/11 in Troupsville (3-12/25)
3097. Fitzhugh, Rennet C. of Sodus m 11/18/19 Sarah Phelps, dau of late Davenport Phelps of Pulteneyville, in P; Rev George H. Norton of Waterloo (5-11/24). Bennett C. Fitzhugh (3/12/8). Married in Sodus (5/11/24).
3098. Fitzhugh, Samuel H., Esq. of Wheeling, VA (now West Va.), formerly of Canandaigua, NY, m 6/13/20 Mary Addison (3-7/26)
3099. Fitzhugh, Sophia (Miss), 20, dau of late Capt. Peregrine, d 7/28/17 near Hagerstown, MD (3-8/27)
3100. Fitz Simmons, Thomas of Newtown, Tioga Co., m 5/18/26 Eliza Waterous of Romulus in R (3-5/31)
3101. Flagg, Edmond M. of Buffalo m Mary Ransford in Lodi, Erie Co. (3-1/14/29)
3102. Flagg, Leantenette, inf dau of Mrs. Rhoda Flagg, d in Bennington (1-9/30/25)

3103. Flagler, Ruth, wf of Rev. Isaac, d 9/25/27 in Fayette (3-10/3)
3104. Flatt, William m Mary Rusenbark in Romulus (3-1/13/30)
3105. Flemens, Primus, 15, d 3/19/16 ("a free black man and faithful servant in the home of Mr. James Davidson;... a member of the New York African Society")  (3-3/27)
3106. Fleming, George (Gen.), 74, (a Rev. officer) d 10/1/22 in Auburn (3-10/16)
3107. Fleming, John B., M.D., m 3/7/49 Hannah C. Brown in Bath; Rev. L. H. Corson. All of Bath (2-3/14)
3108. Fletcher, ____, inf s of Eleazer, d in Harmony (4-10/22/28)
3109. Fletcher, Adelaide Emerson, 4 yrs, dau of A. Fletcher, d 4/12/43 in Jamestown (Funeral from Cong'l. Church)  (4-4/13)
3110. Fletcher, Caroline Elizabeth, inf dau of Adolphus, d 10/12/43 in Jamestown (4-10/12)
3111. Fletcher, Cynthia (Miss), 18, dau of Eleazer, Esq., formerly of Harmony, d in H (4-5/2/45)
3112. Fletcher, J. Warren m 6/5/43 Annie Jean Bailey; Rev. Owen Street (4-6/8)
3113. Flint, Jeremiah of Marion m 7/7/40 Sarah Gibbs of Palmyra in P; Rev. E. M. Galloway (5-7/8)
3114. Flint, John, Jr., 28, d 8/10/22 in Galen (3-8/21)
3115. Flint, Willard, 25, of Canandaigua d 3/10/19 in Geneva (interred with Masonic honors)  (3-3/17)
3116. Flint, William Wallace, 21 mo, s of John and Sally, d 3/26/42 in Jamestown (4-3/31)
3117. Floyd, Joanna, 79, wid of late Gen. William Floyd, one of the signers of the Declaration of Independence, d "lately" in Western, Oneida Co.  (3-12/27/26)
3118. Fluent, Boanerges, about 75, formerly of Cameron, d "in August last" in Elgin, Kane Co., IL (2-9/16/40)
3119. Fluent, Fanny E. (Miss), 22, dau of Joseph and Fanny, d 8/27/47 in Addison (2-9/15)
3120. Fluent, James, 23, d in Bath (3-10/16/22)
3121. Fluent, John, 39, d 5/22/40 in Cameron (2-5/27)
3122. Fluent, Joseph m Fanny Dickerson in Bath; Rev. Higgins (3-2/12/17)
3123. Flynn, Franklin m 8/6/50 Elmira Carter, both of Bennington, at the Eagle Hotel in Batavia; Rev. J. K. Cheesman (1-8/13)
3124. Fogle, George m 11/23/31 Ann W. Metcalfe in Bath; Rev. David Dunham (2-11/30)
3125. Foist, John m 5/26/22 Ruth Miner in Phelps; Rev. Lawrence Riley (3-6/12)
3126. Folger, Charles J., "First Judge of Ontario County", m 6/18/44 Susan H. Worth, dau of late Capt. C. H., in Auburn; Rev. C. D. Lansing (5-7/3)
3127. Folger, Laban (Capt.), formerly of Hudson, d "lately" in Montreal, Canada (3-5/23/10)
3128. Follett, Calvin m 5/13/47 Samanth Peevey, both of Elba, in Byron Centre; L. Hulett, Esq. (1-5/18)
3129. Follett, Frederick, editor of the Times m 8/3/26 Sarah Sutherland, dau of Major Isaac, at the Episcopal Church in Batavia; Rev. Smith (1-8/4). Sarah Southerland (3-8/23)
3130. Follett, Hannah Smith, 13, second dau of Frederick, Esq., d 7/23/46 in Batavia (1-7/28)
3131. Follett, Lewis m 7/8/17 Hilo Anesley in Seneca; John McCullough, Esq. (3-7/23)
3132. Follett, Nathan m Nancy T. Keith in Canandaigua (3-9/16/18)
3133. Follett, Nathan m 7/18/24 Clarissa Miller, both of Batavia; Rev. Lucius Smith (1-7/23)
3134. Follett, Oren of Buffalo m 11/22/32 Eliza G. Ward of Rochester in Fairport, Monroe Co.; Rev. Buck (5-12/12)
3135. Folwell, Thomas I. (Capt.) m 1/31/28 Joan Bainbridge, both of Romulus, in R  (3-2/6)
3136. Fonda, Henry (Gen.) d in Caughnawaga (Fonda) ("an old inhabitant of that place") (3-10/1/28)
3137. Fondey, Stephen, of the house of Ten Eyck and Fondey, merchants, of Geneva m 2/8/20 Lucinda Tanner, dau of C. Tanner, in Geneva; Rev. Axtell (3-2/9)

3138. Foot, Ebenezer, Esq., attorney, d 7/21/14 in Albany (3-8/3)
3139. Foot, Elias m 11/21/25 Almy Thorp in Brighton (3-12/14)
3140. Foot, Frances (Miss), 16, d 4/30/47 in Alexander (1-5/4)
3141. Foot, Harriet Elizabeth, 19, dau of Justin and gr dau of Deacon Isaac,
      d 7/11/46 in Smyrna at the home of Deacon Isaac (1-8/4)
3142. Foote, Anna, 39, consort of Hon. E. T. and dau of Ebenezer Cheney,
      deceased, d 7/7/40 in Jamestown (she a native of Dover, VT; member
      Meth. Episc. Church)(4-7/8)
3143. Foote, Elial T. (Hon.) of Jamestown m 4/27/41 Mrs. Amelia S. L.
      Jenkins of Greenfield, MA in G (4-5/12)
3144. Foote, O. H. m 9/1/39 Lucy M. Crosby at the Presby. Ch. in Jamestown;
      Rev. E. J. Gillet. All of Jamestown (4-9/4)
3145. Foote, R. S. of Buffalo m 4/13/40 Eliza Moses of Palmyra in P;  Rev.
      A. H. Stowell (5-4/15)
3146. Foote, Samuel E. m 10/21/42 Elizabeth Bailey in Dexterville (4-10/27)
3147. Foote, Sybil, 56, consort of Deacon Samuel and mother of E. T. Foote
      of Jamestown, d 3/4/32 in Waterloo (Ellicott) (She a native of
      Hinsdale, NH but for past 35 yrs a resident of NY; surv by husband
      and children) (4-3/7)
3148. Forbes, David D. m 9/7/26 Mary Rumsey, both of Fayette, in F (3-9/20)
3149. Forbes, David S. (Maj.) m 12/29/41 Catharine J. Abell in Fredonia;
      Rev. J. F. Bishop (4-1/20/42)
3150. Forbes, Horace m 12/20/26 Catharine Ann Hoffman at the Glass Factory;
      Rev. Dr. Axtell (3-12/27)
3151. Forbes, Isaac m 2/21/36 Mary Wellington, both of Jamestown, in J; Rev.
      Wilson of Gerry (4-2/24)
3152. Forbes, James H. m 1/17/44 Emily A. Bill in Poland, NY; Amos Feller,
      Esq. All of Poland (4-1/26)
3153. Forbus, John, 70, tavern-keeper, d in Poughkeepsie (3-11/7/27)
3154. Ford, Benjamin, Jr., merchant, m Abigail Pope in Clyde (3-12/5/27)
3155. Ford, Charles m Sally Ellis, both of Palmyra, in P (3-6/3/12)
3156. Ford, Charles B. d 7/11/35 in Palmyra (5-7/17)
3157. Ford, Eli P. m Matilda Bacon, dau of Simeon S., in Howard (3-1/13/30)
3158. Ford, Eliza, 16, dau of Eli of Howard, d 3/2/49 at Alfred University
      (2-3/14)
3159. Ford, George m 1/1/43 Mary Babcock in Jamestown; Rev. Chapin. All of
      Jamestown (4-1/5)
3160. Ford, Henry m 4/10/50 Electa Wilson in Prattsburgh; Rev. B. C. Smith
      (2-4/24)
3161. Ford, John m 9/26/35 Anna Templer, both of Bath, in B; J. D. Higgins
      (2-9/30)
3162. Ford, Lovisa, wf of Dyer, d in Dresden, NY (3-5/6/29)
3163. Ford, Lucius R. m 2/4/37 Almira Hubbard, both of Batavia, in Le Roy;
      Elder Ichabod Clark (1-3/30)
3164. Ford, M. Morris m 1/14/46 Laura Spencer in Bath; Rev. H. Spencer.  All
      of Penn Yan (2-1/28)
3165. Ford, Maria, consort of Hon. James and dau of late Judge Lindsley,
      d 7/26/47 in Lawrenceville, PA (member of Presby. Ch.) (2-8/4)
3166. Ford, Milton of Warren, PA m 3/14/42 Eliza B. Lovell of Jamestown
      in J; Rev. Chapin (4-3/17)
3167. Ford, Nathan, 19, s of late Maj. Mahlan of Ogdensburgh, NY, d 10/1/25
      in Cincinnati, OH (3-11/2)
3168. Ford, Nathan (Hon.), 66, d in Ogdensburgh (3-4/15/29)
3169. Ford, Oliver, Esq. m 6/10/41 Sally Ann Colwell in Byron (1-6/22)
3170. Ford, Richard (Capt.) m 3/29/43 Emily Tingley, both of Palmyra, in
      Phelps; Elder William Rowe (5-4/5)
3171. Ford, Roswell, Esq., formerly of Le Roy, d 7/26/25 in Coffeeville, AL
      (1-9/30)
3172. Fordham, Silas, 46, d 11/29/24 in Le Roy (1-12/3)
3173. Foreman, John W. m 1/11/40 Julietta S. Day; Isaac E. Beecher,Esq.
      (5-1/15)
3174. Forgerson, Stauts M. m 3/17/28 Naomi A. Rice of Athens, PA in Geneva;
      Rev. Dr. Axtell (3-3/19)
3175. Forguson, Solomon m 11/3/46 Susan M. St. John, both of Pulteney, in P;
      Rev. Olney (2-11/18)
3176. Forman, Isaac, 70, d in Romulus (3-6/3/29)

3177. Forman (or Fosman), James m 1/18/44 Lydia A. Young, both of Arcadia,
in Palmyra; Isaac E. Beacher, Esq. (5-1/24)
3178. Forrest, Calden B. of Aurelius m 5/15/41 Mary E. Ongley of Sennett,
Cayuga Co., in S; Rev. Selah Stocking (2-5/26)
3179. Fort, Henry m 8/4/38 Hannah Doane in Orange; John Allen, Esq. (2-8/29)
3180. Fortner, John m 3/1/27 Phebe Hawley in Geneva; Rev. E. W. Martin
(3-3/7)
3181. Fosgate, Bela, 54, d 1/16/30 in Auburn (3-2/3)
Fosman, James. See Forman, James.
3182. Fossett, Molly, 86, d at Mud Creek (3-7/15/29)
3183. Foster, _____, inf ch of Jonathan, d 7/10/25 in Batavia (1-7/15)
3184. Foster, _____ (Mrs.), wf of Zenas, d 2/22/36 in Palmyra (5-3/4)
3185. Foster, Ann Sophia, 3 yrs, dau of Geter (sic), d 6/5/30 in Palmyra
(5-6/11)
3186. Foster, Charles of Penfield m 1/29/29 Julia Ann Wooden of Phelps
(3-2/18)
3187. Foster, Cullen m Betsey Parshal in Palmyra (3-1/16/28)
3188. Foster, Dugald C. of Cohocton m 7/19/46 Laura E. Blinn of Howard in H;
A. S. Phillips, Esq. (2-7/29)
3189. Foster, Edwin S. m 10/5/41 Nancy E. White at the home of Gen. Lyman
Reeves in East Palmyra; Rev. E. A. Platt (5-10/6)
3190. Foster, Elizabeth (Mrs.), 82, d 2/27/22 in Palmyra (5-3/13)
3191. Foster, Hiram m Nancy Reeves, dau of Esquire Reeves; Rev. Jesse Townsend.
All of Palmyra (5-10/13/19)
3192. Foster, Ira m 5/4/31 Amanda Norton, both of Clymer, in Ashville; Rev.
Leonard (4-5/25)
3193. Foster, Jacob m Phebe Crout in Palmyra; H. S. Moore, Esq. (5-11/21/21)
3194. Foster, Jeremiah, Esq., 32, postmaster at Lancaster, Seneca Co., d 4/1/12
in Lancaster (3-4/8)
3195. Foster, Joel, 60, deacon of Presby. Ch., d 2/2/29 in Palmyra (born in
Southampton, Long Island, NY Dec 13, 1768; moved to Palmyra in 1792;
a pioneer settler there; "a number of his children are well settled
in life") (5-2/6)
3196. Foster, Joel m 11/1/36 Mary Jessup, dau of Henry, in Palmyra; Rev.
Shumway (5-11/4)
3197. Foster, John J. m 10/31/42 Mary Ann Hurd of Oxford in O; Rev. Horatio
Bardwell (4-11/17)
3198. Foster, Jonathan B. m 11/18/41 Harriet Campbell; Elder Thomas W. Coleby.
All of Grenwood(?) (2-12/1)
3199. Foster, Joseph L. of Elba m 2/21/38 Jane McRoey of Batavia in B; Rev.
Fister (1-3/1)
3200. Foster, Jubel, s of Jesse, d 6/8/26 in Batavia (1-6/9)
3201. Foster, Lemuel, 60, d 8/25/24 in Elba ("... the youngest of 16 sons all
of whom, together with the father, served in the ... American
Revolution and ... their united services was sixty years." Called
"Judge Foster"; surv by wf and 12 ch.) (1-8/27)
3202. Foster, Mason D. m Romina Bird, dau of John, of Manchester in M;
N. Granger, Esq. (5-9/27/37)
3203. Foster, Robert, 25, s of Cyrus, d 12/29/36 in Palmyra (5-12/30)
3204. Foster, Sophia, 32, wf of Jeter (sic), d 3/7/30 in Palmyra (5-3/12)
3205. Foster, William m 9/20/23 Mary Caward, both of Geneva, in Seneca
(3-10/1)
3206. Foster, Wiliam m 4/2/44 Esther Young in Palmyra; Rev. Harrington. All
of Palmyra (5-4/3)
3207. Foster, William P., 4 mo, s of R. H., Esq., d 10/10/23 in Lyons (3-10/15)
3208. Foster, William S. m 4/2/50 Helen W. Fay in Prattsburgh; Rev. B. C.
Smith (2-4/10)
3209. Fowle, Edward J., editor of the Penn Yan Republican, m 4/1/27 Julia
Smith of Benton in B; Abner Woodworth, Esq. (3-4/18)
3210. Fowler, _____, inf s of John W., Esq., d 4/30/26 in Bath (3-5/10)
3211. Fowler, Hannah, 9, dau of John W., Esq., d 8/3/50 in Bath (2-8/7)
3212. Fowler, Jacob D. m 9/4/27 Ann Eliza Bogert, dau of Nicholas, deceased,
in NYC; Rev. Dr. Brownlee (3-9/12)
3213. Fowler, John, 2 yrs, s of John W., Esq., d 4/19/41 in Bath (2-4/21)
3214. Fowler, Martha, 32, wf of Horace, d 8/15/19 in Goshen, Orange Co.
(3-9/1)

3215. Fowler, Seymour d 12/2/26 (prob. in Geneva) (3-12/13)
3216. Fowler, William McCay, inf s of John W., Esq., d 2/1/38 in Bath (2-2/7)
3217. Fox, David D. of Avoca m 5/28/46 Harriet Dixon of Cohocton in C; Rev.
      S. S. Brown (2-6/3)
3218. Fox, David S. m 4/12/43 Elizabeth Culver, both of Palmyra, in Newark,
      NY; Rev. D. Cushing (5-4/19)
3219. Fox, Major Luster of Cuba, Alleg. Co. m 6/11/45 Hannah Wixon of Wayne
      in W; Elder Ketchum (2-7/2)
3220. Frace, Calvin, 22, d 1/28/50 in Canisteo (2-2/20)
3221. Francis, Chester m 3/12/18 Matilda Bedlack, formerly of Geneva, in
      Phelps; Rev. Gideon Draper (3-3/25)
3222. Francis, James K. m 12/10/35 Catharine Clap at the Franklin House in
      Bath; William Hamilton, Esq. (2-12/16)
3223. Francis, John M., editor of the Troy Budget, m 12/8/46 Harriet E. Tucker
      of Palmyra in P; Rev. D. Harrington (2-12/16)
3224. Francis, Richard, Esq., merchant, formerly of Hammondsport, Steuben Co.,
      d 2/26/30 in Sodus (5-3/10)
3225. Francis, Richard, 83, d 2/12/45 at his home in Prattsburgh (2-2/26)
3226. Francis, Richard, Jr. of Hammondsport m Lidia Wilkinson in Penn Yan
      (3-10/28/29)
3227. Francis, Richard, Jr., 23, d 8/26/30 in Seerleer (East Ridge), Wayne
      Co. (5-9/24)
3228. Francis, Spencer of Prattsburgh m 10/4/35 Eunice Lincoln of Bristol,
      Ont. Co. in Bristol; Rev. McKenny (2-10/14)
3229. Frank, _____, about 12, s of John, killed 6/12/32 "by the falling of
      some lumber which he was engaged in removing" in Busti (4-6/13)
3230. Frank, Charity, wf of Nicholas, d in Busti (4-2/3/41)
3231. Frank, Stewart of Busti m 9/11/35 Polly Edmonds of Jamestown in J; R. Pier,
      Esq. (4-9/16)
3232. Frankenberger, John of Geneva m 12/24/28 Mary Ann Hall, dau of Amasa Jr.,
      of Marion in M; Rev. Seth Mattison (3-1/7/29 and 5-1/9/29)
3233. Franklin, _____ (Mrs.) d 5/28/49 "at an advanced age" in Bath (2-5/30)
3234. Franklin, Charles m 12/15/47 Eliza Ware at St. John's Ch. in Batavia;
      Rev. D. C. Houghton. All of Batavia (1-12/21)
3235. Franklin, Charles, about 35, d 4/9/50 in Bradford (2-4/17)
3236. Franklin, Joseph m Clarissa Bartholomew in Howard, Steuben Co. (3-1/21/29)
3237. Franktin (sic), Walter, Esq., clerk of the U. S. House of Reps., d 9/20/38
      in Lancaster, PA (2-10/3)
3238. Frary, Roswell (Col.), 58, d 12/16/49 in Bethany (1-1/22/50)
3239. Fraser, Alanson m 1/20/25 Sarah Vandebogart in Alexander; E. Smith, Esq.
      (1-2/4)
3240. Frasier, Mary, 1 yr, dau of Joel, d 5/26/27 (prob. in Geneva) (3-5/30)
3241. Frazee, Barnet of the firm of Stow and Frazee, printers, of Geneva
      m 1/7/41 Alice Maria Wheaton, formerly of Seneca Falls, in Geneva;
      Rev. F. G. Hebard (2-1/20)
3242. Frazine, Newton m 1/9/45 Jane Simmons; Rev. O. Street. All of Jamestown
      (4-1/10)
3243. Freeman, Elmur, 2nd, m Nancy Rice in Jamestown (4-1/6/41)
3244. Freeman, George Edwards, 19, d 6/27/30 in Vienna, Ont. Co. (5-7/9)
3245. Freeman, Harriet, 1 yr, dau of Elmer, d 7/2/26 in Jamestown (4-7/5)
3246. Freeman, Horace H., late of Jamestown, m 2/1/38 Clarissa B. Noyes of
      Milwaukee, WI in M; Rev. Goodrich (4-2/21)
3247. Freeman, Hull of Jamestown m 4/5/41 Mary Ann Wood of Westminster, MA
      in Jamestown; Rev. Parmely (4-4/7)
3248. Freeman, John m 2/28/25 Lydia Breese, both of Seneca, in Geneva; William
      Ray, Esq. (3-3/2)
3249. Freeman, Lewis m 8/22/40 Jane Hicks; Henry Pier, Esq. (2-8/26)
3250. Freeman, Remember L. m 12/3/18 Polly M. Janon in Benton; Rev. E. Lazel
      (3-12/9). Correction in same newspaper (12/23): the bride is
      Polly McFarron.
3251. Freer, James m 1/26/23 Lucretai Dexter in Geneva; J. Field, Esq.
      (3-1/29)
3252. Freer, John m Mrs. Delana Haunsom in Benton (3-2/20/28)
3253. French, _____, inf dau of Samuel, d 8/5/27 in Bath (3-8/15)
3254. French, Axtel, 21, d 6/11/32 in Jamestown (4-6/13)

85

3255. French, Benjamin B. m 5/20/46 Miss M. Sattell in Elba; Rev. Dr. Corwin (1-5/26)
3256. French, Betsey Maria, 22, wf of Nathaniel Jr., d 10/9/10 in Junius "leaving an only child 10 days old" (3-10/17)
3257. French, Caleb M., 51, d in Montezuma, NY (3-9/9/29)
3258. French, Catharine Jane, 4, dau of John, d in Bath (3-3/12/28)
3259. French, Catharine R., dau of Samuel, d in Bath (3-8/29/27)
3260. French, John of Cameron m 6/5/49 Mary Overhiser of Big Flats at the Buena Vista Hotel in Big Flats; Rev. Carr (2- 6/27)
3261. French, John F., Esq., 48, d 8/20/49 in South Cameron (2-9/12)
3262. French, Joseph, 33, d 10/16/31 (death place not given) (2-10/19)
3263. French, Uriah m Dimis Rowley in Erwin (3-3/12/28)
3264. Frey, Elisha m 6/15/46 Rhoda Glenn of Urbana, NY; Rev. T. R. Clark (2-7/22)
3265. Frieze, Naomi (Mrs.) (age not given) d 5/1/25 in Geneva (3-5/11)
3266. Frink, Eli, 45, d 3/14/29 in Clyde ("left ten dependent children") (5-3/27 and 3-4/1)
3267. Frink, R. Robie, about 19, d 7/16/47 at the home of his father (not named) in Bath (2-7/21)
3268. Frisbie, Hiram, 45, of Murray, Orleans Co., d 8/7/32 in Palmyra (5-8/15)
3269. Frisbie, Nathaniel m 2/17/18 Myria Olds in Brandford (CT?); "had a daughter born on the 18th, was put in the stocks on the 19th, and committed to gaol in Brandford on the 20th" (3-3/4)
3270. Frost, Nancy, 14, dau of Jacob, d 2/26/50 in Orange (2-3/20)
3271. Frushour, John of Phelps m 1/28/23 Elizabeth Lain of Gorham in G; Rev. Axtell (3-2/5)
3272. Frushour, Solomon of Phelps m 2/8/25 Sophia Wyman of Gorham in G; Rev. Dr. Axtell (3-2/16)
3273. Fry, Ebenezer d in Waterloo (3-2/4/18)
3274. Fuller, _____ (Mr.) d in Pompey, Onon. Co. ("while digging a well the bucket fell on his head and killed him instantly") (3-9/4/16)
3275. Fuller, A. J. m 1/24/39 Polly Ross, both of Carroll, in C; Rev. Bear (4-1/30)
3276. Fuller, Albert G. m 12/24/29 Eunice Lee, both of Palmyra, in Hopewell, Ont. Co. (5-1/1/30 and 3-1/6/30)
3277. Fuller, Clarissa M., 17, d 8/29/43 in Poland, NY (4-9/7)
3278. Fuller, Cyrus of Plymouth, M.T. (Mich. Terr.?) m 5/28/35 Mrs. Lucina A. Haight of Palmyra in P (5-5/29)
3279. Fuller, Hannah (Mrs.), 40, d 5/8/46 in Bradford (2-5/13)
3280. Fuller, Jabez m 3/16/17 Helena Bower, both of Genoa, NY, in G; Rev. L. Merkel (3-5/14)
3281. Fuller, John (Deacon), 87, a Rev. soldier, m 3/4/47 Louise Eastman, 73, both of Oakfield, in O; Eden McIntyre, Esq. (1-3/9)
3282. Fuller, Marjury, 36, wf of Amasa, d 6/2/32 in Chautauqua (4-7/11)
3283. Fuller, Otis (Dr.) m Laura Wiley in Naples, NY (5-12/1/19)
3284. Fuller, Stephen m Mary Green in Manchester (3-10/30/22)
3285. Fullerton, Francis, 63, m 4/15/18 Editha Risley, 60, in Manchester, Ont. Co.; Peter Mitchel, Esq. (5-4/21 and 3-4/29)
3286. Fulling(?), Jacob, in d 11/2/19 in Palmyra (5-11/10)
3287. Fulton, Caleb B. of Bath m 6/3/31 Eliza Simpson of Cameron in C (2-6/8)
3288. Fulton, Robert, 41, the celebrated Mechanician, d 2/23/15 in NYC (3-3/8)
3289. Fulton, Samuel of Gorham m 12/27/21 Jennet H. Simpson of Seneca in S; Rev. Axtell (3-1/2/22)
3290. Furgurson, Hiram, late of Sinclairville, NY, d 10/1/43 in Darien, Wardsworth Co., Wisc. Terr. (4-11/17)
3291. Furman, John, Esq. m 12/31/09 Susan Booth, dau of Jonathan, merchant, of Skaneateles in S; Rev. D. Phelps (3-1/10/10)
3292. Furman, Josiah H. of Bath m 2/8/31 Fanny Wells of Bloomsbury, PA; Rev. Tobias (2-2/16)
3293. Furman, Simeon of Tioga Co., PA m Naomi Babcock in Bath (3-11/25/29)
3294. Fury, Edward m Phebe Haight in Pittsford (3-10/28/29)
3295. Gabriel, Louis(?) m 10/12/43 Eliza Dexter in Canandaigua; Rev. R. Kearny (5-11/1)
3296. Gage, Calvin of Hanover m 8/23/43 Pryphena Jane Bennett of Pomfret in P; A. Hinckley, Esq. (4-8/31)

86

3297. Gage, Edwin Ruthven, 7, s of Martin, Esq., d 12/30/22 in Benton. (On Dec. 28 was pushed off doorsteps at school and struck his back on a stone) (3-1/8/23)
3298. Gage, Samuel G. m 3/11/23 Martha Cole, dau of Mathew, Esq., in Benton; Elder John Goff (3-3/26)
3299. Gaine, Cornelia, 77, wid of Hugh, d in NYC (3-11/6/11)
3300. Gaines, Edmund P. (Maj. Gen.), of U. S. Army, m Barbara G. Blount in Knoxville, TN (3-9/20/15)
3301. Gaines, James of Batavia m 1/23/25 Harriet Wheeler of Churchville in C (1-1/28)
3302. Gale, Elizabeth (Mrs.), 68, mother of Mrs. Sisson of Lyons, d 7/13/26 in Pittsford (3-8/2)
3303. Gallagher, _____, dau of Mrs. Gallagher, d at Fort Utrecht (her clothes caught fire) (3-1/14/29)
3304. Gallagher, James m 12/14/17 Elizabeth Henison in Geneva; J. Dox, Esq. (3-12/17)
3305. Galloway, Almond, formerly of Michigan, m 3/16/37 Celista A. Knowles of East Palmyra; Rev. H. V. Jones (5-3/24)
3306. Galloway, Archer of Marion m 1/30/32 Rosanna Hyde, wid of Dr. Henry Hyde of Arcadia, in A (5-2/7)
3307. Galloway, James D. of Palmyra m 4/19/32 Harriet Springer of Marion in M; Rev. Boyle (5-4/25)
3308. Galloway, John m 6/14/18 Alinda Drake in Palmyra (5-6/30)
3309. Galloway, John H. m 12/19/39 Delia Ann Brown; Rev. Walling. All of Marion (a double ceremony - see marriage of Mathew Hickey) (5-12/20)
3310. Galloway, Rachael, wf of Arthur, d in Marion (3-9/10/28)
3311. Galloway, Samuel, minister, Society of Christians, d 7/16/21 in Williamson (5-7/18)
3312. Gallup, Hiram of Williamson m 9/12/33 Abigail Spear, dau of Lemuel of Macedon, in M; Rev. Hart (5-9/13)
3313. Gallup, James m 9/24/44 Hannah Capron, dau of William P., Esq., in Macedon; Rev. Clark (5-9/25)
3314. Galoway, Milo m 10/27/20 Ann Rowley (5-11/15)
3315. Galusha, Jonas, Esq., governor of VT, m "Mrs. Beach" in Cavendish, VT (3-3/25/18)
3316. Gamage, Lucy, 36, wf of G. A. and last survivor of the numerous family of the late Dr. William Gamage of Cambridge, MA, d 7/28/29 (3-8/12)
3317. Gambe, Gideon m 5/4//20 Sarah Lemmon, dau of Benjamin, in Romulus; Rev. Caton. All of Romulus (3-5/10)
3318. Gamber, William d in Gorham (3-12/3/17)
3319. Gamble, Robert, 23, d 12/31/45 in Bath (2-12/31)
3320. Gamby, Joseph m Lavina Fotsinger in Fayette (3-10/21/29)
3321. Gannett, Enoch m 1/1/18 Elsa Curtis in Penfield (5-1/7)
3322. Gannett, Joseph m Patty Cook in Palmyra (5-6/30/18)
3323. Gannon, David of Wayne m Sally Whitehead "in Jersey" (3-6/3/29)
3324. Gano, Joseph B., merchant, of Wayne m 3/4/27 Adeline Reeder, dau of Stephen, Esq., in Starkey; Rev. White (3-3/7)
3325. Gansevoort, Conrad, 70, of Albany d in Bath (3-8/19/29)
3326. Gansevoort, Elizabeth, 81, relict of late Conrad of Albany and mother of John R., Esq. of Bath, d 1/8/50 in Howard (she died at the home of her son-in-law, Dr. Robert W. Cook in Hollindell, Monmouth Co., NJ (2-1/23)
3327. Gansevoort, Peter, 62, Brig. Gen. of U. S. Army, d 7/2/12 in Albany (3-7/15)
3328. Gansevoort, Peter C. (Capt.), 36, d in Bath (3-6/17/29)
3329. Gansevoort, Susan, 4 yrs, dau of Capt. John, d 7/1/32 in Bath (2-7/4)
3330. Gansevoort, Ten Eyck (Dr.) m 10/14/28 Hellen R. Lyon, both of Bath, in B; Rev. D. Higgins (3-10/22)
3331. Gansevoort, Ten Eyck (Dr.), 39, d 9/24/42 in Bath (2-9/28)
3332. Ganson, Martha Smith, 13 weeks, d 2/23/46 ("only surviving child of Dr. H. and Amanda L. Ganson) (1-3/3)
3333. Gardiner, William m 10/26/17 Mary Lebo in Geneva; Rev. O. Clark (3-10/29)
3334. Gardinier, Barent, Esq., attorney, d 1/10/22 in NYC (3-1/23)
3335. Gardner, Azariah m Samantha Willson in Canandaigua (3-12/10/17)
3336. Gardner, Caleb, 82, d 10/20/19 near Geneva (3-10/27)

87

3337. Gardner, Ebenezer, 8 mo, s of Robert T., d 8/16/22 (1-8/16)
3338. Gardner, Emmor R. m 10/1/50 Ariadne D. Starbuck, both of Somersett,
Niagara Co., in Somersett; Rev. Stimson (1-10/8)
3339. Gardner, Fourman m Betsey Myrtle in Bath (3-7/23/17)
3340. Gardner, Harvey of Pennsylvania m Lydia Linderman in Catharine (3-10/7/29)
3341. Gardner, Henry m 2/15/35 Barbary Maria Todd in Palmyra; Rev. William
Staunton. All of Palmyra (5-2/20)
3342. Gardner, James (Dr.), 60(?), (a Rev. soldier) d in Lynn (MA?) (5-1/24/32)
3343. Gardner, Joseph (Rev.) m 7/1/24 Susan H. Cowing in Geneva; Rev. George
Harmon (3-7/14)
3344. Gardner, Margaretta Ann, 3, dau of Henry, d 1/7/41 (5-1/13)
3345. Gardner, Nicholas D. (Dr.) m Susan Goodwin, dau of Dr. John, in Elmira
(3-7/23/28)
3346. Gardner, Polly (Mrs.), 26, consort of Robert T., d 7/10/25 in Batavia
(1-7/15)
3347. Gardner, Robert B. m 11/28/13 Eunice Cooley, both of Seneca; Rev.
Axtell (3-12/1)
3348. Gardner, Samuel m 12/14/18 Mrs. Sebra Lewis, both of Seneca, in
Geneva; Eli Bannister, Esq. (3-12/16)
3349. Gardner, Wealthy, wf of Col. P. Gardner of West Bloomfield and mother
of the Rev. L. W. Russ of Bath, d 9/12 in Bath ("came here to nurse
her sick daughter") (2-9/23/46)
3350. Gardner, William of Penn Yan m 2/20/31 Emelia C. Bidwell in Prattsburgh;
Rev. G. R. Rudd (2-3/30)
3351. Gardner, William m 11/14/32 Mary Durfee, dau of widow Susan Durfee, in
Palmyra; Rev. B. H. Hickox. All of Palmyra (5-11/21)
3352. Gardner, William B., 25, d 4/6/46 in Le Roy (1-4/14)
3353. Gardner, William H. of Palmyra m 1/1/42 Clarissa Decker of Ontario, NY
in O (5-1/5)
3354. Garez, _____, ch of "Mr. Garez" of the American Mission d 7/3 in Bombay,
(state or country not given) (3-11/30/25)
3355. Garfield, George of Busti m 8/10/34 Ann Hoyt of Ellery in E; R. Pier,
Esq. (4-8/13)
3356. Garfield, Joseph, Jr. m 3/3/41 Lucy Ann Palmer, both of Busti, in Levant;
E. F. Warren, Esq. (4-3/31)
3357. Garfield, Moses, 77, only brother of Joseph and Samuel of Busti, d at
his home in Princeton, MA (4-11/3/43)
3358. Garfield, Nathaniel, Esq., about 80, "brother of the Messrs Garfield
of this vicinity", d 2/9/39 in Hague, Warren Co. (served 7 years
in the Continental Army in the Rev.) (4-9/4)
3359. Garfield, Sally, youngest dau of Joseph, Esq. of Busti, d 4/22/36 in
Jamestown (4-4/27)
3360. Garfield, Samuel, Jr. m 10/8/45 Lucy Ann Pennock in Jamestown; Rev.
O. Street. All of Jamestown (4-10/10)
3361. Garfield, Sherman m 6/15/36 Alvira Pier, both of Busti, in B; Rev.
Gregg (4-6/15)
3362. Garlinghouse, John of Michigan m Mary Jane Benedict of Urbana; Rev.
Mallory (2-12/25/50)
3363. Garlock, Artemas m 5/14/43 Mary Lewis, both of Palmyra; Rev. Fisher
(5-5/31)
3364. Garret, Levi T. of Attica m 9/5/48 Angeline Shadbolt of Alexander at
the American Hotel in Batavia; Rev. Stimson (1-9/19)
3365. Garrett, _____ m 1/2/25 Sophrona McMiltin in Junius (3-1/19)
3366. Garrison, John, Jr. m 12/21/22 Elizabeth Gage in Canandaigua (3-1/1/23)
3367. Garrison, Peter m Cath Korry, both of Romulus, in Canoga (See marr of
William Garrison) (3-3/18/29)
3368. Garrison, Stephen of Benton m Eleanor Brown of Seneca in S; Rev. Nesbit
(3-4/22/29)
3369. Garrison, William m Jane Korry, both of Romulus, in Canoga (3-3/18/29)
3370. Garrow, Nathaniel (Hon.), marshal of the Northern District, d3/3/41
in Auburn ("third attack of apoplexy") (2-3/10)
3371. Gary, Elizabeth (Mrs.) of Batavia, 58, d 2/22/47 in Prairieville, Wisc.
Terr. (1-3/16)
3372. Gary, John m Clarissa Brooks in Elmira (3-4/22/29)
3373. Gasherie, John, Esq, member of State Assembly from Orange Co., d 3/8/12
in Albany (3-3/25)

88

3374. Gaskill, Benjamin m Polly Ryerson in Ulysses (3-2/7/16)
3375. Gates, _____ (Mrs.) d in Ontario, NY (5-9/20/20)
3376. Gates, _____, 1 yr, ch of Amos, d 2/17/25 in Geneva (3-2/23)
3377. Gates, A. (Dr.), about 40, d 8/10/31 in Ovid (5-8/30)
3378. Gates, Benjamin B. of Panama, NY m 6/28/29 Susannah Alvord, dau of Rev.
      Samuel of Clymer, in C; Rev. Palmer Cross (4-7/1)
3379. Gates, Daniel (Capt.), 40, d "lately" in Gorham (3-1/13/13)
3380. Gates, Daniel m 12/3/18 Maria Boyd in Phelps; Rev. Mosier (3-12/9)
3381. Gates, Daniel m Miss _____ Baker in Canandaigua (3-3/12/23)
3382. Gates, Eliza, wf of Hon. S. M., member of Congress, d 8/21/40 in Le Roy
      (5-8/26)
3383. Gates, George W. m 12/27/21 Laura Lelan; Richard Hogarth, Esq.(3-1/16/22)
3384. Gates, Horatio, Esq. of Lockport m 9/7/30 Ann Edmonds of Rochester in
      Rochester; Rev. Whitehouse (5-9/17)
3385. Gates, Increase S. of Gerry, Chautauqua Co. m 11/30/26 Loisa Kinney of
      Phelps in P; Rev. Strong (3-12/6)
3386. Gates, Israel m 10/8/18 Asenath Barber of Scipio in S (3-10/14)
3387. Gates, Jefferson m 7/8/30 Mary Ann Laver; Elder Brown (5-7/30)
3388. Gates, Mary (Miss), 15, sister of the editor of the Waterloo Gazette,
      d 8/8/26 in Hopewell (3-8/16)
3389. Gates, Seth m 10/26/26 Aurelia N. Severance in Phelps (3-11/1)
3390. Gates, Susan Ann Colt, 5 yrs, dau of Horatio, d 12/14/28 in Montreal
      (3-12/31)
3391. Gates, Whitney m Phoebe Ann Street in Painted Post (3-3/11/29)
3392. Gates, William m 1/18/16 Polly Trimmer in Benton; Rev. Chase (3-4/24)
3393. Gates, William (Dr.), 28, s of Solomon of Seneca, d 8/31/22 in Barre,
      Genesee Co. (3-9/11)
3394. Gates, William m 10/16/45 Fanny Pierce, both of Ellington, in Jamestown;
      S. Jones, Esq. (4-10/24)
3395. Gates, Zephaniah, 72, formerly of Chautauqua Co., d 10/6/42 in Perry,
      Delaware Co., IN (4-12/1)
3396. Gautier, Amie (Gen.), 102, d in Elizabethtown ("loyal to the Bourbon
      family during the whole period of his life") (3-12/15/19)
3397. Gavitt, Joseph, 40, of Palmyra d 12/8/34 in Schenectady (5-12/19)
3398. Gay, Joseph, 2 yrs, s of William, d 4/12/41 in Howard (2-4/28)
3399. Gaylord, Homer d in Moscow, NY (3-3/24/19)
3400. Gaylord, Romeo of Benton m 1/27/25 Rachel Coats of Hector in H (3-2/2)
3401. Gear, Ezekiel G. (Rev.), rector of Zion Church in Palmyra m 5/13/29
      Mary Y. Howe of Auburn in A; Rev. Dr. Rudd (3-5/27 and 5-5/22)
3402. Gear, William, 55, d in Whitesborough (3-8/29/27)
3403. Gelston, Phoebe, wf of David, Esq. (he collector of the Port of NY),
      d 3/2/11 in NYC (3-5/8)
3404. Genung, Cornelius, 86, (a Rev. soldier) d in Milo (3-5/21/28)
3405. Genung, John m Abigail Sherwood in Ovid (3-1/17/16)
3406. Geortner, J. P. (Rev.) d in Canajoharie (3-3/18/29)
3407. German, Andrew m Hannah Force in Tyrone (3-2/3/30)
3408. German, Lewis (Lt.) of the U. S. Navy, s of Gen. Obediah, d 4/14/19 at
      Sacket's Harbor (3-4/28)
3409. German, Mary (Miss), 24, d 6/18/29 (3-6/24)
3410. German, Seneca, Esq. m 5/3/43 Ann Ward in Dunkirk, NY; David McDonald,
      Esq. All of Dunkirk (4-5/11)
3411. Gesey, Charles m Lydia Morey "in Jersey" (3-11/19/28)
3412. Gibbons, James, Esq., one of the aldermen of Albany, d 2/10/26 in Albany
      (3-2/15)
3413. Gibbons, Thomas J. (Dr.), 22, d in Albany (3-5/26/19)
3414. Gibbs, Candice B., 6 mo, dau of Anson, d in Ellicottville (3-9/26/27)
3415. Gibbs, Holton G., 6 yrs 11 mo, s of C. D. and Julia A., d 7/17/50 in
      Batavia (1-7/23)
3416. Gibbs, Orrin E. (Dr.), 57, d 5/19/46 in Rochester (1-5/26)
3417. Gibbs, William C. (His Excellency), Gov. of R.I., m Mary Kane, dau of
      Elias, Esq. in Albany (3-6/12/22)
3418. Gibson, John (Gen.) d "at Braddock's Field near Pittsburgh" (a Rev. War
      veteran) (1-5/10/22)
3419. Gibson, John, 28, merchant, d in Sodus (3-4/16/28)
3420. Gibson, William W. m Adeline Merrill in Byron (1-9/6/22)

89

3421. Gidley, John m Eliza Petit in Palmyra; R. M. McLean, Esq. (5-1/16/22)
3422. Giffing, George Hutton, 11 mo., s of William, d 8/2/15 in Geneva (3-8/9)
3423. Giffing, William, Jr. m 2/6/13 Margaret Van Rensselaer Keating in
       Geneva; Rev. Phelps. All of Geneva (3-2/10)
3424. Gifford, Daniel m 10/21/41 Ann M. Shearman, both of Hunt, in Busti;
       E. F. Warren, Esq. (4-10/28)
3425. Gifford, Deborah, about 55, wf of Jeremiah, d 9/13/31 in Busti (4-9/21)
3426. Gifford, Edson m 2/9/43 Lydia B. Whipple in Westfield; Rev. T. M.
       Hopkins (4-2/16)
3427. Gifford, Holder, 27, d 4/2/30 in Ellery (4-4/14)
3428. Gifford, Hubbard, chorister of St. James Church in Batavia, m 2/23/25
       Jane M. Adams of Bates in B; Rev. Sedgwick (1-3/4)
3429. Gifford, John m 9/20/32 Mary Bedell in Batavia; Rev. Smith of St. James
       Ch., Batavia (1-9/25)
3430. Gifford, Luther m Jane Williams in Romulus (3-11/4/29)
3431. Gifford, Matthew C. m 2/22/44 Charlotte E. Cowing, dau of Thompson
       Cowing, in Busti; Rev. E. J. Gillett (4-3/1)
3432. Gifford, Sidney, 29, d 10/1/41 in Busti (4-10/7)
3433. Gifford, Sydney m 12/30/38 Jane Tallman, both of Busti, in Westfield;
       H. Patchin, Esq. (4-1/30/39)
3434. Giffords, John m 6/20/16 Polly Morgan in Benton (3-7/10)
3435. Gilbert, Andrew J., 6, s of Franklin of Cohocton, drowned 9/24/42
       "in attempting to cross the river on a log" (2-9/28)
3436. Gilbert, Charles, late manager of the Bowery Theatre, d 7/30/29 in NYC,
       age 42 (3-8/12 and 5-8/7)
3437. Gilbert, Daniel (Dr.), about 30, d in Benton (typhus fever) (3-4/24/22)
3438. Gilbert, Daniel m 1/10/23 Caty Showerman in Alexander (1-1/17)
3439. Gilbert, Edwin B. m 4/9/29 Margaret Zimmerman in Phelps; Rev. Daniel
       Baker. All of Phelps (3-4/15)
3440. Gilbert, Frances Ann, 3, dau of J. H., d 9/8/34 in Palmyra (5-9/12)
3441. Gilbert, Henry, editor of the Penn Yan Western Star, m 9/27/33 Charlotte
       Case of Canandaigua in C; Rev. Eddy (5-10/4)
3442. Gilbert, Hiram D. m 1/26/45 Emma Borden in Bath; Elias Mason, Esq.
       (2-1/29)
3443. Gilbert, John of Le Roy d 4/6/25 in NYC (1-4/15)
3444. Gilbert, John H., formerly editor of the Wayne Sentinel, m Chloe P.
       Thayer in Palmyra (3-9/19/27)
3445. Gilbert, Joseph m Speedy Tyler in Middlesex (3-5/14/28)
3446. Gilbert, Mason H. of Rushville m 2/9/32 Emily W. Bryant of Manchester
       in M; Rev. Allen (5-2/14)
3447. Gilbert, N. J. (Elder, of the Baptist order) d 7/23/32 in Syracuse
       (5-8/1)
3448. Gilbert, Percis, 21, d 4/18/45 in Stafford (1-4/22)
3449. Gilbert, Polly, 25, wf of John, d 7/19/22 in Lyons (3-8/7)
3450. Gilbert, Richard m Nancy Green in Gorham (3-1/28/18)
3451. Gilbert, Ruth, 11 mo, inf dau of J. H., d 1/11/34 in Palmyra (5-1/17)
3452. Gilbert, Silvester, merchant, m 2/16/18 Lois Ranney in Ogdensburgh
       (3-2/25)
3453. Gilbert, Solomon E. of Lyons d (date and place not given) ("a soldier
       in the U. S. volunteer army"). (3-8/5/12)
3454. Gilbert, Titus m Sarah S. Parker of Gorham (perhaps in Waterloo)
       (3-2/13/28)
3455. Gildersleeve, J. S. m 1/24/31 Belinda McCarthy in Clyde (5-2/4)
3456. Giles, Aquilia (Gen.) (a Rev. officer) d in NYC (3-4/17/22)
3457. Giles, Chauncy G. of Hamilton, Ohio m 9/8/41 Eunice Lakey, dau of
       Abner F., Esq. of Palmyra, in P; Rev. G. R. H. Shumway (5-9/15)
3458. Giles, William B., late Gov. of Virginia, d 12/5/30 (5-12/31)
3459. Gilker, Justus m 6/18/20 Amy Lute in Lyons; John Tibbitts, Esq. (5-6/28)
3460. Gill, Mary, 15, dau of John J., d (date and place not given) (4-7/18/32)
3461. Gillet, Charles m 11/13/13 Polly Newman, both of Benton, in B; Elijah
       Spencer, Esq. (3-12/1)
3462. Gillet, Isaac, 45, postmaster of Port Bay, d in P. B. (3-12/23/29)
3463. Gillet, John m 10/15/26 Martha Liddiard in Geneva; Rev. Orin Clark
       (3-10/25)
3464. Gillet, T. L. m 2/9/32 A. Beckwith in Rushford; Rev. E. J. Gillet of
       Jamestown (4-2/15)

3465. Gillett, William B. m 11/12/45 Catharine Fox, both of Bath, in B; Rev.
L. W. Russ (2-11/19)
3466. Gillette, Isaac, 45, postmaster of Port Bay, d 11/23/29 in P. B.
(5-12/11)
3467. Gilley, John d 7/9/13 in Augusta, ME "at the advanced age of 120 years"
(3-8/25)
3468. Gilliland, Samuel m Jane Van Greson in Fayette (3-1/27/30)
3469. Gillis, Belinda, 36, wf of Samuel and dau of Ezra Willmarth, Esq. of
Clementsville, Keene Co., PA, d in Victor, NY (3-1/27/30)
3470. Gilman, Erastus C. of Jamestown m 10/17/44 Fairanda A. Wright of Ellery
in E; R. Lennox, Esq. (4-10/25)
3471. Gilmore, Perez m Susan Towle, both of Bath, in Livonia (3-10/7/29)
3472. Gilson, Samuel m 11/7/22 Mary Cartright in Phelps; E. S. Stewart, Esq.
(3-11/20)
3473. Gilston, Sally (Mrs.), 32, formerly of Bath, d 11/14/45 in Salina
(2-1/7/46)
3474. Gittig (sic), John m "in Feb. last" Rosana Cone, both of Fayette; Rev.
L. Merkel (3-5/14/17)
3475. Glason, Joseph m Harriet Brown in Palmyra (3-3/11/29)
3476. Glass, ____, 1 yr, ch of Franklin Glass, d in Bath (3-6/11/28)
3477. Glass, Erastus, Esq., 60, d 4/2/41 in Bath (2-4/7)
3478. Glass, Frank d 9/17/38 in Bath (2-9/19)
3479. Glass, Henry B. m 1/1/44 Laura Chapman in Jamestown; S. Jones, Esq.
(a double ceremony - see Washington Boss' marriage this date)
(4-1/12)
3480. Glass, Lydia, about 53, wf of Erastus, d 5/1/35 in Bath (2-5/6)
3481. Glass, Lydia Ann (Miss), 17, dau of late Franklin, d 3/30/47 in
Kennedyville (2-4/21)
3482. Gleason, Benjamin, 22, s of Eleazur of Seneca, d 10/15/14 in Seneca
(3-11/2)
3483. Glen, John V., 55, d 6/19/31 in Schenectady (formerly of the U. S. Army
and an aid-de-camp to Gen. Wilkinson (2-6/29)
3484. Glenn, John, about 63, paper-maker, formerly of Urbana, d 6/1/45 in
Dansville, Liv. Co. (2-6/18)
3485. Glenn, Pierce, 29, d 12/22/44 in Dansville, Liv. Co. (2-12/25)
3486. Glidden, Daniel C., merchant, of Panama, NY m Almira Steward of Harmony
in H; Rev. Best (4-2/6/39)
3487. Glimpse, Cornelius m 7/29/40 Caroline Davis, both of Phelps, at
Nottingham's Hotel in Palmyra; Frederick Smith, Esq. (5-8/5)
3488. Gload, Charles W., 6, s of John, Esq., d 4/2/47 in Pulteney (2-4/7)
3489. Glover, Alexander m Mrs. Abigail Rees (3-8/7/16)
3490. Glover, Andrew, Esq. of Junius m 11/10/24 Phoebe Ann McKinzie of NYC
in NYC; Rev. A. Maclay (3-12/8)
3491. Glover, Mary S., 40, wf of John, d 10/9/45 in Batavia (1-10/14)
3492. Glover, Oliver L. m 12/27/18 Emma Ingraham in Canandaigua (3-1/6/19)
3493. Glover, Philander m 4/16/14 Ruhamah Hall, both of Phelps, in P (3-4/27)
3494. Glover, Polly, 26, wf of P. Glover, d in Phelps (3-9/8/13)
3495. Glowacki, Henry I., Esq. m 2/26/47 Mary Redfield, dau of Heman J., at
St. James Ch. in Batavia; Rev. Bolles (1-3/2)
3496. Godard, E. P. of Palmyra m 1/10/32 Maria Fillmore of Walworth in
Brighton (5-1/17)
3497. Godard, Eliza M., 25, wf of M. J. and dau of William Woodward, Esq.,
formerly of Montgomery Co., d 9/29/36 in Palmyra (surv by husband,
parents, brothers and sisters) (5-9/30)
3498. Godard, Lester O., merchant, of Palmyra m 10/13/36 Mabel Robinson, dau
of Bartlett, Esq. of Macedon (prob. in Macedon); Rev. Jesse Townsend
(5-10/21)
3499. Godard, M. J. of Palmyra m 8/28/37 Adeline Fillmore of Hanover, Chaut.
Co. in H; Rev. Beardsley (5-9/1)
3500. Godard, Marcellus J. of Palmyra m 3/2/36 Eliza M. Woodward, dau of
William, Esq., in Palmyra; Rev. R. G. H. Shumway (5-3/4)
3501. Goddard, William, Esq. d in Baltimore (First editor of the Providence
Gazette which he established in 1762; published newspapers
successively in Providence, NYC, Philadelphia, and Baltimore
(3-1/14/18)
3502. Godfrey, Baily m Rebecca Dolbee in Galen (3-5/12/19)

3503. Godley, Rebecca, 52, d in Ovid (3-10/15/28)
3504. Goff, Alma, 89, widow, d 5/11/32 in Howard (2-5/23)
3505. Goff, Charlotte, 6, dau of Morris, d 2/1/26 in Geneva (3-2/8/26)
3506. Goff, Daniel, 65, d 1/5/16 in Geneva (3-1/10)
3507. Goff, Hiram of Ovid m 12/18/28 Eliza Vincent of Geneva in G; Rev. Dr. Axtell (3-12/24)
3508. Goff, James, Jr. m 7/3/40 Seretta J. Nott, both of Canandaigua; Rev. Isaac C. Goff (5-7/8)
3509. Goff, Jerusha, 22, wf of Nathan, d in Howard (3-12/9/29)
3510. Goff, Job m 11/15/32 Rosilla Hanks inHoward; Asa McConnell, Esq. All of Howard (2-11/28)
3511. Goff, Morris, about 40, of Geneva d 7/16/29 in Butternuts, Chen. Co. (sic) (perhaps intended for Butternuts, Otsego Co.?) (3-7/22)
3512. Goff, Potter D. H. (Dr.) m 6/23/45 Loventia Halsey, both of Cohocton, at St. James Ch. in Bath; Rev. Wilson (2-6/25)
3513. Goff, Sally, 41, wf of Russel, Esq., d in Howard (3-1/9/28)
3514. Gold, Thomas R. (Hon.) d 10/25/27 in Whitesborough (3-11/7)
3515. Golding, Susan, inf dau of Isaiah, Esq., d 9/20/25 in Stafford (1-9/23)
3516. Goldsmith, Abigail, 23, wf of F. A. of Palmyra, d 4/4/37 ("a mother") (5-4/7)
3517. Goldsmith, Benjamin m 4/3/27 Elizabeth Sisco (prob. in Southport, Tioga Co.) (3-4/25)
3518. Goldsmith, Festus A., printer, of Palmyra m 2/14/32 Abigail Munsell of NYC in NYC; Rev. Goodsell (5-3/6)
3519. Goldsmith, Festus A., printer, of Palmyra m Martha Thompson of Manchester in M; Rev. Fuller (5-3/23/42)
3520. Goldsmith, Jane, 30, wf of Thomas, d 11/11/40 in Palmyra (5-11/18)
3521. Goldsmith, Mary, about 69, relict of the late Festus, d 8/17/39 in Palmyra (one of the early settlers in P) (5-8/23)
3522. Goldsmith, Thomas m 8/25/41 Sophia Rich in Palmyra; Rev. Mandaville (5-9/1)
3523. Goldthwait, Harvey of Busti, s of Deacon Goldthwait of Northbridge, MA, m 10/21/30 L. Maria Stow, dau of John of Ashville, NY, recently from Worcester, MA, in Ashville, NY; Rev. J. S. King (4-10/27)
3524. Goldthwait, Laurana Hardy, 29, wife of Constantine of Northbridge (state not mentioned) d 10/24/38 in Shelburne, MA "while on a visit to her father's house" (typhus fever) (4-11/28)
3525. Goldthwait, Nancy, about 48, wf of Obed,d in Northbridge, MA (4-5/30/32)
3526. Goldthwait, Nathan, 76, d in Worcester, MA (4-12/8/42)
3527. Goldthwait, Verry (Mr.), 45, formerly of Jamestown, d in Dexter, MI (4-12/4/39)
3528. Goodale, Daniel d "last week" in Ontario, NY (5-7/18/21)
3529. Goodale, David, 81, m Sarah Colton, 61, in Springfield, MA (3-1/19)
3530. Goodell, Abisha, Esq. of Fairport, Monroe Co., m 6/21/43 Mary Lemon, dau of Dr. Richard, of Palmyra in P; Rev. Piersoll (5-6/28)
3531. Goodell, Andrew P., 18, m Amy Lee, 14, in Canandaigua (3-1/16/11)
3532. Goodell, Betsey (Mrs.), 84, d in Canandaigua (3-12/6/15)
3533. Goodell, Martha (Mrs.), 42, d in Canandaigua (3-2/3/13)
3534. Goodell, Morey m 5/5/36 Charlotte Hall in Palmyra; Rev. Shumway (5-5/6)
3535. Goodfellow, Mary Ann, 1 yr, dau of "Mr. Goodfellow" d 3/30/22 in Geneva (3-4/3)
3536. Goodin, William C. (Dr.) of Canandaigua m Eleanor G. Simmons in Bristol (3-7/23/28)
3537. Gooding, William C. of Canandaigua m Mary R. Winslow, dau of Col. Job, in Bristol (3-1/13/30)
3538. Goodrich, A. M. of Albany m 11/24/50 Amanda C. Reed of Bath in B; Rev. B. R. Swick (2-11/27)
3539. Goodrich, Ansel (Maj. Gen.), 37, d 7/15/19 in Owego (3-7/28)
3540. Goodrich, David, merchant, of Havana, NY m Mary Winton, formerly of Camillus, in Catherine (3-12/23/29)
3541. Goodrich, James, 72, d 1/21/42 in Columbia, Bradford Co., PA (surv by wf of two years, the former Miss Bell) (2-1/26)
3542. Goodrich, Jonas W., Esq. m 4/17/43 Sarah Beaumont in Lyons; Rev. Cook. All of Lyons (5-4/26)

3543. Goodrich, Levi S. (Dr.), 53, d 9/16/46 in Almond, Alleg. Co. ("a husband and a father") (2-9/30)
3544. Goodrich, Louisa M., 1 yr, dau of J. W. of Lyons, d 1/24/31 in Lyons (5-2/4)
3545. Goodrich, Luther of Naples m Clarissa Noble in Cohocton (3-11/11/29)
3546. Goodrich, N. W. of the Warren Bulletin m Sophia P. Young of Fenner, Madison Co. in New Albion, Catt. Co.; H. C. Young, Esq. (4-5/18/36)
3547. Goodrich, Rhoda (Mrs.), 73, d 9/12/50 in Bath (2-9/18)
3548. Goodsell, George m 4/19/38 Sally Ann Folsom in Bath; William Hamilton, Esq. (2-4/25)
3549. Goodsell, Isaac, 51, postmaster of Hornby d 8/25/41 in Port Jefferson, Chemung Co. (2-9/1)
3550. Goodsell, Isaac P. m 8/25/41 Christiana Woodard; Rev. Coriel. All of Hornby (2-9/1)
3551. Goodsell, Jared H. m 12/22/32 Rebecca Ann Crivelling; H. W. Rogers, Esq. (2-12/26)
3552. Goodwin, Charles, 56, d 11/30/25 in Junius (3-12/12)
3553. Goodwin, Daniel (Dr.) of Geneva m "a few days ago" Roxanna Stone in Guilford, CT (3-6/4/17)
3554. Goodwin, Daniel (Dr.), 52, "lately of Geneva", d 11/22/25 near Detroit, Mich. Terr. (surv by wf and several ch) (3-12/12/25)
3555. Goodwin, Fanny, dau of H., d 3/14/14 in Aurelius (3-3/23)
3556. Goodwin, Sarah, wf of L. B., d in De Ruyter (3-1/14/29)
3557. Gookins, Seymour, A.B., principal of Franklin Academy, m 3/31/31 Fidelia Loomis, dau of Gamaliel, Esq., in Prattsburgh; Rev. Rudd. All of P (2-4/6)
3558. Gordon, Archibald m Sarah Ann Tompkins, 3rd dau of late Daniel D., in NYC (3-7/9/28)
3559. Gordon, Eliza (Miss), 18, dau of Robert, d 10/16/22 in NYC (3-11/6)
3560. Gordon, Samuel C., Esq. of Lyons m Mrs. Elizabeth Denny of Sodus in S; Hon. Byram Green (5-12/20/31)
3561. Gordon, Sarah, 40, consort of Elijah H., d 5/3/20 in Geneva (member of Presby. Ch.) (3-5/10 and 5-5/17)
3562. Gordon, Sarah Elizabeth, inf dau of William W. of Jacksonville, IL, d 8/9/33 in Palmyra (5-8/9)
3563. Gordon, Sarah Whiting, about 25, dau of E. H., d 3/24/40 in Geneva (5-4/15)
3564. Gordon, Susan, 70, consort of Peter, Esq. and mother of E. H. of Geneva, d 7/17/23 in Trenton, NJ (3-7/30)
3565. Gordon, Susan Mary, about 5, dau of William W. and Delia M., d 4/5/40 in Palmyra (5-4/15)
3566. Gordon, William Robert, 1 yr, s of Robert, d 8/15/41 in Palmyra (5-8/25)
3567. Gordon, William W., merchant, of Jacksonville, Morgan Co., IL, m 10/7/30 Delia M. Williams of Palmyra in P; Rev. McLaren of Geneva (5-10/8)
3568. Gore, Christopher (Hon.), 69, d 3/1/27 in Waltham, MA (had been a member of the Mass. senate and U. S. senate as well as gov. of Mass.) (3-3/14)
3569. Gorham, James m 11/23/31 Maria Brown in Jamestown; Rufus Pier, Esq. (4-11/30)
3570. Gorham, Nathaniel, Esq., 63, d 10/22/26 in Canandaigua (3-11/8)
3571. Gorham, Sarah, 3, dau of Nathaniel, Esq., d 7/22/15 in Canandaigua (3-8/2)
3572. Gorham, William W. m 4/12/32 Betsey Parrish, dau of Jasper, Esq., in Canandaigua; Rev. A. D. Eddy. All of Canandaigua (5-4/25)
3573. Gorley, Peter, 85, d in NYC (3-11/6/11)
3574. Goss, Ephraim, Esq., attorney, m 11/13/32 Margaret Porter, dau of Chauncey, Esq., in Pittsford; Rev. Buck. All of Pittsford (5-11/28)
3575. Gould, Harry m Sally Wade in Harmony; Rev. Simeon Powers (4-2/21/27)
3576. Gould, Ira of Penn Yan m 11/14/22 Martha Hubbard of Phelps in P; Rev. Brace (3-11/27)
3577. Gould, Isaac m 1/8/26 Aurilla Barber in Elba (a double ceremony - see marr of Isaac N. Howe) (1-1/13)
3578. Gould, John W. m 12/8/50 Jane A. Morgan in Bath; Rev. B. R. Swick. All of Bath (2-12/18)

3579. Gould, Jonathan, 53, d (date and death place not given) (3-4/24/16)
3580. Gould, Ralph F., 14 mo. s of Azel R., d 10/22/47 in Bath (2-10/27)
3581. Goundry, George (Capt.) m 8/14/17 Margaret McDonald in Geneva; Rev.
    O. Clark. All of Geneva (3-8/20)
3582. Goundry, George Mountjoy, "about 3 years", s of George, d 4/10/23 in
    Geneva (3-4/16)
3583. Goundry, Mountjoy Bayly, 10 mo, s of George, d 7/7/19 in Geneva ("The
    father had died but a few days before") (3-7/14)
3584. Gourlay, Janette, wf of Archibald, of Orange Co., d in Albany (3-5/16/27)
3585. Gouverneur, Samuel Lawrence, Esq. of NYC m Maria Hester Monroe, youngest
    dau of J. Monroe, Pres. of U. S., in Washington (3-3/22/20)
3586. Gowdell, Richard (Maj.), 41, agent and keeper of the State Prison,
    d 1/25/26 in Auburn (3-2/8/26)
3587. Gown, _____, inf dau of Hugh W., d in Canandaigua (3-8/9/15)
3588. Grace, Oliver m 8/14/17 Sarah R. Lee, both of Lewiston, Niag. Co.,
    in L (3-8/20)
3589. Grace, William P., 28, d 5/29/49 in Bath (lived in B 6 mos; foreman in
    clothing establishment of Messrs Darling and Proctor; a native of
    Boston, "his mother is still there") (2-5/30)
3590. Graham, _____, 7, ch of Sylvanus, d 3/3/26 in Batavia (1-3/10)
3591. Graham, George P., about 18, d 4/3/40 in Bath (2-4/8)
3592. Graham, Henry A., 17, d 1/3/41 in Bath (2-1/6)
3593. Graham, Henry W. m 7/30/48 Elizabeth Winn in Batavia; Rev. Sunderland.
    All of Batavia (1-8/8)
3594. Graham, John, 65, d 2/6/45 in Bath (2-2/12)
3595. Graham, John B., 31, attorney, of Albany d 7/13/18 in NYC (3-7/22)
3596. Graham, Nancy Electa, 5 yrs, dau of Valentine, Esq., d in Italy, NY
    (3-11/12/28)
3597. Graham, Nathan, 63, d 4/11/46 in Batavia (1-4/14)
3598. Graham, Samuel m 8/20/50 Hannah Wilhelm, both of Woodhull; Esquire
    Persons (2-9/11)
3599. Graham, Sylvanus, 58, d 10/23/45 in Batavia (1-11/4)
3600. Graham, Theodorus V. W., Esq., attorney, d 7/6/22 in Albany (3-7/17)
3601. Gramesley, William S. of Palmyra m 4/28/41 Phebe J. Hildreth, formerly
    of Sag Harbor, L.I., NY, in Palmyra; Rev. G. R. H. Shumway (5-5/5)
3602. Grandin, _____, inf ch of Philip, d 4/9/19 in Palmyra (5-4/14)
3603. Grandin, Andrew Jackson, 6 mo, twin s of Philip, Esq., d 4/2/33 in
    Palmyra (5-4/17)
3604. Grandin, Daniel m 3/8/12 Ann Lewis, both of Pulteneyville, in P; Rev.
    Phelps (3-3/18/12)
3605. Grandin, E. B., editor of the Wayne Sentinel, m 12/23/28 Harriet Rogers,
    dau of William, Jr., in Palmyra; Rev. Davis (3-12/31)
3606. Grandin, Philip, merchant, of Auburn m Amanda Robinson in Palmyra
    (3-1/17/16)
3607. Grandin, Rachel, 12, dau of Daniel, d 12/20/31 in Pulteneyville (5-12/27)
3608. Grandin, William L. m 12/19/18 Phebe A. Wood in Pulteneyville (3-1/6/19)
3609. Granger, Erastus, Esq. of Buffalo m 3/23/13 Elizabeth Sanburn in
    Canandaigua (3-3/31)
3610. Granger, Gideon (Hon.), 55, d 12/31/22 in Canandaigua (born in Suffield,
    CT 19 July 1767; grad from Yale Col. 1787; admitted as a lawyer, 1789;
    member state legislature many years; Postmaster General of U. S.
    until spring 1814 when he moved to NY state. In 1819 elected state
    senator from western district of NY) (3-1/8/23 and 5-1/8/23)
3611. Granger, Hezekiah L., 48, formerly of Geneva, d in Manlius (3-6/11/28)
3612. Granger, John A. m Julia Ann Williams in Geneva (5-4/21/19)
3613. Granger, John A. m Harriet Jackson in Canandaigua (3-5/6/29)
3614. Granger, Ralph, Esq. of Painesville, Granger Co., Ohio, son of Hon.
    Gideon, m 4/16/21 Catherine Van Ness, dau of Hon. W. W., in
    Claverack, Col. Co.; Rev. John G. Gebhard (3-5/2)
3615. Grannis, Samuel m 12/12/16 Sally Barnard, dau of Capt. Foster Barnard,
    in Geneva; Rev. Axtell (3-12/18)
3616. Grant, C.L. of Ithaca m Mary Hargen in Lansing (3-2/3/30)
3617. Grant, Stephen, Esq. of Batavia m 4/26/37 Elizabeth Hunter, late of London;
    Rev. J. A. Bolles (1-4/27)
3618. Graves, _____, 16 mo, s of Samuel, d 7/21 (possibly 7/14)/24 (1-7/23)
3619. Graves, _____, 6 mo, ch of Francis, d 6/16/26 in Geneva (3-6/21)

3620. Graves, _____ (Mrs.), about 65, consort of late Charles of Howard, d 1/15/49 in Howard (2-1/24)
3621. Graves, Augustus, 38, d in Romulus (3-3/18/29)
3622. Graves, Elizabeth, 51, relict of late Randall, Esq., d 4/8/50 in Liberty (2-4/17)
3623. Graves, Horace of Howard m 3/29/50 Dorcas M. Willis of Bath, dau of Orren, in B; W. B. Price, Esq. (2-4/10)
3624. Graves, John, 39, d 7/18/36 in Palmyra (5-8/19)
3625. Graves, John, 78, d 5/23/41 in Palmyra (5-5/26)
3626. Graves, Josiah m Betsey Adams in Canandaigua (3-1/16/22)
3627. Graves, Randall, Esq., late member of the state assembly, d 12/21/31 in Howard (2-12/28)
3628. Gray, _____, inf s of Joshua, d 11/24/24 in Geneva (3-12/1)
3629. Gray, Daniel m 11/19/35 Lydia Myrtle in Wheeler; Rev. Bostwick (2-11/25)
3630. Gray, Elizabeth, 32, wf of Joseph, d 9/9/26 in Seneca (3-9/13)
3631. Gray, John, 18, drowned "in crossing the Niagara River from Canada to Buffalo"(3-10/14/18)
3632. Gray, John m Fanny Walker in Chatham, Col. Co. (3-1/21/29)
3633. Gray, Joseph m 12/31/16 Betsey Blackmer in Seneca (3-1/22/17)
3634. Gray, Riley m 9/21/26 Matilda Stoddard in Busti; Rufus Pier, Esq. (4-9/27)
3635. Gray, William m 7/11/17 Nancy Webb in Seneca; John McCullough, Esq. (3-7/23)
3636. Gray, William of Benton m 10/11/27 Nancy Taylor in Seneca; Rev. Dr. Axtell (3-10/17)
3637. Gray, William, 47, formerly of Flint Creek (in town of Geneva?) d 9/28/28 at York Cross Roads, Ohio (3-10/22)
3638. Gray, William Edward, Esq., "sheriff of the County of Montreal, which office he had held upwards of 40 years", d in Montreal, Lower Canada (3-3/13)
3639. Greely, Leonard of Clymer m Aurelia Madison of Harmony in H; S. Terry, Esq. (4-4/22/29)
3640. Green, Arthur, Esq., clerk of Tompkins County, m 7/31/17 Mrs. Jane Pelton in Ithaca (3-8/13)
3641. Green, Benjamin m 3/2/23 Satira White, both of Macedon; Rev. Snow (5-3/12)
3642. Green, Benjamin T. m 6/11/12 Sally Miller, both of Romulus, in R; Rev. John Caron (3-6/24)
3643. Green, Charles of Bloomfield m 9/10/18 Electa Perrin of Lima in L (5-9/28)
3644. Green, Charles M. m 2/10/42 Elizabeth Cutler in Wolcott; Rev. Mason (5-2/23)
3645. Green, Daniel R. of Utica m Catherine Sawyer of Rochester in R (3-1/21/29)
3646. Green, George H., Esq. m 8/16/17 Ruth Parke in Seneca (3-9/3)
3647. Green, George H., Esq., late of Penn Yan, d 11/25/25 in York, Liv. Co. (3-12/19)
3648. Green, Hannah (Mrs.), 63, d 3/13/41 in Chautauqua (4-3/24)
3649. Green, Haulsey m 4/28/44 Surina Crouch in Jamestown; Rev. Josiah Flowers (4-5/3)
3650. Green, Herrington m Susan Smith; R. Hogarth, Esq. All of Seneca (3-6/12/22)
3651. Green, James B. m 9/8/25 Martha Fisher, both of Geneva, in G; Rev. Dr. Axtell (3-9/14)
3652. Green, John, Jr. of Busti m 10/20/30 Mary W. Arnold, dau of Charles of Fairfield, Herk. Co., in Fairfield (4-11/10)
3653. Green, Joseph, 80, d 6/12/35 in Sodus (a Rev. soldier; father of the Hon. Byram Green of Palmyra)(5-6/26)
3654. Green, Mercy (Miss), 21, dau of Col. John of Fairfield, Herk. Co., d 10/2/31 in Fairfield (deceased is sister of "Messrs Sam'l and John of Jamestown) (4-10/19)
3655. Green, Polly, 22, d 2/8/22 in Milo (3-2/27)
3656. Greene, J. Montagne, M.D., of Southport m Sabrina Hill in Tioga (3-1/27/30)
3657. Greene, Samuel of Jamestown m 5/31/31 Jane Fish, dau of Walter, Esq., of German Flats, Herk. Co. in G. F.; Rev. C. G. Carpenter (4-6/29)

95

3658. Greenfield, H. of Ellicottville m 5/12/36 Mary Hulett of Byron, Gen. Co. in B (4-5/25)
3659. Greenfield, Jerome m 6/27/41 Mary R. Gifford in Bath; Rev. O. Frazer (2-6/30)
3660. Greenvault, Daniel of Lockport m 1/24/37 Mary Price of Farmington in F; Rev. G. R. H. Shumway (5-1/27)
3661. Greenwood, William (Dr.), 37, d 2/12/31 in Ontario, NY (5-3/11)
3662. Grego, John, 63, d 8/28/41 in Bath (2-9/22)
3663. Gregory, ____, about 2 yrs, s of Ralph, d 4/3/13 in Seneca (3-4/7)
3664. Gregory, Benjamin, 16, m Martha Churchill, 11, in Dutchess Co. (3-2/5/17)
3665. Gregory, David (Dr.) m Rachel G. (or O.) Ramsdell in Perinton (5-4/17/22)
3666. Gregory, David, s of Stephen, Esq. of Campbell,m 6/7/40 Julia Miller of Bath in Campbell; Rev. Bebee (2-6/17)
3667. Gregory, Elijah S. m Fanny Fanno in Milo (3-6/13/27)
3668. Gregory, George R., 4, s of Ralph, d 2/24/13 in Seneca (3-3/3)
3669. Gregory, Simeon, 18 mo, s of Stephen, d 7/19/31 at Mud Creek (2-8/24)
3670. Greig, Benjamin of Rochester m 6/22/29 Guliaelena Carpenter of Macedon in M; Rev. Campbell (3-7/15 and 5-7/10)
3671. Grennell, Abel m 11/24/30 Polly Dawley, both of Galen, in Rose; Peter Valentine, Esq. (5-12/3)
3672. Gridley, Norman, 53, d 10/17/35 in Carroll (4-10/21)
3673. Grieve, Janet, 49, wf of Gen. Walter, d 9/18/25 in Geneva (3-9/21)
3674. Grieve, John, 30, s of Gen. Walter, d 8/21/29 in Carlisle (3-8/26)
3675. Grieve, Walter, Esq., 52, (Brig. Gen.) NY State Artillery) d 12/21/26 in Geneva (a native of Dumfrieshire, Scotland; "settled in Geneva 32 years ago" when there were but three houses in town) (3-12/27)
3676. Griffin, Eli B. m Eliza Bundy in Came____(?) (3-8/19/29)
3677. Griffin, Elizabeth (Mrs.), 42, d in Seneca (3-12/3/17)
3678. Griffin, John m 7/28 Clarissa Slaughter in Potter (see also marriages this date of Freeman Soul and of James Slaughter) (5-8/19/36)
3679. Griffing, Edward M., editor of the People's Friend (Little Falls) m 6/8/26 Margaret Van Valkenburgh of Manheim, Herk. Co., in M (3-6/21)
3680. Griffith, David m 5/13/24 Phoebe Sprague in Batavia; D. Tisdale, Esq. (1-5/14)
3681. Griffith, George W. m 11/11/45 Catharine Peterson in Ellery; Rev. H. Martin. All of E (4-11/14)
3682. Griffith, Jediah (sic) m 1/9/45 Sarah Jane Arms of Fluvanna in F; Elder E. H. Halliday (4-1/17)
3683. Griffith, Jeremiah, 84, d 6/10/42 in Ellery (a Rev. soldier) (4-6/16)
3684. Griffith, John, 80, d 12/29/46 in Bath (2-1/6/47)
3685. Griffith, Samuel of Ellicott m 2/14/41 Eliza Pardee of Levant in L; S. B. Winsor, Esq. (4-2/17)
3686. Griffith, William of Rochester m Elizabeth McClary in Lyons (3-4/29/29)
3687. Griffiths, David of Montezuma, NY m 2/24/25 Charlotte Merrill, dau of Capt. Nathaniel, in Phelps; Rev. Strong (3-3/2)
3688. Griffiths, Evan m 7/17/15 Harriet Higgins, both of Sodus, in S; Rev. Powell (3-7/26)
3689. Griffiths, Hyrcanus m Candace Rider in Bath (3-6/11/28)
3690. Griffiths, Joseph m Betsey Storms (3-3/6/16)
3691. Griffiths, Mary Ann, 3, dau of Griffith P., d 5/5/16 in Phelps (3-6/5)
3692. Grimes, George m Mrs. ____ Aldrich in Phelps (3-3/6/16)
3693. Grimes, Jacob, Esq., 37, d in Batavia (3-11/16/25)
3694. Grimwood, Cornelia, 24, wf of Isaac and dau of James McClallen, formerly of Ashville, d 10/24/39 in Bristol, Kane Co., IL (4-11/13)
3695. Griner, Michael m 5/3/20 Lydia Jones at the Glass Factory near Geneva; Rev. Axtell (3-5/10)
3696. Grinold, ____, 23, wf of Levi and dau of William Childon, d 4/14/31 in Troupsburgh (2-4/20)
3697. Griswold, Charles, 19 mo, s of Eber, d in Canandaigua (3-7/17/22)
3698. Griswold, Elijah of Southport m Sylvia Gaylord in Wells, PA (3-9/30/29)
3699. Griswold, George (Rev.), late rector of Christ Ch. in Alexandria, d in Bristol, RI (3-10/14/29)
3700. Griswold, Hermon of Palmyra m 8/2/36 Emily E. Spear of Macedon in M; Rev. H. V. Jones (5-8/5)

3701. Griswold, Seth, 77, d 1/14/47 in Alexander ("Papers in Connecticut, Illinois, and Wisconsin please copy") (1-1/19)
3702. Griswold, Simeon, 66, d 10/1/31 in Galen (5-10/11)
3703. Griswood, Thomas of Perry m 5/31/27 Elizabeth Handley, dau of William "of No. 9" (Seneca) in No. 9 (3-6/6)
3704. Groesbeck, Myndert, Esq., 72, d 10/18/39 in Manchester (formerly of Schaghticoke, Renss. Co.) (5-10/25)
3705. Groot, Edward H. of Auburn m 4/17/44 Sarah A. Smith, dau of F. Smith, Esq. of Palmyra, at Zion Church in Palmyra; Rev. Clark (5-4/24)
3706. Gross, Ezra C. (Hon.), 38, assemblyman from Essex County, d 4/9/29 in Albany (4-4/22)
3707. Grosvenor, Abel M., merchant, of Buffalo d 1/3/13 in Durham, Greene Co. (3-2/3)
3708. Grosvenor, Godfrey J., Esq., attorney, m 7/10/27 Cornelia Bogert, dau of H. H., Esq., in Geneva; Rev. Dr. Axtell (3-7/11)
3709. Grosvenor, Mary Jane, 25, wf of Thomas P., Esq., d at the home of her brother, Alexander C. Hanson, Esq. of Maryland (3-1/3/16)
3710. Grosvenor, Stephen K., merchant, of Buffalo m 2/29/16 Lucretia S. Stanley, adoptive dau of D. W. Lewis, Esq., in Geneva; RevClark (3-3/6)
3711. Grosvenor, T. P., Esq. of Buffalo m 12/28/43 Delia Risley of Fredonia in F; Rev. S. M. Hopkins (4-1/26/44)
3712. Grosvenor, Thomas P. (Hon.), 37, late a representative in Congress from Columbia Co., d 4/24/17 at the home of Judge Hanson near Baltimore (3-5/7)
3713. Grout, _____, 5 mo, inf s of Martin C., d 12/26/44 in Carroll (4-1/3/45)
3714. Grout, Lawson m 12/22/22 Abby Searls in Palmyra; William A. McLean, Esq. (5-12/25)
3715. Grout, Lucinda, 46, wf of Salmon, d 8/17/38 in Schoolcraft, MI (4-9/5)
3716. Grout, Salmon of Schoolcraft, MI m 10/10/42 Flavia Norton of Pomfret, NY in P; Rev. Bishop (4-10/13)
3717. Grove, John m 10/22/12 Alma Blackmore, both of Seneca, in S; Rev. Axtel (3-10/28)
3718. Grove, John m Mary Rippy in Seneca (3-11/18/29)
3719. Grove, Martin m 3/13/28 Ruth Fulton, dau of James, in Seneca; Rev. Nisbet (3-3/19)
3720. Grover, George of Sweden (prob. Sweden, NY) m 3/14/24 Patty Baker of Covington in C; Moses H. Stoddard, Esq. (1-3/19)
3721. Grover, Hiram m Keziah Bird in Southport (3-12/9/29)
3722. Grover, John (Hon.), one of the judges of the common pleas court, d in Cayuga County (3-7/3/11)
3723. Groves, Erastus C. of Angelica m 7/6/46 Theresa R. Harding of Hornells-ville in H; Rev. Lilley (2-7/15)
3724. Grow, William R. m 1/12/43 Harriet Comstock in Wattsburgh, PA; Rev. D. Rowland (4-2/16)
3725. Grummand, Horace m Caroline Balcom in Jamestown; R. Pier, Esq. (4-3/11/35)
3726. Grure, Moses m 9/9/10 Betsey Barrett, both of Ovid, in O; James Van Horn, Esq. (3-9/26)
3727. Guernsey, Hannah, wf of James K., Esq., d 4/7/16 in Lima (3-4/17)
3728. Guernsey, James K., Esq. m Electa Howes in Lima (3-5/9/21)
3729. Guernsey, Solomon C. m 3/28/43 Louisa Melozina Le Fevre in Ellington Center; Rev. William Waitle (4-3/30)
3730. Guernsey, Solomon G., 22, d 10/14/43 in Monticello, Wayne Co., KY (4-11/3)
3731. Guest, Phebe, 46, wf of Richard, d in Junius (3-3/19/28)
3732. Guest, William I., 44, formerly of Albany, d 7/20/23 in Ogdensburgh (3-7/30)
3733. Guille, _____ (Mr.), the aeronaut, and his wife both died the "latter part of March" in Havana (state or country not given) (3-5/1/22)
3734. Guiteau, Norman (Elder), 36, pastor of the Baptist Church, d in Richland, Oswego Co. (3-9/19/27)
3735. Guiwitz, William H. of Wheeler m 8/8/50 Mary J. Kelly of South Dansville in S. D.; Rev. H. Spencer (2-8/21)
3736. Gulick, Peter J. (Rev.) m 9/5/27 Fanny H. Thomas in NYC ("part of the Missionary Family expected to sail for the Sandwich Islands in a few weeks") (3-9/26)

97

3737. Gunn, Alexander (Rev.), D.D., of the Reformed Dutch Church, d in Bloomingdale (3-10/14/29)
3738. Gunn, Dexter C., bookbinder, of Auburn m 9/29/16 Jane Colwell of Owasco in Camillus; Elder Craw (3-10/2)
3739. Gunn, Moses (Dr.), 73, d 11/23/30 in East Bloomfield (a Rev. soldier) (5-11/26)
3740. Gunn, Newton, merchant, m 8/31/24 Eliza Gere, dau of Luther, Esq., in Ithaca; Rev. Wisner (3-9/15)
3741. Gunsolus, Emanuel, 63, d 1/-/46 in Wheeler (2-1/21)
3742. Gunsolus, Roda M., 30, wf of Lombert V., formerly of Bath, d in Portage, Alleg. Co. (2-1/6/41)
3743. Gurley, Royal, M.D., m 7/13/32 Mrs. Hila(?) A. Draper; Rev. Gideon Osborn (5-7/18)
3744. Gurlick, Samuel m 1/3/13 Nancy Sayre, dau of John, Esq. of Romulus in R; Rev. J. Caton (3-1/13)
3745. Gurnee, Lucien m Adeline Schooly in Romulus (3-9/17/28)
3746. Gurney, Abraham m 10/16/31 Eliza Paddock, both of Sodus, in Williamson; Rev. Allen (5-11/1)
3747. Gurney, Phebe, 14, only dau of Thomas W., d 2/14/37 in Palmyra (5-2/17)
3748. Gurnie, Nathan m 1/30/23 Harriet Carr (5-2/5)
3749. Gurnsey, Norman, merchant, m 9/22/33 Julia Palmer, both of Jamestown, in Gerry; Rev. W. R. Babcock (4-9/25)
3750. Gurthrie, Joseph m Mary Cole in Benton (3-2/27/22)
3751. Guyon, Samuel H., 18, oldest s of Elijah, Esq. of Greenwood, d at the home of his uncle, Daniel Jamison, in Canisteo (2-12/7/42)
3752. Gwinn, William R. of Medina m 7/25/48 Emily A. Wells, dau of William H. of Batavia, in B; Rev. Firman (1-8/8)
3753. Hacket, George d in Farmington ... "and his two daughters" (their names not given)(3-3/24/13)
3754. Hackney, Joseph, Esq., "one of the judges of Warren County" (PA) and a "patriot of the Revolution", d in Warren, PA (4-5/23/32)
3755. Hadley, George of Canisteo m 8/15/46 Clarissa Hallett of Cameron in C; George S. Pierson, Esq. (2-8/26)
3756. Hadley, Rhoda, 80, wf of the late James, d 7/9/42 in Canisteo (he was in the first boat of early white settlers that went up the Canisteo River; lived on one farm 52 years) (Elder David Smith of Bath preached the funeral sermon) (2-7/20)
3757. Haff, John P., 68, d 5/1/38 in NYC (5-5/9)
3758. Hagar, Jacob (Capt.), 85, d in Blenheim, Scho. Co. ("served in the French War of 1756 and as a captain during our revolutionary struggle") (3-9/22/19)
3759. Hagerman, Abram of Port Gibson m 12/30/41 Maria Cobb, dau of Elisha W. of Palmyra in P; Rev. A. H. Burlingame (5-1/5/42)
3760. Hagers, John m Hannah Shearman in Williamson (5-4/14/19)
3761. Hahn, Thomas B., Esq., editor of the Ontario Messenger, m 5/16/44 Flora Shepard in Canandaigua; Rev. Goodwin (5-5/29)
3762. Haight, Elizabeth, wf of Fletcher M., d 7/31/27 in Rochester (3-8/1)
3763. Haight, Fletcher M., Esq. of Bath m 10/31/22 Elizabeth McLacklan of Canandaigua in C; Rev. Johns (3-10/16)
3764. Haight, Fletcher M., Esq. m Mary Ann Brown, dau of Dr. M. Brown, Jr., in Rochester (3-10/7/29)
3765. Haight, Horace m Lucinda Soul(?) in Lyons (5-5/12/18)
3766. Haight, Rachel, 76, relict of Benjamin of Albany, d 5/7/20 in Geneva (member, Presby. Ch., Albany) (3-5/10 and 5-5/17)
3767. Haight, Stephen, Esq., 40, d "in Jersey, Steuben County" (3-9/1/19)
3768. Haines, Charles G., Esq., counselor-at-law, d 7/3/25 in NYC (was Adjutant General of State Militia; formerly lived in Batavia for many years) (1-7/15)
3769. Hakes, Jeremiah B.(?), late of Palmyra, m 12/18/29 Maria Smith of Prattsburgh, Steuben Co., in P; Rev. Rudd (5-3/12/30)
3770. Hale, Abraham of Cazenovia d 8/29/22 at the home of Jacob Wright in Lyons (3-9/18)
3771. Hale, Ebenezer, merchant, m 8/20/14 Mary Hayden in Canandaigua; Rev. Torry. All of Canandaigua (3-8/24)
3772. Hale, Ira of Poland, NY m 1/9/34 Eveline Lane of Perry, Gen. Co. in Clear Creek; E. F. Warren, Esq. (4-1/15)

3773. Hale, Lurena, 34, wf of Danford, d 3/10/44 in Pine Grove (4-3/15)
3774. Hale, Sarah, 23, wf of Horace, d 7/29/43 in Westfield (4-8/10)
3775. Halenbake, Isaac Rue, 13, s of Isaac B., d in or near Albany (3-6/27/10)
3776. Hall, _____, inf dau of A. B., d 2/16/15 in Geneva (3-2/22)
3777. Hall, _____, inf s of Moses, d 3/17/19 in Geneva (3-3/24)
3778. Hall, _____, inf ch of William, d in Jamestown (4-8/2/26)
3779. Hall, _____, dau of Philo, d in Wethersfield, Gen. Co. (3-1/14/29)
3780. Hall, Abigail (Mrs.), 79, d 9/21/36 in Jamestown (Printers in
     Brattleboro, VT are requested to insert the above) (4-9/21)
3781. Hall, Abijah, 83, d in Canandaigua (3-12/30/29)
3782. Hall, Adelaide H., about 23, wf of F. A. Hall, principal of Mayville
     Academy, d 5/5/44 in Green, Erie Co., PA (4-5/10)
3783. Hall, Adeline, 17 mo, dau of Austin, d 7/23/42 in Bath "and on the 9th
     ... his consort Rhoda H. Hall aged 28 years, daughter of Elisha
     Hanks, Esq." (2-8/17)
3784. Hall, Amasa, Sr., 82, d 10/29/36 in Marion (5-11/11)
3785. Hall, Ambrose, Esq. of Williamstown, MA m 12/4/17 Clarissa Willcox of
     Palmyra, NY in P; Rev. Townsend (5-12/10)
3786. Hall, Amisa, 2nd, of Marion m 5/16/38 Laura A. Delanoe of Canandaigua
     in C (5-5/23)
3787. Hall, Amos (Maj. Gen.), 66, d 12/28/27 in West Bloomfield (one of the
     earliest settlers in this region) (3-1/2/28)
3788. Hall, Anson m 11/12/15 Lucy Taylor in Hector (3-12/6)
3789. Hall, Charles of NYC m 10/22/27 Sarah W. Lawrence, dau of Col. J. W.
     of Geneseo, in G; Rev. Ball (3-11/14)
3790. Hall, Clarissa, 30, wf of Ambrose, Esq., d in Palmyra (3-7/25/27)
3791. Hall, Clarissa, 4 yrs, dau of William, d 9/15/34 in Jamestown (4-9/24)
3792. Hall, Elisha of Carroll m 6/25/26 Mary D. Foote of Jamestown in J; Rev.
     Eddy (4-6/28)
3793. Hall, Elizabeth, 37, wf of Maj. Joseph, d 4/26/19 in Phelps (3-5/5)
3794. Hall, Enoch A., s of Gen. Hall, m Marietta Shelly in Bloomfield
     (3-3/15/15)
3795. Hall, Eunice, 43, wf of John, d 10/4/28 in Geneva "leaving a large
     family" (3-10/8)
3796. Hall, F. A., principal of Mayville Academy, m 2/22/44 Adelaide H. Lee
     of Green, Erie Co., PA in G; Rev. Dr. Mitchell (4-3/8)
3797. Hall, George A. m 12/18/42 Lydia A. Davis, both of Carroll, in
     Sugargrove, PA; M. Willson, Esq. (4-12/22)
3798. Hall, Harvey m 4/28/22 Eliza Kimball in West Bloomfield; Rev. Ebenezer
     Fitch. All of W. B. (3-5/1)
3799. Hall, Hiland B. m Sophia Hamlin in West Bloomfield (3-3/12/28)
3800. Hall, Isaac (Capt.) of the U. S. Navy m 1/2/13 Ann M. Hart, dau of
     Elisha of Saybrook, CT, in Bloomingdale (state not given) (3-2/17)
3801. Hall, Jacob, 62, d 3/14/17 near Geneva (3-3/19)
3802. Hall, Jacob B. m 11/10/12 Abby Townsend, both of Benton, in B; Rev.
     Alexander (3-12/2)
3803. Hall, James, Esq. m 9/20/29 Abigail Cheney in Carroll; Hon. E.T. Foote
     (4-9/30)
3804. Hall, James, 57, formerly of Stamford, Dutch. Co., d 1/20/42 in Macedon
     (5-2/2)
3805. Hall, Jane, wf of Edward, d 4/4/27 in Seneca (3-4/11)
3806. Hall, John m Nancy Payne in Middlesex (3-9/19/27)
3807. Hall, John m Mary Ann Stewart, both of Howard, in Bath (3-10/21/29)
3808. Hall, John m 9/25/35 Elmira Hall in Painted Post; Jonathan Brown, Esq.
     (2-10/7)
3809. Hall, John m 9/13/45 Helen Wright in Ashville; Rev. T. D. Blin
     (see also the marr of Isaac Benedict) (4-9/26)
3810. Hall, John E., Esq., 45, late editor of the Portfolio, d in Philadelphia
     (3-6/24/29)
3811. Hall, Joseph (Maj.) m 7/25/19 Joanna Swift Northam, both of Phelps, in P
     (3-8/18)
3812. Hall, Joseph m 9/23/19 Susan Howe, both of Cohocton, in C (3-10/6)
3813. Hall, Joseph (Maj.), 45, s of late Capt. William, d 9/14/22 in Phelps
     (3-9/18)
3814. Hall, Joseph, Jr. of Fayette m 11/28/27 Rosalinda Hutchins of Seneca in
     S; Rev. Dr. Axtell (3-12/5)

99

3815.  Hall, Laura Ann, 20, wf of Amasa, 2nd, d 2/23/39 in Marion(5-3/1)
3816.  Hall, Leonard (Rev.) m 10/5/32 Harriet Wells in Hamburgh (4-10/31)
3817.  Hall, Lucinda, 51, wf of Timothy, d 11/28/42 in Troy (2-12/14)
3818.  Hall, Maria, about 17, d 10/4/40 in Kennedyville (2-10/7)
3819.  Hall, Mary, 31, wf of J. A., d 8/5/42 in Batavia (1-8/9)
3820.  Hall, Moses, 18, s of Jonathan of Benton, d 11/11/16 (killed by the
       kick of a horse) (3-11/13)
3821.  Hall, Myron V., printer, of Aurora, IL m 5/11/48 Harriet M. Davis of
       Waterloo, NY; Rev. E. Wheeler (1-5/16)
3822.  Hall, Othniel m 8/16/27 Lamira Glover, dau of Philander of Phelps, in P;
       Rev. Strong (3-8/22)
3823.  Hall, Ransom A. m 1/20/30 Sarah Allen in Geneva; Rev. Eliakim Phelps
       (3-1/27)
3824.  Hall, Richard, 85, of Benton, formerly from New Jersey, d 2/27/12 in
       Seneca Co. (3-3/4)
3825.  Hall, Roslinda, about 26, wf of Joseph, d 4/16/29 in Fayette (3-4/29)
3826.  Hall, Russell m Wattey Crandall in Alfred (3-11/11/18)
3827.  Hall, Ruth, 60, wf of Joseph, d 11/5/18 in Fayette (3-11/18)
3828.  Hall, Samuel m 5/25/14 Catharine Gillet in Phelps; Joseph Hall, Esq.
       (3-6/1)
3829.  Hall, Samuel D. m Louisa Ballard in Warren; William Pier, Esq. (4-11/9/31)
3830.  Hall, Samuel E. of Sugargrove, PA m 2/10/41 Mary Akin of Carroll, NY
       in Sugargrove, PA; M. Wilson, Esq. (4-2/24)
3831.  Hall, Sanford R. of Geneva m 2/1/31 Almira R. Huggins, dau of Zadock
       of Marion, in M (5-2/18)
3832.  Hall, Sarah (Mrs.), mother of ___ (page torn) (died)"at an advanced
       age" ___ (page torn) (3-8/4/24)
3833.  Hall, Sarah W., 15, dau of late Ambrose, d 9/17/42 in Palmyra (5-9/21)
3834.  Hall, Seth m 10/23/16 Mary Secor in Middlesex; Rev. Goff (3-10/30)
3835.  Hall, Stephen, 20, s of Maj. Gen. Hall, d 1/18/17 in Bloomfield (3-1/29)
3836.  Hall, Thomas E., formerly of Palmyra, d 3/26/34 in Rochester (5-3/28)
3837.  Hall, William (Capt.), 82, father of Maj. Joseph, d 8/10/22 in Phelps
       (3-8/14)  Same newspaper dated 8/21: Capt. Hall was a native of Lyme,
       Eng.; orphaned at age 14, "he took to a seafaring life ... for twenty
       years (and) suffered shipwreck and capture five times"
3838.  Halladay, James of Seneca m 1/10/28 Mary Ann Fiero of Gorham in G
       (3-1/16)
3839.  Halleck, Jonathan m 4/13/17 Lucinda Kendal in Wayne (3-4/30)
3840.  Hallet, Nehemiah of Wellsville, Alleg. Co. m 11/17/50 Harriet Smith,
       dau of T. J., Esq., in Bath; Rev. N. Sawyer (2-12/4)
3841.  Hallett, Catharine, 32, wf of Jacob W., Esq., d 12/4/10 in Pulteneyville
       (surv by husband and children)  (3-12/12)
3842.  Hallett, Delavan of Canisteo m 1/8/40 Harriet Swift of Cameron in C;
       E. D. Swartwood, Esq. (2-1/15)
3843.  Hallett, J. W. (Hon.), "late first judge of Wayne County" m 4/14/29
       Margaret Macomb, youngest dau of Alexander, Esq. of Washington, D.C.,
       at St. John's Ch. in NYC; Right Rev. Bishop Hobart (3-4/22 and 5-4/24)
3844.  Hallett, Jacob, 2 yrs, s of Jacob W., Esq., d 11/28/10 in Pulteneyville
       (3-12/12)
3845.  Hallett, Jacob W., Esq. of Pulteneyville m 10/15/11 Gitty Maria Rhea, dau
       of Gen. Rhea of Trenton, NJ, in Trenton (3-10/30)
3846.  Hallock, George W. m 10/13/47 Mary H. Hubbell, oldest dau of Hon. W. S.,
       in Bath; Rev. L. Merril Miller (2-10/20)
3847.  Halsey, Abraham (Dr.) d 5/8/22 in Hopewell, Dutch. Co. ("for many years
       a respectable physician of that place")  (3-5/22)
3848.  Halsey, Amos of Junius m 6/19/23 Caroline Sackett of Aurelius in A; Rev.
       Lane (3-7/9)
3849.  Halsey, Benjamin S., druggist, m Cornelia Evertson, dau of G. B., Esq.,
       in Ithaca (3-6/17/29)
3850.  Halsey, Peter m 5/31/38 Lucia Johnson in Bath; Rev. Isaac W. Platt.  All
       of Bath (2-6/6)
3851.  Halsey, Silas, Esq. m 12/3/15 Mrs. Howell in Ovid (3-12/20)
3852.  Halsey, Silas (Hon.), 89, d 11/19/32 at his home in Ovid (5-12/5/32)
3853.  Halstead, Caleb O., merchant, of NYC m Caroline Louisa Pitney, only dau
       of Dr. Aaron, in Elizabethtown, NJ (3-12/10/23)
3854.  Halsted, Catharine, 35, wf of Robert, d in Waterloo (3-8/29/27)

3855. Halsted, Robert H. m Elizabeth Yandal in Waterloo (3-10/10/27)
3856. Hamersly, Andrew, 94, d in NYC (3-6/2/19)
3857. Hamilton, Harmon M., a teacher in the Haverling School, m 12/23/50 Annis S. Smith, oldest dau of Orrin, Esq.; Rev. A. Lloyd. All of Bath (2-12/25)
3858. Hamilton, Josiah, 40, d in Palmyra (3-3/24/13)
3859. Hamilton, Keziah, 87, wid of Daniel (he a Rev. soldier), d 8/11/49 in Bath (2-8/15)
3860. Hamilton, Lester, 16, s of late John, Esq., d 2/8/47 in Howard (2-2/17)
3861. Hamilton, Lovina, 19, wf of Samuel and dau of John Gilbert of Tully, d 12/22/30 in Rochester (5-1/14/31)
3862. Hamilton, Thomas, 45, d in Palmyra (3-3/24/13)
3863. Hamlin, Horace L., 25, s of Capt. William B., d in East Bloomfield (3-6/24/29)
3864. Hamlin, John m 2/20/29 Almira Sessions in Phelps; Rev. Henry P. Strong (3-3/4)
3865. Hammond, _____, wf of Reuben, d in Howard (3-12/9/29)
3866. Hammond, _____, inf s of Samuel H., Esq., d 2/5/41 in Bath (2-2/10)
3867. Hammond, Asa, 22, of Seneca, s of Joseph, d 3/20/25 in Auburn (3-3/30)
3868. Hammond, Charles D., 7 mo, s of Charles G., d in Canandaigua (3-5/20/29)
3869. Hammond, Charles G. of Canandaigua m Charlotte B. Doolittle in Whites-borough (3-9/19/27)
3870. Hammond, Hannah (Mrs.), 25, d 5/25/23 in Canandaigua (3-6/4)
3871. Hammond, Ira R. of Alexander m 6/7/49 Amelia Pratt, dau of Richard, Esq. of Batavia; Rev. Byron Sunderland (1-6/12)
3872. Hammond, Ira R., 21, s of Jacob, Esq., d 4/28/50 in Alexander (1-5/7)
3873. Hammond, James R. L., 7, s of Samuel, Esq., d 2/25/41 in Bath (2-3/3)
3874. Hammond, Joanna (Mrs.) d in Bloomfield (3-2/5/17)
3875. Hammond, John, 20, d in Bath (3-10/1/17)
3876. Hammond, John S. m 10/17/32 Emily M. Pratt, both of Manchester, in M; Rev. Gideon Osborn (5-10/24)
3877. Hammond, Lazarus, Esq. of Hammondsport m 5/8/32 Mary Prentice of Bath in B; Rev. I. W. Platt (2-5/9)
3878. Hammond, Lebbeus, Esq., 72, one of the earliest settlers on the Chemung River, d 7/12/26 in Southport, Tioga Co. (3-7/26)
3879. Hammond, Luther, 23, d in Canandaigua (3-2/23/20)
3880. Hammond, Nancy, 46, wf of Joseph, d 9/29/28 in Seneca (3-10/8)
3881. Hammond, Samuel S. H., Esq. of Salina, s of Lazarus, Esq. of Urbana, m Emeline Humphrey in Marcellus (3-9/17/28)
3882. Hammond, Thomas (Capt.) of Richmond, NY d in Detroit ("a patriot and soldier; was with Gen. Pike at York and was there wounded) (5-4/7/18)
3883. Hammond, Vincent M., 14, s of Lazarus, Esq., d 5/10/24 in Urbana, Steuben Co. (3-5/19)
3884. Hammond, William C. of Byron m 10/1/50 W. Jane Langdon of North Bergen in Elba; Rev. Dr. Corwin (1-10/8)
3885. Hamot, Peter Simon Vincent, merchant, m 2/1/18 Adeline Woodruff of Lewiston in L (3-2/25)
3886. Hampton, Reuel (Dr.), about 58, d near Hackettstown, Sussex Co, NJ (surv by a wife but no children mentioned) (5-11/27/22)
3887. Hance, Thomas C., merchant, m Esther Lapham in Palmyra (see also marriage of John Lapham this date) (5-1/14/18 and 3-1/21/18)
3888. Hanchet, Oliver, about 12, s of Dr. J. W., drowned in Rochester (3-1/14/29)
3889. Hand, _____ (Mrs.), consort of Abner, d "recently" in Galen (3-9/29/24)
3890. Handee, John M. m "lately" Alta Blake of Dansville in D; Rev. Morison (2-10/14/46)
3891. Handfield, William m 7/19/29 Sarah Wilton in Seneca (3-7/22)
3892. Handley, David, 25, s of William, d 9/14/26 in Seneca (3-9/20)
3893. Handy, Achsah, relict of late Elder Jairus of Fredonia, d 11/1/33 in Hamilton (4-12/4)
3894. Handy, Jairus (Elder), 29, d 11/7/31 in Fredonia (4-11/23)
3895. Handy, P. W. of Palmyra m 1/15/34 Sophronia Gaines of Palmyra, formerly of Bloomfield, in East Bloomfield; Rev. G. D. Simmons (5-1/24)
3896. Handy, Peter W. m 10/10/19 Susannah Whitney, both of West Bloomfield, at the Presby. Church in West Bloomfield; Rev. Dr. Fitch (3-11/3)

101

3897. Hankinson, Joseph m Susan Mirtal in Wheeler (3-1/9/28)
3898. Hanks, Lydia, wf of John, d 3/24/45 in Bath. Their infant son d 3/26
       (2-4/9)
3899. Hanks, Waterman (Dr.) of Marion m 11/17/29 Mary Jane Cramer in Palmyra;
       Rev. Campbell (5-11/20 and 3/11/25)
3900. Hanley, Aaron m 5/31/26 Caroline Smith, oldest dau of Reuben, Esq., both
       of Hector, in Hector; Rev. Chadwick of Burdett (3-6/14)
3901. Hanna, D. T. of Macedon m 3/10/41 Laura H. Nims of Walworth in W; Rev.
       Mandeville (5-3/17)
3902. Hanna, Jane, 75, a native of Scotland, wid of late Capt. William of
       Unadilla, Ots. Co., d 2/24/32 in Bath (2-3/14)
3903. Hanna, John m 4/9/46 Catharine Dunkleburgh in South Dansville; Rev. J.
       Selmser (2-4/22)
3904. Hannah, Alexander, 39, d 3/24/31 in Bath (2-4/6)
3905. Hannom, Timothy, about 25, d 9/3/18 in Ontario, NY (5-9/15)
3906. Hansen, Isaac, Esq., 42, d in Albany (3-3/18/18)
3907. Hanson, Alexander C. (Hon.), 37, U. S. senator, d 4/23/19 at his home
       in Belmont (3-5/5 and 5-5/12)
3908. Hard, Martha, 31, wf of N. P., d 3/1/17 in Geneva (3-3/5)
3909. Hardenburgh, Mariah (Miss), 24, dau of late Col. John L., d 9/21/24 in
       Auburn (3-9/29)
3910. Harding, Oliver, 83, (a Rev. soldier) d 4/8/38 in Hornellsville (one of
       the first settlers in this section and last Rev. War survivor in H)
       (2-4/18)
3911. Harding, William m 12/25/17 Polly ____ in Williamson (5-12/31)
3912. Hare, George m 4/28/29 Jane Prindle in Benton; Rev. Martin. All of
       Geneva (3-5/13)
3913. Harford, Charles m Mrs. Sarah Ewing in Avon (3-2/7/16)
3914. Harlow, Nathaniel W. m 5/18/26 Catharine Johnson in Benton; Rev.
       Campbell. All of Benton (3-5/31)
3915. Harman, Alexander G., s of Philip, Esq. of NYC, m 9/24/49 Martha O.
       Denham, only dau of Francis, Esq. of Brooklyn; Rev. Charles G. Somers
       (2-10/3)
3916. Harmon, Cyrus H. of Andover m 10/2/35 Louisa King, dau of Samuel, in
       Andover; Rev. David Slie (see also the marr of Edgar King) (2-10/14)
3917. Harp, Edward m 5/2/13 Miss McLaughlin in New Town (3-5/12)
3918. Harper, Alexander, 56, d 4/9/25 at his home in Galen (3-4/20)
3919. Harringdeen, Welcom m Phebe Osborn in Palmyra (3-12/10/17)
3920. Harrington, Asa d 3/2/35 in Carroll (thrown from a horse) (4-3/4)
3921. Harrington, Jacob T. d 9/16/18 in Seneca (3-9/23)
3922. Harris, Abigail, 76, wf of Peter H., d 8/9/40 in Palmyra (5-8/12)
3923. Harris, Delpha m Anna Moore in Carroll; Rev. Eddy (4-10/5/31)
3924. Harris, George W., Esq. m 11/24/30 Mrs. Lucinda Morgan, wid of late
       Capt. William, in Batavia; Hon. Simeon Cumings (1-11/26). In 5-12/3:
       Rev. Simeon Cummings with marr date 11/30. See 3927.
3925. Harris, George W. of Elba m 12/24/48 Betsey Hedger of Bergen in B;
       Samuel Richmond, Esq. (1-1/9/49)
3926. Harris, John m Sally Casner in Newark, NY (3-12/23/29)
3927. Harris, John W., Esq. m 11/23/30 Mrs. Lucinda Morgan, wid of late Capt.
       William, in Batavia; Hon. Simeon Cummings (4-12/8). See 3924.
3928. Harris, Joseph of Rochester m 10/20/35 Miss Lucinda Harris of Marion
       at the Eagle Hotel in Palmyra; Elder Henry V. Jones (5-10/23)
3929. Harris, Joseph H. m 6/16/50 Mary Walbridge Cooley, dau of Maj. L. J.
       Cooley, in Elmira; Rev. A. Hull (2-6/26)
3930. Harris, Joseph R., 22, d in West Cayuga (3-9/23/29)
3931. Harris, Peter m 9/31/13 Rachael Folwell, dau of Joseph, in Romulus;
       Rev. Mosher (3-10/13)
3932. Harris, Robert of Phelps m 10/17/26 Elizabeth Norris of Seneca (see
       marr of George Norris this date) (3-11/1)
3933. Harris, Rufus, 35, d in Williamson (3-3/24/13)
3934. Harris, Russel m Rosanah Bosworth in Perinton; Rev. J. Irons (5-11/28/17)
3935. Harris, Seth, 14, d 10/11/29 in Palmyra (3-10/21 and 5-10/16)
3936. Harris, William, 3, s of Martin, d 8/23/19 in Palmyra (5-9/1)
3937. Harrison, ____ (Mrs.), 61, mother-in-law of Mr. H. Dewey, d (prob. in
       Jamestown) (4-7/25/38)
3938. Harrison, Harvey m Catharine Boohall in Benton (3-10/8/28)

3939. Harrison, Hiram m 11/7/32 Jane Jagger in Palmyra (5-11/28)
3940. Harrison, Job m 11/6/32 Eliza Springer, both of Williamson, in W; Rev.
      Cyrus Strong (5-11/14)
3941. Harrison, Joseph, Rev., "minister of Thompson st. church" m 11/7/25
      Margaret Carne in NYC (3-11/16)
3942. Harrison, Julia, 3 yrs, dau of James, d 4/15/41 in Jamestown (4-4/21)
3943. Harrison, Luman, about 55, d 6/28/31 ("an early settler at Palmyra")
      (5-7/1)
3944. Harrison, Rufus m Sarah Sawyer, both of Palmyra, in P (3-6/10/18 and
      5-6/2/18)
3945. Harrison, William L. m 7/1/30 Ann Giberson; D. Grandin, Esq.  All of
      Williamson (5-7/2)
3946. Harrower, Levi B., s of B., Esq. of Lindley, d 1/20/50 in Jacksonville, FL
      (2-3/13)
3947. Harrower, Mary, wf of late Levi B., d 3/20/50 in Big Flats (2-3/27)
3948. Harrower, Susan, 28, consort of Col. G. T. and dau of Alva Thurber, Esq.,
      d 4/20/46 in Lindley (2-5/5)
3949. Hart, _____ (Mrs.), 71, wf of Deacon Joseph, d 12/20/22 in Seneca
      (3-12/25)
3950. Hart, _____ (Mrs.), 42, wf of Ira, d 3/1/42 in Jamestown (4-3/3)
3951. Hart, Eliza, 45, wid of Roswell, d 6/2/32 in Rochester (5-6/11)
3952. Hart, Ephraim, Esq. m Martha Seymour of Hartford, CT in H; Rev. Dr.
      Flint (3-5/16/21) (Ephraim of Utica)
3953. Hart, Henry W. (Dr.) of Avoca m 5/1/45 Sarah Helen Way of South
      Dansville in S. D.; Rev. S. McKinney (2-5/7)
3954. Hart, Ira m 5/27/39 Mrs. _____ Dodge of Harmony, in Jamestown (4-6/5)
3955. Hart, John m Miss _____ Cline in Victor (3-11/22/15)
3956. Hart, Lois, 41, wf of Ira, d in Harmony (4-5/24/37)
3957. Hart, "Mrs. Phi.", 46, d in Palmyra (3-2/3/13)
3958. Hart, Rodman of Junius m 7/28/41 Nancy Lemunyon of Manchester in M;
      Rev. Samuel Wilson (5-8/4)
3959. Hart, Roswell, Esq., 37, merchant, d 8/25/24 in Rochester ("... one of
      the earliest settlers of this village" - from a Rochester newspaper)
      (3-9/8 and 1-9/3)
3960. Hart, Roswell m Polly Ann Stilson, dau of Eli, in Rochester (3-12/29/24)
3961. Hart, Russel, about 24, of Middlebury, Ohio d 3/20/27 at Hemenway's
      Hotel in Geneva ("... had been attending lectures at the 'Vermont
      Academy of Medicine' at Castleton and was on his way home by stage.
      The funeral will be attended from the Hotel.") (3-3/21)
3961. Hart, Samuel, 77, d in Jamestown (4-3/31/42)
3962. Hart, Timothy T. of Bergen m 6/26/47 Susan Ferrell of Rochester; Rev.
      Babcock (1-6/29)
3963. Hart, Truman (Hon.), 54, of Palmyra d 2/7/38 (5-2/14)
3964. Hart, Wealthy Ann, 43, wf of Ephraim, Esq., d in Utica (3-7/28/19)
3965. Harter, Jerod m 6/1/43 Cynthia L. Paddock of Harmony; Rev. N. Norton
      (4-6/8)
3966. Hartford, Philander, merchant, m 3/12/27 Ann Hornell, both of Hornells-
      ville; Rev. Robert Hubbard of Dansville (3-3/21)
3967. Hartman, Mary M. (Mrs.), 36 (or 56?), d 3/16/22 in Geneva.  Her infant
      daughter, Mary M., aged 2 weeks, d 3/24 (3-3/27)
3968. Hartshorn, Jacob, Esq., 72, d 1/30/50 in Lebanon, Mad. Co. (one of the
      first settlers in this town) (3-2/27)
3969. Hartt, Jonathan d in Canandaigua (3-11/12/17)
3970. Hertwell, James L. m 4/14/31 Mary Jane Eaton in Urbana; M. Brink, Esq.
      (2-5/11)
3971. Hartwell, Sophrona, 23 (or 28?), wf of Elijah and dau of Thomas and
      Percey Freeman of Manchester, Washtenaw Co., MI, d 5/12/45 in North
      Cohocton, NY (2-5/21)
3972. Harvey, Asahel, 36, one of the proprietors of the Ontario Repository,
      d 7/19/35 in Canandaigua (5-7/24)
3973. Harvey, Charles Webster, 18 mos, s of Col. C. R., d 8/17/34 in
      Jamestown (4-8/20)
3974. Harvey, Harrison, about 3, s of Stimpson, d 10/21/19 in Palmyra
      (5-10/27)
3975. Harvey, Helen, 16 mo, dau of Col. C. R., d 7/9/38 in Poughkeepsie
      (4-7/18)

3976. Harvey, Henry L., editor of the Watertown Register, m Nancy Ford, dau of
      Capt. Augustus, in Sacket's Harbor (3-4/22)
3977. Harvey, Joseph H. m Mary Harris in Phelps (3-11/5/17)
3978. Hervey, Robert, 32, wagon-maker, d 1/9/30 at the jail in Geneva.
      Committed 6/23/29 ("was to have had his trial at the recent circuit.
      His parents are supposed to reside in Enfield, Tompkins Co.")(3-1/20)
3979. Harvey, Sarah, 1 yr, dau of Uziel, d 3/24/22 (3-3/27)
3980. Harvy, John m 3/2/47 Harriet Crawford in Addison; C. Cole, Esq. (2-3/10)
3981. Harwood, Alpheus m Harriet Goodell, dau of Rev. Goodell, in Bristol;
      Rev. Goodell (5-10/27/18)
3982. Harwood, Archelaus (Dr.) m Parmela Sweatland in Palmyra; A. Spear, Esq.
      (5-11/28/21)
3983. Harwood, John, 94, d in Hopewell (3-2/13/28)
3984. Harwood, John Edmund, formerly of the New Theatre, Asia, comedian, d
      10/21/09 in Germantown, PA (3-10/25)
3985. Harwood, Mary (widow), 91, d in Gorham (3-2/1/15)
3986. Harwood, O. H. Perry m 10/13/42 Janette Ide in Stockton; Rev. E.
      Richmond (4-10/20)
3987. Hasbrouck, Catharine (widow), 83, d in Albany (3-10/13/13)
3988. Hasbrouck, Jeremiah, 60, d in Elmira (3-7/1/29)
3989. Haskell, Andrew L. of Carroll m 8/15/43 Catharine A. Stow of Jamestown
      in J; Rev. A. Chapin (4-8/17)
3990. Haskell, Charles J. m 1/13/45 Phebe Dean in Harmony; M. Norton, Esq.
      (4-2/21)
3991. Haskell, Jeremiah m 9/20/43 Caroline Smith in Canandaigua; Rev. M. L.
      R. F. Thompson. All of Canandaigua (5-10/18)
3992. Haskin, Cyrus m 1/12/32 Betsey Nash, both of Addison, in A; J. Prentiss,
      Esq. (2-1/18)
3993. Hassett, John (Capt.) m 1/9/25 Eliza Kidney in Attica; Rev. Brown
      (1-1/21)
3994. Hastings, Charles of Junius m 1/6/14 Olive Godfrey of Phelps; Joseph
      Hall, Esq. (3-1/12)
3995. Hastings, E. Moore m Mary Ann Fenton, both of Jamestown, in Sugargrove,
      PA; M. Willson, Esq. (4-10/6/42)
3996. Hastings, Eliza, 20, wf of Freeman, d in Canandaigua (3-9/10/17)
3997. Hastings, Elizabeth, wf of O., Esq., d in Geneseo (3-12/16/18)
3998. Hastings, Eunice, 57, wf of Dr. Seth, d 5/2/21 in Clinton (3-5/16)
3999. Hastings, Eurotus P. of Geneva m 1/26/19 Electa Owen, dau of Josiah
      of Cambray, Niag. Co., in Cambray; Rev. Crane (3-2/3)
4000. Hastings, Eurotus P., Esq. of Detroit, Pres. of the Bank of Mich.,
      m 8/23/26 Mrs. Philena Moody of Geneva in G; Rev. Dr. Axtell
      (3-8/30)
4001. Hastings, Freeman, 25, d in Canandaigua (3-8/26/18)
4002. Hastings, Horace of Geneva m 6/7/15 Betsey Hastings of Hatfield, MA in
      H (3-7/5)
4003. Hastings, Isaac, merchant, m Elmira Ward at St. John's Church in
      Canandaigua (3-10/22/28)
4004. Hastings, Jacob, 97, (a soldier in the French and Rev. wars) d in
      Canandaigua (3-6/24/29)
4005. Hastings, Lemuel, merchant, of Hammondsport m 12/13/37 Mary Barnard of
      Geneva in G; Rev. Hay (2-12/27)
4006. Hastings, Perez m 5/6/22 Eunice Hastings in Geneva; Rev. Axtell
      (3-5/8)
4007. Hastings, Thomas of Albany m Mary Seymour in Buffalo (3-10/16/22)
4008. Hastings, Timothy (a Rev. pensioner) of Wayne m 4/7/38 Mrs. Hannah Abel
      of Bath; William Hamilton, Esq. (2-4/11)
4009. Hastings, Truman, Esq. of Geneseo m Elizabeth Vail of Troy in Troy
      (3-8/27/28)
4010. Haswell, Anthony, editor of the Green Mountain Farmer, d in Bennington
      (3-6/5/16)
4011. Hatch, George Whitfield, 58, formerly of Wayne Co., d 2/20/29 at his
      home in Auburn (3-3/18 and 5-3/6)
4012. Hatch, Solomon G. of Busti m 1/24/38 Augusta Ann G. Whitney, adopted dau
      of Thomas Whitney, Esq. of Chautauqua in C; Rev. Dodge (4-2/7 and
      repeated 4-2/14). (In 4-1/31 bride had been listed as "Augusta Green")

104

4013. Hatfield, Richard m 4/2/27 Sally Griswold in Southport, Tioga Co.
(3-4/25)
4014. Hathaway, Gilbert m 6/12/26 Mary Hurd, dau of Gen. Timothy, in Starkey
(3-6/21)
4015. Hathaway, Irena, about 21, wf of Asher, d 6/19/23 in Romulus (3-7/23)
4016. Hathaway, Lucinda, 9, dau of Josiah H., d 8/21/41 in East Palmyra
(5-8/25)
4017. Hathaway, Luther A. m 8/29/42 Clarissa L. Ripley in Macedon Locks;
Rev. Philo Forbes. All of Macedon Locks (See also marr of Adoniram
J. Rice) (5-9/14)
4018. Hathaway, Rebecca, 67, wf of Ebenezer, d 5/29/41 in Palmyra (5-6/2)
4019. Hathaway, Sally, 21, wf of Edward T., d in Addison (surv by husband
and 2 small children) (2-10/13/41)
4020. Hathaway, Salmon of Palmyra d 8/24/34 in Lewiston (5-8/29)
4021. Hausenfrats, Mary, wf of Jacob, d in Rochester (3-1/14/29)
4022. Haven, Curtis (Dr.) m 12/5/33 Elsey Ann King, dau of Elder J. S. of
Silver Creek; Rev. Gillet (4-12/11)
4023. Haven, D. A. m 9/18/38 Minerva Seeley, both of Sinclairville, in S;
Rev. J. Scofield (4-9/26)
4024. Haven, Elias of Jamestown m 4/11/32 Emily N. King, dau of Elder John S.
of Ashville (4-4/16)
4025. Haven, Orlando H. of Joliette, IL m 11/13/38 Eliza Dewey of Jamestown
in J; Rev. Gray (4-11/14)
4026. Haven, Orra, 37, wf of Elias, d 9/5/31 in Jamestown (4-9/7)
4027. Havens, Avery E., 27, d 7/28/37 in Palmyra (5-8/4)
4028. Havens, Eldredge m 6/2/31 Prudence Morgan in Palmyra; F. Smith, Esq.
(5-6/10)
4029. Havens, Elias, 55, d 12/19/43 in Belvidere, IL ("A few weeks before his
death he left his home in Juliet in good health to visit friends
near Fox and Rock Rivers ...") (4-1/1944)
4030. Havens, Eliza M., 26, wf of Orlando and dau of Harvey Dewey of Jamestown,d 8/1/43 in Juliette, IL (4-8/17)
4031. Havens, Ephraim S. m 8/7/43 Mrs. Ann Jane Cowing in Buffalo; Rev. Philo
Wood. All of Buffalo (4-8/17)
4032. Havens, Nancy, consort of E. Havens, d 4/8/30 in Palmyra (5-4/9)(Nancy, 46)
4033. Haverling, Elizabeth, 62, consort of Adam, Esq., d 6/13/41 in Bath
(she is reported as "a mother") (2-6/16)
4034. Haverling, Henry, 19, clerk of the Steuben Bank, d 1/15/35 in Bath
(2-1/21)
4035. Haverly, Rebecca, 28, consort of Adam, d in Bath (3-1/27/19)
4036. Haviland, Ledyard D. m Harriet Tuthill in Elmira (3-10/14/29)
4037. Hawes, Lewis R. (Dr.) of Tyrone m Fanny D. Stewart of Bath in B; Rev.
S. McKinney (2-4/2/45)
4038. Hawkins, _____ m 2/21/26 Mary Ann Parrot in Pittsford; Rev. Knapp
(1-3/10)
4039. Hawkins, Earl of Palmyra m 9/3/20 Phebe Wiser of Penfield in P (5-10/11)
4040. Hawkins, Rodolphus, 89 (a Rev. soldier) d 6/11/47 in Alexander (1-6/15)
4041. Hawks, Ann, wf of Maj. Eleazer, d in Phelps (3-7/9/17)
4042. Hawks, John, M.D., m 7/1/30 Laura Louisa Lathrop, second dau of Leonard
E., Esq.; Rev. Peter Canouse. All of Newark, NY (5-7/16)
4043. Hawks, Jonathan m Clarissa Pease in Victor (3-5/24/20)
4044. Hawks, Nathaniel, Esq., 23, attorney, d 2/17/33 in Jamestown (4-2/20)
4045. Hawley, Adnah S. m 9/6/32 Mary Ann Stocking in Bath; Stephen Willard,
Esq. (2-9/19)
4046. Hawley, Alonzo m 9/24/33 Eliza Chamberlain, dau of Judge Chamberlain
of Great Valley, in G. V.; Rev. Baldwin (4-10/2)
4047. Hawley, Alpheus Fenn m 7/20/43 Lucy Fletcher, dau of A., Esq., in
Jamestown; Rev. Owen Street (4-7/27)
4048. Hawley, Alpheus, 58, merchant d 5/5/44 at his home in Jamestown (surv by
wf. "and family") (4-5/10)
4049. Hawley, Amos Payne (Rev.) of Springville, Erie Co. m 6/4/38 Sarah
Artemesia Harvey, dau of Gen. T. W. of Poughkeepsie, in P; Rev.
Eaton (4-6/20)
4050. Hawley, Anna Mary, 1 yr, dau of Abijah, d 4/21/22 in Geneva (3-4/24)
4051. Hawley, Clara Keziah, 14 mo, dau of John B., d 2/10/45 in Jamstown
(See death of John Jay Hawley) (4-2/14)

4052. Hawley, Daniel, 20, printer, d 4/8/29 in Geneva (3-4/15)
4053. Hawley, Elijah, Esq., one of the judges of the common pleas of Genesee
County, d 4/29/20 in Ridgeway (3-5/10). In 5-5/17 the death date is
4/19/20.
4054. Hawley, George, 10 mo, s of Mr. Comfort Hawley, d 11/11/26 in Geneva
(3-11/15)
4055. Hawley, Harriet, 6 yrs, dau of Mr. Comfort Hawley, d 3/14/28 in Geneva
(3-3/19)
4056. Hawley, Henry of Wayne m 8/13/46 Mariah Lester of Urbana in U; Rev. T. R.
Clark (2-8/19)
4057. Hawley, J. Edwin (Dr.) m Miranda Phillips, oldest dau of Dr. G. W., in
Ithaca (3-9/23/29)
4058. Hawley, Jeremiah M. m Mary Powers in Batavia (3-1/14/29)
4059. Hawley, Jesse m 5/4/12 Betsey R. Tiffany in Canandaigua; Rev. Phelps
(3-5/13)
4060. Hawley, John B., merchant, m 9/24/40 Elizabeth Breed, dau of William
of Jamestown, in J; Rev. Amos P. Hawley (4-9/30)
4061. Hawley, John Jay, 3 yrs, only ch of John B. and Elizabeth, d 3/4/45 in
Hickory Creek, Venango Co., PA ("About three weeks ago, while on a
visit to their friends in Jamestown they lost a ... dau of16 months.
Both children died of a disease resembling the croup.") (4-3/14)
4062. Hawley, Mary, 73, wf of Moses, d in Canandaigua (3-10/1/28)
4063. Hawley, Morse T., 19, d 9/3/24 in Camillus, Cay. Co. (3-9/15)
4064. Hawley, William m Arabella Elizette Wheeler, dau of George A., in
Bloomfield (3-12/23/29)
4065. Haws, Valentine, Jr. m Harriet G. Selby, both of Pulteneyville, in P;
Rev. Harrington (5-1/10/38) (Marr. date: 1/1/38)
4066. Hawse, Charles of Starkey m 5/7/45 Ann Maria Disbrow of Barrington in
Tyrone; Rev. Sunderlin (2-5/14)
4067. Hayden, _____ (Mrs.), 30, d 11/23/25 in Geneva (3-11/30)
4068. Hayden, Peter P. R. m Cynthia Stewart in Manchester (3-9/19/27)
4069. Hayden, William m 11/6/22 Harriet Thomas, both of Alexander, in A
(1-11/22)
4070. Hayes, Alexander m 12/17/27 Susan Sayre Mathews, formerly of Elmira,
dau of Mrs. Henry Towar, in Lyons (3-12/26). Rev. Hubbell, offic.
4071. Hayes, George E. of Canandaigua m Emily H. Hopkins in Prattsburgh
(3-1/9/28)
4072. Hayes, Hector m Lucinda Warren in Bristol (3-2/3/30)
4073. Hayes, Jacob, 62, d in Canandaigua (3-3/17/13)
4074. Hayes, James m 12/6/10 Sophia White, dau of Edward, in Geneva; Rev. A.
Wilson. All of Geneva (3-12/12)
4075. Hayes, James, 59, d 3/17/25 (3-3/23)
4076. Hayes, Margaret (Mrs.), 34, d in Canandaigua (3-6/24/18)
4077. Hayes, Michael, printer, of Auburn m 7/10/16 Letty Bennett of Owasco
in O (3-7/24)
4078. Hayes, Mumford of Bristol m Abigail H. Wilcox, dau of Dr. Ralph, in
East Bloomfield (3-5/14/28)
4079. Hayes, Pliny (Dr.) m 12/21/22 Eliza S. Wells in Canandaigua (3-1/1/23)
4080. Hayes, Pliny, 65, father of Dr. P. Hayes, Jr., d 8/2/31 in Bristol
(5-8/5)
4081. Hayes, Pliny, Jr., 42, of Canandaigua d 7/28/31 in the Medical
Institution in NYC (5-8/5)
4082. Haynes, Peter m 2/27/39 Mrs. Kerlander Havner in Marion; A. H. Dow,
Esq. All of Marion (5-3/8)
4083. Hays, John of Geneva m 8/26/16 Abigail Price of Elizabeth-Town, NJ
in E.-T. (3-9/18)
4084. Hayt, Samuel, 31, d 9/7/47 in Corning ("while at his usual duties at
the store of his brothers") (2-9/22)
4085. Hayward, Charles H. m 4/29/38 Rosetta Ann Woodward, both of Jamestown,
in J; Rev. Gray (4-5/2)
4086. Hayward, John, 32 (or 22) d 7/1/33 in Palmyra (5-7/3)
4087. Hayward, Joseph D. m 12/5/16 Mary Ann Fowle in Geneva (3-12/11)
4088. Hayward, Mary (Mrs.), 68, of Dover, VT d 10/30/31 in Jamestown, NY
(4-11/2)
4089. Hayward, Polly, 19, wf of Asa, d in Canandaigua (3-11/4/29)

4090. Hayward, Samuel, 64, d 3/1/19 in Palmyra (5-3/3 and 3-3/10)
4091. Hayward, Stoughton of East Bloomfield m 10/19/41 Eliza C. Throop of
       Manchester in M; Rev. A. H. Burlingame (5-10/27)
4092. Hayward, William D. m Eleanor Jennings in Macedon (3-7/9/28)
4093. Haywood, William of Rochester m 3/21/21 Almira Taylor, dau of Eliphalet,
       Esq., in Canandaigua (5-4/4)
4094. Hazard, Alse (Mrs.), 70, d in Jerusalem, NY (3-4/30/28)
4095. Hazard, Griffin B., Esq., formerly of Benton, d 7/4/22 in Reading
       (3-8/7)
4096. Hazard, Raymond, about 66, a transient person, d at the home of Francis
       Gragg of Pike Creek, Tioga Co. (3-2/28/16)
4097. Hazeltine, A. (Dr.) m 11/5/38 Jane Morrison in Warren; Rev. Emory
       (4-11/21)
4098. Hazeltine, Abner (Hon.) m 7/21/34 Matilda Hayward, both of Jamestown,
       in J; Rev. Leonard (4-7/23)
4099. Hazeltine, C. G. m 8/23/43 Caroline Bulkley, both of Granville,
       Washington Co., in G (4-10/12)
4100. Hazeltine, Edwin m 1/1/34 Polly Abbot in Busti (4-1/8)
4101. Hazeltine, Gilbert W., M.D., of Jamestown m 6/27/43 Eliza C. Boss of
       Forestville in F; Rev. J. S. Emory (4-7/6)
4102. Hazeltine, Hardin m Polly Stilson in Busti (4-1/8/34)
4103. Hazeltine, Harriet, 27, wf of Pardon, d 2/28/38 in Busti (4-3/7)
4104. Hazeltine, Mary Ann, 12, dau of Daniel, d 1/25/39 in Jamestown (4-1/30)
4105. Hazeltine, Pardon, late of Busti, m 2/17/40 Abigail R. Wheelock, dau of
       Asa, Esq.,of Wardsboro, VT in W (4-3/25)
4106. Hazeltine, Pardon, 42, late of Busti, NY, d 3/12/44 in Worcester, MA
       (4-3/29)
4107. Hazeltine, Peters Oakley, 5, s of Dr. L. Oakley, d 4/30 in Jamestown
       (4-5/6)
4108. Hazeltine, Polly K., 34, wf of Abner, Esq., d 10/14/32 in Geneva
       (4-10/17)
4109. Hazeltine, Robert Falconer, 3 yrs, s of Dr. Laban, d 12/3/34 in James-
       town (4-12/10)
4110. Hazen Edward m Hannah Putnam in Palmyra (3-3/24/19 and 5-3/17/19)
4111. Heacox, _____, 6, a ch of W. B., d 3/9/26 in Batavia. Also, "another
       daughter" of W. B., age 8, d 3/3 (1-3/10)
4112. Heacox, Augustus m 3/13/35 Mrs. Ann Hibbard in Palmyra; F. Smith, Esq.
       (5-3/27)
4113. Heacox, Corintha, 17, d 5/31/49 in Batavia (1-6/5)
4114. Healy, Lois, 90, late a resident of Worcester, MA, relict of Nathaniel
       of Busti, d 9/9/31 in B (4-9/14)
4115. Heartwell, Oliver, Esq. of Canandaigua m 11/18/17 Lucy Hathaway, dau of
       Maj. Thomas of Benton, in B; Rev. Onderdonk (3-12/3)
4116. Heath, B. S. (Dr.) m 10/30/45 Louisa M. Davis, both of Carroll, in Busti;
       Rev. E. R. Swain (4-11/14)
4117. Heath, Elijah m Patience Clark in Geneseo (3-3/29/20)
4118. Heath, John m Sally Hicks in Fayette (3-5/12/19)
4119. Heath, Katharine, 14 weeks, dau of J. C., d 8/1/32 in Palmyra (5-8/15)
4120. Heath, William, 77, d 1/24/14 in Roxbury, MA (a major general in the
       Rev War; "companion in arms of Washington") (3-2/9)
4121. Heck, George m Margaret Hoofstater in Fayette (3-7/15/29)
4122. Hecox, Cyrus, 49, d 6/17/31 in Lyons (5-6/24)
4123. Hedden, Aaron W. of Arcadia m 12/22/42 Ruth Aramantha Harrison of
       Palmyra in P; Rev. D. Cushing (5-12/28)
4124. Hedges, William S. (Dr.) m 9/12/39 Theda C. Parker, both of Jamestown,
       in J; Rev. Gillet (4-9/18)
4125. Heermance, Andries (Col.), 69, formerly of Red Hook, d 8/15/18 in Troy
       (3-9/2)
4126. Heggie, Archibald of Ithaca m Elizabeth Minton in Elmira (3-6/25/28)
4127. Helm, William (Capt.), 66, d 2/23/27 in Bath (3-3/21)
4128. Helmes, Thomas A. (Maj.), formerly of the U. S. dragoons, d 7/26/17
       in New Orleans (3-9/17)
4129. Hemenway, Aaron m 10/27/35 Minerva Mills, both of Bath, in B; John D.
       Higgins, Esq. (2-11/11)
4130. Hemenway, Silas (Maj.) of Geneva m 7/27/29 Mary Ottley, dau of William
       of Phelps, in P; Rev. M. P. Squier (3-7/29 and 5-7/31)

107

4131. Heminway, Truman m 10/22/22 Mary Aldrich in Palmyra (3-11/6)
4132. Hemiup (sic - perhaps handwritten Hemings?), _____ (Mrs.), 65, wf of
        John, d 9/8/17 in Geneva (3-9/10)
4133. Hemiup, _____ (Mrs.), wf of John, d in Geneva (3-6/16/19). See 4132.
4134. Hemiup, Anthony of Geneva m 5/18/23 Phebe Ringer, dau of Jacob, of
        Seneca; Rev. ____ne (blurred) (3-5/21). See 4132.
4135. Hempstead, Charles S., about 1 yr, s of Elisha, d 9/1/31 in Bath
        (2-9/7)
4136. Hempsted, Mary (Mrs.), 75, d 2/13/41 in Erwin (2-2/17)
4137. Hendee, Alva m Mary Wilcox in Palmyra (3-12/20/15)
4138. Hendee, Ariel, 61, d 5/22/41 in West Bloomfield (an early settler there)
        (5-5/26)
4139. Hendee, Edwin A., Esq., 27, late of Bloomfield, d 1/16/42 in St. Croix,
        West Indies, "where he had gone for ... his health" (5-3/2)
4140. Hendee, Mary, 51, wf of Alva and dau of late David Willcox, ("first
  *     female born in Palmyra 'of civilized parents'") died (prob. in
        Palmyra) (5-2/16/42)
4142. Hendee, Mary Ann, wf of Col. Daniel, d 9/9/29 in Lockville (formerly
        of Palmyra) (5-9/18 and 3-9/23)
4143. Henderson, John, 102, d 12/17/11 in Fishkill (a soldier at the Battle
        of Collodon, Scotland (4/17/1746); at Minden, Germany (8/14/1759);
        and at the taking of Quebec under Gen. Wolfe (4/28/1760). After
        that war left the British army and lived mostly in Dutchess Co., NY
        until his death (3-2/26/12)
4144. Hendly, Lester of Alexandria m Sarah Chipman, dau of Samuel, Esq. of
        Madrid, St. Law. Co., in Madrid (5-3/31/18)
4145. Hendricks, Jacob, 55, d 2/24/23 in Fayette (3-3/5)
4146. Hendricks, Jacob m Mrs. Van Cleff in Fayette (3-11/19/28)
4147. Hendricks, Michael m 10/30/23 Anne Hutte, both of Fayette (3-11/12)
4148. Hendricks, Thomas of Penn Yan m Harriet Bishop in Clarksville, Cay. Co.
        (3-10/29/28)
4149. Heney, Samuel m 5/28/15 Harriet Teale, dau of Capt. N., in Junius;
        H. W. Dobbin, Esq. (a double ceremony - see marr of John Maden)
        (3-5/31)
4150. Henion, Ann, 62, wid of David J., d 5/5/26 in Gorham (3-5/10)
4151. Henion, Gerrit m Catharine Provost in Fayette; Rev. Lane (3-9/25/22)
4152. Henion, Jane, wf of John, d 3/12/17 in Romulus (3-3/26)
4153. Henion, Maria, wf of Henry, d 9/27/15 in Fayette and 10/1 Henry, age 64,
        died there (3-10/4)
4154. Hennion, John of Benton m 11/25/13 Jane Dey of Fayette; Rev. Mosier
        (3-12/8)
4155. Henry, Charles W. m 3/15/14 Penelope C. Potter, dau of late Judge
        Potter, in Middlesex (3-3/30)
4156. Henry, Daniel of Rochester m 3/17/25 Mary Melay of Seneca in S; Rev.
        Parker (3-4/13)
4157. Henry, Edward (Dr.), 27, brother of Charles W., Esq. of Geneva, d 11/16/22
        in North Carolina (3-12/11)
4158. Henry, H. O. of Bath m 6/18/35 Phebe Maria Gibson of Rome, Oneida Co.;
        Rev. D. Biddlecom (2-7/1)
4159. Henry, Isaac m Phebe Weaver in Cohocton (3-6/17/29)
4160. Henry, John (Dr.) d 5/17/12 in Geneva (3-5/20)
4161. Henry, John, 60, d 7/22/27 in Geneva (3-7/25)
4162. Henry, John V., Esq. of Albany m 4/31/19 Miss Wilkes, only dau of late
        John, Esq. of. NYC, in NYC (3-5/5)
4163. Henry, John V., Esq., 65, an eminent attorney in Albany, d 10/22/29
        in Albany (4-11/4)
4164. Henry, Josiah m 10/1/35 Mrs. Polly Logan in Bath; John D. Higgins, Esq.
        All of Bath (2-10/7)
4165. Henry, Milton, formerly of Jamestown, m Mrs. Louisa Smith in Blackwell's
        Mills, VA (4-6/30/42)
4166. Henry, William m 12/9/28 Minerva Dinsmore, dau of Thomas, in Seneca;
        Rev. Oliver Ackley (3-12/17)
4167. Henshaw, _____, wf of Madison, d 2/14/44 in Batavia (1-2/20)
4168. Hequembourg, C. L. m 10/25/42 Amelia Williams in Dunkirk; Rev. Stillman
        (4-10/27)
4169. Herbert, John P. m Maria B. Bevier in Fayette (3-5/28/28)
* Number 4141 inadvertently omitted.
                                    108

4170. Herkimer, Abner M. d 2/10/45 in Washington, Arkansas (2-4/16)
4171. Herrick, Arthur, Esq., attorney, m 5/20/28 Hannah M. Haight, dau of Gen
        Samuel S., in Angelica; Rev. Hurd (3-5/28)
4172. Herrick, Arthur, Esq., attorney, of Angelica d 5/9/31 in NYC (2-5/25)
4173. Herrick, Daniel D. of Erwin and B. Rowley of Painted Post drowned in the
        Tioga River at Linsleytown 3/12/32 "while crossing the river in a
        skiff" (the body of D.D.H. "not yet found") (2-4/11)
4174. Herrick, Elijah of Seneca d 3/18/17 in Phelps (3-3/26)
4175. Herrick, Ephraim m Clarinda Williams in Ovid (3-1/16/22)
4176. Herrick, Hannah, 24, wf of Arthur, Esq. and dau of Gen. Samuel S. Haight,
        formerly of Bath, d 4/4/29 in Angelica (3-4/15)
4177. Herrick, S. C. of Barre m 12/5/50 Philena P. Smith of Oakfield in
        Batavia; Rev. S. M. Stimson (a double ceremony - see marr of Henry
        Smith) (1-12/10)
4178. Herring, John H., 22, d in Marcellus (3-9/23/29)
4179. Herring, Joseph, 28, d 9/22/17 in Canandaigua (3-10/1/17)
4180. Herrington, Stacy F. m 8/30/18 Mary B. Chapin, formerly of Geneva, in
        Waterloo; Rev. Axtell (3-9/2)
4181. Hertell, Lorinda, 28, wf of John C., d in Waterloo (3-8/29/27)
4182. Heslop, George, 5, s of John,d 10/16/10 near Geneva (3-10/24)
4183. Heslop, John of Geneva d in Liverpool, England (3-1/20/13)
4184. Heslop, John, about 30, only s of John, Esq. of Geneva, d in Durham,
        England (3-2/3/30)
4185. Hess, Alexander m 1/10/41 Martha T. Seely, dau of late Samuel, at the
        Trinity Church in Elmira; Rev. G. Winslow (2-1/27)
4186. Hess, Hannah Elizabeth, 2 yrs, only ch of Alexander and Martha T.,
        d 1/27/46 in Bath (2-2/4)
4187. Hess, John, Esq., 68?, d 4/12/32 in NYC ("distinguished for his
        connexion with the first Auction House in the Union") (5-4/25)
4188. Hess, Mary, dau of Martha T. and Alexander, d 9/7/50 in Bath (2-9/18)
4189. Hetfield, Aron m 5/2/13 Eunice Seely in New Town (3-5/12)
4190. Heuchan, James, 25, a native of Galway, Scotland, d 12/26/24 in Geneva
        (killed by a fall from a wagon) (surv by wf and one ch) (3-12/29)
4191. Hewett, David, merchant, of Byron m 4/24/31 Olive Hewett of Lewiston
        in Byron; Rev. True (1-4/29)
4192. Hewett, Henry (Hon.) of Marshall, MI m 8/17/41 Alzina Merrill of Byron
        in Batavia; Rev. W. A. Beecher (1-8/24)
4193. Hewett, Russell m 4/10/31 Perlins Smith, both of Middlebury, in M
        (1-5/13)
4194. Hewett, Winter (Dr.), 42, d 8/14/24 in Batavia ("... had resided in this
        village for more than twelve years ... followed the practice of Physic..")
        (1-8/20)
4195. Hewitt, Richard (Dr.) m Hannah Parker in Pulteney (3-11/7/27)
4196. Hewlett. See Hulett also.
4197. Hewlett, Emery, 83, d 5/16/30 in Lyons (5-5/21)
4198. Hewlett, Ira of Byron m Hannah Griswold of Stafford; Stephen Griswold,
        Esq. (1-7/19/22)
4199. Hewlett, John of Onondaga Co. m Angeline Willson of Penn Yan (3-11/5/28)
4200. Hewson, John m 8/7/42 Jane Rogers in Arcadia; M. Rich, Esq. (5-8/10)
4201. Hibbard, Ann (Mrs.), 80, d in Havana, NY (3-5/6/29)
4202. Hibbard, Luther, 45, d in North East, PA (4-3/2/43)
4203. Hibbard, Salmon (Rev.), about 61, d 9/1/24 in Elba (1-9/3)
4204. Hickey, Mathew m 12/19/39 Emily Galloway; Rev. Walling. All of Marion
        (a double ceremony - see marr of John H. Galloway) (5-12/20)
4205. Hickok, Munson, 20, d 8/14/22 in Wolcott (3-8/21)
4206. Hickox, _____, "another child of William B. Hickox" d 3/12/26. "This
        makes the third child he lost during the past week." (1-3/17)
4207. Hickox, Asa, Esq., 74, formerly of Victor, d 5/22/29 in Richmond ("the
        first white person that wintered in the country west of Utica")
        (3-6/3)
4208. Hicks, ----- (Mr.) d 6/6/12 in Canandaigua (3-6/24)
4209. Hicks, Angelica, 36, wf of Joshua, d 7/31/30 in Macedon (5-8/13)
4210. Hicks, B. Schuyler m 4/20/20 Mary Chamberlain in Fayette; Rev. Axtell
        (3-5/10)
4211. Hicks, Benjamin F. of North Bristol m 10/22/45 Margaret Vance of Urbana
        in U; Rev. L. W. Russ (2-10/29)

4212. Hicks, D. C. m 12/20/43 Rebecca Vosburgh in Macedon; Elder McCormack
      (5-1/3/44)
4213. Hicks, David B. m 11/8/25 Jane D. Brevier, both of Fayette, in Geneva;
      Rev. Axtell (3-11/16)
4214. Hicks, Elias, 81?, "the celebrated preacher of the Society of Friends",
      d 2/27/30 at his home in Jericho, L.I., NY (5-3/19)
4215. Hicks, Ellery m Marabe Wilcox, dau of Capt. William, in Palmyra; William
      A. McLean, Esq. (5-5/2/21)
4216. Hicks, Jabez (Deacon), 55, d in Bristol (3-12/6/15)
4217. Hicks, Jacob, 68, (a Rev. soldier) d 9/17/27 in Fayette (3-9/19)
4218. Hicks, John of Fayette m 1/2/29 Mary Greene of Saratoga in S (3-1/7)
4219. Hicks, Joseph m Emeline W. Hill in Lyons (3-1/27/30)
4220. Hicks, Joshua of Macedon m 2/3/31 Adeline Sterns of Gorham in G; Rev.
      Benedict (5-2/11)
4221. Hicks, Orrin of Palmyra m 3/30/42 Maria Pooley of Marion in M; Rev. S. T.
      Griswold (5-4/6)
4222. Hickson, James of Auburn m 12/27/21 Jane Nicholson, dau of Humphrey,
      of Mentz; Rev. Kelly (3-1/16/22)
4223. Higby, Esther, 71, wf of Sylvester, d 4/4/45 in Ellery (4-5/9)
4224. Higby, Hiram M. m 10/6/41 Polly Harris, both of Palmyra, in Geneva;
      M. Hogan, Esq. (5-10/27)
4225. Higby, Lucy (Mrs.), 16, d in Jamestown (4-3/31/41)
4226. Higby, Thomas B. of Chapinville, Ont. Co. m 4/14/42 Mary A. Rogers, dau
      of Shubael G. of Newark, NY, in N; Rev. Lee (5-4/20)
4227. Higday, George m 10/7/40 Lucy Ann Leach, both of Jamestown, in J; Rev.
      Chapin (4-10/14)
4228. Higday, Lucy, 17, wf of George and dau of Stephen Leach, d 3/26/41 in
      Jamestown (4-4/7)
4229. Higgins, _____, inf dau of Dr. John D., d in Bath (3-8/8/27)
4230. Higgins, Cecilia, 53, wf of Hon. David, late of Norwalk, Ohio and formerly
      of Bath, d 11/23/46 in Washington, D.C. (2-12/2)
4231. Higgins, Charles (Capt.) of Sodus m 8/14/29 Eliza Munson of Schenectady
      (formerly of Stockbridge, MA) in Schenectady (3-8/26 and 5-8/28).
      Married in Sodus; Rev. Mason (5-8/28)
4232. Higgins, Charles m 9/11/50 Loana Rice, dau of Seth, Esq., in Howard;
      Rev. N. Sawyer. All of Howard (2-9/18)
4233. Higgins, David, 42, d 4/4/27 in Auburn "leaving a wife and eight
      children" (3-4/11)
4234. Higgins, David C. (Dr.) m 8/7/31 Eliza Smith, an adopted dau of Russell
      Whipple, Esq., in Pulteneyville; Byron Green, Esq. All of Pulteney-
      ville (5-8/12)
4235. Higgins, Helen, 3, dau of James, d in Bath (3-8/1/27)
4236. Higgins, James of Buffalo m Experience Mack in Fredonia (3-12/28/25)
4237. Higgins, James G. m 5/6/35 Maria E. Burns in Bath; Rev. Higgins (2-5/13)
4238. Higgins, James G., Esq., 49, formerly of Bath, NY, d 4/24/40 in Ottawa,
      IL (surv by wf and 7 ch) (2-5/27)
4239. Higley, Hezekiah m Jerusha Clark in Geneseo (3-4/12/15)
4240. Hildreth, John of Boyle m 2/6/14 Susan Hildreth of Phelps in P; Joseph
      Hall, Esq. (3-2/9)
4241. Hildreth, Matthias B., Esq., 48, Attorney General of State of N.Y.
      d 7/11/12 in Johnstown (3-8/5)
4242. Hildreth, Shadrach m 4/28/36 Laura Culver, both of Palmyra, in
      Williamson; Rev. Wilson (5-4/29)
4243. Hildreth, William, Jr. m 11/21/32 Mary Ann Marvin, both of Vienna, in V;
      Rev. Strong (5-11/28)
4244. Hill, _____, s of Stephen, deceased, d 6/21/17 in Caledonia (3-7/9)
4245. Hill, _____ of Wayne Co. m 7/27/42 Mrs. Dillenbeck of Kennedyville in
      Avoca; Rev. J. Shults (2-8/3)
4246. Hill, Arnold m Betsey Brown in Belvidere (3-10/21/18)
4247. Hill, Benjamin (Dr.), 84, d 4/17/49 at the home of his son Ellsworth
      in Le Roy (1-5/1)
4248. Hill, Charles, 21, d in Waterloo (3-8/13/28)
4249. Hill, Charles of Hammondsport m 1/27/41 Eliza Robinson of Addison in A;
      A. F. Lyon, Esq. (2-2/10)
4250. Hill, Charles B. of Newark, NY m 6/3/42 Hester Ann Stiles of Port Gibson
      in P. G. (5-6/15)

110

4251. Hill, Charles D. of Chautauqua m 10/6/31 Marion Wheeler of Westfield
in W; Charles P. Young, Esq. (4-10/12)
4252. Hill, Cornelius, Jr. m 9/7/26 Sally Smith, both of Waterloo, in W
(3-9/20)
4253. Hill, Curtiss, 35, d in Galen (3-8/22/27)
4254. Hill, Eli of Palmyra m 7/4/41 Phebe L. Baker of Farmington in Macedon
Center; Durfee Osband, Esq. (5-7/7)
4255. Hill, Elijah, 50, m 8/5/21 Sophia Allen, 26, in Palmyra (5-8/8)
4256. Hill, Fanny, about 30, consort of Ira, Esq., d 11/7/30 in Macedon
("On the same day, and but a few moments after the death of the
mother, an infant daughter of Mr. Hill, aged 18 months") (5-11/12)
4257. Hill, Francis m Burissa Boynton, dau of Judge Boynton, in Ontario, NY
(3-3/12/28)
4258. Hill, George W. m 12/30/43 Margaret A. Sutton in Ontario, NY; Rev.
Manley. All of Ontario (5-1/10/44)
4259. Hill, Hannah, 22, dau of David, d 6/22/30 in Palmyra (5-7/2)
4260. Hill, Hepzibah, 44, wf of Elijah, d 3/7/19 in Palmyra (5-3/17 and 3-3/24)
4261. Hill, Ira m Fanny Gilbert in Palmyra (5-6/14/20)
4262. Hill, Isaac H. of Dryden, Tompkins Co., m 8/21/41 Elizabeth S. Moore of
Kennedyville in K; Rev. William Hosmer (2-9/1)
4263. Hill, James of the U. S. Army m 3/3/29 Amanda Doyle, "a Creek pupil of
the Institution" at the Ashbury Missionary Institution near Fort
Mitchell, Creek Nation; Rev. Hill (3-4/8)
4264. Hill, James, 26, s of Ephraim, d 2/6/31 in Manchester (5-3/11)
4265. Hill, Milton m Mary Bartlett in Palmyra (3-5/23/27)
4266. Hill, Olba m Ellet Gannet in Palmyra (3-12/10/17)
4267. Hill, Parley (Dr.) m 9/18/31 Mary Ann Stillman in Palmyra (5-9/27)
4268. Hill, Phillip, Jr. of Junius, Seneca Co., m 5/26/31 Barbary Snyder in
Lyons; William Voorheis, Esq. (5-6/10)
4269. Hill, Riley of Walworth m 4/20/37 "Miss R. Sherman" of East Palmyra in
E. P.; Rev. Jonathan Benson (5-4/28)
4270. Hill, William d 12/31/28 in Ontario, NY (5-1/9/29)
4271. Hiller, Samuel, 4, s of Richard, d 8/29/41 in Jamestown (4-9/2)
4272. Hillock, James m Nancy Landon in Ithaca (3-12/28/25)
4273. Hilton, William, 85, m Sally Barber, 50, in Benton (3-5/2/27)
4274. Himrod, Peter, merchant, m 8/8/13 Mabel McMath, dau of John, in Ovid;
Jared Sandford, Esq. All of Ovid (3-8/18)
4275. Himrod, William (Brig. Gen.) d 2/8/13 in Hector (3-2/17)
4276. Hickley, Charles D. m 2/11/35 Margaret Van Wagoner in Walworth (5-2/20)
4277. Hinckley, John G., clerk of Chautauqua Co., m 5/20/42 Mary Minott,
dau of James, Esq. of Fredonia, in F (4-6/9)
4278. Hinckley, Nathan of Hector m Palina (sic) Miller in Lodi (3-11/4/29)
4279. Hind, Henry m 5/3/21 Frances Tuthill, both of Decatursville (Reading)
in D; Rev. Chase (3-5/9)
4280. Hinde. See, possibly, Ninde.
4281. Hines, Paul of Clarkson m 6/4/40 Koziah Crandall of Palmyra in P;
Rev. A. H. Stowell (5-7/8)
4282. Hiney, Garrett Henry m 8/21/42 Sophia Ann O'Neil in Palmyra (5-8/24)
4283. Hinkley, Relief, 30, wf of James, d in Ontario, NY (5-8/1/21)
4284. Hinman, Anna, 54, wf of Harris, d 7/22/29 in Galen (3-8/5 and5-7/31)
4285. Hinman, Daniel Webster, 18 mo, s of Elihu and Calista, d 3/21/39 in
Palmyra (5-3/22)
4286. Hinman, Elihu m 6/30/31 Calista Inman (prob. at the Sulphur Springs
House) in Palmyra; Rev. B. H. Hickox. All of Palmyra (5-7/8)
4287. Hinman, Elijah S., Esq., formerly a member of the state assembly, d in
Catherine, Tioga Co. (3-4/4/27)
4288. Hinman, John E. Esq. of Utica, late sheriff of Oneida Co., m Mary
Scroppel, oldest dau of G. C., Esq. of NYC, in NYC (3-12/26/27)
4289. Hinsdale, Morris, 43, d 2/2/49 at the home of his father (not named)
in Le Roy (1-2/13)
4290. Hippel, George, 26, late of Perry Co., PA, d 2/25/29 in Geneva, NY
(3-3/4)
4291. Hiscock, William H. of Branchport, Yates Co., m 3/14/41 HelenA. Selden
of Cameron in C; H. K. Ketcham, Esq. (2-3/17)
4292. Hitchcock, Amasa of Chautauqua m 1/12/43 Mrs. Mary Ann Worth of Harmony
in H; M. Norton, Esq. (4-1/19)

4293. Hitchcock, Augustus m 9/20/24 JaneAnn Van Buskirk, both of Penn Yan, in Geneva; Rev. Dr. Axtell (3-9/22)
4294. Hitchcock, Luke R. of Canadice, Alleg. Co. m 5/6/46 Susan Ann Gregory, dau of Burr, Esq. of Bath, in B; Rev. E. B. Fuller (2-5/13)
4295. Hitchcock, Samuel, Esq. of Poland, NY d in Cincinnati (4-6/19/33)
4296. Hix, Amos, 36, m 2/17/20 Phebe Schoat, 18, in Farmington (3-3/29 and 5-3/8)
4297. Hoag, Amos, 67, d 3/6/42 in Harmony (4-3/24)
4298. Hoag, Hiram m 10/22/40 Sally Ann Wyman in Macedon, J. McLouth, Esq. (5-10/28)
4299. Hoag, James S. m 11/2/37 Judith Mead of Macedon (See also the marriage of Thomas W. Mead, 11/1/37) (5-11/8)
4300. Hoagland, Abraham , 15, d in Owego (3-9/19/27)
4301. Hoar, Emogene, 11 mo, youngest dau of Leonard and Abby, d 3/4/42 in Busti (4-3/10)
4302. Hobart, _____ (Rt. Rev. - Bishop), 58, d in Auburn (4-9/22/30). See 4304.
4303. Hobart, David m 2/18/16 Mary Williams in Pulteney, Steuben Co. (3-2/28)
4304. Hobart, John Henry, the Right Rev., d 9/12/30 in Auburn ("He ... left a spotless name to his children") (5-9/17). See 4302.
4305. Hobs, Alfred m Polly Hutchinson in Phelps (3-3/6/16)
4306. Hobson, Darius (Col.) of the U. S. Army m Choe (sic) Pi Mackawis, or the Jumping Rabbit, "a belle of the Chickasaw tribe," in Montsville, AL (3-12/23/29)
4307. Hobstrom, Peter m 11/13/30 Polly Hults in Lyons; William Voorhies, Esq. (5-11/26)
4308. Hochstrasser, P., Esq. m Mrs. Olive Sherman of Utica in Troy (3-5/16/27)
4309. Hodges, Allen, about 36, wf of Z, d 2/8/23 in Ontario, NY (5-2/19)
4310. Hodges, Lyman m 9/2/32 Sally Sprague, both of Walworth, in Penfield; Rev. Robert Andrew (5-9/26)
4311. Hodgman, L. D. m 8/5/45 Abigail C. Cook, dau of Constant, Esq., in Bath (2-8/6)
4312. Hoeffer, Christoph Neun, 60, of Ludwigsburg, Suabia, Germany ("after a courtship of six hours") m "the blooming Miss Betsey Marrs, 76," in NYC (3-9/13/09)
4313. Hoff, David D. (Dr.) of Palmyra m 5/19/33 Julia May, dau of E. , Esq. of Westminster, VT in W; Rev. Sylvester Sage (5-5/29)
4314. Hoffman, Chauncey, M.D., 52, late of Chenango Co., NY, d 9/27/47 at his home in Young Hickory, Will Co., IL (2-10/27)
4315. Hoffman, John S. m 2/3/42 Lydia Logan, formerly of Bath, in Elmira; Rev. Spaulding (2-2/16)
4316. Hoffman, Michael, Esq., attorney, of Waterloo m Magdalen Abramse in Herkimer (3-6/12/22)
4317. Hogan, William (Rev.), late pastor of St. Mary's Church in Philadelphia, m Mrs. McKay of Wilmington, NC in W (3-9/15/24)
4318. Hogarth, _____, child of Richard, d 12/28/16 in Geneva (3-1/1/17)
4319. Hogarth, _____, 2 weeks, inf dau of Richard, Esq., d 7/14/23 (prob. in Geneva) (3-7/16)
4320. Hogarth, _____, inf s of John S., d 11/23/24 in Geneva (3-12/1)
4321. Hogarth, John, father of Richard of Geneva, d 11/25/17 in Ovid (3-12/3)
4322. Hogarth, John S. m 8/21/23 Mary Jane Shethar in Geneva; Rev. Orin Clark. All of Geneva (3-8/27)
4323. Hogarth, Richard, 82, "a native of the county of Down, Ireland and grandfather of the Messrs Hogarth of Geneva", d 8/16/19 in Geneva (3-8/18)
4324. Hogeland, Jacob m 7/2/50 Mrs. Harriet Parsons in Prattsburgh; Rev. B. C. Smith (2-7/10)
4325. Hogonin, Hiram of Oswego m 10/27/30 Jane E. Bostwick, dau of late William, in Auburn (5-11/12)
4326. Hoisington, H. E. of Darien m 4/16/46 Priscilla Peck of Alexander in Stafford; Rev. A. P. Ripley (a double ceremony - see marriage of L. L. Lincoln)
4327. Holbrook, Freeman, Esq., 58, d 7/30/43 in Waterloo ("Printers in Worcester, Mass. and Brattleboro, Vt. please copy") (4-8/3)
4328. Holbrook, Isaac, 27, d 2/22/25 in Geneva (3-3/2)
4329. Holbrook, Josiah, merchant, of Panama, NY, m 1/26/35 Cynthia F. Barnes of Ashville in A; Rev. J. S. Emery (4-1/28)

4330. Holbrook, Josiah, 37, d 4/7/39 in Panama, NY (4-4/10)
4331. Holbrook, Levi, 82, d 11/18/49 in Byron (1-11/20)
4332. Holbrook, Ora Lealord of Buffalo m 7/15/45 Louisa M. Guernsey of
       Ellinton in E; Rev. William Waithe (4-7/18)
4333. Holbrook, Selinda, 39, wf of George B., d 11/17/31 in Mayville (4-11/23)
4334. Holden, _____, 2 weeks, inf dau of Marvin, d in Elmira (3-8/26/29)
4335. Holden, A. E., inf s of Marvin, d in Elmira (3-9/17/28)
4336. Holden, Caroline L., 20, wf of Marvin, d in Elmira (3-9/2/29)
4337. Holden, Delia I., 7 yrs, youngest dau of Samuel C. and Delia, d 6/4/49
       in Batavia (1-6/19)
4338. Holden, Giles H. m Susannah Bennett in Perinton; Rev. J. Irons (5-11/28/17)
4339. Holden, Levi, 69, (a Rev. officer) d 4/19/23 in Newark, NJ (a member of
       "George Washington's military family") (3-5/7)
4340. Holdenburg, Justus m 12/12/16 Jane McDowell; Eli Bannister, Esq.
       (3-12/18/16)
4341. Holladay, Lazarus Hammond, 2 yrs, s of E. G., Esq.,d 7/22/35 in
       Hammondsport (2-7/29)
4342. Hollarday, Stephen m Betsey Wilkalaw in Benton (3-10/10/27)
4343. Hollett, Amelia, 18, dau of Mr. Peregrine of Bethel (Gorham),d 4/23/20
       in Geneva (Her funeral from the home of Mrs. Naglee) (3-4/24)
4344. Hollett, Joseph I. m 2/17/31 Sarah Fairbanks, dau of Rev. Ira, in
       Rushville; Rev. Denison Smith (5-3/11)
4345. Holley, _____, inf s of Myron, Esq.,d 7/27/15 in Canandaigua (3-8/2)
4346. Holley, John M., Esq. of Lyons m Mary Kirkland, dau of Gen. Kirkland,
       in Utica (3-6/13/27)
4347. Holley, Noah m Delilah Cain in Elmira (3-1/9/28)
4348. Holliday, Amos m Amanda Fisher; T. S. Bly, Esq. (4-1/23/33)
4349. Holliday, Eliza, 40, wf of Harvey, d 4/12/41 in Cameron (member of
       Bapt. Ch.; surv by husband and 6 ch) (2-4/21)
4350. Holliday, James m Parmelia Bigelow in Farmington (5-1/22/23)
4351. Holling, James m 12/31/29 Rachel Throop in Pulteneyville; Rev. Hubbard
       (3-1/6/30 and 5-1/1/30)
4352. Holling, William L. of Palmyra m 10/14/28 Mary Galloway of Marion in
       M (3-10/22 and 5-10/17)
4353. Hollingshead, Jane (Mrs.), 40, d 10/2/24 in Geneva (3-10/13)
4354. Hollister, Charlotte, 21, wf of H. R., d 2/18/48 in Winchester, Scott
       Co., IL (1-3/21)
4355. Hollister, David, 68, formerly from Delhi, NY, d 7/27/43 in Harmony
       (a Rev. soldier) (4-8/3)
4356. Hollister, Henry of Rutledge m 1/7/41 Maria Rice of Ellington; Rev.
       Waith (4-2/10)
4357. Hollister, Solomon D. m 1/3/38 Phebe Smith, dau of D. K., Esq, in
       Ballston, Sara. Co.; Rev. Davis. All of Ballston (5-1/10)
4358. Holly, Solomon S. m Amanda Baker in Barrington (3-10/17/27)
4359. Holman, Candace, 34, wf of Sanford, d 10/18/32 in Jamestown (4-10/24)
4360. Holman, Mary Jane, 1 yr, only ch of Sullivan Holman d 10/26/28 in Lyons
       (3-11/5)
4361. Holman, Sanford m 2/22/35 Melinda Flint in Jamestown ; Rev. M. Stedman
       (4-2/25)
4362. Holmes, Asa d 11/27/25 in Mulo (3-12/12)
4363. Holmes, Gibson m 10/13/20 Rebecca Gilky in Lyons (5-11/15)
4364. Holmes, Henry G. m Catharine Yawe of Ontario, NY in Wheeler (3-12/23/29)
4365. Holmes, Isaac T m 5/26/22 Lucina Robinson in Farmington (5-5/29)
4366. Holmes, Nathaniel T. m _____ Robinson, both of Palmyra, in P (3-6/3/12)
4367. Holmes, Phillip M. d 12/24/14 in Geneva ("a young man ... left an aged
       father and an affectionate wife) (3-12/28)
4368. Holmes, Polly, wf of Reuben, d 9/16/18 in Ontario, NY (3-10/7 and
       5-9/29)
4369. Holmes, Robert m 1/15/29 Amanda Durfee in Palmya; Rev. Chamberlain.
       All of Palmyra (5-1/16). Marriage performed in Lyons, NY (3-1/21)
4370. Holmes, Samuel S. m 3/10/26 Lorinda Ensign in Stafford; Rev. S. Ensign
       (1-3/10)
4371. Holmes, William F., merchant, of Lyons m 11/28/30 Jane Pierce, oldest
       dau of Dr. Jeremiah B. of Galen, in G; Rev. Hubbell (5-12/3)
4372. Holms Harvey of Tompkins Co. m 2/14/49 Sarah Willour of Bath in B;
       Rev. William Rutherford (2-2/28)

113

4373. Holt, Andrew m 7/13/12 Phebe Swan in Phelps; Rev. Axtell (3-7/15)
4374. Holt, David P. m 11/25/24 Sally M. Huntington; Rev. C. Colton (1-11/26)
4375. Holton, Elisha of Bath m 11/30/50 Mary A. Wright of Grafton, VT in Geneva, NY; Rev. Abel Haskell (2-12/4)
4376. Homan, Daniel m 12/31/29 Sally Avery in Phelps (3-1/13/30 and 5-1/8/30)
4377. Hone, Philip I., 30, d in NYC (3-2/25/18)
4378. Hone, Philip S., 32, d in NYC (3-7/1/18)
4379. Hood, Benjamin of Geneva m 3/28/22 Elizabeth Dubois of Fayette in F; Rev. Axtell (3-4/10)
4380. Hood, Mary, 1 yr, dau of Benjamin, d 9/17/27 in Geneva (3-9/19)
4381. Hoofslater, John m Mary Forbs in Fayette (3-4/1/29)
4382. Hooker, Alfred, merchant, of Prescott, Upper Canada m 7/14/28 Elvira Warner, dau of Maj. Solomon, deceased, in Geneva; Rev. Dr. Axtell (3-7/16)
4383. Hooker, Charlotte, 16, dau of Maj. Hooker, d 9/20/25 in Stafford (1-9/23)
4384. Hooker, Mary Ann (Miss), 15, d 2/25/34 in Vienna, NY (5-3/7)
4385. Hooper, Clarissa, wf of Robert, d 7/27/29 in Seneca (3-7/29)
4386. Hoops, Robert (Maj.), 56, d in Olean (3-9/2/18)
4387. Hoover, Henry d 2/22/13 in Romulus (3-3/3)
4388. Hopkins, Abigail, 71, wf of Elias, Esq., d 9/19/31 in Bath (2-9/21)
4389. Hopkins, Asa Theodore (Rev.) m 2/4/29 Elizabeth Wisner, oldest dau of Asa of Ithaca, in I (3-2/11)
4390. Hopkins, Caleb (Col.), 47, d 1/14/18 in Pittsford (3-2/11)
4391. Hopkins, Caleb, 65, d 7/19/24 at his home in Angelica, Alleg. Co. ("an Episcopalian lately from Pennsylvania") (3-8/25)
4392. Hopkins, Edmund m 8/10/29 Elizabeth Ann Potter, dau of Nathaniel J., in Palmyra; Rev. Pomeroy (5-8/28). Bride is Elizabeth Ann Porter in 5-8/14.
4393. Hopkins, Edward H. of Bath m 5/4/41 Therese Foster of Hammondsport in H; D. Henderson, Esq. (2-5/5)
4394. Hopkins, Elisha m 9/27/23 Jane Aikenhead, dau of Robert, in Lyons (3-10/22)
4395. Hopkins, Elisha G. m Arazetta Skinner in Prattsburgh (3-9/17/17)
4396. Hopkin s, Ezekiel of Cambridge, 80, m "lately" Nancy Davis, 54, of Geneva in G ("The bridegroom was introduced to his bride for the first time about two o'clock of that day, courted and obtained her consent in an hour, entered into an article of agreement, had it ratified, got out License, procured a clergyman, witnesses, etc. and the couple were safely moored in ... conjugal felicity by the hour of four") (3-7/28/13)
4397. Hopkins, Francis m 5/22/26 Eliza Noble in Batavia; C. Carpenter, Esq. (1-5/26)
4398. Hopkins, Gurdon of Mansfield, Catt. Co. m 11/18/42 Caroline Woodford of Mansfield in Jamestown; G. W. Parker, Esq. (4-11/24)
4399. Hopkins, John C. m 1/23/49 Laura B. Butler in Avoca; Rev. H. Spencer (2-1/31)
4400. Hopkins, Joseph of Manchester m 3/15/31 Pamelia Nichols of Pulteneyville; Elder M. Allen (5-3/25)
4401. Hopkins, Joseph E. m 4/1/33 Abigail Swift; Rev. Gillet (4-4/3)
4402. Hopkins, Roswell (Hon.), 73, of Hopkinton, St. Law. Co. d in Chazy (3-9/23/29)
4403. Hopkins, Samuel, Esq., 69, d 3/19/18 in Mount Morris (3-4/15)
4404. Hopkins, Samuel M. (Hon.), a distinguished member of the N.Y. Bar, died (date and death place not given) (formerly a congressman and a state senator) (4-10/18/37)
4405. Hopkins, Stephen m Sally Kent in Palmyra (5-4/21/18)
4406. Hopkinson, George m 5/11/31 Mariah Howell in East Palmyra (5-5/13)
4407. Hornby, J. D. m 10/20/43 Sarah Beaching in Palmyra; Rev. D. Herrington. All of P. (5-10/25)
4408. Hornel, George m 3/17/13 Sally Thatcher in Canisteo; Rev. Hubbard. All of Canisteo (3-3/24)
4409. Hornell, William D., 20, member of Williams College and son of George, Esq. of Canisteo, NY, drowned 5/26/10 at Deerfield, MA (3-6/13)
4410. Horth, Daniel W. m 11/17/42 Mary E. Jackson in Harmony; Rev. Cross (4-12/1)

114

4411. Horton, Allen W., Esq. of Palmyra m 10/21/41 Catherine Knapp, dau of
        Elias, Esq., of Walworth in W; Rev. Mandeville (5-10/27)
4412. Horton, Amy, wf of Nathan, d 4/1/34 in Port Gibson, Ont. Co. (5-4/4)
4413. Horton, Asenath, wf of Eliah (sic), d 2/17/20 in Geneva (3-3/1)
4414. Horton, Barnabas, 76, d 11/3/19 in Palmyra (3-11/17 and 5-11/10)
4415. Horton, Francis, 26, d 6/30/29 in Palmyra (3-7/15 and 5-7/10)
4416. Horton, Franklin m 7/11/41 Betsey Ann Lane, both of Palmyra, at the
        Methodist Chapel in Palmyra; Rev. Bennett (5-7/14)
4417. Horton, James G. of Palmyra m 1/19/32 Mariah Horton of NYC (5-1/31)
4418. Horton, James P. m 2/17/29 Caroline M. Goldsmith; Rev. Campbell. All
        of Palmyra (5-2/20)
4419. Horton, Joseph, about 67, d 7/10/31 in Marion (5-7/15)
4420. Horton, Maria, 23, dau of Samuel T., d 5/28/43 (5-5/31)
4421. Horton, Permelia, 16, dau of Joseph, d 10/7/18 in Palmyra (5-10/13)
4422. Horton, Samuel m Polly Galloway, both of Palmyra, in P (3-6/3/12)
4423. Hortsen, Charles, about 4, s of Dr. William, d 8/19/11 in Phelps
        (3-8/28)
4424. Hortsen, Sarah, 3 yrs, dau of Dr. William, d 9/15/16 (prob. in Geneva)
        (3-9/18)
4425. Hosford, Ashbel, 62, d 3/9/30 in Lyons (5-3/10)
4426. Hosford, E., printer and bookseller, m Eliza Johnston in Albany
        (3-7/28/13)
4427. Hosford, Elisha, of the late firm of E. and E. Hosford, printers and
        booksellers, d 7/28/28 in Albany (3-8/13)
4428. Hosford, Roger, 63, d 8/15/18 in Charlotte, VT (3-10/14)
4429. Hoskins, Samuel Hoskins of Pinegrove, PA m 10/24/44 Corissande P.
        Powell of Jamestown in J; Rev. E. J. Gillett (4-11/1)
4430. Hoskins, Sophia, 26, wf of Charles, Esq., d in Fayette (3-10/1/28)
4431. Hosmer, Aaron, Jr. m 11/16/43 Catherine Sockman, both of Newark, NY,
        in Palmyra; Rev. D. K. Lee (5-11/29)
4432. Hosmer, George, Esq., attorney, m 8/29/11 Mrs. Elizabeth Ellsworth in
        Avon (3-9/11)
4433. Hosmer, Marvin m Mary Parker in Howard (3-1/9/28)
4434. Hosmer, Timothy (Hon.), 70, formerly First Judge of Ontario Co.,
        d 11/23/15 in Avon (3-12/20)
4435. Hossey, William T. d 9/12/31 in Palmyra (5-9/13)
4436. Hostater, Polly, wf of Adam, d 10/15/22 in Fayette (3-11/13)
4437. Hotchkin, Beriah B., editor of the Le Roy Gazette, m Elizabeth A. Fitch
        of West Bloomfield in Buffalo; Rev. Crawford (3-6/13/27)
4438. Hotchkin, Evelyn S., wf of John D., d 2/4/45 in Prattsburgh (2-2/12)
4439. Hotchkin, James H., merchant, m Nancy Elizabeth Jackson, dau of Dr. Z. S.,
        in Prattsburgh (3-7/15/29)
4440. Hotchkin, William H. m 2/27/41 Ann Eliza Perkins, both of Pulteney, in P;
        Rev. James H. Hotchkin (2-3/10)
4441. Hotchkiss, Daniel m Rosannah Turner in Sheldon, Gen. Co. (5-12/12/32)
4442. Hotchkiss, Fordyce m 1/1/41 Eliza Coussen, both of Ellington; Rev. Waith
        (4-2/10)
4443. Hotchkiss, Henry F. m 4/18/43 Maria R. Scovell, dau of Seymour, Esq.,
        in Lewiston; Rev. Murray (5-4/26)
4444. Hotchkiss, Leman (Maj.) of the late firm of Hotchkiss and McNeil
        d 12/31/26 in Vienna (Phelps), NY (3-1/5)
4445. Hotchkiss, Marshall of Wayne m 5/6/32 Maria French of Bath in B; H. W.
        Rogers, Esq. (2-5/9)
4446. Hotchkiss, Polly (Mrs.), 25, wf of Archibald, formerly of Batavia,
        d 2/6/24 in Rochester (1-2/20)
4447. Hotchkiss, Ralph N., 10, only ch of David, d 11/23/36 in Palmyra
        (5-11/25/36)
4448. Hotenbeck, Samuel m 10/17/24 Ann Jolly, both of Fayette, in Vienna, NY
        (3-11/1)
4449. Hotlet, Richard, 3 yrs, s of Mr. Peregrine Hotlet, d 8/15/15 in Geneva
        (3-8/23)
4450. Houck, Abel of Bath m 2/25/47 Angeline Disbrow of Tyrone in T; John
        Chambers, Esq. (2-3/3)
4451. Hough, Daniel m 2/28/22 Elisabeth Lever in Seneca; Rev. H. Axtell (3-3/13)
4452. Hough, Norman of Jamestown m 3/25/45 Mary Smith of Gerry in G; Rev. O.
        Street (4-3/28)

4453. Hough, Richard m 12/31/29 Matilda Plumley in Lyons (5-1/8/30 and 3-1/13)
4454. Houghtaling, Ira m 7/10/42 Jane Sweeny in Bath; William Mulhollon, Esq.
    (2-7/13)
4455. Houghteling, Aaron m 3/8/32 Mary Libbey in Bath; H. W. Rogers, Esq.
    (2-3/14)
4456. Houghteling, Mary Matilda, 16, oldest dau of Dr. James late of Geneva,
    d 5/12/24 in Romulus (3-5/19)
4457. Houghton, Alfred, formerly a teacher in the Select School in Geneva,
    d in Baton Rouge (3-11/4/29)
4458. Houghton, Alured, late Professor in the Baton Rouge Academy died
    (place and date not given - copied from the Baton Rouge (LA) Gazette
    dated 10/3/29) (3-12/9/29)
4459. Houghton, Calista (Mrs.), 23, wf of Nehemiah, Esq., d 4/25/25 in Oak
    Orchard (1-5/6)
4460. Houghton, Sheaver, 87, d 2/8/42 in Palmyra (a Rev. pensioner) (5-2/16)
4461. House, Spencer G. m 5/29/43 Elizabeth Brown; Rev. Clark (5-5/31)
4462. Hover, David of Tyrone m 2/22/35 Sarah Emery of Bristol, CT in Tyrone;
    Rev. Van Rensselaer Wall of Jersey (2-2/25)
4463. Hovey, Arnold m 2/7/39 Deborah Ann Palmer in Alabama, NY; John Crombie,
    Esq.. All of Alabama (1-2/14)
4464. Hovey, Betsy, 8 yrs, d 2/11/46 in Bath (2-2/18)
4465. Hovey, Gershom m 3/22/45 Julia Ann Carter in Panama, NY; Rev.P. H. Pero
    (4-4/4)
4466. How, _____, inf ch of John d 1/19/32 in Bath (2-1/25)
4467. How, Jacob m Candes Adams; Elisha Slocum, Esq. (5-11/28/17)
4468. Howard, _____ m Ellen Duncan in Benton (3-2/19/17)
4469. Howard, Charles m Lydia Page in Owego (3-1/21/29)
4470. Howard, Elizabeth, about 45, consort of Capt. Thomas, d 9/17/10 in
    Benton (3-9/26)
4471. Howard, Hayden N. m 6/9/47 L. Louise Bailey, dau of Erastus, Esq.; Rev.
    G. Crawford. All of Le Roy (1-6/22)
4472. Howard, Henry m 4/3/27 Catharine Henry in Geneseo (3-4/25)
4473. Howard, Hiram of Columbus, PA m Meranda Lucas of Clymer at the Farmers'
    Hotel in Jamestown; Solomon Jones, Esq. (4-9/12/45)
4474. Howard, Isaac m Mrs. Susannah Thompson in Romulus (3-6/17/29)
4475. Howard, Jacob A., merchant, of NYC m 6/6/33 Jane A. Norman of Hudson
    in H; Rev. Andrews (5-7/3)
4476. Howard, John L., 27, d at the Auburn Theological Seminary (5-7/2/30)
4477. Howard, Lewis (Capt.) of the U. S. Artillery d 1/13/11 on the island
    of Michillimackanac (3-5/1)
4478. Howard, Maria Louisa, 15, d 1/11 in Lyons (5-1/24/32)
4479. Howard, Martin of Bloomfield m Laura Morley in Canandaigua (3-12/20/15)
4480. Howard, William m 6/15/19 Hannah Haight in Hopeton; E. Spencer, Esq.
    All of Benton (3-6/30)
4481. Howard, William m 7/21/36 Lucy Ann Phelps; F. Smith, Esq. All of
    Palmyra (5-7/22)
4482. Howe, Count William m 5/30/23 Emiline Waggoner in Penn Yan; A. Waggoner,
    Esq. (3-6/11)
4483. Howe, Elsey (Miss), about 17, d 9/22/17 in Geneva (3-9/24)
4484. Howe, Isaac N. m 1/8/26 Nancy Gould in Elba (a double ceremony - see
    marriage of Isaac Gould) (1-1/13)
4485. Howe, Samuel, Esq., 76, d 1/24/22 in Trenton, Oneida Co. ("Printers in
    New Haven, Conn. and in the Western Division will confer a favor by
    publishing the above") (3-2/13)
4486. Howe, Thomas of Phelps m 1/1/10 Anne Bigelow, dau of Capt. Bigelow of
    Junius, in J (3-1/17)
4487. Howell, _____, inf ch of William, Esq., d 7/29/42 in Bath (2-8/31)
4488. Howell, Charles, 35, d 2/19/32 at his home (prob. in Bath) (2-2/22)
4489. Howell, Cynthia, 53, wf of Col. Gilbert Howell, d 2/15/31 in Ridgeway
    (surv by husband and one son) (5-2/25)
4490. Howell, David W. m 1/4/49 Eliza Elmer, dau of William, in Bergen;
    Samuel Richmond, Esq. All of Bergen (1-1/23)
4491. Howell, Edward m Mrs. Hannah Stout in Bath; Rev. Higgins (3-8/6/17)
4492. Howell, Edward, Jr. m 9/18/50 Mary L. Gansevoort, dau of John, in
    Bath; Rev. L. M. Miller (2-9/25)

116

4493. Howell, Epanetus m 12/22/30 "Miss Soper" in Palmyra; Rev. A. E. Campbell (5-12/24)
4494. Howell, Fanny, 61, wf of Hon. Nathaniel W., d 2/9/42 in Canandaigua (5-2/23)
4495. Howell, Horace of Bath m Caroline Carpenter, dau of Gen. M., in Newtown (3-5/16/21)
4496. Howell, James, about 30, s of late Isaac, d 12/10/32 in Palmyra (5-12/12)
4497. Howell, Jonah, 32, d 2/15/35 in Palmyra (5-2/20)
4498. Howell, Lorenzo, 20 mo, s of Hugh, d 6/2/22 in Lyons (3-6/12)
4499. Howell, Margaret Ann (Miss), 23, d 5/27/40 in Palmyra (5-6/3)
4500. Howell, P. R. m 10/12/37 Alinda Drake in Palmyra; Rev. S. W. Wooster. All of Palmyra (5-10/18)
4501. Howell, William, s of Charles, d in Bath (3-8/29/27)
4502. Howell, William, Esq. of Bath m 4/29/35 Frances Adelphia Adams of West Avon in W. A.; Rev. Kearney (2-5/13)
4503. Howell, William T. m Sophia Brink in Almond (3-6/18/28)
4504. Howes, Benjamin of Phelps m 2/4/16 Esther Whitney, dau of Capt. Joel, in Seneca; Rev. Axtell (3-2/14)
4505. Howes, Rachel, 57, consort of Benjamin, d in Phelps (3-4/12/15)
4506. Howes, William, formerly preceptor of Canandaigua Academy, d in Livonia (3-4/24/16)
4507. Howland, Betsey, 12, dau of Benjamin, of Wolcott d 11/5/17 in Junius (3-11/12)
4508. Howland, George m _____ Robinson in Farmington (5-1/13/19)
4509. Howland, George of Seneca m 12/16/29 Matilda Scott, dau of Capt. Scott, in Phelps; Rev. Strong (3-12/23)
4510. Howland, Hilliard m May Young in Ithaca (3-5/16/27)
4511. Howland, Job m Dolly Fish in Farmington (3-3/10/19 and 5-3/3/19)
4512. Hoxter, Thomas d 2/19/13 in Fayette (3-3/3)
4513. Hoylazts, William of the house of Borrekens and Co. m 5/31/10 Eliza Fitzhugh, dau of Peregrine, Esq. of Troupville, in T; Rev. Phelps of Geneva (3-6/6)
4514. Hoyt, Ard (Rev.), missionary of the American Board of Foreign Missions, d 2/8/28 at Wiltstown, Cherokee Nation (3-4/30)
4515. Hoyt, David P. d in Utica (1-6/18/28)
4516. Hoyt, E. W., Esq. of Little Fort, IL m 6/25/46 Elizabeth Earl, dau of Judge Earl, in Attica; Rev. Cook (1-7/14)
4517. Hoyt, Franklin C. m Isabella Penton in Utica (3-1/14/29)
4518. Hoyt, George m Harriet Skinner in Williamson (See marriage of William Hoyt this issue date) (5-2/25/18)
4519. Hoyt, Isaac Chauncy, 21, s of Minot and Sarah, d 3/21/43 in Ellery (4-4/6)
4520. Hoyt, Robert H. (Dr.) m Mary Easterbrooks in Painted Post; Rev. D. Higgins (2-10/24/32)
4521. Hoyt, Sally, 29, wf of Joseph, d 2/22/42 in Ashville (4-3/3)
4522. Hoyt, Sarah Ann Harrison, 23, wf of Dr. Hoyt, d 2/28/32 in Painted Post (2-3/7)
4523. Hoyt, Timothy m 3/8/24 Sophronia Hammon in Elba (1-3/12)
4524. Hoyt, William m Nancy Harding in Williamson (See marriage of George Hoyt this issue date) (5-2/25/18)
4525. Hoyt, William C. of Coventry, Chen. Co. m 10/1/46 Emeline S. Gilmore of Bath in B; Rev. L. M. Miller (2-10/7)
4526. Hoyt, William H., 26, s of Dr. R. H. of Painted Post, d 5/6/45 in NYC (2-5/21)
4527. Hoyt, William May, 4, s of Dr. D. D., d 2/4/40 of scarlet fever (5-2/5)
4528. Hoyte, Nathan, 92, (a Rev. soldier) d 5/6/48 in Elba (member of Meth. Ch.) (1-5/23)
4529. Hubbard, Eli m 1/12/26 Sophrona Noble in Batavia; D. Tisdale, Esq. (1-1/13)
4530. Hubbard, Alfred m 4/18/37 Lydia P. Shove; Rev. H. K. Ware. All of Palmyra (5-4/21)
4531. Hubbard, Austin m 10/11/38 Laura Chapin in Prattsburg; Rev. Pratt (2-10/17)
4532. Hubbard, Charles of Penn Yan m 7/4/42 Lucy Lamb of Bradford at the Clinton House in Bath; Rev. D. B. Lawton (2-7/6)
4533. Hubbard, Eli, 29, d 8/5/22 in Galen (3-8/21)

4534. Hubbard, Emeline (Miss), 30, dau of Capt. Josiah, d 5/2/38 in Harmony
(surv by father, mother, brothers, and sisters) (4-5/9)
4535. Hubbard, Henry of Penn Yan m 9/7/26 Mary Brooks of Hopewell in H
(3-9/20)
4536. Hubbard, Hiram of Canandaigua m Ruth Corser in Gates, Monroe Co.
(3-3/11/29)
4537. Hubbard, Israel m "within a few days" Polly Card in Snell (3-11/1/09)
4538. Hubbard, James W. m 9/10/45 Angeline Felch in Panama, NY; Rev. A. D.
Olds (4-9/19)
4539. Hubbard, John (Dr.), 92, d 12/5/49 in Batavia (assistant surgeon
during the Rev. War; a Rev. pensioner) (1-1/29/50)
4540. Hubbard, John L. m 12/12/22 Sarah Boothe in Waterloo; Rev. Lane
(3-12/25)
4541. Hubbard, Maria, wf of Patrick, d in Junius (3-10/1/28)
4542. Hubbard, Noadiah. 82. d 8/1/32 in Palmyra (a Rev. pensioner) (5-8/15)
4543. Hubbell, ____, inf ch of Curtis, d in Waterloo (whooping cough)
(3-3/12/28)
4544. Hubbell, ____, inf ch of William S., Esq., d 9/2/31 (prob. in Bath)
(2-9/7)
4545. Hubbell, Harlow m 4/9/28 Almira C. Bailey, dau of Gen. Bailey, in
Hector; Rev. G. Laning. All of Hector (3-4/16)
4546. Hubbell, Jamima, 78, relict of late Nehemiah, of Painted Post d 5/28/42
in Bath (2-6/1)
4547. Hubbell, Levi, Esq., Adjutant General of N. Y. State, m 5/28/36 Susan
De Witt, dau of late Hon. Simeon, in Ithaca (5-6/3)
4548. Hubbell, Maria, about 5, dau of Rev. L., d 5/2/30 in Lyons (5-5/7)
4549. Hubbell, Nehemiah, 71, father of William S., Esq. of Bath, d 6/21/35
in Painted Post (2-6/24)
4550. Hubbell, Philo B., merchant, formerly of Painted Post, m Ann Eliza
Backus, late of Catskill, in Buffalo (3-7/30/28)
4551. Hubbell, Ransom, 36, formerly of Geneva and brother of Walter, Esq. of
Canandaigua, d in Oxford, NC (3-1/23/28)
4552. Hubbell, Sally, 58, wf of Dr. James, d 6/21/44 in East Palmyra (5-7/3)
4553. Hubberd, Pliny m Charity B. Curtiss in Gorham; Rev. W. Brace (3-5/9/21)
4554. Huchinson, John m 11/8/32 Anna Stoughton, both of Bethany; Rev. Jenkins
(1-11/29)
4555. Hudson, ____, inf s of David, Esq., d 12/1/16 in Geneva (3-12/4)
4556. Hudson, ____ (Mrs.), mother of David, Esq., d 9/12/25 "at an advanced
age" in Geneva (3-9/14)
4557. Hudson, ____, 1 yr, youngest ch of Henry, d 10/29/27 in Geneva (3-10/31)
4558. Hudson, C. W. m 9/13/49 Julia Ann Ellas in Bath; Rev. L. H. Corson.
All of Bath (2-9/26)
4559. Hudson, David, Esq. of Geneva m 1/14/16 Hester Dey in Fayette (a double
ceremony - see the marriage of Anthony Dey to Hannah Dey; Hester and
Hannah are both daughters of Peter of Fayette); Rev. Young (3-1/17)
4560. Hudson, David B., 6 mo, s of David, Esq., d 7/30/18 in Geneva (3-8/5)
4561. Hudson, Henry, 42, d 6/19/12 in Geneva (surv by wf and several small
children) (3-6/24)
4562. Hudson, John m 2/27/44 Arvilla Albro, both of Busti, in B; Rev. L. S. Morgan
(4-3/8)
4563. Hudson, Lemuel (Dr.) of Newtown, Tioga Co. m 9/6/18 Maria Woodruff, dau
of Rev. H. N., in Little Falls, Herk. Co.; Rev. H. N. Woodruff (3-9/16)
4564. Hudson, Pliny, Esq., 53, d in Arcadia (5-2/16/42)
4565. Hudson, William, merchant, of Geneva m 7/26/27 Mary Dorsey, youngest dau
of late Daniel, Esq. of Lyons, in L; Rev. Riley (3-8/8)
4566. Hudson, William Henry, 4 mo, s of David, Esq., d 11/9/19 in Geneva
(3-11/10)
4567. Huff, Augustus m 2/7/32 Elsie Lovisa Wiggins, both of Ellery, in
Ellicott; William H. Fenton, Esq. (4-2/15)
4568. Huff, Jacob, 58, d 3/7/19 in Romulus (3-3/31)
4569. Huff, Rozilla, 14, d 12/6/22 (prob.in Geneva) (3-12/11)
4570. Huffman, George m 1/19/16 Sally Kinyon in Phelps; Joseph Hall, Esq.
All of Phelps (3-1/24)
4571. Huffman, William, Esq. of Phelps m 12/22/29 Harriet Beals, dau of Isreal,
Esq. of Junius, in J; Rev. William Kent (3-12/30)
4572. Hughes, Harriet, 26, d in Bath (3-4/22/29)

4573. Hughes, Peter, Esq., 55, of Cayuga m 10/8/09 Naomi Gould, 21, in Canandaigua (3-10/25)
4574. Hughes, Peter (Maj.), 65, formerly clerk of Ontario Co., d 12/26/16 in Cayuga (3-1/8/17)
4575. Hughes, Stephen W., Esq., sheriff of Cayuga Co., d 7/19/26 in Auburn (3-8/2) (Died at age 33)
4576. Hughes, Thomas Pancous of Mud Creek m 7/12/38 Mary French of Bath in B; Rev. Wheeler (2-7/18)
4577. Hughs, John (Capt.), 68, d in Pennsylvania (a Rev. officer) (3-10/21/18)
4578. Huie, James m 5/7/29 Mary Ann Jackson in Seneca; Abraham A. Post, Esq. (3-5/13)
4579. Hulbert, Allen m Sylvia Richardson in Batavia (3-1/14/29)
4580. Hulbert, Charles d 12/24/28 in Waterloo (3-1/7/29)
4581. Hulbert, John T., 1 yr, s of Charles, d in Waterloo (3-8/29/27)
4582. Hulbert, John W., Esq., "celebrated member of the bar", d in Auburn (2-11/2/31)
       Hulett. See also Hewlett.
4583. Hulett, Arnold m 9/1/22 Nancy Tillotson, both of Byron; Stephen Griswold, Esq. (1-9/6)
4584. Hulett, John Hamilton, 42, d 3/8/11 (3-3/13)
4585. Hulett, Mary Ann, 79, relict of William C., d in NYC (3-9/9/18)
4586. Hull, _____, inf s of S. P., d 4/23/19 in Geneva (3-4/28)
4587. Hull, Elias (Capt.) m 9/10/11 Anna Riggs, dau of John, Esq., in Lyons; Hon. P. Swift. All of Lyons (3-9/18)
4588. Hull, Gilbert m 3/31/19 Abigail Harris in Palmyra; Rev. Irons (5-4/7)
4589. Hull, Hannah, 20, d 10/7/13 in Geneva (3-10/13)
4590. Hull, Henry H., editor of the Steuben Courier, m 8/15/50 Clara Williston, dau of Hon. Horace of Athens, in A; Rev. C. Thurston (2-8/21)
4591. Hull, James, editor of the Chautauqua Gazette, m Betsey Crosby in Fredonia (3-12/2/18)
4592. Hull, Jane Ann, 1 yr, dau of Capt. Elias, d 2/6/14 in Lyons (3-2/9)
4593. Hull, Luther m 10/23/50 Louisa E. Smith, both of Howard, in H; Rev. L. Rose (2-10/30)
4594. Hull, Nathan (Capt.), 37, d 7/6/44 in Newark, Wayne Co. (5-7/10)
4595. Hull, Seth m Esther Purdy in Gorham (3-9/15/19)
4596. Hull, William (Gen.), 72, d 11/29/25 in Newton, MA (was a field officer in the Rev. War) (1-12/9)
4597. Hulse, Elisha, 34, d in Canandaigua (3-1/14/18)
4598. Hulse, Ira m 9/27/40 Nancy Doolittle, both of Canandaigua; Rev. Isaac C. Goff (5-9/30)
4599. Hulse, Silas, 18, d in Canandaigua (3-1/14/18)
4600. Hulse, Smith of Starkey m Sophia Mapes of Aurora, Erie Co. in Milo (3-10/3/27)
4601. Humphrey, Friend, Esq. of Albany m Julia Ann Hoyt in Utica (3-11/16/25)
4602. Humphrey, Hannah (Miss), 19, dau of George of Phelps, d 6/10/18 in Newburgh (3-6/24)
4603. Humphrey, Hugh m 3/11/19 Phebe Wiggins in Phelps (3-3/24)
4604. Humphrey, James, 80, d 9/3/34 in Phelps (a Rev. soldier) (5-9/26)
4605. Humphrey, Luke, 40, d 9/4/31 in Elba (1-9/9)
4606. Humphrey, Nathaniel, 65, d 11/11/24 in Pembroke (1-11/26)
4607. Humphreys, Gad (Maj.) of the U. S. Army m Mary S. Larned (3-1/28/18)
4608. Hung____ (blurred), Levi d 9/3/18 in Ontario, NY (5-9/18)
4609. Hunn, John E. of Alexander m 5/6/46 Cornelia K. Churchill of Batavia in B; Rev. B. Sunderland (1-5/12)
4610. Hunn, John S., Esq., cashier of the Newburgh Bank, d "at an advanced age" in Newburgh (3-3/18/29)
4611. Hunn, Samuel C., 11 mo, only s of Samuel W. and Caroline, d 5/13/50 (prob. in Batavia) (1-5/14)
4612. Hunt, _____, 35, a pauper of Cohocton, d 5/12/32 in Bath (2-5/16)
4613. Hunt, Carlton m 7/17/43 Emily Messenger in Harmony; M. Norton , Esq. (4-8/3)
4614. Hunt, Erastus, (age 36, 56, or 86 - blurred) d 12/27/22 in Palmyra (formerly of Bloomfield) (5-1/1/23)
4615. Hunt, Ezekiel, 77, d 3/7/49 in Bath (2-3/14)
4616. Hunt, Joseph (Dr.), 63, d in Fayette (3-9/19/27)
4617. Hunt, Levina, 74, consort of late Ezekiel, d 6/22/49 in Bath (2-6/27)

119

4618. Hunt, Lucius of Coventry, CT m 4/19/41 Susan Morris of Palmyra in P; Rev. G. R. H. Shumway (5-4/21)
4619. Hunt, Lucius O., 24, d in Ithaca (3-5/23/27)
4620. Hunt, Mary (Mrs.), about 80, d 4/6/22 in Milo (3-4/17)
4621. Hunt, Russel m Rebecca Castner in Benton (3-2/19/17)
4622. Hunt, Solomon m Harriet Hopkins in Bath (3-12/9/18)
4623. Hunt, Thomas E., 21, formerly of Geneva, d 9/23/09 in Albany (3-10/11)
4624. Hunt, William m Polly Shadduck in Palmyra (3-12/10/17)
4625. Hunt, William m Nancy McNeil in Argyle, Wash. Co. (3-1/14/29)
4626. Hunter, Elnor, 30, wf of Dr. William, d 11/27/38 in Jasper (2-12/19)
4627. Hunter, Fanny, 5, dau of James and Catharine, d 3/19/49 in Bath (2-4/11)
4628. Hunter, George, Esq., 57, d 10/21/45 in Wayne (an early settler in Wayne; surv by wf "and a large family of children") (2-11/5)
4629. Hunter, Hannah, 56, d 11/17/47 in Bath (2-11/24)
4630. Hunter, James of Bath m 9/21/42 Catharine Velie of Elmira in E; Rev. Bullard (2-9/28)
4631. Hunter, Peter, 25, m Mrs. Meacham, 53 (3-3/15/15)
4632. Hunter, Samuel D., Esq. of the firm of Robie and Hunter m 10/1/46 Augusta A. Whipple, oldest dau of late Rev. P. L. Whipple, at St. Thomas Church in Bath; Rev. L. H. Corson (2-10/7)
4633. Hunter, Sarah F., 14, dau of Peter, Esq., d 4/9/42 in Bath (2-4/13)
4634. Huntington, Eliphalet, 73, d in West Bloomfield (3-10/22/28)
4635. Huntington, Elisha H. m 9/18/25 Phebe White in Geneva; Rev. Dr. Axtell (3-9/21)
4636. Huntington, George m Anna Neally in Bath (3-6/9/19)
4637. Huntington, George, Jr., 20, s of George, Sr. of Rome, NY, d 3/26/28 at the home of B. Wright, Esq. in NYC (buried in Albany) (3-4/2)
4638. Huntington, Jedediah (Gen.), 79, formerly collector at New London, CT, d in N. L. ("a highly disringuished Revolutionary officer") (5-10/20/18)
4639. Huntington, Samuel D. of Palmyra m 12/21/40 Philura Reeves of Arcadia in A; W. Wilcox, Esq. (5-12/23)
4640. Huntley, Elias S., bookbinder, formerly of Canandaigua, m Frances Tooker of Ithaca in Lansing (3-2/3/30)
4641. Hurd, Abner m 12/12/26 Sarah Reeder, dau of Josiah, in Starkey (3-12/27)
4642. Hurd, Betsey, 64, wf of Deacon Thomas, formerly of Litchfield Co., CT d 5/18/48 in Alexander (1-5/30)
4643. Hurd, Byram m Sarah Dey in Almond (3-6/6/27)
4644. Hurd, Gilbert (Gen.) of Lyndon, Whiteside Co., IL m 3/13/42 Sarah Benson of Starkey, Yates Co., dau of late Holbrook, Esq.; Rev. Samuel White (2-4/13)
4645. Hurd, Henry m 5/3/21 Frances Tuthill of Decatursville (Reading) in D(R); Rev. Chase (3-5/16)
4646. Hurd, Isaac Samuel, 11, s of Thomas, d in NJ (3-5/30/27)
4647. Hurd, J. M. m Harriet Barns in Ashville; Rev. Graves (4-5/23/38)
4648. Hurd, Jesse m 1/9/25 Eliza Perkins in Stafford; Oliver Campbell, Esq. (1-1/21)
4649. Hurd, Lovell m 1/15/32 Sally Ann Taber, dau of Capt. B. Taberof Manchester, at Zion Church in Palmyra; Rev. B. H. Hickox (5-1/17)
4650. Hurd, Phebe, wf of Philo, d in Romulus (3-9/26/27)
4651. Hurd, Philena, 63, wf of David H., d in Canandaigua (3-1/14/29)
4652. Hurd, Philo m Ann Vrose in Romulus (3-1/20/30)
4653. Hurd, Rebecca, 35, wf of Ransom, d 5/6/23 in Reading (3-5/14)
4654. Hurd, Rosette of Reading, Steuben Co. m 2/26/23 Abigail Lum of Geneva in G; Rev. Axtel (3-3/19)
4655. Hurd, Sally, 24, wf of Lovewell, d 1/24/29 in Palmyra (5-1/30)
4656. Hurd, Sally Ann, wf of Col. Lovell Hurd, formerly of Palmyra and dau of Capt. Benjamin Taber of Manchester, d 8/14/43 in Hoosick (5-10/11)
4657. Hurd, Zopher of Painted Post m 2/8/41 Elmira Marlatt of Troupsburgh in T; N. D. Ormsby, Esq. (2-3/17)
4658. Hurlburt, Aurelia P., 10, dau of Dr. G. H. Hurlburt, d in Seneca (3-3/31/19)
4659. Hurlburt, Eliza Jane, 1 yr, dau of Truman, d 10/29/45 in Batavia (1-11/4)
4660. Hurlburt, Jeremiah m Cynthia Harris in Palmyra (5-1/12/20)
4661. Hurlburt, John W. (Hon.) d 10/19/31 in Auburn (5-11/1)
4662. Hurlburt, Mary A., 17, d 5/2/38 in Palmyra (5-5/9)

4663. Hurlburt, Mercy, 56, wid of late Truman, d 7/13/42 in Batavia (1-7/19)
4664. Hurlburt, Silas m 9/16/49 Sophia Watkins, both of Cohocton, in C; Rev.
   A. Adams (2-9/19)
4665. Hurlbut, _____ (Rev.) of Natchez, Mississippi m 6/22/26 Jane Eliza Rees
   of Pulteneyville, NY in P (3-6/28)
4666. Hurlbut, Asahel, 57, d 8/23/45 in Le Roy (formerly of Williamstown, MA)
   (1-8/26)
4667. Hurlbut, Charles m 1/29/34 Margaret Gregory in Walworth (5-2/14)
4668. Hurlbut, J. (Capt.) d in Palmyra (3-2/3/13)
4669. Hurley, Miranda, about 37, wf of Samuel, d in Walworth (5-8/15/32)
4670. Husted, Charles m 3/24/25 Mahala Johnson in Batavia; Elder Roach
   (1-3/25)
4671. Husted, Henry m 1/28/34 Susan P. Williams, dau of Richard M., Esq.,
   in Potter, Yates Co.; Rev. Strong (5-1/31)
4672. Husted, John m 3/24/25 Esther Riley in Batavia; Elder Roach (1-3/25)
4673. Huston, James m 4/6/23 Amanda Springsted, both of Geneva, in G; Rev.
   Axtell (3-4/16)
4674. Huston, James, 1 yr, s of James, d 6/19 or 7/19 (blurred)/26 (prob. in
   Geneva (3-7/19)
4675. Hutch, Dexter, Esq. d in the town of Gerry (was postmaster in the village
   of Vermont in the town of Gerry) (4-1/16/28)
4676. Hutchins, George of Marion m 2/26/40 Amanda Philips of Arcadia in A;
   Samuel Moore, Esq. All of Wayne Co. (5-3/4)
4677. Hutchins, Gordon, 36, saddler, d 7/14/17 in Geneva (3-7/23)
4678. Hutchinson, Charles of Fenner, Mad. Co. m 7/6/43 Clarissa M. Woodworth,
   dau of B. Hutchinson of Randolph, in R; S. Scudder, Esq. (4-7/13)
4679. Hutchinson, Clarissa (Miss), 28, dau of John, d in Purinton (5-7/7/18)
4680. Hutchinson, Leonard P., 40, d 7/18/42 in Newark, NY (5-7/27)
4681. Hutchinson, Polly, 53, wf of Luther F., d 3/9/42 in Newark, NY (5-3/23)
4682. Hutchinson, Thomas J. (Dr.) m Eliza Amsden, dau of Isaac of Seneca, in
   Phelps; Rev. Brace (3-4/10/22)
4683. Hyde, _____ (Mr.) m 12/31/22 Mary Stark in Palmyra (5-1/8/23)
4684. Hyde, Elias m 8/7/34 Sarah Woodward, both of Jamestown, in J; Rev. Gillet
   (4-8/13)
4685. Hyde, Ezekiel R., 67, d in Buffalo (3-3/6/16)
4686. Hyde, Harlow, 14, m 7/4/23 Harriet Wisner in Wolcott (3-7/23)
4687. Hyde, Henry (Dr.) d in Arcadia (3-3/12/28)
4688. Hyde, Jabez B., Jr., 24, late printer of the Warren Union, d 4/10/35
   in Mount Pleasant Twp., Warren Co., PA (4-4/22)
4689. Hyde, Jedediah (Capt.), 84, (a Rev. officer) d 4/28/22 in Hyde Park, VT
   (He commenced his military career under Maj. George Washington ... in
   the French War") (3-5/29)
4690. Hyde, John L., 22, printer, d 3/8/19 in Dansville (3-3/24)
4691. Hyde, Sarah, 25, wf of John W., d in Albany (3-1/21/29)
4692. Hyde, William m 12/31/29 Caroline Rose in Palmyra; Rev. Guion (5-1/1/30
   and 3-1/6/30)
4693. Hydes, Harriet, 19, consort of Paris P., d 11/12/15 in Buffalo (3-11/22)
4694. Hyne, Timothy, 60, d 5/12/14 in Farmington ("While moving a hive of bees
   was stung in four or five places on the side of the face and neck ...
   and expired in less than one hour") (3-6/1)
4695. Ide, George m Anna Pettet in Farmington (3-4/8/18)
4696. Ide, John m 3/11/29 Mary Everingham of Fayette in F; Rev. Martin of
   Geneva (3-3/18)
4697. Imlay, Maria, an approved minister of the Society of Friends, d in NYC
   (3-11/25/29)
4698. Impson, Alanson, 17, d 9/25/38 "of the lock jaw" in Palmyra (5-10/5)
4699. Ingals, Solon m 9/11/45 Mary A. Stone, both of Dansville, in D; Rev.
   S. S. Brown (2-9/17)
4700. Ingalsbee, Colby, 21, d 8/12/48 in Alabama, NY. Also Adna Ingalsbee, 55,
   d 8/13 in Alabama and Asa Ingalsbee, 26, d 8/25 in Alabama (1-8/29)
4701. Ingalsbee, Philander, formerly of Pine Grove, PA, d 8/28/38 in Overton,
   Claiborne Parish, Louisiana (4-11/7)
4702. Ingersoll, J. (Capt.) of Batavia m Mary Buckley of Cayuga in C (3-12/6/15)
4703. Ingersoll, Jonathan, Jr., editor of the Seneca Republican, m Eliza Chapman
   in Ithaca (3-2/28/16)

4704. Ingersoll, Nicholas m 12/2/46 Rosanna Scarvel in Bath; Rev. Spencer.
All of Bath (2-12/9)
4705. Ingersoll, William m 3/21/41 Elizabeth M. Lee in Palmyra; RevI. C. Goff
(5-3/24)
4706. Ingham, Ann Maria (miss), 22, niece of the principal of the Le Roy
Female Seminary, d 3/11/48 in Le Roy (1-3/21)
4707. Ingols, Henry m Jane Loom in Seneca Falls; Rev. Merkel (3-1/28/18)
Ireland. See also Irland.
4708. Ireland, David, s of Capt. William, m 4/21/14 Margaret Frantz in Fayette;
Hugh McAlister, Esq. (3-4/27)
4709. Ireland, James, about 25, of Williamson, Wayne Co. d 7/2/26 in Geneva
("Arrived at Williamson two years ago from Edinburgh, Scotland. Had
a circle of friends in this country. Survived by a widowed mother
and one brother beyond the Atlantic and by his widow whose only child
was buried less than two short months since.") (3-7/5)
4710. Ireland, Sophia Agusta Waite, 4 yrs, dau of William B., Esq., d 9/27/29
in Irelandville (Reading) (3-10/14)
4711. Ireland, William (Capt.), 63, a resident of Fayette for 24 years, d 2/11/26
in Fayette (3-2/15)
4712. Ireland, William, Jr. (Ensign), 22, s of Capt. William, d 3/7/13 in
Fayette, Seneca Co. ("This is the seventh member of Capt. Ireland's
company who has died since the 27th October." The others: Thomas
Trotter, Samuel M. Smith, Thomas Barr, David Brown, Benjamin Perrel,
and Aaron Edington, "all young men") (3-3/17)
4713. Irish, Charles G., Jr., merchant, of Buffalo m 9/28/45 Ann Patterson,
dau of R. Patterson, Esq. of Sheldon, Wyoming Co., in Sheldon; Rev.
George Bridgman (1-10/7)
Irland. See also Ireland.
4714. Irland, Joseph of Fayette m 3/7/27 Elizabeth Horton, late of Geneva,
in Romulus; Rev. Dr. Axtell (3-3/14)
4715. Irons, Jeremiah (Elder), 63, pastor of the Bapt. Ch. in Yates, Orl. Co.,
d (date not given) (formerly of Palmyra) (5-3/27/29)
4716. Irwick, John m Diadamie C. Dutton in Lyons (3-9/16/18)
4717. Irwin, Andrew G. m Harriet Blood, dau of Capt. Asa, in Bath (3-10/28/29)
4718. Irwin, Charles m Caroline Hooper, dau of Pontiac, in Waterloo (3-9/15/19)
4719. Irwin, James of Phelps d in Youngstown (a soldier in the U. S. volunteer
army) (3-8/5/12)
4720. Irwin, Robert, 79, d 10/26/42 in Bath (2-11/2)
4721. Isaacs, Hannah (Mrs.), 67, formerly of South Salem, West. Co., d 3/13/42
at the home of N. K. Lamson in Palmyra (5-3/16)
4722. Isenhour, Mary, about 1 yr, dau of Michael, d 8/5/26 in Seneca (3-8/16)
4723. Isenhower, Michael m 8/22/16 Marilla Knickerbocker; Eli Bannister, Esq.
All of Seneca (3-8/28)
4724. Isham, Ebenezer G. m Eliza H. Taylor in Bristol (3-5/2/27)
4725. Isinghour, John m 1/16/20 Lydia A. Smith in Seneca; E. B. Woodworth, Esq.
(3-1/19). Same newspaper dated 2/9: "Correction: The marriage in our
paper of the 19th ult. of Mr. Isinghour to Miss Smith proves to have
been an imposition practiced on us and we are requested to contradict
it ..."
4726. Ives, _____, 3 yrs, dau of Joseph, d 8/28/15 in Geneva (3-8/30)
4727. Ives, Augustus M. m 6/3/40 Caroline Riggs, dau of Dr. Lewis Riggs, in
Homer, Cort. Co.; Rev. Gregory. All of Homer (2-6/24)
4728. Ives, Joseph, 35, d 9/20/15 in Rochester (3-9/27)
4729. Ives, L. S. (Rev.), rector of Trinity Ch., Philadelphia, m 2/15/25 Rebecca S.
Hobart, dau of Bishop Hobart, in NYC; Rev. Berain (1-2/25)
4730. Ives, Lucius, 18, s of Maj. Nathaniel, d 4/25/25 in Black Rock (1-5/13)
4731. Jackson, Amanda E. (Mrs.), wf of Levi F. and only dau of John Clifford
formerly of Batavia, d 12/11/47 in Watertown, W. T. (prob. Wisc. Terr.)
(1-1/4/48)
4732. Jackson, Amasa of NYC m 12/26/31 Jane E, Howell, dau of Hon. N. W., in
Canandaigua (5-1/3/32)
4733. Jackson, Calvin W. of Benton m 10/18/27 Susan Earl of Seneca in S; Rev.
Dr. Axtell (3-10/24)
4734. Jackson, Cornelia, 3, dau of S. Jackson, d 9/6/36 in Palmyra (5-9/9)
4735. Jackson, David m Keziah Peer in Phelps (3-3/17/19)
4736. Jackson, Ellen, 20 mo, dau of Cyrus W., d 9/15/34 in Jamestown (4-9/24)

4737. Jackson, Franklin, 4, s of Widow Jackson, d 3/14/32 in Bath (2-3/21)
4738. Jackson, Giles, merchant, of Lyons d 2/14/20 in Lyons (3-2/16)
4739. Jackson, J. C. of Otis, MA m 11/27/50 H. M. Miller of Rochester in Bath;
       Rev. Miller (2-12/11)
4740. Jackson, Jane, 68, "widow of the late —— Jackson" d 7/2/17 in Geneva
       (3-7/9)
4741. Jackson, John m Damaris Kemble in Jerusalem, NY (3-10/17/27)
4742. Jackson, John d in Bath (3-6/11/28)
4743. Jackson, John F. m 7/4/44 Lucy Ann Pierce in Palmyra; F. Smith, Esq.
       (5-7/10)
4744. Jackson, Mary, 61, relict of Thomas of Yorkshire, England, d 9/14/17
       at Wilson's tavern in Geneva (3-9/17)
4745. Jackson, Nathaniel of Benton m 11/27/25 Harriet Atkins in Milo (3-12/7)
4746. Jackson, Sophia, about 10, d 2/11/31 in Palmyra (5-2/18)
4747. Jackson, William D. of York, Upper Canada m Mrs. Mary Rusco in Ithaca
       (3-1/3/16)
4748. Jackway, Aurelia F., 17, d 9/12/41 (5-9/15)
4749. Jacobs, Joseph, 70, d 9/5/46 in Howard (2-9/16)
4750. Jacobs, Nathaniel, M.D., m 3/8/12 Hannah Sanburn in Canandaigua
       (3-3/18)
4751. Jacobs, Nathaniel m 12/14/33 Rachel Jones of Batavia in B; C. M.
       Russell (1-12/17)
4752. Jacobs, Nicholas of Busti m Sophia Wheeler of Jamestown in Pinegrove, PA
       (4-5/30/32)
4753. Jacobs, Philip, 80, m Eliza Brown, 18; Rev. Schaeffer. All of Geneva
       (3-3/19). (Addendum: Marriage date given as 3/18/17)
4754. Jacobus, Elsey, 25, wf of Josiah, d 4/10/16 in Romulus ("She was the
       first white person born in Seneca County.") (3-4/24)
4755. Jacobus, Gerrit, about 71, d 9/20/14 in Romulus (3-9/21)
4756. Jacobus, John D. of Westchester Co. m 5/23/47 Janett Alderman of Urbana
       in Bath; Rev. E. B. Fuller (2-6/2)
4757. Jacobus, Josiah m 1/2/11 Elsy Fleming in Romulus; Rev. Mosier (3-1/16)
4758. Jacobus, Margaret (Miss), 48, d 10/27/29 at the home of her brother in
       Lodi, Seneca Co. (3-11/4)
4759. Jagger, Jeter m 4/17/39 Ruth Tripp, both of Palmyra, in East Palmyra;
       Rev. Galloway (5-5/3/39)
4760. James, _____ (Mrs.), age 63 or 83, wf of the late Richard, d 1/25/35
       (5-1/30)
4761. James, Lewis M. of Ontario, NY m Abbe Allen of Cayuga Co. in Cayuga Co.
       (5-8/8/21)
4762. James, William (Rev.) m 11/24/24 Mercia L. Ames, dau of E. Ames, Esq.,
       in Albany (3-12/1)
4763. Jameson, Hugh, Esq., 50, d in Canandaigua (3-1/11/15)
4764. Jameson, Hugh, Esq. of Lyons m 6/10/34 Maria Melfier of Phelps in P
       (5-6/27)
4765. Jameson, James m Elizabeth Davis in Junius (3-12/26/27)
4766. Janes, Alonzo m 12/5/24 Mary Ann Disbro in Junius (3-12/22)
4767. Janes, Elijah, Jr., merchant and Pres. of the Lansingburgh Bank,
       d 2/22/23 in Lansingburgh (3-3/5)
4768. Janson, John m 2/24/15 Mrs. Catherine Houselander; Rev. Van Doren.
       Also the same evening, by the same clergyman, the marriage of these
       three children of Catherine: James Crane to Susan Houselander; James
       Terwilliger to Mary Houselander ; and Nicholas Houselander to Polly
       Norris - all of Burlingham (3-3/8)
4769. Janson, Miles H. m 10/30/42 Belinda Betron, both of Bath, in B; Rev.
       Hendrick (2-11/16)
       Jaquay. See Jackway
4770. Jarvis, _____ (Mrs.), wf of William, d 3/6/31 in Palmyra (5-3/18)
4771. Jarvis, William F. of Palmyra m 8/9/31 Harriet Maxon of Buffalo in B;
       Rev. Asa Williams (5-8/16)
4772. Jaughin (sic), Margaret, wid of late Capt. John, d 12/4/25 in NYC
       (3-12/12)
4773. Jenkins, Lewis, merchant, m 2/8/16 Eliza M. Atwater, dau of Hon. Moses,
       in Canandaigua (3-2/21)
4774. Jenkins, Marshal, Esq., 39 or 59, d 10/15/19 in Hudson (3-10/27)

123

4775. Jenkins, Robert, Esq., mayor of Hudson, NY, d 11/10/19 on board the
      steamboat "Richmond" on the Hudson River (had been knocked overboard
      from his own sloop "by some accident" and taken aboard the "Richmond")
      (3-11/24)
4776. Jenner, Asher E. of Belvidere, IL m 8/1/40 Mary Jane Cook of Ashville
      in A; Morris Norton, Esq. (4-8/5)
4777. Jenner, Elias H. m 10/1/44 Louisa E. Pier, dau of Abraham of Busti, in B;
      Rev. A. M. Reed of Jamestown (4-10/4)
4778. Jenner, James m 2/9/32 Sophia Hathaway, dau of Salmon, in Palmyra; Rev.
      Whelpley (5-2/14)
4779. Jennings, Austin, merchant, m 1/7/36 Purlina L. Mitchell, both of
      Stockton, in S; Rev. E. J. Gillet (4-1/13)
4780. Jennings, Elias, 42, m Bellona Chapman, 19, in Palmyra (3-3/10/19 and
      5-3/3/19)
4781. Jennings, James m 9/19/44 Melvina Reynolds, dau of Isaac, in Canandaigua.
      All of Manchester (5-9/25)
4782. Jennings, Samuel, merchant, m 8/30/18 Margaret Todd; Ira Selby, Esq.
      All of Palmyra (3-9/9 and 5-9/1) (a Capt. Sam'l, 40, d 11/26/21 in P 5-11/28)
4783. Jennings, Samuel C. of Palmyra m 3/15/42 Charlotte E. Wood, dau of
      Isaac, Esq. of Aurora, in A; Rev. Matoon (5-3/23)
4784. Jenny, Rhoda (Mrs.), 18, d 8/28/22 in Lyons (3-9/18)
4785. Jerome, Frances Catharine, 2, dau of H. K., Esq., d 8/16/32 in Palmyra
      (5-8/22)
4786. Jerome, Hiram K., Esq. of Palmyra m 1/12/23 Maria Juliana Johnson, dau
      of Col. Amos of Redfield, Oswego Co., in R; Rev. Simeon Bliss
      (5-1/22)
4787. Jerome, Lawrence R. m 8/27/44 Catharine Hall, dau of late Ambrose;
      Rev. G. R. Shumway (5-8/28)
4788. Jerome, Leonard Walter m Clarissa Hall, youngest dau of Ambrose of
      Palmyra, in P; Rev. J. W. French (2-4/18/49)
4789. Jessup, Henry, Jr. of Walworth m 5/29/43 Rebecca F. Seaman of Palmyra;
      Rev. Fisher (5-5/31)
4790. Jessup, Lewis, 44, d 6/1/19 in Lyons (an elder in the Presby. Ch. at
      Lyons) (5-6/9)
4791. Jessup, Mary, wf of Henry, Jr., d in Walworth (5-8/18/41)
4792. Jeudevine, Henry m 1/25/18 Sally Hosford in Geneva; Rev. Axtell
      (3-2/4)
4793. Jewel, Daniel (Deacon) of Greenville, 81, m 5/1/23 Mrs. Mary -----les,
      84, she being his fourth wife; Rev. Beriah Hotchkiss (these persons
      for many years members of the Presby. Ch. in Greenville) (3-6/4)
4794. Jewell, Ezra (Hon.) d 10/20/21 in Lyons (a judge of the court of common
      pleas of Ont. Co. (5-10/31)
4795. Jewell, Joel m 2/20/27 Mary Adriance in Hector; Rev. Tappan (3-2/28)
4796. Jewett, David, Esq., Chief of Div. of the Imperial Brazilian Navy,
      m 11/28/26 Eliza Mactier Lawrence, dau of A. H., Esq., in NYC; Rev.
      Mathews (3-12/6)
4797. Jewett, Lester (Dr.) m 11/11/22 Hannah Southwick in Seneca; Rev. Axtell
      (3-12/18)
4798. Jewett, Neal m 11/12/29 Nancy White in Seneca; Rev. Nisbet (3-11/18)
4799. Jillet, Samuel m Maria Henderson in Milo; Rev. Lanning (3-5/24/20)
4800. Johnson, Abner, 23 mo, s of David, d 12/3/26 (prob. in Geneva) (3-12/13)
4801. Johnson, Anna, 58, wf of John, formerly of Bath, d 2/4/41 in Jasper
      (2-2/10)
4802. Johnson, Austin m Alvira Curtiss in Prattsburgh (3-12/9/18)
4803. Johnson, B. m 12/12/39 Rachel Beal, dau of Caleb; Rev. Osburn. All of
      Palmyra (5-12/13)
4804. Johnson, Barnet B., merchant, of Macedon Center m 12/2/40 Ann Maria
      Hillman, oldest dau of Dr. John of Clyde, in C; Rev. O. Morton
      (5-12/9)
4805. Johnson, Ben, Esq., attorney, of Ithaca m Jane Dey, dau of Peter, of
      Fayette in F; Rev. Young (3-11/26/17)
4806. Johnson, Benjamin m 8/22/26 Dorcas Brown in Lyons (3-8/30)
4807. Johnson, Brian of Sodus m Phebe Perry of Arcadia in A (5-5/14/30)
4808. Johnson, Charles m 1/28/26 Jane Ball in Junius (3-2/8)
4809. Johnson, Corris(?) G. m 1/20/33 Mary Ann White, both of Manchester,
      in M; Rev. G. Osband (5-1/23)

124

4810. Johnson, David m 1/23/25 Roxana Henry; Rev. Dr. Axtell (3-2/2)
4811. Johnson, David of Palmyra m 4/21/36 Mrs. Case of Manchester; Rev.
      Shumway (5-4/29)
4812. Johnson, Dennis, 28, late of Chautauqua, drowned 9/4/28 in Pinegrove
      (4-9/10)
4813. Johnson, Eli of Lyons, NY m Betsey Baldwin in Bristol, CT (3-10/17/27)
4814. Johnson, Ervine of Chester, NY m 10/9/31 Ann Doolittle of Clymer in C;
      Benjamin Sullivan, Esq. (4-10/19)
4815. Johnson, Eunice (Miss), 22, dau of James T., d 1/29/31 in Bath (2-2/2)
4816. Johnson, George m Phebe Drake in Romulus; Rev. Moses Young (3-9/27/15)
4817. Johnson, Gilbert, 27, d 9/1/28 in Geneva (3-9/3)
4818. Johnson, Harriet, 22, dau of David, d 5/25/42 in Palmyra (5-6/1)
4819. Johnson, Hollis of Evans, Erie Co. m 7/3/42 Mary Feesler of Marion in
      East Palmyra; Rev. Ruel Taylor (5-7/13)
4820. Johnson, Holly F., Jr., 21, d 9/20/18in Sodus ("Editors of newspapers
      in Albany, Schenectady, Utica, and Auburn are requested to insert
      the above") (5-9/29). Correction in issue dated 10/6: Name should
      read Holly St. John in place of that stated. But in 3-10/7 the
      name is Holley T. Johnson, Jr., age 23 (d 9/20 in Sodus).
4821. Johnson, James m 4/19/37 Mary Ann Holt in Manchester; Julius N. Granger,
      Esq. (5-4/28)
4822. Johnson, James, about 90, (a Rev. pensioner) d 6/27/42 in Bath (2-6/29)
4823. Johnson, James, Jr. m 7/3/42 Eliza Ann Geralamon, both of Williamsville,
      in Pulteneyville; Rev. Wilkinson (5-7/20)
4824. Johnson, James C., 23, merchant (son of Samuel A., Esq, postmaster of
      Prattsburgh), d 1/7/47 in Prattsburgh (member of Presby. Ch.; surv
      by parents and a brother). Elmira, 47, wf of Samuel A. and dau of
      William Curtiss, Esq., d 1/1/47. Their dau Helen, 21, d 2/3/47.
      All buried in the same grave in Prattsburgh. (2-1/13 and 2/2/10)
4825. Johnson, James H., Jr. of Palmyra m 3/22/29 Rachel Aldrich of Manchester
      in M; _____ Howland, Esq. (5-3/27 and 3-4/1)
4826. Johnson, James W. of Batavia m 12/20/47Sarah H. Walton of Saybrook,
      Ashtabula Co., Ohio in Elba; Rev. S. M. Stimson (1-1/4/48)
4827. Johnson, Joel, 81, m d 4/2/50 in Monterey (2-4/17)
4828. Johnson, John m Olive Metcalf in Avon (3-3/15/15)
4829. Johnson, John, 61, "of the theatre", d in NYC (3-11/3/19)
4830. Johnson, John (Col.), 41, clerk of Tompkins Co., d in Ithaca (3-10/29/28)
4831. Johnson, John, 39, formerly of Port Bay, d 3/20/29 in Penfield, Monroe
      Co. (3-4/15 and 5-4/3)
4832. Johnson, John (Sir, Bart.), 83, d at the home of his dau, "Mrs. Bowes",
      in Montreal (3-1/20/30)
4833. Johnson, John of Ellicott m 3/26/36 Fanny Cade of Busti in B; George
      Martin, Esq. (4-3/30)
4834. Johnson, John Jay m 5/8/43 Susan C. Hequembourg, second dau of William
      Charles, in Buffalo; Rev. Beatty. All of Buffalo (4-5/25)
4835. Johnson, L. B. (Dr.) m 11/30/42 Catherine Hubbard, both of Bath; Rev.
      Wilson of Hammondsport (2-12/7)
4836. Johnson, Lewis, Esq., 33, formerly of Burlington, VT, d 9/10/21 in
      Vienna, NY (5-9/26)
4837. Johnson, Lewis m 2/24/42 Patience Louk in South Danville; Rev. A. Chase.
      All of South Danville (2-3/9)
4838. Johnson, Malinda, 36, wf of William C., d 7/4/42 in Macedon (5-7/20)
4839. Johnson, Milton E., "stranger", d 3/20/23 in Lockport (3-4/9)
4840. Johnson, N____? (Hon.), member of Senate from Palmyra District,
      d 4/4/39 at his lodgings in Albany (5-4/12)
4841. Johnson, Nancy (Mrs.), 30, consort of Daniel,    d 4/29 in Attica
      1-5/27)
4842. Johnson, Nathan, 84, d in Berlin, MA (fought at Bunker Hill) (4-3/6/33)
4843. Johnson, Nathaniel of Manchester m 3/23/36 Ann Sax of Greenfield, Sara.
      Co.; Rev. Barrel (5-3/25)
4844. Johnson, Nelson of Broome Co. m 9/17/45 Lauraett Craig of Jasper;
      Rev. J. Ashworth (2-10/22)
4845. Johnson, Newton m Huldah Kinne in Romulus (3-3/10/19)
4846. Johnson, Nicholas, 21, d 5/2/20 in Geneva (3-5/10 and 5-5/17)
4847. Johnson, Ralph, junior editor of the Norwich Journal, m Mary Randall in
      Norwich, Chen. Co. (3-6/3/29)

4848. Johnson, Samuel S. m Eliza G. Tyler in Benton (3-11/25/29)
4849. Johnson, Sarah, 64, consort of Luther,d in Le Roy (1-8/4/26)
4850. Johnson, Silas L. m Catherine Denwood in Lodi (3-11/4/29)
4851. Johnson, Squire B. m 12/12/39 Rachel Beal, dau of Caleb; Rev. Osburn.
       All of Palmyra (5-12/20)
4852. Johnson, Thomas (Maj.) m 5/9/26 Catharine Ann Cost, oldest dau of late
       Col. Elias late of Phelps, NY, in Newton Trap, MD (3-5/31)
4853. Johnson, William m 11/14/39 Arsena N. Phelps in Palmyra; Frederick
       Smith, Esq. (5-11/29)
4854. Johnson, William, 58, d 7/31/42 in Manchester (5-8/3)
4855. Johnson, William B. m 3/1/42 Clarissa A. Wilder in Bath; Rev. Fraser
       (2-3/9)
4856. Johnson, William R. m 1/17/44 Lucy Willson in Palmyra; Rev. Fisher
       (5-1/24)
4857. Johnson, Zachariah m Hannah Joy; Cyrus Packard, Esq. (5-11/28/17)
4858. Johnston, William Clark of Macedon m 3/19/43 Phebe C. Hine of Palmyra
       in P; Rev. W. Clark (5-3/22)
4859. Jolley, James m 5/20/47 Hannah Baker in Wheeler; Hiram Van Pelt.  All
       of Wheeler (2-5/26)
4860. Jones, _____, inf ch of Edward, s 1/30/22 in Lyons (3-2/13)
4861. Jones, Abigail (Miss), 18, dau of Levi, d 6/18/26 in Busti (4-6/21)
4862. Jones, Albert of Essex Co., NY m 10/15/34 Sarah Jane Bishop of
       Jamestown in J; Rev. Stedman (4-10/22)
4863. Jones, Amos m 10/7/15 Mary Shekel, dau of John, in Clifton Springs;
       Rev. Gideon Draper (3-10/18)
4864. Jones, Andrew B., 64, d 9/18/50 in South Byron (1-9/24)
4865. Jones, Benjamin m Nancy Sherman in Carroll (4-10/14/41)
4866. Jones, Benjamin H., printer, m 10/17/27 Elizabeth Wheeler in Waterloo;
       P. A. Barker, Esq. (3-12/5)
4867. Jones, C. P., A.B., of the Genesee and Wyoming Seminary at Alexander,
       NY, m 8/22/50 Ett Julia Norton, oldest dau of A. Norton, Esq. of
       Groveland, Liv. Co., in Groveland; Rev. H. F. Hill (1-9/3)
4868. Jones, Celestia Priscilla, 3 yrs, dau of Rufus and Emily J. Jones,
       d 2/27/44 in Jamestown (fell into a pail of scalding water) (4-3/1)
4869. Jones, Chloe, 6, dau of Levi, d 8/24/26 in Busti (4-8/30)
4870. Jones, Clement Bishop, 2 yrs 11 mo, s of Albert and Jane, d 7/31/45 in
       Jamestown (4-8/8)
4871. Jones, Daniel K., Esq. of Palmyra m 1/15/23 Serepta St. John of Sodus
       in S (3-1/29 and 5-1/22)
4872. Jones, David (Rev.), 83, chaplain in the Rev. army "and during the late
       war", d 2/5/20 at his farm in Chester Co., PA (3-2/23)
4873. Jones, Ebenezer, 50, "recently from New Portland, Maine where his family
       resides", d 8/13/14 in Troupsville, NY (3-8/17)
4874. Jones, Edmund of Cumberland Co., PA m Theodosia Conkling of Barrington, NY
       in Benton, NY (3-3/11/29)
4875. Jones, Edward m 9/19/19 Ann Hawkins in Lyons; Rev. Riley.  All of Lyons
       (3-9/22)
4876. Jones, Edward, "about 60", d 1/18/23 at the Glass Factory (3-2/12)
4877. Jones, Edward, 9 mo, d in Palmyra (possibly in the household of  Mrs.
       Sarah Jones, 78)  (3-9/20/26)
4878. Jones, Edward m 12/17/28 Ann Newkirk in Seneca; Rev. Dr. Axtell (3-12/24)
4879. Jones, Edward, 38, d in Lyons (one of the earliest settlers in that town)
       (3-9/23/29)
4880. Jones, Elijah, Jr., merchant and Pres. of the Lansingburgh Bank, d 2/22/23
       in Lansingburgh (5-3/12)
4881. Jones, Elizabeth, wf of Joseph, d 11/7/16 (3-11/13)
4882. Jones, Ellic (sic) m Harriet De Jean in Jamestown (4-9/5/32)
4883. Jones, Ezra m 7/29/24 Mary Pinnock, both of Phelps, in Vienna, NY; Rev.
       Dr. Axtell (3-8/4)
4884. Jones, Franklin of Holland, Erie Co. m 6/11/44 Martha N. Carpenter of
       Sinclairville in S; Rev. P. Canfield (4-6/14)
4885. Jones, Gardner(?), 78, d 5/20/23 in NYC (3-5/28)
4886. Jones, George J. of Batavia m Mary Ann Lockhart, dau of William, Esq.
       of Verona, in V; Rev. W. Burnside (1-10/5/47)
4887. Jones, George Tew, 2 yrs, s of Rufus and Emily J., d (date and death
       place not given)  (4-9/12/45)

126

4888. Jones, Hartwell Franklin, 10 mo, s of William and Olive, d 4/6/42 in
      Jamestown (4-4/14)
4889. Jones, Henry C. m 5/22/11 Paulina Clark, both of Geneva, in G; Rev.
      Wilson (3-5/29)
4890. Jones, Henry V. (Elder), pastor of the Bapt. Ch. of Palmyra, m 2/14/36
      Eliza Williams of Groton, Tompkins Co. at the Baptist Meeting House
      in Groton; Elder J. S. Bachus (5-2/19)
4891. Jones, James m 1/20/25 Mary Kip, dau of Nicholas, in Benton; Rev.
      Richard Wil____ (3-1/26)
4892. Jones, James m 4/27/26 Amanda Canfield, dau of Samuel, Esq. of Cortland
      Co., in Phelps; Rev. Henry Strong (3-5/10)
4893. Jones, James E., 35,d in Cameron (killed by a fall of his horse)
      (3-11/25/29)
4894. Jones, Jane E., 22, oldest dau of Isaiah J. Jones of Erwin, drowned
      2/14/35 when the ice broke as her sleigh was crossing the Canisteo
      River ("The body was found two hours after she sunk and was buried
      yesterday.") (2-2/18)
4895. Jones, Jonah Josephus, 20 mo, s of Ellick Jones, d 1/4/41 in Jamestown
      (4-1/6)
4896. Jones, Joseph, 75, m Louisa Smith, 17, in Edenton, NC (3-12/22/24)
4897. Jones, Julius V., 7, s of Albert and Sarah, d 10/16/44 in Jamestown
      (4-10/18)
4898. Jones, Levi m 4/9/27 Elizabeth Brees in Ithaca (3-4/25)
4899. Jones, Louisa, 32, wf of Ellie Jones d 5/18/32 in Jamestown (4-5/23)
4900. Jones, Lydia, wf of Benjamin, d 5/8/40 in Carroll (4-5/13)
4901. Jones, Margaret, 36, consort of Bidcar Jones,d 9/9/42 in Bath (2-9/21)
4902. Jones, Powell m Alzina Blakeman in Clyde (3-1/20/30)
4903. Jones, Richard d 9/17/30 in Lyons (member of Meth. Ch.) (5-9/24)
4904. Jones, Rufus, merchant, m 3/13/32 Emily Tew in Jamestown; Rev. Gillet
      (4-3/14)
4905. Jones, Samuel of Junius m 6/12/17 Harriet Faugkenburgh of Romulus in
      Seneca Falls (3-7/2)
4906. Jones, Samuel, Esq., 79, d in Queens Co., L.I., NY (formerly comptroller
      of this state) (3-12/8/19)
4907. Jones, Samuel m 10/8/48 Mary Spencer, both of Darien, at the Eagle
      Tavern in Batavia; Rev. S. M. Stimson (1-10/10)
4908. Jones, Sarah (Mrs.), 78, d in Palmyra (3-9/20/26)
4909. Jones, Solomon m 11/2/15 Sophia Warner, both of Seneca; Rev. White
      (3-11/8)
4910. Jones, Thomas W. of Bath m 7/26/41 Derinda L. Shideman of Perry in P;
      Rev. Page (2-8/4)
4911. Jones, Uriah m Lavina Patrick in Dansville (3-9/17 and repeated 10/1)
4912. Jones, Whitney, 55, d 8/14/26 in Dover, VT (4-8/30)          (5-8/23)
4913. Jordan Allan A. (Dr.), 26, d 8/17/43 in Macedon (surv by wf and 2 ch)
4914. Joyce, Justice, 20, m 5/18/18 Olica McCumber, 15, in Farmington (5-5/19)
4915. Judd, Levi, Sr. (Deacon), 63, d 9/22/29 in Seneca (a native of South
      Hadley, MA; moved to Seneca about two years ago) (3-9/30)
4916. Judd, William, 36, d in Schoharie Co. (3-12/20/15)
4917. Judd, William P. m Susannah Wood in Milo (3-11/25/29)
4918. Judson, ____, wf of "Mr. Judson, American Missionary to Burmah", d in
      "Burmah" (4-5/9/27)
4919. Judson, David, 28, d in Southport (3-11/4/29)
4920. Judson, Norman m Parthena Beebe in Canandaigua (3-1/16/22)
4921. Judson, Polly, 53, wf of Zephaniah,d in Hartland, Niag. Co. (3-3/1/26)
4922. Judson, Sarah, 70, d in Jerusalem, NY (3-9/10/28)
4923. Judson, Thomas m 1/15/32 Almira Turner in Sodus (5-1/24)
4924. Judson, Thomas, Esq., 32, d 5/7/34 in Sodus (5-5/9)
4925. Kamp, John, 49, L.L.D. and F.R.S.E., professor of math. and natural
      philosophy at Columbia College, d 11/29/12 in NYC (3-12/2)
4926. Kane, Archibald, merchant, late of the house of James and Archibald
      Kane, Albany, d in Port-au-Prince, St. Domingo (3-11/26/17)
4927. Kane, John, Esq., 57, d 4/20/19 in NYC (3-5/5)
4928. Kane, Susan, 7 yrs, d 7/3/49 in Batavia (1-7/10)
4929. Kapple, John L. m 10/13/42 Nancy Blanchard in Harmony; Rev. Stedman
      (4-10/27)
4930. Kapple, Sidney, 34, d 9/29/45 in Fredonia (4-10/10)

4931. Kaush, Christian m 2/4/47 Maria E. Braunschweig, both of South Dansville, in S. D.; Rev. A. Berky (2-2/24)
4932. Kay, William m 5/1/23 Caroline Rice in Seneca; Rev. Nisbet (3-5/7)
4933. Kazort, David m Sally Phelps in Canandaigua (3-11/15/15)
4934. Kealey, Christian, 99, d 5/18/16 in Guilderland, Albany Co. (3-5/29)
4935. Keating, Ruth (Mrs.), 52, d 7/2/14 in Geneva (3-7/6)
4936. Kedzie, William, 46, d in Michigan (3-9/10/28)
4937. Keeler, Zalmon G. m 1/23/40 Joanna B. Crosby, both of Jamestown, in J; Rev. Gillet (4-1/29)
4938. Kees, Abel m Lodamia Vaughn in Big Flats (3-10/14/29)
4939. Keith, Flint m Lavina Flint in West Bloomfield (3-7/1/18)
4940. Keith, Mary, 13, d in Geneseo (3-1/17/27)
4941. Keller, Jacob m Mary Stansell in Lockville; Rev. Alverson (5-7/16/30)
4942. Kelley, Caroline (Miss), dau of Ebenezer, d 8/31/19 in Seneca (3-9/8)
4943. Kelley, William D., 28, formerly of Ovid, d in Ithaca (3-2/11/29)
4944. Kellogg, _____, inf ch of Simeon, d in Batavia (1-7/22/25)
4945. Kellogg, _____ (Mr.) d in Canandaigua (3-12/26/27)
4946. Kellogg, _____, 2 yrs, youngest dau of George W. and Eve E., d 5/19/45 in Rochester (4-5/30)
4947. Kellogg, Augustus, Esq. of Skaneateles m Cornelia C. Hart, dau of Hon. Ephraim, in Utica (3-6/27/27)
4948. Kellogg, Charles (Hon.), 88, late of Kelloggsville, Cayuga Co., d 5/11/42 in Ann Arbor, MI (a pioneer of western NY and a member of Congress) (2-5/25)
4949. Kellogg, Day Otis, Esq. of Cayuga Co. m Eliza Ann Smith in Lansingburgh (3-11/16/25)
4950. Kellogg, Ezekiel, Jr. m 6/11/20 Harriet Fox, both of Williamson, in W; J.L. Powell, Esq. (5-6/14)
4951. Kellogg, George W. m 11/30/34 Eve Kimball in Jamestown; Rev. E. J. Gillett (4-12/3)
4952. Kellogg, James, 54, d 10/14/22 in Elbridge, Huron Co., Ohio (1-11/1)
4953. Kellogg, James H. m 9/2/30 Mary Taylor at Camp Meeting in Sodus (5-9/17)
4954. Kellogg, Joel (Capt.), 68, d in East Bloomfield (3-9/10/28)
4955. Kellogg, Joseph m 9/1/36 Adeline Goodwin in Palmyra; I. E. Beecher, Esq. (5-9/2)
4956. Kellogg, Joseph B., 2 yrs, s of Samuel, d 8/12/29 in Geneva (3-8/19)
4957. Kellogg, Leonard, 36. senior editor and proprietor of the Manlius Times, d 5/22/17 in Manlius "after a long and painful illness" (3-6/4)
4958. Kellogg, Leonard, 18, d in Bath (3-2/13/28)
4959. Kellogg, Lucy (Miss), 18, d 12/7/16 in Hadley, MA (3-1/8/17)
4960. Kellogg, Marcia C. (Miss), 15, d 11/26/41 in Harmony (4-12/2)
4961. Kellogg, Silas D., Esq., a state assemblyman from Washington Co., d "recently" in Buffalo "while employed as Surveyor General of Grand Island preparatory to its sale" (3-10/13/24)
4962. Kellogg, Titus, 66, (a Rev. soldier and father of T. Kellogg, merchant, of Jamestown, NY) d 10/25/31 in Dorset, VT (4-11/23)
4963. Kellogg, Ulysses D. m Mary Livingston in Lodi (3-12/26/27)
4964. Kelly, Ebenezer, about 68, father of Luther of Geneva, d 3/12/29 in Ontario, Wayne Co. (3-3/18)
4965. Kelly, Elizabeth B., wf of Dr. Manning Kelly of Hornellsville, d 8/4/38 in Hornellsville (2-8/22)
4966. Kelly, Sandford of Roxbury, Delaware Co. m 10/23/24 Abigail Pelham of Middletown, Dela. Co. in Fayette (3-11/1)
4967. Kelsey, Harry m Nancy Spencer in Benton (3-12/27/15)
4968. Kelsey, Susannah W., 29, dau of Noah W. and Sally, d 8/14/50 in Batavia (1-8/20)
4969. Kelsie, John, 54, d 3/22/45 in Carroll (4-3/28)
4970. Kendall, George m 7/5/38 Sarah Miller, both of Westminster, MA, in W (4-8/1)
4971. Kendall, Ransom B., 15 mo, s of Salmon B. and Penelope, d 10/27/48 in Batavia (1-11/7)
4972. Kendig, Daniel S. of Waterloo m 4/12/25 Sarah Maria Southwick, dau of Maj. David of Junius; Rev. Lane (3-4/20)
4973. Kendig, Martin, Jr., Esq. of Waterloo m 7/6/23 Mrs. Anna Townsend of Milo in M; Rev. Abner Chase (3-7/16)
4974. Kenneda, Alexander m Margaret McCarther in Penfield (5-4/7/19)

128

4975. Kennedy, Anna, 77, consort of late Henry, Esq., d 9/6/47 in Kennedyville (2-9/8)
4976. Kennedy, Charles m 9/28/43 Alcey E. Keyes; Rev. E. J. Gillett (4-10/5)
4977. Kennedy, Henry (Col.), 61, (a Rev. soldier) d 4/26/26 in Bath (3-5/10)
4978. Kennedy, John (Maj.), 42, d in Dansville, Steuben Co. (lived at Kennedy's Corners in the town of Bath "until about six months since") (2-10/10/32)
4979. Kennedy, Lyman m Mary Newcomb in Canandaigua (3-11/22/15)
4980. Kennedy, William m Maria Sacket in Bath (3-5/20/29)
4981. Kennedy, William, about 32, d 10/2/32 in Bath (2-10/3)
4982. Kent, Abigail, 56, wf of Deacon John, d 6/16/38 in Woodhull (member of Bapt. Ch. nearly 40 yrs.) (2-7/4)
4983. Kent, Alonzo, formerly of VT, m 12/23/33 Mercy Rice of Jamestown in J; Hon. Judge Foote (4-1/29/34)
4984. Kent, John m Clarissa Lamphear in Busti (4-3/28/27)
4985. Kent, Maria Emogene, 3 yrs, dau of Alonzo and Mercy R., d 2/22/42 in Jamestown (4-3/3)
4986. Kenyon, Almond m Bathsheba Tubbs in Southport (3-1/20/30)
4987. Kenyon, Benjamin m 8/22/24 Hannah Clark, both of Phelps, in Waterloo; P. A. Barker, Esq. (3-9/8)
4988. Kenyon, Benjamin, 50, d in Southport (3-4/15/29)
4989. Kenyon, Daniel A. m 12/25/43 Antoinette E. Bartle in Arcadia; Rev. D. K. Lee. All of Newark, NY (5-1/3/44)
4990. Kenyon, Fanny, 35, wf of John, d 5/7/45 in Batavia (1-5/27)
4991. Kenyon, L. M. (Dr.) of Youngsville, PA m 9/23/45 Mercy Ann Mann, dau of David, Esq., in Westfield; Rev. T. P. Tyler of Fredonia (See also the marr. of Jared R. Babcock this date) (4-10/3)
4992. Kerkendall, Jonathan K. m Maria Hanes in Milo (3-9/19/27)
4993. Kerr, William J., Esq. of Niagara, Upper Canada m "lately" Miss Brant, dau of the late Col. Brant, Chief of the Six Nations, at the Head of Lake Ontario (3-10/20/24)
4994. Kerschner, Joseph, Esq. m 5/1/50 Catherine Louisa Kall, dau of J. K., Esq., in Geneseo; Rev. F. D. W. Ward. All of Geneseo (1-5/21)
4995. Kessler, Phelps, 53, d 5/1/44 in Busti (4-5/10)
4996. Ketcham, Joseph (Hon.) m Miss Hannah Davis in Hanover, NH "after a **short** courtship of twelve years" (3-5/11/14)
4997. Ketcham, Morgan L. m 5/1/39 Laura Jenks of Farmington in F; Azel Berry, Esq. (5-5/10)
4998. Ketchum, _____, 13, dau of Joseph, d in Benton (3-10/8/28)
4999. Ketchum, Benjamin, "aged 101 the 19th of Feb., last", d 7/18/16 in Onondaga. "His wife with whom he had lived nearly 80 years died four years ago ... wanting but 8 days of 102 years of age; they had lived to see their fifth generation." (3-7/31)
5000. Ketchum, John, 24, d in Canandaigua (3-3/6/16)
5001. Ketchum, John m 1/12/37 Alma Tedman in Macedon (5-1/20)
5002. Ketchum, Sylvester m 12/5/11 Lucy Woodworth in Benton; D. Brown, Esq. (3-12/11)
5003. Ketchum, William H. m 1/17/38 Ruth E. Gifford in Bath; John D. Higgins, Esq. (2-1/24)
5004. Keyes, Addison, 2 yrs, s of Eber, d 8/16/34 in Dexterville (4-8/20)
5005. Keyes, Clarinda Juliett, 36, wf of Eber, Esq., d 10/23/44 in Busti (4-11/1) (Same newspaper dated 11/8: she d 10/24; member of Cong'l. Ch.; surv by husband and children)
5006. Keyes, Eber of Jamestown m 8/23/31 Clarinda Juliette Gray of Sheridan in S; Rev. B. B. Gray (4-8/31)
5007. Keys, _____ (Mrs.), 26, d in Painted Post (3-3/11/29)
5008. Keys, Chauncey d 7/1/42 in Portsmouth, Ohio "but recently of Natchez, Miss." (1-7/19)
5009. Keyser, Abraham, 73, d in Albany (3-12/21/25)
5010. Kibbe, _____, 4 yrs, ch of Ira, d 12/1/22 in Geneva (3-12/4)
5011. Kibbe, Isaac, Esq., Pres. of the Bank of Niagara, m 9/3/17 Mrs. Serene Grosvenor in Buffalo (3-9/17)
5012. Kidder, Alberoni m 8/23/36 Lucy Emeline Willard, both of Wardsboro, VT, in W; Rev. Bradford (4-8/24)
5013. Kidder, Corbin (Rev.) of Brattleboro, VT m 12/22/40 E. Lorena Wood, dau of Ezra, Esq. of Westminster, MA, in W; Rev, Mann (4-1/20/41)

129

5014. Kidder, Horace J. m 12/15/26 Rachel Jones in Benton; Elder Goff (3-1/5/27)
5015. Kidder, N. B., Esq. m 12/20/26 Rhoda Walbridge in Geneva; Rev. Stockton.
All of Geneva (3-12/27)
5016. Kidder, Nathaniel (Capt.), 78, d at the home of his son, Rev. C. Kidder,
in Brattleboro, VT (lived several years in Jamestown) (4-11/17/43)
5017. Kidder, Paschal P. P. of Branford, CT m 9/21/40 Emeline Burrows, dau of
J. B., Esq., in Mayville; Rev. Lucius Smith (4-9/30)
5018. Kidder, Polly, 66, wf of Capt. Nathaniel, formerly of Wardsboro, VT,
d 5/9/40 in Jamestown (4-5/13)
5019. Kidder, Samuel m 1/9/19 Betsey Belt in Milo (3-1/27)
5020. Kidney, William, 12, s of Jonathan, d in or near Albany (3-6/27/10)
5021. Kierstead, J. F. m 4/10/39 Orissa Wadsworth in Randolph; Rev. Z. Eddy
(4-4/17)
5022. Kimball, Ariel m 2/10/14 Electa Reed, both of Phelps, in P; Joseph Hall,
Esq. (3-3/2)
5023. Kimball, Hannibal m 4/19/35 Orinda C. Blair in Jamestown; R. Pier, Esq.
(4-4/22)
5024. Kimball, John, 10, s of Ebenezer, d 8/29/45 in Jamestown (4-9/5)
5025. Kimberley, Ebenezer C., merchant, of Warsaw, NY m 7/18/22 Corinthia C.
Smith in Caledonia; Rev. Calvin Colton (1-7/26)
5026. Kimble, Daniel J., 33, d in Ovid (3-8/25/19)
5027. King, _____ (Lt.), a wounded prisoner from the British Royal Artillery,
d 2/21/13 at Black Rock (captured 11/28/12)
5028. King, _____ (Mr.), 56, d (prob. in Junius). Also John King, his grandson,
d (prob. in Junius) (3-9/6/26)
5029. King, _____ m Amanda Howard in Starkey, Yates Co. (3-1/14/29)
5030. King, Alanson W. m 12/30/30 Charlotte Bell in Sodus; Rev. Jesse Townsend
(5-1/28/31)
5031. King, Amos (Dr.), lately from New Windsor, Orange Co., d 12/6/18 in
Geneva (3-12/9)
5032. King, Barzillai (Elder of the Bapt. Ch.) d in Covert (3-12/5/27)
5033. King, Bradford of Rochester m Betsey Remington, dau of Col. T., in
Canandaigua (3-11/15/15)
5034. King, Charles, editor of the American, m Henrietta Low, dau of Nicholas,
Esq., in NYC (3-10/18/26)
5035. King, Charles of Greenwood m 8/5/41 Eunice Jeffers of Jasper in J; B. S.
Brundage, Esq. (2-8/18)
5036. King, Cyrus (Maj. Gen.), 44, late a member of Congress, d 4/25/17 in
Saco, ME (3-5/7)
5037. King, David m Heley Smith in Ovid (3-1/16/22)
5038. King, Edgar, s of Samuel late of Ithaca, m 5/28/35 Jemima Harmon of
Andover, NY in A; Rev. David Slie (See also marr of Cyrus H. Harmon)
(2-10/14)
5039. King, Enoch m 11/9/30 Eliza Willis in Lyons; Rev. Tenique (5-11/26)
5040. King, Fanny A., 23, wf of Horace, Esq. of Ithaca, d 6/6/45 (2-6/18)
5041. King, Frederick Gore, M.D., 28, youngest son of late Rufus, d in NYC
(3-5/6/29)
5042. King, George B. m Mary Walling in Urbana (3-2/13/28)
5043. King, George H. m 9/1/45 Amelia Ann Tobias in Bradford; Rev. I. L.
Coffin. All of Bradford (2-9/17)
5044. King, Henry m 4/29/41 Minerva Kingsley, both of Farmington, in Palmyra;
Rev. A. H. Burlingame (5-5/5)
5045. King, Horace of Rochester m Amelia Booth in Brighton (3-5/2/27)
5046. King, John C., 53, d in NYC (3-11/16/25)
5047. King, Joseph m 2/17/20 Serepta Harrington in Farmington (5-3/8)
5048. King, Mary, 50, consort of Hon. Rufus, d 6/5/19 in Jamaica, L. I., NY
(3-6/16)
5049. King, Rufus, (Hon.), 72, L.L.D., d 4/29/27 in NYC ("another of our oldest
statesmen - the favorite of Washington ...") (3-5/9 and 4-5/9)
5050. King, Sarah P., 38, wf of Aaron N., d 7/27/45 in Ashville (4-8/15)
5051. King, Selden, 24, s of Joshua K., d in Manchester (3-8/6/28)
5052. King, Sydney m 2/19/32 Miss Taylor (5-2/21)
5053. King, Theodore F., M.D., of NYC, late of Geneva, m Sarah Arnold, dau of
Col. Robert of Perth Amboy, NJ in P. A.; Rev. J. Chapman (3-6/3/29)
5054. King, William (Dr.), formerly of Alexandria, VA, m 5/14/11 Ann Brazier
in Geneva (3-6/12)

130

5055. King, William (Col.) "a distinguished officer of the U.S. Army during the late war", d 2/1/26 near Mobile (AL?) (3-2/15)
5056. Kingman, George G. m 12/1/31 Elizabeth D. Holley in Lyons (5-12/13)
5057. Kingsbury, Amherst m Betsey Buck in Canandaigua; Rev. Johns (3-7/1/18)
5058. Kingsbury, Cyrus (Col.), 50, late of Alstead, Cheshire Co., NH, d in Aurelius, NY (3-3/23/14)
5059. Kingsbury, Heman W. of Dansville, NY m 3/11/47 Elizabeth Hammond of Elkland, PA in E; Rev. Bronson (2-3/24)
5060. Kingsbury, Horace of Lockport m 5/21/49 Eliza Brace of Shelby, Orl. Co. in Batavia; Rev. S. M. Stimson (1-6/5)
5061. Kingsbury, Oliver, 28, formerly of Penfield, CT, d in Penfield, NY (3-2/7/16)
5062. Kingsbury, Susan (Mrs.), 32, d 6/26/30 in Lyons (5-7/2)
5063. Kingsley, A. S. m Emeline Aldrich in West Bloomfield (3-10/14/29)
5064. Kingsley, Adam m Mrs. Rebecca Gilson in Hector (3-10/21/18)
5065. Kingsley, Alonzo W., type-founder, of Albany d in Savannah, GA "where he had gone for his health" (3-12/9/29). See 5083.
5066. Kingsley, Flavius W. of Urbana m Minerva Larowe (3-3/19/28)
5067. Kingsley, Thurton (sic) W. of Laona m 2/27/43 Polly Maria Willoughby of Sheridan in Pomfret; A. Hinckley, Esq. (4-3/23)
5068. Kinhart, John m 9/1/25 Mary Devall in Junius; Rev. Lane (3-9/14)
5069. Kinnan, Alexander P. W. m 1/13/17 Sophia A. Van Dyck, dau of late James, in NYC; Rev. Dr. Kuypers (3-2/26)
5070. Kinne, ____, dau of John, d in Ovid (3-2/13/28)
5071. Kinnear, Henry of Youngsville, PA m Sally Morgan of Jamestown, NY in J; Rev. Chapin (4-2/28/38)
5072. Kinnear, Sally, 24, wf of Henry P., d in Youngsville, PA (4-6/10/41)
5073. Kinner, Margaret, 55, relict of James and dau of John and Margaret De Bow, d 9/19/41 in Stafford (1-9/21)
5074. Kinney, Alfred B. m 10/10/36 Harriet Bennett, both of Sodus, in Palmyra; Elder Henry V. Jones (5-10/21)
5075. Kinney, Arriette, 20 mo, dau of Hiram, d in Jamestown (4-3/9/31)
5076. Kinney, Daniel, 72, d 6/29/42 in Bath "while hoeing in a field" (2-7/6)
5077. Kinney, Darius F. m 11/26/39 Harriet Rice, dau of William, in Marion; Rev. G. V. Walling. All of Marion (5-12/6)
5078. Kinney, Duane Wing, 3 mo, s of D. F. and Harriet, d 11/21/43 in Williamson (5-11/29)
5079. Kinney, Harriet, wf of Darius F., d 7/16/44 in Williamson (5-7/24)
5080. Kinney, John m Sally Lane of Middlesex in Benton (3-7/15/29)
5081. Kinney, Orville Dwight, 3 mo, s of D. F., d 2/23/41 in Marion (5-3/3)
5082. Kinney, Sally, about 30, wf of Giles, Esq., d 7/7/22 in Jerusalem, NY (3-7/17)
5083. Kinsley, Alonzo W. of the firm A. W. Kinsley and Co., type-founders, of Albany d 11/10/29 in Savannah, GA (5-12/4). See 5065.
5084. Kip, Benjamin H. m 2/26/23 Esther Miller, dau of Capt. Joseph, in Lyons; Rev. J. B. Alverson. All of Lyons (5-3/5)
5085. Kip, Mary A., 11. dau of John L., Esq., d 7/4/30 in Newark, NY (5-7/16)
5086. Kirkham, James m Hannah Dickson in Starkey; Rev. Stephen Lamphire (3-6/21/26)
5087. Kirkpatrick, John d 2/14/13 in Romulus (3-3/3)
5088. Kirkpatrick, William, Esq., supt. of the Salt Springs, m Nancy Duscomb in Salina (3-12/23/29)
5089. Kirtland, John of Hector m Betsey Hinckley in Lodi (3-11/4/29)
5090. Klapp, Edward M., 25, d 4/27/40 at the Palmyra Hotel in Palmyra (Funeral at the Episc. Ch. in Palmyra) (5-4/29)
5091. Knap, Charles m Mary Fuller in Pulteneyville (5-9/19/21)
5092. Knap, William m Betsey Green in Benton (3-1/24/16)
5093. Knapp, Adelia (Miss), 17, dau of Deacon Ezra, d in Galen (3-2/23/20)
5094. Knapp, Daniel, 27, formerly of Otsego, d 2/19/41 in Ellington (4-2/24)
5095. Knapp, G. V., merchant, of Sinclairville d 4/23/44 in Sinclairville (4-5/10)
5096. Knapp, G. W., Esq. m 1/15/24 Evelina Vaill; Rev. True. All of Covington (1-3/26)
5097. Knapp, H. S. of Delaware, Ohio m 8/23/41 Mary J. Magee of the Young Ladies Seminary, Jamestown, in J; Rev. J. F. Hill (4-8/26)

131

5098. Knapp, Ira of Ellington m 8/24/43 Lusina Weaver of Cherry Creek in C. C.;
       Rev. Henry C. Card (4-8/31)
5099. Knapp, James A. m 1/16/18 Margaret Biltibidal, both of Benton, in Geneva;
       John Collins, Esq. (3-1/21)
5100. Knapp, John m 5/15/47 Martha Edson, both of Italy, NY, in Italy; Rev.
       Chapman (2-6/2)
5101. Knapp, Moore, 29, d in Massachusetts General Hospital, Boston (3-7/9/28)
5102. Knapp, O., 30, d 1/12/32 in Sodus (5-1/24)
5103. Knapp, Seth m 12/1/31 Ann Marshal, both of Farmington, in Palmyra;
       F. Smith, Esq. (5-12/6)
5104. Knickerbacker, Guile m Catharine Van Ostrand in Gorham (3-11/19/17)
5105. Knickerbacker, Solomon, about 46, d 2/11/31 in Cameron (2-2/16)
5106. Knickerbaker, James of Cameron m Hannah Hoage in Cohocton (3-4/22/29)
5107. Knight, Daniel m 7/4/38 Emily Warren in Bath; Rev. Wisner. All of Bath
       (2-7/11)
5108. Knight, James m Susan Henion in Ovid (3-1/16/22)
5109. Knight, John, 62, d 7/13/49 in Bath (2-7/25)
5110. Knight, Mehitable, 48, wf of Samuel, d 6/24/41 in Jamestown ("Printers
       in Hartford, CT are requested to insert the above) (See Minerva
       Knight's death) (4-7/1)
5111. Knight, Minerva, 48, wf of Samuel, d 6/24/41 in Jamestown (See Mehitable
       Knight's death) (4-6/24)
5112. Knight, Quartus, 43, d in Waterloo (surv by wf and children) (3-8/1/27)
5113. Knight, Samuel of Jamestown m 10/19/41 Mrs. Zilpah Bostwick of Harmony
       in H; Rev. Norton (4-10/28)
5114. Knight, Solomon, 2 yrs, s of William, d 2/20/35 in Harmony (4-2/25)
5115. Knight, William, 49, d 1/28/43 in Panama, NY (4-2/2)
5116. Knight, Winslow, 2 yrs, s of William, d 4/19/31 in Jamestown (4-4/20)
5117. Knolls, John B. m 6/30/31 Elizah W. Barnhart at the Sulphur Springs
       House (prob. in Palmyra) (5-7/8)
5118. Knower, Charles, 21, s of Benjamin, Esq. and brother-in-law and secretary
       to Gov. Morey, d 11/1/36 in Albany (5-11/4)
5119. Knower, Sarah, 53, wf of Benjamin, Esq. and mother-in-law of Gov. Morey,
       d 2/18/33 in Albany (5-2/27)
5120. Knowles, George W. m 8/28/42 Laura A. Latimer, both of Batavia, in B;
       Rev. A. Steel of St. John's Church (1-8/30)
5121. Knowlton, Sarah, 45, wf of Chester, d 10/25/41 in Hornby (2-3/2/42)
5122. Knox, Edward m 5/9/41 Lutha A. Barager in Macedon; Hon. D. Osband.
       All of Macedon (5-5/12)
5123. Knox, Edward m 4/2/43 Lucinda Pelham, both of Palmyra, in P; F. Smith,
       Esq. (5-4/5)
5124. Kollock, Henry (Rev. Dr.), formerly of Elizabethtown, NJ, d 12/29/19 in
       Savannah (presumably in NY) (3-1/19/20)
5125. Konkle, John, Esq., 72, father of A. Konkle, Esq., d 3/28/28 in Newtown
       (3-4/16)
5126. Korell, John N. m 7/29/32 Angelina Gardner at Zion Church in Palmyra; Rev.
       B. H. Hickes (a double ceremony - see the marr. of John Merrill;
       the genlemen from NYC, the ladies from Boston) (5-8/1)
5127. Kortright, Moses m 5/26/33 Hester Baugher in Poland, NY; Henry McConnell,
       Esq. (4-5/29)
5128. Koutz, William P., Esq. of Logansport, IN m 10/2/50 Julia M. Darby of
       Bethany in B; Rev. R. C. Palmer (1-10/8)
5129. Kromer, Levi Y. m 5/24/46 Lydia Lucretia Perkins in South Dansville;
       Rev. Elder Miner (2-6/3)
5130. Kuhn, Adam (Dr.), 76, d in Philadelphia (PA?) (3-7/23/17)
5131. Kurtz, Coffman of Lancaster, Erie Co., m 6/18/46 Clarissa M. Skidmore of
       Alexander in Batavia; Rev. John Parker (1-6/23)
5132. Kynne, Cyrus m Sarah Dodge in Romulus (3-1/6/30)
5133. Lacy, ____, inf ch of Henry, d in Waterloo (3-3/19/28)
5134. Lacy, Nathan E. m Fanny Genung in Phelps (3-2/19/17)
5135. Lacy, Samuel S. m 1/2/44 Mary A. Akin, both of Chili, Monroe Co., in
       Chili; Rev. Billington (5-1/10)
5136. Laffer, Jacob m Emily Bryan in Mendon, Ont. Co. (3-12/28/25)
5137. La Forge, Charles m 6/30/41 Sally Shaver, both of Savannah, Wayne Co.,
       in Palmyra; F. Smith, Esq. (5-7/7)
5138. Lain, Joseph m Maria Andrews in Middlesex (3-3/12/28)

5139. Laing, Sarah, 21, wf of Webster, d in Junius (3-7/23/28)
5140. Laing, Walter m Jane Renwick in Seneca; Rev. Nisbet (3-2/9/25)
5141. Lake, _____ m Sally Stone in Bloomfield (3-4/3/16)
5142. Lake, David m 10/7/47 Maria Smith at Italy Hill, NY; Rev. W. H. Husted.
       All of Italy, NY (2-10/27)
5143. Lake, James H. m 2/1/43 Eliza M. Blakeslee in Conneaut, Ohio (4-2/16)
5144. Lake, Jesse m Lavina Cook; Elisha Slocum, Esq. (5-11/28/17)
5145. Lake, Nicholas m "within a few days" Oracy Lamb in Snell (3-11/1/09)
5146. Lake, Roxaline, dau of Conrad, d 9/19/24 in Junius (3-9/29)
5147. Lakey, Abner F., Esq. m 12/12/39 Chloe Harris, both of Palmyra; Rev.
       C. M. Butler (5-12/13)
5148. Lakey, Cynthia, 42, wf of Thomas, Esq. of Palmyra, d 8/30/42 (5-8/31)
5149. Lakey, Franklin m 1/26/43 Terrissa Page, both of Palmyra; Isaac E.
       Beecher, Esq. (5-2/1)
5150. Lakey, Lucy, 35, wf of Abner F., d 9/21/29 in Palmyra (3-9/30 and 5-9/25)
5151. Lakey, Rowena (Miss), 16, dau of James, d 11/26/18 in Palmyra (5-12/2)
5152. Lakey, Thomas m 11/16/20 Cynthia Durfee, dau of Pardon, in Palmyra (5-11/22)
5153. Lamb, J. of Auburn m 10/24/45 Margaret Sanderson of Prattsburgh in P;
       Rev. B. C. Smith (2-11/5)
5154. Lamb, Reuben P. of Penn Yan m Diana Roots in Prattsburgh (3-6/11/28)
5155. Lambert, Lydia, widow, 91, d 8/31/20 in Williamson (member of Episcopal
       Church "upwards of 70 years") (5-9/13)
5156. Lamberton, John, Jr. m 10/18/25 Caroline Dunham in Elba - both of Elba;
       C. Woodworth, Esq. (1-11/11)
5157. Lampman, Michael m Lydia Clapper in Canandaigua (3-5/14/28)
5158. Lamson, _____, 5 weeks, ch of Jesse, d 2/26/23 in Geneva (3-3/5)
5159. Lamson, James, 17, s of Miles P. of Le Roy, d 8/7/46 in Rochester
       (1-8/14)
5160. Lamunion, _____ m Polly Popple in Farmington; A. Spear, Esq. (5-10/23/22)
5161. Land, George m 7/7/36 Eveline Hibbard in Palmyra; F. Smith, Esq.  All of
       Palmyra (5-7/8)
5162. Landas, Charles of Newark, NY m 12/25/27 Sarah Forbush of Phelps in
       Vienna, NY; Rev. E. A. Campbell (3-1/2/28)
5163. Landers, Frederick B. of Hornellsville m 6/4/50 Sarah W. Mulhollon of
       Canisteo in C; Rev. H. Pettengill (2-6/19)
5164. Landon, James m Ann Taylor in Ithaca (3-9/19/27)
5165. Lane, A. D. (Rev.) of Waterloo, NY m 10/20/28 Laura Boardman, dau of
       Hon. Homer of New Milford, CT; Rev. Charles A. Boardman (3-10/29)
5166. Lane, Charles, 3 yrs, s of David, d 3/14/41 (prob. in Bath) (2-3/17)
5167. Lane, Edmund m 9/21/31 Melissa Harris in Wheeler; Harry Clark, Esq.
       (2-9/28)
5168. Lane, James of Phelps m 10/14/30 Mrs. Catherine Creger of Lyons in
       Newark, NY; Theodore Partridge, Esq. (5-10/22)
5169. Lang, _____, ch of Alpheus, d in Phelps (3-8/23/15)
5170. Lang, _____, (Mrs.), wf of Alpheus, d in Phelps (3-11/4/18)
5171. Lang, Morgan, about 2 years, s of Alpheus, d 9/23/11 (prob. in Geneva)
       (3-10/2)
5172. Langdon, Lorenzo m Salomi Hinds in Seneca Falls (3-11/25/29)
5173. Langdon, Survina, 38, d 6/8/33 in Sugargrove (possibly in PA?)
       (surv by "numerous children")
5174. Laning (sic), John (Gen.), 40, merchant, d 2/12/20 in Owego (accidentally
       fell 16 feet "through the scuttle of his store") (3-2/23)
5175. Lankford, Samuel A. m 8/28/26 Levina Dimick in Junius (3-9/6)
5176. Lanning, Albert P., Esq. m 9/29/41 E. N. Pulling, only dau of Dr.
       Pulling; Rev. W. W. Bostwick.  All of Hammondsport (2-10/6)
5177. Lansing, Henry R., 81, d in Albany (3-8/18/19)
5178. Lansing, Laura, 28, wf of Rev. D. C. and dau of late Rev. Caleb Alexander,
       d 3/6/31 in Utica (5-3/25).  In 2-3/23 her age at death is given as 37.
5179. Lansing, Mary, 10, dau of Chancellor Lansing, d 10/17/10 in Albany
       (Her clothes caught fire from her "passing too near the fireplace
       on the preceding day") (3-11/7)
5180. Lape, G. W. m 1/1/45 Eliza Ann Parkhill; Rev. Wheeler (2-1/29)
5181. Lapham, Arioch, 28, of Scipio d 10/13/20 in Royalton, Niag. Co. (was in
       a party exploring a northern route for the Erie Canal) ("a father
       and husband") (5-10/25)

5182. Lapham, Elias H., Esq. m 12/4/34 Dirce Ann Brown, both of Farmington, in F; Rev. Shumway (5-12/5)
5183. Lapham, Esther, 66, wf of Abraham, d 5/7/22 in Palmyra (among the earliest settlers there) (5-5/15)
5184. Lapham, Fayette m Lucy Ramsdell; Cyrus Packard, Esq. (5-11/28/17)
5185. Lapham, Hiram, 3, s of A. Lapham, d 10/27/21 (prob. in Palmyra) (5-10/31)
5186. Lapham, John m Salome Porter in Palmyra (5-1/14/18 and 3-1/21/18)
5187. Lapham, William, 74, father of Aretus of Palmyra, d 9/15/41 in Burrillville, RI (newspapers in the western part of this state, NY, and in Ohio are requested to notice the above) (5-9/29)
5188. Larned, Emily, 26, wf of Maj. George B. and oldest dau of Elkanah Watson, Esq. of Albany, d 1/3/17 in Detroit(MI) (3-2/19)
5189. Larned, Simon (Col.), 63, d in Pittsfield, MA ("an officer inthe Revolutionary and late wars") (3-11/26/17)
5190. Larrabee, Adam (Capt.), late of the U.S. Army, m Hannah G. Lester of Groton, CT in G (5-1/21/18)
5191. Larrabee, Charles (Maj.) of the U.S. Army m Elizabeth Hatheway in Rome, Oneida Co. (3-10/20/19)
5192. Larue, George of Cohocton m 10/8/46 Gitty Ann Williamson of Avoca in A; Rev. S. Pitt (2-11/11)
5193. Larzalere, Jacob m 3/28/16 Sally Gardner; Rev. Axtell. All of Geneva (3-4/3)
5194. Larzelere, _____, inf dau of Jacob, d 2/17/17 in Geneva (3-2/19)
5195. Larzelere, Abraham C., 2 yrs, s of Jacob, d 3/7/25 in Geneva (3-3/9)
5196. Larzelere, Anna, 44, consort of Jacob, Esq., d 8/6/22 in Cayuga Bridge (3-8/14)
5197. Larzelere, Harriet, 22, wf of William, d 6/12/26 in Waterloo (3-6/21)
5198. Larzelere, Jacob L., Esq. of Junius m 2/23/23 Sally Maynard, dau of Judge Maynard, of Utica in U; Rev. Frost (3-3/5)
5199. Larzelere, Julia Ann (Miss), 20, d in Junius (3-6/11/28)
5200. Larzelere, Mary, 42, relict of late Richard and dau of Martin Kendig, Sr., d 9/14/19 in Geneva (3-9/22)
5201. Larzelere, Richard (Lt.), 38, d 4/27/10 in Geneva ("... left a wife and six small children...") (3-5/2)
5202. Lascelles, Arthur, 17 mo, s of Henry and Mary P., d 6/21/43 in Pomfret ("scalded from a tea kettle") (4-7/13)
5203. Lathberry, John m 9/12/33 Betsey S. Jones in Manchester; Rev. Gideon Osband (5-9/27)
5204. Lathrop, Elizabeth, 10 mo, only ch of Rev. Eleazer of Elmira,d in Lima (3-9/17/28)
5205. Lathrop, Henry W., 33, formerly of Bethany, d 3/19/48 in Conway, MA (1-5/9)
5206. Lathrop, Homer m 8/18/47 Olive Putnam in Bethany; Rev. L. Richmond. All of Bethany (1-8/24)
5207. Lathrop, John H., Esq., 59, cashier of Ontario Branch Bank, d 6/10/29 in Utica (one of the earliest settlers in U) (5-6/26)
5208. Lathrop, W. W. m 10/8/44 Mary Jane Elizabeth Willson in Jamestown; Rev. George W. Clarke. All of Jamestown (4-10/11)
5209. Latimer, Delausun of Penn Yan m Abigail Smith in Italy, NY (3-1/20/30)
5210. Latta, Moses, 10, s of Samuel, d 8/21/11 in Seneca (3-8/28)
5211. Latten, Wright, Esq., formerly of Palmyra,d in Lockport (5-10/25/43)
5212. Latty, James of Potter Co., PA m Perlina Sears of Cameron, dau of Harley, in Cameron; Harlow Smith, Esq. (2-5/19/41)
5213. Laughry, Charles of Canisteo m 8/14/31 Juliet E. Brown of Cameron in C; H. D. Millard, Esq. (See also marr. of Emmet E. Brown this date) (2-8/24)
5214. Lauton, John of Lyons m Harriet Penier of Arcadia (3-10/28/29)
5215. Law, John m 8/21(36) Caroline Shays in Jamestown; S. Jones, Esq. (4-8/24)
5216. Lawrence, Archy B., Esq. m 1/29/17 Sarah Fairbanks of Pulteneyville in P (3-2/12)
5217. Lawrence, Bigelow (Col.), 78, d in Marcellus (3-2/11/18)
5218. Lawrence, James (Capt.), 32, d 6/5/13 "on board the United States Frigate Chesapeake". (Quoted from a "Boston paper": "On Saturday the flags at the navy yard and forts and upon public and private vessels lying in th harbour were hoisted half mast as a tribute...") (3-7/7)

134

5219. Lawrence, Jemima (Miss), 22, d 8/22/31 in Randolph, Morris Co., NJ
(5-9/13)
5220. Lawrence, John of Mendon m 2/28/38 Catharine Kipp in Macedon (5-3/14); F. Smith, Esq. /
5221. Lawrence, Meletiah m 10/29/11 Mary Alford in Benton (3-11/6)
5222. Lawrence, Richard L. m 2/15/18 Sarah Matilda De Zeng, dau of Maj. F. A.,
in Bainbridge; Rev. Chapin. All of Bainbridge (3-2/25)
5223. Lawrence, Robert, Esq. (age blurred - 70?) d 5/18/26 in Elmira (3-5/31)
5224. Lawrence, Samuel, Esq. m "a short time since" Mrs. Polly Kidder in
Benton (3-8/15/10)
5225. Lawrence, Sylvanus (age blurred) d 8/16/31 in Randolph, Morris Co., NJ
(5-9/13)
5226. Lawson, Peter, 100, d in Ameliasburgh, Upper Canada (3-2/23/20)
5227. Lawson, Susannah, 76, formerly of Virginia, relict of Lawrence, Esq.,
d 3/19/25 in Geneva (3-3/23)
5228. Lawthorp, Mary Ann, 1 yr, dau of Thomas, d 2/28/13 (prob. in Geneva)
(3-3/3)
5229. Lawton, Permelia, 24, wf of Rev. D. B. (he pastor of the Meth. Episc.
Ch. of Bath), d 3/17/42 in Bath (she born in Gouverneur, St. Law. Co.;
surv by husband and two ch) (2-3/23)
5230. Lay, John, 85, d 2/5/45 in Buffalo at the home of his son, Charles
(1-2/11)
5231. Lay, John, Jr. m 6/8/26 Frances E. Atkins in Buffalo (1-6/16)
5232. Lazell, William S. of Carroll m 11/7/41 Lucy E. Hitchcock of Springfield,
MA in Carroll; Rev. J. Wilson (4-11/18)
5233. Leach, Candice (Mr.), 41? (age blurred), d 8/23/30 in Lyons (5-8/27)
5234. Leach, Levi of Ontario m 7/16/21 Eunice Stoddard of Palmyra in Ontario,
NY; Rev. House (5-7/18)
5235. Leach, Lyman, 40, d in Palmyra (3-9/20/26)
5236. Leach, Phineas of Vienna, NY m 11/10/39 Julia Ann Rice of Walworth in
Marion; Rev. J. R. Morrey (5-11/15)
5237. Learn, Levi m 3/17/22 Margaret Shook, both of Phelps, in Lyons; Jacob
Leach, Esq. (3-4/3)
5238. Leavenworth, ____, 3, ch of J., d 4/15/22 in Clyde (3-5/1)
5239. Leavenworth, Alma Ann, 5, dau of Jared, d 4/16/22 in Clyde (3-5/1)
5240. Leavenworth, Harriet (Miss), 15, d in Clyde (3-4/24/22)
5241. Leavenworth, Hiram, editor of the Waterloo Gazette, m 7/4/19 Lavina Holden
in Lansing, Tompkins Co. (3-7/14)
5242. Leavenworth, Jesse. Esq., 86, father of Col. Henry of the 3rd regiment
of U.S. infantry, d 11/21/26 at Sacket's Harbor (he was an officer
in the French War and in the Rev. War) (3-12/6)
5243. Leavenworth, John (Deacon), 47, d 8/27/22 in Galen (3-9/4)
5244. Leavitt, Henry C. m Catharine Thompson in Veteran (3-1/13/30)
5245. Leddick, Jacob m Harriet Bigelow in Fayette (3-4/25/27)
5246. Ledyard, Benjamin, Esq., one of the Masters in Chancery of the State of
NY and secretary of the State Society of the Cincinnati, d 10/24/12
in NYC (3-11/25)
5247. Ledyard, Samuel, merchant, of Pulteneyville m Sophia Childs in Pittsfield
(3-2/7/16)
5248. Lee, ____ (Mrs.), 91, mother of Johnson R. Lee, d 11/1/41 in Jamestown
(one of the earliest settlers in Chaut. Co.) ("The Fredonia Censor
is requested to give this ... an insertion") (4-11/4)
5249. Lee, Ann H. of Georgetown, wid of Gen. Henry Lee of the Rev. War, d 7/26/29
in Ravensworth (3-8/12)
5250. Lee, Avery S. m 12/28/34 Sarah Loop in Urbana; Oliver Rice, Esq. All of
Avoca (2-1/1/35)
5251. Lee, Benjamin, 49, d in Bristol (3-12/26/27)
5252. Lee, Charles, s of Hon. Joshua of Penn Yan, m 9/29/35 Mary M. Hall, oldest
dau of late Ambrose, Esq. of Palmyra, in P; Rev. G. R. H. Shumway
(5-10/2)
5253. Lee, Charles N. B., 12, adopted son of D. J. Lee, d 9/6/48 in Darien
(1-9/19)
5254. Lee, Chester m Sophia Rose in Benton (3-3/24/19)
5255. Lee, Cyrus m 12/4/19 Jane Nichol in Seneca; A. Gage, Esq. (3-12/8)
5256. Lee, David m Sally Van Pelt in Milo (3-7/1/18)
5257. Lee, David J. m 3/7/24 Aurelia Lappin in Pembroke; Sanford Kendrick, Esq.
(1-3/19)

135

5258. Lee, Eli m Laura Ann Phelps in Canandaigua (3-1/9/28)
5259. Lee, Elisha, 58, d in Waterloo (3-9/9/29)
5260. Lee, George m 4/19/37 Cynthia Shearman, both of Busti, in B; John Stow, Jr, Esq. (4-4/26)
5261. Lee, Gideon, Esq., formerly of NYC, d 8/21/41 at his home near Geneva (5-8/25)
5262. Lee, John A., 67, d 10/5/31 in Palmyra (for many years was deacon of the Presby. Church in Cooperstown) (5-10/11)
5263. Lee, Moses, "a man of color", d 4/9/21 in Geneva (3-4/18)
5264. Lee, N. P., merchant, m Zelinda Chamberlain in Waterloo (3-10/10/27)
5265. Lee, Parker Hall, Esq., 70, d 6/20/29 at his home in Deer Creek, Harford Co., MD (a Rev. patriot) (5-6/26)
5266. Lee, Warren F. of Waterloo m Eliza Nelson in Junius (3-10/29/28)
5267. Lee, William, editor of the Curacoa Courant, d 8/8/23 in Curacoa, South America (3-9/17)
5268. Leet(?), Anson, 65, d 6/21/43 in Chautauqua (4-7/13)
5269. Lefferts, John, 43, formerly a senator of this state, d in Flatbush, L.I., NY (3-10/21/29)
5270. Leflen, Azor m 3/22/38 Emeline B . Tracy, both of Palmyra, in P; Rev. Shumway (5-3/28)
5271. Leforge, Martin m 9/2/46 Susan M. Bain of Bath in B; Rev. L. W. Russ (2-9/9)
5272. Legg, Caleb of Benton m Elizabeth Henderson in Milo (3-1/14/29)
5273. Legget. Isaac Whitmore, 22, only s of Allen, d 5/6/45 in Cohocton (surv by wf and parents) (2-5/21)
5274. Legget, John, 84, a native of Ireland, d 4/16/19 in Seneca (3-4/21)
5275. Leggett, Alfred of Bergen m 12/15/47 Helen Howe of Batavia in B; Rev. D. C. Houghton (1-12/21)
5276. Legro, Betsey, 52, wf of Samuel, d 10/20/42 in Bath (2-10/26)
5277. L'Hommedieu, Ezra (Hon.), 77, d in Southold, L.I., NY (surv by wf and one ch) (3-10/23/11)
5278. Leib, Michael, "a leading political character in Pennsylvania", d in Philadelphia, PA (3-1/15/23)
5279. Leland, Belinda P., 39, consort of Hon. Z. A. and dau of Hon. Robert Porter of Prattsburgh, d 3/26/42 in Bath (2-3/30)
5280. Leland, Charles Edward, 2 yrs, s of Judge Leland, d 4/22/41 in Bath (2-4/28)
5281. Lemm, _____, wf of Rouse Lemm of Cameron, d 3/16/32 (2-3/21)
5282. Lemmon, Benjamin of Romulus m 3/19/15 Sally Hudson of Geneva in G; Rev. Axtell (3-3/22)
5283. Lemmon, William m 5/4/20 Amilia Hudson, dau of late Henry, of Geneva in Romulus; Rev. Caton. All of Romulus (3-5/10)
5284. Lemon, John of Romulus m 1/26/28 Maria Priphogle of Fayette in F (3-2/6)
5285. Lemon, Michael, 70, formerly of Howard, NY, d 2/24/47 in Napoleon, MI (2-3/24)
5286. Lemon, Richard m 3/25/44 Mrs. Mary Parshall in Palmyra; Rev. Harrington. All of Palmyra (5-3/27)
5287. Le Monyon, G. (Mrs.), 74, d 7/13/45 at the home of her son, Nathan Follett, Esq. in Batavia (1-7/15)
5288. Lennell, _____ (Mrs.), wf of Washington, d 9/16/29 in Palmyra (5-9/18)
5289. Leonard, Alfred, 3 yrs, and Lucretia Leonard, 18 mo, children of Allen Leonard, d 8/7/15 and 8/8/15 respectively in Canandaigua (3-8/23)
5290. Leonard, Alonzo E., 1 yr, s of J. Leonard, d 11/21/47 in Batavia (1-11/23)
5291. Leonard, Luther m Margaret Gantly in NYC (a member of the U.S. Light Artillery) (3-2/5/17)
5292. Leonard, Marshall, printer, m Polly Posson in Shelby (3-10/21/29)
5293. Leonard, Philip m Polly Moore in Farmington (5-1/12/20)
5294. Leonard, Stephen B., editor of the Owego Gazette, m Henrietta Sperry in Owego (3-3/4/18)
5295. Leonard, Uriah L., merchant, of Augusta, GA, m 4/11/44 Cassarinda M. Drane(?), dau of Col. Stephen of Columbia, GA, in Columbia; Rev. William Steed (5-5/1)
5296. Lesia, Porter James A. m 4/10/48 Martha A. Williams, formerly of Batavia, in Williamsburg, Ingham Co., MI (Martha dau of late Mr. Williams) (1-5/2)

5297. Lessure, John P. m Ruth Franklin in Benton (3-1/19/20)
5298. Lester, David Whitney, nearly 6, only s of David, d 7/30/29 in Benton
(3-8/5)
5299. Lester, Jonathan of "Peth (Wolcott)" m Rachel Hammond of Waterloo in
P (W) (3-5/22/22)
5300. Letch(?), Gurdon C., 29, formerly of Palmyra, d 5/18/41 in Utica, MI
(5-5/26)
5301. Letts, John of Palmyra m Sarah McCombs in Junius (3-4/1/29)
5302. Letts, John, Jr. m 9/2/15 Mary Ann Allen in Romulus; Silas Allen, Esq.
All of Romulus (3-9/27)
5303. Levey, Stephen, Jr. m Sally Gardner of Southport in Jerusalem, NY
(3-1/9/28)
5304. Lewis, Abel m 2/27/42 Mrs. Rhoda Richardson, both of Ellery; Rev. H.
Smith (4-3/3)
5305. Lewis, Abraham Q. m 6/5/50 Catherine B. Downs in Prattsburgh; Rev. B. C.
Smith (2-6/19)
5306. Lewis, Anthony H. m 7/22/18 Polly Cole, dau of Matthew, in Benton; Abner
Woodworth, Esq. All of Benton (3-7/29)
5307. Lewis, Arthur m 11/19/11 Polly Fulton in Seneca; Rev. Wilson (3-11-27)
5308. Lewis, Charles N. m 12/8/39 Hannah Daily, both of Seneca Falls; I. E.
Beecher, Esq. (5-12/13)
5309. Lewis, Elizabeth, 50, wf of Daniel W., Esq., d 9/10/16 in Geneva (3-9/11)
5310. Lewis, Elliot m Orracy Brown in West Bloomfield (3-3/3/19)
5311. Lewis, Ethan of Alleg. Co. m 2/17/25 Violetta Paine of Seneca Co. in
Sen. Co.; Rev. Dr. Axtell (3-2/23)
5312. Lewis, Francis, 93, d in Tisbury, Martha's Vineyard, MA ("...(for) 32
years he dressed as a woman and was supposed as such. After that he
took his proper apparel as a man and passed the remainder of his life
in the marriage state and has left numerous descendants. The family
has always received the respect of those who knew it.") (3-2/12/23)
5313. Lewis, George, editor of the Seneca Patriot, m 8/28/16 Elizabeth L. Madden;
Rev. Porter. All of Ovid (3-9/11)
5314. Lewis, Henry m 8/30/35 Harriet W. Nickerson, both of Penfield, in
Palmyra; F. Smith, Esq. (5-9/18)
5315. Lewis, Holmes, 18, s of Thomas, d 2/2/32 in Williamson (5-2/14)
5316. Lewis, James, 33, d 3/4/40 in Bath (2-3/11)
5317. Lewis, Jasper, 12, of Jasper d 11/18/18 (killed by the fall of a tree)
(3-12/9)
5318. Lewis, John (Dr.) of Clyde m 4/17/22 Eliza Ann Frisbie of Phelps in P;
Rev. S. W. Brace (3-4/24)
5319. Lewis, John m 3/9/43 Mary E. Brigham, both of Sheridan, in Portland;
Rev. Elder La Hatt (4-3/23)
5320. Lewis, John m 10/17/46 Mary Elizabeth Hand, both of Bath, in Avoca
(2-11/11)
5321. Lewis, John V. of Prattsburgh m 12/17/46 Helen Ann Lyon, oldest dau of
Abner P., Esq., of Prattsburgh (2-12/23)
5322. Lewis, M. G., "the celebrated author, well known as 'Monk Lewis'",
died "on his passage from Jamaica to Liverpool" (3-9/9/18)
5323. Lewis, Mary, 35, wf of Darius I., d in Victor (3-10/17/27)
5324. Lewis, Nancy, 23, wf of Charles P., d 7/12/26 in Seneca (3-7/19)
5325. Lewis, Orvil m Diana Griffin in Gorham (3-7/22/29)
5326. Lewis, Philena F., inf dau of Uriah, d 9/14/33 in Williamson (5-9/20)
5327. Lewis, Phones m 7/18/22 Aurilla Sherwood, both of Byron, in B;
Sylvester Willis, Esq. (1-7/26)
5328. Lewis, Polly, 26, of Gorham d at the poor house in Hopewell (3-4/1/29)
5329. Lewis, Ray G. m 11/29/26 Gennet Child, dau of William, Esq., editor of
the Seneca Farmer, in Waterloo; Rev. E. W. Martin (3-12/6)
5330. Lewis, Sally (Mrs.), 33, d 8/3/30 in Palmyra ("she was here on a visit")
(5-8/13)
5331. Lewis, Thomas, about 73, father of D. W., Esq. of Geneva, NY, d in
Lichfield, CT (3-9/13/15)
5332. Lewis, William, 57, formerly of Kentucky, d 1/17/25 near Little Rock,
Arkansas (3-3/30)
5333. Lewis, William, Esq., 38, sheriff of Orleans Co., d 7/25/26 in Clarendon
(3-8/2)

5334. Libby, Joseph m 6/12/47 Elizabeth Warner in Le Roy; A. D. Lampkins, Esq. (1-6/22)
5335. Libhart, Henry V. m Angelina De Lap in Naples, NY (3-1/14/29)
5336. Lidle, William m 6/4/45 Emily Coe, both of Jamestown, in Ashville; Rev. T. D. Blin (4-6/6)
5337. Lilly, ____, 5 mo, inf s of William, d 9/15/14 in Geneva (3-9/21)
5338. Lilly, Asa (Capt.), 67, d 1/26/44 in Palmyra ("moved to this section ... from Ashfield, Mass in 1802." After working as a mechanic he opened a public house. In the War of 1812 Capt. Lilly commanded a company of mounted volunteers on the Niagara frontier.) (5-1/31)
5339. Lilly, Chloe, 60, wf of Enoch, d 5/4/41 in Macedon (5-5/5)
5340. Lilly, Eleazer Bigelow, 17, only s of Capt. Asa, d 9/5/18 in Palmyra (5-9/8)
5341. Lilly, Enoch, 60, d 5/9/41 in Walworth (He and his wife Chloe were among the early settlers of this region) (5-5/12)
5342. Lilly, Lyman, 26, d at the home of Silas Guild in Seneca, Ont.Co. (near Brundage's mill) (Interred by the kindness of the neighboring people; he had said his friends lived near Mansfield, CT) (3-3/10/13)
5343. Lilly, William, merchant, of Geneva m 7/25/13 Catharine Day, dau of John of Romulus, in R; Rev. Clarke (3-7/28)
5344. Limebeck, John m Helen Bradley in Palmyra; Abraham Spear, Esq. (5-5/16/21)
5345. Lincklaen, John (Col.), 53, d 2/9/22 in Cazenovia (3-2/20)
5346. Lincoln, Benjamin (Maj. Gen.), collector of the Port of Boston and Charlestown, d 5/16/10 in Hingham, MA (3-5/23)
5347. Lincoln, L. L. m 4/16/46 Mary Peck, both of Alexander, in Stafford; Rev. A. P. Ripley (a double ceremony - see marr. of H. E. Hoisington) (1-4/21)
5348. Lincoln, William H. L. m 5/20/24 Juliette Pearsons, both of Bethany, in Covington; Rev. Hurd (1-5/28)
5349. Lindsley, Catharine, 10 mo, dau of James, d 9/17/31 in Bath (2-9/21)
5350. Lines, John, 37, m 12/25/17 Louisa(?) Averell, 16, dau of Gen. Averell, in Farmington (5-12/31)
5351. Linnell, ____, wf of Washington, d in Palmyra (3-9/23/29)
5352. Linnell, Haskell m 3/25/29 Melissa B. Morehouse in Palmyra; Rev. Campbell (3-4/1 and 5-3/27)
5353. Liscom, William B., 5 mo, s of George W. d 9/26/28 in Lyons (3-10/15 and 5-10/17)
5354. Liscomb, Lyman m Charity Bronson in Livonia (3-4/12/15)
5355. Liscomb, Parker m 1/19/22 Sally Woods in Geneva; Rev. Orrin Clark. All of Geneva (3-2/6)
5356. Liscomb, Sally, 36, wf of Parker, d 8/29/26 in Geneva (3-8/30)
5357. Little, Catherine, 17 mo, dau of William, d 8/1/47 in Bath (2-8/18)
5358. Little, Francis m 8/26/44 Melinda Langdon; D. Harrington. All of Palmyra (5-8/28)
5359. Little, James, 40, d 3/8/41 in Bath (2-3/17)
5360. Little, John, formerly of Hartford, CT, d 6/3/10 in Troupville (3-6/13)
5361. Little, John (Maj.), 77, d 9/29/22 in Johnstown ("a patriot who commanded the fort at Johnstown during the Rev. War) (3-10/30). In 1-11/8 the death date is 10/19/22.
5362. Little, Norman, merchant, m Jane Lyon in Canandaigua (3-7/30/28)
5363. Little, Sarah (Mrs.), 28, d in Junius (3-9/6/26)
5364. Livermore, Betsey (Mrs.), 35, d in Sing Sing, NY (3-3/11/29)
5365. Livermore, Samuel, Esq., 56, d 4/5/31 in Independence (Born in Mass.; lived a short time in Vermont where he was married; served many years as a magistrate in Madison Co., NY and later moved to Allegany Co. He was "a kind father (and) his family connections live in various parts of this state, Vt., Mass., Penna., and Mich.") (2-4/13)
5366. Livingston, Brockholst, Esq. of NYC m 11/14/12 Catharine Kortright of Newtown, NJ in Newtown; Rev. Wyatt (3-1/6/13)
5367. Livingston, Cornelia, relict of late Walter, Esq. of the Manor of Livingston, d 2/28/22 in NYC (3-3/20)
5368. Livingston, Edward, Esq., attorney, d in Albany (formerly clerk of the state assembly , Representative to Congress from Albany Co, Speaker of the House) (2-6/24/40)
5368a. Livingston, Henry (Gen.), 70, d 5/26/23 at his home in the Manor of Livingston (3-6/11)

5369. Livingston, Henry, Esq., 82, d in Poughkeepsie (3-3/12/28)
5370. Livingston, Johannah, 60, wf of Hon. Peter R. and sister of late
      Chancellor Livingston, d in Rhinebeck, Dutch. Co. (3-3/18/29
5371. Livingston, John H. (Dr.), Prof. of Theology in the Theological
      Seminary of the Reformed Prot. Dutch Ch., d 1/20/25 at his home in
      New Brunswick, NJ (3-2/2)
5372. Livingston, Robert R. (Hon.), 65, d 2/26/13 at his home in Clermont
      (3-3/10)
5373. Livingston, Sarah, 68, wf of Rev. Dr. J. H., Pres. of Queens College,
      d 12/29/14 in New Brunswick, NJ (3-1/25/15)
5374. Livingston, Valentine, formerly of NYC, d in Riga, Gen. Co. (3-1/2/22)
5375. Lloyd, _____ (Mrs.), wf of William R., d in Harmony (4-6/13/32)
5376. Lloyd, Amos G. m Gitty Demerah in Palmyra (5-6/30/18)
5377. Lloyd, Cromwell m 10/21/23 Delia Ann Boughton in Vienna, NY; Rev. Brace.
      All of Vienna (3-10/29)
5378. Lloyd, Joel m 2/23/24 Rachel Lowe, both of Canada, in Batavia; D. Tisdale,
      Esq. (1-2/27)
5379. Lloyd, Nancy (Miss), 17, d in Angelica (3-3/1/26)
5380. Lock, David, 43, d 10/5/22 in Geneva (3-10/9)
5381. Locke, Edwin of Batavia m 3/26/48 Mary Cull of Roanoke in R: Rev. Nettleton
      (1-4/4)
5382. Lockwood, Alanson m 2/17/20 Chloe Booth in Farmington (5-3/8)
5383. Lockwood, Jesse of Upper Canada m Elsey Bartholomew in Ovid (3-2/7/16)
5384. Lockwood, John m 3/4/46 Nancy Glenn in Urbana; Rev. T. P. Clark (2-5/5)
5385. Loder, Job m 6/19/50 Jane Maxwell in Bath; Rev. J. K. Tuttle. All of
      Bath (2-7/3)
5386. Loder, John, just over the line of Pulteney, d 7/12/41 (suicide) (2-7/14)
5387. Logan, George (Dr.), 67, d "at Stanton, near Philadelphia" (3-5/2/21)
5388. Logan, John m 8/27/29 Mary Lacy in Benton; Rev. Eddy (3-9/2)
5389. Logan, John m 2/5/30 Cordelia Howard in Palmyra; F. Smith, Esq. All of
      Canandaigua (5-2/12)
5390. Logan, Robert, 53, d 5/9/31 in Bath (2-5/11)
5391. Logan, William of the Society of Friends d in Kentucky (formerly of the
      national senate from PA; voluntarily visited France and England "in
      preserving peace between them and the U.S.") (3-10/2/22)
5392. Loghry, Jane, about 18, d 8/3/38 in Howard (2-8/8)
5393. Long, Jane, 20, youngest dau of Dr. David, d 8/8/24 in Pembroke (1-8/13)
5394. Longcor, James of Barrington m 7/4/46 Mrs. E. Jane Morse of Bath in B;
      Rev. L. W. Russ (2-7/8)
5395. Longwell, David m 3/25/47 Laura Campbell in Bath; Rev. E. B. Fuller
      (2-3/31)
5396. Longwell, Lewis of Urbana m 1/28/41 Rachel Retan of Pulteney in P;
      Elder Stebbins (2-2/10)
5397. Longyear, Zechariah m Levice Steel in Bloomfield (3-5/5/19 and 5-5/12/19)
5398. Lonnen, Franklin m 8/8/40 Mary Ann Wilcox, both of Mayville, in Ashville;
      Morris Norton, Esq. (4-8/12)
5399. Look, William, 3 yrs, s of S. B., d 3/25/43 in Chautauqua (4-4/6)
5400. Loomis, Chauncey, Esq. of Genesee Co., member of the State Senate,
      d 4/6/17 in Albany (3-4/23)
5401. Loomis, Cornelia, wf of Dr. H. N., d 10/14/31 in Palmyra (5-10/18)
5402. Loomis, Gelina F., dau of Henry, d 9/28/50 in Bath (2-10/2)
5403. Loomis, Henry m 9/18/49 Ann Eliza Swart, dau of P. Swart, in Bath;
      Rev. Corson. All of Bath (2-9/19)
5404. Loomis, Horatio N. (Dr.) of Palmyra m 10/11/30 Cornelia Williams, dau of
      Col. John of Waterville, Oneida Co., in Waterville; Rev. E. S. Barrows
      (5-10/22)
5405. Loomis, Horatio N., M.D., of Palmyra m 6/6/33 Mrs. Mary Ann Mott, dau of
      Col. John Williams of Waterville, Oneida Co., in Waterville (5-6/19)
5406. Loomis, James m Sally Williams in Middlesex (3-6/2/19)
5407. Loomis, Maria, dau of R. Loomis, d in Alexander (1-9/24/24)
5408. Loomis, Roswell m 1/4/26 Sebe Lounsbury in Alexander; Rev. Sampson
      (1-1/13)
5409. Loop, Amos m Cynthia Peck in Ontario, Wayne Co. (3-12/26/27)
5410. Loop, Hector of Elmira m Delina Cummings of Allen in Nunda, Alleg. Co.
      (3-12/7/25)
5411. Loop, Henry m Minerva Calkins in Cohocton (3-11/12/23)

5412. Loop, James L. of Avoca m 8/6/35 Permelia Stevens of Almond in A (2-8/12)
5413. Loop, Mary, inf ch of Christian, d in Elmira (3-9/17/28)
5414. Loper, John H. of Lyons m 1/30/15 Catharine Fisher of Seneca in S; Rev. Axtell (3-2/1)
5415. Lord, E. P. of Dexterville m 12/8/41 Rachel Mather of Sugargrove, PA in S; Rev. Chapin (4-12/16)
5416. Lord, Elmira Almira, 30, wf of William, Esq. d 7/10/25 in Le Roy (1-7/15)
5417. Lord, Hiram m 5/17/40 Sarah Shearman in Busti; George Stoneman, Esq. (4-5/27)
5418. Lord, John J., Esq., attorney, d 5/24/26 in Penn Yan (3-6/7)
5419. Lord, Josiah G., 25, d 9/2/42 in Palmyra (5-9/7)
5420. Lord, Oscar W. m 9/18/50 Minerva L. Holton, both of Batavia; Rev. S. M. Stimson (1-9/24)
5421. Lord, William of Barrington m Nancy Corbet in Reading (3-11/12/28)
5422. Lorin, Anna A., 64, wf of William, d 5/30/41 in Cameron (2-6/2)
5423. Loring, Caleb (Dr.) m 2/8/18 Elizabeth Keeler in Waterloo; Rev. Davis (3-2/18)
5424. Loring, Clarissa, 23, d 5/6/25 in Bergen (1-5/13)
5425. Loring, Lucy, 15, dau of Naham, d in Batavia (3-1/14/29)
5426. Loring, Lydia (Miss), 22, d 3/22/26 in Le Roy (1-3/24)
5427. Losee, Isaac m 2/12/31 Roxy Turrey(?) of Manchester in Lockville; H. Bannister, Esq. (5-2/25)
5428. Loshe _____ m Sally Miller in Bath (3-6/17/12)
5429. Lothrop, John H., Esq., cashier of the Ontario Branch Bank, d in Utica (3-6/24/29)
5430. Lott, James L. of Lottsville, PA m 7/2/39 Sarah M. Barton of Busti in B; Rev. S. W. Parks (4-7/3)
5431. Louck, Jeremiah m 2/8/24 Lucy Britton, both of Elba (1-2/20)
5432. Loucks, J. Perry m 3/10/42 Lucinda Haring in Ellery; Rev. H. Smith (4-3/17)
5433. Loucks, John m 12/30/46 Nancy C. Zielly, both of Avoca, in A; Rev. J. Strough (2-1/6/47)
5434. Loudon, Samuel, 96, formerly of NY, d "lately" in NJ ("an eminent Revolutionary editor and printer") (3-4/7/13)
5435. Louks, Clinton of Ellery m 5/20/42 Hamubital Thrasher of Levant in L; S. B. Winsor, Esq. (4-6/2)
5436. Lounsbury, Thomas (Rev.), pastor of the Presby. Church of Ovid, m "a short time since" Jenet Woodard of Burdette in B; Rev. Chadwick (3-10/25/26)
5437. Lousbury, James m 8/19/24 Melissa Miller in Milo; Abner Woodworth, Esq. All of Milo (3-8/25)
5438. Love, Ichabod m Mercilah(?) Sloan in Palmyra; A. Spear, Esq. (5-1/23/22)
5439. Love, Nelson m 3/5/34 Minerva Butts in Gerry; Rev. Babcock (4-4/2)
5440. Love, Reuben V. m 4/3/42 Sally Annis in Carroll; G. Swift, Esq. (4-4/14)
5441. Love, Thomas C., Esq. of Buffalo m 11/17/24 Maria Maltby of Waterloo in W; Rev. Orton (1-11/26 and 3-11/24)
5442. Lovejoy, _____ (Mrs.), 46, d in Benton (3-5/7/28)
5443. Lovejoy, Henry m 2/17/31 Desire Bly in Harmony (4-3/2)
5444. Lovejoy, William C. m 6/30/31 Emily H. Abbott, both of Newark, NY, in Palmyra; Rev. Alverson (5-7/8)
5445. Lovell, Ann Maria, inf dau of Ovid Lovell,d 5/23/29 in Palmyra (3-6/3 and 5-5/29)
5446. Lovell, Charles, 3 mo, s of Ovid, d 2/20/31 in Palmyra (5-2/25)
5447. Lovell, Gertrude, 27?, wf of Ovid of Palmyra, d 6/12/31 in Albany (5-6/17)
5448. Lovell, Mehitable, 63, wf of Jonathan, d 1/18/42 in Jamestown (4-1/20)
5449. Lovell, Ovid m 6/20/32 Cynthia D. Willcox in Palmyra; Rev. B. W. Whelpley (5-6/27)
5450. Lovell, Ovid, 45, d 3/11/35 in Palmyra (5-3/13)
5451. Lovett, John, Esq., late of Albany, d "recently" at Fort Meigs, Ohio (served on the Niagara Frontier in the campaign of 1812 as "Aid to Gen. Stephen Van Rensselaer (and there) sustained an injury in his sense of hearing.") (3-9/2/18)
5452. Lovett, Joseph Henry, 1 yr, s of Joseph, d 11/1/39 in Palmyra (5-11/8)

5453. Low, Alice, wf of Nicholas, d in NYC (3-4/29/18)
5454. Low, Andrew G., 23, d 11/5/25 in Palmyra (3-11/16)
5455. Low, James (Dr.), 40, d 2/3/22 in Albany (3-2/20)
5456. Low, Nicholas m Sally Ann Walker, both of Poland, NY, in P; Rev. J.
       Flower of Jamestown (4-9/7/43)
5457. Lowe, _____, 23, printer, d 3/3/30 in Galen (5-3/5)
5458. Lown(?), Samuel m 8/20/44 Sarah Allen, both of Sodus, in Palmyra;
       Frederick Smith, Esq. (5-9/4)
5459. Lowndes, William (Hon.) of South Carolina d 10/27/22 in passage from
       Philadelphia to London (5-1/29/23)
5460. Lowry, Ann Eliza, 16, d in Jerusalem, NY (3-10/3/27)
5461. Lowry, Deliah (sic), 9 yrs, d in Jerusalem, NY (3-12/5/27)
5462. Lowry, Elizabeth W., 34, consort of Nathaniel A., Esq., d 9/4/45 in
       Jamestown ("for many years a member of the Presbyterian Church")
       (4-9/5)
5463. Lowry, Harriet, 2 yrs, dau of N. A., d 10/5/35 (4-10/7)
5464. Lowry, Helen Therina Rachel, 8 mo, dau of N. A. and E. W. Lowry,
       d 4/20/41 (prob. in Jamestown) (4-4/21)
5465. Lowthrop, Charles William, 13 mo, s of Thomas, d 8/30/15 in Geneva
       (3-9/6)
5466. Lucas, Harry, 76, d 2/7/45 in Bath (He was emancipated from slavery
       "with some 30 others about 28 years ago"; member of Bapt. Church;
       surv by wf and children ) (2-2/12)
5467. Lucas, Samuel, 64, of Broome Co. d 3/14/19 at the home of Aaron Rice
       in No. 9 (Seneca) (a Rev soldier throughout the war) (3-3/24)
5468. Luce, Henry m 2/15/20 Diantha Colwell; E, B. Woodworth, Esq. All of
       Seneca (3-2/23)
5469. Luck, Edward, 10, s of William, late of Buffalo, d 3/5/31 in Palmyra
       (5-3/11)
5470. Lucup, John, 23, m Sarah Beals, 44, in Williamson (5-3/3/19).
       Married "in Williamstown" (3-3/10)
5471. Ludlow, Henry G. (Rev.) m Abigail Woolsey Welles, dau of Noah, formerly
       of Kinderhook, in NYC (3-11/25/29)
5472. Ludlum, Timothy m 1/17/15 Terressa Beach in Romulus "at Beachtown";
       Isaac Whitehead, Esq. All of Romulus (3-1/25)
5473. Lukins, William, about 21, d 1/7/14 in Geneva ("an honest, industrious
       mechanic and of respectable parents who reside in Philadelphia")
       (3-1/12)
5474. Lum, _____, 1 yr, s of Henry, d 2/21/13 in Geneva (3-2/24)
5475. Lum, _____, wf of Matthew, d 2/25/13 in Geneva (3-3/3)
5476. Lum. Abraham Henry, 1 yr, s of Charles, d 7/14/26 in Geneva (3-7/19)
5477. Lum, Charles m 11/4/18 Charlotte Osborne, both of Geneva, in G (3-11/11)
5478. Lum, Daniel L. of Geneva m 10/17/26 Hannah M. Dyer of Deerfield, Oneida
       Co. in D; Rev. Frost (3-10/25)
5479. Lum, David, oldest s of Matthew of Geneva, d "lately" in Ogdensburgh
       (3-1/3/10)
5480. Lum, Ellen M., 6 weeks, dau of Daniel L., d 10/20/27 in Geneva (3-10/24)
5481. Lumerox, David m 1/21/30 Margaret Vanlim in Lodi; Rev. Bennett. All of
       Lodi (3-1/27)
5482. Lummis, Sarah Ann, 2 yrs, dau of Dr. W. N., d 2/20/18 in Maxwell (Sodus).
       On 3/13/18 the doctor's son, John Maxwell, 5 yrs, died there (3-3/25)
5483. Lummis, William N., M.D., 58, d 4/10/33 in Sodus (5-5/1)
5484. Lund, Alfred of Palmyra m Mary Antoinette Whitney, dau of James, Esq. of
       Nashua, NH, in N; Rev. Richards (5-5/15/44)
5485. Lund, Samuel m 3/14/24 Nancy Morgan, both of Elba, in E; Rev. Whitcomb
       (1-3/19)
5486. Lundy, Basheba, dau of Samuel, d 8/4/22 in Junius (3-8/21)
5487. Lunt, Reuben L. m 7/13/42 Sarah Palmer in Jamestown; Rev. Hill (4-7/14)
5488. Lush, John (Maj.) of Albany d 4/10/22 in Albany (3-4/17)
5489. Lush, Richard, Esq., 70, d in Albany (3-6/11/17)
5490. Lutkins, John m Catharine Van Blaicom in Fayette (3-5/20/29)
5491. Lutz, John, 25, d 5/2/28 in Geneva (3-5/7)
5492. Lyell, Julia Ann, wf of Rev. Thomas Lyell, D.D.,(rector of Christ Church)
       and dau of the late Jonathan Rhea, Esq. of Trenton, NJ, d 7/21/24 in NYC
       (3-7/28)

5493. Lyle, Thomas (Rev.) of NYC m 1/12/23 Juliana Rhea, youngest dau of
late Col. Jonathan of Trenton, NJ, in St. Michael's Ch., Trenton
(3-2/5)
5494. Lyman, Elias of Burlington, VT m 4/14/42 Cornelia J. Hall, dau of
Timothy, in Troy; Rev. S. S. Beman (2-4/20)
5495. Lyman, Joseph (Hon.), 36, "a member of the last congress", d in
Cooperstown (3-4/18/21)
5496. Lyman, Joseph (Rev.), D. D., father of Mrs. Evans Johns of Canandaigua,
d in Hatfield, MA (3-4/16/28)
5497. Lyman, Levi, Esq. of Penn Yan m Betsey Buckbee in Prattsburgh (3-9/19/27)
5498. Lynch, Henry C., 15, s of Albert and Mary C, d 4/16/50 in Orange,
Steuben Co. (2-5/1)
5499. Lyon, _____ of Bath m 9/28/14 Sally Benton, dau of David of Seneca,
in S; Rev. Higgins (3-10/5)
5500. Lyon, Abner P. of Prattsburgh m 3/4/47 Laura Sheldon in Huron, Wayne Co.;
Rev. William C. Clark (2-3/17)
5501. Lyon, ("Charles" inked in) of Tompkins Co. m 9/12/39 Hester Ann R. Chapin
of Carroll in C (4-9/25)
5502. Lyon, David W. (Capt.) of Bath, NY m 9/22/46 Hopey Fay of Uniontown, PA
in U; Rev. G. Owen (2-10/7)
5503. Lyon, Elizabeth (Mrs.), 53, d 9/7/22 in Prattsburgh (3-9/18)
5504. Lyon, James m 11/9/19 Lydia Moseley in Canandaigua (3-11/24 and 5-12/1)
5505. Lyon, James m 5/12/46 Harriet Robie in Bath; Rev. W. D. Wilson. All of
Bath (2-5/20)
5506. Lyon, Moses, 60, d 5/2/23 in Prattsburgh (3-5/14)
5507. Lyon, Newton m Caroline Smith in Walworth; Rev. William Young. All of
Walworth (5-1/10/44)
5508. Lyon, Robert of Ogdensburgh (formerly of Canandaigua) m Catharine Bacon
in Bath (3-11/20/22)
5509. Lyon, William B., 18, s of Capt. Moses H. of Bath, d 1/1/35 in Litchfield,
CT (2-1/14)
5510. McAuley, James of Seneca m Mrs. Hannah Laman in Benton (3-11/5/28)
5511. McBeth, Charlotte, wf of James, formerly of NYC, d 11/15/47 in Bath
(2-11/17)
5512. McBurney, Hannah, wid of late Thomas, Esq., of Painted Post d in Bath
(3-10/14/29)
5513. McBurney, John m 8/29/17 Jemima Patterson in Bath (3-9/10)
5514. McBurney, John, Esq. m Almira Knox in Painted Post; Rev. David Higgins.
All of P. P. (2-11/16/31)
5515. McBurney, Lucretia, 50, wf of Col. James, d 2/8/32 at her residence in
Hornellsville (2-2/15)
5516. McBurney, Samuel, youngest s of Thomas, Esq., d in Painted Post (3-6/18/28)
5517. McBurney, Sarah, 84, mother of late Thomas, Esq., d in Painted Post
(3-5/6/29)
5518. McBurney, Thomas, (Hon.) d in Painted Post (3-9/10/28)
5519. McBurney, Thomas (Col.) of Painted Post, NY m 6/4/40 Jane A. Mills,
dau of late Elisha T., in Fairfield, CT; Rev. Atwater (2-6/17)
5520. McBurnie, Thomas, Esq. m 10/5/18 Hannah True in Bath (3-10/21)
5521. McCain, _____ m 3/23/25 Deborah Ann Garrison in Benton; Elder Goff
(3-3/30)
5522. McCall, Ancel (Mr.) d 8/31/15 in Painted Post (3-9/20)
5523. McCalla, Nancy, 69, d 3/23/50 in Bath (2-3/27)
5524. McCallum, Nathaniel H. d 7/11/33 in Maumee, Ohio (5-8/9)
5525. McCann, _____ m 3/30/16 Susannah Adams in Elmira (3-4/17)
5526. McCarn, John, 80, d 2/20/42 in Newark, NY (a Rev. soldier) (5-3/2)
5527. McCarroll, John, about 40, d at the Ontario (NY) Poor House (3-11/28/27)
5528. McCartee, William J., bookseller, of Geneva d 11/24/13 in Geneva "in an
epileptic fit" ("survived by an amiable wife and four sweet babes")
(3-12/1)
5529. McCarthy, James m 9/4/40 Christiana Thompson in Palmyra; F. Smith, Esq.
(5-9/16)
5530. McCarty, Thomas, 45, d 8/15/23 in Dresden(?) (3-8/27)
5531. McCauley, Thomas m 1/6/32 Mrs. Bridget Farley in the town of Greece, NY;
Esquire Warner. All of Rochester (5-1/31)
5532. McCay, James of Woodhull m 11/6/42 Sarah A. Miller of Pulteney "in Church";
Rev. J. H. Hotchkin (2-11/16)

142

5533. McCay, James Stewart, late of Moss-side in the County of Antrim, Ireland, m 3/12/40 Hester Hamlin, ward of W. W. McCay, Esq., at the home of the latter; Rev. Platt (2-3/18)
5534. McCay, William m Margaret Carmer in Newtown (3-6/13/27)
5535. McCay, William B. of Bath m 9/29/46 Sabra Ellsworth, niece of the Hon. S. Ellsworth, of Penn Yan in P. Y.; Rev. James Richards (2-10/7)
5536. McCay, William W. m 5/19/16 Sally M. Barton in Cayuga; Rev. Woodruff (3-6/5)
5537. McCebbin, Howard,5, only s of James, d 9/26/42 in Howard. Howard's sister, age 7, had died 9/2. "In a brief space they (the parents) have been called on to bury five children." (2-10/5). See 5640.
5538. McChain, James m 2/4/29 Julia Wisner, oldest dau of Rev. William, in Ithaca; Rev. Wisner. All of Ithaca. (3-2/11)
5539. McChesney, Hugh of Howard m 10/7/45 Mary Ann Davison of Bath in B; Rev. Platt (2-10/15)
5540. McClallen, Edith S., 24, wf of James, Jr. and dau of late Daniel Shearman of Busti, d in Kane Co., IL (4-4/18/38)
5541. McClallen, Fanny, 52, wf of James, Esq. formerly of Ashville and sister of A. Fletcher of Jamestown, d 2/27/44 in Jamestown (4-3/1)
5542. McClallen, James, Jr. m 10/13/35 Edith Shearman of Busti in B; Rev. Graves (4-10/21)
5543. McClandish, Alexander m 2/12/29 Nancy Trumbull in Seneca; Rev. Nesbit (3-2/18)
5544. McCleary, Daniel (Dr.), "Representative-elect from Niagara County in the next Legislature", d 1/2/16 in Clarence (3-1/17)
5545. McCleary, David C., 22, d 2/11/31 in Rupert, VT (late editor and joint proprietor of the People's Press in Batavia, NY (1-3/4)
5546. McClellan, Leonard E., m 12/1/41 Cornelia Seeley in Bristol, Kendall Co., IL; Rev. Cotton (4-2/24/42)
5547. McClentick, Susan (Miss) d in Pulteneyville (3-12/9/18)
5548. McClerk, Joseph (Gen.), about 60, postmaster of Franklinville, Catt. Co., d 9/14/33 in Wales, Erie Co. (5-9/27)
5549. McCloud, James, 45, of Geneva d 5/22/28 at the poor house in Hopewell. "First interred at the poor house but later buried in Geneva through the kindness of some of his friends." (3-5/28)
5550. McCluer, John m 3/20/32 Mary Lyon in Erwin; J. Morgan, Esq. All of Erwin (2-4/11)
5551. McClure, _____ (Mrs.), about 80, d in Bath (3-6/11/28)
5552. McClure, Archibald m 6/19/28 Mary Newkirk, dau of Hendrick, in Seneca; Rev. Nesbit (3-7/16)
5553. McClure, Finla (sic), 47, oldest s of Gen. George, formerly of Bath, d 10/28/47 in Canisteo (2-11/3)
5554. McClure, James, merchant, of Geneva m 8/17/26 Elizabeth Pohlman of Albany; Rev. Dr. Chester (3-8/23)
5555. McClure, James B., 26, s of Gen McClure, d 5/6/26 in Bath (3-5/17)
5556. McClure, Joseph L. m Clarissa Barrett in Ovid (3-2/7/16)
5557. McClure, Robert (Col.). 57. attorney and member of Pennsylvania senate, (father of Wm. of Elmira) d in Williamsport, PA (3-12/30/29)
5558. McClure, V.C., M.D., of Bath m 3/4/46 Caroline S. Graves of Howard in H; Rev. Wheeler (2-3/11)
5559. McClure, William m 12/23/22 Mary Stevens at the Ontario Glass Factory; Rev. Axtell (3-12/25)
5560. McCollum, Joel m 8/30/18 Rachael Scovell in Palmyra; Rev. Townsend (3-9/9 and 5-9/1)
5561. McCollum, Robert, 71, d 2/11/35 in Sodus (5-2/20)
5562. McComb, James of the ship "Triton" m in May, 1811 at Canton, China Chi Altangi Hoam,"youngest dau of Altangi Hoam, a mandarin of immense wealth, residing near the English Factory." (3-12/4/11)
5563. McCombes, William m 3/29/49 Marietta M. Rowe, wid of Rev. G. M. Rowe, in Alabama, NY; Rev. R. C. Palmer. All of Alabama, NY (1-4/3)
5564. McConnell, Mathew, 77, d in Elmira (3-7/2/17)
5565. McCord, Andrew, Esq. d 4/22/10 in Wallkill (3-5/9)
5566. McCord, Laura (Mrs.), 28, dau of Daniel and Bethia Hibbard, d 2/19/42 in North East, PA (4-2/24)
5567. McCormick, _____, wf of William, d 9/27/15 near Geneva (the result of an accidentally self-inflicted gunshot wound received 9/22; this accident reported in newspaper dated 9/27) (3-10/11)

143

5568. McCormick, Abraham of Painted Post d in Bath (3-1/24/10)
5569. McCormick, Henry, s of Col. H., d in Owego (3-8/22/27)
5570. McCormick, Samuel d 5/29/16 (prob. in Geneva) (3-6/5)
5571. McCoy, Jonathan of Tyrone m Marietta Griffith in Wayne (3-11/12/28)
5572. McCoy, Samuel M. m 8/17/26 Susan Isenhour, both of Seneca, in Canandaigua (3-8/23)
5573. McCracken, Asa, 32, d 12/16/11 in Batavia (3-1/1/12)
5574. McCracken, Henry William, s of William J., Esq. of Rochester, d 9/2/25 in Bethany (1-9/2)
5575. McCrackern, William of New Haven, CT m Mary G. Jenkins of Canandaigua in C (3-4/29/18)
5576. McCreery, Rebecca L., 19, d 9/14/44 in Ontario, NY (5-9/25)
5577. McCulley, Pamelia, 40, wf of Thomas, d 9/9/25 in Batavia (1-9/16)
5578. McCullough, _____, consort of John and dau of Seth Stanly, d 2/6/15 in Seneca (3-2/8)
5579. McCullough, John, Esq. m Mary Parke in Seneca (3-2/7/16)
5580. McCullough, John, Esq., about 50, d 11/15/26 in Seneca (fell off a wagon and broke his back)(3-11/22)
5581. McCully, Thomas of Batavia m Sally Hollister in Pembroke (1-1/20/26)
5582. McCurdy, James, 15, s of John, d 11/15/17 in Junius (3-11/26)
5583. McCurdy, Susan (Mrs.) d 8/3/22 (1-8/9/22)
5584. McCurdy, William m 1/18/18 Hulda Briggs, both of Junius, in Geneva; Eli Bannister, Esq. (3-1/28)
5585. McCurdy, William m Fanny Bill in Canandaigua (3-5/24/20)
5586. McDavid, James m 2/20/26 Elizabeth O'Donaghey in Batavia; Rev. Smith. All of Batavia (1-2/24)
5587. McDole, James of the Society of Shakers (sic) m 2/22/30 Mrs. Betsey George in Clyde; Frederick Bogher, Esq. (5-3/10)
5588. MacDonald, Daniel (Rev.), D.D., 44, professor of languages in Geneva College, d 3/25/30 "at his residence near Geneva" (5-4/9)
5589. McDonald, Frederick, 11, s of Rev. Dr. McDonald, d 3/23/28 in Geneva (3-4/2)
5590. McDonald, James m 5/12/22 Catharine Green in Seneca; Richard Hogarth, Esq. (3-5/15)
5591. McDonald, S. (Lt.), 106, d "in the Isle of Tikes", NY. "He left three children under ten years of age." (5-2/25/31)
5592. McDonald, Stephen, 37, d in Palmyra (3-10/3/27)
5593. McDougal, _____, 2 weeks, ch of William, d (prob. in Geneva) (3-9/17/23)
5594. McDowall, William P., Esq., late "Prothonotary" of Warren Co., d 4/20/39 in Warren, PA (4-4/24)
5595. McDowel, John of Ithaca m 12/19/15 Laurinda Lowman in Chemung (3-1/3/16)
5596. McDowell, Edward m 6/16/12 Margaret Cook in Phelps; W. Barnet, Esq. (3-6/24)
5597. McDowell, James m 2/14/31 Lucretia Hawser in Lockville; Rev. B. Earley (5-2/25)
5598. McDowell, Samuel m Delilah E. Beardsley in Palmyra; Rev. Jeremiah Irons (3-10/6/19 and 5-9/29/19)
5599. McDowell, Thomas of Howard m 1/4/42 Felinda Sickford of Cohocton in C (2-1/5)
5600. McElwain, James of Lyons m 3/29/42 Susan F. Durfee, dau of Mrs. Susannah Durfee of Palmyra, in Zion Church, Palmyra, NY (5-3/30)
5601. McElwee, James m Savanna Seamans, both of Bath, in Hornby (2-12/28/31)
5602. McEwen, Charles, late a ward justice of the City of NY, died "last week" at his home in NYC ("He was in Palmyra in June and July last on a visit to a daughter residing here.") (5-1/15/36)
5603. McEwing, Hiram m Nancy Smith in Waterloo (3-11/4/29)
5604. McFall, Robert m Polly Denison in Benton; Abner Woodworth, Esq. (3-3/17/19)
5605. McFall, William, 106, d in Pelham, Westchester Co. (3-1/17/16)
5606. McGlashan, Charles, Esq. m 9/25/43 Mrs. Sophia McGlashan, wid of late Gen. James, in Rutledge; Rev. William Waitbe (4-9/28)
5607. McGonegal, Ira m 3/2/50 Mary Owen in Bath; Rev. R. R. Swick. All of Bath (2-3/6)
5608. McGowen, William m 2/15/18 Nancy Hanney, both of Farmington, in Geneva; Jacob Dox, Esq. (3-2/18)
5609. McGraw, _____, inf ch of "Mr. McGraw", d 10/25/26 in Geneva (3-11/1)

5610. McGraw, Aaron of Lyons m 2/21/33 Laura Huggins of Marion in M; Seth
      Eddy, Esq. (5-3/6)
5611. McGraw, Henry m Mrs. Wilson, wid of late J., in Benton (3-7/1/18)
5612. McGuier, _____ (Mr.), 65, d in Benton (3-7/29/18)
5613. McGuire, Sally (Mrs.), 35, d 9/15/24 in Junius (3-9/29)
5614. McHenry, Abraham m Ruth H. Brewster in Elmira (3-5/12/19)
5615. McHenry, Daniel of Almond m 5/9/22 Mary Magee late of Bath (3-5/29)
5616. McHenry, James, 52, d 6/16/41 in Almond, Alleg. Co. (2-6/23)
5617. McHenry, Mary M., 30, wf of Daniel, Esq., sheriff of Alleg. Co., d 3/25/31
      in Angelica (2-3/30)
5618. McIntire, Joseph m 12/16/47 Zilpah M. Mills, dau of Joel, in Elba; Rev.
      I. W. Vaughan. All of Elba (1-12/21)
5619. McIntosh, John m Deborah Eaton in Friendship, Alleg. Co. "after a
      courtship of six hours with very little intermission" (3-9/2/18)
5620. McIntosh, John (Gen.), 70, d "at his plantation in McIntosh Co.,
      Georgia" (3-12/6/26)
5621. McIntosh, Jno. m Cornelia M. Guion of Owego in O (3-1/21/29)
5622. McIntyre, _____, inf s of Dr. A. McIntyre, d 10/9/21 in Palmyra
      (5-10/10)
5623. McIntyre, Alexander (Dr.) m 12/20/18 Ann Beckwith in Palmyra; Rev.
      Townsend (5-12/23)
5624. McIntyre, Allen m Sally Vroman in Syracuse (3-1/14/29)
5625. McIntyre, Jerah d 4/6/24 in Batavia (1-4/9)
5626. McIntyre, Loren m 12/16/45 Cynthia Blasdell in Batavia; Rev. John
      Parker. All of Batavia (1-1/20/46)
5627. McKain, De Witt, s of Capt. James, d 7/22/22 in Batavia at age 5
      (1-7/26)
5628. McKann, William m Sally Smith at Catlin (h. I.) (sic) (3-1/14/29)
5629. McKay, Jennet, 78, wid of Robert, died - (She a native of Sutherland-
      shire, Scotland; came to the U.S. in 1773; was left a widow in 1785;
      member of Presby. Church in Geneva; surv by 8 children) (3-7/2/17)
5630. McKay, Rachael, mother of William W., Esq. of Bath, d in Pittsford
      (3-8/6/28)
5631. McKay, Robert of Caledonia m 8/29/16 Alida Fort of Geneva; Rev. Axtell
      (3-9/4)
5632. McKay, Sophia, 31, wf of Robert, d in Caledonia, NY (3-2/24/13)
5633. McKee, William of Seneca Falls m Catherine Mead in Tyre (3-12/23/29)
5634. McKeen, Marcellus m 10/12/41 Clarissa Robinson in Walworth; Rev. D.
      Lyon. All of Walworth (5-10/13)
5635. McKenneff, Isaac, Esq. m 1/1/23 Eleanor James in Geneva; J. Field, Esq.
      (3-1/8)
5636. McKenney, Mathew, between 60 and 70, d in the Orange County jail.
      "He had been in the Ulster and Orange jail about 50 years for a single
      debt. The debt was at first small and he has been a man of considerable
      property; but of late his children have had possession ..." (3-5/16/21)
5637. McKenny, Philip m 7/17/28 Freelove Crosby, both of Seneca Falls, at the
      Franklin House in Geneva; Rev. Dr. Axtell (3-7/23)
5638. McKenzie, John m 8/18/16 Deborah Gruning; Eli Bannister, Esq. of Seneca
      (3-8/28)
5639. McKenzie, John, 82, d 1/28/25 near Geneva (3-2/2)
5640. McKibbin, Dorothy, wf of James, d 11/28/42 in Howard. "(She) is the
      mother who buried her five children as noticed in our No. of Oct 5."
      (2-11/30). See 5537.
5641. McKinster, Joseph P. of Junius m Sally Ellis in Fayette (3-7/9/28)
5642. McKinstry, Charles (Gen.), 64, d 12/30/18 in Hillsdale, Columbia Co.
      (3-1/20/19)
5643. McKinstry, John (Col.), 77, d 6/23/22 in Livingston. In the Rev. War
      at the Battle of the Cedars (30 mi. above Montreal on the St. Lawrence)
      then-Capt. McKinstry was twice wounded and taken prisoner. Reportedly
      his life was saved through his giving the masonic sign to "Warrior
      Brant" as he was being tied to the stake for burning. (3-6/26)
5644. McKinstry, Willard, senior editor of the Fredonia Censor, m 12/1/43
      Maria A. Durlin in Fredonia; Rev. S. M. Hopkins. All of Fredonia
      (4-12/8)
5645. McKnight, Ann Maria, 30, wf of Orlando, formerly of Westfield, NY
      d 12/10/42 in Sandusky, Ohio (4-12/22)

5646. McKnight, George H., 18, d 9/28/43 in Rochester (5-10/4)
5647. McKnight, James of Palmyra m 10/7/41 Nancy Thatcher of Albion in A;
    Rev. Jackson (5-10/20)
5648. MacKnight, John of Romulus m 4/4/27 Elizabeth Stanley, dau of late
    Deacon Seth, in Seneca; Rev. Dr. Axtell (3-4/11)
5649. McKnight, Orlando, Esq. of Sandusky, Ohio m 6/13/43 Sarah Sophia Deming
    in Westfield; Rev. C. B. Stout (4-6/22)
5650. McKnight, Robert m 12/18/16 Eliza Combs; Rev. Moses Young. All of
    Romulus (3-12/25)
5651. McKnight, William A. m 10/8/29 Mary Cook, dau of Jesse of Fayette in F;
    Rev. Barton of Romulus (3-10/28)
5652. McKnutt, William, Jr., 18, d 9/7/42 in Manchester (5-9/21)
5653. McLallen, John, 2nd, of Trumansburgh m Eunice Holmes in Covert (3-10/22/28)
5654. McLaren, M. N. (Rev.) of Geneva m 7/25/27 Susan Y. Patty, dau of John
    of Auburn, in A; Rev. Johnson (3-8/8)
5655. McLaughlin, William L., 21, m Lucetta Warner, 13, in NYC (3-1/27/19)
5656. McLean, ____, 9, s of Hon. John, d "in Cincinnati" (3-12/23/29)
5657. McLean, Andrew of Orange Co. d in Waterloo (3-10/8/28)
5658. McLean, George of Benton m 11/19/15 Betsey Sebring of Ovid in Ovid
    (3-12/6)
5659. McLean, John (Gen.), 66, d 3/2/21 in NYC (5-3/21)
5660. McLean, John, Esq., "first Judge of Seneca Co.", m 9/23/22 Maria
    Blanchard of Salem, Wash. Co. in S (3-10/16)
5661. McLean, Julius m 1/3/42 Jane D. Eggleston in Palmyra; Rev. A. H.
    Burlingame. All of Palmyra (5-1/5)
5662. McLean, William (Rev.) of the Redstone Presbytery m Mary Miller of
    Sugargrove in S; Rev. Parmely of Jamestown (4-5/19/41)
5663. McLean, William A., 25, d 12/6/24 in Palmyra (3-12/8)
5664. McMaster, Adeline A., 34, wf of David, Esq. of Bath and only child of
    Mrs. A. Humphreys who has long been a widow, d 10/7/41 (member of
    Presby. Ch.) (2-10/13)
5665. McMaster, David, Esq. of Bath m Adeline A. Humphreys in Marcellus
    (3-2/20/28)
5666. McMaster, De Witt Clinton, 2 yrs, s of Capt. James W., d 4/21/27 in
    Benton (3-5/2)
5667. McMasters, James W. m 10/22/18 Jemima Haight in Benton; Rev. Thomas
    White. All of Benton (3-11/11)
5668. McMath, Alla (sic) of Romulus m 3/26/29 ____ Homan of Phelps in P;
    Rev. H. P. Strong (3-4/8/29)
5669. McMichael, Joseph, 86, d 9/12/41 in Palmyra (a Rev. patriot; was a waiter
    to Gen. Washington in that war)(5-9/22)
5670. McMillan, Margaret (Mrs.), 84, d 2/5/49 in Gilead, MI (1-2/20)
5671. McNab, Andrew, Esq., 45, d 10/26/29 at the home of Miss McKay in Geneva
    (a native of Scotland; emigrated to the U.S. in 1806; In 1812 came to
    Geneva as assistant agent in the land office of the Pulteney estate)
    (3-10/28 and 5-11/6)
5672.* McNair, Ann Eliza, 9, dau of Hugh, d 8/11/15 in Canandaigua (3-8/23)
5673. McNair, Hugh, Esq. m 11/12/18 Mrs. Elizabeth Dungan in Canandaigua
    (3-11/25)
5674. McNair, Phebe, 50, wf of Hugh, Esq., d in Canandaigua (3-5/14/17)
5675. McNair, William of Groveland m Amanda Warner in Lima (3-4/17/22)
5676. McNair, William W. of Groveland m Sarah Pierpont of Connecticut in Clyde,
    NY (3-10/28/29)
5677. McNaughton, Duncan of Wheatland m Caroline Marsh of East Bloomfield in
    Rochester (3-5/20/29)
5678. McNeall, John, 70, d 8/23/22 in Junius (3-9/4)
5679. McNeer, Nicholas, 28, of Genesee Co. m 3/26/29 Eunice Burns, 14, of Seneca
    in Geneva; S. G. Gage, Esq. (3-4/15)
5680. McNeil, David, one of the judges of the Ontario County courts, m 12/7/35
    Sarah Young in Phelps (5-12/25)
5681. McNilan, Amy, 1 yr, dau of James, d 4/25/22 in Junius (3-5/8)
5682. McNorton, ____ (Mrs.), 92, d 2/24/35 in Howard (2-3/4)
5683. McPherson, Adaline, about 27, wf of James and dau of William Pardee, Esq.,
    d 3/9/29 in Gorham (3-3/11)
5684. McPherson, William (Gen.), 57, d 11/5/13 in Philadelphia ("a distinguished
    Revolutionary War officer") (3-12/8)
*5672a. McNair, David, Esq., 45, d in Sparta, NY (3-6/11/17)

5685. McQuhae (sic), John, 83 or 33, d 8/12/49 in Danville, PA (2-8/29)
5686. McWhorter, John m 3/24/22 Betsey Cumings in Warsaw, NY; Rev. Smith
       (1-3/29)
5687. Mabee, Israel, 35, of Glen, Mont. Co. d 12/8/36 in Palmyra en route to
       Rochester (buried in the Palmyra burying ground) (5-12/9)
5688. Machin, Thomas (Capt.), 72, member of the order of the Cincinnati,
       d 4/3/16 ("The chain across the Hudson at West Point, in the Rev.
       War, was constructed under his direction ...") (surv by wf and 2 ch)
       (3-5/8)
5689. Mack, Ebenezer, editor of the American Journal (Ithaca) m 2/9/20 Ellinor
       Dey, dau of Peter of Romulus, in R; Rev. Young (3-2/23).  Correction
       in newspaper dated 3/1/20:  The marriage place should read Fayette,
       not Romulus.
5690. Mack, Elisha of South Dansville m 3/2/47 Hannah Niles of Bath in B
       (2-3/10)
5691. Mack, Ransee (Miss), 11, d 9/8/17 in Canandaigua (3-10/1)
5692. Mack, Stephen, Esq. d 4/16/14 in Owego (He was "First Judge of the Court
       of Common Pleas, Broome County, and editor of the American Farmer")
       (3-5/4)
5693. Macomber, Marvin of Williamson m 7/7/41 Eliza Octavia Sears, oldest dau
       of Elder John of Palmyra, in Palmyra (5-7/14)
5694. Macombs, Michael Josiah, 3 yrs, s of John, d 5/3/41 in South Dansville
       (2-5/19)
5695. Madden, Abigail (Mrs.), 79, d in Naples, NY (3-4/12/15)
5696. Maden, John m 5/28/15 Phebe Elmira Teale, dau of Capt. N., in Junius
       (a double ceremony - see marr. of Samuel Heney) (3-5/31)
5697. Magee, Charles, 7, s of John, Esq., d 2/26/41 (prob. in Bath) (2-3/3)
5698. Magee, Jane, 43, wf of Thomas J., d 11/25/50 in Hornellsville (2-12/4)
5699. Magee, John (Hon.), member of Congress from the Steuben Co. region
       m 2/22/31 Mrs. Arabella Snowden of Washington, D.C. in W; Rev. Hawley
       (2-3/9)
5700. Magee, John, 18 mo, s of John, Esq., d 3/13/41 in Bath (2-3/17)
5701. Magee, Sarah, wf of Hon. John of Geneva, d 5/16/28 at the home of her
       father, Judge McBurney,in Painted Post.  Her husband arrived from
       Washington, D.C. on the morning of her funeral (3-5/28)
5702. Magown, Grace, 54, wf of Philip, d in Junius (3-10/1/28)
5703. Magown, Philip, Jr. m Elsy Bradt in Junius (3-4/23/28)
5704. Maiden, John m 6/24/28 Mrs. Mary McCabe, wid of late Michael, in Geneva
       (3-7/2)
5705. Main, Polly, 64, wf of Thomas T., d 12/26/37 in Clarendon, Orleans Co.
       (1-1/4/38)
5706. Main, S. U. m 1/13/49 Adaline Botsford in Castile; Rev. J. S. Brown
       (1-1/23)
5707. Maish, David m 11/1/45 Charlotte Anderson in Le Roy; Rev. Houghton
       (1-11/4)
5708. Maker, Archilus m 11/3/38 Mary Ann Williamson; Rev. McKenney (2-12/5)
5709. Malcolm, William, merchant, of Canaseraga m AnnThompson of Rhinebeck
       in Canaseraga (3-12/23/18)
5710. Maley, John, about 26, d in Canandaigua (3-1/6/13)
5711. *Mallery, John m Mary Lovy in Benton; Rev. Todd (3-8/5/29)
5712. Mallory, James (Hon.), late a member of the state senate, d 2/20/27 in
       Troy (3-2/28)
5713. Mallory, John m 8/20/29 Mary S. Lacey (or Lacky) in Benton; Rev. Eddy
       (3-8/26)
5714. Mallory, Russel of Lyons m 11/20/25 Harriet Taft in Williamstown, MA
       (3-12/7)
5715. Mallory, Samuel m Mrs. Nichols in Canandaigua (3-2/11/18)
5716. Maltby, Alanson T. of Cayuga Co. m 2/23/30 Priscilla G. Gray of
       Alexander; Rev. Allen Crocker (1-2/26)
5717. Maltby, Benjamin of Waterloo m Mary Warner in Hatfield, MA (3-11/12/28)
5718. Maltby, Isaac (Gen.) d in Waterloo ("late from Massachusetts") (3-9/15/19)
5719. Maltby, Isaac Murray, 2 yrs, only ch of S. M., d in Waterloo (3-9/30/29)
5720. Maltby, Seth M., merchant, of Waterloo m Mrs. Abigail Buchanan in
       Geneva (1-3/10/26)
5721. Maltby, William m 11/12/29 Cynthia Carr in Canandaigua; Rev. Eddy
       (3-11/25 and 5-11/27)
* 5711a Mallory, Erastus T. m 10/9/45 Mary J. Kelley in Jasper; Rev. Ashworth(2-10/22)

5722. Maltby, William of Hopewell, Ont. Co. m 9/3/35 Delia W. Chapin in
Palmyra; Rev. Townsend (5-9/18)
5723. Manchester, Adam d in Canandaigua (3-11/5/17). Correction same newspaper
dated 11/12: "We were wrongly informed... Mr. Manchester still lives
and we understand likely to recover although his leg has been amputated
a second time." In the issue of this paper dated 11/19 the death of
Mr. Manchester is confirmed.
5724. Manchester, William W., Esq. of Venice, NY m 9/26/43 Martha Glover
Billings of Macedon in M; Rev. D. Herrington of Palmyra (5-10/4)
5725. Manderville, Homer, Esq., attorney, m 7/17/31 Abigail Manley, both
formerly of Chenango Co., in Addison; Elder Aaron Baxter (2-8/3)
5726. Mann, James, 53, d 4/25/22 in Geneva (3-5/1)
5727. Mann, John Milton, physician, drowned in crossing the Hudson River from
Hudson to Athens, NY (3-10/25/09)
5728. Mann, Mary, 45, wf of James, d 9/25/12 in Seneca (3-10/7)
5729. Mann, Moses m 6/15/16 Abigail Paine, both of Geneva; Rev. Henry Axtell
(3-6/26)
5730. Manning, Joseph m 8/19/29 Jane Johnson, both of Fayette, in F; Rev. M.
Martin (3-8/26)
5731. Manning, Rockwell of Geneva m 2/27/29 Margaret Cowen of Waterloo in W;
Rev. Lane (3-3/11)
5732. Mapes, Benjamin, "near 80", m Mary Wilson, "near 74", in Orange Co.
(3-11/17/13)
5733. Mapes, Jonas (Maj. Gen.), 67, d 7/10/27 in NYC (3-7/25)
5734. Maples, George W., 4 yrs, s of Charles G. and Ruth, died (death place
not given) (4-10/10/45)
5735. Mappa, Adam G. (Col.) d 4/18/28 in Trenton, Oneida Co. (a native of
Holland) (3-4/30)
5736. Marble, John, M.D., of Marion m 1/21/41 Sarah Whitman, dau of John, Esq.
of Lenox, Madison Co., in Lenox; Rev. A. P. Mason (5-1/27)
5737. March, George, 36, d 3/29/50 at his home in Caryville (was of the firm
of Burden, March and Co., mercantile; member of Meth. Episc. Ch.
and trustee of Cary Collegiate Seminary) (1-4/2)
5738. Marcy, Henry K. m Ruth Ann Spalding in Bath; Elder Savage (3-1/23/28)
5739. Markham, Caroline (Miss), 17, d in Auburn (3-3/1/26)
5740. Markham, Henry, Esq., formerly of Bath, d 3/30/42 in Houston, Texas (2-5/4)
5741. Markham, Norris of Cohocton m 11/8/41 Mary Jane Patterson of South
Dansville in S. D. (2-12/15)
5742. Marlatt, Christopher, merchant, m 10/7/32 Cynthia Tubbs in Woodhull;
David Edwards, Esq. (2-10/10)
5743. Marsh, ____, ch of "Mr. Marsh", d 8/8/15 in Canandaigua (3-8/23)
5744. Marsh, Balorman m Mary Hellar, dau of Michael, in Elmira (3-6/25/28)
5745. Marsh, Elvira, 1 yr 11 mo, dau of Asa B., d 2/14/35 in Carroll (4-2/18)
5746. Marsh, Frances, 40, wf of Dr. Marsh of Arcadia, d 3/23/42 in Arcadia
(5-3/30)
5747. Marsh, Jasper of Carroll (a Rev. soldier) m 7/16/35 Mrs. Sarah Sherwin
in Jamestown; R. Pier, Esq. (4-7/22)
5748. Marsh, Jasper, 80, d 4/29/41 in Carroll (a Rev. Soldier) (4-5/5)
5749. Marsh, Joshua of Brattleboro, VT, formerly of Jamestown, NY, m Nancy
Rice of Milbury, MA in M (she dau of Capt. Daniel Rice) (4-7/5/26)
5750. Marsh, Justin (Rev.), pastor of the Cong'l. Ch. in Mina, m 9/14/30
Jane Deming, dau of Fenn of Westfield, in W; Rev. Oaks (4-9/22)
5751. Marsh, Lucinda, 43, wf of Joel, d 1/1/42 in Carroll (4-1/6)
5752. Marsh, Moses, 47, of Jamestown, NY d 6/10/33 in Pittsburgh (PA?)
("Printers in Worcester, Mass. are requested to publish this death")
(4-6/19)
5753. Marsh, Salt, Esq. d at Tioga Point (3-11/29/15)
5754. Marsh, Thomas of Romulus m Caroline Matilda Howe in Ovid (3-1/16/28)
5755. Marsh, Thomas m Mrs. Abigail Arnold in Romulus (3-1/13/30)
5756. Marshall, ____, 1 yr, ch of Jacob, d 9/11/22 in Geneva (3-9/18)
5757. Marshall, Andrew G. m 11/12/23 Mary Cock, both of Reading, in R (3-11/26)
5758. Marshall, Elihu F., editor of the Album m Mary May in Rochester (3-9/19/27)
5759. Marshall, Elihu W., 14 mo, s of Chauncy, d at Seneca Falls (3-3/4/29)
5760. Marshall, Erastus m 11/4/30 Lucy Pitts, both of Arcadia, in Lyons
(5-11/19)
5761. Marshall, Frederick N., 4 yrs, s of O. F., Esq., d 5/6/26 in Wheeler
(3-5/17)

5762. Marshall, James I. of Reading m 1/31/22 Harriet Bouker of Scipio in S;
E. Sawyer, Esq. (3-2/13)
5763. Marshall, Jennet, 3, dau of Jacob, d 10/27/22 ("... being the third
child he has lost within a few weeks") (3-10/30)
5764. Marther, Ebenezer, 36, formerly of Bath, d 2/14/31 in Mich. Terr.
(2-3/30)
5765. Martignon, Francis Anthony, D.D., for 26 yrs pastor of the Roman Cath.
Ch. in Boston, d 9/19/18 in Boston (3-10/7)
5766. Martin, Abram m 9/23/35 Esther Chadwick in Palmyra; Rev. Staunton (5-9/25)
5767. Martin, Abram m 2/4/45 Mary E. Burnham in Jamestown; Rev. E. J. Gillett.
All of Jamestown (4-2/7)
5768. Martin, Adin m Catherine Hicks in Fayette (3-4/21/19)
5769. Martin, Alpheus of Canandaigua m 3/5/29 Sarah Beebe of Palmyra in P;
Rev. Campbell (5-3/6 and 3-3/11)
5770. Martin, Christian (Mrs.), 94, d in NYC (3-1/3/16)
5771. Martin, Dorace, 32, wf of Charles d in Pembroke (1-6/16/26)
5772. Martin, Elisha, about 65, d 7/5/50 in Bath (2-7/17)
5773. Martin, George m Sally Woodruff in Lyons (3-4/8/29)
5774. Martin, Lorenzo m 12/16/41 Mercy Jenkins in Carroll; E. Bradley, Esq.
(4-12/23)
5775. Martin, Thomas, 2nd, m 1/8/45 Marcia Grosvenor, both of Pinegrove, PA,
in Jamestown; Rev. O. Street (4-1/10)
5776. Marvin, Dudley, Esq. m Mary Whalley in Canandaigua (3-1/28/18)
5777. Marvin, Erastus, Esq., 30, d in Kennedyville (4-8/29/32)
5778. Marvin, Henry A. of West Bloomfield m Drusilla Mills in Windsor, CT
(3-9/24/17)
5779. Marvin, Moses, 85, d 10/-/31 in Bethany (formerly from Lyme, CT)
(1-11/25)
5780. Marvin, Richard P., Esq. m 9/8/34 Isabella Newland, dau of David, Esq.
of Albany, in A; Rev. James (4-9/17)
5781. Mason, Anthony m Nancy Mace in Prattsburgh (3-6/14/26)
5782. Mason, Betsey, 42, wf of Wheaton, d 7/29/25 in Batavia (1-7/29)
5783. Mason, Caroline, 4, dau of B. B. and M., d 11/21/44 in Jamestown
(4-11/22)
5784. Mason, Chloe, 26, wf of Capt. F., d in Bristol (3-2/13/28)
5785. Mason, George W. of Wayne, Steuben Co. m Almira Bliss, dau of Capt.
Jeremiah, in Newport (3-7/23/28)
5786. Mason, George W., editor of the Elmira Gazette,m 3/25/49 Elizabeth
Collingwood in Elmira; Rev. A. M. Ball (2-4/4)
5787. Mason, James, 105, d in Greenbush (3-2/11/29)
5788. Mason, James of Palmyra m 2/19/32 Henrietta Harmsley of Sodus at St.
John's Ch., Sodus; Rev. B. H. Hickox (5-2/21)
5789. Mason, Jemima, 41, wf of Elliot, d 11/5/50 in Hornellsville (2-11/13)
5790. Mason, John, about 40, drowned 11/13/31 in Pulteneyville harbor
"leaving a numerous family" (5-11/22)
5791. Mason, Luke (Elder) of Palmyra m Naomi Rew of Newark, NY in N (3-8/6/28)
5792. Mason, Marie Antoinette, 2 yrs, dau of B. B., d 2/19/36 in Jamestown
(4-2/24)
5793. Mason, Thomas L. of Manchester, formerly of Palmyra, m 10/5/28 Sarah
Dobbin, dau of Gen. Dobbin, in Junius; Rev Tucker (3-10/29 and
5-11/7)
5794. Massett, B. W. C. of the Alexander Classical School m 2/17/38 Harriet
Hart of Alexander at St. John's Ch., Batavia; Rev. Bowles (5-3/7)
5795. Masters, Josiah, Esq., first judge of Rensselaer Co., m Ann Smith of
Hamilton, Mad. Co. at the home of A. B. Johnson, Esq. in Utica;
Rev. Baldwin (3-3/25/18)
5796. Masters, Josiah (Hon.), 57, of Schaghticoke, Renss. Co., late member
of Congress and first judge of the court of common pleas, Renss.
Co., d 6/30/22 in Fairfield, CT (3-7/17)
5797. Mather, Hiram F. (Hon - Senator) of Elbridge, Onon. Co. m 11/20/31
Mary P. Cole, dau of Dr. Joseph of Auburn (5-12/27)
5798. Mathews, Fletcher, 38, potmaster of Lancaster, d 2/15/14 in L (3-3/2)
5799. Mathews, James (Maj.) d in Elmira (3-11/26/17)
5800. Mathews, Thomas m 3/19/17 Rebecca Mathews, dau of Vincent, Esq., in Bath
(3-4/2)
5801. Mathews, Peter, about 36, d 10/26/26 in Southport (3-11/8)

149

5802. Mathews, Vincent (Hon.), 80, formerly Counsellor in Elmira, then in Bath, and finally in Rochester, d in R ("left an amiable family") (2-9/30/46)
5803. Mathewson, George m 12/11/22 Betsey Grandee in Ontario, NY; H. S. Moore, Esq. (See the marr. of Ashbel Scott) (5-12/18)
5804. Mathewson, George, Esq., 69, d 4/3/44 in Walworth (a native of R. I.; one of the first settlers in Walworth, then called Ontario; a practical land surveyor for more than 40 yrs) (5-4/10)
5805. Mathewson, Henry of Walworth m 4/22/41 Ruth Tiffany of Canandaigua in C; Rev. Thomas Castleton (5-5/26)
5806. Matteson, Allen m 7/18/22 Mercy Jourdan, both of Byron, in Elba; Charles Woodworth, Esq. (1-7/26)
5807. Matteson, John H. m Hannah Hurlbut in Harmony (4-2/7/27)
5808. Matthews, Henry Lorenzo, 9 mo, s of Lorenzo and Elizabeth, d 5/11/42 in Busti (4-5/19)
5809. Matthews, Jesse, Esq. d 4/9/22 in Wolcott (3-4/24)
5810. Matthews, Samuel R. m 4/9/32 Caroline McBurney in Painted Post; Rev. David Higgins (2-4/11)
5811. Matthies, J. L. D. (Mr.) d 11/24/34 in Rochester (5-12/5)
5812. Mattison, Henry, printer, m Margaret Bogue in NYC (3-5/14/28)
5813. Maud, William of Tioga Co. m Arville Winslow in Whitestown (3-11/16/25)
5814. Maxfield, Ruth (Mrs.), about 63, d 3/23/22 in Stafford (1-3/29)
5815. Maxon, Long John m 11/4/32 Phebe Filmore, both of Bennington in B; C. Wilder, Esq. of Sheldon (1-11/13)
5816. Maxwell, Charles m 11/22/27 Elizabeth Sayre, dau of Capt. Ebenezer, in Elmira; Rev. Williams (3-12/5)
5817. Maxwell, Guy, 43, d 2/23/14 in Elmira (3-3/2)
5818. Maxwell, Hugh m Lucy Blake in Stafford; Stephen Griswold, Esq. (1-7/19/22)
5819. Maxwell, Julia, 24, consort of Thomas and dau of James Sayre, d 8/10/18 in Elmira (3-8/26)
5820. Maxwell, Samuel H. m 10/21/18 Rebecca Conkling in Elmira (3-11/4)
5821. Maxwell, Thomas m 11/17/12 Julia Sayre, dau of James, in Elmira; Rev. Simeon R. Jones (3-12/9)
5822. Maxwell, Thomas, Esq. m 9/12/19 Mariah Purdy, both of Spencer, in S (3-9/29/19)
5823. Maxwell, William m 9/15/14 Zerviah Baldwin, dau of Capt. William, in Elmira; Hon. Caleb Baker. All of Elmira (3-10/5)
5824. May, Amos, 5 yrs, s of James, d 2/7/26 in Bath (3-2/15)
5825. May, Eleazer Huntington, 7 mo, s of Dr. William of Palmyra, d 1/31/40 of scarlet fever (5-2/5)
5826. May, Eli, about 25, committed suicide in early August in Vernon, NY while hunting (8/14/11)
5827. May, Hannah, 70, d 12/9/40 in Bath (2-12/16)
5828. May, Joseph Adams (Dr.), 24, oldest son of James of Bath, NY, d 10/22/40 at Red River Landing, Louisiana (had been settled in his profession there about 2 yrs; surv by wf and parents) (2-11/25)
5829. May, William, M.D., m 10/1/38 Elizabeth Thayer, dau of Levi, Esq., in Palmyra; Rev. Butler. All of Palmyra (5-10/5)
5830. Maydole, Cornelius m Sally Rathbun in Howard (3-1/22/17)
5831. Mayhorn, Charles of Chautauqua Co. m 9/29/29 Mary Orr of Geneva; Rev. Martin (3-9/30)
5832. Maynard, _____ of Canandaigua m Mary Ann Clark in Farmington (3-11/15/15)
5833. Maynard, Charles m 10/28/41 Maria Carey, both of Hopewell, Ont. Co.; F. Smith, Esq. (5-11/3)
5834. Maynard, Elisha B. of Arcadia m 2/2/30 Delila Ray of Lyons in L (5-2/19)
5835. Maynard, Peter m Rachel Maria Gorham in Fayette (3-7/23/28)
5836. Mayors, Josiah m 1/1/45 Susan Legare in Cohocton; Dan H. Davis, Esq. All of Cohocton (2-1/8)
5837. Mazeen, Ezekiel, 27, great grandson of the GREAT UNCAS, died and was buried on May 2 "in the Royal burial place of the Mohegans" in Norwich, CT (3-5/24/26)
5838. Meach, Henry m 5/12/42 Luthera Chapin in Hume, Alleg. Co. (2-6/15)
5839. Mead, George, 4 mo, s of William, d 9/9/23 (prob. in Geneva) (3-9/17)
5840. Mead, Harvey of Reading m 4/29/18 Elizabeth Van Gorder of Catharine, Tioga Co. in C; Samuel Winton, Esq. (3-5/13)
5841. Mead, John m Anna Tinbrook (perhaps intended for Ten Broeck?) in Elmira (3-11/12/17)

5842. Mead, Judah m 11/24/25 Belinda Cook at Big Flats (3-12/21)
5843. Mead, Robert of Butler, Wayne Co. m 3/18/33 Harriet Brown of Penn Yan
in P. Y.; Rev. Crosby (5-4/3)
5844. Mead, Stephen P., Esq. m 5/23/44 Susan W. Barker, dau of Gen. L., in
Fredonia; Rev. Tyler (4-5/31)
5845. Mead, Thomas W. m 11/1/37 Sarah Hoag, both of Macedon, at the Friends
Meeting house in Macedon (See also marr. of James S. Hoag 11/2)
(5-11/8)
5846. Mead, Walter m Sarah Allen in Canandaigua (3-8/29/27)
5847. Meade, Henry M., 54, d 3/25/49 in Jersey City, NJ (served in U.S. Army
in War of 1812; a Lt. at age 19 about; was stationed in Batavia then)
(1-4/3)
5848. Means, George W. m 2/10/23 Harriet Reed, dau of Josiah, in Seneca; Rev.
Axtell (3-2/12)
5849. Means, James m 1/6/25 Hannah Densmore in Seneca; Rev. Nesbit (3-1/12)
5850. Means, James, 76, an officer in the Pennsylvania line in the Rev. War
"and an early settler of this country", d 7/3/28 in Geneva (thrown
from his one-horse wagon when the harness broke) (3-7/9)
5851. Means, John of Seneca m Parmelia Woodworth of Benton in B (3-11/19/17)
5852. Means, William, Jr., s of William, Esq. of Towanda, m 3/1/20 Lydia F.
Mathewson of Tioga Point, PA in T. P.; Abraham Minner(?), Esq.
(5-3/15)
5853. Mears, John m Lydia Devore in Bath (3-1/13/30)
5854. Mecarg, J. B. of Candor m 10/1/45 Sophiah T. Patterson of Erwin in E;
Rev. William Hosmer (2-10/8)
5855. Medbery, Maria, 49, wf of Orson, both formerly of Otsego Co., d 7/19/40
in Tyrone (2-8/19)
5856. Medbury, Nathaniel, Esq. d 2/2/13 in Albany (a state assemblyman from
Chenango Co., NY)(3-2/17)
5857. Meech, Dennis, 2, only s of Horace, d 4/8/21 in Geneva ("they lost their
only two sons in the short space of nine days") (3-4/11)
5858. Meech, Henry Edwin, 4 yrs, s of Asa B. and Elizabeth, d 1/18/30 in Geneva
(funeral from the home of Horace Meech "in Water Street") (3-1/20)
5859. Meech, Rufus of the firm of Dows, Meech, and Cary, m 3/22/25 Eliza
Ensworth, dau of Dr. Azel, in Rochester (3-3/30)
5860. Megis, Benjamin H., Esq., formerly of Albany, d 12/11/18 in Augusta, GA
(3-1/6/19)
5861. Megrady, Biny, 23, d 1-29/47 in Prattsburgh (2-2/10)
5862. Meigs, Josiah, Esq., commissioner of the general land office, d 9/4/22
in Washington, D .C. (3-9/25)
5863. Meigs, Return J. (Hon.), formerly governor of Ohio and Postmaster General
of the U.S., d 3/20/25 in Marietta, Ohio (1-4/28 and 3-4/20)
5864. Mellish, John, 55, "the celebrated geographer", d 12/30/22 in Philadelphia
(3-1/15/23)
5865. Melony, Francis F. of Byron m 2/9/47 Helen M. Woodruff, dau of Dr. L. J.
of Byron; Rev. Babcock (1-2/16)
5866. Melony, Mary, 20, wf of W. Francis and youngest dau of L. J. Woodruff, M.D.,
d 8/24/50 in Canandaigua (2-9/11)
5867. Melvin, Alexander G. of Webster, Monroe Co. m 5/8/44 Emeline M. Foster,
dau of Cyrus, of Palmyra in P; Rev. H. Harrington (5-5/15)
5868. Melvin, Melinda, dau of Jonathan, d in Manchester (3-6/17/29)
5869. Mentor, Elijah, 45, d in Gorham (3-9/3/17)
5870. Mentor, Robert, about 35, d 1/24/13 in Seneca (3-1/27)
5871. Merchant, Samuel, 29(?), s of George, d in Albany (3-12/29/19)
5872. Meredith, Samuel M., 51, d 5/30/46 in Alexander (1-6/2)
5873. Merrel, Charles m Julia A. Seeley; Rev. Pember. All of Harmony (4-8/24/43)
5874. Merrell, Andrew, bookseller, 34, d 1/25/26 in Utica (3-2/8)
5875. Merrell, Bradford S. m Ayres M. Stewart in Ithaca (3-1/6/30)
5876. Merrell, Jeremiah, about 35, d 2/14/26 in Batavia (1-2/17)
5877. Merrell, Joseph M., 36, d 11/9/44 in Jamestown (4-11/15)
5878. Merell, Lucy (Miss), 20, dau of Isaac, d in Utica (3-11/4/29)
5879. Merrell, Thaddeus, 7 mo, s of John, d 12/14/43 in Palmyra (5-12/20)
5880. Merriam, Sumner, 15 mo, s of Abel and Mary, d 3/21/42 in Jamestown
(4-3/24)
5881. Merrifield, Alpheus M. of Jamestown, NY m 2/21/31 Emily A. Norton of
Worcester, MA in W (4-3/16)

5882.  Merrill, Abraham, 81. m 12/16/18 Mrs. Huldah Rowe, 83, in Amherst; Rev.
       Parsons (3-1/6/19)
5883.  Merrill, Alexander M. W. of Manlius, about 28, d 11/18/13 in Geneva
       (interred with masonic honors) (3-11/24)
5884.  Merrill, Archibald C. m 8/15/37 Emily C. Goodwin, both of Jamstown, in J;
       Rev. G. Lane (4-8/16)
5885.  Merrill, Elisha, 78, d 9/22/50 in Benton, MI (father of John, Esq.;
       formerly of Batavia)(1-10/8)
5886.  Merrill, Eliza Melvina, 4, dau of John, d 11/29/38 in Palmyra (5-11/30)
5887.  Merrill, George H., 18, d 3/3/49 at his father's home in Howard (2-3/7)
5888.  Merrill, Hannah, 46, wf of the Rev. Joseph, d 4/27/21 in Gorham (3-5/9)
5889.  Merrill, Jesse, 80, d 3/15/33 in Busti (a Rev. soldier) (4-3/27)
5890.  Merrill, John (?) H. m 7/29/32 Eliza Gardner at Zion Church in Palmyra;
       Rev. B. H. Hicks (a double ceremony - see marriage of John N. Korell)
5891.  Merrill, Joseph (Rev.) of Hopewell m 10/31/22 Margaret Shepard, dau of
       William, Esq. of Canandaigua)in C; Rev. Taylor (3-11/6)
5892.  Merrill, Joseph (Rev.) of Junius m 5/13/28 Philomela Billings of Phelps
       in P; Rev. Strong (3-5/28)
5893.  Merrill, Joseph m 7/4/32 Asenath Phillips in Jamestown (4-7/11)
5894.  Merrill, Mary, 34, consort of Nathaniel, d 7/15/19 in Geneva. Their
       infant child, age 20 days, d 7/20. (3-7/21)
5895.  Merrill, Riley, 17, m 2/23/34 Charlotte Hubbard, 16, in Butler (5-2/28)
5896.  Merrill, Silas L. d in Avon (3-10/17/27)
5897.  Merrill, Simon m Mary K (or R) Harris in Olean (3-3/17/19)
5898.  Merrill, William, 70, (a Rev. soldier) d 2/8/28 in Geneva (3-2/20)
5899.  Merrit, Joseph of Barrington m 4/7/27 Amanda Townsend in Benton (3-4/25)
5900.  Merrit, Robert H. (Capt.) m 4/7/13 Phebe Oliver in Brdgeport, Seneca Co.
       (3-4/14)
5901.  Merritt, Mary (Mrs.), 22, d in Canandaigua (3-2/3/13)
5902.  Merry, Constant m Lucy Brown in Palmyra (3-5/23/27)
5903.  Merry, Festus m 1/5/14 Pirsis Catlin, both of Phelps in P; Joseph Hall,
       Esq. (3-1/12)
5904.  Mervin, Charles, 8 yrs, d in Havana, NY (3-1/27/30)
5905.  Merwin, Sheldon of Geneseo m 12/8/27 Emily H. Blossom of Seneca in Geneva;
       Rev. Nesbit (3-1/16/28)
5906.  Mesier, Peter, Esq., for many years an alderman in NYC, d in NYC (3-12/22/19)
5907.  Messenger, Eland, 32, formerly of Cleveland, Ohio, d 2/27/41 in Orange,
       Steuben Co., NY (2-3/17)
5908.  Metcalf, D. W. of Palmyra m 11/18/41 Cornelia L. Marcy of Brighton in B;
*      Rev. Gray (5-12/1)
5910.  Metcalf, Franklin, merchant, m 9/4/32 Mary Ann Hess in Bath; Rev. David
       Higgins (2-9/5)
5911.  Metcalfe, John, Esq., clerk of Steuben Co., d 5/8/29 in Bath (3-5/13)
5912.  Metcalfe, Nancy, 58, consort of Thomas, d 3/4/46 in Bath (She was one
       of the earliest settlers in Bath) (2-3/18)
5913.  Metcalfe, Nancy (Miss), 82, d 3/6/50 in Bath (2-3/20)
5914.  Metcalfe, Susan, 20, dau of Thomas, d in Bath (3-8/29/27)
5915.  Metcalfe, Thomas Jefferson m Elizabeth Cary in Seneca Falls (3-11/25/29)
5916.  Metcalfe, Thomas J., 20, d 6/23/45 in Bath (2-6/25)
5917.  Metz, William, late of Corning, m 2/13/45 Adaline Dunton of Avoca in
       Mud Creek; Rev. Elias Hicks (2-2/19)
5918.  Metzger, John m 5/4/17 Sephronia Stiles, both of Junius, in J; Rev. L.
       Merkel (3-5/14)
5919.  Michael, Mary (Mrs.), 32, d 9/16/26 in Fayette (3-9/20)
5920.  Micks, William G., M.D., of Portsmouth, VA m 5/7/40 Cornelia M. Rathbone
       in Rathboneville, NY; Rev. Dr. Bush (2-5/13)
5921.  Middaugh, Benjamin m Fanny English in Elmira (3-11/12/17)
5922.  Middaugh, Mary, 76, d in Big Flat (3-2/15/26)
5923.  Mighella, Sally, 34, wf of Eleazer, d 2/27/30 in Arcadia (5-3/19)
5924.  Miles, Charles, 29, d in Lyons (3-10/1/28)
5925.  Miles, Daniel, 30, d 7/13/29 in Macedon (5-7/17)
5926.  Miles, Henry of Carlton, Orleans Co. m 10/19/36 Hannah Clark of East
       Palmyra in E. P.; Rev. G. R. H. Shumway (5-10/21)
5927.  Miles, Jared of Mayville m 5/9/44 Martha E. Wood of Ellery in E; Rev. H.
       Smith (4-5/17)
* Number 5909 inadvertently omitted.

152

5928. Miles, Milo N. of Newstead, Gen. Co. m 9/19/39 Mary K. Keyes of Jamestown in J; Rev. Gillet (4-9/25)
5929. Miles, Sarah (Mrs.), 33, consort of Samuel, d 9/23/24 in Byron (1-10/1)
5930. Millar, Cytherea L., 24, consort of Robert Millar, Esq., d 2/24/25 in Pembroke (1-3/4)
5931. Millard, Charlotte, 36, wf of Timothy A., d 3/15/22 in Benton (3-3/27)
5932. Millard, Edward m 2/18/31 Eliza Laycost in Campbelltown; Daniel Clark, Esq. All of Campbelltown (2-3/9)
5933. Millard, Mary Ann, 8, dau of Asahel, d 8/14/36 in Palmyra (5-8/19)
5934. Miller, _____ (Mr.) of Junius m 7/4/16 Catharine Speaker of Seneca; Rev. Henry Axtell (3-7/10)
5935. Miller, Alexander (Rev.), 80, d in Hague, St. Lawrence Co (sic) (But Hague, NY is in Warren Co.) (3-2/16/20)
5936. Miller, Alvin S. m Betsey Hawley in Canandaigua (3-12/26/27)
5937. Miller, Amasa O. m 4/16/44 Amanda Lewis, both of Williamson, in W; Rev. C. A. Smith (5-5/1)
5938. Miller, Andrew m 12/24/14 Catharine Smith in Seneca; Rev. Axtell (3-12/28)
5939. Miller, Angeline, 24, d 11/1/45 at the home of her father in Stafford (1-11/4)
5940. Miller, Arthur m Betsey Hammel, both of Ithaca, in Newtown (3-2/13/28)
5941. Miller, Benjamin of Geneseo m 11/5/11 Rhoda Arnold of Bloomfield in Cayuga; William P. Bennett, Esq. (3-11/13)
5942. Miller, Catherine. 21, wf of Andrew, d 1/23/19 in Geneva (3-1/27)
5943. Miller, Charles W., Esq., 23, editor of the Advocate, d in Batavia (4-12/7/31)
5944. Miller, Cyrus m Margaret Larzalere in Benton (3-8/5/29)
5945. Miller, Daniel (Gen.) of Homer m 12/7/25 Harriet Hale in Ithaca (3-12/21)
5946. Miller, David m 11/14/23 Anne Maria Smith, both of Seneca, in Geneva; Rev. Dr. Axtell (3-11/26)
5947. Miller, David A. m 2/24/46 Matilda Coss (sic) in Bath; Rev. L.W. Russ. All of Bath (2-3/4)
5948. Miller, Dorcase, 71, wf of Moulton, d 3/23/46 in Great Bend, Jeff. Co. (See also death of Moulton Miller) (1-4/21)
5949. Miller, Ebenezer A. m Betsey Ann Brown in Bachelor's Lane; Elder Gillett of Elmira (3-3/11/29)
5950. Miller, Edward (Dr.), one of the editors of the Medical Repository and an eminent physician, d 3/17/12 in NYC (3-4/1)
5951. Miller, Elizabeth, wf of Jonathan M., d 2/16/17 in Elmira ("also, a few days since, two children of Mr. Miller") (3-2/26)
5952. Miller, Fanny S., 12, dau of Deacon Miller, d 6/15/17 in Seneca Falls ("Her death was occasioned by eating green currants") (3-7/2)
5953. Miller, Franklin G., printer, 20, s of Col. D. C., proprietor of the Republican Advocate, d 11/30/25 in Batavia (3-12/7)
5954. Miller, Franklin R. m 1/19/46 Clarinda M. Tirrell in Bath; Rev. L. W. Russ. All of Bath (2-1/21)
5955. Miller, George R., 29, d 1/13/44 in the City of Detroit (5-1/24)
5956. Miller, Hannah, wf of Elijah, Esq., formerly of Geneva, d in Massachusetts (3-4/3/11)
5957. Miller, Hannah, 48, wf of Judge Miller formerly of Elmira, NY, d in Utica, Indiana (3-4/15/29)
5958. Miller, Harry of Barne, MI m 8/27/38 Jane F. G. Stanley "by the Rev. E. Everett at his residence in Avoca"(2-8/29)
5959. Miller, Harvey m 10/17/39 Sally Bancroft in Walworth; Elder A. P. Draper (5-10/18)
5960. Miller, Henry of Rensselaer Co. m Mrs. Polly Stokes in Penn Yan (3-10/22/28)
5961. Miller, Hezekiah, 83, d 5/21/35 in Palmyra (an early settler there) (5-5/22)
5962. Miller, Hiram m 3/25/41 Harriet Smith, dau of Elder David of Bonny Hill, in Bath; Harlow Smith, Esq. (2-5/19)
5963. Miller, Horace B. m Olive Stokes in Penn Yan (3-12/5/27)
5964. Miller, J. P., late agent of the N. Y. Greek Committee at Greece, m 7/26/28 Sarah Arms, dau of Capt. Jonathan, in Montpelier, VT (3-8/13)
5965. Miller, James H. C. (Dr.) of Rushville m 9/24/26 Calista E. Story of Geneva in G; Rev. Dr. Axtell (3-10/4)
5966. Miller, Jesse, 46, d 8/19/22 in Wolcott (See death of Mary, his wife) (5-8/28 and 3-9/4)

153

5967. Miller, Jesse 66, d 3/9/23 in Canandaigua (one of the early settlers there)(3-3/19)
5968. Miller, Jonas m 4/14/42 Sarah J. Walker in Sodus; Nathan Leighton, Esq. All of Sodus (5-4/27)
5969. Miller, Joseph (Capt.), about 65, d 1/5/31 in Arcadia (an early settler in Genesee Co.) (5-1/14)
5970. Miller, Kingsley, merchant, of Palmyra m 1/14/21 Ann Cole of Canandaigua in C (5-1/17)
5971. Miller, Lewis T. m Mary Delavan in Romulus (3-2/7/16)
5972. Miller, Louise, 32, wf of Joseph A., d 10/22/36 in Newark, NY (5-11/4)
5973. Miller, Mark of Towanda m 8/30/38 Sarah Stewart, dau of Richard B., in Bath; Rev. J. H. Hotchkin (2-9/12)
5974. Miller, Mary (Mrs.), 35, d in Wolcott (3-8/21/22)
5975. Miller, Mary, about 40, wf of Jesse, d 8/14/22 in Wolcott (5-8/28)
5976. Miller, Mary Elizabeth, 7 mo, dau of Kingsley, d 6/25/22 in Palmyra (funeral sermon by "Mr. Hopkins") (5-6/26)
5977. Miller, Michael m 5/21/26 Lydia Dorsey in Lyons; Rev. Smith (3-5/31)
5978. Miller, Morris H., Esq. (Hon.), 44, first judge of Oneida Co., d 11/16/24 in Utica (interred in Albany) (1-11/26 and 3-11/24)
5979. Miller, Moses m Cynthia Scofield in Benton (3-1/19/20)
5980. Miller, Moulton, 75, d 4/13/46 in Great Bend, Jeff. Co. (See also death of Dorcase Miller) (1-4/21)
5981. Miller, Peter m Lydia Kronck in Benton (3-5/28/28)
5982. Miller, Robert m Susan Wagener in Penn Yan; Abner Woodworth, Esq. (3-2/27/22)
5983. Miller, Samuel, 62, d 11/8/28 in Phelps (3-11/12)
5984. Miller, Samuel S., 28, d 2/20/26 in Batavia (1-2/24)
5985. Miller, Solomon of Waterloo m Evelina Bigelow in Fayette (3-11/4/29)
5986. Miller, William, 24, d 1/17/17 in Geneva (3-1/22)
5987. Miller, William m 4/26/25 Abigail Wolcott, dau of Erastus, Esq., in Elba; Rev. S. Whitcomb. All of Elba (1-4/29)
5988. Miller, William m 7/24/42 Lydia Stout of Mt. Washington in Avoca; Rev. S. Pitt (2-8/3)
5989. Miller, William B. m 12/12/13 Caty Ann Goble in Geneva; Jacob Dox, Esq. (3-12/15)
5990. Millett, John of Ontario, NY m Mary Smith of Williamson at the Bunker Hill Hotel in Palmyra; George W. Cuyler, Esq. (5-3/29/43)
5991. Milligan, Rosanna, 7 yrs, dau of Thomas, d 10/16/42 near Kinderhook, Columbia Co. (run over by an ox cart)(2-10/26)
5992. Mills, Abigail, 48, wf of Elisha M., d in Canandaigua (3-4/11/21)
5993. Mills, Alexander (Col.), 61, d in Stamford, CT (a Rev. soldier or officer) (3-1/8/23)
5994. Mills, Daniel m 2/9/40 Polly Borden in Kennedyville (2-2/12)
5995. Mills, Isaac of Galen m 10/19/23 Mrs. Lydia Trotter of Fayette in Waterloo (3-10/29)
5996. Mills, James, 64, d while "removing from Massachusetts to Batavia, NY" (3-3/23/14)
5997. Mills, John H. m 7/4/47 Amelia I. Blood, both of Liberty, at the Bapt. Church in Bath; Rev. H. Spencer (2-7/7)
5998. Mills, Peter (Capt.), 103, d 11/10/30 in Washington, D.C. (a Rev. officer) (5-12/10)
5999. Millspaugh, Peter, 68, father of Mrs. Hall and Mrs. Wight of Geneva, d in Thompson, Sullivan Co. (killed by the falling branch of a tree) (3-4/15/29)
6000. Milner, Joseph C. of Kinderhook, Col. Co. m Polly Mundell in Chatham, Col. Co. (3-1/21/29)
6001. Milo, Asa of Buffalo m Permelia Sisson in Ithaca (3-11/26/28)
6002. Miner, Amasa, 81, d 11/11/36 in Palmyra (a native of New London, CT; a Rev. soldier for 7 yrs) (5-11/18)
6003. Miner, Chauncey m 1/13/42 Sally McKnutt, dau of Archibald, in Macedon; Rev. A. H. Burlingame (5-1/19)
6004. Miner, John of Le Roy m 10/4/42 Martha Hayes, oldest dau of Deacon Jonathan of Bethany; Rev. Jacob Hart (1-10/11)
6005. Mingus, John m Lucy Stanley in Waterloo; James Scott, Esq. (3-9/9/29)
6006. Minor, Maria, consort of James and only dau of George and Betsey Spencer of Farmington, d 7/14/38 in F (surv by husband and 2 inf ch) (5-7/18)

154

6007.  Minor, Maria (Mrs.), 43, d 4/24/41 in Campbell (2-4/28)
6008.  Minzey, Alexander m 8/6/27 Susan Finch in Geneva; Rev. G. Laning
        (3-8/8)
6009.  Minzey, James m 4/6/40 Welthy Huntington, both of Palmyra, in P;
        Frederick Smith, Esq. (5-4/15)
6010.  Mitchel, Harlow m 6/27/44 Olive A. Kidder, dau of Ezbai (sic), Esq., in
        Busti (4-7/12)
6011.  Mitchel, William S., Esq., assistant Indian agent, m 7/14/18 "Miss Jenney,
        eldest daughter of the celebrated Creek warrior, Gen. William
        McIntosh in Thea-catck-kah near Fort Mitchell, Creek Nation"(3-8/26)
6012.  Mitchell, Caroline C., 7 yrs, dau of Thomas S., d 3/26/45 in Jamestown
        (4-3/28)
6013.  Mitchell, Charles m 3/22/45 Clarissa Davis in Carroll; Rev. Granville.
        All of Carroll (4-4/4)
6014.  Mitchell, David (Gen.), "one of the fathers of the republic", d 5/27/18
        in Pennsylvania (3-7/8)
6015.  Mitchell, Dexter m Milanda Kingman in Palmyra (3-3/10/19 and 5-3/3/19)
6016.  Mitchell, Eliphalet m 4/17/39 Sophronia Slayton in Jamestown; Solomon
        Jones, Esq. (4-4/24)
6017.  Mitchell, James, 70, of Southport, Tioga Co. "was burned to death by
        falling in the fire on the 19th ult. He was addicted to intemperance."
        (2-3/2/31)
6018.  Mitchell, John of Benton m Merinda Sherwood in Romulus (3-1/13/30)
6019.  Mitchell, John, 50, d 4/18/45 in Carroll (4-5/2)
6020.  Mitchell, Lewis, Esq., 36, of Troy, an eminent counsellor, d in
        Wethersfield, CT (4-7/19/26)
6021.  Mitchell, Samuel L. (Dr.), about 70, d 9/9/31 in NYC (2-9/14)
6022.  Mitchell, William, 59, d 9/9/19 in Farmington (3-10/6)
6023.  Mix, Ann (Miss), 24, d 1/5/22 in Geneva (3-1/16)
6024.  Mix, Daniel, 26, d 10/8/28 in Seneca (3-10/15)
6025.  Mix, Thomas (Capt.), 38, d 12/28/22 in Hamburgh, NY (3-3/26/23)
6026.  Mizner, ____, 3 mo, s of Lansing B., d 11/14/22 (3-11/20)
6027.  Mizner, Daniel m 8/31/26 Polly Sayre in Geneva (3-9/6)
6028.  Mizner, Henry Rutgers, 9 mo, s of L. B., d 5/4/23 in Geneva (3-5/7)
6029.  Mizner, Lansing B., Esq. m 2/24/18 Mary Gouverneur Rutgers, dau of
        Anthony A. of NYC, in Geneva; Rev. Orrin Clark (a double ceremony -
        see marr. of Robert Rumney) (3-2/25)
6030.  Mizner, Sarah (Mrs.), 49, d 4/3/20 at the home of Mrs. Nicholas in Geneva
        (Funeral from the house of the Rev. Henry Axtell) (3-4/5)
6031.  Moass, Hiram m 11/20/17 Maria Silence, both of Seneca Falls, in S. F.;
        Rev. L. Markel (3-11/26)
6032.  Moncrief, Peter, 73, m 12/9/31 Eliza McWattey, 15, in Adolphstown,
        Upper Canada (5-1/24/32)
6033.  Monell, Oliver m 7/20/47 Mary Ann Skinner; James Shannon, Esq. All of
        Bath (2-7/28)
6034.  Monier, James L. m 12/6/42 Margaret Andrews; Rev. Evarts. All of
        Naples, NY (2-12/14)
6035.  Monroe, Ebenezer, 88, d in Lexington, MA ("...one of the remaining few who
        composed the company of militia ... on the plains of Lexington,
        19 Apr. 1775.") (3-9/6/26)
6036.  Monroe, Jeremiah, 21, d 12/13/42 in Macedon (5-12/28)
6037.  Monroe, Jones B. m 9/23/24 Clarissa Thomas in Batavia; Rev. L. Smith
        (1-10/1)
6038.  Monroe, Seymour m 1/1/35 Mary Brockway in Palmyra; Frederick Smith,
        Esq. (5-1/9)
6039.  Montague, Elijah (Rev.), 63, father of H. of Jamestown, d 9/8/31 in
        North Leverett, MA (4-10/19)
6040.  Montague, Erastus m 9/20/32 Mary Pennington in Warsaw, NY; Rev. Doolittle
        (1-9/25)
6041.  Monteith, Alexander (Rev.), pastor of the Presby. Church in Schenectady,
        d 1/29/15 in Schenectady (3-2/8)
6042.  Montgomery, Augustus m 1/14/30 Esther Brewster in Lodi; Rev. Bennett
        (3-1/27)
6043.  Montgomery, Harvey of Bath m 5/19/12 Mary E. Rochester, dau of Col. N.
        of Dansville, in D (3-6/17)
6044.  Montgomery, Henry, about 56, d 1/22/29 in Lodi, Seneca Co. (3-1/28)

6045. Montgomery, John, 24, d 8/18/22 in Pembroke (1-8/23)
6046. Montgomery, Johnson of Bennington, Genesee Co. m 11/9/30 Elvira Dudley of Jamestown in Ellington (4-11/17)
6047. Montgomery, Mary, 53, wf of Reuben, d 6/20/32 in Wheeler (2-6/27)
6048. Montgomery, Robert, 23, a native of Pennsylvania, d 2/20/12 in Geneva (3-2/26)
6049. Moodie, James (Col.), late of Milton, PA, d 11/7/17 in Canandaigua (3-11/19)
6050. Moody, Caleb C. m Philena Field in Albany (3-5/6/18)
6051. Moody, Caleb C., 30, formerly of Albany, d 7/29/22 in Geneva (interred with masonic honors) (3-7/31)
6052. Moon, A. C. (Dr.) m 10/10/44 Ann Thompson of Uniontown, PA in Knoxville, Ohio (4-11/8)
6053. Moon, E. P., one of the editors of the Waterloo Observer, m 6/18/29 Elizabeth G. Sholes, oldest dau of John, Esq., in Waterloo; Rev. A. D. Lane (5-6/26 and 3-7/1)
6054. Moon, Jasper C. (Col.) m Lydia Lathrop in Milo (3-10/8/28)
6055. Moon, Lyman T. m 11/23/45 Mahala Clark in Jamestown; Rev. A. Handy (4-11/28)
6056. Moon, Salma m Caroline Norton, both of Gorham, in Waterloo (3-8/29/27)
6057. Moon, Stewart C., Esq., merchant, of Nunda m 2/1/23 Mary Ann Snyder, dau of John of Gorham, in G; Rev. Merrill (3-2/19)
6058. Moon, Velina O., 34(?), wf of James, d 11/9/33 in Jamestown (4-11/20)
6059. Mooney, George E. m 1/10/43 Climena Landon, dau of Jervis, Esq., in Lyons; Rev. Day K. Lee. All of Lyons (5-1/18)
6060. Mooney, Richard, 37, a soldier in the U.S. Army and a native of Gibralter, d 2/22/13 in Geneva (3-2/24)
6061. Moor, Amanda (Mrs.), 39, d 8/13/22 in Wolcott (3-8/21)
6062. Moor, James m Christiana Wise in Prattsburgh (3-4/1/29)
6063. Moor, James m 12/25/45 Jane Goodsell in Bath; Elder Kinney (2-12/31)
6064. Moor, Stephen m Mary Ann Drake in Prattsburgh (3-4/1/29)
6065. Moore, Aaron, 34, d 6/26/16 in Geneva (3-7/3)
6066. Moore, Albert Augustus, 7 yrs, twin son of Israel G. and Abigal H., d 5/13/41 in Ellicott (4-5/19)
6067. Moore, Alvira, 18, d in Canandaigua (3-3/18/18)
6068. Moore, Anne (Mrs.), 50, "the fasting woman" of Tetbury, Stafford, England "who existed 4 years without eating any food and nearly 3 years without even drinking so much as a glass of water .." died in England (3-10/23/11)
6069. Moore, George m 9/20/39 Jane Vandine, both of Jamestown, in J; Rev. Gillet (4-9/25)
6070. Moore, Harry S. m Sarah Douglass in Ontario, NY; Abraham Spear, Esq. (5-9/20/20)
6071. Moore, Henry m 9/9/27 Elizabeth Armstrong, both of Geneva, in Lyons; Rev. Hubbell (3-9/12)
6072. Moore, Hugh m Rebecca Woodmancy in Palmyra (3-12/10/17)
6073. Moore, Isaac, Jr. of Busti m 9/6/43 Sylvia Fletcher of Ashville in A; Rev. Radliff (4-10/5)
6074. Moore, Isaac, Jr. m Sarah H. Moore in Panama, NY; Rev. O. Sanderson. All of P (4-10/31/45)
6075. Moore, James m Phebe Hufman in Auburn (3-4/25/27)
6076. Moore, John m Abigail Smith in Angelica; Rev. Hubbard (3-12/22/19)
6077. Moore, Joseph K. m 12/23/34 Betsey Akin in Carroll; Rev. Peck (4-1/7/35)
6078. Moore, Maria Isabella, 9 mo, dau of Samuel, d 5/13/41 at French Creek (4-5/19)
6079. Moore, Oliver W., Esq. of Ann Arbor, MI m 10/24/49 Aurelia Whitney of Le Roy at St. Mark's Church in Le Roy; Rev. T. R. Chipman, Rector (1-10/30)
6080. Moore, Polly, 34 or 54, wf of Thomas, d in Perinton (5-9/26/21)
6081. Moore, Polly, 70, wf of Phineas and dau of David De Camp of Rahway, NJ (where she formerly lived) d 9/10/39 in Farmington (5-9/13)
6082. Moore, Samuel (Dr.) of Marion m 3/31/31 Ruth Sherman, wid of Stephen Sherman of Palmyra, in P; Rev. Abner Chase (5-4/15)
6083. Moore, Samuel, 34, d 1/11/45 in Panama, NY (4-1/24)
6084. Moore, Sarah (Mrs.), 43, d in Hopewell (3-11/16/21)
6085. Moore, Stephen, 32, d in Canandaigua (3-2/3/13)

156

6086. Moore, Sylvia, 19, wf of Isaac, Jr. and dau of E. Fletcher, formerly of Harmony, d 10/31/44 in Busti (4-11/8)
6087. Moore, William, 42, d 2/28/13 in Troupville "leaving a wife and four children" (3-3/17)
6088. Moore, William of Phelps m 1/8/40 Sarah Ann Bolckom, formerly of Palmyra, in Orleans, Ont. Co.; Elder Rice (5-1/22)
6089. Moore, William D. m 1/1/23 Etna Castle in Canandaigua; Rev. George Harman (3-1/22)
6090. Moores, Phineas of Farmington m 11/24/42 Mary Johnson of Palmyra in P; Rev. Fisher (5-11/30)
6091. Moores, Sally, 37, dau of Phineas and Polly, formerly from Westfield, NJ, d 1/18/41 in Farmington (5-1/20)
6092. More, George, 28, d 9/7/22 in Phelps (3-9/18)
6093. More, Peter V. of Palmyra m 8/24/37 Maria H. Selby of Williamson in W; Rev. Jonathan Benson of Walworth (a double ceremony - see marr. of Daniel Ward) (5-9/1)
6094. Morehouse, Elizabeth, 71, d 12/30/21 in Brighton (5-1/16/22)
6095. Morey, Freeland m 1/8/44 Lucy Akin in Busti; G. W. Parker, Esq. (4-1/26)
6096. Morey, William H. of Chili, Monroe Co. m 1/5/34 Mary Gibbs of Palmyra in P; Rev. Doolittle (5-1/10)
6097. Morgan, ____, 4 yrs, ch of Philo, d in Jamestown (4-1/27/41)
6098. Morgan, Abel, 25, d 1/7/44 in Jamestown (4-1/12)
6099. Morgan Chauncey, printer, m Betsey N. Bessac at Chenango Point, Broome Co.; Rev. Palmer (3-12/1/13)
6100. Morgan, Cordelia, 8, dau of Henry, d 4/18/31 in Busti (4-5/4)
6101. Morgan, Eugen L. of Palmyra m 8/5/34 Dorotha Armington of Manchester in M; Rev. Staunton (5-8/8)
6102. Morgan, Eugene L., 24, d 12/1/34 in Palmyra (5-12/5)
6103. Morgan, Jedediah (Hon.) d 12/9/26 in Aurora, Cayuga Co. (3-12/20)
6104. Morgan, John, about 22, from Long Meadows, MA d 7/9/16 in Clifton Springs, NY ("His death was occasioned by the falling of his horse on his return from a camp meeting in Phelps, ... had been in this country only a few weeks") (3-7/24)
6105. Morgan, Mumm m 9/9/30 Angeline Safford in Rochester; Rev. Penny (5-9/24)
6106. Morgan, Russell m 8/4/42 Clarissa A. Palmer in Jamestown; Rev. Chapin (4-8/4)
6107. Morgan, Wakeman, 39, d 3/16/35 in Bath (2-3/25)
6108. Morison, Clark m 11/25/29 Jane Anderson in Geneva; Rev. Tooker (3-12/2)
6109. Morley, Diar m 5/11/43 Ann Eddy in Mayville; Rev. Dodge. All of Mayville (4-5/25)
6110. Morley, Frederick of the Wayne County Whig m 1/12/43 Eleanor Ninde, dau of Rev. William of Baltimore, in Lyons; Rev. C_____? (5-1/25)
6111. Morley, Horace (Capt.) m 11/14/19 Polly Kellogg in Pulteneyville; Rev. White (5-11/17)
6112. Morley, Joseph of Walworth m 3/17/31 Margaret Calhoun of Williamson; Elder M. Allen (5-3/25)
6113. Morley, Luke m 12/25/30 Sarah Cooper, both of Palmyra; Elder Powell (5-2/18/31)
6114. Morley, Obediah, 71, d 4/30/45 in Harmony (4-5/9)
6115. Morrell, David, 16, of Milfordsville m 10/24/25 widow Emma Brewer, 45, of Davenport, Delaware Co.; Daniel Babcock, Esq. (3-11/16 and 11/23)
6116. Morrin, Adelaide, 39, d 3/19/42 (5-3/23)
6117. Morris, ____, inf s of Israel, d 12/13/46 in Bath (2-12/23)
6118. Morris, David m Susan Smith in Junius (3-3/11/29)
6119. Morris, Henry, Esq. of Buffalo m 11/1/31 Mary Natalie Spencer, dau of Hon. John C., (prob. in Canandaigua); Rev. R. Kearny (5-11/1)
6120. Morris, John m Lucinda Sackett in Jersey (3-10/22/28)
6121. Morris, John, Jr. m 6/19/50 Phebe W. Buck, dau of E. S., Esq. of Elba; Rev. Coleman (1-6/25)
6122. Morris, Lorenzo, Esq. of Jamestown m 10/5/43 Fanny E. Strong of Nettle Hill, NH; Rev. E. B. Sparks (4-10/12)
6123. Morris, Richard Valentine, Esq. d 5/14/15 in Westchester ("Commodore Morris was appointed under Adams' administration to the command of the squadron of the Mediterranean"(3-5/31)

6124.   Morris, Thomas, 64, d 4/27/24 in Morrisville, Mad. Co. ("... originally
        from Dudley, Mass. (and) came into this part of the state about
        thirty years since...(was) the first person who made a settlement
        in this village ... has left an aged widow and a large family.")
        (3-5/19)
6125.   Morrison, Jane T., 34, consort of James, Esq., secretary of state
        and formerly of Bath, d 3/29/31 in Indianapolis, IN (2-4/27)
6126.   Morrison, Jeremiah (Dr.), 92, d in Danby (3-3/19/28)
6127.   Morrison, John, Jr. m 8/25/17 Sally Harding in Canisteo (3-9/10)
6128.   Morrison, Thomas, 51, d 6/11/23 in Geneva (3-6/18)
6129.   Morrow, Henry m 3/15/45 Harriet A. Tolls in Urbana; H. L. Comstock, Esq.
        (2-3/19)
6130.   Morse, A_____? m 12/24/39 Lucina Finley in Walworth; Rev. Murray. All
        of Walworth (5-12/27)
6131.   Morse, Charles Augustine, 2 yrs, s of Charles B., d 3/19/35 in Gerry
        (4-3/25)
6132.   Morse, Chauncey m 4/4/18 Ann Williams in Canandaigua; Rev. Onderdonk
        (3-4/15)
6133.   Morse, David, 51, d in Milo (3-10/15/28)
6134.   Morse, Elizabeth Ann, 61, wid of Jedidiah, d in New Haven (3-6/18/28)
6135. Morse, James O. (Hon.), first judge of Otsego Co., d 12/4/37 ("Known in
        Chautauqua County 'as a proprietor of lands purchased by the Cherry
        Valley Company'") ("husband and parent") (4-12/20)
6136.   Morse, Jedediah d 4/9/17 in Gorham (3-4/23)
6137.   Morse, Jedediah (Rev.), 65, D.D., L.L.D. d 6/9/26 in New Haven (3-6/21)
6138.   Morse, John of Waterborough m Margaret Morgan of Panama, NY in P; Rev.
        Gray (4-3/6/33)
6139.   Morse, Louis Le Grand, one of the editors of the Ontario Messenger,
        m 3/4/29 Mahala Pierce, dau of John, Esq. of Geneseo, at St.
        Michael's Church in Geneseo; Rev. Bayard (5-3/13). Bride's name
        is Frances Mahala Pierce in 3-3/18.
6140.   Morse, Newman m 6/20/16 Polly Spangler in Benton (3-7/10)
6141.   Morse, Orlando m Sarah Hawley in Canandaigua (3-2/7/16)
6142.   Morse, William m 10/24/33 Mahala P. Freeman in Walworth (5-11/1)
6143.   Morton, Washington, Esq. of NYC d 5/3/10 "in Paris" (3-8/22)
6144.   Moseley, Leander P. of Marion m 12/29/42 Elizabeth Dewey, dau of
        Jedediah of Manchester, in M; Rev. Miner (5-1/18/43)
6145.   Moseley, Lois (Mrs.) d 3/14/42 (5-3/23)
6146.   Moses, Emma J., 25, wf of Marcus, d 12/28/30 in Rochester (5-1/14/31)
6147.   Moses, Randolph of Palmyra m Eliza Anders of Williamson in W (5-1/21/18)
6148.   Mosher, Charles (Rev.), 56, of Junius d in Reading (surv by wf and 7 ch)
        (3-11/19/28)
6149.   Moss, Jacob m Mary Bush in Junius (3-1/9/28)
6150.   Moss, John m Hannah Brockway in Williamson (5-2/25/18)
6151.   Moss, William, Esq. of Reading m 12/25/11 Betsey Ball, dau of Moses, Esq.,
        of Wayne; Richard Laucin, Esq. (3-1/29/12)
6152.   Mott, Cornelia Maria, 10 weeks, dau of Samuel, Esq. of Geneva, d 6/21/29
        (3-6/24)
6153.   Mott, Samuel, Esq., attorney, m 1/2/28 Margaret Wilson, only dau of late
        Rev. Andrew Wilson, in Geneva; Rev. Dr. Orin Clark. All of Geneva
        (3-1/9)
6154.   Mott, Samuel, Esq., 38?, d 7/29/35 in Geneva (5-8/7)
6155.   Moulton, Stephen (Col.), 64, d in Floyd, Oneida Co. (a Rev. officer)
        (3-4/8/18)
6156.   Moultroup, Phelps m Catharine Ward in Benton (3-10/21/29)
6157.   Mount, Matilda, 1 yr, dau of Randolph, d 2/24/27 (prob. in Geneva)
        (3-2/28)
6158.   Mount, Randolph, merchant, of Geneva m 10/30/24 Lydia Hunt of NYC in
        Waterloo; Rev. Lane (3-11/1)
6159.   Mower, Ellen, 32, wf of James B., Esq., d 6/11/11 in Canandaigua
        (3-7/3)
6160.   Mower, James B. of Canandaigua m 11/15/15 Mary Kip, dau of late Samuel,
        Esq. of Kip's Bay, in NYC (3-11/29)
6161.   Mower, John H. of Canandaigua d 4/3/22 in NYC (age 23) (1-4/12).
        John H. is son of James B. (3-4/17)

6162. Mower, Mary B., wf of Peter A., Esq. and dau of late Zachariah Seymour, Esq., d 11/14/28 in Canandaigua (3-11/19 and 5-11/21)
6163. Mower, Peter A. m Mary B. Seymour, dau of late Z, in Canandaigua (3-9/26/27)
6164. Mower, Peter A., Esq., 27, d 9/18/31 in Canandaigua (5-9/27)
6165. Mowers, Matthias m 8/24/40 Mary Coon, both of Bath (2-8/26)
6166. Mowry, George A. m Nancy Jack in Cameron (3-4/30/28)
6167. Mulford, Miller D. of Warsaw, NY m 7/4/22 Mary Munson of East Bloomfield in E. B.; Rev. Steel (1-7/12)
6168. Mulholland, John E. m Olive Millard in Painted Post (3-3/26/17)
6169. Mullard, Elizabeth Clinton, 8 mo, dau of Asahel and Aurelia, d 10/6/41 in Palmyra (5-10/13)
6170. Mullender, Isaac, 86, "a native of Scotland but for many years a resident of this neighborhood", d 6/1/23 in Seneca (3-6/4)
6171. Mullender, John of Angelica, s of Isaac of Seneca, d 11/25/13 in Middlesex ("... while passing in the road a tree lodged in the crotch of another accidentally fell on him") (interred in Geneva; surv by a wf and 3 ch) (3-12/1)
6172. Mullender, Joseph, s of Isaac, d 4/13/13 in Seneca (3-4/21)
6173. Mullhollon, Jane, 65, consort of William S., Esq., d 2/6/49 in Bath (2-2/7)
6174. Mumford, George m 11/20/19 Mary O'Carr, both of Geneva; Jacob Dox. Esq. (3-11/24)
6175. Mumford, George d 7/7/27 (prob. in Geneva) (killed by the accidental discharge of a fowling piece) (a native of England; lived many years in Geneva, NY (3-7/11)
6176. Mumford, George H., Esq. of Rochester m 5/24/36 Ann Elizabeth Hart, dau of Hon. Truman Hart of Palmyra, in P (5-5/27)
6177. Mumford, Mary, 25, dau of George Huntington, Esq., d 8/31/26 in Rome, NY (3-9/16)
6178. Mumford, Thomas, Esq., 62, d 12/13/31 at his home in Cayuga, NY (5-1/10/32)
6179. Mun, Stephen B., Jr., merchant, m Adeline Keyes in Ithaca (3-12/5/27)
6180. Munday, David of Wheeler m 8/28/31 Ann Wood in Prattsburgh; Rev. Chase (2-9/7)
6181. Munger, A. m 12/31/26 E. Finn, both of Auburn; Rev. Dr. Rudd (3-1/10/27)
6182. Munger, Elmira, 19, d 8/10/22 in Alexander (1-8/23)
6183. Munger, Jasper m Gilletly Purdy in Ithaca (3-10/10/27)
6184. Munn, Rachael, 73, wf of Asa, formerly of Greenfield, MA, d in Bath (3-7/9/28)
6185. Munroe, Sarah (Mrs.), 93, d in Bristol, RI "from her clothes accidentally taking fire" (3-11/6/11)
6186. Munson, Elias Y. of Wolcott m Elizabeth Brown in Waterloo (3-6/24/29)
6187. Munson, Mary Ann, 27, wf of E. Y., d in Wolcott (3-3/12/28)
6188. Murdoch, James d in Schenectady (3-12/25/11)
6189. Murdock, Aaron of Attica m 6/30/31 Charlotte Pratt of Jamestown in J; Rev. Gillet (4-7/13)
6190. Murdock, Alice, 28, wf of Jonathan, d in Reading (3-12/28/14)
6191. Murdock, Eliphalet of Le Roy m 3/20/34 Sally Hall of Palmyra in P; Rev. Samuel Moore (5-3/21)
6192. Murdock, G. J. m 2/13/41 Marinda Niloo in Poland, NY; S. B. Winsor, Esq. (4-2/17)
6193. Murphy, Daniel d "at an advanced age" in Junius (3-10/17/27)
6194. Murphy, Hugh, 66, d 7/29/26 in Le Roy (a Rev. soldier) (1-8/4)
6195. Murphy, Jeremiah of Illinois m 12/21/37 Clarissa Ann Velie of Cameron in C; Rev. Wisner (2-12/27)
6196. Murphy, Royal, 17, m Mary Ann Warren, 15, both of South Pembroke, in S. P. (3-9/23/29)
6197. Murray, _____, _____, and _____, three children of Mrs. William Murray died in Gorham (3-8/9/15)
6198. Murray, Barnabas, about 85, (a Rev. pensioner) d 9/7/28 in Seneca (served in 24 battles) (3-9/10)
6199. Murray, Daniel R. of Pike, Wyoming Co. m 5/17/48 Alzira Bailes of Oakfield in O; Rev. B. Fancher (1-5/30)
6200. Murray, David S. of Geneva m 12/13/09 Sally Russell of Gorham in G (3-1/17/10)
6201. Murray, David S. d 2/10/19 in Ovid (3-2/24)

159

6202. Murray, Elijah m 9/23/13 Mrs. Elizabeth Benham in Gorham (3-10/6)
6203. Murray, Elijah (Maj.), 60, d 6/28/16 in Canandaigua (3-7/17)
6204. Murray, Mercey, 43, wf of Major Elijah, d in Gorham (3-7/3/11)
6205. Murray, William, 44, formerly of Bath, NY, d 9/28/45 in Juliet, IL
       (surv by wf and 5 ch) (2-10/29)
6206. Muzzy, Sarah, 77, wid of late Col. Amos of Attica and mother of Amos W.,
       Esq. of Panama, NY, d 8/27/38 in Panama, NY (4-9/5)
6207. Muzzy, Susan, 40, consort of Amos W., d 8/9/40 in Panama, NY (member of
       Meth. Episc. Ch.) (4-8/12)
6208. Myers, Hannah, 33 or 83, wf of John, d 1/7/18 in Gorham (3-1/21)
6209. Myers, Henry J. m 2/18/48 Marianne Rolfe, both of Bethany, in B; Rev.
       H. Blackmar (1-3/7)
6210. Myers, Isaac m 11/18/19 Lydia Creigher in Seneca; Jacob Dox, Esq.
       All of Seneca (3-11/24)
6211. Myers, Joseph, a licentiate of the Presbytery of Troy, m 10/14/24 Lydia
       Hall, formerly of Geneva, in Canandaigua; Rev. Dr. Axtell (3-10/20)
6212. Myers, M. S., Esq., attorney, of Aurora m 12/31/26 S. Cornell of
       Auburn; Rev. Dr. Rudd (3-1/10/27)
6213. Myers, William M., 27, printer, late of Palmyra, d 9/27/38 in Detroit,
       MI (5-10/12)
6214. Mynderse, John, 74, d in Schenectady (3-11/15/15)
6215. Myron, John J. m 3/4/30 Orelia Stalp in Williamson; A. Cornwall, Esq.
       (5-3/12)
6216. Myrtle, Benjamin m 11/14/38 Arabella Smith; Rev. McKenney (2-12/5)
6217. Myrtle, Phillip, 75, d 3/28/50 in Wheeler (was born in Pennsylvania;
       one of the earliest residents of this county - lived here nearly
       half a century) (2-4/3)
6218. Naglee, _____, 7 mo, dau of David, d 6/1/10 in Geneva (3-6/6)
6219. Naglee, _____, inf dau of David, d 9/20/14 (prob. in Geneva) (3-9/21)
6220. Naglee, David, 46, d 9/12/16 in Geneva (3-9/18)
6221. Nares, Francis of Geneva m 12/25/19 Nancy Wood, dau of R. T., in Phelps;
       Rev. Clark (3-12/29)
6222. Nares, Nelson, 18 mo, s of Francis, d 8/22/28 in Geneva (3-8/27)
6223. Nash, Adam m 6/29/42 Mary Johnson, both of Williamson, in W; Rev.
       Wilkinson (5-7/6)
6224. Nash, Daniel (Rev.) d 12/21/31 in Verona ("long known in the western
       part of the state as a devoted evangelist") (5-1/24/32)
6225. Nash, John, 58, d 8/5/22 in Batavia (interred with masonic honors)
       (1-8/9)
6226. Nash, Rier, Esq. of Bath m 4/20/35 Mrs. Anna Scott of Benton in B;
       Rev. Johnson (2-4/29)
6227. Nash, William W. m 9/1/30 Lucy E. Green, dau of Byram, Esq., in Sodus;
       Rev. Jesse Townsend (5-9/3)
6228. Neally, Elizabeth (Mrs.), 84, d 3/20/41 in Bath (2-4/7)
6229. Neally, Mathew, 86, (a Rev. soldier) d 9/22/41 in Bath (2-9/29)
6230. Neally, William, 6 yrs, s of Samuel, d 8/23/41 in Bath (2-9/1)
6231. Needham, John, 55. d in Junius (surv by wf and several small ch)
       (3-8/22/27)
6232. Neele, Thomas, merchant, m 11/10/35 Laura A. Wolcott at St. John's Ch
       in Canandaigua; Rev. Pound. All of Canandaigua (5-11/13)
6233. Neely, James D. m 2/26/46 Maranda Hamilton of Howard in H; A. A. Olmsted,
       Esq. (2-3/4)
6234. Neice, Lyman m Margaret Drowne in Canandaigua (3-2/11/18)
6235. Neilsen, Catherine, 73, dau of the late Earl of Sterling and relict
       successively of Col. W. Duer and of W. Neilson, Esq., d 7/25/26 in
       NYC (3-8/2)
6236. Neilson, William of Angelica m Mrs. Sarah Peacock of Almond in A
       (3-6/18/28)
6237. Nelson, _____ of Dutchess Co. m 12/1/30 Maria Ostrom of Macedon in M;
       Elder Powell (5-12/3)
6238. Nelson, Hannah, about 30, consort of Capt. James, d 8/10/23 in Galen
       (3-8/20)
6239. Nelson, Henry m 9/15/31 Marietta Brown in Macedon (5-9/27)
6240. Nelson, John J. of Newark m Cornelia Low of Poughkeepsie in P; Rev. Dr.
       Cuyler (5-7/23/30)

6241. Nelson, Robert m 12/23/39 Catherine Bedell, both of Greene Co.,
in Palmyra; Frederick Smith, Esq. (5-12/27)
6242. Nelson, Upton m 3/26/29 Charlotte Standish, both of Junius, in Vienna,
NY; Rev. Strong (See also the marr. of D. P. Standish this date)
(3-4/8/29)
6243. Nelson, William, 72, d 9/28/24 in Alexander (1-10/1)
6244. Nethaway, ____, ch of James, d ("a casualty") (3-2/14/16)
6245. Nevetts, Robert m 2/7/25 Lydia Fairfield in Batavia; C. Carpenter, Esq.
(1-2/11)
6246. Nevins, Minerva, 22, wf of T. J., Esq. of PennYan and dau of Nathan
Loomis, Esq. of Middlesex, d in Middlesex (3-5/16/27)
6247. Nevins, Thomas J., Esq., attorney, of Penn Yan m 11/23/25 Minerva
Loomis in Middlesex (3-12/7)
6248. Nevins, Thomas J., Esq. m 10/3/29 Caroline S. Clark in Penn Yan; Rev.
C. Eddy (3-10/7)
6249. Nevitt, C. R. of Buffalo m 5/28/48 Issabella Cutler of Batavia at St.
John's Church in Batavia; Rev. D. C. Houghton (1-5/30)
6250. Newbol, John m Mary E. Underhill, both of Phelps, in Penn Yan (3-6/17/29)
6251. Newbury, Anna C., wf of Sylvester B., d 12/23/44 in Ellery (age 30)
(4-1/3/45)
6252. Newbury, Fanny A., 1 yr, d 10/11/41. Henry D., 6 yrs, d 10/14. Malvina,
9 yrs, d 10/18. All three children of Garret and Abigail of Ellery.
(4-10/28/41)
6253. Newcomb, George W., editor of the Chautauqua Phoenix, m Lodoiska Philena
Keeney in Bloomfield (3-9/23/29)
6254. Newcomb, Harvey, late editor of the Buffalo Patriot, m 5/19/30 Alithea
Wells, late of Auburn, NY, in New Albany, IN (4-6/16)
6255. Newcomb, Wesley, M.D., of Albany m 2/20/38 Helen Post of Palmyra in P
(5-2/21)
6256. Newell, A. B. m 3/10/25 ____ry Hornell in Hornellsville; A. S. Smith,
Esq. (3-3/30)
6257. Newell, Chauncey m 11/28/25 Samson (sic) A. Stone, dau of Rev. William,
in Sodus (3-12/21)
6258. Newell, Daniel m Jemima Paily in Ulysses, both of Ulysses (3-7/21/19)
6259. Newell, John of Phelps m 6/4/29 Mary Elizabeth Underhill, dau of P.
B., Esq. of Phelps, in Penn Yan; Rev. Eddy (5-6/26)
6260. Newhall, John (Capt.), 47, d 10/4/10 in Phelpstown (3-10/10)
6261. Newkirk, Charles (Col.), 70, d 11/14/22 in Palatine, NY (a Rev. officer)
(3-12/4)
6262. Newkirk, Isaac W. m 11/6/25 Mary B. Dobbin in Geneva; Rev. Axtell
(3-11/9)
6263. Newkirk, Nathan m 8/15/29 Eunice Parmalee in Arcadia (5-8/28)
6264. Newland, ____ (Mr.) m Diana True in Perinton (5-4/17/22)
6265. Newland, George m 2/11/41 Lodemia P. Davenport, both of Palmyra; Rev.
I. C. Goff (5-2/17)
6266. Newland, George Henry, only ch of George, d 2/5/40 (5-2/12)
6267. Newland, Margaret, inf dau of George and Mary, d 2/1/31 in Palmyra
(5-2/4)
6268. Newland, Mary, wf of George, d 7/13/37 in Palmyra (5-7/21)
6269. Newman, Nathaniel m Maria Applegate in Ulysses, both of U (3-7/21/19)
6270. Newman, Willis m 1/30/23 Sarah Sawtell in Gorham; Rev. Merrill (3-2/12)
6271. Newton, Curtis m 11/8/32 Susan Prentiss in Batavia; C. M. Russell, Esq.
All of Stafford (1-11/13)
6272. Newton, George S., 15 mo, s of Butler, d 9/26/43 in Palmyra (5-10/4)
6273. Newton, Henry, merchant, m 10/20/16 Harriet Walbridge; Rev. Axtell.
All of Geneva (3-10/23)
6274. Newton, Hobart m 11/26/26 Pamela Carpenter, dau of Comfort of Ellington,
in E; Rev. Blasdell (4-12/6)
6275. Newton, Ira m 7/7/25 Mary Ann Loomis in Alexander; Rev. Elder Brown
(1-7/8)
6276. Newton, Olive (Mrs.), 42, consort of Joseph, d 5/2/22 in Batavia
(1-5/3)
6277. Neysmith, John, Esq. of Caledonia, Liv. Co. m 10/24/22 Mercy Price of
Phelps in P (3-11/13)
6278. Nichelson, Wesley of Howard m 3/15/46 Jane Leonard of Hechter in H;
Rev. West (2-3/25)

6279. Nicholas, George W., 20, s of Hon. John, Esq. of Geneva, d 1/11/19 in
Savannah, GA "where he had gone for his health" (3-2/3)
6280. Nicholas, John (Hon.), 55, d 1/7/20 in Seneca ("late first judge of this
county, formerly a member of Congress from Virginia, and a senator in
the legislature of this state") (5-1/12)
6281. Nicholas, Mary, 12, dau of late Judge Nicholas, d 1/11/23 near Geneva
(3-1/15)
6282. Nicholas, Robert C. m 11/16/26 Mary Rose, dau of Robert S., Esq. of
Fayette, at the Trinity Church in Geneva; Rev. Norton (3-11/22)
6283. Nicholas, Sarah, 7, dau of Hon. John, d 7/12/14 in Seneca (3-7/20)
6284. Nichols, _____, a dau of Benjamin, d in Canandaigua (3-1/6/13)
6285. Nichols, _____, ch of Rev. J. Nichols of the American mission, d 7/30/25
in Bombay (state or country not given) (3-11/30)
6286. Nichols, Amos H., merchant, of Geneva m 9/1/24 Marian Paine, dau of Judge
Paine of Auburn, in A; Rev. D . C. Lansing (3-9/8)
6287. Nichols, Benjamin m 1/12/32 Keturah Chesebro of Farmington in Palmyra;
F. Smith, Esq. (5-1/17)
6288. Nichols, Chester m 4/4/24 Elizabeth Childs in Pembroke; Sanford Kendrick,
Esq. (1-4/9)
6289. Nichols, Egbert m 3/1/27 Katharine Hoover in Geneva; J. L. Smith, Esq.
All of Geneva (3-3/7)
6290. Nichols, Erastus N. (Rev.) of Hector m 11/1/27 Margaret Litell of
Auburn in A; Rev. Dr. Lansing (3-12/12)
6291. Nichols, George of the firm of Wasson and Nicols of Augusta, GA, m 5/1/26
Mary Slosson Smith, dau of Reuben, Esq. of Waterloo, NY, in Waterloo;
Rev. Lane (3-5/3)
6292. Nichols, Henry m 11/3/28 Rosannah Stanton in Palmyra; A. R. Tiffany, Esq.
(3-11/12 and 5-11/7)
6293. Nichols, Isaac, 82, d 12/23/29 at his home in Milo (a member of the
Society of Friends; one of the earliest settlers in Genesee Co.)
(3-1/6/30)
6294. Nichols, John m Harriet Olds in Gorham; Rev. Merril (5-9/12/21)
6295. Nichols, Samuel m Clarissa Lee in Bloomfield (3-3/15/15)
6296. Nichols, Sylvester J. m Susan Crane in Milo (3-1/13/30)
6297. Nichols, Thomas(?), 48, d 5/2/25 in Geneva (3-5/4)
6298. Nichols, William, s of Judge Nichols of Bath, m 4/20/31 Adeline Bennett,
dau of Jacob of Howard, in H; Daniel Bennett, Esq. (2-4/27)
6299. Nicholson, Ambrose of Howard m 3/27/49 Sophia Ellis of Lodi in L; Rev.
Davis (2-4/4)
6300. Nicholson, William, 49, d 11/13/22 (3-11/20)
6301. Nichoson, James, 37, d 5/6/47 in Elmira (2-5/12)
6302. Nickols, Roswell of Polteneyville m Mary Durfee, dau of Lemuel, in
Palmyra; A. Spear, Esq. (5-8/28/22)
6303. Niles, Allen m 11/16/30 Betsey Wilder, both of Pembroke; Rev. I. B.
Louckton (1-11/26)
6304. Niles, Benjamin, Sr., 41, pastor of the Presby. Church in Binghamton,
d in B (3-7/30/28)
6305. Niles, Frederick M., 3 yrs, s of Hiram, d 5/9/35 in Palmyra (5-5/15)
6306. Niles, Hiram m 3/2/31 Chloe Robinson, dau of Dr. Gain Robinson; Rev.
A. E. Campbell. All of Palmyra (5-3/4)
6307. Niles, Martha, 30, wf of Dr. Addison Niles, d 3/14/45 in Bath (2-3/19)
6308. Niles, Noah (Dr.), 61. d 6/3/40 at his home in Prattsburgh (born in
Colchester, CT; moved to Prattsburgh, NY in 1809; one of the
earliest settlers in P; ordained as a preacher in the Meth.Episc.
Society in 1836) (2-6/10)
6309. Niles, Oliver of Royalton, Niag. Co. m 4/27/34 Hannah A. Gardner of
Varick, Seneca Co. in Palmyra; Rev. William Staunton (5-5/2)
6310. Nims, Hezro m 5/29/43 Sylvia Rice in Marion; Rev. Gideon Osborn
(5-5/31)
6311. Ninde(?), George W. (Rev.), 24, d 9/6/42 in Lyons (5-9/14)
6312. Nixon, George C. m Harriet A. Burns in Bath (3-10/17/27)
6313. Nixson, William, 4 yrs, s of Dr. Joseph, d 2/19 in Batavia (1-2/20/24)
6314. Noble, _____, inf ch of Nathaniel, d 11/27/13 in Geneva (3-12/1)
6315. Noble, Asenath, 37, wf of Elnathan,d 9/6/22 in Geneva (3-9/11)
6316. Noble, Joel of Batavia m 7/5/25 Marian Dewy of Alexander inBrockport
(1-7/15)

162

6317. Noble, Mary W., 36, wf of W. O., d 6/12/47 in Bath (2-6/16)
6318. Noble, Nancy Eliza, 28, wf of Isaac, d 1/27/39 in Fluvanna (4-1/30)
6319. Noble, Sophia, dau of Harvey of Urbana, Steuben Co., d 8/15/50 at the
      home of her sister (not named) at White Deer Mills, Union Co., PA
      (2-9/4)
6320. Nobles, Harry, "a young man of Victor", committed suicide by hanging
      8/17/15 in Victor (3-8/30)
6321. Nobles, Isaac m 1/1/34 Nancy Jacobs in Jamestown; Rev. Gillet (4-1/8)
6322. Nobles, Jonathan m Hyla Tracy in Angelica (3-11/11/18)
6323. Noon, Darby (Maj.) d 9/9/23 in NYC (3-9/17). Same newspaper dated 10/1:
      Maj. Darby came from Ireland at an early age. In Rev. War at his own
      expense he raised and equipped a company of infantry which he commanded.
6324. Norman, John L. m 11/11/27 Mary Ann Scot, both of Benton, in B; Abner
      Woodworth, Esq. (3-11/14)
6325. Norman, William E., 51, bookseller, d in Hudson "leaving a numerous family"
      (3-11/26/28)
6326. Norris, Abraham m 1/12/37 Cynthia Horton, dau of Col. Samuel T., in
      Palmyra; Rev. H. V. Jones (5-1/20)
6327. Norris, Catherine, 3 yrs, dau of John, d 10/24/17 in Seneca (3-11/5)
6328. Norris, Daniel m Julia Ann Stoddard in Milo (3-8/1/27)
6329. Norris, De Witt C. of Walworth m 9/10/37 Mrs. Lucy Rood of Ontario, NY;
      John McCloth, Esq. (5-9/22)
6330. Norris, George of Seneca m 10/17/26 Elizabeth Harris of Phelps (See also
      the marr. of Robert Harris this date) (3-11/1)
6331. Norris, Henry m 4/29/50 Lucy Wheeler in Bath; Rev. A. Wright (2-5/8)
6332. Norris, John of Geneva m 7/4/13 Rachael Fisher, dau of Adam, in Seneca;
      Orin Aldrich, Esq. (3-7/14)
6333. Norris, John B. m 10/24/18 Betsey Gage in Gorham; Rev. Axtell (3-11/11)
6334. Norris, Josiah m Lydia Colton in Brighton (3-12/28/25)
6335. Norris, Mary Elizabeth, 9 mo, dau of Abram, d 10/5/38 in Palmyra
      (5-10/12)
6336. Norris, Moses, 73, d 3/12/41 in Palmyra (5-3/17/41)
6337. Norris, Polly (Mrs.) d in Canandaigua (3-1/29/17)
6338. North, Charles, 2 yrs, s of Linus, d 6/25/31 (5-7/1)
6339. North, Mary, 8 mo, dau of Rev. Samuel, d in Junius (3-9/17/28)
6340. North, Noah, Esq., 39, d 9/23/24 (1-10/1)
6341. North, Olive, 62, wid of Noah, Esq. late of Alexander, d 3/11/49 while
      on a visit to her daughter in Colebrook, Ashtabula Co., Ohio
      (In 1808 she settled with her husband in what was then Batavia,
      now Alexander) (1-4/10)
6342. North, Robert, 72, d 3/15/18 in Poughkeepsie (3-4/8)
6343. North, Samuel, Esq., 26, late clerk to the State Assembly, d 1/16/13
      in Walton, Delaware Co. (3-2/17)
6344. Northrop, Eaton B., 28, principal of Macedon Academy, d 10/17/43 in
      Macedon (5-10/25)
6345. Northrop, Joseph, Jr. of Elk, Warren Co., PA m 6/25/36 Amie E. Shearman,
      dau of Oliver, Esq. of Busti, in B; Abner Lewis, Esq. (4-6/29)
6346. Northrup, Burr m Sally Fisk in Perinton (5-4/17/22)
6347. Northum, David m Julia Moreland in Geneva; Eli Bannister, Esq. (3-11/11/18)
6348. Northum, Epaphroditis m 11/16/17 Joanna Masters in Geneva; Rev. Clark
      (3-11/19)
6349. Norton, _____ m "Mrs. Smith" in Palmyra (5-2/11/18)
6350. Norton, Aaron, 86, (a Rev. officer) d in East Bloomfield (3-12/17/28)
6351. Norton, Ann, 24, wf of Joseph, d 6/29/31 in Palmyra (5-7/1)
6352. Norton, Benjamin, 9, s of Ira, d 3/16/25 in Bethany (1-3/25)
6353. Norton, Birdsey, Esq., 48, of Canandaigua (late of the firm of Birdsey
      and Nathaniel Norton) d 3/27/12 in Goshen, CT (3-4/22)
6354. Norton, Charles of Buffalo m Julia Ann Maltby, dau of late Gen. Maltby
      of Waterloo, in W; Rev. Lane (3-1/14/29)
6355. Norton, Elijah, 37 or 57. formerly of Richfield, d 4/10/39 in Ellington
      (4-4/10)
6356. Norton, Frances Ann Steele, 8 weeks, dau of Joseph A., d in Palmyra
      (5-8/16/31)
6357. Norton, Frederick A., 10 mo, s of Augustus, d 8/21/30 in Palmyra
      (5-8/27)

163

6358. Norton, George (Dr.) of Shelby, Orleans Co. m 11/17/41 Sarah Ellas, dau of Dr. Simpson Ellas of Bath, in B; Rev. Whipple (2-11/24)
6359. Norton, George Hatley (Rev.) of Waterloo m 12/6/19 Maria Gault of Brooklyn at the Trinity Church in Geneva; Rev. Clark (3-12/8)
6360. Norton, Laurin, 28, merchant, d 7/6/17 in Angelica (3-7/23)
6361. Norton, O. W. of Buffalo m 3/20/34 Hannah Wood of Seneca in S (5-4/4)
6362. Norton, Philander, merchant, of Tyrone m Jane Shepherd in Reading (3-1/20/30)
6363. Norton, Reuben m 4/18/25 Mrs. Alice McIntyre (prob. in Elba); Rev. Howe (1-4/22)
6364. Norton, Seth, professor of languages in Hamilton College, died at Hamilton College in Oneida Co. (3-12/23/18)
6365. Norton, William, 56, d in Canandaigua (3-2/3/13)
6366. Norton, Willis m Phebe Gregory in Catharine (3-4/1/29)
6367. Nott, Amasa m Lavinia Hotchkiss in Canandaigua (3-12/17/17)
6368. Nottingham, Henry m 4/9/40 Mary Jane Hathaway in Palmyra; Rev. C. M. Butler. All of Palmyra (5-4/15)
6369. Noxen, Benjamin (Col.), 73, d in Beekman, Dutchess Co. (3-2/18/18)
6370. Noye, Elias, 22, d 7/24/31 in Campbelltown (2-7/27)
6371. Noyes, Enoch m 12/19/40 Catharine Lord in Lyme, CT; Rev. Chester Colton (5-1/6/41)
6372. Noyes, Selden, 29, d 3/7/29 in Manchester (3-3/18 and 5-3/13)
6373. Noyes, Thomas J., 42, d 10/24/44 in Acton, MA (4-11/15)
6374. Noyes, Warren of Ohio m Amy Johnson in Farmington (3-1/21/29)
6375. Nutting, Orton m 7/4/39 Lucy Fisher in Randolph; Rev. Zachariah Eddy (4-7/10)
6376. Nye, _____ (Mrs.) d 8/24/20 in Penfield (5-8/30)
6377. Oak, Emeline, 17, d 11/18/30 in Athens, VT ("Printers in western New York are requested to copy this") (5-12/10)
6378. Oakley, Charles of Sempronius m Ellen Margaret Knox, dau of Hon. John, in Waterloo (3-4/23/28)
6379. Oakley, Jesse, Esq., 79, father of Thomas J., Esq., d in Poughkeepsie (3-11/21/27)
6380. Oakley, Lydia S., 43, wf of Thomas J., Esq., d in Poughkeepsie (3-10/17/27)
6381. Oakley, Nehemiah m 1/29/20 Rhoda Bates in Benton (3-2/9)
6382. Oaks, Esther (Mrs.), 36, wf of Austin and dau of Benjamin Tuttle, d 5/27/22 in Seneca (3-6/5)
6383. Obookiah, Henry, 26, a native of Owyhee (Hawaii perhaps?) and a member of the foreign mission school, d 3/17/18 in Cornwall, CT (3-4/1)
6384. O'Brien, Jeremiah, Esq., 75, collector of the customs for the district of Machias, d 10/5/18 in Machias, Maine (5-10/27)
6385. O'Carr, John, about 25, son of Mrs. George Mumford, drowned 5/21/23 in Seneca Lake ("fell off the docks into the lake at Seeley's Creek"(3-5/28)
6386. Odell, Arthur m 5/12/29 Sarah Wilson in Prattsburg; A. H. Deyo, Esq. (3-6/1)
6387. Odell, David, Jr., 3 yrs, d in Junius (3-8/1/27)
6388. Odeon, Ebenezer m 2/11(?)/24 Lucretia Filmore in Bethany; Elder Segar (1-2/20)
6389. O'Donoughue, John of Rochester m 8/13/33 Ann Clary of Geneva in G (5-8/30)
6390. Ogden, Benjamin, 24, d in Catharine (3-9/9/29)
6391. Ogden, David A., Esq., late first judge of St. Lawrence Co., d in Montreal (3-6/24/29)
6392. Ogden, Lewis Morris, Esq., 27, d in Ogdensburgh (3-1/16/11)
6393. O'Handland, Owen m Anna Fitz-Simmons in Elmira (3-6/9/19)
6394. O'Hara, Margaret, 47, wf of Capt. William, d 5/17/30 in Canandaigua (5-5/28)
6395. Oldfield, Jeremiah d 7/10/18 in Benton (kicked by a horse)(3-7/15)
6396. Olds, Arvilla, 8, dau of David, d 12/4/22 in Geneva (died "of severe burns received by her clothes taking fire while at school") (3-12/11)
6397. Olds, Hamilton, 23, of Batavia d 2/3/25 in Buffalo (1-2/4)
6398. Olds, Ira M., pastor of the churches in Lenox and Sullivan, Madison Co., m 12/16/13 Phoebe Young of Phelps in P; Rev. Axtell (3-12/22)
6399. Olds, William m 4/17/26 Sarah Palmer; Benjamin Stetson, Esq. (1-4/21)
6400. Olin, Henry, 93, m Miss Sally Aylesworth, 75, in East Greenwich, RI (3-6/27/10)

6401. Oliphant, D. S. (Dr.) m 4/22/47 Marinda Hall in Warsaw, NY (1-5/11)
6402. Oliver, Amos S. m 9/27/26 Mary Ann Metzger, both of Junius; Rev. Axtell
(3-10/4)
6403. Oliver, Elizabeth, 74, wf of Rev. Andrew and mother of W. M. and A. F.,
Esqs. of Penn Yan, d in Springfield, NY (3-9/10/28)
6404. Oliver, Elizabeth E., consort of Gilbert of Palmyra and dau of Herman
Judson of Canandaigua, d 5/22/44 in C (5-6/12)
6405. Oliver, Gilbert of Palmyra m 3/19/42 Elizabeth Judson of Canandaigua
in C; R. B. Johnson, Esq. (5-3/30)
6406. Oliver, Margaret, wf of Dr. A. F., d 6/13/29 in Penn Yan (3-6/24)
6407. Oliver, Stephen, about 45, d 3/19/43 in Mayville (4-3/23)
6408. Olmstead, Aaron, Esq. d 1/26/13 in Albany (a state assemblyman from
Columbia Co., NY) (3-2/17)
6409. Olmstead, Clara, 33, wf of Colman, d in Havana, NY "at the head of
Seneca Lake"(3-7/23/28)
6410. Olmstead, James, 44, formerly of Hartford, CT, d 9/9/23 in NYC (3-10/8)
6411. Olmstead, William m Catharine Lockerby, both of Catlin, in Veteran, NY
(3-7/23/28)
6412. Olmsted, Elijah, 76, d 3/10/48 in Pavilion (1-3/21)
6413. Olmsted, William m 1/29/39 Maria Morehouse in Le Roy; Rev. Latimer.
All of Le Roy (1-2/14)
6414. Olney, William A., about 25, editor and proprietor of the Voice of the
People, d 10/12/35 in Warren (4-10/21)
6415. Ongley, Mary S. H., 10 wks, only dau of W. H., d 9/29/42 in Buffalo
(2-10/19)
6416. Ongley, William H. of Jefferson, Chemung Co. m 10/17/40 Mary H.
Hickmott of Lockport, Niagara Co. in Sennett, Cayuga Co.; Rev. Selah
Stocking (2-10/28)
6417. Oram, James, 66, printer and bookseller, d 10/27/26 in NYC (3-11/8)
6418. Orcutt, Moses, 92, (a Rev. soldier) d 2/27/27 in Richmond, Ont. Co.
(was a soldier in the French War also; was taken prisoner by the
Indians and for two days was confined without food with his legs wedged
in notches cut in a tree) (3-3/14)
6419. O'Reilly, Alcina Anne, mother of the editor of the Rochester Republican,
d in NYC (3-8/19/29)
6420. O'Reilly, Henry F., editor of the Rochester Republican, m 12/3/29 Marcia
F. Brooks, dau of Gen. Micah, in East Bloomfield; Rev. U. M. Wheeler.
(5-12/11) also (3-12/23)
6421. Orme, Priscilla (Mrs.), 69, formerly from the state of Maryland, d 1/25/12
in Farmington (moved from MD "about five years ago") (3-2/5)
6422. Ormsby, A. F., printer, m Margaret Hollenbeck in Utica (3-11/4/29)
6423. Ormsby, William of Wheeler m 1/21/32 Minerva Gardner of Urbana in Wheeler;
Otto F. Marshall, Esq. (2-1/25)
6424. O'Rorke, Pat, 50, d in Buffalo (3-12/21/25)
6425. Orr, _____ (Mrs.) d in Palmyra (3-2/3/13)
6426. Orr, R. S. m 1/8/39 Jane Bostwick in Busti; E. F. Warren, Esq.(4-1/9)
6427. Orsin, Cornelius, 36, d in Bath, Rensselaer Co. (sic) (3-11/11/18)
6428. Orton(?), Gerrit V. Z., merchant, of Winfield, Herk. Co. m 5/28/26
Rosamond Cook, dau of Philip, Esq. of Cohocton, in C (3-6/14)
6429. Orton, Horatio W. m 3/15/25 Sarah Carson in Seneca; Rev. Nisbet (3-3/23)
6430. Orton, James, 4 yrs, s of Rev. A. G., d in Seneca Falls (3-12/9/29)
6431. Orton, Samuel, 7, s of Samuel A., d 7/10/44 in Jamestown (4-7/12)
6432. Orwan, Rebecca (Mrs.), 28, d in Elmira (3-10/1/17)
6433. Osband, Marietta, 26, wf of Durfee Osband, d 3/10/34 in Macedon (5-3/21)
6434. Osband, William m 4/23/20 Martha Reeves in Palmyra (5-4/26)
6435. Osband, Willson m Susan Shearman in Palmyra (3-1/17/16)
6436. Osborn, Chauncey m 3/27/37 Deborah P. Hawfer(?);Rev. G. R. H. Shumway.
All of Palmyra (5-3/31)
6437. Osborn, Elijah, 26, d in Manchester (5-6/12/22)
6438. Osborn, Hezekiah of New Lebanon, "a shaking quaker", 77, m 12/25/16
Mrs. Hepzibah Willson, 64, of Windsor, Broome Co. in W (3-1/22/17)
6439. Osborn, Horatio L. of Olean m Sophia Moore in Angelica (3-4/14/19)
6440. Osborn, James of Dansville m 3/27/42 Julia Allen of Howard in H; Rev.
Wickes (2-3/30)
6441. Osborn, John H., 42, d 9/12/31 "at the head of Seneca Lake" (2-9/28)

6442. Osborn, Marcus B. of Ithaca m Eliza A. H. Grant of Hector in H; Rev. William Wisner (3-8/1/27)
6443. Osborn, Oliver m 1/23/22 Patty Rollins; Erastus Fuller, Esq. All of Wolcott (3-2/6)
6444. Osborn, Selleck, Esq., a poet and former editor of the American Watchman, d in Philadelphia (3-11/8/26)
6445. Osborn, Sheldon, 56, d 9/19/46 in Wisconsin (formerly of Alfred, Alleg. Co., NY, he had "left for the west in August last ...") (2-11/11)
6446. Osborne, John, , 16, only son of Mary E., formerly of Jamestown, d in Lockport (4-7/8/40) and (4-7/22/40)
6447. Osborne, Levi m Mrs. Polly Hosier in Harmony; I. S. Fitch, Esq. (4-1/3/27)
6448. Osborne, Samuel W. m 10/26/35 Ann Goldsmith in Palmyra (5-10/30)
6449. Osborne, T. A. (Hon.) m 1/3/39 Eliza Jane Huston in Mayville; Rev. Baldwin (4-1/30)
6450. Osburn, David, Esq. m 11/24/25 Catharine McIntosh, formerly of Batavia, in Albany; Rev. James Martin (1-12/9)
6451. Osgood, ____, wf of Levi, d in Junius (3-10/8/28)
6452. Osterhout, John C. m 6/12/50 Mary Kelly, both of Corning, in Albany; Parker Sargent, Esq. (2-6/19)
6453. Ostram, Lucy Jane, 1 yr, dau of William, d 3/18/23 in Geneva (See also the death of Sarah Ann Ostram) (3-3/26)
6454. Ostram, Sarah Ann, 3 yrs, dau of W, d 3/19/23 in Geneva (see also the death of Lucy Jane Ostram) (3-3/26)
6455. Ostrom, Daniel Z. m 9/22/31 Olive Bixbe in Macedon; Rev. R. Powell (5-10/11)
6456. Ostrom, S. Z. m 2/24/31 Relief Brown in Macedon; Rev. A. E. Campbell. All of Macedon (5-2/25)
6457. Otis, Harrison Gray, Jr., Esq. of Boston d in Springfield, MA (3-1/17/27)
6458. Otis, Joseph of Deriter (sic), Cort. Co. m 9/30/28 Cynthia Smith of Farmington in F (3-10/8/28 and 5-10/3)
6459. Otis, Ralph of Almond m 8/25/38 Mary Smith ("after a courtship of 20 minutes") in Hornellsville; Rev. Russell (2-9/12)
6460. Otis, Sarah, 101, d in Lime (3-6/23/19)
6461. Otley, William, 21 mo, only s of William, d 5/2/22 in Phelps (3-5/8)
6462. Ottley, Deborah (Mrs.), 78, mother of Capt. William, d 4/2/28 in Phelps (a native of Yorkshire, England) (3-4/9)
6463. Ottley, William, 62, (a native of England but many years a resident in this country) d 6/4/15 in Phelps (3-6/7)
6464. Otto, Jacob S., Esq., 49, d 5/2/27 (local agent of the Holland Land Co.; surv by wf and 5 ch) (4-5/9)
6465. Ovenshire, Priscilla, dau of Charles, d in Ovid (3-9/17/28)
6466. Ovett, Milton m 2/22/31 Polly Daymonth; H. L. Arnold, Esq. All of Jersey (2-3/2)
6467. Owen, Asel L. of Albion m 9/21/26 Lucy Beach of Geneva in G (3-10/4)
6468. Owen, Eliphalet m 11/17/25 Clarissa Hayden in Alexander; Rev. E. Spencer (1-11/25)
6469. Owen, James R. (Dr.), about 25, lately of Peekskill, d 10/9/10 at the home of Major Dobbins in Junius (3-10/24)
6470. Owen, John L., 15, s of Mowbray, d in Hector (3-5/13/29)
6471. Owen, Margaret H., wf of Anson and dau of Joseph E. Rumsey of Stafford, d 7/27/45 in East Bethany (1-7/29)
6472. Owen, Samuel, 74, d 1/23/32 in Newstead (a Rev. soldier) (5-1/24)
6473. Owen, Sarah, 29, dau of Daniel formerly of Dutchess Co., d 2/3/26 in Ledyard, Cay. Co. (3-2/15)
6474. Owen, Simeon m Eliza Carnike in Tyre (formerly Junius) (3-5/6/29)
6475. Owen, Terry, 60, d 7/1/22 in Milo (3-7/17)
6476. Owen, Timothy, 81, formerly of Orange Co. and a soldier in the Rev. War, d in Hector (3-10/30/22)
6477. Owens, Ira m 8/22/24 Lu____a Ayers in Benton, both of Milo (3-8/25)
6478. Owens, John d 7/19/12 in Geneva (for many years a bricklayer in Geneva; "killed by the falling of a house under which he was working") (3-7/22)
6479. Oxtoby, George m 3/17/25 Mary Hughs in Benton; S. G. Gage, Esq. (3-3/23)
6480. Oxtoby, Robert, 57, d 7/27/19 in Benton (3-8/4)
6481. Oxtoby, William, about 25, d 7/23/29 in Benton (3-8/12)

6482. Pace, David m 2/7/29 Melinda Clapp in Waterloo (3-2/18)
6483. Packard, Clark, 21, s of Philander, d 8/21/29 in Cummington, MA (5-9/18)
6484. Packard, Philander m 11/29/21 Minerva Lapham in Palmyra; A. Spear, Esq. (5-12/12)
6485. Packer, Jesse of Galen m Mary Carnrike in Waterloo (3-2/13/28)
6486. Packer, William S. of NYC m 7/26/42 Harriet L. Putnam of Morrisville, Mad. Co. (formerly of Palmyra) in Morrisville; Rev. Benjamin F. Putnam (5-8/17)
6487. Padden, Robert m Levina Todd in Wayne (3-5/29/22)
6488. Paddleford, Reuben d in Canandaigua (3-2/22/15)
6489. Paddock, Charles m 5/31/43 Sarah Newman in Harmony; Rev. N. Horton. All of Harmony (4-6/8)
6490. Paddock, Ira R., 55, d 3/9/42 in Sodus ("left a large family") (5-3/30)
6491. Paddock, Stephen. Esq., 85, d in Hudson ("one of the founders of that city and late Pres. of the Bank of Columbia") (3-2/23/14)
6492. Page, Adelaide R., 3 yrs, dau of John, d 10/22/47 in Bath (2-10/27)
6493. Page, Charles H. of Almond m 12/25/44 Matilda Margison of Urbana in U; Rev. Mallory (2-1/8/45)
6494. Page, James m 4/2/50 Lucinda A. Loomis, both of Cohocton, in C (2-4/10)
6495. Page, KilbornC., 17, d in Dresden, NY (3-5/13/29)
6496. Page, Thomas, 18, recently from Middlebury, VT, d 9/17/19 in Rochester, NY (5-9/29)
6497. Page, William (Rev.) of Fredonia, Chaut. Co. m 9/6/24 Frances S. Durand in Whitesborough; Rev. Frost (3-9/22)
6498. Paige, Phineas H. m 3/12/39 Polly Cushing, both of Harmony (4-3/20)
6499. Paine, Elizabeth Weeks, 2 yrs, dau of Dr. Martyn Paine, d 1/30/29 in NYC (3-2/4)
6500. Paine, Martin (Dr.), formerly of Geneva, m 11/23/25 Mary Ann Weeks, dau of Ezra, Esq., at St. John's Ch., NYC; Rt. Rev. Bishop Hobart (3-12/7)
6501. Paine, William, 24, d 2/4/42 in Lyons (5-2/16)
6502. Palmer, Catharine, 9 mo, dau of Benjamin d in Canandaigua (3-9/17/17)
6503. Palmer, Charles of Carroll m 1/22/32 Esther Ann Thompson, dau of late Judge Thompson, in Pinegrove (PA?); Rev. Eddy (4-1/25)
6504. Palmer, Charles, about 20, d in Busti (4-5/28/34)
6505. Palmer, Friend, 40, formerly of Canandaigua, d in Detroit, MI (3-6/13/27)
6506. Palmer, G. W. m 9/17/40 Eunice Burdon, both of Howard; Rev. P. Norris (2-9/23)
6507. Palmer, George m Harriet Foster in Palmyra (3-12/10/17)
6508. Palmer, Henry of Fluvanna m 12/31/40 Clarissa Penhollow of Ellington in E; Rev. Waith (4-2/10/41)
6509. Palmer, Henry F., merchant, m 9/30/29 Emma E. Beckwith in Le Roy; Elder Beckwith (5-10/16)
6510. Palmer, James m Dorothy Case in Canandaigua (3-12/23/29)
6511. Palmer, James H. of Alabama, NY m 12/30/47 Sarah Ann Dustin of Batavia at the Baptist Ch. in Batavia; Rev. S. M. Stimson (1-1/4/48)
6512. Palmer, James M. of Linden, Orl. Co. m 9/9/41 Hannah Louiza Tice of Palmyra; Rev. G. R. H. Shumway (5-9/15)
6513. Palmer, John m Catharine Mullender in Angelica (3-1/16/22)
6514. Palmer, Jonathan, Jr., 39, d 12/26/44 in Jamestown (4-12/27)
6515. Palmer, Joseph E. of Erwin m 12/7/46 Elizabeth M. Vance of Dansville in D; Rev. W. Curry (2-12/16)
6516. Palmer, Lucius S., 23, d 7/29/31 in Jamestown (4-8/10)
6517. Palmer, Nathaniel, 76, d 7/12/40 in Walworth (5-7/22)
6518. Palmer, Noah, Jr. m 12/8/36 Louisa Davenport, both of Macedon, (prob. in Williamson) (a double ceremony - see marr. of Philip Palmer) (5-12/9)
6519. Palmer, Oliver H. (Hon.) of Palmyra m 11/2/43 Susan Hart, dau of Hon. Truman, in Rochester; Rev. Eighenbradt (5-11/8)
6520. Palmer, Philip of Macedon m 12/8/36 Lucinda Potter of Williamson in W; Rev. H. V. Jones (a double ceremony - see marr. of Noah Palmer) (5-12/9)
6521. Palmer, Samuel m 4/28/33 Julia Decker in Macedon; Elder Robert Powell (5-5/1)
6522. Palmer, Whitman m 10/2/31 Tabitha Stearns in Busti; J. Garfield, Esq. (4-10/5)
6523. Palmer, William of Macedon m 4/16/29 Matilda Skinner of Marion in M; Rev. E. Blakesley (3-5/6 and 5-4/24)

6524. Palmer, William of Perinton m 2/15/37 Pamelia Heath of Penfield in P;
Rev. Miner (5-2/17)
6525. Palmer, William Marshall, 1 yr, only son of Amos, d 3/15/43 in Busti
(4-3/23)
6526. Palmeter, Alsa E., 16, dau of Josiah, d 8/15/26 in Busti (4-8/23)
6527. Palmeter, Joanna (Miss), 19, dau of Josiah, Esq., d 12/25/38 in Busti
(4-1/2/39)
6528. Palmeter, Joanna C., 45, wf of Josiah, Esq., d 12/27/33 in Busti (surv
by husband and 6 ch) (Editors in Herkimer County are requested to
publish the above)(4-1/8/34)
6529. Palmeter, Lucy A. (Miss), 19, d in Busti (4-2/23/44)
6530. Palmiter, _____, inf s of Capt. Phineas, Jr., d 8/3/31 in Jamestown
(4-8/10)
6531. Palmiter, Jason of Jamestown m 1/1/44 Ann Bowen of Chautauqua in C;
Rev. J. E. Chapin (4-1/12)
6532. Palmiteer, _____ m Diana Potter in Bath (3-3/26/17)
6533. Panbury(?), George R. of Comack, L.I., NY m 10/16/37 Frances Ann Cole,
dau of the late Abner of Palmyra, in Port Ontario, NY (5-11/15)
6534. Pangburn, Edward S. m 7/4/50Catharine Small in Wheeler; Rev. B. C. Smith
(2-7/10)
6535. Parce, Anthony m Mrs. Amanda Dolph in Hector (3-12/6/15)
6536. Pardee, Amos, Jr., 24, d 9/5/23 at the Glass Factory (in Seneca?)
(3-9/10)
6537. Pardy, Chester m 1/24/41 Rhoda Mitchell; Rev. Samuel Wilson. All of
Palmyra (5-1/27)
6538. Parish, Caleb B. m 1/24/25 Lucinda Moulton in Alexander; Cyrenus Wilber,
Esq. (1-1/28)
6539. Parish, Elijah (Rev.), 63, D.D., d in Byfield (3-11/23/25)
6540. Parish, Elisha, Esq. of South Bristol m Allice Phillips, wid of late
Col. Phillips, in Bristol (3-11/26/28)
6541. Parish(?), Josiah D. (Rev.) of Pike, Alleg. Co. m 9/26/33 Elizabeth Winn
of Palmyra in P; Rev. Gideon Osband (5-9/27)
6542. Park, Henri of Addison m 6/6/50 Mary E. McNulty of Big Flats in Elmira;
Rev. P.H. Fowler (2-6/19)
6543. Parke, _____, about 25, wf of Samuel, d 9/25/29 in Geneva (3-9/30)
6544. Parke, Eliza Ann, 15, dau of William, d 10/8/28 in Palmyra (5-10/10)
6545. Parke, Moses of Sodus m 8/14/33 Harriet Eliza Badger of Geneva in G;
Rev. Bruce (5-8/16)
6546. Parke, Robert, 55, d 9/16/13 in Seneca (3-9/29)
6547. Parke, Russell m Grace Ann McCandlish, both of Seneca (3-3/14/27)
6548. Parke, William F. m 4/22/40 Mary Jane Foster, dau of Cyrus, Esq., in
Palmyra; Rev. Stowell (5-4/29)
6549. Parker, Alexander L. of Pultney m 12/8/41 Sarah Townsend, dau of Rev. Joel
of Jerusalem, NY, in J; Rev. Gould (2-12/22)
6550. Parker, Allen J. of Dansville (late of Bath) m 3/25/47 Harriet M. Ashley
of Springwater in S; Rev. W. F. Curry (2-4/7)
6551. Parker, Ansel m 4/29/40 Elizabeth G. Niles, both of Bath, in Kennedyville;
Harlow Smith, Esq. (2-5/6)
6552. Parker, Charlotte, 56, relict of James, Esq., d 3/18/43 in Frewsburgh,
Chaut. Co. (a native of Framingham, MA; moved to Chautauqua Co. "about
35 years ago"; member Cong'l. Ch. 40 yrs) ("Massachusetts Spy and
printers in Maine please copy") (4-3/23)
6553. Parker, Darius m Sally Whally in Avon (3-4/12/15)
6554. Parker, Eleazer, 45, d 3/31/47 "at his residence in Byron" (1-4/6)
6555. Parker, Elizabeth J., 15, d 2/27/48 in Elba (dau of Nelson and Almira E.)
(1-3/7)
6556. Parker, Emily, 27, wf of George, d 2/23/39 in Fluvanna (4-2/27)
6557. Parker, Ephraim, 23, of Pultney d in Benton (3-10/27/19)
6558. Parker, Eugenia, 9 mo, dau of Horace, d 3/31/22 in Geneva (5-4/17).
In 3-4/10 her death place is listed as "Clyde (Galen)" and her father
as Harris Parker.
6559. Parker, Harriet, inf dau of Rev. Parker, d in Rochester (3-12/5/27)
6560. Parker, Ira, 42, d in Frewsburgh (4-6/16/42)
6561. Parker, Ira, 52, formerly of Port Gibson, d in Lyons (5-10/26/42)
6562. Parker, James, Esq., 86, (a native of R. I.) d 4/24/29 in Benton
(3-5/13)

168

6563. Parker, Jason, 67, d 9/28/30 in Utica (a pioneer settler there; "one of the principal contractors for carrying and running the western line of stage") (5-10/22)
6564. Parker, Jedediah m 2/24/25 Irena Barber in Junius (3-3/9)
6565. Parker, John of Hamburg, Erie Co. m 1/6/25 Sally Maria Johnson of Junius in J (3-1/19)
6566. Parker, Mahitable, 52, wf of Joshua, d in Palmyra (3-7/2/28)
6567. Parker, Martin V. B., 10 mo, s of James and Sabra, d 4/11/42 in Frewsburgh (4-4/21)
6568. Parker, Moses, 53, a transient born in North Carolina, d 8/18/11 in Warsaw, Gen. Co. (At age 14 as a seaman he was "pressed aboard a British Man of War until 2 years previous to the close of the war when he escaped and enlisted in the American service") (3-9/4)
6569. Parker, Perry m 10/28/40 Narcissa Lapham; Rev. Shumway. All of Palmyra (5-11/6)
6570. Parker, Preston R. m Delema Sandford in Palmyra (3-1/17/16)
6571. Parker, Samuel (Rev.) m 12/11/15 Jerusha Lord in Danby (3-1/3/16)
6572. Parker, Samuel C. (Dr.) d in Waterborough (4-6/10/40)
6573. Parker, Stillman of Silver Creek m 1/1/44 Tryphena Gibbs of Ellery in E; Elder Frink (4-1/5)
6574. Parker, William m Mary Cobb in Palmyra (3-7/9/28)
6575. Parkerson, Thomas m Jemima Richardson in Jerusalem, NY (3-7/22/29)
6576. Parkess, _____ (Mr.) d in Palmyra (3-2/3/13)
6577. Parkhurst, Lemuel, Esq., 28, postmaster of Palmyra, d 9/12/18 in P (a native of Milford, MA) (3-9/23 and 5-9/15)
6578. Parkhurst, Seneca of Cayuga Co. m 6/25/10 Rebecca Yates of Geneva in G; Rev. Wilson (3-6/27)
6579. Parkinson, George m 1/20/16 Jane Doyle in Geneva; Jacob Dox, Esq. (3-1/24)
6580. Parkison, Robert, 19, m 12/5/18 Mrs. Sarah Coe, 30, wid of late Halstead Coe, Esq.; Rev. Samuel Pelton. All of Haverstraw, Rockland Co. (3-12/30)
6581. Parks, Amos m 4/9/50 Mary Jane Lafurge in Prattsburgh; Rev. B.C. Smith (2-4/17)
6582. Parks, Jonathan m 12/25/12 Welthy Rinders, dau of Isaac, in Benton; Abraham Wagener, Esq. (a double ceremony - see marr. of Isaac Rinders) (3-1/13/13)
6583. Parks, S. W. (Rev.), formerly of Jamestown, m 6/25/38 Maria A. Carter of Randolph in R; Rev. R. A. Aylworth (4-7/4)
6584. Parks, Ward m Roxana Gooding in Canandaigua (3-2/14/16)
6585. Parmele, Abiel (Rev.), pastor of the Presby. Church in Fredonia, m Nancy Barns in Fredonia (3-1/13/30)
6586. Parmelee, Edward, 18. s of Gen. John H., d 10/2/49 in Le Roy. Gen. John H., 57, d 10/8 (resident of Batavia 30 yrs). John, 14, son of Gen. JohnH., d 10/9. (1-10/16)
6587. Parmer, Elias of Hammondsport m 7/3/49 Hannah Aulls of Bath in B; Rev. B. R. Swick (2-7/11)
6588. Parrish, Hannah (widow), 82, mother of Capt. J., d in Canandaigua (3-10/23/11)
6589. Parrish, Isaac m 11/23/25 Dolly Root in Canandaigua (3-12/7)
6590. Parshall, Israel, 84, d 8/4/43 in Palmyra (a Rev. soldier) (5-8/9)
6591. Parshall, Nathan, 69, d 1/12/36 in Palmyra (an early settler there) (5-1/15)
6592. Parshall, Schuyler R. of Palmyra m 10/9/39 Mary Perkins of Saratoga in S; Rev. Wescott (5-10/18)
6593. Parsley, Thomas m 1/7/30 Jane Adams in Arcadia; Rev. R. Benton (5-1/8). In 3-1/13 the marriage place is Newark, NY.
6594. Parsol, William m 4/4/27 Mary Munger in Ithaca (3-4/25)
6595. Parsons, Charles m 1/12/15 Rebecca Ann Lewis in Seneca; Rev. Axtell (3-1/18)
6596. Parsons, Darwin A. of Bath m 1/15/50 Lucy Sane Walling of Campbelltown in Bath; Rev. H. Spencer (2-1/23)
6597. Parsons, Horace m Polly Loveless in Harmony (4-2/21/27)
6598. Parsons, James P. m 6/21/49 Clara Rich, dau of Calvin, Esq., in Batavia; Rev. Byron Sunderland. All of Batavia (1-6/26)
6599. Parsons, Samuel m 8/12/23 Mary Bragg in Waterloo; Rev. McDonald (3-8/20)

6600. Parsons, Samuel W. of Perry m 12/6/29 Caroline Lewis of Seneca in S; E. Hastings, Esq. (3-12/23)
6601. Parsons, Sarah (Miss), 17, d in New Haven ("Her brother scared her to death with a horrid face mask intended as a sport to him.") (3-5/16/27)
6602. Parsons, Thomas, editor of the Jefferson County Post, m Lovina Collins (3-9/26/27)
    Partridge. See also Patridge
6603. Partridge, ____, inf ch of Joel, d 5/23/41 in Jamestown (4-5/26)
6604. Partridge, Adelia Mehetabel, 9 mo, dau of Almon and Mehetabel, d in Jamestown (4-1/24/39)
6605. Partridge, Almon of Jamestown d in Worcester, MA (4-8/15/38)
6606. Partridge, Azuba, 28, wf of Joel and dau of Paul Goodale of Worcester, MA, d 4/26/41 in Jamestown (4-4/28)
6607. Partridge, Charles, 2 yrs, s of Joel, d 5/5/41 in Jamestown (4-5/12)
6608. Partridge, Charles Edward, 9 mo, s of Joel and Mary R., d 9/18/45 in Jamestown (4-9/26)
6609. Partridge, Deborah H., 62, mother of Joel of Jamestown, d 12/2/38 in Worcester, MA (4-12/12)
6610. Partridge, Dwight, merchant, d 11/12/17 in Vienna, NY (3-11/26)
6611. Partridge, George A., 8 mo, s of Albert A., d 3/20/43 in Boston, MA (4-4/6)
6612. Partridge, Joel m 12/30/41 Mary R. Pennock at the Congregational Ch. (prob. in Jamestown); Rev. Chapin (4-1/6/42)
6613. Partridge, Lorenzo A., 11 mo, s of Almond, d in Jamestown (4-12/28/36)
6614. Partridge, Mary W., 30, wf of Elbridge G., d 9/13/38 in Worcester, MA (4-9/26)
6615. Pasley, Betsey, 56, d in Canandaigua (3-2/3/13)
6616. Patchin, Harriet Douglass, inf dau of T. W., Esq. of Jamestown, d 8/30/39 in Troy (4-9/11)
6617. Patchin, Myron, Esq. m 12/23/46 Rozilla Parmater in Cohocton; Rev. S. S. Brown (2-1/6/47)
6618. Patchin, T. J. m 3/19/45 Sophrona Sutton in Bradford; Rev. J. L. Coffin. All of Bradford (2-3/26)
6619. Paterson, Mathew, Esq., 85, d 2/18/17 in Paterson, Putnam Co.(3-3/12)
6620. Patrick, Benjamin D. of Norwalk m 6/28/49 Eliza P. Maxwell, dau of Hon. Thomas of Elmira, in Milan, Ohio; Rev. J. R. Taylor (2-7/18)
6621. Patridge, Daniel m Almira Aldrich in Manchester (3-7/9/28)
6622. Patridge, George (Hon.), 89, unmarried, (a Rev. soldier) d in Duxbury (Bequeathed $2000 to the Plymouth Bible Soc.; $2000 to theTheological School of Cambridge; $10,000 for a high school in Duxbury; and $10,000 to the Congregational Soc. in Duxbury) (3-7/30/28) (All towns in MA?)
6623. Pattent, Alexander, 64, d 7/2/47 at his home in Wayne (2-7/21)
6624. Patterson, Benjamin, 22, d in Galen (3-4/9/28)
6625. Patterson, Cynthia, 42, wf of Eli, d in Romulus (3-6/11/28)
    Patterson, Cyrus A. See also Batterson, Cyrus A.
6626. Patterson, Cyrus A. m Marcia Dawson in Ithaca (3-1/14/29)
6627. Patterson, Ebenezer, 62, d 8/8/33 in Peacham, VT (1-8/27)
6628. Patterson, Elizabeth, 65, relict of late Ezra, Esq. of Geneva, d 9/17/15 in Ravenna, Ohio (3-10/4)
6629. Patterson, Ezra, Esq., , 54, of Geneva, NY d 8/15/10 in Pensacola, West Florida (3-11/21)
6630. Patterson, Horace m 1/19/23 Emiline Tubbs in Waterloo; Rev. Dr. McDonald (3-1/29)
6631. Patterson, Mungo m 3/23/42 Agnes Clow, dau of Robert, Esq., in Sodus; A. B. Williams, Esq. (5-4/6)
6632. Patterson, Robert, L.L.D., 81?, d 7/22/24 in Philadelphia (3-8/4)
6633. Patterson, Robert, 78, (a Rev. soldier) d 10/2/40 at his home in Lindley (2-10/14)
6634. Patterson, S. A. of Dansville m 1/18/47 Rhoda Ann Canfield of Hornells-ville in H; Rev. Asa Upson (2-1/27)
6635. Patterson, Sarah, 86, of Bath d 7/6/49 while on a visit at the home of her son (not named) in Painted Post (2-7/25)
6636. Patterson, William m 2/22/16 Rachel Ireland in Benton (3-2/28)
6637. Pattingal, Hiram of Aurora d 3/31/46 in Aurora (suicide) (2-4/1)
6638. Patton, Evert m Elizabeth Young in Lyons (3-3/11/29)
6639. Paul, _____ (Mrs.), wf of William, d in Farmington (3-12/20/15)

170

6640. Paul, Lemuel d in Bloomfield (3-3/22/15)
6641. Paulding, John (Maj.), 64 or 84, one of the captors of Major Andre
during the Rev. War, d 12/30/19 in Staatsburgh, NY (3-1/19/20).
See 6642.
6642. Paulding, John (Maj.), one of the captors of Major Andre in the Rev.
War, d 2/19/18 in Yorktown, Westchester Co., NY (3-3/11/18)
See 6641.
6643. Pawling, Henry, Jr., 33, d 7/9/46 in Avoca (2-8/12)
6644. Pawling, Henry, 59, d 10/17/47 in Avoca (2-10/20)
6645. Pawling, Margaret, 33, d in Prattsburgh (3-5/16/27)
6646. Payne, Bushnell of Caledonia m Elizabeth Brownell of Canandaigua in C
(3-1/27/19)
6647. Payne, Charles T. of Palmyra m 4/5/32 Rebecca Pudney, formerly of
Waterford, in Lyons; Rev. Lucas Hubbell (5-4/11)
6648. Payne, Franklin m 7/11/32 Octavia J. Lewis in Palmyra; Rev. B. H.
Hickes (5-7/18)
6649. Payne, Gideon R. m 12/4/34 Mary B. Smith, both of Farmington (5-12/5)
6650. Payne, Joseph m Orrill Buck, both of Palmyra, in Vienna, NY (3-8/27/28)
6651. Payne, Niles m 9/1/47 Patty Lewis in Orange; Rev. Bryant R. Hurd
(2-9/15)
6652. Payne, Susannah, 60, of Victor d at the poor house (3-1/6/30)
6653. Payne, Syrus m 9/12/11 Lavinia Northam, dau of David, in Phelps;
William Burnet, Esq. All of Phelps (3-10/2)
6654. Payne, Th_____, 57, d 1/20/35 in Lyons (5-1/30)
6655. Payson, Edward (Rev.), 44, D.D., d in Portland, ME (3-11/28/27)
6656. Peabody, Calvin, 40, d in Rushville (3-7/9/28)
6657. Peak, Charles, about 29 or 23, d 2/8/40 in Avoca (2-2/12)
6658. Pearce, Pardon, 50, d 3/27/22 "in Clyde (Galen)" (3-4/10)
6659. Pearce, Willis m Elsie Sprague in Jerusalem, NY (3-12/5/27)
6660. Pearsall, _____ (Rev.) of Wellsboro, PA m Orinda Andrews in Chemung
(3-10/22/28)
6661. Pearsall, George, 67, d 1/26/44 in Williamson (His funeral was held at
the Friends Meeting House in Williamson) (5-1/31)
6662. Pearse, James m 3/19/44 Mary Sheckel in Palmyra; Rev. William Fergeson.
All of Palmyra (5-3/27)
6663. Pearson, Henry of Avon m 6/27/27 Grace B. Plumb, dau of late Rev. Elijah
of Northumberland, PA, in Geneseo, NY; Rev. Salmon (3-7/4)
6664. Pearson, Hepzibah, 65, relict of Pool Pearson of Seneca Co. and mother
of Mrs. D. S. Skaats, of Geneva d 9/14/23 (3-9/17)
6665. Pearson, Horatio m Sally Turner in Avon (3-12/27/15)
6666. Pease, Chester m Eunice Church in Somers, CT "after a courtship of
thirty five (not minutes but) years." (3-9/16/18)
6667. Pease, John H. S., about 2 yrs, s of Jabez, d 5/29/16 in Geneva
(3-6/5)
6668. Pease, Lucy, 46, consort of Abel, d 7/15/12 in Lyons (3-7/22)
6669. Pease, Lucy, 39, wf of Ammi, d in Junius (3-4/30/28)
6670. Pease, Phinehas, Jr., 25, d in Rochester (3-9/16/18)
6671. Pease, Samuel, editor of the Massillon Whig, m 5/7/35 Ann Louisa
Shepherdson of Spring Hill, Ohio in S. H.; Rev. T. M. Hopkins
(bride formerly of Palmyra, NY) (5-5/29)
6672. Pease, Sarah E., 5 yrs, dau of Jabez, d 12/24/22 in Auburn (3-1/1/23)
6673. Pease, William of Reading m 12/29/14 Electa Crittenden in Seneca
(3-1/4/15)
6674. Peck, Asa of Alexander m 1/2/48 Eliza Van Tassel of Tyre, Seneca Co.
in Batavia; Rev. S. M. Stimson (1-1/4)
6675. Peck, Chloe, wf of Everard, d 12/5/30 in Rochester (5-12/24)
6676. Peck, Enoch (Dr.) of York, Liv. Co. m 5/10/27 Julia Ann Jones, dau of
Ezra of Phelps, in P; Rev. Dr. Axtell (3-5/16)
6677. Peck, George W., about 41, d 11/19/44 in NYC (brother of Asahel Peck
of Batavia) (1-12/10)
6678. Peck, Joslius (sic) m 7/17/34 Amelia Bushel in Washington (5-8/8)
6679. Peck, Juliet, 3 yrs, dau of John, d 11/16/24 (prob. in Geneva) (3-11/17)
6680. Peck, R. C. of Avoca m 10/12/45 Eliza Davis, dau of D. H., Esq. of
Cohocton, in C; Rev. Brown (2-10/15)
6681. Peck, Samuel, (Capt.), 85, d 6/13/22 in Milford, CT (a Rev. officer)
(3-7/3)

6682. Peck, Thomas K. (Rev.), formerly pastor of Zion Church in Onondaga, d in Norwich, CT (3-8/22/27)
6683. Peck, Virgil m 12/18/17 Mary Phillips, dau of late Col. Phillips, in West Bloomfield (3-1/21/18)
6684. Peck, William C., 14 mo, s of Everard of Rochester, d in Avon (3-7/26/26)
6685. Peckham, Charles m Jerusha Kellogg, both of Palmyra, in P (3-6/3/12)
6686. Peckham, Margaret, 47, wf of Dr. William, d 5/7/32 in Ontario, NY (5-5/23)
6687. Peckham, William A. m 2/11/36 Lydisette Chapin in Ontario, NY (5-3/11)
6688. Peckins, Alexander m 11/16/25 Susan Clark in Benton (3-12/14)
6689. Peek, Samuel, about 26, senior editor of the Cornucopia, d 10/27/11 in Batavia (3-11/6)
Peet, Capt. Ebenezer. See Capt. Ebenezer Post.
6690. Peet, Ezra M. m 11/24/25 Clarinda Fabrigue in Lyons (3-12/7)
6691. Peet, Hiram m Candace Mason in Penfield (3-4/8/18)
Peet, M. A. See M. A. Post.
6692. Peirce, Luther m 9/6/29 Ardilla Wolcott; S. Cowan, Esq. (4-9/30)
6693. Pelham, John of Wheeler m 2/24/42 Susan Warner of Urbana; John Randel, Esq. (2-3/2)
6694. Pelham, Joseph, 21, m 4/23/14 Mrs. _____ Rundell, 51, a sister of the groom's father's second wife, in Lyons (3-5/4)
6695. Pember, Alfred, merchant, of Attica d 5/25/26 in Batavia (1-6/2)
6696. Pember, John P. m 1/13/42 Almira Ransom in Sugargrove, PA; Mark Willson, Esq. (4-1/27)
6697. Pemberton, Thomas, 75, d 11/24/25 in Elmira (3-12/21)
6698. Pembroke, _____, _____, and _____, three young children of widower John Pembroke of Benton, were reportedly murdered 4/2/12 by John's housekeeper of three years, Sally Chris, about age 20. Reportedly, immediately after killing the children, Sally killed herself. (3-4/8)
6699. Pembroke, Joseph m 6/18/22 Sally Cole in Benton; A. Woodworth, Esq. (3-6/26)
6700. Pendleton, Charles H. m 6/10/38 Charity Sears in Greenwood; Rev. Roswell Clark (2-6/13)
6701. Penfield, Henry F., Esq. m Harriet Seymour in Canandaigua (3-2/10/13)
6702. Penfield, Mary, 65, wf of Daniel, Esq., d in Penfield (3-9/10/28)
6703. Penick, Deborah, 31, d 1/11/18 in Geneva "after a lingering illness of two years" ("schirrous enlargement of the liver. After death she was opened by Dr. Pitney, assisted by Doctors Wm. C. Bennet, Cooley, and Lawrence... the liver weighed 34 lbs. 4 oz. (ordinary weight is from three to four lbs.)") (3-1/28)
6704. Penn, Richard, Esq., formerly governor of Pennsylvania, d 5/17/11 in Richmond, England (3-8/14)
6705. Penniman, Anna, 22, wf of William and dau of Capt. Aaron Gates of Phelps, d 6/7/22 in Shelby (3-6/19)
6706. Pennock, _____ (Mr.), 59, d 3/4/39 in Jamestown (4-3/6)
6707. Pennock, _____ and _____, two inf twin daus of Alvin, d "during the last week" in Jamestown (4-4/14/41)
6708. Pennock, Alvin, 41, d 2/22/42 (prob. in Jamestown) (4-3/31)
6709. Pennock, Edward, 1 yr, s of Thomas, d 11/8/24 in Geneva (3-11/17)
6710. Pennock, Juliet, 2 yrs, dau of Thomas J., d 10/13/26 (3-10/18)
6711. Pennock, Peter m 2/10/41 Phinetta Southwick in Busti; George Stoneman, Esq. (4-2/17)
6712. Pennhollow, _____, 6 yrs, ch of Mr. Pennhollow d "lately" in Black Rock of hydrophobia "from having been bitten by a dog in March" (2-8/3/31)
6713. Penny, Joseph (Rev.), pastor of the Presby. Church of Rochester, m Margaret Sterling in NYC (3-6/12/22)
6714. Penoyer, Reuben of Waterloo m Calista Christopher in Canoga (3-12/26/27)
6715. Pepper, Elnathan m Polly Rafter, both of Manchester, in Palmyra (3-6/25/28)
6716. Perine, David m 9/25/11 Margaret --ed in Lyons (both of Lyons) (3-10/2)
6717. Perine, Henry W. m 8/18/47 Elizabeth S. Read, youngest dau of James, in Bath; Rev. Corson. All of Bath (2-8/25)
6718. Perine, Lucy B., 23, wf of P. S. and dau of Whittington Sayre recently from Southport, Chemung Co., d 7/2/45 in Bath (2-7/9)
6719. Perine, Rachel Elizabeth, 21, wf of P. S. and dau of late John Brown of Bath, d 1/4/49 in Bath (2-1/10)

6720. Perine, William E. m 8/21/23 Mary W. ____mpson; Rev. Axtell. All of Lyons (3-8/27)
6721. Perkins, Benjamin D. of the house of Collins and Perkins of Geneva, d 10/13/10 at the home of John Murray, Jr. (Benjamin was a member of the Society of Friends) (3-11/7)
6722. Perkins, Calvin, about 40, d 9/25/28 in East Palmyra (formerly of the village of Palmyra) (3-10/8 and 5-10/3)
6723. Perkins, Clarissa, 23, wf of Septimus formerly of Broome Co.,d 5/17/36 in Jamestown (4-5/25)
6724. Perkins, Henry, M.D., of Oswego m Sarah Jones in Geneseo (3-7/8/29)
6725. Perkins, James, Esq., 61, of Boston d 8/1/22 at his home in Roxbury (state not given) (3-8/14)
6726. Perkins, James H., 24, s of Capt. John, d 12/11/48 in Pulteney (2-12/27)
6727. Perkins, John (Capt.), 66, d 3/27/50 in Pulteney (an early settler there - lived there 40 years) (2-4/17)
6728. Perkins, Lemuel of Campbell m 4/17/42 Orpha Maria Loop of Lenox, Mad. Co. in Cameron; Rev. P. L. Whipple of Cameron (2-4/27)
6729. Perkins, Phebe S., dau of William d 4/14/22 in Galen (3-5/1)
6730. Perkins, Rufus W., 30, a native of Massachusetts, d 3/31/19 in Waterloo (3-4/14)
6731. Perkins, Simeon L., late a merchant in Ovid, d 6/12/22 in Liverpool, Nova Scotia (3-7/31)
6732. Perkins, Thomas C., Esq. of Hartford, CT? m Mary F. Beecher, dau of Rev. Dr. Beecher, in Boston, MA (3-11/28/27)
6733. Perrin, Glover, 67, d 11/12/30 in Pittsford (one of the first settlers there) (5-12/10)
6734. Perrin, Jesse m ____ Burd in Palmyra; Rev. Townsend (3-12/10/17)
6735. Perry, Edward of Middlesex m 2/22/29 Harriet Woodworth of Benton in B; Rev. Ackley (3-2/25)
6736. Perry, Ezra m 6/28/31 Roxana Watson in Le Roy; Rev. Rogers (1-7/1)
6737. Perry, Freeman (Hon.), 83, d 10/15/13 in South Kingston (state not given) ("grandfather of the gallant Com. Perry") (3-12/8)
6738. Perry, Henry E. m Angeline B. Stillman, both of Palmyra, in Manchester; Rev. Draper (5-12/11 and 3-12/23) (marr. 12/6/29)
6739. Perry, John, Esq. m Rebecca Gleason in Middlesex (3-1/19/20)
6740. Perry, Jonathan m Theoda Brown in Milo (3-10/14/29)
6741. Perry, Joseph (Rev.), 52, d in New Haven (state not given) (3-12/23/29)
6742. Perry, Norman m 3/17/25 Susannah Scott, dau of Capt. David (both bride and groom of Covington and married there) (1-3/25)
6743. Perry, Rachel, 57, wf of Alanson, d 10/6/42 in Troupsburgh (surv by husband and children) (2-10/12)
6744. Perry, Roswell m 6/13/18 Sally Newhall, both of Vienna, NY, in V (3- 6/17)
6745. Perry, Susan (Miss), 31, dau of Capt. Rouse Perry, d 10/5/26 in Middlesex (3-10/11)
6746. Perry, Valentine (Deacon) of Perinton m 3/14/41 Abigail Gannett of Macedon in M; Rev. John Sears (5-3/24)
6747. Perry, William m 9/12/41 Harriet E. Selden in Cameron (both of Cameron) (2-9/15)
6748. Persons, ____, wf of Abram, d in Waterloo (3-10/20/19)
6749. Persons, ____ (widow), 76, d in Waterloo (3-7/18/27)
6750. Persons, Harry H. m 1/22/43 Esther Ann Ferris in Aurora, Erie Co. (4-3/2)
6751. Persons, Theophila m Eliza Baker in Ithaca (3-6/11/28)
6752. Persons, William of Woodhull m 6/30/50 Amy McPherrons of Cameron in Jasper; Elder J. B. McKenny (2-9/11)
6753. Peters, John m Polly Carpenter in Perinton (5-4/17/22)
6754. Peters, Joseph of Erwin m Eliza Corey in Angelica (3-5/14/28)
6755. Pettibone, Martha, 45, wf of Levi of Bowling Green and dau of Mr. Lowry late of Chautauqua Co., NY, d 4/15/45 in Louisiana, Pike Co., MO (4-5/9)
6756. Pettit, S. Smith, Esq. of Le Grange, Dutch. Co. m 6/5/44 Gertrude Everitt, dau of the late Richard, of Poughkeepsie in Palmyra (5-6/12)
6757. Pettit, William m 1/18/12 Delia Bateman in Benton (3-1/22)
6758. Pettys, Peleg m 10/20/22 Lavinia Powers, both of Galen in G (3-11/6)
6759. Pew, Sylvester, one of the publishers of the Seneca Falls Democrat, m 4/6/43 Electa Cox, dau of William, Esq. of Seneca Falls, in S. F. (5-4/26)

6760. Phaling, Philip (Capt.), 77, (a Rev. soldier) d 5/16/42 in Jasper (2-5/25)
6761. Phelps, _____, a child of Jon.,d in Canandaigua (3-1/6/13)
6762. Phelps, _____, inf dau of Dan d 8/4/27 in Bath (3-8/15)
6763. Phelps, Davenport (Rev.), 57, d 6/27/13 in Pulteneyville (a husband and father) (3-7/7)
6764. Phelps, Fanny Charlotte, 8 mo, dau of Barney of Jamestown, d 10/3/34 in Gerry (4-10/8)
6765. Phelps, Henry of Pulteneyville m 11/24/41 Martha Moses of Palmyra in P; Rev. Spaulding (5-12/1)
6766. Phelps., Jemima, wf of Calvin, d in Phelps (3-2/5/17)
6767. Phelps, John m 3/9/23 Hetty Mchorter (sic), both of Fayette, in F; Rev. Lane (3-3/19)
6768. Phelps, John F., Jr., publisher of the Mayville Sentinel, m 8/9/43 Julia A. Walter of Lyme, Huron Co., Ohio in Mayville; Rev. Hollis (4-8/24)
6769. Phelps, Joseph Augustus m 1/18/29 Ruth Ann Howard, both of Williamson, at St. John's Church in Sodus; Rev. Hubbard (5-1/23)
6770. Phelps, Luke, 82, d in Williamson (3-2/3/13)
6771. Phelps, Luman, 45, d 2/27/19 in Penn Yan (3-3/10)
6772. Phelps, Lyman m Anne Bristol in Canandaigua (3-11/15/15)
6773. Phelps, Lyman Monroe m 1/1/44 Harriet Angeline Hunt; Rev. D. Harrington. All of Palmyra (5-1/3)
6774. Phelps, Mary, 73, relict of late Oliver, Esq., one of the first settlers and proprietors of Ontario Co., d 9/13/26 in Canandaigua (3-9/27)
6775. Phelps, Nathan, 78, d in Hopewell (3-1/9/28)
6776. Phelps, Oliver, Esq. m 11/27/21 Laura Chapin in Canandaigua; Rev. Johns (5-12/12)
6777. Phelps, Oliver L. (Col.), 37, only son of O. Phelps, Esq., d 3/11/13 in Canandaigua (3-3/24)
6778. Phelps, Paul m 8/21/36 Polly Drake in Palmyra; F. Smith, Esq.(5-8/26)
6779. Phelps, Philo m 9/4/42 Emeline Dewey, both of Manchester, in Newark, NY; Rev. Lee (5-9/7)
6780. Phelps, Polly, 24, dau of Cornelius, d 8/21/13 in Seneca (3-8/25)
6781. Phelps, Stephen, Esq., 73, d 9/13/41 in Lewiston, Fulton Co., IL (Judge Phelps was among the earliest settlers in Palmyra, NY and opened the first public house; moved first to Canandaigua and to Illinois in 1821 (5-10/13)
6782. Phelps, Thomas J., 14, s of Luman of Benton, d 8/8 in B (killed by a tree falling on him in a gale) (3-8/20/17)
6783. Phetteplace, John m 11/19/45 Hercelia Sherwin; Rev. G. W. Clark. All of Jamestown (4-11/28)
6784. Philip, Daniel H. m 5/30/35 Charlotte Becker, both of Valatie, Col. Co., in V; Rev. L. H. Van Dyck (5-6/12)
6785. Philips, Eli m 12/25/28 Vesta Arnold in Macedon (5-12/26)
6786. Philips, Nicholas m 3/9/17 Catharine Foster in Wayne (prob. a double ceremony - see marr. of William Foster) (3-3/19)
6787. Phillips, Alanson m Eliza H. Walker in Bristol (3-1/20/30)
6788. Phillips, Daniel m 1/1/10 Eunice Howe, dau of Dr. Howe of Ovid, in Ovid; Rev. Clark (3-1/17)
6789. Phillips, Jared of Ellery m 8/18/36 Nancy Babcock of Busti in Jamestown; Elder J. E. Church (4-8/24)
6790. Phillips, John m 3/27/31 Betsey Madole in Howard (2-3/30)
6791. Phillips, Moses, 77, d in Phillipsburgh, Orange Co. (a Rev. officer) (3-1/20/19)
6792. Phillips, Pearly, 53, formerly of Geneva, d 11/4/16 in West Bloomfield (interred with masonic honors) (3-11/20)
6793. Phillips, Stephen of Jamestown m 6/28/29 Prudence Shearman, dau of Oliver, Esq. of Busti, in Harmony; Theron Bly, Esq. (4-7/1)
6794. Phillips, Thomas m 5/22/48 Nancy Pease, both of Canawagus, at the home of and by Rev. K. D. Nettleton of the village of Roanoke (1-5/30)
6795. Phillips, William (Hon.), 78, d 5/26/27 inBoston, MA (was gov.of Mass. for 11 years) (3-6/6)
6796. Phinney, Elihu, Esq., 58, d 7/12/13 in Cooperstown (editor of the Otsego Herald for 18 years) (3-8/11)
6797. Pickard, Conrad, 100, d in Owasco (3-8/22/27)

6798. Pickard, John m Irene Near in Ellery; Rufus Pier, Esq. (4-12/30/35)
6799. Pickard, Peter M. m 5/5/44 Malinda A. Decker, both of Ellery, in Gerry; Robert Lenox, Esq. (4-5/10)
6800. Pickard, William, 7, s of John, drowned 6/2/26 in Jamestown (4-6/21)
6801. Pickens, _____ (Gen.) d 8/11/17 in Tumasee, SC (a distinguished Rev. patriot) (3-9/17)
6802. Pickering, Timothy, (Col.) (Hon.), 84,(a Rev. war veteran and national senator) d 2/5/29 in Salem, MA (5-2/6 and 4-2/18)
6803. Picket, Thomas, formerly of Busti, d 12/7/38 in Montezuma, Pike Co., IL (4-2/6/39)
6804. Pickett, William E. of Sodus m 8/14/39 Mary Kellogg of Palmyra in P; Rev. Shumway (5-8/16)
6805. Pickle, Peter m 12/6/46 Clarissa Clark in Howard; Elder E, Bronson (2-1/20/47)
6806. Pier, David, 41, of Jamestown d 5/5/44 in Perrysburgh, Catt. Co. (4-5/10)
6807. Pier, Elizabeth (Mrs.), 75, mother of Henry, Esq., d 1/28/40 in Bath (2-2/5)
6808. Pier, George (Maj.), 36, d 7/13/31 in Cooperstown (4-7/27)
6809. Pier, Rhoda Ann, 4 mo, dau of Norman and Mary Ann, d 11/16/45 in Jamestown (4-11/28)
6810. Pier, Rufus W. of Jamestown m 9/11/45 Martha G. Bailey of Milwaukee, WI in M; Rev. Lord (4-9/26)
6811. Pierce, Abner m 2/12/14 Mary Ann Cane, both of Benton, in B; Morris F. Shepperd, Esq. (3-3/2)
6812. Pierce, Abner, 63, d in Penn Yan (one of the first settlers there) (3-10/3/27)
6813. Pierce, Asa of the Johnson House d 1/19/44 in Fredonia (4-1/19)
6814. Pierce, Benjamin, 49, m 12/4/17 Angeline Oliverson, 18 in Perinton; C. Packard, Esq. (5-12/10)
6815. Pierce, Catharine (Mrs.), 22, d 9/16/31 in Sodus (5-9/27)
6816. Pierce, Ezra m Eliza Gurley in Manchester (3-5/9/27)
6817. Pierce, George I. m 10/20/42 Louisa Sheldon in Randolph; Rev. E. Taylor. All of Randolph (4-11/3)
6818. Pierce, Isaac, 51, d in Canandaigua (3-5/10 and 5-5/17)
6819. Pierce, John, 24, d 3/23/40 in Jamestown (4-3/25)
6820. Pierce, Lurana, 47, consort of Abner, d 1/21/13 in Benton . See 6825. (3-2/10)
6821. Pierce, Nathan, Esq., 44, d 5/25/14 in Farmington (one of the earliest settlers "of this country") (3-6/1)
6822. Pierce, Pardon, 50, d 3/27/22 in Geneva (5-4/17)
6823. Piercem Sarah, about 60, d 9/9/23 in Junius (3-10/1)
6824. Pierce, Sarah, 67, d in Canandaigua (3-5/30/27)
6825. Pierce, Susan, 47, consort of Abner, d 1/21/13 in Benton. See 6820. (3-2/3)
6826. Pierce, William m 1/18/18 Sally Jacobus in Geneva; Rev. Goff. All of Benton (3-1/28)
6827. Pierce, William Leigh, Esq. d 12/18/14 in Canandaigua (3-12/21)
6828. Pierpont, J. E. m 5/16/50 Caroline Hawkins , only dau of the late Harvey, Esq., in Alexander; Rev. Nichols. All of Alexander (1-5/28)
6829. Pierson, Cyrus H. m 1/1/27 Zilpha Hicks in Fayette; Rev. Dr. Axtell (3-1/17)
6830. Pike, Salmon m Sarah Bean in Bath (3-6/13/27)
6831. Pilsbury, Mrs. David d 5/29/30 in West Bloomfield (5-6/4)
6832. Pinkney, _____ (Col.) of the U.S. Army d 12/16/25 in Baltimore (MD?) (3-12/28)
6833. Pinneo, James R. (Rev.) m 2/21/50 Melissa E. Linsley in Prattsburgh; Rev. B. C. Smith (2-2/27)
6834. Pinto, Rachel (Miss), 95, d in NYC (3-11/15/15)
6835. Piper, _____ m 11/5/39 Mrs Hibban in Manchester; Rev. Shumway (5-11/15)
6836. Piper, John m 12/25/17 Madulah Scott in Farmington (5-12/31)
6837. Piper, John m Mrs. Root in Farmington (5-1/12/20)
6838. Piper, John d 3/5/43 in Palmyra (5-3/8)
6839. Piper, Nathaniel m 6/23/29 Harriet Johnson in Palmyra; William Willcox, Esq. (5-7/31). Bridegroom listed as Nathan Piper in 3-8/5).

6840. Pitcher, Anna (Mrs.), 18, of Cayuga d in Canandaigua (3-9/17/17)
6841. Pitkin, Theodore, 67, d in Rochester (3-1/14/29)
6842. Pitney, Betsey, 21, wf of Dr. J. T. and dau of Col. John Harris,
       d 5/4/14 in Auburn (3-6/1). See 6843.
6843. Pitney, Joseph T. (Dr.) of Junius m 11/21/10 Betsey Harris, dau of
       Col. John of East Cayuga, in E. C.; Rev. Stewart. See 6842.
       (3-12/12)
6844. Pitts, Gideon, Esq., 62, of Richmond d 7/29/28 (among the pioneers of
       this county in 1792; member of state legislature and a magistrate)
       (3-8/13)
6845. Pitts, Job, 35, d 6/28/25 in Batavia (1-7/1)
6846. Pitts, Samuel of Canandaigua m Rhoda P. Wells in Richmond (3-10/15/28)
6847. Pitts, William R., 33, d in Richmond (3-4/1/29)
6848. Pixley, Chester m 10/30/50 Rosett Brundage, dau of Henry, in Bethany;
       Rev. A. H. Starkweather (1-11/5)
6849. Pixley, Harlow, 37, d 8/4/41 in Batavia (1-8/10)
6850. Place, John, Jr. m Margaret Truax in Cameron (3-1/9/28)
6851. Plate, Joseph m Sally Manger in Fayette (3-1/20/30)
6852. Platner, Luther m 11/13/42 Sarah Slater in Jamestown; Rev. Hill
       (4-11/17)
6853. Platt, Benjamin, Jr., 21, d 4/22/40 in Bradford (2-4/29)
6854. Platt, Ezra, Esq., about 60, first judge of Genesee Co., d 9/15/11 in
       Le Roy (3-10/2)
6855. Plimpton, Henry of Penn Yan m Maria Ann Warden in Clarkson (3-11/30/25)
6856. Ploss, James m Annis Simmons in Ellicott (4-8/16/26)
6857. Plum, John G., 1 yr, s of C. P. Plum, d in Ithaca (3-9/2/29)
6858. Plumb, Alvin m 12/20/32 Mary Ann Davis of Westfield in W; Rev. Parmlee
       (4-12/26)
6859. Plunket, _____ (Dr.), 89, titular bishop of Malth (sic), d in Dublin, NY
       (3-5/2/27)
6860. Polhemus, Benjamin m Lucina Shepherd in Sennett, Cayuga Co. (3-1/14/29)
6861. Polk, Lucius J. (Hon.), member of Congress from Tennessee, m 4/10/32
       Mary A. Easton, niece of Gen. Jackson, in the President's home,
       Washington, D.C. (5-5/2)
6862. Polk, William (Hon.), "chief judge of the 5th Judicial District",
       d in Maryland (3-2/10/13)
6863. Pollard, Nathaniel m Dorothy Pitcher in Aurelius (3-5/2/27)
6864. Pomeroy, George E. m 8/5/33 Helen E. Robinson, dau of the late Gain
       Robinson, M. D., in Palmyra (5-8/9)
6865. Pomeroy, Helen Augusta, 16 mo, dau of George E., d 9/2/35 in Palmyra
       (5-9/4)
9866. Pomeroy, Hunt of Ithaca m Orlina R. White, dau of Dr. A. G., in
       Southport (3-4/16/28)
6867. Pomeroy, Robert m Elizabeth Rogers in Riga, Monroe, Co. (5-9/18/35)
6868. Pond, Hubbard d in Newark, NY (3-12/23/29 and 5-12/11/29)
6869. Pond, Stillman m 4/18/49 Jane Ann Joyce in Alabama, NY; Rev. R. C.
       Palmer (1-5/1)
6870. Poor, John M., merchant, m2/9/31 Harriet Townsend, both of Carbondale,
       Luzerne Co., PA, in C; Rev. Nobles (5-2/25)
6871. Pope, Samuel, about 25, d 11/28/12 in Campbletown, Steuben Co. "He was
       a stranger in that town" arriving there 12/10. "...said he was from
       Ontario (next word blurred) and had a family." (3-12/16)
6872. Poppino, Daniel, 64, a judge of Wayne Co., d 7/4/41 at his home in
       Williamson (an early settler in that region) (5-7/14)
6873. Poppino, Daniel R. of Williamson m 1/2/32 Sarah L. Green of Troupsville
       in T (5-2/14)
6874. Porhemus, John m 5/7 Catharine Waugh in Seneca; Rev. William Nesbit
    *  (3-5/21/28)
6875. Porter, Benoni of Geneva m 11/18/16 Fanny Long of Phelps in P (3-11/27)
6876. Porter, Chauncey, 58, d 5/18/36 in Pittsford (5-5/20)
6877. Porter, David S., one of the publishers of the Utica Sentinel, m
       Charlotte A. Olmstead in Hartford, CT (3-5/27/29)
6878. Porter, James, Esq. m 12/24/11 Eliza Vredenburgh, dau of Col. Vredenburgh,
       in Skaneateles (3-1/8/12)
6879. Porter, James G. of Skaneateles m Sarah S. Grosvenor, dau of Capt.
       Grosvenor, of Nachitoches (state not given) (3-10/28/29)
*6880. Porter, Albert of Niagara Falls m Julia Matthews, dau of Vincent, Esq., in
       Rochester (3-10/28/29)   176

6881. Porter, Letitia P., 43, wf of Gen. Peter B., d in Black Brook (5-8/5/31)
6882. Porter, Moses (Gen.), 66, of the U.S. Army d in Cambridge, MA (5-5/29/22)
6883. Porter, Peter B. (Maj. Gen.) of New York State m 10/16/18 Laticia P.
       Grayson of Kentucky, dau of the Hon. John Breckenridge, formerly
       Attorney General of the U.S., in Princeton, NJ; Pres. Smith officiating
       (3-10/28)
6884. Porter, Robert H., 3 yrs, youngest s of William L. and Olive L., d 11/5/41
       in Prattsburgh (scarlet fever) (2-11/17)
6885. Porter, Robert L., 27, s of Judge Porter, d 5/29/38 in Prattsburgh
       (2-5/30). Same paper dated 6/6: age 28, served the Presbyterian
       Church in Branchport.
6886. Porter, Rosannah, 67, consort of Benjamin, d 3/25/30 in Batavia
       (1-3/26)
6887. Porter, Roxana, 71, consort of Robert of Prattsburgh, d 10/24/35
       (2-11/4)
6888. Porter, Silas, 25, d in Waterloo (3-10/27/19)
6889. Porter, Thomas (Midshipman), son of the Commodore, d in Madalina,
       Mexico (3-7/23/28)
6890. Porter, Timothy H. (Hon.), 59, d 12/19/45 in Olean, Catt. Co. (4-12/26)
6891. Porter, William, 46, of Palmyra d 3/11/19 in Williamson (5-3/17 and
       3-3/24)
6892. Porter, William N. of New Hartford m Marian Higby, dau of E., Esq., in
       Hopewell (3-5/14/28)
6893. Porter, William G., 32, d 8/5/49 at his home in Woodhull (surv by wf
       and 3 ch) (2-8/15)
6894. Posey, Thornton A. (Col.), 29, late of the U.S. Army, d in Wilmington, NC
       (3-10/8/17)
6895. Posley, George of Palmyra m 10/12/43 Mary Ann Clinton of Black Rock in
       B. R.; Rev. Hawke (5-10/18)
6896. Posson, Peter W. m 1/15/23 Polly Bartholomew in Shelby; Rev. Pratt.
       All of Shelby (1-1/17)
6897. Post, _____, Sr., 77, d in NYC (3-2/5/17)
6898. Post, Abraham m Lorinda Oaks in Angelica (3-7/22/29)
6899. Post, Henry m 12/24/40 Ann Jennett Saulpaugh, dau of Philip, in
       Manchester; Rev. William Roe (5-1/6/41)
6900. Post, Henry John, 49, merchant, formerly of NYC, d 9/18/22 in Woodville,
       Mississippi (3-10/30)
6901. Post, J. W. m 2/21/39 Jane A. Mott, both of Macedon, in M; Rev. Church
       (5-3/1)
6902. Post, M. A. (or Peet, M. A. - copy is blurred), son of Capt. Ebenezer,
       d 9/7/20 in Penfield (surv by wf and an infant child) (5-9/27)
6903. Post, Rachel (Mrs.), 62, d 2/16/25 in Batavia (1-2/18)
6904. Post, Samuel H. m 5/4/30 Elizabeth C. Hathaway in Palmyra; Rev. Campbell
       (5-5/14)
6905. Post, Stephen m 3/13/42 Sarah Ann Gifford, both of Palmyra, in P; Rev.
       Wilson Osborn (5-3/30)
6906. Post, Thomas m 1/7/36 Miranda Chapman in Harmony; Clinton Marcy, Esq.
       All of Harmony (4-1/13)
6907. Post, William m 11/15/27 Phebe McConnel, dau of Judge McConnel; Elder
       P. D. Gillett (3-12/5)
6908. Post, William, Esq. of Newark, NY m 9/1/45 Susanna Hazeltine, dau of
       Daniel of Jamestown, in J; Rev. Carpenter of Sinclairville (4-9/5)
6909. Post, William S. of the firm of Gurney and Post of Palmyra m Helen H.
       Wells of Aurora, Cay. Co. in A (5-2/14/34)
6910. Post, William S., 28, late of the firm of Gurney and Post, d 2/8/35
       in Palmyra (5-2/13)
6911. Post, Wright (Dr.), 63 or 68 d 6/14/28 in NYC (3-7/9)
6912. Potter, _____ (Mr.), 93, father of the late Arnold, Esq., d in
       Middlesex (3-6/8/14)
6913. Potter, Arnold, Esq. of Middlesex d "a few days since" near Lancaster, PA
       (3-1/24/10)
6914. Potter, Arnold, 23, s of Arnold, Esq. of Middlesex, d 7/14/22 in
       Jersusalem, NY (3-7/17)
6915. Potter, Benjamin, 34, d in Ovid (3-12/30/18)
6916. Potter, Benjamin (Dr.), 38, d in Sheldon (1-3/10/26)
6917. Potter, Bradford A., 56, d 2/23/50 in Corning (2-2/27)

6918. Potter, Chester W. m Marietta Abel in Wheeler (3-12/23/29)
6919. Potter, Cornelius m 5/2/22 Rebecca Rose in Wheeler (3-5/29)
6920. Potter, Gifford, 42, d 10/25/41 in Wheeler (2-10/27)
6921. Potter, Jeremiah m Widow Martha Bidwell in Prattsburgh (3-9/17/17)
6922. Potter, Milton E. (Dr.) of Cowlesville m 9/12/48 Sarah L. Bass, adopted
        dau of Ziba Durkee, Esq. of Alden, in A; Rev. Remmington (1-9/19)
6923. Potter, Philomela, 8 yrs, dau of Jeremiah, d in Prattsburgh (3-9/17/28)
6924. Potter, Sally Maria, 14, dau of Anselm, Esq., d in Mayville (4-4/27/31)
6925. Potter, Tabor m Harriet Squier in Junius (3-6/12/22)
6926. Potter, William of Middlesex m 3/26/18 Hannah Chissom of Penn Yan in
        P. Y.; Rev. Merrill (3-4/1)
6927. Poucher, Charles, editor and proprietor of the Western Argus at Lyons,
        m 5/6/41 Mary E. Wales, dau of George, Esq. of Scriba, Oswego Co.,
        in Scriba; Rev. J. Gridley (5-5/19)
6928. Poucher, Harriet W., 1 yr, dau of Charles and Mary, d 10/27/43 in Lyons
        (5-11/1)
6929. Pound, Elizabeth, 43, wf of Thomas, d in Galen (3-3/12/28)
6930. Pound, Thomas m Betsey Harper in Marengo (Galen) (3-11/12/28)
6931. Pow, Thomas, about 50, d 10/6/12 in Geneva (3-10/14)
6932. Powel, Richard m Ruth Staples; Elisha Slocum, Esq. (5-11/28/17)
6933. Powell, _____, 2 mo, s of John, d in Penn Yan (3-1/20/30)
6934. Powell, Catharine, 48, relict of late Thomas, formerly of Geneva,
        d 5/1/28 in Schenectady (3-5/7)
6935. Powell, David N., 22, s of Rev. Howell R. of Phelps, d in NYC (3-10/27/13)
6936. Powell, Emily, 24, consort of John and dau of Jared Patchen, Esq.,
        d 7/16/26 in Penn Yan (3-7/26)
6937. Powell, Jonathan, s of Rev. H. R., m 2/3/11 Sophronia Glover in Phelps;
        Col. Burnet (3-10/9)
6938. Powell, Lurany, 78, consort of late Stephen, Esq. of Dansville, d 11/14/46
        in Bath (2-11/25)
6939. Powell, Thomas, 55, formerly of Geneva, d 2/27/25 in Schenectady (3-3/9)
6940. Powell, William Henry m 11/9/25 Margaret Louisa Van Ingen in Schenectady;
        Rev. Lacey (3-11/23)
6941. Power, Abiather m 2/5/29 Susan Rapalye in Farmington; Rev. A. D. Eddy
        (5-2/6)
6942. Power, Nicholas, formerly editor and proprietor of the Poughkeepsie
        Journal, d in Poughkeepsie (3-10/23/11)
6943. Powers, _____, about 7, dau of Roswell, d 12/14/16 in Fabius.
        A ten-year-old son of Roswell d 12/15. On 12/17 Roswell's wife died
        along with her infant child. (3-1/22/17)
6944. Powers, _____ and _____, age 5 and 11, daus of James of Sempronius,
        drowned 4/25/18 in a neighborhood creek "while seeking leeks"
        (5-5/12)
6945. Powers, Arthur m Mary Dillingham in Farmington (a Quaker marriage)
        (5-3/8/20 and 3-3/29/20)
6946. Powers, Charles H. d in Corning ("a worthy ... brother laborer in the
        cause of Temperance") (2-3/31/47)
6947. Powers, Ep (sic) m 2/26/24 Harriet Case, both of Batavia; S. S. Butler,
        Esq. (1-3/5)
6948. Powers, Calvin m 9/12/35 Maria Emeline Cory, both of Farmington;
        F. Smith, Esq. (5-9/18)
6949. Powers, Gersham d 6/25/31 in Auburn ("late a member of Congress from
        Cayuga County") (5-7/8)
6950. Powers, John m 6/3/10 Lavina Stone in Bath; Rev. G. McClure (3-8/15)
6951. Powers, Jonathan m 8/12/21 Olive Perry in Lyons; J. Tibbitts, Esq.
        (5-8/15)
6952. Powers, Luther m Polly Rundell in Harmony (4-2/7/27)
6953. Powers, Polly, 41, consort of Blanchard Powers, Esq., d 8/21/22 in
        Batavia (1-8/23)
6954. Powers, Warren m 4/6/42 Jane C. Schermerhorn, both of Lyons, in
        Newark, NY; Rev. William F. Davis (5-4/13)
6955. Powers, William R. m Thankful Rowland in Seneca; Rev. Axtel (3-12/30/12).
        In the same paper dated 1/13/13 the bride's name is corrected to
        read Thankful H. Howland.
6956. Pratt, Abraham d in Palmyra (3-2/24/13)

6957. Pratt, Almond (Dr.) of Palmyra m 1/10/33 Mary Boynton, dau of Hon.
Jonathan of Walworth, in W; Rev. Gideon Osband (5-1/16)
6958. Pratt, Alvah of Williamson m 10/18/21 Ann Peck of Ontario, NY in O
(5-10/31)
6959. Pratt, Bartholomew (Rev.) of Mount Morris m Susan McNair, dau of Hugh,
Esq., in Canandaigua (3-4/17/22)
6960. Pratt, Cephleact(?), 15, dau of Elkanah, d 1/12/29 in Manchester
(5-1/16)
6961. Pratt, Claudius B. of Marshall, MI m 10/12/46 Mary E. Phelps, dau of
H. G., Esq., of Corning,in C; Rev. E. B. Fuller (2-10/21)
6962. Pratt, David (Rev.) of Oak Orchard m 11/7/19 Philena Brown of Palmyra
in P; Rev. Jesse Townsend (3-11/17 and 5-11/10)
6963. Pratt, Elijah m 6/16/45 Eliza Tarney in Bath; Elder Rowley (2-7/2)
6964. Pratt, Elisha Willis of Ontario, NY m 5/13/41 Alantha Jackways, dau of
David S., of Palmyra; Rev. Samuel Wilson (5-5/19)
6965. Pratt, Eliza (Miss), 21, dau of Jared, d in Prattsburgh (3-7/15/29)
6966. Pratt, Ezilum m 5/25/26 Perlina Chapin, both of Bath, in B (3-6/7)
6967. Pratt, George m Mrs. Gee in Ovid (3-2/7/16)
6968. Pratt, Hiram, merchant, of Buffalo m Maria Fowle in Northampton
(3-12/21/25)
6969. Pratt, Ira F. of Gainesville m 10/10/24 Phoebe Locke of Covington in C;
Rev. E. M. Spencer (1-10/22)
6970. Pratt, Joel, 19, s of Elisha, Esq., d 3/14/41 in Prattsburgh (2-3/17)
6971. Pratt, John m Sally Potter in Manchester (3-1/19/20)
6972. Pratt, Lorenzo, merchant, m 9/12/27 _____ (page mutilated) in
Milo; Rev. Alverson (3-9/19)
6973. Pratt, Nathan, Jr. m Clarissa Catlin in Middlesex (3-3/24/19)
6974. Pratt, Polly (Mrs.), 57, d in Gorham (3-4/23/17)
6975. Pratt, Rebecca, 35 or 55, wf of Ira, d 1/21/22 in Bath (3-2/6)
6976. Pratt, Shumway m 9/13/35 Anna Warren in Bath; Rev. Platt (2-9/30)
6977. Pratt, Stephen, about 50, formerly of Victor, drowned in Lake Erie near
Buffalo ("His effects are in the hands of Mr. Welcome Wood of Buffalo.")
(3-8/30/15)
6978. Pray, David m 3/14/39 Pernia Miner; T. S. Bly, Esq. (prob. all are of
Harmony) (4-3/20)
6979. Pray, John m 10/23/45 Laura Clark, both of Panama, NY; Rev. O. Sanderson
(4-10/31)
6980. Prendergast, Martin, 66, d in Mayville (4-6/24/35)
6981. Prendergast, Matthew (Hon.) d in Chautauqua (4-2/28/38)
6982. Prendergast, Nancy, wf of James, Esq. and for many years a resident of
Jamestown, d 1/4/39 in Ripley (4-1/9)
6983. Prendergast, Thomas, about 90, d in Ripley (one of the earliest settlers
in Chautauqua Co. (4-6/9/42)
6984. Prentice, Henry, 73, d 2/3/35 in Jasper (surv by wf and a family)
(2-2/18)
6985. Prentice, Polly (Mrs.), 35, d 10/19/30 in Palmyra (5-10/29)
6986. Prentiss, Azariah, formerly of Hartford (state not given), m 6/18/30
Almira C. Brown in Galen; Rev. Merrill (5-7/16)
6987. Prentiss, Daniel m 11/8/32 Patty Clapp in Batavia; C. M. Russell, Esq.
(1-11/13)
6988. Prentiss, George W., 37, late one of the editors of the New York
Statesman, d in Keene, NH (3-3/18/29)
6989. Prentiss, J. G., merchant, of Angelica m 10/11/35 Frances Rolo of
Cortlandville in C; Rev. Foot (2-11/4)
6990. Prentiss, J. H. (Col.), editor of the Freeman's Journal, m 6/3/28 Urilla
Shankland in Cooperstown; Rev. John Smith (3-6/18)
6991. Prentiss, John A. m 5/11/26 Thankful Hotchkin in Pulteney; Rev. Beriah
Hotchkin (3-5/24)
6992. Prescott, Joel (Dr.), 53, d 2/5/11 in Phelpstown (A native of Massachusetts;
one of the first settlers "25 years ago" in the Phelpstown area; for
many years town supervisor and justice of the peace; surv by wf and
6 ch) (3-10/9)
6993. Prescott, Reed, 19, s of late Dr. Joel, d 12/1/17 in Phelps (3-12/10)
6994. Preston, _____, 3 mo, ch of Silas, d in Waterloo (3-1/9/28)
6995. Preston, Benjamin (Rev.), 28, of Cleveland, Ohio d 3/10/41 at the home of
his father in Harmony (Before age 21 had been licensed to preach by the
Pittsburgh Conference of the Meth. Episc. Church (4-3/17)

6996. Preston, Foster D m Clarissa Locke in Farmersville; J. Hazelton, Esq.
(Remarried the following day by Rev. S. Hubbard of Centerville)
(3-4/1/29)
6997. Preston, Henry m 10/21/49 Harriet E. Taft in East Bethany; Rev. Jacob
Hart. All of Batavia (1-11/6)
6998. Preston, Joseph, 20, s of Rev. David, d 4/16/41 in Harmony ("In a few
weeks from the family of the Rev. D. Preston, his aged companion and
his two sons, Benjamin and Joseph, both in the ministry, have been
taken away by death") (4-4/28)
6999. Preston, Joseph W. m 2/4/41 Sophia Muzzey in Panama, NY; Rev.E. J. L.
Baker. All of Harmony (4-2/10)
7000. Preston, William H. m 6/16/50 M. E. A. Plato; Rev. Allen Steele. All of
Batavia (1-6/25)
7001. Price, Abigail, 36 or 38, consort of Benjamin, d 8/30/30 in Lyons
(5-9/3)
7002. Price, Benjamin, 27, formerly of Rhinebeck, was "killed in a duel after
the exchange of six shots"in NYC (3-5/29/16)
7003. Price, Daniel m Rebecca Barrick, both of Clyde, in Waterloo (3-3/18/29)
7004. Price, David C., 29, d 10/14/23 in Lyons (3-10/22)
7005. Price, James H., Esq., attorney, d 6/25/29 in Mayville ("a poet of much
promise - one frailty destroyed his usefulness; through unrestrained
indulgence (he) has found a premature grave...") (4-7/1)
7006. Price, R. of Lockville m 2/22/31 Ruth Ann Crosby of Phelps; Rev. Strong
(5-2/25)
7007. Price, Tobias m Eunice Fellows in Mendon (3-10/28/29)
7008. Price, William m 7/10/14 Betsey Whaley, both of Seneca, in S; Oren
Aldrich, Esq. (3-7/20)
7009. Prichard, James, 31, d 10/7/26 in Geneva (3-10/11)
7010. Prime, Henry L. m Alsma Brewer in Jerusalem, NY (3-1/6/30)
7011. Prime, William m 8/21/32 Eliza Ann Newbury in Palmyra; Rev. Jesse
Townsend (5-8/29)
7012. Pringle, Elizabeth (Mrs.), upwards of 80, (a native of Fredericktown)
d 1/22/29 in Geneva (3-1/28)
7013. Prior, John, 67, d 6/6/24 in Elba (1-6/11)
7014. Prior, Mahetable, 42, wf of Jesse, d 5/18/26 "at the White Springs in
Seneca" (3-5/24)
7015. Prior, Orlo m 2/2/34 Amanda Demmon, both of Jamestown, in J; Rev. W. R.
Babcock (4-2/5)
7016. Prior, Wells, 24, d 2/24/27 in Geneva (3-2/28)
7017. Pritchard, Nathaniel d in Canandaigua (3-1/8/13)
7018. Proctor, Mary, 62, d 6/6/24 in Batavia (1-6/11)
7019. Prosser, David B., Esq., attorney, of Penn Yan m 6/10/41 Loisa H. West
of Milo, late of Bath, in Milo; Rev. Richards (2-6/30)
7020. Prosser, Lydia, 27, consort of Isaac, d 11/17/09 in Snell (3-12/20)
7021. Prossons(?), Gertrude (Miss), 14, d 2/15/40 in Sodus (5-2/19)
7022. Proudfit, James (Dr.) d 8/8/13 in Philadelphia, PA ("a physician of
eminence") (3-8/25)
7023. Proudfit, John m 12/3/29 Eliza Frushour in Hopewell; Rev. Nisbet
(3-12/9)
7024. Proudfit, William P. (Dr.) m 11/8/32 Maria Freeman, both of Jamestown,
in J; Rev. Gillet (4-11/14)
7025. Proudfit, William P. (Dr.), 39, d 3/18/43 in Milwaukee, Wisc. Terr.
(Lived in Jamestown for 5 years and there married "the daughter
of E. Freeman" and also joined the local Presbyterian Church)
(4-4/6)
7026. Prouty, John, brother of Phineas of Geneva, d 4/29/20 in Schenectady)
(3-5/10)
7027. Prouty, Margaret M., 34, consort of Phineas and youngest dau of the
late Rev. Nicholas Van Vranken of Fishkill, Dutchess Co., died
(death date not given) (5-9/17/30)
7028. Prouty, Phineas, merchant, of Geneva m 9/29/19 Margaret M. Van Vranken*
of Schenectady in S; Rev. Van Vechten (3-10/13)
7029. Provost, Augustine Palmer (Rev.), 36, rector of St. John's Church,
Canandaigua in the diocese of western NY, d 11/15/43 at the home of
his father-in-law in Philadelphia (state not given) (5-11/29)
7030. Provost, George W. of Victor m 5/1/31 Rebecca Lambright in Newark (5-6/10)
* - Margaret is dau of "late Nicholas Van Vranken of Fishkill, Dutchess Co."

7031. Provost, Samuel (Right Rev.), D.D., 72, Bishop of the Protestant Episc.
Church of the State of New York, d in NYC (3-9/20/15)
7032. Prusia, Jesse B. m 5/20/46 Olive H. Truman in South Dansville; Rev.
Selmser (2-6/3)
7033. Pulling, Abel, 82, d 10/14/42 at the home of his son, Dr. E. B., in
Hammondsport (Abel was a member of the Episcopal Church) (2-10/26)
7034. Pulling, Mary Frances E., 2 yrs, dau of Dr. E. B. and Mary, d 1/27/45
in Bath (2-2/26)
7035. Pulver, Jacob m 5/1/26 Belinda Brown in Seneca; Rev. Nesbit (3-5/10)
7036. Pumpelly, John, 85, d in Danby, Tioga Co. (3-7/21/19)
7037. Punchis, G. W. of Cameron m 2/18/47 Martha Dennis of Jasper in J; Rev.
Everest (2-2/24)
7038. Punderson, William, formerly of Junius, m Mercy Jenny near Marengo
(3-11/5/28)
7039. Purdy, Allen m Temperance Gillis in Wayne (3-3/24/19)
7040. Purdy, Fay H. of Penn Yan m 6/9/41 Caroline Hall of Palmyra; Rev. Hibbard
of Geneva (5-6/9)
7041. Purdy, Jonathan (Dr.) m 2/4/29 Frances L. Satterlee in Elmira (3-2/25)
7042. Purdy, Lysander., 27, d 4/13/39 in Harmony (4-4/17)
7043. Purdy, Mary Lurany, 3 yrs, dau of Charles and Harriet L., d 4/2/42 in
Bath (2-4/6)
7044. Purdy, P. B. (Capt.), 69, d 11/17/28 in Springfield, Ohio (surv by ch)
(3-12/24)
7045. Purdy, William m 7/15/17 Mrs. Betsey Carpenter in Bath (3-7/23)
7046. Purier, William m Phebe Macumber in Canandaigua (3-3/13/16)
7047. Puriner(?), David m 12/25/17 Polly Curtis(?) in Farmington (5-12/31)
7048. Putman, Myron m 11/3/42 Betsey Lord, both of Bethany, in Batavia
(1-11/8)
7049. Putnam, Aaron (Rev.), 45, d 12/28/31 in Owego (2-1/4/32)
7050. Putnam, Chester, 27, d 2/28/14 in Claremont, NH along with Elisha Putnam,
his brother (both suffocated in a closet room, "recently plastered,
in which a kettle of burning charcoal was put" (3-3/2)
7051. Putnam, Cornelius, Esq. of Marion m 7/15/42 Matilda Bradley of Palmyra
in Lyons; Rev. Ira Ingraham (5-7/27)
7052. Putnam, Dorcas, 42, wf of Stephen, d 2/21/34 in Macedon ("She has left
a large family to lament her loss") (5-3/14)
7053. Putnam, Eliza, 20, wf of William of Painsville, Ohio and dau of Rowell
Buck of Jamestown, d 6/17/45 in Union, PA (4-6/27)
7054. Putnam, Happy (Mrs.), wf of Cornelius, d in Palmyra (5-10/31/21)
7055. Putnam, Peter Schuyler, Esq., youngest son of the late Gen. Israel of
Conn., d in Williamstown, MA (3-11/14/27)
7056. Putnam, Susan (Mrs.), consort of the late Peter, Esq. of Bethany,
d 5/11/22 (1-5/24)
7057. Putnam, Tacy, 34, wf of Newel, Esq., d 1/24/33 in Stockton (4-1/30)
7058. Putnam, Warren m 11/17/42 Susan Carpenter in Ellery; Rev. H. Smith
(4-11/24)
7059. Putnam, William of Painsville, Ohio m 6/4/45 Eliza Buck of Jamestown,
NY in Ashville, NY; Rev. T. D. Blin (4-6/6)
7060. Putnam, William of Pembroke m 5/12/46 Emily Wood of Batavia in B; Rev.
S. M. Stimson (1-5/19)
7061. Pyerson, Lucius C., 17, s of Samuel, d 5/31/26 in Junius ("Neighboring
printers will confer a favor by publishing the above") (3-6/14)
7062. Quackenboss, James m Mary Ann Englehart in Phelps; M. Musselman, Esq.
(3-5/10/26)
7063. Quick, John m 8/23/18 Diadamia C. Dutton in Lyons (5-9/8)
7064. Quimby, Jacob, late professor of Latin and Greek Languages ...at the
Univ. of Maryland, d 2/6/38 in Baltimore (formerly of Palmyra, NY)
(5-2/21)
7065. Quin, Dominic, 32, d 1/5/29 in Bath (3-1/21)
7066. Quin, Edward, Esq. of Tioga Co. m 1/5/31 Margaret Mary Kernan, dau of
Gen. William, in Tyrone; Rev. M. McNamard (2-1/12)
7067. Quin, George E. Esq. of Jefferson m 1/20/46 W. E. Kernan of Tyrone in T;
Rev. John Sheridan (2-2/4)
7068. R_____ett, W. (Rev.) of Wayne m 2/8/38 Mary Ann Mitchell, dau of John
B., Esq. of Wayne in W; Rev. White (2-2/14)

7069. Racife, Hartman of the U.S. Army m Maria del Carmen Meade, dau of late
Richard W. Meade, in Philadelphia (state not given) (3-3/18/29)
7070. Rain, _____ (Mrs.), wf of William,d 1/16/13 "near Geneva" (3-1/20)
7071. Ralph, John (Rev.), D.D., 67, d 3/6/19 in Sheldon, Gen. Co. (3-3/31)
7072. Ramsay, _____, a ch of John d in Canandaigua (3-1/6/13)
7073. Ramsay, John, Esq., 80, d in Westchester Co. (3-11/29/15)
7074. Ramsdell, Gannet m Ann Perin in Perinton (5-4/17/22)
7075. Ramsdell, Nathan m 2/16/32 Mary Ann Hoag in Macedon; A. Purdy, Esq.
(5-3/6)
7076. Rand, Electa, 23, wf of Samuel, d in West Macedon (5-6/11/30)
7077. Rand, James m Clarissa Wilbur in Pembroke; Elder Throop (1-8/13/24)
7078. Randall, Elizabeth (Mrs.), 80?, d in Boston (3-5/20/29)
7079. Randall, Ira M. of Chili, NY m 4/7/47 Mary A. Fish of Batavia in B;
Rev. Bolles (1-4/13)
7080. Randall, Miles m 5/5/25 Betsey Melvin in Attica (1-5/6)
7081. Randall, Samuel B. (Maj.) of Palmyra m 7/4/42 Maria M. Dates of Fishkill,
Dutch. Co. in F; Rev. W. F. Collins (5-7/20)
7082. Randall, Sarah, 31, wf of Maj. Samuel B., d 6/28/41 in Palmyra (5-6/30)
7083. Randall?, Willard m 12/25/17 Rebecca McCollum in Farmington (5-12/31)
7084. Randall, Zadock m 10/6/13 Hannah Hatt; Rev. John Caton (3-10/13)
7085. Randel, _____, ch of Daniel,d in Canandaigua (3-2/14/16)
7086. Randel, William, merchant, of Hammondsport m 11/22/35 Hnnah Read in Urbana;
J. Larrowe, Esq. (2-11/25)
7087. Randolph, Benjamin H., 25, s of Reuben of Ontario, NY d 9/4/21 at
Alexander Rapids (5-11/14)
7088. Randolph, Charlotte (Mrs.), 62, d 7/27/29 in Ontario, NY (5-8/7 and
3-8/19)
7089. Ranney, Assenah, 18, d in Sangerfield, Oneida Co. (3-2/15/26)
7090. Ranney, Thomas S., printer, formerly of Ithaca, m Maria Gager of Albany
in A (3-8/29/27)
7091. Ransom, J.Orville m 5/10/43 Mary R. Talcott in Smyrna; Rev. A. B. Engle(?)
(4-6/8)
7092. Ransom, Norman K. m 9/20/32 Maria Alger; Rev. Gillet. All of Jamestown
(4-9/26)
7093. Ransom, Owen (Lt.) of the U.S. Army m Charlotte W. Perkins in Norwich, CT
(3-3/26/17)
7094. Ransom, Silas, 79, d in Palmyra (3-9/8/19)
7095. Raplee, _____ (Mr.) m 7/1/27 Sally Dean, both of Milo, in Benton;
Elder Ezra Crane (3-7/11/27)
7096. Rappleye, Peter m Ann Wheeler in Ovid (3-3/17/19)
7097. Rash, Jacob, 74, d 3/4/28 in Seneca (3-3/5)
7098. Rathbon, Dobson m 6/9/22 Hannah Green; R. Hogarth, Esq. (3-6/12)
7099. Rathbone, John m Polly Leonard in Romulus (3-2/21/16)
7100. Rathbone, Lucy, 58, wf of Israel, d 11/21/49 in Le Roy (she "a devoted
mother") (1-11/27)
7101. Rathbun, Charlotte, 43, consort of Moses, Esq. of Buffalo, d 7/21/25
in Batavia (1-7/22)
7102. Rathbun, Cornelius m Clara Rathbun in Howard (3-1/22/17)
7103. Rathbun, Hiram m 10/11/49 Louisa Shearer, dau of Robert, in Howard;
W. B. Rice, Esq. All of Howard (2-11/21)
7104. Rathbun, Joanna L., wf of Ammi Rand and dau of Capt. Guy Wheeler of
New London, CT, d in Howard (3-12/23/29)
7105. Rathbun, Lydia, 37, wf of L. S., Esq., d in Almond (3-6/6/27)
7106. Rathbun, Moses, Esq. of Buffalo m 5/2/24 Mrs. Charlotte Moore of New
Lebanon Springs, "in N. L. S."; Rev. Jones (1-5/28)
7107. Rathbun, Thomas R. m 3/20/38 Aurelia Elizabeth Howe in Jamestown;
Rev. Chapin (4-3/21)
7108. Rawson, Jonathan, 77, (a Rev. soldier) d in Victor (3-10/22/28)
7109. Rawson, Mary, 20, dau of late Dr. Thomas Rawson, d 9/18/18 in
Canandaigua (3-9/30 and 5-10/6)
7110. Rawson, Philo S. of Geneseo m 12/27/31 Charlotte Dobbin in Canandaigua
(5-1/3/32)
7111. Rawson, Silas, 79, d 8/26/19 in Palmyra (5-9/1)
7112. Rawson, Thomas H. (Dr.), late of Onondaga, d in Canandaigua (3-8/10/14)
7113. Rawson, Thompson m Keziah Tobey, both of Carroll, in C; James Hall, Esq.
(4-2/18/29)

7114. Ray, David, 70, (a native of Dungamrou, Ireland) d at the home of John R. Barnes in Seneca (3-1/28/29)
7115. Ray, William (Maj.), 54, "the celebrated poet", d 7/29/26 in Auburn (1-8/4)
7116. Raymond, John C. m 1/6/47 Sarah A. Cory, both of Italy, Yates Co., in I; Rev. Chatman (2-1/20)
7117. Raymond, Lucy, 86, wf of Raymond, d 12/31/41 in Cohocton (2-1/12/42)
7118. Raymond, Rufus m 7/12/10 Ruhemma Aulls in Bath; Rev. John Miles. All of Bath (3-8/15)
7119. Raynor, Charles of Lyons m 8/16/18 Mehitabel Clark of Palmyra in P (3-9/16 and 5-9/8)
7120. Rea, Alexander (Gen.), 43, of Genesee Co. d 11/29/13 in Canandaigua (3-12/8)
7121. Read, Darius m 6/24/10 Hannah Montgomery in Bath; Rev. G. McClure (3-8/15)
7122. Read, Elijah m Sally Brundage in Pleasant Valley (3-4/2/17)
7123. Read, Elizabeth, about 1 yr, dau of Lazarus, d 7/14/45 in Bath (2-7/23)
7124. Read, James, 17 mo, s of L. H., d 9/11/42 in Bath (2-9/14)
7125. Read, James H., 27, M.D., s of Capt. James of Bath, d 7/15/50 in Coloma, California (2-9/18)
7126. Reading, George (Capt.) d in Junius (3-9/10/28)
7127. Rector, Andrew m Betsey Coon in Benton (3-2/13/28)
7128. Rector, Coonrod m Mary Wheeler in Benton (3-4/1/29)
7129. Redding, Abel W. of NYC m 9/1/45 Mary Jane Williams, dau of late Oswald of Batavia, at St. James Church, Batavia; Rev. James A. Bolles (1-9/2)
7130. Reddington, Thomas m 10/4/46 Marian Pierson in Canisteo; E. D. Swartwood, Esq. All of Cameron (2-10/14)
7131. Redfield, George of St. Joseph, Mich. Terr. m 6/10/35 Julia Ann Mason of Palmyra; Rev. Staunton (5-6/12)
7132. Redfield, Heman J., Esq. m Abigail Gould in Canandaigua (3-1/22/17)
7133. Redfield, Heman J. (Hon.) m 4/14/46 Constance Collins, dau of Ephraim Bolles, Esq. of Newark, NJ at St. James Church, Batavia; Rev. James A. Bolles (1-4/21)
7134. Redfield, Lewis H., editor of the Onondaga Register, m 2/7/20 Ann Maria Tredwell, dau of Nathaniel H. of Plattsburg, in Clinton, Oneida Co.; Rev. Dr. Davis (3-2/23)
7135. Redfield, Maning, 22, s of Hon. Heman J., d 10/6/48 in Madison, WI (1-10/17)
7136. Redpath, Charles m Jane More in Bath (3-4/14/19)
7137. Ree____r, ____ m Mrs. Jane Crandle of New Paltz "he being her seventh husband" (3-9/23/18)
7138. Reed, _____ (Mrs.), wf of _____ Reed, d 3/23/25 in Seneca (3-3/30)
7139. Reed, Amos H. of Palmyra m 1/1/18 Catherine Brockway of Williamson in W (5-1/7)
7140. Reed, Asa W. m 3/8/18 Lucy Loomis; Dr. Woodworth. All of Seneca (3-3/11)
7141. Reed, Carlo of Gorham m 9/26/27 Mrs. Sally Murray in Hopewell (3-10/17)
7142. Reed, David, 26, d 4/2/33 in Hopewell, Ont. Co. (5-4/17)
7143. Reed, Dustin m 8/27/29 Malinda Cromwell in Seneca; Rev. Tooker (3-9/9)
7144. Reed, Hannah, 74, wf of John, d 12/1/18 in Seneca (3-12/16)
7145. Reed, Hannah, 36, wf of William, d 5/18/19 in Palmyra (3-6/2/19 and 5-5/26/19)
7146. Reed, Hugh m 3/24/42 Sarah Mills, both of Farmington, in Palmyra; I. E. Beecher, Esq. (5-3/30)
7147. Reed, Jacob m 1/13/25 Martha Rippey, dau of John, Sr., in Seneca; Rev. Nisbet (3-1/19)
7148. Reed, John m 2/18?/14 Rebecca Reed, both of Seneca, in S; Rev. Axtell (3-3/9)
7149. Reed, Lazarus, Esq., attorney, of Hammondsport m 4/3/38 Elizabeth Woods, dau of late William, Esq., in Bath; Rev. Platt (2-4/11)
7150. Reed, Lorin W. m 10/22/45 Amanda M. F. Macomber, both of Alabama, NY, in A; Rev. J. Mallory of La Grange (1-10/28)
7151. Reed, Martha, 28, wf of Carlo, d 8/27/27 in Gorham (3-10/17)
7152. Reed, Mary H. E., 28, wf of Rev. Royal (formerly a resident of Palmyra), d 4/27/41 in Cummington, CT (5-6/9)

7153. Reed, Nathaniel, about 70, d 8/22/30 in Manchester (5-8/27)
7154. Reed, Peter m 11/10/40 Ann Maria Thurston, dau of Isaac of Macedon,
in M; Rev. Parker (5-11/25)
7155. Reed, Prescott m 1/28/29 _____ Halladay, dau of C. Halladay; C. Shekell,
Esq. All of Seneca (3-2/4)
7156. Reed, Randall (Dr.) of Allegany Co. m 8/7/38 Eliza Ann Allen of Fleming,
Cay. Co. in F; Elder Plumb (2-8/22)
7157. Reed, Rebecca, 50, wf of Taft Reed, d 5/14/17 in Seneca (3-6/11)
7158. Reed, Riley of Farmington m 2/16/36 Caroline Jackson of Walworth (5-3/11)
7159. Reed, Ward m 2/23/28 Matilda Tallman, both of Seneca, in Geneva; Rev.
Axtell (3-2/27)
7160. Reed, Welcome m 3/4/41 Sarah Booth, both of Manchester, in Palmyra;
F. Smith, Esq. (5-3/17)
7161. Reed, William (Gen.), Adjutant General of the Pennsylvania Militia,
d in New Alexandria, PA (3-7/28/13)
7162. Reed, William m 1/14/19 Betsey Rial in Milo (3-1/27)
7163. Reed, William m Dolly Eggleston in Palmyra; Rev. J. Irons (5-4/11/21)
7164. Reed, Zerviah, 26, dau of Nathan, d 11/1/22 near Geneva "after a
lingering illness of 4 years" (3-11/13)
7165. Reeder, Josiah, 58, d in Reading (3-4/1/29)
7166. Reelman, George, 112 yrs, d 10/2/19 at Settle's Hill, town of Guilderland
(born in Landau in Alsace, Germany 8 Mar 1707; had 4 ch in Germany
three of whom died "before his emigration". His wife died at sea and
with his son he arrived in Philadelphia in 1740; this son survives
his father) (George died at his son's home) (3-11/3)
7167. Rees, Charles W. m 1/8/32 Catharine Hallett at Trinity Church in Geneva;
Rev. Bruce (a double ceremony - see marr. of Charles A. Roe) (5-1/24)
7168. Reese, Frances E., 6 yrs, dau of E. D., d 8/24/48 in Batavia (1-8/29)
7169. Reeve, Harriet, 47, d in Bath (3-11/25/29)
7170. Reeve, Isaac of Bath m 11/3/31 Ann Arnold of Penn Yan in P. Y. (2-11/9)
7171. Reeve, J. V. D. (Lt.) of the U.S. Army m 9/27/42 Elizabeth Shepard, dau of
late Joshua, in Dansville, Liv. Co.; Rev. Walker (2-10/19)
7172. Reeves, _____ (Mrs.) d in Palmyra (3-2/3/13)
7173. Reeves, Charles, about 8 mos, s of Zebulon, d 7/30/18 in Palmyra (5-8/4)
7174. Reeves, David m Tamar Stephens in Caroline, Tompkins Co. (3-1/14/29)
7175. Reeves, Edwin, Esq., 27, oldest son of Zebulon of Palmyra, d 7/3/42
in Du Buque, Iowa Terr. (5-7/27)
7176. Reeves, Elias, 80, d 6/4/43 in Palmyra ("...was the first who emigrated
from Long Island (NY) to this country - at that time a wilderness
(51 years earlier). The year previous he had associated with a
company of woodsmen who explored the country near Turkey Bottom
(now Cincinnati, Ohio)") (5-6/14)
7177. Reeves, George W., 8, d 1/9/21 in Palmyra (5-1/10)
7178. Reeves, Howell m 12/7/22 Phebe Howell in Palmyra; Rev. H. R. Powell
(5-12/18)
7179. Reeves, James m 9/24/35 Caroline Sanford, dau of Luther; Rev. Merrit.
All of Palmyra (5-10/2)
7180. Reeves, Luther, 46, d 2/25/42 in Palmyra (5-3/2)
7181. Reeves, Mahitable, 67, wf of James, Esq., d 12/15/34 in Palmyra
("... emigrated from Southampton, L.I. (NY) to Palmyra ... in 1792")
(5-12/19)
7182. Reeves, Rufus d in Williamson (3-3/24/13)
7183. Reeves, Sayre m Betsey Youngs in Barrington (3-1/13/30)
7184. Reeves, Stephen (Deacon), 86, d 4/13/20 in Palmyra (5-4/26)
7185. Reid, Jasper, 41, d 6/16/30 in Canandaigua (5-7/2)
7186. Reifsneider, James m Phebe Young in Fayette (3-2/13/28)
7187. Reighter, Walter m Polly __eseller in Milo (3-7/12/26)
7188. Reitz, George, 28 or 31, of the firm of T. and G. Reitz of Geneva,
d 9/3/29 in Clyde (3-9/9 and 5-9/11)
7189. Remer, Banjamin M. m Ann Townsend (3-4/8/29)
7190. Remer, George J. m 8/28/19 Arabella Babcock in Milo (3-9/8)
7191. Remer, Lawrence T. of Penn Yan m Sarah Sears in Elmira (3-10/14/29)
7192. Remington, Thaddeus, Jr. m Rhoda Root in Canandaigua (3-2/18/18)
7193. Renwick, George, Jr. m Mary Norton, both of Angelica, in A (3-8/4/19)
7194. Rew, John, 32, d in Bloomfield (3-3/18/18)

184

7195. Rexford, Alanson of Troupsburgh m 11/14/41 Martha Ann Griggs of
        Greenwood; B. S. Brundage, Esq. (2-12/1)
7196. Rexford, Charles m 11/5/40 Lavina Jeffers in Troupsburgh; B. S.
        Brundage, Esq.  All of Troupsburgh (2-11/11)
7197. Reynard, Andrew M. m 7/23/43 Eunice Burnett, both of Arcadia, in
        Palmyra; Rev. J. Pearsall (5-7/26)
7198. Reynear, William, 83, d 7/7/36 in Manchester (5-7/8)
7199. Reynier, Lettis (Mrs.), 80?, d 2/22/43 in Manchester (5-3/1)
7200. Reynolds, _____ (Mrs.), wf of Henry, d in Junius (3-9/6/26)
7201. Reynolds, Abraham of NYC m 1/30/34 Amanda Purdy of Venice, Cay. Co.,
        in V (5-2/7)
7202. Reynolds, Enos m Almyra McKenzer in Pulteney (3-10/8/28)
7203. Reynolds, Jeremiah, 79, d in Avon (3-10/10/27)
7204. Reynolds, Julius A. m 12/24/46 Mary Elizabeth Conklin at the Clinton
        House in Bath; Rev. L. W. Russ (2-12/30)
7205. Reynolds, Martin, 22, formerly of Jamestown, d in Griggsville, IL
        (Martin was principal of Griggsville Academy; two months prior to
        his death he married "a resident of Griggsville") (4-10/14/41)
7206. Reynolds, Nancy (Mrs.), 51, wf of William, d 5/20/45 in Jamestown
        (4-5/30)
7207. Reynolds, Oliver (Dr.) m 12/17/16 Betsey Marlett in Penfield (3-1/15/17)
7208. Reynolds, S. H. of Utica m Elizabeth G. Babcock in Whitesborough
        (3-5/2/27)
7209. Reynolds, Uriah m 12/5/11 Mary Rolson, dau of John, in Seneca; Orin
        Aldrich, Esq. (3-12/11)
7210. Rh____?, Paris A. m Sally Cole in Manchester (3-8/19/29)
7211. Rhea, James (Capt.), late of the U.S. Army and formerly from New Jersey,
        d in Dayton, Ohio (3-4/22/18)
7212. Rhea, Nicholas, Esq., youngest son of late Gen. Jonathan of Trenton, NJ,
        d "lately" in the state of Ohio (3-11/19/17)
7213. Rhoad, Henry of Lockport m Margaret Miller in Fayette (3-12/26/27)
7214. Rhode, Frederick H. m Betsey Dean, both of Milo, in Bethel (3-1/5/20)
7215. Rhodes, Amasa J. m 12/28/34 Elmira Wilcox in Painted Post; Jonathan
        Brown, Esq.  All of Painted Post (2-1/7/35)
7216. Rhodes, Asaph (Dr.) m 11/26/39 Ann Maria Stewart, both of Jamestown,
        in J; Rev. Parmely (4-11/27)
7217. Rhodes, Charles, Esq. of Pulaski, Oswego Co. m 5/21/45 Algenia Knox,
        dau of Gen. John J. of Augusta, Oneida Co.; Rev. Orlo Bartholomew
        (4-6/27)
7218. Rhodes, Maria (Miss), 16, d 9/1/16 in Geneva (3-9/4)
7219. Rhodes, Richard m 11/1/32 Nancy Sherwin in Jamestown; Rev. Z. M. Palmer.
        All of Jamestown (4-11/7)
7220. Rhodes, William C., junior editor of the Elmira Gazette, m 1/7/45 Fanny
        P. Maxwell, dau of Thomas, Esq., in Elmira; Rev. Vanzandt. All of
        Elmira (2-1/29)
7221. Rice, _____ (Lt.) of the New York Volunteers d 9/9/14 in Buffalo (3-9/21)
7222. Rice, _____, 5 mo, dau of Joel, d in Geneva (3-8/5/18)
7223. Rice, _____, child of Joel, d "a few days ago" in Geneva (3-5/12/19)
7224. Rice, _____, (Mrs.), wf of A. E. of Palmyra, d 2/20/39 in Palmyra
        (5-2/22)
7225. Rice, Abigail, 18 mo, dau of late Joel, d 8/12/26 in Geneva (3-8/16)
7226. Rice, Adoniram J. of Newport, Herk. Co. m 8/31/42 Ann S. Ripley of
        Macedon Locks in M. L.; Rev. Philo Forbes (See marr. of Luther A.
        Hathaway dated 8/29/42) (5-9/14)
7227. Rice, Anna Mariah (Mrs.), 27, d 1/1/47 (her birthday) in Avoca (2-1/6)
7228. Rice, Arnold E., proprietor of the Bunker Hill Hotel, d 12/12/38 in
        Palmyra (5-12/14)
7229. Rice, Burrage, Esq., 57, d 4/3/41 in Prattsburgh (2-4/7)
7230. Rice, Caleb, 32 or 37, d 5/9/15 in Seneca (surv by wf and 5 ch) (3-5/17)
7231. Rice, Caroline (Miss), 24, oldest dau of William and Anna, d 5/16/39 in
        Marion (member of Cong'l. Ch. in Marion) (5-5/24)
7232. Rice, Catharine, 25, wf of James, d 7/4/40 in Pinegrove, PA (4-7/8)
7233. Rice, Charles, 22, d 9/1/09 in "Number Nine" (3-9/6)
7234. Rice, Chester m 10/23/23 Mary Head in Howard (3-11/12)
7235. Rice, Clark of Seneca m 1/31/28 Temperance Beman of Cayuga in C; Rev.
        Pomeroy (3-2/6)

7236. Rice, Darius W. of Geneva m 4/8/28 Fanny Mabee of Phelps in P; Rev. John Bogerly (3-4/23)
7237. Rice, Eliphalet (Deacon), 75, d in Homer (3-11/24/19)
7238. Rice, Eunice Biscoe, 2 yrs, dau of J. C., d 11/11/41 in Spencer, MA (4-11/25)
7239. Rice, Gilbert J. of Logansport, IN m Julia M. Potter of Mayville in M; Rev. A. Handy of Jamestown (4-10/17/45)
7240. Rice, Grover E., 1 yr, youngest son of Joel H. and Caroline L., d 9/15/46 in Bath (2-9/23)
7241. Rice, Harriet, 23, wf of Sylvanus, d in Wheeler (3-8/29/27)
7242. Rice, Horace m 1/19/34 Julia Ann Wheat in Phelps, Ont. Co. (5-1/31)
7243. Rice, Jairus S. m Susan Shepardson, dau of Pliny, in Gerry (See also the marr. of John A. Rice) (4-1/8/40)
7244. Rice, Jairus S. m 6/20/44 Lurinda Rogers, both of Ellery in E; Robert Lenox, Esq. (4-6/28)
7245. Rice, James, 67, (a Rev. soldier) d 7/11/22 in Seneca (3-7/17)
7246. Rice, James, Sr., 69, d 6/13/27 at his home in Seneca (3-6/20)
7247. Rice, James of Seneca m 10/14/29 Elizabeth Dickerson of Gorham in Bethel (3-10/21)
7248. Rice, James, Jr., s of James, d 9/5/13 in Seneca (3-9/15)
7249. Rice, Joel B., 6 yrs, d 6/26/16 - also Zebina H. Rice, 2 yrs, d 6/1; both died in Geneva and both were sons of Zebina Rice (3-7/3)
7250. Rice, Joel H. of Jackson, MI m 11/9/41 Caroline L. Butler, only dau of Joseph, formerly of Bath, in Avoca; Rev. O. Johnson (2-11/17)
7251. Rice, Joel H. of Bath m 8/18/50 Mrs. C. A. Turner of Waterloo in W (2-8/21)
7252. Rice, John, Esq. of NYC m 9/4/38 Sarah Smith of Hammondsport in H; Rev. Hubbell of Lyons (2-9/5)
7253. Rice, John A. m 1/2/40 Amanda Shepardson, dau of Pliny, in Gerry; Rev. Wilson (See also the marr. of Jairus S. Rice in Jan 1840) (4-1/8)
7254. Rice, Jones H. of Rochester m Charlotte Skinner in Hopewell (3-1/9/28)
7255. Rice, Josiah of Marion m 2/17/31 Betsey Bennett of Sodus in S; Rev. Marvin Aller (5-3/4)
7256. Rice, Lewis m Nancy Hart in Ontario, NY (5-12/16/18)
7257. Rice, Orrin F. m Sarah Morse in Bath; Rev. O. Frazer. All of Bath (2-6/30/41)
7258. Rice, Sarah H., 20, dau of Ebenezer of Prattsburgh, d 4/9/42 in Bath (2-4/13)
7259. Rice, Seth H. m 2/12/40 Gratia Wheeler, dau of Jeremiah, Esq. of Bath, in B; Rev. M. L. Wisner (2-2/19)
7260. Rice, Sylvanus of Prattstown m Harriet Shaw in Jerusalem, NY (3-6/18/28)
7261. Rice, Wheeler m 9/18/42 Elizabeth Furlow, both of Carroll, in Ellery; Rev. H. Smith (4-9/22)
7262. Rice, Zalmon of Lyons m 9/20/41 Eliza Ann Bleecker of Salina in S; Rev. Myres (5-9/29)
7263. Rice, Zalmon, 55, of Lyons d 6/18/44 in New Brunswick, NJ (5-7/3)
7264. Rich, Amos (Capt.), 46, d 5/26/13 in Galen (surv by wf and 8 ch) (3-6/9)
7265. Rich, Andrew J., Esq. m 8/12/46 Mary W. Townsend, dau of Hon. Charles, in Buffalo; Rev. J. B. Shaw. All of Buffalo (1-8/18)
7266. Rich, David of Caroline m 10/30/26 Hester K. Scovill of Hector in H; Rev. Chadwick (3-11/15)
7267. Rich, Hiram, 22, s of Hiram M. of Marion, d 10/22?/43 in Manchester, CT (5-11/8)
7268. Rich, James De Long, 3 mo, s of C. B. and D. A., d 5/21/45 in Akron (1-5/27)
7269. Rich, Nelson m 3/10/34 Matilda Palmeter in Palmyra; F. Smith, Esq. (5-3/14)
7270. Rich, Noah m Jane Goodwin in Waterloo (3-10/3/27)
7271. Rich, Richard m Hannah Bishop in Junius (3-9/9/29)
7272. Richards, Alpheus, 30, d 12/24/14 in Canandaigua (3-1/11/15)
7273. Richards, Elias m 7/15/35 Matilda Barnhart, both of Palmyra (5-7/17)
7274. Richards, Eliza A., 3 yrs, dau of Charles G., d 9/30/40 in Williamson (5-10/7)
7275. Richards, Fitch, merchant, of Salina m 6/2/22 Harriet Delia Dole, dau of James, Esq. of Troy, in Batavia; Rev. Calvin Colton (1-6/7)

7276. Richards, John, formerly a merchant, of Geneva d 9/24/11 in Geneva (3-10/2)
7277. Richards, Mary Levantle(?), 23, wf of Jefferson C., d 1/7/44 at Little Cannadaway Creek (4-1/26)
7278. Richards, Robert Alsop, 7 mo, s of Charles G., d 8/5/41 in Williamson (5-8/11)
7279. Richards, William (Dr.) of Clarence m 9/29/22 Perses Peters in Batavia; Rev. Hibberd (1-10/18)
7280. Richards, William, 30, d 6/9/32 in Palmyra (formerly of New London, CT) (5-6/11)
7281. Richardson, A. I. (Lt.) of the U.S. Army m 9/20/30 Sylvia R. Porter, dau of Chauncey, Esq., in Pittsford; Rev. Mahan (5-9/24)
7282. Richardson, Amanda R., 20, wf of Thomas J., d 5/28/45 in Bath (2-6/4)
7283. Richardson, Andrew S. m Sarah Nash in Canisteo (3-12/9/18)
7284. Richardson, Christopher of Geneva m 4/6/19 Sarah Adams of Albany in A (3-4/14)
7285. Richardson, E. G., proprietor od the Dansville Weekly Chronicle, m 7/22/49 Mary Ann Stryker, both of Dansville, in Oak Hill, Steuben Co.; Esquire Babcock (2-8/15)
7286. Richardson, Gould m 2/7/22 Clarissa Simmons, both of Victor, in V (5-2/13)
7287. Richardson, Humphrey, Jr. m Julia Cross, dau of Elder Cross, in Harmony (4-1/23/33)
7288. Richardson, Joseph, 63, a native of Yorkshire, England, d 10/27/22 near Geneva, NY (3-11/6)
7289. Richardson, Joseph M., 35, d in Perinton (3-4/30/28)
7290. Richardson, Manning m 10/17/22 Nancy Curtis, both of Stafford, in Batavia; C. Carpenter, Esq. (1-10/18)
7291. Richardson, Nancy, 29, d 4/6/40 of consumption at Mount Washington, NY (2-4/8)
7292. Richardson, Thomas J. m 1/14/47 Amanda Aber in Bath; Elder Carr (2-1/27)
7293. Richardson, William, 8 yrs, s of Joseph, d 8/19/13 in Seneca (3-8/25)
7294. Richardson, William of Owego m Hannah Cozzens in Springport (3-1/14/29)
7295. Richardson, William P. (Dr.) m Mary Porter in Palmyra (3-1/17/16)
7296. Richardson, William P. (Dr.), 43, d 2/23/33 in Macedon (5-2/27)
7297. Richman, Charles L., merchant, of Naples, NY m Amanda M. Sibley (3-5/21/28)
7298. Richmond, _____, 17 mo, ch of John, d 4/14/22 in Clyde (3-5/1)
7299. Richmond, Cyrus m 11/3/42 Caroline Willey in Batavia; S. Wakeman, Esq. All of Batavia (1-11/8)
7300. Richmond, Jonathan d 3/26/13 in Lyons (3-3/31)
7301. Ricker, Joseph m 6/12/17 Sally Lisenring, both of Romulus, in R; Rev. L. Merkel (3-6/25)
7302. Ricker, Stephen B. m 12/31/40 Julia Ann Hubbard, youngest dau of J. Hubbard, at the Temperance House in Busti; E. Davis, Esq. (4-1/6/41)
7303. Rickley, Stephen, 29, d in Elmira (3-7/2/17)
7304. Riddle, George, 49, d 7/26/45 in Canisteo (2-8/6)
7305. Rider, Ira S. of Warren, PA m 6/15/46 Mary Ann Beverly of Howard in H; Rev. S. Brown (2-6/17)
7306. Ridge, Benjamin F. m Agnes Freeman in Batavia; Daniel Tisdale, Esq. (1-12/16/25)
7307. Ridge, David (the marriage of): "At Cornwall, Conn, on the 17th Jan by the Rev. Mr. Smith, the pious and delicate Miss Sally B Northrop, daughter of Mr. John B. Northrop, (was married) to a full blooded Cherokee Indian, late a member of the foreign mission school in that town. His present name is Mr. David Ridge - his true Indian name we have not learned. Those white ladies who are in want of Indian husbands must apply soon or there will not be any copper faces left. They must send in their proposals (post paid) to the trustees of the Cornwall School who have an assortment of unmarried Indians on hand." (underlinings and final parentheses in the original) (1-3/5/24)
7308. Rigels, Daniel of Geneva m 2/13/27 Catharine Frushour of Phelps in P; Rev. Dr. Axtell (3-2/21)
7309. Riggle, John m 2/24/25 Polly Bachman in Fayette; James Huff, Esq. (3-3/9)
7310. Riggs, John, formerly of Lyons, m 5/8/26 Alma Crowl of Allen in A; Elias Hull, Esq. (3-5/24)

7311. Riggs, William m 2/25?/16 Eunice Brown in Benton (3-3/6)
7312. Rigs, Galen, 17, s of Solomon, d in Galen (3-6/11/28)
7313. Riker, _____, 1 yr, dau of "Mr. Riker" d 8/8/15 in Geneva (3-8/16)
7314. Riker, Catharine, about 57, wf of Thomas, d near Waterloo (3-8/27/28)
7315. Riker, George L., 1 yr, s of John and Mary T., d 8/3/43 in Ontario, NY (5-9/13)
7316. Riker, Israel m Elizabeth Adams in Catlin (3-1/13/30)
7317. Riker, James, Jr., 21, d in Big Flats (3-3/12/28)
7318. Riley, Sarah Jane, 22, d 4/29/42. Also Janette, 16 mo, d 7/29 and Levi W., 9 yrs, d 9/11. All three are ch of Abram of Jamestown (4-9/15)
7319. Rinders, Isaac m 12/25/12 Mrs. Mary Langdon,"after a tedious courtship of nineteen years", in Benton; Abraham Wagener, Esq. (a double ceremony - see the marr. of Jonathan Parks) (3-1/13/13)
7320. Rine, Stiles m Maria Vanlieu in Ovid (3-1/16/22)
7321. Ring, E. Ferdinand (Rev.) of Conneaut, Ohio m 3/7/44 Miss E. Greenlief Bates of Cummington, MA (5-3/20)
7322. Ringer, George of Seneca m 3/25/17 Polly Cheaffy of Fayette (3-4/16)
7323. Ringer, John, Sr., 76, a native of Frederick Co., MD, d 7/7/27 in Seneca (3-7/11)
7324. Ringer, Solomon m 3/14/13 Elizabeth Elyea in Seneca; Rev. Axtel (3-3/17)
7325. Ripley, Hiram L. of Rochester m Lucia Wells in Port Byron (3-5/23/27)
7326. Rippey, Joseph m 5/5/25 Elizabeth Smith, dau of Capt. William, in Seneca; Rev. Nisbet (3-5/11)
7327. Rippey, Mathew, about 27, d 4/14/14 in Benton "leaving an aged father and mother" (3-4/20)
7328. Risingh, Leonard P., Esq. of Pittsburgh, PA m 10/29/40 Harriet J. Lathrop of Williamson in W; Rev. Lathrop (5-11/6)
7329. Risley, Elijah, Sr., 81, d 1/11/39 in Pomfret (4-1/24)
7330. Risley, Seth of Catharine m 8/19/24 Mrs. _____nn of Geneva in G; Rev. Orin Clark (3-8/25)
7331. Roach, Cynthia H. (Miss), 20, d in Canandaigua (3-4/23/17)
7332. Robb, William, 10 mo, s of William, d in Canandaigua (3-8/23/15)
7333. Robbins, Edward, 75, of Guilford, Chen. Co. d 1/25/41 in Caton, Steuben Co. (2-2/24)
7334. Robbins, Hiram m 6/28/21 Almy Strong in Bloomfield (3-7/25)
7335. Roberts, _____, 59, d 1/21/25 in Geneva (3-1/26)
7336. Roberts, _____, wf of J., d "recently" in Canandaigua (3-1/14/29)
7337. Roberts, Caroline, about 5, dau of Ezekiel, d 7/25/13 in Geneva (3-7/28)
7338. Roberts, Catherine, about 70, relict of Joseph, d 8/12/47 in Bath (2-8/18)
7339. Roberts, Charles, 30, late of Reading, Steuben Co., d "recently" in California (2-5/1/50)
7340. Roberts, Eliza Ann, 10, dau of Rufus, d 4/28/31 in Harmony (4-5/11)
7341. Roberts, George (Rev.) of the Methodist Church, d in Baltimore (state not given) (3-1/9/28)
7342. Roberts, Henry W. of Wellsburgh m Elizabeth Parshall in Chemung (3-1/27/30)
7343. Roberts, Hugh, 73, a native of Wales, d 7/13/22 in Trenton, NY (3-7/31)
7344. Roberts, Ira m 3/18/41 Hulda Maria Edgar; John Jamison, Esq. All of Reading (2-3/24)
7345. Roberts, James (Deacon), 67, d in Victor (3-10/17/27)
7346. Roberts, Joseph Henry, 3 yrs, oldest son of E.J., drowned 6/3/29 in the canal near his father's home in Rochester (5-6/19)
7347. Roberts, Myron H. m 6/24/45 Polly A. Dinnin in Jamestown; Rev. E. J. Gillett (4-6/27)
7348. Roberts, Purchase of Junius m 12/24/12 Mrs. Susan Inslee of Galen, in Geneva; Rev. Axtel (3-12/30)
7349. Roberts, Truman, 17, m Rebecca Wooden, 15, in Phelps (3-4/16/17)
7350. Roberts, William m 7/4/35 Sophia C. Jeffreys in Jamestown; Rev. Peet (4-7/15)
7351. Robertson, James of Ithaca m Mary Jay in Veteran, NY (3-4/1/29)
7352. Robeson, _____ (Mrs.), wf of Alexander C., d in Geneva (3-10/14/18)
7353. Robie, Jonathan, 75, d 9/31/47 in Corinth, VT (2-10/13)
7354. Robie, Reuben m 4/29/24 Nancy Whiting in Bath (3-5/19)

7355. Robins, Jacob of Palmyra m 9/2/35 Barbara Crater of Batavia in Macedon; D. Osband, Esq. (5-9/4)
7356. Robinson, Clark of Albany, late of Palmyra, m 7/8/30 Delia Strong of Palmyra; Rev. A. E. Campbell (5-7/9)
7357. Robinson, Daniel A. m 5/4/20 Isabella B. P. Richardson of Palmyra at the Friends Meeting House in Palmyra (3-5/17)
7358. Robinson, E. D. m Celesta D. Peck in Palmyra (3-3/11/29)
7359. Robinson, Gain (Dr.), 62, d 6/21/31 in Palmyra (5-6/24)
7360. Robinson, George m 5/2/25 Eliza Thompson in Batavia; Rev. Colton (1-5/6)
7361. Robinson, Henry L., son of Hon. Tracy Robinson of Broome Co., m 8/15/33 Elizabeth Root, dau of Gen. Erastus, in Delhi (1-8/27)
7362. Robinson, Hiram m 2/23/20 Julianna Norton in Farmington (5-3/8 and 3-3/29)
7363. Robinson, Hopkins, comedian, "formerly a performer on the boards of this city" (Geneva), d in NYC. "The manager of the N.Y. theatre generously appropriated the receipts of the house one night, amounting to $1330, for the benefit of his wife and children" (3-12/8/19)
7364. Robinson, James m 11/10/28 Nancy Turner, both of Macedon, in Lockport; Joel McCollum, Esq. (5-12/19)
7365. Robinson, James of Milo m 7/10/18 Susan Stewart of Junius in Phelps; Philetus Swift, Esq. (3-9/22/19)
7366. Robinson, John m 1/26/23 Harriet Clark in Lyons; W. A. McLean, Esq. (5-1/29)
7367. Robinson, Lewis m 10/12/36 Mary Hall (dau of James) both of Macedon, in M; Rev. Jesse Townsend (5-10/21)
7368. Robinson, Mary, 40, wf of Dr. Jedediah H., d 2/26/38 in Howard (surv by husband and 8 ch, "one about 2 years old")(2-3/7)
7369. Robinson, Morgan m 10/20/35 Lucy E. Booth, both of Macedon; Rev. Townsend (5-10/23)
7370. Robinson, Nancy, 36, "a colored woman", d in Canandaigua (3-6/24/29)
7371. Robinson, Noah of Middlesex m Deborah L. Perry of Connecticut in Westerly, RI (3-6/11/28)
7372. Robinson, Philo of Macedon m 2/2/36 Eunice Straight of Palmyra; Rev. Jesse Townsend (5-2/5)
7373. Robinson, Philo m 10/15/38 Janet Thomas, both of Palmyra, in Macedon; Rev. Shumway (5-10/19)
7374. Robinson, Randal m Miranda White in Farmington (5-1/13/19)
7375. Robinson, Richard P., 28, d 9/17/42 in Walworth (5-10/12)
7376. Robinson, Rollin, formerly of Palmyra, m Celestia Corbett in Palmyra, Mich. Terr.; C.C. Robinson. All of the latter place (5-3/13/35)
7377. Robinson, Samuel D., 28, d 8/15/29 in Palmyra (formerly of Pittsburgh, PA) (3-8/26 and 5-8/21)
7378. Robinson, Schuyler m Polly Clarke (prob. in Jamestown); Rev. Gillet (4-7/29/35)
7379. Robinson, Theron m 10/19/41 Sarah Maria Brown in Walworth; Rev. Mandeville. All of Walworth (5-10/20)
7380. Robinson, Walter of Macedon m 1/26/42 Elizabeth O. Johnson, dau of Robert, Esq. of Farmington, in F; Rev. Lucas Hubbell (5-2/9)
7381. Robinson, William m 4/5/30 Mary Horton in Palmyra; Rev. Campbell (5-4/9)
7382. Robinson, William H. m 5/23/43 Alvira Thompson in Busti; Rev. E. J. Gillett (4-6/1)
7383. Robison, James of Guilderland d 4/23/17 at the Geneva Glass Factory (3-4/30)
7384. Robison, Maria (Miss), oldest dau of Gabriel, late of Columbia Co., d 10/22/18 in Farmington (5-10/27)
7385. Roblee, _____, M.D., m 2/9/47 Harriett E. Higgins, both of Kendall, at the home of M. J. Aplin in Batavia; Rev. J. W. Vaughan (1-2/16)
7386. Robords, Ann (Miss), 21, dau of John L., Esq of Avoca, d 4/27/46 in Howard (2-5/5)
7387. Robords, Charles, 59, d in Howard (3-2/3/30)
7388. Robson, Andrew m 12/4/28 Catharine Ann Gibs in Seneca (No. 9); C. Shekell, Esq. (3-2/4/29)

7389. Robson, James m 1/11/22 Margaret Stevenson in Seneca; J McCullough, Esq. (3-1/16)

7390. Robson, Mathew, 56, d 7/2/22 in Seneca (3-7/10)

7391. Robson, Robert m Martha Campbell in Benton (3-12/22/19)

7392. Roby, Joseph, Jr. of the firm of Benedict and Roby in Utica m Margaret Breeze of Sconondaga in S (5-9/25/29)

7393. Rochester, Amanda, 31. wf of Hon. William B., d 1/16/31 in Buffalo (2-1/26). Death date is 1/23 in 5-1/28.

7394. Rochester, Nathaniel (Col.), 80, "founder of that village", d 5/17/31 in Rochester (1-5/27 and 5-5/27)

7395. Rochester, Nathaniel M., 9 yrs, s of Hon. William B., d 2/27/23 in Rochester (3-3/12)

7396. Rochester, Thomas H., Esq. m 9/26/22 Elizabeth P. Cuming at St. Luke's Ch., Rochester; Rev. Francis H. Cuming (3-10/16)

7397. Rochester, William B., Esq. m 1/31/16 Amanda Hopkins, dau of Elias, Esq., in Bath; Rev. David Higgins. All of Bath (3-2/14)

7398. Rochester, William B. of Buffalo m 4/9/32 Mrs. Eliza Powers, wid of Gersham of Buffalo, in Auburn; Rev. Dr. Rudd (2-4/25). William B. is Pres. of the U.S. Branch Bank at Buffalo in 5-4/25.

7399. Rockefeller, Jacob W., 46, d in Milo (3-3/12/28)

7400. Rockwell, Benjamin of the firm of Clark, Rockwell, and Gilbert of NYC m 7/15/35 Lavinia B. Fenton, dau of Joseph S., Esq. of Palmyra, in P; Rev. G. R. H. Shumway (5-7/17)

7401. Rockwell, Ebenezer, Jr., 17, d "in Jersey" (3-3/18/29)

7402. Rockwell, Joseph G., 26, a teacher in the Haverling Union School, d 11/10/49 in Bath (2-12/5)

7403. Rockwell, Noah of Bellona, Yates Co. m 10/18/26 Sally Mariah Stevens of Sodus in S; Esquire Bancroft (3-10/25)

7404. Rodgers, Calvin m 7/11/22 Miss Almeda Rodgers (1-7/26)

7405. Rodgers, Elisha m 6/17/24 Zilph (sic) Dean in Covington; Rev. L. Anson (1-6/25)

7406. Rodgers, Gustavus A. (Dr.) m 4/19/27 Susan Ann Campbell, dau of Robert, in Bath; Rev. David Higgins (3-5/2)

7407. Rodgers, John (Dr.), 83, Senior Pastor of the Presbyterian Churches in NYC, d 5/7/11 in NYC in the 62nd year of his ministry (3-7/10)

7408. Rodgers, Mary, 87, relict of the late Rev. Dr. Rodgers, d 3/15/12 in NYC (3-4/1)

7409. Rodman, Daniel, 32, attorney, d 1/26/16 in Albany (3-2/7)

7410. Rodney, Caesar A. (Hon.), "our minister to that Government (Argentina)" d 6/10/24 "at Buenos Ayres" (1-8/20)

7411. Rodney, Jane (Miss), 18, oldest dau of William, d 3/27/27 (3-3/28)

7412. Roe, Mortimer, 20, formerly of Batavia, d 1/22/47 in Mumford (1-2/16)

7413. Roe, Stephen m 12/31/29 Betsey Smith in Lyons (3-1/13/30 and 5-1/8/30)

7414. Roff, Daniel, 3 ft 8 inches, m Mary Potter, 5 ft 6 inches, in Danube, NY ("communicated by a man 4 ft 11 inches high") (3-5/19/24)

7415. Roff, Frederick, 46, d in Canandaigua (3-5/21/28)

Rogers. See also Rodgers.

7416. Rogers, _____, ch of "Mr. Rogers" d in Phelps (3-8/23/15)

7417. Rogers, _____, m 5/1/25 Mrs. Nancy Hall in Lyons; R. H. Foster, Esq. (3-5/11)

7418. Rogers, _____, merchant, d in Weedsport (3-10/8/28)

7419. Rogers, Bartlet R. (Capt.) m 12/31/29 Belinda Leach in Lyons; Rev. I. Hubbell (5-1/8/30 and 3-1/13/30)

7420. Rogers, Carlton H. m 9/21/43 Sarah A. Perrine, dau of Dr. Henry of
Indian Key, Florida, in Palmyra (5-9/27)
7421. Rogers, Celia L., about 10, dau of David, d 5/15/40 in Palmyra (5-5/20)
7422. Rogers, Charles R. m 3/23/42 Mary Jane Scovil in Macedon; Rev. Forbes.
All of Macedon (5-3/30)
7423. Rogers, Charlotte, 54, wf of Denison, d 12/24/42 in Macedon (5-12/28)
7424. Rogers, Cynthia, 49, wf of Hon. William, Esq., d 7/4/18 in Palmyra
(5-7/7)
7425. Rogers, David m Mara (sic) Conant in Macedon (3-7/9/28)
7426. Rogers, Denison, Esq. m 10/3/43 Elizabeth Scovill, both of Macedon, in M;
Rev. D. Herrington of Palmyra (5-10/4)
7427. Rogers, Freeman of Lyons m 3/5/23 Rachel Smith of Sodus in S (3-3/19)
7428. Rogers, Hazard W. m 11/14/29 Elizabeth Johnson, both of Palmyra; Rev.
Campbell (5-12/18 and 3-12/23)
7429. Rogers, Henry W., Esq., attorney, of Bath m 12/9/28 Harriet K. Adams
of Litchfield, CT in L (3-12/17)
7430. Rogers, Isaac, 59, d 8/30/31 in Lyons (5-9/6)
7431. Rogers, Isaac, 44, d 1/20/35 (5-1/30)
7432. Rogers, J. Clark, merchant, m 6/8/43 Louisa Green, dau of Hon. Byram,
in Sodus; Rev. Mervin. All of Sodus (5-6/21)
7433. Rogers, Jeremiah H. m 3/24/20 Harriet Dunks in Mendon (3-5/24)
7434. Rogers, John, 24, d in Romulus (3-9/27/15)
7435. Rogers, John m Minerva Mason in Palmyra; Rev. J. Irons (3-12/10/17)
7436. Rogers, Jonathan d 2/22/13 in Romulus (3-3/3)
7437. Rogers, Levi m 12/19/22 Abigail Phillips in Fayette; Rev. Axtell
(3-12/25)
7438. Rogers, Lydia, about 26, wf of Stephen, d 7/7/31 in Palmyra (5-7/15)
7439. Rogers, Mary (Mrs.), 26, sister of E. Sheldon of Penn Yan, d in
Weedsport (3-11/26/28)
7440. Rogers, Mary Jane, 19, wf of Charles, d 1/10/43 in Macedon (5-1/18)
7441. Rogers, Mary S. (Mrs.), 23, wf of Hamilton, d 3/28/42 in Newark, NY
(5-4/6)
7442. Rogers, Mima (Mrs.), mother of William R. and S., d 7/6/41 in Ellicott
(more than thirty years a member of the Meth. Episc. Ch.) (4-7/8)
7443. Rogers, Moses, 75, father of Mrs. Samuel M. Hopkins, d in NYC (3-12/21/25)
7444. Rogers, Phebe Ann, 25, wf of Matthew and dau of William and Mary Almy,
d 5/14/45 in Pavilion (1-5/20)
7445. Rogers, Sarah S., 83, relict of Samuel formerly of Unadilla and mother of
Dr. G. A. Rogers of Bath, d 10/2/50 at the home of her dau, Mrs. Mills,
in Alden, Erie Co. (1-10/9)
7446. Rogers, Sidney d 7/6/43 in Brooklyn, Jackson Co., MI (surv by wf and
"numerous children") (4-8/3)
7447. Rogers, Thomas, 3rd m 11/10/31 Jane Thompson in Port Gibson (5-11/15)
7448. Rogers, Thomas, 75, formerly of Palmyra and one of the early settlers
there, d 10/3/35 in Perrysburgh, Ohio (5-10/16)
7449. Rogers, William, Sr., Esq., 82, d 1/14/36 (a pioneer settler in the
Palmyra area; emigrated from RI; funeral in the Presby. Meeting
House in Palmyra) (5-1/15)
7450. Rogers, William, Jr. (Maj.) m 3/19/34 Ruth Throop of Pulteneyville in P;
Rev. Tompkinson (5-3/28)
7451. Rogers, William H. m 1/4/38 Sarah C. Throop in Williamson; Rev. Bateman
(5-1/10)
7452. Roice, Philander B.?, Esq. of Williamson m 1/7/29 Hannah Green of
Palmytra in P; Rev. William Fowler (5-1/16)
7453. Rolfe, Heman B. of Bethany m 5/7/46 Caroline Taber of Alexander in A;
Rev. A. Blackmarr )1-5/19)
7454. Romayne, Nicholas, 61, M.D., d in NYC (3-7/30/17)
7455. Romeyn, Harriet, wid of Rev. John B. and dau of John N. Bleecker of
Albany, d 10/22/25 in NYC (3-11/2)
7456. Romeyn, James T. (Maj.), 28, of the U.S. Artillery d 9/17/18 in NYC
(3-9/30)
7457. Romeyn, Jeremiah (Rev.), 49, "Honorary Hebrew Professor in the Reformed
Dutch Church", d 7/17/18 in Woodstock, Ulster Co. (3-7/29)
7458. Romeyn, John Broadhead (Rev.), D.D., 46, pastor of the Presby. Church,
Cedar Street, NYC, d 2/22/25 in NYC (3-3/2)
7459. Romulus, Timothy m Betsey Patterson in Galen (3-1/16/22)

7460. Ronalds, James, 60, d 5/24/12 in NYC. His widow, Margaret, d 5/26.
(3-6/24)
7461. Rood, Joseph, 94, d 3/31/43 in Pomfret (4-4/6)
7462. Roosevelt, Elizabeth, 26, wf of Nelson, d 7/10/26 in Junius (3-7/26)
7463. Roosevelt, Nelson of Junius m Sally Armitage in Galen (3-7/18/27)
7464. Roosy, Daniel m 12/28/44 Lydia Jane Moore, both of Cameron, in C;
William B. Jones, Esq. (2-1/1/45)
7465. Root, Abraham, 84, d in Canandaigua (3-2/19/17)
7466. Root, Charles, 20, s of Gen. Root of NY, d 12/28/28 on the frigate
"Hudson" at "Rio de Jeneiro" (3-3/4/29)
7467. Root, Francis m 4/9/12 Cynthia Newhall in Phelps (3-5/13)
7468. Root, John, Esq., attorney, of Buffalo m 2/22/24 Elizabeth J. Stewart,
wid of E. S., Esq. of Lyons, in Wolcott, Wayne Co.; William Sisson,
Esq. (1-3/5)
7469. Root, Judah, about 73, father of Mrs. Joel Allen, of Batavia d 1/11/46
in Geneseo (1-1/20)
7470. Root, Loreng (sic) m Phoebe Balcomb in Canandaigua (3-11/25/18)
7471. Root, Nathan of Clarendon m Sally Ann Bishop in South Dansville
(3-6/17/29)
7472. Root, Percy (sic), consort of Eli Root, d 3/12/26 in Murray (1-3/17)
7473. Root, Sally, 60, wf of Aaron, d 1/4/45 in Busti (surv by husband and
3 ch) (4-1/10)
7474. Root, Zadock, Jr. of Busti m 1/15/45 Submit M. Hall of Jamestown in
Busti; Prof. G. W. Clark (4-1/17)
7475. Roreback, John m Anna Spooner in Benton (3-2/19/17)
7476. Rorison, David B. m 1/28/29 Lucinda Yost, dau of Casper. All of
Fayette (3-2/18)
7477. Rorison, John of Fayette m Sarah Clawson, dau of Abraham formerly of
Fayette, in Hartland, Niag. Co. (3-2/3/30)
7478. Rose, _____, inf s of Mrs. Harriet, d in Bath (3-3/10/19)
7479. Rose, Charles A. m 1/8/32 Maria M. Hallett at Trinity Church in Geneva;
Rev. Bruce (a double ceremony - see the marr. of Charles W. Rees)
(5-1/24)
7480. Rose, Daniel H. m 4/28/50 Martha Ann Goff, both of Howard, in H; Wesson
B. Rice, Esq. (2-5/8)
7481. Rose, Elijah, 60, d in Canandaigua (3-12/6/15)
7482. Rose, Elijah m Rebecca Bently in Canandaigua (3-9/3/17)
7483. Rose, Gavin L. (Dr.) m 6/9/29 Mary Ann Granger, dau of Dr. Granger
formerly of Geneva, at Trinity Church in Geneva ; Rev. Mason (3-6/10)
7484. Rose, George m 5/28/16 AnnHuston; ___? Bannister, Esq. All of Geneva
(3-5/29)
7485. Rose, Hiram (Capt.) m Rebecca Hoit in Wheeler (3-5/6/29)
7486. Rose, Jacob, 32, d 12/21/22 (3-12/25)
7487. Rose, John N. of Geneva m 5/26/29 Jane/Macomb, youngest dau of late
John Navarre Macomb of NYC, in NYC; Rev. John A. Clark (3-6/3 and
5-6/12)
7488. Rose, Jonas, Jr. m 11/25/15 Philette Ellis in Hector (3-12/20)
7489. Rose, L. (Rev.) of Howard m 1/17/46 Rachel Bennett of Hornellsville
in H; Rev. F. Lilly (2-1/28)
7490. Rose, Lydia (Mrs.), 71, d 5/1/42 in Wheeler (2-5/4)
7491. Rose, Margaret (Miss), 75, dau of Rev. Robert of Virginia and sister of
the late Mrs. Rawson of Geneva, d 8/12/28 at the home of her niece,
Mrs. Ann Nicholas (3-8/27)
7492. Rose, Martin H., merchant, of Hammondsport m 11/22/38 Eliza Ann Marshall,
dau of Gen. O. F., in Wheeler; Rev. Bostwick (2-11/28)
7493. Rose, Peter m 6/22/15 Charlotte Garry; Celly Smith, Esq. All of Hector
(3-7/5)
7494. Rose, Philip m 2/10/16 Frances Wilson of Geneva; Rev. White (3-2/14)
7495. Rose, Robert L. of Fayette m 9/1/24 Almira Allen, dau of Nathaniel, Esq.,
in Richmond; Rev. George H. Norton (3-9/8)
7496. Rose, Ruth, 50, wf of Nathan, d 2/12/32 in Wheeler (2-2/29)
7497. Rose, S. H., Esq. m 9/17/45 Adaline Barto in Avoca; Rev. J. K. Tuttle.
All of Avoca (2-10/1)
7498. Rose, Samuel, about 90, (a Rev. soldier) d 2/2/35 in Wheeler (2-2/11)
7499. Rose, Sherman, s of Nathan, 2nd, m Mahala Rose, dau of Nathan, in
Wheeler (3-10/14/29)

7500. Rose, Sherman m 3/23/38 Mahala G. Striker in Wheeler; Rev. E. Everett
(2-3/28)
7501. Rose, Silas W., about 40, formerly of Bath d 11/25/44 in Ingham Co., MI
(2-1/1/45)
7502. Rose, William, 109, d 7/4/26 in Wayne Township, PA (a Rev. soldier)
(1-8/4)
7503. Roseboom, Eva, 89, d in Albany (3-1/3/16)
7504. Rosebrugh, Charles W. of Groveland, Liv. Co., son of Judge Rosebrugh,
m 6/5/22 Maria Miles of Sodus in S; Rev. Royal Phelps (3-6/12 and
5-7/3)
7505. Rosecrants, Mortimer, 30, (Brevet Capt., 5th Infantry, Mexican War)
d 10/7/48 in Ypsilanti, MI (1-10/31)
7506. Rosencrantz, William m Priscilla Whitaker in Bath (3-11/16/25)
7507. Rosenkrans, Elijah m 3/16/31 Nancy Dildine in Pulteney; M. Brink, Esq.
of Hammondsport (2-3/30)
7508. Rosenkrans, Simeon (Dr.), 66, formerly of Sussex Co., NJ, d 8/22/41
at his home in Cohocton (2-9/1)
7509. Rosman, Maria, 5, dau of Daniel, d 3/27/42 in Palmyra (5-3/30)
7510. Ross, Alexander, 120, d "in June" in Milton, Sara. Co. (3-9/16/18)
7511. Ross, Horatio (Maj.(, 73, (a Rev. officer) d in Owego (3-11/12/28)
7512. Ross, Jane W. (Miss), 19, dau of Benjamin and Margaret, d 4/12/42 in
Jamestown (4-4/28)
7513. Ross, John m 1/10/22 Amanda Beach, both of Penfield, in New Salem;
D. Allen, Esq. ("The bridegroom is blind") (5-1/16)
7514. Ross, John Z., Esq. of Batavia m 9/20/24 Charlotte Rumsey of Stafford
in S; Rev. L. Smith (1-9/24)
7515. Ross, John Z, first judge of Genesee Co.,d in Batavia (3-11/15/26)
7516. Ross, Mark, 19, m "the blooming Miss Betsey Freelock, aged 70!!"
(3-9/13/09)
7517. Ross, Peleg, 32, d 3/15/20 in Canandaigua (3-3/22)
7518. Ross, William, 38, late from Ireland, d (death place not given)
(5-8/29/21)
7519. Ross, William, 109, (a Rev. soldier) d 7/4/26 in Wayne township, PA
(3-8/2)
7520. Ross, William of Reading m 5/16/50 Sarah C. Reed of Hornellsville
in H; Rev. H. Pettengill (2-6/19)
7521. Rouse, Peter m 11/11/22 Marinda Hawkins in Lyons (3-12/4)
7522. Rouse, Vanrensselaer m 5/30/22 Else Adams in Burt (5-6/5)
7523. Rowe, Cornelia, 24, wf of Anson, d 1/21/42 in Bath of consumption
("...the eighth one of the family who within a few years have died of
this complaint") (2-2/2)
7524. Rowe, Elias m Sally Emmerson in Bath; Rev. Higgins (3-2/12/17)
7525. Rowe, Hippocrates (Rev.), pastor of the Presby. Church in Warsaw, NY,
age 36 or 56, d 6/23/18 in Warsaw (3-7/15)
7526. Rowe, Nelson of Kennedy m 6/17/34 Lovisa Camp of Elk Creek, PA in E. C.
Rev. Murray (4-7/2)
7527. Rowe, Rachel, 40, consort of John S., formerly of Bath, NY d 5/1/41
in Portland, Whiteside Co., IL (2-6/2)
7528. Rowe, Samuel (Col.) of Phelps m 9/19/25 Ann Hooker of New Haven, CT
in Phelps; Rev. Strong (3-9/21)
7529. Rowe, William, 55, d 12/13/40 in Parkhurst, Scott Co., Iowa (2-1/20/41)
7530. Rowland, Robert m 10/17/33 Alzina Winchester in Ellery; Rev. W.R. Babcock
(4-10/23)
7531. Rowley, Francis m 10/28/21 Sally Sherman in Palmyra (5-10/31)
7532. Rowley, Roswell, 45, d 12/15/45 in Fredonia (4-12/19)
7533. Rowley, Samuel, 100, d 12/6/11 in Windsor, CT (3-1/22/12)
7534. Rowley, Sylvester of Manchester m 11/25/41 Mary Ann Drake of Palmyra
in P; F. Smith, Esq. (5-12/1)
7535. Rowley, Timothy, 83, (a Rev. soldier) d in Urbana (3-10/7/29)
7536. Rowlin, David m 1/10/23 Emeline Raymond in Seneca; James Field, Esq.
(3-1/15)
7537. Royce, Caleb, merchant, of Phelps m 5/28/18 Lydia Lothrop of Palmyra
in P (3-6/10 and 5-6/2)
7538. Royce, Elijah, 79, formerly of Lyme, CT,d in West Bloomfield, NY
(3-11/30/25)
7539. Royce, Philander S. of Williamson m 1/17/29 Hannah Green in Lyons
(3-1/21)

7540. Royce, Reuben m 12/2/29 Hannah Squier, both of Seneca, in S; E. Hastings, Esq. (3-12/23)
7541. Rudd, George R. (Rev.) of Fleming m Frances Beardslee in Auburn; Dr. Perrine (3-10/10/27)
7542. Rue, Schuyler m 9/27/35 Hannah Roth in Bath; Oliver Rice, Esq. (2-9/30)
7543. Rugar, John m 7/21/50 Jane Alden in Bath; Elder Mallory (2-7/24)
7544. Rugar, Thomas of Benton m Margaret Briggs of Middlesex in Benton (3-5/20/29)
7545. Ruggles, Philo, Esq., 35, attorney, d in NYC (3-12/23/29)
7546. Ruggles, William (Dr.) m 8/12/19 Mary Benton, dau of David, formerly of Seneca, in Brownstown, IN (3-11/24)
7547. Rumney, Gertrude, 29, consort of Robert and grand daughter of Hugh Gain late of NYC, d 12/12/26 in Geneva (funeral at Trinity Ch. there) (3-12/13)
7548. Rumney, Robert, merchant, m 1/2/28 Catharine Ann Dowers Young, youngest dau of William, Sr., at Trinity Church in Geneva; Rev. Dr. Orin Clark (3-1/9)
7549. Rumney, Robert, merchant, of Geneva m 2/24/18 Gertrude Rutgers, dau of Anthony A. of NYC, in Geneva; Rev. Orrin Clark (a double ceremony - see marr. of Lansing B. Mizner) (3-2/25)
7550. Rumsey, A. R. of Stafford m 11/3/49 Amanda Comstock Dixon, dau of Edward Esq. of East Bethany, in E. B. (1-11/13)
7551. Rumsey, David, Jr. of Bath m 1/19/41 Jane E. Brown, dau of Hon. A. C. of Ogdensburgh, in O; Rev. Savage (2-1/27)
7552. Rumsey, Levi, 57, district attorney of Genesee Co., d 12/27/33 in Batavia (1-12/31)
7553. Rumsey, Louisa D., 39, wf of Alexander R., d 8/7/48 in Stafford (1-8/8)
7554. Rumsey, Lydia, 21, wf of Martin S., d 5/10/32 in Bath (2-5/16)
7555. Rumsey, Lydia S., 54, consort of David, Esq., d 7/28/45 in Bath (2-7/30)
7556. Rundell, Lorenzo C. of Jamestown m 5/26/45 Cornelia Ford of Delanti in D; Rev. Carpenter (4-5/30)
7557. Runyan, Eli m 11/25/30 Sally Ann Gordon in Lyons; William Voorhies, Esq. (5-11/26)
7558. Runyan, Henry M., inf s of Isaac W., d 11/24/25 in Jersey, Steuben Co. (3-12/7)
7559. Runyan, Isaac W. m 2/19/25 Hannah Hollett in Bethel; Rev. Gideon Laning (3-2/23)
7560. Runyan, Philip m Priscilla Brush in Bethel; Rev. Hollett (3-4/15/18)
7561. Runyan, Vincent of Ontario Co. m 6/28/14 Vicey Edington of Fayette in F; Hugh McAlister, Esq. (3-7/6)
7562. Runyon, Aaron of Seneca m 1/14/16 Sally Silvers of Fayette in F; Rev. Young (3-1/24)
7563. Ruppert, _____ (Mrs.), 27, wf of Philip, d 4/27/13 in Geneva (3-5/5)
7564. Ruppert, Philip m 11/16/13 Rebecca Parkhurst in Geneva; Rev. Axtell (3-11/24)
7565. Rushmore, Durant of Farmington m 12/6/37 Eliza Ann Culver of Macedon; F. Smith, Esq. (5-12/20)
7566. Rushmore, William of Farmington m 11/11/41 Jane Hall, dau of James of Macedon, in M; Frederick Smith, Esq. (5-11/17)
7567. Russel, Charity, wf of Perry, d 4/22/21 in Henrietta, Ont. Co. (5-4/25)
7568. Russel, Charles M., Esq., 41, d 11/3/42 in Batavia (1-11/8)
7569. Russel, Melissa, 4 mo, dau of Milden, d in Farmersville (3-9/17/28)
7570. Russel, Perry m 3/7/22 Abigail Church, both formerly of Palmyra, in * Henrietta (5-3/13)
7671. Russell, Barlow, 16, m Caroline Castile, "aged only 42, who surrendered after a siege of three days", in Southborough (3-9/9/18)
7672. Russell, Charles, Esq., 38, d 12/17/16 in Morristown, NJ (3-1/8/17)
7673. Russell, Charles A. m 10/26/48 Mary A. Pratt, dau of Richard, Esq., in Batavia; Rev. B. Sunderland. All of Batavia (1-10/31)
7674. Russell, Daniel of Castleton m 9/23/47 Mariah Hunter of Wayne in W; Rev. B. Russell (2-10/6)
7675. Russell, Ellis m 1/30/17 Eliza Davis in Seneca; Rev. Clark (3-2/5)
7676. Russell, G. W. m Susan Bear in Waterloo (3-7/5/26)
7677. Russell, G. W. of Ellicott m 2/3/41 Abigail Olds of Levant in L; S. B. Winsor, Esq. (4-2/17)
* Numbers 7571-7670 inadvertently omitted.

7678. Russell, James, 43, d in Galen (3-10/1/28)
7679. Russell, James of Dewittville m 3/16/43 Cordelia Kennedy of Ellery in E;
Forbes Johnson, Esq. (4-3/23)
7680. Russell, John, 75, of the Society of Friends, d 2/4/42 in Henrietta
(one of the earliest settlers in Palmyra; killed by the kick of a
horse) (5-3/2)
7681. Russell, Luther, 54, late from Albany, d in Brighton (5-8/29/21)
7682. Russell, Martin W. of Buffalo m 7/10/48 Ann Kinyon of Batavia in B;
Rev. S. M. Stimson (1-7/25)
7683. Russell, Ralph m 2/16/32 Lorinda Smith in Jamestown; Rev. Gillet
(4-2/22)
7684. Russell, Robert, Esq. m 9/17/34 Celia Ann Cook, both of Pinegrove, PA,
in Carroll; Rev. Ammi Bond (4-9/24)
7685. Russell, Samuel m 3/28/32 Esther Hill, both of Newstead, Erie Co.,
in Akron village, town of Newstead; Rev. Stephen H. Weaver (1-4/3)
7686. Rutgers, Cornelia, 47, relict of late Anthony A., Esq. of NYC, d 3/15/18
in Geneva (3-3/18)
7687. Rutgers, Herman G. (Midshipman), 24, d at sea on board the ship
"U.S. Macedonian" ("has left several relatives in and near this
village" (Geneva)) (3-9/25/22)
7688. Rutherford, Adam of Palmyra m 9/16/42 Sarah Reed of Williamson in
Pulteneyville; Rev. Moses Butts (5-9/28)
7689. Rutherford, Elizabeth, 73, wf of Edward, d 6/13/42 in Bath (2-6/15)
7690. Rutherford, George m 1/4/46 Lyda (sic) French in Bath; Elder Sager.
All of Bath (2-1/21)
7691. Rutherford, James M., about 38, d 4/22/42 in Bath (fell off his
high-loaded wagon near the plaster mill) (2-4/27)
7692. Rutherford, Nancy (Mrs.), dau of Henry McElwee, d 1/12/50 in Bath
(2-1/16)
7693. Rutherford, Thomas m 4/29/27 Isabella Cameron in Bath (3-5/9)
7694. Rutherford, Thomas, about 22, s of William, d 2/9/35 in Bath (scarlet
fever) (2-2/11)
7695. Rutherford, Turzah, 12 yrs, dau of Edward of Thurston, d 6/16/47 in
Thurston (2-6/23)
7696. Rutherford, William M. m 12/2/32 Margaret Crivelling; Henry W. Rogers,
Esq. (2-12/5)
7697. Rutledge, Edward A., 23, s of Maj. H. M. of Nashville, Tennessee and
grandson of one of the signers of the Declaration of Independence,
d 7/16/26 in Saratoga, NY (3-8/2)
7698. Ryan, James W. (Gen.), 107, d in Brunswick, ME leaving a wife, aged 98,
"in perfect good health" (He was a Rev. officer) (3-2/12/23)
7699. Ryerson, Lucius C. See, possibly, Pyerson, Lucius C.'s entry.
7700. Ryerson, Samuel. See, possibly, Pyerson, Lucius C.'s entry.
7701. Ryno, William Rapplye, 8 mo, s of Smith Ryno, d in Farmersville
(3-9/17/28)
7702. Sabin, Elizabeth, wf of Rev. Benjamin of the Meth. Ch. and lately of
Ithaca, d in Ontario, Wayne Co. (3-7/2/28)
7703. Sabins, John, Esq. of Ovid m Nancy Black, dau of Michael, in Elmira
(3-4/1/29)
7704. Sacket, G. V., Esq. of Seneca Falls m 2/6/26 Harriet Haig of Aurora
in A (3-2/15)
7705. Sacket, Nancy T., 24, wf of Gary V., Esq., d 7/30/20 in Seneca Falls
(3-8/2)
7706. Sacket, Nathaniel, 47, d 11/5/17 in Tioga (3-11/19)
7707. Sackett, H.A. (Rev.) of Henrietta m 6/25/39 D. E. Gray, dau of Hon.
John D. of Sheridan, in S; Rev. A. F. Gray (4-7/3)
7708. Sadler, Deborah, 11 mo, dau of "Mr. Sadler", d 7/12/23 in Geneva
(3-7/16)
7709. Safford, _____ m Mahala Heacock in Canandaigua (3-9/2/18)
7710. Safford, Betsey, 29, wf of Darius, Esq., d 11/10/24 (surv by husband
and 2 ch) (1-11/19)
7711. Safford, Darius m 4/19/25 Eliza Everett in Barry; Rev. Buel (1-4/22)
7712. Safford, Sherebiah m Mary Westfall, both of Lyons, in Waterloo (3-10/28/29)
7713. Sage, James m Adah Baker in Ulysses (3-2/7/16)
7714. Sage, Phineas m 2/28/43 Cynthia M. Smith, both of Laona, in L; Rev. L. M.
Hopkins of Fredonia (4-3/23)

7715. Sager, Elias m 4/3/22 Hannah Abrahams "near the Glass Factory"; Rev. Axtell (3-4/10)
7716. Sager, Philip m 2/29/30 Sally Riggs in Arcadia; Rev. J. R. Alverson (5-3/10)
7717. St. Clair, Arthur (Maj. Gen.) d 8/31/18 in Laurel Hill, Somerset Co., PA (a Rev. officer "and distinguished patriot") (3-9/16)
7718. St. Clair, Sarah S., consort of Com. Arthur of the U.S. Navy, d in Norfolk (state not given) (3-9/19/27)
7719. St. John, Alexander, 50, d in Northampton, NY (3-11/16/25)
7720. St. John?, Ancel m 7/9/23 Isabella Powell, dau of Thomas?, in Schenectady (3-7/23)
7721. St. John, Holly. See Holly F. Johnson, Jr.
7722. St. John, Jasper m Julia Ann Reynolds in Milo (3-1/13/30)
7723. St. John, Solomon, formerly of Palmyra, d 1/24/35 in Buffalo (5-2/13)
7724. St. Johns, Andrew J. m 10/23/38 Eliza Ann Warner in Panama, NY (4-11/7)
7725. Salisbury, Betsey, 36, wf of H. A., Esq., editor of _____ (page torn), d in Buffalo (3-10/3/27)
7726. Salisbury, Charles Andrew, 6 yrs, s of Tobias and Mary, d 2/26/50 in Urbana (2-3/6)
7727. Salisbury, H. A., Esq., proprietor of the Buffalo Patriot, m 9/6/29 Phoebe Osborne, dau of Elias, Esq., in Clarence; Rev. Safford (3-9/16)
7728. Salisbury, Smith H., Esq., 46, editor of the Rochester Daily Advertiser, d 1/24/32 in Rochester (One of the earliest settlers in the "Genesee Country". When Buffalo was burned in the War of 1812 "he was then conducting a paper there") (5-1/31 and 2-2/8)
7729. Salmon, Mary Ann (Miss), 25, d 1/8/50 in Avoca (2-1/23)
7730. Salmon, Sally, wf of Rev. R., d in Medina, Orleans Co. (3-5/13/29)
7731. Salpaugh, Peter B. (Capt.), formerly of Rensselaerville, Albany Co., m 9/25/36 Sabrina Bird, dau of John, in Manchester; Rev. Rowe. All of Manchester (5-10/21)
7732. Saltonstall, Dudley, Esq., 54, formerly of Canandaigua, NY and a native of New London, CT, d 4/26/24 in Nixonton, NC (1-5/14 and 3-5/19)
7733. Salyer, Daniel m 2/21/31 Luthena Salyer in Tyrone; H. L. Arnold, Esq. All of Tyrone (2-3/2)
7734. Sambre, Peter, "founder of the Roustigouche Society, celebrated for the agility of its members; no person was permitted to participate in the gymnastics that could not throw a javelin of 100 lbs a distance of 26 yards", died in Quebec, Lower Canada (3-11/5/17)
7735. Sample, George m 10/15/29 Louisa Barber in Geneva; Rev. Squier (3-10/21)
7736. Sampson, George m 12/10/38 Eliza Walker, both of Palmyra, in P (5-12/14)
7737. Sampson, William C., printer, m 7/7/31 Mary Barker in Utica; Rev. Dr. Lansing. All of Utica (2-7/27)
7738. Sanborn, John, 57, m Lydia Stanyon, 83, in Hampton Falls, NH (3-2/3/19)
7739. Sanburn, Nathaniel, 57, d 6/25/14 in Canandaigua (formerly of Wethersfield, CT and one of the first settlers in Ontario Co., NY)(3-7/6)
7740. Sanders, Belarmine T. m 7/4/25 Philomena Preston (1-7/8)
7741. Sanders, David H. m 4/13/39 Maryann Barns in Russellsburg, PA; Rev. Smith of Jamestown, NY (4-4/17)
7742. Sanders, Joseph m 9/20/32 Elizabeth Patterson in Batavia; Rev. Smith of St. James Church, Batavia (1-9/25)
7743. Sanderson, Elvira, 9 yrs, d 1/22/13 in Geneva (3-1/27)
7744. Sanderson, Sylvester m Mary Ann Child, dau of William, in Waterloo (3-3/18/29)
7745. Sanderson, William A. m 1/19/35 Maglen Allen, both of Prattsburgh, in P; Rev. Rudd (2-2/18)
7746. Sandford, Jared (Dr.) d 8/18/17 in Ovid (3-8/20)
7747. Sandford, Malachi of Phelps m 12/10/22 Elcy Hardenbrook of Lyons in L (3-12/25)
7748. Sandford, Russell of Wayne m 9/30/47 Laura Chapman of Pulteney in P; Rev. P. Olney (2-10/6)
7749. Sands, Harvey m Sarah Haus in Milo (3-3/13/22)
7750. Sands, Henry B., 25, a master's mate in the U.S. Navy, d 5/4/18 at Sackett's Harbor ("... attended to the grave by all the naval and military officers on that station") (3-5/27)

7751. Sands, Phoebe, 78, consort of Robert, Esq., d 11/23/19 in Rhinebeck (3-12/15)
7752. Sanford, _____ (Maj.) m 3/30/32 Emeline Pratt of Williamson in W; (a double ceremony - see the marr. of John Sheffield) (5-4/4)
7753. Sanford, Abel, Esq., 77, formerly of Wallingford, CT, d 9/10/43 at his home in Marion (5-9/13)
7754. Sanford, Arden m 10/23/49 Betsey E. Bosworth in North Bergen; Rev. Clute. All of Bergen (1-10/30)
7755. Sanford, Giles, merchant, of Erie, PA m 10/5/16 Laura Goodwin of Aurelius, Cayuga Co.; Rev. Axtell (3-10/16)
7756. Sanford, James, Esq. d 1/31/42 in Wayne (from the "fall of a horse he was riding") (2-2/9)
7757. Sanford, John L., 72, d 7/13/43 in Palmyra (5-7/19)
7758. Sanford, Laura, 31, wf of D. M., d 9/16/17 in Canandaigua (3-10/1)
7759. Sanford, Luther, Jr. of East Palmyra m 4/14/41 Ruth Culver, dau of Cooper Culver, Esq. of Arcadia, in A; Rev. David S. Cushing (5-4/21)
7760. Sanford, Nathan (Hon.) of NY state m 5/27/28 Mary Buchanan, dau of late Andrew, Esq. of Baltimore, MD, in B; Rev. Dr. Hyatt (3-6/11)
7761. Sanford, Stephen m Emma Russel in Williamson (3-1/6/19)
7762. Sanford, Thomas m Amelia Wood "in Jersey" (3-4/22/29)
7763. Sanger, Jedediah (Hon.) m Fanny Dench, late of Washington, D.C., in New Hartford, Oneida Co. (3-10/17/27)
7764. Sanger, Jedediah, 78, d 6/6/29 at his home in New Hartford ("one of the first settlers of the 'Whitestone Country'") (3-6/17)
7765. Sanger, Jonathan, 64, d in Canandaigua (3-9/1/19)
7766. Santee, Nancy, 46, wf of Isaac, Esq., d 7/15/40 in Cameron (2-7/22)
7767. Sargeant, Ezra, late a bookseller of NYC, d in Hudson, NY "on his way to Lebanon Springs for benefit of his health" (3-7/15/12)
7768. Sargeant, Henry (Dr.) of Warren, PA m 10/19/36 Mercy W. Adams of Jeffrey, NH in Jamestown, NY; Rev. Gillet (4-10/26)
7769. Sargent, James R. m 4/20/47 Permelia Whittemore in Jasper; Rev. G. T. Everest (2-4/28)
7770. Sartwell, _____ (Deacon), about 70, d in Busti (4-7/18/32)
7771. Sartwell, Henry P. (Dr.) of _____el m 1/20/25 Rebecca Stewart of Junius (3-1/26)
7772. Saunders, John m 5/13/30 Nancy Gage in Gorham, Ont. Co. (5-5/14)
7773. Saunders, Mary, 4 yrs, dau of Anthony, d in Galen (3-9/4/22)
7774. Savage, Almond m 8/18/22 Sally Southerland in Seneca; Jacob Dox, Esq. All of Seneca (3-8/21)
7775. Sawdy, Cyrus m Pamelia Burdick in Pulteney (3-8/29/27)
7776. Sawtell, H. H. of Palmyra m 7/12/40 Elizabeth Mason of Pulteneyville; Rev. Alfred C. Lathrop (5-7/15)
7777. Sawyer, A. P. of Macedon m 1/15/40 Fanny Rice, dau of Charles, Esq. of Pineville, in P; Rev. Robinson of Pulaski (5-1/22)
7778. Sawyer, Adaline, 26, wf of J. A. Sawyer, A.M., and dau of Nathaniel Cady, d 5/10/49 in Alexander (one child living at time of her death) (1-5/22)
7779. Sawyer, Corner (sic) m "within a few days" Margaret Salisbury in Snell (3-11/1/09)
7780. Sawyer, Hooker, 71, formerly of Manchester, d in Middlebury, Summit Co., Ohio (5-5/18/42)
7781. Sawyer, J. A., A.B., of Austerlitz, Columbia Co. m 6/14/47 Adaline Cady of Alexander; Rev. R. L. Waite (1-6/22)
7782. Sawyer, Jeremiah m Esther Pratt in Palmyra (3-1/17/16)
7783. Sawyer, Luke, about 50, d 8/13/31 in Manchester (5-8/16)
7784. Sawyer, Norris m 10/24/43 Caroline Johnston (dau of Robert, Esq.), both of Farmington, in F; Rev. Fisher of Palmyra (5-10/25)
7785. Sawyer, Prescott m Jemima Buckley in Middlesex (3-1/28/18)
7786. Sawyer, William m Mary Bellows in Penn Yan (3-9/17/28)
7787. Saxton, George J. m 9/24/44 Caroline P. Root in Westfield; Rev. T. Hopkins (4-10/4/44)
7788. Saxton, George W. m 11/30/25 Julia Willson in Benton (3-12/21)
7789. Saxton, Paulina, 15, dau of Col. A., d 11/15/12 in Bloomfield (3-12/2)
7790. Sayles, Scott William m 6/18/26 Rhoda F. Ballard, dau of Capt. Gilbert, in Jamestown; Rev. Eddy (4-6/21)

7791. Sayles, Stephen, 54, m 7/3/42 Eunice Rathbun, 21, in Howard; A. M. Leigh, Esq. (2-7/6)
7792. Sayre, Abigail (Miss), 20, d 5/27/16 in Elmira (3-6/19)
7793. Sayre, Coe B. m Mrs. Pamelia Warden in Chemung (3-2/20/28)
7794. Sayre, Daniel (Col.) d 2/22/13 in Junius (3-3/3)
7795. Sayre, Daniel, 17, s of Abner, d 8/31/26 in Ovid (3-9/13)
7796. Sayre, James, 76, a native of Orange Co. and one of the first settlers in Elmira, d 6/4/26 in Elmira (3-6/21)
7797. Sayre, James, 52, d in Elmira (3-7/25/27)
7798. Sayre, Jeremiah (Capt.) m 2/27/44 Maria C. Payne in Sag Harbor, L.I., NY (5-3/13)
7799. Sayre, Mathew m Fanny Bennett in Elmira (3-1/29/17)
7800. Sayre, Whittington, Esq., 64, of Elmira died (date not given) in Jefferson, Wisconsin. ("Left home on a visit to the West some three weeks ago ... while fulfilling a promise to a dying brother-in-law on his deathbed in Geneva that he would see his wife and daughter safe home.") (2-8/29/49)
7801. Scantling, Stephen m Louisa Cooper, both of Palmyra (or Canandaigua?) in Canandaigua; "Mr. Parker" (5-10/24/34)
7802. Schenandoh (sic), the Indian chief, 113, d at Oneida Castle (as agreed many years earlier he was "buried beside the Rev. Mr. Kirkland") (copied from the Utica Patriot and Patrol) (3-3/20/16)
7803. Schenck, William C., pastor of the Presbyterian Congragation of Princeton, NJ, d in Princeton (3-11/11/18)
7804. Schermerhorn, _____, inf dau of John V. R., d 7/12/28 at the Glass Factory near Geneva (3-7/23)
7805. Schermerhorn, Catharine, 4 yrs, dau of John V. R., d 2/8/27 in Geneva (fell backward into a kettle of hot water) (3-2/14)
7806. Schermerhorn, Isaac M. of Canandaigua m 7/18/43 Maria Barkley of Geneva in G; Rev. P. C. May (5-7/26)
7807. Schermerhorn, M. L., Esq. of Hammondsport, Steuben Co. m 5/6/33 Elizabeth Colt, oldest dau of late Major Joseph of Palmyra (5-5/8)
7808. Schoolcraft, Abraham S. m 1/9/22 Alida Herrington "at the Ontario Glass Factory"; Rev. Axtell. "All of that place." (3-1/16)
7809. Schott, Daniel (Capt.) m 5/30/26 Nancy Best(?), both of Fayette (3-6/14)
7810. Schureman, John (Rev. Dr.), 39, professor of pastoral theology in the theological college at New Brunswick, NJ and formerly one of the ministers of the Reformed Dutch Church in NYC, d 5/15/18 (3-6/3)
7811. Schuyler, Caroline, about 30, wf of Peter and dau of late Capt. Valentine Brother, died (date and place not given) (3-12/3/28)
7812. Schuyler, George m 12/21/31 Susan Prindle of Wayne in Bath; Henry W. Rogers, Esq. (2-1/4/32)
7813. Schuyler, Harmanus P., Esq., formerly of Albany, about 55, d 10/20/22 at Locust Grove in the town of Niskayuna (3-10/23)
7814. Schuyler, Lucas, 25, d 10/25/09 in Albany (3-11/1)
7815. Schuyler, Mary, 78, relict of Capt. Peter, d in Newark, NJ (3-9/9/18)
7816. Schuyler, Peter m 11/10/14 Caroline Brother, dau of Capt. Valentine Brother, in Seneca; Rev. White. All of Seneca (3-11/16)
7817. Schuyler, Peter (Capt.), about 41, d 8/9/29 in Seneca (member of the Associated Reformed Church)(3-8/12)
7818. Schyem(?), Peter m Betsey Baldwin in Benton (3-7/17/16)
7819. Scidmore, George B. m 5/20/42 Sarah Ann Wing of Cohecton in C; Rev. G. S. Northrop (2-5/25)
7820. Scofield, Abner (Capt.) m 11/23/25 Elizabeth Redfield in Nunda, Alleg. Co. (3-12/7)
7821. Scofield, Betsy, wf of P., d 3/1/43 in Ellery (4-3/23)
7822. Scofield, David, 46, d 5/18/45 in Elba (1-6/3)
7823. Scofield, David S. m 7/4/42 Lucretia Mattison of Harmony in Sugargrove, PA; "Mr. Wilson, Esq." (4-7/14)
7824. Scofield, John m Clarissa Pember in Sugargrove, PA (4-1/27/42)
7825. Scofield, Seth m 1/25/44 Rua Scofield; Rev. H. Smith (4-2/16)
7826. Scot, Jennet, 16, oldest dau of Robert, Esq., d 7/10/22 in Geneva (3-7/17)
7827. Scot, Robert, 40, d 8/4/14 in Geneva (3-8/10)
7828. Scott, _____, 16 mo, dau of John, d 8/20/30 in Palmyra (5-8/27)

7829. Scott, Ashbel m 12/12/22 Fanny Grandee (prob. in Ontario, NY) (See also George Mathewson's marriage) (5-12/18)
7830. Scott, Charles of Phelps m 11/19/26 Mrs. Phebe Church, wid of late Adonijah, Esq. of Sodus, in S; Byram Green, Esq. (3-11/29)
7831. Scott, Daniel O. of Arcadia m Susan E. Meeker of Elizabethtown, NJ in E; Rev. Nicholas Murray (5-11/25/40)
7831a. Scott, George W. m 2/9/50 Alice Denison, dau of John, in Darien; Rev. Bond (1-2/12)
7832. Scott, Jacob m Charlotte Brink in Tyre (3-1/13/30)
7833. Scott, James (Capt.), 68, d in Boston ("He had crossed the Atlantic 111 times!") (3-10/25/09)
7834. Scott, James m Margaret Covert in Ovid (3-5/27/29)
7835. Scott, John, 82, d 5/23/19 in Cambridge, Wash. Co. ("... a native of Peterborough, N. H. from whence he moved to Cambridge about 1769; ... (a soldier) in the old French and Revolutionary Wars. At age 18 joined 'the Seceder church'.") (3-6/9)
7836. Scott, John m 11/17/22 Mrs. Harriet S. Jordan in Manchester (5-11/20)
7837. Scott, John m 9/13/24 Olive Ransom in Batavia; C. Carpenter, Esq. (1-9/17)
7838. Scott, John m 8/24/31 Almina Eddy, dau of Rev. Isaac, in Jamestown (4-8/31)
7839. Scott, John, V.D.S. (Hon.), 47, first judge of Greene Co., d 11/3/27 in Catskill (3-11/14)
7840. Scott, Leonard J. "from Vermont" d in Arcadia (3-8/22/27)
7841. Scott, Olive, 42, consort of Ethel (sic) Scott, d 3/22/39 in Stafford (1-3/28)
7842. Scott, Rachel (Miss), 20, dau of James, d 9/26/18 in Seneca (3-9/30)
7843. Scott, Thomas m Louisa Davenport in Ithaca (3-4/30/28)
7844. Scott, William (Col.), 70, d 7/11/15 in Greenfield, NY (emigrated to America "about 10 years previous to the commencement of the revolutionary war in which he took an early and active part; received 38 wounds) (3-8/9)
7845. Scotten, Daniel of Palmyra m 9/9/44 Elizabeth H. Perine, dau of Major John of Princeton, NJ, in P; Rev. Samuel Starr (5-9/25)
7846. Scotten, George of Geneva m 5/31/40 Caroline Smith of Palmyra in P; Rev. A. H. Stowell (5-6/10)
7847. Scovell, ____, inf ch of Seymour, d 4/13/19 in Palmyra (5-4/21)
7848. Scovell, Halsey B. m 1/30/21 Ann McCollum in Palmyra; Rev. Charles J. Cook (5-2/7)
7849. Scovell, Horace, s of Ephraim of Palmyra, d 9/28/20 near Edwardsville, IL ("... (Horace) with five other young men accompanied the Rev. Townsend and family who all left (Palmyra) last spring to the state of Illinois") (5-12/20/20)
7850. Scovell, Roxcena (Miss), 20, recently from Orwell, VT, d 5/23/19 in Palmyra (5-5/26 and 3-6/2). Death date is 5/25 in 3-6/2.
7851. Scrantom (sic), Edwin, one of the editors of the Monroe Republican, m 10/26/26 Mary Ann Sibley, both of Rochester, in R (3-11/8)
7852. Scraw, Peter of Seneca m Rachael Rosecrans in Benton (3-2/11/29)
7853. Scudder, Elial, 23, student of law, d 7/5/27 in Geneva (3-7/11)
7854. Seaburn, John of Galen m 1/9/22 Vilena Ford of Seneca in S; Rev. Riley (3-1/23)
7855. Seager, Aurora (Rev.), 24, methodist missionary, died "in Montreal" (3-2/9/20)
7856. Seaman, Andrew, Esq., cashier of the Manhattan Bank, d in NYC (3-10/6/19)
7857. Seaman, Valentine (Dr.), 47, d in NYC (3-7/9/17)
7858. Searing, Augustin P. of the firm of Mack and Searing m Delia Butler in Ithaca (3-6/16/19)
7859. Searles, William m 9/22/38 Sybia Hadden in Pulteney; John Gulick, Esq. (2-10/10)
7860. Searls, Lemuel B., Esq. of Addison m H. E. Carpenter in Bainbridge (3-6/24/29)
7861. Sears, Betsey, about 30, wf of John, d in Bristol (3-12/20/15)
7862. Sears, Caroline Calista, 71, dau of Ebenezer and Diana, d in Dover, VT (4-2/16/43)
7863. Sears, Deborah, 24, wf of Nathan L., d 8/1/36 in Jamestown (4-8/3)

7864. Sears, Harriet, 18, wf of Eli, d 4/3/22 "of consumption" in Galen
(3-4/10)
7865. Sears, James of Elmira m Charity Ann Gould, formerly of Ithaca, in
Catlin (3-8/27/28)
7866. Sears, James, 48, d in Penn Yan (3-10/15/28)
7867. Sears, James C. of Arcadia m 2/10/31 Lydia Elmira Howland, dau of David,
Esq., in Manchester (5-2/25)
7868. Sears, Nathan L. of Jamestown m Polly Marsh of Carroll in C; Rev. D.
Smith (4-6/27/38)
7869. Sears, Rufus (Rev.), 25, d 4/7/42 in Bath ("He had just finished his
education for the ministry at the Seminary in Hamilton, Madison
County" and at time of death was en route to settle in Kentucky.)
(2-4/13)
7870. Sears, Sophia d in Montgomery (3-11/16/25)
7871. Seaver, James E. m 8/24/48 Nancy K. Follett at St. James Church in
Batavia; Rev. J. A. Bolles (a double ceremony - see the marr. of
Lucas Seaver) (1-8/29)
7872. Seaver, Lucas m 8/24/48 Olive M. Hall at St. James Church in Batavia;
Rev. J. A. Bolles. All of Batavia (a double ceremony - see the
marr. of James E. Seaver) (1-8/29)
7873. Seaver, Naomi, 57, wf of Col. William, d 5/23/46 (funeral at the Episc.
Church in Batavia) (1-5/26)
7874. Seaver, William (Col.), editor of the Spirit of the Times, m 4/22/48
Mary M. Morrison at St. James Church in Batavia; Rev. James A. Bolles.
All of Batavia (1-5/2)
7875. Sebbins, Almirah (Miss), 22, dau of late Hezekiah, d "recently" in
Gorham (3-1/28/29)
7876. Sedgwick, Henry D., Esq., 46, d 12/23/31 in Stockbridge, MA ("a
conspicuous ornament to the bar") (2-1/4/32)
7877. Sedgwick, Robert m 5/31/25 Sarah Bixby in Batavia; Daniel Tisdale, Esq.
(1-6/3)
7878. Sedgwick, Theodore m 1/6/29 Hannah C. Finch in Rochester (3-1/21)
7879. Seegins, Ebenezer m 2/15/29 Deborah Pixley in Jamestown; T. W. Harvey,
Esq. All of Jamestown (4-2/18)
7880. Seeley, Bartlett m 1/23/25 Elizabeth Whiteford; P. A. Barker, Esq. All
of Junius (3-2/2)
7881. Seeley, George of Athens, Greene Co. m Jane A. Ransom in Canandaigua
(3-2/13/28)
7882. Seeley, Harvey m Elizabeth Voorhies in Romulus (3-3/10/19)
7883. Seeley, Thomas, about 5 yrs, s of "Mrs. Seeley", d 9/18/17 in Geneva
(3-10/15)
7884. Seeley, William P., Esq., 32, d in Ovid (3-5/24/20)
7885. Seely, _____ (Mr.) d 10/22/21 "at the mission station near the Great
Osage village ... and on the 27th of the same month Mrs. Montgomery,
wife of the Rev. Mr. Montgomery (died)..." (3-2/13/22)
7886. Seely, Charlotte, wid of late Joseph B., printer, d 3/1/30 in
Rochester (5-3/10)
7887. Seely, Eleanor, 9, dau of Joseph B., d 2/22/15 in Geneva (3-3/8)
7888. Seely, Elizabeth, wf of Henry, d 10/3/13 in Hector, Sen. Co. (3-10/20)
7889. Seely, George W, m Sally Brooks in Elmira (3-3/12/28)
7890. Seely, Harry of Seneca Co. m 6/22/15 _____ Meeker of Tioga Co.; Squire
Barnes (3-7/5)
7891. Seely, Joel m 12/31/09 Patty Lewis in Ovid; Rev. Clark. All of Ovid
(3-1/17/10)
7892. Seely, Joseph B., 34, d 6/17/15 in Geneva "leaving a wife and 5 children"
(3-6/28)
7893. Seely, Joseph B., 26, printer, formerly of Geneva, d 9/23/29 in Rochester
(3-9/30)
7894. Seely, Kezia, 59, d in Prescott (3-5/30/27)
7895. Seely, Nelson, 7 mo, s of James, d 9/9/32 in Palmyra (5-9/12)
7896. Segar, Thomas O. m 4/18/36 Mary R. Curtis in Union Ellery; Rev. Jonathan
Wilson (4-4/20)
7897. Selby, Charity (Mrs.) d 11/12/29 in Williamson (5-11/27 and 3-12/9)
7898. Selby, Ira, Jr., 25, oldest son of Ira, Esq., formerly of Palmyra,
d 6/7/29 in Pittsburgh, PA (5-6/26 and 3-7/15)

7899. Selden, J. F. of Stockbridge, Ingham Co., MI m 8/4/49 Eliza Davidson of Henrietta, Jackson Co., MI in Stckbridge, MI; Rev. S. Carey (2-10/17)
7900. Selfridge, Sally, wf of Col. John, d in Galen (3-4/23/28)
7901. Sellon, _____, inf ch of Rev. John, d in Canandaigua (3-3/18/29)
7902. Selover, John R. m 2/27/50 Mary Frances Lewis in Prattsburgh; Rev. B. C. Smith (2-3/6)
7903. Sentell, John M., 26, d 4/19/42 in Sodus (5-5/4)
7904. Serross, Paris m 1/5/40 Harriet M. Wellman in Harmony; M. Norton, Esq. (4-1/15)
7905. Service, William m 7/9/30 Ann Bulrees in Canandaigua; Rev. A. D. Eddy (5-7/16)
7906. Serviss, Nelson of Palmyra m 8/3/30 Martha W. Chandler of Schenectady in S; "Doct. Nott" (5-9/3)
7907. Severs(?), James MacKnight of Canandaigua m 5/27/41 Maria Angelica Brady of Palmyra in P; Rev. Samuel Wilson (5-6/2)
7908. Sew_____, Henry L. of Weedsport m Lucinda Hocum in Waterloo (3-8/19/29)
7909. Sewall, Henry D. of NYC m Mary C. Norton in Bloomfield (3-2/7/16)
7910. Sewall, Samuel (Hon.), 57, Chief Justice of the Supreme Judicial Court of Massachusetts, d 6/22/14 in Wiscasset, MA (3-6/29)
7911. Seward, Asahel, printer, of Utica m 10/14/12 Martha Williams of Cazenovia in C (3-11/25)
7912. Seward, B. J., Esq. of Westfield m Maria Louisa Mumford, dau of J. I., Esq., in NYC (4-1/20/41)
7913. Seward, Calvin of Le Roy m 2/13/25 Nancy McKain in Elba; J. Wilford, Esq. (1-2/18)
7914. Seward, Charles of Alexander m 2/23?/24 Almy B. Allen of Batavia in B; Eben North, Esq. (1-2/27)
7915. Seward, Marcia, 45, wf of B. J., Esq., d 10/25/39 in Westfield (4-11/6)
7916. Seward, Nathan (Col.), 56, d 11/9/15 in New Hartford (a Rev. officer) (3-11/22)
7917. Sexton, Duncan M., 13 mo, youngest child of William S., d 10/15/18 in Palmyra (5-10/20)
7918. Sexton, James of Buffalo m 7/6/45 Emily L. Norton, dau of Ira of Bethany, in B; Rev. Taylor (1-7/8)
7919. Sexton, James K. of Port Gibson m 1/30/44 R. Augusta Jewell of Sodus in S (5-2/7)
7920. Sexton, Margaret, 33, wf of Pliny, a member of the Society of Friends, d 5/27/31 in Palmyra (5-6/3)
7921. Sexton, Margaret, 18, dau of Jeremiah, d in Busti (4-6/30/42)
7922. Sexton, Pliny m 1/2/22 Margaret Turner, both of Palmyra, in P (a Quaker marriage) (5-1/9)
7923. Sexton, Pliny, merchant, of Palmyra m 11/1/32 Susan Aldrich in the Friends Meeting House in Palmyra (11/14)
7924. Sexton, Susan, 37, wf of Pliny, d 8/18/35 in Palmyra (5-8/21)
7925. Sexton, William, 28, of Palmyra d 9/8/22 in Johnstown (5-9/25)
7926. Seybolt, William H., Esq. m 4/23/31 Sally Woodard in Jersey, NY; H. Switzer, Esq. (2-5/4)
7927. Seymour, _____, about 2 yrs, s of "Mr. Seymour", d 7/30/15 in Geneva ("... given laudanum instead of tincture of rhubarb by mistake") (3-8/2)
7928. Seymour, Chloe, 32, wf of Smith Seymour, d 10/11/40 in Jamestown (4-10/14)
7929. Seymour, Dorcas, 23, wf of Joseph W., d 5/5/22 in Canandaigua (5-5/15)
7930. Seymour, Eli, 81, d 4/1/43 in Palmyra (5-4/5)
7931. Seymour, Gurdon I., a native of Hartford, CT, "for many years the editor and proprietor of a public journal in the City of Savannah", d in Savannah, GA (3-11/16/14)
7932. Seymour, Hannah, 53, mother-in-law of Ethan B. Allen, d in Batavia (3-10/10/27)
7933. Seymour, Harris, merchant, of Canandaigua m 4/10/15 Lucretia P. Williams, dau of John C. of Pittsfield, MA, in P; Rev. Punderson (3-4/19)
7934. Seymour, Henry m 10/15/44 H. Jeannette Hinsdill, both of Grand Rapids, MI, in G. R.; Rev. James Ballard (4-11/1)
7935. Seymour, Irving Wattles, 12 yrs, only son of Lorenzo and Phebe Ann, d 9/7/45 in Corning (2-9/24)

7936. Seymour, Joseph W., printer, m 10/8/22 Sophia Hall, both of Canandaigua, in Victor (3-10/30)
7937. Seymour, Orlando m 6/6/22 Mary Carter of Camillus in C; Rev. Beebe (3-6/26)
7938. Seymour, Orson of Canandaigua m 4/24/19 Caroline Maria Clarke, dau of Peter, Esq. of Montezuma, in M (3-5/5 and 5-5/12)
7939. Seymour, Orson, Esq., 58, cashier of the Utica Branch Bank, d 10/11/24 in Canandaigua (3-10/20)
7940. Seymour, Polydore, 25, d in Aurora, Niag. Co. (3-11/24/19)
7941. Seymour, Sidney S., 21, d 3/13/30 in Palmyra (5-3/19)
7942. Seymour, Smith, Esq. m 11/10/41 Mrs. Lucy L. Barrett at the Presby. Ch. in Jamestown; Rev. E. J. Gillett (4-11/11)
7943. Seymour, Stephen P., merchant, of Erie, PA (formerly of Palmyra) m 10/6/35 Almira Norton of Canandaigua in C; Rev. Green (5-10/30)
7944. Seymour, Sybil, 7 yrs, d 5/29/41 in Jamestown (4-6/2)
7945. Seymour, Walter M. m Eliza M. Otto, dau of late Jacob, Esq., in Batavia (3-8/27/28)
7946. Seymour, William m 9/14/43 Melissa McClallan, both of Stockton, in S; Rev. H. Smith of Ellery (4-10/5)
7947. Seymour, Zachariah H., Esq., 63, Pres. of the Utica Branch Bank, d 7/2/22 in Canandaigua ("one of the earliest settlers in that village") (3-7/10, 1-7/12, and 5-7/17)
7948. Shaddock, Daniel of Phelps m Chloe Crittenden of Junius in J; Rev. Mosher (3-11/3/19)
7949. Shadduck, Freelove, 5, dau of Abraham, d 5/20/22 (5-5/22)
7950. Shade, Abraham of Junius m Mary Leddick in Fayette (3-8/6/28)
7951. Shafer, Edward m 3/4/46 Mary Conner, both of Avoca, in A; Rev. L. Rose (2-3/11)
7952. Shaff, William, 76, (a Rev. pensioner), late of Junius, d in Middlesex (3-7/15/29)
7953. Shaffer, Charles __?__rce, printer, m 9/16/11 Elizabeth __?__man (perhaps Slowman), both of Charleston, SC, in C (3-10/23)
7954. Shannon, James, Esq. of Bath m 11/22/42 Lucy Roseboom of Cherry Valley, Otsego Co. in C. V.; Rev. Lusk (2-11/30)
7955. Sharland, Maria (Mrs.), 30 or 50, d 10/19/17 in Benton (3-11/5)
7956. Sharp, Mary (Mrs.) d "of a cancer" in Painted Post (3-8/19/29)
7957. Shattuck, John Tyler, 20, s of Lucius, d 11/5/42 in Cohocton (2-11/16)
7958. Shattuck, Mary, 35, wf of William, Esq., d 7/4/22 in Penn Yan (3-7/17)
7959. Shattuck, William, 50, d in Canandaigua (3-9/3/17)
7960. Shaut, Clarinda, 33, wf of Joseph, d 9/24/40 in Bath (member of Presby. Church) (2-9/30)
7961. Shaut, Joseph m 4/22/41 Jane Ann Hendryx; Rev. Orris Frazer (2-4/28)
7962. Shaver, Alford m 11/21/41 Eleanor Hauber of Greenwood in Canisteo B. S. Brundage, Esq. (2-12/1)
7963. Shaver, Jeremiah of Canisteo m 5/30/46 Ursula Sawtell, formerly of Greene, Chen. Co., in Canisteo; D. D. Davis, Esq. (2-6/17)
7964. Shaver, John m Lucinda Drown; Elder Chase (2-2/2/31)
7965. Shaver, John F. of Howard m 9/12/49 Amanda Loucks of Avoca in A; Rev. H. Spencer (2-9/19)
7966. Shaver, John L. of Lodi m 4/25/46 Polly Rose, dau of J., Esq. of Greenwood, in Canisteo; D. D. Davis, Esq. (2-6/17)
7967. Shaver, Joseph m 2/22/31 Paulina West in Lyons; William Voorhies, Esq. All of Arcadia (5-3/4)
7968. Shaw, ____, wf of Jonathan, d "on Seely Creek" (3-9/17/28)
7969. Shaw, Alpha H., Esq., attorney, of Ludlowville, NY m Almira Phelps, dau of Oliver, Esq. of Centreville, Grantham, Upper Canada, in C; Rev. Russel of Stamford (U.C.?) (3-11/28/27)
7970. Shaw, Benjamin (Capt.) d "a few days since" in Benton (3-4/11/27)
7971. Shaw, Benjamin Warner, 2 yrs, s of Warner D., d 4/21/41 (prob. in Jamestown) (4-4/21)
7972. Shaw, Catherine (Miss), 23, d 6/7/29 in Marion (5-6/19 and 3-6/24)
7973. Shaw, Cornelius m 11/13/28 Betsey Phelps, formerly of Chenango, in Phelps; Rev. Case (3-11/19)
7974. Shaw, D.J., Jr. (Col.) m 12/30/46 Harriet A. Davenport, dau of Col. Lemuel, in Elkland, PA; Rev. E. Bronson. All of E. (2-1/27/47)
7975. Shaw, Elmira, 44, wf of James, d in Fluvanna (4-3/20/39)

7976. Shaw, James m 11/20/42 Mary Tisdale in Carroll; Rev. Hibbard (4-11/24)
7977. Shaw, John (Com.), 50, of the U.S. Navy d 9/10/23 in Philadelphia (PA?)
       (3-10/1)
7978. Shaw, M. H., M.D., of Carroll m 11/17/40 Almira Richmond of Sinclairville
       in S; Rev. J. S. Emory (4-11/25)
7979. Shaw, Warner D., merchant, of Fluvanna m 6/16/33 Lucina Runnyan of
       Ellery in E; William H. Fenton, Esq. (4-7/3)
7980. Shaw, William, 17, s of Thomas, d 7/26/43 in Westfield (4-8/10)
7981. Shay, Asa (Rev.), pastor of the Baptist Church in Manchester, m Lucy
       Baker in Hopewell; Rev. Elder Brown (3-2/21/27)
7982. Shays, Daniel, 84, d 11/19/25 in Sparta, Liv. Co. ("an officer in the
       Revolution and subsequently the leader of a party in Massachusetts
       called 'Shay's Men'") (3-12/19)
7983. Shear, Blaker L. of Floyd, Oneida Co. m 1/11/44 Phebe Ann Eastwood of
       Macedon in Palmyra (5-1/17)
7984. Shearman, Abraham, Jr. m 1/1/41 Mariette Tallman of Harmony in H;
       M. Norton, Esq. (4-1/13)
7985. Shearman, Alden, late of Busti, d 12/20/41 at his home in Youngsville
       (4-12/30)
7986. Shearman, Daniel, Esq., 49, late sheriff of Chautauqua Co., d 4/11/34
       in Busti (4-4/16)
7987. Shearman, David, merchant, of Stockton, m 10/5/30 Melinda Hanchett of
       Chautauqua in C; Rev. O. C. Beardsley (a double ceremony - see the
       marr. of Hiram Whitman - the females are twin sisters, daughters of
       Zacheus Hanchett of Chautauqua) (4-10/13)
7988. Shearman, Gideon m Mercy Eddy in Palmyra (3-1/17/16)
7989. Shearman, Humphrey (Dr.) m 2/11/45 Maria Therza Eaton, dau of S. Eaton,
       M.D., in Irving, NY; Rev. Campbell (4-2/21)
7990. Shearman, Humphrey G. of Jamestown m 5/3/35? Caroline M. Fenton, dau of
       William H. of Fluvanna, in F; Elder E. Beardsley (4-5/6)
7991. Shearman, Jesse m Eunice Williams in Ovid; Rev. Porter (3-11/25/18)
7992. Shearman, Joseph Osgood, 1 yr, s of Loring, d 7/18/26 in Jamestown
       (4-7/19)
7993. Shearman, Myron, 26, d 8/5/43 in Westfield (4-8/24)
7994. Shearman, Robert, merchant, of Penn Yan m 1/6/19 Eliza Kidder in Benton;
       A. Wagner, Esq. (3-1/20)
7995. Shearman, Samuel, 65, d in Milo (3-12/28/25)
7996. Shearman, William Pitt, merchant, of Rochester, formerly of Utica "to
       which place his remains were removed and interred", d 9/9/24 in NYC
       (3-9/22)
7997. Shears, Martha, 19, wf of John and dau of Benjamin Runyan of Jamestown,
       d 2/28/41 in Mayville (4-3/3)
7998. Shears, Platt m 9/29/41 Caroline Runyan in Jamestown; Rev. Dodge
       (4-10/7)
7999. Shears, Spencer of Erie, PA m Minerva Bugbee of Stockton in Gerry; Rev.
       H. Smith (See also the marr. of Israel M. Strong) (4-4/19/44)
8000. Sheather, John (Capt.), 84, d 6/19/35 in Geneva (a Rev. officer) (5-6/26)
8001. Sheats, Joseph of Erie, PA m 9/17/34 Eveline Rawson of Walworth in W;
       Rev. Joseph Gould (5-9/19)
8002. Sheffield, John of Buffalo m 3/30/32 Mary Pratt of Williamson in W;
       Rev. Fairbank (a double ceremony - see the marr. of Major Sanford)
       (5-4/4)
8003. Sheffield, Mary, wf of Nathan, (age blurred), d 8/24/20 in Penfield
       (5-8/30)
8004. Sheffield, Nathan M. m 12/31/29 Maria Stalp in Pulteneyville; George
       D. Phelps, Esq. (5-1/8/30 and 3-1/13/30)
8005. Sheffield, Paul, 75, d 3/24/37 in Macedon (a Rev. soldier; formerly of
       Groton, CT; emigrated to the Macedon area in 1818) (5-3/31)
8006. Shekell, Ann, nearly 80, wid of late Capt. Samuel, formerly of Prince
       George's Co., MD, d 7/17/29 in Phelps, NY (3-7/22 and 5-7/31)
8007. Shekell, Cephas, merchant, of Waterloo m 12/31/18 Matilda Warner, dau of
       late Maj. Solomon, in Seneca; Rev. Axtell (3-1/6/19)
8008. Shekell, Horace m 9/25/19 Content E. Standisn in Waterloo; G. Wells, Esq.
       (3-10/20)
8009. Shekell, John of Phelps m 2/7/16 Betsey Russell in Junius; Rev. Wells
       (3-2/14)

8010.  Shekell, John, "an aged inhabitant of Sulphur Springs" in Manchester, NY
       and native of Frederick County, MD, d 3/4/23 at Sulphur Springs
       (3-3/19)
8011.  Shekell, John, 54, d 7/5/29 in Manchester (Sulphur Springs) (5-7/17 and
       3-7/22)
8012.  Shekell, Samuel, 5, s of Cephas, d 9/26/24 (prob. in Geneva) (3-9/29)
8013.  Shekell, Samuel (Capt.), 78, formerly of Prince George's County, MD,
       d 10/14/26 at his home in Phelps (3-10/25)
8014.  Sheldon, Benjamin F. of Phelps m 10/8/15 Charlotte Patton of Lyons in L
       (3-10/18)
8015.  Sheldon, Benjamin, Jr. m 1/23/23 Minerva Cooley in Canandaigua (3-2/5)
8016.  Sheldon, George A. m 12/31/40 Margery Sample, dau of John, Esq., in
       Randolph; G. A. Bush, Esq. (4-1/13/41)
8017.  Sheldon, Henry B., 17, s of Wareham, d 1/1/28 in Port Bay, Wayne Co.
       ("The editor of the Albany Argus is requested to insert the above")
       (3-1/23)
8018.  Sheldon, John P., one of the editors of the Detroit Gazette, m Eliza
       Whiting in Rochester, NY (3-11/11/18)
8019.  Sheldon, M. Luther of Cincinnati, Ohio m 5/30/44 Cynthia Electa Spencer
       of Jamestown in Utica; Rev. Theodore Spencer (4-6/7)
8020.  Sheldon, Margaret (Mrs.), about 30, d 3/9/29 in Port Bay (5-3/27)
8021.  Sheldon, Samuel of Palmyra m 2/26/29 Elvira Brown of Newark, NY in Lyons;
       Rev. Roe (5-3/13 and 3-3/18)
8022.  Sheldon, T. S., merchant, m 5/2/39 B. Rosetta Crowley, only dau of Walter,
       Esq., in Randolph; Rev. A. Frink (4-5/8)
8023.  Shelly, Thomas of Galen m 1/19/17 Sarah Miller of Seneca; John Freligh,
       Esq. (3-1/22)
8024.  Shepard, ____, inf s of Henry, d 7/25/26 (3-8/2)
8025.  Shepard, D. A. (Rev.) of Owego m Maria R. Robie in Westmoreland, Oneida
       Co. (3-11/26/28)
8026.  Shepard, Daniel, Esq., 48, attorney, d 9/22/19 in Aurora (3-10/6)
8027.  Shepard, Eltzur W. m 2/19/27 Mary Brundage in Ithaca; Rev. Phinney
       (3-2/28)
8028.  Shepard, Erastus of Ithaca m 12/5/17 Eliza M. Carpenter, dau of Gen. (3-12/17)
       M. Carpenter of Elmira, in E (Erastus a printer of the American Journal)
8029.  Shepard, Henry of Dansville m 1/6/25 Catharine Faulkner, dau of William
       of Geneva, in G; Rev. Dr. Axtell (3-1/12/25)
8030.  Shepard, Henry m 10/24/27 Mary Watson, wid of late Samuel, in Geneva;
       Rev. Dr. Axtell (3-10/31)
8031.  Shepard, Irene, 62, mother of Fitch, d 12/5/34 in Jamestown "while on a
       visit with her son having intended to return to her friends in
       Albany" (member of Bapt. Church) (4-12/10)
8032.  Shepard, John, merchant, of Scottsburgh, Liv. Co. m 11/6/46 Lydia Ann
       Blake of Batavia in B; Rev. John Parker (1-11/10)
8033.  Shepard, Joshua, 50, d 9/12/29 in Dansville (3-9/23)
8034.  Shepard, Nathaniel, 58, d in Bloomfield (3-4/15/29)
8035.  Shepard, William (Maj.), 62, d 7/13/23 in Canandaigua (3-7/16)
8036.  Shepardson, Ezra, Esq., 38, postmaster of Palmyra, d 8/31/19 in P
       (surv by wf and children) (5-9/1 and 3-9/8)
8037.  Shepardson, Zebediah of Starkey m Joannah Sayres in Seneca Falls
       (3-4/29/29)
8038.  Shepherd, Alexander H. m 7/8/32 Eliza Van Deusen, both of Ashville, in
       Busti; Josiah Palmeter, Esq. (4-7/11)
8039.  Shepherd, Delia Maria, wf of Fitch and dau of late Paul Dennis, Esq.
       of Washington Co., d 3/15/43 in NYC (4-4/6)
8040.  Shepherd, Niram (sic) m 12/11/25 Eliza Sherwood in Lyons (3-12/21)
8041.  Shepherd, William (Gen.), 81, a Rev. officer and for many years a
       member of Congress, d 11/16/17 in Westfield, MA (3-12/10 and 5-12/10)
       Deathplace listed as Westfield, CT in 3-12/10)
8042.  Shepard, Ezra of Cohocton m Sally Lovejoy of Benton in B; Abner
       Woodworth, Esq. (3-9/15/19)
8043.  Sheppard, John S., 21, s of Morris F., Esq., d 3/2/28 in Penn Yan
       (Joined Presby. Church "about three years ago") (3-3/5)
8044.  Sheppard, Morris P. (Hon.), 72, d 11/18/46 in Penn Yan (2-12/2)
8045.  Sheridan, Daniel, Jr. m Elizabeth Frantz, both of Fayette, in Canoga
       (3-12/9/29)

Sherman. See also Shearman.
8046. Sherman, _____ (Mr.) of Farmington, "lately from Dutchess Co. committed suicide July 16 by hanging himself ... in his barn - (from the Ontario Repository) (5-7/18/34)
8047. Sherman _____, about 3, s of Loring, d in Jamestown (4-3/4/35)
8048. Sherman, Albert H., 1 yr, s of Durfee A. and Susannah H., d 9/4/39 in East Palmyra (5-9/13)
8049. Sherman, Amanda (Miss), 17, sister of Mrs. Gibson of Canandaigua, d in Utica (5-8/29/21)
8050. Sherman, Augustus, 1 yr, s of Alanson, d 3/4/32 in Palmyra (5-3/6)
8051. Sherman, Bradley of Angelica m 10/6/46 Adelia Brown of Bath in B; Rev. Corson (2-10/7)
8052. Sherman, Charles B. m 9/16/29 Lucinda Allen in Rose; E. Flint, Esq. All of Rose (5-9/25 and 3-9/30)
8053. Sherman, David, 16, m Parmelia Reeves, 15, in Palmyra (5-3/17 and 3-3/24)
8054. Sherman, David H. of Palmyra m 1/14/30 Mrs. Valina Marsh of Phelps in P; Rev. Bagley (5-1/22 and 3-1/27)
8055. Sherman, Durfee A. m 2/9/37 Susan H. Fish of Pulteneyville in P; Rev. T. J. Carlton (5-2/17)
8056. Sherman, Francis, 45, d 3/7/46 in Urbana (surv by wf "and a large family") (2-3/11)
8057. Sherman, Gilbert of Arcadia m 1/27/36 Hannah Rowley of Palmyra (5-2/5)
8058. Sherman, Henry, 24, of the firm of Sherman and Townsend d 4/15/21 in NYC (5-4/25)
8059. Sherman, J. Nelson of Palmyra m 4/22/40 Harriet Myres of Lyons in L: Rev. Hall (5-4/29)
8060. Sherman, Jacob m Sarah Lawton in Palmyra (3-10/3/27)
8061. Sherman, John, 56, d 8/2/28 in Trenton Falls, NY, a hotel-keeper there (3-8/13)
8062. Sherman, John, Jr. m 5/14/18 Patience Terry, both of Palmyra (5-5/26)
8063. Sherman, John W. m Rebecca Magee, dau of Thomas C., Esq., in Junius (3-9/19/27)
8064. Sherman, John W. m 4/26/31 Jerusha L. Pratt, both of Williamson, in W; Rev. John Parker (5-4/29)
8065. Sherman, John Warren, 14 mo, s of Silas, d 9/19/34 (4-9/24)
8066. Sherman, Mary (Miss), 77, d in Milo (3-10/15/28)
8067. Sherman, Merritt m 12/23/19 Emily Rich, both age 19, in Palmyra (5-2/9/20)
8068. Sherman, Nelson m 1/24/33 Temperance Goldsmith, both of Palmyra, in Newark, NY (5-1/30)
8069. Sherman, Phineas L. of Palmyra m 8/17/30 Eveline Robinson of Plainfield, Otsego Co., in P (5-9/3)
8070. Sherman, Rhodes H. m 7/4/40 Elizabeth Craig, both of Palmyra, in P; Rev. A. H. Stowell (5-7/8)
8071. Sherman, Samuel m 11/5/20 Hannah Tiney in Palmyra (5-11/29)
8072. Sherman, Stephen, 40, d 2/28/29 in Palmyra (5-3/13)
8073. Sherman, William P. m Mariette Andrews in Rochester (3-10/6/19)
8074. Sherwin, Levi, 34, d 10/25/31 in Jamestown (4-10/26)
8075. Sherwood, Ebenezer m Amelia Barger in Friendship, Alleg. Co. (3-10/17/27)
8076. Sherwood, Elce, widow, 100, d 5/20/14 in Pompey, NY (3-6/1)
8077. Sherwood, Henry of Marcellus m 8/10/41 Sarah A. Benham of Jamestown in J: Rev. E. J. Gillett (4-8/12)
8078. Sherwood, Isaac, 70, stage proprietor and mail carrier, d 4/24/40 in Auburn (5-5/6)
8079. Sherwood, Janett (Miss) d 7/5/40 in Texas at the home of her sister, Mary Wightman, both formerly of Wayne, NY (2-9/9). Same newspaper dated 9/16: "(She) died in Wightman, Texas. The last five years of her history is identical with that of Texas... She went there at the commencement of their struggle for liberty and shared in the difficulties and dangers of those who retreated before the Mexican army."
8080. Sherwood, Jeremiah of Geneva m 2/8/18 Mary Buckley of Cayuga in C; William Sisson, Esq. (3-2/11)
8081. Sherwood, Micajah d 5/6/42 in Woodhull (2-5/11)
8082. Sherwood, Morris m Nelly Skinner in Ovid (3-1/17/16)
8083. Sherwood, William m 8/6/26 Huldah Williams in Pembroke; Reuben Palmer, Esq. (1-8/18)

8084. Shethan, John m 3/27/23 Sally Ensworth, dau of Dr. A. of Rochester, in R;
Rev. Penney (3-4/9)
8085. Shields, Mercy, wf of Cato, d in Canandaigua (3-12/8/19)
8086. Shinabarger, George m 10/1/49 Harriet Hall, both of Hornellsville, in H;
H. Bennett, Esq. (2-10/17)
8087. Shinabarger, William m 9/16/49 Phebe Coburn, both of Hernellsville, in H;
H. Bennett, Esq. (2-10/17)
8088. Shipman, D. (Dr.) m 2/21/38 Sarah C. Townsend; Rev. Platt. All of Bath
(2-2/21)
8089. Shippy, Emer (sic) m 5/13/24 Desire Griffith in Batavia; D. Tisdale, Esq.
(1-5/14)
8090. Shockey, John, 72, d 9/12/41 at his home in Elmira (2-9/22)
8091. Shocky, John L. m Betsey Laura Saunders, dau of John, in Elmira (3-11/4/29)
8092. Shoecraft, _____ m Laura Brown in Palmyra (3-12/20/15)
8093. Shoemaker, Elisha, Esq., sheriff of Tioga Co., m Catharine Floyd in
Chemung (3-2/20/28)
8094. Shoemaker, Phebe, 40, wf of Col. Elijah, d in Nichols, Tioga Co (3-8/22/27)
8095. Shoethread, Adam m 1/26/20 Eliza Nelson in Benton (3-2/9)
8096. Shook, Jacob m 8/24/43 Maria Chapman of Jamestown in J; George W. Parker,
Esq. (4-8/31)
8097. Shores, James m Henrietta Phillips in Syracuse (3-1/14/29)
8098. Short, _____ (Mrs.), consort of George, d 3/13/19 in Junius (3-3/31)
8099. Short, David, 31, d 1/19/42 in Manchester (5-1/26)
8100. Short, Leonard, 27, s of Theodore, d in Manchester (3-8/8/27)
8101. Short, Nicholas, 35, d 1/8/11 in Geneva (3-1/16)
8102. Shotwell, Nathaniel W. of Henrietta m 11/20/50 Sarah T. Brown of Pembroke
in Batavia; Rev. S. M. Stimson (1-11/26/50)
8103. Shove, Isaac m 3/26/43 Phebe Fairbanks at the home of Jesse Eddy; George W.
Cuyler, Esq. All of Palmyra (5-3/29)
8104. Showerman, _____, 10, s of John, d 9/28/24 (1-10/1)
8105. Showerman, Caty (Mrs.), 38, wf of John, d 3/8/24 in Alexander (1-3/12)
8106. Showerman, David m 11/17/25 Lovisa Bradway in Batavia; D. Tisdale, Esq.
(1-11/18)
8107. Showerman, Simeon m 1/3/25 Maria Gordon in Batavia; Eben North, Esq.
(1-1/7)
8108. Showers, Polly, 32, wf of Capt. James S. Showers, d in Newark, NY (3-5/2/27)
8109. Shriner, Cornelius m Catharine Baker in Jersey, NY (3-10/22/28)
8110. Shriner, jacob d 11/21/17 in Fayette ("his death was occasioned by a
small wound in the knee made with a carpenter's adze") (3-11/26)
8111. Shufeldt, Jeremiah m 5/17/41 Ann Edginton, both of East Palmyra, on the
"Oak Ridge" (Palmyra); Rev. B. H. Durfee of Marion "according to the
Levitical Law" (5-6/9)
8112. Shults, Addison J. m 1/1/45 Lucretia S. Havens in Bath; Elder I. Brown
(2-1/8)
8113. Shults, George m 7/16/46 Susan Cornelia Hoes, both of Prattsburgh,
Steuben Co.; Rev. A. R. Palmer of Hornellsville (2-7/22)
8114. Shults, William m Jemima Culver in Milo (3-3/12/28)
8115. Shumway, G. R. H. (Rev.), pastor of the Presby. Church of Palmyra, m
2/17/35 Emily C. Ford, dau of Hon. James of Lawrenceville, PA, in L;
Rev. E. D. Wells (5-2/20 and 2-2/25)
8116. Shumway, Leavins m Betsey Hyde in Victory (3-4/1/29)
8117. Shurtleff, J. B., editor of the Tioga County Gazette, m 5/11/31 Elizabeth
C. Taylor, dau of George W., in Wheeler; Rev. David Higgins (2-5/18)
8118. Sibley, Abbey, 37, wf of Derick, d in Rochester (3-12/26/27)
8119. Sibley, Derick, Esq. of Rochester, former editor of the Republican,
m Rachael Roberts of Ohio in Canandaigua (3-7/23/28)
8120. Sibley, Hannah, 82, mother of James, d 4/2/31 in Canandaigua (5-4/8)
8121. Sibley, Mark H., Esq. m 11/28/21 Maria G. Clark in Canandaigua; Rev.
Barlow (5-12/12)
8122. Sibley, Oscar E. m 10/7/28 Mary A. Wells, dau of Dr. R., in Canandaigua
(5-10/10 and 3-10/15)
8123. Sickles, Aaron m 9/1/36 Harriet M. Salley in Palmyra; Elder Miner
(5-9/2)
8124. Sickles, Richard m Sarah Tryon in Utica (3-1/13/30)
8125. Siggins, John m 7/4/38 Eliza Morgan of Jamestown in Youngsville; C. V.
Kinnear, Esq. (4-7/11)

206

8126. Sill, George G., Licentiate of the Presbytery of Rochester, m 9/19/24
Louisa Lord, dau of Diodate, in Sweden, NY; Rev. Darwin (1-10/8)
8127. Sill, Joseph, formerly of Black Rock, NY d in June in Jonesville, MI
(his wife died one day later) (Joseph was a member of the Presby.
Church; surv by 5 ch) (4-7/13/43)
8128. Silsbe, Edward Clark, 4, oldest s of Alfred T. and Jane, d 10/3/41 in
Avoca (2-10/13)
8129. Silsbe, John of Wayne m Mary Wright in Hammondsport (3-11/25/29)
8130. Silsbe, Sarah Jane, 2, dau of A. H., d 11/17/50 in Bath (2-11/27)
8131. Silvers, Samuel T., 24, d 12/10/22 in Junius (3-12/25)
8132. Sim, Peter, 87, d in Lansingburgh, Renss. Co. (3-6/16/19)
8133. Simmes, James m Clarissa Parker, both of Pulteney, in Bath (3-12/22/19)
8134. Simmons, Alonzo m 2/25/27 Ann Huson, dau of Nathaniel; Rev. White. All
of Starkey (3-3/7)
8135. Simmons, Calvin, 60, d 11/29/50 in Bath (2-12/4)
8136. Simmons, Jenks, Esq., 61, m 7/27/21 Mrs. Barnet, 73, in Hartland, Niag.
Co. (5-8/29)
8137. Simmons, Orson of Fredonia m 6/9/41 Maria E. Gould of Prattsburgh in P;
Rev. William Goodell of Howard (2-6/23)
8138. Simmons, T. G. of Westfield m 6/29/43 Jane Mayborn of Mayville in W;
A. L. Wells, Esq. (4-7/13)
8139. Simmons, Thomas (Elder), 104, d in Rehoboth, MA ("He supported a pulpit
until upwards of ninety ...") (3-1/5/27)
8140. Simms, Charles (Col.) d "at Alexandria, collector of that port ... since
the administration of Washington." (3-9/15/19)
8141. Simons, Elijah G. m Eliza Shaw in Benton (3-6/18/28)
8142. Simpson, _____, inf ch of Henry, d in Ovid (3-9/26/27)
8143. Simpson, Alexander d in Romulus (3-2/21/16)
8144. Simpson, Andrew, 84, (a Rev. soldier) d 8/11/45 in Jasper, Steuben Co.
(2-8/27)
8145. Simpson, Henry of Ovid m 1/26/26 Martha Seely, dau of Maj. Jonas, in
Romulus (3-2/8)
8146. Simpson, Margaret, 15, dau of George, d 10/4/28 in #9 (Seneca) (3-10/8)
8147. Simpson, Robert of Geneva m 4/17/28 Julia Ann Pow of Benton in B; Rev.
Todd (3-4/23)
8148. Simpson, Samuel, Jr. m Miss Robbins of Hector in Ovid (3-1/17/16)
8149. Singer, John Sedgfield, 8, oldest son of John and Susanna S. Singer of
Geneva, d 5/2/19 (3-5/5)
8150. Sink, Freeman of Charlotte m 12/30/37 Abigail Will of Stockton in S;
S. B. Forbush, Esq. (4-1/3/38)
8151. Sisson, _____ (Mrs.), 52, consort of George, d 8/8/11 in Benton (3-8/21)
8152. Sisson, Elisha (Capt.), 80, father of Hon. William of Lyons, d 4/23/44
in Lyons(5-5/8)
8153. Sisson, Thomas D. G., 21, s of Hon. William, d 2/16/44 in Lyons (5-2/28)
8154. Sisson, William, Esq. of Cayuga m 2/26/14 Betsey Gale of Union Village,
Cayuga Co. in U. V. (3-3/16)
8155. Siverson, William of Walworth m 9/28/36 Catherine Grove of Walworth in
Palmyra; Isaac Beecher, Esq. (5-9/30)
8156. Sizer, Asa B. (Maj.) of the 29th Regiment of U.S. Infantry in the War of
1812 d in Trenton, Oneida Co. (3-12/23/29)
8157. Skaats, Lydia Ann, 9 mo, dau of D. S., d 7/18/22 in Geneva (3-7/24)
Skidmore. See also Scidmore.
8158. Skidmore, Delia (Mrs.), dau of Timothy of Dutchess Co., d 11/10/38 in
Walworth (5-11/17)
8159. Skinner, Daniel G., Esq. m 5/20/32 Laura Glass, dau of Erastus, Esq.,
in Bath; Rev. Bostwick. All of Bath (2-5/23)
8160. Skinner, Eliza, 15, dau of Col. D. S., d 1/15/49 in Avoca (2-1/24)
8161. Skinner, Henry G. of Prattsburgh m 6/20/47 Mary Jane Waddell of Pulteney;
Rev. S. White of Pulteney (2-6/23)
8162. Skinner, Joshua G. of Ovid m Sally Blouvelt in Covert (3-2/3/19)
8163. Skinner, Thomas, 17 mo, s of T. M., editor of the Cayuga Republican,
d 10/21/22 in Auburn (3-10/30)
8164. Skinner, Thomas M., printer, of Auburn m Elizabeth Durnford of St.
George's, Bermuda in Colchster, CT (3-12/3/17)
8165. Slade, _____ (Mrs.), about 60, d 6/18/22 in Palmyra (5-6/26)

8166. Slaughter, James m 7/28/36 Elizabeth Stiles in Potter (See also this
       date the marriages of Freeman Soul and of John Griffin) (5-8/19)
8167. Slayton, Washington, s of Reuben of Dexterville, d 7/20/40 in Portsmouth,
       Ohio (4-8/5)
8168. Sleeper, Joseph A., Esq. m 5/29/46 Mary J. Townsend, only surviving
       dau of late Nathan, in Batavia; Rev. J. A. Bolles (1-6/2)
8169. Sleeper, Reuben (Col.) m 4/3/27 Lucretia Caroline Lyman in NYC (3-4/25)
8170. Slider, Abraham m 3/25/28 Prudence Backenstose in Geneva; Rev. Dr. Adams
       (3-4/9)
8171. Sloan, Franklin, junior editor of the Erie Observer, m 4/3/45 Elizabeth
       Maria Barr of Erie at the Associate Reformed Church in Waterford;
       Rev. John J. Findly, pastor (4-4/4). Correction: Name is B. Franklin Sloan
8172. Sloan, James m 12/22/31 Diantha A. Hill in Macedon (5-12/27)
8173. Sloan, John m 10/25/15 Betsey Black, dau of Hugh, in Seneca; Rev. White
       (3-11/1)
8174. Sloan, Rachel, consort of Hon. James, d "at an advanced age" in Southport
       (3-8/13/28)
8175. Sloan, William A., 75, father of the junior editor of the Erie Observer,
       d 3/1/45 in Springfield, PA (4-3/14)
8176. Sloane, Harriet D. (Miss), 18, dau of Douglas W. formerly of Palmyra,
       d 8/12/35 in Cleveland, Ohio (5-8/21)
8177. Slocum, Abraham m Lavina Deo in Waterloo (3-7/11/27)
8178. Slocum, Edward Lloyd Garrison, 3, s of William, d 11/28/38 in Busti
       (fell into a kettle of boiling water)(4-12/5)
8179. Slocum, Joseph m 12/13/31 Hannah Davis in Macedon (5-12/27)
8180. Slossen, Belden, Esq. m Abigal Miller, dau of Maj. Fred, in Williamsville
       (3-9/17/17)
8181. Sly, Elizabeth (Miss), 21, dau of John, d 1/5/27 in Southport, Tioga Co.
       (3-1/17)
8182. Sly, George of Southport m Rachael Berry in Willardsburgh, PA (3-7/18/27)
8183. Sly, Hammond of Southport, Tioga Co. m Sally Ann Wisner, dau of Jeffrey,
*Smalley*-)   Esq., in Warwick, Orange Co. (3-11/4/29)
8184. Smead, Cornelia M., 11 mo, dau of T. H. and M. E., d 7/28/41 in Ohio
       City (2-8/11)
8185. Smead, David, 74, "brother of the editor", d 1/8/35 in Greenfield, MA
       (In 1835 Henry D. Smead was editor of the Steuben Farmers Advocate
       published in Bath, NY) (2-3/4)
8186. Smead, Henry D., printer, of Bath, Steuben Co., m Mary B. Smith of Utica
       (5-2/25/31)
8187. Smedley, Alonzo m 9/29/34 Sylvia King, both of Palmyra, in P; Rev.
       Shumway (5-10/10)
8188. Smedley, James, Esq. m 1/23/15 Ann Hastings, late of Herkimer, in
       Canandaigua (3-2/1)
8189. Smedley, Polly, 42, wf of James, Esq., d in Canadaigua (3-6/8/14)
8190. Smellagen, Jacob m 1/1/15 Nancy Cobb in Bath; Rev. D. Higgins (a double
       ceremony - see the marr. of Samuel Cobb) (3-1/18)
8191. Smelt(?), William m 10/14/41 Margaret Hortman, both of Alloway, in Palmyra;
       F. Smith, Esq. (5-10/20)
8192. Smiley, Asel m Charlotte Johnston, dau of Deacon William. All of Harmony
       (4-1/23/33)
8193. Smiley, Eunice, 31, consort of Orlando M., d 1/20/50 in Le Roy (member
       of Meth. Episc. Church; a mother) (1-2/12)
8194. Smiley, John (Hon.), about 74, d 12/30/12 in Washington, D.C. (for many
       years a congressman from PA) (3-2/3/13)
8195. Smith, _____, inf ch of Alva Smith, d 11/15/25 in Batavia (1-11/18)
8196. Smith, _____, 24, wf of Dr. R. S. Smith, d in Junius (3-10/8/28)
8197. Smith, Adoniram of Youngsville, NY m Emily Strong of Waterford, PA in W
       (4-3/16/31)
8198. Smith, Albert G. of the firm of E. F. Smith and Co., Rochester, m 5/12/30
       Julia A. Burrows of Groton, CT in G (5-5/28)
8199. Smith, Albert M., 18, s of Asa and Hannah, d 8/12/42 in Busti (4-8/18)
8200. Smith, Alfred, "late of the Chautauque Republican," m 8/26/34 Isabella
       Cooke, dau of Dr. Robert of Argyle, Wash. Co., in A (4-9/17)
8201. Smith, Alfred, 23, printer, formerly of Chautauqua Co., NY, d 9/24/37
       in Columbus, GA (was editor of the Chautauque Republican prior to age
       21; lived in Jamestown, NY for three years prior to Nov 1836; surv by
       wf (4-10/18).
*Smalley 8183a - bottom of pg. 209        208

8202. Smith, Alva P., 22, d 5/1/50 at the home of his father (name not given) in Batavia (1-5/7)
8203. Smith, Ammi C. of Walworth m 3/16/37 Lydia Eddy of Macedon; Rev. Jonathan Benson (5-3/31)
8204. Smith, Ann, 58, d 10/31/15 in Seneca (3-11/8)
8205. Smith, Anson, 12, s of Capt. S. T., d in Owego (3-8/22/27)
8206. Smith, Asa m 3/15/17 Esther Thorp in Geneva; Jacob Dox, Esq. (3-3/26)
8207. Smith, Asahel M. m 2/6/44 Betsy C. Hills; Rev. H. Smith (4-2/16)
8208. Smith, Augustus D., 21 mo, s of Jared, d 8/25/50 in Bath (2-8/28)
8209. Smith, Burrage, formerly of Rochester, d "in New Orleans" ("said to have been an active agent in Morgan's abduction") (3-9/30/29 and 5-10/2)
8210. Smith, Calvin W. (Dr.), 60, d 8/21/39 in Little Falls (4-8/28)
8211. Smith, Cassandra, about 28, d 10/15/38 in Kennedyville (2-10/24)
8212. Smith, Catharine, 83, wid of Henry, d 11/19/27 in Seneca (3-12/5)
8213. Smith, Catharine N., 6, dau of Nathaniel and Mary, d 7/24/29 in Gorham (3-8/5 and repeated 8/19)
8214. Smith, Cephas A. of Le Roy m 9/4/25 Sophia Bradley of Middlebury, dau of Rev. J. Bradley, in Middlebury; Rev. J. Bradley (1-9/9)
8215. Smith, Charles of Benton m 5/10/24 Thalia Ann Owen of Geneva; S. G. Gage, Esq. (3-5/19)
8216. Smith, Charles, 70, d in Macedon (3-12/26/27)
8217. Smith, China (Capt.), 93?, d 12/17/31 in Paris, Oneida Co. (a Rev. patriot) (5-1/24/32)
8218. Smith, Conrad m 3/13/17 Sally Smith in Seneca; Rev. Axtell (3-3/19)
8219. Smith, Cornelius V. V. of Geneva d "a few days ago" in Albany (3-5/14/17)
8220. Smith, Cyrenus m 6/27/16 Margaret Yetten in Benton (3-7/10)
8221. Smith, Cyrus of Ballston m 8/17/42 Jane Thompson Sherman of Charlton, Sara. Co. in C; Rev. Ira Chancy (5-10/5)
8222. Smith, Cyrus m 8/3/43 Harriet Allen in Harmony; D. Williams, Esq. (4-8/31)
8223. Smith, Daniel, 20, d in Bath (3-10/6/19)
8224. Smith, Daniel m 11/3/20 Betsey Puffer in Farmington; Rev. H. B. Powell (5-12/6)
8225. Smith, Daniel C., 26, d 1/8/46 in Bath (See death of his dau Fidelia 1/2/46) (2-1/21)
8226. Smith, David, 85, d 2/1/16 near Geneva (among the first settlers "in the Genesee Country where he has resided for the last 24 years") (3-2/21)
8227. Smith, David m Mary Barnes in Benton; Rev. Williams. All of Benton (3-1/30/22)
8228. Smith, David, Esq., merchant, of New Orleans "and brother of the Rev. Mr. Smith of Batavia", d 10/31/25 in New Orleans (LA?) (1-12/9)
8229. Smith, David of Palmyra m 4/5/29 Eliza Howe of Port Gibson in P. G. (5-4/24 and 3-5/6)
8230. Smith, David m Keziah Blowers in Ellery; R. Pier, Esq. (4-9/16/35)
8231. Smith, David, 3 yrs, s of Orrin, d 5/17/42 in Bath (2-5/18)
8232. Smith, David M. of Hector m 1/12/22 Emeline Rowland of Seneca in Geneva; Rev. Axtell (3-1/16)
8233. Smith, Denison (Rev.) m 7/27/23 Louisa Hawks in Phelps; Rev. Alverson. All of Phelps (3-8/13) (Louisa is dau of Maj. E. Hawks)
8234. Smith, Ebenezer, 86, d 3/17/44 in Arcadia (a Rev. soldier) (5-3/27)
8235. Smith, Edward C., inf s of Albert and Elizabeth, d 5/25/31 in Batavia (1-5/27)
8236. Smith, Egbert, 17 mo, s of Orrin, d 2/28/42 in Bath (2-3/2)
8237. Smith, Electa (Miss), 20, d 10/27/38 in Kennedyville (2-11/14)
8238. Smith, Elizabeth, consort of Hon. Peter, of Madison Co. d in Utica (3-9/9/18)
8239. Smith, Elizabeth (Mrs.), 99, d 10/12/18 in Albany (3-10/21)
8240. Smith, Elizabeth (Mrs.), 76, d 9/27/28 (3-10/1)
8241. Smith, Elizabeth (Mrs.), 36, d in Wheeler (3-10/8/28)
8242. Smith, Elizabeth, 29, wf of late Jarvis I., Esq., d 6/23/29 in Geneva (funeral in Episc. Ch.; surv by 5 young ch) (3-6/24)
8243. Smith, Elizabeth (Mrs.), 53, mother of Frederick Ward of Bath, d 8/28/50 in Owego (2-9/4)
8244. Smith, Ezra m 1/21/29 Hannah Peck, both of Jamestown, in J; Rev. Eddy (4-1/28)
* 8183 a  Smalley, Chilion m 12/6/15 Catharine Smalley in Romulus (3-12/20)

8245. Smith, Fidelia, 6 mo, dau of Daniel C., d 1/2/46 in Bath (See his death 1/8/46) (2-1/21)
8246. Smith, Frederick M. of Palmyra m 10/31/42 Delia F. McKnight, youngest dau of Judge McKnight of Watertown, Jeff. Co., in W; Rev. J. Fish (5-11/9)
8247. Smith, Freeman, 31, formerly of Ontario, NY, d 6/13/39 in Detroit (MI?) (5-8/2)
8248. Smith, George m 10/14/35 Sophia Hoffman in Rochester; Rev. Whitehouse (5-10/23)
8249. Smith, George, 24, d 2/13/43 in Jamestown (4-2/16)
8250. Smith, George, 2 yrs, youngest s of Rev. H., d 10/7/43 in Ellery (4-10/12)
8251. Smith, Gilbert D. (Maj.) m 9/30/44 Charlotte Hazeltine in Jamestown; Rev. O. Street. All of Jamestown (4-10/4)
8252. Smith, Griffin of Bath m 2/13/31 Elizabeth Fluent of Canisteo in C; Rev. J. Powers (2-2/16). Notice repeated 3/3.
8253. Smith, Hannah, 64, wf of Joseph, d 5/10/41 in Bath (2-5/26)
8254. Smith, Hannah, 51, wf of Ava, d 9/9/42 in Busti (4-9/29)
8255. Smith, Hannah Catherine, 30, wf of Lucius A. and dau of late Jacob S. Otto, Esq., d 5/15/47 in Batavia (1-5/18)
8256. Smith, Harvey, 26, d in Southport (3-2/13/28)
8257. Smith, Harvey A. m 9/25/44 Mary Broadhead of Busti in B; Prof. Clark of Allegany College (4-9/27)
8258. Smith, Henrietta, wf of Cephas, late of Palmyra, d 5/1/43 in Newport, Herk. Co. (5-5/10)
8259. Smith, Henry, father of William and Leonard, d 7/29/20 in Seneca (3-8/2). Henry died at age 92.
8260. Smith, Henry (Rev.), pastor of the Presby. Church of Camden, NY, d 7/19/28 in Camden (3-7/30)
8261. Smith, Henry of Oakfield m 12/5/50 Caroline A. Ballou of Barre in Batavia; Rev. S. M. Stimson (a double ceremony - see the marr. of S. C. Herrick) (1-12/10)
8262. Smith, Hervey of Seneca m Mary Risley in Junius (3-11/19/28)
8263. Smith, Hiram B. of Royalton, Niag. Co. m Betsey Peck of Phelps in P; W. Sisson, Esq. (3-4/23/23)
8264. Smith, Howell (Rev.) of Penn Yan m 12/12/48 Frances De Golia of Prattsburgh in P; Rev. Purington (2-12/27)
8265. Smith, Ira m Jane Simpson in Troupsburgh (3-10/16/22)
8266. Smith, Ira H. (Dr.) of Auburn m 8/15/24 Ann Goodwin, dau of Dr. Daniel of Geneva, in G; Rev. Dr. Axtell (3-9/8)
8267. Smith, Isaac m Beula Beal in Jerusalem, NY (3-5/14/28)
8268. Smith, Isaac, 50, d 6/18/50 in Bath (2-6/26)
8269. Smith, Isaac E. m Laura Langworthy in Chatham, Columbia Co. (3-1/21/29)
8270. Smith, Isaac I. (or L.) of Walworth m 12/15/40 Charlotte Nichols of McConnellsville, Oneida Co. in Palmyra; Rev. S. Wilson (5-12/23)
8271. Smith, Isaac W. (Dr.), 58, d 3/31/42 in Lockport (5-4/13)
8272. Smith, Israel (Capt.) m 12/24/29 Hannah Heartwell in Pittsford; Rev. Mahan (5-1/1/30)
8273. Smith, Jacob of Waterloo m Sally Bigelow of Fayette in Waterloo (3-12/5/27)
8273a. Smith, Jacob m 3/11/38 Deborah Weeks, both of Palmyra; F. Smith, Esq. All of Palmyra (5-3/14)
8274. Smith, James, M.D., 74, d in NYC (Dr. Smith is son of the Hon. William Smith, formerly one of the judges of the Supreme Court of the Colony of NY) (3-5/13/12)
8275. Smith, James m Phebe Brown in Hector (3-10/8/28)
8276. Smith, James, 50, d in Ellery (4-4/20/31)
8277. Smith, James m 9/8/31 Sarah Irwin in Bath; Henry W. Rogers, Esq. (2-9/14)
8278. Smith, Jarvis L. m 7/9/16 Elizabeth Hitchcock; Rev. Clark. All of Geneva (3-7/17)
8279. Smith, Jarvis L., Esq., 38, d 1/24/29 in Geneva ("an old inhabitant") (for many years magistrate of the town of Seneca within which Geneva lies; surv by wf and 5 ch) (3-1/28 and 5-1/30)
8280. Smith, Jedediah, 66, d in Perry village, Genesee Co. (late of Cooperstown, Otsego Co.) (1-8/21/32)

8281. Smith, Job A., editor of the Elmira Gazette, m Susan Fulton of Orange Co. in Elmira; Rev. Barton (3-12/2/29)
8282. Smith, Joel, 79?, d 6/3/29 in Evans Mills, Jeff. Co. (a Rev. patriot) (5-6/26)
8283. Smith, John (Gen.), 60, late senator from NY in Congress and Marshal of this district, d 6/25/16 in Mastic, L.I., NY (3-7/10)
8284. Smith, John, Esq., 50, d 4/26/17 in Groveland, Ont. Co. ("an old settler there") (3-5/21)
8285. Smith, John (Rev.), 68, d 5/20/17 in Newtown, Tioga Co. (3-6/4)
8286. Smith, John m "Miss Burt" in Ovid (3-3/17/19)
8287. Smith, John of Ontario, NY m Amanda Flint in Palmyra (3-7/9/28)
8288. Smith, John, Jr. (Maj.), 40, a native of Gloucester, MA and "for several years past" a resident of Geneva, NY, d 1/4/28 in Geneva (surv by wf and 4 young ch) (3-1/9)
8289. Smith, John, Jr. of Marion m 6/17/30 Ann Johnson of Williamson in W; D. Grandin, Esq. (5-6/25)
8290. Smith, John L. (Capt.) m 3/4/47 Lois M. Legro in Bath; Rev. Sawyer. All of Bath (2-3/10)
8291. Smith, Jonathan, 50, m 6/29/20 Mrs. Elizabeth Olmsted, 70, in Penfield (5-7/12)
8292. Smith, Jonathan, Esq., 64, d 10/16/30 in Farmington ("one of the first settlers of this part of the country") (5-11/12)
8293. Smith, Jonathan, Jr. m 10/29/35 Lorinda De Mott of Gerry in Sinclairville; W. B. Plato, Esq. (4-11/18)
8294. Smith, Joseph G., 26, d 10/8/40 in Bath (2-10/14)
8295. Smith, Joshua, 89, (a Rev. soldier) d 2/7/49 at the home of his son, John, in Oakfield (1-2/13)
8296. Smith, Junius Augustus, 15 mo, s of Junius A., Esq., d 8/27/48 in Batavia (1-8/29)
8297. Smith, Justice M. of Painted Post m 1/20/46 Rebecca Y. Davis of Hornellsville in H; Rev. F. Lilly (2-1/28)
8298. Smith, Laura, 30, d at the home of Chauncey Metcalf, Esq. in Geneseo (1-10/29/44)
8299. Smith, Leonard of Seneca m 10/20/25 Ann Simmons of Phelps in P; Rev. Axtell (3-10/26)
8300. Smith, Leonard d 12/10/25 in "No. 9" (Geneva area) (3-12/21). Correction in same newspaper dated 12/28: Died at age 23; given name should read Silas, not Leonard.
8301. Smith, Letetia, 19, wf of Isaiah, d 6/19/16 in Romulus (3-6/26)
8302. Smith, Lucius A. m 1/14/45 Hannah C. Otto, dau of late Jacob S., Esq.; Rev. Sunderland (1-1/21)
8303. Smith, Lysander C., 30, d 5/1/43 (5-5/3)
8304. Smith, Martha, 5, dau of J. P., d 4/20/26 in Batavia (1-4/21)
8305. Smith, Mrs. Mary, 78, formerly of Barre, Worcester Co., MA and consort of Stephen, d 8/31/42 in Bath, NY (2-9/7)
8306. Smith, Mason m 11/8/32 Hannah Watson in Batavia; C. M. Russell, Esq. (1-11/13)
8307. Smith, Melancton (Col.), 38, late of the 29th Regiment of the U.S. Infantry, d 8/28/18 in Plattsburgh, Clinton Co. (3-9/16 and 5-9/22)
8308. Smith, Melancton S. m Prua Hanford in Rochester (3-12/30/18)
8309. Smith, Melancton, Esq., merchant, d 7/23/29 in Rochester (an officer in the War of 1812) (3-7/29)
8310. Smith, Minard (deaf and dumb), formerly of Hector, Tompkins Co., m 4/5/35 Hannah Brunk of Walworth in W. (5-4/17)
8311. Smith, Moses m 4/4/32 Lanah Ann Broat in Bath; H. W. Rogers, Esq (2-4/11)
8312. Smith, Nancy (Miss), 35, sister of Mrs. Nicholas Ayrault, d 8/10/26 in Geneva (3-8/16)
8313. Smith, Nathan, Jr. d 5/3/25 in Lyons (3-5/11)
8314. Smith, Nathan T., merchant, of Batavia m 7/28/48 Loraine Dygert of Detroit, MI in D; Rev. Samuel Haskell (1-8/8)
8315. Smith, Peter, 52, d in Milo (3-11/18/29)
8316. Smith, Phelps of Rochester m "Miss Eddy Vosburgh" of Penfield in P (3-5/24/20)
8317. Smith, Phidelia, 21, dau of Edward, d 5/10/40 in Bath (2-5/13)

211

8318. Smith, R. G. m Susan M. Tompkins, dau of the late Governor, in NYC
      (3-12/9/29)
8319. Smith, Ralph of Ovid m Eliza Ann Banker in Hector (3-12/23/29)
8320. Smith, Ransom m 3/26/20 Ruth Gannett in Palmyra; Abraham Spear, Esq.
      (5-4/5)
8321. Smith, Ransom J. m 1/13/39 Lucinda Davis in Busti; Rev. Stoddard
      (4-1/24)
8322. Smith, Reeder of Geneva m 9/13/26 Aurelia Keeny of Braintrin (sic) in B;
      Rev. Loring Grant of Erie District, formerly of Geneva (3-10/4)
8323. Smith, Reuben, 56 d 4/14/35 in Bath (2-5/6)                    in B;
8324. Smith, Richard, Esq. m 7/10/41 Mrs. Kingsbury, both of Batavia/ Rev.
      J. A. Bolles, pastor of St. James Ch. (1-7/13). (St. James prob. Episc.)
8325. Smith, Robert of Palmyra m Patty Jackson of Boyle in B  (3-6/3/12)
8326. Smith, Russel M. m 1/6/29 Amelia Ann Armitage in Waterloo (3-1/21)
8327. Smith, Russel O. m 1/26/23 Abigail Mathewson in Ontario, NY; H. S.
      Moore, Esq. (5-2/5)
8328. Smith, S. Melancton, 38, merchant, d 7/25/29 in Rochester (5-7/31)
8329. Smith, Sally (age blurred - perhaps 24 or 34), wf of Farrington(?)
      d 6/7/19 in Palmyra (5-6/9)
8330. Smith, Salmon m Polly Patterson in Benton (3-12/27/15)
8331. Smith, Samuel Stanhope (Rev.), D. D., LL. D., late Pres. of Princeton
      College, d in Princeton, NJ (3-9/1/19)
8332. Smith, Sarah L., 6 mo, dau of J. L. d 4/2/22 (prob. in Geneva) (3-4/10)
8333. Smith, Sidney m 4/23/36 Catharine F. Farnham in Jamestown; Rev. Gregory.
      All of Westfield (4-4/27)
8334. Smith, Silas m Abigail Aldrich in Burt? (5-6/5/22)
8335. Smith, Silas of Manchester m 3/25/30 Julia Savage of Palmyra in P;
      William Willcox, Esq. (5-3/26)
8336. Smith, Solomon m 12/30/30 Eliza Emery in Urbana; M. Brink, Esq. (2-1/12/31)
8337. Smith, Thomas, Esq., attorney, m "last week" Sophronia Abbey in Vienna, NY
      (3-6/5/22)
8338. Smith, Thomas m 4/10/28 Betsey Coats in Hector; Rev. G. Laning (3-4/16)
8339. Smith, Thomas J. m 2/4/46 Harriet Eliza Ingall in Liberty Corners; Rev. S.
      S. Brown. All of Liberty Corners (2-2/18)
8340. Smith, Vivus W., one of the editors of the Onondaga Standard, m 2/16/31
      Clarissa Caroline Earl, dau of the Hon. J. Earl, Jr., in Onondaga;
      Rev. Beardsley (5-2/25)
8341. Smith, Waterman, 2 yrs, s of Orrin, d 3/15/32 (2-3/21)
8342. Smith, William of Seneca, a private in the NY Volunteers, d in Clarence,
      Niag. Co. (3-10/19/14)
8343. Smith, William, 24, d 3/24/43 (5-3/29)
8344. Smith, William, M.D., of Oswego, IL m 9/9/49 Rebecca P. Blood, dau of
      late Capt. Blood of Bath, in B; Rev. L. M. Miller (2-9/12)
8345. Smith, William of Troupsburgh m 8/10/50 Lucinda H. Persons of Woodhull;
      J. Ashworth (2-9/11)
8346. Smith, William B. of Palmyra m 12/5/39 Lucy Yeomans of Walworth in W;
      Rev. Shumway (5-12/13)
8347. Smith, William Henry of Rochester m 6/6/43 Sarah Ann Salard of Palmyra
      in P (5-6/7)
8348. Smith, William M. (Dr.) m 1/8/32 Mary A. Gildersleeve, both of Clyde,
      in C; Rev. Boyle (5-1/31)
8349. Smith, William R. m Jerusha Burgess in Romulus (3-1/6/30)
8350. Smith, William S. (Col.), 60, d 6/10/16 in Lebanon (3-6/26)
8351. Smolton, John m 11/9/38 Lovina Walton in Palmyra; F. Smith, Esq.
      (5-11/17)
8352. Smook, Jacob, 38, d in Waterloo (3-9/17/28)
8353. Smyth, Charles, Jr. of Rochester m 6/13/31 Catharine Colt, dau of late
      Maj. Joseph of Palmyra; Rev. B. H. Hickox (5-6/17)
8354. Snell, William m Joan Watkins in Bethany; Henry Rumsey, Esq. (1-6/28/22)
8355. Snider, Daniel m 6/7/40 Betsy Ann Southard in Howard; J. W. Whiting, Esq.
      (2-6/10)
8356. Snook, _____, about 45, wf of Matthias, d 5/11/40 in Campbell (member of
      Presby. Church) (2-5/13)
8357. Snow, _____ (Mr.) m "Mrs Thompson" in Ulysses (3-2/7/16)
8358. Snow, Sally, 24, wf of James and dau of Luther Root, d 7/3/27 inPhelps
      (3-7/4)

212

8359. Snyder, Anthony m "lately" Eliza Smith in Italy, NY; Rev. Hustead. All of Italy, NY (2-11/18/46)
8360. Snyder, Hiram m 7/1/47 Elsa A. Smith, both of Bath (2-7/14)
8361. Snyder, Joseph R., 92, d 9/9/26 in Geneva (3-9/13)
8362. Snyder, Mary, 1 yr, dau of Walling R., d 8/19/26 in Geneva (3-8/23)
8363. Sober, Martin, 19, d 10/9/41 in Bath (2-10/13)
8364. Somers, Daniel, 8, s of Jacob, d 10/11/22 in Geneva (3-10/16)
8365. Soper, Timothy, 42, d in Benton (3-9/10/28)
8366. Soul, Freeman m 7/28/36 Mariah Slaughter in Benton (See also the marriages of John Griffin and James Slaughter) (5-8/19)
8367. Soule, John m 1/7/29 Phebe Burden in Palmyra; William Willcox, Esq. (5-1/23)
8368. Soules, Rufus of Boston m 2/12/32 Ursula Turner; Hon. Byram Green (5-2/21)
8369. Southard, Henry, merchant, d 7/18/27 in Clyde (surv by wf and 7 ch) (3-7/25)
Southerland. See also Sutherland.
8370. Southerland, David, Esq., 71, (a Rev. soldier "who has filled several important offices",d in Benton (3-10/15/28). Earlier (10/8) this newspaper had reported the death place as Middlesex.
8371. Southerland, Isaac, 65, d 11/19/38 at his home near the village of Batavia (2-12/12)
8372. Southerland, Lucretia (Mrs.), 56, wf of David S., d in Gorham (3-7/1/18)
8373. Southerland, Smith drowned 1/8/17 "in the inlet of Seneca Lake" (3-1/29)
8374. Southerland, William m 8/27/29 Roxana Henry, both of Geneva, at the Franklin House in Penn Yan; Abner Woodworth, Esq. (3-9/9)
8375. Southwell, Asa B. m Phoebe Ann Culver in Tyre (3-1/27/30)
8376. Southwell, John B. of Monterey m 6/13/47 Jane Goodon of Corning in C; Rev. E. Hotchkiss (2-6/30)
8377. Southwick, Chade (sic), 67, d 3/16/42 in Palmyra (5-3/23)
8378. Southwick, David of Pinegrove, PA m 7/7/33 Laura Brown of Busti in B; George Martin, Esq. (4-7/10)
8379. Southwick, Heman m Achsah Wellman in Busti (4-3/28/27)
8380. Southwick, William H., merchant, of Palmyra m 6/23/41 Henrietta A. Chapman, dau of William, Esq. of Macedon, at the Zion Church; Rev. T. S. Britton or Brittan (5-6/30)
8381. Southworth, Deborah (Miss) d 1/19/36 in Palmyra (5-1/22)
8382. Southworth, Lavina, wf of Dr. S. Southworth of Geneva and dau of Moses Van Campen, Esq., d 7/15/26 in Angelica while visiting friends there (surv by "her partner, babes, and friends") (3-8/2)
8383. Southworth, Mary, 64, wf of Eleazer, d 9/4/48 in Elba (1-9/5)
8384. Southworth, Samuel (Dr.) m 10/2/26 Mrs. Clarissa Rice, wid of late Joel, in Geneva; Rev. Dr. Axtell (3-10/4)
8385. Sowles, Charles E., Esq. of East Hamburg, Erie Co. m 9/13/48 Elizabeth Palmer of Lockport in L; Rev. Murdoch (1-9/19)
8386. Spafford, Charles, merchant, m 12/4/25 Maria King in Onondaga (3-12/14)
8387. Spafford, Horatio Gains, Esq., about 60, d in Lansingburgh (author of the Universal Gazette) (5-8/15/32)
8388. Spafford, Samuel m 1/28/49 Jane Merrill, both of Byron, in B; Rev. Preston (1-2/13)
8389. Spafford, William m 9/9/18 Shelomy Barnet, both of Murray, Genesee Co., in M (5-9/29)
8390. Spalding, Ormond, 24, one of the editors of the Album, d 6/27/26 "in the stage while passing from Avon Springs (whither he had been for his health) to Rochester" (3-7/12/26)
8391. Spalding, Philo B. m 1/27/31 Catharine Metcalfe in Bath; Rev. D. Higgins (2-2/2)
8392. Spanbeck, Martin m Lucy Willmarth in Perinton (5-4/17/22)
8393. Spaulding, Erastus, 55, of Lockport, a member of the Society of Friends, d 7/16/30 "near Schenectady" (5-7/30)
8394. Spaulding, Harry m 2/11/24 Lucy Stocking of Byron (1-2/20)
8395. Spaulding, Thomas, formerly in the employment of A. P. Tillman in Geneva, d at Faulkner's Boarding House in NYC (3-11/21/27)
8396. Spear, Alfred m 1/21/35 Catharine Shirts, both of Lockville, in Palmyra; Rev. G. R. H. Shumway (5-1/23)

213

8397. Spear, Clarissa (Miss), 19, dau of Abraham, Esq., d 11/14/32 in Macedon (5-11/21)
8398. Spear, Erastus m Rebecca Hill in Macedon (3-6/20/27)
8399. Spear, Erastus R. m 1/24/33 Elizabeth Van Allen; Rev. Hart (5-1/30)
8400. Spear, Henry, 21, s of Isaac, d 10/26/31 in Macedon (5-11/8)
8401. Spear, Isaac, 51, d 11/8/33 in Macedon (formerly of Boston, MA) (5-11/8)
8402. Spear, Jacob, 46, d 6/3/31 in Macedon (5-6/24)
8403. Spear, Lemuel H. m 4/19/38 Matilda Hart, dau of Gen. Hart, in North Penfield; Rev. J. S. Woodward. All of North Penfield (5-4/25)
8404. Spear, Lorenzo m 1/1/29 Lydia Winslow in Macedon; Rev. Campbell. All of Macedon (5-1/2 and 3-1/14)
8405. Spear, Lorenzo of Michigan Territory, formerly of Macedon, NY, d "last week on his passage from Buffalo to Detroit"(5-8/29/34)
8406. Spear, Lucy, 6 mo, only dau of Erastus R., d 9/15/32 in Macedon (5-9/19)
8407. Spear, Philetus B. of the Hamilton Institution m 8/29/38 Esther Jackson, dau of R. C. Esq. of Palmyra, in P; Prof. G. W. Eaton (5-9/7)
8408. Spear, Rebecca, 31, wf of Erastus R., d 9/10/32 in Palmyra (5-9/12)
8409. Spear, Ruth (Mrs.), 83, d 9/7/32 in Macedon (5-9/12)
8410. Spear, Stephen of Michigan m 2/14/33 Lucinda Powel, dau of Rev. R. of Macedon, in M; Rev. J. D. Hart (5-2/20)
8411. Spear, William R. of Michigan m 2/14/3? Maria Foster, dau of Cyrus, Esq. of Palmyra; Rev. H. V. Jones (5-2/17)
8412. Spencer, _____ m Almira Fleming in Canandaigua (3-3/18/18)
8413. Spencer, Allen of Jasper m Elizabeth Strickland of Howard in H (3-1/21/29)
8414. Spencer, Ambrose, Esq. (Hon.) m "in Sept." Mrs. Norton, relict of Samuel and sister of De Witt Clinton, Esq. (3-10/25/09)
8415. Spencer, Bethiah, 40, wf of Jonathan, d in Busti (4-3/3/42)
8416. Spencer, Clement Ames, 3 mo, s of Henry and Diana, d 10/25/39 (Clement A. was the "only remaining child of the above parents") (See death of Mary Joannah 10/19/39) (5-11/1)
8417. Spencer, David D., one of the editors of the Republican Chronicle at Ithaca, m 5/5/23 Melissa Lord of Onondaga town, Ohio (3-5/14)
8418. Spencer, Elijah m "within a few days" Sally Beaumont in Snell (3-11/1/09)
8419. Spencer, Gordon m 1/23/23 Samantha Baker in Canandaigua (3-2/5)
8420. Spencer, Henry of NYC m 10/23/36 Diana Williams of Brooklyn, Ohio in B; Rev. E. Boyden (5-11/4)
8421. Spencer, Isaiah J. of Alabama, NY m 4/16/48 Amy Landon of Newstead; Rev. Smith (1-4/25)
8422. Spencer, J. S. (Rev.) of Canandaigua m Hannah Hagoffin in NYC (3-6/13/27)
8423. Spencer, John (Rev.), 68 (a Rev. soldier) d 8/25/26 (a Presbyterian clergyman; served in the Connecticut Missionary Soc., primarily in the western part of that state) (4-8/30 and 3-9/6)
8424. Spencer, Joseph (Hon.), 32, of Rochester d 5/2/23 in Albany (3-5/?)
8425. Spencer, Mary Joannah, 2 yrs, dau of Henry and Diana, d 10/19/39 in Palmyra (See death of Clement Ames Spencer 10/25) (5-10/25)
8426. Spencer, Nelson E. (Rev.) d 2/23/37 in Gambier, Ohio (principal of Senior Dept. of the Grammar School connected with Kenyon College and formerly assistant teacher in the Academy in Palmyra, NY)(5-3/17)
8427. Spencer, Thomas m Hannah W. Phelps in Canandaigua (3-3/20/16)
8428. Spicer, Thomas S. m 3/3/38 Elizabeth Crans in Bath; J. D. Higgins, Esq. All of Bath (2-3/7)
8429. Spooner, Alden, 70, d in Windsor, VT (one of the oldest printers in that state) (3-5/30/27)
8430. Spooner, Benjamin m Lucy Chase in Milo (3-11/25/29)
8431. Spooner, Isaac, 21, d in Phelps (3-12/23/18)
8432. Spooner, William, 63, d in Milo (3-8/26/29)
8433. Spoor, Abraham D., 75, d 1/26/22 (prob. in Phelps) (5-1/30)
8434. Spore, John, about 89, d ?/12/49 at his home in Italy, Yates Co. (2-7/25)
8435. Sprague, Abigail (Mrs.), 23, d in Lyons (3-10/1/28)
8436. Sprague, Charles, s of John, Esq., m 1/11/44 Maria Kendall, dau of Charles, Esq., in Bethany; Rev. Beecher. All of Bethany (1-1/16)
8437. Sprague, Daniel N., printer, of Rochester m 1/1/29 Roda Thompson of Fredonia in F (3-1/14)
8438. Sprague, David (Dr.) m Polly Raymond in Gorham (3-2/7/16). Her surname Rayment in same newspaper dated 2/14.
8439. Sprague, Jeremiah, Jr. m Precilla Ferguson in Penn Yan (3-11/25/29)

8440. Sprague, Joel m 6/6/50 Abigail Adelia Warner in Batavia; Rev. Allen
Steele (1-6/25)
8441. Sprague, Jonathan m 5/3/31 Mary Smith in Farmington (5-5/6). Same
newspaper (6/10) shows this marriage date: 5/5.
8442. Sprague, Nehemiah of Lyons m Sophia Patrick in Sullivan, Madison Co.
(3-4/1/29)
8443. Sprague, Philander m 1/9/44 Hannah T. Bristol in Pomfret; Rev. Tyler,
rector, Trinity Church, Pomfret (4-1/26)
8444. Sprague, Seth of Aurora m 12/12/33 Hannah McKillips of Wales in W; Rev.
Whalings (1-12/17)
8445. Sprague, Stephen, 16, s of John S., d 4/6/50 in Bradford (2-4/17)
8446. Springer, Israel m Nancy Lawson in Marion (3-3/12/28)
8447. Springer, Sarah, 23, wf of Richard, d 5/12/40 in Palmyra (5-5/20)
8448. Springstead, George, 67, formerly of Blooming Grove, d in Columbia Co.
(a Rev. soldier) (3-7/4/27)
8449. Springstead, Jesse m 12/16/17 Anna Smith in Geneva; Jacob Dox,Esq.
(3-12/24)
8450. Springstead, John m 3/12/29 Elizabeth Sigley, both of Geneva; Rev.
Martin of Geneva (3-3/18)
8451. Springstid, James, Sr., 73, d 1/29/13 in Benton (3-2/24)
8452. Springstid, Robert Nelson, 1 yr, s of Jonathan, d 9/16/11 in Seneca
(3-9/18)
8453. Sproule, John (Maj.) of the 2nd U.S. Infantry m 5/5/17 Eliza Cuyler,
youngest dau of late Henry, Esq., in Greenbush (3-6/11)
8454. Sprout, Hosea B. m Saloma Stanhope in Attica (1-6/17/25)
8455. Spurr, _____ (Mr.), 52, d 10/27/33 in Jamestown (4-10/30)
8456. Spurr, Lovisa, about 60, d 5/26/42 in Jamestown (4-6/2)
8457. Spurr, Merick m 3/20/42 Polly Wilcox in Cherry Creek; S. Grosvenor, Esq.
(4-3/31)
8458. Squier, _____ d 10/5/13 in Seneca (3-10/20)
8459. Squier, Maria (Miss), 19, niece of Artemus Stone, d 3/4/27 in Geneva
(3-3/7)
8460. Squier, Miles P. (Rev.) of Buffalo m 2/26/20 Catharine Seymour of Rome, NY
in R (3-3/15)
8461. Squier, Sturges m Polly Caulkins in Hopeton (3-10/21/18)
8462. Squier, Thomas, 33, carpenter, d 11/16/29 in Geneva (3-11/18)
8463. Squire, Matilda Ann, 10 mo, dau of Thomas, late of NYC, d 5/20/26 in
Geneva (3-5/24)
8464. Squire, Seth W. m 1/23/45 Catharine Allen; Rev. Vanzandt (2-1/29)
8465. Squires, Ezra S., 23, d 7/1/29 in Canandaigua (5-7/17 and 3-7/22)
8466. Squires, George W., 6, oldest s of Nathaniel and Eliza Ann, d 6/2/42
in Bath (2-6/29)
8467. Squires, Phile (sic) m 1/23/45 Harriet Davis; Rev. Vanzandt. All of
Avoca (2-1/29)
8468. Staats, Peter, merchant, m 9/27/09 Catherine Voorhees, dau of Capt.
John, in New Brunswick, NJ (3-10/25)
8469. Staats, Wealthy (Mrs.), 38, formerly of Paris, Oneida Co., d 7/6/43
in Fredonia (4-7/13)
8470. Stacy, Edwin m 6/1/43 Caroline Luce, both of Palmyra, in P; Rev. Fuller
(5-6/7)
8471. Stacy, John (Capt.) of Port Gibson m 5/21/40 Dorothy McDuffie of Palmyra;
Rev. Shumway (5-5/27)
8472. Stafford, Abraham, about 50, d 1/24/31 in Manchester (5-1/28)
8473. Stafford, Eliza, 13, dau of A. Stafford, d 12/1/21 in Farmington (5-12/5)
8474.* Stafford, George m Sarah Warren in Manchester (3-1/9/28)
8475. Stafford, Harvey G. m Eliza Booth in Starkey (3-9/19/27)
8476. Stafford, Jedediah Sanger, inf s of Spencer, Jr., d in Albany (3-3/12/28)
8477. Stafford, Job, merchant, m Amelia Gibbons, dau of late James, in Albany
(3-10/3/27)
8478. Stage, Newton m 4/7/22 Murry (sic) Peck in Lima, NY (1-4/12)
8479. Stahl, Jacob of Romulus m Rebecca Gutman in Fayette (3-1/20/30)
8480. Stanbrough, Ira m 3/9/31 Eliza K. Van Waggenen in Arcadia; Rev. Boyle
(5-3/18)
8481. Stanbury, Josiah m Phebe Cornwall, both of Lyons, in L (5-6/30/18)
8482. Stancliff, Elias, 24, d in Canandaigua (3-3/24/13)
* 8474a. Stafford, George, merchant, m 12/24/27 Charlotte H. Beddoe, dau of John,
Esq. of Eldorado, Yates Co., in Geneva; Rev. Dr. McDonald (3-1/30/28)

215

8483. Standish, D. P. m 3/26/29 Elizabeth Allen, both of Waterloo, in Vienna, NY; Rev. Strong (See also the marr. of Upton Nelson this date) (3-4/8)
8484. Stanfield?, ____, ch of Benjamin, d in Canandaigua (3-2/14/16)
8485. Stanley, ____, inf dau of Col. Asa of Canandaigua d in Sulphur Springs (3-9/10/17)
8486. Stanley, Catharine (Miss), 30, dau of Seth of Seneca, d 3/7/11 in Canandaigua (3-3/20)
8487. Stanley, Cruger, 39, s of Seth of Seneca, d in Canandaigua (3-6/14/15)
8488. Stanley, Frederick G. m Julia F. Perkins, only dau of Philetus, in Ithaca (3-10/10/27)
8489. Stanley, Helen, about 70, consort of late Deacon Seth, d 6/29/23 in Geneva (3-7/2)
8490. Stanley, John m Clarissa Beach in Mount Morris (3-5/23/27)
8491. Stanley, Jonathan, 32, "late of this county", d 8/6/17 in New Madrid, LA (3-1/28/18)
8492. Stanley, Lucius of Seneca m 5/1/17 Sally Runyan of Gorham in G (3-5/28)
8493. Stanley, Martha, 10 mo, dau of Maj. Salma, died (death date and place not given) (3-3/22/20)
8494. Stanley, Sally, 31, wf of Seth, Jr., formerly of Canandaigua, d 12/18/19 in Buffalo (3-12/29)
8495. Stanley, Sarah, about 35, wf of Maj. Salma, d 4/19/28 in Seneca (3-4/23)
8496. Stanley, Seth (Deacon), 73, d 5/5/23 in Geneva. Same newspaper dated 5/21: a native of Farmington, CT; moved to this country about 27 years ago during all which period , except one year, he resided on his farm in this town; member of Presby. Ch. (deacon) - was recording votes with pen in hand as clerk of the school district at the moment of his death (3-5/7)
8497. Stanley, Whiting D. m Maria Castle in Canandaigua (3-3/4/18)
8498. Stannard, Edward of Pavilion m 10/8/48 Eunice Kendall, dau of Charles, Esq., in Bethany (1-10/10)
8499. Staple, Emmings m 7/9/26 Susanna Hill in Alexander; Rev. N. Brown (1-7/14)
8500. Star, Anne, 58, consort of William, d 1/17/40 in Howard (2-1/22)
8501. Stark, ____, "the immortal General", d 5/8/22 at age 93 (1-5/24)
8502. Stark, Henry L. m 6/30/50 Almira Stark in Bath; Rev. B. R. Swick. All of Bath (2-7/3)
8503. Stark, Jedadiah H. m Maria Wightman in Gorham (3-9/17/28)
8504. Stark, John (Gen.), 93, "the hero of Bennington", d 5/8/22 in Manchester, NH (5-5/29)
8505. Starks, Archibald, 17, "and weighing 99 pounds" m Rhoda How, 13, "and weighing 101 pounds - total 200 pounds", in Penfield (3-3/4/18)
8506. Starks, Elijah, 36, d in Waterloo (3-3/12/28)
8507. Starks, Reed m 5/9/24 Eliza Brownell in Junius (3-5/19)
8508. Starkweather, Sarah, 23, step-dau of Deacon Julius Bartlett of Pratts- burgh, d 6/6/50 (2-7/3)
8509. Starner, John m Jane Moore in Seneca Falls (3-11/25/29)
8510. Starr, D. (Dr.) of Wisconsin m 8/15/49 Ann D. Abbott of Michigan in Howard, NY; Rev. D. M. Root (2-9/5)
8511. Starr, Elisha, one of the publishers of the Le Roy Gazette, m 10/8/29 Sarah E. Hosmer, dau of A., in Le Roy; Rev. Beardsley. All of L. R. (5-10/9 and 3-10/14)
8512. Starr, Ephraim, Esq., Deputy Comptroller of NY (state), d in Buffalo en route home from a visit in Ohio (3-8/27/28)
8513. Starrow, ____, 9 mo, s of Joseph, d 7/8/22 (3-7/17)
8514. Staughton, ____ (Rev. Dr.), formerly pastor of a Baptist church in Philadelphia and lately Pres. of Columbia College in Washington, d 12/12/29 in Washington City "while on his way to take charge of a college in Kentucky"(5-12/25)
8515. Stearns, Erasmus D. m 2/4/41 Sarah M. Cole, formerly of Palmyra, in Pulaski, Oswego Co.; Rev. William S. Bowdish (5-2/10)
8516. Stearns, Joel, Jr. (Col.), formerly of Palmyra, m 11/26/33 Mrs. C----? Hotchkiss in Vienna, NY (5-12/6)
8517. Stearns, John Calvin, 5, only s of William, d 3/18/43 in Busti (4-3/23)
8518. Stearns, Joseph H., 40, d 7/28/42 in Jamestown (4-8/4)
8519. Stearns, Marcus C. (Col.), formerly of Bath, m 3/28/42 Margaret Elizabeth Clarke of Chicago, IL in C (2-4/13)

216

8520. Stearns, Mary Ann, 35, wf of John R., d in Busti (surv by husband and 2 ch) ("Printers of Montgomery Co., NY are requested to notice the above") (4-7/28/42)
8521. Stearns, Royal (Capt.), 51, d in Gorham (3-12/26/27)
8522. Stearns, William, 59, a native of Massachusetts, d in Busti (surv by wf and 5 ch) ("Printers in Montgomery Co, NY and Worcester,Mass. will please ...") (4-6/9/42)
8523. Stebbin, Harrison P. of Batavia m 11/7/25 Roxana Loring in Bergen (1-11/11)
8524. Stebbins, Cynthia (Miss) d 10/2/18 in Ontario, NY (5-10/6)
8525. Stebbins, Horace of Middlesex m 12/26/28 Helena Lewis in Seneca (3-1/7/29)
8526. Stebins, Handy (Dr.) m 3/22/45 Watie Litle in Panama, NY; Rev. P. H. Pero (4-4/4)
8527. Steddiford, Gerard (Maj. Gen.), 68, a Rev. officer and generalof a division of NY infantry, d in NYC (3-4/19/20)
8528. Steel, Daniel, 56, late bookseller, d in Albany (3-7/23/28)
8529. Steel, George Warner, 22, s of William, Esq., d 10/10/26 in Painted Post, Steuben Co. (3-10/25)
8530. Steel, Nathaniel m Clarissa A. Gunn, dau of Linius in East Bloomfield (3-5/14/28)
8531. Steele, Harvey m 3/29/29 Anna Perkins at the Presby. Ch. in Palmyra; Rev. Campbell (5-4/3 and 3-4/8)
8532. Steele, James, 76, m Deborah Iron, 71, in Isle of Wight Co., MD (5-6/7/20)
8533. Steele, William m 11/1/30 Almira Rice in Marion; Rev. Boyle. All of Marion (5-11/19)
8534. Stephens, Alfred, 58, formerly of Tompkins Co., d 9/29/45 in Cameron (2-10/1)
8535. Stephens, Alfred Walter, 2 yrs, s of Walter, d 5/30/41 (prob. in Jamestown)(4-6/2)
8536. Stephens, Asa, 22, d 8/4/43 in Ripley (4-8/17/43)
8537. Stephens, Charles C. m 2/9/45 Martha A. Chapman in Greenwood; S. Amidon, Esq. All of Greenwood (2-2/26)
8538. Stephens, Elizabeth, 85, wf of Uriah, d 3/30/49 in Canisteo (2-6/6)
8539. Stephens, John of Canisteo m Sally Yaples in Howard (3-4/14/19)
8540. Stephens, Lawrence Lambertson, 1 yr, s of Walter and Matilda B, d 4/30/45 in Jamestown (4-5/2)
8541. Stephens, Nathan m Lucinda Bostwick in Canisteo (3-12/9/18)
8542. Stephens, Nathan of Thurston m 1/6/47 Ellen Schenck of Bath in B; Rev. L. W. Russ (2-1/13)
8543. Stephens, Rachel, 67, wf of Capt. Nathan, d 2/8/50 in Canisteo (2-2/20)
8544. Stephens, Rachel Celestia, 10, dau of Franklin D. and Sophrona, d 5/16/49 in Canisteo (2-6/6)
8545. Stephens, Samuel m Mrs. Lucy Bracy in Caroline, Tompkins Co. (3-1/14/29)
8546. Stephens, Walter m 12/9/34 Matilda Tew, both of Jamestown, in J (4-12/10)
8547. Stephenson, _____ d in Perrysburg, Catt. Co. (a Rev. soldier) (5-1/24/32)
8548. Stephenson, Almira Gertrude, 17 mo, dau of James, d 9/5/41 in Jamestown (4-9/9)
8549. Stephenson, D. D., editor of the Palmyra Freeman m 6/19/28 Maria Gibbs in Palmyra; A. R. Tiffany, Esq. (3-7/9)
8550. Sterns, Charles m 2/26/45 Elvira Jones in Jamestown; Rev. O. Street (4-2/28)
8551. Sterrett, Henry, 84, m 6/3/22 Mrs. Lany Rey, 75, "after a tedious courtship of three hours ... half way between Bath and Cohocton"; John Slack, Esq. (3-6/19)
8552. Sterrett, Henry, 87, d 8/26/22 in Bath (3-9/4)
8553. Stetler, Abraham m Susan Shepherd in Benton (3-11/5/28)
8554. Stevens, David of Pembroke m 10/25/26 Nancy Nichols of Attica in A; Rev. Cochrane (1-10/27)
8555. Stevens, Ebenezer (Maj. Gen.), 71, d 9/2/23 in Rockaway, L.I., NY "where he had gone for benefit of his health" (Lt. Col. in Rev. War) (3-9/17)
8556. Stevens, Gilbert, 12, s of Phineas, d in Canandaigua (3-12/26/27)
8557. Stevens, Horatio, 42, d 3/25/46 in Oneida Castle, NY (1-4/14)

8558. Stevens, John (Dr.) d 3/3/24 in Oak Orchard ("buried in the Masonic form") (1-3/12)
8559. Stevens, John Abbot, editor of the Genesee Messenger, m 5/16/10 Phebe Bates in Canandaigua (3-5/30)
8560. Stevens, Joseph, 77, d in Wheeler (3-1/6/30)
8561. Stevens, Mary, 60, wf of Stephen, d 1/5/30 at the Ontario Glass Factory (born in South Wales; "emigrated to this country in 1801") (3-1/20)
8562. Stevens, Phineas, Jr., 21, m 11/7/17 Rhoda Glover, 35, in Phelps (3-12/17)
8563. Stevens, Walter of Richmond, Ont. Co. m Lucy Osgood in Almond, Alleg. Co. (3-11/28/27)
8564. Stevens, Walter, about 30, s of Daniel, was accidentally killed by a rifle shot by Cabot Barlow while deer hunting in Pleasant Prairie, Wisconsin ("The parties were formerly from Chautauqua County, NY") (4-6/30/42)
8565. Stevenson, David m Phebe Allen in Howard (3-5/6/29)
8566. Stevenson, Dorothy, 76, d 8/21/28 in Seneca (3-9/3)
8567. Stevenson, Margaret (Miss), 29, dau of John, d 5/26/40 in Howard (2-5/27)
8568. Steves, Lockwood d in Ashville (4-2/28/38)
8569. Steward, Curtis P. m Eliza Mallett in Catlin (3-7/23/28)
8570. Steward, John of Harmony m 9/15/31 Joanna Glidden of Clymer in C (4-9/21)
8571. Steward, Sardius m 3/15/32 Rhoda Ward in Harmony; Elder J. S. King (4-3/21)
8572. Steward, Stephen W. m 10/4/35 Olive Dexter, both of Harmony, in H; Abner Lewis, Esq. (4-10/7)
8573. Stewart, _____, inf s of G. D. of Bethel, d 7/21/22 in Penn Yan (3-7/31)
8574. Stewart, _____, 26, wf of R. B. and dau of Thomas and Nancy Metcalfe, d 8/5/46 in Bath (member of Episc. Ch.) (2-8/12)
8575. Stewart, Andrew m Sophrona Stanley in Geneseo (3-11/17/19)
8576. Stewart, Andrew of Howard m 2/3/49 Susan Beacher of Bath in B; Rev. L. Miller (2-2/7)
8577. Stewart, Charles F. of Griswold, CT m 5/9/42 Tryphena Wall, "a Government instructress in the Choctaw nation", in Doaksville, Arkansas (4-7/28)
8578. Stewart, Charles H., 43, d 4/19/45 in Bath (2-4/23)
8579. Stewart, Edward S., Esq., attorney, 35, d 5/9/23 in Lyons (3-5/21)
8580. Stewart, Eleazer m 8/8/40 Lorinda Barton in Bath; Henry Pier, Esq. All of Bath (2-8/12)
8581. Stewart, Elizabeth, 33, wf of Samuel 3rd and dau of John and Elizabeth McElwain, d 1/8/50 in Howard (2-1/23)
8582. Stewart, Frederick m Mary Ann Besley, dau of Samuel, in NYC (3-10/7/29)
8583. Stewart, George, 54, d 6/5/41 in Howard (2-6/9)
8584. Stewart, George D., 44, formerly of Penn Yan, d 12/15/25 in Bethel (Gorham) (3-12/21)
8585. Stewart, James m Hannah Hight in Jersey, NY (3-10/28/29)
8586. Stewart, James, a native of Ireland, d 9/3/32 in Palmyra ("was supposed to be recovering (from an illness) - was imprudent in his conduct and died - neglected the directions of his physician - drank large quantities of ice water ...") (5-9/5)
8587. Stewart, James, 32, d 10/18/47 in Howard (2-10/20)
8588. Stewart, Jerusha, 38, wf of James F., d 6/22/49 in Elba (1-7/3)
8589. Stewart, John, 17, s of late John, d in Newtown (3-8/29/27)
8590. Stewart, John W. of Elba m Julia Knapp in Wallkill, Orange Co. (1-5/7/24)
8591. Stewart, Joseph, 86?, d 8/20/43 in Pulteney, Steuben Co. (a Rev. soldier) (5-9/6)
8592. Stewart, Oliver m 11/21/31 Abigail Parker, both of Bath, in B; Elder S. S. Parker (2-11/23)
8593. Stewart, Robert m 8/9/40 Fanetta Aber of Bath; J. W. Whiting, Esq. (2-8/12)
8594. Stewart, Samuel, 40, postmaster in Bethel, d in B (3-10/22/28)
8595. Stewart, Sylvanus of Cameron m Jerusha Mott at Mud Creek (3-12/9/29)
8596. Stewart, Taylor m 1/18/23 Nancy Brown in Romulus; Elder Caton (3-1/29)
8597. Stiles, _____ (Mrs.), mother of William, d in Junius (3-10/1/28)
8598. Stiles, Calvin, 16, m Roxana Chenay, 15, in Danville, VT (3-12/22/24)
8599. Stiles, John m 1/28/29 Mary Magown, dau of Philip, in Seneca Falls. All of Junius (3-2/18/29)

8600. Stiles, Loring m 8/13/16 Keziah Stout in Lyons; Rev. Riley (3-8/21)
8601. Stiles, Samuel, 55, d in Canandaigua (3-3/27/16)
8602. Still, ____, inf ch of "Mr. Still" d in Ontario, NY (5-9/6/18)
8603. Still, Calvin m 1/1/18 Deborah Shippy in Palmyra (See marr. of Ebenezer Still) (5-1/7)
8604. Still, Ebenezer m 1/1/18 Belinda Robinson in Palmyra (See marr. of Calvin Still and Miles Vanduzer this date) (5-1/7)
8605. Stillwell, Anna, 89, d in Bath (3-7/15/29)
8606. Stillwell, Hamlin m Lydia Byington in Rochester (3-1/21/29)
8607. Stillwell, Jacob of Lyons m 12/7/30 Delilah Harmon of Galen in G; William Voorhies, Esq. (5-12/10)
8608. Stillwell, Stephen m 10/26/15 Polly Swartout in Hector (3-11/15)
8609. Stilwell, Obadiah m Mary Dunn in Covert (3-5/24/20)
8610. Stimers, Frances Antoinette, o, dau of John, d 10/18/45 in Alexander
8611. Stimers, Isaac, 1 yr, s of Philip and Emeline, d in Alabama, NY (1-3/17/46)
8612. Stinsen, George of Mud Creek m 4/11/49 Catharine Johnson of Dansville in Bath; Rev. L. M. Miller (2-4/18)
8613. Stivers, Emily M., 13, d 10/3/50 in Riga (1-11/5)
8614. Stockbridge, Levi of North Hadley, MA m 1/20/41 Syrena Lamson of Jasper in J; Rev. Crissy (2-1/27)
8615. Stockholm, Andrew (Col.), 69, d in NYC (3-4/21/19)
8616. Stocking, John A. m 11/30/42 Betsy Butler in Cameron; J. S. Depuy. All of Cameron (2-12/7)
8617. Stocking, Julius m Emeline Whittlesey in Aurelius (3-1/14/29)
8618. Stockton, Isaac m 5/17/40 Fanny Goodrich in Palmyra; F. Smith, Esq. (5-5/20)
8619. Stockton, James of Vienna, NY m 4/14/16 Martha Hughs of Geneva; Rev. Hollett (3-4/17)
8620. Stoddard, Ansel A. m 9/1/44 Harriet E. Frank, dau of John, in Busti (4-9/6)
8621. Stoddard, Bethsheba, 83, wf of Silas, d 11/30/41 in Macedon (5-12/8)
8622. Stoddard, Calvin W., 35, d 11/19/36 in Macedon (5-12/2)
8623. Stoddard, E. V. m 5/9/32 Mary S. Allen, both of New London, CT, in N. L.; Rev. Judd (5-5/30)
8624. Stoddard, Messrs. Eleazer and Josiah, both 27, twin brothers of Rupert, VT, m 5/9/14 Emily and Almira Hill, both 15, twin sisters, of Moreau, Saratoga Co., NY ("The eldest brother took the youngest sister and vice versa. All four were united in one ceremony by Rev. Armstrong." Copied from the Waterford Gazette. (3-5/11)
8625. Stoddard, Henry m 7/2/18 Minerva Hayden; Rev. Townsend (5-7/7)
8626. Stoddard, Ichabod B., 77, d 2/4/26 in Bethany (a Rev. soldier) (1-3/17)
8627. Stoddard, James S. (Col.) of Macedon m 10/8/23 Hannah Hall of Palmyra in P (3-11/5)
8628. Stoddard, Oren m 9/28/42 Catharine Matilda Smith in Busti; RevI. C. Stoddard (4-9/29)
8629. Stoddard, Peter m 2/10/50 Thankful Welch, both of Wheeler, in W; A. P. Lyon, Esq. (2-2/20)
8630. Stoddard, Philip K., M.D. m 7/4/50 Sarah Jane Lewis; Rev. B. C. Smith (2-7/10)
8631. Stoddard, Richard M., 34, late of Le Roy, d 4/24/10 in NYC (3-5/16)
8632. Stoddard, Silas, 1 week, s of F. U. d 12/3/34 in Macedon (5-12/5)
8633. Stoddard, Simeon A., 45, formerly of New London, CT, d 5/10/18in Palmyra ("left a numerous and worthy family") (5-5/12 and 3-5/20)
8634. Stoddard, William, about 35 d 6/27/42 in Painted Post (2-6/29)
8635. Stone, ____ m Sarah Heacock in Canandaigua (3-9/2/18)
8636. Stone, ____, inf s of Jason H., d 9/8/31 in Kennedyville (2-9/14)
8637. Stone, Amos m 6/17/30 Hannah Carpenter in Jamestown (4-6/23)
8638. Stone, Charles V. m Nancy Wyckoff in Romulus (3-3/12/28)
8639. Stone, Charles V., 25, d 3/10/41 in Prattsburgh (2-3/17)
8640. Stone, Dolphus J. of Stafford m 7/15/49 Lorana A. Perkins of Elba in Bergen; Samuel Richmond, Esq. (1-9/4)
8641. Stone, Ebenezer G., about 26, brother of one of the editors of the New York Commercial Advertiser, d 12/11/28 at the home of his father in East Ridge, Wayne Co. (3-1/7/29 and 5-1/9/29). Ebenezer B. Stone in 5-1/9/29.

8642. Stone, Jason H. m 3/13/35 Harriet Smith in Bath; Rev. Bronson (2-3/25)
8643. Stone, Jesse m 1/1/18 Eliza Stuart, dau of Dennis, in Benton (3-1/21)
8644. Stone, John of Waterloo m Achsa Geer of Seneca (3-1/16/22)
8645. Stone, John (Rev.), "Tutor of Geneva College", m 5/2/26 Sophia Adams of
    Rochester in R; Rev. F. H. Cuming (3-5/10)
8646. Stone, John of Gorham m Martha Rogers in Canandaigua (3-12/30/29)
8647. Stone, Leicester m 12/12/24 Elizabeth Wallace in Batavia; Rev. C. Colton
    (1-12/17)
8648. Stone, Lot m Sarah Barber in Palmyra (3-1/17/16)
8649. Stone, Lot m Birenus (sic) Gannett, both of Palmyra, in P (5-7/7/18)
8650. Stone, Lott (Mr.) d 8/27/32 in Palmyra (5-8/29)
8651. Stone, Mary, 35, wf of Maj. Orange Stone, d in Brighton (3-3/10/19)
8652. Stone, Sally, 29, wf of Lott, d 12/25/17 in Ontario, NY (5-1/7/18)
8653. Stone, Samuel m Caroline Allcott in Rochester (1-5/5/26)
8654. Stone, Samuel (Capt.), 70,(served in Rev. War and War of 1812) d in
    Hector (3-10/15/28)
8655. Stone, Samuel M., 25, s of Rev. William of Sodus, d in Galen (3-11/11/18)
8656. Stone, Simon, 2nd, clerk of Monroe Co., d in Pittsford (3-7/9/28)
8657. Stoothoff, Peter B., printer, of Rochester m Julia G. Penfield in P
    (3-10/7/29)
8658. Storey, William F., 22, s of E. C. and Phila, late of Harmony,NY,
    d 10/27/38 in Wyoming, Iowa Terr. (4-1/9/39)
8659. Storms, Jeremiah m 7/30/29 Marian Peeler of Palmyra in Sodus; James
    Edwards, Esq. (5-8/7). Bride's given name is Maria in 3-8/12.
8660. Story, Asa, editor of the Lockport Journal m Minerva Davis of Cazenovia
    in C; Rev. Ira Fairbanks (3-7/9/28)
8661. Stout, Amos (Maj.), 45, d 3/5/13 (surv by wf and 6 ch) (3-3/10)
8662. Stout, Jesse L. m Olive Abbey in Richmond (3-3/12/28)
8663. Stout, Margaret, 62, consort of late Amos of Lyons, d 2/1/26 in Geneva
    (3-2/8)
8664. Stout, Simon V. W., Esq., sheriff of Wayne Co., m 4/17/43 Caroline Cole,
    both of Lyons, in Waterloo (5-4/26)
8665. Stout, Z. Barton? of Richmond, Ont. Co. m 7/21/24 Jane Caldcleugh, dau
    of Robert A., Esq. of Philadelphia, in Hamiltonville (3-8/4)
8666. Stow, Charity, 6, dau of John formerly of Busti, d in Youngsville, PA
    (4-2/6/39)
8667. Stow, John, 74, formerly of Worcester, MA, d 11/9/37 in Busti (4-11/15)
8668. Stow, Joseph, Jr., one of the publishers of the Geneva Advertiser,
    m 4/20/43 Mary Robinson Bourn?, dau of Peter, in Geneva (5-4/26)
8669. Stow, Samuel, 85, m Judith Scarborough, 23, in Kunakeet, NY (5-8/29/31)
8670. Stow, William S., Esq. of Bainbridge, Chen. Co. m 9/12/25 Maria Augusta
    De Zeng of Bainbridge in Geneva; Rev. Orin Clark (9/14)
8671. Stowell, Avery W. of Syracuse m 5/2/38 Louisa Gardner of Palmyra in P;
    Rev. Jesse Townsend (5-5/9)
8672. Stowell, Avery W., 30, formerly of Palmyra, d 7/5/44 in Syracuse (5-7/31)
8673. Strachan, Alida, 26, oldest dau of Capt. William (a Rev. soldier) d 3/26/13
    in NYC (3-4/7)
8674. Strachan, David R., one of the printers of the St. Lawrence Gazette,
    m 8/15/17 Hester Frazeer, both of Ogdensburg, St. Law. Co., in
    Ogdensburg (3-8/27)
8675. Strachen Stephen, Esq., 74, d in Virginia (3-6/16/19)
8676. Straight, _____, widow, 99, d in Canandaigua (3-3/27/11)
8677. Straight, Elijah, 71, d 9/12/47 in Avoca (member of Bapt. Ch.) (2-9/15)
8678. Straight, Enoch of Macedon m 8/30/42 Elizabeth M. Whitfield of Farmington
    in Palmyra; F. Smith, Esq. (5-8/31)
8679. Straight, Nehemiah, 70, d 11/18/40 in Walworth (5-11/25)
8680. Stranahan, Farrand, Esq., "late a senator from Otsego County", d 10/23/26
    in Cooperstown (3-11/8)
8681. Stratton, Daniel m 12/1/38 Eliza Hawkenburgh; Rev. McKenney (2-12-5)
8682. Stratton, David m 4/29/46 Esther Ann Emerson in Bath; Rev. L. W. Russ.
    All of B (2-5/5)
8683. Straw, Liberty N. m 1/29/31 Lucy Philips, both of Arcadia, in Lyons;
    William Voorhies, Esq. (5-2/4)
8684. Strawn, H. T. of Ogden, Monroe Co. m 6/6/49 Amanda E. Phillips, dau of
    Samuel of Tyrone, in T; Rev. B. Russell (2-6/13)

8685. Street, Owen (Rev.) of Jamestown m 11/29/41 Eliza H. Bolles of Brooklyn, L.I., NY in B; Rev. Dr. Spencer (4-1/6/42)
8686. Strickland, Harley m 4/18/44 Charlotte Andrew of Ontario, NY in Walworth; Rev. Young (5-4/24)
8687. Strickland, Samuel m Martha Turner in Ontario, NY (5-1/27/19 and 3-2/3/19)
8688. Strickland, Samuel of Warren, Ohio m 6/20/32 Emily Keyes of Newfane, VT in N; Rev. Charles Brown (4-7/25)
8689. Stringer, Samuel (Dr.), 85, d in Albany (3-7/23/17)
8690. Strong, Abby L., 25, wf of Hon. Theron R. of Palmyra (member of Congress) died in Palmyra (funeral at Episc. Ch., Palmyra) (5-4/29/40)
8691. Strong, Calvin m 2/2/42 Emeline O. Putnam in Bathany; S. Wakeman, Esq. All of Bethany (1-2/8)
8692. Strong, Delia, 14, youngest dau of Cyrus, Esq., d 9/12/31 in Norwich (5-9/20)
8693. Strong, Edwin, 5, s of T. C., "editor of this newspaper", d 5/28/22 in Palmyra (5-5/29)
8694. Strong, Elisha B., Esq. m Dolly Hooker in Windsor, CT (3-7/14/13)
8695. Strong, Flavilla, 26, wf of Rev. N. D. Strong, d 11/9/26 in Auburn (3-11/15)
8696. Strong, Horace m 7/23/46 Betsey Ann Calkins in Batavia; Rev. Stimson (1-7/28)
8697. Strong, Israel M. of Ellery m 3/14/44 Charity Bugbee of Stockton in Gerry; Rev. H. Smith (See marr. of Spencer Shears) (4-4/19)
8698. Strong, John, 33, d 10/12/31 in Bath (2-10/19) (5-3/10)
8699. Strong, Julia Maria, 8 mo, dau of T. R., Esq., d 3/4/37 in Palmyra/
8700. Strong, Lucius m 2/13/40 Hannah E. Fillmore in Walworth; Rev. West. All of Walworth (5-2/19)
8701. Strong, Lydia, wf of Rev. Noble D., d 6/24/21 in Homer (5-7/11)
8702. Strong, Sarah, consort of Hon. Caleb, d 2/12/17 in Northampton, MA (3-3/12)
8703. Strong, Theron R., attorney "and editor of this paper", m 6/4/33 Abby L. Hart, dau of Hon. Truman, in Zion Ch., Palmyra; Rev. Jesse Pound. All of Palmyra (5-6/5)
8704. Strong, Theron R. (Hon.) of Palmyra m 12/15/41 Cornelia Barnes, dau of Wheeler, Esq., in Oswego; Rev. Condit (5-12/22)
8705. Strong, William, Jr. m 1/6/39 Mary Ann Stetson of Jamestown in Gerry; Willard Bucklin, Esq. (4-1/9)
8706. Strunk, Anna, 36, wf of Henry, d 3/15/42 in Jamestown (4-3/24)
8707. Strunk, Elizabeth, 65, relict of Jacob, d 3/17/36 in Jamestown (4-3/23)
8708. Strunk, Elmira, 36, wf of Henry, 2nd, d 4/12/43 in Jamestown (4-4/20)
8709. Strunk, Henry m 11/16/43 Jemima Ward in Jamestown; Rev E. J. Gillett. All of Jamestown (4-11/24)
8710. Strunk, Lucinda, about 50, wf of John, Sr., d 12/23/31 in Jamestown (4-12/28)
8711. Strunk, William H. m 3/26/34 Jane Ann Van Vleck in Jamestown; Rev. Gillet (4-4/2)
8712. Stryker, Benjamin F. m 10/31/36 Jane Lewis in Wheeler; Rev. McKenney (2-12/5)
8713. Stubbs, Michael P. m Mary Ann H. Evans in Painted Post (3-1/27/19)
8714. Sturges, Daniel froze to death 2/22/11 in Pulteney, Steuben Co. (3-3/13)
8715. Sturges, Ebenezer (Capt.) m 11/3/25 Mary Howard in Livonia (3-11/16)
8716. Styles?, George of Albion m 1/8/32 Harriet Rose of Palmyra in P; F. Smith, Esq. (5-1/10)
8717. Suckley, Catharine Rutson, 57, wf of George, d 11/26/25 in NYC (buried in Rhinebeck, Dutchess Co.)
8718. Sullivan, James m 8/1/32 Freelove Johnson in Palmyra; F. Smith, Esq. (5-8/15)
8719. *Summer, Abigail, 57, wf of George P., d in Ithaca (3-5/2/27)
8720. *Summer, Darius, 59, d 6/16/45 in Ellery (4-6/20)
8721. Summers, Rezin C., 21, m 2/25/17 Lorinda Jones, 14, in Dansville (3-3/19)
8722. Sunderlin, D. of Tyrone m 1/17/41 Lydia Wolverton of Bradford in B; Elder Wall of Tyrone (2-1/27)
8723. Supplee, Achsah, 60, d in Milo (3-9/23/29)
Sutherland. See also Southerland.

*Surname perhaps Sumner

221

8724. Sutherland, Castle of Batavia m 11/11/13 Nancy Gardner of Geneva in G;
Rev. Axtell (3-11/17)
8725. Sutherland, Chauncey m 10/2/44 Margaret Gennette Briggs in Batavia; Rev.
R. L. Waite. All of Batavia (1-10/15)
8726. Sutherland, John m Orline Bell in Ovid (3-12/26/27)
8727. Sutherland, Laura, 7, dau of Isaac, Esq., d 12/16/24 in Batavia (1-12/17)
8728. Sutherland, Lemuel of Palmyra m 9/25/31 Laura Atwater of Newark, NJ in
Pittsford, NY; Rev. Laning (5-10/11)
8729. Sutherland, Reuben, 71, d 6/1/39 in Canandaigua (an early settler there)
(5-6/14)
8730. Sutherland, William D., 29, d 3/4/29 in Canandaigua (5-3/13 and 3-3/18)
8731. Sutton, Elizabeth, 10 mo, dau of William, d 12/30/22 (prob. in Geneva)
(3-1/1/23)
8732. Sutton, Jacob, 21, d 5/7/42 in Hornellsville (2-5/11)
8733. Sutton, James H. m 10/16/25 Delia Dowd in Stafford; Rev. Huxley (1-10/21)
8734. Sutton, John J., 23, printer, formerly a partner with Mr. Bennett in the
Penn Yan Democrat office, d 1/23/27 in Jerusalem, Yates Co. (a member
of the Methodist Society) (3-2/7)
8735. Sutton, Lewis, 20, d in Jerusalem, NY (3-5/14/28)
8736. Sutton, Mary, 116, of Bladen, NC (a native of Culpepper Co., VA) d 1/22/11
(had 5 sons and 7 daus "all now living"; "her descendants amount to
1492". "She has been at the births of 1121 children") (3-5/8)
8737. Sutton, Mary, 49, wf of Benjamin, d in Romulus (3-5/28/25)
8738. Suydam, Abraham m 2/4/22 Ann Duskam in Geneva; Jacob Dox, Esq. All of
Geneva (3-2/13)
8739. Swan, Henry R. m Mary H. Merrell in Utica (3-1/13/30)
8740. Swance, Ambros m 4/14/47 Grace Jones of Batavia; Rev. Babcock (1-4/20)
8741. Swart, Clarissa Marie, inf dau of Peter, d 10/13/45 in Bath (2-10/15)
8742. Swarthout, Lydia, 64, wf of Aaron, d 1/11/32 in Barrington (2-1/18)
8743. Swartout, Anthony, about 100, d 11/20/15 in Ovid (3-12/6)
8744. Swartwout, Abigail, wf of Col. Banardus, d in Hector (3-9/17/28)
8745. *Sweat, Emilous m 11/3/39 Phebe Warren in Palmyra; Frederick Smith, Esq.
(5-11/8)
8746. Sweat, Sarah M. (Mrs.), 29, wf of Jonathan and sister of Mrs. G. B.
Hulburt of Batavia, d in Ridgeway, Orleans Co. (1-1/18/48)
8747. Sweatland, Harvey, Esq., 61, d 3/24/49 in Stafford (1-4/3)
8748. Sweeney, Elizabeth, 29, consort of Col. John of Geneva and dau of Ralph
T. Wood, d 9/27/28 in Tonawanda, Niag. Co. (buried in Geneva)
(3-10/1)
8749. Sweeney, Hugh, about 45, d 2/7/23 "at the Glass Factory" (3-2/12)
8750. Sweeney, James of Buffalo m Moicah Vandercourt of Carmel, Putnam Co.
in C (3-10/16/22)
8751. Sweeney, Rufus of Palmyra m 10/17/33 Philena Wait of Marion in M; Dr.
E. W. Wright (5-10/25)
8752. Sweet, Edward A. of Urbana m 3/3/49 Meribah Gregory of Avoca in A; Rev.
H. Spencer (2-3/14)
8753. Sweet?, Henry (Col.) m Juley Baker in Sodus; Israel Arms, Esq. (5-1/3/32)
8754. Sweeting, Rufus of Paris, Oneida Co. m 4/27/35 Lucy Tucker of Walworth
in W; Rev. Turck (5-5/1)
8755. Swegles, Coe S. m 12/7/27 Polly Tucker in Hector (3-12/26)
8756. Swezey, _____, 11 mo, dau of Walter F., d 2/5/40 in Bath (2-2/12)
8757. Swick, Benjamin, 78, d 5/6/42 in Cold Spring Mills, Urbana (2-5/11)
8758. Swick, Hily Ann, 44, wf of Rev. B. R., d 4/2/50 in Bath (2-4/10)
8759. Swift, _____, (Mrs.), 35, wf of Elisha, d in Palmyra (3-2/3/13)
8760. Swift, Betsey, 27, wf of Judah, d 7/28/34 in Jamestown (4-7/30)
8761. Swift, Daniel, merchant, of Jamestown, m 9/17/33 Julia Ann Swift of
Walworth, Wayne Co. in W (4-10-2)
8762. Swift, Dean, 25, only s of Hon. Philetus, d 5/9/18 in Phelps (5-5/12).
The father is listed as Gen. Philetus in 3-5/20.
8763. Swift, Elizabeth, 36, consort of Charles, d 2/21/20 in Waterloo (3-3/1)
8764. Swift, Heman, Esq., 55, d 2/26/13 in Junius (surv by wf and children)
("Within the short span of six weeks Mrs. Blackman, Mrs. Hart, Mr.
E. Swift, and Mr. H. Swift - all brothers and sisters - have departed
this life") (3-3/10)
8765. Swift, Henry C. of Phelps m 3/17/36 Mary Swift of Waterloo in W; Rev.
J. Chase (5-3/18)

222

8766. Swift, Hetty M., 21, wf of Moses and dau of late Col. Septimus Evans,
       d 2/3/27 in Waterloo (3-2/7)
8767. Swift, James F., U.S. civil engineer, m 1/2/30 Maria Farquhar Jephson
       in NYC; Rev. George Upfold (3-1/13)
8768. Swift, John H., merchant, m 9/10/27 Mary E. Hortsen, dau of Dr. W., in
       Geneva; Rev. Dr. Clark. All of Geneva (3-9/12)
8769. Swift, Judah, merchant, of Jamestown m 10/22/33 Betsey Hyde of Richfield
       in R; Rev. Van Valkenburg (4-10/30)
8770. Swift, Judah, 35, d 8/18/41 in Jamestown (4-8/19)
8771. Swift, Lucinda, 45, wf of Reuben, Esq. of Waterloo, d 5/15/22 in
       Fairfield, CT (surv by husband and children) (3-5/29)
8772. Swift, Lyman m 11/22/24 Aurelia Wright in Batavia; D. Tisdale,Esq.
       (1-11/26)
8773. Swift, Marcus m Anna Orsburn, both of Palmyra, in P (3-6/3/12)
8774. Swift, Moses H., merchant, of Perry, Gen. Co. m 11/9/24 Hetty M. Evans,
       dau of Col. Septimus of Geneva, in Trenton, NJ (3-11/24)
8775. Swift, Philetus (Gen.) of Phelps m 11/13/23 Mrs. Fanny Swift, wid of late
       Capt. Asa R. of Palmyra, in P (3-11/26)
8776. Swift, Philetus (Gen.) d 7/24/28 in Phelps (buried in Vienna, NY)
       ("emigrated to this region above thirty years ago"; in the War of 1812
       commanded a regiment on the Niagara frontier; "has served in the
       state assembly and senate") (3-7/30)
8777. Swift, Reuben, Esq. of Waterloo, NY m 10/19/23 Mrs. Harriet Maria
       Taylor, dau of Homer Boardman, Esq. of New Milford, CT, in N. M.
       (3-11/12)
8778. Swift, Sally, consort of Gen. Philetus, d 5/9/23 in Phelps (3-5/21)
8779. Swift, Thomas Delano, 16, s of Gen. J. G., d 9/2/29 in Geneva (3-9/2)
8780. Swift, William Taylor, 8, s of Mrs. Reuben, d in Waterloo (3-9/6/26)
8781. Switzer, Elizabeth, about 72, wf of Henry, Esq., d 2/6/46 in Bradford
       (2-3/18). See his death in 8783.
8782. Switzer, George (Rev.), late of the Kentucky Annual Conference of the
       Meth. Episc. Church, m 4/13/43 Lucy Armington, dau of Benjamin, Esq.
       of Manchester, in M; Rev. W. H. Goodwin (5-4/26)
8783. Switzer, Henry, Esq., about 78, late of Bradford, Steuben Co., d 12/20/45
       in Illinois (See death of his wife Elizabeth 2/6/46) (2-3/18/46)
8784. Symms, John Cleives (Capt.), a native of NJ and an officer in the War
       of 1812, d 5/19/29 in Hamilton, Butler Co., Ohio (3-6/17). Author
       of A Theory of Open Poles and Concentric Spheres; "fought bravely
       in the Revolutionary War" (5-6/19)
8785. Symonds, Daniel, Esq., 67, d in Beverly, MA (a Rev. officer) (3-10/30/22)
8786. Symonds, Jonas (Col.), late of the 6th Infantry, d 7/15/16 in St. Louis,
       Missouri Terr. (3-8/21)
8787. Taber, Gaylord of Manchester m 4/12/31 Louisa Willcox of Palmyra in P;
       F. Smith, Esq. (5-4/15)
8788. Tabor, James m Elizabeth Applegate in Ulysses, both of Ulysses (3-7/21/19)
8789. Taft, H. N. of Lyons m 11/12/41 Mary M. Cook, dau of Capt. Halsey of Sag
       Harbor, L.I., NY; Rev. Gilder (5-12/1)
8790. Taft, James m 12/28/19 Marina Thayer in Palmyra (See marr. of Job Taft)
       (5-1/5/20 and 3-1/19/20).
8791. Taft, Job m Savannah Thayer in Palmyra (5-1/?7/19 and 3-2/3/19). See 8790.
8792. Taft, Newel m 11/15/18 Jane Sterret in Lyons; Rev. Pomeroy. All of Lyons
       (3-11/18)
8793. Taggart, Frances Alma, 23, wf of Moses, Esq. of Batavia and dau of
       Nathaniel Henshaw of Aurora, d 5/14/32 in Batavia (1-5/15)
8794. Taggart, Samuel (Rev.), 71, d 4/25/25 in Colrain, MA (for 14 yrs a member
       of Congress)(1-5/13)
8795. Talbot, Silas, Esq., late Capt. in U.S. Navy, d 6/30/13 in NYC (3-7/14)
8796. Tallmadge, Ann, 73, mother of Gen. Tallmadge, d in Poughkeepsie
       (3-7/25/27)
8797. Tallmadge, Charles Matthias, 1 yr, only s of James, Lt. Gov. of NY,
       d 9/9/26 in Poughkeepsie (3-9/20)
8798. Tallmadge, John S. (Hon.), first judge of Wayne Co., m 10/28/23 Ann
       Eliza Smith, oldest dau of Maj. Smith of Albany, in A (3-11/5)
8799. Tallmadge, John S., Esq., late first judge of Wayne Co., d 12/17/25 in
       Lyons (3-12/19)

223

8800. Tallmadge, Matthias B. (Hon.), late judge of the U.S. district court for this state, d in Poughkeepsie (3-10/20/19)

8801. Talmadge, William S. (Col.), 38, formerly of the U.S. Army, d 8/15/22 in Moscow, NY (3-8/28)

8802. Tallman, David m Miss _____ Brownson in Palmyra (3-1/17/16)

8803. Tanner, Alvenzo of Palmyra m 1/4/36 Mary Wentworth of Manchester in M (5-1/15)

8804. Tanner, Joseph G. m 6/15/47 Olive O. Seward, both of Alexander; Rev. R. L. Waite (1-6/22)

8805. Tannerill, James m 2/27/42 Altha Norton, both of Ovid, in Palmyra; Rev. K. Townsend (5-3/2)

8806. Tappan, Rachel, 3 mo, dau of William, d 5/14/21 in Geneva (3-5/16)

8807. Tappan, William, 24, d 10/2/28 in Fayette (3-10/8)

8808. Tayler, _____, consort of John, d 6/22/16 in Phelps (3-7/10)

8809. Tayler, John, 86, "a chief in the Revolution", d 3/26/29 in Palmyra (a delegate to the Provincial Congress, 1776; committee of safety, 1777; member of convention on first state constitution; state senator prior to 1813; Lt. Gov. by 1813) (5-3/27)

8810. Tayler, Sarah (Mrs.), about 25, consort of Erastus, d 5/17/10 in Gorham (surv by husband and 3 small daus) (3-5/23)

8811. Taylor, _____ (Mrs.), consort of Dr. Taylor, d in Phelps (3-1/20/13)

8812. Taylor, _____ m 1/17/22 Miss _____ Barnes, dau of Thomas (3-1/23)

8813. Taylor, Abraham, 40, d 4/12/10 in Seneca ("left a large family") (3-5/2)

8814. Taylor, Archibald, Esq. m 4/23/26 Abigail Moffitt in Orangeville; Stephen King, Esq. (1-5/5)

8815. Taylor, Charles of Seneca Falls m Margaret Pierson in Tyre (3-1/20/30)

8816. Taylor, Charles m 5/6/45 Sarah Booty; Rev. G. W. Clarke. All of Jamestown (4-5/16)

8817. Taylor, Christina, 43, consort of George W., formerly merchant of Bath,
   * d 11/12/41 in Wheeler (member of Presby. Church; a mother) (2-11/17)

8818. Taylor, Elijah m Clarissa Hartgrove in Jerusalem, NY (3-1/20/30)

8819. Taylor, Eliphalet d 9/1/30 in Canandaigua ("an old settler of that village") (5-9/3)

8820. Taylor, Elizabeth, 85 or 35, wf of G. W., d 7/5/50 in Bath (2-7/17)

8821. Taylor, Ellicott W. of Alabama, NY m 2/20/50 Sarah Norris of Batavia; Rev. C. R. Palmer (1-2/26)

8822. Taylor, Erastus, 30, d 1/6/13 in Gorham. Samuel, 53, father of Erastus, d 1/13 in Gorham. (The latter was survived by a widow and the former by "four little orphans") (3-1/27)

8823. Taylor, Evander T. of Batavia m 1/14/46 Isabel Ervin of Alabama, NY in A; Hiram Gugg(?) (1-1/20)

8824. Taylor, Giles m Anny Cook, both of Middlesex, in Palmyra (3-10/17/27)

8825. Taylor, Horace, 29, d 9/27/28 in Geneva (3-10/1)

8826. Taylor, James, Esq., attorney, m Maria Wickes in Reading (3-2/3/19)

8827. Taylor, John (Gen.) d 12/4/11 (prob. in Bath) (a Rev. patriot) (3-12/25)

8828. ** Taylor, John (Col.), formerly of Pendleton, SC, d in Cahawa, AL (5-8/29/21)

8829. Taylor, John W. Tobbitt, formerly of Canada, m Pamela McKinstry in Catharine, NY (3-6/27/27)

8830. Taylor, Jonathan m Lydia Crowell in Seneca (3-6/11/28)

8831. Taylor, Joseph m 9/10/09 Miss Percy (sic) Lawrence in Marcellus (See marr. of Phineas Taylor this date) (3-9/13)

8832. Taylor, Lucy, consort of John, d 9/19/18 in Phelps (3-9/23)

8833. Taylor, Lucy Bliss, 36, wf of Rev. Ephraim, d 10/20/41 in Longmeadow (4-11/11)

8834. Taylor, Mary, 29, d 3/25/45 in Fredonia (4-4/4)

8835. Taylor, Othniel m 6/5/14 Miranda Taylor, both of Phelps, in P; Joseph Hall, Esq. (3-6/22)

8836. Taylor, Othniel, 67, d 8/6/19 in Canandaigua (3-8/11)

8837. Taylor, Othniel J. W., 23, s of Gen. O. Taylor, d 11/20/17 in Canandaigua (suicide by taking opium) (3-12/3)

8838. Taylor, Phineas m 9/10/09 Electa L. Lawrence in Marcellus (See marr. of Joseph Taylor this date) (3-9/13)

8839. Taylor, Preserved B. m 4/18/22 Catharine Robson, both of Seneca, in S; Rev. Merrill of Gorham (3-4/24)

* 8817a. Taylor, Dorothy, 68, wid of late Gen. Othniel, d in Canandaigua(3-11/16/25)
** 8827a. Taylor, John m 11/7/16 _____ Prescott, both of Phelps, in P 3-11/13)

8840. Taylor, Stephen, Esq. of Naples, NY m 3/12/40 Mary E. Magowan of
      Jerusalem, NY; Rev. Morgan (2-3/25)
8841. Taylor, Stewart m Roxena M. Wheat, both of Phelps, in P; Elder Brown
      (3-2/6/28)
8842. Taylor, Thankful (Mrs.), 64, d 7/13/22 in Palmyra (5-7/17)
8843. Teachout, Alonzo m 6/2/40 Anna Dewey, both of Manchester, in M; Rev. K.
      Townsend ("the bride is the fourth generation now living in the same
      town") (5-6/10)
8844. Teller, J. V. C. of Massillon, Ohio m 10/12/31 Lydia Ann Shepherdson
      of Palmyra in P; Rev. Whelpley (5-10/18)
8845. Ten Broeck, Abraham (Gen.), 76, d 1/19/10 in Albany (3-1/31)
8846. Ten Broeck, Elizabeth, 78, relict of the late George Abraham of Albany,
      d 7/4/13 (3-7/28)
8847. Ten Eyck, Anthony, Esq. (Hon.), 66, of Schodack d 1/4/16 in Albany ("an
      active magistrate during the Revolution; a member of the convention
      that ratified the constitution; member of the state senate 8 years")
      (3-1/31)
8847a. Ten Eyck, Herman, merchant, m 5/8/21 Eliza Bogert, dau of H. H., Esq.,
       in Geneva; Rev. Lane of Waterloo (3-5/16)
8847b. Ten Eyck, Mary (Mrs.), 58, d in Albany (3-3/25/18)
8848. Tennery, William, 32, recently from Utica, d 2/26/19 in Geneva (3-3/3)
8849. Terrell, ____, inf ch of Miles, d 7/29/42 in Bath (2-8/31)
8850. Terry, Daniel m 8/22/35 Catharine McLaughlan, both of Urbana; William
      Hamilton, Esq. (2-8/26)
8851. Terry, George W. m 10/28/45 Emily White in Batavia; Rev. J. Parker.
      All of Batavia (1-10/28)
8852. Terry, Henry m Delpha Montgomery in Sodus; James Edwards, Esq. All of
      Sodus (5-7/30/30)
8853. Terry, Jane (Miss), 19, d 8/7/37 in Palmyra (5-8/11)
8854. Terry, Lucy, 31, wf of Constant, died (death date and place not given)
      (surv by husband and 3 young sons) (5-12/29/41)
8855. Terry, Milton of Harmony m 1/19/37 Hannah Green of Jamestown in J;
      Rev. Almond Lewis (4-1/25)
8856. Terry, Simcoe John, s of William, Esq., m 2/10/31 Elizabeth G. Talbot,
      dau of late Thomas, Esq. of London, Upper Canada, in L; Rev. Edward
      Jackes Boswell (5-4/15)
8857. Terry, Solomon m 4/30/26 Polly Smith in Orangeville; Donald A. Ward, Esq.
      (1-5/5)
8858. Terwiliger, Alexander R. m Rebekah C. Lemon; D. H. May. All of Palmyra
      (5-5/1/44)
8859. Terwilliger, Martin m 8/29/41 Sylvia Prentiss, both of Ontario, NY, in
      Pulteneyville; A. Cornwall, Esq. (a double ceremony - see marr. of
      Horton Faulkner) (5-9/8)
8860. Terwilliger, Phebe (Mrs.) d 3/2/19 in Dryden (3-3/24)
8861. Tetar, Peter B. m Ann Campbell in Independence, Alleg. Co. (3-5/14/28)
8862. Tew, Albemarle H. m 11/12/45 Susan Fletcher, dau of A., in Jamestown;
      Rev. O. Street (4-11/14)
8863. Tew, George W., Esq. m 6/4/40 Mrs. Caroline Reynolds in Chautauqua; Rev.
      Montgomery (4-6/10)
8864. Tew, Mary, 37, wf of George W., d 8/30/39 in Mayville (4-9/4)
8865. Tew, William H. of Jamestown m 4/12/29 Rhoda Burnham of Pomfret in P
      (4-4/22)
8866. Thallhimer, Margaret (Mrs.), 81, formerly of Montgomery Co., d 3/27/37
      at the home of William Woodward, Esq. in Palmyra (5-3/31)
8867. Tharp, Joseph m 10/31/47 Mary Towle in Bath; Rev. S. W. Alden. All of
      Bath (2-11/3)
8868. Thatcher, Eran, 28, d in Lodi, Erie Co. (3-1/14/29)
8869. Thatcher, Harriet, dau of Thomas, d in Williamson (3-4/30/28)
8870. Thatcher, Mowry m Melinda B. Livermore in Hornellsville; Rev. George
      Hornell (3-5/14/28)
8871. Thayer, ____, ch of "Mr. Thayer", d in Phelps (3-8/23/15)
8872. Thayer, Amasa (Mr.), 43, formerly of Palmyra, d in Waterloo (5-8/29/21)
8873. Thayer, Barack, 62, d 3/12/26 (a Rev. soldier) (1-3/17)
8874. Thayer, Charlotte Eaton, 16, dau of Levi, d 7/19/43 in Palmyra (5-7/26)
8875. Thayer, Christopher E., 4, s of "late lamented Christopher", d 3/3/43
      in Palmyra (5-3/8)

225

8876. Thayer, Clarissa, 43, consort of Levi and dau of Edward and Sibyl Selden, died (death date and place not given) (Clarissa was born in Haddam, CT in June 1787 - her parents members of the Cong'l/ Church. "While she was yet young her parents removed to Windsor (CT) where she remained until her marriage.") (5-12/3/30)
8877. Thayer, Clarissa, 4, dau of Joel, d 10/5/35 in Palmyra (5-10/9)
8878. Thayer, Christopher E. m 3/10/36 Prudence Rogers; Rev. Jesse Townsend; All of Palmyra (5-3/11)
8879. Thayer, Delia Hart, 10, only ch of Charles and Mary Ann formerly of Palmyra, d 2/1/37 in Ann Arbor, MI (5-3/3)
8880. Thayer, Elizabeth, 37, wf of Smith Thayer and oldest dau of Stephen Durfee, d 3/3/36 in Palmyra (5-3/4)
8881. Thayer, Hannah (Mrs.), 80, d 2/13/32 in Palmyra (5-2/14)
8882. Thayer, Henry, 1 yr, s of Levi, d 8/13/31 in Palmyra (5-8/16)
8883. Thayer, Hiram P. m 12/24/31 Sarah E. Williams at the Zion Church in Palmyra; Rev. B. H. Hickox (5-12/27)
8884. Thayer, Joel of Vienna, NY m Nancy Sheldon of Windsor, CT in W (3-10/29/23)
8885. Thayer, Levi, merchant, of Palmyra m 3/23/19 Clarissa Selden of Windsor, CT in Palmyra, NY (5-3/24)
8886. Thayer, Levi of Palmyra m 10/22/32 Elizabeth Selden of Middle Haddam, CT in M. H.; Rev. Bentley (5-10/31)
8887. Thayer, Levi m 8/6/34 Susan Wescott; Rev. Jesse Townsend. All of Palmyra (5-8/8)
8888. Thayer, Mary, 7, dau of Joel, Esq., d 4/22/34 in Palmyra (5-5/2)
8889. Thayer, Reuben of Cameron m 7/1/41 Julia Fife of Jasper in J; B. S. Brundage, Esq. (2-7/7)
8890. Thayer, Sally, 47, relict of Amasa formerly of Palmyra, d 5/4/33 in Palmyra (a Presbyterian) (5-5/8)
8891. Thayer, Smith m Eliza Durfee in Palmyra (3-12/10/17)
8892. Thomas, _____ (Mrs.), wf of David, d 4/9/14 in Phelps (3-4/13)
8893. Thomas, _____ (Dr.) of Ulysses m Harriet Wheeler of Ovid in O (3-1/17/16)
8894. Thomas, Ansel of Utica m Delia Burr (prob. in NYC) (3-5/9/27)
8895. Thomas, Asa, 32, d 9/19/20 in Palmyra (5-9/27)
8896. Thomas, E. H., merchant, m Susan Mills, dau of George, Esq., in Havana (3-6/24/29)
8897. Thomas, Ebon N. of Rose m 10/30/36 Lucy Ann Davis, only dau of Paul H. of Butler; Rev. McKoon (5-11/4)
8898. Thomas, Elizabeth, widow, 106, d 1/1/16 in Rowe (3-1/17/16)
8899. Thomas, Elizabeth (Mrs.), 26, d 9/16/29 in Skaneateles (3-9/30)
8900. Thomas, Emily, 15, dau of Daniel, d in Utica (3-5/23/27)
8901. Thomas, George, 18, m Maria W. Foster, 20, in Kingston, MA (3-10/3/10)
8902. Thomas, Isaiah, Esq., 82, "the patriarch of the American printers", d 4/4/31 in Worcester, MA. "He was the founder of the American Antiquarian Society." (2-4/20)
8903. Thomas, Isaiah, Jr., 44, bookseller, d 6/25/19 in Boston, MA (3-7/7)
8904. Thomas, James (Dr.) m Harriet Wheeler in Ovid (3-2/7/16)
8905. Thomas, James m 3/4/23 Mary _____, both of Fayette in F; Rev. Lacy or Lace? (3-3/12)
8906. Thomas, John (Dr.), 60, d in Poughkeepsie (3-11/11/18)
8907. Thomas, John m Catharine White in Bath (3-8/5/29)
8908. Thomas, John m 5/6/42 Caroline Hill in Bath; Rev. Isaac Platt. All of Bath (2-5/11)
8909. Thomas, Levi E. m 1/24/46 Margaret E. Willour in Bath; Rev. L. M. Miller. All of Bath (2-2/4)
8910. Thomas, Nehemiah m Letice Moore in Canisteo (3-3/17/19)
8911. Thomas, Obed S. (Capt.) m 2/15/32 Lowty Andrews, dau of Ichabod, Esq., in Reading; Rev. Eld. Martin (2-2/22)
8912. Thomas, Peter R. m 8/21/19 Hannah Wilson in Geneva; Rev. Axtell (3-9/1)
8913. Thomas, Reuben, 17, s of James, d in Canandaigua (3-10/28/29)
8914. Thomas, Solomon m 4/6/34 Margaret Wilson in Jamestown; Rev. W. R. Babcock (4-4/16)
8915. Thomas, William of Fayette m 6/14/27 Sophia Creager in Galen (3-6/27)
8916. Thomas, William, 29, d in Fayette (3-9/19/27)
8917. Thomas, William W. m 12/13/31 Maria Gilmore in Coventry, Chenango Co.; Rev. Rugar (2-1/11/32)

8918. Thompson, _____, ch of Capt. Thompson of Lewiston, d 2/4/13 in Geneva (3-2/17)
8919. Thompson, Abigail, wf of Henry, d in Owego (3-10/8/28)
8920. Thompson, Caleb m 2/22/37 Lydia S. Goddard; Rev. G. R. H. Shumway. All of Palmyra (5-2/24)
8921. Thompson, Charles (Maj. Gen.) d in Ovid (3-9/6/26)
8922. Thompson, Charles, youngest s of William, Esq., d in Ovid (3-8/13/28)
8923. Thompson, Charles B., editor of the Le Roy Gazette, m 7/8/42 Elizabeth L. Baldwin, dau of the late Frederick, Esq. of Washington, D. C., in W (1-7/12)
8924. Thompson, Christopher C. of Palmyra m 7/12/43 Caroline G. Gibson of Penfield in P; Rev. H. N. Laver (5-7/19)
8925. Thompson, Daniel,48, d 11/18/29 in Geneva (3-11/25)
8926. Thompson, Henry Allen, 6 mo, s of Allen B., d 10/9/26 in Geneva (3-10/18)
8927. Thompson, John (Col.) d in Opelousas, "N. O. Territory" (N. O. - New Orleans?) "late register and commissioner of land claims" - shot himself with a pistol (3-5/9/10)
8928. Thompson, John, printer, of Batavia m 12/15/47 Mary L. Leonard of Rochester in R; Rev. Church (1-12/21)
8929. Thompson, John, 32, d 9/6/50 in Rochester - "...was a resident (Of Batavia) and for a number of years had been employed in the office of the Spirit of the Times (1-9/10)
8930. Thompson, Jno. W. (Dr.), formerly of Bath, m 4/8/40 Cordelia Jackson. dau of Gen. D., in Burdett, Tompkins Co. All of Burdett (2-4/29/40)
8931. Thompson, Jonathan F., 37, merchant, d in Ithaca (3-1/9/28)
8932. Thompson, Lydia Selina, 28, wf of Caleb, d 6/1/41 in Palmyra (funeral at Presby. Meeting House) (5-6/2)
8933. Thompson, Mary, 84, consort of William, Esq., formerly first judge of Orange Co., d in Goshen, NY (she a member of the Episc. Church for 60 years)(3-9/5/27)
8934. Thompson, Mary Jane, 25, wf of John of Batavia, d 2/9/49 in Rochester (1-2/20)
8935. Thompson, Patrick, 48, of Poughkeepsie m Margaret Bruce, 14, in NYC (3-4/12/15)
8936. Thompson, Robert H. m Almira Carpenter, dau of Gen. M., in Elmira (3-1/6/19)
8937. Thompson, Samuel (Capt.), 60, d in Buffalo (3-11/16/25)
8938. Thompson, Samuel, 73, (a Rev. soldier) d in Bath (2-11/25/40)
8939. Thompson, Samuel R., 89, formerly a resident of Wayne Co., (a Rev. soldier) d 12/18/39 in Shelby, Orleans Co. (5-12/27)
8940. Thompson, Tallmadge m Eliza Eggleston in Middlesex (3-6/24/18)    (3-2/24)
8941. Thompson, Timothy m 2/7/19 Jane Irvine in Phelps; William Burnet, Esq./
8942. Thompson, Wheeler, Esq. m 4/3/40 Hester Ann Stryker in Wheeler; Rev. Nelson Hoag (2-4/8)
8943. Thompson, Zachariah I., 45, late of Dutchess Co., d 1/8/29 in Lyons (3-1/21)
8944. Thompsons, Smith m 2/22/31 Angelina Jordan; Elder Bigelow (2-3/2)
8945. Thomson, Elizabeth L., 31, wf of C. B., editor of the Le Roy Gazette, d 2/2/50 in Le Roy (1-2/12/50)
8946. Thorn, Eber m 2/28/30 Emily Thorp in Arcadia (5-3/5)
8947. Thorn, Stephen (Col.) of the 1st Artillery, d in Granville (3-4/7/13)
8948. Thorn, Stephen m 10/27/30 Mary Kean in Newark, NY; Rev. Benton (5-11/12)
8949. Thornton, Ezra of Meredith, Dela. Co. m Charity Runyan of Fayette in F; Joseph Pixley, Esq. (3-2/3/13)
8950. Thorp, Charles (Rev.) of the Congregational Church d in Brighton (3-9/19/27)
8951. Thorp, Daniel m 6/29/43 Priscilla Carter, both of Sugargrove, PA, in Harmony; Rev. Hinebaugh (4-7/6)
8952. Thorp, John m Mrs. Mary Ann Lewis in Alfred (3-3/11/29)
8953. Thorp, John, about 71, d 10/23/45 in Alexander (member of Episc. Church) (1-11/4)
8954. Thorp, Russell of Batavia m 5/4/48 Ann Maria Foot, dau of Charles, Esq. of Mendon, in M (1-5/9)
8955. Thorp, Thomas (Rev.) d in NYC (3-1/27/19)
8956. Thorp, William m Betsey Young in Canandaigua (3-1/16/22)
8957. Thrasher, Sally (Miss), 25, d 3/6/21 in Palmyra (5-3/21)

227

8958. Throckmorton, B. of the house of Jones, Benjamin and Co. m 2/20/40
Sarah Maria Grandin, dau of P., Esq., in NYC; Rev. Joel Parker. All
of NYC (5-3/4)

8959. Throckmorton, Sarah Maria, 23, wf of B. and dau of Philip Grandin of NYC,
d 3/28/43 in Freehold, NJ (5-4/12)

8960. Throop, Abigail H. (Mrs.), 32, wf of George B., Esq., d 2/4/25 in Batavia
(1-2/11)

8961. Throop, Benjamin (Col.), 80, d 5/16/22 in Oxford, NY (a Rev. officer
promoted from Capt. to Col.; in 1776 led a hundred warriors of the
Mohegan tribe to Canada "who chiefly fell in that unfortunate
campaign.." Fought in the Battles of Long Island, White Plains,
Saratoga, and Monmouth) (3-5/29)

8962. Throop, Benjamin, Esq., 87, d at his home in Manchester, NY (a Rev.
soldier) ("born in Lebanon, CT where he married in the May preceding
the Declaration of Independence Rachel Smith, still living") (5-1/26/42)

8963. Throop, Benjamin, Jr. (Capt.), 50, d 2/8/34 in Palmyra (5-2/14)

8964. Throop, Emily Maria, 17 mo, dau of Benjamin, d 12/21/31 in Palmyra
(5-1/3/32). Corrections in same newspaper dated 1/10/32: Emily
Maria is dau of Benjamin Jr. and age 6 mo, 14 days at time of death.

8965. Throop, Enos T., Esq. of Auburn m 7/19/14 Evelina Vredenburgh of
Skaneateles in S; Rev. W. A. Clark (3-7/27)

8966. Throop, Evaline E., 37, wf of ex-governor Enos T., d 6/28/34 in NYC
(5-7/11)

8967. Throop, George B., Esq. of Auburn m 4/10/26 Frances Hunt, dau of Montgomery
of Utica, in U; Rev. Anthon (sic) (3-5/3)

8968. Throop, Horatio N. m 7/7/34 Mary F. Ledyard, dau of Samuel L. of
Pulteneyville in P; Rev. Hurlburt (5-7/11)

8969. Throop, James m 3/7/24 Hannah Button in Pembroke; Sanford Kendrick, Esq.
(1-3/19)

8970. Throop, Jesse m Zuba Howell in Palmyra (5-3/3/19 and 3-3/10/19)

8971. Throop, Robert, (Col.), 75, d 1/14/32 in NYC (5-1/24)

8971. Throop, William H. m 11/1/43 Jane A. Granger in Palmyra; Rev. J. W.
Clark. All of Palmyra (5-11/8)

8972. Thurber, ____ (Mrs.), wf of Abner, d 9/6/35 in Erwin (2-9/9)

8973. Thurston, Nathaniel, 58, formerly a senator in the New Hampshire
legislature, d in NH ("His remains were interred at Bradford by the
side of 6 deceased wives, leaving the 7th to lament the loss...")
(3-12/11/11)

8974. Tibbits, John, 79, father of Hon. George of Troy, d 1/26/17 in Lisbon,
St. Lawrence Co. (3-2/19)

8975. Tice, John m Mary Shappee, dau of Jesse, in Erin (3-11/4/29)

8976. Tickener, ____ m 9/26/31 Mary Rounds in Macedon; A. Purdy, Esq.
(5-10/11)

8977. Tickner, Jane, 62, wf of Roswell, d 9/12/42 in Bath (2-9/14)

8978. Tiffany, ____, ch of Israel, d 10/27/38 (prob. in Jamestown) (4-10/31)

8979. Tiffany, Albert m Louisa Dexter, dau of John, Esq., in Jamestown; Rev.
Gillet (4-7/29/35)

8980. Tiffany, George of Ohio m 4/21/44 Angeline Cady of Ontario, NY in
Walworth; Rev. Young (5-4/24)

8981. Tiffany, Harriet Janette, 1 yr, dau of Silas and Lucy, d 7/19/42 in
Jamestown (4-7/21)

8982. Tiffany, Hiram of Prattsburgh m 1/5/30 Nancy S. Demming of Phelps in P;
Rev. H. P. Strong (3-1/13)

8983. Tiffany, James, 64, father of the Messrs. Tiffany of Jamestown, d in
Pembroke, Gen. Co. "while returning from Brockport with a loaded
wagon" (fell from the load and broke his neck) (4-6/30/30)

8984. Tiffany, Lawrence, 7 mo, s of Silas and Lucy, d 8/5/45 in Jamestown
(4-8/8)

8985. Tiffany, Louisa, wf of Albert W. and dau of John Dexter, Esq., recently
from Chautauqua Co., d 11/19/38 in Pleasant Prairie, Wisc. Terr.
(4-12/5)

8986. Tiffany, Louisa, 4 yrs, dau of Jehial, d 12/27/40 in Jamestown (4-12/30)

8987. Tiffany, Lucius F. of Buffalo m 4/27/37 Maria L. Patchin of Albany in A;
Rev. Alonzo Potter (4-5/3)

8988. Tiffany, Maria Louisa, 34?, wf of L. F., d 5/24/44 in Buffalo (4-5/31)

228

8989. Tiffany, Norman, 18, s of W. N. of Bath, d 2/17/41 in New Lebanon, Columbia Co. (2-3/3)
8990. Tiffany, Silas, merchant, m 9/25/31 Lucy Hyde in Jamestown; Rev. Eddy (4-9/28)
8991. Tiffany, Silvester, 51, d 3/24/11 in Canandaigua (3-4/3)
8992. Tiffany, Zachariah, Jr. m Nancy Jameson in Canandaigua (3-6/11/17)
8993. Tilbury, ____, inf s of George,d in Owego (3-8/22/27)
8994. Tillinghast, Eliza C., wf of John L., Esq., d 9/27/17 in NYC (3-10/8)
8995. Tillinghast, Maria C. (Miss), 13, oldest dau of John L., Esq., d 12/23/26 in NYC (3-1/17/27)
8996. Tillitson, Robert, Esq. m Emily Gouverneur, dau of late Nicholas, Esq., in NYC; Bishop Hobart (3-2/26/17)
8997. Tillman, John, 75, father of A. P., d 6/30/22 in Geneva (3-7/3/22)
8998. Tillman, William C. m 4/2/27 Harriet Hall, dau of Moses, in Geneva; Rev. Dr. Axtell (3-4/4)
8999. Tillotson, Elias m Sarah Tooker in Ithaca (3-6/11/28)
9000. Tillotson, John (Gen.), 70, (a Rev. soldier) d 7/12/26 at his home in Genoa, Cayuga Co. (3-8/2)
9001. Tillotson, Lewis m Mrs. Eliza Clark in Lyons (3-1/14/29)
9002. Tilton, Daniel m Fanny Spalding, dau of Jared, Esq., in Bath (3-5/16/27)
9003. Tinbrook, Peter B. m 12/25/28 Frances Glodsmith (sic) in Elmira (3-1/7/29)
9003. Tingley, Sarah, 12, dau of Daniel, d 8/12/35 (5-8/21)
9004. Tingley, Sarah (Mrs.), 81, mother of Daniel, d 3/14/44 in Palmyra (5-3/20)
9005. Tinkelpaugh, Adam m 7/31/21 Harriet Allen of Sodus in Williamson; Rev. Howell R. Powell (5-8/8)
9006. Tinker, Daniel m Sophia Lowell in Mendon (3-4/12/15)
9007. Tinker, M. T., M.D., of Perinton m 3/7/44 Harriet Culver of Macedon in M; Rev. D. Harrington of Palmyra (5-3/13)
9008. Tinkham, Desire, 54, d 11/10/32 in Batavia ("... born in Bridgewater, Mass. ... moved first to Middlebury (Middleborough), Mass" where she married Isaac Tinkham. "Buried her husband in Sharon, N. Y.") (1-11/13)
9009. Tinkley, Reuben of Seneca Co., 85, m Widow Pinkney, 82, "late of Putnam County", in Wayne; William Kernon, Esq. (3-7/16/17)
9010. Tinney, Hiram m 11/22/24 Arminda Sprague in Batavia; D. Tisdale, Esq. (1-11/26)
9011. Tinsler, Lawrence, 27, drowned in the Genesee River at Clyde, NY (5-8/29/21)
9012. Tippetts, Stephen, 55, d 4/24/24 in Newtown, L.I., NY ("a native of this state but for many years a resident of Alexandria on the Red River, Louisiana. Mr. T. left home for the benefit of his health and to visit relatives in this place (Geneva, NY) ... (but) when he arrived at Newtown he closed his earthly career. He has left a wife and 2 children at his late residence.") (3-5/19)
9013. Tippetts, William, merchant, of Geneva m 6/13/11 Mary Ashly, dau of Dr. Ashly of Deerfield, MA, in Lyons; Rev. Andrew Wilson (3-6/19)
9014. Tisdale, Henry, merchant, of Pembroke m 8/20/24 Jane Eliza Wilcox of Batavia in East Bloomfield; Rev. Norton (1-9/3)
9015. Tisdale, Sophronia, 44, wf of James, Esq. and dau of Mrs. Susannah Durfee of Palmyra, d 1/1/42 in Castor, Upper Canada (5-1/26)
9016. Tisdale, William Thorp, 5, youngest s of Ira J. and Rhoda M., d 4/21/48 in Alexander (1-4/25)
9017. Titcomb, Daniel m 12/27/19 Jane Dexter in Geneva; Jacob Dox, Esq. (3-1/5/20)
9018. Titsney, William m 10/18/18 Dolly Dickinson in Phelps; Rev. Mosher (3-10/21)
9019. Titus, Lucius B. of Ontario, NY m 4/12/40 Sophia M. Smith of Walworth in W; Rev. D. Lyon (5-5/6)
9020. Tobey, Silas m 12/12/25 Julia Harding in Elba; C. Woodward, Esq. All of Elba (1-12/16)
9021. Toby, Samuel m 9/30/40 Charlotte Spencer in Caton; Rev. Ambrose Abbot. All of Caton (2-10/7)
9022. Todd, Alanson of Bath m 7/4/34 Mary R. Bingham of Palmyra in P; Rev. Richards (5-7/11)
9023. Todd, Catharine (Mrs.), 87, d in Palmyra (3-4/30/28)

229

9024. Todd, Jonathan, about 45, d 2/14/23 in Palmyra (5-2/26)
9025. Todd, Margaret (Miss), 19, d 1/9/36 in Palmyra (5-1/15)
9026. Tolbert, Asa, about 50, of Geneva drowned in the Susquehannah River
       near Tunkhannock, PA (3-6/25/28)
9027. Tolford, Oscar, 4, s of William and Mary, d 9/26/31 in Penn Yan (5-10/11)
9028. Tolford, Thomas W., 4, s of David, d 6/30/16 in Geneva (3-7/3)
9029. Toliver, T. D. m 11/29/48 Elizabeth Nichols in Kennedyville; Rev. L.
       Merill Miller. All of Bath (2-12/13)
9030. Toll, Jane Ann, 18 mo, dau of Philip R., d in Ovid (3-4/9/28)
9031. Tompkins, Calvin D. m 8/15/22 Eliza Fields in Galen; James Dickson, Esq.
       (3-8/21)
9032. Tompkins, Catherine, 73, d 2/6/47 in Le Roy (1-2/16)
9033. Tompkins, Charles S. of Dundee m 6/7/46 Susan Rouse of Barrington at the
       Eagle Tavern in Bath; Rev. L. W. Russ (2-6/10)
9034. Tompkins, Hannah, relict of late Daniel D., d 12/18/28 in NYC (3-3/4/29)
9035. Tompkins, Ira G. of Canandaigua m 3/22/29 Hannah Edington of Seneca
       in S; Rev. Tooker (3-4/22)
9036. Tompkins, Jonathan, 80, father of Gov. Tompkins, m 3/31/14 Mrs. Phoebe
       Reynolds, 36, in Mamaroneck, Westchester Co. (3-5/4)
9037. Tompkins, Jonathan Griffin, 86, father of the Vice Pres. of the U.S.,
       d "at his residence in Westchester County" (3-6/11/23)
9038. Tompkins, Moses (Dr.) m 9/12/27 Mary Ann Smith, dau of Reuben, Esq.;
       Rev. Chadwick (3-9/19)
9039. Tompkins, Nathaniel m 11/20/31 Paulina Dexter in Gerry; Elisha Tower,
       Esq. (4-11/23)
9040. Tompkins, Sarah (Mrs.), wf of Hon. Jonathan Griffin Tompkins and mother
       of "His Excellency the Governor", d in Scarsdale, Westchester Co.
       (3-5/9/10)
9041. Tomson, Tommy, 130 yrs, balck-man, d "a few days since" in Loudon Co.,
       VA (5-8/28/29)
9042. Tooker, Charles K. m 8/25/31 Cornelia L. Clark in Seneca; Rev. John A.
       Clark (5-9/13)
9043. Topping, Perry of Bath m 2/23/45 Elizabeth Bundy, dau of Nathaniel of
       Cameron,in C; Rev. Carle (2-2/26)
9044. Toppins, Moses, 78, m 1/5/23 Judith Mishell, 23, in Canandaigua; S. T.
       Kibbe, Esq. (3-1/22)
9045. Torrance, Asher m 1/30/20 Cynthia Cowing, dau of James, in Seneca;
       Rev. Merrill (3-2/16)
9046. Torrance, Ezra B. (Capt.), 55, d 9/28/28 (3-10/1)
9047. Torrance, William H., 41, d in Jerusalem, NY (3-9/10/28)
9048. Torrey, Augustus m Altha Wilder in Gorham (3-1/28/18)
9049. Torrey, Olive, 27, wf of Henry, d in Gorham (3-8/29/27). Record repeated
       thus in the issue of 9/19: Mrs. Olive Torrey, 27, d in Gorham.
9050. Torry, Edward of Bethany m 2/17/25 Adeline Foster of Elba in E; Rev. C.
       Colton (1-2/18)
9051. Torry, William T. (Rev.) of Canandaigua m Betsey James of Scituate, MA
       in S (3-7/6/14)
9052. Totten, Joseph G. of the U.S. Engineers, m Catalina Pearson in Waterford
       (3-2/28/16)
9053. Tourtellot, S. K. of Hammondsport m 11/22/31 Eleanor McClure, dau of
       Gen. George, in Bath; Rev. Platt of Bath (2-11/30)
9054. Tousley, Emily Frances, 5 yrs, d 1/17/44 in Canandaigua (5-2/7)
9055. Towar, _____ (Mrs.), consort of Capt. Henry, d 3/3/14 in Phelps (surv by
       husband and children) (3-3/9)
9056. Towar, Charles of Phelps m 11/19/18 Mary Leonard of Ovid in O; Rev.
       Porter (3-11/25)
9057. Towar, Henry (Capt.) of Phelps m 1/10/15 Mrs. Sayre, wid of late Col.
       Sayre of West Cayuga, in W. C.; Rev. Axtell (3-1/25)
9058. Towar, Henry m 5/19/22 Polly Glover in Phelps (3-6/5)
9059. Towar, Henry (Capt.) of Lyons m 9/28/24 Mrs. Elizabeth Mathews in Elmira;
       Rev. Henry Ford (3-10/13)
9060. Towar, Henry Thompson, 26, late of Wayne County, d 9/27/28 in Greensburg,
       Dauphin Co., PA (3-10/15/28 and 5-10/17/28)
9061. Towar, Susan, 56, wf of Capt. Henry, d 2/18/23 in Phelps (she a member
       of Presby. Church, Lyons) (3-3/5)
9062. Towar, Z., 14, dau of Capt. Henry of Lyons, d 6/27/12 in Geneva (3-7/1)

230

9063. Tower, Susan, 56, wf of Capt. Henry Towar, d 3/3/23 in Phelps (5-3/12)
9064. Towle, Hester Ann, 19, d 2/11/32 in Howard. Her husband, John, d 2/16 "leaving an infant son of 15 months" (2-2/22). John, age 21 at death.
9065. Town, Mary, 27, wf of Orlando, d 5/12/32 in Elba (1-5/15)
9066. Town, Norman of Canandaigua m 5/1/22 Sarah G. Lyon in Prattsburgh (3-5/29)
9067. Towner, _____ (Mrs.), consort of Gen. E. Towner, d 4/10/32 in Batavia (1-4/17)
9068. Towner, Gersham, 79, for many years of Steuben Co., d 3/4/29 near Bath (3-3/4)
9069. Towner, John m Hannah Loop in Bath (3-1/22/17)
9070. Townsand, Samuel m Maria Dedrick, both of Geneva, in Seneca (3-1/12/25)
9071. Townsend, Abraham m "within a fewdays" Sabra Lawrence in Snell (See marr. of Dr. Joel Dorman) (3-11/1/09)
9072. Townsend, Abraham of Tyrone d 11/29/38 ("While hauling logs with his team he slipped and a log fell on him. Death was instant.") ("one of the oldest citizens of Tyrone") (2-12/5)
9073. Townsend, David m Catharine Dedrich in Seneca; Rev. Nisbet. All of Seneca (3-2/3/30)
9074. Townsend, Edward, 26, s of Henry A., Esq. of Urbana, d 11/25/25 in Athens, PA (3-12/14)
9075. Townsend, Edward S., s of Rev. Jesse, m 12/8/19 Maria Durfee, dau of Pardon, Esq., in Palmyra (5-12/15)
9076. Townsend, Edwin of Townsend Prairie, IL, s of Rev. Jesse, m 3/28/22 Harriet Durfee, dau of Pardon, Esq., in Palmyra (5-4/3)
9077. Townsend, Eliza, 20, wf of Samuel, d 3/28/31 in Carroll (Printer of Berkshire Journal, Lenox, MA, is requested to publish this death) (4-4/6)
9078. Townsend, Eliza Ann, 18 mo, youngest ch of Eleazer M., d 10/8/18 in Palmyra (5-10/13)
9079. Townsend, Elizabeth, 39, wf of Henry A., Esq., d 8/5/13 in Bath ("...a mother") (3-8/25)
9080. Townsend, Henry A. of Bath, member of the Council of Appointment, m Eliza Hull of Troy in NYC (3-12/28/14)
9081. Townsend, Hezekiah, Esq., 60, d in Milo (3-11/28/27)
9082. Townsend, Ira L. of Prattsburgh m 3/27/32 Catherine De Long of Hammondsport in H; Rev. Johnson (2-4/4)
9083. Townsend, Isaiah, Esq., merchant, d in Albany (4-2/28/38)
9084. Townsend, Jeremiah, 26, d 6/28/45 in Batavia (1-7/1)
9085. Townsend, Peter, Jr. m Caroline Parish, dau of Jasper, in Canandaigua (3-7/23/28)
9086. Townsend, Solomon, Esq., member of the NY legislature from NYC, d 4/27/11 in Albany (3-5/1)
9087. Townsend, Thankful, relict of Nathan, d 7/30/46 in Batavia (1-8/4)
9088. Tracy, _____ m Annis Holcomb in Canandaigua (3-2/11/18)
9089. Tracy, Albert H., Esq. m Harriet Norton in Buffalo (3-11/16/25)
9090. Tracy, Elias, Jr. (Col.) m 11/15/32 Mary Ann Forbes in Jamestown; R. Pier, Esq. (4-11/28)
9091. Tracy, Felix, Esq. m 4/6/24 Miss _____ Wilmingding in Moscow, NY; Rev. Mills (1-4/9)
9092. Tracy, Isaac m Anna Sheppard in Angelica (3-9/26/27)
9093. Tracy, Lucy Ann (Miss), 23, dau of Elias of Jamestown, d in Ashville (4-8/1/38)
9094. Tracy, Roby, 2 yrs, only ch of Hatch Tracy, d 11/27/34 in Fluvanna (4-12/3)
9095. Tracy, Wayne m 2/21/36 Emily P. Clark, both of Poland, NY; J. Wait, Esq. (4-2/24)
9096. Traphagen, Harriet Ann (Mrs.), 24, d 11/18/22 in Scauyas (sic) (3-11/27)
9097. Traver, Delia Maria, 4, dau of Levi and Susan, d 12/29/39 (5-1/8/40)
9098. Traver, John m Mary Chamberlain in Waterloo; Rev. Lane (3-2/27/22)
9099. Traver, Thomas m Phebe Munson in Junius (3-1/16/28)
9100. Treat, Cornelius m 1/5/23 Amanda Skinner in Palmyra (5-1/22)
9101. Treat, H. H. of Palmyra m 1/16/30 Addela Bosworth of Pennsylvania in Palmyra, NY; Rev. Henry Davis (5-1/22 and 3-1/27)
9102. Tremper, J. of Philadelphia (state not given) m Susan P. Wells in Jerusalem, NY (3-8/29/27)

231

9103. Tremper, John, 29, late of the city of Philadelphia, d 8/31/22 at the home of Capt. A. Remer in Benton (3-9/11)
9104. Trimmer, Francis of Benton m 5/1/28 Catharine Smith of Seneca in S; Rev. William Nesbit (3-5/21)
9105. Tripp, Henry G. of Hammondsport m 12/29/44 Alcina Foster of Cohocton in Kennedyville; Elder Case (2-1/1/45)
9106. Tripp?, John T. of Palmyra m 9/10/40 Eliza Mott of Macedon in M; F. Smith, Esq. (5-9/16)
9107. Trobridge, _____, inf ch of "Mr. Trobridge" d 4/5/17 in Geneva (3-4/9)
9108. Trobridge, _____ (Mrs.), 28, d in Gorham (3-9/10/17)
9109. Trobridge, Samuel m 1/1/17 Abigail Baker in Phelps; Joseph Hall, Esq. (3-3/12)
9110. Troup, Robert (Col.), 74, d 1/14/32 in NYC (member of the bar and of the Society of Cincinnati)(2-1/25)
9111. Troup, Ruth, inf dau of Azel, d 7/29/21 in Farmington (5-8/1)
9112. Trowbridge, _____ (Mrs.), wf of Daniel, Esq. of Newstead, Erie Co., d 3/19/32 in Newstead (1-4/3)
9113. Trude, William J., 22?, formerly of Jamestown, d 1/3/43 in Middleport, Niag. Co. ("Papers of Chautauqua and Jefferson counties requested to insert ...") (4-1/19)
9114. Truesdale, Elizabeth, 19, oldest dau of Gershom, d 11/19/19 in Wayne (3-12/1)
9115. Truesdell, Peleg m Lucinda Perce in Canandaigua (3-8/27/28)
9116. Trumbull, Eldad B. m 3/27/34 Marilla Ann Silvernail; Rev. Babcock (4-4/2)
9117. Trumbull, John (Hon.), 81, d 5/10/31 in Detroit ("author of McFingal") (5-5/27)
9118. Truxton, Thomas (Com.), late of the U.S. Navy, d 5/5/22 in Philadelphia (state not given) (5-5/29)
9119. Tryon, Amos S., merchant, m 5/2/18 Sally Barton, dau of Benjamin, Esq., in Lewiston; Rev. Smith (3-5/20)
9120. Tubbs, David of Macedon m 9/5/41 Mary Everts of Marion in Pulteneyville; A. Cornwall, Esq. (5-9/8)
9121. Tucker, A. W. of Walworth m 5/9/32 Frances E. Allen of New London, CT in N. L.; Rev. Judd (5-5/30)
9122. Tucker, Abner m 10/18/35 Ann Asa (sic) in Walworth (5-10/30)
9123. Tucker, Calvin of Walworth m 1/11/43 Uretta Knapp of Macedon in M; Rev. Ira Bennett (5-1/18)
9124. Tucker, Daniel m 9/29/50 Susannah C. Brink, both of Mud Creek, in M. C.; Rev. J. C. Mallory (2-10/9)
9125. Tucker, Daniel W., 23, d (death date and place not given). "Mr. Tucker was married the Sabbath evening preceding to a sister of D.(or B.) Fillemore, Esq.; was taken sick on Tuesday evening following and died on Wednesday evening." (5-11/15/20)
9126. Tucker, Edward Augustus, 7 mo, s of A. W., d 1/28/41 in Palmyra (5-2/3)
9127. Tucker, Eliphalet S. of Hector m 12/14/15 Sally Smith in Ovid (3-1/3/16)
9128. Tucker, Erastus m 10/20/42 Sybil Boyd in Ellery; Rev. Smith (4-10/27)
9129. Tucker, Frances Ann, 26, wf of Luther, Esq. and dau of Denison Smith of Groton, CT, d (death date and place not given) (surv by husband and one dau) (5-4/22/31)
9130. Tucker, George (Hon.), 77, d in Virginia (3-12/5/27)
9131. Tucker, George A., 3, s of Albigence W., d 2/25/40 in Palmyra (5-2/26)
9132. Tucker, John, 21, d 8/4/20 (5-8/9)
9133. Tucker, Luther, one of the editors of the Rochester (NY) Daily Advertiser, m 11/19/27 Naomi Sparhawk, dau of Eben, Esq. of Rochester, VT in Rochester, VT; Rev. Hurlbut (3-12/5). See 9136.
9134. Tucker, Luther D., 2 mo, s of Luther, d 11/21/28 in Ontarioville (5-11/28)
9135. Tucker, Luther, merchant, m 4/26/32 Elmira Kent, dau of Elijah, Esq., in Walworth; Rev. Whelpley (5-5/2)
9136. Tucker, Luther, editor of the Rochester (NY) Daily Advertiser, m 10/11/33 Mary Sparhawk, dau of E. Esq., in Rochester, VT; Rev. Kellogg. See 9133. (5-10/25)
9137. Tucker, Luther, 40, of Walworth d at the Bloomingdale Lunatic Asylum in NYC (his obit. included) (5-11/2/38)

9138. Tucker, Mary S., wf of Luther, Esq., d 3/8/44 in Albany (interred in Mt. Hope Cem., Rochester, NY) (5-3/13)
9139. Tucker, Morris H. of Lockport, Niag. Co. m 6/23/22 Esther C. McLean of Windsor, CT in Geneseo, NY (1-6/28)
9140. Tucker, Naomi S., 95?, wf of Luther, one of the publishers of the Rochester Republican and Daily Advertiser, d 8/4/32 in Rochester, NY (5-8/15)
9141. Tucker, Pomeroy, editor of the Wayne Sentinel, m Lucy Rogers, dau of Maj. William, in Palmyra (3-12/29/24)
9142. Tucker, Seth (Dr.), formerly of Woodstock, CT, d 6/30/42 in Marion (a physician in Marion for 40 yrs) (5-7/6)
9143. Tucker, Thomas, Esq., 77, born in NYC "and educated a merchant", d 4/14/20 in Danbury, CT (After the Rev. War he moved to Danbury) (In the Rev. served as a soldier from NY) (3-5/17)
9144. Tucker, Thomas Tudor, 84, Treas. of U.S., d 5/1/28 in Washington, D.C. (3-5/14)
9145. Tucker, William L. of Palmyra m 12/22/41 Maretta Barnhart, dau of Isaac of Macedon, in M; Rev. Ira Bennett (5-12/29)
9146. Tudor, William (Hon.), 69, d in Boston (state not given) (3-7/21/19)
9147. Tuell, Samuel R., Esq. m 12/23/45 Sarah Potter in Bath; Rev. L. W. Russ. All of Bath (2-12/24)
9148. Tufts, James (Rev.), the first ordained pastor of the Congregational Church in Wardsboro, VT, d 8/10/41 in Wardsboro (ordained in 1795) (4-8/26)
9149. Tupper, Jacob m Margaret Rowley in Canandaigua (3-12/20/15)
9150. Tupper, Samuel, Esq., 52, d 12/30/17 in Buffalo (first judge of Niagara County) (3-1/14/18)
9151. Turck, Aaron m 1/27/28 Mary Draper at the Methodist Chapel in Geneva (3-1/30). Correction in issue dated 2/6: name should read Anthony Turck, Jr. Further correction in issue dated 2/13: correct name is neither Aaron nor Anthony but Abraham Turck, Jr.
9152. Turck, Catharine, 56, wf of Anthony, d 6/23/29 in Geneva(3-7/1)
9153. Turk, Archibald J. m 9/24/43 Caroline S. Stanton, both of Jamestown, in Olean; Rev. J. I. Akin (4-10/5). Bride's name is Caroline O'Strander in 4-10/12.
9154. Turk, Caroline, 26, wf of Archibald J., d 10/8/44 in Jamestown (4-10/11)
9155. Turner, _____ (Mr.) d in Williamson (3-3/24/13)
9156. Turner, Alvah R. of Macedon m 7/4/27 Christina Rippinburgh in Lyons (3-7/11)
9157. Turner, Bela (Mr.), 32, d in Palmyra (5-10/17/21)
9158. Turner, Chipman P. m Lovina Bush in Batavia (5-9/18/35)
9159. Turner, Frederick m 2/9/20 Elizabeth Emson (sic) in Seneca; Rev. Axtell (3-2/23)
9160. Turner, George W. (Dr.), 28, d 7/17/27 in Wayne (3-7/25)
9161. Turner, Hector m 12/8/21 Daphne Robinson in Palmyra; A. Spear, Esq. (5-12/12)
9162. Turner, Hezekiah, 55 or 35, d 6/19/23 in Waterloo (3-7/23)
9163. Turner, Jonathan of Macedon m 7/4/44 Betsey M. Dumond of Walworth; F. Smith, Esq. (5-7/10)
9164. Turner, Lois, 29, dau of Capt. Enoch, d 5/10/31 in Sodus (5-6/10)
9165. Turner, Orasmus, Esq. of Lockport m Julia Bush in Batavia (5-2/21/34)
9166. Turner, Royal of Elba m 11/13/32 Julia Hubbard of Batavia in B; Rev. Charles Fitch (1-11/29)
9167. Turner, William, Jr., 24, d 3/7/43 in Canandaigua (for a short time one of the editors of the Ontario Messenger and later, for one year, of the Wayne Sentinel) (5-3/15)
9168. Turner, William Harrison m 2/24/42 Phebe S. Winchester in Ellery; Rev. H. Smith. All of Ellery (4-3/3)
9169. Tuthill, David m 9/11/44 Annis H. Francis in Prattsburgh; Rev.F. A. Weidman. All of Prattsburgh. (5-9/18)
9170. Tuthill, Harriet Melvina, 3, only dau of Mrs. Esther, d 6/8/50 in Tyrone (2-6/19)
9171. Tuthill, Mandeville, 29, d 10/16/47 in Prattsburgh (member of Prattsburgh Lyceum)(2-10/27)
9172. Tuttle, _____, 77, m Miss Jane Weed, 63, in La Fayette (3-11/4/29)

9173. Tuttle, _____ (Dr.) of Indiana m 11/17/39 Sarah M. White of Panama, NY in P; Rev. A. W. Gray (4-11/20)
9174. Tuttle, Benjamin m 12/1/17 Fanny Parke in Seneca; Rev. White (3-12/10)
9175. Tuttle, John L., 39, Lt. Col. of the 9th Regiment, U.S. Army, d 7/23/13 in Watertown near Sacket's Harbor (3-8/25)
9176. Tuttle, Joseph H. m 10/11/26 Sarah Griffin in Seneca; Rev. Axtell (3-11/1)
9177. Tuttle, Levi, 53, d in Clyde (3-5/20/29)
9178. Tuttle, Myron J., 22, d 2/6/39 in Williamson (5-2/15)
9179. Tuttle, Truman of Williamson m 3/24/22 Catherine Butler of Penfield (5-4/3)
9180. Twaddle, Daniel m 1/1/18 Mrs. Peckham in Williamson (5-1/7)
9181. Twaits, _____ (Mr.), "the Celebrated Comedian", d 8/22/14 in NYC (3-9/21)
9182. Tyler, A. S., merchant, of Buffalo m 7/21/41 Frances C. Robson of Palmyra (5-7/28)
9183. Tyler, Asahel of Bloomfield m Maria A. Barnard, dau of Capt. Erastus (3-12/16/18)
9184. Tyler, Comfort (Col.), 64, d 8/6/27 in Montezuma, NY (3-8/15)
9185. Tyrrel, Noah m 10/2/22 Hannah Jinks in Farmington; A. Spear, Esq. (5-10/23)
9186. Underhill, Charles m Portia Brooks in Bloomfield (3-7/4/27)
9187. Underhill, George A., Esq. m 11/24/29 Mary Frances Octavio Seguin, both of New Orleans, in N. O. (3-12/30/29)
9188. Underhill, Henry of Bath m 3/4/45 Henrietta S. Scott of Vienna, NY in V; Rev. L. Hubbell (2-3/12)
9189. Underhill, Punderson B., 55, d 6/14/41 at his home in Orleans, Ont. Co. (2-6/23)
9190. Underwood, Thomas of Washington City (D.C.?) m 9/9/50 Ann E. Wilson, dau of John, Esq. of Batavia; Rev. James A. Bolles (1-9/10)
9191. Upham, Alonzo S., 18 mo, s of Hon. A. S. Upham, d 10/26/48 in Le Roy (Alonzo is the fifth of six children of the Hon. A. S. to die young) (1-10/31)
9192. Upham, Ebenezer P., M.D., 50, d 5/21/42 in Mayville (4-5/26)
9193. Valentine, James m 4/3/14 Louiza Bidwell, both of Galen, in G; W. B. Dickson, Esq. (3-4/13)
9194. Van Alen, James L., Esq. d 5/19/22 at his home in Kinderhook, Col. Co. ("had been a member of the legislature of this state and a representative to the U.S. Congress") (3-5/29)
9195. Van Alen, Peter, Esq., 72, d 12/29/21 at his home in Red Hook (3-1/16/22)
9196. Van Allen, Cornelius, about 50, d 5/24/45 in Stafford (1-5/27)
9197. Van Allen, William H. of Scio, Alleg. Co. m 11/19/50 Nancy M. White, dau of Luther, Esq. of Dansville, in D; Rev. J. Chapman (2-11/27)
9198. Van Alstyne, Leonard of Victory, Cayuga Co. m 3/4/41 Tabitha H. Preston of Palmyra in P; Rev. G. R. H. Shumway (5-3/10)
9199. Van Alstyne, Thomas m 10/20/30 Mary Coslere in Palmyra; A. R. Tiffany, Esq. All of Arcadia (5-10/22)
9200. Van Amber, _____ (Mrs.), wf of Mathew, d in Palmyra (5-10/3/21)
9201. Vanamburg, Mathew m 8/26/19 Wealthy Southard in Palmyra (5-9/8)
9202. Van Antwerp, Margaret, 87, d 6/1/10 in NYC (3-6/13)
9203. Vanauken, George (Maj.) of Phelps m 1/30/28 Elizabeth Bainbridge of Romulus in R (3-2/6)
9204. Van Aukin, _____, inf ch of Simeon and Lydia, d 9/2/26 in Rose. See the death of the mother in entry 9205. (3-9/20)
9205. Van Aukin, Lydia, 33, grandchild of Rev. Thomas Potwine of East Windsor, CT, d 9/9/26 (presumably in Rose, NY). See entry 9204. (3-9/20)
9206. Van Benthuysen, John, Esq., clerk of Dutchess Co., d 10/6/19 (3-10/20)
9207. Van Brunt, William, 22, d 12/27/29 in Geneva (3-12/30)
9208. Van Buren, Abraham (Capt.), 80, d in Kinderhook (3-4/23/17)
9209. Van Buren, Hannah, 35 or 55, wf of Hon. Martin, Esq., d 2/5/19 in Albany (3-2/17)
9210. Van Buren, Henry, 1 yr, d 4/2/22 in Galen (3-5/8)
9211. Van Buren, Mariah, wf of M. R., youngest s of the Hon. Martin, d 6/4/32 in London (5-6/11)
9212. Vanbuskirk, John, 45, d in Bath (3-12/9/29)
9213. Van Buskirk, Richard, 62, d 10/22/50 in Avoca (2-10/30

9214. Van Camp, Abraham I. m 11/15/29 Almira Rawson in Palmyra; William Willcox, Esq. (5-11/27)
9215. Van Camp, William, printer, m 12/25/43 Margaretta Williams in Sodus; Rev. C. Moshier. All of Sodus (5-1/3/44)
9216. Van Campen, Moses, Esq. of Angelica m 12/16/18 Mary Stout of Sparta in S (3-1/6/19)
9217. Van Campen, William R. of Almond m 1/31/47 Harriet A. Howard in Howard; Rev. L. Rose (2-2/17)
9218. Van Cleef, Lawrence, 76, (a Rev. soldier and one of the first settlers in the county) d in Seneca Falls (3-1/27/30)
9219. Van Cleve, Peter d 2/22/26 in Bethany (1-2/24)
9220. Van Clure, Isaac m Ellen Burroughs in Fayette (3-3/11/29)
9221. Van Cortland, _____ (Capt.), 33, of the 33rd British Regiment and son of "old Capt. Van Cortland" of Cortlandt's Manor, NY, was killed in a military action in Portugal (had been in 23 engagements) (3-1/22/12)
9222. Van Cortlandt, Catherine, wf of Col. Pierre and oldest dau of the Hon. George Clinton, Vice Pres. of the U.S., d 1/10/11 in Peekskill (3-3/13)
9223. Van Cortlandt, Philip (Gen.), 82, d 11/19/31 at his home on the North River (includes an obit. detailing the Rev. War battles in which the general participated) (5-11/22)
9224. Vandebogert, Myndert, 95, d 5/4/16 in Poughkeepsie (3-5/8)
9225. Van De Mark, Silas m 1/4/27 Eliza Bannister, youngest dau of Samuel, Esq. of Phelps,in P; Rev. Lane (3-1/17)
9226. Van Der Bump, Frederick, 63, m Amy Joy, 71, in Pleasant Valley, Ohio; Dr. Johannes Wilhelmus (3-12/4/11)
9227. Vander Heuvel, Charles m Mary Morris, dau of Thomas, Esq., in NYC (3-1/6/19)
9228. Vanderheyden, Derick L., Esq. d 2/8/26 in Albany (3-2/15)
9229. Vanderheyden, John G. d 1/5/29 in Troy (3-1/21)
9230. Vanderhoof, Daivid m 10/24/33 Sarah Jane Shirts, both of Arcadia, in Palmyra; Judge Baldwin (5-11/15)
9231. Vanderhoof, John m 12/6/28 Mrs. G. Vandeusen in Manchester (3-12/17)
9232. Vanderhooven, Elizabeth, 10 mo, dau of Jesse and Annis, d 8/29/49 in Bath (2-9/5)
9233. Van Der Kemp, Francis Adrian, LL. D., a distinguished native of Holland, d in Oldenbarneveld (Trenton), Oneida Co. (3-9/16/29)
9234. Van Derlip, Lewis m 10/11/18 Angelina Phelps in Penn Yan (3-10/21)
9235. Vander Veer, _____ (Mrs.), formerly of Waterloo, d 9/29/24 in Clyde (3-10/13)
9236. Vanderveer, Helen Mary, 7 weeks, dau of M. B., d 2/23/30 in Clyde (5-3/10)
9237. Vandervoort, Thomas of Orange Co. m 1/1/28 Elenor Horton in Phelps; Rev. Strong (3-1/9)
9238. Vanderwarken, Jacob m 3/3/49 Temma Elliot, both of Wheeler, in W; Rev. H. Spencer (2-3/14)
9239. Vandeusen, Henry C. of Ashville m 1/1/39 Eunice Ette Brown of Ellington in E; Rev. Covill (4-1/16)
9240. Van Deusen, Loyal E. of Ashville m 6/4/42 Phebe L. Sweet of Utica in U; Rev. Grash (4-6/16)
9241. Van Deusen, Lucia, 39, wf of J. B., d 6/3/33 in Ashville (surv by her husband, children, father, and mother)(4-6/12)
9242. Vandine, Abram m 12/1/38 Loretta Tinny, both of Palmyra, in P; I. E. Beecher, Esq. (5-12/7)
9243. Van Dine, Peter of Phelps m 11/20/31 Mary Redfield in Palmyra; M. W. Willcox, Esq. (5-11/22)
9244. Van Dozen, Edmund of Pulteney m Phila Parmelee in Prattsburgh (3-4/1/29)
9245. Van Dusen, William Henry m 10/17/50 Nancy Bellinger in Wheeler; Rev. Jno. Selmser (2-10/23)
9246. Van Duzer, Ashley m Maria Chattin of Salem in S (5-9/8/19)
9247. Van Duzer, Joseph m 9/19/35 Mrs. Sarah McMellen; F. Smith, Esq. (5-9/25)
9248. Van Duzer, Miles m 1/1/18 Anna Robinson in Palmyra (See marr. of Ebenezer Still this date) (5-1/7)
9249. Van Dyke, B. W., Esq., attorney, about 30, d 9/26/28 in Medina (3-10/15)

9250. Van Fleet, _____ (Mrs.), 48, wf of Joshua, d in Gorham - "also two sons aged 7 and 4 years" (3-9/10/17)
9251. Van, Fleet, Garet, 26, d in Cameron (3-1/13/30)
9252. Vanfoffen (sic), Levi, about 50, d 11/16/11 in Livonia ("accidentally fell into a kettle of melted potash and, though immediately withdrawn, expired in a few minutes") (3-12/4)
9253. Van Gelden, _____ (Mr.), 116, d 2/28/18 in Piscataway, NJ (3-4/1)
9254. Van Gelder, Abraham, 95, d 4/13/12 in NYC (3-5/6)
9255. Vangelder, Barney m 6/8/45 Hannah Parker in Urbana; Rev. Bebee. All of Urbana (2-6/18)
9256. Vangelder, Benjamin m 1/15/45 Lucy E. Look in Bath; Rev. Ferris. All of Bath (2-1/22)
9257. Van Gelder, Henry m 10/31/50 Polly Veley in Bath; Rev. B. R. Swick. All of Bath (2-11/13)
9258. Vangelder, Jonathan of Bath m 2/15/46 Semantha Silsbe of Wayne in W; Rev. Mallory (2-2/18)
9259. Van Gelder, Polly, 44, d 3/13/45 in Bath (2-3/19)
9260. Van Hoosen, Abraham H. m 12/11/44 Mary Ann Jones in Howard; Rev. Rose. All of Howard (2-12/18)
9261. Van Horn, Levi m Rachael Corkendool in Friendship, Alleg. Co. (3-10/17/27)
9262. Van Housen, Adaline Rebecca, 33, wf of Jonn and dau of late Beriah Hotchkin of Prattsburgh, d 5/13/46 in Prattsburgh (2-5/20)
9263. Van Housen, Henry, 74, formerly of Howard, d 2/2/50 in Prattsburgh (2-2/13)
9264. Van Housen, Joseph H. of Prattsburgh m 10/16/50 Catharine Van Wie of Howard in H; Rev. L. Rose (2-10/23)
9265. Vanhusen, Caleb of Knowlesville, Orleans Co. m 2/11/36 Catharine Jackson, dau of R. C., Esq. of Palmyra, in P; Rev. Henry V. Jones (5-2/12)
9266. Van Keusen, E. Benedict, 20, d 1/27/46 in Howard (2-2/11)
9267. Van Lew, John m 1/15/16 Catharine Meyers in Phelps; Joseph Hall, Esq. (3-1/24)
9268. Van Meter, Joseph, 28, of Moorfield, VA d in Elmira, NY (3-8/5/29)
9269. Van Ness, _____, wid of late Judge William P., d 9/6/29 in NYC (3-9/16)
9270. Van Ness, David (Gen.) d 10/4/18 in Troy (3-10/14 and 5-10/20)
9271. Van Ness, Jeremiah m Hester Rouse in Jerusalem, NY (3-11/28/27)
9272. Van Ness, William Cantine, oldest s of late Judge William W., d 7/17/28 in Warren, Trumbull Co., Ohio (3-7/30)
9273. Van Ness, William P., U.S. Judge for the southern district, d 9/6/26 at the home of J. O. Hoffman, Esq. in NYC (3-9/13)
9274. Van Ness, William W. (Hon.), late one of the judges of the Supreme Court of NY, d 2/27/23 in Charleston, SC (3-3/19)
9275. Van Norman, _____ d "at an advanced age" in Canandaigua (3-3/31/13)
9276. Van Orden, Samuel, Esq., attorney, d 7/10/22 in Catskill (3-7/17)
9277. Van Orman, Joseph m Rhoda Case in Canandaigua (3-12/27/15)
9278. Van Ostrand, Jeremiah m 1/1/30 Jane Beckwith in Arcadia; Rev. R. Benton (5-1/8). The marriage place is Newark, NY in 3-1/13.
9279. Van Pelt, _____, 30, wf of Capt. John, d 9/1/28 in Penn Yan (3-9/3)
9280. Van Pelt, John of Onondaga m 5/26/14 Mary S. Annin of East Cayuga in E. C. (3-6/1)
9281. Van Pelt, John, 70, (a Rev. soldier) d in Milo (3-5/7/28)
9282. Van Rensselaer, Jeremiah (Hon.), late Lt. Gov. of NY, d 2/19/10 in Albany (3-3/7)
9283. Van Rensselaer, Jeremiah, Esq., 60, formerly of Utica, d 1/29/29 in Canandaigua (3-2/4 and 5-2/6)
9284. Van Rensselaer, Killian N. of Greenbush m 1/29/22 Jane Bogart, dau of late Capt. Isaac, in Albany (3-2/6)
9285. Van Rensselaer, Philip P., 44, d 2/17/27 in his home at Cherry Hill in Bethlehem, NY (3-2/28)
9286. Van Rensselaer, Philip S. (Hon.), 58, d 9/25/24 in Albany (a lengthy obit. accompanies this death announcement) (3-10/6)
9287. Van Rensselaer, Sabella Adeline, 54, relict of the late Jeremiah, Esq., d 3/4/29 in Canandaigua (5-3/13 and 3-3/18)
9288. Van Schaack, Maria Wilhelmina, 66, youngest dau of the late Rev. Johannes Ritzema, d 1/28/13 in Kinderhook (3-2/24)

236

9289. Van Schaic, Martin, about 45, d 12/19/22 at the home of Edward White
in Geneva (a mason by occupation; fell 10/12/22 from near the top of
a two story building; "has a family residing in Ulster County")
(3-12/25)
9290. Van Schaick, John, Esq., Pres. of the Bank of Albany, d 3/1/20 in Albany
(3-3/8 and 5-3/15)
9291. Van Schaick, John B. (Col.), editor of the **Albany Daily Advertiser**,
d 12/31/38 in Albany (4-1/24/39)
9292. Van Schaick, V. W., Esq., 59, d in Lansingburg ("many years cashier of
the Albany Bank")(3-1/8)
9293. Van Scoter, Elias of Dansville m 9/7/45 Jane Foot of Grove, Alleg. Co.
in Dansville (2-9/17)
9294. Van Scoy, Cornelius, 105, d 4/20/27 in Milo (3-5/2)
9295. Van Sickle, John W. m Susan Dickenson in Ovid (3-11/19/28)
9296. Van Tuyl, Amos, about 28, a soldier in the U.S. Army, d 2/11/13 in
Geneva (formerly of Orange Co.) (3-3/10)
9297. Van Tuyl, Nathaniel m Martha Smith in Jerusalem, NY (3-1/19/20)
9298. Van Tyce, Peter m 2/22/25 Mrs. Anna Britton in Elba; C. Woodworth, Esq.
(1-3/4)
9299. Van Vechten, Cuyler and John, sons of Teunis, d 11/8/25 in Albany
(3-11/16)
9300. Van Vleck, Volkert, about 66, d in Jamestown (4-5/24/37)
9301. Vanvorst, Cornelius, 90, the proprietor of the town of Jersey,d in
Harsimus (sic), NJ "leaving property to the amount of half a million
dollars" (3-10/14/18)
9302. Van Vranken, Nicholas, 2 yrs, s of Phineas Prouty Van Vranken d 8/24/22
in Geneva. Nicholas' brother Charles, 1 yr, died the same day.
These were the only sons of Phineas. (3-8/28)
9303. Van Wart, Isaac, 71, one of the captors of Major Andre, d 5/23/28 at
his home in Geneva. He was a ruling elder in the Greenburgh
(Westchester Co.) Presby. Church. (3-5/28)
9304. Van Wickle, John, 81, d 12/25/29 in Lyons (5-1/1/30 and 3-1/6/30)
9305. Van Winkle, Simeon of Bath m 6/24/46 Mary Jane Look, dau of Dr.S.
Look of Prattsburgh, in Bath; Rev. L. W. Russ (2-7/1)
9306. Van Woert, Henry, 65, father of William of Geneva, d 2/4/13 in Albany
(3-2/24)
9307. Van Woert, Henry, 29, d 6/21/14 in Albany (3-6/29)
9308. Van Woert, William, 40, "for some years a resident of Geneva", d 7/26/29
in Albany (3-8/5)
9309. Van Wyck, Francis H., 41, late of Dutchess Co., d 4/21/27 in NYC
(3-5/9)
9310. Van Wyck, Isaac, Esq. of Fishkill d 9/10/11 in Red Hook (a member of
the state assembly) (3-9/18)
9311. Van Wyck, Pierre C. (Hon.), 48, formerly recorder of NYC, d 4/4/27
in NYC (3-4/11)
9312. Van Wye, John d 5/8/14 in Geneva "leaving a wife and seven children"
(3-5/11)
Vares. See Wares.
9313. Varick, Richard (Col.), 79, d 7/30/31 in Jersey City, NJ (a Rev. soldier;
private secretary to Gen. George Washington; former mayor of NYC)
(5-8/12)
9314. Varnum, George of Wisconsin, formerly of Peacham, VT, m Harriet Brown,
dau of Heman, of Bethany in Bethany; Rev. Hiram Blackmarr (1-6/23/46)
9315. Vasopolos, Nicholas, 21, a native of Ithaca, Greece, d 3/7/27 in Monson,
MA ("one of eleven Greek youths ... in a course of education under
the patronage of the American Board of Com.for Foreign Missions")
(3-3/28)
9316. Vaughan, Mercy Ann, 14, dau of John, d 5/28/19 in Benton (3-6/2)
9317. Vaughan, Roderick m 8/27/15 Clarissa Stebins in Phelps; Joseph Hall, Esq.
(3-9/6)
9318. Vedder, Abraham (Maj. Gen.), 68, 4th Division of NY State Militia,
d 1/27/14 in Johnstown (3-2/23/14)
9319. Vedder, Jemima, 36, wf of William, d 12/13/41 in Prattsburgh (surv by
husband and 6 ch) (2-1/19/42)
9320. Verplanck, Elizabeth, 15 mo, dau of J. V. D., d 10/22/45 in Batavia
(1-11/4)

9321. Verplanck, Ethan Allen, 9, s of Gen. Isaac A., d 1/16/48 in Batavia
       (1-1/18)
9322. Verplanck, Johnston, 41, d 7/8/29 at his home "near Belleville" (3/7/22)
9323. Vickery, Ebenezer (Capt.), sheriff-elect of Tompkins Co., m 11/17/25
       Esther Sheldon in Ithaca; Rev. Wisner (3-11/30)
9324. Vickery, George W. m Lois Cartwright in South Bristol (3-1/27/30)
9325. Viele, John L., Esq. d 10/19/32 in Albany (5-10/24)
9326. Vine, Daniel of Palmyra m 3/10/41 Emily Howland of Manchester in Palmyra;
       Rev. Samuel Wilson (5-3/31)
9327. Vine, Jesse m 3/4/41 Lucy Ann Chafee; Rev. Samuel Wilson. All of
       Palmyra (5-3/10)
9328. Vine, John of Palmyra m Harriet N. Robinson of Newark, NY in N; Rev.
       David Cushing (5-4/13/42)
9329. Vining, William H., Esq., 28, of Waddington, St. Lawrence Co. d 8/10/22
       in NYC (3-8/28)
9330. Volk, Cornelius G. m 6/8/45 Martha Louisa Barlow, dau of Dr. Jonathan K.,
       in Bethany; Rev. Sunderland. All of Bethany (1-6/10)
9331. Volney, Homer, 2, s of Abner Pratt, d 6/2/26 in Batavia (1-6/9)
9332. Voorhees, Derick m Mrs. Sally Calkins (3-11/29/15)
9333. Voorhees, James m Patty Swartout in Ovid (3-1/17/16)
9334. Voorhies, _____, inf ch of Capt. William, d 2/7/13 in Lyons (3-2/17)
9335. Voorhies, _____ (Mrs.), wf of Capt. William, d 9/11/18 in Lyons (5-9/15)
9336. Voorhies, James, about 3, s of Capt. William, d 1/20/11 in Geneva
       (3-1/30)
9337. Voorhies, Sarah, 30 or 50, consort of Capt. William and dau of Maj. Ez.
       Price, d 9/5/18 in Lyons (3-9/9)
9338. Voorhies, William m 11/11/19 Nancy Ranor in Lyons; Rev. Pomeroy. All of
       Lyons (3-11/24)
9339. Vorce, Zebulon, 91, d 2/10/20 in Milo (3-2/23)
9340. Vorse, John O. m 10/24?/32 Rosetta Voorhies, dau of William, Esq., both
       of Lyons (prob. in Lyons); Rev. L. Hubbell (5-10/31)
9341. Vorse?, Lucretia, 72, wf of Charles, d 7/20/44 in Windham, Greene Co.
       (5-8/7)
9342. Vosburgh, Abraham P., Esq., attorney, of Penn Yan m 9/7/22 Elizabeth
       Henry of Bath in B (3-9/18)
9343. Vosburgh, Abraham m 4/16/44 Louisa Foot in Macedon; Benjamin Billings, Esq.
       (5-4/24)
9344. Vosburgh, Abraham P., Esq., attorney, d 3/1/27 in Penn Yan (3-3/7)
9345. Vosburgh, John m 6/12/22 Betsey Tucker in Ontario, NY (5-6/19)
9346. Vosburgh, Kellogg m Sally Norton in Pittsford (3-4/12/15)
9347. Vosper, Thomas m 7/24/50 Mary E. Blakeny, both of Batavia; Rev. J. K.
       Cheesman (1-8/13)
9348. Vought, John G. (Dr.) m 3/31/14 Helen Frances Mumford, dau of Thomas,
       Esq., in Cayuga; Rev. Axtell (3-4/6)
9349. Vought, John G., 45, d 7/22/32 in Harlem "near NYC" (formerly of Rochester)
       (5-8/1)
9350. Vredenburgh, Sarah S., 6 mo, dau of John, d 7/22/29 in Geneva (3-8/5)
9351. Vredenburgh, William I. (Col.), 52, d 5/9/13 in Skaneateles (3-5/26)
9352. Vreedenburgh, John Varick of Norwalk, Huron Co., Ohio m 12/4/25 Marianna
       Schuyler, dau of late Harmanus P., Esq. of Locust Grove, near
       Schenectady; Rev. Proal (3-12/19)
9353. Wade, Anna, 38, wf of Jonathan, d 8/24/24 in Stafford (1-9/3)
9354. Wade, C. B. m 1/16/39 Esther Allen, both of Williamson, in W; E. L.
       Phelps, Esq. (5-1/18)
9355. Wade, Lysander m 1/1/45 Lucinda Seeker in Pinegrove, PA; M. Fish, Esq.
       (4-1/10)
9356. Wadsworth, David of Steuben Co. m 2/1/20 Caroline Phillips of Seneca
       (3-2/9)
9357. Wadsworth, Frederick, 25, d in Canandaigua (3-8/13/17)
9358. Wadsworth, James (Gen.), 83, father of Gen. William and James, Esq. of
       Ontario Co., died (death place and date not given) (3-10/29/17)
9359. Wadsworth, John m Nancy Parker in Canandaigua (3-9/1/19)
9360. Wadsworth, Naomi, 53, wf of James, Esq., d 3/1/31 in Geneseo (1-3/4)
9361. Waeir, William C. m 12/17/15 Mary Jones in Elmira (3-12/27)
9362. Wagener, Jacob of Pulteney m 11/3/42 M. Orrelia Butts of Newark, NY in
       Pulteney; Rev. Wheeler (2-11/16)

238

9363. Wagener, Mary, 36, consort of Abraham, Esq., d 6/3/11 in Benton (3-6/12)
9364. Wagener, Samuel, 23, d in Milo (3-5/23/27)
9365. Wagener, William, 19, s of A. Esq., d 8/24/22 in Penn Yan (3-9/4)
9366. Wager, Nathan, 3??, d in Lyons (3-9/23/29)
9367. Waggoner, Harriet, 4 mo, dau of James, d 6/3/42 in Bath (2-6/8)
9368. Waggoner, Peter, 61, d in Palatine, Mont. Co. (a Rev. soldier) (3-8/13/17)
9369. Wait, Elihu m 5/13/22 Mrs. Sophia Wait in Prattsburgh (3-5/29)
9370. Wait, Franklin H., Esq. m 6/12/44 Adeline Holman in Jamestown; Rev. E. J.
        Gillett (4-6/14)
9371. Wait, John m Betsey Scidmore in Cohocton (3-7/1/29)
9372. Wait, John B. m 11/1/49 Mary Upton; Rev. J. M. Short. All of Genesee Co.
        (1-11/6)
9373. Wait, Lewis m 4/13/34 Maria Cannon in Gerry; Rev. Babcock (4-4/23)
9374. Walbridge, Charles H., about 20, d 9/27/18 in Geneva (3-9/30)
9375. Walbridge, Cornelia, 13 mo, dau of Henry, d 4/8/27 (prob. in Geneva)
        (3-4/11)
9376. Walbridge, Henry S. of Ithaca m Susan H. Dana in Owego (3-1/14/29)
9377. Walbridge, Hiram of the firm of Has___ and Walbridge m 1/24/25 Sally
        Ann Rose; Rev. Dr. Axtell. All of Geneva (3-1/26)
9378. Walden, Catharine, 7, dau of Ebenezer of Buffalo, d 10/2/22 in Geneva
        (3-10/9)
9379. Waldo, Daniel (Hon.) d in Worcester, MA (4-7/18/45)(Age 84 at death)
9380. Waldo, Ducinea, 44, wf of Hiram and dau of/Lemuel Foster, Esq., d in Elba
        (1-4/1/45)
9381. Waldo, Jesse, Esq., 65, d in Prattsburgh (a Rev. soldier) (3-1/17/27)
9382. Waldo, Nathan (Capt.), 78, d 12/20/40 in Elba (a Rev. soldier) (1-1/12/41)
9383. Waldo, Otis H., Esq. of Milwaukie, Wisc. m 4/20/50 Gertrude C.Valkenburgh,
        dau of J., Esq., in Oakley, Oakland Co., MI; Rev. Hyde (2-5/1)
9384. Waldron, Benjamin, 60, m Sally Hawkins, 22, in Ovid (3-1/15/17)
9385. Waldron, Henry m 11/29/27 Polly Robinson in Hector (3-12/26)
9386. Waldron, James m 12/30/24 Jane Rice, both of Geneva, in G; Rev. Clark
        (3-1/5/25)
9387. Wales, Arvine of the vicinity of Massillon, Ohio m (prior to June 6)
        Mrs. Nancy Shepherdson of Palmyra (5-6/19/33)
9388. Walker, ____ m Clarissa Norton in Bloomfield (3-4/3/16)
9389. Walker, ____ (Mrs.), 63, wf of Col. Benjamin, d in Utica (3-7/2/17)
9390. Walker, Abraham m 1/4/37 Mrs. Betsey Newton, both of Farmington, in
        Palmyra; Frederick Smith, Esq. (5-1/6)
9391. Walker, Benjamin (Col.), Pres. of Ontario Branch Bank,d 1/13/18 in Utica
        (a Rev. officer; an aide to Baron Steuben and afterwards toGeneral
        Washington) (3-1/28)
9392. Walker, Benjamin (Col.), 64, d 1/21/18 at his home in Whitestone
        (5-1/28)
9393. Walker, Bradford of Bristol m Eliza Holcomb in Canandaigua (3-3/22/15)
9394. Walker, Calvin, 29, s of St. John of Lexington, KY,d 9/28/31 in
        Jamestown, NY (4-10/5)
9395. Walker, Carmine W. m 4/26/40 Keziah Bristol in Jamestown; E. F.Warren, Esq.
        (4-4/29)
9396. Walker, Elam? H. (Rev.) of Fowlersville m 11/6/32 Alice F. Bacon, dau of
        late Rev. David of West Bloomfield, in W. B.; Rev. Silas C. Brown
        (5-11/14)
9397. Walker, Gideon, 80, formerly of Hartford, CT, d 10/25/50 in Bath (3-10/30)
9398. Walker, Helen Amelia, 3, dau of Hiram and Nancy, d 8/21/41 in Bath
        (2-8/25)
9399. Walker, Hiram P. of Bath m 1/27/46 Sarah Ann Sheffield of Jasper in Bath;
        Rev. L. W. Russ (2-2/4)
9400. Walker, John (Hon.), 53, of Champlain, state assemblyman from Clinton Co.,
        d 1/21/32 in Albany (2-1/25 and 4-1/25)
9401. Walker, John m 3/14/50 Mary Bishop in Bath; Rev. Wilbur (2-3/27)
9402. Walker, Lydia, wf of John, d 3/23/45 in Bath (2-3/26)
9403. Walker, Nancy, 31, wf of Hiram, d 8/31/45 in Bath (2-9/3)
9404. Walker, Nathaniel m 11/10/35 Louisa Wright in Jamestown; R. Pier, Esq.
        (4-11/25)
9405. Walker, Robert of Jasper m Mrs. Adnes Logry in Cameron (3-7/23/28)
9406. Walker, Sarah Mariah, 14, dau of James, d 5/20/38 in Bath (2-5/23)

239

9407. Walker, William m 11/10/31 Alcenath Dawly, both of Jamestown, in Westfield;
Rev. Murry (4-11/16)
9408. Wall, John m Sophia Boiler of Brown, Mercer Co., IN (2-11/25/40)
9409. Wallace, Austin m Hannah Judd in Bethany; Rev. Ensign (1-2/11/25)
9410. Wallace, Cidney m 11/5/40 Mary Ann Jones in Hornellsville; RevS. C.
Church (2-11/25)
9411. Wallace, James of Pembroke m 11/15/32 Maria Kendrick of Batavia in B;
Rev. J. Elliott of Wyoming, NY (1-11/29)
9412. Wallace, William m Paulina Brayton in South Dansville (3-6/17/29)
9413. Wallace, William A. (Dr.) m 9/17/42 Sarah D. Marshal, dau of Gen. O. F.,
in Wheeler; Rev. Gaylord (2-10/19)
9414. Wallis, Ira m 4/17/26 Louisa Olds in Batavia; D. Tisdale, Esq. (1-4/21)
9415. Wallis, John m 5/17/34 Annie? C. Howland, both of Palmyra, in Canandaigua;
Rev. R. C. Shimcall (5-5/23)
9416. Walsh, Dudley, Esq., late Pres. of the Bank of Albany, age 54,d 5/24/16
in Albany (3-6/5)
9417. Walsh, Margaret (Miss), dau of late Dudley Walsh, Esq.,d in Albany
(3-11/19/17)
9418. Walsh, Sarah, wid of late Dudley Walsh, Esq. of Albany d 6/22/16 in
Peekskill (3-7/3)
9419. Walters, Daniel D. (Dr.) d in NYC (3-11/23)
9420. Walters, Lurancey, 34, wf of Jacob, d in Bath (3-10/29/28)
9421. Walters, Parmelia, 33, consort of John, d 5/11/22 in Bath (3-5/29)
9422. Walton, Andrew, 55, d 9/1/24 in Batavia (1-9/3)
9423. Walton, Horace m 3/23/25 Aurelia Clark in Batavia; Daniel Tisdale, Esq.
(1-3/25)
9424. Walton, Rhoena (Mrs.), 18, d 4/2/24 in Batavia (1-4/9)
9425. Walton, William m 2/25/41 Susan Ann Carpenter, dau of George S. of
Palmyra; Rev. T. S. Brittan. All of Palmyra (5-3/3)(Married in Palmyra)
9426. Wannenberg, Francis, Jr. m 3/11/32 Sophronia Page in Cohocton; Olive
Rice, Esq. (2-3/21)
9427. Ward, Alexis, Esq., attorney, m 1/11/26 Laura Goodrich, both of Newport,
in N; Rev. Smith, rector of St. James Church, Batavia (1-1/13)
9428. Ward, Archibald m 8/9/26 Sally Patterson in Orangeville; Rev. Ward. All
of Orangeville (1-8/18)
9429. Ward, Daniel of Palmyra m 8/24/37 Phebe Ann Selby of Williamson; Rev.
Jonathan Benson (a double ceremony - see marr. of Peter More)
(5-9/1)
9430. Ward, Henry Dana, one of the editors of the New York Whig, m Mrs. Abby P.
McGlassin of NYC in NYC; Rev. Somers (4-11/30/31)
9431. Ward, James F. m 4/15/42 Lydia Ann Wheeler in Cohocton; Rev. Story
(2-4/20)
9432. Ward. Levi of Ontario, NY m 12/6/25 Lillis Barton of Lansingburgh; Rev.
Wightman (3-12/19)
9433. Ward, Lucinda, 29, wf of Deacon John, d 8/1/46 in Bergen (1-8/14)
9434. Ward, Lucy Jane, 19, consort of Joseph and dau of Rufus, d 9/4/30 at
Wolcott Furnace. "Her infant child died 30 August previous, age
10 days." (5-9/17)
9435. Ward, Ransom, 39, d in Butler, Wayne Co. (3-5/2/27)
9436. Ward, Samuel m Harriet Warren in Groveland, Liv. Co. (3-10/10/27)
9437. Ward, Samuel C. of the firm of J. D. Bemis and Co. m 4/5/21 Emily
Stanley, dau of Col. Asa, in Canandaigua; Rev. Barlow (3-4/18 and
5-4/25)
9438. Ward, Smith, 45, d in Junius (3-4/23/28)
9439. Ward, William (Rev.),a missionary of the Baptist Church,d 3/27/23 in
Serampore, India (3-9/17)
9440. Warden, George of Arcadia m 2/27/42 Hannah Eliza Moore of Lyons in L;
Rev. Ingraham (5-3/6)
9441. Warden, John, 78, d 9/30/41 in Bath (one of the earliest settlers there)
(2-10/6)
9442. Warden, Phoebe, 19, dau of John, d 7/16/11 in Seneca (3-7/31)
9443. Warden, Sylvester m 2/7/44 Eliza Scott; Amos Feller, Esq. (4-2/16)
9444. Ware, Mary, 5 mo, inf ch of Rev. Joseph K., d 3/31/38 in Palmyra
(5-4/4)
9445. Wares (or Vares), John, 8 mo, s of Francis, d 7/13/23 (prob. in Geneva)
(3-7/16)

9446. Warne (sic), Israel m Elizabeth Hurlbut in Erin (3-11/26/28)
9447. Warnee, Pyncheon m 1/3/27 Prudence H. Goodwin in Geneva; Rev. Dr. Axtell (3-1/17)
9448. Warner, Aaron (Rev.) m 7/4/28 Mary Hardy in Haverhill, MA . Also, Rev. Bates of Newton to Emily Atwood. "These ladies are daughters of the late Mr. Moses Atwood and sisters of Mrs. Harriet Newell, the first martyr to the missionary cause from America." (3-7/9)
9449. Warner, Archelaus, 25, d 4/24/49 in Le Roy (1-5/1)
9450. Warner, David of Palmyra m 6/27/22 Dulcena Stetson of Pittsford in P; (5-7/3)
9451. Warner, David, 75, d 5/23/40 in Macedon (5-5/27)
9452. Warner, Frances, 25, wf of Riel and dau of late William Shepard, Esq., d 12/6/30 in Canandaigua (5-12/10)
9453. Warner, Frederick m Deborah Evans in Lima (3-7/1/18)
9454. Warner, George, Esq., 74, d 1/4/25 in NYC (3-1/19)
9455. Warner, Hiel, merchant, m Frances Shepard in Canandaigua (3-9/19/27)
9456. Warner, Hiram m 10/14/29 Mary Jane Knapp in Hopewell; Rev. Elder Rice (3-10/21)
9457. Warner, Hiram of Wheeler m 3/28/47 Susan Osterhout of Urbana in Bath; A. D. Read, Esq. (2-3/31)
9458. Warner, Levi m 4/8/35 Ann Jagger; Rev. Merrit. All of Palmyra (5-4/10)
9459. Warner, Lewis, Esq., 40, d 2/26/13 in Phelps (surv by wf and "several young children"; interred with Masonic honors) (3-3/3)
9460. Warner, Miranda, 12, dau of Samuel, d 11/21/13 in Seneca (3-11/24)
9461. Warner, Rice m 9/10/18 Rebecca Carson in Phelps (3-9/23)
9462. Warner, Royal D. m 9/1/35 Amanda Palmiter, dau of Phineas, Jr., in Jamestown; A. Lewis, Esq. (4-9/2)
9463. Warner, Ruth, 46, wf of David, d 11/18/21 in Palmyra ("a mother") (5-11/21)
9464. Warner, Seth A. L., Esq. m 9/7/15 Sally Wixom in Hector; Hon. Richard Smith (3-9/27)
9465. Warner, Solomon, Maj.), about 50, d 3/22/13 in Seneca (3-3/24)
9466. Warner, William m 9/24/31 Naomi Chase; S. A. Johnson, Esq. (2-9/28)
9467. Warren, _____ (Mrs.), wf of William, and her infant child d in Canandaigua (3-3/17/13)
9468. Warren, Alice Anna, inf dau of E. F., Esq., d 10/17/39 in Jamestown (4-10/23)
9469. Warren, Charles Joseph, 7, s of Nathaniel, d 5/14/40 in Palmyra (5-5/20)
9470. Warren, David P. m 5/18/50 Alethea Emerson, both of Brockport, in Roanoke; A. D. Lampkins, Esq. of Le Roy (1-5/28)
9471. Warren, Edward (Rev.), 32, grad of Middlebury (VT) College and American Missionary, d 8/11/18 in Ceylon (5-1/27/19)
9472. Warren, Elijah (Capt.), about 70, d 10/15/24 in Canandaigua (3-10/20)
9473. Warren, Emory F., Esq. of Kennedy m 12/24/33 Timandea Sackett of Fredonia in F; Rev. Joy Handy (4-1/1/34)
9474. Warren, Gamaliel m Patience Burden in Palmyra; William A. McLean, Esq. (5-3/27/22)
9475. Warren, Job m 1/4/23 Miss _____ Burden in Palmyra; William A. McLean, Esq. (5-1/8)
9476. Warren, Joseph Butler m 3/11/50 Elizabeth Brooks in Bath; Rev.J. R. Tuttle. All of Bath (2-3/20)
9477. Warren, Laura Ann, 28, wf of Nathaniel, d 3/31/40 in Palmyra (5-4/15)
9478. Warren, Lucretia, 4, dau of J. W. and Sarah, d 9/20/41 in Bath(2-9/22)
9479. Warren, Marcus C. m 9/23/41 Nancy Logan in Bath; Rev. Frazer (3-9/29)
9480. Warren, Maria L., 21, relict of late Stewart K., d 5/13/42 in Bath (2-5/25)
9481. Warren, Matson m 12/2/29 Phebe Gleason in Manchester; Esq. VanFleet (5-12/25 and 3-12/30)
9482. Warren, Phineas, 65, d 3/4/42 in Bath (2-3/16)
9483. Warren, Rachel Amelia, dau of late Steward K., d 1/18/42 in Bath (2-2/2)
9484. Warren, Reuben B. of Alabama, NY m 8/29/48 Huldah E. Spafford of Brighton, C.W. (Canada West?) in Brighton; Rev. John Bridges (1-9/12)
9485. Warren, Samuel m 1/11/29 Sarah Sharp of Baldwinsville in Cicero (3-1/21)
9486. Warren, Sarah (Miss), 20, d 7/25/21 in Palmyra (5-8/1)

9487. Warren, Sarah B., 38, wf of Jonathan and only dau of J. T. and Lucretia
      Johnson of Bath, d 8/25/50 in Bath (2-9/4)
9488. Warren, Steward K, m 3/25/40 Maria L. Willour in Bath; H. Pier, Esq.
      (2-4/8)
9489. Warren, Steward K., 26, d 5/31/41 in Bath (2-6/2)
9490. Warren, William (Capt.), 80, nephew of Gen. Joseph and father of Oliver
      W. L. of Bath, d 7/29/31 in Worcester, MA (a Rev. soldier "wounded at
      Bunker's Hill"; later commanded an armed vessel) (2-9/14 and 5-8/30)
9491. Warring, Michael, 42, d 9/9/26 in Milo (3-9/20)
9492. Washburn, Hiram m 7/4/21 Amanda Hill in Palmyra (3-7/25)
9493. Washburn, Jonn R. m 12/8/33 Amanda Wire, both of Aurora, Erie Co., in A;
      Rev. Whalings (1-12/17)
9494. Washington, John A., "the proprietor of Mt. Vernon, died week before last"
      (2-7/4/32)
9495. Washington, William (Gen.) d 5/16/10 in Sandy Hill, SC (3-5/23)
9496. Washington, William Augustine (Col.), 52, d in Georgetown; buried in the
      vault at Mt. Vernon near his "illustrious relative" (3-11/7/10)
9497. Wass, Adam, about 70, d 9/29/38 in Jasper (2-10/17)
9498. Waterman, Curtis m Betsey Thayer in Palmyra (3-2/3/19)
9499. Waterman, E. S. of Lodi m 2/28/39 D. M. Brown of Ellington in E; Rev.
      Morse (4-3/6)
9500. Waterman, Joshua W., Esq. of Detroit, MI m 7/4/49 Eliza Cameron Davenport,
      dau of Ira, Esq. of Bath, at the Episcopal Church in Bath; Rev.
      Corson (2-7/11)
9501. Waterman, Rollin of Byron m 9/5/48 Hannah Bostwick of Le Roy at the
      Genesee House, Batavia (1-9/19)
9502. Waters, Cassa, "the black woman sentenced to be executed in February
      next" died in the Canandaigua jail (3-10/19/14)
9503. Waters, Daniel D., M.D., d 11/15/25 in NYC "of a lingering illness"
      (1-11/25)
9504. Waters, Eber, 16, d 7/17/27 in Geneva (3-7/18)
9505. Waters, Samuel m 2/14/27 Nancy Masters, both of Rochester, in R
      (3-2/21)
9506. Waterson, John m 3/16/25 Sarah Jones at the Glass Factory; Rev. Dr.
      Axtell (3-3/23)
9507. Watkins, _____ of Gorham m 2/4/15 Deborah Whitney, dau of Rascum of
      Geneva, in G; Rev. Axtell (3-2/8)
9508. Watkins, Agatha, widow, "a colored woman", d 11/28/45 in Bath (2-12/3)
9509. Watkins, Alexander m Pede Legg in Naples, NY (3-2/25/29)
9510. Watkins, Edmund G. m 3/3/31 Catharine Strong in Bath; D. G. Skinner,
      Esq. (2-3/2?/31)
9511. Watkins, Harriet, 58, wf of Simon, d 12/20/49 in Bath (member of
      New School Presby. Church, Bath (2-12/26)
9512. Watkins, John, Esq. m 11/9/10 Polly Keeler of Junius in J; Rev. Stewart
      (3-11/14)
9513. Watkins, John D., Esq. of Petersburgh, GA m 12/18/25 Anna A. Yates, dau
      of Gov. Yates, in Schenectady (3-12/19/25)
9514. Watkins, Simon, 64, "a colored man", d 8/22/50 in Bath (born a slave in
      Virginia "and came to this country with his master, Capt. Helm, more
      than 40 years ago and was held in bondage by several different
      masters ... when by the interference of the Hon. John C. Spencer
      who instituted legal proceedings on behalf of Simon he obtained his
      freedom") (2-8/28)
9515. Watkinson, Harriot, 13, oldest dau of William and Sarah, d 4/20/18 in
      Benton (3-4/22)
9516. Watson, _____, 2 yrs, ch of Mr. Watson, d 7/26/24 in Geneva (3-7/28)
9517. Watson, Charlotte M., 19, wf of William W. and dau of Jeremiah Sherwood,
      d 11/15/22 in Geneva (surv by husband) (3-11/20)
9518. Watson, Elizur m Rebecca Holloway in Almond (3-6/18/28)
9519. Watson, George E. of the house of Decuyer and Watson, oldest s of
      Elkanah, Esq. of Albany, d 6/13/19 in Detroit, Mich. Terr. (3-7/7)
9520. Watson, Joseph m Keziah Redfield in Junius (3-1/16/22)
9521. Watson, Margaret, widow, 74, d 12/6/46 in Bath (2-12/9)
9522. Watson, Samuel, 32, ornamental painter, d 9/4/26 in Geneva (3-9/6)
9523. Watson, Seneca m 8/12/50 Lydia Mills in Bath; Rev. B. R. Swick. All of
      Bath (2-8/14)

9524. Watson, Susan, 7 mo, only ch of William, d 5/7/21 in Geneva (3-5/9)
9525. Watson, Thomas M., 30, of the Arcade House, d 5/16/42 in Rochester (5-5/25)
9526. Watson, William R. m 2/21/44 Elizabeth Walbridge in Kalamozoo (MI?); Rev. O. P. Hoyt (4-3/15)
9527. Watson, William W. m 8/9/19 Charlotte Sherwood, dau of Jeremiah, in Geneva; Rev. Axtell (3-9/15)
9528. Watson, William W. m 10/25/25 Eliza Goundry, dau of Col. George, in Geneva; Rev. Orin Clark (3-10/26)
9529. Watson, Winslow C., Esq., attorney, s of Elkanah, Esq., m 5/28/28 Frances Skinner, dau of Chief Justice Skinner, late Gov. of VT, in VT (3-6/18)
9530. Watterman, Curtis m 1/26/19 Betsey Thayer in Palmyra; Rev. Jeremiah Irons (5-1/27)
9531. Wattles, Mason, Esq., 68, d in Nanticoke, Broome Co. (a Rev. officer) (3-8/4/19)
9532. Watts, _____ (Mr.), 46, d 11/29/40(prob. in Jamestown) (4-12/2)
9533. Watts, John (Dr.), eminent physician and president of the College of Physicians, d in NYC (5-2/18/31)
9534. Way, Andrew, 83, d in Summerset, PA (a Rev. soldier) (5-1/24/32)
9535. Way, Asa, late of Saratoga Co., m 9/5/40 Fanny Beckwith in Bath; Rev. Wing (2-9/9)
9536. Way, Chancey m 4/25/34 Sophronia Trask in Harmony; John Stow, Jr., Esq. (4-5/14)
9537. Weare, Benjamin C., 27, d 10/11/25 in Geneva (3-10/12)
9538. Weatherly, Warren W. of Jamestown m 8/13/43 Mary E. Austin of Concord, Erie Co.; Rev. Zachariah Eddy (4-8/31)
9539. Weaver, David m 11/11/24 Lucinda Richards in Stafford; Rev. Anson (1-11/19)
9540. Weaver, Joseph m 9/18/10 Kitty Spinner of Milford, Bucks Co., PA (3-10/3)
9541. Webb, Erastus (Dr.) m 12/5/11 Ruby Benton, both of Benton (3-12/11)
9542. Webb, James m 1/1/44 Charlotte Hersey, both of Palmyra; Rev. D. K. Lee of Newark, NY (5-1/3). (Married in Palmyra)
9543. Webb, John of West Bloomfield m Nancy Gillet of Detroit (MI?) in Lima, NY (3-3/3/19)
9544. Webb, Joseph, 20, d in Middlesex (3-7/23/17)
9545. Webb, Stephen, Jr. m Hannah Travace in Arkport (3-4/2/17)
9546. Webb, Thomas S., author of the Mason's Monitor, d 5/6/19 in Cleveland, Ohio "on a journey from Boston to the western country" (3-8/11)
9547. Weber, Eunice, 42, wf of Joseph, formerly of Busti, and sister of Pearl Johnson of Jamestown, d 2/4/44 in Hillsboro, Mont. Co., IL (4-3/8)
9548. Weber, Margaret, 8, d 6/16/31 and Martha, 6, d 6/20, both of Busti and both daus of Joseph (4-6/22)
9549. Weber, Nicholas, 78, formerly of Busti, d 2/28/44 in Hillsboro, Mont. Co., MI (4-3/29)
9550. Weber, Sally, 50, wf of Michael formerly of Busti and sister of Pearl Johnson of Jamestown, d 9/19/44 in Hillsboro, Mont. Co., MI (4-11/1)
9551. Webster, Aden of Truxton m 1/18/14 Charlotte Bacon of Phelps in P; Joseph Hall, Esq. (3-1/26)
9552. Webster, Asher B. m 2/25/36 Susan Duer; Rev. Moore. All of East Palmyra (perhaps a double wedding - see marr. of Abraham Woodbeck) (5-3/4)
9553. Webster, Caleb, 72, of Alden m 9/28/24 Mrs. Lydia Rice, 62, of Pembroke in P; Rev. Hugh Wallace (1-10/1)
9554. Webster, Charles J. m 5/24/17 Oravilla Fish, both of Cayuga Co; Jacob Dox, Esq. (3-5/28)
9555. Webster, Daniel (Hon.) of Boston m Caroline Le Roy, youngest dau of Herman, Esq., in NYC; Rev. Dr. Wainright (3-12/23/29 and 5-12/25/29)
9556. Webster, Edward, Esq. of Cuba, NY m 10/31/50 Polly Ann Andrews of Bethany in B; Rev. A.H. Starkweather (1-11/5)
9557. Webster, Fanny Delphene, 9 mo, dau of James and Caroline, d 3/24/47 in Bath (2-3/31)
9558. Webster, George, printer and bookseller, m 10/20/10 Sarah Rush of Massachusetts in Albany (3-11/7)
9559. Webster, George, 60, bookseller and one of the editors and proprietors of the Albany Gazette and Daily Advertiser, d 2/21/23 in Albany (surv by "a large family") (3-3/5 and 5-3/12)

9560. Webster, Horace, Esq., Professor of Math. and Natural Philosophy in Geneva College, m 3/27/27 Sarah M. Fowler, dau of William, Esq. of Albany, in A; Rev. Weed (3-4/4)
9561. Webster, Ithamar m 8/23/49 Harriet Nixon in Bath; Rev. L. M. Miller. All of Bath (2-8/29)
9562. Webster, Ithamar, 25, d 6/23/50 in Bath (2-6/26)
9563. Webster, James R. of Phelps m 7/2/29 Eliza N. Mullender of Seneca; Rev. Strong (3-7/22)
9564. Webster, Noah, Esq., 91, d 11/9/13 in Hartford, CT (3-12/1)
9565. Webster, Sarah, 76, relict of Noah, Esq., d in Hartford, CT (3-6/23/19)
9566. Webster, William Fowler, 1 yr, s of Prof. Webster of Geneva College, d 4/13/29 in Geneva (3-4/15)
9567. Wedge, Benjamin m 6/8/46 Polly Star, both of Howard, in H; John L. Roberds, Esq. (2-6/10)
9568. Wedge, Joseph m Sophia Winslow, both of Lyons, in Rochester (3-9/18/22)
9569. Wedge, Olive (Miss), 14, d in Hector (3-8/25/19)
9570. Weed, _____ (Mrs.), consort of Israel, d 9/16/24 in Junius (3-9/29)
9571. Weed, George of the house of G. Weed and Co. of Buffalo and son of Smith Weed of Albany, d in Auburn (3-9/10/28)
9572. Weed, Thaddeus m Louisa M. Chapin in Buffalo (3-10/29/23)
9573. Weed, Walter, merchant, of Albany m 12/21/10 Cornelia Vredenburgh, dau of William J., Esq. of Skaneateles in S (3-1/9/11)
9574. Weeks, Clark T. m 7/1/47 Levina Lewillin in Bergen; Samuel Richmond, Esq. All of Bergen (1-7/20)
9575. Weeks, Joshua m Sarah Birdsell in Olean (3-12/9/18)
9576. Weeks, William m 3/28/47 Margaret Brazee, both of Barre, in Pine Hill; Rev. D. F. Hutchinson (1-4/13)
9577. Weitzel, Isaac m Charlotte Rathbon, both of Waterloo, in W (3-7/5/26)
9578. Welch, Adolphus m 7/29/49 Hellen Marr Graham, both of Starkey, at the Clinton House in Bath; A. D. Read, Esq. (2-8/1)
9579. Welch, Daniel, Esq., 78, of Mendon d in Ontario, NY (3-9/19/27)
9580. Welch, Ebenezer, 40, of Canandaigua d in Catskill (3-6/20/27)
9581. Welch, Samuel, 112, d 4/5/23 in Bow, NH (3-5/7)
9582. Welch, Stephen, 69, formerly of Trenton, NJ, d 4/19/27 in Seneca, NY (3-5/2)
9583. Weller, Amos R. m 1/3/38 Maryann D'Lamatter in Jamestown; S. Jones, Esq. (4-1/10)
9584. Weller, Amos R., 30, d 11/2/45 in Jamestown (4-11/7)
9585. Weller, Dorliska Angelia, 2 yrs, only child of Amos R. and Mary Ann, d 4/25/41 in Jamestown (4-4/28)
9586. Welles, Henry S. m Margaret Haight, dau of Gen. S. S. Haight (3-1/27/19)
9587. Welles, Randolph of Clyde m 6/17/19 Betsey Rathbone of Junius (3-7/14)
9588. Welles, Silvester, s of Dr. Benjamin, m 6/23/10 Jemima Holdridge in Wayne; Dr. Benjamin Welles (3-8/15)
9589. Welles, William E. of Wayne m 1/1/17 Harriet Prentiss of Pulteney in P (3-1/22)
9590. Wellington, James m 1/1/44 Catharine Dow; Rev. O. Street (4-1/12)
9591. Wellington, James D. of Ashville m 4/28/31 Lucinda Nichols of Ripley in R; Rev. Gregory (4-5/4)
9592. Wellman, Harvey m 9/22/42 Emily Van Deuzen in Busti; D. Williams, Esq. (4-9/29)
9593. Wellman, Henry of Ashville m 12/8/39 Elvira Blodget of Busti in B; Jonathan Bullock, Esq. (4-12/11)
9594. Wellman, James, 58, d 2/24/42 in Ashville (4-3/3)
9595. Wellman, Stephen m Charlotte Blanchard (4-1/23/33)
9596. Wells, Benjamin, 53, d in Chemung (3-4/16/28)
9597. Wells, Benjamin (Gen.), 72, (a Rev. officer and one of the earliest settlers in Steuben Co.) d 6/4/28 in Hopewell (3-6/25)
9598. Wells, Chester, 34, merchant, late of Binghamton, d in Jersey, NY (3-10/22/28)
9599. Wells, David (Capt.) of Howard m 10/6/31 Polly Hanna of Bath in B; Rev. Lyman Barritt (2-10/12)
9600. Wells, Henry m Sarah Daggert in Palmyra (3-9/19/27)
9601. Wells, Henry m 3/13/39 Eliza Cutler; Rev William Butts. Probably all are of Harmony (4-3/20)

9602. Wells, Isaac of Truxton, Cort. Co. m 7/12/25 Sarah Wells of Attica in A;
Judge Robert Earll (1-7/15)
9603. Wells, James m Jane Hapgood, both of Harmony, in Mayville (4-1/10/27)
9604. Wells, James D., 35, printer, d 12/8/25 in Rochester (3-12/21)
9605. Wells, John, Esq., 52, attorney, d 9/7/23 in NYC (surv by wf and at least
one child) (3-9/17)
9606. Wells, Lauren m Laura Dimmick in Junius (3-3/1/20)
9607. Wells, Luke m 3/25/30 Permelia A. Piper in Palmyra; William Willcox, Esq.
(See marr. of George Cooley this date) (5-3/26)
9608. Wells, Luke m 9/22/31 Samantha Coon in Palmyra; M. W. Willcox,Esq.
(5-9/27)
9609. Wells, Maria, 50, wf of Dr. Richard, d 7/25/31 in Canandaigua (5-8/5)
9610. Wells, Marsh, 25, d 10/9/44 in Alexander (1-10/15)
9611. Wells, Rachel, 21, wf of William H., merchant, of Batavia and dau of
James Ganson, Esq. of Livingston Co. d 7/31/22 (1-8/2)
9612. Wells, Randolph (Dr.), 30, d 11/19/25 in Junius (3-11/30)
9613. Wells, Walter m Abigail Lockwood in Gorham (3-12/17/17)
9614. Wells, Willard (Dr.) m Loa Dickinson in Vienna, NY (3-9/17/17)
9615. Welsh, Abraham m 1/20/25 Lydia Taylor in Seneca; Rev. O. Clark(3-1/26)
9616. Welton, Alanson W. (Rev.), late of Richmond, Ontario Co,, d 9/30/22 in
Detroit, Mich. Terr. (3-10/23)
9617. Welton, Alfred T. m Semantha Miller in Canandaigua (3-2/10/13)
9618. Welton, Cyrus m 10/2/26 Agnes Hover in Batavia; C. Carpenter, Esq.
(1-10/6)
9619. Welton, Walter V. P., 10, s of Elias, d in Bath (3-11/4/29)
9620. Wentworth, A. H. of Manchester m 11/20/42 Mary Hine of Palmyra (5-11/30)
9621. Wentworth, Abigail, 41, wf of Uriah, d in Fredonia (3-5/2/27)
9622. Wentworth, Chester, about 35, d 5/13/46 in Bath (2-5/20)
9623. Wentworth, Edward D. m 2/8/38 Mary McNutt, both of Manchester, in
Palmyra; F. Smith, Esq. (5-2/14)
9624. Wentworth, George m 1/13/47 Eunice Cruttenden in Burns, Alleg. Co.; Rev.
Twitchel. All of Burns (2-2/17)
9625. Wentworth, Renning, 60, d 2/9/35 in Kennedyville (2-3/11)
9626. Werks, Sarah, 17 mo, dau of I., d 4/4/22 in Geneva (5-4/17)
9627. Wescott, ____, 2 yrs, ch of "Mr. Wescott", d 6/27/29 (3-7/1)
9628. Wescott, Leonard of Palmyra m 9/25/23 Elizabeth Carpenter of Vernon
in V (3-10/8)
9629. Wescott, Leonard, about 40, d 3/20/32 in Albany (formerly a merchant
in Palmyra) (5-3/28)
9630. West, ____ of Rochester m 11/25/17 Huldah Green of Orleans in O; Rev.
Axtell (3-12/3)
9631. West, A. H. m 10/15/20 Sally Pierce in Farmington (5-10/18)
9632. West, Daniel (Deacon), 73, of Brighton m Miss Lydia Ingersol, 65, of
Victor in V; Rev. Raymond (3-12/4/22)
9633. West, Eleazer m 4/7/14 Amanda Flint, both of Phelps, in P (3-4/13)
9634. West, Elias m Cynthia Cooper in Farmington (5-1/12/20)
9635. West, Ira, 46, d 6/4/32 in Rochester (one of the earliest settlers and
merchants of Rochester - opened a store there in 1812) (5-6/18)
9636. West, James, 5, s of "Mrs. Betsey" d 3/26/22 in Clyde (Galen) (3-4/10).
Death place is Geneva in 5-4/17.
9637. West, John P., formerly of Brutus, m 2/19/22 Rachel Pratt of Williamson
in W (3-2/27)
9638. West, Lebbeus, 19, d in Palmyra (3-1/24/16)
9639. West, Mary, 1 yr, dau of Xenocrates, d 2/24/32 in Bath (2-3/14)
9640. West, Nancy, 29, wf of Henry, d in Galen (3-1/8/23)
9641. West, Pelatiah, 43, d 2/6/36 in Palmyra (an elder in the Presby. Church;
surv by wife and several children) (5-2/12)
9642. West, Samuel H., 22, s of X. West, d "in Natchez" (3-12/23/29)
9643. West, Stephen (Rev.), D.D., d 5/15/19 in Stockbridge, MA (pastor of
Presby. Church there for more than 50 years)(3-6/9)
9644. West, Susannah, 2 yrs, dau of Henry, d 4/4/22 in Clyde (Galen) (3-4/10)
9645. West, William m 12/21/14 Polly Ross in Gorham (3-12/28)
9646. Westcott, Thomas F. m Mrs. Sarah Soper in Benton (3-3/11/29)
9647. Westfall, Edward, 25, d 10/17/43 in Palmyra (funeral at home of J.
Westfall, father of the deceased) (5-10/18)

9648. Westfall, James, 2nd, m 5/22/14 Hannah Middaugh in Phelps; Joseph Hall, Esq. (3-6/1)
9649. Westfall, James m Ann Humphrey, both of Phelps; Rev. Lane of Waterloo (3-10/17/27)
9650. Westfall, James, 78, d 12/30/29 in Phelps ("one of the earliest inhabitants of that town") (5-2/5/30)
9651. Westfall, Uriah, 28, d 3/3/40 in Palmyra (5-3/4/40)
9652. Westlake, Abraham m 1/27/28 Elizabeth Maynard, both of Junius, in Geneva; Eurotus Hastings, Esq. (3-2/13)
9653. Westlake, John m Betsey Harrison in Elmira (3-5/12/19)
9654. Westover, Hiram of Randolph m 9/14/35 Onlelia Gleason of Napoli, NY in N; Rev. Cowles (4-9/16)
9655. Wetherbee, Judah (Capt.), 77, d in Stow, MA (a Rev. soldier) (5-1/24/32)
9656. Wetmore, Anna, 58, wf of Ebenezer, d 5/11/36 in Carroll (4-5/25)
9657. Wetmore, Edmund A., Esq. m Mary A. Lothrop, dau of J. H., Esq., in Utica (3-6/17/29)
9658. Wetmore, Moses B. m 12/24/27 Dorothy Edmonston, dau of Thomas, Esq., in Vienna, NY (3-12/26)
9659. Wetsell, Christian, 99, d 2/7/34 in Ellery (a Rev. soldier) ("Editors in Genesee, Madison, and Saratoga counties please give this an insertion") (4-2/12)
9660. Wey, William H., Esq., cashier of the Catskill Bank, m 5/7/15 Caroline L. Stanley at St. Luke's Church in Catskill; Rev. Prentice (3-5/24)
9661. Weyburn, Jacob, 23, d 9/24/29 (3-9/30)
9662. Whaley, Christopher of Shelby m 3/16/24 Mary Ann Smith, second dau of Ralph Coffin Smith, Esq. of Batavia,in B; Rev. Lucius Smith (1-3/19)
9663. Whaley, James m 3/22/17 Eleanor Wood of Geneva (3-3/26)
9664. Whaley, Robert, innkeeper, d 2/3/18 in Perry, Genesee Co. ("He was apparently in his usual health, sitting by the fire, when he fell from his chair and instantly expired.") (3-2/18)
9665. Whartenby, Benjamin F. m Mrs. Elizabeth Todd in Waterloo (3-11/26/28)
9666. Wharton, Franklin (Col.), commandant of the U.S. Marine Corps,d in NYC (3-9/9/18)
9667. Wheat, John S. m Ursula Cole in Benton (3-9/15/19)
9668. Wheaton, Cyrus m 7/29/42 Julia Chase in Prattsburgh; Seth Wheeler, Esq. (2-8/3)
9669. Wheaton, Jonathan, s of Syrenus, d 8/26/26 in Junius (3-9/6)
9670. Whedon, Mary, 4, dau of Capt. Calvin, d 2/8/23 in Seneca (3-2/12)
9671. Whedon, Alphonso m 5/29/28 Frances Park; Rev. Nisbet. All of Seneca (3-6/18)
9672. Whedon, Samuel, 88, father of Marcena, d 1/14/22 in Seneca (3-1/16)
9673. Whedon, Samuel, Esq., formerly of Geneva, m 8/4/24 Mary Lockman, both of Brownstone, Indiana, in B (3-10/6)
9674. Wheeler, _____ (Mr.) of Richfield m about 2/24/42 Rhoda Mack of South Dansville (2-3/9)
9675. Wheeler, Charles Edward, 3 yrs, s of Elias of the Sinclairville House d in Sinclairville (scalded in a vessel of boiling water) (4-1/26/44)
9676. Wheeler, Elizur, 57, d 5/6/15 in Windham, Greene Co. (died from the bite of a wolf - "ill but 4 days") (3-5/31)
9677. Wheeler, George m Mary Wilson in Palmyra (3-12/10/17)
9678. Wheeler, James m Sally Chambers in Ovid (3-1/16/22)
9679. Wheeler, James Monroe, 2 yrs, s of James, d in Carroll (4-3/12/34)
9680. Wheeler, John, 16, m 10/10/18 Elizabeth Temple, 30, in Ovid; Rev. A. Brocaw (3-10/21)
9681. Wheeler, John G., formerly of Bath, m 1/8/50 Emily E. Wait of Janesville, Wisconsin in J (2-1/30)
9682. Wheeler, Joseph m 2/5/22 Allida Jackson in Palmyra; William A. McLean, Esq. (5-2/13)
9683. Wheeler, Joseph, Esq., merchant, of Augusta, GA m Julia Knox Hull, seventh dau of Gen. William, in Newton, MA (3-9/28/25)
9684. Wheeler, Josiah (Capt.) m 9/22/31 Anna Maria Parker in Carroll; Rev. Eddy (4-9/28)
9685. Wheeler, Josiah m 1/8/42 Mary Wallace, both of Carroll, in Sugargrove, PA; M. Willson, Esq. (4-1/13)
9686. Wheeler, Laura (Miss), 21, d 12/29/44 in Jamestown (4-1/3/45)

9687. Wheeler, Mary and Betsey, daus of David, d "the week previous"
near Junius (3-9/29/24)
9688. Wheeler, Mary, 89, consort of Jeremiah, d 11/28/50 in Bath (2-12/11)
9689. Wheeler, N. Sanger m 1/7/47 Barbary Lewis in Bath; Rev. C. Wheeler.
All of Bath (2-1/13)
9690. Wheeler, Noah d in Junius (3-6/11/28)
9691. Wheeler, O. P. m 12/11/42 Mary Erwin in Bath; Rev. Brown (2-12/14)
9692. Wheeler, Robert B. m 2/25/36 Hannah Doolittle in Branchport, Yates Co.;
Rev. Thomas J. Champion. All of Penn Yan (5-3/4)
9693. Wheeler, Sally, 66, wf of Capt. Silas, d in Wheeler (3-10/8/28)
9694. Wheeler, Salmon of Ithaca m Alica Babcock of Starkey, Yates Co.
(3-1/14/29)
9695. Wheeler, Sarah, 73, wf of Zenas, d 4/20/42 in Fluvanna (4-4/28)
9696. Wheeler, Silas m 11/28/41 Fidelia Frisbee in Wheeler; J. Larrow, Esq.
(2-12/15)
9697. Wheeler, William F., 52, late of NYC, d 9/7/35 in Fluvanna("Printers in
Mass. and N.H. will confer a favor by noticing the above") (4-9/9)
9698. Wheeler, William F. of Jamestown m 7/31/44 Martha R. Houghton; Rev.
S. M. Hopkins (4-8/9)
9699. Wheeler, Zachariah, 44, d 4/13/21 in Jerusalem, NY (3-4/23)
9700. Wheelock, Horace m 1/2/40 Lydia Walker, both of Poland, NY, in
Jamestown; Rev. A. Hall (4-1/8)
9701. Wheelock, Randilla (Miss), 32, d 3/23/43 in Fredonia (4-4/6)
9702. Whelpley, Samuel (Rev.), 50, d 7/15/17 in NYC (3-7/23)
9703. Whicher, Harriet N., 16, late of Westfield, NY, d 11/26/32 in Cicinnati,
Ohio (4-1/9/33)
9704. Whicher, Samuel m 7/8/35 Harriet Pierce; Rev. Kingsley (4-7/15)
9705. Whipple, _____, 14 mo, s of Charles, d 6/13/28 in Geneva (3-6/25)
9706. Whipple, _____, wf of Luther, d in Barrington; the same day her infant
dau, aged 4 weeks, died (3-10/29/28)
9707. Whipple, Abraham, 86, a native of R.I. and "the first naval commander
who fired a shot in the Revolutionary War", d in the state of Ohio
(3-7/14/19)
9708. Whipple, Benjamin, 63, "for many years door-keeper to the house of
assembly of this state", d in Albany (3-5/26/19)
9709. Whipple, Charles D., m Altha B. Werner in Palmyra (5-1/14/18). See 9716.
9710. Whipple Henry m 2/22/20 Elizabeth Nichols; Jacob Dox, Esq. All of
Geneva (3-3/1)
9711. Whipple, Lydia, wf of Robert, d in Whitesborough (3-5/2/27)
9712. Whipple, Newman m 2/15/40 Harriet, Chappel, both of Busti, in B; George
Stoneman, Esq. (4-2/19)
9713. Whipple, Simeon D., 16, d in Almond (3-5/7/28)
9714. Whipple, William H. of Wyoming Co. m 9/20/43 Susan H. McUmber of
Palmyra in Marion; Rev. S. F. Griswold (5-9/27)
9715. Whippo, Ann, 22, dau of James and Hannah, d 3/9/16 in Geneva (3-3/13)
9716. Whippo, Charles T. (Dr.) m Altha B. Warner in Palmyra (3-1/21/18). See 9709.
9717. Whitaker, Hester D., 38, wf of John, d 6/12/45 at Mud Creek (2-6/25)
9718. Whitaker, Stephen m 5/20/11 Mary Hall, both of Benton, in B; Rev. Lindley
(3-5/29)
9719. Whitcome, M. C. of Howard m 8/26/46 Lusina Hoadly of Avoca in A; H. S.
Rose, Esq. (2-9/2)
9720. White, _____, widow of late Rev. Thomas, d 12/28/27 in Geneva (3-1/2/28)
9721. White, _____, inf dau of Job, d in Waterloo (Job's son, Samuel, age 2,
died two days later - both children died of whooping cough) (3-3/12/28)
9722. White, Albert H. of Albion m 11/21/32 Lydia M. Porter of Macedon in M
(5-11/28)
9723. White, Alexander m 10/25/31 Esther Cornell in Bath; Henry W. Rogers, Esq.
(2-11/2)
9724. White, Betsey, 31, wf of James, d 2/11/31 in Jamestown (4-2/16)
9725. White, Charity (Mrs.), 24, d 7/30/22 in Galen (3-8/21)
9726. White, Daniel (Lt. Col.) of the 29th Regiment and a native of NY,
d 7/8/11 in Elvas Portugal "of the wound he received in battle at
Albuhers, the 16th May..." (3-10/2)
9727. White, Edward, 65, d 8/23/27 in Geneva (lived in this town 34 years)
(3-8/29)
9728. White, Elisha M., printer, d 3/12/42 in Southport (5-5/18) (age 30 at death)

9729. White, Elvira, 11 mo, dau of James, d in Jamestown (4-8/2/26)
9730. White, George, merchant, of Albany m 9/9/41 Helen Ann Taylor, dau of
George W. of Wheeler, in the Presby. Church of Bath; Rev. Platt
(2-9/15)
9731. White, George, 20, d 10/26/43 in Jamestown (4-10/26)
9732. White, Henry F., 3, s of Dr. James, d 1/30/35 (5-2/13)
9733. White, Horace (Capt.) m Polly Kellogg in Pulteneyville (3-11/24/19)
9734. White, Horatio, merchant, of the firm of Jackman and White d 2/21/38
in Columbus, Warren Co., PA (4-2/28) (Died at age 26)
9735. White, Hugh, Esq., 80, a native of Middletown, CT, d 4/16/12 in
Whitestown ("He may justly be considered the Patriarch who first
led the children of New England into the wilderness of present-day
central N.Y." In 1788 when the town of German Flats was divided,
the town of Whitestown (named for this man) which then housed fewer
than 200 persons covered all of New York west of Utica.) (3-5/6)
9736. White, Hugh, 85, late of Whitesborough, d in Shrewsbury, NJ (3-5/2/27)
9737. White, Ira, merchant, of Palmyra m 2/5/29 Jane Ranie in Geneva; Rev.
Mason (3-2/11)
9738. White, Ira of the firm of Zuill and White of Palmyra m 6/25/32 Esther
Bates, dau of Stephen, Esq. of Hopewell, in H (5-6/27)
9739. White, Ira A. (Capt.) m 2/15/31 Fidelia Johnson of Cedarville, Herk. Co.
in C; Rev. Hovey (2-3/2)
9740. White, Jane G., 33, consort of Ira, d 3/22/30 in Palmyra (5-3/26)
9741. White, Oren, merchant, m 1/1/18 Ann Thayer, dau of Nathan, in Palmyra;
Rev. J. Townsend. All of Palmyra (5-1/7)
9742. White, Polly, 11, youngest dau of Edward of Geneva, d 1/26/17 (3-1/29)
9743. White, Samuel of Tonawanda, PA m Elizabeth McDuffee of Palmyra, NY in
Athens, Bradford Co., PA; Rev. Cofee(?) (5-2/15/39)
9744. White, Samuel B. of Starkey m 6/24/47 Amanda Tomer of Pulteney in P
(2-6/30)
9745. White, Sophia (Miss), 17, dau of Nehemiah, d in Bath (3-4/1/29)
9746. White, Thomas (Rev.), 44, "pastor of the Associate Reformed Church
in No. 9", d 2/17/20 in Seneca (3-2/23)
9747. White, Thomas of Tyre m Mrs. Sophrona Garret in Junius (3-1/13/30)
9748. White, William of Macedon m 4/14/31 Jane A. Alexander of West Bloomfield
in W. B. (5-5/6)
9749. White, William, late of Bath, m 2/13/47 Angeline Hilton of Oakland Co.,
MI in O; Rev. John Smith (2-3/24)
9750. Whiteford, ____ (Mrs.), wf of Thomas, innkeeper, d 7/15/11 in Junius
(3-7/17/11)
9751. Whiteford, Thomas d 5/9/19 in Junius (3-5/12)
9752. Whitefield, James m 6/21/46 Jane Buck, both mutes, in Penn Yan; Rev.
Isaiah McMahon (2-7/1)
9753. Whiting, Anna, widow of Maj. Eb. and mother of Gen. B. Whiting of Genoa,
formerly of Norwich, CT, d in Norwich (3-7/11/27)
9754. Whiting, Bowen, Esq. of Geneva m 9/13/18 Nancy McKinstry, dau of Gen.
McKinstry of Hillsdale, Col. Co., in H (3-9/23)
9755. Whiting, Catharine (Miss), 19, dau of Capt. Augustus, d in Stuyvesant
(3-6/20/27)
9756. Whiting, Edward, 3, s of B. Whiting, Esq., d 6/5/26 (3-6/7)
9757. Whiting, Henry (Capt.) of the U.S. Army m Nancy Goodwin in Hudson
(3-3/11/18)
9758. Whiting, Jacob, 67, m D. Sabin, 19, his niece, in Halifax, VT (3-12/27/26)
9759. Whiting, James Adgar, 18, s of Gen. Charles, d in Kinderhook (3-12/23/29)
9760. Whiting, John m 12/5/13 Catharine Westfall in Phelps; Joseph Hall, Esq.
All of Phelps (3-12/15)
9761. Whiting, Levi C., Esq. m 11/23/42 Pamelia N. Woods, dau of late William,
Esq., in Bath; Rev. I. W. Platt (2-11/30)
9762. Whiting, Mariana, 2, ch of L. C., d 5/25/47 in Bath (2-6/16)
9763. Whiting, Nancy (Miss), 21, oldest dau of Gen. John, d 8/4/27 in Great
Barrington, MA (3-8/22)
9764. Whiting, Pamelia, 24, wf of late Hon. William Woods, d 7/29/47 in Bath
("Her widowed mother has in a few short years followed to the grave
a ... husband and all her children excepting two married daughters
and a son.") (2-8/4)
9765. Whiting, Sarah (Mrs.), "above 60 years", of Le Roy, Gen. Co. d 10/10/13
(3-10/13)

9766. Whiting, T. W. m 5/21/50 M. J. Lambert at the Methodist Church in Bath;
      Rev. D. Nutten (2-5/22)
9767. Whiting, William, 61 d in Le Roy, Gen. Co. (3-8/9/09)
9768. Whitlock, Thaddeus, 23, d 8/19/18 in Ovid (3-9/2)
9769. Whitman, Hiram m 10/5/30 Clarinda Hanchett, both of Chautauqua, in C;
      Rev. O. C. Beardsley (4-10/13)(a double ceremony - see marr. of David Shearman)
9770. Whitman, John Winslow, Esq., editor of the Boston Bachelors Journal,
      m Sarah Halen Power of Providence, RI in Jamaica RI (3-7/23/28)
9771. Whitmore, _____, relict of the late Deacon Oliver, d in Wolcott, Sen. Co.
      (3-9/22/19)
9772. Whitmore, Electa, 6 mo, dau of Seth, d 9/30/15 in Wolcott (3-10/18)
9773. Whitmore, Oliver (Deacon), 85, "formerly of this neighborhood", d 9/3/19
      in Wolcott, Sen. Co. (3-9/15)
9774. Whitmore, William of Columbia Co. m 8/6/42 Fanny Van Riper of Washington
      Co. (prob. in Palmyra); Frederick Smith, Esq. (5-9/7)
9775. Whitney, _____ (Mrs.), wf of Samuel W., d 7/27/22 in Rochester (5-8/21)
9776. Whitney, Benjamin m Mary Stark in Elmira (3-11/12/17)
9777. Whitney, David (Gen.), 62, m Eliza Wilson, 16, in Addison, VT (3-7/1/18)
9778. Whitney, Ebenezer, 60, d 8/27/24 , "late of Hopbottom", Susque.Co., PA
      (1-9/3)
9779. Whitney, Ephraim J., editor of the Lyons Advertiser, m Susan J. Perine,
      dau of Peter, Esq., in Lyons (3-10/31/27)
9780. Whitney, Franklin, merchant, of Chenango Point, Broome Co. m 9/12/26
      Eliza Cameron, dau of D. Cameron, Esq.; Rev. William W. Bostwick
      (3-9/20)
9781. Whitney, Henry, 48, merchant, of NYC d 3/14/12 in NYC (3-4/1)
9782. Whitney, Joel, Jr. m 4/3/17 Esther Belding, dau of Selah, in Seneca;
      Rev. Axtell (3-4/9)
9783. Whitney, John S., 29, d in Hopewell (3-9/12/27 and 2-9/19/27)
9784. Whitney, Jonas, 48, brother of Joel and Nathan, d 9/17/23 in Hopewell
      ("funeral attended with masonic honors") (3-10/8)
9785. Whitney, Jonas of Barre m 7/17/42 Julia E. Pollay of Batavia in B; Rev.
      A. Handy (1-7/19)
9786. Whitney, Joshua (Gen.) of Binghamton m Julia Crooker in Cairo, NY
      (3-10/3/27)
9787. Whitney, Lorenzo of Fairport m 1/19/43 Mary A. Johnson? of Farmington
      in F; Hon. P. Mitchell (5-1/25)
9788. Whitney, Nathan, Jr. m 12/12/11 Sarah Gray in Seneca; Rev. Wilson. All
      of Seneca (3-12/18)
9789. Whitney, Olive, about 70, wf of Lt. Nathan, d 11/17/29 in Seneca
      (3-11/18)
9790. Whitney, Otis m 3/1/15 Betsey Hawley in Seneca; Rev. Axtell (3-3/8)
9791. Whitney, Washington, merchant, m 12/17/26 Caroline Park, dau of Rufus,
      in Binghamton; Rev. Huse (3-1/5/27)
9792. Whitney, William W. m 3/9/36 Harriet B. Moore in Lyons; Rev. L. Hubbell
      (5-3/18)
9793. Whiton, John, Esq., 63, formerly of Stockbridge, MA, d 3/23/27 in Ithaca,
      NY (3-4/4)
9794. Whittemore, Moses F., publisher of the Constitutionalist, of Bath
      m 4/8/41 Sarah Webster in Bath; Rev. O. Frazer (2-4/14)
9795. Whittemore, Myra Hall, 10, adopted dau of S. and S. F., d 3/26/42 in
      Fluvanna (4-3/31)
9796. Whorton, William m 10/8/26 Phebe Loucks in Ellery; Peter Loucks, Esq.
      (4-10/18)
9797. Wicker, Joel F., 50, a local preacher of the Meth. Episc. Church , d in
      Floyd, Oneida Co. (3-12/23/29)
9798. Wicks, John m 9/13/35 Sarah Hoags in Macedon (5-9/18)
9799. Wier, Hugh m Nancy Chatham in Fayette (3-1/9/28)
9800. Wiggins, John m Amanda Cook in Seneca Falls (3-1/13/30)
9801. Wight, George m 2/25/29 Susan Milspaugh, both of Geneva, in G; Rev.
      Barton (3-3/4)
9802. Wilber, Abigail (Miss), 32, d 1/23/49 in Bath (2-1/31)
9803. Wilber, Benjamin S. m 3/3/35 Sophia Towl in Howard; S. T. Babbitt
      (2-3/18)
9804. Wilber, Elmira, 27, wf of Hoxy H., d 7/26/38 in Bath (2-8/1)
9805. Wilber, Hoxey H. m 4/12/42 Patience Legro in Bath; Rev. Fraser (2-4/20)

9806.  Wilber, John, 86, (a Rev. Soldier) father of Samuel, Esq. of Bath, d 11/9/46 in Troy, PA (2-12/9)
9807.  Wilber, Joseph m 3/26/20 Elizabeth Decker in Williamson (5-4/5)
9808.  Wilber, Samuel m 11/22/42 Sarah Allen, both of Palmyra (5-11/30)
9809.  Wilbur, Isaac Underhill m 9/13/43 Welthy Ann Thomas in Palmyra; Rev. D. Harrington. All of Palmyra (5-9/20)
       Wilcox. See also Willcox.
9810.  Wilcox, ____ m 2/12/40 Betsey Cogswell, both of Marion, in M; Rev. Stowell (5-2/19)
9811.  Wilcox, Bordon, 87, (a Rev. soldier) d 4/22/48 in Caryville, Gen. Co. (born in RI; moved to Colrain, MA first and then to MadisonCo., NY; in Batavia by 1812) (1-5/2)
9812.  Wilcox, Charles (Rev.), late of Hartford, CT, d in Danbury, CT (3-6/20/27)
9813.  Wilcox, Earl m Jane Stewart in Palmyra (3-12/20/15)
9814.  Wilcox, Frances R., 3 yrs, dau of A. G., d 6/27/45 in Napoli, Catt. Co. (4-7/4). Same newspaper dated 7/11: "...her death was occasioned by a bean in her trachea". A writer identified as "J. Uncles" furnishes here a lengthy account of the physicians' trials in their attempts to operate on the proper segment of the trachea. (4-7/4)
9815.  Wilcox, George m 3/2/23 Julia Stoddard, both of Palmyra, in Macedon; Rev. Snow (5-3/12)
9816.  Wilcox, George m Anna Johnson in Bath; Rev. Higgins (3-1/23/28)
9817.  Wilcox, Gideon m Mercy Harringdeen in Palmyra (3-12/10/17)
9818.  Wilcox, Hazard R. m Elizabeth Goss in Palmyra (3-10/17/27)
9819.  Wilcox, Hazard R., 36, d 11/1/38 in Palmyra (5-11/24)
9820.  Wilcox, Hiram m 10/15/24 "Miss Huntley" in Le Roy; S. Skinner, Esq. (1-10/22)
9821.  Wilcox, Irene, 33, wf of Freeborn, d 1/4/19 in Phelps (3-1/13)
9822.  Wilcox, John S. (Capt.) m 11/22/38 Polly Carpenter in Harmony; T. S. Bly, Esq. (4-12/5)
9823.  Wilcox, Joseph (Gen.), a Rev. officer, d in Marietta, Ohio (3-2/19/17)
9824.  Wilcox, Joseph, Esq. m 1/11/38 Eliza Barrows?; Rev. Wooster. All of Palmyra (5-1/17)
9825.  Wilcox, Joseph of Troupsburgh m 7/4/47 Jane Webster of Jasper in J; Elder William G. Raymond (2-7/21)
9826.  Wilcox, Luranel G., 62, wf of late Rev. William J., d 7/10/45 in Napoli, Catt. Co. (4-7/18)
9827.  Wilcox, Moses and Aaron, both age 54, both formerly of Middletown, CT, d in Twinsburgh, Ohio (Both were married the same day, their wives were sisters, both taken sick at the same time, both buried in the same grave) (3-11/7/27)
9828.  Wilcox, Samantha, 27, wf of Thomas A., d 8/13/46 in Bath (2-8/19)
9829.  Wilcox, Wilbur of Buffalo m 6/21/43 Mary Bowtel of Fredonia in F; Rev. S. M. Hopkins (4-7/13)
9830.  Wilder, Gamaliel, Esq., 75, a native of CT, d in Bristol (3-2/19)
9831.  Wilder, Julia, 10, dau of late Col. Joseph, d 4/12/41 in Attica (1-4/27)
9832.  Wilder, Rastus of Galen m 1/25/30 Katharine Meade of Lyons in L; Rev. Hubbell (5-3/5)
9833.  Wiley, Alexander m 12/24/28 Mahala Tibbets in Ontario, NY; Jonathan Boynton, Esq. (5-1/2/29)                                      (2-12/26)
9834.  Wilhelm, Isaac m 12/20/32 Betsey Campbell in Bath; H. W. Rogers, Esq./
9835.  Wilhelm, John m 8/13/49 Emeline Nobles in Bath; Rev. B. R. Swick. All of Bath (2-8/15)
9836.  Wilhelm, Joseph m 12/22/45 Sarah Campbell in Bath; Elder Rutherford (2-12/31)
9837.  Wilhelms, George m Miss Bailey in Benton (3-12/27/15)
9838.  Wilkes, James, 2 yrs, s of B. Wilkes, merchant, d 1/20/38 in Bath (2-1/24)
9839.  Wilkinson, James (Gen.), about 56, m Mademoiselle Trudeau, about 26, in New Orleans (3-5/23/10)
9840.  Wilkinson, Jemima, "near 70, styled by herself and her followers as the UNIVERSAL FRIEND," d 7/1/19 in Jerusalem, NY ("The singular character and strange pretensions of this female fanatic are very generally known ...") (3-7/7 and 5-7/21)
9841.  Wilkinson, Samuel C. m 6/22/40 Rachael Butler in Sodus; Rev. Gould (5-7/8)

9842. Willard, Herbert, 2 yrs, s of Harmis (sic) Willard of Jamestown, NY d in Wardsborough, VT (4-8/7/33)
9843. Willard, John N. of Troy m 12/28/37 Margaret Maria Townsend, dau of William, Esq. of Springfield, PA, in S; Rev. Danforth (4-1/10/38)
9844. Willard, Peter R. m 10/11/38 Jane Hunt in Greenwood; B. S. Brundage, Esq. All of Greenwood (2-10/17)
9845. Willard, Timothy P. m 1/13/12 Elizabeth Hinckley, both of Geneva, in Hopston or Hopeton(?) (3-1/22)
9846. Willcox, Durfee of Palmyra m 9/23/28 Semanthe Wells of Livonia in Palmyra; F. Smith, Esq. (5-9/26)
9847. Willcox, Hiram m 12/25/28 Lucy Brown in Palmyra (5-12/26)
9848. Willcox, Sylvester, 69, formerly and for 20 years a resident of Albany, d 7/30/44 in Palmyra ("Albany papers please copy") (5-7/31)
9849. Willen, James (Dr.), 29, d in NYC (3-11/6/11)
9850. Willett, William m Altha Pratt in Palmyra; John Longley, Esq. (5-11/28/21)
9851. Williams, _____ m "Mrs. Knight" in Palmyra (3-1/17/16)
9852. Williams, Abram of Hector m 12/21/35 Elizabeth Havens of Pulteney at the Franklin House in Bath; William Hamilton, Esq. (2-12/23)
9853. Williams, Alexander B. m 2/19/32 Sarah R. McCarty in Sodus; Israel Arms, Esq. (5-2/21)
9854. Williams, Allyn m 12/31/29 Delia Payne in Palmyra; Rev. Campbell (5-1/1/30 and 3-1/6/30)
9855. Williams, Benjamin, 30, d in NYC (3-11/16/25)
9856. Williams, Charles of Busti m 9/20/31 Matilda Shepardson of Gerry in G; J. M. Edson, Esq. (4-10/5)
9857. Williams, Charles, 82, d 2/10/42 in Alexander (a Rev. soldier) (1-2/15)
9858. Williams, David, 78, d 8/11/31 ("the last of the captors of Major Andre") (buried in Livingstonville, Schoharie Co.) (5-8/12)
9859. Williams, Elvira, 45, wf of John, d 9/28/49 in Alexander (1-10/2)
9860. Williams, Emily, 15 mo, dau of Daniel S. and Sabrina, d 5/1/41 in Jamestown. Also, Juliette, 2 yrs, sister of Emily, d 5/17 in Jamestown (4-5/19)
9861. Williams, George W., 18, brother of D. S., d 11/26/40 in Jamestown (4-12/2/40 and 3/3/41)
9862. Williams, Harvey E. of Fort Plain m 10/1/44 Frances E. Riggs, youngest dau of Timothy, Esq. of Saratoga, in S; Rev. Hill (4-10/18)
9863. Williams, Henry S., 46, d 5/27/44 at his home in Tyrone (for many years one of the judges of the court of common pleas of Steuben Co.; surv by wf and 6 ch) (2-6/1)
9864. Williams, James, inf s of Richard S. formerly of this village (Palmyra), d 8/28/33 in Pittsford (5-8/30)
9865. Williams, James m 9/13/34 Sarah Osborn in Palmyra; Rev. Shumway (5-9/26)
9866. Williams, Jennette, 5, dau of Daniel S. and Sabrina, d 6/16/42 in Jamestown (4-6/23)
9867. Williams, John, 63?, d 8/23/42 in Sodus (5-10/5)
9868. Williams, John of Jamestown m 9/2/45 Betsey Ann Cowden of Poland, NY in Kennedyville; N.S. Lake, Esq. (4-9/12)
9869. Williams, John, Jr. of Salem, Wash. Co. m 9/9/35 Harriet B. Martin of Auburn in A; Rev. Bethune (5-9/18)
9870. Williams, John H. of Corning m 10/29/50 Eliza B. Coleman of Batavia; Rev. Gibbon Williams of Wyoming, NY (1-11/5)
9871. Williams, John Warner, 12, only s of Daniel S. and Sabrina, d 3/1/41 in Jamestown (4-3/3)
9872. Williams, Jonas, Esq., 36, d in Williamsville, Niag. Co. (3-11/3/19)
9873. Williams, Joseph of Seneca m 2/2/15 Amy Woodworth of Benton in B; Rev. Clark (3-2/8)
9874. Williams, Levi m 12/12/31 Nancy Twenty Canoes, of the Christian Party of Indians, in Buffalo (5-12/27)
9875. Williams, Lucinda, 21, wf of Dr. William A., d 5/16/10 in Canandaigua (3-5/30)
9876. Williams, Lucy, wf of John, d 6/17/18 in Palmyra (5-7/7)
9877. Williams, M. M., one of the publishers of the Geneva Courier, m 8/17/35 Caroline Tippets in Geneva (5-9/25)
9878. Williams, Marquis De La Fayette of Hector m 10/21/18 Mrs. Nancy Powell (3-11/11)
9879. Williams, Marvin m Hannah Lincon in Canandaigua (3-3/11/29)

9880. Williams, Nathan T., Esq., cashier of the Madison County Bank, m 5/9/33 Margaret Williams, dau of John (5-5/22)
9881. Williams, Nathan (Hon.), one of the clerks of the Supreme Court, d 9/25/35 in Geneva (5-10/2)
9882. Williams, Nathaniel S. m 5/16/38 Elizabeth Quick in Hammondsport; Rev. C. Wheeler (2-5/23)
9883. Williams, Oliver, 40, d in Perry (1-4/27/41)
9884. Williams, Richard S. of Palmyra m 5/4/30 Olive Ann Porter, dau of Chauncey, Esq. of Pittsford, in P; Rev. Mahan (5-5/7)
9885. Williams, Robert, Esq., 49, late senator from the Middle District of NY, d 3/5/13 in Poughkeepsie (3-3/24)
9886. Williams, Roger m 2/27/18 Mary Ann Bardwell, dau of Dr. Reuben, in Vienna, NY; Rev. Mosier. All of Vienna (3-3/4)
9887. Williams, Ryan m 4/17/25 Lura Studley in Elba; Rev. Howe (1-4/22)
9888. Williams, Samuel, 98, d in Orange, NJ (3-5/6/12)
9889. Williams, Samuel (Rev.), LL.D. d in Rutland, VT (3-1/22/17)
9890. Williams, Sanford, Jr. m 1/6/19 Ann Strong in Sodus (3-1/13)
9891. Williams, Seth, 20 or 30, d 9/17/39 in Palmyra (5-9/19)
9892. Williams, Solomon, 38, of the house of Williams and Whiting, booksellers, d 10/5/10 in NYC (3-10/17)
9893. Williams, Thomas, 63, of Cazenovia d in Utica (3-8/13)
9894. Williams, Thomas, 72, d in Ithaca (3-5/16/27)
9895. Williams, Thomas m Renewed Willcox of Friendship, Alleg. Co., in Angelica (3-6/18/28)
9896. Williams, W. A. (Dr.), 47, m 9/3/09 Lucinda Barlow, 21, in Canandaigua (3-9/13)
9897. Williams, William A., M.D., 70, d 9/4/34 in Canandaigua (5-9/26)
9898. Williams, William A., Jr. of Canandaigua m 2/5/17 Olive Howes of Phelps in P (3-2/19)
9899. Williams, Winny, 119, "a colored woman", d 10/12/26 in Alexandria, D. C. (3-10/25)
9900. Williams, Z., merchant, of Palmyra m 1/2/38 Amanda M. Collins of Sodus in Sodus; Rev. Merrill (5-1/10)
9901. Williams, Zebulon, 59, d 11/22/25 in Palmyra (3-12/7)
9902. Williamson, Abigail, 68, relict of Col. Charles, "formerly chief Agent of the Pulteney Estate in this country", 4 8/31/24 in Geneva (3-9/8)
9903. Williamson, Charles A., Esq. m 5/10/27 Catharine A. Clark of NYC at St. John's Church in NYC; Rev. Berrian (3-5/16)
9904. Williamson, Daniel B. of Fayette m Catharine Hall in Waterloo (3-7/8/29)
9905. Williamson, John D. m 2/7/46 Betsey M. Smith, dau of Rev. David, in Bath; Rev. T. McElheney. All of Bath (2-2/11)
9906. Williamson, John J. of Avoca m 10/24/46 Sarah Jane Larue of Cohocton in Avoca; Rev. S. Pitt (2-11/11)
9907. Williamson, William C. m 10/3/46 Malissa Phoenix in Rathbonville; C. H. Coal, Esq. (2-10/7)
9908. Williston, Lester of Lima m 11/4/22 Ann Tilton of Canandaigua in Middlesex (3-11/27)
9909. Williston, N. B. of Brattleboro, VT m 11/20/45 Caroline Brewster of Hartford (state not given) in H; Rev. G. A. Calhoan (4-12/5)
9910. Willits, Hyram m 12/29/36 Lydia R. Lapham, both of Macedon, in the Friends Meeting House in Farmington (5-12/30)
9911. Willoughby, R. (Rev.) of Little Valley m 7/6/43 Catherine L. Upham, formerly a teacher in Jamestown Academy; Rev E. J. Gillett (4-7/6)
9912. Willour, _____ (Mrs.), wf of Jacob, d 3/25/50 in Bath (2-3/27). In the issue dated 4/3 this announcement is repeated with her age at death listed as 52.
9913. Willour, Charles G., 3 yrs, and Hannah M., 5 yrs, son and dau of Jacob and Rachel, d 2/9/42 in Bath (2-2/23)
9914. Willour, James H. m 6/20/45 Lydia Palmer in Bath; Rev. Ferris. All of Bath (2-7/23)
9915. Willour, Nancy Adaline, 21, wf of Alonzo, d 6/10/50 in Bath (2-6/26)
9916. Willsie, Thomas m 8/1/30 Sally Ann Harrington in Carroll; Samuel Cowan, Esq. (4-8/18)
9917. Willson, David m 12/25/44 Keziah Collins in Jamestown; Rev. E.J. Gillett (4-1/3/45)

9918. Willson, Delia, 46, wf of Jared, Esq., d 4/26/42 in Canandaigua (5-5/4)
9919. Willson, James H. m 4/11/41 Rachael Booth, both of Manchester; F. Smith, Esq. (5-4/14)
9920. Willson, Jared, Esq. m Delia Williams in Canandaigua (3-10/29/17)
9921. Willson, Lucinda, wf of Dr. Nathaniel, d in Mendon (3-9/23/29)
9922. Willys, _____ (Mr.), keeper of one of the hotels at Bennett's Flats, d 6/4/41 in Howard (2-6/9)
9923. Wilmarth, Otis m 7/4/21 Sophronia Boughton in Victor (3-7/25)
9924. Wilmer, Christian m 2/22/25 Anna Schott, both of Fayette, in Junius; B. Hendricks, Esq. (3-3/9)
9925. Wilmer, William H. (Rev.), D.D., President of William and Mary College and for many years rector of St. Paul's Church in Alexandria, D. C., d in Virginia (3-8/22/27)
Wilson. See also Willson.
9926. Wilson, Adoniram, 38, d 2/25/38 in Palmyra (5-2/28)
9927. Wilson, Alexander, Esq., author of the American Ornithology, d in Philadelphia (state not given) (3-10/13/13)
9928. Wilson, Amzi, printer, m Philena Wetherby in Abington, PA (3-8/29/27)
9929. Wilson, Andrew (Rev.), 39, pastor of the Associate Reformed Church in Seneca, d 6/26/12 in Geneva (a native of Ireland; educated at the Univ. of Glasgow; came to America in 1801; surv by a wf and children) (3-7/1)
9930. Wilson, Charity, dau of David, d 8/1/43 at the home of Henry P. Wilson in Macedon ("New York papers please copy") (5-8/9)
9931. Wilson, Cyrus m Anna Miliman in Geneseo (3-3/29/20)
9932. Wilson, David m 3/24/25 Mary Adams of Hopewell in Canandaigua (3-4/6)
9933. Wilson, Frances Ann, 4, dau of "Mrs. Wilson", d 8/7/13 in Geneva (3-8/11)
9934. Wilson, George m 9/8/50 Harriet Brown, both of Roanoke; Rev. Hager (1-9/24)
9935. Wilson, Henry P. of Macedon m 12/16/40 Emily Bickford of Victor in V; Rev. Bartholomew (5-12/16)
9936. Wilson, James m 11/18/41 Marion Lidle in Poland, NY; S. B. Winsor, Esq. (4-11/25)
9937. Wilson, Jane, 16, wf of Russell and dau of Phineas Palmiter, Esq., d 3/1/41 in Jamestown (4-3/3)
9938. Wilson, John m 5/16/24 Anna Maria Thompson, both of Batavia; Rev. Calvin Colton (1-5/21)
9939. Wilson, John S., Esq., 50, clerk of Steuben Co., d 2/8/17 in Bath (3-2/19)
9940. Wilson, Mary, 34, wf of Johnson Wilson, d in Penn Yan (3-7/4/27)
9941. Wilson, Merverick of Pembroke m 2/8/24 wid Caty North of Elba; Rev. Salmon Hebard (1-2/20)
9942. Wilson, Phebe (Mrs.), 41, d 8/18/22 in Wolcott (3-9/4)
9943. Wilson, Russell m 12/23/41 Cordelia Schoonmaker in Jamestown; Rev. E. J. Gillett (4-1/6/42)
9944. Wilson, Samuel of Rochester m Elizabeth Saxton of Canandaigua in Brighton (3-8/19/29)
9945. Wilson, Samuel R. m Mary A. Spear, dau of Harry, Esq., in Warren Co., GA (5-2/7/44)
9946. Wilson, Wareham (Capt.) of Whitehall m 1/8/35 Cordelia Gardner, dau of Isaac of Palmyra, in P; Elder Richards (5-1/9)
9947. Wilson, William, M.D., formerly President of the Medical Society of the State of NY, d 12/20/28 in Clermont, Col. Co. (for many years first judge of common pleas, Columbia Co.) (3-1/14/29)
9948. Wilson, William m 10/3/41 Lurany Cutting in Gerry; Rev. Wilson (4-10/7)
9949. Wiltsey, William H. of Barrington m 11/6/45 Caroline Houch of Wayne in W; Rev. H. Spencer (2-11/12)
9950. Wiltsie, Alvin m 3/12/41 Mary Card, dau of Stephen; M. Norton, Esq. All of Harmony (4-3/31)
9951. Wiltsie, Martin, 94, d in Fishkill (3-12/26/27)
9952. Wimple, Harry A. m 5/28/45 Betsey P. Smiley, both of Busti, in B; Rev. T. D. Blin (See marr. of Isaac Woodin this date) (4-6/6)
9953. Winans, Clark (Dr.), 22, d 3/30/16 in Big Flats (3-4/10)

9954. Winans, Jeremiah m 8/13/26 Chloe Wilcox in Junius (3-8/30)
9955. Winants, Rebecca (Mrs.), 76, d in Benton (3-5/14/28)
9956. Winchester, Berry H. of Ellery m 9/17/45 Malona L. Clark of Jamestown in J; S. Jones, Esq. (4-9/19)
9957. Winchester, Frances Elizabeth, 2 yrs, dau of Ebenezer and Elizabeth N., d 1/17/43 in Brooklyn (4-1/26)
9958. Wing, Elnathan H. of Cohocton m 2/1/47 Sally Oliver of Dansville in D; Charles Oliver, Esq. (2-2/17)
9959. Wing, Sylvanus m Margaret Sickles in Marion (3-9/19/27)
9960. Wing, Thomas, 19, d 4/17/20 in Geneva (3-4/19)
9961. Winship, Joseph of Palmyra m 8/23/34 Nancy Belden of NYC in NYC (5-8/29)
9962. Winship, Mary, 32, wf of Joseph, d 5/21/33 in Palmyra ("Also recently an infant daughter of the same") (5-5/22)
9963. Winslow, Catharine (Mrs.) d in Pennsylvania Hospital ("she had resided in the hospital upwards of 27 years in a state of insanity") (3-5/8/11)
9964. Winsor, Abraham, Esq., 68, d 5/23/44 in Wales, Erie Co. (an early inhabitant of Chautauqua Co. and for many years a resident of Jamestown) (4-6/7). See 9967.
9965. Winsor, Abraham, Jr. m Merinda Stedman in Jamestown (4-7/18/32)
9966. Winsor, Nancy, wf of Henry, late of Westfield, NY, d 6/11/39 in Pleasant Prairie, Wisc. Terr. (4-7/10)
9967. Winsor, Sophia, 61, wf of Abraham, Esq., d 5/20/44 in Wales, Erie Co. (4-6/7). See 9964.
9968. Winston, Horatio N. m 4/5/34 Minerva Carpenter in Palmyra; F. Smith, Esq. (5-4/11)
9969. Winter, Garret of Waterloo m 3/13/28 Jane Bourhite of Geneva; Rev. E. W. Martin (3-3/19)
9970. Wire, Delight, 26, d 6/27/27 in Middlesex (3-7/11)
9971. Wisner, _____, inf ch of P. B., Esq., d 10/21/10 (3-10/24)
9972. Wisner, Henry A., Esq. of Penn Yan m 8/31/26 Susan Hathaway, dau of Maj. Thomas of Milo, in M; Rev. Alfred Campbell (3-9/6)
9973. Wisner, Maria, relict of late Polydore B., Esq. of Geneva, d 10/3/25 in Schenectady (3-10/12)
9974. Wisner, Polydore B., Esq., 44, of Geneva d 7/15/14 at the home of Spencer Coleman, Esq. of Geneva (born in Orange Co. and lived in G about 16 yrs; at time of death was district attorney for the four western counties of NY; surv by wf and 3 ch) (3-7/20)
9975. Witbeck, Gertrude (Mrs.), 72, d in Greenbush (3-7/21/19)
9976. Withers, Mary Elizabeth, 6, dau of Robert and Mary Ann of Palmyra, d 12/25/37 (5-12/27)
9977. Witmer, Peter of Seneca Falls m Eliza Ann Miller in Fayette (3-7/15/29)
9978. Wixom, Elizabeth, 21, wf of William, d 9/16/41 in Prattsburgh (2-9/22)
9979. Wixom, William of Prattsburgh m Elizabeth Gulick of Pulteney in P; Rev. Southerland (2-9/23/40)
9980. Wixom, William, M.D., m 2/15/46 Semantha Doubleday, dau of Hon. E., in the Meth. Church at Italy Hill; Rev. Nutting. All of Italy, NY (2-2/18)
9981. Wixton, Robert of Hector m 2/20/17 Mrs. Ruth Marshall of Phelps (3-3/12)
9982. Wolcott, Eleanor (Mrs.), 77, wid of late Oliver, d 8/25 in Oakfield (1-8/29)
9983. Wolcott, George m Sally Baird in Painted Post (3-1/7/29)
9984. Wolcott, James m Maria Glassby of Jersey, NY in J (3-1/13/30)
9985. Wolcott, John S. of Shelby m 2/19/26 Maria A. Wilford of Elba in E; Rev. Colton (1-2/24)
9986. Wolcott, Mercy, wf of John S., d 8/12/24 in Shelby (1-8/27)
9987. Wolcott, Oliver, Esq., 73, "for several years governor of CT", d 6/1/33 in NYC (5-6/19)
9988. Wolcott, Rhoda, 38, wf of Caleb, d 4/27/32 in Bath (2-5/2)
9989. Wolcott, Solomon (Dr.), 49, d 10/30/18 in Utica (3-11/11)
9990. Wolloben, Edward of Fredonia m 7/4/43 Clara Priscilla Hebard of Dunkirk in D; Rev. C. L. Hequembourg (4-7/13)
9991. Wolsey, Mary (Mrs.), formerly of Albany, d in Gorham (3-12/23/29)

9992. Wolsey, Sampson of Providence, Saratoga Co. d 9/28/37 in Galway, NY ("choked on a piece of beef lodged in his windpipe; left a large family") (4-10/18)

9993. Wolstoncroft, Charles (Maj.) of the corps of artillery, d in New Orleans (state not given) (3-11/19/17)

9994. Wolven, Levi, about 35, d in Seneca (3-10/1/28)

9995. Wood, _____ (Mrs.), mother of Ralph T., a native of England, d 10/22/18 near Geneva (3-10/28)

9996. Wood, Abigail, 63, consort of Capt. John, d 2/17/14 in Junius ("Newspapers in Northampton, Mass. are requested to insert this notice") (3-2/23)

9997. Wood, Benjamin of Aurora m Helen Ann Townsend, dau of H. A., Esq., in Bath (3-10/27/19)

9998. Wood, Benjamin H., about 50, formerly of Bath, d 2/28/46 in Washington, D.C. "while waiting to receive a continuance of his patent right to the iron plough invented by his father" (2-3/18). See 10015.

9999. Wood, Berry C. m Mary Ann Fegals in Painted Post; Edward Bacon, Esq. (2-9/16/40)

10000. Wood, Betsey, 28, wf of Henry, d in Waterloo (3-5/24/20)

10001. Wood, Betsey, 74, wf of Charles, d 2/6/40 in Jamestown (4-2/12)

10002. Wood, Charles, 84, "for a number of years resident of Jamestown" d 2/4/44 in Harlinsburgh, Mercer Co., PA (a Rev. pensioner; member of Bapt. Church) (4-2/23)

10003. Wood, Cylvander (sic) m 3/22/25 Mary Ann Bennett in Attica; Elder Cheney (1-4/22)

10004. Wood, David (Capt.) m Patience Rolfe in Jersey, NY (3-5/20/29)

10005. Wood, Doane (sic) (Miss), 20, dau of William, d in Canandaigua (3-8/9/15)

10006. Wood, Emanuel m 1/11/17 Jane Barkenstose in Seneca (3-1/22)

10007. Wood, Ezra, Jr. of Jamestown m 9/9/32 Mary Williams of Boston (state not given) in Boston; Rev. Cyrus Mann (4-9/26)

10008. Wood, George of Junius m 11/19/22 Eliza C. Buck of Palmyra in P; A. R. Tiffany (5-11/20)

10009. Wood, Halsey A., 33, pastor of the Presby Church of Amsterdam, NY d 11/26/25 in Amsterdam (3-12/21)

10010. Wood, Harrison m Jane Klock, both of Ellery, in E; Rev. H. Smith (4-1/5/43)

10011. Wood, Heslop T., 18 mo, s of Ralph T., d 9/19/15 in Phelps (3-9/27)

10012. Wood, Jacob, Jr. m 12/30/24 Clarinda Andrews in Attica; Rev. Amos P. Bowen. All of Attica (1-1/7/25)

10013. Wood, Jane (Mrs.), dau of Mrs. Elizabeth Backenstose, d 11/27/17 in Geneva ("Her death was occasioned by her clothes catching fire...") (3-12/3)

10014. Wood, Jason, 70, (a Rev. soldier) d in Italy, NY (3-11/12/28)

10015. Wood, Jethro, 60?, inventor of the cast iron plough, d 9/29/34 at his home in Ledyard, NY ("Few men have contributed so much to the advancement of agriculture") (5-10/17). See 9998.

10016. Wood, John m Betsey Cline in Farmington (5-1/12/20)

10017. Wood, John, s of Jethro, m 1/17/22 Belya Sherwood, dau of late Judge Sherwood, in Scipio; Rev. Johnson (3-1/23)

10018. Wood, John O. (Rev.) m 2/4/38 Electa Crane in the Methodist Chapel in Jamestown (4-2/7)

10019. Wood, Joseph, 34, d in Geneva (3-2/4/18)

10020. Wood, Orsamond B. m 10/28/32 Julia Ann Frazier in Alexander; Rev. Cheney. All of Alexander (1-10/30)

10021. Wood, Phebe, 68, wf of Capt. Thomas, d 8/21/22 in Bellona (surv by her children) (3-8/28)

10022. Wood, Philander m 7/5/35 Sophronia Winchester in Ellery; J. W. Barney, Esq. (4-7/15)

10023. Wood, Rachel, 36, wf of Capt. William, d 6/20/27 in Lyons (3-7/11)

10024. Wood, Rebecca, widow, 114, native of Ireland, d in Richmond, Ontario Co. (3-3/31/19)

10025. Wood, Samson Sober (Rev.), only surviving son of late Samson Tickel Wood, Esq., d 10/1/28 at the Hermitage, Beaumaristone (perhaps in England?) (deceased is grandson of "late Cumberbatch Sober, Esq., late of upper George-st Byranstone") (3-12/24)

Wood, Sylvester. See, possibly, Wood, Cylvander
10026. Wood, Tabor m 5/3/41 Almira Chapman, both of Jamestown, in J; Rev. Parmely (4-5/5)
10027. Wood, Thomas, about 1 yr, s of Ralph T., d 7/4/13 (3-7/7)
10028. Wood, Thomas, 38?, d in Geneva (3-3/13/16)
10029. Wood, Thomas m Esther Pate in Addison (3-1/9/28)
10030. Wood, Walter (Hon.), 62, d in Sempronius (3-9/19/27)
10031. Wood, William of Addison m 2/21/41 Nancy Holden of Bath in B; Henry Pier, Esq. (2-2/24)
10032. Wood, William I. of Batavia m 11/11/24 Catharine Ann Wilcox of Le Roy; Rev. Colton (1-11/12)
10033. Wood, William W. m Sally Ann Hempstead in Waterloo (3-1/13/30)
10034. Woodard, Jonas of Palmyra m 10/21/30 Eliza S. Davis at the Bapt. Church in Brockport; Rev. H. Davis (5-11/12)
10035. Woodard, Joseph, 79, d 9/14/47 in Avoca (2-9/22)
10036. Woodard, Levi m Nancy Brocklebank in Manchester (5-3/31/18 and 3-4/8/18)
10037. Woodard, Martin m 9/7/29 Mary Willis in Phelps; Elder Case (3-9/30)
10038. Woodbeck, Abraham m 2/25/36 Mary Ann Duer; Rev. Moore. All of East Palmyra (Perhaps a double ceremony — see marr. of Asher Webster) (5-3/4)
10039. Woodcock, Aaron of Carroll m 5/23/41 Almira H. Higby of Ellery in E; Elder H. Smith (4-5/26)
10040. Woodcock, David, Esq., 50, d 9/18/35 in Ithaca (5-10/2)
10041. Wooden, Rachael (Miss), 18, dau of _____ Wooden, Esq., d in Rochester (3-12/24/28)
10042. Woodhull, Benjamin, 21, d 8/23/20 in Penfield (5-8/30)
10043. Woodhull, John (Rev.), D.D., 82, d 11/22/24 at his home in Freehold, NJ ("late and for many years Pastor of the Presbyterian Church in that place") (3-12/8)
10044. Woodhull, Nancy, 19, d 10/7/19 in Phelpstown (5-10/13)
10045. Woodin, Isaac of Jamestown m 5/28/45 Almira Smiley of Busti in B; Rev. T. D. Blin (See marr. of Harry A. Wimple this date) (4-6/6)
10046. Woodman, John m Esther McIntyre in Farmington; P. Mitchell, Esq. (5-9/8/18)
10047. Woodruff, Adam, 21, d 11/23/30 in Lyons (5-11/26)
10048. Woodruff, Amos m Eliza Potter in Lyons (3-4/8/29)
10049. Woodruff, Daniel d in Ithaca (3-1/14/29)
10050. Woodruff, Edwin, late of Canandaigua, m 1/1/32 Lydia A. Gilmore of Coventry, Chen. Co.; Elder Birdsall (2-1/11)
10051. Woodruff, Fenn C. d 3/31/43 in Pomfret (4-4/6)
10052. Woodruff, James, about 47, d 7/3/20 in Fayette (probably died of acute alcoholism as explained in great detail in the death notice; "he has left a wife and a number of small children, fortunately in good circumstances.") (3-7/26)
10053. Woodruff, Jerry m Almira Dunks in Canandaigua (3-4/17/22)
10054. Woodruff, Milo m 10/19/24 Mary Philips in Fayette (3-11/1)
10055. Woodruff, Oliver, 90, (a Rev. soldier) d 12/24/45 in Livonia (2-1/7/46)
10056. Woods, _____, 9 mo, s of William, Esq., d 3/17/32 in Bath (2-3/21)
10057. Woods, James Lyons, 15, oldest s of William, Esq. of Bath, d 7/5/31 (funeral in the Presby. Church) (2-7/6)
10058. Woods, James S., Esq. of Elmira m 6/19/49 Susan Van Duser, dau of William of Veteran, Chemung Co.; Rev. C. C. Carr (2-7/4)
10059. Woodside, James m 2/3/42 Susan Miller, both of Sugargrove, PA, in S; Rev. O. D. Hibbard (4-2/10)
10060. Woodward, _____ (Mrs.), wf of John, d 8/24/21 in Palmyra (5-8/29)
10061. Woodward, John m 8/15/25 Sally Eddy in Stafford (1-8/19)
10062. Woodward, John D. m 8/8/40 Elvira Rice in Jamestown; E. F. Warren, Esq. (4-8/19)
10063. Woodward, Marianna Cornelse, 20, d 4/26/43 in Palmyra (5-5/3)
10064. Woodward, Marvin, 18, d 12/21/39 in Palmyra (5-12/27)
10065. Woodward, Moses Lyon, 3, s of William A. and Sally, d 2/22/46 in Bath (2-2/25)
10066. Woodward, Thomas, 22, d 7/12/50 in Bath (2-7/17)
10067. Woodward, Walter, editor of the Freeman, m Eliza Ann Henderson in Watertown (3-8/1/27)

10068.  Woodworth, Abner (Capt.) of Benton m 1/18/16 Isabella Black, dau of
        Hugh, in Seneca; Rev. White (3-1/24)
10069.  Woodworth, Ariel, 24, d in Canandaigua (3-1/6/13)
10070.  Woodworth, Charles (Dr.) m 7/14/18 Eleanor Winans in Elmira (3-7/29)
10071.  Woodworth, Jonathan, 19, m Ellen Cummings, 11, in Scipio, NY (3-10/3/10)
10072.  Woodworth, Josephus m 12/22/49 Ann Eliza Aqur (sic) in Covert, Seneca
        Co.; Rev. Jonathan Woodworth.  All of Covert (1-2/12/50)
10073.  Woodworth, Sarah, wf of Samuel, d 7/20/21 in Mayfield (5-8/8)
10074.  Woolbert, Elijah m 10/8/46 Hannah Vanorman of Genesee, PA in Canisteo;
        E. D. Swartwood, Esq. (2-10/14)
10075.  Woolsey, Melancthon Lloyd, 61, d in Trenton, Oneida Co. (an officer
        throughout the Rev. War) (3-7/14/19)
10076.  Woolsey, Melancton L., 23, printer, (formerly of Canandaigua) d 1/17/32
        in NYC (5-1/31)
10077.  Woolsey, Melancton T. of the U.S. Navy m Esther Blain, both of South
        Carolina, in Cambridge, MA (3-11/19/17)
10078.  Woolworth, Richard, Esq. m Delia A. Forman in Syracuse (3-1/14/29)
10079.  Wooster, L. N., 20, printer, d 8/2/29 in Bay of St. Louis (formerly
        of Rochester but for two years past of New Orleans)(state not given)
        (5-9/18)
10080.  Worden, H. m P. Reeves in Macedon (3-4/1/29)
10081.  Worden, Justice, Jr. m 2/4/44 Hannah Priest in Poland, NY; Amos Feller,
        Esq. (4-2/16)
10082.  Woren, John G. m 8/7/34 Lois P. Howland, formerly of Palmyra, in Seneca
        Falls (5-8/8)
10083.  Work, Edward m 10/27/41 _____ Jeffres, both of Worksburg, in W; Rev.
        John Broadhead (4-10/28)
10084.  Work, Jane, 55, wf of Edward, d 9/19/33 in Jamestown (4-9/25)
10085.  Work, Jane (Miss), 21, only dau of Edward, d 1/23/41 in Jamestown
        (4-1/27)
10086.  Works, Sarah, 17 mo, dau of I. Works, d 4/4/22 in Clyde (Galen)
        (3-4/10)
10087.  Worth, William J. of the U.S. Navy m Margaret Stafford in Albany
        (3-10/7/18)
10088.  Worthington, Mary, 14 mo, twin dau of G. B., d 8/31/48 in Batavia
        (1-9/5)
10089.  Worthington, Thomas (Hon.), late governor of Ohio, d in NYC (3-7/11/27)
10090.  Wride, _____ (Miss), 21, d 10/18/29 in Geneva (3-10/21)
10091.  Wright, Amasa of Canandaigua m 10/22/22 Jane Rogers of Gorham in G
        (3-11/6)
10092.  Wright, Chauncey L. of Albany m 3/3/31 Louisa Griswold of Lyons in L;
        Rev. I. Hubbell (5-3/4)
10093.  Wright, Clark m 7/8/30 Polly Hammond, both of Palmyra, in Seneca;
        E. Hastings, Esq. (5-7/30)
10094.  Wright, E. Monroe of Northampton m Martha P. Graves of Easthampton, MA
        in E; Rev. Payson Williston (4-7/29/41)
10095.  Wright, James of the house of Wilbur and Wright m 7/15/29 Sarah Markoe,
        dau of Francis, Esq., in NYC; Rev. Cyrus Mason (3-7/22)
10096.  Wright, Joel m 7/5/29 Emily Phelps, dau of Stephen, Esq., formerly of
        Canandaigua, in Lewiston, IL (3-8/19).  In 5-8/28 Stephen, Esq.
        is listed as "formerly of Palmyra" and the marriage place just
        Lewiston (state not given).
10097.  Wright, Luther (Capt.), merchant, of Trumansburgh m Lucinda Smith in
        Smithville, Jefferson Co. (3-2/13/28)
10098.  Wright, Moses C. m 11/6/28 Abigail Judd in Seneca; Rev. Dr. Axtell
        (3-11/12)
10099.  Wright, Samuel, Esq., 64, d in Bloomfield (3-12/6/15)
10100.  Wright, Silas, Jr. (Hon.), senator in Congress, m Clarissa Moody, dau
        of late Medad of Canton, St. Law. Co., in Canton (5-9/20/33)
10101.  Wyckoff, James S. m 4/10/27 Henrietta M. Beebe in Syracuse (3-4/25)
10102.  Wyckoff, Joseph m 1/8/29 Elizabeth Baldridge in Romulus; Rev. Barton
        (3-2/4)
10103.  Wylie, Philo m 4/10/28 Maria How in Chenango Point; Rev. Lockwood
        (3-4/16)
10104.  Wylie, William D. m 1/1/23 Demaries D. Empie(?) (surname blurred)
        in Ontario, NY (5-1/1)

10105. Wylie, William D., Esq. of Walworth, Wayne Co. m 1/22/37 Eliza Ann
Lewis, formerly of Clyde, at the Presbyterian Meeting House in
Vienna, NY; Rev. Porter (5-2/24)
10106. Wyman, Hannah, 78, widow, d in Penn Yan (3-12/9/29)
10107. Wynaugle, Jonas m 1/23/23 Elvila Chapman in Geneva; Elder Goff
(3-1/29)
10108. Wynkoop, _____ (Mrs.), wf of Major Wynkoop of Elmira, d 9/27/12 in
Elmira (3-10/7)
10109. Wynkoop, Peter, 68, d at his home near Flint Creek in Seneca (3-8/20/28)
10110. Wynkoop, Tobias m Eleanor Wells in Seneca (3-11/3/19)
10111. Yakley, H. m 2/28/30 Calista Harwood in Rushville (5-3/5)
10112. Yates, Christopher C. (Dr.) m Mrs. Emma Willard, Preceptor of the Troy
Female Academy, in the chapel of the Academy in Troy, NY ("Except
for a few of her friends, some 200 of her scholars tastefully
dressed in white with bouquets of flowers were the only witnesses")
(2-10/3/38)
10113. Yates, Jerome Whitney, 10 mo, s of John S., d 10/25/38 in Jamestown
(4-10/31)
10114. Yates, John, 66, brother of Robert Yates, formerly chief justice of
this state, d 12/19/26 in Schenectady (3-1/5/27)
10115. Yates, John S. m 11/29/32 Salina Jones in Jamestown; Rev. Barrows
(4-12/5)
10116. Yates, John W., Esq., 58, cashier of the New York State Bank, d 3/29/28
in Albany (3-4/9)
10117. Yates, Louisa Adelaide, 2 yrs, dau of John S., d 5/30/42 in Jamestown
(4-6/9)
10118. Yates, Thomas m 7/14/42 Julia D. Mix, both of Batavia; Rev. Allen
Steele (1-7/19)
10119. Yayn, Joseph N. m Susan Crane in Tyrone (3-10/14/29)
10120. Yeckley, Adam A., 48, d 5/3/19 in Seneca (3-5/12)
10121. Yeomans, Theron G., merchant, of Walworth, Wayne Co. m 9/28/37 Lydia A.
Stearns of Gorham, Ontario Co.; Rev. Galston (5-10/4)
10122. Yeomans, Vaniah m 1/20/31 Alzorah Boynton, dau of Hon. Jonathan, in
Walworth; Elder Blakesley. All of Walworth (5-1/28)
10123. Yeomans, Vaniah, 37, d 4/1/42 in Walworth (5-4/6)
10124. Yerkes, _____ m Elmira Brown in Romulus (3-1/6/30)
10125. York, Joseph, Esq., formerly a state assemblyman "and late sheriff of
St. Lawrence Co.", d in Ogdensburgh (3-5/16/27)
10126. York, M. M. (Rev.), pastor of the Presby. Church (27th year of his
ministry) d in Wysox (3-2/3/30)
10127. Yortan, James m 3/15/47 Laura M. Smith, both of Howard, in H; Rev. L.
Rose (2-3/24)
10128. Youker, William G. of Ellery m 5/8/38 Mrs. Eliza McNette of Jamestown
in J; Solomon Jones, Esq. (4-5/9)
10129. Youmans, Isaac, 37, d in Penn Yan (3-3/12/28)
10130. Youmans, Jonas, 92, (a Rev. soldier) d 3/28/50 in Thurston (2-4/10)
10131. Youmans, Mary Jane Elizabeth, 14, d 8/19/50 in Bath (2-8/28)
10132. Young, Aaron m Electa Doty in Phelps (3-2/21/16)
10133. Young, Albert m 7/4/41 Mary Butler in Ellery; Rev. H. Smith (4-7/8)
10134. Young, Anderson, civil engineer on the Ohio Canal, m Jane M. Brown
(sic), dau of Daniel Penfield, Esq. of Penfield, in St. Luke's
Church, Rochester (3-10/8/28)
10135. Young, James m 6/3/27 Mary Smith near Geneva; Rev. Dr. Axtell (3-6/6)
10136. Young, James m Betsey Stroup in Canoga (3-3/18/29)
10137. Young, John, Jr. (Rev.) "one of the missionaries of the U.D.MS.,
formerly of Otsego County, N.Y.", d 8/16/25 in Vincennes, Indiana
(3-11/9)
10138. Young, John S. of Geneva m 2/8/27 Elizabeth Smith of Seneca in S; Rev.
Dr. Axtell (3-2/14)
10139. Young, Joseph (Dr.), 81, of NYC d 4/18/14 at the home of Thomas Hertell,
Esq. in Rye, Westchester Co. (For many years a prominent physician
in Albany and NYC. During the Rev. War was a member of the Secret
Committee of Public Safety in Albany. Also "was Chief Prescribing
Physician in the General Military Hospital of the U.S. from its
establishment until its dissolution at the close of the Rev. War."
(3-5/11)

10140. Young, Josiah of Penn Yan m Julia Ann Marther in Bath (3-11/4/29)
10141. Young, Julia, 33, d 8/20/40 in Benton Centre, Yates Co. (2-8/26)
10142. Young, Lydia, consort of Rev. Moses of Romulus, d 5/6/16 in Romulus (3-5/8)
10143. Young, Moses (Rev.), 38, pastor of the Presby. Church in Romulus, d 10/15/24 in Romulus (surv by wf and 8 ch) (born in Morris, NJ; moved to Ontario Co., NY in Oct 1811; licensed to preach by Presbytery of Geneva in Sept 1814; was ordained and installed as pastor of the Presby. Church of Romulus in March 1815) (3-10/20)
10144. Young, Nelson D. of Marion m 3/8/36 Achsah M. Kingsley of Sodus in S (5-3/11)
10145. Young, Peter m Sally Acker in Benton (3-1/21/18)
10146. Young, Samuel m 8/16/18 Priscilla Van Scoy in Milo (3-9/2)
10147. Young, Samuel (Hon.) of Saratoga Co. m 3/28/27 Mrs. Sarah Lasher of New Hurley, Ulster Co. in NYC (3-4/11)
10148. Young, Samuel m 1/1/29 Mary Dean in Canandaigua (3-1/14)
10149. Young, Samuel (Hon.), about 72, d 11/3/50 in Ballston (death discovered by his son John "who occupied an adjacent apartment") (2-11/6)
10150. Young, Seth m 9/10/09 Betsey Crosset in Manlius (3-9/13)
10151. Young, Stephen m 12/23/13 Harriet Doty, both of Phelps, in P; Rev. Henry Axtell (3-1/5/14)
10152. Young, Stephen, 22, editor of the Geneva Palladium, d 9/16/16 (3-9/18)
10153. Young, William (Capt.), 65, formerly of Boston (state not given), d 5/4/19 in Sodus (3-5/12)
10154. Young, William, 60, d 1/23/22 in Phelps (5-1/30)
10155. Younger, Clarendon, formerly of the island of Jamaica, d 9/18/10 in Canandaigua (3-9/19)
10156. Younglove, Aaron, Esq., 80, d 1/9/44 at his home in Gorham, Ontario Co. (a Rev. soldier) (5-1/24)
10157. Younglove, John (Rev.), pastor of the Presby. Church in Brunswick, Renss. Co., d 12/29/27 (3-1/23/28)
10158. Youngs, Archibald m Eleanor Quick in Elmira (3-3/12/28)
10159. Youngs, Hannah, 82, relict of late John, d 9/3/30 in Lyons (5-9/17)
10160. Youngs, Peter m 6/26/22 Hannah Green in Milo (3-7/10)
10161. Youry, John m Nancy Brewster in Junius (3-1/9/28)
10162. Zielley, Thomas H. of Peterborough m 7/15/50 Ann Tooker of Elmira in Avoca; Rev. N. Sawyer (2-7/17)
10163. Ziellie, Sally (Mrs.), 60, d 5/18/42 in Oil City, Crawford Co., PA (2-6/22)
10164. Zimmerman, John, 80, d in Ithaca (3-8/1/27)

APPENDIX

MARRIAGE OFFICIALS

Name; religious affiliation (if applicable and given); residence town; date
span of ceremonies performed; number of ceremonies performed.

(Probably all persons with the title "esquire" are local justices of the peace)

___ds, James (Elder); ___; Charlestown; 1811; 1
___ne, ___ (Rev.); ___; Geneva; 1823; 1
Abbot, Ambrose (Rev.); ___; Caton; 1840; 1
Abeel, ___ (Rev.); ___; Geneva; 1836; 1
Abell, A. (Elder); ___; Campbell?; 1841; 1
Ackley, ___ (Rev.); ___; Benton; 1829; 1
Ackley, Oliver (Rev.); ___; Seneca?; 1828; 1
Adams, ___ (Rev.); ___; Carroll; 1839; 1
Adams, ___ (Rev. Dr.); ___; Geneva; 1821; 1
Adams, A. (Rev.); ___; Cohocton; 1849; 3
Adgate, ___ (Rev.); ___; Reading; 1822; 1
Akin, J. I. (Rev.); ___; Olean; 1843; 1
Alden, S. W. (Rev.); ___; Bath or Urbana; 1847; 3
Aldrich, Oren, Esq.; Seneca; 1811-14; 4
Alexander, ___ (Rev.); ___; Benton; 1812; 1
Allen, ___ (Rev.); ___; Manchester?; 1832; 1
Allen, ___ (Elder); ___; Marion; 1830; 1
Allen, ___ (Elder); ___; Sodus; 1829; 1
Allen, ___ (Rev.); ___; Williamson; 1831; 2
Allen, Daniel, Esq.; New Salem; 1821-22; 2
Allen, John, Esq.; Orange; 1838; 1
Allen, M. (Elder); ___; Pulteneyville-Sodus-Williamson area; 1831; 3
Allen, Silas, Esq.; Romulus; 1815; 1
Aller, Marvin (___); ___; Sodus; 1831; 1 (See Allen, M. above)
Alsop, Robert, Esq.; Sodus-Williamson area; 1829-31; 2
Alverson, ___ (Rev.); ___; Lockville; 1830; 1
Alverson, ___ (Rev.); ___; Milo; 1827; 1
Alverson, ___ (Rev.); ___; Palmyra; 1831; 1
Alverson, ___ (Rev.); ___; Phelps; 1823; 1
Alverson, J. B. (Rev.); ___; Lyons; 1823-30; 2
Alverson, J. R. (Rev.); ___; Arcadia; 1830; 1
Amidon, S., Esq.; Greenwood, 1845; 1
Anson, L. (Rev.); ___; Covington; 1824-25; 2
Andrew, Robert (Rev.); ___; Penfield; 1832; 1
Andrews, ___ (Rev.); ___; Hudson?; 1833; 1
Andruss, William (Rev.); ___; Prattsburgh; 1845; 1
Anson, ___ (Rev.); ___; Stafford?; 1824; 2
Anthon, ___ (Rev.); ___; Utica; 1826; 1
Arms, Israel, Esq.; Sodus; 1832; 2
Arnold, H. L., Esq; Tyrone-Reading area; 1831-32; 3
Ashworth, J. (Rev.); ___; Jasper-Woodhull area; 1845-50; 3
Atwater, ___ (Rev.); ___; Fairfield, CT; 1840; 1
Axtell, Henry (Rev. Dr.); Presby.; Geneva; 1810-28; 137 (d 1829)
Axtel, ___ (Rev.); ___; Jamestown?; 1845; 1
Aylworth, ___ (Rev.); ___; Jamestown?; 1838; 1
Aylworth, R. A. (Rev.); ___; Randolph; 1838; 1
Babbitt, S. T. (Rev.); ___; Howard; 1835; 3
Babbitt, Samuel T. (Rev.); ___; Avoca; 1844; 1
Babcock, ___ (Rev.); ___; Alexander; 1847; 1
Babcock, ___ (Rev.); ___; Batavia; 1847; 2
Babcock, ___ (Rev.); ___; Byron; 1847; 1
Babcock, ___, Esq.; Oak Hill, Steuben Co.; 1849; 1
Babcock, ___ (Rev.); ___; Rochester?; 1847; 1
Babcock, Daniel, Esq.; Davenport, Delaware Co.; 1825; 1
Babcock, G. G., Esq.; South Dansville; 1846; 1
Babcock, W. K. (Rev.); ___; Stafford, 1846; 1
Babcock, W. R. (Rev.); ___; Ellery-Gerry-Jamestown-Poland area; 1833-34; 9

261

Bachus, J. S. (Elder); Bapt.; Groton?; year lacking; 1
Bacon, ___ (Rev.); ___; Waterloo; 1818; 1
Bacon, Edward, Esq.; Erwin-Painted Post area; 1840; 3
Badger, ___, Esq.; Alden?; 1824; 1
Baggerly, John (Rev.); ___; Phelps?; 1843; 1
Bagley, ___ (Rev.); ___; Phelps?; 1830; 1
Bailey, Benjamin (Rev.); ___; Palmyra; 1819; 1
Baker, Caleb, Esq.; Elmira; 1813-14; 2
Baker, Daniel (Rev.); ___; Phelps; 1829; 1
Baker, E. J. L. (Rev.); ___; Harmony; 1841; 1
Baker, Nathan (Rev.); ___; Lyons; 1842; 1
Baker, P. A., Esq.; Seneca; 1821; 1
Baker, S. (Rev.); ___; Busti; 1841; 1
Baldwin, ___ (Rev.); ___; Great Valley; 1833; 1
Baldwin, ___ (Rev.); ___; Mayville; 1839; 1
Baldwin, A. G. (Rev.); ___; Utica; 1818; 2
Baley, Thomas W., Esq.; Troupsburg; 1841; 1
Ball, ___ (Rev.); ___; Geneseo; 1827; 1
Ball, A. M. (Rev.); ___; Elmira?; 1849; 1
Ballard, James (Rev.); ___; Grand Rapids, MI?; 1844; 1
Bancroft, ___, Esq.; Sodus?; 1826; 1
Bannister, Eli, Esq.; Geneva; 1816-18; 9
Bannister, H., Esq.; Lockville; 1831; 1
Bardwell, Horatio (Rev.); ___; Oxford; 1842; 1
Barker, P. A., Esq.; Fayette-Junius-Waterloo area; 1822-27; 4
Barlow, ___ (Rev.); ___; Canandaigua; 1821; 2
Barlow, ___ (Rev.); ___; Syracuse?; 1827; 1
Barnes, ___, Esq.; Tioga County?; 1815; 1
Barnet, William, Esq.; Phelps; 1812; 2
Barney, J. W., Esq.; Ellery; 1835; 1
Barr, ___ (Rev.); ___; Gerry; 1831; 1
Barrel, ___ (Rev.); ___; Greenfield, Saratoga Co.; 1836; 1
Barrie, J. S. (Rev.); ___; Alexander-Middlebury area; 1847; 2
Barritt, Lyman (Esq.?); Bath; 1831; 1
Barrows, ___ (Rev.); ___; Jamestown?; 1832; 1
Barrows, E. S. (Rev.); ___; Waterville?; 1830; 1
Bartholomew, ___ (Rev.); ___; 1840; 1
Bartholomew, Orlo (Rev.); Augusta; 1845; 1
Barton, ___ (Rev.); ___; Cayuga?, 1828; 1
Barton, ___ (Rev.); ___; Elmira; 1829; 1
Barton, ___ (Rev.); ___; Geneva; 1829; 1
Barton, ___ (Rev.); ___; Romulus; 1829; 2
Bateman, C., Esq.; Williamson; 1837-38; 2
Baxter, Aaron (Elder); ___; Addison?; 1831; 1
Bayard, ___ (Rev.); ___; Geneseo; 1829; 2
Beach, R. M. (Rev.); ___; Campbell?; 1850; 1
Bear, ___ (Rev.); ___; Carroll?; 1839; 1
Beardsley, ___ (Rev.); ___; Hanover; 1837; 1
Beardsley, ___ (Rev.); ___; Le Roy; 1829; 1
Beardsley, ___ (Rev.); ___; Onondaga; 1831; 1
Beardsley, E. (Elder); ___; Ellington-Fluvanna area; 1835-38; 2
Beardsley, O. C. (Rev.); ___; Chautauqua; 1830; 2
Beatty, ___ (Rev.); ___; Buffalo; 1843; 1
Bebee, ___ (Rev.); ___; Campbell-Urbana area; 1840; 2
Beckwith, ___ (Elder); ___; Le Roy; 1829; 1
Beebe, ___ (Rev.); ___; Camillus; 1822; 1
Beebee, ___ (Rev.); ___; Bath; 1841; 1
Beecher, ___ (Rev.); ___; Bethany; 1844; 1
Beecher, Isaac E., Esq.; Palmyra; 1836-44; 11
Beecher, L. E., Esq.; Sodus; 1841; 1
Beecher, W. A. (Rev.); ___; Batavia; 1841; 1
Beers, Smith (Rev.); ___; Dresden?, 1840 ; 1
Beman, S. S. (Rev.); ___; Troy; 1842; 1
Benedict, ___ (Rev.); ___; Gorham; 1831; 1
Bennett, ___ (Rev.); ___; Lodi; 1830; 2
Bennett, ___ (Rev.); ___; Walworth; 1841; 1

262

Bennett, Daniel, Esq.; Howard; 1831; 1
Bennett, H., Esq.; Hornellsville?; 1849; 1
Bennett, Ira (Rev.); Meth.; Palmyra-Macedon area; 1841-43; 2
Bennett, William P., (Esq.?); Cayuga; 1811; 1
Benson, Jonathan (Rev.); ___; Palmyra-Walworth-Williamson area; 1837; 4
Bentley, ___ (Rev.); ___; Middle Haddam, CT; 1832; 1
Benton, R. (Rev.); ___; Arcadia-Newark area; 1830; 3
Berain (also Berrian), ___ (Rev.); ___; New York City; 1825-27; 2
Berky, A. (Rev.); ___; South Dansville?; 1847; 1
Berrigan, William (Rev.); ___; New York City; 1822; 1
Berry, Azel, Esq; Farmington; 1839; 1
Best, ___ (Rev.); ___; Harmony; 1839; 1
Bethune, ___ (Rev.); ___; Auburn?; 1835; 1
Biddlecom, D. (Rev.); ___; Rome, NY; 1835; 1
Bigelow, ___ (Elder); ___; Bath; 1831; 1
Billings, Benjamin, Esq.; Macedon?; 1844; 1
Billington, (Rev.); ___; Chili, NY; 1844; 1
Birdsall, ___ (Elder); ___; Coventry; 1832; 1
Bishop, J. F. (Rev.); ___; Fredonia-Pomfret area; 1841-42; 2
Blackmarr, A. (Rev.); ___; Alexander; 1846; 1
Blackmarr, Hiram (Rev.); ___; Bethany?; 1846-48; 2
Blakesley, E. (Rev.); ___; Marion-Palmyra-Walworth area; 1829-31; 3
Blaskell, ___ (Rev.); ___; Ellington, 1826; 1
Blin, T. D. (Rev.); ___; Ashville-Busti area; 1845; 6
Bliss, Simeon (Rev.); ___; Redfield, Oswego Co.; 1823; 1
Bly, Theron S., Esq.; Harmony-Jamestown area; 1829-39; 5
Boardman, Charles A. (Rev.); ___; New Milford, CT?; 1828; 1
Bogerly, John (Rev.); ___; Phelps?; 1828; 1
Bogher, Frederick, (Esq.?); Clyde; 1830; 1
Bolles, ___ (Rev.); ___; Stafford; 1837; 1
Bolles, James A. (Rev.); Episc.; Batavia; 1837-50; 16
Bond, ___ (Rev.); ___; Darien?; 1850; 1
Bond, Ammi (Rev.); ___; Pinegrove, PA?; 1834; 1
Bordwell, Enoch, Esq.; Middlesex; 1816; 1
Bostwick, William W. (Rev.); Meth.; Auburn-Bath-Geneva-Hammondsport; 1826-41;
Boswell, Edward Jackes (Rev.); ___; London, Upper Cananda; 1831; 1
Wowdish, William S. (Rev.); ___; Pulaski?; 1841; 1
Bowen, Amos P. (Rev.); ___; Attica; 1824-32; 2
Bowers, ___ (Rev.); ___; Canisteo; 1831; 1
Bowles, ___ (Rev.); ___; Batavia?; 1838; 1
Boyden, E. (Rev.); ___; Brooklyn, Ohio?; 1836; 1
Boyle, ___ (Rev.); ___; Marion; 30-32; 5
Boynton, Jonathan, Esq; Ontario, NY; 1822-28; 2
Brace, S. W. (Rev.); ___; Lyons-Phelps-Vienna; 1821-23; 7
Bradford, ___ (Rev.); ___; Wardsboro, VT?; 1836; 1
Bradley, E., Esq.; Carroll; 1841; 1
Bradley, J. (Rev.); ___; Middlebury; 1825; 1
Bradley, William (Rev.); ___; Fredonia?; 1835; 1
Bradley, William (Rev.); ___; Bath; 1850; 1
Bridges, John (Rev.); ___; Brighton, Canada West?; 1848; 1
Bridgman, George (Rev.); ___; Sheldon?; 1845; 1
Brink, M., Esq.; Hammondsport-Urbana area; 1830-31; 3
Brittan (also Britton), T. S. (Rev.); ___; Macedon-Palmyra area; 1841; 4
Broadhead, John (Rev.); ___; Worksburg; 1841; 1
Brocaw, A. (Rev.); ___; Ovid?; 1818; 1
Bronson, E. (Rev.); ___; Avoca-Bath area, NY and Elkland, PA; 1835-47; 5
Brooks, A. L. (Rev.); ___; Corning; 1850; 1
Brooks, W. R. (Rev.); ___; Harmony; 1843; 1
Brown, ___ (Rev.); ___; Attica; 1825; 3
Brown, ___ (Elder); ___; Hopewell; 1827; 1
Brown, ___ (Rev.); ___; Kennedyville; 1846; 1
Brown, ___ (Rev.); ___; Le Roy?; 1841; 1
Brown, ___ (Elder); ___; Palmyra?; 1830; 1
Brown, ___ (Rev.); ___; Perry; 1825; 1
Brown, ___ (Elder; ___; Phelps; 1828; 1
Brown, ___ (Rev.); ___; Romulus?; 1819; 1

Brown, A., Esq; Fluvanna; 1843; 1
Brown, Charles (Rev.); ___; Newfane, VT?; 1832; 1
Brown, D., Esq.; Benton; 1811; 1
Brown, Ira (Elder); ___; Bath; 1845-46; 2
Brown, J. S. (Rev.); ___; Castile?; 1849; 1
Brown, John, Esq.; Lyons; 1813; 1
Brown, Jonathan, Esq.; Painted Post; 1834-35; 2
Brown, N. (Rev.); ___; Alexander; 1825-26; 2
Brown, S. (Rev.); ___; Howard?; 1846; 1
Brown, S. S. (Rev.); ___; Chocton (Liberty Corners) and Dansville; 1845-46; 8
Brown, Silas C. (Rev.); ___; West Bloomfield?; 1832; 1
Brown, Zurial, Esq.; Farmington?; 1840; 1
Brownlee, (Rev. Dr.); ___; New York City; 1827; 1
Brownson, James (Rev.); ___; Cohocton?; 1841; 1
Bruce, ___ (Rev.); ___; Geneva; 1832-33; 2
Bruce, Nathaniel F. (___); Angelia?; 1838; 1
Brundage, B. S., Esq.; Canisteo-Greenwood-Jasper-Troupsburgh; 1838-41; 7
Buck, ___ (Rev.); ___; Fairport-Pittsford-Sodus area; 1832-33; 3
Bucklin, Willard, Esq.; Gerry?; 1839; 1
Buel, ___ (Rev.); ___; Barry; 1825; 1
Bullard, ___ (Rev.); ___; Elmira?; 1842; 1
Bullock, ___ (Elder); ___; Jamestown; 1843; 1
Bullock, Jonathan, Esq.; Busti?; 1839; 1
Burbank, ___ (Rev.); ___; Marion?; 1830; 1
Burbank, Jacob (Rev.); ___; Sodus?; 1840; 1
Burgess, ___ (Rev.); ___; Hartford, CT?; 1846; 1
Burlingame, A. H. (Rev.); Bapt.; Palmyra; 1841-42; 10
Burnet, William, Esq.; Phelps; 1811-19; 3
Burnside, W. (Rev.); ___; Verona?; 1847; 1
Bush, ___ (Rev. Dr.); ___; Rathbonville?; 1840; 1
Bush, A. G., Esq.; Poland, NY; 1845; 1
Bush, G. A., Esq.; Randolph?; 1841; 1
Butler, ___ (Rev.); ___; Cohoes?; 1819; 1
Butler, C. M. (Rev.); ___; Palmyra; 1838-40; 5
Butler, S. S., Esq.; Batavia?; 1824; 1
Butts, Moses (Rev.); ___; Pulteneyville?; 1842; 1
Butts, William (Rev.); ___; Harmony?; 1839; 1
C___, ___ (Rev.); ___; Lyons; 1843; 1
Calhoan, G. A. (Rev.); ___; Hartford (State not given); 1845; 1
Camburn, L. (Rev.); ___; Palmyra?; 1821; 1
Campbell, ___ (Rev.); ___; Benton; 1826; 1
Campbell, ___ (Rev.); ___; Irving, NY?; 1845; 1
Campbell, A. E. (Rev.); Presby.; Palmyra; 1828-31; 20
Campbell, Alfred (Rev.); ___; Milo?; 1826; 1
Campbell, E. A. (Rev.); ___; Vienna, NY?; 1827; 1
Campbell, Oliver, Esq.; Stafford; 1825; 1
Canfield, P. (Rev.); ___; Sinclairville; 1844; 1
Canouse, Peter (Rev.); ___; Newark, NY; 1830; 1
Card, Henry C. (Rev.); ___; Cherry Creek?; 1843; 1
Carey, S. (Rev.); ___; Stockbridge, MI?; 1849; 1
Carle, ___ (Rev.); ___; Cameron?; 1845; 1
Carlton, T. J. (Rev.); ___; Pulteneyville; 1837; 1
Carpenter, ___ (Rev.); ___; Delanti?; 1845; 1
Carpenter, ___ (Rev.); ___; Sinclairville; 1845; 1
Carpenter, C., Esq.; Batavia; 1822-30; 7
Carpenter, C. G. (Rev.); ___; German Flats?; 1831; 1
Carpenter, Elijah, Esq.; Bennington?; 1825; 1
Caron, John (Rev.); ___; Romulus; 1812; 1
Carr, ___ (Elder); ___; Bath?; 1847; 1
Carr, ___ (Rev.); ___; Big Flats?; 1849; 1
Carr, C. C. (Rev.); ___; Veteran, Chemung Co.?; 1849; 1
Case, ___ (Rev.); ___; Bath?; 1838; 1
Case, ___ (Rev.); ___; Phelps?; 1828-29; 2
Case, J. (Rev.); ___; Kennedyville; 1844-47; 2
Castleton, Thomas (Rev.); ___; Canandaigua; 1841; 1
Caton, J. (Rev.); ___; Romulus; 1813-23; 4 (See Caron, J. above)

Chadwick, ___ (Rev.); ___; Burdette-Hector area; 1826; 3
Chadwick, ___ (Rev.); ___; Geneva?; 1827; 1
Chaise, ___ (Rev.); ___; Farmington; 1820; 1
Chamberlain, ___ (Rev.); ___; Palmyra; 1829; 1
Chambers, John, Esq.; Tyrone?; 1847; 1
Champion, Thomas J. (_?_); Penn Yan; 1836; 1
Chancy, Ira (Rev.); ___; Charlton?; 1842; 1
Chapin, ___ (Rev.); ___; Bainbridge; 1818; 1
Chapin, A. (Rev.); Congregational; Jamestown; 1838-43; 11
Chapin, J. E., Esq.; Westfield; 1843; 1
Chapman, ___ (Rev.); ___; Geneva?; 1811; 1
Chapman, ___ (Rev.); ___; Italy, NY?; 1847; 1
Chapman, ___ (Rev.); ___; Prattsburgh?; 1847; 1
Chapman, C. R. (Rev.); ___; Panama, NY?; 1845; 1
Chapman, J. (Rev.); ___; Dansville?; 1850; 1
Chapman, J. (Rev.); ___; Perth Amboy, NJ?; 1829; 1
Chase, ___ (Elder); ___; Bath?; 1831; 1
Chase, ___ (Rev.); ___; Benton; 1816-27; 2
Chase, ___ (Rev.); ___; Decatursville (town of Reading); 1821; 2
Chase, ___ (Rev.); ___; Prattsburgh?; 1831; 1
Chase, A. (Rev.); ___; South Dansville; 1840-42; 2
Chase, Abner (Rev.); ___; Milo and Palmyra; 1823-31; 2
Chase, J. (Rev.); ___; Waterloo; 1836; 1
Chatman, ___ (Rev.); ___; Italy, NY?; 1847; 1
Cheeseman, Lewis (Rev.); ___; Albion?; 1828; 1
Cheesman, J. K. (Rev.); ___; Batavia; 1850; 4
Cheever, George B. (Rev.); ___; New York City?; 1843; 1
Cheney, ___ (Rev.); ___; Alexander-Attica area; 1825-32; 2
Chester, ___ (Rev. Dr.); ___; Albany?; 1820; 1
Chidsey, S. B., Esq.; Romulus?; 1830; 1
Chipman, T. R. (Rev.); Episc.; Le Roy; 1849; 1
Church, J. E. (Elder); ___; Jamestown?; 1836; 1
Church, S. C. (Rev.); ___; Hornellsville; 1840; 1
Clark, ___ (Rev.); ___; Benton?; 1815; 1
Clark, ___ (Prof. - Allegany College); ___; Busti?; 1844; 1
Clark, ___ (Rev.); ___; Ovid; 1809-10; 2
Clark, ___ (Rev.); ___; Perry?; 1836; 1
Clark, ___ (Rev.); ___; Phelps; 1819; 1
Clark, ___ (Rev.); ___; Wolcott; 1822; 1
Clark, Daniel, Esq.; Campbelltown; 1831; 2
Clark, G. W. (Rev.); ___; Jamestown?; 1845; 1
Clark, Harry, Esq.; Wheeler?; 1831; 1
Clark, Ichabod (Elder); ___; Le Roy?; 1837; 1
Clark, J. W. (Rev.); ___; Palmyra; 1843-44; 5
Clark, John A. (Rev.); ___; New York City and Seneca?; 1829-31; 3
Clark, Oren or Orrin (Rev.); ___; 1816-28; 27
Clark, Roswell (Rev.); ___; Greenwood?; 1838; 1
Clark, T. P. or T. R. (Rev.); ___; Urbana; 1846; 5
Clark, W. (Rev.); ___; Palmyra?; 1843; 1
Clark, W. A. (Rev.); ___; Skaneateles?; 1814; 1
Clarke, ___ (Rev.); ___; Romulus?; 1813; 1
Clarke, George W. (Rev.); ___; Jamestown; 1844-45; 2
Clary, ___ (Rev.); ___; Cohocton?; 1826; 1
Clute, ___ (Rev.); ___; Bergen; 1849; 1
Coal, C. H., Esq.; Rathbunville; 1846; 1
Cochrane, ___ (Rev.); ___; Attica?; 1826; 1
Cofee, ___ (Rev.); ___; Athens, Bradford Co., PA?; 1839; 1
Coffin, I. L. or J. L. (Rev.); ___; Bradford (state not given); 1845; 2
Cole, C., Esq.; Addison?; 1847; 1
Coleby, Thomas W. (Rev.?); ___; Greenwood?; 1841; 1
Collier, John D., Esq.; Howard; 1831; 1
Collins, John, Esq.; Geneva?; 1818; 1
Collins, W. F. (Rev.); ___; Fishkill?; 1842; 1
Colman, ___ (Rev.); ___; Jamestown?; 1834; 1
Colman or Coleman, M. (Rev.); ___; Elba; 1848-50; 2
Colton, ___ (Rev.); ___; Le Roy?; 1824; 1

Colton, Calvin (Rev.); ___; Batavia; 1822-26; 15
Colton, Chester (Rev.); ___; Lyme, CT?; 1840; 1
Comstock, H. L.,Esq.; Urbana?; 1845; 1
Condit, ___ (Rev.); ___; Oswego?; 1841; 1
Conklin, William (Rev.); ___; Pike; 1841; 1
Cook, ___ (Rev.); ___; Attica?; 1846; 1
Cook, ___ (Rev.); ___; Jamestown; 1842; 1
Cook Charles J. (Rev.); ___; Palmyra?; 1821; 1
Cook, Constant, Esq.; Cohocton; 1840; 1
Cook, M. (Rev.); ___; Lyons; 1842-43; 2
Coriel, ___ (Rev.); ___; Hornby; 1841; 1
Corning, A. (Rev.); ___; Sharon?; 1843; 1
Cornwall, A., Esq.; Williamson-Pulteneyville area; 1830-42; 5
Corson, L. H. (Rev.); ___; Bath; 1846-49 8
Corwin, G. S. (Rev. Dr.); ___; Elba-Pine Hill area; 1844-50; 5
Cotton, ___ (Rev.); ___; Bristol, IL?; 1841; 1
Covill, ___ (Rev.); ___; Ellington?; 1839; 1
Cowan, Samuel, Esq.; Carroll-Jamestown area; 1829-30; 2
Cowdin, A., Esq.; Bethany; 1846; 1
Cowles, ___ (Rev.); ___; Napoli, NY; 1835; 1
Cox, ___ (Rev.); ___; New York City?; 1829; 1
Crane, ___ (Rev.); ___; Cambray; 1819; 1
Crane, Ezra (Elder); ___; Benton; 1827; 1
Crane, W. I. (Rev.); ___; Hartland; 1840; 1
Craw, ___ (Elder); ___; Camillus?; 1816; 1
Crawford, G. (Rev.); ___; Le Roy; 1847; 1
Crissy, ___ (Rev.); ___; Jasper?; 1841; 1
Crocker, Allen (Rev.); ___; Alexander?; 1830; 1
Crombie, John, Esq.; Albama, NY; 1839; 1
Crosby, ___ (Rev.); ___; Penn Yan?; 1833; 1
Cross, Palmer (Rev.); ___; Clymer-Harmony area; 1829-42; 3
Cuming, Francis H. (Rev.); ___; Rochester; 1822-26; 3
Cummings, Simeon (Hon.); Batavia; 1830; 3
Curry, W. F. (Rev.); ___; Springwater-Dansville area; 1846-47; 2
Cushing, David (Rev.); ___; Arcadia-Newark area; 1841-43; 4
Cuyler, C. C. (Rev. Dr.); ___; Poughkeepsie; 183031; 2
Cuyler, George W., Esq.; Palmyra; 1843; 2
Danforth, ___ (Rev.); ___; Springfield, PA?; 1837; 1
Danforth, William, Esq.; Marion; 1843; 1
Darwin, ___ (Rev.); ___; Riga-Sweden area; 1824; 2
Dashiell, George (Rev.); ___; Seneca Falls?; 1835; 1
Davis, ___ (Rev.); ___; Ballston; 1838; 1
Davis, ___ (Rev. Dr.); ___; Clinton; 1820; 1
Davis, ___ (Rev.); ___; Lodi?; 1849; 1
Davis, ___ (Rev.); ___; Palmyra; 1828; 1
Davis, ___ (Rev.); ___; Waterloo; 1818; 1
Davis, D. D., Esq.; Canisteo; 1846; 1
Davis, D. D., Esq.; Greene?; 1846; 1
Davis, Dan H., Esq.; Cohocton; 1845; 3
Davis, Emry, Esq.; Busti; 1831-41; 4
Davis, H. (Rev.) Bapt.; Brockport; 1830; 1
Davis W. H. (Rev.); ___; Brooklyn?; 1848; 1
Davis, W. P. (Rev.); ___; Geneva?; 1839; 1
Davis, William F. ( ? ); Newark, NY; 1842; 1
Delavan, George E. (Rev.); ___; Wayne?; 1835; 1
Depue, J. S., Esq.; Cameron-Thurston area; 1842-46; 2
Deyo, A. H., Esq.; Prattsburgh; 1829; 1
Dickson, James, Esq.; Galen; 1821-22; 2
Dickson, W. B., Esq.; Galen?; 1814; 1
Dobbin, H. W., Esq.; Junius?; 1815; 1
Dodge, ___ (Rev.); ___; Chautauqua?; 1838; 1
Dodge, ___ (Rev.); ___; Jamestown?; 1841; 1
Dodge, ___ (Rev.); ___; Mayville; 1842-44; 3
Dodge, J. (Rev.); ___; Starkey; 1849; 1
Dodge, John R. (Rev.) Bapt.; Brockport; 1829; 1
Dodge, Jonas (Rev.); ___; Arcadia; 1840; 1

Doolittle, ___ (Rev.); ___; Palmyra; 1834; 1
Doolittle, ___ (Rev.); ___; Warsaw?, 1832; 1
Dorman, Joel, Esq.; Penn Yan?; 1824; 1
Douglas, W. H. (Rev.?); ___; Palmyra; 1843; 1
Dow, A. H., Esq.; Marion; 1839; 1
Dox, Jacob, Esq.; Geneva; 1813-22; 24
Draper, ___ (Rev.); ___; Manchester?; 1829; 1
Draper, A. P. (Elder); ___; Walworth?; 1839; 1
Draper, Gideon (Rev.); ___; Clifton Springs and Phelps?; 1815-18; 2
Dunham, David (Rev.); ___; Bath?; 1831-41; 2
Dunham, Hezekiah, Esq.; Arcadia?; 1830; 1
Dunlap, Ledley (sic), Esq.; Ovid?; 1822; 1
Durfee, B. H. (Rev.); ___; Marion; 1841; 1
Earley, B. (Rev.); ___; Lockville?; 1831; 1
Earll, Robert (Judge); Attica?; 1825; 1
Eaton, ___(Rev.); ___; Poughkeepsie?; 1838; 1
Eaton, G. W. (Prof.); ___; Palmyra?; 1838; 1
Eddy, ___ (Rev.); ___; Benton; 1829; 3
Eddy, ___ (Rev.); ___; Jamestown; 1826-32; 6
Eddy, A. D. (Rev.); ___; Canandaigua; 1826-33; 5
Eddy, C. (Rev.); ___; Penn Yan; 1826-29; 3
Eddy, Isaac (Rev.); ___; Carroll; 1830-32; 5
Eddy, Seth, Esq.; Marion; 1833; 1
Eddy, Zachariah (Rev.); ___; Randolph and Concord, Erie Co.; 1839-43; 3
Edson, J. M., Esq.; Gerry?; 1831; 1
Edwards, David, Esq.; Woodhull?; 1832; 1
Edwards, James, Esq.; Sodus; 1829-30; 2
Edwards, Jesse (Rev.); ___; Dansville?; 1849; 1
Eighenbradt, ___ (Rev.); ___; Rochester?; 1843; 1
Elliot or Elliott, J. (Rev.); ___; Wyoming and Middlebury area; 1832-48; 2
Elliot, Joseph (Rev.); ___; Batavia?; 1829; 1
Ely, T. S., Esq.; Harmony; 1833; 1
Emmons, ___ (Rev.); ___; Elba?; 1839; 1
Emory, ___(Rev.); ___; Warren?; 1838; 1
Emory, J. S. (Rev.); ___; Forestville-Sinclairville area; 1840-43; 2
Engle, A. B. (Rev.); ___; Smyrna?; 1843; 1
Ensign, ___ (Rev.); ___; Bethany?; 1825; 1
Ensign, S. (Rev.); ___; Stafford?; 1826; 1
Eustace, ___ (Rev.); ___; Palmyra?; 1829; 2
Evarts, ___(Rev.); ___; Naples; 1842; 1
Everest, G. T. (Rev.); ___; Jasper?; 1847; 2
Everett, E. (Rev.); ___; Avoca-Wheeler area; 1838; 2
Fairbank, ___ (Rev.); ___; Williamson?; 1832; 1
Fairbanks, Ira (Rev.); ___; Cazenovia?; 1828; 1
Fancher, B. (Rev.); ___; Oakfield?; 1848; 1
Farley, ___ (Rev.); ___; Benton; 1817-19; 3
Farley, ___ (Rev.); ___; Phelps?; 1829; 1
Feller, Amos, Esq.; Jamestown-Poland area; 1844; 3
Fenton, William H., Esq.; Ellicott-Ellery area; 1832-38; 4
Ferguson or Fergeson, William H. (Rev.); Meth.?; Palmyra; 1843-44; 3
Ferguson, W. M. (Rev.); ___; Pittsford?; 1850; 1
Ferris, ___ (Rev.); ___; Albany?; 1825; 1
Ferris, ___ (Rev.); ___; Bath-Cameron area; 1845; 4
Fiddle, ___ (Rev.); ___; China Grove?; 1818; 1
Field, James, Esq.; Geneva; 1821-23; 6
Fifield, Jesse, Esq.; ___; 1833;1
Fillmore, ___ (Rev.); ___; Williamson?; 1835; 1
Findly, John J. (Rev.); ___; Waterford; 1845; 1
Firman, ___ (Rev.); ___; Batavia?; 1848; 1
Fish, J. (Rev.); ___; Watertown?; 1842; 1
Fish, M., Esq.; Pinegrove, PA?; 1845; 1
Fisher, N. W. (Rev.); ___; Palmyra; 1842-44; 8
Fister, ___ (Rev.); ___; Batavia?; 1838; 1
Fitch, Charles (Rev.); ___; Batavia; 1832; 1
Fitch, Ebenezer (Rev. Dr.); Presby.; West Bloomfield; 1819-22; 2
Fitch, Isaac S., Esq.; Ashville-Harmony area; 1826-38; 3

Flint, ___ (Rev. Dr.); ___ Hartford, CT?; 1821; 1
Flint, E., Esq.; Rose; 1829; 1
Flint, Elijah, Esq.; Pembroke?; 1824; 1
Flower, J. (Rev.); ___; Jamestown or Poland, NY?; 1843; 1
Flowers, Josiah (Rev.); ___; Jamestown?; 1844; 1
Foot, ___ (Rev.); ___; Cortlandville; 1835; 1
Foote, E. T. (Judge); Busti-Carroll-Jamestown area; 1829-33; 3
Forbes, Philo (Rev.); ___; Macedon Locks; 1842; 3
Forbush, S. B., Esq.; Stockton?; 1837; 1
Ford, Henry (Rev.); ___; Elmira; 1824; 1
Foster, R. H., Esq.; Lyons?; 1825; 1
Fowler, P. H. (Rev.); ___; Elmira?; 1846-50; 2
Fowler, William (Rev.); ___; Palmyra?; 1829; 1
Frazer, Orris (Rev.); ___; Bath; 1841-42; 8
Frelich, John, Esq.; Seneca?; 1817; 1
French, J., Esq.; Gorham?; 1813; 1
French, J. W. (Rev.); ___; Palmyra?; 1849; 1
Frink, ___ (Elder); ___; Ellery?; 1844; 1
Frink, A. (Rev.); ___; Randolph?; 1839; 1
Frost, ___ (Rev.); ___; Utica-Whitesborough-Deerfield area; 1823-26; 3
Fuller, ___ (Rev.); ___; Manchester; 1842; 1
Fuller, ___ (Rev.); ___; Palmyra?; 1843; 1
Fuller, ___ (Rev.); Port Gibson?; 1842; 1
Fuller, Ames, Esq.; Poland, NY; 1845; 1
Fuller, E. B. (Rev.); ___; Palmyra?; 1819; 1
Fuller, E. B. (Rev.); ___; Bath; 1846-47; 6
Fuller, Erastus, Esq.; Wolcott; 1822; 1
Fuller, H. (Rev.); ___; Palmyra; 1843; 1
Fuller, William A.; (_?_); Ontario, NY; 1836; 1
Gage, Anthony, Esq.; Seneca?; 1819-22; 2
Gage, A. D., Esq.; Macedon; 1840; 1
Gage, Samuel G., Esq.; Geneva, Benton, and Bellona; 1823-29; 10
Galloway, E. M. (Rev.); ___; Palmyra?; 1839-40; 2
Galston, ___ (Rev.); ___; Gorham?; 1837; 1
Garfield, J., Esq.; Busti?; 1831; 1
Gaylord, ___ (Rev.); ___; Wheeler?; 1841-42; 2
Gear, ___ (Rev.); ___; Palmyra?; 1829; 2
Gear, E. G. (Rev.); ___; Painted Post?; 1828; 1
Gebhard, John G. (Rev.); ___; Claverack?; 1821; 1
Gelston, ___ (Rev.); ___; Rushville?; 1841; 1
Gilder, ___ (Rev.); ___; Sag Harbor?; 1841; 1
Gildersieve, ___ (Rev.); ___; Wilkes Barre, PA?; 1826; 1
Gillam, W. C. (Rev.); ___; Franklinville; 1841; 1
Gillett, ___ (Elder); ___; Elmira; 1829; 1
Gillett, E. J. (Rev.); Presby.; Jamestown; 1831-45; 51
Gillett, P. D. (Elder); ___; Geneva?; 1827; 1
Gillmore, J. (Rev.); ___; Geneva?; 1828; 1
Gload, John, Esq.; Pulteney?; 1840; 1
Goff, ___ (Elder); ___; Geneva; 1822-23; 2
Goff, ___ (Rev.); ___; Middlesex; 1816; 1
Goff, Isaac C. (Rev.); ___; Canandaigua, Marion, Arcadia and  Palmyra; 1840-41; 6
Goff, John (Elder); ___; Benton; 1818-26; 4
Goodell, ___ (Rev.); ___; Bristol?; 1818; 1
Goodell, William (Rev.); ___; Howard; 1840-41; 3
Goodrich, ___ (Rev.); ___; _?_; 1832; 1
Goodrich, ___, Esq.; Barcelona, NY?; 1849; 1
Goodrich, ___ (Rev.); ___; Milwaukee, WI?; 1838; 1
Goodsell, ___ (Rev.); ___; New York City?; 1832; 1
Goodwin, W. H. (Rev.); ___; Manchester-Canandaigua area; 1843-44; 2
Gould, ___ (Rev.); ___; Sodus; 1840; 1
Gould, ___ (Rev.); ___; Jerusalem?; 1841; 1
Gould, Joseph (Rev.); ___; Walworth?; 1834; 1
Grandin, D., Esq.; Williamson; 1830; 3
Granger, Julis N., Esq.; Manchester; 1837-43; 3
Grant, Loring (Rev.); ___; "Erie District, formerly of Geneva"; 1826; 1
Granville, ___ (Rev.); ___; Carroll; 1845; 1

Grash, ___ (Rev.); ___; Utica; 1842; 1
Graves, ___ (Rev.); ___; Ashville-Busti area; 1835-38; 2
Graves, ___ (Rev. Dr.); ___; Corning?; 1845; 2
Gray, ___ (Rev.); ___; Batavia?; 1831; 1
Gray, ___ (Rev.); ___; Jamestown; 1838; 3
Gray, A. F. (Rev.); ___; Sheridan?; 1839; 1
Gray, A. W. (Rev.); ___; Panama-Harmony area; 1826-39; 4
Gray, Levi, Esq.; Wheeler?; 1841; 1
Green or Greene, ___ (Rev.); ___; Canandaigua?; 1835-36; 2
Green, Byram (Hon.); Sodus-Palmyra area; 1826-32; 3
Green, Byron, Esq.; Pulteneyville; 1831; 1
Green, George, Esq.; Benton?; 1813; 1
Gregg, ___ (Rev.); ___; Urbana?; 1850; 1
Gregory, ___ (Rev.); ___; Homer; 1840; 1
Gregory, ___ (Rev.); ___; Ripley-Westfield area; 1831-36; 2
Gregory, Almon (Rev.); Episc.; Bath; 1850; 1
Gridley, J. (Rev.); ___; Scriba?; 1841; 1
Griswold, ___ (Rev.); ___; Palmyra?; 1822; 1
Griswold, S. F. or S. T. (Rev.); ___; Marion?; 1842-43; 2
Griswold, Stephen, Esq.; Byron-Stafford area; 1822-25; 4
Grosvenor, S., Esq.; Cherry Creek?; 1842; 1
Gugg, Hiram (_?_); Alabama, NY?; 1846; 1
Guion, ___ (Rev.); ___; Palmyra?; 1829; 1
Hager, ___ (Rev.); ___; Roanoke?; 1850; 1
Hall, ___ (Rev.); ___; Lyons?; 1840; 1
Hall, ___ (Rev.); ___; Victor; 1836; 2
Hall, A. (Rev.); ___; Jamestown?; 1840; 1
Hall, James, Esq.; Carroll?; 1829; 1
Hall, Joseph, Esq.; Phelps; 1813-17; 14
Halliday, ___ (Rev.); ___; Ellery; 1844; 1
Halladay, E. H. (Elder); ___; Fluvanna?; 1845; 1
Hamilton, William, Esq.; Bath; 1835-38; 5
Hamilton, William, Esq.; Hamburgh?; 1839; 1
Hammond, ___ (Rev.); ___; Pittsford?; 1844; 1
Handy, A. (Rev.); ___; Batavia?; 1842; 1
Handy, A. (Rev.); ___; Jamestown; 1845; 2
Handy, Joy (Rev.); ___; Fredonia?; 1
Harman, George (Rev.); ___; Canandaigua?; 1823; 1
Harmon, George (Rev.); ___; Geneva?; 1824; 1
Harrington, D. (Rev.); ___; Pulteneyville and Palmyra; 1838-46; 14
Harrington, H. (Rev.); ___; Palmyra; 1844; 1
Hart, J. D. (Rev.); ___; Palmyra-Macedon area; 1833; 3
Hart, Jacob (Rev.); ___; Batavia-Bethany area; 1842-49; 2
Harvey, T. W., Esq.; Jamestown; 1829; 1
Haskell, Abel (Rev.); ___; Geneva; 1850; 1
Haskell, Samuel (Rev.); ___; Detroit, MI?; 1848; 1
Hastings, Eurotus, Esq.; Geneva; 1828-30; 7
Hathaway, David, Esq.; Napoli, NY; 1835; 1
Wawks, ___ (Rev. Dr.); ___; New York City?; 1839; 1
Hawley, ___; Rev.); ___; Washington, D.C.; 1831; 1
Hawley, Amos P. (Rev.); ___; Jamestown?; 1840; 1
Hay, ___ (Rev.); ___; Geneva?; 1837; 1
Hazelton, J., Esq.; Farmersville?; 1829; 1
Hebard, F. G. (Rev.); ___; Geneva?; 1841; 1
Hebard, Salmon (Rev.); ___; Elba?; 1824; 2
Hedley, ___ (Rev.); ___; Walton, Delaware Co.; 1825; 1
Henderson, D., Esq.; Hammondsport; 1841; 1
Hendrick, ___ (Rev.); ___; Bath?; 1842; 1
Hendricks, B., Esq.; Junius?; 1825; 1
Henry, ___ (Rev.); ___; Ithaca?; 1849; 1
Hequembourg, C. L. (Rev.); ___; Dunkirk?; 1843; 1
Heustice, ___ (Rev.); ___; Palmyra?; 1837; 1
Hibberd, ___ (Rev.); ___; Attica; 1822; 1
Hibberd, ___ (Rev.); ___; Batavia?; 1822; 1
Hibberd, ___ (Rev.); ___; Geneva; 1841; 1
Hibberd, O. D. (Rev.); ___; Sugargrove, PA and Carroll, NY; 1842-44; 4

Hickes, B. H. (Rev.); ___; Palmyra; 1831; 1
Hickox, B. H. (Rev.); ___; Palmyra; 1831-32; 17
Hicks, Elias (Rev.); ___; Mud Creek?; 1845; 1
Higgins, ___ (Rev.); ___; Bath?; 1828; 1
Higgins, ___ (Rev.); ___; Seneca?; 1814; 1
Higgins, D. (Rev.); ___; Auburn; 1811; 1
Higgins, David (Rev.); ___; Bath; 1815-35; 19
Higgins, John D., Esq.; Bath; 1835-38; 5
Hill, ___ (Rev.); ___; Fort Mitchell, Creek Nation; 1829; 1
Hill, ___ (Rev.); Saratoga?; 1844; 1
Hill, H. F. (Rev.); ___; Groveland?; 1850; 1
Hill, J. F. (Rev.); ___; Jamestown; 1841-42; 3
Hinckley, Allen, Esq.; Fredonia-Pomfret area; 1843-44; 4
Hinebaugh, ___ (Rev.); ___; Harmony, NY and Sugargrove, PA; 1842-43; 4
Hoag, N. (Rev.); Meth.?; Avoca?; 1840; 1
Hoag, Nelson (Rev.); ___; Wheeler?; 1840; 1
Hobart, (Rt. Rev. Bishop); ___; New York City; 1817-29; 4
Hoffman, Charles O., Esq., Arcadia-Lyons area; 1842; 2
Hogaboom, ___ (Rev.); ___; Arcadia; 1843; 1
Hogan, M., Esq.; Geneva?; 1841; 1
Hogarth, Richard, Esq.; Geneva-Seneca area; 1821-23; 7
Holland, ___ (Rev.); ___; Delanti; 1843; 1
Holland, David, Esq.; Manchester; 1829; 1
Hollett, ___ Rev.); ___; Bethel; 1818; 1
Hollett, ___ (Rev.); ___; Geneva?; 1816; 1
Hollis, ___(Rev.); ___; Mayville?; 1843; 1
Holmes, Simeon, Esq.; Cohocton; 1842; 1
Hood, George (Rev.); ___; Urbana?; 1850; 1
Hopkins, ___ (Rev.); ___; Auburn?; 1840; 1
Hopkins, A. (Rev.); ___; Walworth?; 1839; 1
Hopkins, S. M. (Rev.); ___; Fredonia and Jamestown; 1843-44; 5
Hopkins, T. B. (Rev.); ___; Westfield; 1840-44; 3
Hopkins, T. M. (Rev.); ___; Spring Hill, Ohio?; 1835; 1
Hopkins, T. M. (Rev.); ___; Westfield, NY; 1843; 1
Hornell, George B. (Rev.); ___; Hornellsville?; 1828; 1
Horton, N. (Rev.); ___; Harmony; 1843; 1
Hosmer, William (Rev.); ___; Erwin; 1845; 1
Hosmer, William (Rev.); ___; Kennedyville; 1841; 1
Hotchkin, ___ (Rev.); ___; Campbell; 1838; 1
Hotchkin, ___(Rev.); ___; Painted Post?; 1838; 1
Hotchkin, Beriah (Rev.); ___; Pulteney?; 1826; 1. See also Rev. Beriah Hotchkiss.
Hotchkin, James H. (Rev.); ___; Bath and Pulteney; 1838-42; 3
Hotchkiss, Beriah (Rev.); Presby.?; Pulteney; 1823; 1. See also Beriah Hotchkin.
Hotchkiss, E. (Rev.); ___; Corning?; 1847; 1
Houghton, D. C. (Rev.); ___; Batavia; 1845-48; 7
House, ___ (Rev.); ___; Ontario, NY?; 1821; 1
House, Elisha (Rev.); ___; Montezuma?, 1822; 1
Hovey, ___ (Rev.); ___; Cedarville, Herkimer Co.; 1831; 1
Howe, ___ (Rev.); ___; Elba?; 1825; 2
Howell, ___ (Rev.); ___; Palmyra?; 1834; 1
Howland, David, Esq.; Manchester; 1829-30; 3
Hoyt, O. P. (Rev.); ___; Kalamazoo, MI?; 1844; 1
Hubbard, ___ (Rev.); ___; Angelica?; 1819; 1
Hubbard, ___ (Rev.); ___; Canisteo; 1813; 1
Hubbard, ___ (Rev.); ___; Sodus?; 1829; 1
Hubbard, Robert (Rev.); ___; Dansville; 1827; 1
Hubbard, S. (Rev.); ___; Centerville; 1829; 1
Hubbell, Lucas (Rev.); ___; Lyons and Farmington?; 1826-42; 17
Hubbell, L. (Rev.); ___; Vienna, NY?; 1845; 1
Huff, James, Esq.; Fayette?; 1825; 1
Hulett, L., Esq.; Byron Center?; 1847; 1
Hull, A. (Rev.); ___; Elmira?; 1850; 1
Hull, Elias, Esq.; Allen?; 1826; 1
Hunter, ___ (Rev.); ___; Stockton?; 1841; 1
Hurd, ___ (Rev.); ___; Angelica; 1828; 1
Hurd, ___ (Rev.; ___; Bethany?; 1824; 1
Hurd, ___ (Rev.); ___; Covington; 1824; 1

Hurd, B. (Rev.); ___; Reading?; 1846; 1
Hurd, Bryant R. (Rev.); ___; Orange?; 1847; 1
Hurlburt, ___ (Rev.); ___; Palmyra?; 1841; 1
Hurlburt, ___ (Rev.); ___; Oulteneyville?; 1834; 1
Hurlbut, ___ (Rev.); ___; Rochester, VT?; 1827; 1
Huse, ___ (Rev.); ___; Binghamton; 1826; 1
Hustead, W. H. (Rev.); ___; Italy, NY; 1846-47; 2
Hutchinson, D. F. (Rev.); ___; Barre (Pine Hill)?; 1847; 1
Huxley, ___ (Rev.); ___; Stafford?; 1825; 1
Hyatt, ___ (Rev. Dr.); ___; Baltimore, MD?; 1828; 1
Hyde, ___ (Rev.); ___; Oakland Co., MI?; 1850; 1
Ingraham, Ira (Rev.); ___; Lyons; 1842; 3 (Surname also Ingram)
Irons, J. (Rev.); ___; Perinton; 1817; 2
Irons, Jeremiah (Rev.); ___; Palmyra; 1817-21; 5
Irons, Jeremiah (Rev.); Bapt.; Yates ("formerly of Palmyra"); 1829; 1
Ives, Almon, Esq.; Ellery?; 1832; 1
Jackson, ___ (Rev.); ___; Albion?; 1841; 1
James, ___ (Rev.); ___; Albany?; 1834; 1
Jamison, John, Esq.; Reading; 1841; 1
Jenkins, ___; Rev.); ___; Bethany?; 1832; 1
Johns, ___ (Rev.); ___; Canandaigua; 1818-22; 4
Johnson, ___ (Rev.); ___; Auburn?; 1827; 1
Johnson, ___; Rev.; ___; Benton?; 1835; 1
Johnson, ___ (Rev.); ___; Hammondsport?; 1832; 1
Johnson, ___ (Rev.); ___; Scipio?; 1822; 1
Johnson, Forbes, Esq.; Ellery?; 1843; 1
Johnson, O. (Rev.); ___; Avoca?; 1841-42; 2
Johnson, R. B., Esq.; Canandaigua?; 1842; 1
Johnson, S. A., Esq.; Bath?; 1831; 1
Jones, ___ (Rev.); ___; Lyons; 1830; 1
Jones, ___ (Rev.); ___; New Lebanaon Springs?; 1824; 1
Jones, Henry V. (Rev.); ___; Palmyra; 1835-37; 8
Jones, Simeon R. (Rev.); ___; Elmira; 1812-16; 4
Jones, Solomon, Esq.; Jamestown; 1836-45; 9
Jones, William B., Esq.; Cameron?; 1844; 1
Judd, ___ (Rev.); ___; New London, CT; 1832; 2
Kanouse?, Peter (Rev.); ___; Newark, NY; 1830; 1
Kearney or Kearny, R. (Rev.); ___; Canandaigua-West Avon area; 1831-43; 5
Keefe, Jacob, Esq.; ___; 1812; 1
Kellogg, ___ (Rev.); ___; Rochester, VT?; 1833; 1
Kelly, ___ (Rev.); ___; Auburn or Mentz?; 1821; 1
Kelly, ___ (Rev.); ___; Geneva; 1822; 1
Kelsy, ___ (Rev.); ___; Lansing, Tompkins Co.; 1817; 1
Kendrick, Sanford, Esq.; Pembroke; 1824; 3
Kent, William (Rev.); ___; Junius?; 1829; 1
Kernon, William, Esq.; Wayne?; 1817; 1
Ketcham, H. K., Esq.; Cameron; 1841; 2
Ketchum, ___ (Elder); ___; Barrington; 1841; 1
Ketchum, ___ (Elder); ___; Wayne; 1845; 1
Ketchum, J. K., Esq.; Cameron?; 1841; 1
Kibbe, S. T., Esq.; Canandaigua?; 1823; 2
Kidder, A. (Rev.); ___; Alexander?; 1850; 1
King, J. S. (Rev.); ___; Ashville-Harmony area; 1830-32; 2
King, Jonas (Rev.); Egina, Greece?; 1829; 1
King, Stephen, Esq.; Orangeville; 1826; 1
Kingsley, ___ (Rev.); ___; Jamestown; 1835; 1
Kinnear, C. V., Esq.; Youngsville?; 1838; 1
Kinney, ___ (Elder); ___; Bath?; 1845; 1
Kinney, J. (Rev.); ___; Williamson; 1822-23; 2
Knapp, ___ (Rev.); ___; Pittsford?; 1826; 1
Kneeland, A. (Rev.); ___; Prattsburgh; 1845; 1
Kuypers, ___ (Rev. Dr.); ___; New York City?; 1817; 1
Lace or Lacy, ___ (Rev.); ---; Fayette?; 1823; 1
Lacey, ___ (Rev.); ___; Schenectady?; 1825; 1
Lacy, (Rev. Dr.); Episc.: Albany; 1830; 1
La Hatt, ___ (Rev.); ___; Portland; 1842-43; 3

Lake, N. S., Esq.; Kennedyville?; 1845; 1
Lakin, L., Esq.; Ashville-Busti area; 1839; 2
Lamb, ___ (Elder); ___; Saratoga?; 1824; 1
Lamberton, John, Esq.; Elba?; 1825; 1
Lamphire, Stephen (Rev.); ___; Starkey, 1826; 1
Lampkins, A. D., Esq.; Le Roy; 1847-50; 2
Lane, ___ (Rev.); ___; Aurelius?; 1823; 1
Lane, ___ (Rev.); ___; Fayette; 1822-25; 3
Lane, ___ (Rev.); ___; Geneva?; 1822; 1
Lane, ___ (Rev.); ___; Junius; 1825-28; 3
Lane, ___ (Rev.); ___; Phelps?; 1827; 1
Lane, ___ (Rev.); ___; Tyre?; 1834; 1
Lane, A. D. (Rev.); ___; Waterloo; 1819-29; 15
Lane, G. (Rev.); ___; Jamestown?; 1837; 1
Laning, ___ (Rev.); ___; Pittsford?; 1831; 1
Laning, G. (Rev.); ___; Geneva; 1825-28; 3
Laning, G. (Rev.); ___; Hector; 1827-28; 3
Laning, Gideon (Rev.); ___; Bethel?; 1825; 1
Laning, Gideon (Rev.); ___; Stafford; 1841; 1
Lanning, ___ (Rev.); Milo?; 1820; 1
Lansing, C. D. (Rev.); ___; Auburn?; 1844; 1
Lansing, D. C. (Rev. Dr.); ___; Auburn; 1818-27; 3
Larrowe, J., Esq.; Urbana-Wheeler area; 1835-42; 3
Lathrop, Alfred C. (Rev.); ___; Pulteneyville-Williamson area; 1840; 2
Latimer, ___ (Rev.); ___; Le Roy; 1839; 1
Laucin, Richard, Esq.; Wayne; 1811; 1
Laver, H. N. (Rev.); ___; Penfield?; 1843; 1
Lawrence, A. B. (Rev.); ___; New Orleans, LA?; 1837; 1
Lawton, D. B. (Rev.); Meth.; Bath; 1842; 1
Lazel, E. (Rev.); ___; Bath-Pulteney area; 1817-18; 2
Leach, Jacob, Esq.; Lyons?; 1822; 1
Lee, Day K. (Rev.); ___; Newark-Lyons-Palmyra area; 1842-44; 6
Leigh, A. M., Esq.; Howard?; 1842; 1
Leighton, Nathan, Esq.; Sodus; 1842; 1
Lennox or Lenox, Robert, Esq.; Jamestown-Ellery area; 1844; 5
Leonard, ___ (Rev.); ___; Ashville; 1831; 2
Lewis, Abner, Esq.; Jamestown-Harmony-Busti area; 1835-36; 4
Lilley or Lilly, F. (Rev.); ___; Hornellsville; 1846; 3
Lindley, ___ (Rev.); ___; Benton?; 1811; 1
Lloyd, A. (Rev.); ___; Bath; 1850; 1
Lockwood, ___ (Rev.); ___; Chenango Point?; 1828; 1
Longley, John, Esq.; Palmyra?; 1821; 1
Loomis, E. (Rev.); ___; Fredonia?; 1843; 1
Lord, ___ (Rev.); ___; Milwaukee, WI?; 1845; 1
Loucks, Peter, Esq.; Ellery?; 1826; 1
Louckton, I. B. (Rev.); ___; Batavia?; 1830; 1
Lounsbury, Thomas (Rev.); ___; Ovid; 1826;28; 2
Lucky, ___ (Rev.); ___; Palmyra?; 1836; 1
Lusk, ___ (Rev.); ___; Cherry Valley?; 1842; 1
Lyon, A. F., Esq.; Addison; 1840-41; 2
Lyon, Daniel (Rev.); ___; Walworth; 1840-42; 3
McAlister, Hugh, Esq.; Fayette; 1814; 2
McCloth, John, Esq.; Ontario, NY?; 1837; 1
McClure, G. (Rev.); ___; Bath; 1810; 2
McCollum, Joel, Esq.; Lockport?; 1828; 1
McConnell, Asa, Esq.; Howard; 1832; 1
McConnell, Henry, Esq.; Poland, NY?; 1833; 1
McCormack, ___ (Elder); ___; Macedon?; 1843; 1
McCreedy, ___ (Rev.); ___; Erie, PA?; 1831; 1
McCullough, John, Esq.; Seneca; 1817-22; 2
McDonald, ___ (Rev. Dr.); ___; Geneva-Waterloo area; 1822-27; 5
McDonald, David, Esq.; Dunkirk; 1843; 1
McElhana or McElheney, T. (Rev.); ___; Bath-Thurston area; 1846-47; 2
McIlvaine, Charles P. (Rev.); ___; West Point, NY; 1824; 1
McIntyre, Eden, Esq.; Oakfield?; 1847; 1
McKenney, ___ (Rev.); ___; Bath-Wheeler area; 1838; 5

McKenny, ___ (Rev.); ___; Bristol?; 1835; 1
McKenny, J. B. (Elder); ___; Jasper?; 1850; 1
McKinney, S. (Rev.); ___; Bath-South Dansville area; 1845; 2
McKoon, ___ (Rev.); ___; Butler?; 1836; 1
McLaren, ___ (Rev.); ___; Geneva; 1830; 1
McLaren, William (Rev.); ___; Caledonia; 1849; 1
McLean, R. M., Esq.; Palmyra?; 1822; 1
McLean, William A., Esq.; Palmyra; 1822-23; 9
McLouth, John, Esq.; Marion?; 1842; 1
McMahon, Isaiah (Rev.); ___; Penn Yan?; 1846; 1
McMurray, ___ (Rev.); ___; ___; 1818; 1
McNamard, M. (Rev.); ___; Tyrone?; 1831; 1
McNeal, ___ (Rev.); ___; Owasco?; 1827; 1
Maclay, A. (Rev.); ___; New York City; 1824; 1
Mahan, A. (Rev.); ___; Pittsford; 1829-30; 4
Mairs, George, Jr. (Rev.); ___; Argyle, Washington Co.?; 1828; 1
Mallory, A. C. (Rev.); ___; Bath-Wayne-Urbana area; 1844-50; 7
Mallory, J. (Rev.); ___; Alabama, NY?; 1845; 1
Mallory, J. C. (Rev.); ___; Bath, Campbell, Mud Creek, Savonia; 1850; 5
Mallory, S. C. (Rev.); ___; Wayne; 1847; 1
Mandeville, ___ (Rev.); ___; Walworth; 1841; 3
Manley, ___ (Rev.); ___; Ontario, NY; 1843; 1
Mann, ___ (Rev.); ___; Westminster, MA?; 1840; 1
Mann, Cyrus (Rev.); ___; Boston (state not given); 1832; 1
Mann, R. (Rev.); ___; Palmyra?; 1841; 1
Marcy, Clinton, Esq.; Harmony; 1836; 1
Markel, L. (Rev.); ___; Seneca Falls?; 1817; 1
Marshall, Otto F., Esq.; Wheeler?; 1832; 1
Martin, ___ (Rev.); ___; Palmyra?; 1827; 1
Martin, ___ (Elder); ___; Reading?; 1832; 1
Martin, E. W. (Rev.); ___; Geneva-Waterloo area; 1826-29; 12
Martin, George, Esq.; Busti; 1833-36; 3
Martin, H. (Rev.); ___; Ellery; 1845; 1
Martin, James (Rev.); ___; Albany?; 1825; 1
Martin, M. (Rev.); ___; Fayette?; 1829; 1
Mason, ___ (Rev.); ___; Geneva; 1829; 2
Mason, ___ (Rev.); ___; Sodus; 1829; 1
Mason, ___ (Rev.); ___; Wolcott?; 1842; 1
Mason, A. P. (Rev.); ___; Fenner-Lenox area; 1840-41; 2
Mason, Cyrus (Rev.); ___; New York City?; 1829-32; 2
Mason, Elias, Esq.; Bath?; 1845; 1
Mason, Octavus (Rev.); ___; Williamson?; 1843; 1
Matthews, ___ (Rev. Dr.); ___; New York City; 1826-28; 2
Matoon, ___ (Rev.); ___; Aurora; 1842; 1
Mattison, Seth (Rev.); ___; Marion?; 1828; 1
May, D. H., (_?_); Palmyra; 1844; 1
May, P. C. (Rev.); ___; Geneva?; 1843; 1
Merkel, L. (Rev.); ___; Fayette, Junius, Romulus, Seneca Falls; 1817-18; 6
Merrill, ___ (Rev.); ___; Galen?; 1830; 1
Merrill, ___ (Rev.); ___; Gorham; 1821-23; 4
Merrill, ___ (Rev.); ___; Penn Yan; 1818; 1
Merrill, ___ (Rev.); ___; Seneca; 1814-25; 4
Merrill, ___ (Rev.); ___; Sodus; 1838; 1
Merrit, ___ (Rev.); ___; Palmyra; 1835; 2
Mervin, ___ (Rev.); ___; Sodus; 1843; 1
Merwin, C. P. (Rev.); ___; Williamson?; 1843; 1
Massler, ___ (Rev. Dr.); ___; Somerville, NJ?; 1844; 1
Miles, John (Rev.); ___; Bath; 1810; 1
Millard, H. D., Esq.; Cameron?; 1831; 1
Millard, H. D., Esq.; Canisteo?; 1831; 1
Miller, C. K., Esq.; Erwin; 1838-41; 2
Miller, L. Merrill (Rev.); ___; Bath; 1846-50; 17
Mills, ___ (Rev.); ___; Moscow, NY?; 1824; 1
Miner, ___ (Rev.); ___; Jamestown?; 1842; 1
Miner, ___ (Rev.); ___; Macedon and Palmyra; 1836; 2
Miner, ___ (Rev.); ___; Manchester?; 1842; 1

Miner, ___ (Rev.); ___; Penfield?; 1837; 1
Miner, ___ (Rev.); ___; South Dansville?; 1846; 1
Miner, O. (Rev.); ___; Penn Yan?; 1841-42; 2
Minner, Abraham, Esq.; Tioga Point?; 1820; 1
Mitchell, ___ (Rev. Dr.); ___; Green, Erie Co., PA?; 1844; 1
Mitchell, Peter, Esq.; Farmington-Manchester area; 1818-22; 5
Mitchell, P. (Hon.); Farmington; 1843; 1
Montgomery, ___ (Rev.); ___; Chautauqua; 1840; 1
Moore, ___ (Rev.), ___; East Palmyra; 1836; 1
Moore, H. S., Esq. Ontario-Palmyra area; 1821-23; 3
Moore, Samuel (Rev.); ___; Palmyra area; 1834-40; 2
Morgan, ___ (Rev.); ___; Attica?; 1850; 1
Morgan, ___ (Rev.); Jerusalem?; 1840; 1
Morgan, J., Esq.; Erwin; 1832; 1
Morgan, L. S. (Rev.); ___; Busti; 1842-44; 2
Morrey, J. R. (Rev.); ___; Marion?; 1839; 1
Morse, ___ (Rev.); ___; Ellington?; 1839; 1
Morse, Lemuel, Esq.; Rushville?; 1828; 1
Morton, O. (Rev.); ___; Clyde?; 1840; 1
Moses, O. (Rev.); ___; Williamson?; 1843; 1
Mosher, Moser, Moshier, Mosier, ___ (Rev.); ___; Romulus, Fayette, Phelps,
    Vienna, and Junius; 1811-1819; 10
Moshier, C. (Rev.); ___; Sodus; 1843
Mulhollon, William, Esq.; Bath?; 1842; 1
Mulligan, ___ (Rev.); ___; Rochester; 1823; 1
Murdoch, ___ (Rev.); ___; Lockport?; 1848; 1
Murray, ___ (Rev.); ___; Elk Creek, PA?; 1834; 1
Murray, ___ (Rev. Dr.); ___; Geneva?; 1826; 1
Murray, ___ (Rev.); ___; Lewiston?; 1843; 1
Murray, ___ (Rev.); ___; Walworth; 1839; 1
Murray, Nicholas (Rev.); ___; Elizabethtown, NJ?; 1840; 1
Murry, ___ (Rev.); ___; Westfield?; 1831; 1
Musselman, ___, Esq.; Phelps?; 1826; 1
Myres, ___ (Rev.); ___; Salina?; 1841; 1
Nash, Ira, Esq.; Mud Creek?; 1840; 1
Nesbit or Nisbet, William (Rev.); ___; Seneca; 1825-30; 25
Nettleton, K. D. (Rev.); ___; Roanoke; 1848; 2
Nichols, ___ (Rev.); ___; Alexander; 1850; 1
Nobles, ___ (Rev.); ___; Carbondale, PA?; 1831; 1
Norris, P. (Rev.); ___; Howard?; 1840; 1
North, Eben, Esq.; Batavia; 1824-25; 2
Northrop, ___ (Rev.); ___; Greenwood?; 1846; 1
Northrop, G. S. (Rev.); ___; Cohocton; 1842; 1
Norton, George H. (Rev.); ___; Waterloo-Geneva- East Bloomfield-Richmond area;
    1819-26; 5
Norton, Morris, Esq.; Ashville-Harmony-Jamestown area; 1840-50; 10
Norton, N. (Rev.); ___; Harmony; 1841-43; 2
Norton, Seba (Rev.); ___; Sodus?; 1819; 1
Nott, ___ (Dr.); ___; Schenectady?; 1830; 1
Nutten, D. (Rev.); Meth.; Bath-Canisteo area; 1850; 2
Nutting; ___ (Rev.); ___; Italy, NY; 1846; 1
Oaks, ___ (Rev.); ___; Westfield?; 1830; 1
Olds, A. D. (Rev.); ___; Panama, NY?; 1845; 1
Oliver, Charles, Esq.; Dansville?; 1847; 1
Olmsted, A. A., Esq.; Howard?; 1846; 1
Olney, P. (Rev.); ___; Pulteney; 1845-47; 3
Onderdonk, ___ (Rev.); ___; Benton?; 1817; 1
Onderdonk, ___ (Rev.); ___; Canandaigua?; 1817-18; 2
Onderdonk, H. U. (Rev.); ___; Pennsylvania; 1827; 1
Ormsby, N. D., Esq.; Troupsburgh?; 1841; 1
Orton, ___ (Rev.); ___; Ripley?; 1843; 1
Orton, ___ (Rev.); ___; Waterloo-Seneca Falls area; 1824-27; 2
Osband, ___ (Rev.); ___; Canandaigua; 1832; 1
Osband, Durfee, Esq.; Macedon; 1835-41; 6
Osband, Gideon (Rev.) ___; Manchester-Palmyra-Walworth area; 1832-34; 5
Osband, G (Rev.); ___; Arcadia; 1842; 1

274

Osborn, Gideon (Rev.); ___; Manchester, Palmyra, and Marion; 1832-43; 3
Osborn, Wilson (Rev.); ___; Palmyra; 1842; 2
Osburn, ___ (Rev.); ___; Palmyra; 1839; 2
Owen, G. (Rev.); ___; Uniontown, PA?; 1846; 1
Packard, C., Esq.; Perinton?; 1817; 1
Packard, Cyrus, Esq.; Palmyra; 1817; 2
Packard, J. F., Esq.; Macedon; 1832; 1
Page, ___ (Rev.); ___; Perry?; 1841; 1
Palmer, ___ (Rev.); ___; Chenango Point?; 1813; 1
Palmer, A. R. (Rev.); ___; Hornellsville; 1846; 1
Palmer, C. R. (Rev.); ___; Batavia?; 1850; 1
Palmer, R. C. (Rev.); ___; Alabama-Bethany area; 1849-50; 3
Palmer, Reuben, Esq.; Pembroke?; 1826; 1
Palmer, Z. M. (Rev.); ___; Jamestown; 1832-40; 2
Palmeter, Josiah, Esq.; Busti?; 1832; 1
Parker, ___ ("Mr."); Canandaigua?; 1834; 1
Parker, ___ (Rev.); ___; Macedon?; 1840; 1
Parker, ___ (Rev.); ___; Seneca?; 1825; 1
Parker, George W., Esq.; Jamestown-Busti area; 1841-44; 6
Parker, J. (Rev.); ___; Batavia; 1845; 1
Parker, Joel (Rev.); ___; New York City; 1840; 1
Parker, John (Rev.); ___; Batavia; 1845-6; 4
Parker, John W. (Rev.); ___ Williamson; 1831; 1
Parker, S. S. (Rev.); ___; Bath; 1831; 2
Parker, S. W. (Rev.); ___; Jamestown-Busti area; 1839-45; 3
Parmelee, ___ (Rev.); ___; Westfield; 1831-32; 1
Parmely, ___ (Rev.); ___; Jamestown-Busti area; 1838-41; 8
Parsons, ___ (Rev.); ___; Amherst?; 1818; 1
Partridge, Theodore, Esq.; Newark, NY?; 1830;1
Patchin, H., Esq.; Westfield?; 1838; 1
Pattengill, H. (Rev.); ___; Hornellsville; 1850; 1.  See Pettengill, H.
Pearsall, ___ (Rev.); ___; Palmyra?; 1843; 1
Peck, ___ (Rev.); ___; Carroll?; 1835; 1
Peet, ___ (Rev.); ___; Jamestown; 1834-35; 2
Pelton, Samuel (Rev.); ___; Haverstraw; 1818; 1
Pember, ___ (Rev.); ___; Harmony; 1843; 2
Penney or Penny, ___ (Rev.); ___; Rochester; 1823-30; 2
Perkins, ___ (Rev.); ___; Hawley; 1838; 1
Perkins, A. (Rev.); ___; Poughkeepsie; 1831; 1
Pero, P. H. (Rev.); ___; Panama, NY; 1845; 2
Perrine, ___ (Dr.); ___; Auburn; 1827; 1
Persons, ___, Esq.; Woodhull?; 1850; 1
Pettengill, H. (Rev.); ___; Canisteo-Hornellsville area; 1850; 2.  See Pattengill.
Pettibone, ___ (Rev.); ___; Hopkinton?; 1827; 1
Phelps, ___ (Rev.); ___; Canandaigua?; 1812; 1
Phelps, ___ (Rev.); ___; Geneva; 1809-13; 4
Phelps, ___ (Rev.); ___; Pulteneyville; 1812; 1
Phelps, D. (Rev.); ___; Skaneateles?; 1809; 1
Phelps, Eliakim (Rev.); ___; Geneva; 1830; 1
Phelps, George D., Esq.; Pulteneyville?; 1829; 1
Phelps, Royal (Rev.); ___; Sodus?; 1822; 1
Phillips, A. S., Esq.; Howard?; 1846; 1
Phinney, ___ (Rev.); ___; Ithaca?; 1827; 1
Pier, Henry, Esq.; Bath; 1840-42; 9
Pier, Rufus, Esq.; Jamestown and vicinity; 1833-35; 16
Pier, William, Esq.; Warren?; 1831; 1
Pierpont, ___ (Rev.); ___; Geneseo; 1846; 1
Piersoll, ___ (Rev.); ___; Palmyra?; 1843; 1
Pierson, George S., Esq.; Cameron?; 1846; 1
Pitt, S. (Rev.); ___; Avoca; 1842-46; 4
Pixley, Joseph, Esq.; Fayette-Junius area; 1813-18; 3
Plato, W. B., Esq.; Sinclairville?; 1835; 1
Platt, ___ (Rev.); ___; Homer?; 1842; 1
Platt, E. A. (Rev.); ___; East Palmyra?; 1841; 1
Platt, Isaac W. (Rev.); Presby.: Bath; 1831-45; 16
Plumb, ___ (Elder); ___; Fleming?; 1838; 1

Pomeroy, ___ (Rev.); ___; Cayuga?; 1828; 1
Pomeroy, ___ (Rev.); ___; Lyons; 1818-22; 5
Poppino, Daniel, Esq.; Williamson-Pulteneyville area; 1832-40; 2
Porter, ___ (Rev.); ___; Ovid; 1816-19; 4
Porter, ___ (Rev.); Presby.; Vienna, NY; 1837; 1
Post, Abraham A., Esq.; Seneca?; 1829; 1
Potter, Alonzo (Rev.); ___; Albany?; 1837; 1
Pound, ___ (Rev.); ___; Canandaigua; 1835; 1
Pound, Jesse (Rev.); ___; Palmyra; 1833; 1
Powell, ___ (Rev.); ___; Sodus?; 1815; 1
Powell, ___ (Rev.); ___; Palmyra-Macedon area; 1830; 4
Powell, H. B. (Rev.); ___; Farmington?; 1820; 1
Powell, Howell R. (Rev.); ___; Williamson and Palmyra; 1817-22; 4
Powell, J. L., Esq.; Williamson?; 1820; 1
Powell, Robert (Rev.); ___; Macedon; 1830-33; 3
Powers, ___ (Rev.); ___; Bath?; 1817; 1
Powers, J. (Rev.); ___; Canisteo; 1831; 1
Pratt, ___ (Rev.); ___; Prattsburgh?; 1838; 1
Pratt, ___ (Rev.); ___; Shelby; 1823; 1
Prentice, ___ (Rev.); ___; Catskill?; 1815; 1
Prentiss, J., Esq.; Addison; 1832; 1
Preston, ___ (Rev.); ___; Byron; 1849; 1
Price, W. B., Esq.; Bath?, 1850; 1
Proal, ___ (Rev.); ___; Schenectady?; 1825; 1
Punderson, ___ (Rev.); ___; Pittsfield, MA?; 1815; 1
Punnell, R.; (Rev.); ___; Gerry?; 1845; 1
Purdy, A., Esq.; Macedon and Pittsford; 1831-32; 3
Purdy, C. C., Esq.; Hartsville?; 1850; 1
Purington, ___ (Rev.); ___; Prattsburgh?; 1848; 1
Putnam, Benjamin (Rev.); ___; Morrisville?; 1842; 1
Quackenbush, Abraham I., Esq.; Cohocton?; 1832; 1
Randel, John, Esq.; Urbana; 1841-42; 3
Rathbun, L. (Rev.); ___; Phelps?; 1843; 1
Ray, William, Esq.; Geneva?; 1825; 1
Raymond, ___ (Rev.); ___; Victor?; 1822; 1
Raymond, William G. (Elder); ___; Jasper?; 1847; 1
Read, Arnold D., Esq.; Bath; 1822; 1
Read, A. D., Esq.; Bath; 1845-49; 4
Reed, ___ (Rev.); ___; Orange County?; 1818; 1
Reed, ___ (Rev. Dr.); ___; Poughkeepsie; 1813-27; 3
Reed, A. M. (Rev.); ___; Jamestown; 1844; 2
Remmington, ___ (Rev.); ___; Alden?; 1848; 1
Reynolds, James (Rev.); ___; Ulysses?; 1815; 1
Rice, ___ (Elder); ___; Hopewell-Orleans area; 1829-40; 2
Rice, Oliver, Esq.; Cohocton, Avoca, and Bath; 1832-35; 3
Rice, Wesson B., Esq.; Howard; 1849-50; 2
Rice, William, Esq.; Clymer?; 1829; 1
Rich, M., Esq.; Arcadia?; 1842; 1
Rich, Marvin S. (_?_); Marion?; 1829; 1
Richards, ___ (Rev.); ___; Palmyra; 1834-35; 2
Richards, ___ (Rev.); ___; Milo; 1841; 1
Richards, ___ (Rev.); ___; Nashua, NH?; 1844; 1
Richards, Charles, Esq.; Williamson; 1844; 1
Richards, James (Rev.); ___; Penn Yan; 1846; 1
Richardson, R. (Rev.); ___; Middlebury?; 1842; 1
Richmond, E. (Rev.); ___; Stockton?; 1842; 1
Richmond, L. (Rev.); ___; Bethany; 1847; 1
Richmond, Samuel, Esq.; Bergen; 1847-49; 5
Riley, Lawrence (Rev.); ___; Lyons?; 1815-27; 4
Riley, ___ (Rev.); ___; Seneca?; 1822; 1
Riley, Lawrence (Rev.); ___; Phelps?; 1822; 1
Ripley, A. P. (Rev.); ___; Phelps; 1822; 1
Ripley, A. P. (Rev.); ___; Stafford; 1846; 2
Roach, ___ (Elder); ___; Batavia; 1825; 2
Robinson, ___ (Rev.); Pulaski; 1840; 1
Robinson, C. C. (_?_); Palmyra, Michigan Territory; 1835; 1

276

Robords, John L., Esq.; Avoca and Howard; 1846; 2
Roe, ___ (Rev.); ___; Lyons-Newark area; 1829-31; 2
Roe, William (Rev.); ___; Manchester?; 1840; 1
Rogers, ___ (Rev.); ___; Le Roy?; 1831; 1
Rogers, Henry W., Esq.; Bath; 1831-32; 15
Root, D. M. (Rev.); ___; Howard; 1849; 1
Rose, ___ (Rev.); ___; Howard; 1844; 1
Rose, H. S., Esq.; Avoca?; 1846; 1
Rose, L. (Rev.); ___; Bath and Howard; 1846-50; 8
Rowe, ___ (Rev.); ___; Manchester; 1836; 1
Rowe, William (Elder); ___; Arcadia and Phelps; 1830-43; 2
Rowland, D. (Rev.); ___; Wattsburgh, PA; 1842-43; 2
Rowley, ___ (Elder); ___; Bath?; 1845; 1
Roy, ___ (Rev.); ___; Freehold, NJ; 1829; 1
Rudd, ___ (Rev. Dr.); ___; Auburn; 1826-32; 5
Rudd, G. R. (Rev.); ___; Prattsburgh; 1829-35; 5
Rugar, ___ (Rev.); ___; Coventry?; 1831; 1
Rumsey, Henry, Esq.; Bethany; 1822-24; 2
Russ, L. W. (Rev.); ___; Bath-Hammondsport-Urbana area; 1845-50; 17
Russel, ___ (Rev.); ___; Stamford, Upper Canada; 1827; 1
Russell, ___ (Rev.); ___; Hornellsville?; 1838; 1
Russell, B. (Rev.); ___; Tyrone?; 1849; 1
Russell, C. M., Esq.; Batavia-Stafford area; 1832-33; 5
Rutherford, William (Rev.); ___; Bath; 1845-49; 3
Safford, ___ (Rev.); ___; Clarence?; 1829; 1
Sagar, ___ (Rev.); ___; Bath; 1845-46; 2
Sage, Sylvester (Rev.); ___; Westminster, VT?; 1833; 1
Salisbury, ___ (Rev.); ___; Clyde?; 1831; 1
Salisbury, A., Esq.; Palmyra?; 1835; 1
Salisbury, Aaron, Esq.; Evans, Erie Co.; 1825; 1
Salmon, ___ (Rev.); ___; Geneseo?; 1827; 1
Sampson, ___ (Rev.); ___; Alexander?; 1826; 1
Sampson, ___ (Rev.); ___; Greece, Monroe Co.?; 1829; 1
Sanderson, O. (Rev.); ___; Panama, NY; 1845; 2
Sandford, Jared, Esq.; Ovid; 1813; 1
Sargent, Parker, Esq.; Albany?; 1850; 1
Savage, ___ (Rev.); ___; Modina?; 1830; 1
Savage, ___ (Rev.); ___; Ogdensburgh?; 1841; 1
Sawyer, E., Esq.; Scipio?; 1822; 1
Sawyer, N. (Rev.); ___; Bath-Howard area; 1846-50; 6
Schaeffer, ___ (Rev.); ___; Geneva; 1817; 1
Schofield, James (Rev.); ___; Charlotte-Sinclairville area; 1838-40; 2
Scott, James, Esq.; Junius-Waterloo area; 1829; 2
Scudder, S., Esq.; Randolph?; 1843; 1
Seager, Schuyler (Rev.); ___; Lima; 1842; 1
Segar, ___ (Elder); ___; Bethany?; 1824; 1
Sears, ___ (Rev.); ___; Palmyra?; 1837; 1
Sears, John (Rev.); ___; Macedon?; 1841; 1
Seaver, H. N. (Rev.); Meth.; Elmira; 1849; 1
Seaver, H. N. ( ? ); Wales, NY; 1847; 1
Sebring, ___, Esq.; Lancaster, Seneca Co.; 1809; 1
Sedgwick, ___ (Rev.); ___; Bates?; 1825; 1
Selby, Ira, Esq.; Palmyra; 1818-19; 2
Selmser and Selsmer, Jno. (Rev.); ___; South Dansville-Wheeler area; 1846-50; 4
Shannon, James, Esq.; Bath; 1847; 1
Shart, D. (Elder); ___; Addison?; 1832; 1
Shaw, J. B. (Rev.); ___; Buffalo; 1846; 1
Shekell, Cephas, Esq.; Geneva area; 1828-29; 9
Shephard, W. (Elder); ___; Ellington?; 1843; 1
Shepperd, Morris F., Esq.; Benton?; 1814; 1
Sheridan, John (Rev.); ___; Tyrone?; 1846; 1
Shimcall, R. C. (Rev.); ___; Canandaigua?; 1834; 1
Short. See, possibly, Shart.
Short, J. M. (Rev.); ___; Genesee County; 1849; 1
Shults, J. (Rev.); ___; Avoca?; 1842; 1
Shumway, ___ (Rev.); ___; Farmington?; 1834; 1

Shumway, G. R. H. (Rev.); ___; Palmyra; 1834-44; 41
Simmons, G. D. (Rev.); ___; East Bloomfield; 1834; 1
Sisson, William, Esq.; Cayuga?; 1818; 1
Sisson, W., Esq.; Phelps?; 1823; 1
Sisson, William, Esq.; Wolcott; 1824; 1
Skinner, D. G., Esq.; Bath-Cameron area; 1831; 2
Skinner, S., Esq.; Le Roy-Stafford area; 1824; 2
Slack, John, Esq.; Geneva?; 1822; 1
Slie, David (Rev.); ___; Andover; 1835; 2
Slocum, Elisha, Esq.; Palmyra; 1817; 6
Smith, ___ (Rev.); ___; Auburn?; 1822; 1
Smith, ___ (Rev.); ___; Benton; 1829; 2
Smith, ___ (Rev.); ___; Campbelltown; 2
Smith, ___ (Rev.); ___; Cornwall, CT?; 1824; 1
Smith, ___ (Rev.); ___; Dunkirk?; 1839; 1
Smith, ___ (Rev.); ___; Howard?; 1841; 1
Smith, ___ (Rev.); ___; Jamestown; 1839; 1
Smith, ___ (Rev.); ___; Lewiston?; 1818; 1
Smith, ___ (Rev.); ___; Lyons; 1826; 1
Smith, ___ (Rev.); ___; Newstead?; 1848; 1
Smith, ___ (Rev.); ___; Warsaw, NY; 1822; 1
Smith, A. S., Esq.; Hornellsville?; 1825; 1
Smith, B. C. (Rev.); ___; Bath?; 1850; 1
Smith, B. C. (Rev.); ___; Italy, NY?; ? ; 1
Smith, B. C. (Rev.); ___; Prattsburgh; 1845-50; 10
Smith, B. C. (Rev.); ___; Wheeler?; 1850; 1
Smith, Celly, Esq.; Hector; 1815; 1
Smith, Clark A. (Rev.); ___; 1842-44; 4
Smith, D. (Rev.); ___; Carroll; 1831-38; 2
Smith, David (Rev.); ___; Cameron; 1845-50; 3
Smith, Denison (Rev.); ___; Rushville?; 1831; 1
Smith, E. (Rev.); Episc.; Batavia; 1825-32; 7
Smith, Frederick, Esq.; Palmyra; 1820-44; 71
Smith, H. (Rev.); ___; Ellery and Jamestown; 1841-44; 21
Smith, Harlow, Esq.; Bath-Cameron area; 1840-41; 4
Smith, J. L., Esq.; Geneva; 1827; 1
Smith, John (Rev.); ___; Cooperstown; 1828; 1
Smith, John (Rev.); ___; Painted Post?; 1840; 1
Smith, John (Rev.); ___; Oakland County, MI?; 1847; 1
Smith, Lucius (Rev.) ___; Batavia; 1824; 7
Smith, Lucius (Rev.); ___; Mayville?; 1840; 1
Smith, Richard (Hon.); Hector?; 1815; 1
Smith, S. (Rev.); ___; Aurora, Cayuga Co.; 1831; 1
Smith, Thomas, Esq.; Phelps?; 1819; 1
Smith, Thomas, Esq.; Vienna, NY?; 1827; 1
Smith, William W. (Elder); ___; Batavia?; 1837; 1
Smuller, H. W. (Rev.); ___; Fowlerville; 1848; 3
Snow, ___ (Rev.); ___; Macedon; 1823; 2
Somers, ___ (Rev.); ___; New York City; 1831; 1
*Somers, Charles G. (Rev.); ___; Brooklyn; 1849; 1
Sparks, E. B. (Rev.); ___; Jamestown? or Nettle Hill, NH?; 1843; 1
Spaulding, ___; Rev.); ___; Elmira?; 1842; 1
Spaulding, ___ (Rev.); ___; Palmyra?; 1841; 1
Spear, A., Esq.; Farmington?; 1822; 2
Spear, Abraham, Esq.; Ontario, NY; 1820; 1
Spear, Abraham, Esq.; Palmyra; 1820-22; 8
Spencer, ___ (Rev.); ___; Batavia; 1826; 1
Spencer, ___ (Rev.); ___; Bath; 1846; 1
Spencer, ___ (Rev. Dr.); ___; Brooklyn?; 1841; 1
Spencer, ___ (Rev.); Lodi?; 1829; 1
Spencer, E. (Rev.); ___; Alexander; 1825; 1
Spencer, E. (Rev.); ___; Bethany; 1826; 1
Spencer, E. M. (Rev.); ___; Covington-Middlebury area; 1824-25; 2
Spencer, E. M. (Rev.); ___; Westville, Otsego County; 1844; 1
*Southerland, ___ (Rev.); ___; Pulteney?; 1840; 1
Spacer, ___ (Rev.); ___; Palmyra?; 1822; 1

278

Spencer, Elijah, Esq.; Benton; 1813-19; 5
Spencer, H. (Rev.); Bapt.; Bath area; 1845-50; 14
Spencer, John, Esq.; Hector?; 1820; 1
Spencer, Theodore (Rev.); ___; Utica?; 1844; 1
Squier, ___ (Rev.); ___; Geneva?; 1829; 1
Squier, M. P. (Rev.); ___; Phelps?; 1829; 1
Starkweather, A. H. (Rev.); ___; Bethany; 1850; 2
Starr, Samuel J. (Rev.); ___; Princeton, NJ?; 1844; 1
Staunton, William (Rev.); ___; Palmyra; 1834-35; 5
Staunton, ___ (Rev.); ___; Manchester?; 1834; 1
Stebbins, ___ (Elder); ___; Pulteney?; 1841; 1
Stedman, M. (Rev.); ___; Jamestown-Harmony area; 1834-42; 3
Steed, William (Rev.); ___; Columbia, GA?; 1844; 1
Steel, ___ (Rev.); ___; East Bloomfield; 1822; 1
Steel or Steele, Allen (Rev.); ___; Batavia; 1842-50; 5
Stephens, Elias, Esq.; Greenwood-Canisteo area; 1842; 2
Stetson, Benjamin, Esq.; Pembroke-Batavia area; 1825-26; 2
Stevens, John, Esq.; Walworth; 1833; 1
Stewart, ___ (Rev.); ___; Junius?; 1810; 1
Stewart, E. S., Esq.; Phelps?; 1822; 1
Stillman, T. (Rev.); ___; Dunkirk; 1837-42; 2
Stimson, S. M. (Rev.); Bapt.; Batavia; 1846-50; 19
Stocking, Selah (Rev.); ___; Sennett; 1840-41; 2
Stoddard, I. C. (Rev.); ___; Busti; 1839-42; 2
Stoddard, Moses H., Esq.; Covington?; 1824; 1
Stone, ___ (Rev.); ___; Bath?; 1826; 1
Stone, ___ (Rev.); ___; Litchfield, CT?; 1828; 1
Stoneman, George, Esq.; Busti; 1840-41; 2
Story, ___ (Rev.); ___; Cohocton?; 1842; 1
Stout, C. B. (Rev.); ___; Westfield?; 1843; 1
Stow, John, Jr., Esq.; Harmony and Busti; 1834-37; 2
Stowell, A. H. (Rev.); ___; Palmyra; 1839-40; 9
Street, Owen (Rev.); ___; Jamestown; 1843-45; 10
Strong, ___ (Rev.); ___; Potter?; 1834; 1
Strong, ___ (Rev.); ___; Vienna, NY; 1829-32; 3
Strong, Cyrus (Rev.); ___; Williamson?; 1832; 1
Strong, Henry P. (Rev.); ___; Phelps; 1825-31; 17
Strough, J. (Rev.); ___; Avoca; 1845-47; 3
Strough, J. (Rev.); Wheeler?; 1845; 1
Stuart, ___ (Rev.); ___; Gananoque, Upper Canada; 1826; 1
Sullivan, Benjamin, Esq.; Clymer?; 1831; 1
Sunderland, Byron (Rev.); ___; Batavia; 1845-49; 11
Sunderlin, ___ (Rev.); ___; Tyrone?; 1845; 1
Swain, E. R. (Rev.); ___; Busti; 1843-45; 4
Swartwood, E. D., Esq.; Cameron-Canisteo area; 1840-46; 3
Swick, B. R. (Rev.); ___; Bath; 1849-50; 14
Swift, G., Esq.; Carroll; 1840-42; 2
Swift, P. (Hon.); Lyons; 1811; 1
Swift, Philetus, Esq.; Phelps; 1816-18; 3
Switzer, H., Esq.; Jersey, NY; 1831; 1
Taggert, ___ (Rev.); ___; New Lebanon Springs?; 1826; 1
Tappan, ___ (Rev.); ___; Hector?; 1827; 1
Taylor, ___ (Rev.); ___; Bethany?; 1845; 1
Taylor, ___ (Rev.); ___; Canandaigua?; 1822; 1
Taylor, ___ (Rev.); ___; Jamestown?; 1835; 1
Taylor, E. (Rev.); ___; Randolph; 1842; 1
Taylor, J. R. (Rev.); ___; Milan, Ohio?; 1849; 1
Taylor, Ruel (Rev.); ___; East Palmyra; 1842; 1
Tenique, ___ (Rev.); ___; Lyons?; 1830; 1
Terry, S., Esq.; Harmony?; 1829; 1
Thompson, J. D., Esq.; Rochester?; 1831; 1
Thompson, M. L. R. F. (Rev.); ___; Canandaigua; 1841-43; 2
Throop, ___ (Elder); ___; Pembroke?; 1824; 1
Thurston, C. (Rev.); ___; Athens, NY?; 1850; 1
Tibbitts, John, Esq.; Lyons-Palmyra area; 1820-21; 3
Tiffany, A. R., Esq.; Arcadia-Palmya area; 1822-31; 5

Tinney, ___ (Rev.); ___; Pittsford?; 1828; 1
Tisdale, Daniel, Esq.; Batavia; 1824-26; 17
Tisdale, William H., Esq.; Batavia; 1822-23; 2
Tobias, ___ (Rev.); ___; Bloomsburg, PA?; 1831; 1
Todd, ___ (Rev.); ___; Benton; 1828-29; 2
Todd, ___ (Rev.); ___; Seneca?; 1827; 1
Todd, ___ (Rev.); ___; Stamford, CT?; 1838; 1
Todd, ___ (Rev.); Sugargrove, PA; 1845; 1
Tompkinson, ___ (Rev.); ___; Pulteneyville?; 1834; 1
Tooker, ___ (Rev.); ___; Geneva area; 1829; 3
Torry, ___ (Rev.); ___; Canandaigua; 1814; 1
Tower, Elisha, Esq.; Gerry?; 1831; 1
Townsend, ___ (Rev.); Phelps?; 1818; 1
Townsend, Hezekiah, Esq.; Milo?; 1822; 1
Townsend, Jesse (Rev.); Palmyra; 1817-38; 20
Townsend, K. (Rev.); ___; Arcadia; 1842; 1
Townsend, K. (Rev.); ___; Manchester; 1840; 1
Townsend, K. (Rev.); ___; Palmyra?; 1842; 1
True; ___ (Rev.); ___; Byron; 1831; 1
True, ___ (Rev.); ___; Covington; 1824; 2
Tucker, ___ (Rev.); ___; Junius?; 1828; 1
Turck, ___ (Rev.); ___; Walworth?; 1835; 1
Tuttle, J. K. (Rev.); ___; Avoca, Prattsburgh, and Bath; 1845-50; 5
Tuttle, J. R. (Rev.); ___; Bath; 1850; 1
Twitchel, ___ (Rev.); ___; Burns, Allegany Co.; 1847; 1
Tyler, ___ (Rev.); Episc.; Pomfret; 1844; 1
Tyler, J. E. (Rev.); Windham, CT?; 1841; 1
Tyler, T. P. (Rev.); ___; Fredonia; 1844-45; 3
Upfold, George (Rev.); ___; New York City; 1830; 1
Upson, Asa (Rev.); ___; Hornellsville; 1847; 1
Valentine, Peter, Esq.; Rose?; 1830; 1
Van Doren, ___ (Rev.); ___; Burlingham; 1815; 1
Van Dyck, L. H. (Rev.); ___; Valatie, Columbia County; 1835; 1
Van Fleet, ___, Esq.; Manchester; 1829; 2
Van Fleet, Joshua, Esq.; Farmington?; 1821; 1
Van Horn, James, Esq.; Ovid?; 1810; 1
Van Pelt, Hiram (?); Wheeler; 1847; 1
Van Valkenburgh, ___ (Rev.); ___; Richfield?; 1833; 1
Van Vechten, ___ (Rev.); ___; Schenectady?; 1819; 1
Vanzandt, ___ (Rev.); ___; Avoca; 1845; 2
Van Zandt, W. (Rev.); ___; Elmira-Corning area; 1845-46; 2
Vaughan, I. W. or J. W. (Rev.); ___; Elba and Batavia; 1847?; 2
Vining, ___ (Rev.); ___; Ellicotville?; 1833; 1
Voorhies, William, Esq.; Lyons; 1830-31; 8
Wagener, Abraham, Esq.; Benton; 1812; 1
Wagener, Abraham, Esq.; Geneva?; 1812; 1
Waggoner, A., Esq.; Penn Yan?; 1823; 1
Wainright, ___ (Rev. Dr.); ___; New York City?; 1829; 1
Wait, Joseph, Esq.; Gerry-Poland area; 1836; 2
Waite, R. L. (Rev.); ___; Alexander and Batavia; 1838-47; 5
Waitbe. See also Waith and Waitle.
Waitbe, William (Rev.); ___; Rutledge?; 1843; 1
Waith. See also Waitbe and Waitle.
Waith, William (Rev.); ___; Ellington and Rutledge; 1840-45; 5
Waitle. See also Waitbe and Waith.
Waitle, William (Rev.); ___; Ellington Center?; 1843; 1
Wakeman, S., Esq.; Bethany and Batavia; 1842-49; 3
Walden, S. (Rev.); ___; Bath; 1849; 1
Walker, E. H. (Rev.); ___; Dansville; 1842-47; 2
Wall, ___ (Elder); ___; Bradford?; 1841; 1
Wall, ___ (Elder); ___; Tyrone; 1841; 1
Wall, Van Rensselaer (Rev.); ___; Jersey, NY; 1835; 1
Wallace or Wallis, Hugh (Rev.); ___; Pembroke; 1824-26; 3
Walling, G. V. (Rev.); ___; Marion; 1839; 3
Ward, Donald A. (Rev.); ___; Orangeville; 1826; 2
Ward, F. D. W. (Rev.); ___; Geneseo; 1850; 1

Ward, Z., Esq.; Harmony?; 1833; 1
Ware, H. K. (Rev.); ___; Palmyra; 1837; 1
Warner, ___, Esq.; Rochester; 1832; 1
Warren, E. F., Esq.; Kennedyville, Busti, Jamestown, Levant; 1832-41; 8
Weaver, Stephen H. (Rev.); ___; Akron?; 1832; 1
Weed, ___ (Rev.); ___; Albany?; 1827; 1
Weidman, F. A. (Rev.); ___; Prattsburgh; 1844; 1
Welles, Benjamin (Dr.); ___; Wayne?; 1810; 1
Wells, ___ (Rev.); ___; Junius; 1816; 1
Wells, ___ (Rev.); ___; Seneca Falls?; 1815; 1
Wells, A. L., Esq.; Westfield; 1842-43; 2
Wells, E. D. (Rev.); ___; Lawrenceville, PA?; 1835; 1
Wells, G., Esq.; Waterloo; 1819; 1
Wells, Henry, Esq.; Elmira; 1811; 1
Welton, ___ (Rev.); ___; Geneva?; 1815; 1
Wescott, ___ (Rev.); ___; Saratoga?; 1839; 1
West, ___ (Rev.); ___; Hector; 1846; 1
West, ___ (Rev.); ___; Walworth; 1840; 1
Whalings, ___ (Rev.); ___; Aurora?; 1833; 1
Whalings, ___ (Rev.); ___; Wales, NY; 1833; 1
Whedon, S., Esq.; Seneca?; 1910; 1
Wheeler, ___ (Rev); ___; Canandaigua?; 1829; 1
Wheeler, ___ (Rev.); ___; Howard?; 1838-46; 2
Wheeler, ___ (Rev.); ___; Pulteney?; 1842; 1
Wheeler, C. (Rev.); ___; Hammondsport and Bath; 1838-47; 6
Wheeler, E. (Rev.); ___; Waterloo?; 1848; 1
Wheeler, George, Esq.; Bath?; 1841; 1
Wheeler, George, Esq.; Kennedyville?; 1835; 1
Wheeler, James, Esq.; Wheeler?; 1831; 1
Wheeler, Obediah, Esq.; Urbana?; 1835; 1
Wheeler, Seth, Esq.; Wheeler-Prattsburgh area; 1841-42; 3
Wheeler, U. M. (Rev.); ___; East Bloomfield?; 1829; 1
Whelpley, B. W. (Rev.); ___; Palmyra-Walworth area; 1831-32; 4
Whillers, ___ (Rev.); ___; Romulus?; 1826; 1
Whipple, P. L. (Rev.); ___; Bath-Cameron area; 1841-42; 2
Whitcomb, S. (Rev.); ___; Elba; 1824-25; 3
White, ___ (Rev.); ___; Benton; 1817; 1
White, ___ (Rev.); ___; Pulteneyville?; 1819; 1
White, ___ (Rev.); ___; Seneca; 1814-19; 6
White, ___ (Rev.); ___; Wayne?; 1838; 1
White, S. (Rev.); ___; Pulteney; 1847; 1
White, Samuel (Rev.); ___; Starkey; 1813-27; 3
White, Samuel (Rev.); ___; Bath?; 1842; 1
White, Solomon C., Esq.; Canandaigua; 1842; 1
White, Thomas (Rev.); ___; Benton; 1818; 1
Whitehead, Isaac, Esq.; Romulus?; 1815; 1
Whitehouse, ___ (Rev.); ___; Rochester; 1830-35; 2
Whiting, J. W., Esq.; Bath-Howard area; 1840-41; 3
Whiting, S. (Rev.); ___; Salem, Washington Co.?; 1833; 1
Wickes, ___ (Rev.); ___; Howard?; 1842; 1
Wightman, ___ (Rev.); ___; Lansingburgh?; 1825; 1
Wilber, Cyrenus, Esq.; Alexander?; 1825; 1
Wilbur, ___ (Rev.); ___; Bath?; 1850; 1
Wilcox, ___ (Rev.); ___; Napoli, NY; 1831; 1
Wilcox, W., Esq.; Arcadia?; 1840; 1
Wilder, C., Esq.; Sheldon; 1832; 1
Wilford, J., Esq.; Elba; 1825; 2
Wilhelmus, Johannes (Dr.); ___; Pleasant Valley, Ohio?; 1811; 1
Wilkinson, George (Rev.); ___; Pulteneyville-Williamson area; 1842-43; 3
Willard, Stephen, Esq.; Bath-Cameron area; 1832; 2
Willcox, M. W., Esq.; Palmyra; 1831; 2
Willcox, William, Esq.; Palmyra; 1829-30; 6
Williams, ___ (Rev.); ___; Benton?; 1822; 1
Williams, ___ (Rev.); ___; Elmira?; 1827; 1
Williams, Alexander B., Esq.; Sodus; 1842; 2
Williams, Asa (Rev.); ___; Buffalo?; 1831; 1

Williams, D., Esq.; Busti-Harmony area; 1842-43; 4
Williams, Gibbon (Rev.); ___; Wyoming, NY; 1850; 1
Williams, M. W., Esq.; Palmyra?; 1832; 1
Willis, Sylvester, Esq.; Byron?; 1822; 1
Williston, Payson (Rev.); ___; East Hampton, MA?; 1841; 1
Wilson, ___ (Rev.); ___; Campbell?; 1845; 1
Wilson, ___ (Rev.); ___; Gerry; 1836-41; 3
Wilson, ___ (Rev.); ___; Hammondsport; 1842-50; 2
Wilson, ___ (Rev.); ___; Williamson?; 1836; 1
Wilson, A. (Rev.); ___; Geneva; 1810-11; 5
Wilson, Andrew (Rev.); ___; Lyons?; 1811; 1
Wilson, Jonathan (Rev.); ___; Ellery-Carroll area; 1839-41; 2
Wilson or Willson, Mark, Esq.; Sugargrove, PA; 1841-42; 6
Wilson, Samuel (Rev.); ___; Manchester?; 1841; 1
Wilson, Samuel (Rev.); ___; Palmyra; 1840-41; 6
Wilson, W. D. (Rev.); ___; Bath?; 1845-46; 2
Wing, ___ (Rev.); ___; Bath; 1840; 2
Winslow, G. (Rev.); ___; Elmira; 1841; 1
Winsor, S. B., Esq.; Jamestown-Poland-Levant area; 1840-43; 7
Winton, Samuel, Esq.; Catharine; 1818; 1
Wisner, M. L. (Rev.); ___; Cameron and Bath; 1837-40; 4
Wisner, William (Rev.); ___; Hector?; 1827; 1
Wisner, William (Rev.); ___; Ithaca; 1824-29; 3
Wood, Philo (Rev.); ___; Buffalo; 1843; 1
Wood, S. (Rev.); ___; Schroon, Essex County; 1845; 1
Woodruff, ___ (Rev.); ___; Cayuga; 1813-16; 2
Woodruff, H. N. (Rev.); ___; Little Falls?; 1818; 1
Woodward, C., Esq.; Elba; 1825; 1
Woodward, J. S. (Rev.); ___; North Penfield; 1838; 1
Woodworth, Abner, Esq.; Benton-Penn Yan area; 1818-29; 11
Woodworth, Charles, Esq.; Elba; 1822-25; 3
Woodworth, E. B., Esq.; Seneca; 1820; 2
Woodworth, Jonathan (Rev.); ___; Covert; 1849; 1
Wooster, S. W. (Rev.); ___; 1837-38; 3
Worthington, D. L., Esq.; Bethany; 1850; 1
Wright, ___ (Rev.); ___; Bethel?; 1821; 1
Wright, A. (Rev.); ___; Bath; 1850; 2
Wright, E. W. (Dr.); ___; Marion; 1833; 1
Wyatt, ___ (Rev.); ___; Newtown, NJ; 1812; 1
Young, ___ (Rev.); ___; Fayette; 1816-20; 4
Young, Charles P., Esq.; ___?___; ?; ?
Young, H. C., Esq.; New Albion, Cattaraugus County?; 1836; 1
Young, Moses (Rev.); Presby.; Romulus; 1815-16; 2
Young, William (Rev.); ___; Walworth; 1844; 3
Young, Z. C., Esq.; Westfield?; 1845; 1
Youngs, ___ (Rev.); ___; Painted Post; 1850; 1

Arnold, Mary W. 3652
Arnold, Rhoda 5941
Arnold, Robert 5053
Arnold, Sarah 5053
Arnold, Vesta 6785
Asa, Ann 9122
Ashley, Harriet M. 6550
Ashley, Sophronia 1565
Ashly, ___ (Dr.) 9013
Ashly, Mary 9013
Aspell, Phebe 1809
Aspell, Richard 1809
Atkins, Frances E. 5231
Atwater, Eliza M. 4773
Atwater, Laura 8728
Atwater, Moses 4773
Atwood, Emily 9448
Atwood, Moses 9448
Aull, Isabel 1016
Aulls, Hannah 6587
Aulls, Ruhemma 7118
Austin, Francis 260
Austin, Mary E. 9538
Austin, William 261
Averell, ___ (Gen.) 5350
Averell, Louisa 5350
Averill, Gideon 265
Avery, Betsey 2056
Avery, Calista 62
Avery, Cyrus 270
Avery, Fanny 2889
Avery, Sally 4376
Axtell, Henry (Major) 278
Axtell, Henry (Rev.) 278,
  279, 280, 6030
Axtell, Hiram 277
Axtell, Rebecca 275
Axtell, Sally 209, 273
Ayer, Eliza 1080
Ayers, Lu___a (Miss) 6477
Aylesworth, Sally 6400
Aylsworth, Levi D. 282
Ayrault, Nicholas 8312
Babbet, ___ (Mr.) 288
Babbit, John 289
Babbit, Nathaniel 292
Babbit, Olive 292
Babcock. See also Bobcock.
Babcock, Alica 9694
Babcock, Ann 1336
Babcock, Arabella 7190
Babcock, Asa 305
Babcock, Asa (Capt.) 2904
Babcock, Bathia 531
Babcock, Edith 2145
Babcock, Elizabeth G. 7208
Babcock, Henry 304
Babcock, Mary 3159
Babcock, Nancy 6789
Babcock, Naomi 3293
Babcock, Samuel 306
Bachman, Polly 7309
Backenstose. See also
  Barkenstose.
Backenstose, Clarissa 2606
Backenstose, Eliza 1541
Backenstose, Elizabeth (Mrs.)
  10013
Backenstose, Frederick 670,
  1541
Backenstose, Henry 319
Backenstose, Joseph 317
Backenstose, Prudence 8170
Backenstose, Sarah 670
Backus, Ann Eliza 4550
Backus, Azul (Dr.) 320
Bacon, Alice F. 9396
Bacon, Angeline 1576
Bacon, Catharine 5508

Bacon, Charlotte 9551
Bacon, Cole S. 1576
Bacon, David 9396
Bacon, Horace 326
Bacon, Matilda 3157
Bacon, Noah 333
Bacon, Olive 2569
Bacon, Simeon 3157
Badger, Harriet Eliza 6545
Bailes, Alzira 6199
Bailey, ___ (Miss) 9837
Bailey, ___ (Mrs.) 2473
Bailey, Almira C. 4545
Bailey, Annie Jean 3112
Bailey, Elizabeth 3146
Bailey, Erastus 4471
Bailey, L. Louise 4471
Bailey, Martha G. 6810
Bailey, Nicholas 1748
Bailey, Sarah 1748
Baily, Lorinda 347
Baily, Thomas 347
Bain, Susan M. 5271
Bainbridge, Elizabeth 9203
Bainbridge, Joan 3135
Baird, Sally 9983
Baker, ___ (Miss) 3381
Baker, Abigail 9109
Baker, Adah 7713
Baker, Amanda 4358
Baker, Andrew, Jr. 354
Baker, Catherine 8109
Baker, Eliza 6751
Baker, Experience M. 2435
Baker, Hannah 4859
Baker, Henry (Maj.) 353
Baker, James 363
Baker, Juley 8753
Baker, Lucy 7981
Baker, Nancy 2555
Baker, Patty 3720
Baker, Phebe L. 4254
Baker, Roswell 366
Baker, Semantha 8419
Balcom, Caroline 3725
Balcom, Leafa 2094
Balcomb, Phoebe 7470
Baldridge, Elizabeth 10102
Baldwin, Alcinoe 1684
Baldwin, Alfred 394
Baldwin, Augustin U. 384
Baldwin, Benjamin 378
Baldwin, Betsey 4813, 7818
Baldwin, Elizabeth L. 8923
Baldwin, Elvira 1497
Baldwin, Frederick 8923
Baldwin, Isaac 1684
Baldwin, Mary R. 1052
Baldwin, Susan R. 1563
Baldwin, William 5823
Baldwin, Zerviah 5823
Baley, Betsey 1788
Ball, Betsey 6151
Ball, Calvin S. 400
Ball, Jane 4808
Ball, Lucy 623
Ball, Moses 6151
Ballard, Gilbert 7790
Ballard, James 408
Ballard, Louisa 3829
Ballard, Rhoda F. 7790
Balloo, Mary 2377
Ballou, Caroline A. 8261
Bancroft, Orpha 1653
Bancroft, Sally 5959
Bancroft, Thadeus 415
Bancroft, Willard 414
Banister, Electa 2542
Banker, Eliza Ann 8319

Banker, Margaret 346
Bannister, Eliza 9225
Bannister, Samuel 9225
Barager, Lutha A. 5122
Barber, Asenath 3386
Barber, Aurilla 3577
Barber, Irena 6564
Barber, Louisa 7735
Barber, Sally 4273
Barber, Sarah 2354, 8648
Bardeen, Mary C. 1763
Bardwell, Mary Ann 9886
Bardwell, Reuben (Dr.) 9886
Barger, Amelia 8075
Barkenstose, Jane 10006
Barker, L. (Gen.) 5844
Barker, L. (Mr.) 441
Barker, Mary 7737
Barker, Samuel S. 451
Barker, Silas 445
Barker, Susan W. 5844
Barker, William 438
Barkley, Maria 7806
Barlow, Ahaz 454
Barlow, Cabot 8564
Barlow, Joel 453
Barlow, Jonathan K. 9330
Barlow, Lucinda 9896
Barlow, Martha Louisa 9330
Barlow, Mary 2075
Barlow, Nathan 452
Barnard, Erastus 9183
Barnard, Foster 462, 3615
Barnard, Maria A. 9183
Barnard, Mary 4005
Barnes, ___ (Miss) 8812
Barnes, Cornelia 8704
Barnes, Cynthia F. 4329
Barnes, David 475
Barnes, Huldah 2375
Barnes, James 474, 2537, 2539
Barnes, John R. 7114
Barnes, Joseph 477
Barnes, Lorinda L. 185
Barnes, Margaret 2672
Barnes, Mary 8227
Barnes, Sherman 476
Barnes, Thomas 8812
Barnes, Wheeler 8704
Barnet, ___ (Mrs.) 8136
Barnet, Shelomy 8389
Barney, Nelson 478, 486
Barnhart, Christian 491
Barnhart, Elizah W. 5117
Barnhart, Fidelia (Mrs.) 440
Barnhart, Isaac 9145
Barnhart, Maretta 9145
Barnhart, Matilda 7273
Barnhart, Polly 2805
Barns, Eben 495
Barns, Ebenezer 501
Barns, Harriet 4647
Barns, Maryann 7741
Barns, Nancy 6585
Barnum, Isaac 504
Barnum, Philo B. 503
Barnum, Thomas P. 502
Barr, Elizabeth Maria 8171
Barr, Thomas 4712
Barret, Cornelius 509
Barrett, Betsey 3726
Barrett, Clarissa 5556
Barrett, Lucy L. 7942
Barrett, Samuel 511, 514
Barrick, Rebecca 7003
Barrit, Hildah 344
Barrow, Mary 214
Barrows, ___ (Mr.) 519
Barrows, Eliza 9824

Bartholomew, Clarissa 3236
Barhtolomew, Elsey 5383
Bartholomew, Julia 250
Bartholomew, Polly 6896
Bartle, Antoinette E. 4989
Bartlett, Julius 8508
Bartlett, Mary 4265
Barto, Adaline 7497
Barton, Benjamin 542, 544, 1969, 9119
Barton, Lillis 9432
Barton, Lorinda 8580
Barton, Mary 1263
Barton, Sally 9119
Barton, Sally M. 5536
Barton, Sarah M. 5430
Barton, Susan S. 1969
Bass, Mary Ann 554
Bass, Samuel 547
Bass, Sarah L. 6922
Bateman, Delia 6757
Bateman, Eleazer 555
Bateman, Phebe 857
Bates, ___ (Rev.) 9448
Bates, Alvah (Mr.) 559
Bates, E. Greenlief (Miss) 7321
Bates, Esther 9738
Bates, P. P. 568, 570,
Bates, Phebe 8559
Bates, Philo 571
Bates, Phineas 557
Bates, Phineas P. 569
Bates, Rhoda 6381
Bates, Stephen 556, 569, 9738
Baugher, Hester 5127
Baxter, Mary 2398
Bayles, Euphemy 64
Beach ___ (Mrs.) 3315
Beach, Clarissa 8490
Beach, Israel 589
Beach, Jefferson 582, 591
Beach, Lucy 6467
Beach, Lurany 56
Beach, M. J. (Miss) 15
Beach, Teressa 5472
Beacher, Susan 8576
Beaching, Sarah 4407
Beaden, Martha 618
Beal, Beula 8267
Beal, Caleb 4803, 4851
Beal, Dolly 1112
Beal, Rachel 4803, 4851
Beall, Sally T. 1872
Beall, Tam'l. 1872
Beals, B. (Mr.) 853
Beals, Deborah 853
Beals, Delia 736
Beals, Harriet 4571
Beals, Israel 4571
Beals, James 599
Beals, Josiah 598
Beals, Rosannah 1923
Beals, Sarah 5470
Bean, George 609
Bean, Isabella 1752
Bean, Sarah 6830
Bear, Susan 7676
Beardslee, Frances 7541
Beardsley, Delilah E. 5598
Beardsley, Ruth 1235
Beaumont, Sally 8418
Beaumont, Sarah 3542
Beavers, Betsey 558
Beck, Eliza Ann 933
Beck, William 933
Becker, Charlotte 6784
Beckwith, A. (Miss) 3464
Beckwith, Amasa 626

Beckwith, Annn 5623
Beckwith, Emma E. 6509
Beckwith, Fanny 9535
Beckwith, George 630
Beckwith, Jane 9278
Beckwith, N. H. (Col.) 633
Beckwith, Nathaniel 627
Beckwith, Nathaniel H. 628, 634
Beckwith, Philancy T. (Miss) 484
Beckwith, Samuel 2048
Beckwith, Stella 2048
Beddoe, Charlotte H. 8474a
Beddoe, John 8474a
Bedell, Catherine 6241
Bedell, Mary 3429
Bedell, Susan 769
Beden, Smithfield 640
Bedlack, Matilda 3221
Beebe, Fanny 2590
Beebe, Gabriel 646
Beebe, Harriet 3
Beebe, Henrietta M. 10101
Beebe, Joseph L. 645
Beebe, Parthenia 4920
Beebe, Sarah 5769
Beebe, Zaccheus 647
Beecher, ___ (Rev. Dr.) 6732
Beecher, Caroline E. 815
Beecher, Mary F. 6732
Beecher, Randal F. 649
Beggerly, Cynthia 2103
Belcher, Polly 1949
Belden, Nancy 9961
Belding, Abigail 1492
Belding, Azor 665, 1492
Belding, Esther 9782
Belding, Selah 666, 668, 9782
Belknap, Lydia 426
Bell, ___ (Miss) 3541
Bell, Benjamin P. 672, 676
Bell, Charlotte 5030
Bell, Orline 8726
Bell, William 673
Bellinger, Nancy 9245
Bellows, Isaac 682
Bellows, Mary 7786
Belt, Betsey 5019
Beman, Temperance 7235
Bemis, J. D. (Mr.) 691
Bemus, Eliza 487
Bemus, Jane 2073
Bemus, Mary 2246
Bemus, Thomas 487
Benedict, Betsey (Mrs.) 697
Benedict, Eleazer 698
Benedict, Hiram 696
Benedict, Isaac 697
Benedict, Mary Jane 3362
Benham, Amanda 731
Benham, Celestia 303
Benham, David 704
Benham, Elizabeth 6202
Benham, S. (Mr.) 706
Benham, Sally 704
Benham, Sarah A. 8077
Benjamin, Samuel 711
Benn, V. M. (Mrs.) 2040
Bennet, Catharine 1335
Bennet, Emily 2768
Bennet, Ephraim 1554
Bennet, Maria S. 699
Bennet, Peggy 1554
Bennet, Phineas 715
Bennet, Sally 276
Bennet, William C. (Dr.) 6703
Bennett, ___ (Mr.) 8734
Bennett, Adeline 6298
Bennett, Ann 1203

Bennett, Ann 1203
Bennett, Betsey 2410, 7255
Bennett, Fanny 7799
Bennett, H. (Mr.) 8087
Bennett, Harriet 5074
Bennett, Huldah A. 1353
Bennett, Jacob 6298
Bennett, Mary Ann 10003
Bennett, James 733
Bennett, Joseph 726
Bennett, Letty 4077
Bennett, Pryphena Jane 3296
Bennett, Rachel 7498
Bennett, Reuben 732
Bennett, Susannah 4338
Bennott, Mary 2595
Benson, Holbrook 4644
Benson, Sarah 4644
Bentley, Uriah 752
Bently, Rebecca 7482
Benton, David 5499, 7546
Benton, George 759
Benton, Henry 756
Benton, Levi 760
Benton, Mary 7546
Benton, Ruby 9541
Benton, Sally 5499
Bergstroser, Sarah 661
Berry, Arathusa D. (Miss) 365
Berry, Martha 2598
Berry, Nancy 1834
Berry, Rachael 8182
Berry, William 765
Besley, Jane 376
Besley, Mary Ann 8582
Besley, Samuel 376, 1183, 8582
Besley, Susan 1183
Bessac, Betsey N. 6099
Best, Nancy 7809
Betron, Belinda 4769
Beverly, Mary Ann 7305
Bevier, Catharine 1091
--(This entry purposely deleted)--
Bickford, Emily 9935
Bidwell, Amelia C. 3350
Bidwell, E. R. (Capt.) 777, 1530
Bidwell, Edwin R. (Capt.) 780
Bidwell, Eli 781
Bidwell, Louisa 9193
Bidwell, Martha (Widow) 6921
Bigelow, ___ (Capt.) 4486
Bigelow, Anne 4486
Bigelow, Eliza 2228
Bigelow, Evelina 5985
Bigelow, Harriet 5245
Bigelow, John 785
Bigelow, Parmelia 4350
Bigelow, Sally 8273
Bignall, Buliff 790
Bigsby, Mary Jane 2439
Biles, Maria 243
Bill, Emily A. 3152
Bill, Fanny 5585
Billings, James A. (Dr.) 795, 802
Billings, Martha Glover 5724
Billings, Philomela 5892
Billings, William 800, 801
Billson, Helen Ann 2030
Biltibidal, Margaret 5099
Bingham, Mary R. 9022
Birchard, Asahel 812
Birchard, Sophia 632
Bird, Eliza 686
Bird, John 3203, 7731
Bird, Keziah 3721
Bird, Lydia 687
Bird, Romina 3203
Bird, Sabrina 7731
Birdsall, Daniel 821

Birdsall, Eliza 822
Birdsall, John (Hon.) 816
Birdsall, Mary Ann 1096
Bishop, Harriet 4148
Birdsall, Samuel 817
Birdsall, Sutton, Sr. 822
Birdsall, Sutton 823
Birdsell, Sarah 9575
Bishop, Amy 829
Bishop, Elijah 829
Bishop, Hannah 7271
Bishop, Martha 1897
Bishop, Mary 1594, 9401
Bishop, Phebe 2018
Bishop, Sally Ann 7471
Bishop, Sarah Jane 4862
Bissel, Moses 831
Bissell, Mary 2480
Bixbe, Olive 6455
Bixby, Sarah 7877
Black, Aaron 844
Black, Betsey 8173
Black, Hugh 846, 8173, 10068
Black, Isabella 10068
Black, Jane 1829
Black, Jeremiah 849
Black, Michael 7703
Black, Nancy 7703
Black, Olive 744
Blackford, Huldah 3065
Blackman, ___ (Mrs.) 8764
Blackman, Ransom 851
Blackman, Ruby 2896
Blackmer, ___ (Mr.) 859
Blackmer, Betsey 3633
Blackmore, Alma 3717
Blain, Esther 10077
Blair, Abby 865
Blair, Jane 1567
Blake, Alta 3890
Blake, Lucy 5818
Blake, Lydia Ann 8032
Blake, Sarah 2416
Blakely, Amanda 2927
Blakeman, Alzina 4902
Blakeman, Joel 870
Blakeny, Mary E. 9347
Blakeslee, Eliza M. 5143
Blakesley, J. M. (Dr.) 871
Blanchar, Orinda 447
Blanchard, Charlotte 9595
Blanchard, Harriet 448
Blanchard, Maria 5660
Blanchard, Nancy 4929
Blasdell, Cynthia 5626
Blauvelt. See Blouvelt.
Bleecker, Eliza Ann 7262
Bleecker, J. L. (Mr.) 883
Bleecker, John N. 7455
Blinn, Laura E. 3188
Bliss, Almira 5785
Bliss, Jeremiah 5785
Blodget, Elvira 9593
Blodgett, Heman 897
Bloget, Rufus 899
Blood, ___ (Capt.) 905, 8344
Blood, Amelia I. 5997
Blood, Asa 906, 4717
Blood, Asa (Capt.) 2083
Blood, Ellen (Mrs.) 903
Blood, Harriet 4717
Blood, Indiana (Miss) 2083
Blood, Rebecca P. 8344
Bloodgood, Francis 908
Bloom, ___ (Gen.) 909
Blossom, Emily H. 5905
Blossom, Ezra 912
Blossom, William 912
Blount, Barbara G. 3300

Blouvelt, Sally 8162
Blowers, Keziah 8230
Bly, Desire 5443
Boardman, Elizabeth C. 1831
Boardman, Homer 5165, 8777
Boardman, Laura 5165
*Bobcock, Warden 922
Bogardus, Sarah 1650
Bogart, Gerrit 2646
Bogart, Isaac 9284
Bogart, Jane 9284
Bogart, John 927
Bogart, Magdalena 2646
Bogart, Peter J. 926
Bogart, Susan )Mrs.) 926
Bogert, Ann Eliza 3212
Bogert, Cathalina 1261, 2441
Bogert, Cornelia 3708
Bogert, Eliza 8847a
Bogert, H. H. 929, 935, 2441,
   2442, 3708, 8847a
Bogert, Isaac 1261
Bogert, Nicholas 930, 932,
   1135, 3212
Bogert, Rodolphus B. 939
Bogert, Rudolphus 940
Bogert, Stephen (Dr.) 941
Bogue, Laura G. 21
Bogue, Margaret 5812
Boiler, Sophia 9408
Bolckom, Sarah Ann 6088
Bollard, Harriet 2227
Bolles, Eliza H. 8685
Bolles, Ephraim 7133
Bond, J. R. (Mr.) 2980
Boogher, Frederick 950
Boohall, Catharine 3938
Boorman, Brazilla 954
Booth, Amelia 5045
Booth, Chloe 5382
Booth, Eliza 8475
Booth, Jonathan 3291
Booth, Lucy E. 7369
Booth, Rachael 9919
Booth, Sarah 7160
Booty, Sarah 8816
Booth, Susan 3291
Boothe, Sarah 4540
Borden, Eliza C. (Mrs.) 966
Borden, Emma 3442
Borden, Isaac 966
Borden, Polly 5994
Borrekens, ___ (Mr.) 968
Borrowe, ___ (Dr.) 970
Bortles, J. H. 976
Bortles, Mary 2468
Boss, Eliza C. 4101
Bostwick, ___ (Maj.) 979
Bostwick, Elmira 652
Bostwick, H. W. 981
Bostwick, Hannah 9501
Bostwick, Jane 6426
Bostwick, Jane E. 4325
Bostwick, Lucinda 8541
Bostwick, Polly 238
Bostwick, William 1905, 4325
-(Entry purposely deleted)-
Bosworth, Addela 9101
Bosworth, Betsey E. 7754
Bosworth, Rosanah 3934
Botsford, Adaline 5706
Botsford, Luther H. 988
Boughton, Delia Ann 5377
Boughton, Sophronia 9923
Bouker, Harriet 5762
Boulbear, Lucy 2636
Bourhite, Jane 9969
Bourn, Mary Robinson 8668
Bourn, Peter 8668
*Bockover, Hannah 2917

Bouton, Delia 63
Bovier, Sally 1548
Bowdoin, ___ (Gov. - MA) 1000
Bowdoin, James (Hon.) 2418
Bowdoin, Margaret 348
Bowdoin, Sarah (Mrs.) 2418
Bowen, Ann 6531
Bower, Helena 3280
Bowes, ___ (Mrs.) 4832
Bowlby, James 1523
Bowlsby, Catharine 2220
Bowtel, Mary 9829
Boyd, Elsy 418
Boyd, James I. 1013
Boyd, Maria 3380
Boyd, Mary 2562
Boyd, Robert 1009, 2276
Boyd, Sybil 9128
Boyer, Letitia 1359
Boyle, Ann 496
Boyle, Betsey 432
Boynton, ___ (Judge) 4257
Boynton, Alzorah 10122
Boynton, Burissa 4257
Boynton, Jonathan 6957, 10122
Boynton, Mary 6957
Brace, Charles 1019, 1021
Brace, Eliza 5060
Brace, Ruth (Mrs.) 990
Bracy, Lucy (Mrs.) 8545
Bradish, Harriet 1303
Bradish, John 1024, 1025
Bradley, Edwin D. 1030
Bradley, Eliza 1181
Bradley, Hel4n 5344
Bradley, J. (Rev.) 8214
Bradley, Luanna 1038
Bradley, Matilda 7051
Bradley, Sophia 8214
Bradley, Zera 1033, 1036
Bradt, ___ (Mr.) 1042, 2163
Bradt, Catherine 2163
Bradt, Elsy 5703
Bradway, Lovisa 8106
Brady, Maria Angelina 7907
Bragg, Mary 6599
Brainard, Lovina Ann 541
Bramble, Samantha B. 24
Brant, ___ (Col.) 4993
Brant, ___ (Miss) 4993
Brant, "Warrior" 5643
Brantley, Mary Ann 2052
Brantley, W. T. (Rev.) 2052
Braunschweig, Maria E. 4931
Brayton, Paulina 9412
Brazee, Margaret 9576
Brazier, Ann 5054
Breck, A. Y. (Mr.) 1050
Breck, George W. 1051
Breck, Joseph 1050
Breckenridge, John 6883
Breed, Elizabeth 4060
Breed, J. C. 1053
Breed, W. (Mr.) 1053
Breed, William 4060
Brees, Elizabeth 4898
Breese, Lydia 3248
Breeze, Margaret 7392
Brevier, Jane D. 4213
Brewer, Alsma 7010
Brewer, Emma (Mrs.) 6115
Brewer, Martha 2086
Brewster, Caroline 9909
Brewster, Esther 6042
Brewster, Nancy 10161
Brewster, Ruth H. 5614
Bridge, Lydia 2719
Bridgen, Anna M. 2507
Bridges, James W. 1062

Bridges, Sophia 1088
Bridgman, Lewis H. 1063
Briggs, Adelia 1003
Briggs, Hulda 5584
Briggs, Margaret 7544
Briggs, Margaret Gannette 8725
Briggs, Molly 532
Brigham, James 1078
Brigham, Mary E. 5319
Brinckerhoff, Catharine 2931
Brink, Charlotte 7832
Brink, Sophia 4503
Brink, Susannah C. 9124
Bristol, Anne 6772
Bristol, Aurilla 3092
Bristol, Frances 1508
Bristol, Hannah T. 8443
Bristol, Josiah W. 1508
Bristol, Keziah 9395
Bristol, Mary 2742
Britton, Angeline Gennette 1161
Britton, Anna (Mrs.) 9298
Britton, Emeline 1507
Britton, Lucy 5431
Brizse, Henry 1103
Broadhead, Mary 8257
Broat, Lanah Ann 8311
Brockelbank, Lima 620
Brocklebank, Nancy 10036
Brockway, Amy 1216
Brockway, Ann 2915
Brockway, Catherine 7139
Brockway, Gamaliel 1109
Brockway, George 1111
Brockway, Hannah 529, 6150
Brockway, Mary 6038
Brockway, Mercy 1762
Bronk, Judith 2504
Bronson, Charity 5354
Bronson, Phebe 2857
Brooks, Clarissa 3372
Brooks, Elizabeth 9476
Brooks, Harriet E. 2224
Brooks, Marcia F. 6420
Brooks, Mary 4534
Brooks, Micah (Gen.) 1123, 6420
Brooks, Moses 1124
Brooks, Portia 9186
Brooks, Samuel 1124
Brooks, Sally 7889
Brother, Caroline 7816
Brother, Valentine 7811, 7816
Brower, Cornelia L. 2634
Brower, Theophilus 1134
Brower, William 1134
Brown, ___ (Maj. Gen.) 1106
Brown, A. C. (Mr.) 7551
Brown, Adelia 8051
Brown, Almira C. 6986
Brown, Ann 1299
Brown, Arva L. 49
Brown, Barney 1137
Brown, Belinda 7035
Brown, Benjamin 228
Brown, Bethia 2247
Brown, Betsey 4246
Brown, Betsey Ann 5949
Brown, D. M. (Miss) 9499
Brown, Daniel 1142
Brown, Daniel Penfield 10134
Brown, David 4712
Brown, Delia Ann 3309
Brown, Dirce Ann 5182
Brown, Dorcas 4806
Brown, Ebenezer 1168
Brown, Eleanor 3368
Brown, Eliza 838, 4753
Brown, Elizabeth 4461, 6186
Brown, Elmira 10124

Brown, Elvira 8021
Brown, Eunice 7311
Brown, Eunice Ette 9239
Brown, Ezra W. 1141
Brown, F. E. (Miss) 2189
Brown, George M. 1149
Brown, Hannah 1656
Brown, Hannah C. 3107
Brown, Harriet 3475, 5843, 9314, 9934
Brown, Heman 9314
Brown, Henry 838
Brown, Jane Ann 2240
Brown, Jane E. 7551
Brown, Jane M. 10134
Brown, John 1165, 6719
Brown, John A. 2189
Brown, Juliet E. 5213
Brown, Laura 8092, 8378
Brown, Lucy 5902, 9847
Brown, M., Jr. (Dr.) 3764
Brown, Maria 3569
Brown, Marietta 6239
Brown, Mary Ann 3764
Brown, Mary Skinner 1106
Brown, Nancy 8596
Brown, Nelson 1157
Brown, Orracy 5310
Brown, P. O. (Mrs.) 1187
Brown, Penelope 228
Brown, Phebe 8275
Brown, Philena 6962
Brown, Phineas 1197
Brown, Relief 6456
Brown, S. A. (Mr.) 1143, 1151, 1187
Brown, S. A. (Mrs.) 1857
Brown, Sarah 2011
Brown, Sarah M. 782
Brown, Sarah Maria 7379
Brown, Sarah T. 8102
Brown, Theoda 6740
Brown, Thomas 1166
Brownell, Eliza 8507
Brownell, Elizabeth 6646
Brownell, Mary 2310
Brownson, ___ (Miss) 8802
Bruce, Margaret 8935
Bruce, Sarah 189
Bruen, Gabriel 1214
Brumfield, A. D. 2206
Brumfield, Andrew D. 1217
Brumfield, James I. 1217
Brumfield, Louisa 2206
Brundage, Abram (Capt.) 1224, 1225
Brundage, B. S. (Mr.) 41
Brundage, Henry 6848
Brundage, Mary 355, 8027
Brundage, Rosett 6848
Brundage, Sally 7122
Brundage, William 355
Brunk, Hannah 8310
Brunning, Patty 2252
Brush, Priscilla 7560
Bruyn, Mary 2045
Bryan, Emily 5136
Bryan, J. B. 1234
Bryant, Emily W. 3446
Bryant, Mary 257
Bryant, Sally 862
Bryden, James 2040
Bryner, R. W. 1238
Buchanan, Abigail (Mrs.) 5720
Buchanan, Andrew 7760
Buchanan, Mary 7760
Buchanan, Mohent 2599
Buchanan, William 1240
Buck, Betsey 5057
Buck, Cynthia 1777

Buck, E. S. (Mr.) 6121
Buck, Eliza 7059
Buck, Eliza C. 10008
Buck, Hannah 1254
Buck, Jane 9752
Buck, Orrill 6650
Buck, Phebe W. 6121
Buck, Roswell 1250
Buck, Rowell 7053
Buck, Sarah 1279
Buck, William H. 1280
Buckbee, Betsey 5497
Buckingham, Hannah 2076
Buckley, Jemima 7785
Buckley, Mary 4702
Buckley, Mary 8080
Buckley, Robert 1264
Budd, Eliza Ann 1741
Budd, Joseph 1741
Budlong, ___ (Mrs.) 1268
Budlong, Benjamin 1269
Budlong, Judiah E. 1270
Budlong, Martha J. 104
Budlong, Samuel 1268
Buell, A. K. (Rev.) 1272
Bugbee, Charity 8697
Bugbee, Minerva 7999
Bulkley, Caroline 4099
Bull, Asher 1276
Bull, Ruth 1471
Bullock, L. M., 16
Bulrees, Ann 7905
Bump. Lilly 362
Bunce, Ruth 1253
Bundy, Cynthia 2891
Bundy, E. (Mr.) 2891
Bundy, Eliza 3676
Bundy, Elizabeth 9043
Bundy, Nathaniel 1660, 9043
Bunnel, Abner 1290
Bunnell, Ann Eliza 2994
Bunnell, Miles 1292
Burbank, Solomon M. 1294
Burd, ___ (Miss) 6734
Burden, ___ (Miss) 9475
Burden, Patience 9474
Burden, Phebe 8367
Burdick, Pamelia 7775
Burdon, Eunice 6506
Burge, Eunice 401
Burgess, Jerusha 8349
Burgess, John 1298
Burhans, Mary Ann 1186
Burick, Bet ___ 2156
Burket, William 1304
Burley, Daniel 1306
Burlingame, A. H. (Rev.) 1310
Burlingham, Amanda 500
Burnet, ___ (Gen.) 1316
Burnet, Eleanor 999
Burnet, William (Gen.) 1318
Burnett, Eunice 7197
Burnett, Roenna 350
Burnham, Mary E. 5767
Burnham, Rhoda 8865
Burns, Adaline 428
Burns, Eunice 5679
Burns, Harriet A. 6312
Burns, Maria S. 4237
Burr, Delia 8894
Burr, Joseph 1328
Burrel, Edward 1332
Burrel, Margaret 1333
Burrell, Mary W. 2167
Burroughs, Ellen 9220
Burrows, Emeline 5017
Burrows, Julia A. 8198
Burrows, Ransom 1340
Burt, ___ (Miss) 8286
Burt, Hannah 1575

Burt, Oliver 1344
Burtch, Malcolm H. 1346
Burton, Elizabeth 1450
Burton, G. E. (Mr.) 1457
Burton, S. Louisa 1457
Bush, James 2385
Bush, Julia 9165
Bush, Lovina 9158
Bush, Lucinda 2385
Bush, Mary 12, 6149
Bush, Oscar 2385
Bush, Polly 1552
Bush, Rachael 1351
Bush, Sally 2383
Bush, Sally M. 1446
Bush, Selden F. 1349
Bush, Solon 2385
Bushel, Amelia 6678
Buskirk, Susannah 367
Butler, ___ (Dr.) 1380
Butler, A. R. (Mr.) 1380
Butler, Betsy 8616
Butler, C. (Mr.) 2119
Butler, C. N. (Mr.) 1381
Butler, Caroline L. 7250
Butler, Catherine 9179
Butler, Charles 1363
Butler, Charles 1384
Butler, Clarissa 2119
Butler, Delia 7858
Butler, Delin (Miss) 2099
Butler, G. J. 1379
Butler, Joseph 7250
Butler, Laura B. 4399
Butler, M. A. (Mrs.) 1381
Butler, Mary 10133
Butler, Mary E. (Mrs.) 1385
Butler, Medad 2119
Butts, Orrelia M. 9362
Butler, Orville L. (Mrs.) 1380
Butler, Rachael 9841
Butler, Sarah 2691
Butler, Solomon S. 1385
Button, Hannah 8969
Butts, Minerva 5439
Buzzell, Roba (Mrs.) 1394,
   1395
Buzzell, S. D. (Dr.) 1394
Byington, Lydia 8606
Byron, ___ (Lord) 841
Cade, Fanny 4833
Cady, Adaline 7781
Cady, Angeline 8980
Cady, Ichabod 1399
Cady, Lucinda 237
Cady, Nathaniel 7778
Cain, ___ (Mrs.) 1402
Cain, Delilah 4347
Caldcleugh, Jane 8665
Caldcleugh, Robert A. 8665
Caldwell, Letty 535
Caldwell, William 1404
Calhoon, Erastus R. 1408
Calhoon, Hannah 1310
Calhoon, Mary 2085
Calhoon, Nathan 1310
Calhoun, Celista M. 2166
Calhoun, James 1410
Calhoun, Margaret 6112
Calhoun, Nathan 2166
Calkins, Betsey Ann 8696
Calkins, Minerva 5411
Calkins, Sally (Mrs.) 9332
Cameron, Charles 1427
Cameron, D. (Mr.) 9780
Cameron, Dugald 1419, 1420,
   1421, 1424, 1425, 2095,
   2343
Cameron, Eliza 9780

Cameron, Isabella 7693
Cameron, Lydia 2343
Camp, ___ (Mrs.) 2887
Camp, Clarissa 498
Camp, Eliza M. 1846
Camp, Hermon 1435
Camp, Lovisa 7526
Camp, William 1846
Campbell, Alfred E. (Rev.) 1440
Campbell, Ann 8861
Campbell, Anna (Mrs.) 1462
Campbell, Archibald 1451
Campbell, Betsey 9834
Campbell, Charles W. 1456
Campbell, Christina 588
Campbell, Christopher 1438
Campbell, Harriet 3198
Campbell, John 1453, 1455
Campbell, Laura 5395
Campbell, Lydia 710
Campbell, Martha 7391
Campbell, Rebecca 2971
Campbell, Robert 7406
Campbell, Sarah 9836
Campbell, Susan Ann 7406
Cane, Mary Ann 6811
Canfield, Amanda 4892
Canfield, Rhoda Ann 6634
Canfield, Samuel 4892
Cannon, Harriet M. 763
Cannon, Maria 9373
Cantine, Moses I. 1470
Cappell, Harriet 286
Capron, Ann 2477
Capron, C. M. (Miss) 2393
Capron, George 1480
Capron, Hannah 3313
Capron, Samuel 1476
Capron, William P. 1474, 1476,
   3313
Card, Louisa 1482
Card, Mary 9950
Card, Polly 4537
Card, Stephen 9950
Card, Timothy 1482
Carey, Maria 5833
Carlisle, David 1486
Carlow, Roxina 2029
Carmer, Margaret 5534
Carnahan, Susan 1308
Carne, Margaret 3941
Carnike, Eliza 6474
Carnike, Mary 6485
Carpenter, Almira 8936
Carpenter, Betsey (Mrs.) 7045
Carpenter, Caroline 4495
Carpenter, Catharine T. 641
Carpenter, Comfort 6274
Carpenter, Eliza M. 8028
Carpenter, Elizabeth 613, 9628
Carpenter, George 1492
Carpenter, George S. 9425
Carpenter, Guliaelema 3670
Carpenter, H. E. (Miss) 7860
Carpenter, Hannah 2833, 8637
Carpenter, Jesse 1505
Carpenter, Julia Ann 91
Carpenter, M. (Gen.) 4495,
   8028
Carpenter, Martha N. 4884
Carpenter, Minerva 9968
Carpenter, Nancy 2496
Carpenter, Pamela 6274
Carpenter, Polly 6753, 9822
Carpenter, Susan 7058
Carpenter, Susan Ann 9425
Carpenter, William (Capt.) 1497
Carr, Cynthia 5721
Carr, Harriet 3748

Carrier, Hannah 1434
Carroll, ___ (Judge) 1520
Carroll, Charles 3095
Carroll, Elizabeth 3095
Carruthers, Cameron 1523
Carson, Peter 1524
Carson, Rebecca 9461
Carson, Sarah 6429
Carter, Elmira 3123
Carter, Julia Ann 4465
Carter, Maria A. 6583
Carter, Mary 7937
Carter, Priscilla 8951
Cartwright, Lois 9324
Cartwright, Mary 3472
Cary, Betsey 1198
Cary, Cordelia 617
Cary, Ebenezer 1539
Cary, Elizabeth 5915
Cary, Margaret 1977
Cary, Trumbull 1539
Case, ___ (Mrs.) 4811
Case, Charlotte 3441
Case, Dorothy 6510
Case, Harriet 6947
Case, Laura 332
Case. Rhoda 9277
Cash, Betsey 1178
Casner, Sally 3926
Cassleman, Harriet 57
Caster, Catharine 2658
Castile, Caroline 7671
Castle, Maria 8497
Castner, Rebecca 4621
Catlin, ___ (Judge) 1554
Catlin, Clarissa 6973
Catlin, Pirsis 5903
Catlin, William, Jr. 1558
Caton, John (Elder) 1559
Caulkins, Polly 8461
Caward, George 1560, 1561
Caward, Mary 3205
Caykendall, Gehiel 586
Chadwick, Jabez 1566
Chafee, Lucy Ann 9327
Chamberlain, ___ (young male)
   2674
Chamberlain, ___ (Judge) 4046
Chamberlain, Angeline 1571
Chamberlain, Calvin T. 1572
Chamberlain, Eliza 889, 4046
Chamberlain, Henry W. 1571
Chamberlain, Joseph 1574
Chamberlain, Mary 4210, 9098
Chamberlain, W. W. (Mr.) 1570
Chamberlain, Zelinda 5264
Chambers, Sally 9678
Champron, Rebecca 1417
Chandler, Martha W. 7906
Chapin, Ann 140
Chapin, Cynthia 1604
Chapin, Cyrenius 1596, 1610
Chapin, Delia W. 5722
Chapin, Ezra 1614
Chapin, Henry 1604, 1622
Chapin, Hester Ann R 5501
Chapin, Israel 1599
Chapin, Jane, Aurelia 643
Chapin, Laura 6776
Chapin, Laura L. 4531
Chapin, Louisa M. 9572
Chapin, Luthera 5838
Chapin, Lydisette 6687
Chapin, Mary B. 4180
Chapin, Perlina 6966
Chapin, Silas 1609, 1621
Chapin, Vistus 1602
Chapman, Almira 10026
Chapman, Bellona 4780

Chapman, Elisha (Dr.) 3029
Chapman, Eliza 4703
Chapman, Elvila 10107
Chapman, Ezekiel 1640
Chapman, Guy R. 1642
Chapman, Henrietta A. 8380
Chapman, J. T. 1628
Chapman, Jedediah (Rev.) 275
Chapman, John 2962
Chapman, John T. 1627
Chapman, Joseph (Rev.) 2834
Chapman, Laura 3479, 7748
Chapman, Louisa A. 3029
Chapman, Maria 8096
Chapman, Martha A. 8537
Chapman, Mary 2834, 2962
Chapman, Miranda 6906
Chapman, Thomas 1643
Chapman, William 1636, 8380
Chapman, Zyporah 2020
Chappel, Harriet 9712
Charles, Lewis 1645
Chase, Charles 1660
Chase, Eliza 1658
Chase, Eunice 607
Chase, George 1652
Chase, John 1658
Chase, Julia 9668
Chase, Laura 575
Chase, Lucy 8430
Chase, Mary 19
Chase, Mary A. 1652
Chase, Naomi 9466
Chase, Pamela 1553
Chase, Phebe 995
Chase, Polly 383
Chatfield, John 1671, 1672
Chatfield, Mary Ann 1672
Chatham, Nancy 9799
Chatten, Elizabeth 1128
Chatter, Elizabeth 1128
Chattin, Mary 9246
Chauncey, ___ (Mr.) 1673
Cheaffy, Polly 7322
Cheeny, William 1675
Chenay, Roxana 8598
Cheney, Abigail 3803
Cheney, Ebenezer 3142
Chesebro, Keturah 6287
Chidsey, Augustus 2088
Chidsey, Sally 2088
Child, Elias 1689
Child, Gennet 5329
Child, Lyvonia 1689
Child, Mary Ann 7744
Child, William 1688, 5329,
    7744
Childon, William 3696
Childs, Elizabeth 6288
Childs, Joel 1693
Childs, Sophia 5247
Chipman, Samuel 4144
Chipman, Sarah 4144
Chissom, Hannah 6926
Chittenden, Ebenezer 3024
Chittenden, Sally 2026
Chodwick, Esther 5766
Chris, Sally 6698
Christopher, Calista 6714
Church, Abigail 7570
Church, Adonijah 7830
Church, Alonzo 1717
Church, Chauncy 1719
Church, Eunice 6666
Church, John B. 1713
Church, Permelia 2591
Church, Phebe (Mrs.) 7830
Church, Sibel 1398
Church, Warner 1718

Churchill, Cornelia K. 4609
Churchill, Josiah 1721
Churchill, Martha 3664
Clackner, John B. 1723
Clackner, John S. 1724
Clap, Catharine 3222
Clapp, Melinda 6482
Clapp, Patty 6987
Clapper, ___ (Mr.) 1730
Clapper, Lydia 5157
Clark, ___ius 1739
Clark, Almira 2982
Clark, Alonzo 1754
Clark, Aurelia 9423
Clark, Betsey 221
Clark, Calvin 1736
Clark, Caroline 6248
Clark, Caroline (Mrs.) 1769
Clark, Catharine A. 9903
Clark, Cazia 284
Clark, Charlotte
Clark, Clarissa 6805
Clark, Cornelia L. 9042
Clark, Elisa J. 58
Clark, Eliza (Mrs.) 9001
Clark, Emeline 2774
Clark, Emily P. 9095
Clark, Ezekiel 1765
Clark, G. W. (Prof.) 7474
Clark, Gaius 1732, 1734, 1812
Clark, Hannah 1562, 4987,
    5926
Clark, Hannah Mariah 1913
Clark, Harriet 7366
Clark, Hiram 1735
Clark, J. A. (Mr.) 1769
Clark, Jane 1399
Clark, Jerusha 4239
Clark, Jesse 1795
Clark, John 1749
Clark, Jonas 1759
Clark, Jonathan 1785
Clark, Joseph P. 1779
Clark, Laura 6979
Clark, Mahala 6055
Clark, Malona L. 9956
Clark, Maltby C. 1784
Clark, Margaret (Mrs.) 2140
Clark, Maria G. 8121
Clark, Martha (Mrs.) 2837
Clark, Mary (Mrs.) 1855
Clark, Mary Ann 5832
Clark, Mahitabel 7119
Clark, O (Rev.) 1808
Clark, Orin (Rev.) 1733,
    1753
Clark, Patience 4117
Clark, Paulina 4889
Clark, Peter 1783
-(Entry purposely deleted)-
Clark, Prudence 198
Clark, Samuel 1731, 1797
Clark, Susan 6688
Clark, Thomas B. 1786
Clark, William 1399
Clark, William (Capt.) 1745
Clark, William H. 1782
Clarke, Caroline Maria 7938
Clarke, Charity P. 2629
Clarke, Eliza A. 1819
Clarke, James C. 1819
Clarke, Margaret Elizabeth
    8519
Clarke, Peter 7938
Clarke, Polly 7378
Clary, ___ (Rev.) 1956
Clary, Ann 6389
Clary, Elizabeth 2772
Clawson, Abraham 7477

Clawson, Magdalena 2783
Clawson, Sarah 7477
Clemons, Hannah G. 2667
Cleveland, Stephen B. 1835
Clifford, John 4731
Cline, ___ (Miss) 3955
Cline, Betsey 10016
Clinton, ___ (Gov.) 1844
Clinton, ___ (V. Pres. of U.S.)
    1843
Clinton, De Witt 8414
Clinton, George (V. Pres. of U.S.)
    9222
Clinton, Mary Ann 6895
Clizbe, Joseph 1848
Closson, Samuel (Dr.) 1853
Clow, Agnes 6631
Clow, Robert 6631
Coates, Angeline 1691
Coats, Betsey 8338
Coats, Leonard 1860
Cobb, Adam B. 1870
Cobb, Elisha W. 3759
Cobb, Lucy 1104
Cobb, Maria 3759
Cobb, Mary 6574
Cobb, Nancy 8190
Cobb, Thetis 1870
Coburn, Charlotte 524
Coburn, Phebe 8087
Cochran, Schuyler 1871
Cock, Margaret 102
Cock, Mary 5757
Codding, George 1875
Codding, William T. 1876
Coe, ___ (Rev.) 1882
Coe, Cyrus 1880
Coe, Emily 5336
Coe, Halstead 6580
Coe, John 1884
Coe, Sarah (Mrs.) 6580
Coffin, Sarah Ann 2323
Coffman, Norris 1887
Cogswell, Betsey 9810
Cogswill, Rachel 2654
Colburn, Abigail 2222
Colcord, Joseph 1898
Cole, Abigail 267
Cole, Abner 6533
Cole, Ann 5970
Cole, Aurelia J. 68
Cole, Caroline 8664
Cole, Catherine 2745
Cole, Cyrene 3033
Cole, Edward 1928
Cole, Ehoda 2012
Cole, Frances Ann 6533
Cole, Hezekiah M. 1929
Cole, J. (Dr.) 1906
Cole, Joseph (Dr.) 5797
Cole, Luther 1909, 1924
Cle, Lydia A. 1490
Cole, Lydia S. 907
Cole, Martha 3298
Cole, Mary 3750
Cole, Mary Ann 2751
Cole, Mary P. 5797
Cle, Mathew 3298
Cole, Matthew 5306
Cole, Phebe 1116
Cole, Polly 5306
Cole, Reuben 1907
Cole, Rhoda 1046 (See, possibly,
    "Cole, Ehoda" above)
Cole, Sally 6699, 7210
Cole, Samuel 1910, 1927
Cole, Sarah Ann 233
Cole, Sarah M. 8515
Cole, Ursula 9667

Coleman, Ambrose 1934
Coleman, Eliza B. 9870
Coleman, Elizabeth 411
Coleman, Spencer 9974
Coles, Alva 1939
Coles, Tamor 2544
Collier, John A. 1944
Collingwood, Elizabeth 5786
Collins, Amanda M. 9900
Collins, Constance 7133
Collins, John 1948
Collins, Keziah 9917
Cook, Lovina 6602
Collins, Moses P. 1950
Collver, Phineas 1954
Colt, Catharine 8353
Colt, Elias 1963
Colt, Elizabeth 7807
Colt, Joseph 1958, 1962, 7807, 8353
Colt, Joseph (Maj.) 977
Colt, Joseph S. 1960
Colt, Mary 977
Colt, S. (Mr.) 969
Colt, Samuel (Gen.) 1964
Colton, Calvin (Rev.) 1965
Colton, Lydia 6334
Colton, Sarah 3529
Colville, William, Jr. 1966
Colvin, Anna S., 1893
Colwell, Diantha 5468
Colwell, Jane 3738
Colwell, Sally Ann 3169
Combs, Eliza 5650
Compton, James 1972
Compton, Jonathan 1975
Compton, Peter 1974
Comstock, Amy 574
Comstock, Darius 1023
Comstock, Edwin P. 1988
Comstock, Harriet 3724
Comstock, Jared 574
Comstock, Moses 1984
Comstock, Rachael 596
Comstock, Roby S. 1023
Conant, Mara 7425
Cone, Eli 1992
Cone, Rosana 3474
Conklin, Frances Ann 2999
Conklim, Mary Elizabeth 7204
Conklin, Sophia A. 1167
Conkling, Rebecca 5820
Conkling, Theodosia 4874
Conner, Betsey 1122
Conner, Harriet 252
Conner, Mary 7951
Connet, Nancy 489
Converse, John P. 2006
Cook, Abigail C. 4311
Cook, Adeline 66
Cook, Amanda 9800
Cook, Anna Marie 2016
Cook, Anny 8824
Cook, Bates 2007
Cook, Belinda 5842
Cook, Betsey 2989
Cook, Celia Ann 7684
Cook, David 1436, 2022, 2023
Cook, Eliza 946
Cook, Ellen C. 2039
Cook, Halsey 8789
Cook, Harriet 1184
Cook, Henrietta 2116
Cook, Henry 2035
Cook, Henry (Rev.) 2016
Cook, Janet M. 565
Cook, Jesse 5651
Cook, Julia Ann 2164
Cook, Lavina 5144

Cook, Margaret 5596
Cook, Mary 5651
Cook, Mary Caroline 1436
Cook, Mary Jane 4776
Cook, Mary M. 8789
Cook, Metila 1674
Cook, Nathaniel 2008
Cook, Patty 3322
Cook, Philip 1184, 1674, 6428
Cook, Robert (Dr.) 565
Cook, Robert W. (Dr.) 3326
Cook, Rosamond 6428
Cook,Sheldon 2028
Cook, Titus R. 2037
Cooke, Adriana Maria 2642
Cooke, Isabella 8200
Cooke, Robert (Dr.) 8200
Cooley, ___ (Dr.) 6703
Cooley, Edwin A. 1722
Cooley, Eunice 3347
Cooley, James 2046
Cooley, Jerusha 342
Cooley, John 2047
-(Entry purposely deleted)-
Cooley Mary Walbridge 3929
Cooley, Melissa Jane 1722
Cooley, Minerva 8015
Coon, Betsey 7127
Coon, Elizabeth 26
Coon, Mary 6165
Coon, Samantha 9608
Cooper, Cynthia 9634
Cooper, Emeline 405
Cooper, Griffith M. 1475, 2062
Cooper, Hepsebeth 3093
Cooper, Louisa 7801
Cooper, Rebecca M. 1475
Cooper, Richard F. 2058
Cooper, Sarah 6113
Cooper, Thomas J. 2067
Coppeck, F. (Mr.) 2074
Copps, Elizabeth B. 461
Corbet, Nancy 5421
Corbin, Sarah 2944
Corey, Eliza 6754
Corkendool, Rachael 9261
Cornell, Esther 9723
Cornell, S. (Miss) 6212
Cornice, Elizabeth 2668
Corning, Alexander (Rev.) 2083
Corning, Erastus 2083
Corning, Mary 40
Cornwall, Phebe 8481
Cornwell, Ann 789
Cornwell, Elizabeth Ann 22
Corser, Ruth 4536
Corwin, Isaac 2091
-(Entry purposely deleted)-
Cory, Sarah Ann 7116
Coryell, V. M. 2095
Coslere, Mary 9199
Coss, Lyman 2692
Coss, Matilda 5947
Cost, Catharine Ann 4852
Cost, E. (Capt.) 2100
Cost, Elias 2102, 4852
Cotton, E. (Mr.) 2110
Cotton, Henry G. 2107
Cottrell, Phebe Jane 3052
Couch, Ira 2112
Coussens, Eliza 4442
Covell, Esther L. 2130
Covell, Sally Maria 2129
Covert, Margaret 7834
Covert, Tunis, Sr. 2120
Covey, Amos (Deacon) 948
Covey, Betsey 1342
Covey, Sybil 948

Covian, Maria Del Refugio ... 2081
Cowan, Ephraham 2131
Cowden, Betsey Ann 9868
Cowdin, A. (Mr.) 2136
Cowdrey, John (Col.) 2440
Cowdrey, Sarah E. 2440
Cowen, Margaret 5731
Cowing, Ann Jane (Mrs.) 4031
Cowing, Calvin 2146
Cowing, Charlotte E. 3431
Cowing, Cynthia 9045
Cowing, James 9045
Cowing, Polly 281
Cowing, Susan H. 3343
Cowing, Thompson 3431
Cowles, Abbey 424
Cowles, Lovisa 1229
Cox, Electa 6759
Cox, Thomas 2150
Cox, William 6759
Cozzens, Hannah 7294
Craft, Dorcas (Mrs.) 2199
Craft. Edward 2199
Crafts, Charlotte 225
Craig, Elizabeth 8070
Craig, Lauraett 4844
Cramer, Mary Jane 3899
Crandall, Adovestus 2165
Crandall, Ann P. (Mrs.) 2165
Crandall, Clara 1532
Crandall, Ezra 451
Crandall, Jane 893
Crandall, Koziah 4281
Crandall, Sarah 451, 2909
Crandall, Wattey 3826
Crandle, Jane (Mrs.) 7137
Crane, Amanda 2545
Crane, Betsey 1107
Crane, Electa 10018
Crane, James 4768
Crane, Lyman 2170, 2172
Crane, Susan 6296, 10119
Crane, Sylvia 2487
Crans, Elizabeth 8428
Cranston, Sally 2080
Crater, Barbara 7355
Craw, Abigail 1317
Crawford, Harriet 3980
Creager, Sophia 8915
Creger, Catherine (Mrs.) 5168
Creigher, Lydia 6210
Critchell, Ann Eliza 2413
Crittenden, Chloe 7948
Crittenden, Electa 6673
Crittenden, Inmer (Mr.) 2195
Crittenden, Lots (Mrs.) 956
Crittenden, Mary 1117
Crivelling, Margaret 7696
Crivelling, Rebecca Ann 3551
Crocker, Jane R. 2203
Crocker, Wickham R. (Dr.) 2203
Cromwell, Benjamin 199
Cromwell, Catharine 199
Cromwell, Malinda 7143
Cronkite, Mary 1634
Crooke, John 709
Crooke, Margaretta L. 709
Crooker, Cordelia J. 2417
Crooker, George A. S. 2417
Crooker, Julia 9786
Crosby, Betsey 754, 4591
Crosby, Eliakim 2214
Crosby, Freelove 5637
Crosby, Henry S. 2218
Crosby, Joanna B. 4937
Crosby, Lucy M. 3144
Crosby, Mary 183
Crosby, Mary Ann 644

Crosby, Ruth Ann 7006
Cross, ___ (Elder) 7287
Cross, E. T. (Mr.) 2225
Cross, Edward 2221
Cross, Julia 7287
Cross, Lydia 1
Crosset, Betsey 10150
Crouch, Surina 3649
Crout, Phebe 3193
Crowell, Lucy 2939
Crowell, Lydia 8830
Crowell, Solomon, Sr. 2235
Crowl, Alma 7310
Crowley, B. Rosetta 9022
Crowley, Walter 8022
Cruger, Daniel 2238
Cruttenden, Eunice 9624
Cull, Mary 5381
Culver, Cooper 7759
Culver, Eliza Ann 7565
Culver, Elizabeth 3218
Culver, Harriet 9007
Culver, James H. 2248
Culver, Jemima 8114
Culver, John 2249
Culver, Laura 4242
Culver, Lucretia 994
Culver, Phoebe Ann 8375
Culver, Ruth 7759
Cuming, Elizabeth P. 7396
Cuming, F. H. (Rev.) 2255
Cumings, ___ 2257
Cumings, Betsey 5686
Cumings, Chauncy 2259
Cumings, Simeon 2257
Cummings, Delina 5410
Cummings, Ellen 10071
Curtis, Alpheus 2267
Curtis, Elsa 3321
Curtis, Hiram W. 2269
Curtis, Mary R. 7896
Curtis, Nancy 7290
Curtis, Polly 7047
Curtis, Susan 1129
Curtiss, Alvira 4802
Curtiss, Azor 2275
Curtiss, Charity B. 4553
Curtiss, Samuel F. 2276
Curtiss, William 4824
Cushing, John 2279
Cushing, Polly 6489
Custor, Mary 2126
Cutler, Eliza 9601
Cutler, Elizabeth 3644
Cutler, Isabella 6249
Cutting, Lurany 9948
Cuyler, Eleanor (Mrs.) 396
Cuyler, Eliza 8453
Cuyler, Eliza (Mrs.) 2297
Cuyler, Henry 2291, 8453
Cuyler, William H. 2297
Cuyler, William Howe 2292
Cyrene, ___ (Miss) 2396
Dabole, Ansen 2301
Daggert, Nancey 814
Daggert, Sarah 9600
Dagget, Betsey 2746
Dagett, Levi 2305
Daggett, William H. 2304
Daily, Hannah 5308
Dana, Susan H. 9376
Danforth, Thomas 2317, 2318
Daniell, Ramania 576
Daniels, Mary D. 761
Daniels, Norman 2322
Danielson, Mary
Darby, Julia M. 5128
Darling, ___ (Mr.) 3589
Darling, Susan W. 106

Darrow, Ann 955
Darrow, Jared 2330
Darrow, Orinda 2332
Darrow, Prudence 1755
Dart, Jonathan 2333
Dascam, Henry 2334
Daskam, Nathan 23352336, 2337
Dates, Maria M. 7081
Dautremor, Caroline 1221
Davenport, Eliza Cameron 9500
Davenport, Harriet A. 7974
Davenport, Ira 9500
Davenport, Lemuel 7974
Davenport, Lodemia P. 6265
Davenport, Louisa 6518, 7843
Davenport, Squire 2345
Daves, John P. 2346
Davids, John 2347
Davidson, ___ (Mrs.) 1786
Davidson, Eliza 7899
Davidson, James 1786, 2349, 3105
Davidson, Roderick 2674
Davidson, Susan 1682
Davies, ___ (Rev.) 2352
Davies, Charlotte 1330
Davies, William 2355
Davies, William (Capt.) 2357
Davis, Aaron 2380
Davis, Betsey 921
Davis, Caroline 3487
Davis, Clarissa 6013
Davis, D. H. (Mr.) 6680
Davis, Diana 1012
Davis, Eliza 6680, 7675
Davis, Eliza S. 10034
Davis, Elizabeth 4765
Davis, Emry 2385
Davis, George R. (Gen.) 2365
Davis, Hannah 4996, 8179
Davis, Harriet 8467
Davis, Harriet M. 3821
Davis, J. (Mr.) 2374
Davis, James J. 2359
Davis, James, Jr. (Dr.) 2371
Davis, Jerusha 1223
Davis, John 921
Davis, Louisa M. 4116
Davis, Lucinda 8321
Davis, Lucy Ann 8897
Davis, Lydia A. 3797
Davis, Mary Ann 6858
Davis, Minerva 8660
Davis, Nancy 4396
Davis, Paul H. 8897
Davis, Rachel 2070
Davis, Rebecca Y. 8297
Davis, Samuel 2382
Davis, William 2379
Davis, William H. 2388
Davison, Mary Ann 1488, 5539
Daw, Clarinda 2180
Dawley, Polly 3671
Dawly, Alcenath 9407
Dawson, Marcia 6626
Dawson, Margaret 2835
Day, Catharine 5343
Day, Elijah 2401
Day, Jackson 2404
Day, John 5343
Day, Julietta S. 3173
Day, Nathaniel 2397
Daymonth, Polly 6466
Dean, Betsey 7214
Dean, Mary 10148
Dean, Pamela 1573
Dean, Patience 631
Dean, Phebe 3990
Dean, Robert 2414

Dean, Sally 7095
Dean, Zilph 7405
Deane, Dolly 597
Dearborn, ___ (Gen.) 2420
De Bow, John 2423, 2425, 5073
De Bow, Margaret (Mrs.) 5073
De Camp, David 6081
Decker, ___ 2432
Decker, Bethsheba 2064
Decker, Clarissa 3353
Decker, Elizabeth 9807
Decker, Julia 6521
Decker, Malinda A. 6799
Decker, Richard 2432
Dedrich, Catharine 9073
Dedrick, Maria 9070
De Forrest, Delia 2366
De Forrest, William 2366
De Golia, Frances 8264
De Golyer, Rensselaer 2438
De Jean, Harriet 4882
D'Labar, Sophia 2748
Delamater, John (Dr.) 2371
Delamatter, George C. 2443
D'Lamatter, Maryann 9583
De Land, Eunice A. (Mrs.) 2448
Deland, Julia 2884
Deland, William (Deacon) 2449
De Land, William F. 2448
Delano, Israel 2453
De Lano, Lorinda E. 1401
Delano, Louisa 1262
Delany, James 2455
De Lap, Angelina 5335
Delavan, Henry W. 2456
Delavan, Mary 5971
De Long, Catherine 9082
Demerah, Gitty 5376
Deming, ___ (Dr.) 2467
Deming, Fenn 5750
Deming, Fenn (Dr.) 2464
Deming, Jane 5750
Deming, Nancy S. 8982
Deming, Sarah Sophia 5649
Demmon, Amanda 7015
De Mott, Lorinda 8293
Dench, Fanny 7763
Denham, Francis 3915
Denham, Martha O. 3915
Denison, Alice 7831a
Denison, John 7831
Denison, Polly 5604
Dennis, Martha 7037
Dennis, Paul 8039
Denniston, ___ (Judge) 1676
Denny, Elizabeth (Mrs.) 3560
Densmore, Hannah 5849
Denton, Eliza Jane 241
Denwood, Catherine 4850
Deo, Lavina 8177
Derby, John K. 2488
De Riemer, Peter 2490
Deusenbery, Polly 219
Devall, Mary 5068
Devore, Lydia 5853
Dewey, Anna 8843
Dewey, Eliza 4025
Dewey, Elizabeth 6144
Dewey, Emeline 6779
Dewey, H. (Mr.) 3937
Dewey, Harvey 4030
Dewey, Jedediah 6144
Dewey, William 3057
De Witt, Harriet 1854
De Witt, Simeon 2509, 4547
De Witt, Susan 4547
Dewy, Marian 6316
Dexter, Eliza 3295
Dexter, Jane 9017

291

Dexter, John 8979, 8985
Dexter, Louisa 8979
Dexter, Lucretae 3251
Dexter, Olive 8572
Dexter, Paulina 9039
Dexter, Samuel 2516
Dexter, Sarah 1862
Dey, Anthony 2522
Dey, Anthony 2527
Dey, Ben 2528
Dey, David 2523, 2525
Dey, Ellinor 5689
Dey, Hannah 2527, 4559
Dey, Hester 3559
Dey, Jane 4154, 4805
Dey, Peter 4805, 5689
Dey, Philip (Dr.) 2521, 2524
Dey, Sarah 4643
Dey, Susan 2530
Deyo, Ruth 1883
Deyoe, Charity 1390
De Zeng, F. A. (Mr.) 5222
-(Entry purposely deleted)-
De Zeng, Sarah Matilda 5222
De Zeng, William S. 2531, 2532
Dibble, Polly 2479
Dible, Peter 2535
Dickenson, Susan 9295
Dickerson, Elizabeth 2188, 7247
Dickerson, Fanny 3122
Dickerson, Lyman 2537
Dickerson, Mary Jane 1179
Dickinson, Dolly 9018
Dickinson, E. A. 2548
Dickinson, Julia 658
Dickinson, Loa 9614
Dickinson, Sarah 2706
Dickinson, William 2543
Dickson, Hannah 5086
Dickson, Nancy 703
Didama, Simon (Dr.) 2559
Dildine, Nancy 7507
Dillenbeck, ___ (Mrs.) 4245
Dillingham, Mary 6945
Dimick, Levina 5175
Dimmick, Laura 9606
Dinnin, James 2564
Dinnin, Polly A. 7347
Dinsmore, Minerva 4166
Dinsmore, Thomas 4166
Disbro, Mary Ann 4766
Disbrow, Angeline 4450
Disbrow, Ann Maria 4066
Dixon, Amanda Comstock 7550
Dixon, Edward 7550
Dixon, Harriet 3217
Dixon, Mary 919
Doane, Hannah 3179
Dobbin, ___ (Gen.) 5793
Dobbin, Charlotte 7110
Dobbin, H. W. (Col.) 2581
Dobbin, Hugh W. 2579
Dobbin, Justus 2577
Dobbin, Mary 2578
Dobbin, Mary B. 6262
Dobbin, Phebe 1102
Dobbin, Sarah 5793
Dobbins, ___ (Maj.) 6469
Dodd, Elizabeth 1538
Dodge, ___ (Mrs.) 3954
Dodge, Bethia 1388
Dodge, Sarah 5132
Dolbear, Lucy 2636
Dolbee, Rebecca 3502
Dole, Harriet Delia 7275
Dole, James 7275
Dolloff, Elizabeth 338
Dolph, Amanda 6535

Donahe, John 649
Donahe, Welthy 649
Doolittle, Ann 4814
Doolittle, Charlotte B. 3869
Doolittle, Hannah 9692
Doolittle, Nancy 4598
Doremus, ___ (Deacon) 2608
Dorman, Joel (Dr.) 2610
Dorman, Temperance 1195
Dorr, James D. (Dr.) 2612
Dorrance, Harriet Augusta 227
Dorrance, Trumbull (Dr.) 227
Dorsey, Daniel 1620, 4565
Dorsey, Deborah 1620
Dorsey, Lydia 5977
Dorsey, Mary 4565
Doty, Abel 2622
Doty, Electa 10132
Doty, Eliza 728
Doty, Harriet 10151
Doty, John 2620
Doubleday, Semantha 9980
Doubleday, U. F. 2628
Douglas, Stephen 2631
Douglass, Sarah 6070
Dow, Catharine 398, 9590
Dow, Lorenzo 2637
Dowd, Delia 8733
Downing, Nathaniel 2639
Downs, Catherine B. 5305
Dox, Jacob 2645
Dox, Peter 2652
Dox, Thomas 2651
Doyle, Amanda 4263
Doyle, Jane 6579
Drake, ___ (Deacon) 2663
Drake, Alinda 3308, 4500
Drake, Allen 2655
Drake, G. W. (Mr.) 2666
Drake, Gideon 2661
Drake, Hannah 2928
Drake, Harriet 1409
Drake, John 2664
Drake, Mary Ann 6064, 7534
Drake, Phebe 4816
Drake, Polly 6778
Drane, Cassarinda M. 5295
Drane, Stephen 5295
Draper, Hila A. 3743
Draper, Mary 9151
Driscoll, John 2674
Drown, Lucinda 7964
Drown, Samuel 2676
Drowne, Margaret 6234
Dubois, Elizabeth 4379
Dudley, Benjamin F. 774
Dudley, Elvira 6046
Dudley, John (Deacon) 2686
Dudley, Louisa 774
Duer, Mary Ann 10038
Duer, Susan 9552
Duer, W. (Col.) 6235
Duffee, Olive 2690
Duggan, Della C. 2662
Duggan, Nathaniel 2662
Dumond, Betsey M. 9163
Dunbar, Angeline 1001
Duncan, Ellen 4468
Duncan, William C. 2692
Dungan, ___ (Dr.) 2694
Dungan, Elizabeth (Mrs.) 5673
Dunham, Caroline 5156
Dunham, Timothy 2697
Dunkleburgh, Catharine 3903
Dunks, Almira 10053
Dunks, Harriet 7433
Dunlap, E. A. 2701
Dunn, Alice 387
Dunn, Mary 8609

Dunning, Martin 2714
Dunton, Adaline 5917
Durand, ___ (Miss) 1291
Durand, Frances S. 6497
Durfee, Abel 2732
Durfee, Amanda 4369
Durfee, Ann 1864
Durfee, Cynthia 5152
Durfee, Delia 1587
Durfee, Elihu 2725, 2743
Durfee, Eliza 8891
Durfee, Harriet 9076
Durfee, Innocent 1919
Durfee, James (Dr.) 2737
Durfee, Lemuel 2740, 6302
Durfee, Maria 9075
Durfee, Mary 3351, 6302
Durfee, Pardon 5152, 9075, 9076
Durfee, Stephen 2724, 2738, 8880
Durfee, Susan (Mrs.)3351
Durfee, Susan F. 5600
Durfee, Susannah (Mrs.) 5600, 9015
Durfee, William 2736
Durkee, Ziba 6922
Durlin, Maria A. 5644
Durnford, Elizabeth 8164
Ducomb, Nancy 5088
Duskam, Ann 8738
Dustin, Sarah Ann 6511
Dutcher, Jane N. 397
Dutton, Austin 2757
Dutton, Diadamia C. 4716, 7063
Dyer, Hannah M. 5478
Dygert, Loraine 8314
Dygert, Mary Ann 2766
Earl, ___ (Judge) 4516
Earl, Clarissa Caroline 8340
Earl, Elizabeth 4516
Earl, J. Jr. (Hon.) 8340
Earl, Susan 4733
Earll, Daniel 2775
Earll, Jephthah 1231, 2775
Earll, Laura 1231
Eason, Hart 2779
Easterbrooks, Mary 4520
Eastman, ___ (Mr.) 2780
Eastman, Louise 3281
Easton, Mary A. 6861
Eastwood, Phebe Ann 7983
Eaton, Amos 2784, 2790
Eaton, Benjamin 2788
Eaton, Deborah 5619
Eaton, Maria Therza 7989
Eaton, Mary Jane 3970
Eaton, S. 7989
Eaton, William (Gen.) 2787
Ebberts, John 2792
Eckley, Thomas 2795
Eddy, ___ (Mr.) 2152
Eddy, ___ (Mrs.) 1745
Eddy, Almina 7838
Eddy, Ann 6109
Eddy, David 2801
Eddy, Isaac 7838
Eddy, Jesse 8103
Eddy, John 2808
Eddy, Joseph 2797
Eddy, Lydia 8203
Eddy, Mercy 7988
Eddy, Sally 10061
Eden, Benjamin 2556
Edgar, Hulda Maria 7344
Edginton, Ann 8111
Edington, Aaron 4712
Edington, Hannah 9035
Edington, Vicey 7561
Edmonds, Ann 3384
Edmonds, John L. 2818

Edmonds, Polly 3231
Edmonston, Dorothy 9658
Edmonston, Thomas 9658
Edson, Martha 5100
Edwards, Amelia Ann 1444
Edwards, Catherine J. 2429
Edwards, George 2839
Edwards, George C. 2831
Edwards, Jeremiah 2829
Edwards, Martha 2839
Edwards, Ogden 2830
Eggleston, Dolly 7163
Eggleston, Electa 1218
Eggleston, Eliza 8940
Eggleston, Helen Cornelia 2895
Eggleston, J. S. (Dr.) 2845, 2846
Eggleston, Jane D. 5661
Eggleston, Mary Ann 450
Eggleston, Patience 2124
Eggleston, Phebe Ann 2105
Elbridge, Roby 1820
Elderkin, Vine (Dr.) 2848
Eldred, Cooper 2850
Ellas, Alva 2860
Ellas, Henry 2855, 2861
Ellas, Julia Ann 4558
Ellas, Sarah 6358
Ellas, Simpson (Dr.) 6358
Elliot, Temma 9238
Elliott, Jane 2187
Elliott, Mary 1704
Ellis, Ella (Mr) 2872
Ellis, Jane 2872
Ellis, Jason 2874
Ellis, Philette 7488
Ellis, Sally 3155, 5641
Ellis, Sophia 6299
Ellison, Ann 2973
Ellsworth, Elizabeth (Mrs.) 4432
Ellsworth, Sabra 5535
Ellsworth, Sally Ann 2000
Elmer, Eliza 4490
Elmer, William 4490
Elyea, Elizabeth 7324
Emans, Julia Ann 1247
Embree, Sarah 215
Emerick, Polly 2043
Emerson, ___ (Miss) 1358
Emerson, Alethea 9470
Emerson, Esther Ann 8682
Emerson, Harriet 2847
Emerson, Joseph 2899
Emery, Amelia 2342
Emery, Eliza 8336
Emery, Sarah 4462
Emmerson, Sally 7524
Emmons, Esther 2836
Emmons, George (Rev.) 2904
Emmonsm Hannah 1527
Emory, Angeline 2213
Emott, ___ (Judge) 2905
Empie, Demaries D. 10104
Emson, Elizabeth 9159
Engelbrecht, ___ (Mr.) 2907
Englehart, Mary Ann 7062
English, Charles 2908
English, Fanny 5921
Ensign, Lorinda 4370
Ensign, William 739
Ensworth, A. (Dr.) 8084
Ensworth, Azel (Dr.) 1441, 5859
Ensworth, Eliza 5859
Ensworth, Sally 8084
Ensworth, Sophronia 1441
Ervin, Isabel 8823

Erwin, Adeline 2750
Erwin, F. E. (Gen.) 2920, 2922
Erwin, Mary 9691
Estelow, Betsey 86
Evans, Ann Eliza 2778
Evans, David E. 2932, 2936
Evans, Deborah 9453
Evans, Harriet (Mrs.) 136
Evans, Hetty M. 8774
Evans, Mary Ann H. 8713
Evans, Septimus 8766, 8774
Everess, Olive 1170
Everett, Eliza 7711
Everingham, Mary 4696
Everitt, Gertrude 6756
Everitt, Richard 6756
Everts, Mary 9120
Evertson, Cornelia 3849
Evertson, G. B. (Mr.) 3849
Ewing, Sarah (Mrs.) 3913
Eyneuf, Ann 1397
Fabrique, Clarinda 6690
Fairbank, Patty 1544
Fairbanks, Eleazer 2947
Fairbanks, Harriet S. 544
Fairbanks, Ira (Rev.) 2710, 4344
Fairbanks, Joshua F. 544
Fairbanks, Lucina 2710
Fairbanks, Miranda 2376
Fairbanks, Phebe 8103
Fairbanks, Sarah 4344, 5216
Fairchild, Lydia 467
Fairchild, Sarah T. 359
Fairfield, Lydia 6245
Falls, Louise 1676
Fanning, Phineas 2958
Fanno, Fanny 3667
Farely, Millins 2959
Farewell, Sophronia 1517
Fargo, Emeline 542
Farley, Bridget (Mrs.) 5531
Farnham, Aaron (Deacon) 2968
Farnham, Caleb 2966
Farnham, Catharine F. 8333
Farr, Clarinda 1077
Faugkenburgh, Harriet 4905
Faulkner, Catharine 8029
Faulkner, J. W. 2974
Faulkner, John 2975
Faulkner, William 8029
Fay, Europe (Mr.) 2981
Fay, Helen W. 3208
Fay, Hopey 5502
Fay, Louisa 96
Fay, Roxana 2871
Featherly, Henry 2987
Featherly, Peter 2986
Feesler, Maru 4819
Fegals, Mary Ann 9999
Felch, Angeline 4538
Fellows, Eunice 7007
Fenton, Caroline M. 7990
Fenton, J. S. 1801
Fenton, Joseph S. 2996, 7400
Fenton, Julia A. 1801
Fenton, Lavinia B. 7400
Fenton, Mary Ann 3995
Fenton, R. E. 2998
Fenton, R. F. (Mr.) 2997, 3005, 3006
Fenton, William H. 3004, 7990
Ferguson, Precilla 8439
Ferre, Gideon 3009
Ferrell, Susan 3962
Ferris, Esther Ann 6750
Ferris, James 3015
Ferris, James C. 3011
Fessendon, Ruthanny 1392

Field, Calvin 3025
Field, Clary 2351
Field, David 3023, 3024, 3028
Field, Deborah 2563
Field, Peter 2563
Field, Phila 3030
Field, Philena 6050
Fields, Eliza 9031
Fields, Oliver 3032
Fiero, Magdalena 2817
Fiero, Mary Ann 3838
Fiero, William 2817
Fife, Julia 8889
Fillemore, B. 9125
Fillemore, D. (Mr.) 9125
Fillmore, Adeline 3499
Fillmore, Hannah E. 8700
Fillmore, Mary 3496
Filmore, Lucretia 6388
Filmore, Phebe 5815
Finch, Daniel G. 3043, 3044, 3045
Finch, Hannah C. 7878
Finch, Susan 6008
Finley, Lucina 6130
Finn, E. (Miss) 6181
Finney, Amanda 144
Fish, Cyrus 3051
Fish, Dolly 4511,
Fish, E. H. (Mr.) 3057
Fish, Isaac 734
Fish, Jane 3657
Fish, Libbeus 3058
Fish, Mary A. 7079
Fish, Mary E. 734
Fish, Oravilla 9554
Fish, Susan 2118
Fish, Susan H. 8055
Fish, Walter 3657
Fisher, Adam 3064, 6332
Fisher, Amanda 4348
Fisher, Catharine 5414
Fisher, Christina A. 1714
Fisher, Elizabeth 653
Fisher, George 3069
Fisher, Henry 3066
Fisher, Lucy 6375
Fisher, Martha 3651
Fisher, Matilda 2406
Fisher, Rachael 6332
Fisher, Rebecca 1323
Fisher, Samuel 2674
Fisk, Ellen M. 902
Fisk, Hannah 173
Fisk, Sally 6346
Fitch, Clark 3087
Fitch, Elizabeth A. 4437
Fitzgerald, Elizabeth 1799
Fitzhugh, Bennett C. 3097
Fitzhugh, Eliza 4513
Fitzhugh, F. (Col.) 322
Fitzhugh, Maria 2843
Fitzhugh, Peregrine 2843, 3099, 4513
Fitzhugh, Rebecca 322
Fitz-Simmons, Anna 6393
Flagg, Rhoda (Mrs.) 3102
Flagler, Dorcas 818
Flagler, Isaac (Rev.) 3103
Fleming, Almira 8412
Fleming, Elsy 4757
Fletcher, A. 5541
Fletcher A. (Mr.) 3109, 4047, 8862
Fletcher, Adolphus 3110
Fletcher, E. (Mr.) 6086
Fletcher, Eleazer 3108, 3111
Fletcher, Lucy 4047
Fletcher, Susan 8862

Fletcher, Sylvia 6073
Flint, Amanda 8287, 9633
Flint, John 3116
Flint, Lavina 4939
Flint, Melinda 4361
Flint, Sally 2502, 3116
Flower, Hannah (Mrs.) 768
Flower, Martha A. 1778
Floyd, Catharine 8093
Floyd, William (Gen.) 3117
Fluent, Elizabeth 8252
Fluent, Fanny 3119
Fluent, Joseph 3119
Fluent, Lucy E. 1995
Fluent, Susan 1489
Follett, Frederick 3130
Follett, Nancy K. 7871
Follett, Nathan 5286
-(Entry purposely deleted)-
Folwell, Joseph 3931
Folwell, Rachael 3931
Foot, Ann Maria 8954
Foot, Charles 8954
Foot, Isaac 3141
Foot, Jane 9293
Foot, Justin 3141
Foot, Louisa 9343
Foote, E. T. (Mr.) 2215, 3142, 3147
Foote, Mary Ann 2215
Foote, Mary D. 3792
Foote, Samuel 3147
Foote, Sedate 2144
Forbes, Mary Ann 9090
Forbs, Mary 4381
Forbush, Elizabeth 534
Forbush, Sarah 5162
Force, Elizabeth 1150
Force, Hannah 3407
Ford, Anna 916
Ford, Augustus 3976
Ford, Cornelia 7556
Ford, Dyer 3162
Ford, Eli 3158
Ford, Emily C. 8115
Ford, James 3165, 8115
Ford, Mahlan 3167
Ford, Nancy 3976
Ford, Phineas 916
Ford, Sarah 2540
Ford, Vilena 7854
Forman, Delia 10078
Forsyth, Abba J. 2749
Fort, Alida 5631
Foster, Alcina 9105
Foster, Adeline 9050
Foster, Almira 550
Foster, Augusta 505
Foster, Catharine 6786
Foster, Cyrus 3203, 5867, 6548, 8411
Foster, Electa 1032
Foster, Emeline M. 5867
Foster, Geter 3185
Foster, Harriet 6507
Foster, Isaac 2981
Foster, Jesse 3200
Foster, Jeter 3204
Foster, Jonathan 3183
Foster, Lemuel 9380
Foster, Maria 8411
Foster, Maria W. 8901
Foster, Mary Jane 6548
Foster, Miranda 1326
Foster, R. H. (Mr.) 3207
Foster, Therese 4393
Foster, Zenas 3184
Fotsinger, Lavina 3320
Fowle, Maria 6968

Fowle, Mary Ann 4087
Fowler, Horace 3214
Fowler, John W. 3210, 3211, 3213, 3216
Fowler, Sarah M. 9560
Fowler, William 9560
Fox, Betsey 2952
Fox, Catharine 3465
Fox, Harriet 4950
Fox, Sylva 1727
Francis, Annis H. 9169
Frank, Emma D. 14
Frank, Harriet E. 8620
Frank, John 3229, 8620
Frank, Nicholas 3230
Frank, Polly 2394
Frank, William 14
Franklin, Arlow 2734
Franklin, Benjamin 1528
Franklin, Fanny S. 1830
Franklin, Hannah 2079
Franklin, Mary 572
Franklin, Ruth 5297
Frants, Margaret 4708
Frantz, Elizabeth 8045
Frasier, Joel 3240
Frazeer, Hester 8674
Frazier, Julia Ann 10020
Freelock, Betsey 7516
Freeman, Agnes 7306
Freeman, Dinah 1147
Freeman, E. (Mr.) 7025
Freeman, Elmer 3245
Freeman, Mahala P. 6142
Freeman, Maria 7024
Freeman, Percey 3971
Freeman, Thomas 3971
French, Charlotte J. 1289
French, John 3258
French, Lyda 7690
French, Maria 4445
French, Mary 4576
French, Nathaniel, Jr. 3256
French, Samuel 3253, 3259
Frew, Jane 3002
Frew, John 3002
Frisbee, Eliza G. 1814
Frisbee, Fidelia 9696
Frisbie, Eliza Ann 5318
Frost, Eliza M. 669
Frost, Jacob 3270
Frushour, Catharine 7308
*Frushour, Eliza 7023
Fuller, Amasa 3282
Fuller, Mary 5091
Fuller, Orrin J. 2674
Fuller, Sarah 2741
Fullington, Editha (Mrs.) 2141
Fulton, Polly 5307
Fulton, Ruth 3719
Fulton, Susan 8281
Fulton, Elizabeth 7261
Gage, Betsey 6333
Gage, Elizabeth 3366
Gage, Martin 3297
Gage, Nancy 7772
Gager, Maria 7090
Gain, Hugh 7547
Gaine, Hugh 3299
Gaines, Bathsheba 2983
Gaines, Sophronia 3895
Gale, Betsey 8154
Gallagher, ___ (Mrs.) 3303
Galloway, Archer 3310
Galloway, Emily 4204
Galloway, Julia A. 126
Galloway, Mary 4352
Galloway, Polly 4422
Galusha, Almira E. 808
* Fuller, ___ (Mr.) 2674

Gamage, William (Dr.) 3316
Gannet, Ballona 566
Gannet, Ellet 4266
Gannett, Abigail 6746
Gannett, Birenus 8649
Gannett, Ruth 8320
Gansevoort, Conrad 3326
Gansevoort, John 3329, 4492
Gansevoort, John R. 3326
Gansevoort, Mary L. 4492
Ganson, Amanda L. 3332
Ganson, Eliza Ann 1496
Ganson, H. (Dr.) 3332
Ganson, James 1496, 9611
Gantly, Margaret 5291
Gardner, Abigail 458
Gardner, Almira 764
Gardner, Angelina 5126
Gardner, Cordelia 9946
Gardner, Eliza 5890
Gardner, Elizabeth 205
Gardner, Emily A. 329
Gardner, Hannah A. 6309
Gardner, Henry 3344
Gardner, Isaac 9946
Gardner, Isaac (Mrs.) 1518
Gardner, Louisa 8671
Garner, Lucinda 584
Gardner, Mary 130
Gardner, Minerva 6423
Gardner, Nancy 8724
Garner, P. (Col.) 3349
Gardner, Phoebe 918
Gardner, Robert T. 3337, 3346
Gardner, Sally 5193, 5303
Garez, ___ (Mr.) 3354
Garfield, ___ (Mr.) 3358
Garfield, Joseph 3357, 3359
Garfield, Lydia 2452
Garfield, Samuel 3357
Garlock, Maria 2687
Garner, Mary 2270
Garret, Sophrona (Mrs.) 9747
Garrison, Catharine 1678
Garrison, Deborah Ann 5521
Garrison, Lavina 650
Garrison, William 650
Gates, Aaron 6705
Gates, Amos 3376
Gates, Horatio 3390
Gates, S. M. (Mr.) 3382
Gates, Solomon 3393
Gates, Susan 2547
Gault, Maria 6359
Gay, William 3398
Gaylord, Sylvia 3698
Gee, ___ (Mrs.) 6967
Geer, Achsa 8644
Geer, Samuel F. (Capt.) 1671
Gelston, David 3403
Genung, Abigail 947
Genung, Ann 2497
Genung, Fanny 5134
George, Betsey (Mrs.) 5587
Geralaman, Eliza Ann 4823
Gere, Clorinda 1971
Gere, Eliza 3740
Gere, Luther 3740
German, Obediah 3408
Germond, Mary T. 531
Gerry, Charlotte 7493
Gibbons, Amelia 8477
Gibbons, James 8477
Gibbs, Anson 3414
Gibbs, C. D. 3415
Gibbs, Julia A. 3415
Gibbs, Maria 8549
Gibbs, Mary 6096
Gibbs, Mary Ann 203

Gibbs, Sarah 3113
Gibbs, Tryphena 6573
Giberson, Ann 3945
Gibs, Catharine Ann 7388
Gibson, ___ (Mrs.) 8049
Gibson, Caroline G. 8924
Gibson, Jane 2078
Gibson, Mary 1868
Gibson, Phebe Maria 4158
Giffing, William 3422
Gifford, Alice 753
Gifford, Deborah 42
Gifford, Jeremiah 3425
Gifford, Mary R. 3659
Gifford, Sarah Ann 6905
Gifford, Ruth E. 5003
Gilbert, Clarissa 2265
Gilbert, Fanny 4261
Gilbert, Franklin 3435
Gilbert, J. H. (Mr.) 3440, 3451
Gilbert, John 3449, 3861
Gildersleeve, Mary A. 8348
Gilky, Rebecca 4363
Gill, John J. 3460
Gillet, Nancy 9543
Gillimand, Margaret 1968
Gillis, Jane 258
Gillis, Samuel 3469
Gillis, Temperance 7039
Gilmore, Emeline S. 4525
Gilmore, Lydia A. 10050
Gilmore, Maria 8917
Gilson, Rebecca 5064
Giltson, Hannah 1364
Giraud, Sarah 674
Glass, Adelia A. 978
Glass, Erastus 3480, 8159
Glass, Franklin 3476, 3481
Glass, Laura 8159
Glassby, Maria 9984
Gleason, Eelazer 3482
Gleason, Onlelia 9654
Gleason, Phebe 9481
Gleason, Rebecca 6739
Gleason, Susan 2838
Glenn, Nancy 5384
Glenn, Rhoda 3264
Glidden, Joanna 8570
Gload, John 3488
Glodsmith, Frances 9003
Glover, John 3491
Glover, Lamira 3822
Glover, Mary 797
Glover, Milly 2800
Glover, P. (Mr.) 3494
Glover, Philander 3822
Glover, Polly 9058
Glover, Rhoda 8562
Glover, Sophronia 6937
Goble, Anna M. 1926
Goble, Caty Ann 5989
Godard, M. J. 3497
Goddard, Lydia S. 8920
Goddard, Emeline 1275
Godfrey, Olive 3994
Goff, Harriet M. 714
Goff, Martha Ann 7480
Goff, Morris 3505
Goff, Nathan 3509
Goff, Russel 3513
Golding, Isaiah 3515
Goldsmith. See also
    Goldsmith.
Goldsmith, Ann 6448
Goldsmith, Caroline M. 4418
Goldsmith, F. A. (Mr.) 3516
Goldsmith, Festus 3521
Goldsmith, Temperance 8068

Goldsmith, Thomas 3520
Goldthwait, ___ (Deacon) 3523
Goldthwait, Constantine 3524
Goldthwait, Obed 3525
Goodale, Paul 6606
Goodell, ___ (Rev.) 3981
Goodell, Harriet 3981
Goodfellow, ___ (Mr.) 3535
Gooding, Roxana 6584
Goodon, Jane 8376
Goodrich, Almira 1825
Goodrich, Fanny 8618
Goodrich, J. W. 3544
Goodrich, Laura 9427
Goodrich, Rachel 1994
Goodsell, Jane 6063
Goodwin, Adeline 4955
Goodwin, Ann 8266
Goodwin, Daniel (Dr.) 8266
Goodwin, Emily C. 5884
Goodwin, H. (Mr.) 3555
Goodwin, Jane 7270
Goodwin, John (Dr.) 3345
Goodwin, L. B. (Mr.) 3556
Goodwin, Laura 7755
Goodwin, Mary B. 945
Goodwin, Nancy 9757
Goodwin, Prudence H. 9447
Goodwin, Susan 3345
Gordon, Delia M. 3565
Gordon, E. H. (Mr.) 3563, 3564
Gordon, Elijah H. 3561
Gordon, Maria 8107
Gordon, Peter 3564
Gordon, Robert 3559, 3566
Gordon, Sally Ann 7557
Gordon, William W. 3562, 3565
Gorgas, Elizabeth A. 1631
Gorgas, Joseph 1631
Gorham, Nathaniel 3571
Gorham, Rachel Maria 5835
Goss, Elizabeth 9818
Goss, Maria 184
Gould, Abigail 7132
Gould, Azel R. 3580
Gould, Catharine 2605
Gould, Charity Ann 7865
Gould, Maria E. 8137
Gould, Nancy 4484
Gould, Naomi 4573
Gould, Sophia 896
Goundry, Eliza 9528
Goundry, George 3582, 9528
Gourlay, Archibald 3584
Gouverneur, Emily 8996
Gouverneur, Nicholas 8996
Gown, Hugh W. 3587
Gragg, Francis 4096
Graham, Hellen Marr 9578
Graham, Valentine 3596
Grandee, Betsey 5803
Grandee, Fanny 7829
Grandin, Daniel 3607
Grandin, P. (Mr.) 8958
Grandin, Philip 3602, 3603, 8959
Grandin, Sarah Maria 8958
Granger, ___ (Dr.) 7483
Granger, Gideon 3614
Granger, Jane A. 8971
Granger, Mary Ann 7483
Grant, Eliza A. H. 6442
Grant, Nancy W. 1859
Grant, Stephen 1860
Graton, Parmelia 101
Graves, Abigail 141
Graves, Armenia 352
Graves, Caroline S. 5558

Graves, Charles 3620
Graves, Francis 3619
Graves, Harriet 1542
Graves, Martha P. 10094
Graves, Randall 3622
Graves, Samuel 3618
Grawbadger, Jane 3036
Gray, Clarinda Juliette 5006
Gray, D. E. (Miss) 7707
Gray, Eliza 838
Gray, Elizabeth 2676
Gray, John D. 7707
Gray, Joseph 3630
Gray, Joshua 3628
Gray, Priscilla G. 5716
Gray, Sarah 9788
Grayson, Leticia P. 6853
Green, Agnes 2659
Green, Augusta 4012
Green, Betsey 5092
Green, Byram 3653, 6227, 7432
Green, Catharine 3590
Green, Hannah 7098, 7452, 7539, 8855, 10160
Green, Huldah 9630
Green, John 3654
Green, John, Jr. 3654
Green, John W. 2659
Green, Lorany 3046
Green, Louisa 7432
Green, Lucy E. 6227
Green, Mary 1522, 3284
Green, Nancy 3450
Green, Penelope 413
Green, Samuel 3654
Green, Sarah L. 6873
Greene, Mary 4218
Greenleaf, Emily 1503
Gregg, Louisa J. 811
Gregory, Burr 4294
Gregory, Caroline E. 2111
Gregory, Margaret 4667
Gregory, Meribah 8752
Gregory, Phebe 6366
Gregory, Ralph 3663, 3668
Gregory, Stephen 3666, 3669
Gregory, Susan Ann 4294
Grieve, Walter (Gen.) 3674
Griffin, Diana 5325
Griffin, Sarah 9176
Griffith, Desire 8089
Griffith, Helen 2866
Griffith, Marietta 5571
Griffith, Thomas (Dr.) 2866
Griffiths, Griffith 3691
Griggs, Martha Ann 7195
Grimes, Parmelia 1547
Grimwood, Isaac 3694
Grinold, Levi 3696
Griswold, caroline 1163
Griswold, Eber 3697
Griswold, Hannah 4198
Griswold, Louisa 10092
Griswold, Mary L. 2538
Griswold, Sally 393, 4013
Griswould, Olive S. 791
Grosvenor, ___ (Capt.) 6879
Grosvenor, Marcia 5775
Grosvenor, Sarah S. 6879
Grosvenor, Serena (Mrs.) 5011
Grosvenor, Thomas P. 3709
Grout, Martin C. 3713
Grout, Salmon 3715
Grove, Catherine 8155
Grow, Nancy 1957
Gruning, Deborah 5638
Guernsey, James K. 3727
Guernsey, Louisa M. 4332
Guest, Richard 3731

Guild, Silas 5342
Guille, ___ (Mrs.) 3733
Guion, Cornelia M. 5621
Gulick, Elizabeth 9979
Gunn, Clarissa A. 8530
Gunn, Lineus 8530
Gusolus, Lombert V. 3742
Guptyl, Lucia 1858
Gurley, Eliza 6816
Gurlinghouse, Jane 1987
Gurney, Thomas W. 3647
Gutman, Rebecca 8479
Guyon, Elijah 3751
Hadden, Sybia 7859
Hadley, James 3756
Hagaman, Catharine 364
Hager, Jerusha 1516
Hagoffin, Hannah 8422
Haig, Harriet 7704
Haight, Brnjamin 3766
Haight, Fletcher M. 3762
Haight, Hannah 4480
Haight, Hannah M. 4171
Haight, Jemima 5667
Haight, Lucina A. (Mrs.) 3278
Haight, Margaret 9586
Haight, Phebe 3294
Haight, S. S. (Gen.) 9586
Haight, Samuel S. 4171, 4176
Hale, Charlotte 2036
Hale, Danford 3773
Hale, Harriet 5945
Hale, Horace 3774
Halenbake, Isaac B. 3775
Hall, ___ (Gen.) 3794
Hall, ___ (Maj. Gen.) 2300, 3835
Hall, ___ (Mrs.) 5999
Hall, A. B. 3776
Hall, Amanda 2460
Hall, Amasa 3815
Hall, Ambrose 3790, 3833, 4787, 4788, 5252
Hall, Augustus 1695
Hall, Austin 3783
Hall, C. Lasira (Miss) 356
Hall, Caroline 7040
Hall, Catharine 4787, 9904
Hall, Charlotte 3534
Hall, Clarissa 4788
Hall, Cornelia J. 5494
Hall, Edward 3805
Hall, Elmira 3808
Hall, F. A. (Mr.) 3782
Hall, Hannah 8627
Hall, Harriet 8086, 8998
Hall, J. A. 3819
Hall, James 7367, 7566
Hall, Jane 7566
Hall, John 3795
Hall, Jonathan 3820
Hall, Joseph 3793, 3825, 3827, 3837
Hall, Lydia 1074, 6211
Hall, Maria 463
Hall, Marinda 6401
Hall, Mary 695, 1334, 7367, 9718
Hall, Mary Ann 3232
Hall, Mary M. 5252
Hall, Moses 3777, 8998
Hall, Nancy (Mrs.) 7417
Hall, Olive M. 7872
Hall, Philo 3779
Hall, Rhoda H. 3783
Hall, Richmond 3493
Hall, Sally 6191
Hall, Sophia 7936
Hall, Submit M. 7474

Hall, Timothy 3817, 5494
Hall, William (Capt.) 2037, 3778
Hall, William 3791, 3813
Halladay, ___ (Miss) 7155
Hallett, Catharine 7167
Hallett, Clarissa 3755
Hallett, Jacob W. 3841, 3844
Hallett, Maria M. 7479
Hallock, Martha T. 2954
Hallock, Mary P. 138
Hallock, Nancy 1087
Halsey, Loventia 3512
Halstead, Mary Ann 1121
Halsted, Robert 3854
Hamilton, Daniel 3859
Hamilton, Jane 577
Hamilton, John 3860
Hamilton, Maranda 6233
Hamilton, Rebecca 50
Hamilton, Sally 1257
Hamilton, Samuel 3861
Hamilton, Sarah H. 1140
Hamilton, William 1140
Hamlin, Hester 5533
Hamlin, Sophia 3799
Hamlin, William B. 3863
Hammel, Betsey 5940
Hammon, Ester 2054
Hammon, Sophronia 4523
Hammond, Betsey 2431
Hammond, Catharine 371
Hammond, Charles G. 3868
Hammond, Elizabeth 5059
Hammond, Jacob 3872
Hammond, Joseph 3867, 3880
Hammond, Lazarus 3881, 3883
Hammond, Minerva 2977
Hammond, Polly 10093
Hammond, Rachel 5299
Hammond, Reuben 3865
Hammond, Samuel 3873
Hammond, Samuel H. 3866
Hammond, Sarah 1851
Hanchet, J. W. (Dr.) 3888
Hanchett, Clarinda 9769
Hanchett, Melinda 7987
Hanchett, Zacheus 7987
Hand, Abner 3889
Hand, Mary Elizabeth 5320
Handley, Elizabeth 3703
Handley, William 3703, 3892
Handy, Cordelia A. 1509
Handy, Jairus (Elder) 3893
Hanes, Maria 4992
Hanford, Prua 8308
Hanks, ___ (young male) 3898
Hanks, Elisha 3783
Hanks, John 3898
Hanks, Rosilla 3510
Hanna, Polly 9599
Hanna, William 3902
Hanney, Nancy 5608
Hannibal, Ellen 3079
Hanson, ___ (Judge) 3712
Hanson, Alexander C. 3709
Hapgood, Jane 9603
Hard, N. P. (Mr.) 3908
Hardenbrook, Elcy 7747
Hardenburgh, John L. 3909
Harding, Julia 9020
Harding, Nancy 4524
Harding, Sally 2137, 6127
Harding, Theresa R. 3723
Harding, Mary 9448
Hargen, Mary 3616
Haring, Lucinda 5432
Harman, Philip 3915
Harmon, Delilah 8607

Harmon, Jemima 5038
Harmon, Martha (Mrs.) 334
Harmsley, Henrietta 5788
Harper, Betsey 6930
Harringdeen, Mercy 9817
Harrington, Amelia 2135
Harrington, Sally Ann 9916
Harrington, Serepta 5047
Harris, Abigail 4588
Harris, Betsey 6843
Harris, Chloe 5147
Harris, Christiana 2713
Harris, Cynthia 4660
Harris, Elizabeth 6330
Harris, Jacobus 2713
Harris, John 6842, 6843
Harris, Lucinda 3928
Harris, Lucy 2561
Harris, Martin 3936
Harris, Mary 3977
Harris, Mary K. 5897
Harris, Mary R. 5897
Harris, Melissa 5167
Harris, Peter H. 3922
Harris, Polly 1863, 4224
Harris, Roxcenia (Mrs.) 1980
Harrison, Betsey 9653
Harrison, Eunice 1818
Harrison, James 3942
Harrison, Ruth Aramantha 4123
Harrower, B. (Mr.) 3946
Harrower, G. T. (Mr.) 3948
Harrower, Levi B. 3947
Hart, ___ (Gen.) 8403
Hart, ___ (Mrs.) 8764
Hart, Abby L. 8703
Hart, Adelia 3062
Hart, Ann Elizabeth 6176
Hart, Ann M. 3800
Hart, Cornelia C. 4947
Hart, Elisha 3800
Hart, Ephraim 3964, 4947
Hart, Harriet 5794
Hart, Ira 3950
Hart, Ira 3956
Hart. Joseph 3949
Hart, Matilda 8403
Hart, Mary E. 1026
Hart, Nancy 7256
Hart, Peter G. 1026
Hart, Roswell 3951
Hart, Sally 2550
Hart, Susan 6519
Hart, Truman 6176, 6519, 8703
Hartgrove, Clarissa 8818
Hartman, Mary M. 3967
Hartwell, Elijah 3971
Harvey, C. R. (Col.) 2869
Harvey, C. R. (Mr.) 3973, 3975
Harvey, Marcia Lorette 2869
Harvey, Sarah Artemesia 4049
Harvey, Stimpson 3974
Harvey, T. W. (Gen.) 4049
Harvey, Uziel 3979
Harwood, Calista 10111
Harwood, Eliza 525
Haskins, Eliza Ann 828
Hastings, Ann 8188
Hastings, Betsey 4002
Hastings, Cynthia 25
Hastings, Electa 3021
Hastings, Eunice 4006
Hastings, Freeman 3996
Hastings, O. (Mr.) 3997
Hastings, Seth 3998
Hatch, Laurena 2185
Hathaway, Asher 4015
Hathaway, Ebenezer 4018
Hathaway, Edward T. 4019

Hathaway, Elizabeth C. 6904
Hathaway, J. T. (Mr.) 802
Hathaway, Josiah H. 4016
Hathaway, Lucy 4115
Hathaway, Mary Jane 6368
Hathaway, Salmon 4778
Hathaway, Sophia 4778
Hathaway, Susan 9972
Hathaway, Thomas 4115, 9972
Hatheway, Elizabeth 5191
Hathorn, Ann 1807
Hatt, Hannah 7084
Hauber, Eleanor 7962
Haunsom, Delana (Mrs.) 3252
Haus, Sarah 7749
Hause, Mary Jane 2567
Hasenfrats, Jacob 4021
Haven, Elias 4026
Havens, Ann Maria 120
Havens, E. (Mr.) 4032
Havens, Elizabeth 9852
Havens, Lucretia S. 8112
Havens, Orlando 4030
Haverling, Adam 4033
Haverly, Adam 4035
Havner, Kerlander (Mrs.) 4082
Hawes, Ascenith 564
Hawfer, Deborah P. 6436
Hawkenburgh, Eliza 8681
Hawkes, Elizabeth E. 1043
Hawkins, Ann 4875
Hawkins, Caroline 6828
Hawkins, Harvey 6828
Hawkins, Marinda 7521
Hawkins, Sally 9384
Hawks, E. (Maj.) 8233
Hawks, Eleazer 4041
Hawks, Louisa 8233
Hawley, Abijah 4050
Hawley, Alpheus 2802
Hawley, Amos (Deacon) 2108
Hawley, Asenith 1996
Hawley, Betsey 5936
Hawley, Betsey 9790
Hawley, Comfort 4054, 4055
Hawley, Elizabeth 1204
Hawley, Elizabeth L. 2802
Hawley, Elizabeth (Mrs.) 4061
Hawley, John B. 4051
Hawley, Moses 4062
Hawley, Phebe 3180
Hawley, Sarah 6141
Hawser, Lucretia 5597
Hayden, Clarissa 6468
Hayden, Mary 1177, 3771
Hayden, Mary Ann 2777
Hayden, Minerva 8625
Hayden, Strong 2777
Hayes, Elizabeth A. 861
Hayes, Jonathan 6004
Hayes, Martha 6004
Hayes, P. Jr. (Dr.) 4080
Haynes, Mary 843
Haynes, Nathan 843
Hayt, Sally Ann 2399
Hayward, Asa 4089
Hayward, Matilda 4098
Hazard, Nancy 236
Hazeltine, Abner 4108
Hazeltine, Charlotte 8251
Hazeltine, Daniel 4104
Hazeltine, Daniel 6908
Hazeltine, Laban (Dr.) 4109
Hazeltine, Pardon 4103
Hazeltine, Susanna 6908
Hazen, Elizabeth 2678
Hazzard, Phebe Ann 2134
Heacock, Mahala 7709
Heacock, Sarah 8635

Heacox, W. B. (Mr.) 4111
Head, Mary 7234
Healy, Nathaniel 4114
Heartwell, Hannah 8272
Heath, Elmira 1970
Heath, J. C. (Mr.) 4119
Heath, Pamelia 6524
Hebard, Clara Priscilla 9990
Hecox, Polly 2761
Hecox, Sophia 2618
Hedger, Betsey 3925
Hellar, Mary 5744
Hellar, Michael 5744
Helm, ___ (Capt.) 9514
Hemings, John 4132
Hemings, John 4133
Hemiup, John 4132
Hemiup, John 4133
Hempstead, Elisha 4135
Hempstead, Sally Ann 10033
Hempsted, Ann 2933
Hendee. See, possibly,
    Hendree also.
Hendee, ___ 681
Hendee, Alva 4140
Hendee, Daniel 4142
Henderson, Eliza Ann 10067
Henderson, Elizabeth 5272
Henderson, Maria 4799
Hendree. See, possibly,
    Hendee also.
Hendree, John, Jr. 2674
Hendricks, Sally 311
Hendrix, Nelle 2243
Hendryx, Jane Ann 7961
Henion, ___ (Mr.) 2911
Henion, David J. 4150
Henion, Henry 4153
Henion, John 4152
Henion, Susan 5108
Henison, Elizabeth 3304
Henman, Eunice 1322
Henries, Hannah 875
Henman, C. W. 2346
Henry, Catharine 4472
Henry, Charles W. 4157
Henry, Elizabeth 9342
Henry, Hannah 433
Henry, Roxana 4810
Henshaw, Madison 4167
Henshaw, Nathaniel 8793
Henyon, Catharine 2912
Hepburn, Harriet Jane 456
Hequembourg, William Charles
    4834
Hequembourg, Susan C. 4834
Herbert, Elizabeth 1582
Herrick, Arthur 4176
Herrington, Alida 7808
Herrington, Ann 952
Hersey, Charlotte 9542
Hertell, John C. 4181
Hertell, Thomas 10139
Heslop, John 4182
Heslop, John, Sr. 4184
Hess, Alexander 4186, 4188
Hess, Martha T. 4186, 4188
Hess, Mary Ann 5910
Hewett, Olive 4191
Hibban, ___ (Mrs.) 6835
Hibbard, Ann (Mrs.) 4112
Hibbard, Bethia 5566
Hibbard, Daniel 5566
Hibbard, 5161
Hickmott, Mary H. 6416
Hickox, William B. 4206
Hicks, Catherine 5768
Hicks, Ellen 35
Hicks, Hannah 2147

Hicks, Jane 3249
Hicks, Joshua 4209
Hicks, Maria 1579
Hicks, Mary E. 1630
Hicks, Sally 4118
Hicks, Zilpha 6829
Higby, Almira H. 10039
Higby, E. (Mr.) 6892
Higby, Marian 6892
Higby, Sylvester 4223
Higday, George 4228
Higgins, David 4230
Higgins, Harriet 3688
Higgins, Harriett E. 7385
Higgins, James 4235
Higgins, John D. (Dr.) 2615,
    4229
Hight, Hannah 8585
Hildreth, Phebe J. 3601
Hildreth, Ruth 2303
Hildreth, Susan 4240
Hildruth, Amanda 1249
Hill, Almira 8624
Hill, Amanda 9492
Hill, Ann M. 2097
Hill, Caroline 8908
Hill, Charlotte 2309
Hill, David 4259
Hill, Diantha A. 8172
Hill, Elijah 4260
Hill, Elsworth 4247
Hill, Emeline W. 4219
Hill, Emily 8624
Hill, Ephraim 4264
Hill, Estehler 7685
Hill, Ira 4256
Hill, Loisa 1159
Hill, Rebecca 8398
Hill, Sabrina 3656
Hill, Stephen 4244
Hill, Susan 1692
Hill, Susanna 8499
Hill, Richard 4271
Hillman, Ann Maria 4804
Hillman, John (Dr.) 4804
Hillman, Mary 2696
Hills, Betsy C. 8207
Hilton, Angeline 9749
Hilton, Betsey E. 1066
Himrod, Elnor 654
Hinckley, Betsey 5089
Hinckley, Elizabeth 9845
Hinckley, Juliana 798
Hinds, Mary 470
Hinds, Salomi 5172
Hine, Laura 998
Hine, Mary 9620
Hine, Phebe C. 4858
Hinkley, James 4283
Hinman, Calista 4285
Hinman, Elihu 4285
Hinman, Harris 4284
Hinman, James 2674
Hinsdill, Jeanette 7934
Hitchcock, Elizabeth 8278
Hitchcock, Harmony 1429
Hitchcock, Lucy E. 5232
Hoadly, Lusina 9719
Hoag, Anna (Mrs.) 2730
Hoag, Matilda 105
Hoag, Mary Ann 7075
Hoag, Sarah 5845
Hoage, Hannah 5105
Hoags, Sarah 9798
Hoam, Altangi 5562
Hoam, Chi Altangi 5562
Hoar, Abby 4301
Hoar, Leonard 4301
Hoar, Sarah (Mrs.) 2320

Hobart, ___ (Bishop) 4729
Hobart, Rebecca S. 4729
Hobart, Sarah B. 1612
Hocum, Lucinda 7908
Hodge, Lucy 863
-(Entry purposely deleted)-
Hoe, Caroline A. 2890
Hoe, Robert 2890
Hoes, Susan Cornelia 8113
Hoffman, Catharine Ann 3150
Hoffman, H. S. (Mr.) 2674
Hoffman, J. O. (Mr.) 9273
Hoffman, Sophia 8248
Hogarth, ___ (Mr.) 4323
Hogarth, Jane 2469
Hogarth, John 2469
Hogarth, John S. 4320
Hogarth, Richard 4318, 4319,
    4321
Hogarth, Isabella 1211
Hoit, Rebecca 7485
Holbrook, George B. 4333
Holcomb, Annis 9088
Holcomb, Eliza 9393
Holcomb, Rhoda 1849
Holden, Delia 4337
Holden, Lavina 5241
Holden, Marvin 4334, 4335,
    4336
Holden, Nancy 10031
Holden, Samuel C. 4337
Holdridge, Jemima 9588
Holladay, E. G. (Mr.) 4341
Hollenback, Delia 343
Hollenbeck, Margaret 6422
Hollett, Hannah 7559
Hollett, Peregrine 1230,
    4343
Hollett, Sarah Ann 1230
Holley, Clarissa G. 619
Holley, Elizabeth D. 5056
Holley, Myron (Hon.) 619,
    4345
Holliday, Harvey 4349
Holling, Mary 2960
Hollister, H. R. (Mr.) 4354
Hollister, Sally 5581
Holloway, Rebecca 9518
Holman, Adeline 9370
Holman, Sanford 4359
Holman, Sullivan 4360
Holmes, Cyrenius 1618
Holmes, Eunice 5653
Holmes, Reuben 4368
Holmes, Ruth 480
Holmes, Simeon 3018
Holmes, Sophronia 3018
Holmes, Sylvia (Mrs.) 1618
Holt, Mary Ann 4821
Holton, Minerva L. 5420
Homan, ___ (Miss) 5668
Hone, Catharine 1839
Hone, John 1839
Hood, Benjamin 4380
Hoofstater, Margaret 4121
Hooker, ___ (Maj.) 4383
Hooker, Ann 7528
Hooker, Dolly 8694
Hooper, Caroline 4718
Hooper, Pontiac 4718
Hooper, Robert 4385
Hoover, Katharine 6289
Hopkins, ___ (Mr.) 5976
Hopkins, Amanda 7397
Hopkins, Charlotte A. 612
Hopkins, Elias 4388, 7397
Hopkins, Emily H. 4071
Hopkins, Esther 2782
Hopkins, Eunice 1256

Hopkins, Harriet 4622
Hopkins, Lucinda 1130
Hopkins, Samuel M. (Mrs.)
    7443
Hopkinson, Jane 772
Hornell, ___ry (Miss) 6256
Hornell, Ann 3966
Hornell, George 4409
Horner, Sally M. 542
Hortman, Margaret 8191
Horton, Cynthia 6326
Horton, Electa 2161
Horton, Elenor 9237
Horton, Eliah 4413
Horton, Elizabeth 4714
Horton, Joseph 4421
Horton, Mariah 4417
Horton, Mary 7381
Horton, Nathan 4412
Horton, Samuel T. 4420, 6326
Hortsen, Mary E. 8768
Hortsen, W. (Dr.) 8768
Hortsen, Wm. (Dr.) 4423,
    4424
Hosford, Sally 4792
Hosier, Polly 6447
Hoskins, Charles 4430
Hoskins, Eliza J. 1148
Hosmer, A. (Mr.) 8511
Hosmer, Sarah E. 8511
Hostater, Adam 4436
Hotchkin, Beriah 9262
Hotchkin, James H. (Rev.)1614
Hotchkin, John D. 4438
Hotchkin, Thankful 6991
Hotchkiss, Archibald 4446
Hotchkiss C. (Mrs.) 8516
Hotchkiss, David 4447
Hotchkiss, Lavinia 6367
Hotlet, Peregrine 4449
Houch, Caroline 9949
Hough, Polly 1712
Houghton, Clarissa 9
Houghton, Martha R. 9698
Houghton, Nehemiah 4459
Houghteling, James (Dr.) 4456
Hover, Agnes 9618
Houselander, Catherine (Mrs.)
    4768
Houselander, Mary 4768
Houselander, Nicholas 4768
Houselander, Susan 4768
How, John 4466
How, Maria 10103
How, Rhoda 8505
Howard, Amanda 5029
Howard, Cordelia 5389
Howard, Harriet A. 9217
Howard, Mary 8715
Howard, Ruth Ann 6769
Howard, Thomas 4470
Howe, ___ (Dr.) 6788
Howe, Aurelia Elizabeth 7107
Howe, Caroline Matilda 5754
Howe, Eliza 8229
Howe, Eunice 6788
Howe, Helen 5275
Howe, Mary Y. 3401
Howe, Susan 3812
Howell, ___ (Mrs.) 3851
Howell, Charles 4501
Howell, Gilbert 4489
Howell, Hugh 4498
Howell, Isaac 4496
Howell, Jane E. 4732
Howell, Mariah 4406
Howell, Mary Ann 1708
Howell, N. W. 4732
Howell, Nathaniel W. 4494

Howell, Phebe 7178
Howell, R. (Rev.) 6935
Howell, William 4487
Howell, Zuba 8970
Howes, Electa 3728
Howes, Olive 9898
Howland, Annie C. 9415
Howland, Benjamin 4507
Howland, David 7867
Howland, Emily 9326
Howland, Lois P. 10082
Howland, Lydia Elmira 7867
Howland, Maria 2727
Howland, Mary 1201
-(Entry purposely deleted)-
Howley, Zilpha 611
Hoxter, Harriet 196
Hoyt, ___ (Dr.) 4522
Hoyt, Amanda 1664
Hoyt, Ann 3355
Hoyt, Anna 2935
Hoyt, D. D. (Dr.) 4527
Hoyt, Joseph 4521
Hoyt, Julia Ann 4601
Hoyt, Minot 4519
Hoyt, R. H. (Dr.) 4526
Hoyt, Sally 606
Hoyt, Sarah 4519
Hoyt, Sarah E. 2856
Hubbard, Almira 3163
Hubbard, Catherine 4835
Hubbard, Charlotte 5895
Hubbard, Harriet (Mrs.) 1184
Hubbard, J. (Mr.) 7302
Hubbard, Josiah 4534
Hubbard, Julia 9166
Hubbard, Julia Ann 7302
Hubbard, Martha 3576
Hubbard, Patrick 4541
Hubbard, Sarah Maria 3072
Hubbell, Curtis 4543
Hubbell, Frances 766
Hubbell, James (Dr.) 4552
Hubbell L. (Rev.) 4548, 9340
Hubbell, Mary H. 3846
Hubbell, Nehemiah 4546
Hubbell, W. S. (Mr.) 3846
Hubbell, Walter 4551
Hubbell, William S. 4544
Hubbell, William S. 4549
Hudson, Amilia 5283
Hudson, David 4555, 4566
Hudson, David, Sr. 4560
Hudson, Henry 4557, 5283
Hudson, Sally 5282
Huested, Tamma 2910
Huff, Hannah 314
Hufman, Phebe 6075
Huggins, ___ (widow) 2470
Huggins, Almira R. 3831
Huggins, Laura 5610
Huggins, Zadock 3831
Hughs, Martha 8619
Hughs, Mary 6479
Hulbert, Charles 4581
Hulburt, G. B. (Mrs.) 8746
Hulett, Mary 3658
Hulett, William C. 4585
Hull, Elias 4592
Hull, Eliza 9080
Hull, Julia Knox 9683
Hull, S. P. (Mr.) 4586
Hull, William (Gen.) 9683
Hults, Polly 4307
Hultz, Rebecca 2433
Humphrey, Ann 9649
Humphrey, Emeline 3881
Humphrey, George 4602
Humphreys, A. (Mrs.) 5664

Humphreys, Adeline A. 5665
Hunn, Caroline 4611
Hunn, Samuel W. 4611
Hunt, Electa 1459
Hunt, Ezekiel 4617
Hunt, Frances 8967
Hunt, Harriet Angeline 6773
Hunt, Jane 9844
Hunt, Lydia 6158
Hunt, Susan 2475
Hunter, Catharine 4627
Hunter, Elizabeth 3617
Hunter, James 4627
Hunter, Mariah 7674
Hunter, Peter 4633
Hunter, William 4626
Huntington, Frances 2491
Huntington, George 6177
Huntington, George, Sr. 4637
Huntington, Henry 2491
Huntington, Joseph 1835
Huntington, Sally M. 4374
Huntington, Welthy 6009
Huntley, ___ (Miss) 9820
Hurd, David 4651
Hurd, Ebenezer 2082
Hurd, Harriet 2082
Hurd, Laura 848
Hurd, Lovell 4656
Hurd, Lovewell 4655
Hurd, Mary 4014
Hurd, Mary Ann 3197
Hurd, Philo 4650
Hurd, Ransom 4653
Hurd, Sarah 2194
Hurd, Thomas 848, 4646
Hurd, Thomas (Deacon) 4642
Hurd, Timothy 4014
Hurlburt, Caroline A. 2256
Hurlburt, G. H. (Dr.) 4658
Hurlburt, J. W. (Mr.) 2256
Hurlburt, Truman 4659, 4663
Hurlburt, Elizabeth 9446
Hurlbut, Hannah 5807
Hurley, Sally 2880
Hurly, Samuel 4669
Huson, Ann 8134
Huson, Nathaniel 8134
Hussey, Mary (Mrs.) 1057
Husted, Mary 1048
Huston, Ann 7484
Huston, Eliza Jane 6449
Huston, Elizabeth 2903
Huston, James 4674
Huston, John 2903
Hutchins, Rosalinda 3814
Hutchinson, Eliza 2773
Hutchinson, John 4679
Hutchinson, Luther F. 4681
Hutchinson, Polly 4305
Hutte, Ann 4147
Hyde, Betsey 8116
Hyde, Betsey 8769
Hyde, Henry (Dr.) 3306
Hyde. Lucy 8990
Hyde, John W. 4691
Hyde, Rosanna 3306
Hyde, Silas 1564
Hyde, Paris P. 4693
Ide, Cordelia A. 2995
Ide, Janette 3986
Ingall, Harriet Aliza 8339
Ingalls, Jane 1804
Igalsbee, Adna 4700
Ingalsbee, Asa 4700
Ingersol, Lydia 9632
Ingraham, Emma 3492
Inman, Calista 4286
Inslee, Susan (Mrs.) 7348

Ireland, Rachel 6636
Ireland, William 4708, 4712
Iron, Deborah 8532
Irons, Pamelia 1145
Irvine, Jane 8041
Irwin, Laura Ann 1295
Irwin, Sarah 8277
Irwin, William P. 1294
Isenhour, Michael 4722
Isenhour, Susan 5572
Ives, Joseph 4726
Ives, Nathaniel 4730
Jack, Nancy 6166
Jackson, ___ (Gen.) 6861
Jackson, ___ (Mr.) 4740
Jackson, ___ (widow) 4737
Jackson, Allida 9682
Jackson, Caroline 7158
Jackson, Catharine 9265
Jackson, Cordelia 8930
Jackson, Crus W. 4736
Jackson, D. (Gen.) 8930
Jackson, Esther 8407
Jackson, Giles 1774
Jackson, Harriet 3613
Jackson, Levi F. 4731
Jackson, Mary 1646
Jackson, Mary Ann 1493
Jackson, Mary Ann 4578
Jackson, Mary E. 4410
Jackson, Mary Elizabeth 4439
Jackson, Olive 1774
Jackson, Patty 8325
Jackson, R. C. (Mr.) 8407, 9265
Jackson, S. (Mr.) 4734
Jackson, Thomas 4744
Jackson, Z. S. (Mr.) 4439
Jackways. See also Jaquay.
Jackways, Alantha 6964
Jackways, David S. 6964
Jacobs, Nancy 6321
Jacobus, Josiah 4754
Jacobus, Sally 6826
Jagger, Ann 9458
Jagger, Jane 3939
Jagger, Prudence 537
James, Betsey 9051
James, Eleanor 5635
James, Richard 4760
Jameson, Nancy 8992
Jamison, Daniel 3751
Janon, Polly M. 3250
Jaquay. See also Jackways.
Jaquay, Harriet 2897
Jarvis, William 4770
Jaughin, John 4772
Jay, Mary 7351
Jeffers, Eunice 5035
Jeffers, Lavina 7196
Jeffres, ___ (Miss) 10083
Jeffreys, Sophia C. 7350
Jenkins, Amelia S. L. 3143
Jenkins, Elizabeth A. 457
Jenkins, Mary G. 5575
Jenkins, Mercy 5774
Jenks, Laura 4997
Jenner, Emeline 825
Jennings, Eleanor 4092
Jenny, Mercy 7038
Jephson, Maria Farquhar 8767
Jerome, H. K. (Mr.) 4785
Jessup, Henry 3196
Jessup, Henry, Jr. 4791
Jessup, Mary 3196
Jewell, Augusta 7919
Jinks, Hannah 9185
Johns, Evans (Mrs.) 5496
Johnson, A. B. (Mr.) 5795

Johnson, A. B. (Mrs.) 55
Johnson, Amos 4786
Johnson, Ann 8289
Johnson, Anna 9816
Johnson, Catharine 3914, 8612
Johnson, Charlotte 2660
Johnson, Daniel 4841
Johnson, David 4800, 4818
Johnson, Eliza 2852
Johnson, Elizabeth 7428
Johnson, Elizabeth O. 7380
Johnson, Elmira 4824
Johnson, Fidelia 9739
Johnson, Freelove 8718
Johnson, Harriet 6839
Johnson, Helen 4824
Johnson, Holley T., Jr. 4820
Johnson, J. T. (Mr.) 9487
Johnson, James T. 4815
Johnson, Jane 5730
Johnson, John 4801
Johnson, Lucia 3850
Johnson, Lucretia (Mrs.) 9487
Johnson, Luther 4849
Johnson, Mahala 4670
Johnson, Maria Juliana 4786
Johnson, Mary 164, 3000, 6090, 6223
Johnson, Mary A. 9787
Johnson, Pearl 9547, 9550
Johnson, Philena 3086
Johnson, Robert 7380
Johnson, Sally Maria 6565
Johnson, Samuel A. 4824
Johnson, William C. 4838
Johnston, Caroline 7784
Johnston, Charlotte 8192
Johnston, Eliza 4426
Johnston, Robert 7784
Jolly, Ann 4448
Jolly, Hanna Susanna 313
Jones, ___ (Mr.) 2674
Jones, Abigail 507
Jones, Albert 4870, 4897
Jones, Ann (Mrs.) 1608
Jones, Anna 2546
Jones, Benjamin 4900
Jones, Betsey S. 5203
Jones, Bidcar 4901
Jones, Catharine 1840
Jones, Edward 1907, 4860
Jones, Elizabeth 1907
Jones, Elizabeth B. 3022
Jones, Ellick 4895
Jones, Ellie (Mr.) 4899
Jones, Elvira 8550
Jones, Emily J. 4868, 4887
Jones, Ezra 6676
Jones, Grace 8740
Jones, Isaiah J. 4894
Jones, Joseph 4881
Jones, Julia Ann 6676
Jones, June 4870
Jones, Levi 4861, 4869
Jones, Lorinda 8721
Jones, Lydia 3695
Jones, Malinda 2671
Jones, Mary 1907, 2481, 9361
Jones, Mary Ann 9260, 9410
Jones, Olive 4888
Jones, Rachel 4751, 5014
Jones, Rufus 4868, 4887
Jones, Salina 10115
Jones, Sarah 4897, 6724, 9506
Jones, Sarah (Mrs.) 4877
Jones, Sarah J. 2816
Jones, Thomas (Dr.) 1840
Jones, William 4888
Jordan, Angelina 8944

Jordan, Harriet S. (Mrs.) 7836
Jourdan, Mercy 5806
Joy, Amy 9226
Joy, Hannah 4857
Joyce, Jane Ann 6869
Judd, Abigail 10098
Judd, Hannah 9409
Judson, ___ (Mr.) 4918
Judson, Elizabeth 6405
Judson, Herman 6404
Judson, Zephaniah 4921
Kall, Catherine Louisa 4994
Kall, J. K. 4994
Kane, Dorothy 1683
Kane, Elias 3417
Kane, Eliza 1173
Kane, Mary 3417
Kast, Nancy 2328
Katner, Catharine 601
Kean, Mary 8948
Keating, Margaret Van
  Rensselaer 3423
Keeler, Elizabeth 5423
Keeler, Polly 9512
Keeney, Ladoiska Philena 6253
Keeny, Aurelia 8322
Keith, Nancy T. 3132
Keith, Susannah H. 958
Kelley, Ebenezer 4942
Kelley, Mary J. 5711a
Kellogg, Eve E. 4946
Kellogg, George W. 4946
Kellogg, Jerusha 6685
Kellogg, Mary 6804
Kellogg, Mary F. 2948
Kellogg, Polly 6111, 9733
Kellogg, Samuel 4956
Kellogg, Sim eon 4944
Kellogg, T. 4962
Kellogg, Titus 2948
Kelly, Harriet 1355
Kelly, Luther 4964
Kelly, Manning (Dr.) 4965
Kelly, Mary 6452
Kelly, Mary J. 3735
Kelsey, Noah W. 4968
Kelsey, Sally 4968
Kemble, Demarius 4741
Kempshall, Jane 90
Kendal, Eliza 1205
Kendal, Lucinda 3839
Kendall, Charles 8436, 8498
Kendall, Eunice 8498
Kendall, Maria 8436
Kendall, Penelope 4971
Kendall, Salmon B. 4971
Kendig, Martin 5200
Kendig, Sarah (Mrs.) 1060
Kendrick, Maria 9411
Kennedy, Cordelia 7679
Kennedy, Henry 4975
Kennedy, John 2038
Kennedy, John P. (Dr.) 813
Kennedy, Mary Ann 813
Kennedy, Saphronia 2038
Kenny, Elizabeth 446
Kent, Alonzo 4985
Kent, Elijah 9135
Kent, Elizabeth 2253
Kent, Elmira 9135
Kent, John 4982
Kent, Mercy R. 4985
Kent, Sally 4405
Kenyon, John 4990
Kenyon, Nancy 1993
Kernan, Margaret Mary 7066
Kernan, W. E. (Miss) 7067
Kernan, William (Gen.) 7066
Ketchum, Joseph 4998

Ketchum, Martha S. 4
Ketchum, Nancy 2702
Ketchum, Rachel 2854
Keyes, Adeline 6179
Keyes, Alcey E. 4976
Keyes, Eber 5004, 5005
Keyes, Emily 8688
Keyes, Mary K. 5928
Keyes, Melissa M. 2972
Kibbe, Abigal 2084
Kibbe, Gaius 738
Kibbe, Ira 5010
Kibbe, Isaac 2084
Kibbe, Lucy T. 1611
Kibbe, Mary 712, 738
Kibbe, William 712
Kidder, C. (Rev.) 5016
Kidder, Desdemona 721
Kidder, Eliza 7994
Kidder, Ezbai 6010
Kidder, J. B. (Mr.) 5017
Kidder, Lyman 547
Kidder, Nathaniel 5018
Kidder, Olive A. 6010
Kidder, Polly (Mrs.) 5224
Kidney, Eliza 3993
Kidney, Jonathan 1730, 5020
Kies, Hannah (Mrs.) 2570
Kimball, Almira 609
Kimball, Ebenezer 5024
Kimball, Eliza 3798
Kimball, Eve 4951
Kimball, Mary 336
King, Aaron N. 5050
King, Elsey Ann 4022
King, Emily N. 4024
King, Horace 5040
King, J. S. (Elder) 4022
King, John 5028
King, John S. (Elder) 4024
King, Joshua K. 5051
King, Louisa 3916
King, Maria 8386
King, Rufus 5041, 5048
King, Samuel 3916, 5038
King, Sylvia 8187
Kingman, Milanda 6015
Kingman, Minerva 2739
Kingsbury, ___ (Mrs.) 8324
Kingsley, Achsah M. 10144
Kingsley, Minerva 5044
Kinne, Huldah 4845
Kinne, John 5070
Kinnear, Henry P. 5072
Kinner, James 5073
Kinney, D. F. 5078, 5081
Kinney, Giles 5082
Kinney, Harriet (Mrs.) 5078
Kinney, Hiram 5075
Kinney, Loiisa 3385
Kinney, Mary 2216
Kinyon, Ann 7682
Kinyon, Sally 4570
Kip, John L. 5085
Kip, Mary 4891
Kip, Mary 6160
Kup, Nicholas 4891
Kip, Samuel 6160
Kipp, Catharine 5220
Kirkland, ___ (Gen.) 4346
Kirkland, ___ (Rev.) 7802
Kirkland, Mary 4346
Kittle, Charles 2674
Klock, Jane 10010
Klock, Rosanna 2133
Knap, Lavina 2568
Knapp, Catherine 4411
Knapp, Elias 4411
Knapp, Ezra 5093

Knapp, Julia 8590
Knapp, Mary Jane 9456
Knapp, Matilda 1856
Knapp, Uretta 9123
Knickerbocker, Maria 3020
Knickerbocker, Marilla 4723
Knight, ___ (Mrs.) 9851
Knight, Eliza 226
Knight, Minerva 234
Knight, Olive 124
Knight, Samuel 5110, 5111
Knight, William 5114, 5116
Knower, Benjamin 5118, 5119
Knowles, Celista A. 3305
Knowles, Fanny F. C. 2424
Knowlton, Chester 5121
Knox, Algenia 7217
Knox, Almira 5514
Knox, Ellen Margaret 6378
Knox, John 6378
Knox, John J. 7217
Konkle, A. (Mr.) 5125
Korry, Cath 3367
Korry, Jane 3369
Kortright, Catharine 5366
Kronck, Lydia 5981
Lacey, Mary S. 5713
Lacky, Mary S. 6713
Lacy, Henry 5133
Lacy, Laura 206
Lacy, Mary 5388
La Due Clarissa F. 1405
Lafayette, Marquis de 481
Lafurge, Mary Jane 6581
Lain, Elizabeth 3271
Laing, Webster 5139
Lake, Conrad 5146
Lke, Phebe T. 834
Lakey, Abner F. 3457, 5150
Lakey, Eunice 3457
Lskey, James 5151
Lakey, Thomas 5148
Lalliet, Emma 1120
Laman, Hannah 5510
Lamb, Lucy 4532
Lamb, Oracy (Miss) 5145
Lambert, M. J. (Miss) 9766
Lambright, Ebecca 7030
Lamphear, Clarissa 4984
Lamphier, Lois 1869
Lamphier, Rhoda 2273
Lamphier, Sally 2128
Lamson, Jesse 5158
Lamson, Miles P. 5159
Lamson, N. K. 4721
Lamson, Syrena 8614
Landon, Amy 8421
Landon, Climena 6059
Landon, Jervis 6059
Landon, Nancy 4272
Lane, Betsey Ann 4416
Lane, C. (Col.) 540
Lane, David 5166
Lane, Eveline 3772
Lane, Lydia Jane 540
Lane, Sally 5080
Lang, Alpheus 5169, 5170, 5171
Langdon, ___ (Judge) 2929
Langdon, Caroline 2929
Langdon, Jane 3884
Langdon, Mary (Mrs.) 7319
Langdon, Melinda 5358
Langhorne, ___ (Mr.) 5
Langworthy, Laura 8269
Lansing, ___ (Chancellor) 5179
Lansing, D. C. (Rev.) 5178
Lapham, A. (Mr.) 5185
Lapham, Abraham 5183
Lapham, Aretus 440, 493, 5187

Lapham, Esther 3887
Lapham, Fidelia 440, 493
Lapham, Lydia P. 1282
Lapham, Lydia R. 9910
Lapham, Minerva 6484
Lapham, Narcissa 6569
Lappin, Aurelia 5257
Laraby, Mary 1352
Larned, George B. 5188
Larned, Mary S. 4607
Larowe, Minerva 5066
Larrowe, Sally 117
Larue, Sarah Jane 9906
Larzalere, Margaret 5944
Larzelere, Jacob 5194, 5195, 5196
Larzelere, Richard 5200
Larzelere, William 5197
Larzelerf, Julia Ann 2582
Lascelles, Henry 5202
Lascelles, Mary P. (Mrs.) 5202
Lasher, Sarah (Mrs.) 10147
Lathrop, Eleazer (Rev.) 5204
Lathrop, Harriet J. 7328
Lathrop, Laura Louisa 4042
Lathrop, Leonard E. 4042
Lathrop, Lydia 6054
Latimer, Laura A. 5120
Latta, Samuel 5210
Laughry, Mary 1154
Laver, Mary Ann 3387
Lawrence, ___ (Dr.) 6703
Lawrence, A. B. (Rev.) 2593
Lawrence, A. H. (Mr.) 4796
Lawrence, C. M. P. (Miss) 2593
Lawrence, Electa L. 8838
Lawrence, Eliza Mactier 4796
Lawrence, Fanny B. 1900
Lawrence, J. W. (Col.) 3789
Lawrence, Marianne 3001
Lawrence, Olive 2609
Lawrence, Percy (Miss) 8831
Lawrence, Sabra 9071
Lawrence, Sarah W. 3789
Lawson, Lawrence 5227
Lawson, Nancy 8446
Lawthorp, Thomas 5228
Lawton, D. B. (Rev.) 5229
Lawton, Sarah 8060
Lay, Charles 5230
Laycost, Eliza 5932
Leach, Aleymena 180
Leach, Belinda 7419
Leach, Lucy Ann 4227
Leach, Stephen 4228
Leake, Temperance 2635
Leavenworth, Henry 5242
Leavenworth, J. (Mr.) 5238
Leavenworth, Jared 5239
Lebo, Mary 3333
Leddick, Mary 7950
Ledyard, Mary F. 8968
Ledyard, Samuel L. 8968
Lee, Adelaide H. 3796
Lee, Amy 3531
Lee, Clarissa 6295
Lee, D. J. (Mr.) 5253
*Lee, David R. 1219
Lee, Elizabeth M. 4705
Lee, Esther 33
Lee, Eunice 3276
Lee, Francis 1775
Lee, Henry (Gen.) 5249
Lee, Johnson R. 5248
Lee, Joshua 5252
Lee, Joshua (Dr.) 820
Lee, Martha Ann 637
Lee, Mary 1775
* Lee, Eliza 1041

Lee, Mary Jane 820
Lee, Sarah Jane 1219
Lee, Sarah R. 3588
Le Fevre, Elizabeth 1189
Le Fevre, Louisa Melozina 3729
Le Furgey, Catherine 1546
Legare, Susan 5836
Legg, Pede 9509
Legget, Allen 5273
Legro, Lois M. 8290
Legro, Patience 9805
Legro, Samuel 5276
Lelan, Laura 3383
LeLand, ___ (Judge) 5280
Leland, Z. A. (Mr.) 5279
Lemm, Rouse 5281
Lemmon, Benjamin 3317
Lemmon, Sarah 3317
Lemon, Mary 3530
Lemon, Rebekah C. 8858
Lemon, Richard (Dr.) 3530
Lemoreau, Sally 2941
Lemunion, Celista 1297
Lemunion, Priscilla 1918
Lemunyon, Nancy 3958
Leonard, Allin 5289
Leonard, Alonzo 2541
Leonard, Charlotte 2541
Leonard, Cyrus 2541
Leonard, Deborah 1338
Leonard, Ischa 1067
Leonard, J. (Mr.) 5290
Leonard, Jane 6278
Leonard, Lucretia 5289
Leonard, Mary 9056
Leonard, Mary L. 8928
Leonard, Olive 2534
Leonard, P. (Deacon) 826
Leonard, Polly 7099
Leonard, Semantha 826
Leonard, Susan P. 1545
Le Roy, Caroline 9555
Le Roy, Herman 9555
Lesieur, Joanna 2815
Lester, Christian 2362
Lester, David 5298
Lester, Hannah G. 5190
Lester, Mariah 4056
Lever, Elisabeth 4451
Lewillin, Levina 9574
Lewis, ___ (Mrs.) 7
Lewis, A. (Mr.) 2913
Lewis, Amanda 5937
Lewis, Ann 407, 3604
Lewis, Barbary 9689
Lewis, Caroline 6600
Lewis, Charles P. 5324
Lewis, D. W. (Mr.) 3710, 5331
Lewis, Daniel W. 5309
Lewis, Darius I. 5323
Lewis, Electa (Mrs.) 1465
Lewis, Eliza Ann 10105
Lewis, Emeline 2913
Lewis, Emily 2277
Lewis, Helena 8525
Lewis, Jane 2926, 3073, 8712
Lewis, Joseph 2926
Lewis, Laura 149
Lewis, Mary 983, 3363
Lewis, Mary Ann (Mrs.) 8952
Lewis, Mary Frances 7902
Lewis, Nancy 2389
Lewis, Octavia J. 6648
Lewis, Ozias 983
Lewis, Patty 6651, 7891
Lewis, Rebecca Ann 6595
Lewis, Sarah Jane 8630
Lewis, Sebra (Mrs.) 3348
Lewis, Sophrona 2571

Lewis, Thomas 5315
Lewis, Uriah 5326
Libbey, Mary 4455
Liddiard, Martha 3463
Lidle, Marion 9936
Lilly, Asa 5340
*Lilly, Chloe 5341
Lilly, Enoch 5339
Lilly, Mary A. 2268
Lilly, William 5337
Lincoln, Arietta 2760
Lincoln, Eunice 3228
Lincon, Hannah 9879
Linderman, Lydia 3340
Lindsey, Elmira E. 1430
Lindsley, ___ (Judge) 3165
Lindsley, James 5349
Linkletter, Sarah 1847
Links, Diana 2486
Linn, ___ (Dr.) 2509
Linn, Susan 2508
Linn, William (Rev.) 2508
Linnell, Washington 5351
Linsley, Melissa E. 6833
Liscom, George W. 5353
Liscomb, Parker 5356
Lisenring, Sally 7301
Litell, Margaret 6290
Litle, Watie 8526
Little, William 5357
Livermore, Melinda B. 8870
Livingston ___ (Chancellor) 5370
Livingston, J. H. (Rev.) 5375
Livingston, Mary 4963
Livingston, Peter R. 5370
Livingston, Serena 2204
Livingston, Walter 5367
Lloyd, Elizabeth Ann 530
Lloyd, William R. 5375
Lobdell, Rebecca 1192
Lock, Sally 1772
Locke, Clarissa 6996
Locke, Phoebe 6969
Lockerby, Catharine 6411
Lockhart, Mary Ann 4886
Lockhart, William 4886
Lockman, Mary 9673
Lockwood, Abigail 9613
Lockwood, Diadama 160
Lockwood, Laura 3007
Logan, Lydia 4315
Logan, Nancy 9479
Logan, Polly (Mrs.) 4164
Logry, Adnes 9405
Lomiston, Ruth 1393
Long, David 5393
Long, Fanny 6875
Look. Lucy E. 9256
Look, Mary Jane 9305
Look. S. (Dr.) 9305
Look, S. B. 5399
Loom, Jane 4707
Loomis, Amanda D. 2858
Loomis, Anna 2625
Loomis, Fidelia 3557
Loomis, Gamaliel 3557
Loomis, H. N. (Dr.) 5401
Loomis, Henry 5402
Loomis, Lucinda A. 6494
Loomis, Lucy 7140
Loomis, Mary Ann 6275
Loomis, Minerva 6247
Loomis, Nathan 6246
Loomis, R. (Mr.) 5407
Loop, Christian 5413
Loop, Hannah 9069
Loop, Orpha Maria 6728
Loop. Sarah 5250
Lord, Betsey 7048
*Lilly, Emily 975

Lord, Catharine 6371
Lord, Eunice B. 222
Lord, Jerusha 6571
Lord, Louisa 8126
Lord, Melissa 8417
Lord, Sarah Ann 548
Lord, William 5416
Lorin, William 5422
Loring, Naham 5425
Loring, Roxana 8523
Loring, Sally 1817
Lothrop, J. H. (Mr.) 9657
Lothrop, Lydia 7537
-(Entry purposely deleted)-
Lott, Betsey 2921
Louck, Patience 4837
Loucks, Amanda 7965
Loucks, Phebe 9796
Lounsbury. Elizabeth 2511
Lounsbury, Sebe (Miss) 5408
Lovejoy, Sally 8042
Loveless, Polly 6597
Lovell, Eliza B. 3166
Lovell, Ovid 5445, 5446, 5447
Loverhill, Sarah 2951
Loverhill, Susan 2952
Lovett, Joseph 5452
Lovy, Mary 5711
Low, Cornelia 6240
Low, Henrietta 5034
Low, Nicholas 5034, 5453
Lowe, Rachel 5378
Lowell, Sophia 9006
Lowman, Laurinda 5595
Lowry, ___ (Mr.) 6755
Lowry, E. W. 5464
Lowry, N. A. 5463, 5464
Lowry, Nathaniel A. 5462
Lowthrop, Thomas 5465
Lucas, Meranda 4473
Luce, Caroline 8470
Luck, William 5469
Lum, Abigail 4654
Lum, Charles 5476
Lum, Daniel L. 5480
Lum, Henry 5474
Lum, Matthew 5475, 5479
Lum, Sally 717
Lumbard, Betsey 29
Lummis, Elizabeth F. 2862
Lummis, John Maxwell 5482
Lummis, W. N. (Dr.) 5482
Lummis, William N. (Dr.) 2862
Lundy, Samuel 5486
Lute, Amy 3459
Lyell, Thomas (Rev.) 5492
Lyle, Sally 549
Lyman, Lucretia Caroline 8169
Lynch, Albert 5498
Lynch, Mary C. 5498
Lyon, Abner P 5321
Lyon, Helen Ann 5321
Lyon, Hellen R. 3330
Lyon, Jane 5362
Lyon, John 2674
Lyon, Mary 5550
Lyon, Moses H. 762, 5509
Lyon, Sarah G. 9066
McAuley, Mary R. 409
McBeth, James 5511
McBurney, ___ (Judge) 328, 5701
McBurney, Carolyn 5810
McBurney, Eliza 328
McBurney, Harriet E. 2602
McBurney, James 5515
McBurney, Maria 2106
McBurney, Thomas 2107, 2602, 5512, 5516

McCabe, Mary (Mrs.) 5704
McCabe, Michael 5704
McCandlish, Grace Ann 6547
McCarther, Margaret 4974
McCarthy, Belinda 3455
McCarty, Sarah R. 9853
McCay, W. W. (Mr.) 5533
McCebbin, James 5537
McClallan, Melissa 7946
McClallen, James 3694, 5541
McClallen, James, Jr. 5540
McClary, Elizabeth 3686
McClure, ___ (Gen.) 5555
McClure, Eleanor 9053
McClure, George (Gen.) 5553, 9053
McClure, William 5557
McCollum, Ann 7848
McCollum, Mary 1251
McCollum, Rebecca 7083
McComb, John N. 1793
McComb, Sarah L. 1793
McComber, Mary 75
McCombs, Sarah 5301
McConnel, ___ (Judge) 6907
McConnel, Phebe 6907
McCornell, Ann 980
McCowlan, Jane 1252
McCracken, William J. 5574
McCulley, Thomas 5577
McCullock, Lucretia 830
McCullough, John 1577, 5578
McCullough, Mary (Mrs.) 1577
McCumber, Olica 4914
McCurdy, Elizabeth 2832
McCurdy, John 5582
McDonald, ___ (Rev.) 5589
McDonald, Margaret 3581
McDougal, William 5593
McDowell, ___ (Mrs.) 385
McDowell, Eluza Ann 3017
McDowell, Jane 4340
McDowell, Thomas 2674
McDuffee, Elizabeth 9743
McDuffie, Dorothy 8471
McElwain, Elizabeth 8581
McElwain, John 8581
McElwee, Henry 7692
McEntee, Marian 2877
McFarron, Polly 3250
McGlashan, James (Gen.) 5606
McGlashan, Sophia (Mrs.) 5606
McGlassin, Abby P. (Mrs.) 9430
McGowen, Nancy 594
McGraw, ___ (Mr.) 5609
McHenry, Almond 5616
McHenry, Betsey 635
McHenry, Daniel 5617
McHenry, Mary S. 3081
Mchorter, Hetty 6767
McInstry, Betsey 444
McIntosh, Catharine 6450
McIntosh, Jenney 6011
McIntosh, William (Gen.) 6011
McIntyre, A. (Dr.) 5622
McIntyre, Alice (Mrs.) 6363
McIntyre, Esther 10046
McIntyre, Isabella 2885
McKain, James 5627
McKain, Nancy 7913
McKay, ___ (Miss) 2608, 5671
McKay, ___ (Mrs.) 4317
McKay, Robert 5629, 5632
McKay, William W. 5630
McKeen, Frances Maria 2919
McKenzor, Almyra 7202
McKibbon, James 5640
McKillips, Hannah 8444
McKinney, ___ (Mrs.) 2887

McKinstry, ___ (Gen.) 9754
McKinstry, Nancy 9754
McKinstry, Pamela 8829
McKinzie, Phoebe Ann 3490
McKnight, ___ (Judge) 8246
McKnight, Delia F. 8246
McKnight, Orlando 2467, 5645
McKnutt, Archibald 6003
McKnutt, Sally 6003
McLacklan, Elizabeth 3763
McLaughlan, Catharine 8850
McLaughlin, ___ (Miss) 3917
McLean, Esther C. 9139
Mclean, John 5656
McMaster, David 5664
McMaster, James W. 5666
* McMasters, Mary 845
McMillen, Sarah (Mrs.) 9247
McMiltin, Sophrona 3365
McNair, Hugh 5672, 5674, 6959
McNair, Susan 6959
McNaughton, D. 1445
McNeil, Mary Jane 232
McNeil, Nancy 4625
McNette, Eliza (Mrs.) 10128
McNiel, Polly 2758
McNilan, James 5681
McNulty, Mary E. 6542
McNutt, Mary 9623
McPherrons, Amy 6752
McPherson, James 5683
McPherson, Nancy 213a
McRoey, Jane 3199
McUmber, Eleanor 2500
McUmber, Susan H. 9714
McWattey, Eliza 6032
McWhorter. See Mchorter.
McWhortle, Ann 483
Mabbet, Charlotte 1649
Mabee, Anna 741
Mabee, Fanny 7236
Mace, Lucinda 2262
Mace, Nancy 5781
Machi, Tereza 841
Mack, Abigail 1414
Mack, Experience 4236
Mack, Rhoda 9674
Mack, Sarah Ann 2109
Mackawis, Choe Pi 4306
Macomb, Alexander 3843
Macomb, Jane Eliza 7487
Macomb, John Navarre 7487
Macomb, Margaret 3843
Macomber, Amanda M. F. 7150
Macombs, John 5694
Macumber, Phebe 7046
Madden, Elizabeth L. 5313
Madison, Aurelia 3639
Madole, Betsey 6790
Magee, John 5697, 5700, 5701
Magee, Mary J. 5097
Magee, Rebecca 8063
Magee, Thomas C. 8063
Magee, Thomas J. 5698
Magowan, Mary E. 8840
Magown, Mary 8599
Magown, Philip 5702, 8599
Main, Philura 1018
Main, Thomas T. 5705
Mallett, Eliza 8569
Mallory, Carolyn Matilda 923
Mallory, Leah 170
Maltby, ___ (Gen.) 6354
Maltby, Julia Ann 6354
Maltby, Maria 5441
Maltby, S. M. (Mr.) 5719
Manger, Sally 6851
Manley, Abigail 5725
Manley, L. D. C. (Miss) 2237
* McMath, John and Mabel 4274

Mann, ___ (Dr.) 1331
Mann, Adelia H. 302
Mann, David 302, 4991
Mann, James 5728
Mann, Mercy Ann 4991
Mann, Sarah J. 1331
Mansfield, Jared 2353
Mansfield, Mary Ann 2353
Mapes, Sophia 4600
Maples, Charles G. 5734
Maples, Ruth 5734
Marcy, Cornelia L. 5908
Margison, Matilda 6493
Markham, Anna (Mrs.) 984
Markoe, Francis 10095
Markoe, Sarah 10095
Marlatt, Elmira 4657
Marlett, Betsey 7207
Marrs, Betsey 4312
Marsh, ___ (Dr.) 5746
Marsh, ___ (Mr.) 5743
Marsh, Caroline 5677
Marsh, E. C. 2296
Marsh, Elizabeth C. 2296
Marsh, Joel 5751
Marsh, Polly 7868
Marsh, Valina (Mrs.) 8054
Marshal, Ann 5103
Marshal, O. F. (Gen.) 9413
Marshal, Sarah D. 9413
Marshall, Chauncy 5759
Marshall, Eliza Ann 7492
Marshall, Jacob 5756, 5763
Marshall, O. F. (Gen.) 7492
Marshall, O. F. (Mr.) 5761
Marshall, Ruth (Mrs.) 9981
Marther, Julia Ann 10140
Marther, Margaret M. 248
Martin, Charles 5771
Martin, Eliza 3019
Martin, Harriet B. 9869
Martin, Sarah Jane 1824
Marvin, Mary Ann 4243
Marvin, Ruth S. 2888
Mason, B. B. 5783, 5792
Mason, Candace 6691
Mason, Elizabeth 7776
Mason, Elliot 5789
Mason, F. (Capt.) 5784
Mason, Julia Ann 7131
Mason, M. (Mrs.) 5783
Mason, Minerva 7435
Mason, Wheaton 5782
Masters, Joanna 6348
Masters, Nancy 9505
Mather, Rachel 5415
Mathews, Elizabeth (Mrs.) 9059
Mathews, Rebecca 5800
Mathews, Sally 1998
Mathews, Smith 2674
Mathews, Susan Sayre 4070
Mathews, Vincent 5800
Mathewson, Abigail 8327
Mathewson, Lydia F. 5852
Matteson, Hannah 172
Matthews, Elizabeth 5808
Matthews, Julia 6880
Matthews, Lorenzo 5808
Matthews, Vincent 6880
Mattison, Lucretia 7823
Maxon, Harriet 4771
Maxwell, ___ (Mrs.) 1402
Maxwell, Eliza P. 6620
Maxwell, Elizabeth T. 389
Maxwell, Fanny P. 7220
Maxwell, Jane 5385
Maxwell, S. H. (Mr.) 389
Maxwell, Thomas 5819, 6620, 7220

May, E. (Mr.) 4313
May, James 5824, 5828
May, Martha Ann 719
May, Mary 5758
May, Nancy 1389
May, William (Dr.) 5825
Mayborn, Jane 8138
Maynard, ___ (Judge) 5198
Maynard, Elizabeth 9652
Maynard, Sally 5198
Meacham, ___ (Mrs.) 4631
Mead, Catherine 5633
Mead, Judith 4299
Mead, William 5839
Meade, Katharine 9832
Meade, Maria del Carmen 7069
Meade, Richard W. 7069
Means, William 5852
Medbery, Orson 5855
Meech, Asa B. 5858
Meech, Elizabeth 5858
Meech, Horace 5857
Meeker, ___ (Miss) 7890
Meeker, Susan E. 7831
Melay, Mary 4156
Melfier, Maria 4764
Melony, W. Francis 5866
Melvin, Betsey 7080
Melvin, Jonathan 5868
Merchant, George 5871
Merell, Isaac 5878
Merfields, Anna 1309
Merill, ___ (Mrs.) 416
Merrell, John 5879
Merrell, Mary H. 8739
Merrell, Matilda 2363
Merriam, Abel 5880
Merriam, Harriet Y. 2501
Merriam, Mary 5880
Merrill, Aurissa V. 2765
Merrill, Adeline 3420
Merrill, Alzina 4192
Merrill, Carolyn 2196
Merrill, Cecilia 1945
Merrill, Charlotte 3687
Merrill, Jane 8388
Merrill, John 5885, 5886
Merrill, Joseph (Rev.) 5888
Merrill, Nathaniel (Capt.) 2196, 3687, 5894
Merriman, Lucy 2946
Merriman, Sylvester 2946
Mesick, Eliza 965
Mesick, Henry 965
Messenger, Emily 4613
Messenger, Laura 876
Metcalf, Chauncey 8298
Metcalf, Eliza 2630
Metcalf, Olive 4828
Metcalfe, Ann W. 3124
Metcalfe, Catharine 8391
Metcalfe, Nancy (Mrs.) 8574
Metcalfe, Thomas 5912, 5914, 8574
Metzger, Mary Ann 6402
Metzger, Rachel 2458
Meyers, Catharine 9267
Middaugh, Hannah 9648
Mighella, Eleazer 5923
Miles, Clarissa 603
Miles, Esther 1386
Miles, Maria 7504
Miles, Parmelia 1764
Miles, Samuel 5929
Miliman, Anna 9931
Millar, Robert 5930
Millard, Asahel 5933
Millard, Olive 6168
Millard, Timothy A. 5931

Miller, ___ (Deacon) 5952
Miller, ___ (Judge) 5957
Miller, Abigal 8180
Miller, Adeline 855
Miller, Andrew 5942
Miller, Clarissa 3133
Miller, Cornelia 2798
Miller, D. C. (Col.) 5953
Miller, Elijah 5956
Miller, Eliza Ann 9977
Miller, Esther 5084
Miller, Fred 8180
Miller, H. M. (Miss) 4739
Miller, Hezekiah 2808
Miller, Jesse 5975
Miller, Jonathan M. 5951
Miller, Joseph 5084
Miller, Joseph A. 5972
Miller, Kingsley 5976
Miller, Margaret 8, 7213
Miller, Martha 1665
Miller, Mary 2072, 2796, 2806, 2824, 5662
Miller, Melissa 5437
Miller, Moulton 5948
Miller, Palina 4278
Miller, S. (Capt.) 2824
Miller, Sally 1702, 3642, 5428
Miller, Sarah 4970, 8023
Miller, Sarah A. 5532
Miller, Semantha 9617
Miller, Sophia 2068
Miller, Susan 10059
Milligan, Thomas 5991
Mills, ___ (Mrs.) 7445
Mills, Drusilla 5778
Mills, Elisha M. 5992
Mills, Elisha T. 5519
Mills, Eunice H. 283
Mills, George 8896
Mills, Jane A. 5519
Mills, Joel 5618
Mills, Louisa M. 2319
Mills, Lydia 9523
Mills, Mariam 1431
Mills, Minerva 4129
Mills, Phebe Jane 1432
Mills, Sarah 7146
Mills, Susan 8896
Mills, Zilpah M. 5618
Milspaugh, Susan 9801
Miner, Pernia 6978
Miner, Ruth 3125
Minor, James 6006
Minott, James 4277
Minott, Mary 4277
Minton, Elizabeth 4126
Minzie, Charlotte 2879
Mirtal, Susan 3897
Mishell, Judith 9044
Mitchell, Freelove 268
Mitchell, Helena Ann 2177
Mitchell, John 7068
Mitchell, John B. 2177
Mitchell, Mary Ann 7068
Mitchell, Purlina L. 4779
Mitchell, Rhoda 6537
Mitchell, Thomas S. 6012
Mix, Julia D. 10118
Mizner, L. B. 6028
Mixner, Lansing B. 6026
Moe, John (Capt.) 1850
Moe, Matilda 1850
Moe, Phebe 254
Moffitt, Abigail 8814
Moffitt, Mary T. 1274
Mondy, Polly 773
Monell, Louisa 2918
Monroe, J. (Pres. of U.S.) 3585

Monroe, Maria Hester 3585
Montague, H. (Mr.) 6039
Montgomery, ___ (Mrs.) 7885
Montgomery, ___ (Rev.) 7885
Montgomery, Cynthia 1312
Montgomery, Delpha 8852
Montgomery, Hannah 7121
Montgomery, Reuben 6047
Moody, Clarissa 10100
Moody, Jemima 1738
Moody, Medad 10100
Moody, Philena 4000
Moon, James 6058
Moore, Abigal, H. 6066
Moore, Anna 3923
Moore, Charlotte (Mrs.) 7106
Moore, Elizabeth (Mrs.) 2539
Moore, Elizabeth S. 4262
Moore, Hannah Eliza 9440
Moore, Harriet 1811
Moore, Harriet B. 9792
Moore, Isaac, Jr. 6086
Moore, Israel G. 6066
Moore, Jane 8509
Moore, Letice 8910
Moore, Lois 2327
Moore, Lydia Jane 7464
Moore, Martha 497
Moore, Mary 786
Moore, Mary Ann 1670
Moore, Phineas 6081
Moore, Polly 5293
Moore, Sally 705
Moore, Sally Ann 2450
Moore, Samuel 6078
Moore, Sarah H. 6074
Moore, Sarah Maria 2624
Moore, Sophia 6439
Moore, Thomas 6080
Moores, Phineas 6091
Moores, Polly 6091
More, Jane 7136
Morehouse, Caroline M. 147
Morehouse, Maria 6413
Morehouse, Melissa B. 5352
Moreland, Julia 6347
Morey, ___ (Gov.) 5118, 5119
Morey, Lydia 3411
Morey, Melissa 1391
Morey, William L. 2674
Morgan, Eliza 8125
Morgan, Harriet Eliza 1967
Morgan, Henry 6100
Morgan, Jane A. 3578
Morgan, Julia E. 1146
Morgan, Lucinda (Mrs.) 3924, 3927
Morgan, Margaret 6138
Morgan, Nancy 5485
Morgan, Peter B. 1967
Morgan, Polly 3434
Morgan, Prudence 4028
Morgan, Sally 5071
Morgan, William 3924, 3927
Morison, James 6125
Morley, Laura 4479
Morris, ___ (Mr.) 739
Morris, Israel 6117
Morris, Mary 9227
Morris, Susan 4618
Morris, Thomas 9227
Morrison, Eliza 1028
Morrison, Jane 4097
Morrison, Mary M. 7874
Morse, Charles B. 6131
Morse, Clarissa 2003
Morse, E. Jane (Mrs.) 5394
Morse, Eliza C. 1615
Morse, Jedidiah 6134

Morse, Sarah 7257
Morton, Margaret 931
Moseley, Lydia 5504
Moses, Eliza 3145
Moses, Marcus 6146
Moses, Martha 6765
Moses, Mary E. 776
Moss, Irene 1196
Mott, Eliza 9106
Mott, Elizabeth R. 1061
Mott, Jane A. 6901
Mott, Jerusha 8595
Mott, Mary Ann (Mrs.) 5405
Mott, Samuel 1061, 6152
Moulton, Lucinda 6538
Mount, Caroline 2978
Mount, Randolph 6157
Mower, James B. 6159, 6161
Mower, Peter A. 6162
Mudge, Deborah 1911
Mullard, Asahel 6169
Mullard, Aurelia 6169
Mullen, Malvina 1931
Mulleneder, Catharine 6513
Mullender, Eliza N. 9563
Mullender, Isaac 6171, 6172
Mullhollon, Srah W. 5163
Mullhollon, William S. 6173
Mumford, George (Mrs.) 6385
Mumford, Helen Frances 9348
Mumford, J. I. (Mr.) 7912
Mumford, Maria Louisa 7912
Mumford, Mary 2312
Mumford, Thomas 2312, 9348
Mundell, Polly 6000
Munger, Amanda 2113
Munger, Mary 6594
Munn, Asa 6184
Munsell, Abigail 3518
Munson, E. Y. (Mr.) 6187
Munson, Eliza 4231
Munson, Mary 6167
Munson, Phebe 9099
Murdock, Jonathan 6190
Murray, Elijah 6204
Murray, John, Jr. 6721
Murray, Lucretia 1452
Murray, Sally (Mrs.) 7141
Murray, William (Mrs.) 6197
Muzzey, Sophia 6999
Muzzy, Amos 6206
Muzzy, Amos W. 6206, 6207
Myers, John 6208
Myres, Harriet 8059
Myrtle, Betsey 3339
Myrtle, Lydia 3629
Naggs, Betsey 197
Naglee, ___ (Mrs.) 4343
Naglee, David 6218, 6219
Nares, Francis 6222
Nash, Betsey 3992
Nash, Caroline S. 3041
Nash, Sarah 7283
Neally, Anna 4636
Neally, Samuel 6230
Near, Irene 6798
Neilsen, Earl 6235
Neilson, W. (Mr.) 6235
Nelson, Eliza 5266, 8095
Nelson, James 6238
Nethaway, James 6244
Newbury, Eliza Ann 7011
Newbury, Garret 6252
Newbury, Henry D. 6252
Newbury, Malvina 6252
Newbury, Sylvester B. 6251
Newcomb, Mary 4979
Newell, Harriet (Mrs.) 9448
Newell, Laura Ann 689

Newhall, Cynthia 7467
Newhall, Sally 6744
Newkirk, Ann 4878
Newkirk, Hendrick 5552
Newkirk, Mary 5552
Newland, David 5780
Newland, George 6266, 6267, 6268
Newland, Isabella 5780
Newland, Mary (Mrs.) 6267
Newman, Betsey 79
Newman, Polly 3461
Newman, Sarah 6489
Newton, Betsey (Mrs.) 9390
Newton, Butler 6272
Newton, Joseph 6276
Newton, Lucinda 1407
Newton, Rebecca 1377
Nichol, Jane 5255
Nicholas, ___ (Judge) 430, 6281
Nicholas, ___ (Mrs.) 6030
Nicholas, Ann (Mrs.) 7491
Nicholas, Ann C. 2644        6283
Nicholas, John 1808, 2644, 6279 /
Nicholas, Susan L. 1792
Nichols, ___ (Judge) 6298
Nichols, ___ (Mrs.) 5715
Nichols, Benjamin 6284
Nichols, Charlotte 8270
Nichols, Elizabeth 9029, 9710
Nichols, J. (Rev.) 6285
Nichols, Lucinda 9591
Nichols, Mary 561
Nichols, Nancy 8554
Nichols, Pamelia 4400
Nicholson, Elizabeth 2506
Nicholson, Humphrey 4222
Nicholson, Jane 4222
Nickerson, Harriet W. 5314
Niles, Addison (Dr.) 6307
Niles, Elizabeth G. 6551
Niles, Hannah 5690
Niles, Hiram 6305
Niles, Marinda 6192
Nims, Laura H. 3901
Ninde, Eleanor 6110
Ninde, William (Rev.) 6110
Nixon, Harriet 9561
Nixson, Joseph (Dr.) 6313
Noble, Clarissa 3545
Noble, Eliza 4397
Noble, Elnathan 6315
Noble, Harvey 6319
Noble, Isaac 6318
Noble, Lucy V. 2552
Noble, Nathaniel 6314
Noble, Roxana L. 1180
Noble, Sarah Ann 1302
Noble, Sophrona 4529
Noble, W. O. 6317
Nobles, Emeline 9835
Norman, Jane A. 4475
Norris, ___ (Mrs.) 3016
Norris, Abram 6335
Norris, Elizabeth 3932
Norris, John 6327
Norris, Polly 4768
Norris, Sarah 8821
North, Caty 9941
North, Linus 6338
North, Noah 6341
North, Samuel (Rev.) 6339
Northam, David 6653
Northam, Joanna Swift 3811
Northam, Lavinia 6653
Northrop, John B. 7307
Northrop, Sally B. 7307
Northrup, Mary 256
Northrup, R. K. (Mr.) 256
Norton, ___ (Mrs.) 8414

Norton, A. (Mr.) 4867
Norton, Almira 7943
Norton, Altha 8805
Norton, Amanda 3192
Norton, Augustus 6357
Norton, Caroline 6056
Norton, Clarissa 9388
Norton, Emily A. 5881
Norton, Emily L. 7918
Norton, Ett Julia 4867
Norton, Flavia 3716
Norton, Harriet 9089
Norton, Ira 6352, 7918
Norton, Joseph 6351
Norton, Joseph A. 6356
Noton, Julianna 7362
Norton, Lavantia 749
Norton, Mary 7193
Norton, Mary C. 7909
Norton, Sally 9346
Norton, Samuel 8414
Nott, Seretta J. 3508
Nottingham, Catharine (Mrs.) 89
Noyes, Clarissa B. 3246
Oakley, Jonathan 3077
Oakley, L. (Dr.) 4107
Oakley, Tydia 3077
Oakley, Thomas J. 6379, 6380
Oaks, Austin 6382
Oaks, Fanny (Mrs.) 2101
Oaks, Loronida 6898
Oaks, Thaddeus 2101
O'Carr, Mary 6174
O'Donaghey, Elizabeth 5586
Ogden, Abraham 1362
Ogden, Eliza A. 1362
O'Hara, William 6394
Olds, Abigail 7677
Olds, David 6396
Olds, Harriet 6294
Lods, Louisa 9414
Olds, Myria 3296
Oliver, A. F. (Dr.) 6406
Oliver, A. F. (Mr.) 6403
Oliver, Andrew (Rev.) 6403
Oliver, Gilbert 6404
Oliver, Phebe 5900
Oliver, Sally 9958
Oliver, W. M. 6403
Oliverson, Angeline 6814
Olmstead, Charlotte A. 6877
Olmstead, Colman 6409
Olmsted, Elizabeth (Mrs.) 8291
Olmsted, Jane 1284
O'Neil, Sophia Ann 4282
Ongley, Mary E. 3178
Ongley, W. H. (Mr.) 6415
Orr, Mary 5831
Orsburn, Anna 8773
Orton, A. G. (Rev.) 6430
Orton, Samuel A. 6431
Osband, Durfee 6433
Osband, Marietta 80
Osband, Rowena L. 1341
Osband, Wilson (Rev.) 80, 1341
Osborn, Juliet 2722
Osborn, Lorinda 2776
Osborn, Louisa 2149
Osborn, Lucy 485
Osborn, Phebe 3919
Osborn, Rebecca 285
Osborn, Sarah 9865
Osborne, Caroline 2098
Osborne, Charlotte 5477
Osborne, Mary E. 6446
Osborne, Phebe 7727
Osgood, Levi 6451

Osgood, Lucy 8563
Osterhout, Susan 9457
Ostram, W. (Mr.) 6454
Ostram, William 6453
O'Strander, Caroline 9153
Ostrom, Maria 6237
Otis, Jabez 2225
Otley, William 6461
Ottley, Mary 4130
Ottley, William 4130, 6462
Otto, Eliza M. 7945
Otto, Hannah C. 8302
Otto, Jacob 7945
Otto, Jacob S. 8255, 8302
Ovenshire, Charles 6465
Overhiser, Mary 3260
Overton, Maria 885
Owen, Anson 6471
Owen, Betsey A. 216
Owen, Daniel 6473
Owen, Electa 3999
Owen, Josiah 3999
Owen, Mary 5607
Owen, Mowbray 6470
Owen, Thalia Ann 8215
Packard, Philander 6483
Paddock, Cynthia L. 3965
Paddock, Eliza 3746
Page, Caroline 1661
Page, John 6492
Page, Lydia 4469
Page, Sophronia 9426
Page, Terrissa 5149
Paily, Jemima 6258
Paine, ___ (Judge) 6286
Paine, Abigail 5729
Paine, E. L. (Maj.) 737
Paine, Elizabeth S. 737
Paine, Marian 6286
Paine, Martyn (Dr.) 6499
Paine, Violetta 5311
Palmer, Amos 6525
Palmer, Arraminta 713
Palmer, Benjamin 6502
Palmer, Clarissa 264
Palmer, Clarissa A. 6106
Palmer, Deborah Ann 4463
Palmer, Elizabeth 8385
Palmer, Julia 3749
Palmer, Lucy Ann 3356
Palmer, Lydia 9914
Palmer, Sally 3071
Palmer, Sarah 5487, 6399
Palmeter, Josiah 6526, 6527, 6528
Palmeter, Matilda 7269
Palmiter, Amanda 9462
Palmiter, Ann 2721
Palmiter, P. (Mr.) 2192
Palmiter, Phineas 9937
Palmiter, Phineas, Jr. 6530, 9462
Palmiter, Sevila 2192
Pardee, Eliza 3685
Pardee, William 5683
Parish, Caroline 9085
Parish, Cornelia 1861
Parish, J. (Capt.) 1861
Parish, Jasper 9085
Parish, Meriam 1827
Park, Caroline 9791
Park, Frances 9671
Park, Rufus 9791
Parke, Fanny 9174
Parke, Mary 5579
Parke, Ruth 3646
Parke, Samuel 6543
Parke, William 6544
Parker, ___ (Rev.) 6559

Parker, Abigail 8592
Parker, Almira E. 6555
Parker, Ann 161
Parker, Anna Maria 9684
Parker, Clarissa 8133
Parker, Elvira 1114
Parker, George 6556
Parker, Hannah 4195, 9255
Parker, Harris 6558
Parker, Horace 6558
Parker, James 6552, 6567
Parker, Joshua 6566
Parker, Lucy 186
Parker, Mary 4433
Parker, Nancy 9359
Parker, Nelson 6555
Parker, Sabra 6567
Parker, Sarah S. 3454
Parker, Theda C. 4124
Parkhill, Eliza Ann 5180
Parkhurst, Amanda 1679
Parkhurst, Rebecca 7564
Parks, Delphena S. 2640
Parks, Nancy 1889
Parmalee, Eunice 6263
Parmater, Rozilla 6617
Parmele, Mary E. 2338
Parmelee, John 6586
Parmelee, John H. (Gen.) 6586
Parmelee, Phila 9244
Parrish, Betsey 3572
Parrish, J. (Capt.) 6588
Parrish, Jasper 3572
Parrot, Mary Ann 4038
Parshal, Betsey 3187
Parshall, Elizabeth 7342
Parshall, Mary (Mrs.) 5286
Parsons, ___ (Judge) 2498
Parsons, Catherine Victoria 2372
Parsons, David 2372
Parsons, Harriet 2316
Parsons, Harriet (Mrs.) 4324
Parsons, Jane 2226
Partridge, Albert A. 6611
Partridge, Almon 6604
Partirdge, Almond 6613
Partridge, Joel 6603, 6606, 6607, 6608, 6609
Partridge, Louisa 1433
Partridge, Mary R. (Mrs.) 6608
Partridge, Mehetabel (Mrs.) 6604
Passage, Margaret 1321
Patchen, Jared 6936
Patchin, Maria L. 8987
Patchin, T. W. (Mr.) 6616
Patchin, Thaddeus W. 2365
Pate, Esther 10029
Patrick, Lavina 4911
Patrick, Sarah 1007
Patrick, Sophia 8442
Patten, Polly 83
Patterson, Ann 4713
Patterson, Betsey 7459
Patterson, David 2303
Patterson, Eli 6625
Patterson, Elizabeth 7742
Patterson, Ezra 6628
Patterson, Jemima 5513
Patterson, Louisa 1892
Patterson, Mary Jane 5741
Patterson, Polly 8330
Patterson, R. (Mr.) 4713
Patterson, Sally 9428
Patterson, Sophiah T. 5854
Patterson, Theodosia 323
Patton, Charlotte 8014
Patty, John 5654
Patty, Susan Y. 5654
Paul, William 6639

305

Pauling, Betsey 1426
Payne, Delia 9854
Payne, Maria 1360
Payne, Maria C. 7798
Payne, Mary 2090
Payne, Nancy 3806
Peacock, Sarah (Mrs.) 6236
Pearson, Catalina 9052
Pearson, Pool 6664
Pearsons, Juliette 5348
Pease, Abel 6668
Pease, Ammi 6669
Pease, Clarissa 4043
Pease, Dorcas 300
Pease, Harriet 1090
Pease, Jabez 6667, 6672
Pease, Nancy 6794
Peck, Ann 6958
Peck, Asahel 6677
Peck, Betsey 2114, 8263
Peck, Caroline 1227
Peck, Celista D. 7358
Peck, Cynthia 5409
Peck, Everard 6675, 6684
Peck, Hannah 8244
Peck, John 6679
Peck, Mary 5347
Peck, Murry (Miss) 8478
Peck, Orilla M. 1144
Peck, Priscilla 4326
Peckham, ___ (Mrs.) 9180
Peckham, Henrietta L. 1961
Peckham, William (Dr.) 6686
Peeb, Hannah P. 2182
Peed, Hannah P. 2182
Peeler, Maria 8659
Peeler, Marian 8659
Peer, Kaziah 4735
Peet, Ebenezer 6902
Peet, M. A. 6902
Peevey, Samanth 3128
Pelham, Abigail 4966
Pelham, Lucinda 5123
Pelton, Jane (Mrs.) 3640
Pelton, Nancy 1125
Pember, Clarissa 7824
Pembroke, John 6698
Penfield, Daniel 1158, 2830, 6702
Penfield, Jane 1158
Penfield, Julia G. 8657
Penhollow, ___ (Mr.) 6712
Penhollow, Clarissa 6508
Penier, Harriet 5214
Penniman, William 6705
Pennington, Mary 6040
Pennock, Alvin 6707
Pennock, Lucy Ann 3360
Pennock, Mary R. 6612
Pennock, Thomas 6709
Pennock, Thomas J. 6710
Penton, Isabella 4517
Perce, Lucinda 9115
Perin, Ann 7074
Perine, Elizabeth H. 7845
Perine, John 7845
Perine, P. S. 6718, 6719
Perine, Peter 9779
Perine, Susan J. 9779
Perkins, Ann Eliza 4440
Perkins, Anna 8531
Perkins, Betsey 67
Perkins, Charlotte W. 7093
Perkins, Eliza 4648
Perkins, John 6726
Perkins, John (Capt.) 2223
Perkins, Julia F. 8488
Perkins, Lorana A. 8640
Perkins, Louise 2223

Perkins, Lydia Lucretia 5129
Perkins, Mary 6592
Perkins, Parmilla 2174
Perkins, Philetus 8488
Perkins, Septimus 6723
Perkins, William 6729
Perrel, Benjamin 4712
Perrin, Electa 3643
Perrine, Elizabeth 2478
Perrine, Hannah 41
Perrine, Henry (Dr.) 7420
Perrine, Sarah A. 7420
Perry, ___ (Com.) 6737
Perry, ___ (Miss) 1985
Perry, Alanson 6743
Perry, Deborah L. 7371
Perry, E. A. (Miss) 1002
Perry, Louisa 2360
Perry, Olive 6951
Perry, Phebe 4807
Perry, Rouse (Capt.) 6745
Persons, Abram 6748
Persons, Harriet 688
Persons, Lucinda 8345
Peters, Harriet 1118
Peters, Perses 7279
Peterson, Catharine 3681
Petit, Eliza 3421
Pettet, Anna 4695
Pettibone, Levi 6755
Pfouts, Mercy 2814
Phelps, ___ (Rev.) 2870
Phelps, Almira 7969
Phelps, Angelina 9234
Phelps, Arsena N. 4853
Phelps, Barney 6764
Phelps, Betsey 7973
Phelps, Betsey Ann 1651
Phelps, Calvin 6766
Phelps, Cornelius 6780
Phelps, Dan 6762
Phelps, Davenport 3097
Phelps, Emily 10096
Phelps, H. G. (Mr.) 6961
Phelps, Hannah W. 8427
Phelps, Harriet 683, 684
Phelps, Jon 6761
Phelps, Laura Ann 5258
Phelps, Lucy 2870
Phelps, Lucy Ann 4481
Phelps, Luman 6782
Phelps, Mary E. 6961
Phelps, O. Esq. 6777
Phelps, Oliver 6774 , 7969
Phelps, Sally 4933
Phelps, Sally M. 1015
Phelps, Sarah 3097
Phelps, Stephen 10096
Phelps, Susan 3050
Phelps, Thankful 1105
Philips, Amanda 4676
Philips, Lucy 8683
Philips, Mary 10054
Phillips, ___ (Col.) 6540, 6683
Phillips, Abigail 7437
Phillips, Allice 6540
Phillips, Amanda E. 8684
Phillips, Asenath 5893
Phillips, Betsey 1287
Phillips, Caroline 9356
Phillips, G. W. (Dr.) 4057
Phillips, Henrietta 8097
Phillips, Mary 229
Phillips, Mary 6683
Phillips, Miranda 4057
Phillips, Samuel 8684
Phoenix, Malissa 9907
Pickard, John 6800

Pickett, Levina T. 2560
Picksley, Olive 1894
Pier, Abraham 4777
Pier, Alvira 3361
Pier, Henry 6807
Pier, Louisa E. 4777
Pier, Mary Ann (Mrs.) 6809
Pier, Norman 6809
Pierce, Abner 6820, 6825
Pierce, Fanny 3394
Pierce, Frances Mahala 6139
Pierce, Harriet 9704
Pierce, Jane 4371
Pierce, Jeremiah B. (Dr.) 4371
Pierce, John 6139
Pierce, Lucy Ann 4743
Pierce, Mahala 6139
Pierce, Margaret R. 1069
Pierce, Sally 9631
Pierpont, Sarah 5676
Pierson, Margaret 8815
Pierson, Marian 7130
Pike, ___ (Gen.) 3882
Pinkney, ___ (widow) 9009
Pinnock, Mary 4883
Piper, Harriet C. 2044
Piper, Nathan 6839
Piper, Permelia A. 9607
Pitcher, Dorothy 6863
Pitney, ___ (Dr.) 6703
Pitney, Aaron (Dr.) 3853
Pitney, Caroline Louisa 3853
Pitney, J. T. (Dr.) 6842
Pitts, Lucy 5760
Pixley, Deborah 7879
Pixley, Joseph 1770
Pixley, Lucinda 1770
Plate, Elizabeth 1976
Plato, M. E. A. (Miss) 7000
Platt, Anna 2716
Platt, William 2714
Plough, Eliza 1468, 1469
Plum, C. P. (Mr.) 6857
Plumb, Alvin 3083
Plumb, Anna Mary 3082
Plumb, Elijah (Rev.) 6663
Plumb, Grace B. 6663
Plumb, J. (Mr.) 3082
Plumley, Matilda 4453
Pohlman, Elizabeth 5554
Poillon, Margaret 2092
Polley, Julia E. 9785
Pomeroy, George E. 6865
Pond, Catharine 985
Pooley, Maria 4221
Pope, Abigail 3154
Popple, Polly 5160
Porter, ___ (Commodore) 6889
Porter, ___ (Judge) 6885
Porter, Benjamin 6886
Porter, Caroline 2293
Porter, Chauncey 2293, 3574, 7281, 9884
Porter, Elizabeth Ann 4392
Porter, Lydia M. 9722
Porter, Margaret 3574
Porter, Mary 7295
Porter, Olive Ann 9884
Porter, Olive L. (Miss) 6884
Porter, Peter B. (Gen.) 6881
Porter, Robert 5279, 6887
Porter, Salome 5186
Porter, Sephronia 2276
Porter, Sylvia R. 7281
Porter, William L. 6884
Posson, Polly 5292
Post, Ebenezer 6902
Post, Helen 6255
Post, Mary J. 636

Potter, ___ (Judge) 4155
Potter, Anselm 6924
Potter, Arelia 115
Potter, Arnold 6912, 6914
Potter, Diana 6532
Potter, Eliza 10048
Potter, Elizabeth Ann 4392
Potter, Hannah 1955
Potter, Hiram 339
Potter, Jeremiah 6923
Potter, Julia M. 7239
Potter, Louisa 339
Potter, Lucinda 6520
Potter, Mary 587. 7414
Potter, Nathaniel J. 4392
Potter, Penelope C. 4155
Potter, Phebe 2656
Potter, Sally 6971
Potter, Sarah 9147
Potwine, Thomas (Rev.) 9205
Poucher, Charles 6928
Poucher, Mary 6928
Pound, Sarah 2307
Pound, Thomas 6929
Pow, Julia Ann 8147
Powel, Lucinda 8410
Powell, Corissande P. 4429
Powell, Elizabeth (Mrs.) 1460
Powell, H. R. (Rev.) 6937
Powell, Isabella 7720
Powell, John 6933, 6936
Powell, Nancy (Mrs.) 9878
Powell, Stephen 6938
Powell, Susan 1510
Powell, Thomas 6934
Power, Sarah Halen 9770
Powers, Blanchard 6953
Powers, Caroline (Mrs.) 2902
Powers, Eliza (Mrs.) 7398
Powers, Gersham 7398
Powers, James 6944
Powers, Lavinia 6758
Powers, Mary 4058
Powers, Philander (Rev.) 2902
Powers, Roswell 6943
Powley, Susan 1922
Pratt, Abner 9331
Pratt, Altha 9850
Pratt, Amelia 3871
Pratt, Charlotte 6189
Pratt, Cornelia R. 592
Pratt, Electa 2173
Pratt, Elisha 6970
Pratt, Elkanah 6960
Pratt, Emeline 7752
Pratt, Emily M. 3876
Pratt, Esther 7782
Pratt, Harriet A. 1089
Pratt, Ira 583, 6975
Pratt, Jared 6965
Pratt, Jerusha L. 8064
Pratt, Mary 1343, 8002
Pratt, Mary A. 7673
Pratt, Naomi 2991
Pratt, Rachel 9637
Pratt, Richard 3871, 7673
Prendergast, James 6982
Prentice, Mary 3877
Prentis, Eliza 2886
Prentiss, Harriet 9589
Prentiss, Susan 2976, 6271
Prentiss, Sylvia 8859
Prescott, ___ (Mrs.) 8827a
Prescott, Benjamin 1831
Prescott, Joel (Dr.) 6993
Preston, Amos 1904
Preston, Benjamin 6998
Preston, David (Rev.) 6998
Preston, Joseph 6998

Preston, Philomena 7740
Preston, Roena 2853
Preston, Sarah A. 2572
Preston, Sials 6994
Preston, Tabitha H. 9198
Price, Abigail 4083
Price, Benjamin 7001
Price, Ez 9337
Price, Mary 3660
Price, Mercy 6277
Priest, Hannah 10081
Prindle, Jane 3912
Prindle, Susan 7812
Prior, Jesse 7014
Priphogle, Maria 5284
Pritchard, Elsey (Mrs.) 685
Proctor, ___ (Mr.) 3589
Prosser, Isaac 7020
Prouty, Phineas 7026, 7027
Provost, Catharine 4151
Pruyn, Alida 920
Pudney, Rebecca 6647
Puffer, Betsey 8224
Puffer, Mary 827
Pullen, ___ (Mrs.) 2549
Pulling, ___ (Dr.) 5176
Pulling, E. B. (Dr.) 7033, 7034
Pulling, E. N. (Miss) 5176
Pulling, Mary 7034
Pullman, Joseph 664
Pullman, Louisa 664
Purdy, Amanda 7201
Purdy, Charles 7043
Purdy, Esther 4595
Purdy, Gilletly (Miss) 6183
Purdy, Harriet L. 7043
Purdy, Mariah 5822
Putnam, Cornelius 7054
Putnam, Elisha 7050
Putnam, Emeline O. 8691
Putnam, Hannah 410
Putnam, Harriet L. 6486
Putnam, Israel (Gen.) 7055
Putnam, Mary 663
Putnam, Newel 7057
Putnam, Olive 5206
Putnam, Peter 7056
Putnam, Sarah 2033
Putnam, Stephen 7052
Putnam, William 7053
Pyerson, Samuel 7061
Quant, Cornel a 1305
Quick, Eleanor 10158
Quick, Elizabeth 9882
Race, Jane 953
Rafter, Polly 6715
Rain, William 7070
Ramsay, John 7072
Ramsdell, Lucy 5184
Ramsdell, Rachel G. 3665
Ramsdell, Rachel O. 3665
Rand, Ammi 7104
Rand, Samuel 7076
Randall, Lovisa (Mrs.) 2153
Randall, Mary 4847
Randall, Samuel B. 7082
Randel, Daniel 7085
Randolph, Reuben 7087
Ranie, Jane 9737
Rankin, Mary 1750
Ranney, Lois 3452
Ranor, Nancy 9338
Ransford, Mary 3101
Ransom, Almira 6696
Ransom, Jane A. 7881
Ransom, Olive 7837
Rapalye, Susan 6941
Rathbon, Charlotte 9577

Rathbone, Betsey 9587
Rathbone, Cornelia M. 5920
Rathbone, Israel 7100
Rathbone, Laura 2350
Rathbone, R. (Gen.) 3074
Rathbun, Amy 2274
Rathbun, Clara 7102
Rathbun, Eunice 7791
Rathbun, Frances B. 1710
Rathbun, L. S. (Mr.) 7105
Rathbun, Moses 7101
Rathbun, Sally 5830
Rawson, ___ (Mrs.) 7491
Rawson, Almira 9214
Rawson, Eveline 8001
Rawson, Hila 602
Rawson, Rebecca 2168
Rawson, Thomas (Dr.) 7109
Ray, Delila 5834
Rayment, Polly 8438
Raymond, Emeline 7536
Raymond, Polly 8438
Raymond, Raymond 7717
Razey, Betsey Maria 156
Read, Elizabeth S. 6717
Read, Hannah 7086
Read, James 6717, 7125
Read, L. H. (Mr.) 7124
Read, Lazarus 7123
Read, Maria 925, 1220
Rector, Adaline 1543
Redfield, Elizabeth 7820
Redfield, Heman J. 3495, 7135
Redfield, Keziah 9520
Redfield, Mary 3495, 9243
Reed, ___ (Capt.) 3012
Reed, ___ (Mr.) 7138
Reed, Amanda C. 3538
Reed, Carlo 7151
Reed, Catharine 3012
Reed, Electa 5022
Reed, Fanny 2626
Reed, Harriet 5848
Reed, John 7144
Reed, Josiah 5848
Reed, Laura 708
Reed, Martha Ann 375
Reed, Nathan 7164
Reed, Rebecca 7148
Reed, Rhoda 377
Reed, Royal (Rev.) 7152
Reed, Sarah 7688
Reed, Sarah C. 7520
Reed, Taft 7157
Reed, William 7145
Reeder, Adeline 3324
Reeder, Josiah 4641
Reeder, Sarah 4641
Reeder, Stephen 3324
Rees, ___ (Maj.) 2645
Rees, Abigail 2729
Reed, Abigail (Mrs.) 3489
Rees, Carolyn 2533
Rees, James 2533, 2647
Rees, Jane Eliza 4665
Rees, Mary Ann 2647
Reese, E. D. (Mr.) 7168
Reeves, ___ (Mr.) 3191
Reeves, Celinda 345
Reeves, James 7181
Reeves, Luther 345
Reeves, Lyman 3189
Reeves, Martha 6434
Reeves, Nancy 3191
Reeves, P. (Miss) 10080
Reeves, Parmelia 8053
Reeves, Philura 4639
Reeves, Ruth 718
Reeves, Zebulon 7175

Remer, A. (Capt.) 9103
Remer, Abraham 2641
Remer, Henrietta 2641
Remington, Betsey 5033
Remington, T. (Col.) 5033
Renwick, Jane 5140
Retan, Rachel 5396
Rew, Naomi 5791
Rey, Lany (Mrs.) 8551
Reynolds, ___ (Miss) 1536
Reynolds, Caroline (Mrs.) 8863
Reynolds, Henry 7200
Reynolds, Isaac 4781
Reynolds, Julia Ann 7722
Reynolds, Melvina 4781
Reynolds, Phebe (Mrs.) 9036
Reynolds, William 7206
Rhea, ___ (Gen.) 3845
Rhea, Gitty Maria 3845
Rhea, Jonathan 5492, 5493
Rhea, Jonathan (Gen.) 7212
Rhea, Juliana 5493
Rhodes, Amelia 2961
Rial, Betsey 7162
Rice, A. E. (Mr.) 7224
Rice, Aaron 5467
Rice, Almira 8533
Rice, Anna 7231
Rice, Caroline 4932
Rice, Caroline L. 7240
Rice, Charles 7777
Rice, Clarissa (Mrs.) 8384
Rice, Daniel 5749
Rice, Ebenezer 7258
Rice, Elizabeth M. 1383
Rice, Elvira 10062
Rice, Fanny 7777
Rice, Harriet 5077
Rice, J. C. (Mr.) 7238
Rice, James 7232
Rice, James, Sr. 7248
Rice, Jane 9386
Rice, Joel 7222, 7223, 7225,
  8384
Rice, Joel H. 7240
Rice, Julia Ann 5236
Rice, Loana 4232
Rice, Lucy 488
Rice, Lydia (Mrs.) 9553
Rice, Maria 4356
Rice, Mary (Mrs.) 839
Rice, Mercy 4983
Rice, Nancy 839, 3243, 5749
Rice, Naomi A. 3174
Rice, Oliver 488
Rice, Seth 4232
Rice, Sylvanus 7241
Rice, Sylvia 6310
Rice, William 5077, 7231
Rice, Zebina, Sr. 7249
Rice, Zebina H. 7249
Rich, C. B. (Mr.) 7268
Rich, Calvin 6598
Rich, Clara 6597
Rich, D. A. (Mrs.) 7268
Rich, Emily 8067
Rich, Hiram M. 7267
Rich, Sophia 3522
Richards, Charles G. 7274,
  7278
Richards, Jefferson C. 7277
Richards, Lucinda 9539
Richardson, Isabella B. P.
  7357
Richardson, Jemima 6575
Richardson, Joseph 7293
Richardson, Rhoda (Mrs.) 5304
Richardson, Sylvia 4579
Richardson, Thomas J. 7282

Richmond, Almira 7978
Richmond, John 7298
Rider, Candace 3689
Riggs, Anna 4587
Riggs, Caroline 4727
Riggs, Frances E. 9862
Riggs, John 4587
Riggs, Lewis (Dr.) 4727
Riggs, Sally 7716
Riggs, Timothy 9862
Rigs, Solomon 7312
Riker, ___ (Mr.) 7313
Riker, Abigail 2514
Riker, John 7315
Riker, Mary T. 7315
Riker, Thomas 7314
Riley, Abram 7318
Riley, Esther 4672
Riley, Janette 7318
Riley, Levi W. 7318
Rinders, Isaac 6582
Rinders, Welthy 6582
Ringer, Jacob 4134
Ringer, Phebe 4134
Riordan, John 2674
Ripley, Ann S. 7226
Ripley, Clarissa L. 4017
Rippenburgh, Christina 9156
Rippey, Isabella 846
Rippey, John 846
Rippey, John, Sr. 7147
Rippey, Martha 7147
Rippey, Mary 3718
Risley, Delia 3711
Risley, Editha 3285
Risley, Mary 8262
Ritzema, Alida 930
Ritzema, Johannes (Rev.) 930,
  9288
Robb, William, Sr. 7332
Robbins, ___ (Miss) 8148
Robbins, Hannah M. 2892
Robbins, Tryphena 778
Roberts, Abigail 2053
Roberts, E. J. (Mr.) 7346
Roberts, Ezekiel 7337
Roberts, J. (Mr.) 7336
Roberts, Joseph 7338
Roberts, Rahael 8119
Roberts, Rufus 7340
Robeson, Alexander C. 7352
Robie, Harriet 5505
Robie, Maria R. 8025
Robins, Thankful 2412
Robinson, ___ (Miss) 4366,
  4508
Robinson, Amanda 3606
Robinson, Anna 9248
Robinson, Belinda 8604
Robinson, Charlotte 989
Robinson, Chloe 6306
Robinson, Clarissa 5634
Robinson, Daphne 9161
Robinson, Delia 1222
Robinson, Eliza 4249
Robinson, Emma A. 1940
Robinson, Eveline 8069
Robinson, Gain (Dr.) 6306,
  6864
Robinson, Harriet 370
Robinson, Harriet N. 9328
Robinson, Helen E. 6864
Robinson, Jedediah H. (Dr.)
  7368
Robinson, Lucina 4365
Robinson, Lucy 1491
Robinson, Lydia 1758
Robinson, Mabel 3498
Robinson, Polly 2587, 9385

Robinson, Tracy 7361
Robison, Gabriel 7384
Robords, John L. 7386
Robson, Catharine 8839
Robson, Eliza 2573
Robson, Frances C. 9182
Rochester, ___ (Col.) 1690
Rochester, Mary E. 6043
Rochester, N. (Col.) 6043
Rochester, Sophia E. 1690
Rochester, William B. 7393, 7395
Rockwell, Phoebe Ann 2849
Rodgers, (Rev.) 7408
Rodgers, Almeda 7404
Rodney, Caesar A. 2923
Rodney, Eliza 2923
Rodney, William 7411
Rogers, ___ (Mr.) 7416
Rogers, Charles 7440
Rogers, Cynthia 1500
Rogers, David 7421
Rogers, Denison 7423
Rogers, Elizabeth 6867
Rogers, G. A. (Dr.) 7445
Rogers, Hamilton 7441
Rogers, Harriet 3605
Rogers, Jane 4200, 10091
Rogers, John 2062
Rogers, Letty 1199
Rogers, Lucy 9141
Rogers, Lucinda 7244
Rogers, Martha 8646
Rogers, Mary A. 4226
Rogers, Matthew 7444
Rogers, Prudence 8878
Rogers, Rebecca 443
Rogers, S. (Mr.) 7442
Rogers, Samuel 7445
Rogers, Sarah W. 2062
Rogers, Shubael G. 4226
Rogers, Sophia 2744
Rogers, Stephen 7438
Rogers, William 7424, 9141
Rogers, William (Judge) 2453
Rogers, William, Jr. 2744, 3605
Rogers, William R. 7442
Rolfe, Marianne 6209
Rolfe, Patience 10004
Rollins, Patty 6443
Rolo, Frances 6989
Rolson, John 7209
Rolson, Mary 7209
Romeyn, John B. (Rev.) 7455
Ronalds, Margaret (widow) 7460
Rood, Lucy 6329
Roosevelt, Nelson 7462
Root, ___ (Gen.) 7466
Root, Aaron 7473
Root, Caroline P. 7787
Root, Dolly 6589
Root, Eli 7472
Root, Elizabeth 7361
Root, Erastus (Gen.) 7361
Root, Luther 8358
Root, Patty 2482
Root, Rhoda 7192
Root, Sally 1467
Roots, Diana 5154
Rose, Caroline 4692
Rose, Harriet 8716
Rose, Harriet (Mrs.) 7478
Rose, J. (Mr.) 7966
Rose, Mahala 7499
Rose, Maroa 716
Rose, Mary 6282
Rose, Nathan 7496
Rose, Nathan, 2nd 7499
Rose, Polly 7966
Rose, Rebecca 6919

Rose, Robert (Rev.) 7491
Rose, Robert S. 6282
Rose, Sally 964
Rose, Sally Ann 9377
Rose, Sophia 5254
Roseboom, Lucy 7954
Rosebrugh, ___ (Judge) 7504
Rosecrans, Rachael 7852
Rosenkrans, Margaret 2032
Rosman, Daniel 7509
Ross, Benjamin 7512
Ross, Margaret 7512
Ross, Polly 3275, 9645
Roth, Hannah 7542
Rounds, Mary 8976
Rouse, Hester 9271
Rouse, Susan 9033
Rowe, Anson 7523
Rowe, Catharine H. 2801
Rowe, Epicratus (Rev.) 2801
Rowe, G. M. (Rev.) 5563
Rowe, Huldah 5882
Rowe, John S. 7527
Rowe, Marietta M. 5563
Rowland, Emeline 8232
Rowland, Thankful 6955
Rowley, Ann 3314
Rowley, B. 4173
Rowley, Dimis 3263
Rowley, Hannah 1943, 8057
Rowley, John S. 605
Rowley, Margaret 9149
Rowley, Martha 605
Royer, Catharine 1378
Rubles, Sarah 1720
Ruger, Eliza Ann 671
Rumney, Robert 7547
Rumney, Sarah 1920
Rumsey, Alexander R. 7553
Rumsey, Charlotte 7514
Rumsey, David 7555
Rumsey, Joseph E. 6471
Rumsey, Julia F. 3091
Rumsey, Martin S. 7554
Rumsey, Mary 3148
Rundell, ___ (Mrs.) 6694
Rundell, Polly 6952
Runnyan, Lucina 7979
Runyan, Benjamin 7997
Runyan, Caroline 7998
Runyan, Charity 8949
Runyan, Isaac W. 7558
Runyan, Patty 2707
Runyan, Sally 8492
Ruppert, Philip 7563
Rusco, Mary (Mrs.) 4747
Ruscoe, Eliza 552
Rusenbark, Mary 3104
Rush, Roxana 439
Rush, Sarah 9558
Russ, L. W. (Rev.) 3349
Russel, Alida Lucretia 961
Russel, Charles 961
Russel, Emma 7761
Russel, Milden 7569
Russel, Perry 7567
Russell, Betsey 8009
Russell, Elinda 2554
Russell, Mary 2867
Russell, Melinda 2554
Russell, Phebe 2415
Russell, Polly 3054
Russell, Sally 6200
Rutgers, Anthony A. 6029,
 7549, 7686
Rutgers, Eliza Ann 1791
Rutgers, Gertrude 7549
Rutgers, Mary Gouverneur
 6029

Rutherford, Edward 7689, 7695
Rutherford, William 7694
Rutledge, H. M. (Maj.) 7697
Ryerson, Polly 3374
Ryno, Smith 7701
Sabin, Benjamin 7702
Sacket, Gary 7705
Sacket, Maria 4980
Sackett, Caroline 3848
Sackett, Lucinda 6120
Sackett, Timandea 9437
Sadler, ___ (Mr.) 7708
Safford, Angeline 6105
Safford, Darius 7710
Sage, Pamela 391
Saibley, Maria 412
St. Clair, Arthur (Commodore)
 7718
St. John, Harriet 2461
St. John, Holly 4820
St. John, Serepta 4871
St. John, Susan M. 3175
Salard, Sarah Ann 8347
Salisbury, Ambrose 2254
Salisbury, Eunice 2289
Salisbury, H. A. (Mr.) 7725
Salisbury, Helen Mar 2254
Salisbury, Margaret 7779
Salisbury, Mary (Mrs.) 7726
Salisbury, Tobias 7726
Salley, Harriet M. 8123
Salmon, R. (Rev.) 7730
Salyer, Luthena 7733
Sample, John 8016
Sample, Margery 8016
Sanburn, Elizabeth 3609
Sanburn, Hannah 4750
Sanderson, Margaret 5153
Sandford, Delema 6570
Sandford, Melissa J. 595
Sandford, Sally R. 2781
Sands, Robert 7751
Sanford, Amelia 2364
Sanford, Caroline 7179
Sanford, D. M. (Mr.) 7758
Sanford, Luther 7179
Sanger, Amelia 2791
Sanger, Lucy 1511
Santee, Isaac 7766
Saterly, Caroline 2604
Sattell, M. (Miss) 3255
Satterlee, Frances L. 7041
Satterlee, Rachael 2711
Saunders, Anthony 7773
Saunders, Betsey Laura 8091
Saunders, John 8091
Saulpaugh, Ann Jennett 6899
Saulpaugh, Philip 6899
Savacool, Peggy 1601
Savage, Julia 8335
Savage, Polly 292
Sawtell, Sarah 6270
Sawtell, Ursula 7963
Sawyer, Catherine 3645
Sawyer, J. A. (Mr.) 7778
Sawyer, Sarah 3944
Sax, Ann 4843
Saxton, A. (Col.) 7789
Saxton, Elizabeth 9944
Sayre, ___ (Col.) 9057
Sayre, ___ (Mrs.) 9057
Sayre, Abner, 7795
Sayre, Ebenezer 5816
Sayre, Elizabeth 5816
Sayre, James 381, 5819, 5821
Sayre, John 3744
Sayre, Julia 5821
Sayre, Myrilla 381
Sayre, Nancy 3744

Sayre, Polly 6027
Sayre, Whittington 6718
Sayres, Joannah 8037
Scarborough, Judith 8669
Scarvel, Rosanna 4704
Schenck, Ellen 8542
Schermerhorn, Jane C. 6954
Schermerhorn, John V. R. 7805
Schoat, Phebe 4296
Schooly, Adeline 3745
Schoonmaker, Cordelia 9943
Schoonmaker, Cynthia 2565
Schott, Ann 9924
Schram, William 138
Schuyler, Harmanus P. 9352
Schuyler, Marianna 9352
Schuyler, Peter 7811, 7815
Schuyler, Philip (Gen.) 1713
Scidmore, Betsey 9371
Scofield, Ann (Mrs.) 358
Scofield, Caroline Amelia 1479
Scofield, Charlotte 92
Scofield, Cynthia 5979
Scofield, Marlin 697
Scofield, P. (Mr.) 7821
Scofield, Rua 7825
Scot, Mary Ann 6324
Scot, Robert 7826
Scott, ___ (Capt.) 4509
Scott, Anna (Mrs.) 6226
Scott, David 6742
Scott, Eliza 88, 9443
Scott, Ethel (Mr.) 7841
Scott, Henrietta S. 9188
Scott, James 7842
Scott, John 7828
Scott, Madulah 6836
Scott, Mary 404
Scott, Matilda 4509
Scott, Susannah 6742
Scovell, Cynthia R. 1132
Scovell, Elvina 1301
Scovell, Ephraim 7849
Scovell, Maria R. 4443
Scovell, Rachael 5560
Scovell, Seymour 1132, 4443,
 7847
Scovell, Sylvia 1481
Scovil, Mary Jane 7422
Scovill, Elizabeth 7426
Scovill, Hester K. 7266
Scroppel, G. C. (Mr.) 4288
Scroppel, Mary 4288
Scudder, Betsy 3003
Scudder, Hannah 974
Scudder, Laura 1020
Seaman, Rebecca F. 4789
Seamans, Savannah 5601
Searls, Abby 3714
Sears, Charity 6700
Sears, Diana (Mrs.) 7862
Sears, Ebenezer 7862
Sears, Eli 7864
Sears, Harley 5212
Sears, John 5693, 7861
Sears, Martha (Mrs.) 2580
Sears, Nathan L. 7863
Sears, Perlina 5212
Sears, Sarah 7191
Seaver, Maria 39
Seaver, William 7873
Sebbins, Hezekiah 7875
Sebring, Betsey 5658
Sebring, Jane 2263
Secor, Mary 3834
Sedgwick, ___ (Judge) 2498
Seeker, Lucinda 9355
Seeley, ___ (Mrs.) 7883
Seeley, Cornelia 5546

309

Seeley, Julia A. 5873
Seeley, Minerva 4023
Seeley, Sally 2123
Seely, Eunice 4189
Seely, Henry 7888
Seely, Jonas (Maj.) 8145
Seely, Joseph B. 7886, 7887
Seely, Martha 8145
Seely, Martha T. 4185
Seely, Samuel 4185
Seely, Stella 600        9187
Sequin, Mary Frances Octavio
⌄Selby, Hannah 805
Selby, Ira 7898
Selby, Maria H. 6093
Selby, Phebe Ann 9429
Selden, Clarissa 8885
Selden, Edward 8876
Selden, Elizabeth 8886
Selden, Harriet E. 6747
Selden, Helen A. 4291
Selden, Sibyl (Mrs.) 8876
Selfridge, John 7900
Selleck, Betsey 799
Selleck, Harriet 1644
Sellon, John (Rev.) 7901
Sental ___, (Mrs.) 7927
Servis, Katharine 2716
Sessions, Almira 3864
Sessions, Amasa 724
Sessions, Sila (Miss) 724
Severance, Aurelia N. 3389
Sewall, ___ (Judge) 2498
Seward, B. J. 7915
Seward, Olive O. 8804
Sexton, Catherine T. 82
Sexton, Jeremiah 7921
Sexton, Pliny 82, 7920, 7924
Sexton, William S. 7917
Seymour, ___ (Mr.) 7927
Seymour, Catharine 8460
Seymour, Eliza 1623
Seymour, Harriet 6701
Seymour, Joseph 7929
Seymour, Lorenzo 7935
Seymour, Martha 3952
Seymour, Mary 4007
Seymour, Mary B. 6163
Seymour, Phebe Ann (Mrs.) 7935
Seymour, Smith 7928
Seymour, Z. (Mr.) 6163
Seymour, Zachariah 6162
Shadbolt, Angeline 3364
Shadduck, Abraham 7949
Shadduck, Philena 3059
Shadduck, Polly 4624
Shadduck, Roxcenia 1418
Shankland, Urilla 6990
Shappee, Jesse 8975
Shappee, Mary 8975
Sharp, Sarah 9485
Shattuck, Lucius 7957
Shattuck, William 7958
Shaut, Joseph 7960
Shaver, A. 3014
Shaver, Sally 5137
Shaw, Amelia 2922
Shaw, Eliza 8141
Shaw, Harriet 7260
Shaw, James 7975
Shaw, Mary Ann 1406
Shaw, Thomas 7980
Shaw, Warner D. 7971
Shays, ___ (Gen.) 1354
Shays, Caroline 5215
Shays, Rhoda 1354
Shearer, Louisa 7103
Shearer, Robert 7103
Shearman, Amie E. 6345
* Selby, Harriet G. 4065

Shearman, Ann M. 3424
Shearman, Cynthia 5260
Shearman, Daniel 5540
Shearman, Edith 5542
Shearman, Hannah 3760
Shearman, Loring 7992
Shearman, Oliver 6345, 6793
Shearman, Prudence 6793
Shearman, Sarah 5417
Shearman, Susan 6435
Shears, John 7997
Sheckel, Mary 6662
Shed, Betsey 1580
Sheffield, Nathan 8003
Sheffield, Sarah Ann 9399
Shekel, John 4863
Shekel, Mary 4863
Shekell, Cephas 8012
Shekell, Ruth 2616
Shekell, Samuel 8006
Sheldon, E. (Mr.) 7439
Sheldon, Esther 9323
Sheldon, Laura 5500
Sheldon, Louise 6817
Sheldon, Nancy 8884
Sheldon, Wareham 8017
Shelly, Marietta 3794
Shepard, Elizabeth 7171
Shepard, Fitch 8031
Shepard, Flora 3761
Shepard, Frances 9455
Shepard, Henry 8024
Shepard, Joshua 7171
Shepard, Lydia Ann 1946
Shepard, Margaret 5891
Shepard, William 5891, 9452
Shepardson, Amanda 7253
Shepardson, Matilda 9856
Shepardson, Pliny 7243, 7253, 7259
Shepardson, Susan 7243
Shepherd, Fitch 8039
Shepherd, Jane 6362
Shepherd, Lucina 6860
Shepherd, Lydia 1526
Shepherd, Maria 2529
Shepherd, Mary 2158
Shepherd, Susan 8553
Shepherdson, Ann Louisa 6671
Shepherdson, Lydia Ann 8844
Shepherdson, Nancy (Mrs.) 9387
Sheppard, Anna 9092
Sheppard, Morris F. 8043
Sherman. See also Shearman.
Sherman, Alanson 8050
Sherman, Amy W. 1666
Sherman, Anna 1045
Sherman, Durfee 8048
Sherman, Jane 1485
Sherman, Jane Thompson 8221
Sherman, Loring 8047
Sherman, Nancy 4865
Sherman, Nicholas 1666
Sherman, Olive (Mrs.) 4308
Sherman, R. (Miss) 4269
Sherman, Ruth 6082
Sherman, Sally 218, 7531
Sherman, Silas 8065
Sherman, Stephen 6082
Sherman, Susannah H. (Mrs.) 8048
Sherrill, Amelia 2627
Sherwin, Hercelia 6783
Sherwin, Nancy 7219
Sherwin, Sarah (Mrs.) 5747
Sherwood, ___ (Judge) 10017
Sherwood, Abigail 3405
Sherwood, Aurella 5327

Sherwood, Belya 10017
Sherwood, Charlotte 9527
Sherwood, Eliza 8040
Sherwood, Elizabeth 546
Sherwood, Isaac 2127
Sherwood, Jeremiah 9517
Sherwood, Mary 2127, 2239
Sherwood, Mary Ann 957
Sherwood, Meranda 6018
Shethar, Mary Jane 4322
Shideman, Derinda L. 4910
Shields, Cato 8085
Shippey, Susan 2930
Shippy, Deborah 8603
Shirts, Catharine 8396
Shirts, Sarah Jane 9230
Shoemaker, Elijah 8094
Sholes, Elizabeth G. 6053
Sholes, John 6053
Shook, Margaret 5237
Short, George 8098
Short, Georgianna 1751
Short, Sabrina 1246
Short, Theodore 8100
Short, Theophilus 1246
Shove, Lydia P. 4530
Showerman, John 8104, 8105
Showerman, Katy 3438
Showers, James S. 8108
Shuler, Marthalane 410
Shutts, Nelly 2251
Sibley, Amanda 7297
Sibley, Derick 8118
Sibley, James 8120
Sibley, Mary Ann 7851
Sickford, Felinda 5599
Sickles, Margaret 9959
Sigley, Elizabeth 8450
Silence, Maria 6031
Sill, Elizabeth L. 1194
Silsbe, A. H. (Mr.) 8130
Silsbe, Alfred T. 8128
Silsbe, Caroline 1320
Silsbe, James 1320
Silsbe, Jane (Mrs.) 8128
Silsbe, Semantha 9258
Silsbee, Lorinda 1182
Silvernail, Marilla Ann 9116
Silvers, Sally 7562
Simmons, A. (Capt.) 420
Simmons, Ann 8299
Simmons, Annis 6856
Simmons, Clarissa 7286
Simmons, Eleanor G. 3536
Simmons, Jane 3242
Simmons, Rebecca 420
Simpson, Eliza 3287
Simpson, George 8146
Simpson, Henry 8142
Simpson, Jane 8265
Simpson, Jennet H. 3289
Simpson, Polly 2483
Singer, John 6149
Singer, Susanna S. 8149
Sisco, Elizabeth 3517
Sisson, ___ (Mrs.) 3302
Sisson, Anna 771
Sisson, George 8151
Sisson, Permelia 6001
Sisson, William 8152, 8153
Skaats, D. S. (Mr.) 8157
Skaats, D. S. (Mrs.) 6664
Skidmore, Clarissa M. 5131
Skidmore, Timothy 8158
Skinner, ___ (Chief Justice) 9529
Skinner, Amanda 9100
Skinner, Arazetta 4395
Skinner, Charlotte 7254

310

311

Sprague, John S. 8445
Sprague, Maria 1365
Sprague, Phoebe 3680
Sprague, Sally 4310
Springer, Eliza 3940
Springer, Harriet 3307
Springer, Richard 8447
Springsted, Amanda 4673
Springstid, Jonathan 8452
Spurr, Sarah 1313
Squier, Charlotte 3085
Squier, Hannah 7540
Squier, Harriet 6925
Squier, Thirza 2881
Squire, Thomas 8463
Squires, Caroline 1936
Squires, Eliza Ann (Mrs.) 8466
Squires, Nathaniel 8466
Stacey, Nancy 403
Stafford, A. (Mr.) 8473
Stafford, Marcia 361
Stafford, Margaret 10087
Stafford, Spencer, Jr. 8476
Stalp, Maria 8004
Stalp, Orelia 6215
Standish, Charlotte 6242
Standish, Content E. 8008
Stanfield, Benjamin 8484
Stanley, Asa 8465, 9437
Stanley, Caroline L. 9660
Stanley, Elizabeth 5648
Stanley, Emily 9437
Stanley, Hulda 1555
Stanley, Jane F. G. 5958
Stanley, Lucretia 3710
Stanley, Lucy 6005
Stanley, Salma (Maj.) 8493,
  8495
Stanley, Seth 1555, 5578
  5648, 8486, 8487, 8489,
  8494
Stanley, Sophrona 8575
Stansell, Mary 4941
Stanton, Caroline S. 9153
Stanton, Rosannah 6292
Stanyon, Lydia 7738
Staples, Ruth 6932
Star, Polly 9567
Star, William 8500
Starbuck, Ariadne D. 3338
Stark, Almira 8502
Stark, Mary 1595, 4683, 9776
Stark, Pamilla 2728
Starks, Catharine 1113
Starks, Eliza 2236
Starkweather, Lucinda 2198
Starkweather, Maria 1463
Starkweather, Samuel 1463
Starret, Catharine 2122
Starrow, Joseph 8513
Stautice, Louise 1207
Stearns, John R. 8520
Stearns, Lydia A. 10121
Stearns, Tabitha 6522
Stearns, William 8517
Stebbins, Martha 1307
Stebins, Clarissa 9317
Stedman, Merinda 9965
Steel, Levice 5397
Steel, William 8529
Steele, Chloe 3067
Stephens, Eliza 2503
Stephens, Emeline 357
Stephens, Franklin D. 8544
Stephens, Matilda B. 8540
Stephens, Nathan 8543
Stephens, Pamelia 294
Stephens, Sophrona 8544
Stephens, Tamar 7174

Stephens, Uriah 8538
Stephens, Walter 8535, 8540
Stephenson, James 8548
Sterling, Margaret 6713
Sterns, Adeline 4220
Sterret, Ann 2619
Sterret, Jane 8792
Stetson, Almira G. 3060
Stetson, Dulcena 9450
Stetson, Mary Ann 8705
Steuben, ___ (Baron) 9391
Stevens, ___ (Mr.) 2674
Stevens, Daniel 8564
Stevens, Lucinda 1525
Stevens, Mary 5559
Stevens, Permelia 5412
Stevens, Phineas 8556
Stevens, Sally Mariah 7403
Stevens, Stephen 8561
Stevenson, John 8567
Stevenson, Margaret 7389
Stevenson, Martha Washington
  1699
Steward, Almira 3486
Stewart, Ann Maria 7216
Stewart, Augusta 2519
Stewart, Ayres M. 5875
Stewart, Calcina E. 1188
Stewart, Catharine 2793
Stewart, Cynthia 4068
Stewart, E. S. (Mr.) 7468
Stewart, Eliza 1101
Stewart, Elizabeth 171
Stewart, Elizabeth J. 7468
Stewart, Fanny D. 4037
Stewart, G. D. (Mr.) 8573
Stewart, James 8588
Stewart, Jane 9813
Stewart, John 8589
Stewart, Loisa 963
Stewart, Marian 2284
Stewart, Mary Ann 3807
Stewart, R. B. (Mr.) 8574
Stewart, Rebecca 7771
Stewart, Richard B. 5973
Stewart, Samuel 8581
Stewart, Sarah 5973
Stewart, Susan 7365
Stickney, Rosanna 38
Stiles, Elizabeth 8166
Stiles, Hester Ann 4250
Stiles, Sephronia 5918
Stiles, William 8597
Still, ___ (Mr.) 8602
Stillman, Angeline B. 6738
Stillman, Mary Ann 4267
Stilson, Eli 3960
Stilson, Polly 4102
Stilson, Polly Ann 3960
Stimers, Emeline (Mrs.) 8611
Stimers, John 8610
Stimers, Philip 8611
Stocking, ___ (Mr.) 1235
Stocking, Abbey Jane 1677
Stocking, Lucy 8394
Stocking, Mary Ann 4045
Stockwell, Elizabeth C. 2313
Stodard, Lucy 2819
Stoddard, Betty 1138
Stoddard, Eunice 5234
Stoddard, F. U. (Mr.) 8632
Stoddard, Josiah 8624
Stoddard, Julia 9815
Stoddard, J lia Ann 6328
Stoddard, Matilda 3634
Stoddard, Silas 8621
Stoddard, Tabitha Frances
  1477
Stoddard, Wait 1480

Stoddard, Wealthy 255
Stokes, Olive 5963
Stokes, Polly (Mrs.) 5960
Stone, ___ 681
Stone, ___ (Col.) 923
Stone, Artemus 8459
Stone, Asahel 3013
Stone, Celeste A. 1890
Stone, Ebenezer B. 8641
Stone, Jason H. 8636
Stone, Lavina 6950
Stone, Lott 8652
Stone, Mary A. 4699
Stone, Orange 8651
Stone, Roxana 3553
Stone, Sabra 3013
Stone, Sally 5141
Stone, Samson A. (Miss) 6257
Stone, Sarah 2755
Stone, William (Rev.) 6257,
  8655
Stoneman, Catharine C. 1495
Stoneman, George 88
Storey, E. C. (Mr.) 8658
Storey, M. A. (Miss) 1361
Storey, Phila (Mrs.) 8658
Storms, Betsey 3690
Story, Calista E. 5965
Stoughton, Anna 4554
Stout, Amos 8663
Stout, Hannah (Mrs.) 4491
Stout, Keziah 8600
Stout, Lydia 5988
Stout, Mary 9216
Stow, Catharine A. 3989
Stow, John 3523, 8666
Stow, L. Maria 3523
Strachan, William 8673
Straight, Eunice 7372
Strait, Alvira 1022
Strait, Betsey Ann 2155
Street, Emily Ann 1082
Street, Phoebe Ann 3391
Strickland, Elizabeth 8413
Strickland, Lucia Ann (Mrs.)
  2493
Strickland, Sarah 2367
Striker, Mahala G. 7500
Stringer, Irena 2244
Strong, Almy 7334
Strong, Ann 9890
Strong, Caleb 8702
Strong, Catharine 9510
Sttong, Cyrus 8692
Strong, Delia 7356
Strong, Emily 8197
Strong, Fanny E. 6122
Strong, John W. 2950
Strong, Julia 2950
Strong, N. D. (Rev.) 8695
Strong, Noble D. (Rev.) 8701
Strong, T. C. (Mr.) 8693
Strong, T. R. (Mr.) 8699
Strong, Theron R. 8690
Stroup, Betsey 10136
Strunk, Henry 8706
Strunk, Henry, 2nd 8708
Strunk, Jacob 8707
Strunk, John 8710
Stryker, Hester Ann 8942
Stryker, Mary Ann 7285
Stuart, Dennis 8643
Stuart, Eliza 8643
Studley, Laura 9887
Stull, Zemanda 395
Sturges, Lewis B. 330
Sturgess, Almyra 787
Suckley, George 8717
Summer, George P. 8719

312

Sutherland, Isaac 3129, 8727
Sutherland, Sarah 3129
Sutland, Almira 1588
Sutton, Benjamin 8737
Sutton, Margaret A. 4258
Sutton, Sophrona 6618
Sutton, William 8731
Swan, Ann F. 181
Swan, Phebe 4373
Swn, Sybil 1815
Swart, Ann Eliza 5403
Swart, P. (Mr.) 5403
Swart, Peter 8741
Swarthout, Aaron 8742
Swarthout, Hannah 1162
Swarthout, Isabel 2271
Swarthout, Levina 1633
Swartout, Patty 9333
Swartout, Polly 8608
Swartwout, Banardus 8744
Sweat, Jonathan 8746
Sweatland, Parmela 3982
Sweeney, John 8748
Sweeny, Jane 4454
Sweet, Harriet 1537
Sweet, Phebe L. 9240
Swezey, Walter F. 8756
Swick, B. R. (Rev.) 8758
Swift, Abigail 4401
Swift, Ann (Mrs.) 2400
Swift, Asa R. 8775
Swift, Charles 8763
Swift, E. (Mr.) 8764
Swift, Elisha 8759
Swift, Fanny (Mrs.) 8775
Swift, H. (Mr.) 8764
Swift, Harriet 578, 3842
Swift, J. G. (Gen.) 8779
Swift, Judah 8760
Swift, Julia Ann 8761
Swift, Mary 8765
Swift, Moses 8766
Swift, Philetus 8762, 8778
Swift, Reuben 578, 8771
Swift, Reuben (Mrs.) 8780
Switzer, Henry 8781
Taber, B. (Capt.) 4649
Taber, Benjamin 4656
Taber, Carolyn 7453
Taber, Sally Ann 4649
Taft, Harriet 5714
Taft, Harriet E. 6997
Taft, Harriet J. 1209
Taggart, Moses 8793
Tailor, Sarah 651
Talbot, Elizabeth G. 8856
Talbot, Thomas 8856
Talcott, Mary R. 7091
Tallmadge, ___ (Gen.) 8796
Tallmadge, James 8797
Tallman, Jane 3433
Tallman, Mariette 7984
Tallman, Matilda 7159
Tanner, C. (Mr.) 3137
Tanner, Lucinda 3137
Tappan, William 8806
Tarney, Eliza 6963
Tayler, Erastus 8810
Tayler, John 8808
Taylor, ___ (Dr.) 8811
Taylor, ___ (Miss) 5052
Taylor, Almira 4093
Taylor, Ann 5164
Taylor, Eliphalet 4093
Taylor, Eliza H. 4724
Taylor, Elizabeth 1747
Taylor, Elizabeth C. 8117
Taylor, Ephraim 8833
Taylor, G. W. (Mr.) 8820

Taylor, George W. 8117, 8817, 9730
Taylor, Graty 2586
Taylor, Harriet Maria (Mrs.) 8777
Taylor, Helen Ann 9730
Taylor, Jane E. 2632
Taylor, John 8832
Taylor, Lucy 3788
Taylor, Lydia 9615
Taylor, Mary 4953
Taylor, Miranda 8835
Taylor, Nancy 3636
Taylor, O. (Gen.) 8837
Taylor, Othniel (Gen.) 8817a
Taylor, Samuel 8822
Teale, Harriet 4149
Teale, N. (Capt.) 4149, 5696
Tedman, Alma 5001
Temple, Elizabeth 9680
Ten Broeck. See also, possibly, Tinbrook.
Ten Broeck, Anna 5841
Ten Broeck, George Abraham 8846
Terrell, Miles 8849
Terrill, Unsuna 1867
Terry, Patience 8062
Terry, William 8856
Terwilliger, James 4768
Tew, Ann Maria 2031
Tew, Emily 4904
Tew, George W. 8864
Tew, Matilda 8546
Tews, ___ (Mr.) 3005
Thatcher, Nancy 5647
Thatcher, Sally 4408
Thatcher, Thomas 8869
Thayer, ___ (Mr.) 8871
Thayer, Amana 8890
Thayer, Ann 9741
Thayer, Betsey 9484, 9530
Thayer, Charles 8879
Thayer, Chloe P. 3444
Thayer, Christopher, Sr. 8875
Thayer, Elizabeth 5829
Thayer, Joel 8877, 8888
Thayer, Levi 5829, 8874, 8876, 8882
Thayer, Marina 8790
Thayer, Mary Ann (Mrs.) 8879
Thayer, Mary Emeline 2387
Thayer, Nathan 9741
Thayer, Savannah 8791
Thayer, Smith 8880
Thomas, Clarissa 6037
Thomas, Daniel 8900
Thomas, David 8892
Thomas, Elinor 1255
Thomas, Ellen B. 2953
Thomas, Fanny H. 3736
Thomas, Harriet 4069
Thomas, James 8913
Thomas, Janet 7373
Thomas, Perisses 2280
Thomas, Welthy Ann 9809
Thompson, ___ (Capt.) 8918
Thompson, ___ (Judge) 6503
Thompson, ___ (Mrs.) 8357
Thompson, Allen B. 8926
Thompson, Alvira 7382
Thompson, Ann 5709, 6052
Thompson, Anna Maria 9938
Thompson, Caleb 8932
Thompson, Catharine 5244
Thompson, Christiana 5529
Thompson, Eliza 7360
Thompson, Esther Ann 6503
Thompson, Henry 8919

Thompson, Jane 7447
Thompson, John 8934
Thompson, Lucy G. 2258
Thompson, Maria 251
Thompson, Martha 3519
Thompson, Martha C. 624
Thompson, Paulina 2339
Thompson, Roda 8437
Thompson, Susannah 4474
Thompson, T. C. (Mr.) 905
Thompson, William 8922, 8933
Thomson, C. B. (Mr.) 8945
Thornton, Virginia S. 335
Thorp, Almy 3139
Thorp, Emily 8946
Thorp, Esther 8206
Thrall, Mary 1228
Thrasher, Hamubital 5435
Thrasher, Mahitable 84
Throckmorton, B. (Mr.) 8659
Throop, Benjamin, Jr. 8964
Throop, Eliza C. 4091
Throop, Enos T. 8966
Throop, George B. 8960
Throop, Rachel 4351
Throop, Ruth 7450
Throop, Sarah G. 7451
Thurber, Abner 8972
Thurber, Alva 3948
Thurbur, Maria H. 2422
Thurston, Ann Maria 7154
Thurston, Isaac 7154
Tibbets, Mahala 9833
Tibbets, Rebecca 1176
Tibbetts, Mahala 1017
Tibbits, George 8974
Tice, Abigail 806
Tice, Hannah Louiza 6512
Tice, Lydia Ann 807
Tice, Rebecca 3048
Tice, Rhoda 1760
Tickner, Roswell 8977
Tiffany, ___ (Mr.) 8983
Tiffany, Albert W. 8985
Tiffany, Betsey 1034
Tiffany, Betsey R. 4059
Tiffany, Israel 8978
Tiffany, Jehial 8986
Tiffany, L. F. (Mr.) 8988
Tiffany, Lucy (Mrs.) 8981, 8984
Tiffany, Ruth 5805
Tiffany, Silas 8981, 8984
Tiffany, W. N. (Mr.) 8989
Tilbury, George 8993
Tilden, Clarissa 434
Tillinghast, John L. 8994, 8995
Tillman, A. P. (Mr.) 8395, 8997
Tillotson, Nancy 4583
Tilton, Ann 9908
Tinbrook. See also, possibly, Ten Broeck.
Tinbrook, Anna 5841
Tinbrook, Catharine 3084
Tiney, Hannah 8071
Tingley, Daniel 9003, 9004
Tingley, Emily 3170
Tinkham, Isaac 9008
Tinney, Hannah M. 109
Tinny, Loretta 9242
Tippets, Caroline 9877
Tippetts, Polly 2201
Tirrell, Clarinda M. 5954
Tisdale, Ira J. 9016
Tisdale, James 9015
Tisdale, Jane 2444
Tisdale, Mary 7976

Tisdale, Rhoda M. (Mrs.) 9016
Tobey, Keziah 7113
Tobias, Amelia Ann 5043
Todd, Barbary Maria 3341
Todd, Elizabeth (Mrs.) 9665
Todd, Harriet 2014
Todd, Levina 6487
Todd, Margaret 4782
Todd, Mary Ann 2093
Todd, Sarah Ann 1412
Tolbert, Mary Ann 2459
Tolford, David 9028
Tolford, Mary (Mrs.) 9027
Tolford, William 9027
Toll, Philip R. 9030
Tolls, Harriet A. 6129
Tolsday, Elizabeth 1416
Tomer, Amanda 9744
Tompkins, ___ (Gov.) 8318, 9036, 9040
Tompkins, ___ (Vice Pres. of U. S.) 9037
Tompkins, Daniel D. 3558, 9034
Tompkins, Frances (Mrs.) 94
Tompkins, Jonathan Griffin 9040
Tompkins, Sarah Ann 3558
Tompkins, Susan M. 8318
Tooker, Ann 10162
Tooker, Frances 4640
Tooker, Sarah 8999
Torrance, Sally 2139
Torrey, Henry 9049
Towar, Henry 9055, 9061, 9062, 9063
Towar, Henry (Mrs.) 4070
Towl, Sophia 9803
Towle, Celia 1075
Towle, Elizabeth B. 1648
Towle, John 9064
Towle, Mary 8867
Towle, Susan 3471
Town, Orlando 9065
Towner, E. (Gen.) 9067
Towner, Mary 2764
Townsend, ___ (Rev.) 7849
Townsend, Abby 3802
Townsend, Amanda 5899
Townsend, Ann 1258, 7189
Townsend, Anna 4973
Townsend, Charles 7265
Townsend, Eleazer M. 9078
Townsend, H. A. (Mr.) 9997
Townsend, Harriet 6870
Townsend, Helen Ann 9997
Townsend, Henry A. 9074
Townsend, Henry A. 9079
Townsend, Jane 1206
Townsend, Jesse (Rev.) 9075, 9076
Townsend, Joel (Rev.) 6549
Townsend, Margaret Maria 9843
Townsend, Martha 247
Townsend, Mary J. 8168
Townsend, Mary W. 7265
Townsend, Nathan 8168, 9087
Townsend, Samuel 9077
Townsend, Sarah 6549
Townsend, Sarah C. 8088
Townsend, Uriah 1206
Townsend, William 9843
Towsley, Amelia 2447
Tracy, Elias 9093
Tracy, Emeline B. 5270
Tracy, Hatch 9094
Tracy, Hyla 6322
Tracy, Jane L. 380
Trask, Sophronia 9536

Travace, Hannah 9545
Traver, Levi 9097
Traver, Susan (Mrs.) 9097
Tredwell, Ann Maria 7134
Tredwell, Nathaniel H. 7134
Trimmer, Polly 3392
Tripp, Ruth 4759
Trotter, Lydia (Mrs.) 5995
Trotter, Thomas 4712
Troup, Charlotte 1092
Troup, Robert 1092
Trowbridge, ___ (Mr.) 9107
Trowbridge, Daniel 9112
Trowbridge, Hetty 1787
Truacs, Fulena 1781
Truax, Gertrude B. 867
Truax, Margaret 6850
Trudeau, ___ (Mademoiselle) 9839
True, Diana 6264
True, Hannah 5520
Truesdale, Gershom 9114
Truesdel, Phidelia 2747
Truman, Olive H. 7032
Trumbull, Dorothy 615
Trumbull, Nancy 5543
Trusdell, Mary Ann 1054
Tryon, Sarah 8124
Tubbs, Bathsheba 4986
Tubbs, Cynthia 5742
Tubbs, Emiline 6630
Tucker, Achsah Maria 2812
Tucker, Albigence W. 9131
Tucker, Betsey 9345
Tucker, Harriet E. 3223
Tucker, Lucy 8754
Tucker, Luther 9129, 9134, 9140
Tucker, Nancy 1190
Tucker, Polly 2840, 8755
Tudor, Mary 2938
Tuell, Mary 309
Turck, Abraham, Jr. 9151
Turck, Anthony 9152
Turck, Anthony, Jr. 9151
Turck, Abram (Capt.) 2176
Turk, Archibald J. 9154
Turk, Maria 2176
Turner, Almira 4923
Turner, Amanda 1662
Turner, C. A. (Mrs.) 7251
Turner, Caroline 2472
Turner, Enoch 2472, 9164
Turner, Margaret 7922
Turner, Martha 8687
Turner, Melissa 1564
Turner, Nancy 7364
Turner, Noah (Capt.) 1662
Turner, Rosannah 4441
Turner, Slly 6665
Turner, Ursula 8368
Turrey, Roxy 5427
Tuthill, Esther (Mrs.) 9170
Tuthill, Frances 4279, 4645
Tuthill, Harriet 4036
Tuthill, Mariah 740
Tuthill, Samuel (Capt.) 740
Tuttle, Benjamin 6382
Twenty Canoes, Nancy 9874
Tyler, Eliza G. 4848
Tyler, Harriet 360
Tyler, Nancy 1403
Tyler, Rhoda 874
Tyler, Speedy 3445
Umstead, Esther 2883
Uncles, J. 9814
Underhill, Caroline S. 1502
Underhill, Mary E. 6250
Underhill, Mary Elizabeth 6259

Underhill, Mary Jane 266
Underhill, P. B. 6259
Upham, A. S. 9191
Upham, Catharine L. 9911
Upson, Susan 1813
Upton, Mary 9372
Van Allen, Elizabeth 8399
Van Alst 2489
Van Amber, Mathew 9200
Van Amburg, Sarah F. 20
Van Aukin, Lydia (Mrs.) 9204
Van Aukin, Simeon 9204
Van Blaicom, Catharine 5490
Van Brunt, Phoebe 2526
Van Buren, James 2674
Van Buren, M. R. (Mr.) 9211
Van Buren, Margaret 1035
Van Buren, Martin (Hon.) 9209
Van Buskirk, Jane Ann 4293
Van Campen, Moses 8382
Van Clief, A. (Miss) 794
Van Cliff, ___ (Mrs.) 4146
Van Cortland, ___ (Capt.) 9221
Van Cortlandt, Pierre 9222
Vandebogart, Sarah 3239
Vandercourt, Moicah 8750
Vanderhooven, Annis (Mrs.) 9232
Vanderhooven, Jesse 9232
Vandoren, Eliza C. 150
Van Deusen, Charlotte 2231
Van Deusen, Eliza 8038
Van Deusen, G. (Mrs.) 9231
Van Deusen, J. B. (Mr.) 9241
Van Deusen, John 2826
Van Deusen, Mary Jane 2826
Van Deuzen, Emily 9592
Van Dine, Anna 1798
*Vandine, Jane 6069
Van Duser, Susan 10058
Van Duser, William 10058
Van Duzer, Isabel 536
Van Dyck, Eleanor 2408
Van Dyck, James 2408, 5069
Van Dyck, Sophia A. 5069
Van Fleet, Joshua 9250
Van Gelder, Catharine 301
Vangelder, Eliza 539
Van Gorder, Elizabeth 5840
Van Greson, Jane 3468
Van Hoosen, Ann 121
Van Horn, Margaret 527
Van Housen, John 9262
Van Ungen, Margaret Louisa 6940
Vanlieu, Maria 7320
Vanlim, Margaret 5481
Van Ness, Catharine 116, 3614
Van Ness, W. W. 3614
Van Ness, William P. (Judge) 9269
Van Ness, William W. (Judge) 9272
Van Nostrand, Bethiah 692
Vanorman. See also Venorman.
Vanorman, Hannah 10074
Vanornam, Rosana 1568
Van Ostrand, Catharine 5104
Van Pelt, John 9279
Van Pelt, Sally 5256
Van Rensselaer, Alida Maria 1521
Van Rensselaer, Jeremiah 1521, 9287
Van Rensselaer, Stephen (Gen.) 5451
Van Ri___, Catharine 1584
Van Riper, Eliza 2681
Van Riper, Sally 9774
Van Riper, Sophia 2021
Van Scoy, Priscilla 10146
* Vandorn, Anna (Mrs.) 2121

Van Sickle, Hannah A. 1226
Van Tassel, Eliza 6674
Van Valkenburgh, Margaret 3679
Van Vechten, John 9299
Van Vechten, Teunis 9299
Van Vleck, Jane Ann 8711
Van Vranken, Charles 9302
Van Vranken, Margaret 7028
Van Vranken, Nicholas (Rev.)
  7027, 7028
Van Vranken, Phineas Prouty
  9302
Van Waggenen, Eliza K. 8480
Van Wagoner, Margaret 4276
Van Wie, Catharine 9264
Van Woert, William 9306
Van Wormer, Rachael 1119
Vail, Elizabeth 4009
Vail, Mary 1267
Vaill, Eevelina 5096
Valkenburgh, Gertrude C. 9383
Valkenburgh, J. (Mr.) 9383
Vance, Elizabeth M. 6515
Vance, Margaret 4211
Vares, Francis 9445
Vaughan, John 9316
Vaughan, Rebecca 3076
Vaughn, Lodamia 4938
Vedder, William 9319
Veley, Polly 9257
Velie, Catharine 4630
Velie, Clarissa Ann 6195
Venorman. See also Vanorman.
Venorman, Phoebe 1047
Verplanck, Isaav A. 9321
Verplanck, J. V. D. (Mr.)
  9320
Viles, Catherine 1583
Vincent, Charlotte Ann 1873
Vincent, Eliza 3507
Voorhees, Catherine 8468
Voorhees, John 8468
Voorhies, Elizabeth 7882
Voorhies, Rosetta 9340
Voorhies, William 9334, 9335,
  9336, 9337, 9340
Vorse, Charles 9341
Vosburgh, Eddy (Miss) 8316
Vosburgh, Rebecca 4212
Vredenburgh, ___ (Col.) 6878
Vredenburgh, Cornelia 9573
Vredenburgh, Eliza 6878
Vredenburgh, Evelina 8965
Vredenburgh, John 9350
Vredenburgh, William J. 9573
Vroman, Sally 5624
Vrose, Ann 4652
Waddell, Mary Jane 8161
Waddum, Sally 197
Wade, Jonathan 9353
Wade, Mary Helen 466
Wade, Sally 3575
Wadsworth, James 9358, 9360
Wadsworth, Orissa 5021
Wadsworth, William (Gen.)
  9358
Wagener, A. (Mr.) 9365
Wagener, Abraham 9363
Wagener, Susan 5982
Waggoner, Emiline 4482
Waggoner, James 9367
Wait, Emeline M. 784
Wait, Emily E. 9681 Wait, Ira
  (Judge) 784
Wait, Philena 8751
Wait, Sophia (Mrs.) 9369
Waite, Augusta 4710
Waite, Chester 1498
Waite, D. D. (Mrs.) 163, 165,
  167

Waite, Elizabeth 1498
Waite, William B. 4710
Wake, Jane 2157
Wakeman, Laura 1504
Walbridge, Elizabeth 9526
Walbridge, Harriet 6273
Walbridgem Henry 9375
Walbridge, Rhoda 5015
Walcott, Ellen Marion (Mrs.)
  560
Walden, Ebenezer 9378
Wales, George 6927
Wales, Mary E. 6927
Walker, Benjamin 9389
Walker, Eliza 7736
Walker, Eliza H. 6787
Walker, Elizabeth (Mrs.) 1725
Walker, Fanny 3632
Walker, Hiram 9398, 9403
Walker, James 9406
Walker, John 9402
Walker, Lurena 1337
Walker, Lydia 9700
Walker, Nancy 9398
Wlaker, St. John 9394
Walker, Sally Ann 5456
Walker, Sarah J. 5968
Wall, Tryphena 8577
Wallace, Desdemona 604
Wallace, Elizabeth 8647
Wallace, James 660
Wallace, M. C. (Miss) 660
Walling, Amanda M. 1632
Walling, Lucy Sane 6596
Walling, Mary 5042
Walsh, Catharine 459
Walsh, Dudley 459, 9417, 9418
Walter, Julia A. 6768
Walters, Jacob 9420
Walters, John 9421
Walton, Anna Maria 621
Walton, Lovina 8351
Walton, Sarah H. 4826
Ward, Ann 3410
Ward, Catharine 6156
Ward, Eliza G. 3134
Ward, Elmira 4003
Ward, Emily 1005
Ward, Frederick 8243
Ward, Jemima 8709
Ward, John (Deacon) 9433
Ward, Joseph 9434
Ward, Nancy 971
Ward, Rhoda 8571
Warden, Eliza 842
Warden, John 9442
Warden, Maria Ann 6855
Warden, Pamelia (Mrs.) 7793
Ware, Ann Maria 1484
Ware, Eliza 3234
Ware, Harriet 2457
Ware, Joseph K. (Dr.) 9444
Wares, Francis 9445
Warner, Adelia 8440
Warner, Altha B. 9716
Warner, Amanda 5675
Warner, Asenith 368
Warner, David 9463
Warner, Eliza Ann 7724
Warner, Elizabeth 5334
Warner, Elvira 4382
Warner, Lucetta 5655
Warner, Mary 5717
Warner, Matilda 8007
Warner, Nancy 1095
Warner, Riel 9452
Warner, Samuel 9460
Warner, Solomon 4382, 8007
Warner, Sophia 4909

Warner, Susan 6693
Warren, ___ (Miss) 2272
Warren, Anna 6976
Warren, E. F. (Mr.) 9468
Warren, Emily 5107
Warren, Harriet 9436
Warren, J. W. (Mr.) 9478
Warren, Jemima 523
Warren, Jonathan 9487
Warren, Joseph (Gen.) 9490
Warren, Laura Ann 642
Warren, Lucinda 4072
Warren, Mary Ann 6196
Warren, Nathaniel 9469, 9477
Warren, Oliver W. L. 9490
Warren, Phebe 8745
Warren, Phineas (Col.) 2325
Warren, Samuel 1175
Warren, Sarah 8474
Warren, Sarah (Mrs.) 9478
Warren, Sarah H. 2325
Warren, Steward K. 9483
Warren, Stewart K. 9480
Warren, William 9467
Warson, ___ (Mrs.) 648
Washburn, Hannah 747, 1193
Washington, ___ (Gen.) 3096,
  5669
Washington, George 4689
Washington, George (Gen.) 9313,
  9391
Waterman, Caroline 949
Waterman, Eliza Ann 2510
Waterman, Jedediah 2510
Waterous, Eliza 3100
Waterous, Maria 1914
Waters, Maria 1914
Waters, Rose 1185
Waters, Sally 518
Watkins, Almina 1191
Watkins, Andrew 1789
Watkins, Joan 8354
Watkins, Simon 9511
Watkins, Sophia 4664
Watkins, Zilpha 1789
Watkinson, Sarah (Mrs.) 9515
Watkinson, William 9515
Watrous, Polly 1098
Watson, ___ (Mr.) 9516
Watson, Alkanah 5188, 9519,
  9529
Watson, Hannah 8306
Watson, Mary 8030
Watson, Roxana 6736
Watson, Samuel 8030
Watson, William 9524
Watson, William W. 9517
Waugh, Catharine 6874
Way, Eliza 1902
Way, Laura 123
Way, Sarah Helen 3953
Weaver, A. (Mr.) 3038
Weaver, Lucena 3038
Weaver, Lusina 5098
Weaver, Phebe 4159
Webb, Nancy 3635
Weber, Joseph 9547, 9548
Weber, Martha 9548
Weber, Michael 9550
Webster, ___ (Prof.) 9566
Webster, Caroline (Mrs.) 9557
Webster, James 9557
Webster, Jane 9825
Webster, Noah 9565
Webster, Sarah 9794
Weed, Israel 9570
Weed, Jane 9172
Weed, Smith 9571
Weeks, Deborah 2979, 8273

Weeks, Ezra 6500
Weeks, Mary Ann 6500
Welch, Joseph 2674
Welch, Thankful 8629
Weller, Amos R. 9585
Weller, Mary Ann (Mrs.) 9585
Welles, Abigail Woolsey 5471
Welles, Benjamin (Dr.) 9588
Welles, Noah 5471
Wellington, Mary 3151
Wellman, Achsah 8379
Wellman, Harriet M. 7904
Wells, Alithea 6254
Wells, Eleanor 10110
Wells, Eliza S. 4079
Wells, Emily A. 3752
Wells, Fanny 3292
Wells, Harriet 3816
Wells, Helen H. 6909
Wells, Lucia 7325
Wells, Mary A. 8122
Wells, R. (Dr.) 8122
Wells, Rhoda P. 6846
Wells, Richard (Dr.) 9609
Wells, Sarah 9602
Wells, Semanthe 9846
Wells, Susan P. 9102
Wells, William H. 3752, 9611
Welton, Elias 9619
Wentworth, Mary 804, 8803
Wentworth, Uriah 9621
Werks, I. (Mr.) 9626
Werner, Altha B. 9709
Wescot, Laura A. 516
Wescot, Pauline E. 99
Wescott, ___ (Mr.) 9627
Wescott, Susan 8887
West, Betsey (Mrs.) 9636
West, Elizabeth 2154
West, Eveline 1260
West, Henry 9640, 9644
West, Loisa H. 7019
West, Paulina 7967
West, X. (Mr.) 9642
West, Xenocrates 9639
Westfall, Catharine 9760
Westfall, J. (Mr.) 9647
Westfall, Mary 7712
Wetherby, Philena 9928
Wetmore, Ebenezer 9656
Whaley, Betsey 7008
Whalley, Mary 5776
Whally, Sarah 6553
Wheat, Julia Ann 7242
Wheat, Roxena M. 8841
Wheaton, Alice Maria 3241
Wheaton, Syrenus 9669
Whedon, Calvin 9670
Whedon, Marcena 9672
Wheeler, Ann 7096
Wheeler, Arabella Elizette
4064
Wheeler, Betsey 9687
Wheeler, David 9687
Wheeler, Dorcas 854
Wheeler, Elias 9675
Wheeler, Eliza 212
Wheeler, Elizabeth 4866
Wheeler, George 1036
Wheeler, George A. 4064
Wheeler, Gratia 7259
Wheeler, Grattan H. 212,
1224
Wheeler, Guy 7104
Wheeler, Harriet 3301, 8893,
8904
Wheeler, James 9679
Wheeler, Jeremiah 7259,
9688

Wheeler, Lucy 6331
Wheeler, Lydia Ann 9431
Wheeler, Marion 4251
Wheeler, Mary 7128
Wheeler, Mary Ann 1040
Wheeler, Sally Ann 2965
Wheeler, Sarah 1224
Wheeler, Silas 9693
Wheeler, Sophia 4752
Wheeler, Zenas 9695
Wheelock, Abigail R. 4105
Wheelock, Asa 4105
Whipple, Augusta A. 4632
Whipple, Charles 9705
Whipple, Luther 9706
Whipple, Lydia B. 3426
Whipple, P. L. (Rev.) 4632
Whipple, Robert 9711
Whipple, Russell 4234
Whippo, Hannah 9715
Whippo, James 9715
Whitaker, John 9717
Whitaker, Priscilla 7506
White, A. G. (Dr.) 9866
White, Catharine 8907
White, Edward 4074, 9289,
9742
White, Emily 8851
White, Fanny A. 510
White, Ira 9740
White, James 9724, 9729
White, James (Dr.) 9732
White, Job 9721
White, Julia Ann 2985
White, Luther 9197
White, Mary 2737
White, Mary Ann 1108
White, Mary Ann 4809
White, Miranda 7374
White, Nancy 4798
White, Nancy E. 3189
White, Nancy M. 9197
White, Nehemiah 9745
White, Orlina R. 9866
White, Patty 1877
White, Phebe 4635
White, Samuel 9721
White, Sarah M. 9173
White, Satira 3641
White, Sophia 4074
White, Thomas (Rev.) 9720
Whiteford, Elizabeth 7880
Whiteford, Thomas 9750
Whitehead, Sally 3323
Whitehouse, L. I. (Miss) 1093
Whiteside, Ann 819
Whitfield, Elizabeth M. 8678
Whiting, Augustus 9755
Whiting, B. (Gen.) 9753
Whiting, B. (Mr.) 9756
Whiting, Charles (Gen.) 9759
Whiting, Eb (Maj.) 9753
Whiting, Eliza 8018
Whiting, Hannah 1068
Whiting, Harriet 1413
Whiting, John 1281
Whiting, John (Gen.) 9763
Whiting, L. C. (Mr.) 9762
Whiting, Nancy 7354
Whiting, Sabin 9758
Whiting, Sarah 1281
Whitman, John 5736
Whitman, Sarah 5736
Whitman, Oliver (Deacon) 9771
Whitmore, Seth 9772
Whitney, Abraham I. 2138
Whitney, Augusta Ann 4012
Whitney, Aurelia 6079
Whitney, Betsey 1514

Whitney, Deborah 9507
Whitney, Emeline 2138
Whitney, Esther 4504
Whitney, James 5484
Whitney, Joel 4504, 9784
Whitney, Mary Antoinette 5484
Whitney, Nathan 9784, 9789
Whitney, Rascum 9507
Whitney, Samuel W. 9775
Whitney, Susannah 3896
Whitney, Thomas 4012
Whittemore, Permelia 7769
Whittemore, S. (Mr.) 9795
Whittemore, S. F. (Mrs.) 9795
Whittlesey, Emeline 8617
Wickes, Maria 8826
Wiggins, Elsie Lovisa 4567
Wiggins, Phebe 4603
Wight, ___ (Mrs.) 5999
Wightman, Maria 8503
Wightman, Mary 8079
Wilber, Hoxy H. 9804
Wilber, Lucinthia 553
Wilber, Samuel 9806
Wilbur, Clarissa 7077
Wilbur, Laura 482
Wilber, Phoebe 1592
*Wilcox, A. G. (Mr.) 9814
Wilcox, Aaron 9827
Wilcox, Abigail H. 4078
Wilcox, Almira 2484
Wilcox, Chloe 9954
Wilcox, Diantha 750
Wilcox, Elmira 7215
Wilcox, Freeborn 9821
Wilcox, Jane Eliza 9014
Wilcox, Marabe 4215
Wilcox, Mary 4137
Wilcox, Mary Ann 5398
Wilcox, Polly 8457
Wilcox, Prudence 1011
Wilcox, Ralph (Dr.) 4078
Wilcox, Thomas A. 9828
Wilcox, William 4215
Wilcox, William J. (Rev.) 9826
Wilder, Altha 9048
Wilder, Ann (Mrs.) 960
Wilder, Betsey 6303
Wilder, Clarissa A. 4855
Wilder, Joseph 9831
Wiley, Laura 3283
Wilford, Maria A. 9985
Wilhelm, Hannah 3598
Wilkalaw, Betsey 4342
Wilkes, ___ (Miss) 4162
Wilkes, B. (Mr.) 9838
Wilkes, John 4162
Wilkie, Harriet 563
Wilkie, Mary 836
Wilkin, Peggy 153
Wilkinson, ___ (Gen.) 3483
Wilkinson, Lidia 3226
Will, Abigail 8150
Willard, Clarissa 580
Willard, Emma (Mrs.) 1012
Willard, Harmis 9842
Willard, Lucy Emeline 5012
Willcox, Clarissa 3785
Willcox, Cynthia D. 5449
Willcox, David 4140
Willcox, Louisa 8787
Willcox, Renewed 9895
Willey, Caroline 7299
Williams, ___ (Mr.) 5296
Williams, Amelia 4168
Williams, Ann 6132
Williams, Anna 2704
Williams, Benjamin 944
Williams, Clarinda 4175
*For Wilcox see also Willcox.

Williams, Cornelia 5404
Williams, D. S. (Mr.) 9861
Williams, Daniel S. 9860,
  9866, 9871
Williams, Delia 9920
Williams, Delia M. 3567
Williams, Diana 8420
Williams, Eliza 4890
Williams, Elizabeth 2369
Williams, Emeline 2391
Williams, Emily 3075
Williams, Eunice 7991
Williams, Harriet Love 159
Williams, Huldah 8083
Williams, Jane 3430
Williams, John 5404, 5405,
  9859, 9876, 9880
Williams, John C. 7933
Williams, Julia Ann 3612
Williams, Juliette 9860
Williams, Lucretia P. 7933
Williams, Margaret 9880
Williams, Margaretta 9215
Williams, Martha 7911
Williams, Martha A. 5296
Williams, Mary 4303
Williams, Mary Jane 7129
Williams, Oswald 7129
Williams, Richard M. 4671
Williams, Richard S. 9864
Williams, Ruth 2752
Williams, Sabrina (Mrs.) 9860,
  9866, 9871
Williams, Sally 2600, 5406
Williams, Sarah E. 8883
Williams, Susan May 944
Williams, Susan P. 4671
Williams, William A. (Dr.)
  9875
Williamson, Charles 9902
Williamson, David 1703
Williamson, Gitty Ann 5192
Williamson, Mary Ann 5708
Williamson, Ruth 1703
Willis, Dorcas M. 3623
Willis, Eliza 5039
Willis, Mary 10037
Willis, Orren 3623
Willis, Rhoda 2767
Williston, Clara 4590
Williston, Horace 4590
Willmarth, Ezra 3469
Willmarth, Lucy 8392
Willoughby, Polly Maria 5067
Willour, Alonzo 9915
Willour, Hannah M. 9913
Willour, Jacob 9913
Willour, Margaret E. 8909Wil
Willour, Maria L. 9488
Willour, Rachel (Mrs.) 9913
Willour, Sarah 4372
Willson, Angeline 4199
Willson, Hepzibah 6438
Willson, Jared 9918
Willson, Julia 7788
Willson, Louisa 2162
Willson, Lucy 4856
Willson, Martha 1076
Willson, Mary Jane Elizabeth
  5208
Willson, Nathaniel (Dr.) 9921
Willson, Samantha 3335
Willys, Laura S. 996
Wilmingding, ___ (Miss) 9091
Wilson. See also Willson.
Wilson, ___ (Mrs.) 5611, 9933
Wilson, Andrew (Rev.) 6153
Wilson, Ann E. 9190
Wilson, Betsey 1156

Wilson, David 9930
Wilson, Electa 3160
Wilson, Eliza 9777
Wilson, Frances 7494
Wilson, Hannah 8912
Wilson, Henry P. 9930
Wilson, Isabella 2827
Wilson, J. (Mr.) 517, 5611
Wilson, John 9190
Wilson, Johnson 9940
Wilson, Margaret 6153, 8914
Wilson, Mary 5732, 9677
Wilson, Mary Ann 517
Wilson, Russell 9937
Wilson, Sarah 6386
Wilton, Sarah 3891
Wiltsie, Hannah 351
Wiltsie, Thomas (Capt.) 351
Winans, Betsey Maria 108
Winans, Eleanor 10070
Winchell, Sally 2027
Winchester, Alzina 7530
Winchester, Ebenezer 9957
Winchester, Elizabeth N. (Mrs.)
  9957
Winchester, Harriet M. 2589
Winchester, Mary Ann 667
Winchester, Phebe S. 9168
Winchester, Sophronia 10022
Windsor, ___ (Elder) 2191
Windsor, Roxana 2191
Wing, Lydia 166
Wing, Sarah Ann 7819
Winn, Elizabeth 3593, 6541
Winne, Mary (Mrs.) 1049
Winship. See also Wynship.
Winship, Catharine 1647
Winship, Joseph 9962
Winslow, Arville 5813
Winslow, Job 3537
Winslow, Lydia 8404
Winslow, Mary R. 3537
Winslow, Sophia 9568
Winsor, Abraham 9967
Winsor, Henry 9966
Winton, Mary 3540
Wire, Amanda 9493
Wise, Christiana 6062
Wiser, Phebe 4039
Wisner, Asa 4389
Wisner, Elizabeth 4389
Wisner, Harriet 4686
Wisner, Jeffrey 8183
Wisner, Julia 5538
Wisner, P. B. (Mr.) 9971
Wisner, Polydore B. 9973
Wisner, Sally Ann 8183
Wisner, William (Rev.) 5538
Withers, Mary Ann (Mrs.) 9976
Withers, Robert 9976
Wixom, Sally 9464
Wixom, William 9978
Wixon, Hannah 3219
Wolcott, Abigail 5987
Wolcott, Ardilla 6692
Wolcott, Caleb 9988
Wolcott, Deziah 991
Wolcott, Elsa 1411
Wolcott, Erastus 991, 5987
Wolcott, John S. 9986
Wolcott, Laura A. 6232
Wolcott, Oliver 9982
Wolcott, Silvena 2680
Wolverton, Lydia 8722
Wood, ___ (young male) 2674
Wood, Amelia 7762
Wood, Ann 6180
Wood, Charles 10001
Wood, Charlotte 4783

Wood, E. Lorena 5013
Wood, Eleanor 9663
Wood, Eliza Jane 727
Wood, Emily 7060
Wood, Ezra 5013
Wood, Hannah 6361
Wood, Henry 10000
Wood, Isaac 4783
Wood, Jethro 10017
Wood, John 9996
Wood, Loretta 2670
Wood, Martha E. 5927
Wood, Mary Ann 3247
Wood, Nancy 6221
Wood, Phebe A. 3608
Wood, R. T. 6221
Wood, Ralph T. 8748, 9995,
  10011, 10027
Wood, Samson Tickel 10025
Wood, Susannah 4917
Wood, Thomas 10021
Wood, Welcome 6977
Wood, William 10005, 10023
Woodard, Christiana 3550
Woodard, Jenet 5436
Woodard, Sally 7926
Woodcock, D. (Mr.) 1944
Wooden, ___ (Mr.) 10041
Wooden, Julia Ann 3186
Wooden, Rebecca 7349
Woodford, Caroline 4398
Woodmancy, Rebecca 6072
Woodruff, Adeline 3885
Woodruff, H. N. (Rev.) 4563
Woodruff, Helen M. 5865
Woodruff, L. J. (Dr.) 5865,
  5866
Woodruff, Maria 4563
Woodruff, Matilda R. 437
Woodruff, Sally 5773
Woods, Elizabeth 7149
Woods, Mary 2753
Woods, Pamelia N. 9761
Woods, Sally 5355
Woods, William 2753, 7149,
  9761, 9764, 10056, 10057
Woodward, Eliza M. 3500
Woodward, Harriet H. 1153
Woodward, Rosetta Ann 4085
Woodward, Sally (Mrs.) 10065
Woodward, Sarah 4684
Woodward, William 3497, 3500,
  8866
Woodward, William A. 10065
Woodworth, Amy 9873
Woodworth, B. Hutchinson
  4678
Woodworth, Charles 296
Woodworth, Clarissa M. 4678
Woodworth, Harriet 6735
Woodworth, Lucy 5002
Woodworth, Parmelia 5851
Woodworth, Samuel 10073
Work, Edward 10085
Works, I. (Mr.) 10086
Worth, C. H. (Capt.) 3126
Worth, Mary Ann (Mrs.) 4292
Worth, Susan H. 3126
Worthington, G. (Mr.) 1099
Worthington, G. B. (Mr.)
  10088
Worthington, Mary A. 1099
Wooster, Ann (Mrs.) 492
Wright, Aurelia 8772
Wright, B. (Mr.) 4637
Wright, Eunice 1933
Wright, Fairanda A. 3470
Wright, Helen 3809
Wright, Jacob 3770

Wright, Louisa 9404
Wright, Mary 8129
Wright, Mary A. 4375
Wright, Roxana 872
Wyatt, Ann 629
Wyckoff, Nancy 8638
Wygant, Mary (Mrs.) 2050
Wyman, Polly 2151
Wyman, Sally Ann 4298
Wyman, Sophia 3272
Wynkoop, ___ (Maj.) 10108
Wynkoop, Jane 1999
Wynship, Lucy 1663
Yandel, Elizabeth 3855
Yaples, Sally 8539
Yates, ___ (Gov.) 9513
Yates, Anna A. 9513
Yates, John S. 10113, 10117
Yates, Rebecca 6578
Yates, Robert 10114
Yawe, Catharine 4364
Yeomans, Lucy 8346
Yerrington, Amanda 562
Yetten, Margaret 8220
York, Naomi (Mrs.) 1133
Yost, Casper 7476
Yost, Lucinda 7476
Yost, Mercy 2786
Youmans, Catharine 1540
Young, Betsey 8956
Young, Catharine 2285
Young, Catharine Ann Dowers
    7548
Young, Elizabeth 6638
Young, Esther 3206
Young, John 10149
Young, Lydia A. 3177
Young, May 4510
Young, Moses (Rev.) 10142
Young, Phebe 7186
Young, Phoebe 6398
Young, Rosetta 1039
Young, Sarah 5680
Young, Sophia 3546
Young, William, Sr. 7548
Youngs, Betsey 7183
Youngs, John 10159
Youngs, Maria 2087
Youngs, Polly 1757
Zielly, Nancy C. 5433
Zimmerman, Margaret 3439